Cases and Concepts in Corporate Strategy

ROBERT L. KATZ

President, U.S. Natural Resources, Inc.

Prentice-Hall, Inc. • Englewood Cliffs, New Jersey

PRENTICE-HALL INTERNATIONAL, INC., *London*
  PRENTICE-HALL OF AUSTRALIA, PTY. LTD., *Sydney*
PRENTICE-HALL OF CANADA, LTD., *Toronto*
  PRENTICE-HALL OF INDIA PRIVATE LTD., *New Delhi*
PRENTICE-HALL OF JAPAN, INC., *Tokyo*

Foreword

This book is the outcome of more than twenty years of college teaching and business practice. It is intended primarily for advanced students in the art of total enterprise management. It is dedicated to our good friend and great example, Ernest C. Arbuckle. As dean of the Stanford Business School, he gave us much encouragement in our attempts to bring reality, complexity, and a general management point of view into the classroom. As chairman of the board of a great bank and director of many leading corporations, he has shown us the power of this viewpoint in overall corporate affairs.

Preface

This book is designed for advanced work in the management of the total enterprise. It emphasizes the effective development and implementation of overall corporate strategy, in relation to the efficient operation of any of its parts.

Simple but powerful conceptual frameworks are presented to help the student increase his personal skills in identifying and describing a company's actual strategic posture, in evaluating past strategy and present prospects, and in planning the company's future direction so as to best match its resources and its opportunities. Case materials provide a firsthand familiarity with the problems and opportunities of total enterprise management. The cases provide contexts in which to experience and practice the skills of dealing with these kinds of complex data; they lead from relatively simple, narrow-scope companies to large, and complicated, diversified enterprises. (A companion volume, *Management of the Total Enterprise,* utilizes the same conceptual tools but provides a less complex range of case materials in which to employ them.)

The cases and concepts here are largely the outgrowth of an eight-year program of course development at the Stanford Business School. Each case has been tested thoroughly for its contribution in a variety of the school's educational programs. Each concept has been similarly tested for its utility in the classroom, as well as for practicality and relevance in "real life." In fact, since the manuscript was originally submitted, the author has been actively "practicing what he preaches" as the president and chief executive officer of a rapidly growing international company employing several thousand persons and generating several million dollars in operating profits.

There are three cumulative parts. Part I highlights the difference between strategy and operations, and presents a number of relatively narrow-scope company situations for introductory skill development and practice. Part II increases the complexity. Frameworks are presented for analysis and evaluation of company strategy, while case materials enable the student to compare and contrast the differing strategies of various companies facing the same industry characteristics. Part III introduces the final dimension: the multimarket, multiproduct diversified firm. Concepts in this section help in planning strategy and organizing its implementation. The Boise Cascade cases are sequential, covering an extensive time period. They allow the student to analyze the growth and development of a major company from its modest beginnings. At each point in time, the student has the opportunity to develop a plan, contrast it with actual company performance, and then develop a new plan in the light of additional data and changed circumstances. The Castle & Cooke series provides the student with a chance to deal with a far-flung, loosely related, widely diversified company, while the Applied Power series presents a tightly knit group of units serving vastly different markets with vastly different products. These organizational alternatives can stretch the analytical capabilities and challenge the ingenuity of even the most experienced practitioners of corporate strategy.

Many persons have contributed to the development of these materials. Paul R. Johnson, Director of Case Development at the Stanford Business School, not only supervised the various casewriters who worked with us over the eight year period but also wrote a number of the cases himself. Our colleagues in the business policy course at Stanford—Professors Carleton A. Pederson, Gayton E. Germane, Jack D. Steele, Gail M. Oxley, Henry S. Eyring, and the late Mason Smith—all contributed much to the development of these concepts and cases. Charles A. Anderson, now president of Stanford Research Institute but formerly associate dean and our colleague in business policy, gave generously of his wisdom and support. Former Dean Ernest C. Arbuckle, now chairman of the board of Wells Fargo Bank, gave us encouragement in our darkest hours.

We pay special tribute for his conceptual contribution to Professor Edmund P. Learned, Professor (emeritus) at Harvard Business School.

Stephen E. Halprin, now associated with Ocean Science Capital Corp., contributed enormously to the principal case series, in this book—the airlines and forest products industries, the Castle & Cooke and the Applied Power series, Paul Johnson worked on the Castle and Cooke series and wrote the Pioneer Brass and Burns Corp. cases. He was also the major author of the Forest Products Industry and the Boise Cascade cases, assisted by Lawrence S. Ward and Noel Fenton.

Peter M. Oliver, now associated with Arthur D. Little Co., was responsible for the Mitchell Nursery Co. case, while Michael Tennican, now assistant professor at the Harvard Business School wrote Morgan Corp. La Plant-Choate Manufacturing Co., Inc., is reproduced here through the courtesy of Professor C. R. Christensen of Harvard.

We received many good suggestions and very helpful assistance from a number of reviewers, including Professor Edward Watson of Northwestern University, Dr. Donald Grunewald of Suffolk University, Professor William D. Guth of Columbia University, Professor Jack Holland of San Jose State College, Mr. Kenton L. Anderson of Peat, Marwick, Mitchell & Co., Professor Chester F. Healy, Jr., of Sacramento State College, Professor W. F. Rabe of San Fernando Valley State College, Professor William E. Rogers of San Francisco State College, and Professor Louis J. Shuster of the University of Missouri. Professor William H. Newman of Columbia University was especially helpful in clarifying the textual material.

To all of these many people, we extend our thanks and gratitude. To them belongs whatever credit is due this volume. Its shortcomings remain the responsibility of the author.

ROBERT L. KATZ

Stanford, California

Contents

chapter 3

97 ... The General Management Functions

DEFINITION OF GENERAL MANAGEMENT FUNCTIONS. THE MANAGER'S JOB. DIFFERENCES AND SIMILARITIES BY ORGANIZATIONAL LEVEL. STRATEGIC VARIABLES. STRATEGIC CRITERIA. OPERATING VARIABLES. OPERATING CRITERIA. RELATING THE STRATEGIC PLAN AND OPERATIONAL PERFORMANCE. COMMITMENT AND COMPETENCE.

chapter 4

193 ... The Concept of Corporate Strategy

ACTUAL STRATEGIC POSTURES AND INTENDED STRATEGIC PLANS. THE COMPONENT ELEMENTS OF CORPORATE STRATEGY. IDENTIFYING, EVALUATING AND PLANNING CORPORATE STRATEGY. STRATEGIC VARIABLES AND OPERATING VARIABLES. THE IMPORTANCE OF THE CONCEPT OF CORPORATE STRATEGY.

part III

**DETAILED ANALYSIS,
PLANNING AND DEPLOYMENTS
IN COMPLEX, MULTI-DIVISIONAL
ENTERPRISES**

chapter 7

**345 ... Planning
Corporate Strategy**

*STEPS IN PLANNING CORPORATE STRATEGY. THE FINAL PLAN. STRA-
TEGIC MODE. MODIFYING THE BASIC STRATEGIC PLAN.*

CASES:

chapter 8

501 ... Corporate Strategy and Organizational Form

*STAGES OF GROWTH AND DEVELOPMENT. SIGNIFICANCE OF ORGANIZA-
TIONAL FORM. BASIC OBJECTIVES. PERFORMANCE CRITERIA. STRA-
TEGIC MODE. STRATEGY AND STRUCTURE. SKILL REQUIREMENTS. THE
ORGANIZATIONS OF THE FUTURE.*

CASES:

LIST OF CASES

part I

INTRODUCTION TO
CORPORATE STRATEGY

chapter 1

Introduction

THE PURPOSE OF THIS BOOK

This book is concerned with the management of the total enterprise, with the basic strategic issues which provide the framework and direction for over-all company operations: In what business should a specific firm be (in terms of its products, services, and customers)? What should be its performance criteria (in terms of the objectives of owners, managers, and employees, and the requirements of the marketplace, society, government, and other relevant institutions)? What should it emphasize in establishing a competitive advantage or "distinctive competence"? What strategy should it pursue (in terms of emphasis, priorities, and timing in the allocation of its resources and its efforts)? What must be done to assure competent, committed, creative, and socially responsible performance as resources are continuously deployed and redeployed?

Such courses, most commonly called "Business Policy," or "General Management," or "Top Management Decision-making," usually are intended to provide a "capstone," "unifying," "integrating," "coordinating" opportunity to tie together concepts, principles, and skills learned separately in other, more specialized courses. A second—and even more important—objective may be to provide the context for developing the special skills and ways of thinking which are uniquely appropriate to total enterprise management.

As any experienced executive knows, the requirements, problems, and opportunities of the total enterprise are fundamentally different from those of any of its parts. They extend far beyond the mere summing of the situations and characteristics of the various functions, departments, or divisions.

Management of the total enterprise demands a different way of thinking, application of different criteria, and the exercise of different skills than are required for the management of any part. Many companies can, and do, survive without doing anything more than operating each part efficiently. However, such companies lose much of the opportunity to choose and change their own destinies. They surrender the initiative and, instead, change only in defensive response to external pressures and events. Unable to initiate an offensive strategy, they become highly dependent for long-term success upon luck—the occurrence of favorable external circumstances over which they have no control. This book provides materials which make it possible for a student to see how a company can become the master of its own situation, rather than the captive of it—consciously seeking and pursuing objectives, rather than being shaped by outside influences or "happenstance."

For Whom is the Book Intended?

This book was written primarily for advanced students in business administration: those who are near the completion of an extended educational experience, or those who have had substantial firsthand management experience. The cases and concepts presented here have been tested in many different situations, ranging from groups of young men and women without any firsthand business experience to groups composed solely of seasoned corporate presidents.

Groups of students have included executives from government, education, hospital administration, and other nonbusiness contexts. They have included executives from service industries and from manufacturing companies; from giant enterprises and from small ones; from multinational companies and from single-location, domestic operations. Some groups came wholly from the United States, while other groups represented more than 30 different nations.

Our experience has been that these very different sets of students have all been able to use these materials effectively.

Specific practices, customs, alternatives, and constraints may vary from nation to nation, and from one type of enterprise to another. Competitive contexts may differ, as do the objectives and strategies of individual enterprises. But it has been our experience that the *concepts* presented here are *universal*. They apply as well to the Persian carpet industry as to the U.S. airlines industry; they can be learned and utilized by inexperienced college students as well as by seasoned senior executives. The emphasis assigned to each variable will differ among situations, but the basic conceptual schema have universal utility in analyzing, evaluating, and dealing with virtually all total enterprise situations.

Prerequisites

The cases and concepts presented here require a familiarity with, understanding of, and competence in the application of concepts, techniques, knowledge, skills, and points of view of the various functional aspects of an enterprise: marketing, finance, production, accounting, personnel, and purchasing. They also demand a basic understanding of economics, organizational behavior, and quantitative and statistical techniques.

In studying these materials, a student is not likely to learn more about any of the functional subjects or basic disciplines. But working with these cases and concepts should enable him to learn more about the *relationships* among the various functional areas and among the foundation disciplines: the limits of application of specialized knowledge; the innate conflicts in objectives and points of view; the tradeoffs which are necessary among competing goals in order to preserve the health and vigor of the enterprise. While maintaining respect for the indispensable contributions of specialized knowledge to complex endeavors, the student may also gain an awareness of the essential requirements for blending, coordinating, and integrating these separate inputs, and for establishing an over-all guiding direction to the total effort.

THE NEED FOR A COURSE IN GENERAL MANAGEMENT

The extensive study of American business education sponsored by the Ford Foundation and conducted by Professors Robert Aaron Gordon and James E. Howell states eloquently the need for such an integrating course in every curriculum:

> The capstone of the core curriculum should be a course in "business policy" which will give the students an opportunity to pull together what they have learned in the separate business fields and utilize this knowledge in the analysis of complex business problems.
>
> The business policy course can offer the student something he will find no-where else in the curriculum: consideration of business problems which are not prejudged as being marketing problems, finance problems, etc.; emphasis on the development of skill in identifying, analyzing, and solving problems in a situation which is as close as the classroom can ever be to the real business world; opportunity to consider problems which draw on a wide range of substantive areas in business; opportunity to consider the external, nonmarket implications of problems at the same time that internal decisions must be made; situations which enable the student to exercise qualities of judgment and of mind which were not explicitly called for in any prior course. Questions of social responsi-

bility and of personal attitudes can be brought in as a regular aspect of this kind of problem-solving practice. Without the responsibility of having to transmit some specific body of knowledge, the business policy course can concentrate on integrating what already has been acquired and on developing further the student's skill in using that knowledge. The course can range over the entire curriculum and beyond.[1]

The other major study of business education, the Carnegie Foundation-sponsored project conducted by Professor Frank C. Pierson, is equally emphatic about the need for a course in every business curriculum which "serves as a focus for the student's entire studies" and which stresses "the role of management in coordinating internal operations and in adapting to change in the external environment." [2] In the same study, Professor George Leland Bach, then Dean of the Graduate School of Industrial Administration at Carnegie Tech, underscored the need for a course which provided "a more advanced, integrating approach to a wide variety of business policy and administrative problems, mainly at the upper management level. Stress would be on integrated use of *both* the analytical tools from the three major foundation areas *and* knowledge from the various functional fields of business, in making company-wide policy decisions and getting these decisions carried out effectively." [3]

There has been a growing trend in recent years to offer such courses in more and more educational programs—at the graduate level, at the end of an undergraduate curriculum, and in executive development programs for practicing businessmen. But as Gordon and Howell point out, there have been some difficulties:

> If the argument for a policy course is so strong, why do so few schools require it? First, some faculties have a bias against the use of cases—a "sine qua non" of a policy course. While we have stressed the need to teach principles, there is no doubt that the development of problem-solving skill requires the use of cases, particularly in the latter part of the student's program. Second, some deans report that their requirements already are "too tight"—there is no room. This argument also can be brushed aside. Reduction of the excessive amount of specialization required by virtually every school using this argument would provide room for several policy courses.
>
> The next two arguments are somewhat more serious. The first of these concerns staffing. Some deans have argued that policy courses require instructors who are well-trained in all areas of business and have a substantial amount of business experience. We cannot agree with this description of what is needed, although we admit that such courses do pose staffing problems if they must be of-

---

[1] Robert Aaron Gordon and James Edwin Howell, *Higher Education for Business* (New York: Columbia University Press, 1959), pp. 206-207.

[2] Frank C. Pierson, *The Education of American Businessmen* (New York: McGraw-Hill Book Co., 1959), p. 257.

[3] *Ibid.*, p. 333.

fered on a multi-section basis. The instructor in a policy course should have a technical background at least equal to what most of his students possess; this is surely not a restrictive condition. In addition (and this is the major difficulty), he must have the maturity, sophistication, and mental poise so that he can approach problems in a variety of ways and not merely from the viewpoint of the particular area in which he may be a specialist. He must be able to admit he does not always or even usually know "the" answer and that he can think of problems as having indeterminate and conditional solutions—e.g., he does not think in terms of "black and white." This prescription should not be too restrictive for most faculties.

The last objection to a requirement in business policy is that its role can be played equally well by other courses in the curriculum, perhaps after some slight modifications in the latter. We do not believe that this is true, ... In addition, as we have already noted, there is some hazard involved in relying heavily on cases in the basic functional fields.

While this evidence is not conclusive, we should also cite our conversations with students in a large number of schools. Students are unqualifiedly in favor of such courses, even in schools where we suspect they were only moderately well taught. Student opinion, of course, is an insufficient reason for including a new course in the curriculum; but it is not without weight when added to the other evidence that has been presented.[4]

GENERAL MANAGEMENT AS A FIELD FOR TRAINING

Historically, the "Business Policy" or "General Management" area has been ill-defined. So long as it was viewed wholly as an integrating experience, it was difficult to establish a coherent structure of subject matter or a meaningful conceptual framework. Individual courses in various programs and institutions were dependent on the personal skill and experience of their specific instructors, and varied widely in content and concept.

In recent years, it has become clear that, while there may not be an independent body of general management knowledge, per se, there are distinct skills and ways of thinking unique to the general management function. Dealing with the total enterprise provides challenges and opportunities which do not exist in the management of a single part. As Professor Jay Forrester has pointed out, "the great complexity of the total enterprise as a functioning system does not merely extend the phenomena of simpler situations; entirely new phenomena take place." [5]

Outstanding business executives such as Alfred P. Sloan, Jr., Robert McNamara, and Crawford Greenewalt have repeatedly suggested the existence of a

---

[4] Gordon and Howell, *Higher Education for Business, op. cit.,* pp. 207-208.

[5] Jay W. Forrester, "The Structure Underlying Management Processes," in *Evolving Concepts in Management,* Proceedings of the 24th Annual Meeting of the Academy of Management, New York, December 28-30, 1964.

unique general management skill. A perceptive review of the book *My Years with General Motors* emphasized Mr. Sloan's clear "conviction that there is such a thing as general management ability which has a 'logic' quite distinct from any specific knowledge of the business or any of its functions. And while Sloan was the first to admit that experience in the business might be useful to the general executive, he insisted that there was a clear distinction between the two. . . . above all else, he regarded himself as 'a specialist in management.' Ponder the impact on a company of the fact that its chief executive affirms that his forte is neither sales nor production, neither finance nor law, but management. And, as GM's affairs progressed, Sloan and his close associates never missed an opportunity to attribute each corporate achievement to the manner in which the company was managed." [6]

Thus, in recent years, innovative general management courses have begun to focus on the distinctive aspects of total enterprise management. The need for competence in these skills and ways of thinking is enormous in our increasingly complex and competitive society, and the task of developing this competence cannot be left to chance.

Consequently, great efforts are being made to develop an acceptable, explicit conceptual framework for learning about, and dealing with, the crucial elements of total enterprise management. This book represents a beginning effort toward the construction of such a framework.

THE GENERAL MANAGEMENT POINT OF VIEW

The basic objective is to help the student to develop a personally useful, explicit way of thinking about the business enterprise as a total system in a total environment: to enable him to identify the crucial elements and relationships in a situation, analyze systematically and rigorously the basic opportunities, constraints, and issues, and trace out the impact of an action in any one part upon the other parts and upon the totality. His analysis is subjected to tests of utility, reality, multidimensionality, emphasis, and focus. His action recommendations face criteria of relevance, emphasis, ingenuity, feasibility, timing, and adequacy. He soon learns that what is best for the *total* enterprise is *always* suboptimal from the point of view of an individual unit or function. Thus he must be able to predict consequences accurately, choose which outcomes he is willing to live with, and be satisfied with less than perfect, but workable, plans and programs.

Management of the total enterprise involves dealing with an enormous quantity of information, activities, and events. The man who tries to deal with the individual elements one at a time will be inundated. The man who deals only with "problems" as they arise, the "squeaky wheel" approach, is likely to emphasize the things which are merely urgent and to ignore the issues which are truly

---

[6] Harold Wolff, "The Great GM Mystery," *Harvard Business Review* (Sept.-Oct. 1964).

important. What is needed is the ability to perceive the crucial patterns among the various bits, pieces, and mountains of information, activities, and events. This point of view is complementary to (not competitive with) the point of view of individual functions, fields, or departments which deal with parts of the whole. It emphasizes the relations between parts and their impacts on one another and on the totality.

With such a viewpoint, one can identify, and accept, the limits of what is realistically possible, as well as the imminence of what will probably occur unless overt action is taken. The utility of such a "general management point of view" is not limited to persons holding the position of General Manager. It should be immediately helpful to *anyone* actively engaged in a business situation, regardless of his organizational position, in sharpening his awareness and understanding of what is going on around him.

CONCEPTUAL STRUCTURE

The development of a personally useful "general management point of view" is greatly abetted by an explicit conceptual structure. Grasping the structure of total enterprise management enables the student to learn more readily. It makes possible the understanding of many situations as specific instances of more general cases, without losing sight of the unique aspects of the situations examined.

This book presents a few basic observable or measurable concepts: objectives, scope, performance specifications, competitive advantage, and resource deployment. These concepts are combined in different ways to provide separate frameworks for identifying and describing a company's total situation; evaluating past performance and future prospects; planning the company's future competitive posture and allocating its resources.

A few second-order concepts for describing complex multidimensional uniformities are utilized heavily. The principal second-order concept is, of course, *corporate strategy. The distinction between* strategic *variables and* operating *variables is the underlying structural theme of this book.*

The conceptual structure is developed in a spiral pattern. The few important basic concepts are introduced at the very beginning, then returned to again and again, with increasing scope and depth. New ideas are introduced—effectiveness and efficiency; environmental requirements and market opportunities; resource availability and investment opportunities; membership patterns and commitment opportunities; integrated enterprises and conglomerates; synergistic combinations and debilitating ones; phases of organizational growth and development; adaptations and tradeoffs.

Throughout, an attempt is made to differentiate among the general management *point of view* (useful for all), the general management *functions* (performed by many), and the *position* of general manager (to which only a few will ascend). It would be unrealistic to assume that very many of the students using this book will become general managers. But most will be in a position to influence strategic choices. Hopefully, the conceptual structure presented here will help them to identify these opportunities with confidence and to assess the alternatives accurately.

HOW THE BOOK IS ORGANIZED

This book attempts to deal continuously and consistently with the total enterprise as a unitary whole. It does not offer different types of functional policy issues which can be resolved by specialist talent. It does not fragment or splinter the enterprise into component functional parts for analysis or action. Nor does it provide individual incidents or problems for solution or decision-making. All of these would be contrary to the main purpose, which is to focus on those conditions which are unique to *total* enterprise management and to the *total* enterprise's situation.

Neither does this book break down the general management job into separate "planning" and "implementing" aspects. Each situation is viewed as requiring a cyclical process of broad-gauge assessment, planning, deployment, operation, reassessment, replanning, and so on. Most *strategic* deployments can be accomplished without requiring significant changes in the behavior of those charged with operating responsibility. On the other hand, operating viability *requires* the continuous delineation of strategic emphasis, priorities, timetables, and assignments.

This book is divided into five parts. Part I introduces the basic conceptual structure and provides a group of cases on which the student can begin to practice and develop his skill in identifying, describing, analyzing, and evaluating company strategy. Each of these companies is a single unit, with a relatively limited product line, operating in relatively limited, well-defined markets.

Part II introduces much greater complexity. Conceptual materials provide more explicit frameworks for analysis and evaluation. The case materials demand rigorous analysis of entire industries and provide data for evaluating the strategies of a broad range of individual companies competing within each industry.

Part III introduces much greater complexity. Conceptual materials provide more explicit frameworks for analysis and evaluation. The case materials demand rigorous analysis of entire industries and provide data for evaluating the strategies of a broad range of individual companies competing within each industry.

The intent is to provide a cumulatively deepening experience, using the same basic tools and concepts in increasingly complex situations, with progressively intricate and sophisticated requirements.

The case materials contained in this book are extensive and pervasive, since it is necessary to present data affecting every aspect of a company's situation.

Even so, these apparently iong cases have been greatly distilled from the actual data available in the situation.

The cases are not intended as illustrations, or as springboards for generalized discussion on some specific management topic. They are not cases "of" something or "in" something. They are descriptions of actual situations, reported as faithfully as possible, and presented in as much (or little) detail as we felt necessary for the role which the case is expected to play in the concept of the book. The choice and sequence of cases is not random. Their order is consistent with the book's conceptual structure.

These cases do *not* have clearly defined and specified "issues" or "problems" which allow for simplification of data and generalization of response. Many of them do contain issues and problems, but they require the student to separate the crucial from the trivial, to define and treat only those elements which are paramount to the company's present strength and future success.

In dealing with the cases, the student should be concerned primarily with understanding the situation. He should try not to spend his time looking for problems, or applying some arbitrary standard of "right," "wrong," "good," or "bad." Rather he should try to distinguish among relevant facts, opinions, and assumptions; marshal evidence to support his view and to take account of the contradictory evidence; reason logically about the data, and where essential information is missing; indicate what he needs and how to get it; assess the principal trends, risks, and opportunities in the industry and the economy; assess the major human, physical, and financial resources available to the firm; make clear choices among alternatives which capitalize on company strengths and minimize weaknesses; avoid obvious inconsistencies among various objectives, policies, and resources; distinguish between the urgent and the postponeable, the important and the trivial; plan actions which are clearly consistent with company resources, industry trends, owners' or managers' objectives, and are logically and sequentially related to one another; foresee accurately what the consequences of his proposed actions are likely to be; and explicitly choose the risks which he is willing to accept.

All who use these materials are partners in a process of examining the same body of complex materials and trying to learn from it. While there is no *single* "right" answer to any of these situations, it should be obvious that not *all* proposed programs are of equal value.

Many of the cases are undisguised, making it possible for the student to collect data on his own to add to those presented in the book. In this way, company progress can be continually updated and new analyses made.

We would hope that, as the student works through the cases and concepts presented here, he will feel a sense of progress, despite the increasingly difficult material confronting him. He will have repeated opportunities to identify many different companies' strategies, to assess their past performance and future prospects, and to plan for their future activities. Continued practice, under guidance, should lead to improved skills and greater personal competence.

chapter 2

The General Management Point of View

We are concerned in this book with helping the student to comprehend accurately the enterprise's present posture, strengths, and opportunities, and to assess realistically the balance between available resources and environmental requirements. This means thinking always in terms of relative *emphasis* and *priorities* among multiple units, activities, objectives, and criteria, and being willing to shift the emphasis or rearrange the schedule of priorities as conditions change, either within the enterprise or in its external environment.

"The general management point of view" is a matter of both *judgment* and *attitude*. Judgment is required in identifying and assessing which variables are crucial, and in predicting the future consequences of action alternatives. Attitude is important in being *willing* to choose among competing activities and programs and to accept the inevitable antagonisms and disappointments of those whose situations receive lower priorities or lesser emphasis than their proponents believe they deserve.

Every strategic action must strike a balance among so many conflicting values, objectives, and criteria that it will *always* be suboptimal from any single viewpoint. *Every* decision or choice affecting the whole enterprise has negative consequence for some of the parts. A man with a "general management point of view" will perceive the conflicts and trace accurately their likely impact throughout the organization. Reluctantly, but wittingly, he will sacrifice a single unit or part for the good of the whole. He will deliberately accept conflict by committing himself to the welfare of the total enterprise, placing its interests ahead of personal gain or the special interests of any unit or group. He will be satisfied to achieve what is *adequate* and feasible in the situation, rather than what, from one single point of view, may be *elegant* or *optimum.*

This point of view stands in sharp contrast to the viewpoint of the technical specialist, whose major goal is to optimize against a set of limited criteria. Both viewpoints are needed. The latter is essential to the efficiency of the enterprise's operations; the former is essential to the enterprise's effectiveness in relating to the competitive market-environment. The two orientations are complementary, not competitive. Each is appropriate to its own purposes.

THE NEED FOR DIFFERENT FRAMES OF REFERENCE FOR DIFFERENT PURPOSES

Each of us, in attempting to comprehend and deal with situations in which we find ourselves, abstracts certain elements from the situation in accordance with some accustomed way of thinking. This process is most often *implicit,* and therefore unconscious.

The opportunity for comprehending the nature of a situation more accurately and for predicting outcomes more certainly is increased greatly when the way of thinking is made *explicit,* so that it can be subjected to continuous testing and refinement. Man's major gains in knowledge and practice have always resulted from the conceptual breakthroughs of abstracting different elements from the totality and/or perceiving them in new and different relationships.

Moreover, as indicated above, different ways of thinking are appropriate to different situations. The mature, competent individual has a repertoire of frames of reference (or points of view) to choose among, as the phenomena which confront him vary. For example, in most physical activities involving limited time and distance, it is useful for us to think of the earth as if it were not in motion. In building a house or a road, we can view the earth as if it were a relatively flat, steady body of infinite depth. This frame of reference allows us to hit a golf ball, walk a "straight" line, and conduct many other activities which are confined within the spatial limits of the horizon. We could not perform these activities effectively if we were consciously thinking of the earth as a twirling sphere moving through space at a speed of thousands of miles per hour. This latter view, however, is essential in situations involving astronomy, space travel, long-range ballistics, and so on. In each of these instances, we abstract different concepts from our observations of the earth. Each set of abstractions (or frame of reference) is enormously useful for one purpose, but very misleading for the other.

This same versatility in utilizing different points of view when dealing with different situations is crucial to the effective management of a business enterprise.

"ELEMENTAL" AND "SYSTEMIC" FRAMES OF REFERENCE

Renowned physical scientist Irving Langmuir once divided physical phenomena into two different classes.[1] The first type he called *convergent* phenomena, referring to situations in which the fluctuating details of the individual activities of very large numbers of atoms (or other units) averaged out, giving a result that converged to a definite state. For such phenomena, it is possible to limit sharply the number of relevant variables and conditions affecting outcomes, and to derive simple general rules of cause and effect, and of direct relationships among variables. Newton's laws of motion, the actuarial data of insurance companies, Ohm's law of electricity, and Boyle's law of gases are all examples of the kinds of precise rules and laws which can be stated about convergent phenomena. Each rule enables very accurate prediction of the outcomes of certain actions, applied *under closely specified conditions,* which presume that all other conditions are irrelevant or remain constant.

The second type he called *divergent* phenomena, in which, from a small beginning, increasingly large results were produced. These phenomena—typified by the birth, growth, development, and behavior of individual living organisms—could not be described or explained in the usual terms of classical physics, which centered on convergent phenomena and direct cause-effect relationships. Einstein's relativity theory and Planck's quantum theory were the beginning of a new modern physics which attempted to deal with divergent phenomena.

The two basic concepts in understanding divergent phenomena are *probability* (rather than certainty) and *patterns of uniformity in events,* where elements consistently appear or correlate together (rather than clean-cut cause and effect relationships, in which it can be said that one event causes the other). Uncertainty of outcomes and interdependence of elements are, of course, key characteristics of human enterprises.

An "Elemental" Frame of Reference

Most inanimate phenomena can be classified as convergent. In dealing with linear, convergent, cause and effect phenomena, an "elemental" frame of reference can be demonstrated as being most useful (i.e., in describing the phenomena, explaining its characteristics, and achieving desired ends). This frame of reference is based on the so-called "scientific method" and allows the user to apply previously designated concepts, theories, principles, procedures, methods, and techniques to the solution of current problems.

Procedurally, the problem is divided into its component elements in order to make it manageable; the designated principles are applied to the component parts; and then the components are recombined, with appropriate weighting and

---

[1] Irving Langmuir, "Science, Common Sense, and Decency," *Science,* Vol. 97, No. 2505 (January 1943), 1-7.

sequencing, to produce a decision program. This way of thinking is exceedingly useful in dealing with a very wide range of business problems involving the planning and execution of procedures, methods, and techniques. It is also relevant to detecting and correcting deviations from expected outcomes of plans and programs.

A "Systemic" Frame of Reference

In contrast to the elemental frame of reference, so enormously useful when dealing with specified *parts* of a whole, a different way of thinking is required when one deals with the total, unified, interacting, interdependent *systemic* character of a business enterprise. Such divergent phenomena are not susceptible to the same kind of analysis. Here, nothing is designated as separate or separable. Each person is himself deeply involved in the system. His own actions are at least in part shaped by the other aspects in it, and his behavior in turn affects to some degree those aspects and the character of the totality.

A "systemic" frame of reference involves dealing with the whole *Gestalt* of the enterprise. The analyst is obliged to identify his *own* values, feelings, and perceptual biases as influencing which data he abstracts from the totality. The emphasis is on identifying *tendencies and uniformities* in the phenomena, and identifying *patterns of relationships* among the variables comprising the uniformities and tendencies. The *limits* and *constraints* in the situation must also be identified. Within these limits, it is then necessary to predict the expected changes in the total pattern, and in the other components, with changes in any one or more of the component variables. Action programs are then thought of as a cyclical single-step-at-a-time of (a) changing the characteristics of one or more variables; (b) assessing the outcome on the total system and on the other variables; (c) introducing a subsequent multivariable change; (d) testing reactions; (e) reassessing outcomes, and so on.

This frame of reference is unnecessarily complex and too inconclusive for dealing efficiently with the separate convergent parts of a whole, i.e., for solving predefined problems in which external variables remain constant or are irrelevant. It is, however, of great utility in dealing with the system as a whole, in its relationship with an ever-changing, uncertain external environment. This is especially true in planning future strategy, where greatest emphasis should be put on activities which have the greatest strength. Positive feedback of favorable results allows the strategist to put most of his resources into the most productive activities until the opportunity is completely utilized.

SPECIALIST THINKING AND GENERAL MANAGEMENT THINKING

From the foregoing it should be clear that an elemental frame of reference is most relevant to the technical specialist, while a systemic frame of reference is consistent with what we have called "the general management point of view."

It would be helpful if every manager could utilize *both* frames of reference, applying an elemental approach to those problems which can be cleanly separated and defined and a systemic approach to those which cannot. It is rarely easy for the manager to switch frames of reference. Criteria for evaluating specialist results are in terms of the elegance and optimization of the solution, while criteria for evaluating general management results must be in terms of maintaining organizational equilibrium, settling for what is merely feasible and adequate. Moreover, the elemental specialist viewpoint is concerned with reducing the range of relevant variables as much as possible to make the problem more manageable and the outcome more controllable. The systemic view requires keeping the maximum number of possibilities open—considering as many variables as possible in the hope of finding a combination which yields the greatest return from the available resources. The systemic view continually searches for a synergistic effect in which the impact of the combined outcome is greater than that of the sum of the parts. Such an opportunity appears infrequently in dealing with linear, cause and effect situations. In both instances a premium is place on ingenuity, but the kind of ingenuity most helpful to the specialist differs greatly from that most useful to the person dealing with a total system.

DEPARTMENTAL POINTS OF VIEW

This distinction between elemental and systemic thinking becomes further complicated when translated into departmental affiliations within the enterprise. Departments are typically organized by functional specialty. Within each department, some activities call for elemental frames of reference, while others call for sytemic views. However, the systemic view of a situation by a member of one department often will produce a very different analysis from the systemic view of a member of another department.

As every experienced executive knows, each major function of a business (production, sales, finance, research and development, accounting, purchasing, personnel) has its unique values and criteria. Each department may stress "competence" and "loyalty" as the key criteria in evaluating individuals. But "competence" may mean *sociability* in a sales department, *ingenuity* in a production department, and technical *knowledge* in a research and development department. "Loyalty" in a sales department may mean a *personal identification* with the boss; it may mean a commitment to *schedules and efficiency* in a production department; in research and development it may mean scientific integrity and commitment to a *principle*.

Similarly, each departmental point of view tends to put greatest emphasis on a somewhat different set of company objectives and performance criteria.

A *production* point of view will tend to put greatest emphasis on cost reduction, internal operating efficiency, schedule responsibility, simplification, high certainty, and stability in operations.

A *sales* point of view will tend to put greatest emphasis on increasing sales volume, market share, and relationships and reputation with customers.

A *product-development* point of view will tend to emphasize high frequency of invention, elegance in design, and superiority in technical performance of products.

A *financial* point of view will tend to put greatest emphasis on profits, return on investment, and cash flow.

A *purchasing* point of view will tend to put greatest emphasis on shrewdness, timing, and opportunism.

An *accounting* point of view will tend to emphasize accuracy, orderliness, systematization, safety of assets, clarity, and efficiency.

A *personnel* point of view will tend to put greatest emphasis on worker satisfaction, individual growth and development, career certainty, and organizational stability.

Obviously, few persons in any department commit themselves completely to only one set of criteria, without any regard for the others. But the same relative emphasis among these criteria will probably be shared by most persons within a given functional department.

Differences in criteria often lead members of various departments to quite different analyses of shared events. Similarly, each department will tend to form its own evaluations of actions taken, applying its unique criteria of what is "good" or "bad," "necessary" or "desirable." *Every* total enterprise action will be viewed as suboptimal by at least one (and usually more) of the departments involved.

THE GENERAL MANAGEMENT POINT OF VIEW

It should be clear that *all* of the departmental criteria cited above are desirable —each has merit for the enterprise's welfare. However, as anyone with general management experience knows, it is rarely possible to satisfy all of these criteria simultaneously. Every specific action or decision emphasizes some few criteria to the detriment of others. That is why goodwill and integrity are necessary, but not *sufficient,* in dealing with total enterprise situations. Everyone *cannot* be fully satisfied. Choices must be made, *relative* emphasis determined, and priorities ranked.

So we return to the need for a "general management point of view" which seeks a balanced equilibrium among conflicting claims. Whichever criteria an enterprise emphasizes most heavily will determine the company's basic orientation and define its range of acceptable action. Unless this emphasis is given explicit attention in making strategic choices, the current relative power and influence of the various departments may be the sole determinant of corporate emphasis and of the over-all strategic direction which the enterprise takes! What is needed is a way of thinking which allows flexibility from one situation to the next, emphasizing those criteria most relevant to the specific conditions, but never losing sight of the over-all corporate goals.

What is proposed here as an appropriate "general management point of view" is very different from the viewpoint of the trader or the financial manipulator of common stocks. To be effective, a trader cannot allow himself to become involved with the persons and activities which make up the enterprise's internal life. He must remain aloof and external to the enterprise, single-mindedly committed to a solitary criterion—profit on an impersonal, unemotional, in-and-out, buy-and-sell, completed transaction—without becoming affected by what it is he is trading. The manager, on the other hand, is inextricably involved with the persons and activities he supervises.

Department heads are in a particularly difficult position. They must be true to the values and criteria of their departments or lose the respect and support of their subordinates. Equally important, each must argue eloquently for the special point of view of his department, or others will not understand the full consequences of each alternative. But then, after he has championed the cause of his department, the manager is expected to be a "good company man" and sublimate departmental interest to the interests of the total enterprise.

It has been our experience that even chief executive officers frequently think in terms of a single department's criteria. It is only natural that a man whose career has been, for example, in sales will tend to emphasize the values of the sales function. This is probably impossible to change. However, a self-aware executive should be able to *recognize* his innate bias and to compensate for it overtly in his thinking.

What we are suggesting is that there is no such thing as a separate, permanent, "general management" set of values and criteria. Rather, "the general management point of view" involves selecting among differing departmental criteria and emphasizing those which are currently most appropriate to the enterprise's total situation. It is crucial that this emphasis be *shifted* when basic conditions change within the organization or in the competitive market place. Thus, evaluations of the enterprise's situation must be continuous, and establishment of emphases and priorities must never be permanently frozen. Otherwise, the enterprise will sacrifice both its adaptive and its innovative capacities.

The cases included in this book are meant to provide practice, in a wide number of different situations, in determining what the appropriate emphasis should be. Hopefully, working with these materials not only will improve the student's ability to identify what emphasis is needed in a specific circumstance, but also will help the student to identify his own built-in biases and preconceptions.

VIEWING THE TOTAL ENTERPRISE

Every enterprise—no matter how simple its operations, how few its members, or how limited its activities—is a complex entity which defies neat dissection and classification. The framework which we present here, deliberately crude and non-inclusive, offers a few basic constructs which allow a simple, general description of a company's over-all situation without fragmenting its essential unitary characteristics. In collecting, abstracting, and ordering data, we propose three observable, separable, but related, dynamic variables: the business's *environment, resources,* and *members.*

At any point in time, the relationships among these variables may be viewed as describing the enterprise's present condition. These relationships also provide a basis for evaluating the enterprise's future prospects for survival and goal achievement. In a sense, such a description may be thought of as a "snapshot" or "Balance Sheet" of the company at that moment. Each category is deliberately noninclusive; we shall be concerned with only a few items from among the enormous variety possible. We bear in mind that the "general management point of view" concentrates our attention on those few crucial items which make the primary difference in the enterprise's situation. Hence, we view the company as being composed of:

I. A network of *members* who possess differing types and degrees of competence and skill; differing values, personal goals, and commitments; differing degrees of interpersonal contact, cooperation, and influence.

Note that each of these items refers to *actual* characteristics of specific *persons* in the company, and not to prescribed organizational structures or assignments. As we have discussed earlier, the specific combination of member competences, commitments, and influence which exists in the enterprise at any point in time determines the *acceptable* range of alternative actions. This pattern provides the explanation for the specific criteria which have been applied to choices in the past, and allows us to predict with high probability which choices will likely be made in the future.

II. These members have available to them, immediately or potentially, an aggregation of *resources: Capital,* as represented by cash on hand, magnitude of cash flow, debt capacity, equity availability; *Facilities* and capabilities, as represented by existing plant, equipment, raw material holdings, transportation units, distribution outlets, and so on; *Market position,* as represented by product (or service) reputation and acceptance, brand franchises, market penetration and coverage, patent position or know-how, control or ownership of intermediate processors, distributors, or end users; *Supply position,* as represented by control or ownership of important raw material supplies, facilities for creating intermediate components or products, or activities capable of providing needed services.

The magnitude and patterns of the resources in hand or potentially available to the company, at any point in time, determine the range of action alternatives which are realistically *available* to the enterprise at that time.

III. The members operate the resources within an *environment* which provides the enterprise's opportunities for service contributions and which makes certain demands upon the enterprise's performance. Here we are concerned with present and potential *customers'* characteristics, resources, behavior, and preferences; the *supply/demand/price* characteristics of the enterprise's present or contemplated major products or services; existing and potential *competitors'* characteristics, resources, strategic commitments, and activities; present and potential *suppliers'* characteristics, resources, and requirements, and the supply/demand/price characteristics of principal raw materials; *government* constraints, limits, incentives, and assistance; *labor* constraints, demands, and characteristics; the relevant *customs and traditional ways* of doing business in the industry and in the communities and nations in which the enterprise operates; the general *economic conditions* of the relevant communities and nations, affecting employment levels, wage levels, disposable income, and interest rates; the *investment climate,* affecting availability of funds, currently popular investment choices, price/earning ratios, and so on.

The combination of these environmental characteristics determines, within broad limits, what the enterprise *must* do, in order to survive and prosper, and what it *must not* do, except at great peril.

Thus, the environment places certain requirements and constraints upon what the enterprise *must* and *must not* do. The resources available to the enterprise put further limits upon what the enterprise *can* do. Within these limits, the pattern of value commitments, competences, and personal influence among the key members determines what the enterprise *will* do.

In the cases which follow, we will have repeated opportunities to explore the dynamic interplay among a company's environment, resources, and members, in a wide range of different industries and technologies. These three variables give us a convenient way of describing a company's total situation. A "general management point of view" obliges us to focus our attention upon the *relationships* among these variables. We shall continually try to identify the relationships in each situation which are most crucial to the enterprise's survival and success, and to concentrate our efforts upon them. We shall attempt to assign relative emphases and priorities among competing demands and opportunities. Finally, we shall try to make choices and to establish action programs which are consistent with these emphases and priorities. Chapter 3 discusses in some detail the general management functions which are involved in relating environment, resources, and membership to one another.

Mitchell Nursery Company

Mitchell Nursery Company, located in Marysville, California, raised grapevines and fruit and nut trees for sale to commercial farmers and to other nurseries. Marysville, approximately 50 miles north of Sacramento, is situated in one of the nation's largest and most productive agricultural regions.

The material contained in this case is abstracted from an interview, conducted in April, 1961, by Bob Elliott, a Business School casewriter, with Carl Oakes, the general manager of Mitchell Nursery Company. The essence of what Carl Oakes said is presented in his own words.

Oakes: I'd be happy to let you write a case on our company. Besides, I think you can be of real help by letting us know what you think of the way we operate. Ever since I heard Professor Curtis from your School talk a couple of weeks ago on the importance of having definite polices to go by, I realized that this is something we really have to work on. Maybe you can help us there. We have made profits every year, but I can't get away from the feeling that we are always just about to go under. It's this kind of feeling that brings on the ulcers. What I would like to develop is a set of goals and policies on which I can rely to carry us through year in and year out.

As you know, we are in the business of raising fruit and nut trees and grapevines. I would say that 99% of our sales are to farmers and other nurserymen.

John Mitchell and I started the business in 1950 under a partnership agreement. John had been in the nursery business since 1930. He built himself an excellent reputation as a nurseryman over those years. We used his name as the name of the firm in order to build on this reputation.

In 1957 we incorporated, mainly for income tax purposes. We found that we could save on taxes by taxing some of our company income at the corporate rate rather than at our personal income rates. Besides, anything we make outside of our salaries we reinvest in the business.

As an example of our growth, we started with one employee, 50,000 trees, and 25,000 grapevines in 1950. Today we have around 700,000 trees and 500,000 grapevines under cultivation, and a year-round labor force of eleven workers. We have a sales volume of roughly $200,000 a year.

Elliott: What was your background, Carl, before starting in this business?

Oakes: I attended the University of Alaska on the GI Bill and received a Bachelor of Science degree in Business Administration there. I also completed a year of Law School at the University of Washington before coming here.

Elliott: Would you give me an idea of how you're organized?

Oakes: We call this a "ma and pa" organization, meaning that it's family owned. I guess I didn't tell you, John Mitchell is my father-in-law. He's president and chairman of the board. I have the title of secretary-treasurer. To comply with the rules of a corporation, we have also appointed our wives as members of our board of directors. Each of them has the title of vice president. However, most decisions are made by John and myself, and we seldom have board meetings.

I'm in charge of managing the day-to-day operations of the company, including sales. We have no sales force. John used to help out, especially in the sales end of the business, but now he has withdrawn from full-time management of the company. John is 67 years old now. He usually appears at the office every day, though, in order to sign checks. All checks that we issue require the signatures of two of our directors before they will be honored by a bank. John also keeps a close watch on our field operations and helps with the maintenance of our equipment. We rely on him for advice on field problems, since he has faced about all there are in his thirty years in the nursery business.

Reporting directly to me is Steve Taylor, who, if we were to use titles around here, would probably be called the field superintendent. John and I look upon Steve as a partner in the business even though he has no ownership interest. His salary is composed of a fixed amount plus a percentage of sales, and the total usually amounts to more than $10,000 a year. Steve worked for John in John's previous business and came with him to form the new firm in 1950. He was our first employee. I think Steve is an excellent supervisor of our nursery hands, but his chief weakness is that he is reluctant to make decisions on his own. Even though he has enough background in the field to know what to do himself, he refers decisions such as those concerned with soil treatment and purchase of supplies to me. I've been working with Steve to try to get him to make these decisions on his own, and I'm beginning to feel that I can rely on him to assume responsibility for most decisions in the field. The trouble is that John is pretty particular about the way various problems should be tackled. That's the way John operates. I would rather hold Steve accountable for the results and leave the method up to him. What happens now is that Steve usually waits until John tells him what to do before he initiates any action.

Steve relies on two field hands from time to time to act as supervisors. Right now we are renting three fields nearly fifty miles apart for growing our plants. Frequently we have to split our work force to tend two fields on the same day; and this is where our two key hands take over as supervisors. They are paid a salary of $100 a week, while the rest of our field workers are paid wages of from $1.25 to $1.50 an hour.

We have fluctuating employment throughout the year. Spring is our busiest season, so every April we hire from twenty to twenty-five new workers. Out of this group we hope to find four or five dependable workers to take care of the turnover in our year-round working force of eleven or twelve. The grafting techniques which we use in raising our trees require some degree of skill before a worker becomes fully productive. Therefore we want to be fairly certain that a new man can be depended upon as a steady worker. We feel that it is essential that this kind of training be conducted on a continuous basis from job to job. Therefore, we assign the new group of workers each April to planting grapevine cuttings. This work is very tiring. It requires a great deal of bending. By the time all the grapevine cuttings have been planted, all but four or five of the new workers usually have quit. These four or five remaining are then assigned to easier operations such as thinning out seedlings, weeding, pruning, and finally grafting.

Our field workers are either transient Mexicans or whites who you would probably call "Okies." Of the two groups, we have found Mexicans to be the steadiest workers. In fact, one of our two field supervisors is Mexican. We follow the same employment practices as farmers in the area. No fringe benefits are paid. As an incentive to the workers who we want to stay with us, we usually give pay raises in steps of 5¢ or 10¢ an hour above the starting salary of $1.25 an hour.

In our office we have a secretary and a man whom we are training to become office manager. They report directly to me. You have already met Mary, our secretary. She acts as a receptionist and also keeps our account books. The trouble with Mary is that she is pretty rough on some of our customers. I get nervous every time she answers the phone. One day I watched her from my office when the phone rang. She picked up the phone, listened for a few minutes and then loudly said "no" as she slammed the receiver down on the hook. I keep telling her that this kind of behavior certainly won't help our relationship with our customers but it doesn't seem to have any effect on her. Mary is John Mitchell's sister, so I'm afraid this is a situation we're just going to have to live with. You can see some of the difficulties of running a family-owned organization.

Not too long ago, we hired Bill Winters to perform some financial analysis work and to learn the duties of office manager. Bill just finished a commercial high school course in accounting and has a good head on his shoulders. Right now, I have him assigned to a project of compiling and analyzing cost information on the material and labor going into each plant variety that we raise. Since June, a year ago, I've had Steve Taylor turn in a report at the end of each working day which shows the hours and materials spent for each of our varieties. It will take until June 1962 before we obtain all the cost information necessary for this study since it takes two years to process a crop of our yearling trees.

This might be as good a time as any to run down our product line with you, now that you've gotten the picture of our organization. Our products fall into four general categories: grapevines, seedlings, June buds, and yearlings. (See Exhibit 1.)

We grow an annual crop of about 500,000 grapevine plants. These plants are started from cuttings which we obtain from mature vines from vineyards in the area. Except for a few rare varieties we pay nothing for these cuttings, except for the cost of our own labor in obtaining them. We plant these cuttings every April and the plants are ready for sale by the following January. Grapevines account for roughly 10% of our sales.

Seedlings are one year old tree plants which we start from seed each spring. We start about 500,000 each year, and they are ready for transplanting by the following spring. We grow most of our seedlings in order to provide our own rootstock requirements, and sell only a few as seedlings. They only account for 1% or 2% of our sales.

The majority of our trees are propagated by means of a grafting operation called "budding," which is performed on five basic seedling varieties which we term "rootstock." Budding consists of cutting a bud off of a mature tree of the variety we desire and inserting it beneath the bark of the rootstock. After budding has been performed, the tree will take on the characteristics of the tree from which the bud was cut. The rootstock is developed to grow well in given soil conditions and to resist disease. Any one of our rootstocks could form a base for many different trees. For example, a Lovell peach seedling is commonly used as a rootstock for around fifty varieties of trees in the peach, almond, and nectarine families.

June buds are our most important product category. We produce about 300,000 June buds each year. These are budded during a six weeks period, usually starting in late April on rootstock we started from seed the previous year. Once the buds have taken hold, we cut off the stem of the plant directly above the bud in order to force all further growth up through the bud. We sell about 140 total varieties of peach, nectarine,

exhibit 1

MITCHELL NURSERY COMPANY

Summary of Product Line

Product	Number of Basic Varieties	Total Number Produced Each Year	Length of Growing Cycle	% of Total Sales in Dollars	
June Buds	140	300,000	1 year spring to spring	70%	80% to orchardists 20% to nurseries
Yearling Trees	90	200,000	1½ years fall to spring	20%	20% to orchardists 80% to nurseries
Grapevines	5	500,000	9 months Apr. to Jan.	10%	100% to vitaculturists
Seedlings	5	500,000	1 year spring to spring	Intermediate product used for production of June Buds and Yearlings	

300,000
40,000

[1]Summarized by casewriter from information given in the case.

1. *June buds*—trees which are "budded" in late April, May, and early June, on rootstock started from seed the previous year.

After buds are firmly established, the stem of the rootstock above the bud is removed, and subsequent growth is entirely through the bud.

These trees are cared for over the full year following "budding," and are sold in June (hence the name) for immediate transplanting. Such trees will not reach bearing for six to seven years after transplanting in the buyer's orchard.

2. *Yearling trees*—similar to June buds, except that the rootstock is budded in the fall and the

bud is left dormant until the following spring before removing the rootstock stem above it.

These trees are cared for over the full year following removal of the stem and are sold in the late spring for transplanting. After transplanting, they will reach bearing approximately one year sooner than June buds, since the rootstock is six months older at the time of budding and the bud is six months older at the time of transplanting.

3. *Seedlings*—trees started from seed each spring for use as rootstock. "June buds" are grafted, in the spring, onto year-old seedlings. "Yearling" trees are grafted, in the fall, onto year-and-a-half old seedlings.

4. *Grapevines*—rooted plants started from cuttings each April and sold the following January.

and almond June buds each spring and they usually account for about 70% of our total sales volume.

Our other major product category is yearling trees. Each fall, over approximately a two month period, we bud the rootstock which are to form our yearling trees. Generally, about 200,000 trees are budded at this time. The bud is allowed to lie dormant until the following spring. Then we cut off the stem above the bud and allow the tree to grow for a year before it is sold. That's where it gets its name. We sell nearly fifty varieties of almond trees in the yearling form and also about forty total varieties of apple, apricot, cherry, pear, plum, prune, persimmon, and walnut trees. Yearlings account for about 20% of our annual sales.

Elliott: I noticed that some of the varieties you mention could be sold either as June buds or as yearlings. What is the difference between the two?

Oakes: Most of the trees we sell can be sold in either form. Some farmers plant their orchards with yearlings because they are a more mature and slightly larger tree than the June buds. Of course, they also cost a little more than the June buds.

That reminds me, I haven't told you how we break down our sales between the wholesale and the retail portions of our market. We call sales to other nurseries wholesale sales. Direct sales to farmers are called retail sales. Nearly 80% of our June bud volume is sold to retail accounts. On the other hand, only 20% of our yearling sales are sold to retail accounts. However, the retail portion of our business is increasing. I've been working to build up this side of the business, since we have to give a standard discount of 40% on any sales to other nurseries. Of course, they grant us the same terms when we buy trees from them.

One thing that selling to wholesale accounts achieves is a broadening of our market areas. I can hardly keep on top of our local market, which consists of Sutter, Yuba, Colusa, and Butte Counties. What I generally do is see how much retail sales I can generate in this local area and then I sell the rest of the trees to wholesale accounts. Of course, sometimes several nurseries get together and agree to have one of their number supply all of their needs of a variety that is demanded in only small quantities in any one area. Another thing that our wholesale sales do is to compensate for the effects of a bad prediction as to what the market demand for a given variety of tree will be. Sometimes when the demand for a tree is off in one area, it will be high in another.

It is necessary for us to make projections of what the demand will be one year ahead of time in the case of June buds and two years ahead of time in the case of yearlings. It's hard to see just what the demand will be because it is typical of the farmer to plant peach trees, for example, in a year when the market for peaches is particularly good. If the market is bad for peaches, he won't buy peach trees even though it will take from five to seven years before any trees he buys will achieve full production. So what generally happens is that in five or seven years after a good peach year you can expect an over-supply of peaches which will drive peach prices down and cause a poor market both for peaches and for peach trees. I try to convince every farmer I talk to that they should plant the tree that will grow best on their land regardless of the prevailing market conditions. However, I can't say that my efforts have met with any great measure of success.

The penalty for making a bad estimate of market demand is that any tree that we can't sell we burn. If we were to hold our trees over until the next season, they would reach a size that would make it difficult to transplant them successfully. One step which we have recently taken to reduce some of these losses is that we won't dig any trees out of the ground until a firm order for delivery has been placed. Before, we used to dig and tie up all of our plants at the same time. We have found that by working overtime, if necessary, we can still fill any order within twenty-four hours under the new system.

Often, we will also underestimate the demand for a tree. Even if we knew exactly how much of each variety to plant or bud, we never know how much we will be able to harvest because of the factor of disease. We never know when a disease will strike our plants. In some years we have lost as much as $5,000 worth of trees from disease. It was this factor alone that caused our poor profit picture in 1959.

Elliott: How much of your stock do you have to destroy in a given year?

Oakes: Anywhere from 10% in a good year to as much as 50% in some poor years. That is why it is common in the nursery business to offer a 20% discount to anyone who places his order for trees before the trees have been budded. This requires placing your order a year ahead of time for June buds or a year-and-a-half ahead of time in the case of yearlings. I would say that roughly 60% of our June bud sales are contract sales but only 20% of our yearling sales are on a contract basis. The contract method of buying is designed to save us the cost of stock losses, and we make the point that we pass this saving on to the buyer through the discount he receives. (Portions of the 1961 price list appear as Exhibit 2.)

Elliott: Thanks . . . how do you determine what prices to charge?

Oakes: I just copy them from the price list of our largest competitor, the Foothills Nursery located just south of Sacramento. The list prices of all the nurseries in this area are pretty identical, but don't let this fool you. We still have price competition. Each of us adjusts his price to the competitive conditions existing when we are trying to sell our trees. We do this by adjusting the discounts we offer the buyers. For example, a commonly advertised discount on contract orders for June buds is 10% throughout the state. Right now, however, I'm advertising in the *Marysville Weekly* a 20% discount on contract sales because I know the Bischoff Nursery, located on the opposite end of town, is offering a 20% discount.

This whole matter of pricing is a major problem area for us. Once I was approached by several other nurserymen who asked me to hold my price on a certain line of trees. I agreed to do this since I have always tried to keep my prices as stable as possible; but the next thing I found was that my sales volume on this line of trees began to drop off. When I looked into the matter, I found my competitors had simply turned around after visiting me and lowered their prices. The next time they came around, I told them that from now on I will adjust my own prices

exhibit 2

MITCHELL NURSERY COMPANY

Samples of 1961 Price List

SEEDLINGS

No. California Black Walnut

2-3 feet (tall)	$ .30
3-4 feet	.40
4-6 feet	.45
6-8 feet	.50

Chinese Wingnut (Pterocarya Stenoptera

Add 20 ¢ to the above prices

Paradox (Black Walnut Hybrid)

1-2 feet	$1.00
2-3 feet	1.25
3-4 feet	1.50
4-6 feet	1.75
6-8 (up)	2.00

Mazzard—Mahaleb—Pear

1/4"-5/16" (dia. at base of trunk)	$ .20
5/16"-3/8"	.30
3/8"-1/2"	.40
1/2"-5/8"	.45
5/8"-up	.50

JUNE BUDS

Almonds

Lovell Rootstock

Davey—Drake—Mission (Texas) Jordanolo

NePlus—Nonpareil—Peerless varieties

3/16"-1/4" (diameter)	$ .30
1/4"-5!66"	.50
5/16"-3/8"	.60
3/8"-1/2"	.65
1/2"-up	.75

Apples

Apple Rootstock

Red Delicious—Yellow Delicious—Red June

Roman Beauty—Winesap—Red Rome— Jonathan—

Red Gravenstein

5/16"-3/8" (diameter)	$ .65
3/8"-1/2"	.70
1/2"-5/8"	.80
5/8"-3/4"	.90
3/4"-up	1.00

Apricots

Peach—Apricot—Myrobolen 29-c Root Blenheim—Tilton

5/16"-3/8" (diameter)	$ .50
3/8"-1/2"	.65
1/2"-5/8"	.75
5/8"-3/4"	.85
3/4"-up	.90

Grapevines

Rooted Cuttings

Thomoson Seedless—Grenache—Carigane Mission—French Columbard (varieties) No. 1 Well-Rooted Vines

$75.00 per M

YEARLINGS

Almonds

Lovell Rootstock

Davey—Drake—Mission (Texas) Jordanolo

NePlus—Nonpareil—Peerless Varieties

5/16"-3/8" (diameter)	$ .60
1/4"-5/16"	.65
1/2"-5/8"	.75
5/8"-3/4"	.80
3/4"-1"	.85
1"-up	.90

Add 10 cents to above prices for Resistant, Almond, Mariana, and Myro 29-c Root

Plums & Prunes

Mariana 26-24—Myro 29-c Roots

La Roda	Satsuma
Santa Rosa	French Improves

5/16"-3/8"	$ .60
3/8"-1/2"	.70
1/2"-5/8"	.80
5/8"-3/4"	.85
3/4"-up	.90

CONTRACT GROWING	DELIVERY
We grow many special orders and would be happy to handle yours for you. We extend special prices for contract orders. Ask about them. We will grow any amount for you, and you may select your own source of budwood or scion wood or we will furnish it for you from the best sources available. Contract growing saves you money and assures you of the grades and variety you want. No order too small.	Delivery is made on any order where the size of the order and the distance warrant it. Packing is done at cost and where shipping is necessary it is collect by the best methods. *Commercial Prices*—This list applies only to commercial growers and in most cases is for commercial quantities only. Prices subject to change without notice.

any time I see fit. Would it interest you to see the discounts we allowed on last year's sales?

Elliott: Yes, it would.

Oakes called to the next office to Bill Winters and asked him to bring in an analysis which the latter had prepared. Oakes introduced the men, who exchanged greetings. Winters then handed Oakes a sheet of paper which listed various discount categories, the total dollar amounts allowed in each category throughout 1960, and the average discount allowed. Having done this, Winters left. Elliott questioned Oakes as to the basis for each of the discount categories and jotted this down on Winters' analysis sheet. The information he received is shown in Exhibit 3. He then resumed the conversation as follows:

exhibit 3

MITCHELL NURSERY COMPANY

Analysis of Discounts Granted on 1960 June Bud Sales

Discount	Reason for Granting	Dollar Amount of Discount	Average Size of Discount
50%	Replacement sales	$ 1,477.39	$ 48.75
40%	Wholesale customers	1,221.16	384.21
25%	Sales to Co-op groups		43,63
20%	Contract sales	13,722.25	57.65
15%	Negotiated	53.32	53.32
10%	Negotiated	3,228.11	73.37
		$21,360.28	

Total of 1960 June Bud Sales: approximately $125,000, after discounts.

Source: Compiled from company records by Bill Winters.

Elliott: Would you please explain, Carl, the discount category which you call "replacement sales."

Oakes: This is the discount we allow to farmers who buy trees to replace those they lost during the previous year. We adopted this policy two years ago. In other words, we will replace 50% of the trees which are lost during the first year after we sell them. We used to try to judge each case of loss separately on the basis of the cause of the loss. If we could trace the loss to the farmer, for example, if he accidentally cut their roots with a disk harrow, or his plants died through lack of water, he had to buy the replacement trees himself. The trouble with this system was that we often had to rely on the farmer's word as to the cause of loss, and this tended to make liars out of a lot of people. With our present replacement policy, we are sure of at least covering the out-of-pocket costs involved in raising replacement trees.

The whole area of pricing is a real concern to me. I think this is our major problem area. I hate to keep changing my prices from year to year. Yet what happens is that we charge high prices in good years and lower them in poor ones, just as our competitors do. I don't think this helps our customer relations at all. Sometimes I have to lower my prices in the middle of one selling season when I see that the demand for a particular tree is lower than expected. Then what happens is that the farmers who bought this tree earlier in the season hear of the lower price and ask me why I charged them a higher price. I have to make an adjustment on their bills, or else lose them as customers. Another thing I'm faced with is that farmers, who have a large order to place, really shop around to negotiate for a low price. Some nurseries will sell their trees at cost to a volume buyer if they think that otherwise they might have to burn them. The trouble is that once you grant a farmer a lower price he will expect the same price in the future. When a nurseryman does sell at cost he finds it pretty hard to get any cooperation from the rest of us whenever he needs any of our trees. I would rather burn my trees than grant a discount larger than our wholesale discount of 40%.

What I would like to come up with is some form of stable pricing. One possibility I'm considering is a discount schedule which will give recognition to those customers who will agree to place all their business with us as long as we carry the trees they want. Here is one idea I've had on what such a discount schedule would look like. See what you think of it. (Schedule shown in Exhibit 4.)

You'll notice that this schedule shows the same discount that we are presently giving for trees or grapevines grown to order. But it also gives discounts for volume orders. This is designed to keep the farmer from shopping around when he has a large order to place. This schedule of mine also gives recognition to customers who pay their bills on time. Too often a farmer tends to look upon a nurseryman as he would a bank . . . in other words, to help him finance his orchard.

exhibit 4

MITCHELL NURSERY COMPANY

Proposed Discount Schedule

	June Bud		Yearling		Grapevine	
	Size of Order ($)	Discount (%)	Size of Order ($)	discount (%)	Size of Order ($)	Discount (%)
Contract Customers						
Any amount grown to order		20		20		10
Any amount *not* grown to order		10		none		5
Quantity discounts in addition to the above listed discounts	500-999	5	500-999	5	1,000-3,999	5
	1,000-1,999	10	1,000-1,999	10	4,000-up	*
	2,000-4,999	15	2,000-4,999	15		
	5,000-9,999	20	5,000-9,999	20		
	10,000-up		10,000-up	*		
Noncontract Customers						
Any amount grown to order		20		20		10
Any amount *not* grown to order		none		none		none
Quantity discounts in addition to the above listed discounts	1,000-4,999	5	1,000-3,999	5	2,000-3,999	5
	5,000-9,999	10	4,000-4,999	7	4,000-up	*
	10,000-up	*	5,000-9,999	10		
			10,000-up	*		

Conditions: A contract customer is defined as one who agrees to place all of his orders for plants with the Mitchell Nursery. If the Nursery cannot supply him, he may then purchase his plant requirements elsewhere. The contract customer must also fulfill the following conditions: (1) Each order must be firm and not subject to cancellations or changes, unless by mutual consent, and at no loss to the Nursery. (2) The order requires a deposit of 20% of the total order at the time of placing the order. (3) The balance must be paid within 30 days of delivery. If not, all discounts will be forfeited and the account becomes due at the listed price and the purchaser must sign a note at 6% interest for the outstanding balance.

1 By negotiation.

Source: Carl Oakes.

I don't have any idea of whether this idea will work or whether the discounts I've listed are realistic. Several of my customers, however, agreed in principle to the idea, although I didn't go into detail in describing how the discount schedule would look.

Elliott: Would you describe the kind of competition you're faced with, Carl?

Oakes: I would say that our main competition comes from three other nurseries. I think I've already mentioned Foothills Nursery in Sacramento. This is one of the largest nurseries in the state but I think it only has a limited effect on our sales because about 80% of its business is derived from selling ornamental trees. The next largest competitor is a large commercial nursery located in Merced. He sells throughout the state too, but I would say he has only a limited effect in our area because he is fairly far away. Our chief competitor is from the Bischoff Nursery located across the river in Yuba City. I would estimate that they have about three times our sales volume, in other words, around $600,000 a year in sales. However, they don't do as much actual growing as we do. They buy most of their stock from other nurseries. Bischoff employs four salesmen who sell its stock throughout the state.

Elliott: Do you know how well you're doing in relation to these firms in terms of market share and profitability?

Oakes: As far as market share goes, I would say that we obtain 50% to 60% of the sales of June buds, which is our specialty, in our local market area. I don't know what our share of the local yearling market is. There is not much demand for yearlings around here. We sell most of our yearlings through other nurseries.

I don't know how well our competitors are doing in profitability in relation to us. All except Foothills Nursery are family owned and therefore don't publish any financial statements. I never bothered to try to get a financial statement from Foothills Nursery because most of their business is in ornamental trees.

All the competitors I've mentioned are much larger than we are. We feel that we have to keep growing just to remain where we are relative to our competition. Otherwise, I can see no advantage in growth. In fact, there are quite a few disadvantages. For one thing you start losing control of things and for another you probably will start running into labor problems. One thing I know from asking around is that none of our competitors, despite their size, have any idea of what their costs are for each of their products. I think we can learn a lot from this cost study which I have Bill Winters doing.

One thing I'm wondering about is whether we would do any better by employing a salesman. To attract a salesman we would have to pay him a commission of 20%, which is standard for the industry. Right now, I'm doing all the direct selling for the company, but with the other demands on my time, I'm unable to make regular calls on the farmers even in our own local area. Therefore, we try to encourage the farmers through our advertising to stop in at the office to talk to us, and we rely heavily on repeat sales from our customers. Roughly 80% of our sales are repeat business. The trouble is, in a lot of cases, we can't rely on any long standing relationship with the customer to ensure his continued business. I remember one farmer I stopped to chat with last week. When I saw that he had some new trees in his field that weren't ours, I asked him where he got them. He replied that he had purchased them from Bischoff Nursery because they had come directly to him to solicit his business. I told him that I had been planning all along to drop by but that business had me tied up. I told him this knowing that I really hadn't considered calling on him, thinking that it would be unnecessary to do so to get his business. As another example, one of my long standing customers placed a large order with Foothills Nursery because Foothills filled a small order for him several years back when we had run out of the variety he wanted.

One method we use to aid us in selling is to buy our fertilizers and insecticides from local dealers. We split our orders among these dealers hoping they will return the favor by recommending us to the farmers they deal with. Seldom do we have a large enough requirement for these supplies at any one time to make it worthwhile to purchase them out of town or to look for volume discounts by buying from one firm.

Frequently farmers will ask us to recommend a particular variety of tree which would be most profitable for them to grow. Many nurseries take advantage of this to push a particular variety which they want to sell. However, when I consider that a farmer's future livelihood is completely tied up in his orchard, I'm pretty reluctant to make any specific recommendations on the exact variety he should plant in that orchard. Instead I point out the pros and cons of each possible alternative and leave the final decision to him. A sharp businessman could probably have done wonders with this business. We have tended to look at the business, perhaps too much, from the standpoint of the farmer since our business is pretty much of a farming operation in its own right.

Elliott: You mentioned advertising. What kinds of advertising do you use?

Oakes: We have been spending from $2,000 to $3,000 a year on advertising for the past two years. The largest portion of this money was spent on direct mail advertising. We have a mailing list of some 1,500 farmers and we try to send them two mailings a year. One of these mailings is a postcard which asks former customers to give an estimate of the number of trees they would require to replace those they had lost. We ask them to indicate on the card the year the trees were planted. When we receive these cards, we use them to anticipate the stock we must reserve for replacements—the number of free replacements which we will have to provide. You might want to take a look at the other mailing which we send out. We are also using a copy of this letter (see Exhibit 5) as an advertisement in the *Marysville Weekly,* which is the only other advertising outlet that we use. Bischoff Nursery also uses the *Marysville Weekly* for advertising purposes. All of our competitors use newspaper advertising, and the larger ones also run ads in the *Pacific Coast Nurseryman and Supply Dealer* magazine.

Elliott: How do you stand in relationship to your competitors as far as quality goes?

Oakes: I would say that none of our competitors have any better quality than we do. Some have much worse. Quality is a factor which tends to vary in importance with the market conditions in a given year. When the demand for a particular tree is high, quality is not as important a factor as when the demand for that variety is low. In general, I think price is a more important factor than quality. However, I think that farmers are

exhibit 5

MITCHELL NURSERY COMPANY

Sample of Recent Direct Mail Advertisement [1]

April 25, 1961

Dear Mr. ————

In a very few days, we will again be budding. Yes, our June budding is early this season. Our ground is new, and the stock looks exceptionally good. We have nematode resistant rootstocks, Fort Valley and Rancho Resistant, as well as the ever-dependable Lovell on which to bud the varieties of your choice. Or, if you prefer, we can June bud you trees on almond rootstock.

We will use budwood of your choice or supply buds from orchards that we have personally selected as the best available. By working in cooperation with the University of California, the Bureau of Nursery Service, and the U. S. Department of Agriculture, we have selected and indexed many trees that respond negatively to the common virus diseases. We would like to discuss with you our methods of budwood selection, and have you visit our growing grounds. We think you will be impressed with what you see. We are proud of our results.

Important too is the 20% prebud discount on orders placed before June 1st. You will be assured of the trees you want, and we will save by budding the right varieties. We pass the saving along to you.

We would appreciate your call for an appointment if you are interested in placing an order now. We will be glad to call on you at your convenience to talk over your planting plans. Thank you.

Sincerely yours,

MITCHELL NURSERY COMPANY

[1] Text to be reproduced in *Marysville Weekly*.

becoming more quality conscious. To maintain our quality standards, I have Steve Taylor inspect every tree in each order that goes out. This usually requires all of Steve's time in the spring, when we fill nearly all of our orders. To give you an idea of our standards, out of a 5,500 tree order, for example, we provide 5,000 top trees on the average. The remaining 500 trees will be of average quality. To help ensure that a farmer will be satisfied with the quality of trees that we sell him, I have Steve include 5 or 6 extra trees for every 1,000 trees in each order.

The State Department of Agriculture exercises control over the quality of new trees being planted within the State. However, quality inspections are carried out at the county level. Therefore, inspection standards tend to be lenient for trees shipped within a county in which the nursery is located. For any trees we sell outside of this country, inspection standards vary according to the county we are sending the shipment to. We make all of our shipments by truck. While in transit, these shipments are subject to State inspection at any time and we are required to have identification markings for each variety we ship. We always make it a practice to more than fulfill the State's quality standards.

As you probably noticed in that advertisement I showed you, we stress the point that we carefully select the budwood that we use. Obtaining good budwood is the most important factor in determining the quality of trees we sell. If any of our budwood comes from a diseased tree, the disease will be carried over to the new tree formed by the bud. Sometimes the effect of these diseases won't show up for five or seven years after we have budded a tree. To obtain the budwood required for a particular variety of tree, I look for the best producing orchard of that variety in the State. One or two years before we cut the budwood from that orchard, I call the "pathology boys" from the California Department of Agriculture and ask them to test the trees for virus infections. This testing is necessary because often a tree will not show symptoms of a virus which it is carrying. The tests which are performed are similar to a battery of allergy tests for humans. The pathology boys mark each symptomless carrier that they find with white paint. Right now, I'm working on a system of indexing all the acceptable trees for budwood selection in the orchards that we use. Here is an example of what we're doing. (Oakes showed Elliott a map he had drawn of an orchard with each tree numbered and X's drawn over the diseased trees.) The trouble is that even after I have shown my workers how to use an index map and how to spot a tree that shows every symptom of having a disease, I still find it necessary to keep a close check on the men cutting budwood to make sure that they're not cutting from the wrong tree. The average worker simply will not concern himself with the critical importance to our business of obtaining disease-free budwood. I have attempted to find a man whom I can entrust with the responsibility of indexing budwood sources and supervising the cutting operation. For about a year, I trained a man who looked like he could handle this job. He was a graduate of the University of California Agricultural School. Unfortunately, I was unable to keep him with us. It wasn't the fact that he was able to obtain higher wages elsewhere so much as he couldn't cope with the long working hours and six day week which we required him to put in.

In this business we keep the same hours as the farmers in the area. The only holidays we observe are Christmas, New Year's, and the opening day of trout season. I guess that I put in an average of twelve hours a day running the business. After all, I can't quit before the farmers do and they work whenever there is enough light. I try to keep in contact with the farmers by stopping to chat every time I see one working in his fields. Oftentimes, too, a farmer will stop in at night at my home on his way into town.

Elliott: I noticed that somewhere in your price list you mentioned patented tree varieties.

Oakes: Yes, we sell about 23 patented varieties of almond and nectarine trees. We have obtained these varieties on licensing agreements from the patent holders. I am attempting to carry out a program of developing new strains myself, although any work I do is done in my spare time and in a pretty haphazard fashion. As yet, I have developed no patents of my own, but I have several varieties under test. One of the problems associated with developing new stock varieties is that it takes a long testing period to establish what characteristics can be expected from a new tree. It usually takes about seven years of growth in the area where you want to sell the tree before the advantages of a new tree can be completely assessed. I am constantly looking for new varieties to put in our line but before I take any one, I require that it have a seven year history of growth in our region. To help out with this testing program, when I think a new variety might be suited for our area, I try to convince a farmer around here to raise several trees at no cost to him except for the land he uses for growing them.

Every new strain of tree that is developed is patentable. However, it is unusual for a patent holder to obtain a full seventeen year monopoly on his product. It is easy to get around a patent, for example, by changing the ripening period by one day. However, seldom does anyone resort to this. The factor that limits the useful life of a patent most is that even better strains are developed each year.

Besides looking for new strains that will grow well in our area, I also spend a great deal of my time looking for new fertilizers, insecticides, and bactericides. I try to keep in close contact with the California School of Agriculture, the State Agricultural Department, and Shell Oil's Research Laboratory. In fact, I try to pick the brains of anyone I come across who is familiar with developments in any of these areas. I also make my fields available as experimental grounds for testing new products.

I would love to hire a man full time just to do research for us. The problem is finding enough money to carry on this work. If someone came along tomorrow and offered to invest $20,000 in getting our research program under way, I wouldn't hesitate a minute in accepting it. But when it comes to supplying your own money to do this, the question becomes more difficult. You have to ask yourself how long you must wait before you get a return on this money.

Elliott: (Pointing out the window)—Are those some of your growing grounds over there?

Oakes: No, that is just a small plot of trees that we are experimenting with. All of our growing grounds are on land that we rent from farmers in the area. By renting we can rotate our fields whenever the nutrients in the soil need replenishing. If ever our sales volume should increase we can also rent more land to add to our growing grounds. Right now, we have a field on either side of the Sacramento Valley. These two are about 50 miles apart. A third field is located on the Feather River, just east of here. Would it interest you to see some of our field operations?

Elliott: Yes, certainly. Shall we use my car?

Oakes: No, better use mine; the roads are pretty rough.

It was about a half hour drive to one of the company's fields, which was located on the east side of the Sacramento Valley. While they were driving, Oakes told Elliott that the bulk of the work which had to be performed by the laborers in the field was hand labor usually requiring the worker to be on his knees throughout his normal nine hour working day. For operations which were easily mechanized, such as plowing, cultivating, fertilizing, dusting, and digging, the company owned five tractors and auxiliary equipment. He said that the company also owned its own irrigation equipment which included pumps, aluminum pipes, and sprinkler systems. Contrary to what might be expected, he said that the biggest irrigation problem in past years had been encountered on the field nearest the Feather River. The reason for this was that during the dry season the river water used for irrigation built up a salt concentration which was harmful to the plants. The water which they pumped from irrigation ditches for their other fields did not exhibit as great a problem in this regard. Irrigation water was provided to the area free of charge since the cost of providing this service was paid for out of the revenues obtained from the electrical power developed from the system.

When they arrived at the field, Oakes led Elliott over to a group of people working their way on their hands and knees up a row of plants of about 200 yards in length. The group consisted of four men and one woman. As they approached, one of the men stood up and Oakes introduced Elliott to Steve Taylor. Taylor said that the group was performing the budding operation. Elliott observed that each of the men carried a supply of slender branches from which they would cut off a sliver containing a bud with a sharp knife. They would then make a T-shaped incision in the bark on the main stem of each plant and insert the bud. The woman in the group followed behind and tied up each incision with strips of rubber.

Oakes then walked up and down various rows in the field inspecting the growth progress of his plants and checking for signs of disease. He stopped to chat for a few minutes with a tractor operator who was dusting insecticides on one section of the field.

Oakes then drove Elliott to the field which was located on the banks of the Feather River. He inspected several areas of this field and then showed Elliott an orchard he had planted for the farmer who owned the land. He said that the nursery had planted this orchard as payment for the rent charged for the use of the field.

When they had returned to the office, Elliott questioned Oakes as to the company's finances:

Elliott: Are there any financial statements available which I could use for writing this case?

Oakes: The only statements that we draw up are annual income tax statements.

Elliott: Do you have any balance sheets available, say for the last three years?

Oakes: We had a balance sheet drawn up when we incorporated the firm back in 1957. I'll see if I can locate this for you. We haven't had a balance sheet made up since then. Maybe our depreciation schedule will be of help to you. I think I can find a copy of this also.

Elliott: Fine. How do you keep track of the company's financial condition at any one time?

Oakes: I keep tabs on our current finances by cosigning all of our checks and making sure that our bank balance is not overdrawn. Our balance usually varies from about $70,000 at the end of each spring to zero at the end of each fall. We follow a policy of incurring no debts and paying all bills on time and taking all discounts which are allowed for fast payments. I follow up overdue receivables myself. I have only had to sue for payment in court on two or three occasions. Once, however, a man filed bankruptcy, sold his farm, and skipped out of town owing us $5,300. Whenever we need short-term loans in order to pay our bills, either myself or John Mitchell provide these funds from our personal accounts. We charge a 6% rate of interest. Even if we were to discard our policy of not incurring debts, we have very little equity on which to secure a loan.

The company owns no land and our inventory is considered a poor risk by a bank. In fact, we make no attempt to value our inventory at any one time. The growth we have achieved thus far has been out of profits of the firm. We apply these profits toward purchasing new equipment. If we ever feel we have to grow faster than this, John and I might be able to obtain funds from a bank through mortgages on the homes which we own. If we did this, we would probably contribute an equal amount of money since we each have a 50% interest in the company. We would both be reluctant to obtain additional financing through issuing stock since this would impose the risk of losing control of the company. We feel that we want to maintain control of this company in our family. Someday, I hope my son will take over management of the firm.

Elliott: I think I've got a pretty complete picture of your business, Carl. Do you think we have covered all your problem areas?

Oakes: Let me see; I've talked about our pricing difficulties and the question of whether we should hire a salesman. In the production area, I told you about the problem of predicting how much of each variety of tree to grow when you have the factors of disease and fluctuating demand to contend with. We also have the problem of attracting dependable workers and getting them to assume responsibilities. I mentioned the difficulty I have in finding enough time to keep abreast of new developments and to develop our own new strains of trees. John Mitchell doesn't think this is as important as I do. I have a tough time convincing him that the time I spend on research is well worth it. As far as our finances go, I keep wondering whether the company could pull through if we ever lost money for two years in a row. It wouldn't take much for this to happen if our plants are hard hit by disease and we miss on our predictions of the market. Considering the risks that a company like ours has to face, I think we should be earning more money than we have been just to compensate for the risk factor.

Well, I think those are our major difficulties. Don't you think we have enough of them? I'm really anxious to hear the suggestions the students in your business school have for coping with these problems. I especially want their comments on that discount schedule I'm thinking of using. A firm pricing policy, I think, is our most important requirement.

Elliott obtained from Oakes a copy of the company's 1957 balance sheet and a depreciation schedule for its buildings and equipment. He also obtained copies of the tax statements which the company turned in each year since its incorporation. Elliott thanked Oakes for the information he had obtained and told him that he would contact him as soon as he had written a draft of the case.

From Mitchell Nursery's depreciation schedule, Elliott learned that the company valued its buildings, trucks, tractors, and equipment at their original cost of $56,000. Depreciation charges of $31,000 had been applied against this amount giving the buildings and equipment a net value in 1961 of $25,000.

The straight line method for calculating depreciation was used. From the company's income tax statements, Elliott prepared the income statements which are shown in Exhibit 6. The firm's actual 1957 balance sheet and an estimated 1961 balance sheet, prepared by Elliott, are shown in Exhibit 7. Exhibit 8 shows a summary of company personnel records.

Some relevant information on the California nursery industry, gathered by Elliott, is reproduced in Appendix A.

exhibit 6

MITCHELL NURSERY COMPANY

Income Statements for Years Ending June 30

	1960	1959	1958
Sales	$183,427	$198,585	$163,344
Purchased Plants	15,025	43,863	13,001
Gross Profits	$168,402	$154,722	$150,343
Expenses:			
Officers' salaries	$ 30,225[1]	$ 30,000[1]	$ 20,000
Wages	64,810	69,271	50,411
Repairs	2,993	2,912	670
Rent	3,571	2,466	3,084
Interest	488	50	250
Taxes	8,223	10,276	7,072
Depreciation & Amortization	7,402	7,465	6,979
Advertising	2,430	3,211	864
Gasoline & Lubrication	3,331	3,491	2,976
Fertilizer & Insecticides	12,444	12,678	8,415
Machine hire	361	179	190
Dues & Subscriptions	204	244	203
Utilities	622	297	293
Insurance	2,000	1,934	1,423
Legal & Accounting	355	155	225
Office supplies	935	372	313
Supplies & Small tools	9,512	6,103	7,679
Telephone	717	716	397
Miscellaneous	1,037	1,409	1,606
	$151,660	$153,229	$113,050
Net Income before Income Tax	$ 16,742	$ 1,493	37,293
Tax	5,021	448	13,892
Net Income	$ 11,721	$ 1,045	$23,401

[1]Includes a bonus of $5,000 each to John Mitchell and Carl Oakes.

Source: Company income tax returns and compilations of casewriter.

exhibit 7

MITCHELL NURSERY COMPANY

Balance Sheet July 1, 1957

Assets

Noncurrent Assets	Cost	Depreciation	Book Value
Office Equipment	$ 1,094	$ 375	$ 719
Other Equipment	22,756	8,565	14,191
Trucks	6,343	2,301	4,042
Buildings—Portable	5,375	845	4,530
Total	$35,568	$12,086	$23,482
Goodwill			10,000
Total Assets			$33,482

Liabilities and Capital

Liabilities	None	
Capital		
John Mitchell	16,741	
Carl Oakes	16,741	
Total Liabilities and Capital		$33,482

	Cost	Depreciation	Book Value
Capital equipment, buildings, etc.	$56,000	$31,000	$25,000
Goodwill			$10,000
			$35,000
Liabilities			None
Capital			
John Mitchell		$17,500	
Carl Oakes		17,500	
			$35,000

exhibit 8

MITCHELL NURSERY COMPANY

Positions in Company and Salary for Each

Position	Occupied by	Salary in 1960	Years with Firm
President	John Mitchell	$15,000/year	12
Secretary-Treas.	Carl Oakes	$15,000/year	12
Field Supervisor	Steve Taylor	$10,000/year	12
Field Foreman	2 "key" workers	$100/week	7
Office Manager	Bill Winters	$350/month	1
Secretary	Mary Mitchell	$250/month	6
Laborers	5 to 30 workers	$1.25 to $1.50/hour	3 mos. to 5 yrs.
Vice Presidents	Mrs. Mitchell and Mrs. Oakes	$300/year (each)	12

[1]$5,000 of this amount was considered a "bonus." Oakes stated that he could likely earn a salary of $10,000/year working for another nursery.

Source: Oakes.

appendix A

NOTES ON THE CALIFORNIA NURSERY INDUSTRY *

The California nursery industry is an important part of the agricultural economy of the state and nation. According to the 1950 U.S. Census of Agriculture, the state leads in the production of all nursery stock. The wholesale value of the crops grown in 1949 by the 535 producing nurseries (out of 2,500 in the state) that filed returns was $10,789,239 or 15.2 per cent of the national total.[1] This was more than the next two states combined. California also led in the production of ornamental nursery stock (15.0 per cent of the U.S. total); floricultural plants, rooted cuttings, and other material for growing on (17.8 per cent);

---

* These notes are excerpts from the *U.S. System for Producing Healthy Container-Grown Plants,* K. F. Baker (ed), Division of Agricultural Sciences, University of California, September, 1957. Reprinted by permission.

[1] That this figure is very conservative is shown by the 1954 farm valuation ($33,324,980) of nursery stock in 12 southern California counties. This was tenth among 66 farm commodities for the area.

bedding and vegetable plants (16.5 per cent); and lining-out stock (10.9 per cent).

There were 6,676 nurseries and other outlets licensed for plant sales in the state in 1954–55.

EFFECT OF ECONOMIC CHANGES

Recent economic changes in California are making it increasingly important to reduce the cost of fighting diseases, and to avoid the occasional heavy losses they may cause. These changes also make it more important to find ways of cutting labor cost and saving space, and make mechanization more necessary.

Land Values, Tax Rates, and Zoning Restrictions Are Increasing

Increasing population pressure in the state is bringing about real estate development, rising land values, higher taxes, and zoning restrictions. From 1940 to 1950 the population increased by slightly more than one-half, and one-third of the state's dwelling units were constructed. In the Los Angeles and San Francisco–Oakland areas the population increased 37.6 and 41.6 per cent respectively during that period. Growers are finding that these developments collectively create one of the worst pressures they face today, and many are contemplating moving to rural areas.

On the other hand, the larger population will provide an expanding local market and eventually reduce out-of-state shipment. The immediate effect, however, is to sharpen the interest in techniques, such as soil treatment, that will reduce cost of production.

Labor Costs Are Increasing

Labor costs are increasing rapidly because of both increased pay scale and decreased work output. This has led directly to a growing interest in labor-saving methods and devices, mechanization, and reduction of erratic crop losses.

There are many indications that competition is intensifying in the nursery business, and that the financial returns to growers are decreasing. There are two ways nurserymen can meet this situation:

1. They may *reduce production cost* through improved culture, mechanization, and reduction of erratic unnecessary losses from diseases and similar factors.
2. They may *reduce competition* by growing plants that other nurserymen find difficult to produce profitably, rather than those found in most establishments. The "difficult" crop is usually one that requires such painstaking, specialized, or highly skilled techniques for success that most growers are unwilling or unable to produce it profitably. This may be due to the necessity of control-

ling some serious disease, or to the development and exclusive retention of a superior crop variety. Some specialists, for example, grow pathogen-free propagative stock of chrysanthemums, carnations, geraniums, or foliage plants. If the propagator produces healthy stock at reasonable cost, growers come to depend on him as a source of supply. Other specialists are developing hybrid flower and vegetable seed that may be purchased only from the originator.

However accomplished, such specialization leads to a limited natural monopoly and reduced competition. The more difficult the problem, the better the job is done, and the more reasonable the charges for it, the greater the chance of thus reducing competition.

MECHANIZATION AND DISEASE CONTROL

For reasons already mentioned, mechanization is a present and future fact in the nursery industry. This in turn imposes certain demands, most of which are in themselves beneficial. Scheduled production at low cost demands dependable results. Just as assembly-line manufacturing requires that no phase of the process break down, so scheduled mechanized production of plants demands that all possible chances for error or failure be removed. Uncontrolled losses from diseases, such as damping-off in seed flats, must be eliminated or reduced to unimportance, or the rest of the growing procedure may be stopped for lack of material.

Mechanization may lead to bigness, since some kinds of equipment (for example, flat-making or can-filling machines) can profitably be added only when the volume has reached a certain level. This bigness eventually may introduce other problems, as it becomes impossible for the man who built the successful enterprise to maintain personal supervision. The daily application of his knowledge, experience, and foresight often is the price of maintained success, and very large nurseries may exhibit slackness or inefficiency for this reason. Increase in size places ever greater emphasis on assured control of diseases, insects, and soil problems.

LaPlant-Choate Manufacturing Co., Inc.

In February, 1944, the R. G. LeTourneau Company, a leading competitor of LaPlant-Choate in the manufacture of earth-moving equipment, announced that it planned large-scale, postwar production of prime movers (tractors) and that it would distribute these tractors, as well as LeTourneau accessory earth-moving equipment, through its own distributor organization. This announcement, as reported in *Fortune* magazine for January, 1945, abruptly changed the then existing manufacturing and sales relationships throughout the earth-moving equipment industry.

For better or worse, the structure of the industry is set for the duration. But it is not going to stay that way. In February last year, LeTourneau announced that it would no longer sell its earth-moving machines through Caterpillar distributors, and that it was going into the prime-mover business on a big scale. Last May Caterpillar announced that it was going to begin making bulldozers and scrapers to compete with LeTourneau.

These actions made a full break with the past. In the twenties, Caterpillar busied itself exclusively with the crawler tractor and the Diesel engine. It gathered around itself other manufacturers—who came to be known as the Allied Equipment Group—to produce bulldozers, scrapers, winches, and other tractor-operated tools. LeTourneau made most of the scrapers, and LaPlant-Choate and LeTourneau ran neck and neck on bulldozer production, LaPlant-Choate having perhaps a slight edge. Other tractor companies did business in the same way. International Harvester's equipment was chiefly made by Bucyrus-Erie, the big shovel and crane company that had diversified its line.

The LaPlant–Choate Manufacturing Co. Case, No. BP 435, was prepared by Professors George Albert Smith and C. Roland Christenson of the Harvard Business School. Case material of the Harvard Graduate School of Business Administration is prepared as a basis for class discussion. Cases are not designed to present illustrations of either correct or incorrect handling of administrative problems.

Allis-Chalmers got tools for its tractors chiefly from Baker Co., and Gar Wood Industries. Cleveland Tractor Co., now a part of Oliver Corporation, dealt with Heil Co. and others.

Caterpillar, of course, has no desire to see LeTourneau become the only vertically organized company in the industry it pioneered. It has retaliated by designing equipment to compete with LeTourneau. Its first bulldozers and scrapers are now already under test; and it has designed both cable-control and hydraulic units to operate them. Despite its constant emphasis on crawler tractors, Caterpillar added a four-wheeled rubber-tired tractor to its line in 1941. It is entirely possible Caterpillar is planning a two-wheel job to compete with the Tournapull after the war. For Caterpillar, the expansion is natural: it took on a line of motor graders in 1931 and began to make stationary, industrial diesel engines in the same year. Saleswise, Caterpillar has today a distinct advantage over LeTourneau, for its distribution system, a model for the industry, is virtually intact. LeTourneau has had to build up dealers from scratch.

The innocent bystander in the reshuffling is, of course, LaPlant-Choate, which has made Caterpillar equipment exclusively since 1925. Not only does it face competition from both Caterpillar and LeTourneau, it also lacks a prime mover to round out its line, and it has no distributors. . . . Caterpillar recently offered to buy out the company for an undisclosed price, reported to be somewhat above the market value of its stock. But President Roy Choate, who helped found the company thirty-four years ago, turned it down. He believes that LaPlant-Choate has a definite place in the earth-moving industry, regardless of what the bigger companies do. . . .

These new vertical setups clearly mean more competition, and the other companies are following along. International Harvester has reorganized its internal setup, plans to emphasize industrial power units more than ever after the war. Allis-Chalmers has been experimenting with bigger bulldozers and tractors. Oliver Corp., having acquired Cle-Trac, will expand its industrial tractor business.[1]

Following its announced change in policy, the LeTourneau company severed relations with the Caterpillar Tractor Company and set up its own distributor organization. Large-scale production of the LeTourneau motive power unit, the Tournapull—a two-wheel, rubber-tired diesel tractor built in combination with a high-speed scraper—was begun at the conclusion of World War II.

THE INDUSTRY

Prior to the LeTourneau announcement in 1944, the earth-moving equipment section of the construction machinery industry had been divided into two groups: (1) four motive power manufacturers—International Harvester, Allis-Chalmers, Caterpillar Tractor, and the Oliver Corporation (see Exhibit 1), and (2) eight

---

[1] "The Working Front 2: The Big Dirt Diggers," *Fortune* (January, 1945), pp. 135, 136, 138. Reprinted by special permission of the Editors of *Fortune* magazine.

exhibit 1

LAPLANT-CHOATE MANUFACTURING CO., INC.

Sales and Total Assets of Four Major Tractor Manufacturers
(Selected Years, 1938–1946: in millions)

Year	Assets	Sales	Assets	Sales	Assets	Sales	Assets	Sales
1938	$406	$282	$104	$ 77	$52	$ 48	$ 4	$ 4
1942	517	364	184	196	79	142	8	26
1944	566	640	213	379	85	245	50	43
1946	599	482	185	93	63	128	49	50

*Cleveland Tractor Company, manufacturers of the Cle-Trac track-type tractor, merged with the Oliver Corporation in 1944.
Note: All companies manufacture a wide range of products in addition to earth-moving equipment.
Source: Annual reports of respective companies.

Sales Analysis of Four Major Tractor Manufacturers
(1938 = 100)

	(sales index)	(sales index)	(sales index)	(sales index)
1938	100.0	100.0	100.0	100.0
1942	129.1	254.5	295.8	650.0
1944	227.0	492.2	510.4	1,075.0
1946	170.9	120.8	226.7	1,250.0

Source: Prepared from Exhibit 2 by Harvard Business School staff.

major accessory equipment manufacturers [2] (for example, LaPlant-Choate, Le-Tourneau, Gar Wood, Wooldridge, and Heil), who supplied the dozers, scrapers, and other tools attached to the tractors.

Most accessory manufacturers were smaller and less strong financially than the tractor manufacturers. Each of them sold its products through some allied

---

[2] Excluding grader and power-shovel companies.

tractor company's distributor organization. The accessory manufacturer, under this arrangement, shipped his dozers or scrapers directly to the tractor company's distributors upon the latter's order. This distributor (a retail dealer) then himself assembled the equipment for sale to private contractors, construction firms, and governmental agencies.

COMPANY HISTORY

The LaPlant-Choate Manufacturing Co., Inc., of Cedar Rapids, Iowa, was a pioneer manufacturer of heavy, tractor-operated, accessory earth-moving equipment. It had originally (1911–1922) manufactured heavy-duty housemoving equipment. In 1922 Mr. LaPlant and Mr. Choate entered the earth-moving field with the manufacture of a large, steel-wheel dump wagon for hauling earth and, one year later, built what company officials believed was the first real bulldozer. A small hydraulically controlled, two-wheel, tractor-drawn scraper was produced in 1927. In the same year the company was incorporated, and Mr. Choate became president and active manager.

With earth wagons, dozers (steel blades, attached to tractors, which push earth), and scrapers (machines pulled by tractors which dig, carry, and spread earth in one continuous cycle) as original products, LaPlant-Choate, over a period of years, enlarged its earth-moving equipment line. This expansion occurred through increases in the number and sizes of models available on previously designed equipment and by the addition of new products such as rippers, tamping rollers, and side dozers.[3] In addition to earth-moving products, landclearing equipment such as treedozers, brushcutters, and rootcutters was manufactured.

Beginning in 1925, all LaPlant-Choate equipment was designed and manufactured to complement Caterpillar track-type (crawler) tractors as a source of motive power. This equipment was sold and serviced in both the domestic and foreign market exclusively through Caterpillar distributors. In 1936, at the suggestion of the Caterpillar company, the company began to specialize in the manufacture of dozers and landclearing equipment. Production of scrapers was continued, but the manufacture of earth-moving wagons was halted. LaPlant-Choate sales, which reflect the rapid growth of the Caterpillar company as well as of the industry generally, increased from $283,000 in 1926 to a peak of $14,746,431 in 1945 (see Exhibit 2).

In 1947, Mr. Choate and his family owned 17% of the company's outstanding stock. The next largest owner held approximately 1%. The rest was scattered among 1,571 shareholders.

---

[3] A dozer which can push earth to either side of the tractor (bulldozers push earth directly ahead of the tractor).

exhibit 2

LAPLANT-CHOATE MANUFACTURING CO., INC.

Selected Industry Sales Information
(in thousands)

Year	Caterpillar Tractor Co. Net Sales	Profits	R.G. Le Tourneau, Inc. Net Sales	Profits	LaPlante-Choate Manufacturing Co., Inc. Net Sales	Profits
1930	$ 45,355	$8,714	$ 110	$ 34	$ 1,194	$192
1932	13,258	1,616d	207	52	604	30d
1934	23,769	3,651	929	340	584	41d
1936	54,118	9,849	4,392	1,364	1,144	94
1938	48,246	3,235	6,246	1,412	1,523	37
1940	73,062	7,839	10,740	1,858	2,466	271
1942	142,168	7,002	30,060	2,097	5,237	250
1943	173,945	8,195	36,174	2,185	7,596	318
1944	245,949	7,663	42,209	2,094	12,432	405
1945	230,599	6,511	37,654	1,234	14,746	399
1946	128,437	6,111	28,298	670	8,379	209

*Fiscal year ends on June 30.
dDeficit.

Source: Published sources.

(percentages)

	Caterpillar Tractor Co. Net Profit as a Percentage of Net Sales	R.G. Le Tourneau, Inc. Net Profit as a Percentage of Net Sales	LaPlante-Choate Manufacturing Co., Inc. Net Profit as a Percentage of Net Sales
1930	19.2	30.9	16.1
1932	12.2d	25.1	5.0d
1934	15.4	36.6	7.0d
1936	18.2	31.1	8.2
1938	6.7	22.6	2.4
1940	10.7	17.3	11.0
1942	4.9	7.0	4.8
1943	4.7	6.0	4.2
1944	3.1	5.0	3.3
1945	2.8	3.3	2.7
1946	4.8	2.4	2.5

d Deficit.

Source: Prepared from Exhibit 3 by Harvard Business School Staff.

OPERATIONS PRIOR TO MAY 30, 1944

"From 1925 to 1944 we were an industrial tailor-shop, inventing, designing, and manufacturing tractor-operated tools for the Caterpillar Tractor Company," said Mr. Roy Choate, president of the LaPlant-Choate company. During that period the primary emphasis of the company was on production, since, as has previously been stated, LaPlant-Choate equipment was sold through Caterpillar distributors.

Production of scrapers and bulldozers was primarily a fabricating and welding job involving heavy steel plates and channels welded into unit structures. Over a long period of time, LaPlant-Choate had developed to a high state of efficiency the process of fabrication by means of templates from working drawings; also the fabrication of steel plates and shapes with the assistance of rigid welding jigs and fixtures. The company was therefore able to produce a bulldozer or scraper rapidly at low cost. A great deal of precision work was required in the manufacture of the hydraulic pumps, valves, and cylinders which operated the bulldozers and small scrapers. One manufacturing difficulty lay in the fact that Caterpillar made frequent model changes in its eight types of tractors. Any of these changes necessitated revision both in the design of the complementary accessory equipment and in LaPlant-Choate's manufacturing operations.

Plant facilities consisted of six modern one-story buildings equipped with heat-treating, welding, and materials-handling equipment and some machine tools. Most of the factory space was occupied by the heat-treating department, the welding and erection shops, and the storage and shipping departments. There was a labor force of approximately 850 men, primarily welders, assembly men, machine operators, and service personnel.

The executive sales organization before 1944 consisted of a general sales manager aided by an assistant domestic sales manager and an export sales manager. Sales promotion work was done by a group of domestic district representatives (11), export sales representatives (2), and field service representatives (9). The district representatives were essentially missionary salesmen. They called on Caterpillar distributors to explain uses and advantages of LaPlant-Choate equipment. If given permission, they aided the distributors' salesmen in selling LaPlant-Choate equipment. Field service representatives' duties were to aid and instruct the distributors' service departments in servicing LaPlant-Choate equipment.

Advertising of LaPlant-Choate products was limited to pamphlets on the types of equipment manufactured, such as bulldozers, sidedozers, and scrapers. These were distributed to users and prospects by the distributor. A direct-mail advertising program was administered by the Caterpillar company. Inasmuch as Caterpillar controlled the direct-mail program and because of the close relations between LaPlant-Choate and Caterpillar, LaPlant-Choate's customer list was not kept entirely up to date. In fact, during World War II it was completely neglected because of the large number of dozers being shipped to the government and because so few were being shipped directly to civilian customers.

Product development and research work from 1911 to 1935 was carried on under Mr. Choate's personal direction. He succeeded in working out the basic design for company dozers, earth wagons, scrapers, and certain minor products. From 1935 to 1943, company engineers worked in conjunction with the engineering department of the Caterpillar company in improving LaPlant-Choate dozers and in developing effective tractor-drawn scrapers. Mr. Choate, recognizing the increasing importance of developmental work, organized his own research unit in 1943 as a section of the engineering division. This unit consisted of five persons who specialized in hydraulic-control developmental work. Mr. Rockwell, who had been with LaPlant-Choate for ten years, was placed in charge of the research section. He had had considerable experience in scraper design work.

LaPlant-Choate tractor-drawn scrapers were lighter and more compact than competitive models. In addition to dozers and its standard tractor-drawn scrapers (6, 8, and 14 cubic yard), the company had produced 2 cubic yard and 4 cubic yard tractor-drawn scrapers during World War II; it was believed these small units would have peacetime sales potentialities for farms and small contractors. LaPlant-Choate's primary competitive advantage had resulted from the fact that it had pioneered in adapting hydraulic controls to dozers for lowering and lifting the blade and to small tractor-drawn scrapers for operating the cutting edge and the earth-ejection units. The LaPlant-Choate hydraulic unit was recognized by the industry as being superior to other hydraulic control units. It was not yet feasible, however, to apply hydraulic controls to large scraper units. LaPlant-Choate, along with other manufacturers, employed cable-control units on the large models.

Typical LaPlant-Choate prices, f.o.b. Cedar Rapids, were C-114, 14 cubic yard tractor-drawn scraper, $6,300; C-108, 8 cubic yard tractor-drawn scraper, $4,900; B-61, bulldozer, $1,335.

BREAK WITH THE CATERPILLAR COMPANY

During April and May, 1944, Caterpillar attempted, without success, to purchase the LaPlant-Choate company. On May 30, 1944, the Caterpillar company first advertised in trade magazines its intention to manufacture a complete line of its own accessory earth-moving equipment including dozers and scrapers. It announced that these products were to be available after the end of World War II.

LaPlant-Choate, as a result of the new developments, faced several critical problems. (1) The loss of the Caterpillar sales organization, recognized as the best in the industry, would leave it without distributor outlets. (2) LaPlant-Choate dozers and scrapers had been designed for use with Caterpillar equipment. This fact was well known in the trade. LaPlant-Choate scrapers (but not dozers), however, could, by adjustment, be powered by any make tractor. (3) If LaPlant-Choate were to stay in business, it would either have to ally itself with another tractor manufacturer to provide LaPlant-Choate equipment with motive power or have to manufacture its own motive power, a field in which it had neither previous manufacturing know-how nor the necessary physical plant and facilities.

"We could have adopted a sit-down-and-weep policy," said Mr. Choate, "but though the situation was critical, we were not going to be forced out of the earth-moving equipment field." In a letter to company employees, he made the following statement:

> Your company has full confidence in its ability to achieve success in the post-war world as an *independent* company. We have a strong organization of loyal and dependable employees, a proved line of equipment, adequate financial resources, plus one of the finest modern plants in the industry. In addition, new developments and plans are already under way which promise even greater opportunities than ever before for LaPlant-Choate men and women.

DECISION AS TO FUTURE COMPANY POLICY

"The Caterpillar decision to manufacture its own dozers and scrapers," said Mr. Choate, "forced us to consider the following courses of action: (1) liquidate, (2) sell the company, (3) secure another sales outlet for the LaPlant-Choate equipment, if possible, with other motive power manufacturers, and (4) manufacture both motive power units and accessory equipment." Company officials did not believe that an immediate decision was required as of May, 1944, since the industry was still committed to full-scale war production.

Mr. Choate rejected the possibilities of liquidating or selling his company.

During the latter part of 1944 and the first half of 1945, the company attempted to conclude sales agreements with other motive power manufacturers. Satisfactory arrangements, however, could not be made with companies which LaPlant-Choate considered desirable.

On July 26, 1945, the company made its first specific statement of policy. The company announced that it would continue to manufacture accessory earth-moving equipment and that its products would for some time still be handled by Caterpillar distributors.

"We later decided that our company would have to go out on its own," said Mr. Choate. "We faced the job of designing, manufacturing, and selling a complete line of motive power and accessory equipment."

While the previous Caterpillar–LaPlant-Choate sales arrangement had resulted in a substantial sales volume for his company, Mr. Choate believed the severance of this relationship would, in the long run, be a good thing for the company. "We knew enough to get off at the right time," he concluded. Mr. Choate believed that the following disadvantages of the former sales arrangement with Caterpillar far outweighed its advantages: (1) Frequent revision in the design of Caterpillar tractors necessitated design changes in LaPlant-Choate products. This industry design competition forced LaPlant-Choate to carry large inventories which rapidly became obsolete. (2) LaPlant-Choate did not have any control over the Caterpillar distributor organization and had difficulty in securing promotion of its products over competing accessory manufacturers' products also carried by Caterpillar distributors. (3) There was no legal contract between the two companies stating the responsibilities of both parties.

INTERIM PERIOD

After the decision to manufacture and sell both motive power and accessory equipment had been made, LaPlant-Choate was confronted with two major problems: (1) continued profitable operation of the company during the readjustment period; (2) preparation for conversion into an independent manufacturer of both accessory equipment and tractors.

In the interim between May 30, 1944, and the establishment of the company's distributor organization, LaPlant-Choate equipment, by mutual agreement, was sold through the Caterpillar distributor group. After the establishment of a La-Plant-Choate distributor organization (March–June, 1946), company dozers and scrapers were sold through the LaPlant-Choate's own distributor organization. In the few instances where a new distributor had not yet been appointed, Mr. Choate stated, a few dozers and tractor-drawn scrapers were sold through the Caterpillar distributors. As soon as a LaPlant-Choate distributor could be found to replace this Caterpillar distributor, shipments to the Caterpillar distributor were stopped. While a limited drop in sales was expected during this readjustment period, the company felt that government demands during the war, plus the accumulated civilian backlog for the immediate postwar era, would assure LaPlant-Choate of profitable conversion operations.

Manufacturing during the interim period was interrupted by a 90-day strike of the 850 shop employees. It ended in February of 1946. "This strike, the first in company history, cost both our company and its employees a great deal of money," said Mr. Choate. The strike had been called by Local Union 116, CIO, United Farm Equipment and Metal Workers of America, which had organized the plant in 1941. Twice, later in 1946, walkouts by smaller groups of employees occurred, but the company believed its relations with Local 116 were improving. The latest wage negotiations had been settled after only four meetings with union officers; company wages equalled those paid by other firms in the Cedar Rapids area. Employee turnover, however, remained high, a fact which the director of labor relations attributed to veterans shopping for employment.

Wartime expansion of the company had revealed certain inadequacies in some operating procedures. To correct this situation the executive management committee was developing improved scheduling and inventory control procedures which it hoped to put into operation during 1947. Mr. Choate had also been dissatisfied with the operations of the employee wage incentive system, installed in 1941. That program, in the absence of time and methods studies, had been based on past performance data abstracted by the cost accounting department from its records. By 1947, 30% of all manufacturing operations had been time-studied. A restatement of burden rates was also being considered, since actual burden had exceeded standard burden for several years.

In preparation for his company's future role as an independent manufacturer, Mr. Choate contemplated first the development of a 14 cubic yard, two-wheel, rubber-tired tractor-scraper rig. During the latter part of 1945, the R. G. LeTourneau Company began advertising widely the competitive advantages of its Tournapull, a two-wheel, rubber-tired tractor-scraper rig which Mr. LeTourneau had designed in 1939. *Fortune* magazine describes this development as follows:

> It is a 150-horsepower Diesel engine running on two huge tires, each independently controlled by clutches to permit steering. It can travel over paved roads, from which the crawler tractor is barred. More important, it overcomes the chief disadvantage of the tractor-hauled scraper; slow speed. A Tournapull-scraper combination can move as fast as fifteen miles per hour, whereas a comparable tractor-scraper can hit a maximum of only six. In construction work, where time is definitely money, higher speeds mean longer hauls and more pay loads per hour. A rule of thumb in the industry is that tractor bulldozers are economical for dirt moving up to 300 feet, while tractor-scrapers can operate efficiently up to about 2,500 feet. With the development of the Tournapull, hauls of up to two miles are quite possible—a fact that LeTourneau has begun to plug hard in its promotion.[4]

Popularity of the Tournapull forced production of similar rigs by other manufacturers. The Wooldridge Manufacturing Company, for example, introduced a combination two-wheel, rubber-tired tractor-scraper rig in 1945. Two other accessory manufacturers had test models completed, and other motive power and accessory manufacturers were contemplating introducing similar units. Mr. Choate believed that the design and manufacture of a rig to compete with the Tournapull were essential to his company's success.

Competition for the limited number of capable earth-moving equipment distributors became exceedingly keen at the end of World War II. At that time, the four motive power manufacturers had virtually finished postwar expansion of their established dealer organizations, and LeTourneau had completed the appointment of his new distributor group, approximately 65 dealers. Other smaller accessory manufacturers, who hoped to build up and strengthen their own sales organizations, were engaged in the process of securing additional or stronger distributors.

As has been stated, LaPlant-Choate was faced with the necessity of producing

---

[4] "The Working Front 2: The Big Dirt Diggers," *Fortune* (January, 1945), pp. 135-136. Reprinted by special permission of the Editors of *Fortune* magazine.

a tractor. Tractor manufacture was a field in which the company had not had previous experience. Production of dozers was a fairly simple fabricating operation. Manufacture of the new two-wheel tractor, however, would require a great deal of precision machining work and skilled assembly operations. With the exception of the radiator, diesel engine, and tires, all parts of the tractor were to be manufactured by LaPlant-Choate. The scraper used in the new tractor-scraper rig was to be a modified version of LaPlant-Choate's tractor-drawn scraper Model C-114. Since LaPlant-Choate personnel had not had actual tractor manufacturing experience, some of the present labor force would have to be retrained and reassigned for these operations.

LaPlant-Choate would have to expand its existing plant facilities to manufacture efficiently the new tractor-scraper rig, as well as other contemplated products. Any expansion plans would require a sizable new investment. Under the old Caterpillar sales arrangement, the company had been able to operate with a minimum of working capital. The new program, however, would require a large sum to finance increased inventory and sales expenses as well as manufacturing costs. The 1946 strike, plus uncertainty in material shipments, had forced material inventories up to an all-time high.

The procurement of materials for the new program was expected to cause some difficulty. The tractor-scraper combination required more steel and steel of a different weight and size than LaPlant-Choate had formerly used.

PLAN OF ACTION

On August 31, 1944, the company's stockholders elected a new board of directors. Three former members, Mr. Choate, Mr. Coquillette, the company banker, and Mr. Dennis, the company treasurer, were retained. Others on the new board were three executive officers of leading noncompetitive construction machinery firms and the firm's general counsel. The new board supported Mr. Choate's plans for a change in product and sales distribution and provided him with a source of advice in planning the company's conversion. During February of 1947, Mr. E. R. Galvin replaced Mr. Dennis as a member of the board.

Early in 1945, Mr. Choate assigned Mr. Hyler, a LaPlant-Choate development engineer for over four years, to design a 14 cubic yard, 225 horsepower, two-wheel, rubber-tired tractor-scraper rig. Mr. Hyler prior to 1939 had worked with Mr. R. G. LeTourneau on the development of the Tournapull. He had also designed three of LaPlant-Choate's most successful tractor-drawn scrapers, the C-106, C-108, and C-114. Company officials believed that these scrapers were the most modern, fast-loading, tractor-drawn scrapers on the market. In the latter part of 1945, Mr. Choate gave the former head of the engineering department a new assignment in the company and himself temporarily assumed direction of this department until a new director of engineering could be secured. Early in 1946, he increased the size of the development and research section of the engineering department from five to ten men. Mr. Rockwell was instructed to develop a complete line of products, including a four-wheel, rubber-tired tractor, in addition to carrying on hydraulic research.

Recognizing the coming need for intensive sales effort, Mr. Choate made some changes in his executive sales personnel in the summer of 1945; these changes, however, did not prove effective. On March 1, 1946, he brought to the company Mr. E. R. Galvin as his executive vice president and general sales manager. Mr. Galvin, 62 years of age, had 35 years of experience in building distributor organizations in the industry. He had served as general sales manager for both Caterpillar and LeTourneau. He was immediately placed in charge of the LaPlant-Choate drive to secure a distributor organization. Mr. Choate said that Mr. Galvin would personally select the LaPlant-Choate distributor group and that because Mr. Galvin's contacts in the industry were widespread, this selection would assure the company of excellent dealers.

Mr. Galvin stated that to set up his sales organization he had circulated the news that LaPlant-Choate wanted distributors and then had had the district representatives of the company screen the several hundred prospective applicants. Those applicants which the district representatives approved filled out a questionnaire listing their financial status, sales volume, lines of construction equipment handled, property and equipment owned, and personnel employed. They were then brought to Cedar Rapids for a personal interview with Mr. Galvin, Mr. A. D. Dennis, secretary-treasurer, and Mr. J. W. Schoen, credit manager.

While waiting for tractor-scraper production to begin, manufacturing operations were to be concentrated on five sizes of tractor-drawn scrapers. Production of dozers, upon which the company had centered its production during the war, was to be subcontracted to an Omaha firm; all dozer production, however, was to be halted by June of 1947. Mr. C. H. Lage, production manager, surveyed company needs in regard to machine tools and equipment for the new tractor program; initial orders for some equipment were placed immediately. "We are going into tractor production in a small way," stated Mr. Lage. "Later we will have to secure additional space and equipment if we are to achieve maximum production efficiency." Mr. Lage, 57 years of age, had been with LaPlant-Choate since 1943. He had formerly been employed by International Harvester and in the production planning and manufacturing departments of the Caterpillar Tractor Company for over eleven years.

To provide for immediate working capital needs, a million dollar credit line was established late in 1946; $750,000 of this credit was utilized immediately for current operations. The company planned to increase permanent working capital at a later date through the issuance of stock.

OPERATIONS OF THE COMPANY—JANUARY, 1947

By January of 1947 a 14 cubic yard tractor-scraper rig had been designed and tested; in addition to the experimental model, one rig had been manufactured and shipped to a contractor for final "on-the-job" tests. This rig was tentatively priced at $24,500. Preliminary company reports from this test indicated that the LaPlant-Choate rig outperformed other competitive models.

At the same time, Mr. Rockwell's development and research section had completed preliminary design work on a new 225 horsepower, four-wheel drive, rubber-tired tractor with a specially designed dozer. That section further had started design work on a 9 cubic yard tractor-scraper rig and a 20 cubic yard bottom dump wagon. Mr. Hyler, upon completion of his assignment to design the tractor-scraper rig, was placed in charge of the experimental department to build a test model of this machine.

The two tractor-scraper rigs produced by January had been individually assembled; all component parts had been specially manufactured. With dozer production subcontracted, current production was limited to five sizes of tractor-drawn scrapers. All manufacturing changes to complete the shift from dozers to scraper production had been completed, and the factory was running two eight-hour shifts in all departments and three eight-hour shifts in critical departments. Government-owned equipment used by LaPlant-Choate during the war, valued at $200,000, had been purchased by the company.

Arrangements for production of the tractor-scraper rigs were still in the planning stage. For production of the new two-wheel tractor, Mr. Lage planned to use one wing of the weld shop as an assembly plant. Rearrangements for this move, however, were not yet under way, since full production, a minimum of one unit a day, was not expected to start until June of 1947. Some of the additional machine tools required for the tractor program had been secured. After all machine tools had been obtained, machining work on tractor parts would have to be done at various points throughout the factory where space locations for the new machines could be secured. Procurement of steel for the tractor program was proceeding slowly. Company suppliers did not have allotments of steel available in the sizes required. Sufficient radiators, engines, and tires, though in short supply, had been secured. In addition to these items, the company was attempting to purchase temporarily as many additional component tractor parts as possible to speed initial tractor production.

Mr. Galvin, in his campaign to secure dealers, had signed up 65 domestic distributors; he was seeking four more. Twenty-five of the 65 LaPlant-Choate distributors also handled Oliver–Cle-Trac track-type and four-wheeled, rubber-tired tractors, and several others handled J. I. Case and Minneapolis-Moline four-wheeled, rubber-tired tractors. Those distributors with established businesses had had experience in selling earth-moving equipment. The rest of the dealers had not handled track-type or rubber-tired tractors; they were either men who had worked for other earth-moving equipment dealers and were now entering business for themselves or dealers who formerly had handled some lines of construction machinery but not scrapers and dozers. All LaPlant-Choate distributors, in addition to handling LaPlant-Choate equipment, carried five or six noncompetitive lines, such as motor graders and shovels. Although the LaPlant-Choate distributor organization did not yet have either the capital resources or the established distributor-contractor sales relationships which other large manufacturer-distributor organizations had, Mr. Galvin did not believe that this condition was a disadvantage. "I would rather have young, aggressive dealers who will fight for business; older well-established dealers sometimes go to sleep on the job." Analyses of sales by product and by distributor organization are given in Exhibits 3 and 4.

Mr. Galvin hoped that each LaPlant-Choate distributor would have minimum capital resources of $100,000, since distributors had to arrange for financing of contractor equipment purchases. "We did not always get this," he stated.

exhibit 3

LAPLANT-CHOATE MANUFACTURING CO., INC.

Sales Analysis for Two Major Products
(selected months, March—December 1946)

	Percentage of Total Equipment Sales	
1946	*Scraper (%)*	*Dozer (%)*
March	21	79
September	46	54
December	65	35

Source: Company records.

exhibit 4

LAPLANT-CHOATE MANUFACTURING CO., INC.

Sales of LaPlant-Choate Products by LaPlant-Choate and
Caterpillar Distributors (April through December, 1946)

	Domestic Sales		*Export Sales*	
1946	*LaPlant-Choate Distributors (%)*	*Caterpillar Distributors (%)*	*LaPlant-Choate Distributors (%)*	*Caterpillar Distributors (%)*
April-June	42	58		100
July-September	78	22	9	91
October-December	84	16	42	58

Source: Company records.

In January of 1947, the concern was represented by 65 overseas distributors, of which 23 were newly appointed LaPlant-Choate dealers; 42 were Caterpillar dealers who were temporarily handling LaPlant-Choate equipment. Export sales before the war years had averaged between 25% and 30% of the company's total sales volume.

Sales by distributors were made directly to contractors engaged in earth-moving projects. Since the equipment required a large capital investment on the part of the purchaser and could stand constant repair and rebuilding, the frequency of sales was low. Prices for earth-moving machines were approximately equal throughout the industry. Contractors, therefore, purchased equipment on the following bases: (1) efficiency of the unit (measured in cost per yard of earth moved); (2) service and spare-parts facilities maintained by the distributor; (3) distributor-contractor relationships, many of which had been built up over a long period of time; and (4) reputation of the equipment and manufacturer.

LaPlant-Choate discounts were 20% on all rubber-tired equipment and 25% on other products and parts; these discounts followed the general industry pattern.

Distributors were expected to carry an adequate spare-parts inventory. During the depression periods, spare-parts sales frequently were the mainstay of a dealer's business. The company anticipated that as the number of products manufactured by LaPlant-Choate increased, the parts inventory maintained by a distributor would increase from $10,000 (1947) to $20,000. Spare-parts sales currently averaged 20% of distributor sales volume. Each distributor, in addition to a parts department, maintained a service department with facilities and men available to make repairs. The company did not insist that a distributor have a specified number of servicemen; it assumed he would maintain a staff large enough to meet his requirements.

The distributors were supervised by the company's district representatives. District representatives were responsible for the sales and service activities of dealers in their sales districts. They did not set prices for equipment or determine dealer credit lines with the LaPlant-Choate company. Field servicemen and district representatives were supposed to work together whenever they thought it desirable. Twice a year all representatives were brought to Cedar Rapids for a sales conference. A sales training program had been initiated in the latter part of 1946 to assist the new distributors' salesmen in merchandising LaPlant-Choate products.

Mr. Galvin used a minimum of formal procedures to administer his sales organization. "We secure control over our distributors through the district representatives," said Mr. Galvin. "They know our standards and apply them. I plan to do a great deal of personal checking and want to visit each distributor once a year." To check sales operations by districts, Mr. Galvin had each district representative send a weekly resume of his activity as well as a scheduled itinerary for the coming week. In addition, the sales department received a copy of each sales transaction made by a dealer; this record was tabulated by distributor and district.

COMPETITIVE SITUATION—JANUARY, 1947

"Competition in the earth-moving equipment field is going to become increasingly severe," Mr. Choate stated. Industry-wide readjustments in sales distribution methods had increased the number of accessory manufacturers making both motive power and accessory earth-moving equipment. Moreover, established companies manufacturing other construction machinery planned to expand into the production of earth-moving tools. Some new companies as well had already announced their intention to enter the industry and manufacture competitive equipment.

Mr. Galvin considered the Caterpillar Tractor Company with its 109 domestic outlets to be the primary competitor of LaPlant-Choate as far as dealer strength was concerned. Next he rated International Harvester, LeTourneau, and the Oliver Corporation. The Cleveland Tractor Company, predecessor company of Oliver Corporation and manufacturer of the Cle-Trac, had experienced financial difficulties prior to World War II.

With regard to product design, the primary competitor of the LaPlant-Choate company was LeTourneau. Modern earth-moving equipment had largely been developed between World Wars I and II, with the 1930's witnessing the most rapid technological advances. This progress in design improvement had been temporarily halted by the National Defense Program in 1939, at which time the industry's primary effort was directed toward increasing production of already designed models. LeTourneau, a leader in this developmental work, had designed the first successful powered scraper, had introduced the concept of large flotation rubber tires to earth-moving equipment, and in 1939 had developed the first tractor-scraper combination, the Tournapull. By 1947, Mr. LeTourneau was producing a complete line of Tournapull tractor-scraper rigs in several different yardage models, in addition to a complete line of more conventional earth-moving and construction equipment. The Euclid Road Manufacturing Company, a well-established construction machinery firm, had recently developed and produced an automatic type of earth-loading machine which was being closely studied by all members of the industry. All earth-moving machinery firms were either contemplating or producing bigger and more effective earth-moving tools.

Industry information on the number of track-type tractors equipped with earth-moving tools was not available. It was the opinion of Mr. Galvin, however, that approximately 25% of track-type tractor production was used for earth-moving purposes and would therefore be equipped with tractor-operated tools. His formula implied that a maximum of 7,500 track-type tractors would annually be equipped with tractor-operated tools if record peacetime production (30,780 units in 1937) was repeated (see Exhibit 5). "Possibilities for LaPlant-Choate

exhibit 5

LAPLANT-CHOATE MANUFACTURING CO., INC.

Track-Type Tractor Production

Year	Production	Year	Production
1922	4,187	1934	N.A.
1923	5,002	1935	17,145
1924	4,612	1936	26,179
1925	5,282	1937	30,780
1926	7,175	1938	19,801
1927	10,433	1939	20,890
1928	16,762	1940	25,086
1929	25,450	1941	29,378
1930	N.A.	1942	28,616
1931	10,064	1943	24,963
1932	N.A.	1944	44,860
1933	N.A.	1945	44,872

Source: U. S. Department of Census.

expansion rest, therefore, on enlarging the market by development and improvement of rubber-tired, earth-moving tractors and equipment," he concluded. Moreover, since all the unit sales price would now be divided between LaPlant-Choate and its distributors, the company would increase its over-all income on any given number of unit sales. Formerly, a crawler-tractor dozer sale, LaPlant-Choate had received less than 25% of the total sales price paid by the purchaser, inasmuch as the tractor manufacturer had received a substantial amount.

Wartime sales by the construction industry reached a high of $750 million in 1944. Peacetime production during the 1930's had averaged $200 million annually.[5] These wartime increases in production had been made possible by building new facilities, by working additional shifts, and by employing subcontracting facilities.

Whereas the civilian demand, accumulated during wartime years, assured earth-moving machinery companies of capacity production for many months, the industry's hopes for large-scale utilization of these wartime-constructed facilities were based primarily on an expected increase in public construction work. Trade publications [6] estimated a $35 billion backlog of proposed engineering construction work (78% public projects and 22% private construction) existed in early 1947. Although private construction (houses and buildings) had approached

---

[5] Over-all sales of the more than 100 major firms in the construction machinery industry. Separate sales statistics on the earth-moving equipment section of the construction machinery industry are not available.

[6] *Engineering News Record*, February 20, 1947, p. 111.

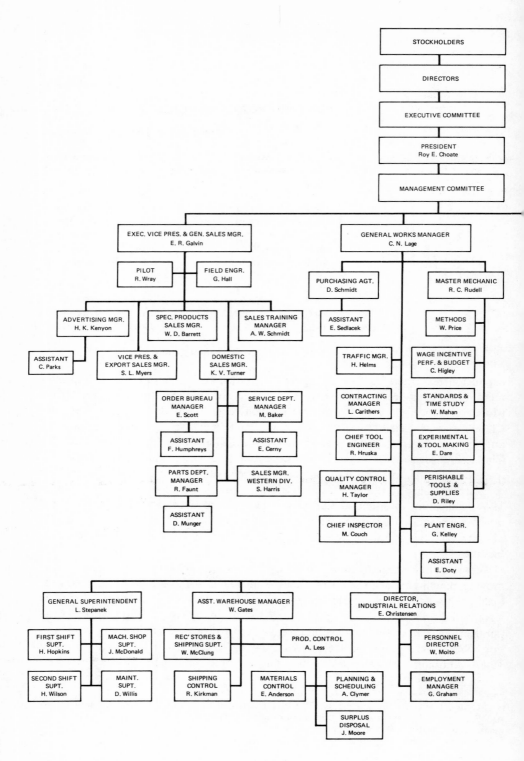

STOCKHOLDERS

DIRECTORS

EXECUTIVE COMMITTEE

PRESIDENT
Roy E. Choate

MANAGEMENT COMMITTEE

EXEC. VICE PRES. & GEN. SALES MGR.
E. R. Galvin

GENERAL WORKS MANAGER
C. N. Lage

PILOT
R. Wray

FIELD ENGR.
G. Hall

PURCHASING AGT.
D. Schmidt

MASTER MECHANIC
R. C. Rudell

ADVERTISING MGR.
H. K. Kenyon

SPEC. PRODUCTS
SALES MGR.
W. D. Barrett

SALES TRAINING
MANAGER
A. W. Schmidt

ASSISTANT
E. Sedlacek

METHODS
W. Price

ASSISTANT
C. Parks

VICE PRES. &
EXPORT SALES MGR.
S. L. Myers

DOMESTIC
SALES MGR.
K. V. Turner

TRAFFIC MGR.
H. Helms

WAGE INCENTIVE
PERF. & BUDGET
C. Higley

ORDER BUREAU
MANAGER
E. Scott

SERVICE DEPT.
MANAGER
M. Baker

CONTRACTING
MANAGER
L. Carithers

STANDARDS &
TIME STUDY
W. Mahan

ASSISTANT
F. Humphreys

ASSISTANT
E. Cerny

CHIEF TOOL
ENGINEER
R. Hruska

EXPERIMENTAL
& TOOL MAKING
E. Dare

PARTS DEPT.
MANAGER
R. Faunt

SALES MGR.
WESTERN DIV.
S. Harris

QUALITY CONTROL
MANAGER
H. Taylor

PERISHABLE
TOOLS &
SUPPLIES
D. Riley

ASSISTANT
D. Munger

CHIEF INSPECTOR
M. Couch

PLANT ENGR.
G. Kelley

ASSISTANT
E. Doty

GENERAL SUPERINTENDENT
L. Stepanek

ASST. WAREHOUSE MANAGER
W. Gates

DIRECTOR,
INDUSTRIAL RELATIONS
E. Christensen

FIRST SHIFT
SUPT.
H. Hopkins

MACH. SHOP
SUPT.
J. McDonald

REC' STORES &
SHIPPING SUPT.
W. McClung

PROD. CONTROL
A. Less

PERSONNEL
DIRECTOR
W. Moito

SECOND SHIFT
SUPT.
H. Wilson

MAINT.
SUPT.
D. Willis

SHIPPING
CONTROL
R. Kirkman

MATERIALS
CONTROL
E. Anderson

PLANNING &
SCHEDULING
A. Clymer

EMPLOYMENT
MANAGER
G. Graham

SURPLUS
DISPOSAL
J. Moore

64

exhibit 6

LAPLANT-CHOATE MANUFACTURING CO., INC.

Organization Chart: April 7, 1947

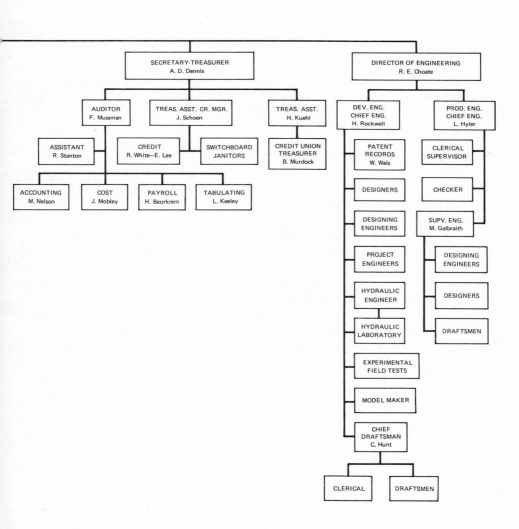

record levels in 1946, public projects (roads, airports, dams), which used the greatest amount of earth-moving equipment, were slow to materialize. The failure of public construction to expand as rapidly as had been anticipated was attributed to (1) higher construction costs at a time when all government agencies were being pressed to cut expenditures; (2) the more critical nature of the delayed private construction; and (3) the reluctance of the Federal Government to engage in large-scale public works program at a time of national prosperity.

During the first quarter of 1947, the whole industry's production of tractor-drawn scrapers had reached a point where orders for new equipment were being filled immediately by direct shipment from the factories. Production of other types of earth-moving equipment, however, had not yet caught up with the backlog of demand.

Mr. Choate, in evaluating his company's progress since 1944, stated, "We have demonstrated that we can design, manufacture, and sell our own products. Originally there were some signs of defeatism; but we soon cleared that out. I did not want anyone working for me who did not believe in our program. We are prepared for the extremely competitive era which is in sight."

To meet competition, Mr. Choate stated, "The company is planning to produce a complete line of products: a 6 cubic yard and a 9 cubic yard tractor-scraper rig (late 1947), a four-wheel, rubber-tired industrial tractor (1948), and a bottom-dump, rubber-tired, earth-moving wagon (1948)." The four-wheel industrial tractor had been designed in conjunction with a new type of LaPlant-Choate bulldozer and would be sold in competition with crawler and rubber-tired tractors. "The most important single factor in our future," said Mr. Choate, "will be the sales of our new two-wheel tractor-scraper rig." Not only was the company expecting to increase the number of products manufactured, but it was considering the establishment of a plant in England.

As of January 31, 1947, the company issued an additional $4/10$ of a share for each share of common stock outstanding and on March 31, 1947, paid a quarterly cash dividend on the increased shares then outstanding. The par value of the common stock was $5 per share; the market price for the stock on February 1, 1947, was approximately $14. Exhibit 6 presents the company's organization chart as of April 7, 1947. Exhibits 7 and 8 provide financial information for the years 1936–1946.

exhibit 7

LAPLANT-CHOATE MANUFACTURING CO., INC.

Balance Sheets as of June 30, 1936–1946 (in thousands)

Assets	1936	1937	1938	1939	1940	1941*	1942*	1943*	1944*	1945*	1946	Jan. 31, 1947
Cash	$ 50	$ 82	$ 47	$ 29	$ 92	$ 168	$ 133	$ 284	$1,500	$1,320	$ 526	$ 607
United States Tax Notes								306	803	1,015		
Receivables—Net	139	138	211	239	321	426	580	1,468	1,638	1,198	575	882
Inventories	193	257	369	370	668	1,038	1,595	2,010	2,213	1,876	2,438	3,411
Total Current Assets	$382	$477	$627	$638	$1,081	$1,632	$2,308	$4,068	$6,154	$5,409	$3,539	$4,900
Land, Buildings, and Equipment—Net	223	231	280	294	472	834	887	870	759	562	776	883
Miscellaneous Assets	13	15	18	22	23	139	31	109	254	131	137	49
Total Assets	$618	$723	$925	$954	$1,576	$2,605	$3,226	$5,047	$7,167	$6,102	$4,452	$5,834
Liabilities and Net Worth												
Banks and Other Loans Payable	$ 53	$ 60	$ 93	$ 9	$ 121	$ 125	$ 625	$1,250	$1,750	$ 750		$1,060
Accounts Payable and Accrued Expenses	20	37	123	121	250	261	321	658	1,019	1,017	1,234	1,030
Reserve for Taxes on Income			27	32	73	146	190	733	1,696	1,285		258
Total Current Liabilities	$ 73	$ 97	$243	$162	$ 444	$ 532	$1,136	$2,641	$4,465	$3,052	$1,234	$2,358
Long-Term Liabilities			37	25	101							
Reserve for Contingent Taxes on Income								153	258	350	350	350
Total Liabilities	$ 73	$ 97	$280	$187	$ 545	$ 532	$1,136	$2,794	$4,723	$3,402	$1,584	$2,708
Capital Stock:												
Preferred Stock	$ 86	$100	$100	$100	$ 100	$ 850	$ 850	$ 850	$ 746	$ 735	$1,040	$1,456
Common Stock	160	160	160	160	704	704	704	704	706	710		
Surplus:												
Paid-In Surplus	6	6	6	6	6	6	6	6	8	15	541	126
Earned Surplus	293	360	379	501	221	513	530	693	984	1,240	1,287	1,544
Total Net Worth	$545	$626	$645	$767	$1,031	$2,073	$2,090	$2,253	$2,444	$2,700	$2,868	$3,126
Total Liabilities and Net Worth	$618	$723	$925	$954	$1,576	$2,605	$3,226	$5,047	$7,167	$6,102	$4,452	$5,834

Source: Company records.

*Figures have been revised to give effect to renegotiation, accelerated amortization of war facilities, and adjusted federal taxes on income.

exhibit 7A

LAPLANT-CHOATE MANUFACTURING CO., INC.

Balance Sheet Analysis (percentages)

Assets	1936	1937	1938	1939	1940	1941	1942	1943	1944	1945	1946	January 31, 1947
Cash	8.1	11.3	5.1	3.0	5.8	6.4	4.1	5.6	20.9	21.6	11.8	10.4
United States Tax Notes	—	—	—	—	—	—	—	6.1	11.2	16.6	—	—
Receivables—Net	22.5	19.1	22.8	25.1	20.4	16.4	18.0	29.1	22.9	19.6	12.9	15.1
Inventories	31.2	35.5	39.9	38.8	42.4	39.9	49.4	39.8	30.9	30.8	54.8	58.5
Total Current Assets	61.8	65.9	67.8	66.9	68.6	62.7	71.5	80.6	85.9	88.6	79.5	84.0
Land, Buildings, and Equipment—Net	36.1	32.0	30.0	30.8	29.9	32.0	27.5	17.2	10.6	9.2	17.4	15.1
Miscellaneous Assets	2.1	2.1	1.9	2.3	1.5	5.3	1.0	2.2	3.5	2.2	3.1	.9
Total Assets	100.0	100.0	100.0	100.0	100.0	100.0	100.0	100.0	100.0	100.0	100.0	100.0
Liabilities and Net Worth												
Banks and Other Loans Payable	—	—	10.1	.9	7.7	4.8	19.4	24.8	24.4	12.3	—	18.2
Accounts Payable and Accrued Expenses	8.6	8.3	13.3	12.7	15.9	10.0	9.9	13.0	14.2	16.7	27.7	17.7
Reserve for Taxes on Income	3.2	5.1	2.9	3.4	4.6	5.6	5.9	14.5	23.7	21.0	—	4.5
Total Current Liabilities	11.8	13.4	26.3	17.0	28.2	20.4	35.2	52.3	62.3	50.0	27.7	40.4
Long-Term Liabilities	—	—	4.0	2.6	6.4	—	—	—	—	—	—	—
Reserve for Contingent Taxes on Income	—	—	—	—	—	—	—	3.1	3.6	5.7	7.9	6.0
Total Liabilities	11.8	13.4	30.3	19.6	34.6	20.4	35.2	55.4	65.9	55.7	35.6	46.4
Capital Stock:												
Preferred Stock	13.9	13.9	10.8	10.5	6.3	32.7	26.4	16.8	10.4	12.1	—	—
Common Stock	25.9	22.1	17.3	16.8	44.7	27.0	21.8	14.0	9.9	11.6	23.4	25.0
Surplus:												
Paid-In Surplus	1.0	.8	.6	.6	.4	.2	.2	.1	.1	.3	12.1	2.1
Earned Surplus	47.4	49.8	41.0	52.5	14.0	19.7	16.4	13.7	13.7	20.3	28.9	26.5
Total Net Worth	88.2	86.6	69.7	80.4	65.4	79.6	64.8	44.6	34.1	44.3	64.4	53.6
Total Liabilities and Net Worth	100.0	100.0	100.0	100.0	100.0	100.0	100.0	100.0	100.0	100.0	100.0	100.0

Source: Prepared from Exhibit 8 by Harvard Business School staff.

LAPLANT-CHOATE MANUFACTURING CO., INC.

Balance Sheet Analysis (index numbers: base year = 1936)

Assets	1936	1937	1938	1939	1940	1941	1942	1943	1944	1945	1946	January 31, 1947
Cash	100.0	164.0	94.0	58.0	184.0	336.0	266.0	568.0	3,000.0	2,640.0	1,052.0	1,214.0
United States Tax Notes								*	*	*	*	*
Receivables—Net	100.0	99.3	151.8	171.9	230.9	306.5	417.3	1,056.1	1,178.4	861.9	413.7	634.5
Inventories	100.0	133.2	191.2	191.7	346.1	537.8	826.4	1,041.5	1,146.6	972.0	1,263.2	1,767.4
Total Current Assets	100.0	124.9	164.1	167.0	283.0	427.2	604.2	1,064.9	1,611.0	1,416.0	926.4	1,282.7
Land, Buildings, and Equipment—Net	100.0	103.6	125.6	131.8	211.7	374.0	397.8	390.1	340.4	252.0	348.0	396.0
Miscellaneous Assets	100.0	115.4	138.5	169.2	176.9	1,069.2	238.5	838.5	1,953.8	1,007.7	1,053.8	376.9
Total Assets	100.0	117.0	149.7	154.4	255.0	421.5	522.0	816.7	1,159.7	987.4	720.4	944.0
Liabilities and Net Worth												
Banks and Other Loans Payable	*	*	*	*	*	*	*	*	*	*	*	*
Accounts Payable and Accrued Expenses	100.0	113.2	232.1	228.3	471.7	492.5	605.7	1,241.5	1,922.6	1,918.9	2,328.3	1,943.4
Reserve for Taxes on Income	100.0	185.0	135.0	160.0	365.0	730.0	950.0	3,665.0	8,480.0	6,425.0	*	1,290.0
Total Current Liabilities	100.0	132.9	332.9	221.9	608.2	728.8	1,556.2	3,617.8	6,116.4	4,180.8	1,690.4	3,230.1
Long-Term Liabilities	*	*	*	*	*	*	*	*	*	*	*	*
Reserve for Contingent Taxes on Income	*	*	*	*	*	*	*	*	*	*	*	*
Total Liabilities	100.0	132.9	383.6	256.2	746.6	728.8	1,556.2	3,827.4	6,469.9	4,660.3	2,169.9	3,709.6
Capital Stock:												
Preferred Stock	100.0	116.3	116.3	116.3	116.3	988.4	988.4	988.4	867.4	854.7	—	—
Common Stock	100.0	100.0	100.0	100.0	440.0	440.0	440.0	440.0	441.3	443.8	650.0	910.0
Surplus:												
Paid-In Surplus	100.0	100.0	100.0	100.0	100.0	100.0	100.0	100.0	133.3	250.0	9,016.7	2,100.0
Earned Surplus	100.0	122.9	129.4	171.0	75.4	175.1	180.9	236.5	335.8	423.2	439.2	527.0
Total Net Worth	100.0	114.9	118.3	140.7	189.2	380.4	383.5	413.4	448.4	495.4	526.2	573.6
Total Liabilities and Net Worth	100.0	117.0	149.7	154.4	255.0	421.5	522.0	816.7	1,159.7	987.4	720.4	944.0

*No base year figures.

Source: Prepared from Exhibit 8 by Harvard Business School staff.

exhibit 7C

LAPLANT-CHOATE MANUFACTURING CO., INC.

Selected Balance Sheet and Operating Ratios

	1936	1937	1938	1939	1940	1941	1942	1943	1944	1945	1946	January 31, 1947
(%) Current Ratio	5.2	4.9	2.6	3.9	2.4	3.1	2.0	1.5	1.4	1.8	2.9	2.1
($) Net Working Capital	$309	$380	$384	$476	$637	$1,100	$1,172	$1,427	$1,689	$2,357	$2,305	$2,542
(R) Acid Test[1]	2.6	2.3	1.1	1.7	0.9	1.1	0.6	0.8	0.9	1.2	0.9	0.6
(%) Current Assets to Total Assets	61.8	65.9	67.8	66.9	68.6	62.7	71.5	80.6	85.9	88.6	79.5	84.0
(%) Fixed Assets to Total Assets	36.1	32.0	30.3	30.8	29.9	32.0	27.5	17.2	10.6	9.2	17.4	15.1
(R) Net Worth to Debt[2]	7.5	6.5	2.3	4.1	1.9	3.9	1.8	0.9	0.5	0.9	2.3	1.3
(%) Net Worth to Total Assets	88.2	86.6	69.7	80.4	65.4	79.6	64.8	44.6	34.1	44.3	64.4	53.6
(%) Long-Term Liabilities to Total Assets	—	—	4.0	2.6	6.4	—	—	—	—	—	—	—
(Days) Receivables Turnover[3]	44	32	50	47	47	39	40	69	47	29	25	46
(%) Total Assets to Net Sales	54.0	46.6	60.7	52.6	63.9	66.2	61.6	66.3	57.4	41.4	53.1	84.4
(%) Fixed Assets to Net Sales	19.5	14.9	18.4	16.2	19.1	21.2	16.9	11.4	6.1	3.8	9.3	12.8
(%) Profit Before Taxes on Income to Net Worth	20.9	25.2	7.3	21.6	33.4	21.7	19.3	42.7	62.2	57.1	4.7	20.2
(%) Net Profit to Net Worth	17.2	19.3	5.7	17.5	26.3	16.2	12.2	12.9	18.0	15.0	7.3	12.3

[1] [Cash + United States Tax Notes & Receivables - Net] /Total Current Liabilities

[2] Debt=Total Current Liabilities + Long-Term Liabilities

[3] Receivables Net X 360/Net Sales

Source: Prepared from Exhibits 8 and 9 by Harvard Business School staff.

exhibit 8

LAPLANT-CHOATE MANUFACTURING CO., INC.

Profit and Loss Statements

(years ended June 30, 1936–1946: in thousands)

	1936	1937	1938	1939	1940	1941[1]	1942[1]	1943[1]	1944[1]	1945[1]	1946[2]	July 1, 1946 to Jan. 31, 1947
Net sales	$1,144	$1,551	$1,523	$1,812	$2,466	$3,933	$5,238	$7,617	$12,485	$14,746	$8,379	$6,915
Cost of sales, operating expense, etc.	997	1,363	1,446	1,610	2,081	3,415	4,669	6,440	10,660	12,879	8,092	6,220
	147	188	77	202	385	518	569	1,177	1,825	1,867	287	695
Depreciation and amortization	33	32	31	35	39	63	159	194	267	298	131	63
	114	156	46	167	346	455	410	983	1,558	1,569	156	632
Add: Interest earned, etc.		2	3	4	3	3	2	4	4	12	7	10
Deduct: Interest paid			2	5	5	9	8	25	43	40	29	11
Profit before taxes on income	114	158	47	166	344	449	404	962	1,519	1,541	134	631
Provisions for:												
Taxes on income	20	37	10	32	73	114	148	518	973	1,043	75[2]	247
Contingent taxes on income								153	105	92		
Net profit	94	121	37	134	271	335	256	291	441	406	209	384
Earnings per share of common stock	$41.75[3]	$71.90[3]	$18.85[3]	$79.45[3]	$1.88[4]	$2.30[4]	$1.50[4]	$1.75[4]	$2.81[5]	$2.60[6]	$0.96[7]	$1.32[8]
Dividends per share of common stock	$3.00	$29.00	$7.00	$3.50	$3.86	$0.15	$0.60	$0.60	$0.75	$0.80	$0.80	

[1] Figures have been revised to give effect to renegotiation, accelerated amortization of war facilities, and adjusted federal taxes on income.

[2] Excess of claim for refund of federal taxes on income arising from carry-back of unused excess profits tax credit over tax payable for year.

[3] Based on 1,600 common shares, $100 par value.

[4] Based on 140,800 common shares, $5 par value.

[5] Based on 141,120 common shares.

[6] Based on 142,024 common shares.

[7] Based on 208,000 common shares.

[8] Based on 291,200 common shares.

[9] Stock dividend.

Source: Company records.

exhibit 8A

LAPLANT-CHOATE MANUFACTURING CO., INC.

Profit and Loss Statement Analysis (percentages)
(index numbers: base year = 1936)

	1936	1937	1938	1939	1940	1941	1942	1943	1944	1945	1946	July 1, 1946 to Jan. 31, 1947
Net sales	100.0	100.0	100.0	100.0	100.0	100.0	100.0	100.0	100.0	100.0	100.0	100.0
Cost of sales, operating expense, etc.	87.2	87.9	95.0	88.9	84.4	86.8	89.1	84.6	85.4	87.3	96.6	90.0
	12.8	12.1	5.0	11.1	15.6	13.2	10.9	15.4	14.6	12.7	3.4	10.0
Depreciation and amortization	2.9	2.1	2.0	1.9	1.6	1.6	3.1	2.5	2.1	2.0	1.6	.9
	9.9	10.0	3.0	9.2	14.0	11.6	7.8	12.9	12.5	10.7	1.8	9.1
Add: Interest earned, etc.	—	.2	.2	.2	.1	.1	.1	.0	.0	.1	.1	.2
Deduct: Interest paid	—	—	.1	.3	.2	.3	.2	.3	.3	.3	.3	.2
Profit before taxes on income	9.9	10.2	3.1	9.1	13.9	11.4	7.7	12.6	12.2	10.5	1.6	9.1
Provisions for:												
Taxes on income	1.7	2.4	.7	1.7	2.9	2.9	2.8	6.8	7.8	7.1	.9	3.6
Contingent taxes on income	—	—	—	—	—	—	—	2.0	.9	.6	—	—
Net Profit	8.2	7.8	2.4	7.4	11.0	8.5	4.9	3.8	3.5	2.8	2.5	5.5

Source: Prepared from Exhibit 9 by Harvard Business School staff.

	1936	1937	1938	1939	1940	1941	1942	1943	1944	1945	1946
Net sales	100.0	135.6	133.1	158.4	215.6	343.8	457.9	665.8	1,091.3	1,289.0	732.4
Cost of sales, operating expense, etc.	100.0	136.7	145.0	161.5	208.7	342.5	468.3	645.9	1,069.2	1,291.8	811.6
	100.0	127.9	52.4	137.4	261.9	352.4	387.1	800.7	1,241.5	1,270.1	195.2
Depreciation and amortization	100.0	97.0	93.9	106.1	118.2	190.9	481.8	587.9	809.1	903.0	397.0
	100.0	136.8	40.4	146.5	303.5	399.1	359.6	862.3	1,366.7	1,376.3	136.8
Add: Interest earned, etc.		*									
Deduct: Interest paid			*	*	*	*	*	*	*	*	*
Profit before taxes on income	100.0	138.6	41.2	145.6	301.8	393.9	354.4	843.9	1,332.5	1,351.8	117.5
Provisions for:											
Taxes on income	100.0	185.0	50.0	160.0	365.0	570.0	740.0	2,590.0	4,865.0	5.215.0	375.0
Contingent taxes on income								*	*	*	
Net profit	100.0	128.7	39.4	142.6	288.3	356.4	272.3	309.6	469.1	431.9	222.3
Earnings per share of common stock	100.0	172.2	45.1	190.3	4.5	5.5	3.6	4.2	6.7	62	2.3
Dividends per share of common stock	100.0	966.7	233.3	116.7	128.7	5.0	20.0	20.0	25.0	26.7	26.7

*No base year figures.
Source: Prepared from Exhibit 9 by Harvard Business School staff.

The Morgan Corporation

The Morgan Corporation was, in 1962, one of the 50 largest industrial companies in the United States. The company was an important defense contractor, ranking within the top 10 firms in total military sales, and was also diversified into a number of important industrial product areas. Morgan was not engaged in the manufacture or sale of any consumer products.

The Morgan Corporation had compiled a record of growth in sales and earnings which was rated "impressive" by investors. Throughout the 1952 to 1962 period, the company had reinvested virtually all of its earnings in the business and had expanded its military and industrial product lines considerably.

The Microwave Components Division of The Morgan Corporation manufactured a broad line of microwave electronic components including waveguides, microwave antennas, and microwave tubes. The bulk of the division's components were sold to manufacturers of military microwave systems for original equipment manufacture; a smaller number were sold to systems users for replacement parts.

The largest of the operating groups within the Microwave Components Division was the Tube Department. The Tube Department produced a wide line of microwave tubes of three major types: magnetrons, klystrons, and traveling wave tubes. In 1962, the Tube Department had total sales of about $25 million.

In 1957, impressed by the potential they saw for microwave cooking, management of The Morgan Corporation decided to produce a magnetron-type microwave "cooker" tube for sale to manufacturers of microwave ovens. In 1960, the Tube Department succeeded in designing a cooker magnetron and, by 1962, was manufacturing about 150 cooker tubes per month—a production volume far below the potential that Morgan had envisioned in 1957.

In late 1962, corporate, divisional, and departmental management were trying to decide how they might best develop

---

© 1965 by the Board of Trustees of the Leland Stanford Junior University.

the market for the microwave cooker tube. Morgan executives saw two broad alternatives available to them:

1. Continue to sell the cooker magnetron to manufacturers of microwave ovens, or
2. Begin to manufacture and sell complete microwave ovens, hoping both to realize a profit on the oven manufacture and to stimulate sale of the Morgan cooker magnetron.

THE TUBE DEPARTMENT

Objectives

Management of the Tube Department stated that their objective was, in general, to continue supplying manufacturers of microwave systems with components related to the department's technological competence in electron devices. The Tube Department produced some accessories closely related to its microwave tubes, but concentrated on the manufacture and sale of tubes for use in systems manufactured by other firms.

According to Mr. George Crawford, the department's Director of Marketing, the Tube Department manufactured systems using microwave tubes only when such systems were not available from any other source. "Manufacture of systems such as radar," he said, "would get us into competition with our own customers. And, other divisions of The Morgan Corporation are better equipped, in terms of both facilities and personnel, to undertake such systems manufacture." Management of the Tube Department stated that manufacture of complete microwave ovens would thus represent a sharp departure from the stated objectives of the Tube Department.

Sales

Historically, magnetrons—one of the several major classes of microwave electron tubes—had been by far the most important product line manufactured by the department. In 1952, magnetrons accounted for almost 100% of total tube sales. According to one engineer, "Until the mid-1950's we produced a relatively narrow line of microwave tubes. Thus, we could capitalize on our extensive background of efficient production techniques."

In the mid-1950's, applications for klystrons and traveling wave tubes began growing rapidly; the Tube Department expanded its product line markedly by research and development concentrating on these newer tube types. In 1962, klystrons and magnetrons each contributed about 45% of total Tube Department sales of $25 million. The cooker tube, which was a magnetron-type tube, accounted for less than 2% of total Tube Department sales.

The engineer commented that "We've probably lost some of the production advantages we used to enjoy when we specialized in magnetrons. Nevertheless, I think that Morgan still gets more results per engineering dollar than the other companies having a tube line as broad as ours."

The basic line of electron tubes was sold to defense contractors by a small group of field sales engineers. Most sales were made on a bid basis and profits on any contracts were subject to government inspection and renegotiation. Government policy set "reasonable" profit margins at about 10% of sales. The cooker magnetron was the only item manufactured by the Tube Department which had a significant commercial market.

Organization

The 1962 formal organization of the Tube Department is shown in the simplified organization chart. The line managers of the Tube Department all had technical degrees, many of them Ph.D.'s in Electrical Engineering or Physics, and considerable experience in engineering development and design work. Most of these managers had published significant technical papers or held patents related to microwave tube design.

In November, 1962, Mr. David Bright, General Manager of the Tube Department, set up an informal committee, with himself as chairman, of the corporate, divisional, and departmental managers having responsibility for the cooker tube. The committee, according to Mr. Bright, was to advise the Tube Department on plans for marketing the cooker tube.

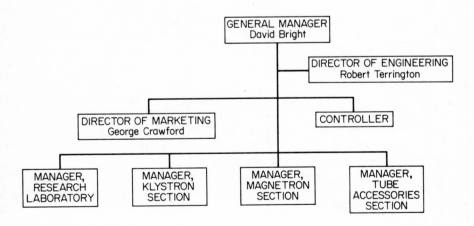

THE MICROWAVE INDUSTRY

The Tube Department's product line, including the microwave cooker tube, belonged to the microwave industry. Generally, the microwave industry was subdivided into two major classifications, components and systems. Although components (including microwave tubes) were sometimes sold for replacement parts, the bulk of component sales were to manufacturers of systems such as radar and electronic countermeasures equipment, communications systems, and scientific and test equipment.

Stanford Research Institute (SRI) predicted an annual growth rate of 6.5% (to $2.8 billion) for all microwave systems and components over the 1961 to 1966 period. The increasing costs of higher power tubes and other advanced components were expected to increase the relative importance of components in total microwave industry sales. SRI predicted annual sales gains of 8.5% for microwave components, from $350 million sales in 1961 to $600 million in 1966. Total tube sales were expected to grow at about the same rate as all microwave components generally.

The table presents estimated industry output from 1954 to 1962 and predictions for 1966 output of the most important tube types. The sale of mag-

Industry Output for Selected Microwave Tubes

(in millions of dollars)

	1954	1955	1956	1957	1958	1959	1960	1961	1962	1966
Magnetrons	51	42	42	44	50	49	45	45	46	50
Klystrons	4	16	21	25	29	40	48	53	55	60
Traveling Wave Tubes		1	2	6	12	17	22	26	48	60

Source: Figures prepared by casewriter from: *Business and Defense Services Administration, U.S. Department of Commerce,* for years 1952 to 1959; *Electronics Magazine* for years 1961 to 1966.

netrons, to which class the microwave cooker tube belonged, was expected to remain fairly static as newer tubes replaced magnetrons in many applications.

In 1962, about 16 companies, including 10 large corporations, manufactured microwave tubes. Some small firms had quickly gained prominence by developing one or two tubes which they could produce better than anyone else. Most of the tube manufacturers specialized in one or a few types of tubes rather than competing across the board in all tube types.

MICROWAVE HEATING

The Microwave Heating Effect

The heating of certain materials exposed to microwave energy was probably first noted in World War II work with the English magnetrons used in radar. Microwaves were known to be reflected by metal objects, and microwaves were observed to pass through many materials, such as air, glass, pottery, paper, etc., without significant attenuation. Thus, neither metal nor paper *absorbed* any heat-producing microwave energy. However, microwave energy was found to penetrate some distance into and be completely absorbed by a class of materials, including foodstuffs, which had electrical properties similar to water. The penetration enabled microwaves to generate heat both at the surface and in the interior of objects in this class of materials.

Most heating methods in general use depend on conduction. The surface of the mass to be heated is exposed to high temperatures; heat is conducted through the mass toward the center. Since conduction is an inherently slow process, the discovery of microwave heating was thought to be an important step toward the rapid heating, from surface to center, of solid materials.

Commenting on the economics of microwave heating, Mr. Bright pointed out that "the relatively high costs of operating microwave equipment limit its application primarily to heating processes where the object to be heated has a high value." In most geographical regions, the cost per unit of heat generated by conventional electric heaters is considerably higher than heating by coal, oil, or gas. Secondly, electronic devices generally have an input/output efficiency of 35% to 60%. "Thus," said Mr. Bright, "even before taking the amortization of complex equipment into consideration, the costs of buying electricity and generating heat through an electronic intermediary are initially much higher than generating an equivalent amount of heat by conventional means." Mr. Bright commented that few products other than food have values greater than the 30 cents to 40 cents per pound he felt necessary to justify the costs of microwave heating.

Industrial Applications

Although microwave energy was seen as a potential solution to numerous industrial heating problems because of its penetration, controllability, and "selective" heating of certain materials, few—if any—industrial applications had, by 1962, proven *economically* feasible.

For example, by replacing the original conventional heaters with microwave heating units, one company achieved a *technically* successful modification of a freeze-dry food processing unit manufactured by another firm. In the freeze-dry process, food was quick frozen and then placed in a vacuum chamber where the ice crystals sublimated until moisture content of the food was down to about 3% by weight. Although the food remained frozen throughout the process, heat was added to speed sublimation. With conventional heating, sublimation took place comparatively easily on the outer surface of the food. However, once these outer surfaces lost their moisture content, they acted as very effective insulation for the interior of the food. In contrast to the conventional conduction heating, microwaves could penetrate through the outer insulating surfaces and cut the whole processing time by a factor of three.

This reduction in time essentially trebled the capacity of a given freeze-dry process unit. The investment in microwave equipment was around $30,000, as compared with $250,000 for the rest of the freeze-dry unit. Morgan executives asked, however, "Who besides the food processor really makes money on the microwave freeze-dry equipment? Unless total sales of freeze-dry foods is more than trebled due to the introduction of the microwave heating, the freeze-dry equipment manufacturer will sell fewer units by using microwaves. And, unless the total market becomes very large, the money to be made on tubes and associated microwave equipment is small."

A number of other applications employing microwaves had been suggested and investigated. A major automobile battery manufacturer was concerned about the storage area required when the epoxy in the batteries was left standing to cure naturally. Morgan developed a heater which cut curing time radically and, because the battery company had only limited plant and property space, the microwave heater was proven economically attractive. However, a cheaper alternative method of heating the epoxy was finally chosen. The use of microwaves has also been suggested for the curing of plywood, foam rubber, and other products. Each of these applications would require specialized microwave engineering and design.

Microwave energy had also been proposed as a means of controlling temperature or moisture with more accuracy than is now feasible. For example, conventional fossil fuels (coal, oil, or gas) would be employed to bring a process close to the critical temperature, at which time microwave energy could be used for fine control.

Other applications would depend on the microwave property of heat generation in specific materials. Grain drying prior to storage has been suggested. In conventional dryers, grain is dropped through a tower where circulating hot air removes some of the moisture on each of several drops. However, this conventional method requires that energy be expended first to heat the air, which then transfers heat to the grain. Microwave heating could be an improvement in that the energy would act only on the grain and not the air, and secondly, would act on the interior of the grain as well as the surface. Mr. Robert Terrington, Tube Department Director of Engineering, thought that the higher cost of electronic energy might well be compensated for by the higher efficiency of its utilization.

Microwave Cooking

Of all the microwave heating applications investigated, food preparation by microwave energy looked most promising. The primary advantage cited for microwave cooking was its speed: food could be cooked in $\frac{1}{10}$ to $\frac{1}{15}$th of the time required in conventional electric or gas ranges. Microwave cooking was noted to have other advantages. Since microwaves did not heat metal, air, or pottery, only the food, or items in direct contact with the food, was heated. Thus, food could be cooked on the same plates used for serving, food splatters could easily be wiped off the cool oven walls, and little heat escaped into the kitchen.

Since cooking times were very short, foods retained their moisture and appearance. Finally, the cook had only to set a timer rather than worry about the twin variables of time and temperature, as in conventional cooking.

However, microwave cooking was said to have some disadvantages. Microwaves did not brown foods as much as conventional ranges; thus, the familiar charred exterior of a steak could not be achieved without using an auxiliary conventional broiler. Since energy tended to concentrate at the interface between meat and fat or meat and bone, meat was somewhat more cooked at these interfaces. Some foods which rose during the cooking process were not heated long enough to allow the protein to set; for example, souffles were a failure. A few freak problems also cropped up. For example, eggs sometimes exploded, since their tough membrances tended to contain rapidly generated steam.

Morgan executives commented that, to gain the full benefits of microwave cooking, one had to match the size of the load to be heated with the amount of microwave power carefully. For example, a 1-kilowatt microwave oven offered little speed advantage over conventional stoves for large loads. In such a unit, one potato would cook in about 3 minutes, but 10 potatoes required 25 minutes. On the other hand, an oven using multiple or high-power cooker tubes was unsuited for small loads since it created high-voltage arcs in the food, which could ruin its taste. In the cooking of large roasts, too much energy input sometimes resulted in the overcooking of the outer 1 inch of meat while the center was left raw.

The low moisture loss of foods during the short time required for microwave heating also suited microwaves to the reheating of leftovers or the reconstitution of prepared foods. In the reconstitution of foods, microwave energy was used only to heat to serving temperature foods, such as the familiar TV dinner, which had already been precooked by conventional means at the food processor's plant. Even with conventional ovens, reconstitution of prepared meals was faster than cooking of raw foods; microwave reconstitution was about 10 times faster than conventional reconstitution.

Frozen foods could also be thawed and heated to serving temperature in one step in the microwave oven. However, reconstitution of a portion of frozen food required about triple the heating time of an equivalent amount of thawed food. Although the use of high-power ovens could hasten the process, one limitation existed. As food defrosted, the thawed portions absorbed energy more quickly than the still-frozen areas. The sudden generation of steam sometimes caused the food to explode.

THE MICROWAVE OVEN

In 1962, the basic elements of a microwave oven were: a power supply for the cooker tube, a tube, a cavity (in which the food was heated), a door, a waveguide (which carried microwaves from the tube to the cavity), an outer cabinet, and a few simple controls, such as a timer. The power supply, operating from a standard low-voltage, low-frequency (220 volt, 60 cycle/second) electrical outlet, delivered high-voltage, low-frequency power to the tube. The tube converted the low-frequency electrical energy into the ultrahigh-frequency microwaves which could heat foodstuffs. Together, a cooker tube and its power supply were often referred to as a microwave heating unit or the "electronic" part of a microwave oven. The waveguide, cavity, and door were all sheet metal items whose primary function was to guide and contain the tube's microwave output around the food.

The Cooker Tube

According to Morgan's executives, the microwave cooker tube was "the vital component which makes the microwave oven operable." The cooker tube was closely related to the magnetrons used extensively in radar. According to one of Morgan's engineers, magnetron design required both a highly skilled microwave tube engineer and a large supporting staff of chemists, metallurgists, and tool and die makers. He commented that there were "perhaps only 10 to 20" engineers in the country able to work on the fine points of microwave tube design. Further, he thought that a "company needs $10 to $20 million in tube sales to support the necessary staff in metallurgy, etc."

Although magnetrons could be designed to operate at a number of frequencies suitable for microwave cooking, Federal Communicatons Commission (FCC) regulations required that microwave ovens be restricted to frequencies of 915 Mc (million cycles/second) or 2450 Mc only, so as not to interfere with communications transmitted at other microwave frequencies. In theory, the 915 Mc frequency had some advantages for microwave heating. Since the wavelength of 915 Mc microwaves was "longer" than 2450 Mc microwaves, energy at the lower frequency penetrated farther into foodstuffs before being completely absorbed. Thus, it was claimed, foods such as large roasts could be cooked from the surface to the center more uniformly. Also, 915 Mc microwaves should have had less tendency to concentrate in those sections of frozen foods which thawed first. Morgan's tube, however, was designed for 2450 Mc because, in practice, the higher frequency had been found to produce more even heating of foods.

Cooker magnetrons could also be designed for a range of output powers. The Morgan Corporation had decided on a 1-kilowatt output primarily because a prospective customer was interested in purchasing a tube of about that power.

Operating life (including the ability to withstand severe or incorrect use) was an important performance parameter in the sale of cooker tubes. Assuming a $136 replacement cost, and assuming 1,000 hours of operating life, tube "amortization" of 13.6 cents per hour (compared to electricity costs of 4 cents to 5 cents per hour) represented the major "operating cost" of a microwave oven. The Morgan Corporation's tube carried up to a 2 year warranty on operating life.

Tube warmup time was also a factor in the sale of cooker tubes, particularly when the tubes were purchased for use in household microwave ovens. Although, after warmup, a 1-kilowatt oven could reconstitute a 12 ounce meal in less than 2 minutes, some magnetron designs required up to 75 seconds before the tube could begin to generate microwave power. In homes where only one or two meals were heated, the warmup time could thus be a significant percentage of total heating time. In restaurants where an oven was in nearly continuous use, warmup time was less important, since the tube could be warmed up, then left in a "standby" (ready for instant use) condition which used only ⅓ as much electricity as when heating food. Morgan's latest cooker tube had a "fast" warmup of only 6 to 8 seconds.

Morgan's cooker tube manufacturing costs, in late 1962, were estimated at about $125 per unit on a volume of 1,500 to 2,000 tubes per year. Of the total cost, about 10% represented the cost of raw materials and purchased parts; the remainder was divided about equally between direct labor and overhead cost. The cooker tubes were produced in two rooms having a total of about 1,200 square feet of floor space. The machinery and equipment used in cooker tube production originally cost approximately $75,000. Mr. Bright estimated that production of up to 3,500 tubes per year could be accomplished with this equipment and production space simply by adding more workers.

Management thought that there were a number of ways in which costs could be reduced. First, the department was gradually substituting unskilled workers for technicians on the parts fabrication and assembly operations. Secondly, the main labor cost, parts fabrication labor, could be reduced "substantially" through automated machinery. Mr. Bright thought that $150,000 would purchase equipment capable of expanding parts production by a factor of 10. Since the Tube Department occupied an old mill building which was broken up into dozens of production areas, it was thought that more modern facilities, enabling efficient production line layout, might reduce cooker tube labor costs by 30% to 50%.

The selling price of Morgan's cooker tube was around $136. However, nearly all cooker tubes were sold as part of a microwave heating unit, named the "Heatwave Electronic Heating Unit," which included the tube's power supply. In 1962, the complete microwave heating unit was quoted at the following prices:

For use in household microwave ovens
(2 year warranty)

Quantity	Price/Unit
1-5 units	$350
20 units	315
100 units	280
5,000 units	206
10,000 units	194

The Cooker Tube Power Supply

The power supply for the Morgan cooker tube consisted of transformers and coils "of fairly simple and routine design," according to the department's engineers, and was built to Morgan's specifications by a major U.S. manufacturer of transformers. Each power supply cost Morgan about $70. Mr. Terrington, director of engineering for the Tube Department, saw "little chance to reduce the price of the power supply below current levels. Most of the inefficiencies in transformer design and manufacture have long since been eliminated and competition keeps margins low."

Although transformer costs were thought to be at a minimum for the current cooker tube–power supply combination, Mr. Terrington commented that "recent advances in electronic component performance have enabled a shift in the state-of-the-art which might cut costs of the complete heating unit in half." The new design concept was based on designing a cooker tube which could operate on the output from an inexpensive power supply, thereby eliminating the need for the expensive transformer power supply.

Equipment Design and Manufacture

Morgan's microwave heating units were sold to equipment manufacturers who fabricated the sheet metal parts, installed the heating units and other purchased parts, and marketed the completed microwave oven. Morgan's engineers stated that "considerable microwave technology is involved in designing the equipment" to ensure proper performance of the tube and proper heating of the food. Morgan's cooker tube applications engineer was continuously called on for assistance in equipment design by manufacturers who purchased the Morgan microwave heating units.

In terms of mechanical design and fabrication, requirements for the oven were not complex. Since the microwaves did not heat either the metal walls of the cavity or the air in the cavity, the oven did not require heavy insulation. The cavity did have to be completely enclosed and made of electrically conductive material. The door had to make a tight seal with the cavity to avoid leakage of microwave energy and to prevent the arcing which could occur where there was not a good metal-to-metal contact. Finally, the unit had to be easy to clean, since not enough heat was generated in the cavity walls to kill bacteria.

According to executives of a leading stove manufacturer who had investigated microwave oven manufacture, the cost of manufacturing a household oven, exclusive of the purchase price of the electronic heating unit, was about $200 per unit at a yearly volume of 1,000 units. However, one Morgan executive commented that $125 seemed a more reasonable cost estimate. Morgan believed that commercial ovens might be $150 more expensive to manufacture than household ovens. Plant and equipment used in the production of conventional electric or gas ranges were used to produce the microwave oven.

In 1962, retail selling prices for microwave ovens ranged from $795 for a single-tube household oven to $2,400 for a double-tube oven designed for commercial or restaurant use.

THE MARKETS FOR MICROWAVE OVENS

Development of Microwave Ovens

Toward the end of World War II, at least two companies—Raytheon and General Electric—became interested in using radar magnetron tubes for heating food. During the war, General Electric had developed an inexpensive 200-watt military magnetron which could operate at the 915 Mc frequency set aside by the FCC for noncommunications use. According to some reports, General Electric succeeded in getting this small magnetron to deliver 600 watts of microwave power into an oven. Although GE was rumored to have continued work on the cooker tube during the postwar period, the company never marketed a cooker tube of its own.

At about the same time, Raytheon also began looking for nonmilitary applications for its radar magnetrons. By 1945, Raytheon had developed a microwave oven, called the "Radarange," which used 2450 Mc radar magnetron tubes. According to one restaurant equipment distributor, this early unit was "bulky, nearly as complex as a radar set, and probably cost $10,000 to produce." In 1946, a number of experimental units were manufactured and started into field testing.

Raytheon continued extensive development work toward a practical microwave oven which could be used in restaurants and other commercial food service applications. During the course of its development work, Raytheon applied for, and was eventually granted, a number of patents covering aspects of tube design, methods of delivering and distributing microwave energy for cooking, and cavity design. In 1949, Raytheon interested the Tappan Company in using Raytheon tubes and power supplies for a domestic microwave oven. The Tappan Company, a large independent manufacturer of household electric and gas ranges, had no experience in microwave design, but, under Raytheon's guidance, began working on a microwave oven in 1951.

In 1955, Raytheon began marketing a Radarange for general purpose cooking in the restaurant industry. The oven delivered about 800 watts of energy at 2450 Mc, had a 1½ minute warmup time, and cost nealry $3,000. The oven was sold directly to potential users by Raytheon teams comprised of a chef and a technical salesman.

The Tappan Company introduced an electronic oven for household use in 1955. Tappan's oven used a Raytheon tube and power supply and was produced under license from Raytheon. To aid in the surface browning of foods a conventional electric broiler was included in Tappan's microwave oven. The oven sold at retail for $1,195 and was distributed to retailers through Tappan's established distribution channels.

Hotpoint, a division of General Electric, also began marketing a domestic microwave oven in 1955. Hotpoint's oven used a Raytheon heating unit and had a conventional electric broiler unit to brown foods. The range sold at retail for $1,395 and was distributed through the same marketing channels used for the company's conventional ranges.

The early microwave ovens were not highly successful in terms of sales. According to a report filed with the FCC by the Tappan Company, its household ovens were "too costly" to gain mass sales. Tappan did envision a market for up to 150,000 ovens per year, however, if the cost of the microwave heating unit could be reduced to $100, or about half of the Raytheon price. Trade reports indicated that Tappan had shelved several planned promotional campaigns because of difficulties with performance and delivery of the Raytheon microwave heating units. Although Raytheon was reported to have sold several thousand Radaranges to restaurants in the first few years of its marketing campaign, Radarange purchasers were not all satisfied with their investments. According to some restaurants, technical problems complicated the use of microwave cooking. Installation and service, which required the skills of a trained technician, were thought to be costly and somewhat slow. Unsatisfactory tube life and replacement costs of $225 per tube or $250 per complete heating unit caused a few firms to drop microwave cooking entirely.

In 1956, Tappan management began talks with the major manufacturers of microwave tubes, including The Morgan Corporation, in hopes of developing a second source of supply for microwave heating units. Morgan began analysis on the feasibility of a cooker magnetron early in 1957. During August, 1957, Morgan's management decided to try to make experimental tubes and power supplies available to Tappan by May, 1958. The target date for finished tube and power supply design was to be January, 1959. $50,000 was budgeted for tube design work.

Early development work proceeded slowly. A number of urgent military projects took priority on engineering time. Morgan engineers experimented with several radical tube designs which depended on materials not then available in quantity. When the initial $50,000 allocation was exhausted without producing a practical cooker magnetron, company management decided to design a tube which could serve as a replacement for Raytheon's tube. Another $100,000 was spent in developing the cooker magnetron and its power supply; design work was completed in mid-1960. The Morgan cooker magnetron delivered about 1 kilowatt of power and had a 75-second warmup time. Although Morgan engineers believed that their heating unit was technically superior to Raytheon's, Morgan's tube manufacturing costs were too high to match the $200 selling price of Raytheon's complete heating unit.

In late 1960, Litton Industries announced development of its "Microtron" microwave heating unit. Litton's magnetron had power output of about 1 kilowatt and a warmup time of 6 to 8 seconds. Once Litton had shown it possible, Morgan engineers redesigned the Morgan tube for fast warmup. Morgan believed that its tube had a longer life and was able to withstand more severe operating conditions.

Litton began supplying Tappan with microwave heating units for a price believed to be $200 per unit for a quantity of 1,000. Despite Litton's selling price of $200, Morgan engineers believed that Litton's production costs were as high as Morgan's costs, if not higher.

In February, 1961, General Electric unexpectedly introduced two commercial microwave ranges as a supplement to its broad line of conventional electric, forced-air, and steam ovens. One of the GE ovens, a single oven designed for countertop uses, sold for about $1,600. The other unit was a free-standing cabinet, with two ovens mounted one above the other, and sold for about $2,800. The basic oven design was quite similar to the previously introduced Hotpoint microwave ovens; both models used Litton microwave heating units.

During 1961, Raytheon introduced a microwave oven similar to its restaurant units which had the added feature of color-coded pushbutton timers. The oven was designed for consumer-operated "sidearm" heating of foods purchased from refrigerated vending machines or self-service cold storage cabinets. In such a system, the customer purchased a prepared meal or sandwich marked with a color code. The customer then placed his own meal in the adjacent sidearm heater and, by punching a pushbutton corresponding to his meal's color code, heated the meal for the correct length of time. Raytheon, in mid-1961, was reported to have replaced conventional cafeterias with microwave sidearm systems in 11 industrial plants. In 1961, the manager of the Raytheon Radarange department estimated that "by 1965 more than 3,000 plants will have electronic cafeterias in order to fill the void between small, vending machine lunchrooms (of the cold sandwich variety) and large cafeterias with on-premise cooking." A Canadian firm which was organized to prepare and distribute complete meals and sandwiches for microwave heating estimated that 2 to 4 Radaranges would serve 200 to 400 employees, 8 to 10 ovens would serve 1,000 to 1,500 employees.

Food Systems

In 1961, the sales departments of microwave oven manufacturers began emphasizing fast reconstitution rather than fast cooking. Earlier that year, a number of food and restaurant trade magazines had pointed out a trend toward the use of convenience foods—foods which required only slight conditioning at the restaurant to be ready for serving. Typically, convenience foods were cooked, packaged either in individual portions or in bulk, and frozen on a mass-production basis by food processors. Since most restaurants utilized their kitchen staff and equipment fully during only one or two peak periods a day and made only limited numbers of each particular food item on the menu, the cost to the restaurant of the additional steps performed at the food processors was thought to be substantially less than the concurrent reduction in the restaurant's labor costs and investment in space and equipment. Further, since the convenience foods were frozen, and meals were heated only as needed, food wastage was said to be reduced drastically.

During 1961, General Foods produced a line of high-quality convenience entrees, but withdrew it in 1962. According to Morgan executives, reconstitution in conventional ovens made it difficult to maintain the quality standards of the original product. General Foods was also reported to believe that "antiquated" regulations on the interstate shipping of frozen foods had vitiated the potential cost savings to customers. However, a number of restaurants which had heated the General Foods entrees with microwave ovens said that they had been most pleased with their results.

Several high-quality restaurants built their entire menu around prepared entrees and used microwave ovens for all heating. These restaurants essentially used the food processor as their kitchens, preparing only items such as vegetables and salads on the premises. Other restaurants used microwave ovens and convenience entrees as a supplement to the on-premise cooking of fast and simple entrees such as steaks and chops.

In 1962, Armour & Company and the Morton Foods Division of Continental Baking were both marketing extensive lines of frozen entrees for reconstitution. Many restaurant industry spokesmen believed that microwave ovens offered advantages of speed and quality retention in the heating of convenience foods. But neither the Morton nor the Armour entrees were packaged in materials especially suited for microwave heating. Mr. Bright thought that these companies, like General Foods, were reluctant to tie their products to microwave heating because of the high cost and newness of the ovens.

Some restaurants and chains developed reconstituted food systems of their own. For example, Buitoni, an integrated food processing and restaurant firm, set up a restaurant which used microwave heating for almost all meal preparation. Buitoni's food plant prepared a variety of complete Italian meals in single portion packages suitable for microwave reheating. These meals were transported to the restaurant, where they were stored in freezers and refrigerators. When a waitress received an order for a specific meal, she could select the proper serving from cold storage, place it in a microwave range for heating, and serve the hot meal— all within a couple of minutes. Any product left unsold at the end of the day could be held for days, if refrigerated, or weeks, if frozen. Similarly, a few restaurant chains set up central commissaries for food preparation employing microwave reconstitution. Some very small restaurants also set up "food systems" using microwave ovens. In such a system, the kitchen staff would use the slack serving hours to precook and refrigerate meals which could be reheated quickly by microwaves when needed.

Microwave ovens were also being used in some restaurants for general purpose cooking. For the most part, these users were small lunch counters which used microwave cooking only when peak serving hour demand exceeded the capacity of their conventional equipment. According to a survey taken by The Morgan Corporation, the firms cooking with microwave ovens were less satisfied with the return on their investment than those firms which used the ovens for reconstitution only.

Opportunities in the Restaurant Industry

The restaurant industry includes restaurants, lunchrooms, cafeterias, refreshment stands, catering firms, etc. The Department of Commerce estimated that total restaurant industry sales were $13.1 billion in 1954 and $15.2 billion in 1958. The National Restaurant Association predicted that 1962 industry sales would reach nearly $19 billion.

From Department of Commerce data for the years 1948, 1954, and 1958, certain trends were evident. Over the 1948 to 1958 period, the *number* of eating and drinking establishments had declined nearly 20% on a per capita basis, from 2.2 per thousand in 1948 to 1.8 per thousand in 1958. Secondly, those restaurants with sales above $100,000 per year had increased in industry importance. By 1954, the $100,000 (and over) class of restaurants had 31.2% of industry sales. During the 1954 to 1958 period, while total industry sales grew 16%, the $100,000 restaurants increased their share of the total market to 36.1%. Between 1954 and 1958, the number of $100,000 restaurants increased to 25,000, a growth of 25%. An even greater percentage growth in number (to 4,300) and share of market occurred in the subgroup of restaurants with yearly sales of over $300,000.

According to data compiled by the National Restaurant Association, the average net income before taxes during the 1955 to 1960 period was 1.4% of sales for all restaurants generally, and 4.0% for those restaurants showing a profit on operations. One of the major differences between the profitable and unprofitable restaurants was that the latter had substantially higher labor costs. A study conducted in conjunction with the industry's 1961 efforts to defeat Federal minimum wage legislation showed that average labor cost was 32% of sales. Students of the industry commented that "labor has for a number of years been taking more and more of the income dollar, to the disadvantage of profits and of the quality and quantity of material in the product sold." Mr. Bright said that chain restaurant operators had found that food *preparation,* rather than serving, accounted for the major part of labor expenses.

Although some speakers at a November, 1962, Cornell University Hotel and Restaurant School conference felt that pressure-steam heating of convenience entrees was a major advance in cutting food preparation costs, most speakers said that no equipment generally available for reconstitution exactly met the needs of a restaurant. According to most speakers, present microwave heaters were too expensive and too slow in heating large volumes of food, and available convenience foods were unsuitable for microwave reconstitution.

Morgan executives thought that, to achieve widespread use of microwave heating, microwave equipment manufacturers would have to combine their technology with that of the food processors and packaging manufacturers. According to Morgan, "No microwave heating equipment firm has established itself as *the* expert to whom restaurants, food processors, and packaging firms can come with their problems. Further, most of the ovens manufactured thus far have been general purpose units. Some unsuccessful oven designs have also hurt the reputation of all microwave ovens." One equipment salesman stated that, although Raytheon was rumored to have invested about $10 million in microwave heating, it had done only limited work with food processors and seemed to be interested primarily in sandwich items.

Mr. Bright believed that chain restaurants offered the greatest potential market for microwave heating. "Chain restaurants," said Mr. Bright, "use such large volumes of food that either food processors or chain-operated commissaries could economically prepare food tailored specifically for reconstitution in microwave ovens. This group is very much aware of the high costs of food wastage and preparation labor. Thus, assuming a good food system, we could show them an economic value of about $1,200-$1,400 for a microwave oven. With 50,000 chain units already in existence and more being added every year, an equipment manufacturer could afford to tailor an oven specifically to fit chain-restaurant needs, since this market segment might absorb 20,000 microwave ovens per year."

Mr. Bright commented that the gourmet, or high-quality, restaurant might be less willing to adopt microwave heating. These restaurants usually were not large enough to develop food systems of their own and food processors tended to concentrate on entrees of medium quality to supply the great majority of restaurants. However, it was thought that, even in the gourmet restaurants, some frozen convenience entrees of high quality could be used to supplement on-premises prepared foods.

Mr. Bright commented that "the time is past when we can afford the luxury of restaurants as inefficient as the 'Mom and Pop' stores. However, there still are a large number of these small restaurants, lunch counters, delicatessens, etc., which may represent a large potential market." Mr. Bright said that these restaurants typically have the "Blue Plate Special" which was prepared during the slack hours and then held on steam tables until served. Although most customers ordered the "Blue Plate," special orders for items which required cooking slowed customer turnover. Microwave heating offered a means of cooking the special orders in the same time cycle required to dish out a serving of the "Blue Plate." Although Morgan management did not believe that the "cook-faster" concept was the real advantage of microwave ovens, they did think that an economic value for the speed of the electronic oven could be shown.

Mr. Bright believed that the "Mom and Pop" restaurant market would be quite varied, with no one use sufficiently large to warrant the manufacturers' tailoring microwave equipment to that specific use. However, he also commented that the largest margin of profit might come from sales to this group.

"A number of glamour applications, such as microwave ovens in airplanes, have been suggested, but don't mean much," said Mr. Bright. "The volume is so low that development costs would be very difficult to amortize."

According to Mr. Bright, "The institutional market is very large, but looks a little remote for microwave heating. In institutions, food is not the main interest of the management, but rather an unavoidable cost and nuisance. Further, a captive market minimizes pressures for quality. Thus, batch feeding has generally been adopted as the cheapest and simplest way of dealing with the nourishment problem. However, some applications for extremely high-power magnetrons and conveyors have been suggested. This market is attractive in that the per unit investment could be very large, perhaps $50,000 per unit."

Opportunities in the Vending Industry

Sales of goods and services by automatic merchandising methods totaled about $2.7 billion in 1961. According to a 1960 Stanford Research Institute prediction, sales might pass the $6 billion mark by 1970. Manufacturers of vending machines had 1962 sales of almost $165 million and were expected to reach sales of $300 million by 1970. In 1962 the structure of the vending industry was:

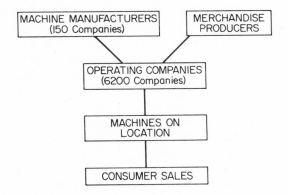

Although most of the operating companies were small (over half had less than 4 employees), several firms had sales of over $50 million, and one predicted 1962 sales of $170 million. Less than 10 companies acocunted for the majority of machine sales; one firm, Vendo Company, accounted for almost a third of total industry sales.

Most of the vending machines in operation sold cigarettes, soft drinks, and candy. In 1961, the vending of ready-to-eat food (other than candy) accounted for only about $80 million in sales; sandwiches ($15 million), other prepared foods ($40 million), canned hot soup ($15 million), and other canned foods ($10 million) were the most important food items. However, the fastest growth in automatic merchandising was expected to be the vending of foods, including complete hot dinners. SRI observed that meal vending machines may be placed in industrial plants, large offices, schools and colleges, hospitals, ball parks, recreational areas, military posts, or any other location where groups of people are likely to want meal facilities. Nearly 150,000 elementary and secondary schools, over 7,000 hospitals, 2,000 colleges and junior colleges, and over 300,000 industrial plants made up a large potential market.

Potential cost savings to be realized from vending ready-to-eat foods were thought impressive. SRI estimated that U.S. industry loses from $50 to $100 million annually subsidizing the operation of in-plant feeding facilities. About 60% of the companies that operated their own cafeterias lost money, and at least 20% of the companies that contracted with concessionaires fail to break even. SRI predicted that, as more plants moved to suburban locations away from commercial eating facilities and as more unions pressed for in-plant feeding as a fringe benefit, industry losses on cafeteria facilities would probably increase.

The introduction of automatic meal vendors could drastically cut these costs. According to one set of figures, a full-line machine array offering sandwiches, hot soup and other canned meals, pastry, and coffee requires only about 200 to 250 patrons daily, spending about 20 cents each, to break even. This compares with 750 to 1,000 employee-patrons needed to make a profit on company-run cafeterias. While the break-even point with the larger, more costly, complete-meal vendors was somewhat higher, costs were still far below those of conventional cafeteria operations.

Several large companies reported substantial savings in feeding employees from the use of machines. Also, many companies were turning to food vending machines for late-shift feeding and for supplementing cafeteria service. However, one survey showed that less than 10% of all plants with 250 or more employees had sandwich and pastry vendors, and fewer than 5% had machines selling hot canned foods.

In addition to industrial plants, SRI predicted that automatic vending of food would be popular in large offices. During the next few years firms such as insurance companies, with large office staffs, were expected to depend increasingly upon vending machines to service coffee breaks, snacks, and, later, complete meals.

Although the elementary and secondary school market was large (total wholesale value of food sold to public schools was over $600 million annually), the advantages of automatic vending appeared to be somewhat smaller. Because the choice of food for students could be limited, food could be prepared in large lots and predictable quantities prior to the meal.

Oil companies were encouraging the placement of a much wider variety of vending machines in company owned service stations because of the proven ability of machines as traffic builders. With automatic meal vendors, a patron was thought likely to make only one stop for food and gasoline.

"However," noted SRI, "the full potential of automatic meal vending will not be realized until some method of 'instantly' cooking refrigerated or frozen meals is generally available." In 1962, complete hot meals of high quality could not be vended conveniently. Most food machines held cooked meals at serving temperature until vended; enzymic action at elevated temperatures caused food quality to deteriorate rather quickly. Thus, any meals remaining unsold after a few hours had to be thrown away.

In contrast, frozen meals could be stored almost indefinitely so that precise estimates of daily sales were not a necessity. Even refrigeration could increase the shelf life of prepared foods up to 4 days. SRI in 1960 noted that microwave heating seemed the most promising method of accomplishing the "instant" heating of cold foods.

Morgan executives thought that "the use of sidearm units is perhaps the quickest and easiest way to combine microwave heaters and vending machines. However, the potential volume for sidearm units is probably quite small. Microwave heating won't come into large-scale vending use until someone develops a machine which can vend directly a meal heated by microwaves." As of 1962, no such machine had been developed.

Perhaps the major technical problem hampering the integral microwave heater was the "slowness" of heating. Although people were willing to be vended a cold meal, then wait up to 1½ minutes while they heated it in a sidearm unit, the vending machine manufacturers found that people were very unwilling to wait for more than 15 to 30 seconds to get something out of a machine. As noted earlier, there were very complex problems involved in trying to use high-power magnetrons to speed up the heating cycle.

Morgan believed that the major vending machine manufacturing companies were reluctant to invest in microwave hot-food vending machine development. SRI noted that "because of rapid machine obsolescence, the large number of companies competing for a modest market, and the high costs of research and development, machine manufacturing has been the least profitable segment of the vending industry." Further, Morgan was aware that one major company had commited substantial funds to development of a vending machine which held meals at serving temperature. This company was thought reluctant to undertake further research which could obsolete its existing line. Another company had been interested in microwave heating until the decline in market value of its stock during early 1962.

Even if a vending machine manufacturer who was interested in microwave heating could be found, Morgan was unsure of how far it would have to go in the manufacture of complete vending machines. On the one extreme, manufacture of a complete hot-food vending machine, to be distributed through the vending machine manufacturers, was thought to involve highly complex mechanical problems which could be solved best by experienced vending companies. On the other extreme, a vending machine manufacturer would have to develop considerable microwave competence to determine how microwave heating could be adapted to a vending machine.

Opportunities in the Household Market

In 1961, there were an estimated 60 million conventional electric or gas ovens in use in homes. The new building market was 1.3 to 1.6 million ranges per year; replacement sales brought industry output to over 4 million units, with gas ranges outselling electric by a ratio of 1.2 to 1. Prices at retail ranged from $100 to $500.

In 1958, a major manufacturer of household ranges and stoves estimated the annual market potential for microwave ovens at various retail prices, assuming "reasonable" amounts of promotional expenditures, as follows:

For use in commercial microwave ovens (1 year warranty) $275/unit in quantities of 500

Price per unit	Potential market
$1,200	3,000 units
1,000	12,500 units
900	25,000 units
750	75,000 units
700	100,000 units
500	300,000 units

Although very little advertising had been done by 1962, the retail price of Tappan's microwave oven had been reduced to $795. However, Tappan's sales of household microwave ovens (which accounted for virtually all sales of household microwave ovens) were thought to be less than 100 units per year.

Although Mr. Bright stated that most of Morgan's market estimates were based on the estimates of household range manufacturers, he cited a number of general reasons for believing that microwave heating had a good future:

To start from the very beginning, everybody has to eat three times a day. The basic population trends make a market for new food preparation equipment a certainty. Further, employment is increasing more rapidly than population. Therefore, if more of the population is employed, something has to happen. I think that the amount of time spent in the home will suffer. Since income is increasing, people will be willing to pay a premium to eat out or to make food preparation in the home quicker and easier. Even at the present time nearly 25% of disposable income is spent on food items, either luxury food items at home or restaurant meals. Microwave heating can make the cook's job simple; in fact, most of the work is done in the kitchens of the food manufacturer.

However, the absolute cost of a microwave range is important in the household market. The housewife doesn't assign a cost factor to her time, so we can't make payout calculations to show that a microwave range has an economic value twice that of a conventional stove.

Morgan executives cited a number of factors they believed important for the success of a household microwave oven. These were: technical criteria (performance, cost, installation, and service); existence of good prepared foods; and education or promotion. According to Mr. Terrington, the ideal household oven would operate from a standard 110-volt electrical outlet and require service no more complicated than present refrigerators. A 110-volt outlet would limit microwave power output to around 500 watts, which level was deemed satisfactory for household ovens. If higher microwave power output was more acceptable to the public, the oven would have to operate from a 220-volt electrical outlet. Mr. Terrington believed that "cost criteria are probably more difficult to establish. My own subjective estimate is that, if the retail price of a microwave oven were $275, sales would reach 500,000 units per year."

Commenting on the availability of good prepared foods, Mr. George Crawford, Tube Department Director of Marketing, said that "to date, food processors have encountered quality control problems after the food leaves the plant. Although food may leave the plant of gourmet quality, the meal as served will be poor unless the distributor, the retailer, and the customer all keep the food at a constant low temperature." However, Mr. Crawford thought that the consumer market, if equipped with microwave ovens, would provide such a large market for prepared foods that quality control throughout the chain of distribution would be forced to improve. Mr. Crawford noted, nevertheless, that the low-quality image of the common TV dinner might make it difficult to convince the household customer that any reconstituted foods could be good enough to warrant his purchasing an oven.

Mr. Crawford thought that "promotion of microwave cooking for the home would have to be extensive. Typically, appliance manufacturers spend 5% or more of sales on advertising; advertising expenditures for new products often run over 25% of sales during introduction. Since microwave heating is a radical innovation, promotional expenses could run higher than appliance industry experience." According to Mr. Crawford, vending installations using sidearm heaters could prove to be an important means of educating the general public about what microwave ovens can do.

Companies Active in Microwave Heating

In late 1962, Raytheon, Litton, and Morgan were the only U.S. companies producing a significant volume of cooker magnetron tubes. Both Litton and Morgan had their manufacturing facilities in the U.S., but Raytheon had shifted its production to an Italian affiliate. According to trade rumors, Raytheon was ready to shift its tube production again, this time to a Japanese affiliate. Some oven manufacturers thought that Raytheon's foreign production was enabling it to exert price pressure on the U.S. manufacturers; the complete Raytheon power unit of 800-watt output was selling for about $150 in quantities of 5,000. The Litton and Morgan heating units, both 1-kilowatt, sold for about $185 and $206 respectively, in quantities of 5,000.

General Electric was reported to have persisted in its efforts to design a workable 915 Mc tube and to be nearly ready for test marketing of a commercial range which incorporated its own tubes. The Franklin Manufacturing Co., a Studebaker subsidiary engaged in the manufacture of private brand appliances, was also known to be working on a microwave tube.

Two European firms had marketed microwave cooker tubes in the United States. Philips of Holland, a very large and diversified electronics company, was producing 2450 Mc tubes of 200-watt, 2.5 kilowatt, and 5-kilowatt power. Reportedly, the company was also experimenting with microwave cooking at different frequencies. Philips tubes were marketed through Amperex Company, its American subsidiary. The other European firm was a small German company, Mikrowellen, which produced a 2450 Mc tube with power output of about 1,300 watts. Mikrowellen tubes were sold primarily to Thermowave Corporation, a small oven manufacturer whose president had been the importer for Mikrowellen tubes.

Raytheon, Tappan, and General Electric were the major manufacturers of microwave ovens. Raytheon was marketing two new commercial ovens designed for either restaurant or sidearm use. One unit used two 800-watt magnetrons and sold for $2,400; the other oven, a single tube model, sold for $1,345. By 1962, Tappan had reduced the price of its household microwave oven to $795 and was also beginning to sell ovens for commercial use. The commercial ovens, one with a manual control for restaurants, the other with pushbutton timers for sidearm use, both used Litton electronic heating units and sold for $1,495. Morgan estimated that Tappan and Raytheon had 1962 microwave oven sales of roughly $750,000 and $2 million respectively. GE was thought to have sold several hundred commercial microwave ovens in 1962. Although GE's Hotpoint Division still carried a household oven, sales were thought to be "insignificant."

By 1962, Raytheon was selling its ovens primarily through hotel and restaurant jobbers. Service was handled through Raytheon service centers located in major cities. According to a survey conducted by The Morgan Corporation, almost ⅓ of the Raytheon oven users were dissatisfied with the cost and speed of service afforded by the centers.

Service for both Tappan's household microwave oven, sold through retailers carrying the Tappan conventional ranges, and its commercial ovens, sold directly to users by factory salesmen, was handled by an extensive factory service organization. However, Morgan executives thought that Tappan's service organization lacked microwave know-how and was at a disadvantage because it was not closely tied to the tube manufacturers' microwave technology.

By 1962, a number of small firms had begun the manufacture of ovens which used purchased tubes. Rudd-Melikian, a vending machine manufacturer with sales of $8 million, had designed an oven similar to an early Raytheon unit for use in conjunction with its vending machines. Rudd-Melikian's sidearm unit used a Raytheon heating unit. Seco Electronics, a Minneapolis-based subsidiary of Di-Acro Corporation, was marketing a unit, incorporating a Philips cooker tube, designed for commercial or sidearm use. The Micro-Dine Corporation, incorporated in late 1961, was marketing a range much like Seco's. Thermowave Corporation, founded in 1960, was marketing a range of unique design which used a Mikrowellen tube. American Monarch Corporation (formerly American Electronics) was producing an electronic oven which could use either a Franklin or a Raytheon tube.

At least three major European companies were interested in microwave oven manufacture. In addition to manufacturing cooker tubes, Philips was also working on oven design, concentrating primarily on high-power ovens for use in mass feeding operations. Since Philips lacked a U.S. marketing organization experienced in large equipment sales, Morgan executives did not think it likely that Philips would compete for the U.S. restaurant market in the foreseeable future. Elektro-Helios of Sweden, one of the largest manufacturers of commercial and domestic conventional heating equipment in Scandinavia, was said to be taking a "very broad approach to new methods of heating." In addition to buying microwave tubes from Philips, Morgan, and others, the company was investigating conventional heating methods such as forced air, steam, etc. Elektro-Helios had done little marketing in the United States. Husqvarna, a Swedish company which was formerly part of Saab, had purchased about 300 tubes from Mikrowellen and was expected to order about 1,000 tubes in 1963. According to Morgan's executives, Husqvarna had decided that there was a specialty market for microwave ovens on the continent, and was aiming for sidearm units, self-service units in motels, etc.

Several Japanese companies were also known to be working with microwave ranges. In early 1961, one of these, Hayakawa Electric, introduced a commercial unit selling for $2,800 to the Japanese market.

ALTERNATIVES

Commenting on the alternatives which the microwave heating committee was considering, Mr. Bright said that a tube manufacturer could only indirectly affect sales volume of microwave ovens and, thus, sales volume of its cooker tubes. Therefore, Morgan thought that manufacture of complete ovens might both produce a profit on the final equipment fabrication and stimulate sale of its cooker magnetrons.

Morgan executives believed that each of the major markets for microwave ovens (the restaurant, vending, and household markets) would involve different equipment design, marketing, and service considerations. Morgan thought that, in the long run, the household market offered by far the greatest volume potential for microwave ovens. Timing of entry was believed to be of vital importance, since "the first few successful entrants into the consumer market can probably establish a strong brand position." However, in 1962, manufacturing costs were thought to be too high for high-volume household oven sales.

Although manufacturing costs for restaurant ovens were roughly similar to household ovens, Mr. Bright felt that the commercial units could command much higher prices. Distribution of the restaurant ovens would be "much less complex since there is an established system of restaurant jobbers. Or, microwave ovens might be sold or leased to restaurants by a food processor wanting to stimulate sales of his line of convenience foods."

In discussing the Tube Department's capabilities, Mr. Bright said that:

Morgan has outstanding microwave technical skills and a fair amount of experience, gained from the equipment manufacturers we sell to, in product requirements. On the other hand, there isn't a division in the entire corporation which has a marketing organization or experience related to the restaurant, vending, or consumer markets.

Although the Tube Department itself has neither the facilities nor the personnel to deal with the sheet metal fabrication and assembly required in equipment manufacture, I think that this is less of a problem. Morgan is so diversified that some other division should be able to help us set up a sheet metal operation. Or, we could depend on subcontractors for a while. Some sort of a joint venture or merger with a manufacturer of conventional ranges is also a possibility. However, conventional ranges are typically manufactured by old-line companies whose managements may be unwilling to get involved with electronic technology.

chapter 3

The General Management Functions

At any point in time, a company's actual strategic posture will be determined by how each of the various managers throughout the total enterprise is performing certain "general management" functions. Although the opportunity to influence strategy may vary with the level of organizational responsibility, *every* manager is viewed as having *some* impact upon the outcome. Three basic general management functions are enunciated; these are in turn described in terms of seven basic policy commitments. An essential distinction is made between the seven *strategic variables* and the *operating variables* with which managers deal, and between four *strategic criteria* and a host of *operating criteria*. Finally, the relationship between strategy and performance is discussed.

DEFINITION OF "GENERAL MANAGEMENT FUNCTIONS"

In Chapter 2 we described a company's present situation in terms of the relationships among its *environment, resources,* and *membership*. This same set of analytical variables may be applied to the job of the individual manager. He is continually involved in relating together the requirements of the *environment* in which he operates, the *resources* available to him, and the capabilities, demands, and behavioral tolerances of the *persons* with whom he deals.

In relating these variables, every manager, within the discretionary limits of his position, performs to some degree the three basic general management functions of:

1. *Defining the scope* of his unit's activity (what it will emphasize).
2. *Specifying performance criteria* for his unit (what standards, limits, policies, and procedures will be enforced and reinforced within his unit, what performance will be rewarded or punished, and how).
3. Procuring, conserving, and then *deploying resources* among competing demands within his unit.

The cumulative performance of these functions by all of the managers within the enterprise, at any point in time, *will determine the company's actual strategic posture.*

THE MANAGER'S JOB

Of course, managers perform a great many other functions as well. But those which are not related to defining scope, specifying criteria, and deploying resources we prefer to classify as *administrative* (*operating* or *technical*) functions.

Some time ago, we suggested that managerial ability could be defined in terms of *technical, human,* and *conceptual* skills.[1] We argued that the relative importance of these skills varied with the level of the manager in the organization.

We proposed that technical skills are concerned with *what* is done; administrative (human) skills are concerned with *how* it is done; and general management (conceptual) skills are concerned with *why* it is done. We suggested that, at low levels of management, technical skills were most important; at intermediate levels, human skill became at least as important as technical; at top levels, conceptual (general management) skills became most important of all. The anvil-shaped diagram is meant to show that, at lowest levels, the manager is most heavily dependent on his technical abilities. As he rises to middle management

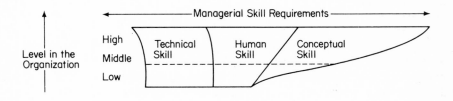

<hr/>

[1] Robert L. Katz, "Skills of an Effective Administrator," *Harvard Business Review,* Vol. 33, No. 1 (January-February 1955).

ranks, his technical skill may increase, but it becomes relatively less important than his ability to work effectively with others. At top management levels, both of these skills stand him in good stead, but his major requirement is for the conceptual ability to view the enterprise as a whole, in strategic terms.

It should be noted that managers are frequently called upon to fill roles requiring very different skill mixtures. The *remedial* role (when the organization is in great difficulty) calls for drastic human action and emphasizes conceptual and technical skills. The *maintaining* role (of sustaining the organization in its present posture) requires only modest technical or strategic changes and emphasizes human skill. But the *innovative role* (developing and expanding the organization) demands high competence in conceptual and human skills on the part of the manager, with the technical contribution being provided primarily by subordinates.

DIFFERENCES AND SIMILARITIES BY ORGANIZATIONAL LEVEL

To carry this analysis one step further, we submit that, from a strategic point of view, the most crucial requirements for a manager are that he be an analyst of conditions affecting his unit; a procurer and allocator of the resources to be used by his unit; and a diagnostician of the interpersonal relationships, values, and norms within his unit. These requirements are *common to all managerial positions,* not just to those jobs called "general management." The relevant characteristics of environment, resources, and people shift with the range of responsibility inherent in each position.

The *environment* of an individual manager coincides with the range of accessible information available to him, which is relevant to the discretionary actions he may take. Thus, the environment of a general manager may include not only the entire enterprise, but also the entire socio-political-economic fabric of the nation or the world. The environment of a division head may include only that part of the world external to the enterprise which relates directly to the activities of his division and, internally, only his own division and those persons and activities in other divisions which directly affect his division. The environment of a department head may be defined still more narrowly as comprising only his own department and those other persons and activities within the enterprise which directly affect his department.

Similarly, the nature and volume of available *resources* will be different at each organizational level, depending on the freedom of choice or degree of decision-making autonomy inherent in the manager's position.

Entrepreneurs bring into the enterprise new, additional resources which it previously did not possess. Only a few top positions in an enterprise normally have discretionary access to sources of outside funds or the right to acquire major phyical resources.

In contrast, *administrators* work with resources already existing within the enterprise, or resources which they generate internally. At his own organizational level, the administrator has a negotiating opportunity to secure for his unit some share of the total discretionary resources of the enterprise. But the volume of resources potentially available to each unit decreases sharply at each successively lower level of the organization.

The *people* with whom the manager is concerned similarly vary with his level of responsibility. The first level supervisor must be concerned, individually and collectively, with each person under his supervision, plus all those individuals directly contacting his unit. Each successively higher level of management needs to concern itself more and more with the *collective* patterns of values, norms, and power relationships among the various units, and *individually* only with those persons who *represent* the units, or who provide staff-level support to the manager.

STRATEGIC VARIABLES

We have described the general management functions as defining scope, specifying performance criteria, and deploying resources, but they can be broken down more specifically in terms of seven basic policy commitments. These seven *strategic variables* are by far the most crucial to the survival and development of the enterprise. They relate the enterprise to its external environment, and are defined in practice, i.e., in how the business actually conducts its affairs. If managers do not continually monitor and consciously modify these parameters, they will soon discover that they have become the captives of their situations, rather than the masters. All of their efforts will be spent in defensive responses to external pressures and events, and they will have forsaken the opportunity to initiate action upon their environments and to plan their own futures.

Carl Oakes, the general manager of Mitchell Nursery Company, is a clear example of an executive who has been unable to identify and control the strategic variables in his company. As a result, although his firm has been consistently profitable, he "can't get away from the feeling that we are just about to go under." This harassed executive feels himself to be at the mercy of his competitors, the weather, and the vagaries of his customers. In fact, this has become a self-fulfilling prophecy. These external factors have, through Oakes' abdication of the initiative, been determining the strategic posture of the company, providing the pressures to which Oakes continually reacts.

Similarly, in Pioneer Brass Co. (a case which appears later in this book) management felt itself completely at the mercy of the residential building cycle, with no opportunity to determine its own destiny. In this instance, the efforts and preferences of jobbers and large customers determined both company product policy and pricing policy, because, here too, management merely responded to immediate external pressures and events.

Inevitably, these strategic parameters will become defined by customers, salesmen, low-level subordinates, competitors, and so on, whenever management fails to maintain the initiative. No business operates without allocating resources, accepting orders, and delivering products or services. The way in which these functions are accomplished—where the emphasis is actually placed, what priority sequence is actually followed, and what criteria are applied—defines the company's strategic posture.

We suggest that only seven key parameters need to be considered on a continuous, universal basis in determining company strategy: product policy, customer policy, distribution and promotion policy, competitive emphasis, pricing policy, financing policy, and investment policy. Other parameters may assume temporary strategic importance to many firms or be of major continuing importance to a single enterprise, e.g., labor relations at a time of intense conflict; plant location (a once-in-a-generation decision); or a major change in the law or in government practice. But each of these later variables becomes so urgent and obvious that it is unlikely to be slighted. Product-market-customer mix, on the other hand, is frequently looked upon as a given rather than as a variable over which management can maintain the initiative.

Let us look at each of the seven key parameters in turn. Whether the enterprise's officers know it or not, their company *always* has a current position along each of these strategic dimensions. The systemic confluence of these seven dimensions (along with those parameters which may have temporary strategic importance) is what we mean by the enterprise's *corporate strategy*.

Product policy. By this we mean the design, specifications, characteristics, and mix of products (or services) offered. Especially important here are the questions of which items or characteristics to emphasize, which lines to add, and which items to drop. In the La Plant-Choate case [found on page 109], that Mr. Choate cited lack of control over this variable as the most unsatisfactory part of his relationship with Caterpillar. Frequently, the personal preferences of field salesmen or sales managers will determine the company's product mix, without any reference to the importance of the different items to over-all profits or company stability—e.g., in Mitchell Nursery. Or, as in Pioneer Brass [page 109], the product mix may be determined wholly by the sequence in which orders are received, without any conscious corporate attempt to influence purchasers' choices. A frequent oversight here is the failure to analyze sales volume by product type. Often a very small number of types comprises the great bulk of a company's business, yet managers continue to think of their companies as having broad-based product lines—e.g., in Morgan Corp. [to be found on page 72], two tube types constituted 90% of Tube Department Sales. Yet management thought of the department as offering a full line of microwave tubes. Hence any item for which there is customer interest could command large sums for product development, regardless of its impact on the rest of the organization.

Explicit attention to product policy requires continually answering the key question: "Where are our principal product/service concentrations?"

Customer policy. This parameter refers to the specific types and characteristics of customers to whom products (or services) are offered. Which markets to enter, which segments to concentrate on, where to place geographic emphasis, are all questions which require continual determination. La Plant-Choate *chose* to sell directly to earth-moving contractors, after a long period of supplying only one customer. On the other hand, we saw Mitchell Nursery selling to whomever sought *them* out. Morgan Corp. tried vigorously to sell their cooker tubes to manufacturers of microwave ovens with such limited success that they were contemplating manufacturing the ovens themselves. Specific salesmen's interests and abilities in gaining acceptance by individual companies was shaping Pioneer's market policy, almost independently of management. Concentrations of customers can determine a company's destiny, if management is not sensitive to this fact and has not created viable relationships.

Explicit attention to our customer policy requires the continual answering of: "Where are our major market opportunities?"

Distribution and promotion policy. By this is meant the manner in which products (or services) are moved from the supplier to the end user, and how prospective users are informed and encouraged to purchase. Key questions here concern choices among distributors, dealers, and direct salesmen in each of the different markets the company serves, and how best to reach the prospective user with product information and promotional material. In La Plant-Choate, direct sales to Caterpillar were replaced by a hastily-formed dealer organization backed up by newly-organized regional sales representatives. However, the strongest dealers were already representing competitors, and La Plant-Choate was left with second-rate sales and service facilities. In Pioneer Brass, stocking and non-stocking jobbers, direct salesmen, product specialists, and sales by officers directly to large customers were all involved. Volume through any of these channels could vary substantially over any time period, but discernible trends caused little change in company behavior. Morgan sold virtually its entire output through sales engineers to defense contractors on a bid basis. Thus they were ill-equipped to enter a line which required widespread consumer distribution.

Explicit attention to distribution policy requires continually answering the question: "How can we best get our products into the hands of our prospective customers?"

Competitive emphasis. By this we mean the distinctive competitive advantage which the company emphasizes in its efforts. La Plant-Choate emphasized design ingenuity and manufacturing efficiency when it was solely a supplier to Caterpillar. Later, the emphasis shifted to the performance characteristics of its products, since dealers had little else to distinguish their line. Morgan emphasized its broad research capability, but actual product sales were concentrated in only two types of tubes. Pioneer relied on its long-standing relationships with municipalities, while Mitchell Nursery, for example, depended on its location for its competitive advantage.

Explicit definition of a firm's competitive advantage focuses efforts on *what the enterprise can do better than anyone else,* and is a primary guide to establishing emphasis and priorities.

Pricing policy. Here we are concerned with how to charge for the various products or services offered. La Plant-Choate priced its equipment on the basis of what competitors charged. Pioneer applied a variable discount policy that makes pricing a function of customer pressure. Mitchell Nursery tried to maintain a constant price, year in and year out. Each of these practices shapes the kind of customer mix and the character of the business which that company conducts.

Explicit attention to pricing policy obliges the enterprise to determine its *qualitative* customer mix and its price/value product mix. If such attention is not given, pricing policy can unduly influence product specifications and customer characteristics.

Financing policy. Where and how to obtain the short-term and permanent capital needed for the enterprise is also a crucial element in defining the character of the company. La Plant-Choate, forced to borrow from banks and to float equity may expect its dealers to be self-financing; this places them at a competitive disadvantage. Mr. Oakes and Mr. Mitchell financed Mitchell Nursery's requirements out of their own pockets, which made them very cautious about new investments. Each of these practices molds the character and scope of the company.

Explicit attention to financing policy obliges the company to consider: "Are we exploiting our available opportunities?" or "Are we unwittingly allowing ourselves to lose competitive flexibility?"

Investment policy. Each of the six variables cited above has an immediate impact on the business. A more delayed impact stems from the funds allocation choices made among discretionary expense items (e.g., product development, sales promotion, equipment maintenance) and among capital budgeting items (e.g., choices among alternate technologies, production processes, major make-or-buy decisions, construction of new facilities). These choices reflect the current relative emphasis being given to the various functions (e.g., engineering, manufacturing, marketing) or to the various product lines or divisions. Their immediate impact is not severe, but, ultimately, they determine the company's long-range strategic posture. La Plant-Choate's early emphasis was consistently in favor of engineering. Later it was obliged to emphasize distribution and manufacturing. Mitchell's major investments in inventories gave it great leverage with customers.

Similarly, *divestment* choices critically affect the direction of a company's operations. Not only do they narrow the company's product/market scope, but they also often provide additional funds whose reinvestment may further emphasize a particular function, product line, or division.

Explicit attention to investment policy obliges the enterprise to continually *define its scope, its competitive advantages, and its greatest areas of opportunity*.

Perhaps key *personnel placement* decisions should be added as an eighth strategic variable. New persons in key job positions will necessarily affect which strategic choices are made and which criteria are honored. Changing the previously existing balance of power among principal executives can influence materially the activities and objectives which are emphasized and the commitments and allocations which are made.

These seven (or eight) strategic variables determine the enterprise's scope and resource allocation; they establish how effective the enterprise will be. Obviously, those in the top organizational positions have both the greatest obligation and the best opportunity to influence these determinations consciously and continuously. However, many others in the organization also affect these variables. If such persons are consciously aware of their impact, they can make major contributions to the enterprise's survival capacity and success. Any of these variables which are *not* given explicit attention at top management levels, will be defined in practice, either at lower levels, or as a consequence of external factors.

STRATEGIC CRITERIA

The strategic variables require criteria if consistent and responsible choices and decisions are to be made. Whether explicitly defined or implicitly inferred, managers making these choices usually act in terms of achieving:

1. A desired *growth rate* for the unit or for the total enterprise (in sales, assets, net worth, or numbers of employees).
2. A desired *market share* or penetration.
3. A desired *tradeoff between risk and reward* (usually measured in terms of profit objectives, such as return on investment, earnings per share, or additions to net worth).
4. A desired *life span* (for perpetuity, or until the occurrence of a specific event).

These specifications can all be expressed in terms of market performance. They can be given numerical values and can serve as indicators of how well the enterprise is responding to the requirements and opportunities of its external environment (*effectiveness*). Evaluative measurements can be made along these four dimensions by comparing present performance with: (a) desired target goals; (b) own past performance; (c) the performance records of competitors; and (d) alternative uses of company resources. *When they are explicitly defined and universally applied, the selected points along these four dimensions become the enterprise's performance objectives.*

OPERATING VARIABLES

Most managers spend the majority of their time on the nonstrategic, operating concerns which affect the *efficiency* of the enterprise, i.e., the degree to which the company is able to maintain high internal performance levels. The crucial internal operating variables are:

1. *Structure:* the assignments of responsibilities, accountabilities, and division of labor; the selection and placement (and replacement) of personnel; the establishment and formalizing of work-flow and communication requirements.
2. *Standards:* the establishment, enforcement, and reinforcement of operating systems, procedures, rules, routines, and policies which govern behavior; the identification and enforcement of desired performance ranges and limits; assuring that performance requirements and standards are consistent with the corporate strategy. (If performance and strategy are not consistent, the actual behavior will produce unanticipated shifts in the existing strategic posture.)
3. *Evaluation:* the measurement of the performance of individuals, groups, departments, divisions, and the total enterprise (as related to strategic requirements); the administration of organizational social and monetary rewards and punishments (relative to the strategic requirements).
4. *Value reinforcement:* the representation of the objectives, values, and sentiments of the organization to employees and community; the legitimatization of procedures, plans, and decisions; the conduct of the expected ceremonies in connection with beginning and ending projects, bestowing rewards, anointing positions, and so on.

These four variables are dimensions along which the organization's work gets done and its strategic objectives and criteria become institutionalized. Whereas the strategic variables give the enterprise its *direction,* the operating variables provide its *control.*

The enterprise can be thought of as being in control of itself when its structure, standards, and values are clear; when its standards are consistent with strategic objectives and are continually enforced and reinforced; when evaluations are consistent with the standards; and when its members are committed to the values and standards. When these conditions are obtained, members become self-regulating, with no need for external policing or threat.

These four basic operating variables determine the organization's *performance levels.* Higher management positions again have the greatest obligation and opportunity to establish limits, standards, and operating philosophy. Lower level managers may become basically reallocators of resources and reinforcers of standards previously set. But if the structure, standards, evaluations, and value reinforcements are *not* set at high levels, then these variables will be defined and established at subordinate levels, either as a consequence of explicit lower management intent or in implicit response to work group norms and pressures.

OPERATING CRITERIA

The operating variables also require criteria to guide choices. Most managers act in terms of achieving:

1. Some specific level of *output* (as measured by manpower productivity or total units produced).
2. Sufficient *satisfaction* to avoid excessive conflict or antagonism, and to preserve stability (in terms of labor turnover and absenteeism).
3. Sufficient *cooperation* and collaboration among individuals and units to get the work done without inordinate slippage.
4. Some degree of *learning,* growth, and individual development (in terms of ability to provide internally for succession and for filling newly developed or expanding positions).
5. Some specific level of total *cost* (relative to own past performance, comparable units' performance, records of competitors).
6. Sufficient levels of *service, delivery,* and *quality* to meet scheduled obligations and customer expectations.
7. Some degree of creativity and *innovation* (in terms of new ideas regarding products, processes, or procedures).

Some of these specifications are quantifiable; some are susceptible only to qualitative judgment. All are measures of *internal* performance, of how *efficiently* the organization is operating. Evaluative measurements of operating efficiency can be made along these seven dimensions by comparing actual performance level with desired goals; own past performance; competitors' performance; or the performance of comparable units.

RELATING THE STRATEGIC PLAN
AND OPERATIONAL PERFORMANCE

The operating performance of an enterprise frequently is at variance with the requirements of chosen strategic performance objectives. This may result from the strategic plan not properly matching the resources of the enterprise with the requirements of the marketplace, or may stem from the behavior of people in the company not being adequate to, or consistent with, the task requirements of the strategy. Sometimes both mismatches are made.

Some managers assume that once a strategy is set, a detailed program should be determined which delineates appropriate behavior for all members of the enterprise. Members are then supposed to be informed, trained, directed, motivated, and controlled so that they will perform precisely according to plan. This assumption sees strategy formulation as exclusively the province of top management and separate from strategy implementation. Implementation is thought of as the responsibility of subordinate managers, whose only job is to assure that all employees perform as planned.

Anyone with organizational experience knows that things *never* work out this way. People's performances are always *different* from what is planned, and the program *always* turns out differently, in some degree, from what was intended.

Similarly, an enterprise's actual strategic posture is *always* determined, at least in part, by the performance of individual salesmen, financial managers, production men, and so on. Often the corporate emphasis is determined by the unrecognized emergence of a power structure which values certain aspects more highly than others. Emphasis on a particular set of values obliges the organization to a specific strategic posture.

Sometimes top management does not develop a clear value orientation, and equal weight is given to all elements of activities. While this posture's apparent fairness to all parties tends to minimize overt disagreement and conflicts, it inevitably creates inequities. Units with different levels of opportunity will always find ways to redress their perceived disadvantages. Differential emphasis will *always* exist among units and activities, whether sanctioned by top management or not. This emergent emphasis will set the strategic posture of the enterprise in a way which was unplanned and unanticipated, but which is nevertheless real and governing.

An enterprise cannot avoid a strategy. If top managers do not make explicit strategic choices of emphasis and priorities, then the strategic posture will emerge from the actual performance of the enterprise's members.

It is the job of the manager at every level simultaneously to deal with *both* the strategic and the operating elements affecting total corporate performance. He must assure that plans fit the capabilities and motivations of the unit's members, and also that the actual behavior is compatible with the plan. Thus, he may be modifying *both* plan and behavior so that they will be compatible. Assuring that these modifications mesh with activities of other units is the job of each successively higher level manager.

All persons and groups have strong value identifications (a product of their past experience) that influence their perceptions of their present situation. They respond positively to outside direction only within their "zones of indifference" —i.e., they will do those things that do not violate greatly their values, their evaluations by their peers, and their beliefs about themselves. People will resist external pressures to do those things which lie outside their "zones of indifference." But for most persons who comprise an organization, this zone is very broad. The aggregate corporate "zone of indifference" is broader still, which is why many organizations can survive inefficient or inappropriate management direction.

Much organizational activity takes place as a result of setting up mutual feelings of *obligation* between enterprise managers and employees (e.g., "a fair day's work for a fair day's pay"—with "fair" defined by each party). We submit that the appropriate managerial function is *not* to elicit performance through obligation, but rather to provide conditions which promote *commitment* and *competence*.

COMMITMENT AND COMPETENCE

Commitment occurs when individuals identify emotionally with an *idea* or *ideal* which is consistent with their own values and aspirations. Commitment may be to a department goal (e.g., meeting production schedules on time and within budget) if that is the basis on which a person evaluates himself. It may be to a personalized "company" image, personified by the top management (e.g., doing whatever will cause the President to think well of me), if the person has high dependency needs. It may be to some intangible corporate goal (e.g., to be the "best" company in the business), when the evaluations of those *outside* the enterprise are most important to the individual. Or it may be a commitment to serving others—providing opportunities for others' growth, development, and understanding—if the person evaluates himself in terms of such contributive criteria.

Competence is an outgrowth of innate ability, education, practice, and experience. High standards of performance, rigorously enforced along dimensions which the persons involved deem important, tend to produce high levels of competence. Enforcement of standards deemed unimportant by those involved produces subterfuges, counterreactions, and other unanticipated and undesired behavior.

The true test of the manager lies in his ability to respond to his people in such a way that he encourages competence (as *they* define it!), and commitment (as *they* define it!) by:

1. Establishing a strategy and a set of limits and standards which are acceptable and meaningful to those people.
2. Deploying resources, measuring performance, and administering rewards and punishments in relation to that strategy.
3. Assuring that the strategy fits the requirements of the environment, the available resources of the unit, and the competences and commitments of the people.

This is an extraordinarily difficult task. It requires special skills and special ways of thinking. But *how* it is performed will determine the survival capacity and developmental capability of each unit and of the total enterprise.

Pioneer Brass Company (A)

INTRODUCTION

The Pioneer Brass Company manufactured a line of bronze valves, fittings, and couplings for the waterworks industry.[1] Located in Chicago, the company had long been an important supplier to waterworks customers in the Illinois-Wisconsin area. Management estimated that, in 1958, Pioneer held a 50% share of the market for products in its line. The company had sales of about $1.5 million and employed over 120 people. But, against a background of 14 consecutive years of profitable operations and peak earnings of over $100,000, Pioneer suffered losses of $9,000 and $22,000 in 1957 and 1958.

COMPANY BACKGROUND

Incorporated in 1892 in the city of Chicago, the Pioneer Brass Company began as a foundry and machine shop for the manufacture of any product involving bronze castings. In 1905, an increased volume of business enabled the company to move to new quarters in downtown Chicago.

By 1919, the company had entered the waterworks business in addition to its job shop operations and, by 1920, had completed a shift to the exclusive manufacture of a catalogued line of waterworks valves and fittings. Although sales declined during the 1919 transition year, Pioneer posted 1920 sales of $205,000, an increase of $60,000 over 1918.

---

[1] See *Note on U.S. Waterworks Industry.*

At the outset, Pioneer sold its products directly to local water companies for use in connecting water service to homes. Since demand was closely related to residential housing starts, volume declined drastically with the start of the 1929 depression and the company suffered losses during the 1931 to 1934 depression years. The firm emerged strongly in the late 1930's and, in 1941, earned record profits and return no net worth with sales of $416,000. With the exception of 1942, when retooling and changeover for wartime production of bronze ship fittings resulted in a loss, Pioneer showed consistent profits for over 20 years.

Accompanying the postwar expansion in housing starts, Pioneer sales and earnings increased in 1946 and 1947. In 1950, "housing starts jumped to a new all-time high," according to company management. Pioneer sales rose to over $1.2 million. In 1952, the company moved to a new plant on the outskirts of Chicago.

Although expanding the size of its product line, Pioneer continued to concentrate on waterworks products. In the 1950's jobbers became increasingly important in the distribution of Pioneer products, and price competition became significant in the company's market.

Operations remained profitable through 1956. In the middle of 1957, the Pioneer Brass workers struck. Management hired an entire new workforce through the picket line and resumed production. Pioneer lost $21,000 (before tax refunds) in 1957 and $41,000 in 1958. A financial summary of operations from 1920 to 1958 is presented as Exhibit 1.

COMPANY ORGANIZATION AND MANAGEMENT

Pioneer's founder, Myron Bransten, operated the company until his death in 1899. Subsequently, his two sons took over management of the company, with the elder serving as president. The younger son, Alan Bransten, worked in various departments within the company and in 1918, at the age of 40, replaced his brother as president and general manager. Over the years of his presidency, Alan Bransten gradually delegated much of the responsibility for operations to Mr. George Cunningham. Mr. Cunningham directed the foundry, machine shop, purchasing, personnel, and design functions. Mr. Mel King, reporting to Mr. Bransten, directed the firm's sales activities. An accountant, Mr. Roberts, handled the bookkeeping and office functions. Total company employment varied; starting at 40 in the 1920's, employment dropped to 32 in the depression and then rose to a prewar high of 77 in 1941. The company provided Alan Bransten with a good income and was able to pay some dividends to the family owners.

Alan Bransten's son, Guy, entered the business on a full-time basis in 1941 after completing three years at the University of Illinois. In 1944, at the age of 24, Guy Bransten was appointed vice president and general manager, but spent the next two years in the service. Returning to the company in 1946, Guy was given full responsibility for management of the company and, in 1949, became

exhibit 1

PIONEER BRASS COMPANY (A)

Historical Financial Summary

Year	Net Sales (000)	Income Before Taxes (000)	Net Income (000)	Earnings as % of Sales	Dividends Paid (000)	Stock * Repurchase (000)	Net Worth (000)	Earnings as % of Net Worth
1920	205	13	12	5.8			158	7.4
1921	160	3	3	2.0	9		152	2.1
1922	220	5	5	2.1			157	3.0
1923	319	22	19	6.0			176	10.6
1924	319	(3)	(3)	(1.0)	28		145	(1.9)
1925	309	10	9	2.9			154	5.6
1926	300	31	27	9.0	9		172	15.1
1927	340	37	32	9.5	25		179	18.0
1928	361	33	29	7.9	56		151	18.9
1929	338	22	20	5.9	18		153	13.1
1930	260	7	7	2.6	10		150	4.6
1931	164	†	†	0.2			150	0.3
1932	88	(11)	(11)	(12.9)			138	(8.2)
1933	102	(2)	(2)	(1.7)			136	(1.3)
1934	108	(1)	(1)	(1.3)			134	(1.0)
1935	142	14	12	8.6			142	8.6
1936	217	29	23	10.4	21		144	15.7
1937	230	16	14	5.9	12		146	9.2
1938	214	22	18	8.6	10		154	11.8
1939	232	30	24	10.4	18		160	15.1
1940	248	34	25	10.0	18		167	14.9
1941	416	81	40	9.5	30		176	22.4
1942	237	(5)	(5)	(1.9)	9		163	(2.8)
1943	491	101	42	8.6	11		194	21.4
1944	457	107	26	5.7	13		207	12.5
1945	400	31	22	5.6	17		213	10.2
1946	613	98	61	9.9	18		255	23.7
1947	814	117	72	8.9	20		306	23.8
1948	752	80	50	6.6	26		331	15.1
1949	669	81	50	7.5	12		369	13.7
1950	1,228	195	99	8.1			469	21.2
1951	1,224	111	61	5.0	2	20	507	12.0
1952	1,221	80	44	3.6		10	541	8.1
1953	1,259	131	68	5.4		10	600	11.4
1954	1,453	172	85	5.9		10	675	12.7
1955	1,816	209	103	5.6		10	768	13.4
1956	1,686	175	88	5.2	5	10	840	10.4
1957	1,440	(21)	(9)	(0.6)	3	10	818	(1.1)
1958	1,485	(41)	(22)	(1.5)	3	10	784	(2.7)

*Repurchase of shares from a minority stockholder.
†Less than $500.

Source: Company records.

president and general manager when his father moved up to chairman of the board. Guy Bransten also held stock control of the company by 1952. Through a series of transactions betwen 1942 and 1952, Alan Branstein gained majority ownership of the company and then, in a step taken to minimize inheritance taxes, placed his shares into an irrevocable living trust, the terms of which assigned voting control of the stock to Guy and dividends to Guy's mother and sister.

George Cunningham left the company immediately following Guy's return from the service. Guy commented that there were a number of experienced people in the plant and market demand was high, so that his own inexperience caused no serious problems. A series of men was hired in an attempt to find a good production manager. One man held the post from 1950 until 1956, but was finally released because Mr. Bransten felt that "we just hadn't been making any progress under him." A successor with an impressive record of education and experience was hired. "After two years," said Mr. Bransten, "I finally realized that this man was an autocrat and just couldn't get along with others, so I had to let him go." Eric Stevens, 35, was promoted from the industrial engineering department to fill the production manager's position.

By 1951, the company's sales activities were directed by Mr. Ray Miller. After serving in World War II as a lieutenant colonel in the Air Force, Mr. Miller joined the company in 1946 as a salesman. Thirty-four years old at the time, his only previous experience was in selling cars. "However," Guy stated, "Ray demonstrated superior ability and advanced rapidly to the position of sales manager." Mr. Miller was named vice president of sales in 1956.

Mr. Roberts continued as the company's accountant and office manager and held the title of vice president—finance and treasurer. Mr. Bart Jacobs was personnel director, a post created in 1955. Mechanical engineering was headed by Mr. Joe Cannon. Guy's brother, Ole Bransten, was a salesman for the company. In 1958, Alan, Guy, and Ole drew salaries of $35,000, $27,500, and $15,500 respectively.

Total employment in the firm was about 120 persons, of whom seven were women. Pioneer's 1958 organization chart is presented as Exhibit 2.

SALES

Municipal waterworks and private and mutual water companies were the end customers for Pioneer Brass products. The company's valves and fittings were used to connect the water main and water meter in supplying water to the home. From the standpoint of the water company, Pioneer Brass products were the last link in water service and, compared to the materials used in providing service, pumping, storage, and distribution of water, probably the smallest in dollar value. Several products, selected by management as typical of their product line, are shown in Exhibit 3.

exhibit 2

PIONEER BRASS COMPANY (A)

Organization Chart and Company Personnel
(with age and length of service)

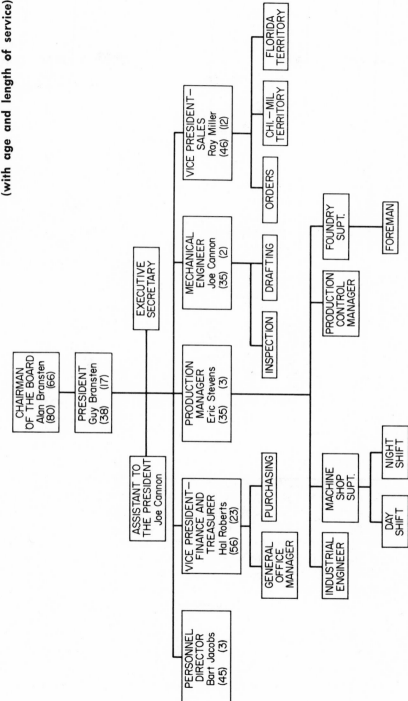

exhibit 3

PIONEER BRASS COMPANY (A)

Selected Company Products

Service   Clamp

Fitting

Ground Key Valve

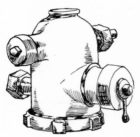

Hydrant

Angle Valve

Pioneer products were sold at or prior to the start of residential construction. Sales potential was determined largely by the number of single and multiple unit housing starts. For example, the jump in Pioneer sales in 1950 paralleled the sharp rise in construction for that year. Management watched closely the statistics for new housing starts, but had not been able to correlate either their dollar or pound sales volume with construction to any useful degree of accuracy. Mr. Bransten noted that, in parallel with a national trend, the ratio of multiple unit construction to total residential construction had increased over a few years from about 3% to nearly 15% in the Pioneer market areas. Since one set of water connections might serve five or ten residential units in a multiple unit, Guy believed that the demand for waterworks products could decrease even during periods of rising total housing starts. Mr. Miller did consider predicted housing starts in assembling his sales forecasts, but relied more heavily on Pioneer's own sales history and trends. Management recognized the cyclical nature of residential construction, but usually classified industry performance only to the extent of "good" or "bad" years.

Pioneer sold its products in 21 states; all but three (Minnesota, Iowa, and Missouri) were east of the Mississippi. In 1957, 75% of sales came from the Illinois-Wisconsin area, 12% from Michigan, Indiana, Ohio, Kentucky, and West Virginia. The company had recently expanded into Florida because of high building activity in that state.

Since bronze valves and fittings are of relatively low value per pound, a manufacturer's geographical market is limited by shipping costs. Pioneer was able to sell in Florida because there were no large plants in the area and all companies marketing there faced similar freight costs. Despite the actions of some companies to the contrary, Pioneer management felt that shipping costs made it unprofitable for a midwestern or eastern manufacturer to compete with western manufacturing operations for the booming California market. In Pioneer's own region, several of the larger companies in the industry established, in the mid-1950's, manufacturing branches to compete for the Chicago market.

Pioneer Brass, in 1959, marketed its products directly and through jobbers. The company sold direct in the Chicago and Milwaukee areas because of the concentration of building activity and long-standing relationships that had developed. The trend toward selling through jobbers had increased, however, particularly where jobbers sold full lines (fittings, pipe, meters, etc.) to contractors who in turn provided and installed the entire water distribution systems for the water companies. Jobbers were classified as either stocking or nonstocking, depending on whether or not they maintained an inventory of products. Stocking jobbers were obviously preferred because they could provide faster customer service and also relieve Pioneer Brass of large inventory requirements.

Nonstocking jobbers played a minor role in distribution and were not considered to be actual representatives of the company. Business coming through nonstocking jobbers usually occurred only when the jobber received an order that specified Pioneer products. Jobber territories were exclusive and jobbers seldom competed for customers to whom Pioneer sold direct. See Exhibit 4 for a diagram of the marketing channels.

In early 1959, 70 stocking jobbers sold Pioneer products. These outlets were usually plumbing supply houses carrying a full line of products which complemented, but did not compete with, Pioneer products. The Pioneer jobber in Detroit, for example, had twelve salesmen calling on potential buyers of meter connections and related products. Theoretically, stocking jobbers operated on a 25% discount (15% for nonstocking jobbers) from Pioneer's trade net price (catalogue price). From Pioneer's point of view, the jobbers should have sold to their customers at trade net price. Price competition, however, greatly limited the amount of this "regular" business. In fact, it was becoming common for the buying units to ask for bids on the larger and more important jobs. When asked for a bid, the jobber had to set a price for the entire package. When the bid package included products other than those of Pioneer Brass, the jobber might, in order to

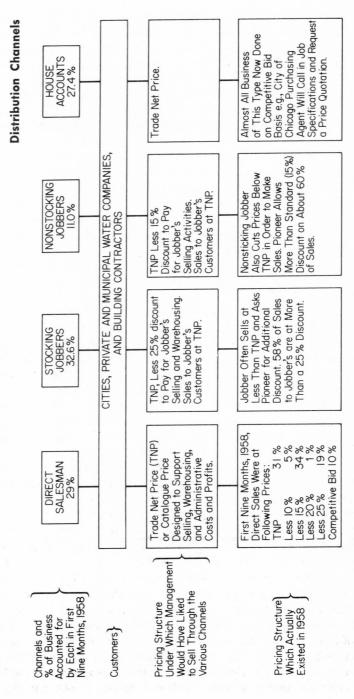

exhibit 4

PIONEER BRASS COMPANY (A)

Distribution Channels

Channels and % of Business Accounted for by Each in First Nine Months, 1958

| DIRECT SALESMAN 29% | STOCKING JOBBERS 32.6% | NONSTOCKING JOBBERS 11.0% | HOUSE ACCOUNTS 27.4% |

Customers

CITIES, PRIVATE AND MUNICIPAL WATER COMPANIES, AND BUILDING CONTRACTORS

Pricing Structure Under Which Management Would Have Liked to Sell Through the Various Channels

Trade Net Price (TNP) or Catalogue Price Designed to Support Selling, Warehousing, and Administrative Costs and Profits.

TNP, Less 25% discount to pay for Jobber's Selling and Warehousing. Sales to Jobber's Customers at TNP.

TNP Less 15% Discount to Pay for Jobber's Selling Activities. Sales to Jobber's Customers at TNP.

Trade Net Price.

Pricing Structure Which Actually Existed in 1958

First Nine Months, 1958, Direct Sales Were at Following Prices:
TNP   31%
Less 10%   5%
Less 15%   34%
Less 20%   1%
Less 25%   19%
Competitive Bid 10%

Jobber Often Sells at Less Than TNP and Asks Pioneer for Additional Discount. 58% of Sales to Jobber's are at More Than a 25% Discount.

Nonsticking Jobber Also Cuts Prices Below TNP in Order to Make Sales. Pioneer Allows More Than Standard (15%) Discount on About 60% of Sales.

Almost All Business of This Type Now Done on Competitive Bid Basis. e.g., City of Chicago Purchasing Agent Will Call in Job Specifications and Request a Price Quotation.

Source: Exhibit prepared by the casewriter from management statements and company records.

get the business, include Pioneer products at their cost to him (trade net less 25%) or slightly above. On these occasions, the jobbers often asked Pioneer Brass for more than the standard discount. Mr. Bransten estimated that, during 1958, close to 60% of the company's sales to jobbers were at prices below the standard discount price.

According to Ray Miller, vice president—sales, the market situation described above did not exist prior to 1955.

> Before 1955, we did 70% of our business direct and, more important, sold our products at full price. We would buy our customers a few drinks, play poker with them, and they would buy our products. We didn't worry about price cutting because no one in the industry would openly engage in this practice.
>
> Conditions started changing in 1955, though, and have been getting worse since. For one thing, our competitors started selling through jobbers and the jobbers were less reluctant to cut prices. About the same time, through growth and mergers, purchasing units became larger and much more aware of their bargaining position. They were also influenced by general demands for price consciousness. Consequently, purchasing agents began asking for bids, or on some jobs (e.g., large tract developments) turned the whole responsibility for buying and installing water service over to outside contractors. In either case, the purchaser became interested in the price advantages of buying all of his plumbing needs from one source. Of course, a company like ours could not satisfy this demand and we were ourselves forced to rely on full line jobbers.
>
> By 1958, very few orders, either direct or through jobbers, sold at list price. For example, in 1954, the city of Milwaukee placed several large orders directly with the company and paid list price. In 1958, when bids were requested, the effective price amounted to list less 25% less 10% if the bid was won. In selling to the city of Chicago, the margin in 1954 on a $100,000 job was 30%. In 1958, the margin could drop as low as 5%.

Near the end of 1958, Messrs. Bransten and Miller thought seriously of discontinuing direct sales altogether and concentrating on selling through jobbers. Subsequently, Mr. Miller prepared the analysis shown in Exhibit 5. He gave the following explanation of his findings:

> It's quite obvious from looking at these figures that our salesmen are showing a definite profit. However, I still plan to drop over 200 accounts which aren't producing enough business to warrant calls. The reduction will leave us with 200 accounts. These will, of course, be the better accounts and therefore too great in number for one man properly to cover.
>
> Notice that, for the first nine months of 1958, 29% of our sales were direct and over 27% were in the category of house accounts. It's my opinion that the house accounts are partly the result of the salesmen's efforts even though they are not credited as such.
>
> I have considered assigning a man to Michigan, Indiana, Ohio, Kentucky, and West Virginia. We are now doing 12% of our total volume in these states. The

exhibit 5

PIONEER BRASS COMPANY (A)

Sales Distribution

Ole Bransten Sales (224) accounts)

Trade Net Sheet	$ 57,797	25% profit	$14,450
less 10%	7,926	15% profit	1,189
less 15%	40,458	10% profit	4,046
less 25%	27,532		
Quoted	5,593		
Totals	$139,306		$19,685

Profit to firm over and above selling through jobbers: $19,685 less salary and expenses of $7,695 leaves total savings of $11,990.

Walt Beeman Sales (185 accounts)

Trade Net Sheet	$ 46,057	25% profit	$11,515
less 10%	8,401	15% profit	1,261
less 15%	72,273	10% profit	7,228
less 20%	3,187	5% profit	160
less 25%	34,720		
Quoted	26,266		
Totals	$190,904		$20,164

Profit to firm over and above selling through jobbers: $20,164 less salary and expenses of $8,329 leaves total savings of $11,835.

Direct Sales Results: First nine months, 1958

Sales Breakdown by Channel of Distribution: First nine months, 1958

Stocking and nonstocking jobber sales	$ 496,244	43.6%
House accounts	311,859	27.4%
Direct sales	330,210	29.0%

Sales Breakdown by Region: 1957 totals

Michigan, Indiana, Ohio, Kentucky, and West Virginia	181,848	12%
Illinois, Wisconsin	1,071,641	75%
All others (total)	186,908	13%

Concentration of Sales

32 Selected accounts: 1957	932,035	64.7%
32 Selected accounts: First nine months, 1958	754,183	66.2%

[1]Ole Bransten's "salary," for the purposes of this calculation, was set equal to Beeman's salary. The remainder of Ole's actual $15,500 salary was charged to the department's administrative expense.

Source: Company records.

fact that 64% of our 1958 business came from the Chicago area *only* is evidence of too great a local concentration of sales.

It is also interesting to note that 32 selected accounts provided 66.2% of our first nine months' 1958 business. This situation can be rectified by establishing additional jobbers as we have done in Florida. We have a company man calling on jobbers and supervising our efforts in that state.

Because of the very high percentage of our total business that is obtained from the Chicago-Milwaukee area and the highly competitive condition that exists at present, I recommend no change in our sales distribution for at least the next six months. However, we may have to reassign our present personnel to different territories, or make my time almost completely available for work in the field if we want to gain the coverage we need. I would like to train a new man to take over my office duties and responsibilities for general liaison between management and sales as well as between salesmen and their customers.

There was no trade association within the industry and no exchange of information among the companies. Consequently, it was difficult to compare operating results directly. However, Mr. Miller estimated that, in the Chicago area, Pioneer Brass still held about 55% of the market, although its percentage share was declining.

In December, 1958, Guy experimented to see if the company could operate by accepting regular business only (trade net price and standard jobber discounts). Bids, when submitted, were calculated to include a profit margin that was in line with the successful period of the mid-1950's. Even with a sharp increase in sales price per pound (from $1.03 to $1.19), total volume fell from $124,000 in November to $89,000 in December. Guy stopped the experiment at the end of the month when the monthly income statement indicated an after tax loss of $20,000.

MANUFACTURING

Manufacturing took place in a modern plant built in 1952 at a cost of $400,000. The 38,000 square foot structure occupied a portion of a four and two-thirds acre site. The foundry and the machine shop were the primary centers of operation. Exhibit 6 illustrates the general plant layout and process flow.

Upon receipt of a customer order, a job ticket was sent to the foundry. The proper pattern was selected from the pattern shop and used to make a sand mold. Bronze or red brass was melted in one of three 2,700-pound capacity furnaces. Transported by the latest conveyorized equipment, the molten metal was poured into the sand mold and left to solidify. After removal from the sand, the cleaned and trimmed castings were transported to the appropriate production line for machining operations.

Most of the machining was carried out on standard turret lathes or drill presses. However, several special purpose machines were also utilized. One of these, manufactured by the Goss and Deleeuw Company, cost $24,000, but was

exhibit 6

PIONEER BRASS COMPANY (A)

Plant Layout and Process Flow

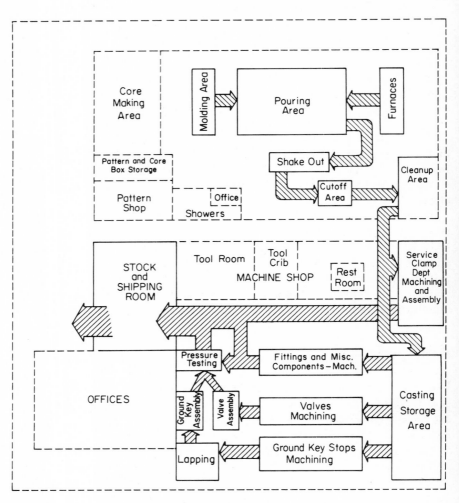

capable of machining T-shaped products at 10% of the direct labor cost of the other equipment in the shop. The production manager, Eric Stevens, said, "We heard about the Goss and DeLeeuw machine back in 1954. The labor savings seemed impressive and we had enough money to buy it. It's too bad we can't do all our machining on equipment like that." An Excello boring machine, purchased at a price of $30,000, was another special purpose machine recently acquired by Pioneer Brass. A summary of manufacturing costs is presented in Exhibit 7.

The strike and other personnel problems had caused Mr. Stevens considerable trouble. Explaining the situation, he said:

> I sure hope we now have good men as machine shop and foundry superintendents. The old foundry superintendent was a bad egg from the beginning. He was replaced at the same time the previous production manager was moved out. Our new machine shop foreman seems to know his job pretty well. He has recommended that we buy $10,000 in tooling equipment so we can repair our own production machinery. I think Guy is going to approve the purchase.
>
> My big problem right now is finding a good production control man to replace a man recently killed in an automobile accident. We need someone to keep track of the orders as they go through the foundry and machine shop. Unfortunately, I have no idea where we stand on customer deliveries.
>
> I've recently had to get on the back of our industrial engineer. That Excello boring machine has been in the shop for six months and we still have no time study on it. However, the I.E. department has been very busy adjusting our incentive program to the new work force. The foundry now has 90% of the

exhibit 7

PIONEER BRASS COMPANY (A)

Cost of Products Sold

	1958 $	1958 %	1957 $	1957 %	1956 $	1956 %	1955 $	1955 %	1954 $	1954 %
Materials										
Beginning inventory	40,474		72,169		67,167		36,790		32,378	
Purchases	591,424		430,989		638,567		774,241		486,445	
	631,898		503,158		705,734		811,032		518,823	
Ending inventory	48,516		40,474		70,169		67,168		36,790	
Total materials used	583,382	49.4	462,684	42.5	633,565	52.4	743,864	57.3	482,033	49.7
Less: Sale of scrap*	86,247	7.3	23,878	2.2	20,654	1.7	17,531	1.4	11,197	1.1
Net materials used	497,135	42.1	438,806	40.3	612,911	50.7	726,333	55.9	470,835	48.6
Direct labor	336,616	28.5	308,452	28.3	295,432	24.4	333,460	25.7	292,209	30.1
Manufacturing expense										
Indirect labor	124,527		108,177		93,566		101,319		99,903	
Taxes	32,650		30,550		24,394		24,431		21,567	
Supplies & tools	78,291		58,361		50,981		52,666		45,279	
Utilities	11,779		9,737		9,991		11,769		11,639	
Repairs	11,828		8,577		3,713		5,885		2,262	
Insurance	18,738		13,043		16,636		15,125		18,633	
Mfg. depreciation	26,200		21,500		21,824		20,962		10,549	
Miscellaneous	11,230		14,927		8,967		2,555		1,792	
Total	315,243	26.6	264,872	24.3	230,072	18.9	234,712	18.1	221,624	22.9
I.E. expense	19,150	1.6	20,075	1.8	19,702	1.6	19,889	1.5	19,390	2.0
M.E. expense	23,233	2.0	9,580	0.9	9,339	0.8	5,933	0.5	—	
Production control expense	15,476	1.3	29,503	2.7	14,873	1.2	—	—	—	
In process inventory (increase)	(25,312)	(2.2)	17,437	1.6	26,703	2.2	(21,464)	(1.7)	(35,285)	(3.6)
Cost of products mfg'd.	1,181,541	100.0	1,088,725	100.0	1,209,032	100.0	1,298,865	100.0	968,774	100.0
Finished goods inventory (increase)	12,251		42,394		(30,128)		(45,971)		4,871	
Cost of products sold	1,193,792		1,131,119		1,178,904		1,252,894		973,646	

*Until 1958, Pioneer remelted the bronze chips resulting from machinery operations. In 1958, management investigations indicated that this practice was uneconomical; therefore, chips were also sold as scrap.

Source: Company annual reports.

workers on an incentive basis, but the machine shop lags and has only 60% on incentive.

The Pioneer Brass workers were organized by the CIO Steelworkers in 1946. By 1957, the majority of the workforce had been with the company for over five years and approximately 25% had been employed for more than ten years. Scrap and rework had never been alarming and production efficiency sustained a high output volume with minimum hours of overtime. After the 1957 strike, management stated that it had become apparent to them that the old workforce had been very stable and that most of their production skills were based on experience and a thorough knowledge of the equipment.

In 1955, Bart Jacobs, newly appointed personnel director, replaced Mr. Bransten as company representative at union bargaining sessions. Both in 1955 and 1956, negotiations ended before agreement was reached, and strikes—three weeks in 1955 and three days in 1956—resulted. "In both instances," commented Mr. Bransten, "the union presented demands for which they were prepared to strike. And, both times, we ended up giving in."

Although the 1957 negotiations were scheduled to deal with wages, Pioneer management did not anticipate any particular problems "because business conditions weren't too good and the union knew we could stand a strike more easily than in the past." Guy Bransten determined the highest figure the company would meet and left with his family for a vacation in Europe.

At the end of negotiations, there remained a significant difference between the company's top figure and union demands. Mr. Jacobs said of the situation:

> Guy set up this department, in part, because he was too involved in the situation to carry on objective negotiations. But, there wasn't much that could be done about this strike. The union wanted an increase of 54¢ an hour. They claimed that this would bring Pioneer Brass to the level of the steel and western aircraft industries. We couldn't see this; even before negotiations we were paying wages equal to or above companies in our own industry (brass valves, fittings, etc.). Our best offer was still 26¢ too low for them.

In looking back, Mr. Bransten commented that:

> The union probably wanted our settlement to set precedent for negotiations with other companies. With a new plant, new equipment, and landscaped grounds, we looked prosperous enough to make them think we could afford the higher wages. And, everybody knew that we had been doing a good business for several years.

When negotiations stalled, Mr. Bransten decided to hire a new labor force:

> We had warned the union that, this time, we weren't going to give in on all demands they cared to make. And, I was sick of strikes. Within a few days we

filled up the plant with practically anyone we could get to come through the picket line.

Within a year, the new workers decertified the union in action taken with the National Labor Relations Board. Mr. Jacobs concluded:

> Now that we have the new labor force, we are going to do everything possible to keep the union out. Each year I make an industry survey so that we can stay at least equal in our wage scale. We extended a 7¢ an hour increase this year. We will have a new union vote in 1960, but I'd say the boys are pretty happy the way things are.

Repercussions from a complete turnover in the labor force were expected, but their severity came as a surprise to management. Exhibit 8 graphically illustrates the sudden change in a number of production statistics which management used as a measure of plant efficiency. Management said that, even at the end of 1958, production efficiency remained below prestrike levels.

Since the strike, the plant had been operating almost continuously at full capacity. The foundry was on one shift operation and the machine shop, to keep up with the foundry output, on two shifts. Mr. Bransten was concerned about overtime, which cost up to $800 per week in premium pay, but realized that this would continue until previous efficiency levels were reached.

MECHANICAL ENGINEERING

Joe Cannon, a graduate engineer, headed the company's mechanical engineering department and also served as assistant to the president. Mr. Bransten said, "I need Joe's technical advice and also want him to broaden his experience beyond just the engineering viewpoint." Mr. Cannon and a draftsman assistant were primarily engaged in providing technical assistance to the sales and production departments. Mr. Cannon said of his responsibilities:

> There are some very basic engineering problems that I have to straighten out, but in the present loss situation all of my time seems to be devoted to meeting emergencies brought to our attention by customers and the sales department. One of our biggest problems is trying to standardize our product line. We have no engineering drawings of our products; but, with better than 5,000 patterns (samples) we can't hope to make up drawings for all of them. What we are doing instead is assigning a part number to each component and drawing up a bill of material for each finished product.
>
> I would also like to devote some more time to equipment replacement analysis. Our machinery is in poor shape, giving us no guarantee of tolerances. Eleven

exhibit 8

PIONEER BRASS COMPANY

Production Statistics

FOUNDRY: Output Per Man Hour* and % Defective

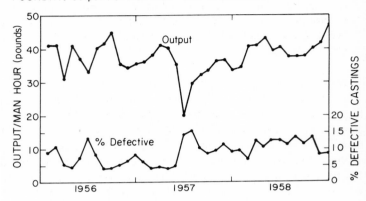

MACHINE SHOP: Output Per Man Hour† and % Defective

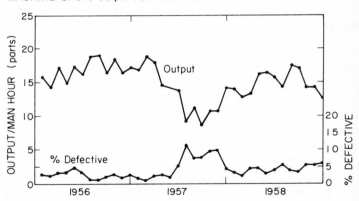

* Foundry output/man hour was measured in pounds of cleaned and trimmed castings *before* inspection for flaws. Defective castings include those castings which were found to have imperfections after one or more machining operations (e.g., subsurface cracks may not have been apparent at foundry inspection).

† Machine shop output/man hour was measured in number of parts completed, before final inspection. Machine shop defectives do not include those parts which, after the start of machining operations, were found to have casting (foundry) flaws.

exhibit 8 (cont'd)

PIONEER BRASS COMPANY (A)

Production Statistics

FOUNDRY: % Overtime Hours‡

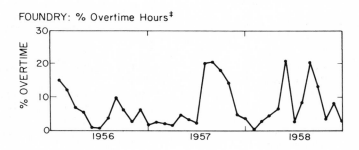

MACHINE SHOP: % Overtime Hours‡

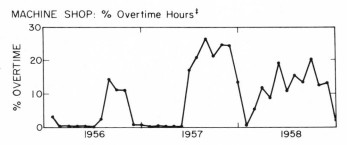

‡ Per cent overtime hours for both foundry and machine shop represents the ratio of overtime to straight-time hours of work.

of our turret lathes were purchased prior to 1943, nine others between 1943 and
1947. Our four drill presses are up to 15 years old. At least 80% of the equipment needs repair. I would venture to say that tooling rather than training is
now our major cause of scrap loss. You can imagine the pressures on the workforce to try to meet the old efficiency levels under these conditions.

Our production standards are also confusing; I have seen one part machined
three different ways. We can't even rely on our inspection because we have no
specifications or gauges—much of the work is entirely subjective. In addition to
my engineering functions, I have also been somewhat concerned about devising
a method for production control and scheduling.

exhibit 9

PIONEER BRASS COMPANY (A)
Year End Balance Sheets

Liabilities and Net Worth

	1957	1956	1955	1954	1953
Current Liabilities					
Notes payable	$ 76,102	$ 26,613	—	$ 11,000	$ 23,000
Accounts payable	69,178	49,310	$ 42,607	85,819	54,215
Accrued wages & salary	4,468	14,336	7,376	14,388	9,654
Accrued vacation pay	10,478	9,890	9,793	9,979	8,569
Payroll taxes	9,440	10,986	7,792	14,968	10,255
Sales tax	5,569	7,480	15,978	14,929	13,261
Income tax	—	—	87,011	101,024	86,634
Long-term debt[1]	4,573	2,712	—	—	14,437
Total current liabilities	179,808	121,327	170,557	252,107	220,025
Long-Term Debt	41,284	51,788	71,386	94,345	109,554
Net Worth					
Capital stock[2]	106,375	110,050	113,725	117,400	121,075
Retained earnings	677,214	708,425	726,513	650,504	554,078
Total net worth	783,589	818,238	840,238	767,904	675,153
Total Liabilities and Net Worth	$1,004,681	$991,590	$1,082,181	$1,114,357	$1,004,732

[1]Portion of long-term debt due within one year.

[2]Par value of capital stock $100 per share. Stock repurchases at a cost of $272 per share.

Source: Company annual reports.

ACCOUNTING AND FINANCE

Mr. Roberts, vice president—finance and treasurer, said of the 1957 and 1958 operating results:

> I believe that we are in a period where several external factors are hurting us, but it is just a matter of time before we are back on our feet. Our financial position is still strong [See Exhibits 9 and 10 for financial statements of the last five years] and our credit is good. We have a $250,000 line of credit established with the bank, but have borrowed only about $75,000. A recent change in the tax law enables us to use $100,000 we had placed in the bank to cover taxes and expenses when Mr. Bransten dies. Raw material inventory doesn't involve a large investment since we purchase our requirements from local branches of national firms and can get fairly prompt delivery.

exhibit 9 (cont.)

Assets	1958	1957	1956	1955	1954
Current Assets					
Cash	$ 19,968	$ 9,952	$ 45,383	$ 109,340	$ 102,509
Bank deposits	110,608	106,920	95,878	52,369	50,583
Accounts receivable	98,413	135,858	145,433	149,473	143,111
	228,989	252,730	286,694	311,182	296,203
Inventories					
Raw materials	48,516	40,474	72,169	67,167	36,790
Work in process	141,591	116,279	133,716	160,419	138,955
Finished goods	75,500	87,751	130,145	100,017	54,046
	265,607	244,504	336,030	327,603	229,791
Prepaid expenses					
Insurance	—	—	—	4,920	5,068
Tax refunds	19,674	12,258	—	—	—
Other	14,593	10,529	7,167	2,799	1,552
	34,267	22,787	7,167	7,717	6,617
Total current assets	528,863	520,021	629,891	646,504	532,614
Other Assets					
Cash value of life insurance	6,235	2,779	—	—	—
Fixed Assets					
Plant & equipment	610,060	580,052	539,079	528,987	509,962
less: depreciation	221,439	192,224	167,751	142,096	120,633
Plant & equipment (net)	388,621	387,828	371,328	386,891	389,329
Patterns	58,743	58,743	58,743	58,743	58,743
Land	22,219	22,219	22,219	22,219	24,046
Total fixed assets	469,583	468,790	452,290	467,852	472,118
Total assets	$1,004,681	$ 991,590	$1,082	$1,114,357	$1,004,732

Guy Bransten made the following comments about the cost accounting system:

Cost accounting is becoming one of my biggest problems. Five years ago most of our business was based on persuasive selling and our trade net price included sufficient cushion to cover any deficiencies in our costing methods. Now most of our jobs are bid, and the competitive requirements don't allow one to be very far off and still make money. We're in a real squeeze between high internal production costs and declining market prices. Up until the time of the strike, we had made no changes in our accounting system for years. Right now our auditor is helping Mr. Roberts tie our cost accounting into pricing.

The costing system in use in 1958 was built around estimated costs based on established direct labor and raw material standards. General overheard expense was assigned to individual items by dividing total overhead expense by total paid hours and multiplying this figure by labor hours for the specific item. Until late 1958, scrap losses had been charged equally to all products. Since scrap loss was found to vary greatly among the company's 5,000 products, all products were divided into several basic product lines, each of which was assigned an estimated scrap loss figure. Mr. Bransten was concerned about the accuracy of the cost estimates and felt that they still had only a rough idea of what production cost of each product was.

The sales department submitted monthly reports recapitulating the selling price and the margin (calculated from estimated production costs) for products sold during the previous month. The table below shows, for products selected by the casewriter as typical of the entire list, the wide variation in calculated margin.

Mr. Bransten was also interested in setting up controls which would enable him to spot production difficulties more quickly. Although such indicators as pounds per man hour were used extensively in the plant, he felt that short-term variations in the product mix might confuse the meaning of the numbers. Since the sale price

exhibit 10

PIONEER BRASS COMPANY (A)

Income Statements

	1958 $	1958 %	1957 $	1957 %	1956 $	1956 %	1955 $	1955 %	1954 $	1954 %
Sales	1,526,415		1,523,973		1,756,441		1,844,082		1,473,430	
Returns & allowances [1]	41,222		83,575		70,588		28,333		20,598	
Net sales	1,485,193	100.0	1,440,398	100.0	1,685,853	100.0	1,815,749	100.0	1,452,832	100.0
Cost of products sold	1,193,792	80.4	1,131,119	78.5	1,178,904	69.9	1,252,894	69.0	973,646	67.0
Gross earnings	291,401	19.6	309,279	21.5	506,949	30.1	562,854	31.0	479,186	33.0
Selling expense	84,306		91,670		82,243		80,577		71,070	
Shipping expense	51,169		54,745		56,049		63,209		51,845	
Administrative expense	167,840		182,969		193,375		176,513		153,012	
Total	303,315	20.4	329,384	22.9	332,667	19.7	320,301	17.6	275,928	19.0
Other income										
Discounts earned	2,654		3,439		3,509		4,168		2,457	
Miscellaneous	3,816		1,457		2,882		1,997		3,294	
	6,470	0.5	4,896	0.3	6,391	0.4	6,166	0.3	5,752	0.4
Other deductions										
Discounts allowed	28,760		—		—		31,380		28,693	
Interest	4,822		4,459		5,651		6,622		7,897	
Miscellaneous	1,478		1,675		225		1,553		306	
	35,060	2.4	6,134	0.4	5,876	0.4	39,556	2.2	36,896	2.5
Earnings before Fed. Inc. Tax	(40,504)	(2.7)	(21,343)	(1.5)	174,797	10.4	209,163	11.5	172,113	11.8
Federal Tax carryback	18,296	1.2	12,258	.9	—	—	—	—	—	—
Federal Income Tax	—	—	—	—	87,011	5.2	106,412	5.9	86,634	6.0
Net earnings	(22,208)	(1.5)	(9,085)	(0.6)	87,786	5.2	102,750	5.6	85,478	5.9
Total depreciation charges	36,671		29,244		28,403		26,241		24,057	
Sales in pounds	1,414,469		1,273,563		1,404,800		1,598,885		1,488,396	
Sales price/pound	1.05		113		1.20		1.14		.98	
Manufacturing cost/pound	.84		.89		.84		.78		.65	
Raw material cost/pound	.35		.36		.43		.44		.32	
Labor & overhead cost/pound [2]	.49		.53		.41		.35		.34	

[1] Discounts allowed of $27,000 in 1957 and $30,000 in 1956 were included in returns and allowances.

[2] Totals do not add due to rounding.
Source: Company records.

Pioneer Brass Company Mark-up on Selected Items

Item	Product Line	Selling Price (each)	Estimated Cost	Mark-up (%)
Corporation Stop	1	2.13	1.69	19
Service Stop	1	1.53	1.206	21
Angle Meter Stop	1	2.31	2.01	13
Angle Meter Stop	1	2.54	2.01	21
Curb Stop	1	2.99	2.14	28
Corporation Stop	1	2.54	1.547	39
Water Meter Coupling	2	No Aug. Sales	1.01	
Water Meter Coupling	2	.59	.50	15
Coupling	2	.715	.40	44
Angle Fire Plug Valve	3	22.78	14.70	35
Fire Hydrant Head	3	78.05	59.91	23
Gate Valve	3	9.91	8.21	17

of company products varied from less than 40¢ to over $1.00 per pound, a "reasonable" poundage output might be profitable or unprofitable, depending on the degree of product complexity. Similarly, with sales price ranging from about $1 to $100 per item, a measurement based on parts per man hour was felt to be imprecise.

GUY BRANSTEN

Mr. Bransten described himself as a man who enjoyed having full responsibility for running Pioneer.

> Although we certainly have a lot of hard work ahead if we are going to get the company turned around, my position gives me advantages that I might not have elsewhere. I wouldn't like to travel all the time or work long hours to the exclusion of time with my family and other interests. Nevertheless, in addition to the factors of personal income and investment in the company, I try to take a professional interest in ensuring that this company makes money. In a sense, return on net worth serves as a scoring device to measure how well we are doing.

On a typical day, Guy Bransten started work at 8:00 A.M. with the checking of his calendar for appointments and a listing of things to do for the day. After checking through the incoming mail, Guy spent most of the time between 8:30 and 10:30 meeting with one of the members of the planning committee. A half-hour plant tour followed the meeting. During the tour he greeted employees and checked cleanliness, scrap, grouping of workers, and inoperative machines. The time before lunch was devoted to miscellaneous duties. Each afternoon, Guy worked on current business problems and projects. His weekly schedule called for a review of weekly reports, a call on one of the top ten local customers, and a Rotary Club meeting. Monthly commitments included a planning committee meeting, a board of directors meeting, a Young Presidents Organization meeting, a bank directors meeting, and a Merchant and Manufacturers directors meeting.

In addition to vacation time, Mr. Bransten usually spent four weeks away from the company on activities relating to business. These activities included conventions and two Y.P.O. seminars. Guy felt that the seminars, where groups of company presidents attended several days of lectures and discussions on new management developments, often provided him with techniques and insights useful in his own business.

Guy believed that the company had some underlying strengths:

> We have a long-established name in a basic industry. There's always going to be a demand for waterworks products. We do compete against some much larger concerns, and their engineering staffs could come up with products which would render ours obsolete overnight. However, our market is slow to accept radically new products; water companies want to make very sure that any product they buy will operate after years of underground service. We watch carefully for any new products on the market. So far, we have always been able to come up with a comparable design. We also watch for possible inroads by companies in other industries. For instance, valves can be molded from some of the newer plastics. Actually, one of my long-range projects is to consider setting up an exclusive sales agreement for a line of plastic products which would both complement and compete with the bronze items we manufacture ourselves.

In relating his views on how the company should be run, Mr. Bransten emphasized the reliance he placed on management personnel.

> I feel that one thing I have to do if we are going to pull out of this situation is to get my key men really interested in the business. My management philosophy could be called participative management. That is, I want my managers to come up with suggestions on how to run the business. If I decide that a proposal seems sound, the man can then put his ideas to work. I try to give everyone an opportunity to make a contribution. This participative method does make the jobs of management personnel harder. Most people find it easier to follow orders; I have often been asked for more directions.
>
> My job involves defining the areas for which each man is responsible. In a company this size, you do have to work closely with the people you have. But, I wouldn't say that it's just like a big happy family, because at some point I have to tell the men "get your job done."

The planning committee, made up of the heads of sales, production, finance, and mechanical engineering, met monthly with Mr. Bransten to review various phases of the business and to outline operations for the coming month. "In order to bring the firm back together," said Mr. Bransten, "I have started to require periodic reports from the major operating departments." Sales, production, and worker efficiency were reported weekly and compared to the same periods for the prvious month and the previous year. Through this series of reports, Guy hoped "to get each department head to take the initiative in recommending action that we can take."

> We have set up moving annual targets for most of the plant activity. Our "Business Position Report" compares actual and target performance for: orders received, invoices issued, orders outstanding, late deliveries, and credit allowed. Also, I have different departments charting various activities under their control. These include actual versus target figures for such items as: hourly employee absenteeism and man hours worked, number of accidents, clean castings, finished parts, and finished parts shipped.
>
> Our financial reporting includes a monthly balance sheet and income statement, a three month cash flow forecast, a recap of the past month's cash flow, and an over-all yearly budget based on variable and fixed expense.
>
> We have also set up a mid-management group as a means of broadening the base of thinking on management problems. The program brings together supervisors from different departments in monthly meetings and helps to build a concept of teamwork by informing each member of the needs, problems, and objectives of other departments.

Guy commented that his father was highly critical of the increased use of reports and charts.

> Dad had never interfered in any way with my methods of running the company and, through the trust, gave me complete control. Under the loss situation, he suddenly realized that he no longer has any real say in the business and he is worried that the whole company will fold.
>
> Although my father is getting old, he still shows up at the plant every day. I have tried routing business transactions through his office for inspection, but rarely got any response. Instead, he walks around the offices or shops trying to find someone with whom he can discuss his latest opinions on how the business should be run. He seems to feel that I have to get out in the plant and personally show the people how to work.
>
> The whole situation is hurting the business to the extent that my efforts have been criticized to both the family and other members of the company. It can't help but shake one's confidence and personal efficiency.

In summarizing why the company was losing money and what had to be done, Mr. Bransten continued:

> If we had stopped to make projections of how much replacing the entire workforce was going to cost us, we probably would have yielded to the union. We still have some distance to go before reaching old levels of plant efficiency.

Moreover, the 1957 strike showed up many weaknesses. The only way we can get back on our feet is to get at the root of the problems.

Mr. Bransten believed that a general tightening of the market and change in methods of selling had contributed to the company's poor results over the past two years. "In fact," he said, "even with the old crew we probably would have done no better than break even."

The strike has caused such a crisis that we are forced to notice things that we could let slide during the easier years through 1956. We are developing a useful set of controls and, when we get costing and pricing more organized, I hope that we will have the tools to cut costs below the market prices we have to meet.

NOTE ON U.S. WATERWORKS INDUSTRY

The U.S. waterworks supply industry, of which Pioneer Brass Co. was a part, served the more than 20,000 water utilities (municipal and private) throughout the nation. Products manufactured by the industry comprised all of the parts necessary to regulate and distribute the water furnished by the utility to its customers. Major items included: water main pipe and the associated valves, fittings, and hydrants for controlling the major flow lines through an area; the clamps, fittings, valves, and pipe necessary for bringing service from the main to the individual building units (residential, commercial, industrial); and meters for measuring the flow of water to the serviced unit. This entire system of water transmission was installed and maintained by the water utility, either directly by its own crews or under contract. Exhibit 1 summarizes the manufacturing and distribution patterns that had developed within the various segments of this industry.

The waterworks supply industry had different manufacturing and distribution characteristics from the plumbing supplies used inside the building. Plumbing products, installed by the building contractor and maintained by the property owner, were made by a relatively few very large companies and sold through plumbing distributors.

As seen in Exhibit 1, several groups of manufacturers were involved in this industry. Main pipe, copper tubing, and meters were manufactured by different companies. In manufacturing valves and fittings, some companies made only parts for the water main system, while others (including Pioneer Brass Co.) made only the service linkage from the main to the meter. One firm, the Mueller Company, manufactured both types. Mueller Company, with estimated annual sales of about $25 million, was by far the largest fittings company in the industry, and was believed to account for about 50% of the total sales of such products in the U.S. The limited product line manufactured by Pioneer Brass Co. (the linkage from the main to the meter, plus some specialty *bronze* hydrants and gate valves) had an estimated annual sales potential in the U.S. of about $15 mil-

exhibit 1

NOTE ON WATERWORKS SUPPLY INDUSTRY

Manufacturing and Distribution Patterns for Industry Products

Products Required by Water Utilities in Providing Water Service	Quantity Required	Manufactured by	Distribution
Water Main System			
Pipe (cast iron, asbestos coated concrete, 2''-12'' in diameter)	Largest $ value in water service system.	A few large firms such as Amer. Cast Iron Pipe Co., U.S. Pipe and Foundry, Johns Mansville. Requires substantial capital investment.	Normally sold directly to user. Some product distributed through jobbers in remote geographical areas.
Valves, fittings, hydrants (Brass and malleable iron— brass used in above ground hydrants only in special situations)	Actual number of items relatively small but is second in $ value in system. High value per item.	Several small firms with annual sales in the range of $10-$25 million. Requires brass and iron processing facilities to provide complete line. Mueller Co. largest in this field.	Sold direct to large water utilities doing their own installation. Sold through waterworks jobbers to smaller water utilities and contractors doing installation for water utilities. It is estimated that 50% or more of sales are through jobbers.
Linkage from Main to Meter Service clamps, fittings, corporation stops, meter setting equipment* (mostly brass to resist corrosion— ½'' to 2'' diameter)	Lowest $ value in system. Approximately $10-$12 per service unit. Total market estimated at about $15 million annually.	Five small companies. The largest, Mueller Co., holds an estimated 50% of market. Other four companies each have annual sales of $2 million or less.	
Copper tubing	Estimated at between $12-$15 per service unit.	Large copper fabricating firms. Requires large volume to offset substantial investment in extruding equipment.	Normally sold directly to user. Some distributed through jobber in remote areas.
Water Measuring System Water meters	One per service unit. Value ranges from $15-$30 per meter.	Three major producers: Hershery Sparling Co., Rockwell Mfg. Co., and Neptune Meter Co. Requires fairly sophisticated design and relatively high capital investment to manufacture meter.	Mostly sold direct to users. Some distributors used in remote areas.

1Product line manufactured by Pioneer Brass Co.

Source: Casewriter exhibits.

lion,[1] of which Mueller was estimated to produce about 40%. The remainder was divided among Pioneer and four other small companies.

Although there were differences in the size of the fittings required to handle different volumes of water flow, only one set of connections was needed for each building unit served, regardless of the purpose for which the building was used.

The buying characteristics of the water utilities varied with their size. For example, the Chicago municipal water company installed its own water service systems and purchased its requirements directly from the manufacturers. Smaller water utilities usually bought main pipe, copper tubing, and meters direct from the manufacturers, and fittings and valves from waterworks jobbers who provided a complete line of these products. Still smaller water utilities would likely contract for the installation services, and the contractor would then be responsible for purchasing the product requirements. The contractor, in turn, would buy either directly from the manufacturer and/or from waterworks jobbers, depending on the

---

[1] These figures are the best estimates of the casewriter. Most of the firms in this industry are privately owned and do not publish data about their operations.

size of the job. Past practice and geographical location factors caused frequent exceptions to these patterns.

Waterworks jobbers, particularly in areas of heavy population concentration, ment used in linking the water meter to the main. Minimum investories of main system and the service clamps, fittings, corporation stops, and meter setting equipment used in linking the water meter to the main. Minimum inventories of main pipe, copper tubing, and meters were sometimes carried. The farther a waterworks jobber was from a center of residential growth, the more likely he was to inventory a complete line of water distribution products. In some of the more remote areas water distribution products were carried by broadline wholesalers who also sold plumbing, heating, and air conditioning products.

Pioneer Brass Company (B)

COMPANY PERFORMANCE 1959–1963

After losses of $21,000 before taxes in 1957, and $40,000 in 1958 [see Pioneer Brass Company (A)], the company reversed this trend in 1959 and showed profits in each subsequent year. The 1954–63, ten year performance record was as follows:

Year	Net Sales ($000)	Gross margin (%)	Income Before Taxes ($000)	Average Sales Price Per Pound ($)	Average Mfg. Cost Per Pound (¢)
1954	1,453	33.0	172	0.98	65
1955	1,816	31.0	209	1.14	78
1956	1,686	30.1	175	1.20	84
1957	1,440	21.5	(21)	1.13	89
1958	1,485	19.6	(41)	1.05	84
1959	1,823	20.3	39	1.12	92
1960	1,512	24.8	58	1.14	83
1961	1,619	25.2	104	1.10	83
1962	1,718	23.8	94	1.13	87
1963	1,928	29.5	173	1.16	83

See Exhibits 1 and 2 for detailed financial statements for the period 1959-1963.

In 1959, housing starts and, consequently, the demands for the types of waterworks fittings made by Pioneer, increased sharply. Although Pioneer's manufacturing costs jumped 10% in 1959, this was more than offset by a 23% increase in sales volume and a 7% price increase. Also in 1959, cost savings of more than $20,000 were effected by reducing executive salaries, and cutting a number of nonoperating expenses.

Late in 1959, two important changes were made in Production top management, and early in 1960 a shift was made from gas-burning to electrical furnaces in the foundry.

Also in 1960 the company reduced its raw material costs by using a higher portion of brass scrap than heretofore.

---

[1] After $59,000 of incentive pay to key executives ($52,000) and salesmen ($7,000). These plans were not in effect in 1962.

Subsequent years saw a major shift in distribution from direct sales to sales through jobbers. This shift resulted in broadening the company's geographical coverage.

Subsequent years saw a major shift in distribution from direct sales through jobbers. This shift resulted in broadening the company's geographical coverage.

The company's product line remained relatively constant throughout the 1954–1963 period, but, beginning in late 1961, some excess foundry and machine shop capacity was utilized in subcontracting for local manufacturers.

By 1964, sales were running at an annual rate of more than $2 million, and pretax profits were estimated at about 7% of sales.

Guy Bransten, president of Pioneer Brass Company, summarized the past five years' operations: "I don't think you will find that our basic operation has changed substantially since 1958, but we are doing a number of things differently. For example, we have made some personnel changes, our control records have been improved, and we made a major investment in electrical furnaces for the foundry. The major difference, though, has been an improved market, and I think equally important, the way we view our market. As you can see from the figures, we have made money in each year since 1958 and will continue this record in 1964, although the results won't be quite as good as they were in 1963."

PIONEER BRASS COMPANY: 1964

Organization and Management

After incurring losses in 1957 and 1958, Mr. Bransten had reduced the salaries of all shareholder executives 10% and of all other executives 5% in April, 1959. These reductions were in effect until April, 1961, and by mid-1964 salaries were no higher than their 1958 level. Mr. Bransten also eliminated a number of company fringe benefits, such as membership in two country clubs, and reduced the amount of charitable contributions. These cost savings amounted to a total of about $20,000 in 1959.

In one of several personnel changes, Mr. Joe Cannon, formerly mechanical engineer and assistant to the president, was named production manager in October, 1959, replacing Eric Stevens, who returned to his former position of industrial engineer. Mr. Cannon subsequently was promoted to vice president—production manager. Stevens resigned from the company early in 1963.

Mr. Hal Roberts, vice president—finance and treasurer, was fired in May, 1960, for making loans to employees, which was contrary to company policy. This event was the last of a long series of infractions, including drinking, which, according to Mr. Bransten, seriously limited Roberts' usefulness to the firm. His functions were taken over in large part by one of the female bookkeepers. Her efforts were supplemented by the company's auditors, who provided technical advice and assistance on a one-day-per-month retainer.

exhibit 1

PIONEER BRASS COMPANY (B)

Income Statements

	1963		1962		1961		1960		1959	
	$	%	$	%	$	%	$	%	$	%
Sales	1,969,185		1,744,169		1,646,638		1,545,002		1,852,914	
Returns and allowances	40,831		25,663		27,616		32,649		30,193	
Net sales	1,928,354	100.0	1,718,506	100.0	1,619,022	100.0	1,512,353	100.0	1,822,721	100.0
Cost of products sold	1,359,044	70.5	1,309,290	76.2	1,211,646	74.8	1,136,645	75.2	1,451,816	79.7
Gross earnings	569,310	29.5	409,216	23.8	407,376	25.2	375,708	24.8	370,905	20.3
Selling expense	115,854	6.0	97,052	5.6	85,084	5.3	83,090	5.5	83,899	4.6
Shipping expense	62,944	3.2	54,812	3.2	51,827	3.2	51,180	3.4	64,819	3.6
Administrative expense	182,605	9.7	128,854	7.5	137,186	8.5	148,766	9.8	148,545	8.2
Total	361,403	18.7	280,718	16.3	274,097	16.9	283,086	18.7	297,263	16.3
Other income										
Discounts earned	4,269		3,945		3,057		2,557		3,789	
Miscellaneous	1,014		625		4,416		1,412		1,516	
	5,283	0.3	4,570	0.3	7,473	0.5	3,969	0.3	5,305	0.3
Other deductions										
Discounts allowed	35,053		31,004		27,925		27,433		32,485	
Interest	5,166		7,783		8,604		11,270		7,130	
Miscellaneous										
	40,219	2.0	38,787	2.3	36,529	2.3	38,703	2.6	39,615	2.2
Earnings before Fed. Income Tax	172,971	9.0	94,281	5.5	104,223	6.4	57,938	3.8	39,332	2.2
Federal Tax carryback										
Federal Income Tax	86,740	4.5	44,290	2.6	41,501	2.6	31,000	2.1	14,300	0.8
Net earnings	86,231	4.5	49,991	2.9	62,722	3.9	26,938	1.8	25,032	1.4
Total depreciation charges	51,143		52,740		63,341		57,310		39,229	
Sales in pounds	1,664,000		1,527,770		1,467,595		1,321,042		1,630,892	
Sales price/pound [1]	1.16		1.13		1.10		1.14		1.12	
Manufacturing cost/pound	.83		.87		.83		.83		.92	
Raw material cost/pound	.36		.35		.33		.28		.38	
Labor and overhead cost/pound	.47		.52		.50		.55		.54	

[1] Includes only those products manufactured by Pioneer Brass.

Source: Company records.

Mr. Alan Bransten, chairman of the board, died in October, 1960. Mrs. Alan Bransten was paid a year's salary of $31,500 as widow's benefits over the next two years.

Pioneer's personnel function was discontinued as a separate department in September, 1963, with the release of Bart Jacobs. Clerical administration of personnel was assigned to the accounting department, and an industrial psychologist was retained for psychological consulting, recruiting advice, and assistance in wage and salary administration.

Also in September, 1963, Mr. Bransten hired Mr. George Starr as marketing manager and assistant to the president. Prior to joining Pioneer, Mr. Starr had had five years of marketing experience with several firms in the consumer products field. Reporting directly to Mr. Bransten, Mr. Starr's major responsibilities were described as: "managing market information available from the field and other sources"; and "being responsible for all of the administrative aspects of Sales." Mr. Bransten explained that by hiring Starr he hoped to greatly strengthen the company's market intelligence and thus provide a basis for current and pro-

exhibit 2

PIONEER BRASS COMPANY (B)

Year End Balance Sheets

Assets

	1963	1962	1961	1960	1959
Current assets					
Cash	$ 165,542	$ 122,386	$ 92,398	$ 61,599	$ 13,522
Bank deposits	111,795	107,526	97,582	82,525	92,219
Accounts receivable	173,447	137,199	139,798	130,742	151,286
Inventories					
Raw materials	77,310	71,007	71,086	64,999	65,958
Work in process	156,410	119,359	123,080	103,336	163,515
Finished goods	128,993	121,169	96,655	93,797	130,971
	362,713	311,535	290,821	262,132	360,444
Prepaid expenses	13,363	11,050	9,722	8,942	11,648
Total current	827,102	689,696	630,321	545,940	629,119
Other assets					
Cash value of life insurance	32,349	26,917	21,635	16,445	11,360
Fixed assets					
Building	317,522	313,430	312,830	312,830	312,611
Machinery and equipment	365,875	355,628	344,643	362,190	259,271
Office equipment	31,152	28,082	18,513	28,565	26,239
Automobiles and trucks	25,580	21,879	27,982	29,205	29,033
	740,137	719,019			
Less: Depreciation	396,505	353,953	308,986	307,917	258,486
Net plant and equipment	343,632	365,066			
Land	24,046	24,046	24,046	22,219	22,219
Patterns	58,143	58,743	58,743	58,743	58,743
Total fixed assets	402,375	447,855	477,771	505,835	449,630
Total assets	$1,285,872	$1,164,468	$1,129,727	$1,068,220	$1,090,109

Liabilities and Net Worth

	1963	1962	1961	1960	1959
Current liabilities					
Notes payable	—	—	—	—	$ 94,682
Accounts payable	$ 76,617	$ 60,192	$ 44,088	$ 34,808	87,142
Accrued wages and salary	15,067	10,576	9,403	7,721	7,738
Accrued incentive bonus	59,221	3,241	10,269	—	—
Accrued vacation pay	10,848	9,609	9,921	8,405	12,162
Payroll and withholding taxes	14,506	10,653	10,551	10,874	14,213
Sales taxes	5,740	5,161	4,357	5,381	6,208
Income tax	84,982	43,346	41,377	31,000	14,300
Long-term debt[1]	17,801	13,891	16,968	17,965	9,153
Total current	284,782	156,669	146,934	120,154	247,858
Long-term debt	30,360	99,527	114,512	132,507	43,630
Net worth					
Capital stock[2]	90,550	91,675	95,350	99,025	102,700
Retained earnings	880,180	816,597	772,931	716,534	695,921
Total net worth	970,730	908,272	868,281	815,559	798,621
Total liabilities and net worth	$1,285,872	$1,164,468	$1,129,727	$1,068,220	$1,090,109

[1]Portion of long-term debt due within one year.

[2]Par value of capital stock $100 per share. Stock repurchases at a cost of $272 per share.

jected sales plans and for defining specific objectives and means of implementation. Mr. Bransten viewed the position as being on trial and had asked Starr "to identify, by the end of his second year, the profit contribution resulting from his planning and efforts."

Ray Miller, vice president and sales manager, who had been responsible previously for the entire sales effort, had his duties shifted to supervision of salesmen and direct contact with customers.

Corporate Objectives and Strategy

The basic objectives of the Pioneer Brass Company (see Exhibit 3) remained unchanged, except that in 1963, a specific goal of doubling net worth over the next ten years was established. Exhibit 4 presents Mr. Bransten's computations of the sales and profit requirements for meeting this objective for the period 1963–1970.

Prior to 1963, Mr. Bransten had been seeking various means of diversification. As a result of a 1963 market forecast by George Starr, Mr. Bransten became convinced that the long-range potential in the waterworks industry was adequate for achieving the company's stated objectives, and diversification efforts were abandoned.

exhibit 3

PIONEER BRASS COMPANY (B)

Basic Objectives

---

1. To produce adequate profits as measured by return on investment.
2. To safeguard company's accumulation of assets and to increase these.
3. To grow soundly through earnings and intelligent financing.
   a. Through this growth provide opportunity for increased responsibility and more jobs.
4. To meet the need for our product and provide it at a competitive price, high in quality, and provide good service through specialization and standardization.
5. To provide a working atmosphere of friendly interest and respect for personal freedom and integrity coupled with good communications and requirements of high efficiency and skill.
   a. Delegation of authority and responsibility backed with controls to evaluate performance.
   b. Link compensation with responsibility and performance.
6. To carry our share of community service and civic responsibility.

---

exhibit 4

Long-Range Plan—10% Increase in Net Worth per Year

$ (000)

Year	Profit $	% Increase	Net Worth	% Increase	Standby $	% Raise	Variable %	Standby & Profit	Required Sales $	$ Increase
1963	90.8	—	908.0	—	520	—	63.5	610.8	1,673.4	—
1964	99.9	10.0	998.8	10.0	590	13.5	63.0	689.9	1,864.5	11.40
1965	109.9	10.0	1,098.7	10.0	650	10.0	62.5	759.9	2,026.4	8.68
1966	120.8	9.9	1,208.7	10.0	700	7.7	62.0	820.8	2,160.0	6.66
1967	132.9	10.0	1,329.4	10.0	735	5.0	61.5	867.9	2,254.2	4.40
1968	146.3	10.1	1,462.3	10.0	770	4.8	61.5	916.3	2,380.0	5.58
1969	160.9	10.0	1,608.6	10.0	810	5.2	61.5	970.9	2,521.8	5.96
1970	177.0	10.0	1,769.5	10.0	850	5.0	61.5	1,027.0	2,667.5	5.78

Formula to calculate Profit before taxes and incentive for a given increase in net worth:

N = Net worth

X = Required increase in net worth

B = Profit before taxes & before incentive adjustment

A = Profit after taxes @52%

F = Depreciation (dividends & payouts)

C = Profit before taxes after incentive adjustment.

1
$$A = .48C$$
$$C = B - Incent.$$
$$I = .4 (B - .1N)$$

so:
$$C = B - I$$
$$= B - .4 (B - .1N)$$
$$= B - .4B + .04N$$
$$= .6B + .04N$$

3
$$X = A + F (A = .288B + .0192N)$$
$$X = .288B + .0192N + F$$
$$B = \frac{X - .0192N - F}{.288}$$

Express X in terms of N
$$X = AN$$
$$B = \frac{AN - .0192N - F}{.288}$$
$$= \frac{N(a - .0912) - F}{.288}$$

If a = 10% increase in net worth
$$B = \frac{N(.1 - .0912) - F}{.288}$$
$$= \frac{.808N - F}{.288}$$

2 and
$$A = 0.48(.6B + .04N)$$
$$= 0.288B + .0192N$$

Until the company's waterworks business employed all of the presently existing plant capacity, however, Mr. Bransten intended to continue a policy of subcontracting foundry and machine shop work as a means of attaining additional profit contribution. He had become convinced of the economics involved in running the plant at full capacity, and the subcontract work seemed to be an excellent way of achieving high utilization of fixed assets without endangering the basic line of business. According to Mr. Bransten, Pioneer would consider any subcontract work which utilized idle equipment and which produced enough revenue to cover all variable costs and make some contribution to standby (fixed) costs. He was well aware of the dangers of the contribution concept, but said that he personally reviewed all subcontract work to insure that added standby costs were not being incurred, and also that the subcontract business was not diverting attention from the company's proprietary waterworks business.

In 1964, the subcontract work fell into categories: miscellaneous, small quantity foundry castings; and manufacturing of longer-run production units such as sprinkler heads and parts, for several small companies in the lawn sprinkler and irrigation business. Subcontracted foundry castings reached an annual rate of $100,000 in sales in July, 1964, and sprinkler parts subcontracting was expected to reach $65,000 for the year. Mr. Bransten estimated that the subcontracting operations would contribute about $30,000 to pretax profits in 1964.

Marketing

Mr. Bransten believed that Pioneer was not big enough to be an innovator in new products. "New product ideas are limited in the waterworks business, and the costs of developing a product and gaining acceptance of it in the market are prohibitive for a company like Pioneer. We prefer to 'wait and see' and jump in after someone else has introduced a new item and proven the demand."

In looking at the market for waterworks products of the type manufactured by Pioneer Brass, Mr. Bransten indicated that nonfarm housing starts provided probably the best single index of current trends. Plotted below are housing starts in Pioneer's primary market area along with company sales and before tax profits for the period 1955 through 1963.

Pioneer Sales, before Tax Profit, and Housing Starts in Primary Market Area, 1955-1963

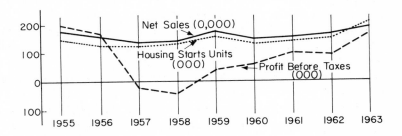

Mr. Bransten cautioned that the increasing percentage of multiple dwelling units, for which the dollar value of waterworks products per dwelling unit was considerably lower than for single homes, could significantly distort these figures.

The study made by George Starr projected continued growth in housing starts in the range of 4% to 8% a year until 1970. After 1970 he predicted that the housing market, particularly in the single home segment, would enter a "boom period occasioned by the needs of the 'war babies' as they reached the home buying age."

Sales territories. Illinois and Wisconsin continued to be Pioneer's major market for waterworks products in 1963, accounting for 60% of the company's total sales dollars compared with 65% in 1958.

Sales coverage in 1964 was provided by five company-employed salesmen:

two in the Illinois-Wisconsin territory; one covering Michigan, Ohio, and Indiana; one in Florida; and one in California. The salesmen in the Michigan-Ohio-Indiana territory had been added early in 1963, and the California man was hired in August, 1963.

According to Ray Miller, the two new salesmen had been added following a break-even analysis of the potential in the territories to which they were assigned. It was Miller's opinion that at least $55,000 in sales volume was required in a new territory to justify placing a salesman in the territory. Miller computed this $55,000 figure by taking the cost of keeping a salesman in the field (estimated at $20,000 per year) and dividing this by 36% (the fixed cost of over-all company operations in 1963). According to Miller's calculations, all sales over $55,000 would contribute directly to profit as long as the price of the products sold maintained the same 64%–36% proportion of variable and fixed costs.

Channels of distribution. In the six years since 1958, Pioneer had come to rely more and more heavily on its jobbers as a primary means of distribution. In 1964, about 68% of the company's sales were through jobbers, compared with only 44% in 1958. Prospective customers (small contractors and water companies) increasingly were demanding a single source for the full line of waterworks products they required. Large water service companies and municipalities operating their own services were the exception to this trend and tended to purchase directly from manufacturers. Most of Pioneer's direct sales were made to such customers, usually on a bid basis.

Whereas in 1958 Pioneer's direct salesmen often competed with jobbers, in 1964 they were expected to work with and support the jobbers in any way possible. Thus the salesmen were doing substantial amounts of missionary sales work for the jobbers to insure that Pioneer products received adequate attention and push.

When the company entered a new territory, the initial effort was usually aimed at direct sales. Mr. Miller explained that many jobbers would not take on a new line until the products were accepted by the purchasing units, be they water companies or contractors working for the water companies. Thus, the procedure was to get the products on the accepted list and then bid on several large jobs where the purchaser was not necessarily interested in a package deal. With several successful bids in hand, the salesman could then begin calling on jobbers and showing them that the line was becoming established in the area.

In one attempt to expand Pioneer's marketing scope, Mr. Bransten had entered an agreement in July, 1963, to sell the company's products through the firm selling water meters in an area Pioneer did not serve. It had been noted that many meter company salesmen called on the same kinds of accounts as Pioneer salesmen. The meter company was to receive jobber prices for Pioneer products which it could then sell along with its own line of water meters. After a year's trial, this arrangement proved highly disappointing to Mr. Bransten, and he discontinued it.

In 1964, as in 1958, Pioneer depended heavily on a few large customers. Twenty of its largest jobbers produced over 55% in sales. The ten largest direct accounts added another 20%. The balance of company sales were scattered among more than 400 accounts.

Pricing. During 1963, 42% of Pioneer's sales were on a bid basis, 39% were at "regular" prices (trade net price on direct sales, and trade net price less 25% on sales through jobbers), 12% were at "special" prices (negotiated with the purchaser), and 7% were at negotiated subcontract prices for the company's miscellaneous manufacturing work. These figures were little changed from 1962. Dollars received per pound of product sold in 1963 had continued a slow but steady rise that began in 1961. Prices for waterworks products had actually increased more than would appear because the larger share of lower priced subcontract sales tended to hold the overall average down.

In new markets where it was necessary to establish the Pioneer line, the company was inclined to take business on an incremental cost basis, even though in some cases a large freight penalty was being incurred. In all cases, the objective was to cover variable costs and to maximize the dollar contribution applied to standby costs and profit.

Manufacturing

Late in 1958, Pioneer's production personnel completed studies on the feasibility of shifting to electric furnaces in the company's foundry operations. The study indicated that, by investing $110,044 in this new equipment, Pioneer could realize cost savings of up to $60,000 per year from: remelting the chips from machining operations, reducing the loss of metal during melting, and reducing the metal content of the slag produced during melting. The project was approved and the installation of the furnaces was completed early in 1960. Joe Cannon, vice president and production manager, indicated that on 1963 volume the company was actually saving about $50,000 per year on chip conversion, lower metal losses, and lower manpower requirements, but that slag savings had not been achieved.

In 1960, Pioneer markedly increased the percentage of scrap brass used relative to refined ingots. Mr. Cannon pointed out that scrap was generally about 4¢ a pound cheaper to purchase than ingot (in mid-1963, scrap was 28¢, ingot 32¢) and was not significantly more expensive to process. During both 1960 and 1961, Pioneer used about 60% scrap. By early 1962, the foundry was using about 80% scrap, at which time, said Cannon, "we ran into the problems associated with scrap: contaminated metal. Somehow, some of the scrap we bought had an impurity in it which made our castings porous. We quickly switched to 100% ingot to get rid of our casting problems, but by the end of the year, we were again operating at about 80% scrap."

Mr. Cannon commented that another major change in manufacturing was the hiring, in November, 1959, of Dick Cole as machine shop superintendent. "The people we had had as previous superintendents were probably capable of general machine shop work," said Cannon, "but we needed someone who was familiar with our equipment and knew how each product should be machined. Dick had this experience because he had worked for Pioneer about ten years ago. We used him part-time during the strike, and finally, in 1959, got him back full-time. Since then Dick has cut our setup times substantially and perhaps has been the biggest single influence in increasing the output of our machine shop." (See Exhibits 5 and 6 for data pertaining to the company's manufacturing operations.)

Another major cost saving move on the production side of the business was the approval, in April, 1964, of an $85,000 expenditure for an improved sand system for foundry castings. This latter project was expected to lower labor and material costs, and increase the quality of the finished castings. On completion of the sand system in September, Mr. Bransten believed that, for a company of its size, Pioneer would have one of the most modern and efficient foundries available.

Prospects for 1964

At the end of July, 1964, it appeared that Pioneer's sales for the full year would slightly exceed those of 1963, but would fall short of the target for the year. Mr. Bransten indicated that a 2¢ per pound decrease in selling prices was partially responsible for the lower than anticipated sales volume. He stated that a mid-year lag in housing starts and increased prices for brass accounted for most of the rest.

Given a continuation of this trend, Mr. Bransten predicted that 1964 profits would be somewhat lower than in 1963. Additionally, the company's standby (fixed) costs had been increased by $60,000. Most of the increase was in the wage and salary account, which was budgeted at $36,000 over 1963, while another $10,000 was earmarked for publishing a new catalog. Increases in travel expense, sales incentives, and nonincome taxes made up the rest.

In 1964, Pioneer accounting information was being processed by an EDP service bureau, and providing rapidly information on sales and contribution by product line, customer, and territory. Mr. Bransten felt that this data would facilitate greatly his control of operations.

FUTURE POSSIBILITIES

In 1964, Guy Bransten saw three principal alternative ways of reaching his stated objective of doubling the company's net worth by 1973.

First and most obvious, Pioneer could continue in its present historical product area—selling the highly specialized brass fittings which connected the individual home with the primary water main. While this was a limited market—perhaps no more than $15 million total in the entire U.S. in 1964—it was a growing market. And Pioneer, with roughly a 60% share of its regional market and 12% of the national market, would undoubtedly share in this growth. The only major

exhibit 5

PIONEER BRASS COMPANY (B)

Cost of Products Sold

	1963	1962	1961	1960	1959
Materials					
Beginning inventory	$ 71,007	$ 71,086	$ 64,999	$ 65,958	$ 48,516
Purchases	627,526	552,514	504,804	388,501	762,699
	698,533	623,600	569,803	454,459	811,215
Ending inventory	77,310	71,007	71,086	64,999	65,958
Total materials used	621,223	552,593	498,717	389,460	745,257
Less: sale of scrap	26,846	14,790	18,631	26,497	126,916
Net materials used	594,377	537,803	480,086	362,963	618,341
Direct labor	206,225	198,926	194,701	169,633	314,563
Outside labor purchased	17,414	23,216	26,996	25,497	54,588
Manufacturing expense					
Indirect labor	211,315	187,276	173,423	157,365	179,783
Labor benefits	75,606	72,028	64,692	62,930	75,986
Property taxes	26,154	25,688	26,065	27,321	22,055
Supplies and tools	68,835	69,838	54,825	44,014	75,768
Utilities	28,365	26,886	24,662	21,354	18,595
Repairs	16,462	26,013	23,038	17,483	20,920
Insurance	1,956	2,300	1,721	1,890	3,904
Depreciation: plant and equipment	41,764	46,050	55,313	46,258	30,670
Miscellaneous	10,539	9,844	9,087	7,572	8,760
Total	480,996	465,903	432,826	386,187	436,441
I.E. expense	27,829	29,936	27,580	28,730	11,849
M.E. expense	8,182	7,575	7,208	6,514	19,386
Production control expense	24,431	24,087	24,534	21,487	27,069
Plant administration	50,465	49,472	46,509	44,791	53,701
	110,907	111,070	105,831	101,522	112,005
Allocated to shipping	(6,000)	(6,835)	(6,192)	(6,540)	(6,727)
In process inventory (increase)	(37,051)	3,721	(19,744)	60,179	(21,924)
Cost of products manufactured	1,366,868	1,333,804	1,214,504	1,099,471	1,507,287
Finished goods inventory (increase)	(7,824)	(24,514)	(2,858)	37,174	(55,471)
Cost of products sold	$1,359,044	$1,309,290	$1,211,646	$1,136,645	$1,451,816

problems Guy Bransten foresaw in limiting his business to this market were: potential price pressures from larger, more diversified competitors, and possible competition from substitute materials (e.g., plastic) in which Pioneer had little know-how.

exhibit 6

PIONEER BRASS COMPANY (B)

Production Statistics

FOUNDRY: Output Per Man Hour and % Defective*

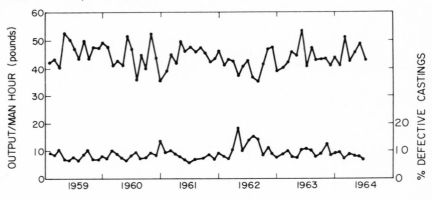

MACHINE SHOP: Output Per Man Hour and % Defective†

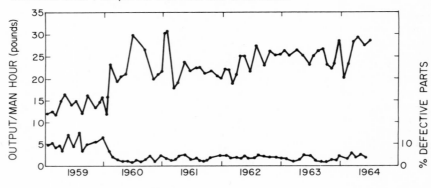

FINISHED PARTS SHIPMENTS

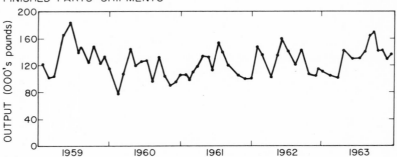

* Foundry output/man hour was measured in pounds of cleaned and trimmed castings *before* inspection for flaws. Defective castings include those castings found to have imperfections after one or more machinery operations (e.g., subsurface cracks may not have been apparent at foundry inspection).

† Machine shop output/man hour was measured in pounds of finished parts before final inspection. Machine shop defectives do not include those parts which after the start of machinery operations were found to have casting (foundry) flaws.

Source: Prepared by casewriter from company records.

Secondly, Pioneer could diversify into other products. These might be defined by channels of distribution: the other types of fittings and materials used in waterworks and plumbing systems. Or they might be defined by Pioneer's manufacturing capabilities: products of brass or similar material, requiring casting and machining.

Thirdly, Pioneer could integrate forward into the jobbing and supply business.

Excerpts from a long-range market study conducted in early 1964 by George Starr, Pioneer's marketing manager, is attached as Appendix A.

appendix A

PIONEER BRASS COMPANY (B)

PIONEER BRASS COMPANY MARKET AND SALES FORECAST, 1964

The first area of study was to be the over-all long-range view of the company's position in its current primary area of sale—the waterworks industry. The highlights of this study are as follows.

I. The Pioneer Brass Company, from 1964 through 1970, should anticipate an average annual sales dollar growth of 9% if the current economic picture remains static. The year 1964 is projected as 16%.
   a. Pioneer's midwestern market accounted for over 19% of the U.S. housing starts in 1963 and should exceed 20% in 1964. The company captured about 58% of this market in 1963 and should take 60% of the 1964 market. This amounts to approximately 12% of U.S. market in 1964 as opposed to 11% in 1963.

II. Gross National Product is the best possible area of study, at present, for long-range future forecasts and expected housing trends.
   a. Because residential construction has maintained such a *very* constant percentage level of total GNP of just over 4% through a ten year period.
   b. This percentage share of GNP is expected to maintain this general level but commence a slow climb until it reaches an 8% share of GNP by 1970.
   c. Housing's real boom will commence soon after 1970 when our "War Babies" reach the home buying age.
   d. GNP is expected to show an average annual increase of 5%, 1962 to 1963 was 4.9% but 1963 to 1964 is forecast for 5.9%. Construc-

tion in 1964 is expected to show an 8% increase by only 3% in residential or $26.5 billion.

The second consideration under study was the potential worth of expanding our product line into other fields or to strengthen our position in the present market. I looked into various outside markets such as mobile homes and marine hardware. Both mobile homes and marine hardware have common faults—highly competitive pricing based on small quantities per account. Major manufacturers tend to use automatic equipment for small fitting volume and so keep prices down. Both OEM and major jobbers are so widespread that it would require additional sales force to meet competitive coverage. There are several areas for additional consideration—air conditioning at OEM level, the gas industry, and additional items for fire safety. Based on the additional investment required for extending our interest into any of these fields, I would prefer that we consider direct acquisition of a company in another field. We would be stepping into a ready-made share of market that needs maintaining rather than starting from scratch with a piecemeal line.

In the meantime we should, and are, working on upgrading the job requirements and controls in our various departments concerned with waterworks products. Warehousing and inventory levels, production control standards, short-run department, foundry modernization, tighter control on salesmen, a performance rated incentive plan for salesmen, constant forecast control and revision, new product catalog, advertising, and better packaging for the entire line are some of the major areas now under consideration.

If our economic growth continues as presently forecast we can expect housing to continue a gradual growth from 4% to 8% as an annual growth rate. Commencing about 1970 the housing market will go into a boom period supplying the needs of the "War Babies" market that will have reached a home buying age. There are several questions that need answering at this point in light of the projected growth rate for housing.

I. Does the company wish to continue upon its current growth rate?
   a. This will give us our 10% annual increase in net worth in less than ten years.
   b. This will not expand the scope of the company. Acquisition would achieve this end and would double net worth in a much shorter period, but would necessitate outside financing. Does the management wish to consider outside financing? If so, when?
   c. If the company prefers to strengthen its position in its present markets only, we should consider expanding our lines and upgrading our production facilities. This decision also involves the question of financing. Type of financing, how much, and when?
   d. If we elect to grow at a rate established by availability of additional

dollars through annual net profits, are we willing to move at the slow pace allowed by this method? Will we be ready for the post-1970 housing boom?

1964 FORECAST

Est. Sales, 1964—$2,232,800   *Actual, 1963—$1,928,383*
Est. Sale Price Per Pound1—$1.20   *Actual, 1963—$1.22*

Projected Sales	*Projected, 1964*	*Actual, 1963*
Waterworks products	$2,087,419	$1,809,977
Foundry castings and miscellaneous manufacturing	145,381	118,376
Totals: 15.8% increase	$2,232,800—1964	$1,928,353—1963

[1] Waterworks products only. Subcontract work excluded.

BASIS FOR 1964 FORECAST

1. Market 1964 vs. 1963, housing starts
   a. The U.S. is expecting an 8% increase in construction with a 3% increase in nonfarm residential.
   b. However, our prime market is still the midwest and it is expected to hold approximately 20% of national starts, with 60% of this in Illinois.
   c. Illinois should easily support a 10% increase.
   d. Our sales in Michigan, Wisconsin, and Ohio showed a 20% increase in 1963 and should have no difficulty in adding another 15% in 1964.
   e. Our Florida sales were up 40% in 1963 and are continuing to grow. We are only asking for 15% increase. Our problem here is high selling cost and low selling price because of a weak market price level.
   f. The Kentucky market is in a decline of 10% to 15% but Ray Miller expects $50,000 in 1964 based on a better jobber situation than in 1963. This is an increase of $8,000.
   g. West Virginia is a slow market and has been very poor for our company. We are targeting $10,000 based on a new jobber. This is an increase of $5,000.
   h. Exports should rise to $39,000 in 1964 from $7,000 in 1963.
   i. Berkeley Co. (subcontract) should maintain its 1963 level of $38,500, while R. L. Jackson Co. (subcontract) continues to rise from $13,600 to $25,000 for an expected total volume of $63,500 from these two accounts.
   j. Our foundry casting subcontracts should increase 15% over 1963, a total of $80,500 for 1964.

k. New products can be expected to return a minimum of $10,000 this year.

l. California is developing nicely and this market is expected to return $75,000 this year.

m. More emphasis on control and forecasting for production control should increase our ability to deliver the maximum share of incoming requests.

2. We are expecting a maximum of $1.20 per pound in 1964, compared to $1.22 in 1963, for several reasons.

a. California and Florida are both cheap price markets and we will tend to price low in California to gain an entry into many accounts there.

b. There is a definite trend in Illinois to a one time, full year supplier type of bid. Because we cannot help but think of this as a one shot, all or nothing bid, we will tend to hold bid prices low. This bid business represents a considerable share of our local dollar volume and will have a strong effect on our final dollar per pound performance.

I am including for your appraisal several other broad analyses.

a. My own break-even estimation for 1964. It is self-explanatory.

b. Some time ago Joe Cannon and Guy Bransten collaborated in determining a formula [Exhibit 4 of case] for arriving at a long-range sales plan based on creating an additional 10% net worth each year. I find no fault with the formula but appreciate the fact that any such analysis must rest on a false static condition for many variables whose normal year to year fluctuations go unheeded, i.e., change in depreciation, dividends, variable percentage, dollar value of standby, etc. In any case, this plan, using 1963 net worth as a base and applying the formula thereafter, would indicate that we are well ahead of our minimum requirement in sales revenue and requires only a 6.06% annual increase to maintain the plan. Our relationship to expected GNP indicates an average growth rate of 8.93%, in which case we should reach our goal well under the ten year proposed plan of action.

George Starr, Assistant to the President/Marketing
2/18/64

	Standby $	Var %	Total Sales $	Break-even $	P.B.T. $
1959	345,011	78.0	1,775,975	1,580,000	47,025
1960	489,364	63.5	1,450,414	1,340,000	61,938
1961	473,307	65.6	1,536,220	1,340,000	82,802
1962	505,742	64.5	1,614,021	1,420,000	104,500
1963	528,555	61.7	1,718,349	1,370,000	210,100
est. 1964	589,000	62.5	1,984,500	1,575,000	248,300

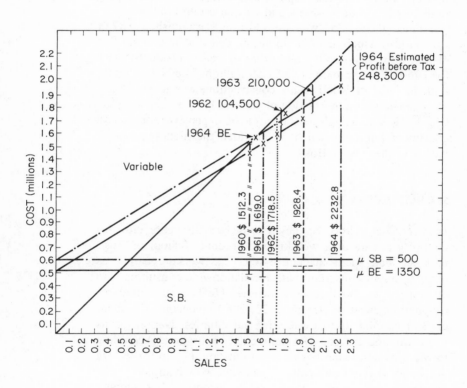

Burns Corporation

On December 26, 1960, the Board of Directors of the Burns Corporation, of Boston, Massachusetts, planned to meet in an all-day session to lay out the general strategy and operating policies for this newly formed company.

Burns Corp. ("Burnsco") was organized in December of 1960, under the laws of the Commonwealth of Massachusetts, by Mr. Stanley Burns and his associates as the vehicle for acquiring the stock of the Napoli Pasta Co., and for developing both Napoli's food business and its real estate holding.

Napoli Pasta Co. was an old-time (established 1875) Boston firm which manufactured and distributed a broad line of macaroni, egg noodle, and other dry paste products. Sales for 1960 were approximately $1.59 million. The Napoli plant, built in 1921 of wood frame construction, was located on a ¾ acre site on the north side of Beacon Hill, overlooking the Charles River, a high-density area of expensive homes and apartment buildings which commanded the highest property values in the city of Boston.

STANLEY BURNS

In December, 1960, Stanley Burns was 35 years old. An honors graduate of a well-known Graduate School of Business, he had spent his entire ten year working career as a management consultant with the nationwide consulting firm of Andrew C. Boyden & Associates. He had submitted his resignation, effective December 31, 1960, to become President of Burnsco and its two operating subsidiaries, Napoli Foods Company and Beacon Development Corporation. According to Mr. Boyden, "Stan has done an outstanding job for us. He has handled many difficult assignments with complete satisfaction by our clients. On several occasions he has actually operated 'sick' subsidiaries or divisions of client companies

---

for some critical period, during which he has 'turned them around.' On one occasion, he arranged the sale of a unit he had nursed back to health, at a substantial profit to the client. I think ever since then he's had the 'bug' to be an entrepreneur and to be in business for himself. We'll miss him very much, and I know he'll do a fine job on his own."

Mr. Burns was married, had two school-age children, and lived in a pleasant, upper middle class suburb in a comfortable, but unassuming, home. In 1960, he anticipated earnings of over $20,000 in salary and bonuses. He had a net worth of approximately $45,000, amassed from the investment and reinvestment of his savings. $25,000 of this was invested in the 25,000 shares of Burnsco stock he had purchased to found the company. Most of the balance was represented by his equity in his home.

Mr. Burns told the casewriter: "I'd been a consultant for ten years, and, while it had been challenging and interesting work, I thought the time had come to make a change. I've made a lot of money for our clients, and I've gotten a pretty good income for it. Now I'd like to try to build up some capital—that's hard to do when you work for someone else. Besides that, I've developed a definite philosophy about how a small business should be run that I want to put to the test. And, of course, the chance to stay put for a while and not do so much traveling is appealing—especially to my wife. I think she's become reconciled to my working very long hours in this business by just knowing that I'll be home every night.

"I've been looking for a good situation for a long time. I guess I studied 50 companies before finding Napoli. This one looks ideal—both to have some fun operating it and to make some real money from it."

THE NAPOLI NEGOTIATIONS

In September of 1960, Burns had learned through a business broker friend of his that the Napoli Pasta Co., founded by, manned by, and owned by successive generations of south-side Italians, might be for sale. The firm employed 61 people, of whom all were Italian. However, most were second or third generation, and all spoke English as their native tongue. The firm's current management had taken over the operation in 1946. According to Burns, by aggressive promotion with many small food markets, plus very tight control over production procedures, the new management had raised sales volume and gross margins, and turned a debt-ridden company into a profitable operation. By 1954, annual sales had reached about $1,500,000, which was then, as in 1960, close to the maximum output which the owners felt the factory could handle comfortably on a three-shift basis. Since 1954, sales and earnings had held to a relatively constant level. Management had used these earnings to replace old machinery, retire all debt, and to call in the stock of all nonemployees.

When Burns asked Napoli's president, Mr. Anthony Salvatierra, why he had not expanded the company's capacity, Salvatierra responded:

Why should I risk everything and expand? I've taken this company from nothing to where we've got a very healthy net worth. I've got all the money I can spend, a $75,000 house in a high class suburb, a summer place on the Cape, and a 30-foot cabin cruiser. I work plenty hard now. Why should I work harder, go into debt for new equipment, go through all the upset of expanding the plant? Why take the risks? Give me a good safe income, an assured principal, and I'll be glad to sell out and spend more time fishing and hunting.

Burns viewed Napoli Pasta as a company heavily influenced by ethnic tradition and by patriarchal authority patterns in its operations. He felt that the president ran a "one-man show" in which virtually nothing happened without his direct order or approval. Burns observed signs in the plant forbidding talking while working, and watched the president personally stand over a group of women packers to assure that the rule was observed.

The company impressed Burns as "a very stable social unit which had successfully resisted the major change demands of its competitive environment, yet which had provided sufficient service and satisfactions to earn good profits and to retain employees with very low turnover. This company," he continued, "has few limits to its growth potential. Its major competitor increased sales from $2,000,000 in 1954 to $10,000,000 in 1959, while Napoli stood still. There would be a real challenge involved in getting this organization off dead center without disrupting all of its present functionality. Many things would have to be done differently, and all under the impact of a new president who knows nothing about the business and has none of the ethnic qualifications which are the standard prerequisites for the job."

After much investigation and analysis, Burns decided to open negotiations with Salvatierra for the purchase of Napoli Pasta Company. Although Burns' personal funds for investment in the venture were limited, he felt confident that, if he could work out a sound financing agreement, adequate funds from other investors could be obtained readily. Napoli's stock was held by six of its employees. The three major shareholders, who held 78% of the stock, were Salvatierra, Louis Rossotti (office manager), and Rudolpho Lombardi (factory superintendent). Burns learned from Salvatierra that he and the two other major stockholders would be most interested in a purchase and sale arrangement that would defer capital gains taxes, would provide a secure income, and would assure each of them of a substantial estate. Salvatierra added that the minor stockholders would probably prefer to get their money out now, but that they would go along with whatever he thought was best.

Salvatierra, who was 50 years old in 1960, had joined Napoli Pasta in 1927, and had been president and general manager since 1946. He had two sons, one in the army and the other a sophomore in high school. Neither was interested in the pasta business, and Salvatierra had no desire "to hand the boys a ready-made job. They ought to have to work for it, like I did," he said. Salvatierra told Burns he'd be willing to stay on as executive vice president for five years or so after he sold the business, if Burns desired. "I don't want to retire," he said, "I just want to take it a little easier."

Lombardi, who was Salvatierra's father-in-law, had been with the company for 50 years and was planning to retire at the end of 1960. Rossotti, age 40, preferred to stay in the business after its sale, and stated that he would be willing to do so if Burns bought the company and became president.

In November, 1960, as a result of considerable negotiation, Burns presented Salvatierra with a letter of intent (shown as Appendix A), outlining his proposed financial arrangements for acquiring Napoli. Since Salvatierra had indicated to Burns that his major interest was in long-term, guaranteed income with relative safety of principal, Burns proposed a purchase price of $750,000 in ten year, 8% notes with certain guarantees. At the insistence of Salvatierra and Rossotti, he agreed that their notes could not be prepaid, so that they could be assured of at least ten years' interest income. Moreover, they were agreeable to a ten year extension of maturity if Burns desired it. As Salvatierra said, "How else can I get 8% on my money with so little risk?"

Burns planned to pay the interest, and ultimately to retire the principal, from earnings generated by expanding the pasta business and by introducing certain cost savings. He also planned to move the outmoded plant, and to develop the present site as residential income property.

Simultaneously, Burns was negotiating with Investment Capital Company (ICC), a privately owned venture capital company, to provide the funds needed for the expansion of the pasta business and the development of the real estate. Burns was well known to the president of Investment Capital Co., Mr. Adams, who on several occasions had told Burns that Investment Capital Company would be willing to back him in an appropriate small business venture. When Burns brought the Napoli opportunity to ICC, Mr. Adams told Burns that ICC had been looking for a food processing operation as part of their diversification program. Adams asked Burns to submit a written proposal stating the amount of money that would be needed to acquire and operate Napoli, how the funds would be used, and describing the program that Burns expected to put into operation. Burns' proposal to ICC appears as Appendix B.

On December 15, Salvatierra and his group accepted Burns' offer, as proposed in Appendix A. Salvatierra and Rossotti both indicated their willingness to continue in the business, if requested, at annual salaries of $13,800 and $12,600 respectively.

On December 19, Investment Capital Company approved the purchase of 50,000 shares of Burnsco common stock at $1 per share and of $325,000 of seven year, 8% subordinated debentures, as proposed in Appendix B, payment to be made immediately.

As a result of these transactions, ICC held a 66⅔% equity interest in Burnsco and anticipated playing a very active role in the formulation and administration of corporate strategy and policies.

THE TAKEOVER

Under the terms of the purchase and sale agreement, Burns Corporation was to take over operating control of Napoli Pasta Company as of January 1, 1961.

As indicated in Appendix B, Burnsco expected to manage the pasta business and develop the property through the medium of two separate, wholly owned subsidiaries. Stanley Burns was to be president of all three corporations. Officers and directors of the subsidiaries had not yet been elected. However, the initial Board of Directors of Burnsco was established as consisting of three members: Stanley Burns, and two staff members of ICC.

These three were to meet on December 26, 1960, to develop the strategy and policies for the three companies.

appendix A

LETTER OF INTENT FROM STANLEY BURNS TO NAPOLI SHAREHOLDERS

STANLEY BURNS
8 NORTHSIDE ROAD
BOSTON, MASSACHUSETTS

November 15, 1960

Mr. Anthony Salvatierra
c/o Napoli Pasta Company
813 Virginia Street
Boston, Massachusetts

Dear Mr. Salvatierra:

This letter will serve as a letter of intent on behalf of my associates and myself concerning the acquisition of the outstanding stock of Napoli Pasta Company.

On the basis of the assets and liabilities of Napoli Pasta Company which have been disclosed to me, we would propose to purchase from the present stockholders of the company all of the outstanding stock for a total purchase price of $750,000.00.

The purchase price would be paid by delivering to each stockholder a promissory note, made by the acquiring corporation, for his proportionate share of the purchase price. Each note would: (i) be payable in full ten (10) years after the date thereof, with the acquiring corporation having an option to extend its maturity for an additional ten years; (ii) bear interest at the rate of 8% per annum, payable monthly; and (iii) be subordinated to all trade and bank creditors of the acquiring corporation. The notes to Messrs. Salvatierra and Rossotti cannot be prepaid. The notes to the other present stockholders can be prepaid at any time after one (1) year, without premium or penalty.

All of the notes would be guaranteed and secured in the following manner:

1. All of the outstanding stock of the acquiring corporation (hereinafter called "the operating company") would be owned by another corporation (hereinafter called "the holding company"), which would also guarantee the notes. The holding company would have initial cash assets of at least $400,000.

2. The operating company would transfer the real estate now owned by Napoli to a wholly owned subsidiary of the holding company (hereinafter called "the realty company"), which would also guarantee the notes. No other assets would be transferred from the operating company, which would be the maker of the notes.

3. To assure continuity of interest payments, the operating company would place in escrow a sum equal to a full year's interest on all of the outstanding notes, in cash or marketable securities, earmarked only for the payment of interest on the notes. Such sum would be kept in escrow at all times until the principal and interest on the notes are paid in full.

4. To further secure the notes beyond the $750,000 assets of the holding company and the realty company, the present stockholders would be given: (i) a first deed of trust on the real estate, subordinated, upon mutually agreeable terms, only to a construction loan and/or permanent mortgage which may be required for the development of the property; (ii) a chattel mortgage on the present equipment of Napoli and on any new equipment which may be purchased by the operating company for the purpose of expanding and modernizing the business; and (iii) an assignment of the leasehold to the new plant into which the business would be moved. This collateral is in addition to the guarantees of the holding company and the realty company.

5. The present stockholders would be entitled to accelerate the maturity of their notes and demand payment of the total principal and all interest which would have been payable thereon if they had gone to maturity in the event any of the following events should occur: (i) the failure to pay any two consecutive monthly installments of interest when due; or (ii) the failure of the operating company, the holding company, and the realty company to maintain a combined audited net asset value of at least $800,000.

"Net asset value" is defined for this purpose as total tangible assets, at depreciated book value, less all liabilities, except for: (a) shareholders' equity; (b) the long-term notes to be held by the present Napoli shareholders; and (c) any subordinated long-term notes which may be held by present or future investors in any of the three companies (operating, holding, or realty). Long-term notes, for this purpose, shall be deemed to be those with maturities of more than one year. The Napoli real estate, for this purpose, would be valued at $300,000.

The contract which would be entered into with the selling stockholders would have the warranties, representations, and other provisions normally contained in agreements to purchase all of the stock of a closely held corporation. In particular, all of the selling stockholders would have to agree to indemnify the operating company against any undisclosed liabilities, and in the event the operating company should be required to pay out any sums as a result of any such undisclosed liabilities, the amount of such payments would be deducted from the interest payments to be paid to the stockholders pursuant to their promissory notes.

This letter is not to be deemed a formal legal offer, but rather a bona fide statement of our intentions. If the terms outlined herein are acceptable to you and the other stockholders, I would appreciate hearing from you as soon as possible, and we can then have our attorneys prepare a formal written contract.

Sincerely,

/s/ *Stanley Burns*

appendix B

PROPOSAL SUBMITTED BY BURNS CORPORATION

to

INVESTMENT CAPITAL COMPANY (ICC)

Burns Corporation (Burnsco) will be a Boston corporation, organized by Stanley Burns, with an initial capital of $25,000, to acquire the stock and operate the assets of Napoli Pasta Company, a pioneer Boston producer and distributor of macaroni and related products.

Burnsco proposes to sell to Investment Capital Company (ICC) 50,000 shares of Burnsco common stock @ $1/share, plus seven year, 8% subordinated debentures in the amount of $325,000.

The total monies invested by ICC, $375,000, would be employed:

1. To relocate the present Napoli macaroni factory and to purchase additional machinery and equipment essential to expanding output and increasing the economy of operations.
2. To develop the present Napoli plant site, when vacated, as income property.
3. To increase working capital in anticipation of a vigorous expansion of Napoli's sales volume and scope of operations.

It is proposed that ICC purchase 50,000 shares of Burnsco stock @ $1/share, the same price as paid by the founder, Stanley Burns. If this proposal is accepted, Burnsco would be owned ⅔ by ICC and ⅓ by Stanley Burns. There is *no* promotional stock to be issued in this corporation or its subsidiaries.

BACKGROUND INFORMATION

Napoli Pasta Company, established in 1875, is the oldest and second largest producer and distributor of macaroni, spaghetti, noodles, and related products in the Boston area. Since 1946, when Mr. Anthony Salvatierra became president, the company has been consistently profitable, with earnings before taxes and bonuses averaging about $50,000 a year. Sales volume has held steadily at between $1.3 and $1.5 million since 1950.

During this decade, the company's factory, located on Beacon Hill in downtown Boston, has operated at close to capacity on a three shift, five days per week basis. Sales promotion has been minimal, since demand for the company's products has consistently exceeded the factory's limited capacity. Numerous large contracts or invitations to bid have been proffered the company and been refused for lack of capacity, including inquiries by the major supermarket chains.

Building code restrictions at the present site make major additions to existing facilities impossible, and present management has been reluctant to undertake the sizeable investment and risk involved in adding a second plant or in relocating and enlarging present operations.

During this same decade, Napoli's principal competitor, Prince Macaroni Company, following an aggressive sales and production expansion policy, has grown from sales volume of approximately $2 million to a present volume of over $10 million. Prince Macaroni now completely dominates the macaroni industry in the Boston area, with 100% distribution through every major supermarket chain, wholesaler, and cooperative. Napoli, on the other hand, has never had, or actively sought, distribution through any of these major outlets, the great majority of its sales being made to small independent grocers, on a drop-ship basis, through company salesmen, with store-door deliveries in company trucks by company drivers.

Napoli quality enjoys an excellent reputation wherever the company has distribution; Napoli products consistently outsell all other competition, including Prince Macaroni, in these locations. All items are sold under the Napoli label, except for about 20% of sales volume, which is sold in bulk to two long-time customers: a large canner of soups and other items utilizing macaroni products, and a medium-sized hotel and restaurant supply house.

Napoli has another valuable asset in its real estate. Although the factory buildings are old and have little value, the land on which they are situated is extremely valuable. Carried on the books at only $18,000, this land has been bid for regularly by prospective developers at prices ranging from $300,000 to

$400,000. (Mr. Salvatierra presently has an open, outstanding offer, available at his option, for $350,000.) The land consists of approximately 33,000 square feet on the north side of Beacon Hill in Boston, located where two streets dead-end, with a panoramic view of the Charles River. Nearby land has sold in the past year at prices ranging from $10 to $17 per square foot. The Napoli property is one of the largest potentially available pieces of land on the Hill, and is ideally suited for development as an apartment site.

Burnsco has been organized by Stanley Burns as a vehicle for acquiring and developing these assets of Napoli Pasta Company. Burnsco proposes to operate these assets through two wholly owned subsidiaries. Napoli Foods Company, of which Mr. Burns will be president and Mr. Salvatierra executive vice president, would conduct, and attempt to expand, the present macaroni business. Beacon Development Corporation would develop the real estate at the present plant site.

Mr. Burns is negotiating an agreement with the present Napoli Pasta Company stockholders, whereby they will sell all of their outstanding shares in exchange for 8%, ten year renewable notes in the amount of $750,000, made by Napoli Foods Company, and secured by certain guarantees of Burnsco and Beacon Development (as described more fully in the attached letter of intent from Stanley Burns to Anthony Salvatierra, dated November 15, 1960).[1]

If ICC acts affirmatively on this proposal, Burnsco, through its subsidiaries, will acquire all of the outstanding stock of Napoli Pasta Company, and commence the operation of both the food company and the realty company as of January 1, 1961.

CAPITAL STRUCTURE

Burnsco has a present capital position of $25,000 in cash and no liabilities. If this proposal is acted upon affimatively, Burnsco would then have a capital structure of:

Cash $400,000	7 year, 8% debentures		$325,000
	Common stock		
	Authorized	500,000	
	Issued	75,000[1]	75,000
			$400,000

1Owned: 25,000 Stanley Burns, 50,000 ICC.

Burnsco would then organize Napoli Foods Company, with an original capital of $10,000, to acquire the Napoli Pasta Company stock, and would also organize Beacon Development Corporation with a similar original capital.

---

[1] This letter appears in the case as Appendix A.

Napoli Foods Company would then purchase all of the outstanding stock of Napoli Pasta Company for 8%, ten year renewable notes, in the amount of $750,000. (As of December 31, 1960, Napoli Pasta Company is expected to show assets of $564,000 and liabilities of $164,000.)

Napoli Foods would then sell the real property to Burnsco in exchange for Burnsco's noninterest-bearing note of $350,000.

Burnsco, in turn, would sell the real property to Beacon in exchange for 350,000 shares of Beacon stock.

After all of these transactions, the capital structure of the three corporations would be as follows:

Burnsco

Cash	$380,000	Notes payable (to	
Napoli Foods		Napoli Foods)	$350,000
capital stock	10,000	7 year, 8% debentures	
Beacon Dev.		(to ICC)	325,000
capital stock	360,000	Capital stock	75,000
	$750,000		$750,000

Napoli Foods Company

Cash	$170,000	Current liabilities	$164,000
Other current assets	225,000	10 year, 8% renewable	
Note receivable		notes	750,000
(from Burnsco)	350,000	Capital stock	10,000
Fixed assets (net)	179,000		
	$924,000		$924,000

Beacon Development Corp.

Cash	$ 10,000	Capital stock	$360,000
Land and buildings	350,000		
	$360,000		

Consolidated Statement

Cash	$ 560,000	Current liabilities	$ 164,000
Other current assets	225,000	10 year, 8% renewable notes	750,000
Fixed assets (net)	529,000	7 year, 8% debentures	325,000
		Capital stock	75,000
	$1,314,000		$1,314,000

USE OF FUNDS

The new funds from ICC and Stanley Burns which, through Burnsco, will be invested in Napoli Foods and Beacon Development, will be allocated as follows:

Napoli Foods	
Cost of:	
1. Moving factory equipment	$ 25,000
2. Flour handling equipment	90,000
3. New press and drying equipment	55,000
4. New packaging unit	30,000
	$200,000
Beacon	
Cash to support construction loan and mortgage on development of real property and/or purchase of new factory building	175,000
Burnsco	
Increase in working capital	25,000
Total	$400,000

Specifically, it is proposed that:

1. Mr. Burns and Mr. Salvatierra will undertake at once to secure contracts and commitments from major chains, wholesalers, and industrial or institutional customers above and beyond present Napoli Pasta Company sales. A tentative commitment from the New England district of A & P, the largest chain in the area, for both private label and Napoli label items has already been secured by Burns. It is estimated that this commitment will cover a beginning quantity of at least four million pounds for 1961. A & P's New England sales of paste products for fiscal 1960 were reported to be 16 million pounds, of which Prince was the dominant supplier.
2. As soon as sufficient commitments have been obtained to assure a production rate by the end of 1961 of at least $2.5 million/year, a suitable factory building will be purchased or leased (depending on the relative attractiveness of the terms) and orders executed for the necessary new equipment, building toward a total company capacity on a three shift/seven day basis of $4.5 million.
3. The new building will commence immediately to serve as a warehousing and distributing depot for the output of both new and old factories. After production lines have been installed and operated successfully in the new plant, the gradual moving of equipment and personnel from old quarters to new will begin. We estimate that this transition may require a year to complete fully so that deliveries to customers are not interrupted and so that the

greatest degree of efficiency in plant layout and production may be achieved. Mr. Burns' experience in the human problems associated with the administration of change, and Mr. Salvatierra's intimate familiarity with the technological factors in macaroni manufacture, hopefully can be integrated to produce a high-productivity, high-efficiency, low-cost production operation.

4. As sales volume increases, a reorganization of Napoli's distribution and promotion methods will be instituted in an attempt to serve customers more effectively and to reduce the extraordinarily high selling expenses involved in Napoli Pasta Company's costly and outmoded procedures. It is anticipated that sales and promotional efforts will be concentrated in the Boston metropolitan area until substantial market coverage has been achieved.

5. After the factory has been relocated, the present Beacon Hill site would be developed by Beacon Development Corporation as income property. . . .

6. As Napoli Foods Company market penetration grows, after the reorganization of the selling and distribution effort, and after production operations are functioning smoothly, an aggressive program of growth through seeking distribution in new market areas and/or development or acquisition of new, related products is contemplated. Obviously, this phase is sufficiently distant that its form is presently quite vague.

Details of the individual aspects of this proposal follow. . . .

NAPOLI PASTA COMPANY AND ITS PRESENT POSITION

Company Products

Currently, the company produces more than 40 different paste products, of which the most important are long spaghetti, elbow macaroni, salad macaroni, egg noodles, coil spaghetti, special shapes for soup (e.g., stars, alphabets, wagon wheels), vermicelli, capellini, and seashell macaroni. These nine items constitute about 75% of total sales.

In addition, the company packages two combination items: macaroni dinner (macaroni with cheese), and a special low-calorie macaroni dinner. These sell currently in very small volume.

Napoli also distributes related items, such as minestrone soup, mushroom sauce, marinara sauce, and a broad line of beans and rice, which are packed for Napoli to their specifications. Beans and rice comprise approximately 10% of total sales volume; other purchased items sell in very small volume.

The company holds the trade name on a quick-cooking slim macaroni with only 103 calories per four oz. serving, but has never really capitalized on the promotion of this product.

Dry paste products are packed in attractive cellophane bags in 8 oz., 12 oz., 14 oz., 1 lb., and 2 lb. packages for consumer sales, and in cardboard boxes for bulk sales in 5 lb., 10 lb., 20 lb., 25 lb., 35 lb., and 50 lb cartons.

Combination products are packaged in colorful 12 oz. and 1 lb. cartons, while related products appear in a variety of can sizes.

Present production is at a rate of about eight million lbs./year. Napoli products contain only the finest ingredients, using 100% first-grade semolina flour, the heart of Durum wheat, in combination with first quality egg solids.

Promotion and Distribution

From 1946 to 1954, sales expanded nearly tenfold. Since that time, with the factory operating at capacity, sales have held steadily between $1.35 and $1.5 million.

Napoli products are sold through Napoli's own sales force, consisting of 14 full-time employees. Products are delivered directly to the stores in Napoli's own trucks by five Napoli teamsters. A very small percentage of output is handled through brokers and wholesalers.

Most of Napoli's accounts are small grocers or operators of single super-markets. While some distribution is achieved throughout the New England states, the Boston area accounts for more than 75% of sales. In the Boston area, 70% of the total grocery business is done by the major chains (A & P, First National, Stop and Shop, Elm Farm, etc.) or by the big wholesalers. Napoli has no representation in any of these. However, wherever Napoli *does* have distribution, it outsells all other competition. Its most dominant position is in areas of high Italian concentration, because Napoli products are *authentic, high-quality, old-fashioned* Italian style pasta. For example, in Boston's south side (including the one A & P store where Napoli has distribution), Napoli products outsell competition two to one and frequently command a higher shelf price.

If the major portion of the Boston area market is to be tapped, Napoli must get distribution in the chains and wholesalers. These new channels will require direct sales to central buying offices and deliveries to central warehouses. Some consideration to store-door delivery will be given, however, for chain stores, since this procedure would enable Napoli salesmen to stock shelves and enhance the merchandise display.

More attention must also be given to expanding bulk or private label sales. Sales volume is at the point where fixed costs are well covered, and subsequent business can be bid on at lower prices and still yield comfortable profits.

Personnel

Present Napoli personnel consist of 60 full-time employees. These are divided as follows:

Factory workers	36
Teamsters	5
Salesmen	14
Office	2
Management	3

Factory workers belong to the Macaroni Workers' Union, affiliated with the Bakery & Confectionary Workers' Union. Teamsters belong to the Teamsters' Union. All employees are organized, except for office, sales, and management personnel.

Most employees are long-service employees, 75% having service of ten years or more with Napoli. Virtually all are second or third generation Italians. Most have substantial family background in the macaroni business.

Management presently consists of three persons:

> Mr. Anthony Salvatierra, president and general manager
> Mr. Louis Rossotti, office manager
> Mr. Rudolpho Lombardi, factory superintendent

Mr. Salvatierra and Mr. Rossotti are both being retained on five year employment contracts, Mr. Salvatierra as executive vice president and general manager, and Mr. Rossotti as secretary-treasurer and office manager of Napoli Foods Company. Mr. Salvatierra may elect after one year to work part-time, as may Mr. Rossotti, and compensation will be scaled accordingly. Mr. Salvatierra's contract will call for $13,800 a year on a full-time basis. Mr. Rossotti's contract will be for $12,600 for the first year, with subsequent years' salaries to be negotiated on the basis of his duties and performance. Both men will sign a noncompetitive agreement.

Mr. Rudolpho Lombardi is retiring on December 31, 1960, after 50 years' employment with Napoli. His place will be filled by Mr. Gino Antionoli, a pressman who has had 25 years' experience in the macaroni business, was at one time in the business for himself, and has been with Napoli for 20 years. No problems are anticipated in this changeover.

The one new person in the company will be Stanley Burns, formerly management consultant for Andrew C. Boyden & Associates. Mr. Burns will serve as president and will be primarily concerned with financial management, sales to chains and wholesalers, administering the relocation and expansion program, and personnel administration. Mr. Salvatierra will supervise purchasing and production, plant engineering, warehousing and shipping, and sales to bulk accounts. Mr. Rossotti will be concerned with all accounting and recordkeeping functions, will supervise the office force, and will lend general assistance to Messrs. Salvatierra and Burns. One of the present salesmen will be assigned the additional responsibility of supervising sales to independent grocers. He will be supported by Messrs. Rossotti, Salvatierra, and Burns. Mr. Burns' salary will be $15,000 a year from Napoli Foods Company, and $10,000 a year from Burnsco.

Facilities

Present company facilities consist of a four story frame factory building and a single story office and warehouse building, both on Virginia Street on the north side of Beacon Hill. These properties are owned outright and are unencumbered.

The factory building contains three large macaroni presses, each capable of producing 800 lbs. of paste per hour under ideal conditions. Each press has its own series of drying ovens. In addition, there are a number of packaging machines of various kinds, a flour sifter, and a blender. The company owns five large trucks and two automobiles.

Napoli also leases, on a year-to-year basis, a small warehouse and production facility in Quincy. This building contains a small press and associated drying units. These are used mostly for production of specialty products under a secondary label. Maximum rated production capacity is 600 lbs. per hour.

Presses are relatively modern and have been maintained in excellent condition. There has been little change in basic design or operation in macaroni presses over the past 20 years.

Industry Conditions

The macaroni industry, in general, has experienced slow but steady growth. Per capita consumption has been increasing gradually, and the advent of new products for quick, complete meals promises to accelerate that trend.

The newest and fastest-growing segments are packaged "heat and eat" macaroni dinners, spaghetti dinners, pizzas, etc., which contain paste, sauce, cheese, etc., in individual sections of a single carton. Canned macaroni type products have not moved ahead as rapidly as these packaged "dinners," but frozen foods offer perhaps the newest and fastest-growing possibilities of all.

Macaroni products compete to some degree with other specialty foods, such as Mexican or Chinese foods, but are much more universally accepted and sell in substantially larger quantities. Specialty products like lasagne, vermicelli, cappelini, egg noodles, etc., are sold primarily on a quality basis for use with meats, sauces, in casseroles, etc. Basic macaroni and spaghetti products are sold as meat substitutes or to accompany meat dishes in place of potatoes or rice. As such, these products are nonseasonal, selling well in every month of the year, and are countercyclical. The more depressed business conditions become, the more the basic macaroni products are consumed.

This steady, nonseasonal, noncyclical consumption pattern, together with the steady increase in population of the Boston area, provides a stable, growing market for Napoli's products.

Limited brand differentiation is possible, particularly on specialty products, where substantial difference exists in appearance and taste between products utilizing the finest quality ingredients and those employing inferior materials. But in most respects, macaroni sales are not unlike coffee sales, where a familiar name is the major prerequisite for sales, and differentiation of brands is more a matter of differences in packaging and advertising than of differences in basic products. Under these circumstances, the familiar private label of a large chain may outsell widely advertised national brands, especially if there is a price differential favoring the private label. Consequently, trade relationships with major chains and wholesalers become the determining factors in distribution, unless a ruinous course of price cutting is to be followed. Napoli's ability to build such relationships is as yet untried.

Competition

Napoli's competition is considerable. The major factor in the Boston area market is Prince Macaroni Company. This aggressive organization captured the market and achieved close to 100% distribution, while other local macaroni producers, of whom Napoli is the largest, stood still. Prince Macaroni is firmly entrenched in A & P, First National, Stop and Shop, and other major outlets. In recent years, however, they have expanded their product line and their areas of distribution with uneven success. There is some reason to believe that acquisitions in the Philadelphia market plus fierce price competition in the New York market have left Prince Macaroni somewhat vulnerable in the Boston area.

NAPOLI PASTA COMPANY

Comparative Balance Sheets: 1954–1959
(December 31)

	1959	1958	1957	1956	1955	1954
Current Assets						
Cash	$151,373	$167,866	$123,333	$108,134	$ 92,277	$ 89,592
Accounts receivable	106,897	97,264	108,895	111,644	111,795	113,001
Inventory	90,572	89,738	90,138	87,929	77,401	75,219
Prepaid expenses	4,272	5,386	3,247	7,018	4,982	5,161
Other assets—deposits and supplies	795	795	6,583	7,804	7,964	10,243
Total current assets	$353,909	$361,049	$332,196	$322,529	$294,419	$293,216
Current Liabilities						
Accounts payable	$128,722	$121,923	$122,044	$163,774	$157,499	$164,476
Notes payable	—	5,512	5,512	5,726	1,656	9,241
Accrued liabilities	37,266	50,051	48,247	38,394	37,924	47,043
Total current liabilities	$165,988	$177,486	$175,803	$207,894	$197,079	$220,760
Net Working Capital	$187,921	$183,563	$156,393	$114,635	$ 97,340	$ 72,456
Land, buildings, and equipment						
Land	$ 18,335	$ 18,335	$ 18,335	$ 18,335	$ 18,335	$ 18,335
Buildings	57,728	57,728	57,728	57,290	55,806	52,149
Automotive	44,429	44,171	40,847	41,088	36,913	36,913
Other machinery and equipment	280,170	240,703	305,802	300,832	281,441	258,588
Total land, buildings, and equipment	$400,662	$360,937	$422,712	$417,545	$392,495	$365,985
Less: accumulated depreciation	260,828	197,948	248,393	218,880	191,608	161,771
Net land, buildings, and equipment	$139,834	$162,989	$174,319	$198,665	$200,887	$204,214
Total working capital and land, buildings, and equipment	$327,755	$346,552	$330,712	$313,300	$298,227	$276,670
Long-Term Liabilities	$8,548	$9,716	$ 15,124	$ 14,554	$ 22,220	$ 25,720
Capital and Surplus	319,207	336,836	315,588	298,836	276,007	250,950
Total long-term liabilities and capital	$327,755	$346,552	$330,712	$313,390	$298,227	$276,670

Napoli is the second largest macaroni manufacturer in the Boston area. Nearly as large is Eastern States Macaroni Co., who produce under the Superior label. Eastern States has distribution in a number of independent chains and markets and produces under private label for the First National chain. Unlike Prince Macaroni, Eastern States' principal entry into stores has been through price cutting, and their financial position is consequently not nearly so strong.

In addition to these two competitors, there are literally two dozen small producers. Most of these are single press, two to five man operations, each capable of producing less than a million lbs. per year, and therefore unable to serve major chains or wholesalers. These small companies tend to concentrate on private labeling, bulk sales, or brand sales in a very limited distribution. They are not regarded as serious factors in Napoli's plans for expansion.

A more difficult and potentially threatening factor is the influx of New York producers into the Boston market. Ronzoni (New York City) and Mueller (New

NAPOLI PASTA COMPANY

Profit and Loss Summaries
(for years ending December 31, 1954–1959, and estimated for 1960)

	1960(est.)	1959	1958	1957	1956	1955	1954
Sales							
City[1]	$ 291,500	$ 260,849	$ 284,414	$ 265,319	$ 237,508	$ 233,119	$ 228,516
Country[2]	1,091,500	1,107,312	1,313,502	1,202,294	1,316,794	1,205,043	1,163,970
Rice and beans	216,240	161,846	—	—	—	—	—
	$1,599,240	$1,530,007	$1,597,916	$1,467,613	$1,554,302	$1,438,162	$1,392,486
Returns and allowances	9,010	8,952	10,563	12,634	11,738	13,210	9,590
Net sales	$1,590,230	$1,521,055	$1,587,353	$1,454,979	$1,542,564	$1,424,95?	$1,382,896
Cost of sales							
Purchases							
Flour	$ 501,380	$ 534,190	$ 596,630	$ 540,339	$ 630,929	$ 575,882	$ 603,607
Egg solids	64,448	71,776	92,234	47,289	55,500	39,142	35,438
Cellophane	64,024	57,868	48,007	64,636	57,090	57,954	43,744
Cases & cartons	45,474	64,995	66,604	75,818	144,985	133,790	112,781
	$ 675,326	$ 728,829	$ 803,455	$ 728,082	$ 888,504	$ 806,768	$ 795,570
Rice and beans for resale	210,940	149,842	128,009	90,001	47,657	39,131	30,104
Total	886,266	878,671	931,464	818,083	936,151	845,899	825,674
Inventory change	32,886	(834)	401	(2,209)	(10,528)	(2,182)	(23)
Total Cost	$ 919,152	$ 877,837	$ 931,865	$ 815,874	$ 925,623	$ 843,717	$ 825,651
Gross profit	$ 671,078	$ 643,218	$ 655,488	$ 639,105	$ 616,941	$ 581,235	$ 557,245
Operating expense							
Manufacturing	$ 325,420	$ 351,695	$ 311,311	$ 331,120	$ 338,634	$ 297,941	$ 289,102
Selling	260,760	224,355	262,146	225,819	194,434	197,302	170,113
General	51,410	53,212	53,167	47,145	51,987	49,944	47,738
Total	$ 637,590	$ 629,262	$ 626,624	$ 604,084	$ 585,505	$ 545,187	$ 506,953
Other income							
Discount	$ 2,650	$ 2,489	$ 2,427	$ 2,469	$ 1,967	$ 1,801	$ 1,463
Other	318	670	795	242	937	256	120
Total	$ 2,968	$ 3,159	$ 3,222	$ 2,711	$ 2,904	$ 2,057	$ 1,583
Net income	$ 36,456	$ 17,115	$ 32,086				
Add back—bonus, officers	11,474	28,726	27,263				
Net income without bonus	$ 47,930	$ 45,841	$ 59,349	$ 37,732	$ 50,314	$ 54,079	$ 67,849
State taxes	1,585	—	962	639	639	639	—
Federal Income Tax—adjusted	18,646	18,008	24,494	26,035	20,019	22,974	29,435
Adjusted net income	$ 27,699	$ 27,833	$ 33,893	$ 35,130	$ 29,656	$ 30,466	$ 38,414

[1]Within Boston and Cambridge city limits.

[2]All sales outside city limits.

Jersey) are the biggest of these. Ronzoni has achieved A & P distribution with at least 14 items (all in boxes), and Mueller is sold in a number of independent markets and chains (also in boxes). In the rapidly growing "packaged dinner" field, Chef Boy-ar-Dee (American Home Products), Kraft (National Dairy), Franco-American (Campbell Soups), and Prince Macaroni have close to 100% distribution for two to three items each. Single item distribution has also been widely achieved by Van Camp (Tenderoni) and Buitoni (Wagon Wheels).

It is our opinion that Napoli can compete very effectively on both a quality and price basis with the New York producers (Ronzoni, Mueller, Buitoni), but that competition with local producers (Prince Macaroni, Eastern States) must be on a different basis which establishes some brand differentiation for Napoli's products. Napoli's excellent reputation for quality, its unusually high acceptance among the Italian population, its Italian name, and its authentic Italian products provide some basis for such differentiation.

Current Limits on Performance

Napoli's principal current limits are:

1. Plant capacity, which makes substantial expansion of sales impossible without plant relocation or additions.
2. Management attitudes and behavior, which have been content to maintain status quo while others captured the increases in the market.
3. Lack of distribution and trade relationships with the major chains and wholesalers. Vis-à-vis these important customers (75% of the total market), Napoli is starting from an absolutely dead stop position. Moreover, its market penetration is less than 25%.
4. Competitors who have filled the void and are, apparently, functioning satisfactorily.
5. Inadequate sales volume to support an effective advertising program to promote the brand.

Napoli's Opportunities

Nonetheless, it is our belief that Napoli has unusual opportunities:

1. Its fine name and high acceptance among those who know good pasta best gives it a superb base from which to promote.
2. It has excellent relations and performance records with present customers.
3. It has highly favorable relationships with at least two major bulk buyers and has been approached by several others in the past year whose business could be added fairly readily.
4. A new plant, as contemplated, would be the lowest cost producer in the industry, enabling Napoli to compete effectively price-wise with entrenched competition.

We are forecasting a rate of growth of $1 million in the first year of new management (reflecting a new plant and the acquisition of at least two major chains or wholesalers as customers) and $800,000 for the next year (reflecting distribution in other principal outlets). Thereafter, growth is contemplated at $600,000 a year for the next two years, allowing only for consumption and population increases.

HISTORICAL FINANCIAL STATEMENTS

Balance Sheets, Profit and Loss Statements, and Source and Application of Funds Statements for the years 1954–1960 are attached. [See pages 167–174.]

These statements are particularly noteworthy for their consistency and stability. They reflect the company's near-capacity operations and the ability of Mr. Salvatierra to improve the financial position of the company without substantial increases in sales.

NAPOLI PASTA COMPANY

Historical Summary—Source and Application of Funds

	Summary: 5 years	1959	1958	1957	1956	1955
Sources of funds were:						
Net profit	$161,866	$17,115	$32,066	$37,846	$34,782	$40,057
Less: Federal Income Tax	56,848	5,135	10,818	13,850	12,045	15,000
	105,018	11,980	21,248	23,996	22,737	25,057
Add: depreciation	155,272	28,757	30,935	32,132	33,612	29,837
Total sources of funds	$260,290	$40,737	$52,183	$56,128	$56,349	$54,994
Funds were applied to:						
Net additions to fixed assets	90,210	4,919	19,607	7,786	31,389	26,510
Acquisition of capital (treasury) stock	37,444	30,290	–	7,155	–	–
Net reduction in long-term debt	17,172	1,168	5,408	(570)	7,666	3,500
Funds applied other than working capital	$144,826	$36,377	$25,015	$14,371	$39,055	$30,010
Resulting in a net increase (decrease) in working capital[1]	115,464	4,360	27,168	41,757	17,294	24,984
Total funds applied	$260,290	$40,737	$52,183	$56,128	$56,349	$54,994

[1]For purposes of analysis, other assets were included with current assets in computing working capital.

NAPOLI PASTA COMPANY

Balance Sheet—October 31, 1960
(prepared from company books, after adjustments, without audit)

Assets

Current Assets:			
Cash			
Bank		$151,290	
Petty cash		768	$152,058
Accounts Receivable			
City		$ 36,596	
Country		107,564	144,160
Inventory (estimated)			89,517
Prepaid expenses			
Insurance		$ 4,361	
Taxes		1,864	6,225
Total current assets			$391,960
Fixed Assets:			
Land		$18,335	
Building	$ 57,728		
Automotive equipment	44,429		
Dies	11,767		
Electric motors	1,018		
Machinery and equipment	238,221		
Factory fixtures	24,361		
Office fixtures	5,486		
	$381,992		
Less: accumulated depreciation	283,524	98,468	
Total fixed assets			116,803
Other Assets:			
Stationery, supplies		$ 424	
Deposit, compensation insurance		371	
Deposit, purchase of machinery		1,060	
Total other assets			1,855
Total Assets			$510,618

Liabilities

Current liabilities:			
Accounts payable			$125,248
Accrued liabilities			
Labor		$ 5,791	
Payroll taxes		5,435	
Other liabilities		2,622	13,848
Total current liabilities			$139,096
Long-term liabilities			
Notes payable			
Bank (secured by mortgage on real property)			2,635
Total liabilities			$141,731

Balance Sheet (cont.)

Capital

Capital stock authorized:		
2,400 shares—par value $25	$63,600	
Premium on capital stock	16,562	
	$80,162	
Less: capital stock in treasury	28,045	
Total capital stock		$ 52,117

Surplus

Surplus:			
Balance—January 1, 1960	$262,894		
Adjustments			
Account receivable credit			
	4,776		
1957	$267,670		
Net profit for period from January			
1, 1960, to October 31, 1960	49,100	$316,770	
Total capital and surplus			368,887
Total Liabilities, Capital, and Surplus			$510,618

PROPOSED PLAN FOR THE GROWTH AND DEVELOPMENT OF THE NAPOLI PASTA COMPANY BUSINESS

Strategy

As outlined in the earlier pages of this prospectus, it is our intention to aggressively solicit business from the major outlets, purchase or lease a new plant, re-equip and add to present machinery, attempt to reduce production and purchasing costs, and follow a program of expansion through further internal growth and acquisition.

The key to success of this program is distribution through the major outlets—especially A & P, which dominates the area. Our strategy will be to avoid pure price cutting as our means of entry, since this is a self-defeating practice. We will, instead, offer to private label for the big chains at a fair price and to offer our Napoli label to them for sale at a price differential of 2 to 3¢ more per package, perhaps in a different package (box vs. cellophane), giving them a substantially higher markup. Store-door delivery is another possibility. Our objective will not be to *replace* Prince Macaroni on the shelves, but to gain equal showing. Therefore, our major attack will be in competition with the small producers (who cannot afford a price war) and the New York manufacturers (who

NAPOLI PASTA COMPANY

Statement of Income for Period from January 1, 1960, to October 31, 1960
(prepared from books, after adjustments, without audit)

Sales:			
City			$ 218,918
Country			889,995
Beans and rice			174,145
Total			$1,283,058
Less: returns and allowances			7,639
Net sales			$1,275,419
Cost of goods sold:			
Inventory—January 1, 1960		$ 90,572	
Purchases			
Flour	$414,114		
Eggs	54,781		
Cellophane	51,818		
Casings and cartons	39,687		
Merchandise purchased for resale			
Beans and rice	153,433	713,833	
Total		$804,405	
Less: inventory—October 31, 1960			
(estimated)		89,518	
Cost of goods sold			714,887
Gross profit			$ 560,532
Operating expenses:			
Manufacturing expenses		$297,707	
Selling expenses		182,325	
General expenses		35,559	
Total operating expenses			515,591
Net profit from operations			$ 44,941
Other income:			
Purchase discounts		$2,169	
Gain on sale of capital assets		24	
Bad debts recovered		303	
Accounts receivable			
balances—adjustment		1,766	
Total other income			4,262
Net income for period from January 1, 1960, to October 31, 1960			$ 49,203

suffer from a considerable cost disadvantage). In the first year, we will use our advertising budget to give advertising allowances to the chains and wholesalers who stock our merchandise. Only after sales volume exceeds $3 million will we undertake any kind of real space (newspaper, radio, TV, etc.) campaign.

Statement of Operating Expenses for Period from January 1, 1960, to October 31, 1960
(prepared from books, after adjustments, without audit)

Manufacturing Expenses	
Fuel, light, water	$ 16,311
Depreciation	21,787
Insurance	10,784
Labor:	
Drivers	32,712
General	112,618
Cellophane	57,650
Building repair	37
Machinery repair	11,305
Fumigation	2,370
Factory expense	4,552
Payroll taxes	10,753
Union pension and trust fund	12,030
Storage and demurrage	4,773
Freight incoming	25
Total manufacturing expenses	$297,707
Selling Expenses	
Advertising	$ 6,316
Brokerage	7,954
Commissions	3,095
Depreciation	868
Drivers' expense	2,832
Freight, prepaid	13,971
Auto, truck, and tractor expense	17,148
Sales discount	23,006
Salesmen's and executive salaries	75,387
Salesmen's health insurance	3,581
Salesmen's automobile expense	15,065
Salesmen's expense	5,384
Teamsters' pension and security fund	1,358
Rent	1,325
Taxes	4,731
Extended duration benefit fund	304
Total selling expenses	$182,325
General Expenses	
Depreciation	$ 322
Dues and subscriptions	830
Interest	183
Office salaries	22,406
Postage	1,242
Professional service	3,648
Licenses and fees	417
Stationery and printing	2,347
Telegraph and telephone	2,221
Taxes	823
General expense	1,120
Total general expenses	$ 35,559

During this period, we will also solicit U.S. Government, State, Army, and other bulk contracts, as well as bulk sales to such prospects as packers who purchase macaroni products.

If we are successful, we may purchase some of the smaller competitors whose business we are taking as a source of qualified personnel, equipment, and some trade relationships.

Timing

The first year is the most crucial one for this new venture. Unless it is clear that distribution can be obtained through the major chains without drastic reductions in gross margins, the expansion of the business will be both slow and limited in scope. Thus, the first year should indicate what the likelihood of success will be. No contracts for new equipment, and no commitments for new facilities, personnel, or moving agreements will be made until *after* major chain and/or wholesaler distribution is assured.

It would be our plan to operate in two locations for about a year, if the sales contracts are forthcoming, and to move piecemeal from the old location to the new one over that period. The new location should be one in which major economies in flour handling and purchasing, packing, and warehousing can be effected. It should be large enough to accommodate our anticipated volume of $4.5 million by 1965, should be located on a rail spur to enable bulk carload flour purchases, and have adequate warehouse and distribution facilities to enable Napoli trucks to serve customers directly.

Costs of Implementing Proposed Plan

In order to carry out this program, substantial costs will be incurred.

1. Flour handling equipment is estimated at $90,000. Such facilities will handle up to at least the $4.5 million volume contemplated and should result in minimum savings of 4¢ per lb. on flour purchase and handling expense. At current levels of 8 million lbs. of flour purchased per year, this is a saving of $32,000 a year. At projected sales for 1961 ($2.5 million), 14 million lbs. of flour would be involved, for a $56,000 saving. Thus, the equipment could pay for itself in less than two years.

2. New presses will be necessary to expand capacity, along with their companion drying units. Two new, high-speed presses are contemplated in 1961–1963: a long paste machine @ approximately $27,500 and a short paste machine @ approximately $17,500. Additional drying units needed for these presses are estimated at $60,000. The new long paste machine would have maximum capacity of approximately 1,500 lbs. an hour, and the short cut approximately 1,200 lbs. an hour.

    The new plant would thus have an ultimate maximum capacity of:

2,400 lbs. an hour from existing presses

plus   600 lbs. an hour from the press now in Quincy

plus   2,700 lbs. an hour from the new presses

for a total of 5,700 lbs. an hour.

Therefore, the company's maximum capacity will be: 5,700 lbs. an hour times 24 hours a day times 300 days a year for a total of 41 million lbs. a year.

Allowing 30% for changeover and shutdown time, the realizable capacity would be approximately 29 million lbs. a year, which is sufficient to support nearly $5 million in sales (target projected for 1965).

Addition of the short paste press and appropriate drying equipment to completely mechanize the existing operations would likely take place in 1961. It is estimated that these additions, aggregating approximately $55,000, would increase present output by over 150%, bringing capacity up to 1962–1963 sales target levels. This mechanization would also make possible the higher output *without* additional pressmen, thereby lowering manufacturing costs substantially.

The long paste press and appropriate dryers would likely be added in late 1962, if sales levels are running as projected. This expenditure of approximately $50,000 is expected to be covered by depreciation cash flow from Napoli Foods operations.

3. A new, flexible, automatic packaging unit is also contemplated in 1961. This unit, estimated to cost $30,000, utilizes polyethylene and makes its own bags, enabling a materials saving over present cellophane of 5¢ per bag, and would be suitable for products presently using 3 million bags per year, for a saving of $15,000 a year. The machine would thus pay for itself in materials savings alone in two years. Additionally, the machine requires only two operators on a single shift to pack the projected output, vs. 11 packers to handle the present output of cellophane-packed products. The displaced packers can be utilized on other items, thus again providing greatly increased output without the need for additional personnel.

4. A new plant building may be purchased or leased, depending on the relative advantage of the terms. If purchased, the building financing would be extended to include flour handling equipment, the packaging unit, and the new short cut press and dryers. The down payment on the building and equipment could thereby be fixed at approximately the same level as the outright purchase of this equipment (approximately $175,000).

5. Costs of moving the equipment from the present site to a new one have been estimated at $25,000. These would be spread out over a year's period.

6. Sales expense would likely decrease as a per cent of sales due to cheaper methods involved in soliciting a few large chains vs. many small independent grocers as the principal basis for expansion of sales volume, but advertising and promotion allowances, plus shorter margins to chains, would likely counterbalance this saving.

7. Some further new automatic packaging equipment will be required ultimately, but it is contemplated that such equipment will be *rented* rather

than purchased in order to allow for replacement as improved machines come on the market in this rapidly changing technology.

8. Some additional financial costs in carrying larger inventories and accounts receivable are inevitable as sales expand. But it is estimated that payroll costs will not increase greatly with improved methods and equipment and seeking a mass distribution market. Few production employees and virtually no salesmen will need to be added. There may have to be a small increase in office personnel, and perhaps one or two additional management members, but personnel increase should be disproportionate to sales increases.

Thus, new funds from ICC and Stanley Burns likely would be partially employed in 1961 as follows:

Moving factory equipment	$ 25,000
Flour handling equipment	90,000
New press and drying equipment	55,000
New packaging equipment	30,000
	$200,000

to provide the base for expansion of the macaroni business.

9. Organizational expenses are estimated at approximately $25,000, including $18,000 finder's fee to Business Brokers, Inc. These expenses, however, will be met by Napoli Foods Company from Napoli Pasta working capital, which is more than adequate to absorb these costs without impairing the company's operation.

Assuming that Napoli can increase its share of a growing market, operating profits are projected for each of the four subsequent years as follows:

	1961	*1962*	*1963*	*1964*
Expected sales volume	$2.5 mil.	$3.3 mil.	$3.9 mil.	$4.5 mil.
Projected operating profit	103,000	174,000	219,000	209,000
Less: interest payments	86,000	86,000	86,000	86,000
Net profit before taxes	$17,000	$88,000	$135,000	$223,000
Est. Fed. Income Taxes	6,000	43,000	65,000	101,000
Net after taxes	$11,000	$45,000	$ 68,000	$122,000
Less: retirement of debentures	—	30,000	40,000	50,000
Excess of earnings over debt requirements	$11,000	$15,000	$ 28,000	$ 72,000

Thus, it is expected that Napoli Foods will be able to earn sufficient income to pay all interest payments, retire the debentures, fund the ICC notes, and add subsequent equipment, without any assistance from Burnsco's other ventures, notably Beacon Development Corporation.

Detailed projections are attached. A most noteworthy item is the fact that these figures show no need for additional outside financing as the scope of operations grows.

BURNSCO

Projected *Pro Forma* Consolidated Balance Sheet
(December 31, 1960–1963)

	1960	*1961*	*1962*	*1963*
Current Assets:				
Cash	$207,000	$ 142,000	$ 181,000	$ 181,000
Accounts receivable	101,000	250,000	300,000	350,000
Inventory	85,000	275,000	330,000	390,000
Prepaid expenses	4,000	10,000	10,000	10,000
Other assets	—	—	—	—
Total current assets	$397,000	$ 677,000	$ 821,000	$ 931,000
Current Liabilities:				
Accounts payable	121,000	190,000	230,000	275,000
Notes payable—current portion	8,000	—	—	—
Accrued liabilities	30,000	70,000	85,000	100,000
Federal and state income taxes	18,000	6,000	43,000	65,000
Total current liabilities	177,000	266,000	358,000	440,000
Net working capital	220,000	$ 411,000	$ 463,000	$ 491,000
Land, Buildings, and Equipment:				
Land	17,000	350,000	350,000	350,000
Buildings	55,000			
Equipment	306,000	379,000	379,000	429,000
Total cost—land, buildings, and equipment	378,000	729,000	729,000	779,000
Less: accumulated depreciation	271,000	40,000	80,000	125,000
Net land, buildings, and equip.	$107,000	$ 689,000	$ 649,000	$ 654,000
Other assets:				
1 yr.'s interest—Napoli shareholders (cash escrow acc't.)	—	60,000	60,000	60,000
Other	1,000	1,000	1,000	1,000
Total other assets	1,000	61,000	61,000	61,000
Total assets less current liabilities	328,000	1,161,000	1,173,000	1,206,000
Less: long-term liabilities debentures (ICC)	—	325,000	295,000	255,000
Due on purchase (Napoli shareholders)	—	750,000	750,000	750,000
Capital	328,000	75,000	75,000	75,000
Surplus	—	11,000	56,000	124,000
Total long-term liabilities and capital	$328,000	$1,161,000	$1,173,000	$1,206,000

[1]Re-evaluations (does not include any possible activity in Beacon Development Corp.).

NAPOLI FOODS COMPANY

Projected Profit and Loss

Year Ended December 31	1961	1962	1963
Sales (net of discounts)	$2,500,000	$3,300,000	$3,900,000
Cost of sales			
Materials	$1,375,000	$1,815,000	$2,145,000
Labor	298,000	399,000	475,000
Fringes	37,000	50,000	59,000
	$1,710,000	$2,264,000	$2,679,000
Gross profit	$ 790,000	$1,036,000	$1,221,000
Expense			
Manufacturing			
Rent	$ 25,000	$ 25,000	$ 25,000
Utilities	30,000	35,000	40,000
Insurance	15,000	25,000	30,000
Repairs and factory expense	25,000	30,000	35,000
Depreciation	40,000	40,000	45,000
	$ 135,000	$ 155,000	$ 175,000
Sales			
Salaries, commissions, and brokerage	$ 300,000	$ 397,000	$ 470,000
Delivery and freight-out	60,000	60,000	60,000
Advertising	75,000	99,000	117,000
Bad debts	3,000	3,000	4,000
Discount and miscellaneous	—	—	—
	$ 438,000	$ 559,000	$ 651,000
General			
Salaries	$ 75,000	$ 99,000	$ 117,000
Taxes	14,000	16,000	20,000
Professional / Other office	25,000	33,000	39,000
	$ 114,000	$ 148,000	$ 176,000
Interest @ 8% on outstanding debt	$ 86,000	$ 86,000	$ 83,600
Total expense	$ 773,000	$ 948,000	$1,085,600
Net before Federal and State Income Taxes	$ 17,000	$ 88,000	$ 135,400
Federal and State Income Taxes	6,000	43,000	65,400
Net income	$ 11,000	$ 45,000	$ 70,000

These figures are conservative on all items except the forecasts of dollar sales. They take account of no anticipated economies in purchasing, production, or distribution. As a contrast, optimistic figures could show earnings of several times the conservative figures.

BURNSCO

Pro Forma **Consolidated Source and Application of Funds Statement for the Years 1960, 1961, 1962, 1963**

	1960	*1961*	*1962*	*1963*
Source of funds:				
Net income after taxes	$27,000	$ 11,000	$45,000	$ 70,000
Add: depreciation	24,781	40,000	40,000	45,000
Total funds provided by operations	$51,781	$ 51,000	$85,000	$115,000
Long-term loans ICC ($325,000) Present Napoli ($750,000) shareholders	—	1,075,000	—	—
Capital investments (ICC and Burns)	—	75,000	—	—
Total funds provided	$51,781	$1,201,000	$85,000	$115,000
Application of funds:				
Purchase of Napoli Pasta Co.				
Land and building	—	$ 350,000	—	—
Equipment	—	179,000	—	—
Working capital	—	220,000	—	—
Other assets	—	1,000	—	—
Total cost		$ 750,000		
Increase in other assets	$ 1,000	—	—	—
Acquire additional equipment	—	200,000	—	50,000
Deposit to cover 1 year's interest	—	60,000	—	—
Retirement of ICC debentures	—	—	30,000	40,000
Reduction—contracts	8,064	—	—	—
Total applications	$ 9,064	$1,010,000	$30,000	$ 90,000
Resulting in a net increase in working capital of	$42,717	$ 191,000	$55,000	$ 25,000

E. Sherlock Mason
Certified Public Accountant

November 6, 1960

I have prepared the following statements of Burns Corp. and Napoli Foods Co., without audit or other verification, based on information furnished to me:

PROJECTED *PRO FORMA* BALANCE SHEETS
December 31, 1960–1963

PROJECTED PROFIT AND LOSS
December 31, 1961–1963

PRO FORMA SOURCE AND APPLICATION OF FUNDS
STATEMENT
For the years 1960–1963

Projected profit and loss were based on the following assumptions:

1. Gross annual volume was estimated by Mr. Burns.
2. Material costs were based on 55%, the approximate past historical average, excluding items purchased for resale.
3. Labor expense is based on 16% of sales, the historical average, minus 3.3% of sales for projected savings in flour handling expenses and $20,000 additional savings in payroll. Fringes are based on labor expenses.
4. Rent paid is estimated rental expense of a new plant. Manufacturing and other expenses were estimated based on volume in past experience.
5. Depreciation was estimated based on 15-year equipment life—straight line.
6. Salaries, commissions, and brokerage are based on 12% of sales.
7. Delivery and freight-out was assumed to remain constant (no increase because additional volume expected to come from different types of sales).
8. Advertising was estimated at 3% of sales.
9. General salaries were estimated at 3% of sales.
10. Professional and other office expense is based on 1% of sales.
11. Federal income taxes were based on current rates.
12. State income tax added as a current year expense and liability.
13. Inventories were projected at 60 day material cost.
14. Accounts receivable projected at 30 day sales.
15. Accounts payable projected at 30 day terms except for purchases at 60 days on flour.

PLAN FOR ACQUISITION OF NAPOLI PASTA COMPANY STOCK

Napoli Pasta Company, as of December 12, 1960, had 1,660 shares of common stock outstanding, owned by six shareholders, all employees of the company. There are no other classes of securities.

Burnsco proposes to purchase all of these shares for ten year notes, bearing 8% interest per annum, made by Burnsco's wholly owned subsidiary, Napoli Foods Company. Notes will be given as follows:

For 700 shares, note to Mr. Anthony Salvatierra	
(President, Napoli Pasta Company)	$316,267
For 276 shares, note to Mr. Louis Rossotti (Office	
Manager, Napoli Pasta Company)	124,695
For 304 shares, note to Mr. Rudolpho Lombardi	
(Mr. Salvatierra's father-in-law)	137,347
For 180 shares, note to Mr. George Gaudino	
(salesman, Napoli Pasta Company)	81,330
For 100 shares, note to Mr. Phillip Pellegrini	
(shipping clerk, Napoli Pasta Company)	45,180
For 100 shares, note to Mr. Jack Teresi	
(salesman, Napoli Pasta Company)	**45,180**
Total	**$750,000**

The notes to Messrs. Salvatierra and Rossotti shall not be prepayable; all other notes may be prepaid without penalty at any time after one year from date of issue. All notes are renewable, at the option of the maker, Napoli Foods Company, for an additional ten years following their present term.

The terms of these notes place certain restrictions on the operations of Burnsco, Napoli Foods Company, and Beacon Development Corporation which are detailed in Exhibit 1.[2] The most important of these are: (1) Burnsco's and Beacon's guarantees of Napoli Foods' notes and their promise to maintain a minimum net asset value greater than the value of the outstanding notes; (2) a year's interest ($60,000) would be placed in escrow in cash or marketable securities and maintained until the notes are retired; (3) trust deeds and chattel mortgages on Napoli Foods and Beacon's physical assets would be assigned to the noteholders; (4) in the event of default on interest or minimum asset level, the principal value of the notes and all interest payable to maturity become immediately payable.

The debentures held by ICC would be junior to these notes in the payment of interest and, in the event of dissolution, in the payment of principal. The ICC debentures, which would bear interest at 8% per annum on the outstanding balance, would be retired only out of earned surplus accumulated after January 1, 1961. This retirement would take place as follows:

On or before December 31, 1962	$ 30,000
On or before December 31, 1963	40,000
On or before December 31, 1964	50,000
On or before December 31, 1965	60,000
On or before December 31, 1966	70,000
On or before December 31, 1967	75,000
	$325,000

---

[2] Appendix A of case.

Following the purchase of the Napoli Pasta Company stock, that corporation will be dissolved and its assets and liabilities assigned to Napoli Foods Company at their estimated present market value, as follows:

Cash	$160,000	Current liabilities	$164,000
Other current assets	225,000		
Land and buildings	350,000		
Machinery, equipment, and autos (net)	179,000		
	$914,000		

Napoli Foods Company will then sell its land and buildings to Beacon Development Corporation in exchange for 350,000 shares of the stock of Beacon. Burnsco, in turn, will give its note (noninterest bearing) for $350,000 to Napoli in exchange for the Beacon stock.

Thus, following all those transactions, the capital structure of the three corporations would be as follows:

Burnsco			
Cash	$380,000	Notes payable (to	
Napoli Foods		Napoli Foods)	$350,000
capital stock	10,000	7 year, 8% debentures	
Beacon Dev.		(to ICC)	325,000
capital stock	360,000	Capital stock	75,000
	$750,000		$750,000
Napoli Foods Company			
Cash	$170,000	Current liabilities	$164,000
Other current assets	225,000	10 year, 8% renewable	
Note receivable		notes	750,000
(from Burnsco)	350,000	Capital stock	10,000
Fixed assets (net)	179,000		
	$924,000		$924,000
Beacon Development Corp.			
Cash	$ 10,000	Capital stock	$360,000
Land and buildings	350,000		
	$360,000		
Consolidated Statement			
Cash	$ 560,000	Current liabilities	$ 164,000
Other current assets	225,000	10 year, 8% renewable notes	750,000
Fixed assets (net)	529,000	7 year, 8% debentures	325,000
		Capital stock	75,000
	$1,314,000		$1,314,000

If this proposal is acted on affirmatively, Burnsco, with 75,000 shares of common stock outstanding, will be owned ⅔ by ICC and ⅓ by Stanley Burns.

Neither party shall offer his shares for sale without first offering them at the same price to the other except:

1. in the event of a public offering;
2. in the event of sale of the entire company to another party; or
3. in the event the options specified below are exercised.

ICC shall grant to Stanley Burns the following options on their Burnsco stock:

1. Beginning two years after the date of organization of Burnsco and running for five years thereafter, Stanley Burns shall have the right, at his option, to purchase up to 10,000 Burnsco shares from ICC at $2 per share.
2. Beginning four years after the date of organization, and running for five years thereafter, Stanley Burns shall have the right, at his option, to purchase up to 10,000 additional Burnsco shares from ICC at $3 per share.

If all of these options were exercised, ICC would have recovered its total investment in Burnsco, and would still own 30,000 shares, or 40%, of Burnsco. Ownership would then be Stanley Burns 60%, ICC 40%.

It is contemplated that Burnsco would have a board of directors of three members: two nominees of ICC and Stanley Burns.

Napoli Foods Company would have a board of seven members, including one nominee of ICC, Stanley Burns, A. Salvatierra, and four men of substantial experience in the food industry.

Beacon Development Corporation would have a board of three members, including one nominee of ICC, Stanley Burns, and an experienced real estate developer.

BEACON DEVELOPMENT CORPORATION

Substantial work has been done by the real estate development firm of Smith, Smith, and Jones in planning the possible development of Beacon's property. While it is likely that a different plan may be followed, employing greater utilization of the site than Smith, Smith, and Jones have contemplated, employing, for example, air space leased over a contiguous building, their projections serve as at least a rough guide to the income potential of the property.

These figures forecast a total cost of approximately $1,110,000 for construction of luxury apartment buildings on the site, which, together with their valuation of the land at approximately $400,000, would give property valued at over $1.5 million. A loan for over $900,000 for 20 years can be negotiated @ 6¼%. Smith and Jones' estimates show a "net cash annual income" of over $70,000 a year *after* loan payments, interest payments, expenses, and a vacancy factor, but before depreciation and taxes. Thus, with an investment of approximately $200,000 in cash (available from Burnsco), Beacon Development in 20 years could have completely paid off the mortgage, own the land and buildings free and clear, and *still* show $71,000 a year pretax cash flow to apply against Burnsco's obligations. These figures are attached as Exhibit A (see page 186).

If these figures are at all accurate, in ten years' time Beacon could have an equity in the property (excluding depreciation) of over $800,000 (more than the amount due to Napoli Foods noteholders, if the notes were not extended), or an equity of over $1.5 million at the end of 20 years, when the extended notes fall due. In addition, Beacon's estimated cash flow more than covers the $60,000 annual interest payments on the Napoli notes.

Thus, according to these figures, Beacon, by itself, could cover all of Burnsco's obligations to the original Napoli Pasta shareholders without assistance from Napoli Foods Company.

This double-pronged earning potential for both Napoli Foods and Beacon Realty presents the possibility of extraordinary capital appreciation for Burnsco, particularly with its highly leveraged position.

The very least that Beacon might do is to sell the property outright and realize a minimum of $350,000 in cash. This cash could then be used to: (1) retire notes; or (2) expand the activities of Napoli Foods and Burnsco.

[A casewriter's exhibit on apartment rentals and operating costs for the Boston area appears on page 193.]

exhibit A

Proposal for Development of Napoli Real Estate

Smith, Smith, and Jones
Architects–Planners–Developers
9 Milk Street
Boston, Massachusetts

Mr. Stanley Burns
John Hancock Building
Boston, Massachusetts

Dear Mr. Burns:

We are enclosing herewith copies of analyses of the projects proposed for construction on the Beacon Hill property of Napoli Pasta Company.

The site plan shows three steel frame buildings, which front on Virginia Street. The contiguous unimproved street will be used only as a pedestrian entrance and for light and air, and will be appropriately landscaped. The apartments vary in size from 700 square feet for one bedroom, one bath apartments, to 1,050 square feet for two bedrooms and two baths. Parking conforms to city planning requirements of one parking space for each apartment. The entire project is based upon strict conformance with present regulations, including the present 40 foot height limit on structures in this area. Possible advantageous variations may result from further consultation with city agencies.

The analyses are based upon information which has been acquired over many months of study and we believe them to be realistic. We hope they are self-explanatory. Should you require additional data, please do not hesitate to call on us.

Very truly yours,

s/*Sam S. Smith,* AIA

for

Smith, Smith, and Jones

Attachments:

    A. Sketch of Proposed Project [Not shown.]
    B. Summary Project Analysis
    C. Analysis of Building #1
    D. Analysis of Building #2
    E. Analysis of Building #3
    F. Analysis of Proposed New Factory
        Building for Napoli Foods Company

Summary Project Analysis

	Building No. 1	Building No. 2	Building No. 3	Total
Building evaluation	$572,040	$480,480	$462,000	$1,514,520
Cash down payment required	68,588	60,137	71,451	200,176
Net cash return/yr. (before depreciation and taxes)	27,097	22,760	21,885	71,742

Loan payment progress schedule

Total loan $908,712 at 6.25%—20 years

Age of Loan	Cumulative Amount Paid Against Loan Principal
1 year	$ 23,626
5 years	134,489
10 years	317,140
15 years	567,036
20 years	908,712

Rental units
    21 one bedroom, one bath ap'ts. at $180/mo.*
    35 two bedroom, one bath ap'ts. at $250/mo.*
    20 two bedroom, two bath ap'ts. at $275/mo.*

*Rental price includes garage (1 car/ap't.), pool, heat, electricity, water, and janitor service.

Napoli Properties—Virginia Street: Project Analysis

Building No. 1:	26,429 sq. ft. at $11.50	$303,933	
	10,640 sq. ft. at 5.00	53,200	
	Elevator	7,500	
	Pool	3,000	
			$367,633
	Architectural fees	25,734	
	Demolition	2,000	
	Construction loan fees and interest	15,445	
	Landscaping	1,000	
			44,179
	Total construction cost		$411,812

Rental schedule:	15 two bedroom, one bath apartments at $250	$ 3,750
	17 one bedroom, one bath apartments at $180	3,060
	Total monthly rentals	$ 6,810
	Gross annual income: %6,810/mo. ✕ 12	81,720
	Annual expenses (@ 30% of gross income)	24,516
	Net annual income	$57,204

Loan schedule: $57,204 ✕ 10 = $572,040 valuation of property
(10 ✕ net income)
60% ✕ $572,040 = $343,224 loan value (60% of total value)

Total construction cost	$411,812
Loan	343,224
Cash required	$ 68,588
Net annual income	57,204
Annual loan payment (principal + interest)	
$343,224 at 6.25% 20 yrs.	30,107
Net cash return	$ 27,097

Napoli Properties—Virginia Street: Project Analysis

Building No. 2:	21,576 sq. ft. at $11.50	$248,124	
	10,416 sq. ft. at 5.00	52,080	
	Elevator	7,500	
	Pool	3,000	
			$310,704
	Architectural fees	21,749	
	Demolition	2,000	
	Construction loan fees and interest	12,972	
	Landscaping	1,000	
			37,721
	Total construction cost		$348,425

Rental schedule:	20 two bedroom, one bath apartments at $250	$ 5,000
	4 one bedroom, one bath apartments at $180	720
	Total monthly rentals	$ 5,720
	Gross annual income: $5,720/mo.✕12	68,640
	Annual expenses @ 30%	20,592
	Net annual income	$48,048

Loan schedule: 48,048 ✕ 10 = $480,480 valuation of property
60% ✕ 480,480 = $288,288 loan

Total construction cost	$348,425
Loan	288,288
Cash required	$ 60,137
Net annual income	48,048
Annual loan payment $288,288 at 6.25% ✕ yrs.	25,288
Net cash return	$ 22,760

Napoli Properties—Virginia Street: Project Analysis

Building No. 3:

21,000 sq. ft. at $11.50	$241,500	
7,650 sq. ft. at $5.00	38,250	
Elevator	7,500	
Pool	3,000	
Street work	3,000	
Soils work	20,000	
		$313,250
Architectural fees	21,927	
Construction loan fees and interest	12,474	
Landscaping	1,000	
		35,401
Total construction cost		$348,651

Rental Schedule:

20 two bedroom, two bath apartments at $275	$ 5,500
Total monthly rentals	5,500
Gross annual income: $5,500/mo. ✕ 12	66,000
Annual expenses @ 30%	19,800
Net annual income	$46,200

Loan Schedule:

46,200 ✕ 10 = $462,000 valuation of property
60% ✕ $462,000 = $277,200 loan

Total construction cost	$348,651
Loan	277,200
Cash required	$ 71,451
Net annual income	46,200
Annual loan payment	
$277,200 at 6.25% ✕ 20 yrs.	24,315
Net cash return	$ 21,885

Analysis of Proposed New Factory Building

Smith, Smith, and Jones
Architects–Planners–Developers
9 Milk Street
Boston, Massachusetts

Mr. Stanley Burns
John Hancock Building
Boston, Massachusetts

Dear Mr. Burns:

We attach herewith a project analysis for a proposed factory building for Napoli Foods Company to replace the present Beacon Hill plant. At the present time, our information on the building itself is sketchy, so we have based our analysis on information supplied to us and as yet not verified.

The land cost shown approximates the cost of similar acreage available in industrial areas in this vicinity. We are at present investigating the possibility of acquiring a site of approximately 2.23 acres in South Boston, adjacent to a railroad spur track.

As noted on the analysis, a small portion of the site could be acquired on a time-payment basis, but should be subject to subordination in conjunction with the major portion.

It is our understanding that the equipment noted can be purchased under a chattel mortgage at the loan percentage shown.

Cost of the building proper is based on a standard type warehouse-factory building with minimum utilities and finishes. Further study of the plant operation and of each department is necessary to establish the detailed requirements of the firm.

Yours very truly,

Sam S. Smith, AIA

for

Smith, Smith, and Jones

Proposed New Factory Building Project Analysis

Factory Building
1.	Land	$125,000
2.	Construction	
	50,000 sq. ft. @ $6.00	300,000
3.	Architectural Fee	21,000
4.	Moving costs	25,000
5.	New press	30,000
6.	Flour handling equipment	90,000
7.	Additional equipment	20,000
	Total construction cost	$611,000

Total construction cost	$611,000
Loan (at 60% of construction cost)	366,600
Cash required	$244,400

The land could be purchased on $90,000 down, with the remainder on time-payment basis, with subordination of entire parcel.

Cash required	$244,400
Less: land Subordination	35,000
Net cash down payment required	$209,400

Annual amortization payment
(366,600 @ 6.25% X 10 yrs.) $48,800

Age of Loan	Amount of Principal Paid Against Loan
1 year	$ 27,128
2 years	56,456
5 years	150,071
8 years	274,216
10 years	366,600

BOSTON, MASSACHUSETTS AREA

Average Income and Operating Costs for Reporting Buildings

	Elevator Buildings	Walkup Buildings (25 units or more)	Garden type Buildings
Number of buildings reporting	7	15	2
Number of rentable rooms	1,005	1,505	948
Number of apartments	307	551	226
Income			
Actual rental collections unfurnished apartments	$365.16/rm./yr.	$310.49/rm./yr.	$414.91/rm./yr.
Average vacancy factor	0.85%	1.38%	0.65%
Average number of new tenants in year per 100 occupants	8.1%	15.7%	7.3%
Average age of buildings	14 yrs.	23 yrs.	8 yrs.
Average Expenses (per room per annum)			
Janitor and cleaning supplies	$ 29.06	$ 33.44	$ 38.46
Electricity, gas, and water	16.10	8.10	12.90
Fuel (inc. ash removal)	20.62	25.39	27.21
Management and administrative	27.14	20.15	33.73
Subtotal operating expenses	$ 92.92	$ 87.08	$112.30
Exterior Maintenance, Repair, and painting	9.47	15.39	2.24
Tenant space decorating	10.38	8.69	3.81
Tenant space maintenance and repair	8.20	10.30	1.43
Public space decorating, maintenance, and repair	4.59	6.89	8.44
Elevator and other mechanical maintenance and repair	4.00	2.50	4.96
Grounds upkeep	1.52	.74	1.59
Subtotal maintenance and repair	$ 38.16	$ 44.51	$ 22.47
Insurance	11.11	7.68	4.38
Taxes, fees, and permits	97.64	72.09	103.48
Average Grand Total, all expenses	$239.83	$211.36	$242.63
Average net operating income, per room per annum (after taxes, but before depreciation)	125.33	99.13	172.28

Note: On this basis, Beacon's proposed one bedroom, one bath apt. would be rated as three rooms; Beacon's proposed two bedroom, one bath apt. would be rated as four rooms; Beacon's proposed two bedroom, two bath apt. would be rated as four and one-half rooms.

Source: Data derived from the *Apartment Building Experience Exchange,* published annually by the *Institute of Real Estate Management* of the National Association of Real Estate Boards; 1960 edition.

chapter 4

The Concept of
Corporate Strategy

After referring continuously to *corporate strategy* in the first three chapters of this book, it is perhaps overdue for us to address this concept rigorously and begin to define our terms. However, our experience has been that students can comprehend and utilize the strategy concept more easily *after* the general management point of view and functions have been presented. All of these ideas are so intimately related that it is impossible to talk about one without referring to the others.

Corporate strategy refers to the relationship between an enterprise and its environment. Strategy has two aspects. *Strategic posture* (or position) refers to an *actual* relationship between enterprise and environment at a specific point in time. The *strategic plan* refers to an intended future relationship; the plan consists of a set of corporate objectives and the proposed conditional action steps to be taken in order to reach those objectives.

All enterprises have identifiable and describable *past* and *present* strategic postures. Only a few have detailed, explicit strategic plans for the *future*. Throughout this book, the single word *strategy* is frequently used in describing both *actual* strategic posture and *intended* strategic plan. The context should make clear to the reader whether reference is being made to past posture, present position, or future plan.

ACTUAL STRATEGIC POSTURES
AND INTENDED STRATEGIC PLANS

In Chapter 2, we proposed that, at any point in time, the total enterprise could be viewed as consisting of: (1) a network of *members,* operating (2) an aggregation of *resources,* within (3) a competitive *environment.* The particular configuration actually existing among these three elements at a point in time is what we mean by an enterprise's strategic posture.

The environment makes certain demands and produces certain constraints which define, within broad limits, what the enterprise *must* do in order to be successful (i.e., to meet customer needs effectively), and *must not* do in order to survive (i.e., to meet the social and political expectations and the legal requirements of the culture in which it operates). The resources presently or potentially available to the enterprise put further limits on what the enterprise realistically *can* do. Then, within these tighter constraints, the particular pattern of value commitments, competences, and personal influence among the key members determines what the enterprise *will* do (i.e., the final choice among alternatives).

A company's actual past or present strategic posture can be *identified* and *described* at the chosen point in time in terms of where the emphasis was placed and what priorities were honored in the allocation of resources and in responding to events in the environment. The particular strategic position taken can be *explained* in terms of the members' values and commitments.

A strategic plan, to be effective as an intended guide to future action, must specify which values of the membership are being emphasized and pursued, and how the resources of the enterprise are to be employed in meeting the requirements and opportunities of the environment. As previously indicated, the intended plan and the actual posture produced are rarely identical. A strategic plan must be viewed as highly conditional and subject to continuous modification and revision as events unfold and conditions change, both in the external environment and in the internal condition of the enterprise. Without a viable explicit plan, it is difficult for the enterprise to maintain its self-directing initiative.

As one noted practicioner of strategic planning has observed:

> There is nothing new about long-range planning, corporate strategy, or corporate development. Only the emphasis is new. By one means or another, all companies in the past have adjusted themselves to changes in competition, markets, and technology. All companies to some degree have always had plans for improving their situation.
>
> A few companies have had impressive success which rapidly brought them fame and profits. Others have had equally spectacular difficulties. For most companies, however, life has consisted of working very hard to produce small differ-

ences in performance. Yet in even the most static industries the perspective of history reveals that different strategies eventually produce quite different consequences.

Corporate success, for any company, must be the result of superior use of that company's distinguishing characteristics. Yet few companies attempt to examine the strategy which brought them success in the past. Moreover, success reinforces the organization's belief in the essential correctness of past methods, philosophy, and competitive posture. So long as the underlying competitive conditions and relationships continue to hold, the corporate success may continue also. But in time, these conditions must change.

This is why strategies become obsolete and inappropriate in a changing world. It is a matter of common observation that more companies seem to fall prey to creeping decline than to identifiable or specific management mistakes in decision.

. . . In the absence of an explicit strategy, the adaptation to changing conditions is almost certain to be deferred until past successful strategies are clearly failing. Intuitive and implied strategy adjustments are apt to be too late, too slow, and even inappropriate to cope with rapid change with a complex organization.

. . . Experience repeatedly demonstrates that conditions change and competitors take the initiative. Not only does new technology provide new means, but the whole market is constantly changing in character. Therefore, an extension of past strategy is essentially a negative course. No matter how well chosen it may be, the fact remains that sooner or later, it will become inappropriate.

Still, successful strategy revision in a going organization is a difficult task. The very lack of explicitness about past and current strategy and its reasons for success can be an obstacle to accepting the need for change. High morale carries with it the implicit assumption that personal competence rather than strategic leverage is the underlying cause for superior performance. In the absence of an explicit analysis and acceptance of the strategies of the past, it is almost a foregone conclusion that any effort to change them will be regarded as a personalized attack upon those who administered them.[1]

THE COMPONENT ELEMENTS OF CORPORATE STRATEGY

For purposes of identifying, describing, evaluating, and planning those configurations among an enterprise's environment, resources, and membership which define strategic posture and strategic plan, we need a few simplified concepts which relate together the fundamental categories of observable data. We propose three basic component elements: *scope, specifications,* and *deployments.*

---

[1] Bruce D. Henderson, "Preventing Strategy Obsolescence," in *Perspectives in Planning* (Boston: Boston Consulting Group, 1966).

Scope may be thought of as the basic definition of the business of the enterprise, while deployments reflect the emphasis and priorities established in resource allocation. As such, they define the interface between environment and resources. Scope indicates the *direction* of corporate activity, while deployments represent the *force*.

Specifications represent the performance characteristics of the enterprise. The actual specifications achieved provide a basis for evaluating the enterprise. Desired specifications are what we mean by corporate *objectives*. As such, specifications define the interface between members' goals and enterprise resources.

These relationships can be diagrammed simply.

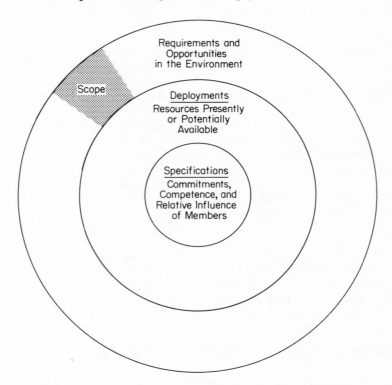

Here we see a scope (depicted by shaded area) which is that part of the total environment that the enterprise serves. To survive and prosper, every business must provide wanted products (or services), delivered at a price the customer is willing to pay, at the time and place that they are wanted. Scope defines the products, customers, location, and competitive emphasis for the enterprise. Resources are deployed in accordance with the specifications of the members and the demands of the environment.

Let us look at each of these concepts in more detail.

Scope

Scope is defined here in terms of:

1. The *markets* and *customers* served and the relative volume of business being done by the company with each identifiable category of user.
2. The various types, models, and characteristics of *products* (or services) being offered and the relative proportion or *mix* of sales among the various offerings.
3. The *basis* on which the company has chosen to compete (e.g., personal relationships, distribution strength and skill, manufacturing efficiency, product design and engineering ingenuity, raw material ownership, customer service, brand franchise, price-quality-value relationships, capital availability).

In each instance we are trying to identify principal concentrations and clusters, rather than to produce an all-inclusive listing. Thus, the scope of Mitchell Nursery Co. in 1961 may be thought of as supplying June buds (70% of total volume), primarily to orchardists (80%) in the Sacramento Valley (90%), basing their competitive posture on product availability.

The scope of La Plant-Choate, in the pre-1945 period, consisted of supplying Caterpillar with tractor-operated bulldozers and scrapers, competing on the basis of design ingenuity and manufacturing efficiency. In the post-1945 period, the scope shifted to supplying contractors with complete tractor-drawn scraper rigs and bulldozers. Competition was based on product design and performance characteristics.

Morgan Corp.'s tube department had a scope of supplying defense contractors with magnetron and klystron tubes (90%). Although strong in research and development, Morgan's primary bases for competing were price and availability.

For all but the largest of enterprises, a rather narrow definition of the company's scope is appropriate. Such a definition affords the company an opportunity to establish a *distinctive competence* which can give it a unique *competitive advantage* in serving its market. But few enterprises would choose such a narrow definition as the production of only a single product for a single customer.

As one prominent writer has indicated:

> Most companies are engaged in a variety of businesses. Either they have a diversified product line, or sell to widely different customer groups (such as domestic and export), or use a number of very different distribution channels (such as to both original equipment and replacement markets). Consequently, before discussing strategy in the context of a company, it is important to look at the range of businesses that the company is engaged in and to consider the strategic issues inherent in each.
>
> . . . Within each of his businesses, the manager has to decide which particular groups of customers are going to represent the focus of his strategy. He can-

not really expect to have an equal chance in going after *all* kinds of customers. He has to select that customer group toward which he is going to offer some specific appeal, and then design a combination of tactics which will give him a competitive edge. The selection of that customer group, and the design of that combination of tactics, are important strategic choices. They will influence his company's performance at least as much as anything else his subordinates can do.

A critical issue in defining a business is to do so at the most meaningful level of generalization. Unfortunately, there is a prevalent notion that if one merely defines one's business in increasingly general terms—such as transportation rather than railroading—the road to successful competitive strategy will be clear. Actually, this is hardly ever the case. More often, the opposite is true. For example, in the case of the railroads, passengers and freight represent very different problems, and short-haul versus longer haul are completely different strategic issues. Indeed, as the unit train demonstrates, just coal handling is a meaningful strategic issue.[2]

On the other hand, very large companies, for whom vastness of resources comprises the principal competitive advantage, may usefully define their scopes somewhat broadly—in terms of multiple product lines and multiple markets—either as integrated, operating entities or as conglomerates of separate operations, each with its own individual definition of scope.

Identification of scope provides the first level of generalization about the company's business. In future planning, scope, whether consciously defined or implicitly inferred, becomes the first order of discrimination as to which tasks and commitments the company will undertake and which it will not. Thus, definition of the enterprise's scope provides a gross, first-level relationship among environmental opportunities, company resources, and member disposition.

Specifications

In addition to its product-market characteristics, every enterprise can be described in terms of certain other measurable parameters which specify important performance characteristics. These measurements are similar to the specifications of an automobile or the measurements of the body. By themselves, they enable one to *describe* the enterprise at that point in time. Comparisons along these dimensions provide a basis for *evaluating* the enterprise's past performance. When desired values (objectives) are established for each parameter, they become a basis for *planning* the future activities of the enterprise.

We alluded to these specifications in Chapter 3, when we presented them as strategic criteria for *evaluating* company performance. Now we note that they

---

[2] Seymour Tilles, "Making Strategy Explicit" (Boston: Boston Consulting Group, 1966).

can also be utilized for *description*. It should be apparent that every enterprise can be characterized in terms of:

1. Its present size and past rate of growth.
2. Its share of present market (or markets) and its historical rate of change in market penetration.
3. Its present degree of profitability (or other measure of effectiveness) and its past history.
4. The range of its future life expectancy.

Size can be specified in terms of sales volume, assets, net worth, and number of employees. Thus, we can say that, in 1946, the La Plant-Choate Mfg. Co., Inc. had sales of about $8 million, assets of about $4.5 million, net worth of $2.9 million, and about 1,000 employees. This gives us a pretty good idea of the *scale* of the company's activities at that time. We can add to this a history of continuous growth in sales over the previous ten years, at a compounded rate of about 26 per cent per year from 1936 to 1945, then a sharp reduction of 43 per cent in 1946. Similarly, assets showed continuous increases from 1936 to 1944, at a rate of over 30 per cent per year, but then sharp declines in 1945 and 1946. Net worth, on the other hand, showed continuous increases through 1946, at a 16 per cent compounded rate. The number of employees remained fairly constant over the 1943–1946 three year period. This history of change gives us some idea of the vigor and activity of the enterprise.

Market share is specified in terms of percentage of total sales of like products or services, within a given user category (e.g., industry, geographical unit, type of end use). Thus Mitchell Nursery had 50 to 60 per cent of the June bud market in the Sacramento Valley. Historically, we see little change over the past several years. La Plant-Choate, on the other hand, began with a major share of all U.S. dozer and scraper blade sales. La Tourneau eroded that position substantially in the prewar period. In 1946, when La Plant-Choate decided to supply a complete earth-moving unit, its market share of such items was under 5 per cent a poor fourth to Caterpillar, Le Tourneau, and Allis-Chalmers. These figures give us some idea of the importance of the enterprise in its industry or to its markets, relative to its competitors.

Profitability is the most widely used measurement of over-all corporate effectiveness, but the abstraction and highly generalized end result of this measurement cautions us to view it in only a *qualitative,* gross way. Profitability can be measured in absolute numbers of monetary units, as a percentage return on net worth, in terms of earnings per share of the company's stock, or in terms of net cash flow retained in the business. Thus we can say that, in 1946, La Plant-Choate earned $209,000 including a tax credit, down 50 per cent from the previous year's after-tax performance, or we can note that pretax operating profits were $134,000, down 90 per cent. The $209,000 results in a 7.3 per cent return on investment (as compared with a historical range of around 15 per cent). This translates into $.96 per share, down substantially from past years. Yet additional cash retained in the business ($168,000) was not greatly different from amounts added in previous years. These figures give us some feeling for the present strength of the enterprise.

In departments, companies, or economies where profits are not relevant because of controlled prices or arbitrarily assigned costs, measures of units of output per unit of input (efficiency) are often substituted for profitability (effectiveness) measures. Note that these internal efficiency measures, by themselves, do *not* indicate how well the company is meeting the needs of its external customer-market environment.

Life expectancy is a wholly qualitative measure of the "staying power" or "survival capacity" of the enterprise. It has to do with the net worth available (the greater the available capital, the greater the survival capacity), the dependence of the enterprise on specific persons and their skills, of Mitchell Nursery Co. of La Plant-Choate Mfg Co. and the dispersion of ownership. Thus, we can conclude that, in 1961, Mitchell Nursery's life expectancy was tied wholly to how long Mr. Oakes continued in the business. La Plant-Choate's survival capacity, previous to 1947, was tied to the success and survival of Caterpillar. On the other hand, Morgan Corp's life expectancy was very high in 1962. With very broad ownership, great size, and net worth of over a billion dollars, its survival appeared assured. Even if it failed in the microwave oven business, the magnitude of its resources would minimize the impact of that failure on the company as a whole. Surely, it would be able to find new opportunities and to redirect its efforts without great strain.

In describing the enterprise, the four dimensions of size, market share, profitability, and life expectancy specify its strength, vigor, and survival capacity. When stated as objectives, these specifications provide a second order of discrimination as to which tasks and commitments the company can and will undertake.

Deployments

The third component element of corporate strategy is the deployment of the company's resources. By this we mean the relative allocation of funds, facilities, equipment, manpower, and management attention among the company's various activities. The priorities, emphasis, and relative weights actually assigned tell us about the real orientation of a company's strategy, which may be quite different from how its executives perceive it. For example, in the Pioneer Brass Co. case, the president, Mr. Bransten, talks about his company as if sales and support of distribution were its most important activities; but, in fact, the bulk of the company's assets had been poured into plant and equipment and the major emphasis in recent years had been upon *manufacturing* standard products.

La Plant-Choate's deployments in the pre-1945 period were wholly towards engineering and manufacturing activities. Subsequently, resources had to be split not only among a major engineering effort and the revamping of manufacturing facilities, but also towards creating a completely new distribution system. This meant *less* emphasis to engineering and manufacturing than heretofore, more to marketing.

Thus the actual deployment of resources adds the necessary third component of the relationship among environmental opportunities, resource availability, and member characteristics. In describing the company, the deployments indicate its true emphasis. In planning, deployments become the final delineation of future commitments.

IDENTIFYING, EVALUATING, AND PLANNING CORPORATE STRATEGY

We will use these three basic component elements—scope, specifications, and deployments—as the major tools for identifying, evaluating, and planning corporate strategy.

Describing the enterprise's present *scope* and *deployments* enables us to *identify* the actual present strategy.

Comparing the enterprise's performance characteristics (*specifications*) with those of competitors, with the values assigned to each parameter by the owners or managers (objectives), and with the characteristics of other industries or activities to which the company's resources and competences could be applied, provides a basis for *evaluating* past performance and future prospects.

Future *planning* for the enterprise necessarily involves defining what the company's *scope* will be; *specifying* what the desired size, market share, risk-reward tradeoff (profit expectation), and life expectancy characteristics will be; and then designating what the necessary procurements and *deployments* of resources shall be in order to reach those objectives.

Later chapters will provide specific conceptual material on identifying a strategic posture, evaluating strategic performance, and planning future strategy.

STRATEGIC VARIABLES AND OPERATING VARIABLES

In Chapter 3 we distinguished between strategic variables (which determined the company's external effectiveness) and operating variables (which affected the enterprise's internal efficiency). It should be clear that what we have called strategic variables refer to the choices and activities which establish scope, define performance specifications, and deploy resources.

An enterprise's scope is determined by its product policy, customer policy, distribution policy, competitive emphasis, and long-term pricing policy. Resource procurement and deployments are embodied in financing policy and investment policy. Specifications can be employed in three distinctly different ways; as:

1. Descriptive parameters.
2. Evaluative criteria.
3. Targets for future performance.

When employed as evaluative criteria or planning targets, they reflect the personal values of key executives in the organization, and hence stem from the company's personnel placement policy.

Those matters which concern cost, delivery, scheduling, service, quality, quantity, employee productivity, satisfaction, turnover, cooperation, training, innovation, organization structure, methods, procedures, standards, and so on, we have called operating variables. These factors certainly will affect corporate performance and may seriously thwart a strategic plan, but they are not sufficient in themselves. Without a clear-cut strategic plan, a highly efficient organization may be critically ineffective. Consider, for example, a well-trained and highly disciplined bomber squadron which flies well and delivers its bombs accurately, but which continually bombs the wrong targets.

Conversely, a company which is well-situated strategically—whose product-market position is strong and whose competitive advantage is clearly exploited—can survive gross internal inefficiencies and still remain effective. Consider the Ford Motor Co. in the 1930's when it underwent violent labor uprisings, including armed battles between workers and company police, yet still remained strong and profitable. Or we may recall the wartime aircraft industry in Southern California, which suffered employee turnover rates and absenteeism which were unprecedented in organizational history, yet still managed to get the job done. Sheer magnitude of available resources often compensates for inefficiency in operations. But there is no compensation for inappropriate strategy!

It has been said that efficiency in operations can affect company performance drastically on the *down*side (i.e., heavy losses), but that its impact on the *upside* (profits) may be "only" on the order of 100 per cent. An ineffective strategy may similarly produce heavy losses (despite efficient operations), but an effective strategy may have an upside potential which represents a gain of 1000 per cent or more. Control Data and Xerox are two excellent examples in recent years of the vast upside impact of an effective strategy.

Thus, the emphasis of this book is upon the strategic variables, rather than the operating ones. These are the variables which have long-term impact upon the company's ability to survive threats and to capitalize upon opportunities.

THE IMPORTANCE OF THE CONCEPT OF CORPORATE STRATEGY

The concept of strategy has great utility for describing and evaluating a company's past and present situation, but its greatest application, after the present situation is clearly understood, is in planning the *future* activities of the enterprise. Only through explicit attention and conscious planning can a company increase its control over its own destiny. Such planning allows the enterprise to determine and alter events, to actively initiate upon its environment, rather than allow itself to be shaped by external factors over which it exercises no control.

Planning reduces the possibility of completely unanticipated events occurring. It permits the preparation of alternative courses of action. The greater the uncertainty in a situation, the more imperative is the need to anticipate possibilities, to assign probabilities to their occurrence, and to have alternative responses available. The more explicit the attention the company has given to where it wants to go and what it wants to be (defining strategy), the clearer will be the choices and their consequences, as the company responds to—and initiates upon —the environment in which it operates.

Strategy definition provides visible goals to which members can commit themselves. The process of determining strategy creates an opportunity for persons with differing personal objectives and conflicting points of view to hammer out their differences and to establish goals which they all wish to pursue. Without a clear definition of strategy, long lead-time commitments (e.g., building a new plant, developing a new product) are difficult to coordinate with shorter-term commitments. Resources are procured and allocated on an ad hoc basis. Strategic posture gets established without anyone having exercised conscious choice. In Chapter 3 we indicated how strategy may accumulate from many apparently finite or low-level functions and activities.

This is not to imply that strategic plans should be immutable. On the contrary, effective planning continually adds new data as events unfold and oblige new choices and revisions. Preserving alternatives is a key aspect of planning. Commitment of a company's full resources to any particular outcome involves a degree of risk that only a professional gambler should take. Survival of the enterprise must always be protected by the prudent, responsible administrator. Strategic plans should be reviewed periodically—every season, every year, and so on to determine how relevant and desirable they continue to be. They should also be reviewed whenever a major change occurs in the environment (competitive action, shifts in customer characteristics or demands, supply changes, government actions), in corporate resources (through new products, major changes in price of stock, catastrophes), or in the roster of key members of the organization (retirements, death, new hires, changes in ownership). Important changes in any of these three basic elements will demand a change in over-all corporate strategy. Such strategic change can be planned by giving it explicit attention; otherwise, it will occur with its consequences and outcomes unchosen and unanticipated.

part II

INDUSTRY ANALYSIS: ESTABLISHING A COMPETITIVE ADVANTAGE

chapter 5

Identifying and Describing
the Total Situation:
Past Strategies and
Present Deployments

In the previous four chapters we have introduced the concept of corporate strategy and its component elements of scope, specifications, and deployments. We have described the enterprise in terms of its environment, resource availability, and membership patterns. We have suggested that the environment determines, within broad limits, what the company's strategy *must be;* the availability of resources more narrowly limits the choices of what the company's strategy *can be;* and the particular balance of power and value commitments among the key members determines which of the alternative strategies available *will be* pursued.

In this and the two subsequent chapters we will present three specific frameworks, utilizing these concepts and categories, for (1) identifying and describing a company's past strategies and present strategic posture; (2) evaluating these strategies; and (3) developing a strategic plan for the future. These three steps are separable but related phases in a continuous cycle of assessment, planning, action, reassessment, and replanning.

The descriptive framework can be thought of as analogous to a balance sheet; it tells the company's situation at a particular point in time. The evaluative framework is similar in function to a profit and loss statement; it gives a measurement of performance over a particular time period. The planning framework is like a funds flow statement; it indicates where and *when* assets will be deployed and where they will come from. Each framework employs the same basic concepts and categories, but uses them in different ways and for different purposes. Just as no single accounting statement can tell the whole story, no one of these frameworks can do the whole job in strategic analysis and planning.

THE CYCLE OF STRATEGIC ANALYSIS, PLANNING, AND ACTION

We think it is desirable for the strategist to view his job as involving a continuous cycle of identification, evaluation, planning, and deployment. At least 12 consecutive steps are involved in each complete cycle.

Identification and Description of Present Strategy (Steps 1 to 4)

1. We begin with an identification of the actual current scope of the company's activities. The delineation of customer/product/market emphasis and concentrations gives us an indication of what kind of a company it is currently.
2. This analysis should be followed by identification of the pattern of actual past and existing resource deployments. This description allows us to determine which functions and activities have received the greatest management emphasis and where the greatest sources of strength currently lie.
3. Given the identification of scope and deployment patterns, we should be able to deduce the actual basis on which the company has been competing. Such competitive advantages or distinctive competences represent the central core of present performance and future opportunities.
4. Next, on the basis of observation of key management personnel, we should be able to determine the actual performance criteria (specifications), emphasis, and priorities which have governed strategic choices in the past.

These four elements *describe* and *explain* the company's current strategic posture. (Note that they *do not* evaluate that posture!)

Evaluation of Past Performance (Steps 5 to 8)

5. The *actual* choice criteria employed should now be compared with management's *stated* targets and goals. How well these match is an indication of management's self-awareness and understanding.
6. Next, past performance records (in terms of (a) size and rate of growth; (b) market share(s); (c) return on investment and risk/reward tradeoff; (d) survival capacity; and (e) any other parameters actually employed by management) should be compared against both previous company performance and also the current targets set by management.

7. The same performance records should then be compared with the records of competitors.
8. Finally, past performance records should be compared with what could reasonably have been expected from liquidating the company and redeploying the funds in other kinds of businesses or investments.

These comparisons, taken together, provide practical yardsticks for evaluating the effectiveness of present strategy.

Planning Future Strategy (Steps 9 to 12)

Description of present strategic posture and evaluation of past performance should now be matched with future expectations.

9. A rigorous examination should be made of the environment to determine important trends and competitors' activities, and to identify the major opportunities which fit the company's resources and the potential threats to the company's current market position and competitive advantage. Especially important are indications of changes in the life-cycle stages of major company products; the imminence of change in customer needs or desires; the likelihood of the emergence of substitute products or services.

From the analysis of opportunities and threats, we should be able to:

10. Define what our future product/market scope should be and, exploiting our present strengths plus those realistically obtainable, what the basis of our future competitive advantages will be.

Given our forecast of the future environment and the resources of our company, we must then:

11. Determine appropriate future performance specifications and choice criteria (objectives).
12. We can now develop a conditional plan for the procurement and allocation of resources, over time, to achieve these objectives within the limits of our human competences and commitments and our material availability of resources.

We now proceed to deploy our resources, according to plan. A *new* identification–evaluation–planning cycle is initiated by each major deployment. Similarly, plans should be reviewed at the end of each major reporting period, as well as whenever a major change takes place in the environment, in the company's resource availability, or in the roster of key executives.

The remainder of this chapter will deal with the identification phase. Chapters 6 and 7 will discuss the evaluative and planning phases of the strategy cycle.

IDENTIFYING A COMPANY'S SCOPE

We start with scope, which establishes the *limits* within which all other data can be confined. The vast quantities of data potentially available demand such restrictions and economies, if we are to avoid inundation and hopeless confusion.

Scope can be determined from a careful analysis of *sales* for the desired period. Preferably, we should have breakdowns of:

1. Sales by customer category.
2. Sales by product category.
3. Sales by channel of distribution.
4. Sales by price/quality category.

Sales by customer category should be grouped according to type, size, location, and other characteristics to determine the relevant *concentrations*. For example, it is crucial in understanding Mitchell Nursery's situation to know that 80 per cent of the company's sales came from small orchardists within a 50 mile radius. Similarly, it can be determined that 90 per cent of Morgan Corporation's tube sales went to very large defense-based customers. La Plant-Choate's greatest challenge was to adjust from serving a single, very large customer (Caterpillar), which specified precisely what its requirements would be, to serving a great number of small contractors, widely scattered geographically, for whom only standard units could be produced. And the shift from a single customer classification (municipalities) to a more diverse buying public (contractors, private companies, etc.) forced Pioneer Brass into a new strategic posture, the consequences of which were only dimly comprehended by the management.

Sales by product category are most typically classified by similarity in manufacturing process or similarity in raw materials or ingredients. While such classification is useful in scheduling the production function, categorization by *usage* is more meaningful in portraying the business accurately. For example, it is more significant for analysis and future planning to know that most June buds sold by Mitchell Nursery were bought as *replacements* for dead trees in existing orchards than to have a year-by-year listing of sales of the various varieties of fruit trees. Similarly, it is more important for Pioneer Brass to differentiate between water works fittings for single family residences and fittings for commercial, industrial or multi-family dwellings than to study sales records of the number of brass fittings versus cast iron or bronze.

Sales by channel of distribution is especially important where many channels are potentially available and their characteristics and requirements are very different, as, for example, in the case of Pioneer Brass. It would be impossible to deal realistically with the company's situation without taking account of the various types of jobbers, agents, and salesmen being utilized. Similarly, in La Plant-Choate and Morgan Corporation, the new channels required by the changes in strategy were the most crucial elements in each company's future success.

Sales by price/quality category is another way of identifying the market segments being served. This breakdown may reveal important characteristics about the company's customers and markets which would be hidden in a classification of sales by other categories.

These four sales analyses enable one to identify the concentrations and clusters of customer/product/market segments which the company is, in fact, serving. Frequently, this characterization is at odds with what some members of management *believe* their markets to be or with their aspirations of what they would *like* them to be. Accurately documenting this scope is essential to understanding the company's situation, evaluating its performance, and planning for its future health and survival.

Up to this point in this book, it has been our deliberate attempt to limit the cases studied to companies with limited product/market scope. Such companies are easier to describe and to plan for than more widely diversified ones. Yet, even with a diversified company, such as Rexall, it is important to analyze the sales pattern for the total company, without regard for divisional boundaries, in addition to giving detailed attention to the concentration patterns within each division.

IDENTIFYING THE PATTERN OF A COMPANY'S DEPLOYMENTS

Once the customer/product/market mix has been identified from sales records, we turn to analysis of *financial records*. Here we are most interested in:

1. The division of the company's total assets among the various units and activities, including the extent of investment in control or ownership of raw materials, intermediate suppliers or processors, distributors, or end users.
2. The division of each year's *discretionary* funds among the various units and activities.
3. The cash flows produced by each of the various units.
4. The division of time, attention, interest, and support by influential members of management.

Division of assets. Analysis of these accounts will indicate how resources have been allocated in the past. Units responsible for the largest asset investments necessarily are the most important units in describing the company's *present* strategic posture. Even though management may want to emphasize new aspects of the business in the future, the continued heavy investment in older units cannot be discounted in assessing the *current* situation.

Division of discretionary funds. While a company may be obliged to sustain its historical investment in existing plants and equipment, marketing organizations, inventories, receivables, and so on, each year there is a substantial amount of new cash available whose distribution among units is discretionary. Such funds —for acquisition, new capital investment, research and development activities, advertising and sales promotion—are rarely assigned equally to each unit. The *relative* division of discretionary funds among units indicates where management is *currently* placing its emphasis.

Cash flows. Cash flow figures for each unit provide us with an indication of the current relative contribution of each unit to the total enterprise. (We use cash flow, rather than earnings, to accommodate differences in age and depreciation of assets and to identify the true sources of funds for company operations.) A company cannot be described in a useful or meaningful way without identifying the *sources* of the cash which keep it alive and provide the basis for its future progress. Cash retained within the unit producing it must be considered as an *allocation,* even though no formal allocation procedure may take place.

Management attention. The relative assignment of outstanding personnel to one unit or another is just as important a deployment decision as the division of funds. In many businesses, outstanding personnel represent a far more crucial scarce resource than the limited availability of capital. Similarly, top management, by giving more time and attention, support, or criticism to one unit than to others, can make a disproportionate "investment" in that unit which gives it greater importance than it would otherwise have had. If top management time actually expended were costed accurately to such a unit, its true allocated share of discretionary funds would be *increased* dramatically, and its indicated cash flow would be *reduced* sharply.

These four analyses, taken together, indicate the company's pattern of resource development and allocation. They show what aspects have received the greatest emphasis historically and currently, and they allow us to see the current sources of the company's strength and vitality.

IDENTIFYING A COMPANY'S COMPETITIVE ADVANTAGE

In a free enterprise society, no business can survive unless it maintains some kind of an advantage over its competitors. That advantage may be only a convenient location relative to certain customer groups (e.g., the neighborhood grocery or drugstore). It may be only a preferential personal relationship with certain friends or relatives (e.g., some types of brokers or salesmen). It may be only the temporary availability of products in short supply (e.g., a marginal producer). But without some advantage, some distinctive competence, no company can induce a customer to do business with it rather than with its competition. In controlled economies, businesses frequently have the advantage of being the *only* available suppliers. Thus, customers are obliged to patronize the company or do without the particular service or product. Such businesses survive and prosper as

long as they are protected (by tariffs, laws, customs and traditions, cartel agreements) from more efficient or responsive competitors, but they are extremely
vulnerable whenever the old, artificial protection breaks down. The lack of a
genuine, market-based competitive advantage is what currently concerns many
European firms, who foresee future inroads by companies from other countries
as the E.E.C. and G.A.T.T. become more workable.

A viable competitive advantage is most frequently related to the excellence of
outstanding personnel. As such, it is expressed in terms of one or more of the
following factors:

1. Excellence in product design and/or performance (engineering ingenuity).
2. Low-cost, high-efficiency operating skill in manufacturing and/or in distribution.
3. Leadership in product innovation.
4. Efficiency in customer service.
5. Personal relationships with customers.
6. Efficiency in transportation and logistics.
7. Effectiveness in sales promotion.
8. Merchandising efficiency—high turnover of inventories and/or of capital.
9. Skillful trading in volatile price movement commodities.
10. Ability to influence legislation.

A competitive advantage may also stem from the company's resource base:

11. Highly efficient, low-cost facilities.
12. Ownership or control of low-cost or scarce raw materials.
13. Control of intermediate distribution or processing units.
14. Massive availability of capital.
15. Widespread customer acceptance of company brand name (reputation).
16. Product availability, convenience.

This listing is obviously not all-inclusive, but it is indicative of the kind of edge
which a company may be able to gain over its competitors.

Once we have identified the company's product/market/customer scope and
the deployment of its resources, we should be able to *infer* the company's competitive advantage by comparing its scope and deployments with those of its
competitors. For example, we can identify Mitchell Nursery's advantage as
readily available, good quality products. La Plant-Choate's competitive advantage
of engineering ingenuity and low-cost manufacturing was sufficient when Caterpillar took all of its output, but was not enough in a free, open market against
equally skillful producers with much greater marketing skills and resources. Morgan Corporation's competitive advantage was its strong R&D staff, while Pioneer
Brass had its advantages in favorable location and in personal relationships with
important customers.

Excellence in any of these functions may be sufficient to give a company some advantage, but not all of these attributes are equally important. Clearly, they vary by industry, and even within industries, over extended time periods, the basis for success is likely to shift so that an old attribute may no longer be relevant.

IDENTIFYING ACTUAL STRATEGIC CHOICE CRITERIA

The company's scope, deployments, and competitive advantage *describe* its strategic posture at any point in time. The question remains, "How did it get that way?" Invariably, the explanation lies in the particular value orientations of the influential owners and/or managers of the business. Their personal values will determine what strategic choices are made: which resources will be divested, which acquired, and how they will be deployed; what kind of a market/product scope will be sought; and what the company's basic competitive emphasis will be.

As Cyert and March point out, "Organizations do not have objectives; only people do." [1] Motivations differ among key managers. Some seek personal reputation (or company reputation which will reflect positively upon them). Some seek personal influence or power (or merely to perpetuate themselves in their present power positions). Some seek affluence and monetary gain, while others seek the esteem of their employees and coworkers. Still others seek altruistic aims above and beyond their own personal gain. Depending upon the pattern of these *personal* objectives among the dominant owners or managers, specific values are placed on the *time horizon* of the business and on the general attitudes toward *risk* and *change*.

Persons most interested in attaining reputation, power, and affluence tend to take a relatively *short-term* view of the business; i.e., they think in terms of profits and achievements within, say, a one to three year span. They are also inclined to be high risk takers and are willing to undertake substantial change. Those who have already attained positions of power and affluence and who seek only to preserve them tend to be highly conservative and to avoid change (perpetuate the status quo). Persons motivated by adulation, esteem, and altruism may take a longer-term view of the business, but tend to be quite cautious as regards major change or risk.

Alert younger managers are quick to catch the appropriate signals from their superiors. They soon learn that compensation and promotion of individuals within units come swiftest for men whose time horizons and attitudes toward risk are compatible with their seniors. They see that disposition of discretionary funds and awarding of amenities and ratings between units and divisions most often reflect the activities, interests, and values of the most powerful senior executives.

---

[1] R. M. Cyert and J. G. March, *A Behavioral Theory of the Firm* (Englewood Cliffs, N.J.: Prentice-Hall, Inc., 1963).

In this way, top management motivations influence subordinate behavior far down the line.

Within these limits, most company managements seek corporate survival, prosperity, and enhancement of the company's situation. Only immoral, unscrupulous managers would deliberately make strategic choices which debilitate the company's present situation for personal gain. By the same token, few would be so oriented to immediate profits (short-run) that they would deliberately compromise the company's future survival. Instead, there are continuous trade-offs made between short-run and long-run profit opportunities.

Much management literature prescribes what a company's objectives *should* be: "maximizing profits"; "profit-constrained maximization of growth"; "maximizing survival capacity"; "balancing the claims of the various interested groups —owners, employees, customers, general public"; "growth"; "stability"; "flexibility." Unhappily, none of these statements offers much help to a manager in choosing among vaguely defined alternatives in unique, only partially-understood, highly-uncertain, specific situations. As much as he might *wish* to fall back on a mathematical computation or a clean-cut formula, inevitably his own experience, judgment, desires, and value structure will come into play.

When confronted with difficult choices, many managers emphasize a particular *functional* point of view. As indicated earlier, men with long experience in the *manufacturing* function tend to emphasize increasing internal operating efficiency, certainty, and stability as criteria for their resource allocation choices. Men with a *sales* point of view might make allocation choices aimed at increasing sales volume, market share, and reputation with customers. The *engineering* or product-development viewpoint tends to emphasize improved product design or performance as the determination of how resources are allocated. The *financial* point of view tries to maximize cash flows, return on investment, and the market value of the company's stock. An *accounting* viewpoint tends to place highest value on liquidity, credit availability, and certainty of profits. A *trader* would view each choice as a completely separable transaction, with a goal of maximum profits in minimum time. A *personnel* viewpoint tends to emphasize employee satisfaction (and the avoidance of conflict) above other variables, while a *public relations* point of view is most concerned with public image, company reputation, and favorable relations with government and other external institutions.

Few managers would support a single functional criterion to the point of ignoring all others. But, in most companies, the emphasis is all too clear. We have no difficulty in seeing La Plant-Choate as emphasizing engineering values in their crucial strategic decisions. It is to Mr. Choate's credit that, in his changed circumstances, he could maintain a long time horizon and willingness to take enormous risks. On the other hand, Guy Bransten in Pioneer Brass was clearly "playing it safe." His time perspective was short; he tried to avoid risk. When faced by crisis (i.e., the strike of his employees), he fell back on manufacturing values in making his choices.

The five major U.S. airlines provide perhaps the clearest example of basic differences in strategic choice criteria. In the period before 1960, all five companies were dominated by strong individuals with long time horizons. They ranged from the conservatism of ex-banker Patterson (United) to the great willingness to take risks of the expansionists Smith (American) and Trippe (Pan American). United's cautious financial policies and strong *accounting* orientation gave them an image of stability and reliability, but American's *sales* emphasis produced greater revenues and earnings. Eastern's single-minded emphasis on *operating* (production) efficiency produced very great short-term profits but ultimately alienated its previously captive customers. TWA in its early stages was governed almost wholly by *engineering* values, as Howard Hughes and Jack Fry sought the latest innovations in aircraft equipment and design. In contrast, Pan American's orientation, from the very start, was *public relations,* as America's "chosen instrument" and ambassador abroad.

Over time, as the companies have grown in size and new management generations have taken the helms, these clear-cut single emphases have become much less distinct. But the same patterns of emphasis can be seen in many other industries, especially those which still are growing rapidly and have not achieved maturity.

The five airlines examples cited companies which were heavily dominated by single individuals. In companies where this kind of dominance is not the case, it is necessary to observe and identify the pattern of relationships among key executives in order to determine the relative balance of power and, therefore, the *relative* emphases given to choice criteria. Such observation and analysis will usually yield a clear explanation of "how the company's present strategic posture got that way." It should allow the observer to predict, with a high degree of accuracy, what the company's response is likely to be to any one of a series of major changes in environmental conditions or resource availability. The emphasis, criteria, and priorities actually honored become clear; the acceptable degree of perceived risk becomes institutionalized; and the degree of innovation or repetition of past policies becomes highly predictable. Increasing size of the firm and maturity of the industry both tend to dampen the degree of risk-taking, but explicit management attention to emphasis and priorities makes flexibility possibile even among giants. IBM, Xerox, DuPont, and ITT are all obvious examples of this flexibility.

SUMMARY

In this chapter we have tried to indicate what data must be gathered, what sources exist for these data, and how they can be put together to *identify, describe,* and *explain* a company's current strategic posture. Exhibit 1 provides a summary check list of the items covered.

The *sales analysis* items identify how the company has *actually* defined its *scope.* The *financial analysis* and *observation* of management time items will

exhibit 1

FRAMEWORK FOR IDENTIFYING A COMPANY'S ACTUAL STRATEGIC POSTURE

1. *Determine SCOPE* (Analysis of Sales Data)
   - (a) Sales by Customer Category
   - (b) Sales by Product Category
   - (c) Sales by Channel of Distribution
   - (d) Sales by Price/Quality Category

   What are the predominant *product/market concentrations?*

2. *Determine Actual Pattern of RESOURCE DEPLOYMENT* (Analysis of Financial and Accounting Data)
   - (a) Division of Assets among Units and Activities
   - (b) Division of Current Discretionary Funds
   - (c) Cash Flows Produced by Each Unit or Activity

   Which units or activities have received the predominant *emphasis?*

3. *Determine Basis of Competitive Advantage(s)* (Deduced from Comparison of Scope and Resources with Those of Competitors)
   - (a) Market Position
   - (b) Supply Position
   - (c) Physical Resources
   - (d) Financial Resources
   - (e) Personnel Competences
   - (f) Personal Relationships

   What is the company's primary *distinctive competence or competitive advantage?*

4. *Determine Actual Strategic Choice Criteria* (Analysis of Behavior and Commitments of Key Executives)
   - (a) Time Horizons
   - (b) Attitude toward Risk
   - (c) Functional Emphasis in Choice Criteria
     - (i)   production (operations) orientation
     - (ii)   sales orientation
     - (iii) product development (engineering) orientation
     - (iv)   financial orientation
     - (v)   trading (purchasing) orientation
     - (vi)   personnel orientation
     - (vii) public relations orientation
     - (viii) accounting orientation

   What is the basis on which resource allocation choices are made?

identify how the company has *actually* allocated its resources and therefore what the true balance of influence is among divisions and/or functions. This allocation indicates how the company's distinctive competence is actually being defined.

The observational data, personnel records, and division of discretionary capital records will identify the *actual* performance criteria being followed (i.e., the actual distribution of rewards and punishments). From these criteria, the *actual objectives* and choice criteria can be deduced.

These definitions of *actual* scope, deployments, distinctive competence, and choice criteria describe a company's present strategic posture. Such description is the starting point for realistic appraisal of the company's present situation and future prospects. It tells us what the company's posture really is—not what its spokesmen hope for it, or, in all good will, believe it to be. Subsequent chapters will discuss the evaluative and planning phases of the strategy cycle.

Competitive Strategies of
Five Major U. S. Airlines

PART I: INDUSTRY ANALYSIS

Introduction

The purpose of this case is to provide data which allow the student to identify the differing strategies followed by each of five major companies in a single industry. Commercial air transportation is a relatively straightforward industry for this purpose, since many of the strategic variables are circumscribed by government regulation. Nonetheless, because of differing histories, differing resource availabilities, and unique emphases by their key executives, United Air Lines, American Airlines, Eastern Airlines, Trans World Airlines, and Pan American Airways have followed surprising divergent competitive courses in relating to the opportunities and problems of a commonly-shared environment.

This case begins with a description of the major regulatory constraints imposed on the industry by the U.S. Government. Next follows a description of the structure of the industry and the functional requirements of an individual operating airline. Thirdly, the physical, technical, financial, marketing, labor relations, and operating expense characteristics of the industry are presented. Fourthly, the principal aspects of intercompany competition are discussed. Finally, each company's activities and characteristics are described. Exhibits 1 through 7b provide historical statistics for the industry including comparative figures for the five major companies.

Government Regulation

Since its inception, the development of U.S. commercial air transportation has been closely tied to governmental super-

---

vision. In 1911, just eight years after the world's first powered flight at Kitty Hawk, North Carolina, the U.S. Post Office Department flew a four pound sack of mail a distance of 20 miles in a French Bleriot monoplane. That flight launched commercial aviation in the U.S.

The following year, 31 mail flights were completed between various eastern cities. In 1918, the Post Office Department began to operate and maintain 17 aircraft, and the next year the American Railway Express (later renamed REA Express) sponsored the first air express shipment.

In 1925, legislation authorized the award of air mail contracts to private organizations, and a number of companies were formed to bid on the service. During the late 1920's and early 30's, the major transcontinental airlines were formed (typically by merger), and their early route patterns were established. These routes were still the major traffic arteries in 1966.

Over the years, commercial air transport grew and several pieces of legislation were enacted to encourage sound development. The two laws which have had the greatest effect upon U.S. commercial air carriers have been the Civil Aeronautics Act and the Federal Aviation Act. The former, enacted in 1938, created the Civil Aeronautics Board (CAB), which remained the primary economic regulatory agency for the air transportation in the U.S. In 1958 the Federal Aviation Act continued the authority of the CAB, and, in addition, created the Federal Aviation Agency (FAA) to administer air safety regulations and air navigational aids. The members of the CAB (four plus a chairman) and the administrator of the FAA were all appointed by the President, with the concurrence of the Congress.

Routes. Certificates of public convenience and necessity, granted by the CAB, were required for all U.S. interstate air carrier operations. This included air freight, air express, and air freight forwarding companies, in addition to passenger carriers. Routes could not be granted or abandoned without the approval of the CAB. The CAB could exempt individual air carriers or groups (such as the nonscheduled operators) from economic regulation. (The Interstate Commerce Commission had no similar power over surface transportation.)

Rates. Air carriers were required by the CAB to charge "just and reasonable rates" and "undue preference and prejudice" were prohibited. The Board had the power to prescribe the lawful rate or a maximum and/or minimum rate for interstate commerce, but had no direct control over rates for foreign or intrastate air service. All rates and fares had to be filed with the Board; they were then published and open to public inspection. Thirty days' notice was required for interstate rate changes, and, after public hearings, such changes could be denied by the Board. As another alternative, the CAB could suspend proposed changes for as much as 180 days.

Service. All carriers were required to provide safe and adequate service, equipment, and facilities, in order to get CAB certification. When a certificate

exhibit 1

VOLUME INDICATORS

Total U.S. Scheduled Air Transportation Industry (1930–1966)

Year	Number of Commercial Fixed-Wing Aircraft in Service	Total Operating Revenues[1] ($ millions)	Passenger Revenues ($ millions)	Passenger Miles (millions)	U.S. Mail Ton-Miles (millions)	Freight Ton-Miles (millions)
1930	497	22	7	104	N.A.	N.A.
1935	363	29	18	361	2	3
1937	291	40	27	550	6	3
1939	347	76	41	729	9	3
1941	370	134	83	1,385	13	19
1943	254	152	105	1,634	36	32
1945	432	280	203	3,336	65	25
1946	799	460	363	5,903	33	54
1948	1,012	692	497	7,872	55	148
1950	1,161	877	608	10,241	69	271
1952	1,323	1,169	914	15,619	93	330
1954	1,443	1,441	1,167	20,653	119	353
1956	1,705	1,898	1,542	27,612	152	504
1958	1,769	2,244	1,828	31,482	177	550
1960	1,842	2,884	2,388	38,863	241	703
1961	1,854	3,064	2,485	39,831	299	794
1962	1,811	3,439	2,763	43,760	340	968
1963	1,821	3,759	3,067	50,362	357	1,097
1964	1,843	4,251	3,483	58,494	371	1,380
1965	1,896	4,958	4,029	68,677	483	1,820
1966	2,022	5,735	4,529	79,889	751	2,150

[1] Including mail pay subsidy.

Sources: FAA, *Statistical Handbook of Aviation* (Washington, D.C., 1966). Annual Report of the CAB, 1966 (Washington, D.C., 1966). Air Transport Association, "Air Transport Fact and Figures," various years. Roadcap, Ray, *Airline Record,* 1948 (Chicago, 1948).

authorized the transportation of mail, the air carrier had to provide adequate facilities for this purpose and had to transport mail whenever required—even if it meant putting off passengers. The CAB decided what interstate routes required air service, what the minimum schedule requirements would be, and what carriers would be allowed to fly the routes.

Safety. Safety regulations, applying to all nonmilitary aircraft, were promulgated and enforced by the Federal Aviation Agency. The FAA also inspected and licensed all civilian aircraft, licensed pilots and aviation mechanics, etc. Air accidents were investigated by the CAB. Aircraft suspected of being unsafe could be grounded by the FAA or the CAB. The FAA also determined the closing of airports, under temporary weather conditions, and the suspension of flight schedules.

Subsidies. All carriers received indirect government subsidy through the FAA's construction and operation of costly air navigation and safety control facilities. The annual total cost of such services for 1966 was estimated by the FAA at $256 million. (The Johnson Administration had hopes of obtaining legislation in 1966 which would assess commercial aviation and its customers for much of this expense. By a proposed combination of taxes on aircraft fuel, air freight, and passenger tickets, the Administration hoped to raise about 90% of FAA's costs. Commercial carriers were strongly opposed to such action, and claimed that military and private aviation were beneficiaries of at least 40% of FAA's services.)

A second form of government subsidy was available through air mail contracts. In the early years of U.S. commercial air transportation, payments for carrying the mail guaranteed the financial success of the carrier. The original laws were still in force in 1966; they were interpreted to mean that mail pay provided to a certificated carrier should be sufficient to enable it to earn a profit, if operated under "honest, economical and efficient management." In actual practice, the principal domestic airlines did not receive a direct subsidy; they were paid on a predetermined realistic rate per ton-mile for air mail actually carried.

Smaller airlines, which required financial support, could, and did, apply for subsidy mail pay rates. These rates, also calculated against ton-miles of mail actually carried, were set individually by the CAB for each applicant. A carrier could apply for subsidy mail pay—or for revision of an existing subsidy rate—whenever it believed that other revenues, plus existing mail compensation, were inadequate to support its operations. In 1966, about 4% of total U.S. airline revenues came from mail payments. Of this amount, the domestic trucklines accounted for only $88 million (2.4% of their total—almost all on a service pay basis). Mail pay subsidies were, however, very important to local service carriers, and most territorial and intrastate operators. Local service carriers were the recipients of $62 million out of total fiscal 1966 subsidy of $74 million. Most of the balance went to Hawaiian and Alaskan intrastate carriers.

COMPETITION AND FINANCE

Consolidation, mergers, and acquisitions of control among air carriers required the consent of the CAB. Interlocking relationships between any air carrier and any other carrier, or with other branches of the aviation industry, were prohibited unless approved by the Board. The Board investigated alleged "unfair or deceptive practices or unfair methods of competition in air transportation," and could order carriers or ticket agents to cease and desist from such practices. This power also extended to foreign air carriers serving points in the United States. (The ICC had no similar power.)

The CAB had the power to prescribe the system of accounts and to require regular reports from the air carriers. It did not, however, have any control over the carriers' issuance of securities (this power was reserved to the Securities and Exchange Commission), except for certain aircraft equipment loans which could be guaranteed by the CAB. Such guarantees were limited by law to $5 million per company, not to exceed 90% of the purchase price of new aircraft, and were available only to local service airlines.

Industry Structure

In 1966, the U.S. air transport industry had domestic and international revenues of about $5.7 billion. Roughly $4.5 billion was from domestic service. The industry consisted of a number of different types of carriers, performing a variety of services.

Domestic trunkline carriers. This group consisted of the 11 so-called "major" domestic airlines, whose revenue accounted for about 64% of the total revenue of the U.S. air transport industry. Generally, they operated on the high-density traffic routes between the principal cities. Some of them also had international routes. In order of size, by 1966 sales revenue, they were: (1) United, (2) American, (3) Trans World, (4) Eastern, (5) Delta, (6) Northwest, (7) Braniff, (8) National, (9) Western, (10) Continental, and (11) Northeast.

Domestic local service carriers. There were 13 smaller airlines in this group. Together, their revenues totaled about 6% of the industry's domestic total. They generally operated between smaller cities, or between small cities and larger ones, where the traffic density did not justify the type of aircraft used on important, long distance routes. In order of size by 1966 revenue, they were: (1) Mohawk, (2) Allegheny, (3) North Central, (4) Piedmont, (5) Ozark, (6) Frontier, (7) Trans-Texas, (8) Southern, (9) Bonanza, (10) Pacific, (11) West Coast, (12) Lake Central, and (13) Central.

All-cargo carriers. Three air carriers made up this group. They operated scheduled flights carrying freight, express, and mail. Passengers were also flown on a charter basis. Their total revenues were about 3% of the domestic air transport industry total. These carriers, in order of 1966 total revenues, were: (1) Flying Tiger, (2) Seaboard World, and (3) Airlift International.

International and territorial carriers. This group included all U.S. Flag airlines operating between the United States and foreign countries other than Canada, and over international waters. Revenues of this group were about ¼ of those for the total U.S. air transport industry. Most of the airlines in this category also belonged to at least one other group. For this reason, the revenue data for International and Territorial Carriers represented a substantial amount of double

exhibit 2

FINANCIAL INDICATORS

Total U.S. Scheduled Air Transportation Industry (1948–1966)

Year	Total Operating Revenues ($000)	Federal Subsidy Received ($000)	Subsidy as a Per cent of Total Operating Revenue (%)	Passenger Revenues ($000)	Domestic Trunkline Passenger Load Factors (%)	Net Income After Interest and Taxes ($000)	Rate of Return on Stockholders' Investment (%)
1948	691,879	62,493	9.0	497,121	59.7	1,032	
1949	769,152	75,732	9.8	549,937	61.3	17,344	
1950	877,372	83,512	9.5	607,937	67.9	39,769	
1951	1,024,045	66,648	6.5	779,820	65.6	54,361	
1952	1,169,268	63,448	5.4	913,771	63.4	60,412	10.9
1953	1,317,398	67,736	5.1	1,043,223	62.5	59,361	9.9
1954	1,440,977	58,418	4.1	1,166,551	63.3	69,781	10.0
1955	1,643,412	39,790	2.4	1,363,579	63.4	77,699	10.0
1956	1,897,867	43,217	2.3	1,541,596	60.8	30,203	8.9
1957	2,128,386	48,626	2.3	1,731,497	59.4	44,202	5.2
1958	2,243,964	52,539	2.3	1,827,811	61.4	52,914	5.5
1959	2,618,471	50,016	2.0	2,167,109	59.5	72,681	6.2
1960	2,884,277	65,735	2.3	2,387,937	56.2	9,140	3.2
1961	3,063,555	72,735	2.4	2,484,650	53.3	(37,881)	2.1
1962	3,438,731	80,877	2.4	2,762,697	53.8	52,319	5.7
1963	3,759,051	82,821	2.3	3,067,193	55.4	78,480	6.5
1964	4,250,838	83,092	2.1	3,482,760	55.2	223,172	10.4
1965	4,957,859	79,473	1.7	4,029,383	58.5	367,783	12.0
1966	5,734,837	68,065	1.2	4,528,549	N.A.	427,572	11.1

Sources: FAA, *Statistical Handbook of Aviation* (Washington, D.C., 1966). (Annual Report of the CAB, 1966 (Washington, D.C., 1966). Air Transport Association, "Air Transport Facts and Figures," various years. (Roadcap, Ray, Airline Record, 1948 (Chicago, 1948).

counting, when compared with totals for other groups. Principal companies in this group included Pan American, TWA, Northwest, and Braniff. Additionally, most of the trunkline carriers had at least one route that qualified in this category, e.g., Hawaii, Puerto Rico, Mexico City, etc.

Supplemental air carriers. Thirteen carriers held certificates (three temporary and ten permanent) issued by the Civil Aeronautics Board authorizing them to perform passenger and cargo charter services, as well as scheduled operations on a limited or temporary basis. They were intended to supplement the scheduled service offered by the certificated route carriers. Their operations varied considerably and statistics were not readily available, but their revenues were estimated at about 3% of the industry total. These carriers had benefited from the

Vietnam buildup, with military revenues reaching 65% of the total supplemental carrier revenues in 1966.

Other groups. Additional classes of air carriers were Intrastate Carriers (such as Pacific Southwest, Hawaiian Airlines, Alaska Airlines, Aloha Airlines, and many smaller lines) and Helicopter carriers operating between airports and surrounding urban areas. These classes accounted for about 1% of the domestic total.

Air carrier associations. The major trade associations of the carriers were the Air Transport Association of America, which represented the U.S. domestic truckline carriers, and the International Air Transport Association, with headquarters in Montreal, which represented most of the world's airlines that operated in international service. These groups were concerned with public policy issues and general industry welfare matters.

Air cargo. As indicated, the overwhelming majority of air carrier revenues, in 1966, was derived from passenger traffic. However, all of the more than 10,000 scheduled flights per day carried some kind of cargo. Despite rapid growth, air carriers moved less than 1% of the 1966 total intercity ton-miles of freight transported in the U.S. It was not expected that air freight would ever account for an important proportion of total intercity freight movement. Rather, it was believed that its importance would be measured in terms of unique benefits arising from its speed.

Patterns of air cargo movement. There were several characteristics of air cargo movements which affected the present operations of air frieght carriers. The major features were:

1. Westbound and southbound movements, consisting mostly of manufactured goods, considerably exceeded eastbound and northbound movements, which were mostly flowers and perishables. This made balanced scheduling difficult.
2. Most cargo had to move at night. It was usually produced or harvested during the day, then moved to the airpost late in the day; and, normally, shipment was expected at the destination by the next morning.
3. Door-to-door service was demanded by customers. Thus, provision had to be made for rapid and efficient ground transportation.
4. Scheduled service had a margin for flexibility. Definite routing, precise arrival times, and the number of intermediate stops was not crucial, so long as total elapsed time was within reasonable limits.
5. High density passenger traffic routes were often completely different from high density freight routes. Hence, freight shipped by passenger planes often required back-up with all-cargo planes.

Air cargo sales. Air cargo space was sold directly by the airline's sales forces, by freight forwarders, and by connecting carriers. Space was sold both on a "reserved" and on a "space available" basis.

Most air freight usage was based upon short delivery times, which could reduce inventory requirements; extend the range of perishable commodities; meet emergencies; etc.

Use of air cargo often implied a major shift in transportation procedures for both the shipper and for the receiver. The use of air transportation on a continuous basis needed to be justified on the basis of lower total cost of distribution, and often required considerable investigation and experimentation.

Freight forwarders. The freight forwarder assembled individual shipments and obtained contracts for carrier space to transport them. His earnings came from charging his customers normal freight rates for the commodities and quantities which they shipped and then consolidating these into one large shipment in order to receive a quantity discount rate from the airline.

The CAB gave approval to the freight forwarder function following World War II. The carriers were opposed to freight forwarders from the start, on the grounds that: (1) use of forwarders would delay the movement of shipments by waiting for consolidation; (2) rate reductions on large quantity shipments would be more difficult because the forwarders' income depended on the spread between small and large shipment rates; (3) freight forwarders represented an unhealthy potential concentration of buying power. Despite this opposition, certain individual freight forwarders, like Emery and Airborne, grew very rapidly. Less-than-planeload traffic continued to account for nearly all air freight business. Although individual airlines would have preferred to handle this business without the use of middlemen, the relatively small volumes and widely divergent destinations involved in individual customers' shipments required the timely availability of more equipment than any single airline could justify.

Air freight forwarding had grown very rapidly. There were 78 companies in 1961, 120 in 1965, and 137 in 1966. While revenues of these companies grew from $66 million in 1961 to $164 million in 1965, the largest 10 companies retained control of 82% of air freight forwarding revenues.

Air-truck service. Northwest Orient Airlines was an industry leader in developing door-to-door joint service with motor carriers serving the area covered by the airline's routes. It provided many of the advantages of air freight service to communities located at a distance from major airports. The shipper paid only one rate, received only one set of papers, and had only one carrier (usually the originating trucker) to deal with the entire operation. However, this service was not widely imitated. Instead, the major airlines formed a joint trucking agency, Air Cargo, Inc. (ACI), which divided its revenues and expenses proportionately among its owners. It acted as an agent for the airlines, and contracted with local truck operators for pickup and delivery, storage facilities, and the issuance of shipment documents.

Air cargo costs. The average charges per ton-mile by Class I Railroads, Class I Truck Companies, and Domestic Scheduled Airlines in 1966 were: 1.26¢,

6.50¢, and 20.21¢. The ton-mile costs of shipping by air, however, were decreasing much faster than costs for other types of transportation. (For example, direct operating costs, which represented about one-half of the total costs of moving freight by air, were 80% less in a pure jet than they were in a DC-3. Ground costs were decreasing at about the same rate.)

In 1965, after 20 years of concerted development efforts, over-all cargo operations were still unprofitable for the airlines. Combination carriers made money on freight operations when the freight was carried in the bellies of passenger planes (since incremental costs were very slight), but they lost money operating all-cargo planes. All-cargo carriers were obliged to add charter passenger operations in order to break even.

As a means of improving aircraft cargo space utilization, and reducing freight costs, TWA introduced the concept of "deferred air freight." This arrangement permitted the airline to move the shipment on a "space available" basis, but assured the shipper of delivery within five days. Rates for large volume shipments over long distances were often substantially below the van load rates of household goods movers.

The CAB remained concerned about air freight operations, but had felt that rate increases would choke off too much traffic, while rate decreases would not expand business enough to make all-cargo operations profitable.

Functional requirements. The major functions of an operating airline included: 1. deciding on route structures, equipment, and schedules; 2. conducting flight operations; 3. maintaining and servicing aircraft; 4. servicing passengers and shippers; 5. advertising, promoting sales, and conducting public relations; 6. dealing with governmental and other public bodies; 7. purchasing and inventory control; 8. financial planning; 9. industrial relations.

While there was no typical pattern, each of the commercial air carriers contained an Operations Division and a Sales Division.

Operations was responsible for completion of the airline's schedules and improvement of operating techniques, and usually included four departments: Flight Operations; Ground Operations; Aircraft Engineering and Maintenance; Airports and Facilities Maintenance.

Sales Division typically included: Agency and Interline Sales, Customer Service, Reservations, Schedules, Tariffs, Mail and Freight, and a number of Regional Traffic Managers, responsible for sales, reservations, ticketing, advertising, publicity, customer relations, and freight activities within their respective regions.

In addition to Operations and Sales, there were usually the following staff departments: Economic Planning; Finance; Industrial Relations; Advertising and Public Relations; Legal; and Purchasing and Stores.

The men originally responsible for the development of the U.S. air transportation industry, all strong individualists, have left indelible impressions on both the strategies and the organizational patterns of the companies which were under their jurisdictions. The influence of Juan Trippe on Pan American; of W. A. Patterson on United; of C. R. Smith, Eddie Rickenbacker, and Howard Hughes on American, Eastern, and TWA respectively will be seen when those airlines are discussed later in this case. A tendency towards more reliance upon formal organizational devices characterizes the present, second generation of airline presidents, who are obliged to deal with very much larger organizations than their predecessors.

Operational Characteristics

Airports. In North America, most public airports were owned by municipal governments. In effect, they represented a subsidy to the users, and were regarded as a form of local business development or advertising. The charge to the airline for using an airport was individually negotiated with the local airport administration. Terminal facilities at the airports were crucial to the speed and convenience with which passengers could be served.

Airlines normally leased sales and administrative space at the terminal, and in other suitable locations in the surrounding communities. Less than 20% of an airline's investment in physical assets typically was represented by land, buildings, and ground support equipment. This investment was dwarfed by the flight equipment requirements.

The airport's runways determined, by their length, number, and orientation, the volume of traffic and kinds of aircraft that could utilize the field. When commercial jet aircraft were first being ordered, there were only a few airports in the country that had runways long enough to permit their operation. This resulted in an extensive program of airport expansion at almost every major city in the nation.

Air navigation and instrument landing facilities at most major airports were provided and operated by the Federal Aviation Agency. This assured a degree of uniformity in practice that would be difficult to achieve if each community were to provide its own.

At an increasing number of airports, income from the airline charges was supplemented by fees from observation decks, view telescopes, concessions to service businesses located at the airport, and ground leases for air transport related business offices. In spite of this, most airports were not financially self-supporting.

Aircraft. Aircraft and flight equipment accounted for 84% of the average carrier's fixed assets in 1966 (25% of an airline's investment in aircraft fleet was represented by spare parts and spare engines). Additionally, the characteristics of its aircraft dictated operating procedures, determined the airline's image, and were important influences on passenger acceptance. Thus aircraft purchase decisions were crucial strategic choices.

The decision by one carrier to purchase newer, faster, or more comfortable

exhibit 3

COMPARATIVE STATISTICS ON FIVE MAJOR U.S. AIRLINES

	1957	1958	1959	1960	1961	1962	1963	1964	1965	1966
United Air Lines										
Operating revenue (in millions)	$281.9	$316.8	$329.2	$379.1	$502.2	$594.3	$622.9	$669.4	$792.8	$ 856.9
Total Assets (in millions)	285.9	332.9	394.6	508.8	644.7	630.8	635.4	730.1	974.7	1,207.7
Net Income (in millions)	7.9	14.3	13.8	11.2	3.7	7.7	14.7	27.3	45.8	38.3
% of Total U.S. Industry Revenues	13%	14%	13%	13%	16%	17%	18%	16%	16%	15%
L.T. Debt as % of Total Capitalization	41%	43%	47%	57%	58%	55%	44%	47%	54%	49%
American Airlines										
Operating revenue (in millions)	$306.0	$317.2	$377.7	$428.5	$421.4	$463.0	$488.1	$544.0	$612.4	$ 727.7
Total Assets (in millions)	285.3	318.1	510.3	536.8	657.3	666.4	702.6	721.1	821.6	1,082.1
Net Income (in millions)	10.9	16.1	21.0	12.9	8.6	7.1	19.7	33.5	39.7	52.1
% of Total U.S. Industry Revenues	14%	14%	14%	15%	14%	13%	13%	13%	12%	13%
L.T. Debt as % of Total Capitalization	32%	33%	56%	56%	63%	62%	57%	53%	50%	58%
Eastern Airlines										
Operating revenue (in millions)	$263.8	$247.5	$300.2	$295.8	$297.3	$290.0	$357.7	$417.8	$511.6	$ 501.0
Total Assets (in millions)	221.2	260.8	308.3	339.9	344.8	331.8	322.4	370.1	449.3	545.5
Net Income (in millions)	13.5	6.9	11.6	(3.5)	(9.7)	(13.3)	(37.9)	(5.8)	29.8	14.7
% of Total U.S. Industry Revenues	12%	11%	11%	10%	10%	8%	10%	10%	10%	9%
L.T. Debt as % of Total Capitalization	43%	52%	49%	55%	65%	69%	81%	85%	66%	65%
Trans World Airlines										
Operating revenue (in millions)	$263.7	$284.8	$348.5	$378.4	$362.5	$403.0	$476.5	$575.0	$672.8	$ 681.6
Total Assets (in millions)	253.6	254.3	254.9	450.3	477.2	531.3	533.9	623.9	688.2	830.4
Net Income (in millions)	1.6	(1.8)	9.4	6.5	(14.7)	(5.7)	19.8	37.0	50.1	29.7
% of Total U.S. Industry Revenues	12%	13%	13%	13%	12%	12%	13%	14%	14%	12%
L.T. Debt as % of Total Capitalization	33%	30%	19%	60%	72%	77%	74%	65%	50%	54%
Pan American World Airways										
Operating revenue (in millions)	$312.7	$313.2	$356.8	$413.1	$460.3	$503.9	$560.9	$604.7	$669.0	$ 841.0
Total Assets (in millions)	296.0	361.8	480.6	585.7	573.1	564.0	552.7	663.1	777.7	1,039.4
Net Income (in millions)	9.9	4.4	7.4	7.1	7.2	15.0	33.6	37.1	52.1	83.7
% of Total U.S. Industry Revenues	15%	14%	14%	14%	15%	15%	15%	14%	13%	15%
L.T. Debt as % of Total Capitalization	42%	56%	62%	65%	63%	58%	44%	46%	47%	49%

Note: In 1966, operating results of United, Eastern, and Trans World Airlines were adversely affected by a 43 day strike by the International Association of Machinists. Results of American and Pan American Airlines might be inflated by the increased revenues resulting from the I.A.M. strike against five U.S. carriers. However, the results for 1966 include payments made by American and Pan Am to the five struck airlines under the Mutual Aid Pact of $29.0 million and $12.4 million respectively.

aircraft placed pressures upon its competitors over the same routes to do the same thing. For example, the DC-7 was less efficient and more costly to operate than the DC-6, and many airlines would have preferred to continue operating their DC-6's until the major conversion to jets became necessary. Nevertheless, since the DC-7 was faster and more comfortable and gained immediate passenger acceptance, many airlines were forced into purchasing DC-7's and replacing their DC-6's prematurely in order to remain competitive.

In 1966, there were a total of 13 air frame manufacturers supplying the U.S. commercial air transport industry. Through the years, the most important had been: (1) Douglas, which built the DC-3 through DC-9 series; (2) Lockheed, which manufactured the Constellation and the Electra during the 1950's, but had chosen not to build a commercial jet; (3) Boeing, which manufactured the Boeing 707, 720, 727, and 737 commercial jet transports; and (4) Consolidated-Vultee Aircraft (Convair), which made the 880 and 990 commercial jet transports. Whenever a major new aircraft type was being designed by a manufacturer, this information was well known throughout the airline industry. Similarly, when a major carrier ordered new planes, this was also well publicized. Thus, it was difficult for an airline to surprise its competition by suddenly introducing a new and faster plane on its routes, but obtaining first delivery of new equipment was frequently an important competitive advantage to a carrier.

Aircraft financing. Prior to World War II, airlines' equipment purchase needs were met primarily through the sale of stock. Following the war, long-term borrowing became necessary to finance the major fleet expansions. Some equity financing was also conducted in the mid-1950's, when carrier earnings and stock prices were up, but subsequently the capital requirements have far exceeded the airlines' retained earnings. Since the introduction of jets, virtually all new aircraft have been purchased through debt instruments. Institutions financing

exhibit 4

COMPARATIVE STATISTICS ON FIVE MAJOR U.S. AIRLINES (1961–1966)

	1961	*1962*	*1963*	*1964*	*1965*	*1966*
United Air Lines						
Passenger Load Factor	58.1%	53.6%	53.7%	53.9%	55.3%	57.6%
Return on Investment[1]	2.0%	2.6%	3.8%	65%	89%	6.2%
Expenses/plane mile	$3.13	$3.06	$3.00	$2.99	$2.93	$3.17
American Airlines						
Passenger Load Factor	61.4%	57.2%	58.7%	59.7%	59.0%	63.1%
Return on Investment[1]	3.3%	3.1%	5.1%	7.8%	8.5%	10.0%
Expenses/plane mile	$3.33	$3.43	$3.30	$3.40	$3.38	$3.28
Eastern Airlines						
Passenger Load Factor	52.2%	49.5%	50.5%	55.5%	57.3%	59.4%
Return on Investment[1]	(1.0%)	(2.4%)	(10.5%)	19%	13.3%	6.8%
Expenses/plant mile	$2.62	$3.07	$3.04	$3.26	$3.29	$3.56
Trans World Airlines						
Passenger Load Factor	55.1%	50.9%	51.0%	56.6%	54.6%	54.4%
Return on Investment[1]	(7.9%)	1.7%	9.1%	11.1%	12.1%	7.6%
Expenses/plane mile	$3.64	$3.58	$3.45	$3.36	$3.25	$3.30
Pan American World Airways						
Passenger Load Factor	59.3%	58.1%	57.2%	58.1%	57.9%	64.1%
Return on Investment[1]	3.7%	4.8%	8.8%	10.6%	11.3%	14.8%
Expenses/plane mile	$4.26	$4.13	$4.12	$4.24	$4.02	$3.90

[1]Net Income including extraordinary items plus minority interest, depreciation, and amortization and fixed charges (less income taxes) divided by total invested capital as of the beginning of the year.

Source: Financial Dynamics Incorporated, 1966.

aircraft purchases were mainly concerned with the practical life of the equipment and its possible use by other airlines if the borrower defaulted. Loans on propeller-driven airline equipment had usually been amortized over a five-year period. Because jets were not expected to become obsolete as quickly as predecessor aircraft, most loans for jet fleets were made for periods of seven to ten years.

Another common method of financing aircraft purchases was through the use of an equipment trust. In this arrangement, title was held by the lending institution, which acted as the trustee for a series of notes given by the carrier. Conditional sales contracts were sometimes used, whereby the aircraft manufacturer retained title to the plane until the entire price had been paid, but the purchaser took possession and operated it.

Marketing. Marketing passenger service was a matter of primary concern for most airline managements. This had not always been the case, however, as stated by Mr. Floyd D. Hall, President of Eastern Air Lines:

> We used to be too enthralled with the helmet and goggle era. In effect, we used to stand around and cheer for 15 minutes every time an airplane took off. Well, we're not doing it any more. We are now an industrial company manufacturing a product. Our product is a seat in motion. And just producing it isn't good enough—it must be marketed. What we are doing at Eastern is to take all the assets of the organization—the planes, the people, the routes, the terminals, the maintenance facilities, everything—and analyze them to see exactly where they can best be used. This is no different from the way one would treat any marketing problem.

According to American's president, Marion Sadler, the major marketing problem facing the industry was "to make air transportation easier to use." TWA's general manager added, "We must put the airplane where the passenger wants it, when he wants it, and make the traveler feel he's wanted."

Said the president of another major airline:

> Our problem now boils down to this: What can we do to accelerate the traffic increases of recent years to insure adequate profits? In my opinion, the answer lies principally in the realm of service. We are entering what might be called "the era of the pampered passenger."

Passenger space on airlines was sold by travel agents, airline ticket offices, and by agents at airport reservation counters. Airlines used their own personnel to man ticket offices and airport reservation counters, and sales forces were used to maintain liaison with travel agents. Sales forces also called directly on large business customers. While it was difficult to establish preferential position with a travel agency, many airlines had been able to do this with a few customers.

Most airlines operated reservation systems which provided control over available space on the aircraft. In the most common system, all seats were controlled by one central reservations office, located near the geographical center of the airline's operations. The job was usually done with an electronic computer, which kept a complete record of the space sold and the space available on every flight from each city. Then, each of the reservations desks throughout the country queried the computer regarding available space. Within seconds the station knew if space was available on the flight in question, and the reservation was recorded at the central reservations office. Central systems were gradually replacing space allocations to individual stations, which required each station to keep track of the number of seats available to it and the number of seats which it had sold on any given flight.

Customer attitudes and preferences. Two sets of customer attitudes had been of continuing concern to the commercial air transport industry. The first was a demonstrable lack of customer loyalty. Because services offered by competing airlines were very similar, passengers tended to fly on whatever airline departed at the time they wanted to leave. Surveys showed that, although a customer might express some preferences for a particular airline, he normally would not wait more than 20 to 30 minutes longer to fly with that particular carrier rather than with any other.

exhibit 5

1966 EXPRESS AND FREIGHT TON MILES

Rank	Airline	Ton-Miles Carried (000)
1	Pan American	525,711
2	Flying Tiger	425,692
3	American	371,358
4	United	344,497
5	Trans World	285,035
6	Seaboard World	234,385
7	Airlift	227,922
8	Northwest	146,420
9	Continental	104,550
10	Delta	72,541
11	Eastern	66,912
12	Braniff	56,491
13	National	28,843
14	Alaska	27,766
15	Western	13,926

Source: "Aviation Week & Space Technology" (March 6, 1967), p. 255.

exhibit 6

PASSENGER TRAVEL BETWEEN THE U.S. AND FOREIGN COUNTRIES *

(thousands of passengers)

	1953	1958	1959	1960	1961	1962	1963	1964	1965	1966
Passengers via Air	1,715	3,402	4,064	4,576	4,954	5,364	5,997	6,905	8,227	9,780
Passengers via Sea	1,112	1,219	1,426	1,474	1,469	1,568	1,639	1,710	1,652	1,549
Total International Passengers by Air and Sea	2,827	4,621	5,490	6,050	6,423	6,932	7,636	8,615	9,879	11,329
Passengers via Air (as % of Total)	60.7%	73.6%	74.0%	75.6%	77.1%	77.4%	78.5%	80.2%	83.3%	86.3%
Passengers via U.S.—Flag Airlines	1,152	2,053	2,348	2,505	2,458	2,680	3,020	3,440	4,032	5,036
Passengers via Foreign—Flag Airlines	563	1,349	1,706	2,071	2,496	2,684	2,977	3,465	4,195	4,744
U.S. Citizens via Air (as % of total Air Passengers)	65.9%	66.0%	64.3%	63.0%	61.2%	61.4%	61.8%	61.8%	60.9%	62.1%
U.S.—Flag Airlines' Share of total Air Passengers	67.2%	60.0%	58.1%	54.8%	49.6%	50.0%	50.4%	49.8%	49.0%	51.5%

*Figures are for fiscal years and are exclusive of: travel over land borders (except Mexican air travel); crewmen; military personnel; and travelers between continental United States and its possessions.

Source: U.S. Department of Justice, Immigration and Naturalization Service, "Report of Passenger Travel Between the United States and Foreign Countries."

A second persistent concern regarded the general public's fear of flying. Even though the fatality rate per 100 million passenger miles was considerably below the auto fatality rate, airline executives believed that it would be a matter of generations before all people came to accept air travel as a truly safe mode of transportation. Surveys showed that many people considered flying at speeds of 600 miles per hour unnatural and somewhat dangerous, and more than 75% of the U.S. public had never been inside an airplane.

In the early 1960's, the carriers assigned greater numbers of people to the marketing efforts, and major reorganizations took place to emphasize the growing importance of the marketing effort to the organization. Airlines were also attempting to find out more scientifically where passengers would like to go and what they expected in the way of service.

Historically, the carriers had used the CAB's origin and destination statistics to determine when new traffic warranted the addition of a flight between any city pair. In the early 1960's, rather than using historical data, market research departments had been attempting to *anticipate* the trends, in order to beat competition to the growing markets.

Increasing attention was also being given to problems which passengers encountered in obtaining reservations, disorganized ticket lines, slow baggage handling, finding informed "information" people, etc.

Operating expenses. Compared with nontransportation enterprises, the airline operated with an extremely high proportion of fixed expenses, Most airlines figured that roughly 50% of their costs were completely fixed at any given point in time, while another 40% varied only with the number of hours of aircraft operation. Only 10% varied with traffic volume—i.e., the number of people or the amount of freight carried per flight. Thus, for any scheduled flight, 90% of costs could be considered as fixed. This overwhelming proportion of fixed (or obligated) expense, combined with the heavy debt burdens imposed by equipment purchases, caused the airlines to be greatly concerned with load factors.

Looking at major operating expense categories, the following approximate breakdown could be made:

Flying operations	28%
Maintenance	18
Aircraft and traffic service	17
Promotion and Sales	13
Passenger service	9
Administration	5
Depreciation	10
Total Expenses	100%

"Flying operations" was the largest single expense for the airlines. This included the direct costs of plane operations, predominantly for wages and fuel. The average consumption of fuel by a DC-8 jet was over 2,000 gallons per hour.

Another large, unavoidable expense was maintenance. This covered the periodic inspection, service, and overhaul required after certain periods of flying time had elapsed. A major overhaul for a DC-8 or 707 airframe cost an airline more than $200,000, not including overhead, or overhaul of the engines.

There were innumerable factors which could cause different operating expenses for similar airlines. One major variable was the average length of the airline's routes. The relationship between short and long flight segments is shown in Exhibits 7A and 7B, which plot costs against the length of flight. These exhibits show that operating costs drop sharply with increasing length of flight segments, up to 500 miles.

Operating expenses also tended to vary with the type of equipment operated (certain aircraft were distinctly more efficient than others for certain route patterns) and the climate in which they flew (freezing climates greatly increased costs).

Utilization of aircraft was an all important profit variable, since planes depreciated rapidly, at least technologically, whether they were used or not. Consequently, most airlines sought to utilize their big jets at least 11 hours a day.

Labor Relations

The airline industry had had a history of difficult labor relations. There had been a number of crippling strikes over the years and individual companies had been compelled to deal with eight or nine different unions. Jurisdictional disputes had been a major source of conflict in labor management relationships. The Air Lines Pilots Association (ALPA) had a reputation for being one of the strongest and best-organized unions in the country, and other "professional" union organizations had also built strong industry positions.

The basic federal legislation providing for labor relations and collective bargaining in the industry was the Railway Labor Act. Under this act, employees were given the right to organize, and carriers were forbidden to interfere. Disagreements were to be settled by conference. When conferences failed, a National Mediation Board was provided to hear grievances. The National Mediation Board was not an enforcement agency. It could not compel either unions or management to do anything. If the Board was unable to effect an agreement between the bargaining parties, it might persuade the parties to submit the case to arbitration. If either party refused to arbitrate, the unions had to wait at least 30 days before striking. If a strike was threatened, and the President of the United States determined that a substantial interruption to interstate commerce was involved, he could appoint an emergency board to hear the dispute. If such a board was appointed, no strike could be called until 30 days after the board issued its report. Although the board had no power to enforce its findings, its influence on public opinion often assisted in the settlement of disputes.

The threat of a strike to the airlines was a particularly onerous one because, as in all service businesses, the business lost during a shutdown is lost forever. There

OPERATING COSTS OF SELECTED PROPELLER DRIVEN AIRCRAFT BY DISTANCE FLOWN

(dollars per thousand passenger-miles, calculated on the basis of a full load)

Distance Flown (miles)

Aircraft	0– 200	200– 400	400– 600	600– 800	800– 1000	1,000– 1,500	1,500– 2,000	2,000– 2,500	2,500 and over [1]
Douglas DC-3	42.41	31.62	30.13						
Martin M-404	34.72	25.16	23.79						
Convair CV-440	33.80	22.55	20.89						
Douglas DC-4	40.89	26.88	24.79	22.14	21.68	21.22			
Douglas DC-6B	45.00	26.93	24.09	21.18	20.56	19.95	19.47		
Lockheed L-1049	53.01	30.62	27.02	23.61	22.81	22.03	21.45	20.83	21.08
Douglas DC-7	62.24	34.01	29.40	25.43	24.42	23.41	22.66	21.17	21.63
Lockheed L-1049H	57.42	32.74	28.80	25.12	24.25	23.41	22.78	21.76	22.00
Douglas DC-7C	65.03	35.09	30.18	26.05	24.28	23.95	23.18	21.67	22.12

[1]3,000 miles is used as midpoint in calculating figures for this class.

Source: Stephen P. Sobotka, et al., *Prices of Used Commercial Aircraft* (Evanston:The Transportation Center, Northwestern University, 1959), Table 14, p. 45.

ESTIMATED OPERATING COSTS, TURBINE AND PRE-1958 AIRCRAFT

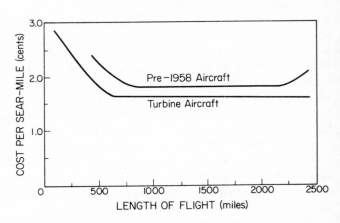

Source: John H. Frederick, *Commercial Air Transportation*, 4th ed. (Homewood, Ill.: Richard D. Irwin, Inc., 1965).

is no way to make up for empty seats. In order to offset losses from one airline to another whenever a single airline is struck, six of the major airlines evolved a Mutual Air Pact in the late 1950's, which was filed with, and approved by, the Civil Aeronautics Board. It provided a method for passing to the struck carrier the additional income accruing to the other carriers by reason of the diversion of traffic. The original parties to the pact were American, Eastern, Capital, Pan American, TWA, and United.

Typical of the complex and difficult labor relations problems of the industry was the bitter battle which occurred between the ALPA and the Flight Engineers International Association (FEIA) in the late 1950's. The issue arose over the make-up of cockpit crews for the new jets. Prior to the jets, most crews consisted of two pilots and a "flight engineer." The latter was concerned with propeller and mixture controls, cowl flaps, engine superchargers, oil cooler flaps, etc. On the jets, these jobs were done electronically or were not required; the only functions left for the flight engineer were fuel management, preflight inspections, and the management of the heating and air conditioning systems, all of which could be easily handled by the pilots. On the other hand, the functions of the pilots had become much more complicated on the jet.

The position of the ALPA was that the third crew member in the jet cockpit should have pilot training, so that he could take over in emergencies. The FEIA's view was that, regardless of the number of pilots, there should be at least one professional flight engineer aboard (who did not have to be a pilot, and who would be a member of the FEIA).

The airlines were caught in a situation in which the engineers threatened to strike unless the company guaranteed them a job on the jets, while the pilots threatened to strike if they did. Negotiations took a different course with each airline.

In 1966, ALPA and the airlines were arguing a new issue concerned with cockpit crew size. Improved electronic equipment on the DC-9 and the BAC-111 had made the third man unnecessary and the CAB had approved a two man cockpit crew. The Boeing 737 had a similar cockpit configuration and was expected to also gain approval for a two man crew. Even though many pilots agreed that two men could handle the physical requirements, they argued that the third man should be retained because increased speeds and density of aircraft near airports required the full attention of at least one man. ALPA wanted this man retained to cope with the increased communications load and for plotting positions of convergent airplane courses.

The Competitive Variables

Competition within a regulated industry, like the airlines, had two major characteristics. First, the competitive alternatives available to the companies within the industry were severely limited. An airline could not change its route structure, its prices, or its basic operating techniques without CAB or FAA approval.

Second, there was little proprietary information that could be kept secret from competitors. Proposed route and rate changes had to be filed with the CAB, and detailed operating and financial statements had to be submitted. Information reported to the CAB became public property, and all competitors had access to it.

There were six major dimensions along which a commercial air carrier potentially could differentiate itself from its competition. These were rates, routes, equipment, schedules, service, and advertising.

1. Rates. For any given class of service between two major traffic centers, it was difficult to sustain a price differential. This is not to say, however, that rates were stable. There was almost continuous downward pressure on rates, as one airline attempted to gain some temporary competitive advantage over another. Most downward pressure came through "promotional" rates (family plans, excursion rates, etc.). Almost invariably, competing airlines would immediately meet price reductions involving comparable equipment and service.

Local service carriers were particularly prone to use rates as a competitive tool, to compensate for equipment, schedule, or route disadvantages. In addition, since they usually received air mail subsidies, local service carriers could afford price reductions somewhat more easily than the trunklines.

In 1966, there were three major classes of passenger service: first class, coach, and an in-between "standard" class. Other categories, such as "Jet DeLuxe Night Coach," "Night Coach," "Economy Coach," "Sky-Bus," "Prop First Class," "Prop Coach," provided at least ten more different service-fare combinations. The percentage of passengers flying first class declined steadily since the introduction of coach fares in 1949. In 1962, coach passengers accounted for 62% of domestic seat-miles and 83% of international. By 1966, these percentages had risen to 76% and 89% respectively.

The general cargo rate in 1966 was about 20¢ per ton-mile, but there were also specific commodity rates, which were usually lower. Additionally, West to East cargo rates were considerably below East to West rates, in an attempt to reduce the usual imbalance in traffic volume. There were also rate variations for different weight and distance categories, ranging from 15.7¢ per ton-mile (for the longest haul and the highest weight category) to 34.3¢. Deferred air freight rates were set at a minimum of 55% of the general commodity rate.

2. Routes. An airline's route structure was perhaps its most important competitive variable, but one which was difficult to change. Route structures had been modified or strengthened through mergers, but it was generally believed that the CAB was unlikely to approve mergers among carriers who were in reasonably strong financial condition. Many carriers felt there was already too much competition between major city pairs.

In some instances, the trunklines had petitioned the CAB to discontinue service to smaller and less profitable traffic centers. Where this service could be satisfactorily carried out by a local service carrier, the CAB had granted such withdrawal.

3. Equipment. The type of aircraft which an airline operated was the variable on which most industry executives placed the greatest emphasis. Passengers tended to select the newest, fastest, and most comfortable planes available if given a choice. Thus most airlines felt that they had to match or surpass their competitors' equipment. As previously noted, the types of aircraft in a company's fleet also determined many of the company's operating requirements.

4. Schedules. Scheduling was a crucial profit variable. Most airlines scheduled their aircraft with a delicate balance between economy of operation and service to the public. The former, of course, points toward high load factors and maximum utilization of the aircraft, while the latter points toward flights and availability of standby facilities. An airline which originated only a few flights from a given station, in order to maximize load factors, might quickly lose many of its customers to competing airlines, whose flights had available seats (more often), or which departed at more convenient times. On the other hand, too many empty seats would quickly plunge the company into heavy losses.

Service provided between any two points on an airline's system was also related to the service provided on other segments. For example, in order to maintain a minimum service pattern of two flights each day between two intermediate cities along a high density route, an airline might have to accept low load factors over these segments; or, in order to avoid disappointing connecting passengers on a through route, schedules between two cities might have to be extended to three flights, thus reducing the average load factor per flight; or, in order to get aircraft back to the home base for overnight maintenance, an off peak flight at a low load factor might have to be scheduled.

In addition to these problems, there were peaks in demand during certain times of the year. In particular, early morning, noon, and early evening departures were much more in demand than mid-morning or afternoon flights. Likewise, demand reached peaks in the summer months and at Christmas time. In its schedule planning, an airline had to take this into account and accept lower load factors during off-peak times.

Still another scheduling problem arose from flight delays and cancellations, due to equipment failures or bad weather. When a flight was late, a decision often had to be made by the dispatcher to either hold connecting flights, snowballing the problem, or to release the connecting flights, and cause missed connections. Similarly, the cancellation of a flight upset crew and equipment availability on the backhaul.

Scheduling alone could establish or destroy customer preference. While most of the scheduling could be done mechanically, the really important choices had to be based upon the informed judgment of management, taking account of their own situation and the scheduling of competitors. Some industry executives estimated that these "exceptional circumstances" occurred in about 10% of all flights.

5. Service. When rates, routes, equipment, and schedules were roughly comparable, customer service became an important distinction between airlines in attracting customers. From the moment a passenger contacted an airline, there were innumerable opportunities for differentiating the company's service. Ticketing procedures, information, baggage handling, boarding, in-flight meals, stewardess attention, off-loading procedures, and baggage claiming were only a few of the passenger services which customers presumed would be handled well.

6. Advertising. Because opportunities for significant competitive advantages in rates, schedules, service, etc., were sometimes limited, advertising and sales promotion efforts received a great deal of management attention. Consumers usually had an active interest in flying, since the service affected their personal plans and comfort, and the purchase of an airline ticket often represented a considerable expenditure. Thus they tended to respond positively to advertising programs. Airline advertising budgets averaged 2.6% of sales in 1966.

Ancillary services. It is interesting to note that the airlines have allowed others to capitalize on ancillary service opportunities related to air travel. By defining their business as *Air Transportation,* the airlines have precluded themselves from highly profitable, nonregulated activities, such as the rent-a-car business, which has been a direct result of increased air travel. (Hertz, in 1966, had sales volume greater than all but six U.S. airlines.)

Other opportunities existed in freight forwarding, trucking, airport limousine and bus services, etc. The airlines had the original, preferred opportunities also to build and/or sponsor development of close-to-airport hotels and motels, and restaurants. Airport food services would have seemed especially logical since the airlines were required to have extensive kitchen facilities at major airports to prepare in-flight meals.

New airports invariably have spawned business centers. Airlines, with great interest in new airport locations, had ready-made opportunities to sponsor industrial park development in connection with new airport construction. After the airports were built, the airlines still could have franchised the airport shops that seem to be an integral part of all airports. This diversification, however, had not been a part of the airlines' growth.

The "Jet Age" and the Future

The greatest change in commercial air transportation was the advent of the big jets. The British introduced the first commercial jet transport, the Comet, in 1952. The Comet, however, was destined for tragedy. First one, and then another, was destroyed while in flight by structural failure before the cause of the accidents was identified.

In the U.S., development of a commercial jet transport was much slower. The widely-used, propeller-driven DC-6 was an economical aircraft, and its 50 to 60 seats were adequate for operating a full pattern of daily schedules. Nevertheless, Boeing proceeded with the development of a commercial jet transport (the Boeing 707, based on their military KC-135 contract) and flew the first prototype in 1954.

Douglas also undertook the development of a commercial jet transport. The DC-8, which was designed completely from scratch, was placed in service about one year later than the Boeing 707.

Spending three times as much for a single airplane as they ever had before (a single Boeing 707 cost over $5,000,000), the airlines committed more than their entire total assets to buy the new jets, which promised to fly twice as many passengers nearly twice as fast as the latest commercial passenger aircraft, the DC-7 and the Lockheed 1649. But, for the first time since the DC-3, the airlines expected to use a new aircraft through its entire depreciation life (about ten years). As a result of the jet acquisition program, investment in the U.S. commercial air transport industry (including equity, long-term debt, and advances) increased 300% between 1953 and 1963. It was not until 1962 that the airlines recovered from this unprecedented financial plunge and began to operate the 600 mile per hour jets at a profit. By 1963, the changeover to jets was largely completed. In that year, 82% of all passenger miles flown by scheduled airlines in the U.S. were flown aboard jets.

In 1963, a Boeing 707, flying an average length trip with 55% of its seats filled, could generate about $1,900 an hour in revenue. Jet utilization varied with the airline, but averaged about 11 hours a day. The 707 produced an available seat mile for approximately 1.5¢ (or, without depreciation, 1¢). The average aircoach fare brought in 5.8¢ per mile in revenues compared to 3.0¢ for rail coach and 2.9¢ for bus.

In the five year period ending with 1965, revenue passenger miles flown increased 130%, cargo ton-miles increased 130%, and total revenues increased 81%. International air travel more than tripled.

The Future

There were a number of factors which certain industry leaders felt might have an adverse affect upon the future expansion of air traffic. For one, the communications industry was developing devices that might make a great deal of business travel unnecessary. A combination of conference telephone calls with large screen phone-vision, instant data transmission facilities via interlocking computers, and fascimile machines for visual transfer of documents were three advances mentioned by certain government officials and airline executives.

Some industry analysts were concerned that large shippers might find an investment in their own cargo aircraft would be more economical than the use of a common carrier. They pointed to this development in the trucking industry.

The rapid increase in the use of private passenger aircraft was also viewed with concern. Some carriers (Pan American was first) even offered business jets for lease or sale.

Two important unknowns were the future impact of the supersonic transport (SST) and the huge 400–500 passenger subsonic aircraft (such as the C5A), which were under development in both Europe and the U.S.

The ultimate development of an SST (capable of three times the speed of sound) posed several major problems to the air transport industry, not the least of which was the requirement for tremendous financial outlays both for aircraft and for airport facilities. With their present huge financial commitment to subsonic jets, the airlines might not be able to sustain the costs of adding SST's to their fleets. This situation might require the FAA to make expenditures aggregating hundreds of millions of dollars, and, as a result, could greatly increase the the federal role in aviation.

1966 airport facilities would not be equal to the strain presented by SST's. Landing facilities would be most affected: they would be too short, too narrow, or too weak to withstand the beating to which a 200 ton transport would subject them.

A Mach III transport would leave a sonic boom 50 miles wide. This would prohibit it from flying at the altitudes used by subsonic jets. The SST would have to climb to about 45,000 feet before accelerating. In this process, much of the plane's original efficiency would be lost, since it would have to fly at subsonic speeds much of the time.

The development costs of the SST could eliminate many of the present aircraft manufacturers as potential suppliers. The costs could, in fact, reduce the U.S. aircraft industry to only two or three manufacturers. For instance, Martin no longer was in the aircraft business; General Dynamics and Lockheed no longer made commercial planes; and Douglas had withdrawn from the Mach III competition.

The problem of convenience had to be solved also before the Mach III could be operated profitably. The facilities necessary to handle such an aircraft could not be located very close to most cities, because of the size of facility required and the potential sonic boom. Thus, the number of potential passengers might be reduced. The probable routes for an SST could take it from one area of low population density to another—not the most desirable locations for air travelers.

The problems were compounded with the development of the giant 500 passenger subsonic planes. Their great cost and size would make enormous demands upon schedulers if they were to operate at efficient load factors. Their slow speed might restrict them to economy flights, so that airlines would still be obliged to offer SST's for first class passengers. And their airport handling facilities might prove incompatible with those required for the SST.

Thus, although the future for air transportation appeared to offer great opportunities for growth and innovation, major problems of vast scale and complexity would have to be resolved.

PART II: COMPANY ANALYSIS

In the early years of their development, each of the major U.S. airlines tended to adopt a strategic posture and character which distinguished it from its competitors. These characteristics tended to persist over long time periods, and have only recently been becoming diffused as a new generation of management replaces the original founders. This section describes the early history and the subsequent strategic emphasis of each of the five largest airlines in the U.S. These five—United, American, TWA, Eastern, and Pan American—accounted for nearly two-thirds of total U.S. Air Transportation revenues in 1966. Among them they flew almost as many passenger miles as all other airlines in the Western world combined.

UNITED AIR LINES

Early Origins

Boeing Airplane Company, a pioneer aircraft manufacturer, formed an airline—Boeing Air Transport—in 1927, which bid for, and received, the Chicago–San Francisco mail route. The following year, Pacific Air Transport, a small airline formed in 1926 to feed mail into the San Francisco–New York route, was merged into Boeing. In 1929 and 1930, three other acquisitions added Midwestern and Eastern routes, which shifted the center of the airline's activities to Chicago (from that time forward, Chicago was the airline's headquarters).

Also, in 1929, the Boeing complex acquired several major aircraft and airplane components manufacturers: Sikorsky Aviation, Chance-Vought, Stearman, Pratt & Whitney, Northrop, United Aircraft, Hamilton Aero, and Standard Steel Propeller Corp.

In 1934, the growth of this group of companies came to an abrupt ending. The U.S. Post Office Department became concerned about alleged "'unfair competition" in bidding for air mail contracts. As a result, all existing contracts were cancelled, and plane makers were ordered to divest their transportation activities. Consequently, on August 31, 1934, the Boeing group was dissolved, and ·its properties were transferred to three new, separate companies: Boeing Airplane Corporation, which acquired the assets of the Western manufacturing companies; United Aircraft Corporation, which acquired the assets of the Eastern manufacturing companies; and United Air Lines Transport Corporation, which received all of the air transport holdings.

As part of this reorganization, a young banker, William A. Patterson, then age 34, entered the United Air Lines Transport Corporation as president. United then bid for new air mail contracts, and was awarded virtually all of its old routes: New York–Chicago; Chicago–San Francisco; Salt Lake City–Seattle–Spokane; and Seattle–San Francisco–Los Angeles–San Diego. One important former route, Chicago–Dallas, was awarded to Braniff. However, TWA and American were also awarded transcontinental routes competitive with United's "mainline," thereby terminating what had once been a United monopoly.

In the years following reinstatement of the main contracts, United's relations with the Federal Government deteriorated. The few routes that the airline applied for were not granted, and United concentrated upon internal growth, leaving the new routes and extensions to American, TWA, and Northwest. Thus, while United concentrated on its northern transcontinental route, American doubled the number of population centers which it served. By 1937, American served 60 major traffic centers, and flew over a territory which blanketed one-third of the country's population. In 1934, United's revenues were three times as large as American's; by 1938, they were less than half.

Route Structure

A proposed purchase of a Milwaukee–Detroit–Washington route in 1936 was blocked by the ICC, but purchase of a Cheyenne–Denver segment was approved. In 1939 United negotiated the purchase of 55% of the stock of the predecessor to Western Air Lines, but this acquisition was disapproved by the CAB. A similar attempt to acquire the predecessor to Capital Air Lines was rejected by that company's shareholders. Finally, in late 1944, the company was allowed to extend its service to Boston, Hartford, Cleveland, and Detroit.

In 1944 and 1945, Patterson directed his staff to study the prospects of the international market, particularly the so-called "blue ribbon" route over the North Atlantic. Several U.S. carriers applied for routes over the North Atlantic, and many foreign carriers indicated that they intended to fly it. Fearing over-competition, United decided not to apply for the route. However, it did bid for an overwater route to Hawaii which it subsequently received. During the same period of time, TWA withdrew its application for U.S.–Hawaii routes, but successfully prosecuted its North Atlantic application.

In 1947, United acquired Western Air Express's Denver–Los Angeles route. This acquisition terminated a series of events which had begun when the CAB denied a Western Air Express–United merger in 1940. Following this denial, both United and Western petitioned for the Denver–Los Angeles route. Western was granted the route in 1944. Then, early in 1947, Western ran into extreme financial difficulty, and was within 30 days of receivership. Patterson approached Terrell C. Drinkwater, new president of Western, and the two decided that $3.75 million was needed to bail Western out. Patterson offered to buy the Denver–Los Angeles route from Western for that exact amount of money. With Western facing bankruptcy, the CAB felt it had no choice but to approve the sale of the route.

In 1960, a merger with Capital Airlines became a possibility, as Capital had begun to experience severe financial difficulties. The company had gone deeply into debt to order English Vickers Viscount turbo-prop airliners, becoming the first U.S. airline to fly with turbine power. The Viscount was fast, quiet, and smooth, but limited in range. In airline operations, the Viscount had no more capacity than the older Convairs, and on many of Capital's short routes the Viscount's speed advantage was not an important factor. On the Washington–Chicago route, however, the Viscount's passenger appeal was tremendous.

With Capital facing bankruptcy, United and Capital started merger negotiations, and eventually reached an agreement. No other airline appeared to be particularly interested in acquiring Capital. Although the CAB had no enthusiasm for the merger, it also had no desire to let an airline go into bankruptcy. The merger was approved, and in June, 1961, Capital Airlines ceased to exist as a separate entity.

The addition of Capital's routes in the east and south completed the structure of United's 1966 route pattern.

In 1966, several applications for additional domestic city pairs were outstanding. Also, along with 17 other airlines, United had applied to serve the Pacific regions, thus extending their Hawaiian service to Hong Kong and Tokyo, and possibly also including Australia, New Zealand, and South East Asia.

Equipment

The equipment race between United and its competition began in the early 1930's when United management placed an order for 60 Boeing 247's. The 247 increased the speed of air travel from 125 miles per hour to 170 miles per hour, and cut coast-to-coast flight time from 27 to 19½ hours. United, by placing an order for so many planes, tied up the facilities of the Boeing plant in Seattle, making certain that its competitors would not obtain this first all-metal airliner. Competitors, particularly TWA, were not content to let United gain such an equipment advantage. TWA and American turned to Douglas and sponsored development of the DC-2. The DC-2 was also an all-metal monoplane, approximately 20 miles per hour faster than the 247, and it carried as many as eight more passengers. Thus, shortly after the 247's were delivered to United, the company found itself at its first important equipment disadvantage. Early delivery to TWA and American of the DC-3, which followed the DC-2 into service in 1936, heightened United's disadvantage. These lines were able to fly between Chicago and New York nonstop in five hours, while United's 247's had to refuel in Cleveland.

In 1936, United finally obtained delivery of a few DC-3's. In order to establish some kind of service differential, some of these new planes were converted into "Skylounges" for the Chicago–New York run. The "Skylounge" was a 14 passenger plane, with swivel chairs. It flew between the two cities in three hours and 55 minutes. However, passengers were not willing to pay the extra fare for this service, and the "Skylounges" were eventually converted into regular 21 passenger planes or into sleepers. The sleepers were used on overnight flights between San Francisco and Chicago.

United suffered losses along with the industry in most years between 1934 and 1938. Not the least of its problems was the crash of a 247 in 1936, and the crash of a DC-3 into San Francisco Bay in early 1937. In one day, following the second accident, United's passenger revenues dropped from $25,000 to $5,000. Many planes flew empty; the Post Office cancelled one of United's mail flights between New York and Chicago, and heavy losses piled up.

This served as an impetus for the company to seek a newer, faster, and safer plane, and to increase its safety standards.

Patterson sought a new airliner that would have four engines, and which would incorporate many of his safety and comfort ideas. United's engineers drew up a set of rough specifications, and took them to several manufacturers around the country. Douglas was selected, and United offered to pay for half the company's engineering cost of $300,000. Later, TWA, Pan American, North American Aviation (of which Eastern Air Lines was then a division), and finally American Airlines also joined in underwriting the project, with United paying 40% of the airlines' share, and the other carriers paying for the balance on a prorated amount. Ultimately, three of the carriers withdrew from the agreement, and only United and American shared with Douglas the development cost, which eventually amounted to $600,000. In June, 1938, a prototype was completed and designated as the DC-4.

Delivery of the DC-4 was delayed by the outbreak of World War II. Subsequent production of that aircraft went directly into military service.

In 1945, following the war, most of the prewar and wartime commercial aircraft were released back to the airlines, and the battle for speed and comfort began anew. TWA had worked with Lockheed before the war in the initial development of the Constellation, and the two companies agreed that the Constellations would not be sold to competitive transcontinental lines. Eastern and several other noncompeting, foreign lines were later allowed to buy them. As soon as the war ended, TWA took delivery of the 300 mile per hour Constellations.

This gave TWA a significant competitive advantage over American and United, who were still flying DC-3's. DC-6's were a year or two in the future, and United, American, and other airlines bought as many surplus military DC-4's as they could get their hands on. DC-4 conversion costs averaged $200,000 per plane, and each plane took four months to go through the conversion program.

Even when United and American had the DC-4's they still suffered from a 70 mile per hour disadvantage. However, when two Constellations crashed, TWA's fleet was grounded until the causes of the crashes were ascertained.

At about this time, United ordered 50 Martin 303's, replacements for the DC-3 over United's shorter runs. Shortly after this, a series of crashes by the 202's (unpressurized version of the 303), coupled with production difficulties at the Martin plant, caused United to have second thoughts. With United losing money in its postwar operations, Mr. Patterson cancelled his $16,000,000 commitment to Martin, and subsequently ordered Convairs for the shorter runs. This cancellation gave an effective two year equipment lead to American, who had tied up Douglas's DC-6 deliveries through their own orders.

United also ordered seven four-engine double deck Boeing Stratocruisers for delivery in 1947 and 1948. These planes were programmed to accommodate 55 passengers, 9,000 pounds of baggage, and would cruise at 340 miles per hour.

Late in 1951, American and several other airlines placed orders for DC-7's at a cost of $1.8 million each. The DC-7 carried the same number of passengers as a DC-6 (58) but traveled at 365 miles per hour, approximately 65 miles per hour faster than the DC-6B's. The increased range and speed of the DC-7 made practical coast-to-coast nonstop flights.

United was against the DC-7 from the start. The company's engineers estimated that its operating costs would be much higher than the DC-6's, and that training and integration costs would also be high. Studies had been conducted on commercial jet transportation, and management felt that a practical jet would be available by about 1958. Mr. Patterson thus hoped to move directly from the DC-6 to jets.

The fact remained that United would be placed at a severe transcontinental speed disadvantage if it did not have the new planes. Accordingly, the company ordered 25 DC-7's from Douglas in mid-1952, financed through a $45 million standby credit arrangement with 38 banks.

Another equipment choice facing United in 1951 and early 1952 was the coming availability of turboprop aircraft. The four-engine Lockheed Electra, which would fly 68 passengers at speeds over 400 miles per hour, was scheduled for introduction several months ahead of the jets. Both American and Eastern Airlines ordered the new Electras, but Mr. Patterson decided to hold out for the jets and thus deliberately gave the advantage to American. As it developed, the advantage was short-lived, since structural difficulties were encountered with the Electras, and they had to fly at reduced speeds for over a year.

By late 1955, jetliner development had proceeded to a point where airlines were ready to place their orders. The choice was between Douglas' DC-8 and the Boeing 707, both at about $5 million. Douglas had started from scratch in designing its DC-8's, while Boeing had evolved the 707 from the Boeing KC-135 military jet tanker, which had already flown thousands of hours. A prototype 707 was flying successfully in early 1955. This meant that the 707 would be available to the airlines a full year before the DC-8.

In October, 1955, Patterson and several of United's engineering and sales staff flew to Seattle to inspect the prototype 707. The group felt that the 707's cabin dimensions were too narrow to accommodate six abreast seating. Patterson asked Boeing if the company would change the cabin dimensions. Boeing engineers indicated that they could lengthen the cabin but not widen it.

The group then flew to Santa Monica, where they talked with Douglas engineers. The DC-8 was still on the drawing boards, and Douglas stated that they would redesign the cabin, making it three inches wider to accommodate six abreast seating in coach sections. The United staff then returned to Chicago to make a decision.

United felt that it wanted a jetliner for both first class patrons, seating four abreast, and coach passengers, seating six abreast. With coach traffic representing 25% of United's revenues, the company felt this was a particularly important consideration. On the other hand, there was Patterson's long-standing opposition to coach travel, and his further belief that six abreast seating might constitute a safety hazard, because it would prevent rapid evacuation.

Still another complicating factor was the relationship of Douglas to its competitors. If Douglas did not receive orders to manufacture a jetliner, it seemed reasonable to assume that the company would divorce itself from the commercial transport industry. Lockheed had already decided not to manufacture a commercial jet. This left only Boeing and Consolidated Vultee (Convair), and it had not been clear what Consolidated Vultee's objectives for the next few years would be.

As United was deliberating on its purchasing decision, President Juan Trippe of Pan American placed the industry's first order for a fleet of jetliners. He ordered the Boeing 707's. Patterson believed that Tripp's order would touch off a wave of jetliner orders by other airlines, and that United should make its decision immediately in order to obtain reasonably early delivery positions.

On October 25, United Air Lines surprised the entire air transport industry by announcing its decision to purchase 30 DC-8's. The purchase contract was signed November 3, 1955. Not long after, Boeing realized that it might be in serious difficulty if it did not widen the 707 fuselage. Therefore, it announced that the fuselage would be widened; and American, TWA, Continental, and National wasted no time in placing orders for 707's.

Late in 1957, American and TWA initiated transcontinental jet flights. Passengers flocked to the Boeing 707's, and United's DC-7 traffic dropped sharply. The company discontinued several of its DC-7 flights, and shunted them into shorter routes such as San Francisco to Denver, New York to Cleveland, and other routes where there was no jetliner competition. It was not until late September of 1959 that United began limited jet service with its newly delivered DC-8's.

In the original jet age planning, United and several other airlines felt that the jetliners would handle long hauls, while the DC-7's, DC-6's, and Convairs would handle the short haul traffic. As it developed, however, passengers preferred to ride in the jet planes, even for short hops, once jets became available. At the Los Angeles International Airport, for example, hundreds of potential customers waited at the gates hoping to catch a jet for San Francisco, while the DC-6's and DC-7's departed with seats to spare. Because of this, preparations for medium and short haul jets were stepped up at both Boeing and Douglas. United increased its order for 11 Boeing 720's to 18 in mid-1959. In addition, during 1960, the airline ordered 20 short range twin jet French Caravelles. Finally, late in 1960, Boeing evolved its 727 model, powered by three jets clustered about the tail.

Cruising at 550 miles per hour, the 727 was designed to carry up to 114 passengers and to operate from mile-long airstrips. On December 5, 1960, United ordered 40 Boeing 727's for delivery late in 1963.

In 1966, United continued its fleet expansion program. It was the first airline to put the 198 passenger Super DC-8 into service and, with outstanding orders for 25 additional "stretched-jets," it expected to fly more of these giant subsonic aircraft than any other airline. Additionally, United had placed orders for five Boeing 747's with a capacity of nearly 400 passengers, for delivery in 1970. The company had also reserved delivery positions for 12 supersonic jets—six Concordes and six Boeing SST's.

At year-end, 1966, United's fleet stood at 318, which included 126 propeller and turboprop aircraft. (These provided only 8.3% of United's available seat miles.) An all-jet fleet was not expected until 50 737's on order were received. Deliveries of the first three planes were expected in 1967.

Operating Emphasis

Throughout Mr. Patterson's 30 years at United's helm, the company was known as a "conservative" airline. Reflecting Mr. Patterson's own background in finance, the primary performance criterion was certainty and stability in earnings. Consequently, United maintained one of the industry's lowest debt to capital ratios, fought vigorously for rate stabilization and against increases in expensive customer services, was consistently slow in placing equipment replacement orders, and was the industry leader in fare increases with the introduction of new equipment.

United also was the industry leader in promoting air safety through equipment design and training of personnel. Less aggressive in passenger services or equipment introduction than American or TWA, United had been more active in soliciting freight business. However, in all major investment decisions, the company had followed a rather cautious path, choosing to wait as long as possible, often until data on markets and on customer preferences could be obtained from competitors' experience.

Mr. Patterson chose not to compete on the strenuous North Atlantic route or in Latin America. In the 1943 Annual Report he supported Pan American's "chosen instrument" position, saying:

> Instead of advocating a free-for-all rush of many domestic airlines into the international field, your management has proposed that one or more chosen instruments should represent this country, under private enterprise, in competing with foreign government-owned monopolies. Our factual studies have shown that even in the choice north Atlantic area there is likely to be a relatively narrow demand for air transportation. It is our considered view that, if more than one U.S. company is to participate in this country's share of north Atlantic business, higher public subsidy than otherwise would be necessary seems inevitable.

The eventual outcome of such an uneconomic system would be to reflect discredit on private enterprise and on the U.S. flag position in international air transportation.

In setting forth this company's views in a letter to the Civil Aeronautics Board, your president served notice that, if a policy of "wide open" competition is adopted by the Board, United will protect its position and prestige by filing applications for routes in both the Atlantic and the Pacific. This safeguard was deemed necessary in view of the fact that 16 domestic airlines and one U.S. flag foreign operator, with United Air Lines dissenting, recommended free and open worldwide air transport competition under private ownership and management. Your company believes implicitly in the competitive system but does not insist on all-out competition when it threatens financial solvency and the standing of U.S. flag aviation in the international field.

In 1949, a few airlines instituted coach-type service, and United began a never-ending battle against lower fares. The following statement appeared in the 1949 annual report:

> Your management has taken the position, while anything that encourages more people to fly may be constructive, a nationwide lowering of air fares at this time can be highly destructive. Our studies have indicated that coach service is unsound economically at this particular period, especially with a considerable number of operators competing for the coach passenger.

Because of competitive considerations, United reluctantly inaugurated air coach service on the Pacific Coast early in 1950. It was extended to transcontinental runs in 1951.

By 1953 coach service produced 21% of company revenue passenger miles, and United continued to oppose extension of this service.

As late as 1962, Mr. Patterson was still battling coach service:

> Financial results would have proved more satisfactory had they not been affected by the continued dilution of revenues through diversion of passengers to coach and the introduction of still more promotional and experimental fares which disregard economics.
>
> Although the burden of evidence shows that promotional fares of recent years have failed to produce the new traffic volumes required to offset price reductions—and indeed serve to draw away established customers from regular areas—these discounts came hard and fast in 1962. Though opposing such fares, the competitive situation compels your company to meet them when and where they occur.

Mr. Patterson's ultimate attack on coach fares was the introduction of "one-class service," priced somewhat below first class but above coach rate. His hopes that this plan "would put an end to the patchwork of fares and discounts" were thwarted when American and TWA, instead of following suit, merely reduced rates on existing first class services. As a consequence, United found itself forced into *three* services (Red, White, and Blue), in place of the original two.

In 1948, and again in 1957, United led the industry in attempting to get approval for fare increases to cover increasing costs. In both instances CAB sanction was given the fare increase, but American and TWA refused to up their rates. Instead, many discounts and "family plan" type arrangements were instituted, and net fares actually were decreased. United reluctantly matched competitive fares.

Mr. Patterson also tried to "retain sanity in the industry" by opposing "premature obsolescence of the DC-6," but was forced ultimately into operating DC-7's when American and TWA provided customers with nonstop transcontinental service (outside the range of the DC-6). Once into DC-7's, he chose to fly them for two years in competition with 707 jets, while he waited for "the ultimate airplane" (the DC-8). Similarly, for three years United deliberately gave up its commanding market share on the important San Francisco–Los Angeles route, refusing to match PSA's lower fares for piston planes, and unable to match other lines' jets until its own 727's could be delivered.

United originally opposed the serving of cocktails aloft, the introduction of gourmet meals, in-flight movies, and other high cost services, on the grounds that they were uneconomic. But in each instance, competitive pressures obliged them to follow suit.

Performance Record

Despite this deliberate conservatism, United's performance had been a creditable one. 1963 and 1964 were years of greatly increasing sales and profits, as equipment replacement, high load factors, and stable prices enabled United to operate its transcontinental "mainline" and its Hawaiian runs under very favorable conditions. In 1964, the return on investment [1] was 7.9%, compared with 5.7% in 1963. It reached 8.6% in 1965, but fell to 5.9% in 1966. This drop in earnings was largely attributed to the 43 day strike by the International Association of Machinists against United, Eastern, Pan American, National, and Northwest Airlines, tying up 60% of the nation's air traffic. As a result of the Capital merger, United in 1966 was the world's largest airline, with revenues of $857 million and net income of $38 million. It operated 318 aircraft, and boasted the industry's most extensive, efficient, and elaborate ground installations. Its operating unit costs were among the lowest in the industry. While its average load factor and

---

[1] The Civil Aeronautics Board had established as a guideline for rate regulation that airlines were entitled to a "fair and reasonable rate of return on investment" of 10.5%. The figure was calculated by dividing net profit after taxes plus interest paid by the airline's total investment. With the industry's highly leveraged position, this guideline allowed a return on equity which was somewhat higher than 10.5%. Exhibit 4 compares the airlines return on invested capital, but these calculations include depreciation in the numerator as well as earnings and interest charges.

return on investment had been consistently lower than American's or Pan American's, they were higher than for many other airlines. (See Exhibit 4 for comparison of these measures for the five airlines examined in this note.) Losses were recorded in only one postwar year (1948), and this was at a modest $1.1 million level. During the decade 1957–66, after tax earnings ranged between $4 million and $46 million, and averaged $18 million per year.

In 1963, Mr. Patterson became Chairman of the Board, and Mr. George E. Keck was made President.

AMERICAN AIRLINES

Early History

American's predecessor company was Aviation Corporation (AVCO), a holding company formed in 1928 to capitalize on market demand for aviation stocks. AVCO raised several million dollars, and bought a number of small airlines. Their operations ran into difficulties, and the company lost $3.4 million in 1930. In 1931, the various domestic transport lines of AVCO were consolidated as American Airways. In 1932, Mr. E. L. Cord gained control of AVCO and split the affairs of American Airways from all of AVCO's other activities.

With the cancellation and reinstallation of mail contracts in 1934, American Airways underwent organizational changes. The name was changed to American Airlines and a young Texan, C. R. Smith, was named president. Smith had been president of Southern Air Transport when it was acquired by AVCO in 1929. He was dedicated to the concept that passengers, rather than mail, offered the greatest future potential for the airlines.

Route Structure

The various companies which were combined into American Airways had a route structure for air mail which spanned from New York to Chicago, Tulsa, and Nashville. As part of the 1934 reassignment of air mail contracts, American was granted (along with TWA and United) the transcontinental Chicago to Los Angeles route as well. During the next three years, other intermediate cities were added, including St. Louis, Dallas, Cincinnati, Cleveland, Washington, and Boston. By 1937, American had become the leading U.S. airline in revenues, surpassing United. (This lead was maintained until the United–Capital merger in 1961.)

The route system expanded gradually to add major population centers in Texas, Arizona, Oklahoma, Arkansas, Tennessee, Kentucky, Ohio, West Virginia, Pennsylvania, and New York.

In 1944, American bid successfully for a North Atlantic international route. In the early postwar years, this route, operated by a subsidiary, American Overseas Airlines, showed losses of about $400,000 per year. Consequently, the line was sold to Pan American in 1947.

Subsequently American was successful in obtaining a Dallas–San Antonio–Mexico City route, as well as a direct Chicago–Mexico City route. The Mexico City terminal was, however, the only nondomestic segment in the entire American system.

In 1964, American and Eastern proposed a merger, but this was disapproved by the CAB. This combination would have been the world's largest airline and would have provided a very dense coverage of eastern population centers, in addition to the basic transcontinental route.

In 1966 American was one of 18 bidders for the certificate to serve Hawaii, Tokyo, and other Pacific points from the Mainland. No other important route applications were outstanding.

Equipment

The first major move made by Mr. Smith, as American's president, was the purchase of ten Convair "Condor" aircraft. These planes, entering service as sleepers in 1934, were slow, but safe, quiet, and comfortable. This first transcontinental sleeper service was very well received, and American began to cut deeply into United's previously exclusive territory.

In 1935, when United preempted the whole year's production of Boeing 247's, American joined with TWA to encourage Douglas to develop a competitive aircraft. The resulting DC-2 proved to be faster and more efficient than the Boeing 247, and American increased its market share at United's expense.

In early 1936, Mr. Smith contracted for enough newly developed DC-3's to re-equip the airline. He arranged a Reconstruction Finance Corporation loan to provide the necessary funds, at a time when other airlines were financing new equipment wholly out of equity.

American joined with United and others to help Douglas develop the four-engine DC-4. When the other companies withdrew from supporting the expanding development costs, United and American ended up with preferred delivery positions on the DC-4. Unfortunately, World War II prevented delivery of the DC-4, and American (like United) flew DC-3's throughout the war.

Following the war, as a substitute for the DC-3 in passenger service, American ordered 75 new Convair 240's at a price of around $225,000 each. (Fourteen years later these aircraft were sold second hand for more than the purchase price.) Smith favored equipment standardization and ordered DC-6's for his long haul routes, specifying that the same Pratt and Whitney engines which powered the Convairs be used.

When TWA brought out its Constellations in 1945, American, like United, was at a serious equipment disadvantage. American met this challenge by ordering DC-6B's and encouraging Douglas to begin development of the DC-7, a plane that could provide coast-to-coast nonstop service.

As DC-6B's were delivered, American proceeded to sell off and retire its DC-

3's. On short routes, the DC-6 could operate at nearly as low a unit cost as the DC-3 and at the same time provide much greater capacity. In a spectacular public relations move, Mr. Smith donated American's last DC-3 to the Smithsonian Institution's national museum, while other airlines continued to use these aircraft as their basic equipment.

Mr. Smith had always been customer oriented. Even though the DC-6 was a very economical aircraft, it could not fly across the U.S. nonstop. Knowing what a great advantage a nonstop flight would give the carrier, Smith persuaded Douglas to build the DC-7, a propeller-driven aircraft that could cross the continent nonstop, and within an eight hour crew shift. Although Douglas had hoped to go directly with the DC-6 to a jet aircraft, it reluctantly delivered the DC-7 to American for service in late 1953. This scheduling advantage enabled American to cut deeply into its competitors' shares of the transcontinental market.

Introduction of the DC-7 created labor problems when the westbound flight (against headwinds) took more than eight hours elapsed time. ALPA protested this extension of working hours, but the CAB upheld the company and allowed the domestic eight hour flight limit to be extended to ten hours for transcontinental flights. ALPA took the case to court, protesting that the CAB was not sufficiently concerned about safety. In the course of the controversy, ALPA went on strike against American Airlines for a three week period. Ultimately, an agreement was reached which permitted nonstop flights between New York and Los Angeles, even when the elapsed time exceeded eight hours.

Believing jets were still some years away, American moved in 1955 to replace some of its DC-7 fleet with the much faster, quieter Lockheed Electras. Although these airplanes were well received at their introduction, crashes and subsequent speed restrictions made them more of a liability than an asset.

By late 1955, American was prepared to make its commitments to purchase jet aircraft. Past history had bound the company more closely to Douglas than Boeing, where United had the preferred position. When United elected to buy the Douglas DC-8, American moved quickly to order a fleet of Boeing 707's. Receipt of these jets in 1957 gave American an important edge over United until late 1959, when the DC-8's were finally delivered. Even then, 707's were faster and easier to service.

During the mid-1960's, American continued an aggressive pattern of jet airplane acquisitions. At the end of 1966, the company had 88 planes on order, costing an anticipated $761 million. This included ten Boeing 747's, each priced at $26 million, but not expected to be in service until 1970.

Operating Emphasis

Mr. Smith consistently stressed customer convenience and service. As he said in the mid-1930's, "There's really no difference between selling an airline ticket and a box of Post Toasties." In each case, it was a matter of serving consumer needs and wants.

In the early 1930's, the company began to experiment with various credit programs (fly now, pay later) and was an industry leader in supporting the Air Credit Card plan and other ways of increasing air travel through ease of payment.

As the major focus of its advertising program, American directly challenged the passenger's fear of flying. This aggressive advertising and sales promotion program which emphasized the safety of air travel was credited with the major impetus in increasing passenger revenues by 330% between 1933 and 1937, as compared with an average of 175% for the other lines.

American consistently led the industry in innovations in improved customer services. Along with TWA, it always led in instituting price reductions and in resisting proposed price increases. American pioneered special lounges for important customers (the Admiral's Club), gourmet meals aloft, coach flights, and special coach services (the "Royal Coachman").

Additionally, American had always been an equipment leader, whenever the new equipment provided improved customer service (speed, comfort, economy, etc.). Moreover, it had become an important air-cargo carrier (third largest after Pan American and Flying Tiger in 1966), being the first airline to file official air freight tariffs (in 1945).

Performance

Although United's 1961 merger with Capital put United's sales volume ahead of American's for the first time in 23 years, American continued to outperform United in earnings, passenger load factor, and return on investment. During the 1957–66 period, American's earnings fluctuated between $7 million and $52 million, with an average of $22 million per year (as compared with United's $18 million). Return on investment averaged around 9% from 1964 through 1966 as compared with about 7% for United. In 1966, the company stood in an exceedingly strong position relative to the quality of its aircraft fleet, its ground facilities, and its reputation with customers. Its operating costs were relatively low, its load factors were relatively high, and its fleet was one of the newest and most modern in the industry.

During World War II, Mr. Smith served as deputy commander of the U.S. Air Transport Command. During his wartime absence, Ralph Damon served as president. When Mr. Smith returned, he became Chairman. But a 1948 dispute with Mr. Damon led to Mr. Damon's resignation from American and subsequent election as president of TWA. In 1964, Marion Sadler became president, and Mr. Smith again moved up as Chairman.

TRANS WORLD AIRLINES

Early History

Trans World Airlines (TWA) began as Transcontinental Air Transport, which was formed in 1928 as a passenger airline. Cooperating with the Pennsylvania and Santa Fe Railroads, it provided combination passenger service between New York and Los Angeles (air by day, rail by night).

In 1932 General Motors acquired control of North American Aviation Company. This company, which had purchased ownership of Eastern Air Transport (predecessor to Eastern Airlines) in 1929, bought Transcontinental (which had merged with Western Air Express) in 1933.

The 1934 air mail contract cancellation and industry shakeup divided the combine into three separate entities: North American, an aircraft manufacturing company; Eastern; and TWA (then Transcontinental & Western Air). Control of this small, fledgling, West Coast line passed to a young pilot, Jack Frye. Frye retained his pilot's view of the line's activities, occasionally captaining scheduled flights for a number of years after becoming president.

In order to pursue his ambitious plans for the airline, Frye sought additional capital from his flying friend, Howard Hughes. Hughes, who had inherited a large fortune based on the Hughes Tool Company (producers of the universally-used rotary oil well drilling bits), was strongly interested in aviation. He piloted "hot ships" in racing competition, was active in aircraft design, and was a frequent sponsor of air shows and exhibitions. Hughes' investments in TWA were gradually increased over the years. He acquired a majority interest in 1939, but, in 1966, his Hughes Tool Company sold its 78% interest in TWA common stock for $566.3 million cash.

Route Structure

TWA's original route was the New York–Los Angeles run. In 1934, following the reassignment of air mail contracts, it added the Chicago–San Francisco leg. Subsequently population centers in the Southwest and in the East were added to augment the main transcontinental route. Kansas City became a central hub around which other routes were added.

During World War II, TWA was called upon to fly men and material to the combat zones and to assist in the formation of the Air Transport Command. Because of its experience in flying for the military during the war, TWA was in an excellent position to be awarded the commercial overseas routes for which it applied. In 1945, TWA was awarded routes across the North Atlantic, extending as far east as Bombay, Bangkok, Manila, Shanghai, and Hong Kong.

It was not until 1966 that TWA commenced service as far east as Hong Kong. Also in 1966, TWA obtained landing rights in Eastern Africa and filed for routes serving the Pacific region. As of 1966, TWA was the only scheduled U.S. carrier with both major domestic routes and routes to Europe.

Equipment

Frye and Hughes took special interest in the type of aircraft flown by TWA. They were continually working on aircraft design to bring out the most advanced aircraft.

After equipping the line with DC-2's in 1934–35, following United's tying up of the Boeing 247, TWA joined the rest of the industry in purchasing DC-3's.

In the late 1930's, Hughes and Frye decided that they could achieve a substantial competitive advantage by pioneering an entirely new type of aircraft. They made arrangements with Boeing to build the Stratoliner—the first four-engine commercial land transport. TWA acquired five Stratoliners in 1940, and was thus able to inaugurate the first one-stop coast to coast service, while its competitors (flying DC-3's) were forced to make several en route fuel stops.

TWA made many technical advances under the leadership of Hughes and Frye. For example, the company's Stratoliners were the first pressurized aircraft in commercial service. This allowed them to fly over poor weather conditions and provide passengers with superior service.

Hughes' interest in the airline was intermittent. While he did not concern himself with day-to-day operational problems of the airline, he was greatly interested in the airline's planes, their radio equipment, and other technical devices. After the Stratoliner, Hughes and Frye sought to obtain a plane that would be technically very advanced. Accordingly, they made secret arrangements with Lockheed for the production of the Constellation. Hughes personally wrote a check for the down payment (reputedly $1 million), and the Board of Directors was not told of the decision for many months, for fear that it would "leak" to the competition. The Hughes-Fry plan to scoop the industry might well have succeeded, but World War II disrupted the plans. Instead of being able to build the Constellation on schedule, Lockheed was diverted to war work. When the Constellations were finally available for commercial service on TWA in 1945, competing carriers were able to buy war surplus DC-4's. The Constellation was a faster, longer range, and more comfortable aircraft than the DC-4, and gave TWA a substantial advantage, but this tended to be reduced by the early development of the DC-6B.

In 1946, when all of the airlines were taking delivery on substantial numbers of four-engine equipment, the Air Line Pilots Association sought higher rates of pay for flying the four-engine planes than they had received for flying the DC-3's. The airline industry took the position that pilots should be paid the same amount of money for flying the larger planes. An industry-wide negotiating committee was formed, headed by Ralph Damon, then president of American Airlines. ALPA selected TWA as the battlefront in this issue. In 1946, TWA was struck by ALPA. Many of TWA's pilots believed that the strike was caused, at least in part, by the fact that TWA's management had lost touch with their pilots.

The strike added to TWA's mounting financial problems. A substantial amount of traffic was diverted to American and United during the strike, and TWA's poststrike recovery was slow. Large numbers of pilots were furloughed (laid off), and morale suffered.

In 1948, Frye left TWA, and the line operated without a president for several months. When C. R. Smith and Ralph Damon had a dispute, Damon resigned as president of American and moved over to head TWA. He inherited many problems: the line was underequipped and underfinanced, and employees' morale was low. Damon's problems were made more difficult because of Hughes' interest in new aircraft. Hughes made many decisions concerning the type and number of new aircraft to be acquired, and these decisions did not always coincide with those that Damon would have made himself. During this period, TWA bought successive models of the Lockheed Constellation, while their major competitors bought DC-4's, DC-6's, DC-6B's, and DC-7's. TWA suffered some competitive disadvantage during the latter part of this period because the Constellations were somewhat slower than the DC-7's in long-range flight, while their operating costs were higher than the DC-6B's in shorter-range operations.

Damon died of a heart attack in 1955. After an interregnum lasting several months, Carter Burgess became president of the line. Burgess made preliminary plans for the operation of jet equipment, but did not remain long enough to see them in operation. He resigned 11 months after taking on the presidency—without ever meeting Hughes or talking with him in person.

Burgess was succeeded by Charles Thomas during a period in which TWA was definitely behind its major competitors in virtually every respect. Thomas followed plans that had been set in motion by Burgess and managed to get some jet equipment in operation. Through a series of intricate financial transactions, TWA managed to order 33 Boeing 707's, 30 Convair 880's, and 13 Convair 990's. (The 990 order was later cancelled.)

Thomas left TWA after serving as president for about two years. Following his departure, a consortium of insurance companies and banks agreed to finance TWA's future purchases of jet equipment on the provision that Hughes give up operating control. An elaborate agreement was worked out whereby Hughes' stock was put in a voting trust and the management of TWA had to be approved by the financial interests. Under this arrangement, Hughes Tool Company had the right to name one trustee while the financial institutions named the other two. Hughes, under severe pressure, reluctantly agreed to these provisions as necessary for the company's massive re-equipment requirements. Ernest Breech, former president of the Ford Motor Company, became Chairman of the Board of TWA. He hired Charles Tillinghast, Jr., as president in 1962.

The financial institutions involved in the trust agreement later sued Hughes, alleging that he had used his influence improperly in the purchase of airplanes; that he had permitted the company to buy only such planes as he had personally purchased; and that he had required the airline to purchase all of its planes from Hughes Tool Company. As of April, 1966, no final disposition of the case had yet been made by the courts.

TWA made dramatic progress under Tillinghast's direction. In 1962, the company did not earn enough to make interest payments on its $6\frac{1}{2}\%$ subordinated convertible debentures. But by 1966, the line was highly profitable. Its stock sold as high as $101 per share and the first cash dividend in 30 years was declared. A few years previously, the stock had sold for as little as $9. The sharp rise in the share price had been attributed not only to improved performance, but also to the anticipated benefits of management autonomy following the 1966 divestiture of TWA shares by Hughes Tool Company. In 1966 the company continued expansion of its fleet by placing an order for $410 million worth of equipment, including

12 Boeing 747's. At the end of 1966, TWA had a fleet of 159 aircraft (17 of which were piston) and had an additional 75 jets on order.

Competitive Emphasis

Throughout its formative years, TWA's major emphasis was on obtaining and flying new, advanced aircraft. During this period, the company prospered and grew rapidly along with the rest of the industry.

After Frye's resignation in 1948, the company was in a virtual hiatus for nearly 14 years. Leadership was uncertain, and policies were unclear. Nonetheless, the company's operating efficiency and momentum were sufficient to enable TWA to survive this period, and even to show profits during some years.

The strength of the operating organization was amply demonstrated as soon as Hughes influence was removed and the leadership situation stabilized.

During the 1960's, the emphasis began to shift to increased customer awareness. TWA actively supported the development of supplemental helicopter service (costing TWA $2.5 million between June, 1965, and June, 1966). The company had entered into an agreement with Piper TWINAIR to "provide commuter air transport between numerous smaller, outlying communities and the major airports of 15 key U.S. and European cities." The company continued to promote reduced fares for youth and excursions. More nonstop service was added, including every hour transcontinental scheduling.

In late 1966, TWA submitted a merger plan with Hilton International Company, owner of 36 Hilton hotels outside the continental U.S.A. Hilton International had 1966 revenues of $47 million and owned and/or operated more than 12,000 rooms in 24 countries plus Hawaii, Puerto Rico, and the Virgin Islands.

EASTERN AIR LINES

Early History

Eastern Air Transport was formed in 1926, and began business with the awarding of the New York to Miami air mail route. In 1929, the company was acquired by North American Aviation. When General Motors acquired control of North American Aviation in 1932, Edward V. Rickenbacker was appointed general manager of Eastern. Rickenbacker was one of the U.S.'s most famous World War I heroes. The leading "ace" in the Hat in the Ring Squadron, he was a glamorous figure and a Congressional Medal of Honor winner.

Eastern had been losing money, and most of its equipment was antiquated, but after two years of hard effort, Rickenbacker succeeded in putting the company into the black. In 1935, Eastern earned $90,000.

Following the cancellation of the air mail contracts in 1934, Eastern was set up autonomously and regained its former North–South routes along the eastern seaboard.

In 1938, General Motors sold Eastern for $4.4 million to a syndicate consisting of Smith, Barney & Co., Laurence Rockefeller, Rickenbacker, and several others.

Route Structure

The original New York–Miami mail route was elaborated over the years with the addition of a large number of intermediate routes in Pennsylvania, Virginia, North Carolina, Georgia, Tennessee, and Florida. Ultimately, the system was expanded northward to Boston, Montreal, and Toronto, westward to Cleveland, Detroit, Chicago, Minneapolis, and St. Louis, and southward to New Orleans and parts of Texas. From headquarters in New York, the line blanketed the densely populated eastern half of the U.S.

Following World War II, Eastern was caught up in the enthusiasm for international expansion. The company bid for a route from Miami to Brazil and across the South Atlantic to Africa. But, after reconsidering the cost, Rickenbacker withdrew the application. Braniff was subsequently awarded the route.

Eastern then applied for, and received, routes from New York to Bermuda, from New York, Washington, and Miami to Puerto Rico, and from New Orleans to Mexico City and Acapulco. These routes, plus Toronto, Ottowa, and Montreal service, represented Eastern's only international flights.

During most of its early years, Eastern faced only limited competition on most of its routes, especially the high density, long haul New York to Miami and New York to San Juan routes. In 1961, Eastern improved its structure by transferring a number of small, upstate New York routes to Mowhawk.

Equipment Decisions

Like most of the other major lines, Eastern's prewar equipment was primarily DC-2's, then DC-3's. Following World War II, Rickenbacker was able to obtain Constellations, after TWA had equipped its fleet, and invested heavily in this aircraft.

Eastern used the Constellation for its long-haul flights until late in the 1950's. DC-7's were added to the fleet in substantial numbers, and Eastern was the leading purchaser of the Lockheed Electra. Eastern expected to be able to serve its routes very efficiently with these fast (400 mph), comfortable aircraft, beating its competition, who were flying DC-7's. Consequently, Rickenbacker felt that he could delay delivery of pure jets and elected to order the Douglas DC-8 for 1959 service.

The unfortunate structural problems of the Electra forced Eastern to fly them at reduced speed during the period when they had anticipated their major advantage. By the time these aircraft had been modified and approved for 400 mph travel, National Airlines was flying 707's on the Miami run. It was a full year later before Eastern was able to compete on an even basis with its new DC-8's.

As of 1961, Eastern was still modifying its fleet of 40 "Super Electras," as well as flying some 40 DC-7B's. It had received 14 DC-8's, and was converting its Constellations into cargo liners and air shuttle planes.

The air shuttle service offered regularly scheduled air transportation at fares lower than the cost of travel by highway bus or the family automobile. This service was instituted on a trial basis between Miami and Pittsburgh, Cleveland and St. Louis; it introduced simplified theater-type ticketing and eliminated the costs of baggage checking, meal service, and other "extras." Load factors were encouraging: 9% of customers using the air shuttle had never used airline service before, a figure three times as high as that registered on Eastern's regular first class and air coach services. Furthermore, some 22% had previously driven their cars to Florida, and over one-third were converted to flying by the low rates offered.

To further develop a larger volume of air travelers, Eastern introduced other "no-frill" services on major high-density routes, using piston-engine equipment, doing away with reservations, and cutting ticketing and baggage-handling costs to the minimum.

By 1964, Eastern was well on its way to retiring piston aircraft in favor of jets. Subsequently equipment purchases were made for additional DC-8B's, and for Boeing 720's and 727's. But Super Electras continued to make up an important part of the company's fleet.

Competitive Emphasis

From the very beginning, "Captain Eddie" focussed his attention on economy and efficiency in operations. For years, Eastern had the lowest operating costs, and the highest percentage of on-time arrivals of any major airline. These were the major criteria by which Rickenbacker evaluated his organization.

Many travelers contended that courteous, thoughtful customer service was not high on Eastern's list of priorities. Although the line's safety record and schedule performance were good, many customers resented the brusque, impersonal treatment they received. It was sometimes said that "Captain Eddie ran the airline for the convenience of the pilots," i.e., that the interests of the employees were put ahead of passenger satisfaction. As one former Eastern executive stated, "Oh, I know we used to treat the passengers badly, but we made money every year."

So long as Eastern's competition was limited—particularly on its key routes— this undivided attention to minimizing operating costs, regardless of customer inconvenience, enabled the company to show one of the best profitability records in the industry. For example, in the period 1953 to 1957, Eastern's aggregate profits of $52.4 million equalled United's, despite Eastern's smaller size.

However, beginning in 1958, increased competition began to be felt. Customer hostility had increased, and alternative service was available. Passenger revenues in 1958 and 1959 were affected by the adverse publicity on the Electras. And, in 1960, National Airline's 707 jets cut deeply into Eastern's Miami market, which was still served by Electras and DC-7B's. In 1960 the company reported its first loss in 26 years.

In the face of these difficulties, Rickenbacker agreed to become Chairman, and turn over operating responsibilities to a new president. Laurence Rockefeller selected Malcolm MacIntyre, who took over during 1960. MacIntyre immediately moved to establish a new public image, to improve passenger service, and to equip Eastern with new jets as soon as possible. He reorganized the airline from top to bottom, changed schedules, and instituted air shuttle service between Boston, New York, and Washington. These flights left every hour from these cities and required no reservations.

In spite of the success of MacIntyre's innovations, Eastern continued to have financial difficulties. The cost of re-equipping and reorganizing the company was heavy, and 1960's loss of $3.6 million expanded to $9.6 million in 1961 and to $13.3 million in 1962.

Conditions became aggravated as an oversupply of airplane space became available on Eastern's routes, as both Eastern and competitors added new equipment. When 1963 losses hit an astronomical $37.8 million, both Rickenbacker and McIntyre resigned.

Floyd Hall, who had been TWA's general manager, was elected president. His strenuous attempts to woo customers back to the airline began to bear fruit. At the same time, the increase in air travel (without much increase in aircraft availability) began to improve Eastern's low load factor. Despite a record year for United, American, and TWA, 1964 brought a $12 million loss to Eastern. But, by 1965, Hall's "new look" had enabled Eastern to return solidly into the black, showing a whopping profit of $29 million, or a return on equity of 24%. In 1966, profits fell to $14.7 million, but management attributed this decline to the 43 day airline strike against Eastern and four of its competitors. In fact, management felt that Eastern had continued its rapid improvement in its competitive position.

The fleet had been expanded to 191 aircraft, 100 of which were pure jet. Eighty per cent of available passenger miles had been provided in pure jet equipment in 1966. This fleet expansion had enabled Eastern to upgrade its air shuttle service almost entirely to Boeing 727 and Douglas DC-9 equipment. To improve the distribution of passenger demand, the company had introduced special prices for off-peak hours.

Whereas Eastern had previously neglected air cargo, in 1966 the company entered this growing business. New 727 aircraft were being delivered with "Quick Change" capability which allowed freight to be carried at night and passengers during the daytime.

In 1966, Eastern acquired Mackey Airlines, thus expanding its route structure to provide service to the Bahamas. It also filed for route expansion westward to Hawaii and the Pacific region.

During the same year, the company also acquired Remmert-Werner, Inc., which held the worldwide sales franchise for North American Aviation's Sabreliner business jet. This 560 mile per hour plane had been the most widely used executive jet in the world.

PAN AMERICAN AIRWAYS

Early History

Pan American was formed in 1927 by Juan Trippe and a group of New York bankers to fly the 90 mile mail run between Miami and Havana. Shortly thereafter, Trippe began obtaining flying permits from the governments of other Latin American countries, throughout the Caribbean.

Once the Caribbean routes were well established, Trippe expanded the company southward into South America. He conceived of Pan Am's operations as not only an essential service, but also as an expression of U.S. foreign economic policy. He felt that the United States government should sanction a single international airline—a "chosen instrument"—which could represent the U.S. abroad by providing service, while remaining a private capitalistic enterprise.

Trippe chose flying boats, rather than land planes, to operate between coastal South American cities. He felt it was much easier to find a sheltered harbor near a city than to carve a runway out of the jungle. He also believed that the flying boats would be safer for overwater flights. Beginning with Sikorsky's S-38's in 1928, Pan Am re-equipped with Consolidated Commodores and Sikorsky's S-42's in 1930 and 1934.

Since no existing aircraft were capable of flying the great transoceanic distances to which Trippe aspired, Pan Am sponsored development of the famous "China Clipper" flying boats designed by Igor Sikorsky and built by Martin. With a plane capable of crossing the oceans, Trippe opened negotiations with the French and British for trans-Atlantic service. Negotiations were slow, however, and Trippe turned to the Pacific while the State Department continued talks with the Europeans.

In the Pacific, Trippe sought the route from San Francisco to the Philippines via Hawaii. Government approval came swiftly, and in 1935 the 25 ton Martin M-130 China Clipper made her first trip from San Francisco to Manila. Carrying 32 passengers, the Clipper traveled the 7,000 miles across the Pacific in 60 hours of flying time on a trip that took six days elapsed time. (Even in 1966 the trip by surface vessel took several weeks.)

In 1935 the State Department reached an agreement with the U.K. providing for twice-weekly service between the U.S. and England, to be shared by American and British airlines for 15 years. However, it was not until 1939 that Pan Am's first Boeing 314 four engine, the "Yankee Clipper," began trans-Atlantic service to England.

In the early 1940's it became obvious to Trippe that several carriers would be in a position to bid for international routes. He fought with every means at his disposal to prevent this. He believed firmly in his "chosen instrument" theory, and he personally crusaded to convince the industry and the government that there was not enough international traffic available to support more than one U.S. airline.

Trippe's efforts to prevent international competition were unsuccessful, and several other airlines were granted certificates to operate overseas following World War II. Pan Am's reaction was two-fold. The company cut its fares in 1948, and it sought vigorously, but unsuccessfully, to obtain domestic routes.

Routes

Each year, Pan Am expanded its overseas route structure: Caribbean, South American, and trans-Pacific route systems were developed around the original key routes; trans-Atlantic routes expanded rapidly in the postwar era. By 1960, Pan Am was flying all around the world.

Even in the mid-1960's, new routes were added: Morocco, Yugoslavia, Czechoslovakia, Tahiti, and other key destinations were opened up; more intercity pairs were added. At the same time, some routes were turned over to other carriers—e.g., Alaskan intrastate operations were sold to Wien Alaska Airlines, and, in 1966, Pan Am's 50% interest in Panagra was sold to Braniff.

As international air travel grew, Pan Am participated fully in the expanded market. During the late 1940's and throughout the 1950's, Pan Am carried one out of every four people traveling to and from the United States, including people traveling by sea.

In 1953, Pan American began to diversify somewhat, obtaining the prime contract from the U.S. Air Force for the management and operation of the Cape Canaveral Missile Test Center and Atlantic Missile Range. By 1963, Pan Am had over 6,000 employees engaged in activities at Cape Kennedy.

Intercontinental Hotels Corporation, a Pan Am subsidiary, was established in 1945 to build and operate hotels at destination cities. By 1966, 39 such hotels were in operation.

During the early 1960's Pan Am was still actively seeking entry into the domestic market. The company developed strong ties with National Airlines, which grew to a point where each airline held substantial amounts of stock in the other, and the two companies used each other's aircraft. However, the CAB stepped in and ordered each airline to divest itself of the other's stock by 1964.

Following this, in 1962, Pan Am concluded a merger agreement with TWA, and submitted the proposal to the CAB. After 11 months without any CAB action, and with a decision in the near future, TWA and Pan Am called the deal off. The intent was to create a single U.S. flag transatlantic carrier (as well as to provide Pan Am with domestic routes). Even though TWA was in financial difficulty, the CAB was reluctant to create a combined domestic-international air carrier of such potentially dominant size.

With the growth of strong competitors such as Air France, British Overseas Airways Corporation (BOAC), Japan Airlines, Royal Dutch Airlines (KLM), and Scandinavian Airlines System (SAS), Pan American was faced with increasing competition in the late 1950's and early 1960's. Significant inroads were being made in the U.S. share of international air transport, and Trippe still supported his "chosen instrument" concept for a single U.S. flag overseas airline.

Equipment

Beginning in 1939, Pan Am began to shift from flying boats to conventional four-engine aircraft. It adopted the Boeing 314 in 1939, and the Boeing 307 in 1940. After World War II, Pan Am re-equipped the line with DC-4's and Constellations in 1945 and 1946. A major re-equipment change was made in 1952, with the introduction of the DC-6. This aircraft served until the advent of the DC-7 in 1955.

Pan Am was the first American carrier to order the Boeing 707, and thus became the first U.S. airline to fly jets (1958). The fleet was rounded out with additional 707's and with DC-8's.

In 1963, Pan Am became the first carrier to order a supersonic transport by making a down payment on six British-French Concordes, and on 15 SST's being developed under the auspices of the U.S. Government. These aircraft were expected to be delivered by 1970, and to fly at 1,800 miles per hour. In 1966, Pan Am concluded negotiations that resulted in the Boeing 747 program and an initial $600 million order for 25 planes. The first 747 service was expected to be launched by Pan Am in September of 1969.

Competitive Emphasis

Pan Am had vigorously cut fares and provided customer services, had continuously reduced unit operating costs, and had been a leader in aircraft development and acquisition. It had been a major force in cargo development, and by 1966 was the leading U.S. air cargo carrier.

Pan Am pioneered international economy class fares and had been a consistent force for increased service and lower fares on the trans-Atlantic routes. It had for several years been the only company in the industry to diversify—into missile site management, hotel management, and even the sale and service of business jets. Like TWA, Pan Am had been a leader in the support of helicopter connecting services and had arranged and underwritten the service by New York Airways (29% owned by Pan Am) between the Pan Am building in downtown Manhattan and the Pan Am terminal at the Kennedy International Airport. These diversified activities had grown to the extent that, by 1966, annual dollar volume (including these activities) exceeded $1 billion.

Nonetheless, the company's principal emphasis had been consistently tied with the "chosen instrument" theme of being the U.S. representative abroad. Route structure had been assiduously developed and vigorously pursued. As the major U.S. overseas operator, Pan Am had built a volume greater than any other international line. 1966 airline sales exceeded $840 million, and earnings reached $83.7 million.

chapter 6

Evaluating

Past Performance and

Present Strategic Posture

In Chapter 5 we indicated in detail the data (and their sources) necessary for identifying, describing, and explaining a company's actual strategic posture. In this chapter, we present a similarly detailed checklist for a rigorous evaluation of past performance and for evaluation of future appropriateness of the present strategic posture.

Rational evaluation requires: (a) *parameters* along which to measure performance; (b) *criteria* as to what constitutes "adequate," "excellent," or "poor" performance on each of these dimensions; and (c) some relative *weighting* of the separate ratings of the various parameters in arriving at an overall judgment.

In Chapters 3 and 4 we indicated four basic parameters (performance specifications) along which we could *measure* past company performance. These were:

1. Present size and historical rate of growth (expressed in terms of sales volume, assets, net worth, or number of employees).
2. Present market share and historical rate of change in market penetration (expressed as a percentage of total unit or dollar sales of like products or services within a specific customer category—e.g., a specific industry, geographical area, or end use market).

3. Present level of profitability and historical trends in the risk-reward tradeoff (expressed in absolute monetary units, as a percentage return on investment, or in earnings per share of the company's stock).
4. Survival capacity (expressed in terms of capital availability, breadth of owner-ship, depth in management).

In evaluating past performance, numerical values can be assigned for each historical period along each of the four performance specifications. The company's record along each of these four parameters can then be compared with:

1. Management's stated targets (or budgets).
2. The company's own past performance.
3. The record of competitors.
4. Probable results of liquidation and redeployment.

Let us look at each of these in turn.

CRITERIA FOR EVALUATING PAST PERFORMANCE

Management's Stated Targets

In evaluating company performance, we must not apply some arbitrary, external standards which may or may not be applicable in the specific situation. Of first importance is what the company's top management wants to achieve. To the degree that these objectives can be translated into operational targets and articulated to the organization, they provide the fundamental standards against which actual performance should be measured.

A company *deliberately* kept small by its management so that they can maintain close personal control over operations should not be evaluated poorly on the parameter of size and rate of growth. Similarly, a company whose management *deliberately* chooses to keep the full complement employed during a sales down turn should not be faulted for the consequent effect upon current profits. Rather, company performance should be assessed in terms of how well these stated targets were achieved.

Most companies have annual budgets which define at least some kind of size objective and profitability target. Comparing actual performance against these targets, if they are thoughtfully constructed, provides a first order generalization of company "success." Use of arbitrary budget figures or mere historical extrapolations of the past, may prove more an indictment of management's way of thinking than a measure of company performance. Thus, the more specific and realistic top management can be in setting performance specifications, the better the opportunity for evaluating that performance effectively.

We ended Chapter 5 with a discussion of the *actual* choice criteria emphasized by key management personnel in their strategic decisions. These actual criteria are frequently implicit and unrecognized, and are often very different from top management's *stated* criteria. To the degree that differences exist, management is either unaware of "what's really going on" or fooling itself about its true objectives.

Part of the problem may result from confusion or disagreement about *what* is being measured (performance specifications). But much of it centers in actual differences among key management members in time horizon, attitudes toward risk and change, and functional orientation. If explicit attention is not given to balancing the tradeoffs among these differing viewpoints, the company's strategy becomes set by default—the strongest and most aggressive members of management attract the choice criteria in their direction.

These "unofficial" choice criteria are rarely articulated and frequently become both a deterrent to employee initiative and a source of widespread frustration and irritation. People don't know "what's expected" of them or "where the company is headed." Some who otherwise might contribute extensively are reluctant to stick their necks out. Those who do try to contribute often encounter unanticipated, hidden power blocs.

Thus, assessment of the company's over-all situation inevitably involves an evaluation of top management itself. The extent of management's competence and sensitivity can be determined by the answers to such questions as follows.

How accurate has top management been in appraising the company's situation and requirements? How realistic have they been in their past estimates of future possibilities? How appropriate to their resources and competitive situation are their capital and physical deployments? To what degree is management limited in their viewpoints by tradition or preconception? Are they flexible enough to assign different emphases to key criteria in each fresh situation?

Are they sufficiently skilled to carry out all major functions satisfactorily? How well are they able to work together for the good of the entire enterprise? What appears to be the relative influence in corporate decisions of the various functions —Marketing? Manufacturing? Engineering? Research and development? Finance? How does this relative balance of power match the needs of the company's competitive situation? How compatible are the personal goals of the various members of management with the performance required of them under present conditions?

What do the chief executive's past performance, plans, and statements, and the evaluations of his associates reveal about his major strengths and weaknesses? Do other members of management possess adequate complementary skills to maintain organizational balance and flexibility? How does his perception of his job match the present leadership requirements of the organization? How appropriate are the criteria by which he evaluates the performance of his associates and the performance of the total company? How aware is he of the power relationships that actually exist and of the balance of power which is most appropriate for carrying out present strategy effectively? To what extent is he perceived as supportive or predictable by his subordinates? Is he aware of his own personal needs (control, perpetuation, growth) and how they affect the scope and nature of company operations? How accurate are his perceptions of how his associates regard him? To what degree is he aware of the effects of his behavior on their performance?

Own Past Performance

At first glance, this second set of measurements is much more straightforward, involving simple comparison of present achievements along each of the four performance parameters with the company's historical record. But evaluation cannot stop there. It is not sufficient to know that the company's market share is shrinking or that its earning power is growing. To be effective in governing future company activities, we must also know why these results are occurring. Hence it is important for us to address such detailed questions as the following.

Financial record. Is the company presently making money? What has been the pattern of its earnings trend? How strong is its present financial condition? Is it getting stronger or weaker? How adequately is it generating the funds to meet its cash outlay requirements? What is its credit availability? How accessible is new equity capital, if and when needed?

Market record. Is this company a leader in its industry? Average? A marginal producer? How do its products or services compare with its competitors'? How has it defined its market(s)? What is its market share? Is this share growing? Declining? Static? What appears to be determining this trend? How strong is the company's hold on present customers? On what does this seem to depend? How strong is the company in the skills and attributes which are particularly critical in this market? What is its reputation with: Customers? Suppliers? Bankers? Labor? Governmental agencies? Competition? The general public?

Physical facilities. How is the company situated relative to its raw materials? Its market? In what condition are its plant(s) and equipment? How do its operating costs compare with competition? In what special manufacturing skills is the company especially strong? How flexible are the facilities? To what other uses can they be put economically? To what extent do present operations utilize potential capacity? What is the approximate break-even point? How does this compare with competition?

External pressures. Are community conditions or governmental activities presently restricting company activities? To what extent do the attitudes of the owners place limits on what can be done? To what degree do well-established traditions or well-entrenched personnel circumscribe the action alternatives? To what extent is labor activity a limiting factor? How rapid are the changes taking place in process technology, product obsolescence, and market buying characteristics? To what degree are substitute products or processes significant?

Answers to questions such as these give us a good basis for evaluating our subject company relative to its own historical performance pattern.

Competitors' Records

Frequently the relative prosperity or poverty of a company is rooted in broad factors which pervade the entire industry. Within the industry, however, there are usually dramatic differences in individual companies' performances. The case data on the five major U.S. airlines provide excellent opportunities for the student to differentiate one company from another in terms of strategic commitments and to evaluate their respective performances.

In addition to the earlier questions about market share, relative costs, and other individual company items, it is also important to assess the entire industry's situation.

Industry trends. Are the markets the industry serves growing? Static? Declining? What has been the pattern of productive capacity, unit and dollar sales, unit prices, and industry earnings over an extended time period? To what extent must markets, raw material supply, or manufacturing facilities be viewed locally, nationally, or internationally? To what extent do other industries offer substitute products or services? In what stage of the product life cycle is each of the company's major product categories?

Present basis for success in this industry. What job functions require particularly competent performance? What characteristics are essential in the products or services offered? To what degree is profitability or stability predicated on: Personal relationships? Product availability and convenience? Marketing services? Manufacturing skill or efficiency? Product design and innovation? Raw material or patent ownership? Massive availability of capital? What are the relative costs of labor, raw materials, capital, distribution, and transportation? Which of these are the most variable? The most crucial?

Once we have gained this kind of understanding of the industry, we should be able to evaluate our subject company relative to its competitors.

Liquidation and Redeployment

In the final analysis, every company should be evaluated in terms of its economic utility. Are its assets earning more money, producing more jobs, and creating lower cost products than they would if liquidated and redeployed in some other line of endeavor?

We must appraise assets at their actual current market resale value (rather than a low depreciated book value or a high replacement cost), and consider the effect of paying out tax money for any capital gains arising from the liquidation. But if the net amount received could be readily reinvested in some activity which would more nearly meet the needs and demands of the company's owners, we would argue that such liquidation and redeployment should be vigorously pursued.

For example, the owners of Pioneer Brass could have received a much higher profit and certainly have been much safer and more secure in their investment by selling (or liquidating) the company and putting the proceeds into government bonds than by continuing to operate it.

WEIGHTING THE VARIOUS RATINGS

As Tilles [1] points out, there are many different audiences continually evaluating a company's performance. *Stockholders* often judge performance only by the price appreciation (or depreciation) of their holdings and/or by the dividend payout. The *labor force* frequently is concerned only with stability of employment, wage levels, and future advancement opportunities. *Customers* judge a company by the value given relative to price for products or services, and by the efficiency and courtesy with which service is rendered. *Suppliers* tend to evaluate a company in terms of the size of its orders and the promptness of its payments, while *competitors* judge a company in terms of its rate of growth in market share, product innovation, and service offerings.

Although each of these evaluations is important, we believe that it is best if the manager confines himself to the four parameters indicated above, comparing performance on each of these against the criteria suggested. Doing this would result in 13 measurable comparison points.[2] A company that scores well on most of these 13 comparisons has clearly been doing a good job, while the one that scores poorly needs some strategic reorientation. Exhibit 1 presents a sample evaluation of La Plant-Choate in 1946.

First consideration should be given to management's stated targets. (La Plant-Choate's 1946 performance was disappointing to management.) Next, we should compare the present record with the company's own past performance (the trends are decidedly downward). Third, we contrast the company with its competitors (on all counts, decidedly poorer than most competitors). When we make the final evaluation of present performance vesus liquidation, we see that this is not nearly so good an alternative as strategic redeployment within the current company framework.

Note that we have withheld any attempt to evaluate performance until *after* we have described the company's strategic posture. Only by a nonevaluative ap-

---

[1] Seymour Tilles, "The Manager's Job—A Systems Approach," *Harvard Business Review,* Vol. 41, No. 1 (January–February, 1963), pp. 111-121.
[2] Size and rate of growth, market share and rate of change, profitability and trend, and survival capacity, each compared with management's stated targets, own past performance, and competitors' record (4 × 3 = 12), plus owners' objectives compared with liquidation and redeployment.

exhibit 1

EVALUATING PAST PERFORMANCE

(LaPlant-Choate, 1946)

Company Performance Specifications	Subject Company's Record	Compared with Own Past Performance	Compared with Management's Stated Targets	Compared with Competitors Record	Compared with Liquidation and Redeployments of Resources
Present size & rate of growth	1946: $8mm. sales. Growth 1936-1945 of 26%/yr.	43% decline from 1945	About same	Poorer than all major competitors	Not applicable
Present mkt. share & rate of change	5% and declining	Declining	Down	Poorer than all major competitors	Not applicable
Present level of profitability & trend	7.3% ROI down from historical range of 15%	Less than half of past	Down	Poorer than most major competitors	Present level higher than sale or liquidation
Survival capacity	Net worth $2.9mm.; limited ownership base; shallow mgt	Up slightly	About same	Lower than most major competitors	Lower than could be achieved by redeployment of assets

proach to description can we be sure of reasonable accuracy and freedom from prejudgment and bias. Moreover, evaluative measurements do *not* give us any clue as to *why* these results have been achieved. There is little value in knowing that a company is doing a "good" or a "bad" job unless we know the reasons for this performance level. Without the reasons, we will not know which aspects should be perpetuated and which need to be changed. Many managements are afraid to make changes in a successful operation because they are uncertain about the basis for their success. They are willing to *evaluate* performance but not to *describe* and *explain* it! It is tough discipline for a mind trained in "problem-solving" to try to describe and understand a situation *before* evaluating it, but only in this way can one be confident about subsequent actions.

Critical self-analysis is always difficult. Not only is it hard for the manager to be objective, it is also hard for him to extricate himself from the pressures and perceptions of current crises in order to take an over-all view.

As Peter Drucker [3] has indicated, the bulk of managers' time, attention, and concern tends to go first to "problems" rather than to opportunities, and second to old, familiar areas where even extraordinarily successful performance is likely to have minimal impact on results. He urges us to remember that a very small number of events (perhaps 10 per cent or less) account for 90 per cent of all results. Economic results are generally proportionate to the *volume* of revenues produced by the event. On the other hand, costs tend to be directly proportionate to the *number* of individual transactions involved. Thus, Drucker exhorts us to give our greatest attention to the 10 per cent of events that make up 90 per cent of the real profit opportunities. He points out that, unless explicit direction is given, people will naturally allocate their time to those events which occur most frequently rather than to those which promise the greatest payoff. They will attack what is difficult rather than what is productive, and try to solve yesterday's problems rather than seek today's and tomorrow's opportunities.

EVALUATING PRESENT STRATEGIC POSTURE

Assessment of past performance leads directly to an appraisal of how effective the company's present strategic posture is likely to be in the future. We must try to forecast the future threats and opportunities which the company is likely to encounter. Their identification will be the keystone for planning the future strategy of the enterprise.

We must seek to determine: (a) if there are major profit opportunities within our present business which we have not exploited; (b) if there are major opportunities in product/market/customer segments, other than the ones we are presently serving, which would fit the company's resources well and utilize its competitive strengths; or (c) if it would be possible to have less exposure to risk and yet still equal or exceed our present level of profitability.

To do this, we must make a careful analysis of the company's environment by asking: *What changes are taking place in this industry or are likely to take place over the next five to ten years?*

What are the new products presently available or in the offing? How significant do they appear? Are new methods and processes being developed? What changes are they likely to make in the cost/price/volume structure? What changes are occurring in the nature of competition, including concentration of firms? Entry of companies from other industries? Changes in public policy? Integration forwards or backwards? Diversification? What segments of the industry seem to be leveling off in demand? What shifts in consumer preference and consumption patterns seem to be taking place? Concentration of buying units? Different bases for purchase? Substitute products or services? New needs and desires? Different

---

[3] Peter F. Drucker, "Managing for Business Effectiveness," *Harvard Business Review*, Vol. I, No. 3 (May–June, 1963), pp. 53-60.

means of distribution? Changes in taste or requirements? What changes are taking place in packaging? Transportation? Presentation or products? What changes are occurring in forms of organization and administration in this industry? What does the future basis for success in this industry appear to be?

What changes are occurring in other industries to whose products our present manufacturing or distribution facilities could be adapted? What changes are occurring in our present markets which provide new product or service opportunities? How do the likely future growth rates and profitability potentials of these alternatives compare with those of our present business?

Then we must contrast these expected threats and opportunities with the company's present resource deployment. How well equipped is this company to face the future? Does it have the necessary qualified personnel? Adequate capital? Adequate physical facilities and resources? Appropriate products and distribution methods? If any of these appear inadequate, can they be bolstered at reasonable cost? Are the attitudes and desires of owners and managers compatible with the patterns of performance which will be necessary in the future? Would the company be strengthened by merger, acquisition, or joint venture? Are such opportunities available? At what cost? Are there alternative uses which can be made of part or all of this company's present resources that would produce a higher net return on the reinvested capital and/or provide greater satisfaction to the owners? Is sale or dissolution possible at a reasonable price? What are the unrecoverable sunk costs which would be sacrificed? What other strengths and advantages would be lost? What are the obvious strengths on which we can build? What opportunities best fit these strengths?

EVALUATING THE PRODUCT LINE

Drucker offers a particularly perceptive breakdown of a company's *product line* into six basic classifications:

——Tomorrow's breadwinners—new products or today's breadwinners modified and improved (rarely today's breadwinners unchanged).

——Today's breadwinners—the innovations of yesterday.

——Products capable of becoming net contributors if something drastic is done; e.g., converting a good many buyers of "special" variations of limited utility into customers for a new, massive "regular" line. (This is the in-between category in terms of contribution potential.)

——Yesterday's breadwinners—typically products with high volume, but badly fragmented into "specials," small orders, and the like, and requiring such massive support as to eat up all they earn, and plenty more. Yet this is—next to the category following—the product class to which the largest and best resources are usually allocated. ("Defensive research" is a common example.)

——The "also rans"—typically the high hopes of yesterday that, while they did not work out well, nevertheless did not become outright failures. These are always minus contributors, and practically never become successes no matter how much is poured into them. Yet there is usually far too much managerial and technical ego involved in them to drop them.

——The failures—these rarely are a real problem as they tend to liquidate themselves.

This ranking suggests the line that decisions ought to follow. To begin with, the first category should be supplied the necessary resources—and usually a little more than seems necessary. Next, today's breadwinners ought to receive support. By then, even a company rich in talent will have to begin to ration. Of the products capable of becoming major contributors, only those should be supported which have either the greatest *probability* of being reformed successfully, or would make an *extraordinary* contribution if the reform were accomplished.

And from this point on there just are no high-potential resources available, as a rule—not even in the biggest, best-managed, and most profitable business. The lower half of the third group and groups four, five, and six, either have to produce without any resources and efforts or should be allowed to die. "Yesterday's breadwinner," for instance, often makes a respectable "milch cow" with high yields for a few more years. To expect more and to plow dollars into artificial respiration when the product finally begins to fade is just plain foolish.

The "also rans," who after four or five years of trial and hard work are still runts in the product litter and far below their original expectation, should always be abandoned. There is no greater drain on a business than the product that "almost made it." This is especially true if everyone in the company is convinced that, by quality, by design, or by the cost and difficulty of making it (that is what engineers usually mean when they say "quality"), the pet product is "entitled" to success.

. . . . And while the job to be done may look different in every individual company, one basic truth will always be present: every product and every activity of a business begins to obsolesce as soon as it is started. Every product, every operation, and every activity in a business should, therefore, be put on trial for its life every two or three years. Each should be considered the way we consider a proposal to go into a new product, a new operation or activity—complete with budget, capital appropriations request, and so on. One question should be asked of each: "If we were not in this already, would we now go into it?" And if the answer is "no," the next question should be: "How do we get out and how fast?"

The end products of the manager's work are decisions and actions, rather than knowledge and insight. The crucial decision is the allocation of efforts. And no matter how painful, one rule should be adhered to: *in allocating resources, especially human resources of high potential, the needs of those ares which offer great promise must first be satisfied to the fullest extent possible.* If this means that there are no truly productive resources left for a lot of things it would be nice, but not vital, to have or to do, then it is better—much better—to abandon these uses, and not to fritter away high-potential resources or attempt to get results with low-potential ones. This calls for painful decisions, and risky ones. But that, after all, is what managers are paid for.[4]

---

[4] Drucker, *op. cit.,* pp. 59-60.

SUMMARY

We will have more to say about *environmental analysis* and *resource analysis* in Chapter 7, where these are listed as the first and second steps in the six part sequence of planning company strategy.

In this chapter we have attempted to present a simple framework for evaluating a company's past performance, and to provide a basis on which future prospects can be explored. Chapter 7 outlines the necessary steps in planning a new strategy and offers some basic rules for resource deployment in situations where previous description and evaluation suggest the desirability of change.

Notes on the U.S. Forest Products Industry,

PART I: INDUSTRY DATA

INTRODUCTION

These notes on the U.S. forest products industry were prepared primarily as background information for study of the Boise Cascade cases. Some of the conclusions presented herein reflect the writers' general impressions of the industry, combining data from published sources with information obtained from interviews with knowledgeable persons. Sources are indicated for information taken directly from published sources, without further interpretation.

The notes are presented in two parts. Part I covers the major strategic factors in the industry. It begins with an overall indication of the importance of forest products in the U.S. economy. Next follows a discussion of the location, ownership, and utilization of U.S. timber resources. Part I concludes with information on production and consumption patterns for each of the industry's three major segments—lumber, plywood, and paper. While the emphasis is on the U.S. forest products industry, the Canadian situation is considered throughout Part I because of its significant influence on domestic planning and action.

Part II of the note is devoted to an examination of the ways in which eight leading forest products companies have chosen to compete.

INDUSTRY DEFINITION

The forest products industry is generally defined as consisting of those companies involved in the manufacturing,

---

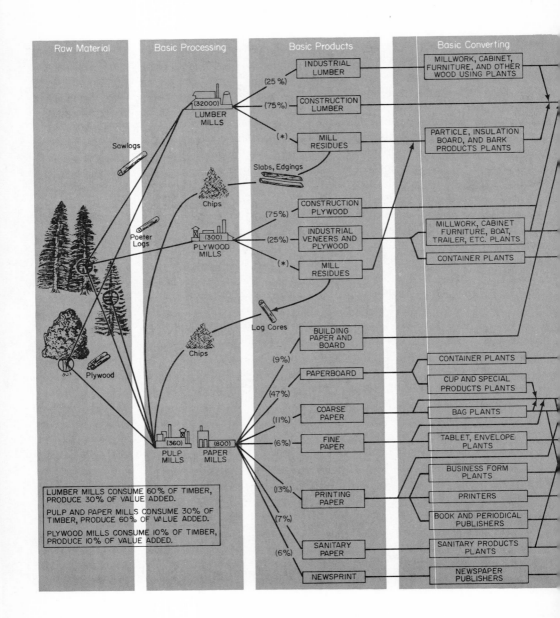

exhibit 1

NOTES ON THE FOREST PRODUCTS INDUSTRY

Products Flow

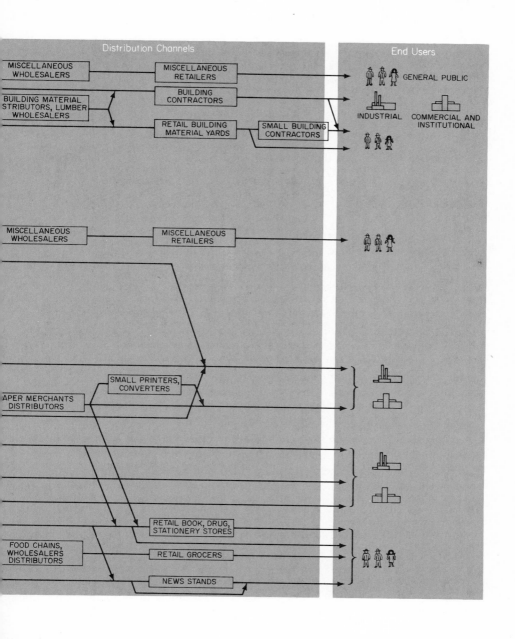

processing, and distribution of products made from trees. Although a very wide range of items falls within this classification, this note is confined to the two major product groups which account for 95% of total industry sales. These are: (1) the Primary Wood Products group, consisting of lumber (20% of total industry sales), plywood (8%), and building board (1%); and (2) the Paper and Paperboard group (66%). The bulk of the remaining 5% is in firewood. Exhibit 1 charts the basic flow of the major product segments from forest to end users.

Total sales of $21 billion in 1964 ranked forest products as the fifth largest industry in the domestic economy. Exhibit 2 shows that, over that last 15 years, the rates of growth of most segments of the industry have about kept pace with the over-all industrial growth of the United States. The most notable exceptions are lumber and plywood. The decline in lumber production during a period of expanding construction activity is explained largely by the encroachment of substitute materials, one of the most important being plywood, whose growth rate has been three times that of total GNP.

INDUSTRY STRUCTURE

Although forest products is one of the oldest industries in the United States, its structure is still in flux.

Since World War II, continuous consolidation, expansion, and both vertical and horizontal integration have blurred traditional industry segmentation by product line. The high level of industrial activity throughout the United States over the past 15 years has created a tremendous demand for paper and paperboard products at the same time that technological advances in the construction industry have developed widespread demand for plywood. The anticipated profit opportunities of these newly developing markets set off a wave of expansions and mergers. These changes took several forms. Whereas traditional paper manufacturers had been chipping up whole logs for pulp production, some timber and plywood manufacturers in the early postwar years began to sell wood chips and sawdust, made from sawmill and plywood mill wastes, for use in pulp production. Thus material which for years had been burned as a space-consuming nuisance became a valuable and extremely low-cost raw material. Upgrading the value of these wastes by integrating forward into pulp manufacture became an obvious profit opportunity for the major lumber producers. The subsequent pressure on the established paper companies caused by the entrance of lumber and plywood companies into pulp production led to backward integration on their part into lumber manufacture. This, in turn, frequently necessitated the acquisition of additional timber. As this pattern of forward and backward integration progressed, many of the small paper companies, faced with requirements for heavy capital outlays in order to maintain their market positions, merged with larger, wealthier companies. This became a favorite means by which pulp manufacturers entered the production and sale of paper products.

exhibit 2

NOTES ON THE FOREST PRODUCTS INDUSTRY

Growth Rates

	1950-55 %	1955-64 %
Gross National Product*	4.3	3.1
Personal consumption expenditures*	3.4	3.5
Industrial production	3.5	3.7
Total construction expenditures*	6.7	3.9
Private residential expenditures*	3.8	2.2
Total paper consumption	2.9	3.3
Newsprint	2.1	2.5
Printing	3.5	4.1
Fine	4.0	5.2
Coarse	2.4	1.8
Tissue	5.1	4.9
All other	5.3	4.3
Paperboard consumption	4.5	3.2
Construction paper and paperboard consumption	4.3	2.1
Total paper and paperboard consumption	3.6	3.2
Dissolving pulp production	7.8	1.3
Lumber production	-.6	-1.0
Softwood plywood production	14.6	9.2

*In constant dollars.

Sources: American Pulp & Paper Assoc.; *Business Statistics 1963,* U.S. Dept. of Commerce, Office of Business Economics; *Construction Review,* U.S. Dept. of Commerce, Business and Defense Service Administration; National Lumber Manufacturers Assoc.; *Survey of Current Business,* U.S. Dept. of Commerce, Office of Business Economics.

The substantial shifts in industry activity soon led to an overexpansion of capacity and to an intensive struggle for markets. This new challenge touched off a scramble to acquire or build converting plants in order to gain captive markets for producers' basic commodity products.

The magnitude of the consolidation is apparent from the record of acquisitions of the ten largest companies during the 1950's. In total, these ten were involved in more than 160 mergers and acquisitions, excluding joint ventures. The situation was further complicated by the diversification into paper products of companies from other industries. Most important of these were American Can, Continental Can, and Owens-Illinois Glass Co., who saw paper as a natural expansion of their basic packaging businesses. A second group of consumer products companies (e.g., Procter & Gamble) also began to enter the manufacture of paper products.

In 1964, the industry was still in the throes of change. Most markets remained highly competitive. As demand crept towards existing supply capacity, extensive additional expansion was being planned, which unquestionably would produce a new overcapacity condition. The realignment had created a substantial number of strong, large, integrated competitors, no one of whom could be considered as the industry leader, and each was battling to maintain or enhance its position.

TIMBER RESOURCES

Timber, unlike most other natural resources, can be easily located, is roughly measurable, and is renewable. It is available in several hundred commercially valuable species, each possessing special characteristics which make it most appropriate for only a few of an enormously wide range of end uses.

There are important differences in the kinds of timber required for lumber, plywood, and paper. Lumber and plywood manufacture in the United States have developed around the use of large-sized virgin timber, because of the economics of harvesting and milling the logs. Since it takes from 80-120 years for most trees of this kind to reach maturity (i.e., an economically good size for harvesting), there has been constant need for new sources of virgin timber. Paper making, on the other hand, is not limited by the size of the tree. If a log is at least four inches in diameter and meets a few other requirements, it is suitable for conversion to paper. The paper industry, unlike lumber and plywood, can therefore be sustained on second-growth timber.

These differing requirements for timber explain, in part, why the lumber segment of the industry is located primarily in the West, where large stands of virgin timber are found, while the paper segment of the industry remains centered in the South and East, where there are substantial supplies of second-growth timber. It was not always this way, however. In the early stages of the industry's development (1600–1874), the timber stands in New England were adequate to meet user requirements for forest products. As virgin timber suitable for conversion to lumber was depleted there, new areas were tapped. In this way the lumber segment of the industry moved into the Lake states in the 1870's, into the South in the early 1900's, and finally into the West in the 1920's. The location of pulp mills has, in the past, tended to follow in the wake of the lumber industry

exhibit 3

NOTES ON THE FOREST PRODUCTS INDUSTRY

Forest Regions of the United States

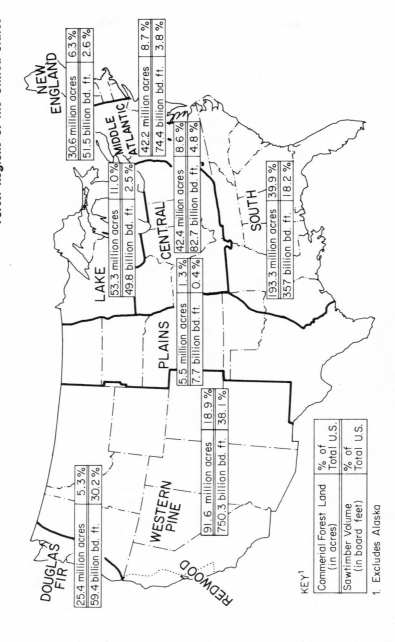

DOUGLAS FIR

25.4 million acres	5.3 %
59.4 billion bd. ft.	30.2 %

NEW ENGLAND

30.6 million acres	6.3 %
51.5 billion bd. ft.	2.6 %

MIDDLE ATLANTIC

42.2 million acres	8.7 %
74.4 billion bd. ft.	3.8 %

LAKE

53.3 million acres	11.0 %
49.8 billion bd. ft.	2.5 %

CENTRAL

42.4 million acres	8.6 %
82.7 billion bd. ft.	4.8 %

PLAINS

5.5 million acres	1.3 %
7.7 billion bd. ft.	0.4 %

SOUTH

193.3 million acres	39.9 %
357 billion bd. ft.	18.2 %

WESTERN PINE

91.6 million acres	18.9 %
750.3 billion bd. ft.	38.1 %

REDWOOD

KEY[1]

Commercial Forest Land (in acres)	% of Total U.S.
Sawtimber Volume (in board feet)	% of Total U.S.

1. Excludes Alaska

Source: Forest Service, Timber Resource Review (U.S. Department of Agriculture).

moves, primarily because of the availability of second-growth timber in cut-over areas. Paper making will probably remain well entrenched in the South, however, because fast-growing timber species in that area are capable of providing an abundant supply of low-cost raw material, and because of the area's favorable location relative to the large paper markets of the East.

Geography of United States Timber Resources

Because the location of timber resources affects the location of producing plants and influences other corporate choices relative to raw material supply, it is necessary to look closely at the geography of the U.S. timber resources. The U.S. Forest Service divides the nation into eight forest regions. Exhibit 3 shows the boundaries of these regions, along with the total acres of commercial forest land [1] and volume of sawtimber [2] existing in each.

Douglas Fir Region. The Douglas Fir region, located in western Oregon and Washington, is probably the most unusual timber producing area in the United States. There, on the slopes of the western coastal mountains, heavy rainfall and rich soils encourage heavy and high-quality growth. As a result of these conditions, the region contains about 30% of the nation's available sawtimber on less than 5% of the total U.S. commercial forest land acreage.

The Douglas fir species, which predominates in this area, is a tall, stately tree that requires about 80 years to reach commercial sawlog size. Its long-fibered wood has exceptional strength, one of the qualities that makes it the most highly prized species for lumber and the most widely used species for softwood plywood. Also, Douglas fir residues are suitable for making paper.

Intermingled in the Douglas fir forests are western hemlock, white fir, and some white pine and sitka spruce. Hemlock is particularly well suited for framing and other house construction trim uses because of its relatively few defects and its high degree of stiffness. It is also a valuable species for pulp production. White fir also has value as lumber and, because it is nonresinous, is considered exceptionally good for producing the sulfite pulp used in making fine papers. White pine and spruce are valuable chiefly as pulpwood.

Much of the timber in the Douglas Fir region grows in very dense, even-aged stands, and thus it can be harvested by clear-cutting selected areas. This is an efficient method of harvesting timber because it produces a high yield per acre

---

[1] Forest land which is producing or is physically capable of producing usable crops of wood. Such areas have to be covered at least 10% by trees capable of producing timber or other wood products. Land which is withdrawn from timber utilization (such as parks) is not included.

[2] Trees of commercial species that contain at least one merchantable sawlog as defined by regional practice and that are of the following minimum diameters at breast height: Eastern Regions (New England, Middle Atlantic, Lake, Central, South, and Plains)—softwoods, 9.0 inches; hardwoods, 11.0 inches; Western regions (Douglas Fir and Western Pine, including Redwood region)—all species, 11.0 inches.

of land and minimizes road building and other installation costs. Since seedlings of these species grow best on open, sunlit land, the clear-cut method also provides excellent conditions for natural or artificial reforestation.

The Douglas Fir region enjoys an additional advantage in its easy access to both rail and ocean transportation.

Western Pine Region.   The Western Pine region covers the 11 western states exclusive of the Douglas Fir region. It has more sawtimber than any other region, 38% of the nation's total. California has 48% of the region's sawtimber, followed by Idaho and eastern Oregon with 13% each. Montana and eastern Washington each contain about 8%.

In contrast to the Douglas Fir region, the Western Pine region has a drier climate, more rugged terrain, and less densely distributed timber. The most abundant species is the ponderosa pine, followed closely by the Douglas fir and white fir. Western white pine and spruce are present in lesser amounts. Most of the species mentioned have value as lumber and are so used. Each species yields sawmill waste suitable for paper making.

The ponderosa pine and other species of the Western Pine region grow slowly, requiring 100 to 120 years to reach sawlog size. The timber stands in the region are of mixed species and size, with younger pines thriving as an understory of tall mature trees. Consequently, in this area, a forester has to select and mark each tree to be harvested. This requirement, combined with the rugged terrain found in much of the region, makes timber harvesting relatively difficult and expensive.

Most of the world's commercial redwood reserves are located in the Western Pine region in a small area along the coast of northern California. Redwood, unique in its beauty, stability, and resistance to fire, insects, and decay, is very limited in supply, relative to the other species.

Southern Region.   The Southern region has the largest supply of hardwoods, in addition to a sizeable quantity of softwood. The softwood is predominantly southern pine, which can be used to manufacture either lumber or paper. In recent years, the rapid growth of the pulp and paper industry in the southern states has caused competition between pulp and lumber mills for the available supply of softwood timber.

In the South, lands capable of growing timber are almost as important as existing timber stands because the rapid growth rate of the southern pine species allows successive harvests of pulpwood in comparatively short intervals of 20 years or less. Since timber cut after this length of time would not be large enough to qualify as sawtimber, the commercial availability of southern softwood is understated in the U.S.F.S. figures.

Southern pine is easy to harvest because it grows in open stands on predominantly flat lands. When this species is grown specifically for pulpwood it is planted in rows, like any other crop.

Southern hardwoods are used primarily in the manufacture of specialty products, such as furniture, where there is need for the strength and surface characteristics inherent in these species. However, increasing quantities of some hardwood species are being used by the southern pulp and paper industry.

Central, Lake, Middle Atlantic, and New England Regions.   These regions are considered as a group because they have basically similar timber resources. Combined, the four regions claim about 14% of the country's sawtimber, of which 80% is in hardwood species. Mature softwoods in this area were mostly depleted prior to 1900 and most of the second-growth timber is claimed by the paper industry long before it qualifies as sawtimber.

Major timber species available in these regions are jack pine, spruce, and hemlock in the softwoods, and oak, birch, and maple in the hardwoods. The eastern softwood species are adequate for lumber production but are considered excellent raw material for paper production. The scarcity of softwood for pulp in these regions has led to an increasing reliance on hardwoods for local paper making.

Alaska.   Alaskan timber resources total about 197 billion board feet of sawtimber (roughly 10% of the nation's supply), of which 167 billion board feet are in softwood species. Spruce is the major softwood species (62% of softwoods), followed by western hemlock (32%). These species as they grow in Alaska have primary value only as pulpwood.

Canada.   Canadian sawtimber resources total roughly one trillion board feet, which is equal to about one-half of the U.S. sawtimber volume. The geographical distribution of this timber is almost the same as that found in the United States: Over 80% of the Canadian sawtimber is in softwood species and 80% of this softwood timber is found in the western part of the country (specifically, British Columbia).

Leading Canadian Softwood Species

Western hemlock	243 billion board feet
Spruces	242 billion board feet
Western red cedar	108 billion board feet
True firs (white fir)	105 billion board feet
Lodgepole pine	63 billion board feet
Douglas fir	58 billion board feet

Most Canadian hardwood consists of cottonwood, aspen, alder, and birch.

As in the United States, the Canadian lumber industry relies on old-growth, virgin timber, such as that found in British Columbia, and the pulp and paper industry uses second-growth and those species not suited for lumber production.

Timber Ownership

One of the most important factors affecting corporate strategy within the forest products industry is timber ownership. In the United States timber ownership falls into two general categories: public and private. A breakdown of ownership by forest regions reveals that in the East and South, where timber stands are largely second-growth, 90% of the timber is privately owned. On the other hand, in the Douglas Fir and Western Pine regions, where the prime virgin softwood timber is concentrated, the percentages of timber publicly owned are 55% and 66%, respectively.

Private ownership. About two-thirds of the privately owned U.S. timber is held by farmers and others not associated with wood producing. The remaining third is owned by a relatively small number of companies actively involved in the forest products industry. In the Douglas Fir and Western Pine regions, about one-half of the privately owned timber is on large tracts of 5,000 acres or more and is controlled by fewer than 500 owners. The Weyerhaeuser Company, for example, owns about 20% of the private timber in the Douglas Fir region, and the Georgia-Pacific and Crown Zellerbach Companies each own another 4% to 5%.

Although the farmers and others not identified with the forest products industry control the majority of the privately owned timber lands, they are not considered a significant source of timber supply. Their lands are largely too remote, too small in area, or too poorly stocked to make timber harvesting economically feasible. There are, however, some large stands of economic timber believed to be currently withheld from use for speculative reasons. It appears reasonable to assume that the private timber owned by the forest products companies will continue to be actively harvested and managed, but that other private timber will not be harvested in appreciable quantities in the foreseeable future.

Public ownership. Publically owned timber can be broadly classified into three groups: state and local governments, the Department of the Interior (National Parks, Indian reservations, etc.), and the U.S. Forest Service (National Forest). As suppliers of timber to the forest products industry, state and local governments play a minor role. The major sources of government timber are the National Forests and, to a much smaller degree, forests under the control of the Department of the Interior.

Historically, the total cut of timber from Federal lands has been much less than from private lands, even in the West. Between 1940 and 1964, however, the percentage of timber cut on Federal lands increased from about 9% to 28% of the nation's total. Some industry leaders expect Federal timber to be an increasingly significant factor in supplying forest product companies in the future. They assert that present timber removal rates from U.S.-owned land is well below the potential cuts consistent with sustained-yield forest management.[3]

---

[3] Refers to a concept of cutting only as much timber from a stand in any year as will be replenished through new growth, so as to assure a constant, perpetual withdrawal rate.

Federal timber is normally made available to private firms by the sale of cutting rights on specific lands. The sale is outright to a single party. Sales of more than $500 are awarded by competitive bid. In addition, the Small Business Administration administers sales of certain parcels of timber set aside exclusively for those forest products companies which qualify as small businesses. When the cutting rights to Federal timber are sold, the timber must be harvested in a relatively short period of time. Virtually all small and medium-sized sales, and many of the large ones, are for periods of less than three years. The harvesting and transport of timber during the contractual period must be in accord with strict government rules and restrictions, designed to guarantee sustained-yield operations, and it is closely supervised. The most important rules have to do with road construction and reforestation programs, as these can add substantial costs not covered in the sales contract.

The present policy of the Forest Service is neither to sell nor otherwise dispose of national forest timberland, nor to acquire more. This is a departure from a long-standing program of land acquisition, and it means greater emphasis on management and development of forest properties. As is the practice with the Bureau of Land Management, only those lands which do not fit into a practical, economic management program are considered for sale or exchange.

The importance of Federal timber ownership, particularly in the West, should not be underestimated. With only one or two exceptions the major Western forest products companies do not own sufficient forest lands to supply all their own needs, at present levels of operations, on a continuous basis. Most companies attempt to keep their own forest lands on sustained-yield and buy sufficient government timber to maintain and expand their markets. If a company chooses this strategy, however, it has to be prepared to draw heavily from its own timber at those times when government timber is not made available, or as a function of competitive bidding when it is priced too high.

In Canada, where the government owns 87% of all sawtimber, the timber disposal methods are slightly different. About one-fourth of the cut made from government lands is made available to wood-using industries and individuals on long-term (usually 21 years) renewable leases. Most of the balance is sold on the basis of cutting rights for three years or less.

Timber Utilization

Prior to the early 1900's, there had been little concern over depletion of this country's timber resources. Many considered the supply of trees inexhaustible. By 1910, however, when timber removal was four times new timber growth, government and industry leaders began to worry about the future availability of this prized natural resource. Consequently, the U.S. Forest Service, which had been established in 1905, began to emphasize sustained-yield forestry methods in its National Forests. And the wood-using industries themselves sought new ways to conserve their timber supplies. As a result of these efforts, by 1944 annual timber growth was about equal to removal. In 1952, U.S. timber growth exceeded removal by about 25%. Nevertheless, in the Pacific Northwest, it was estimated that the wood-using industries were cutting more timber than was being grown each year.

According to many industry leaders, more complete utilization of the timber cut is the best means of ensuring the future supply of U.S. timber. The paper segment of the industry presently affords the best example of high utilization. If whole logs are used to make pulp, all but the bark is consumed. If wood chips made from sawmill or plywood mill residues are used for pulp, products are made from what would otherwise be waste. In addition, the paper industry has made some strides in increasing the use for pulp of tree species which are unsuited for lumber. The greatest waste of wood fibers occurs in converting logs to lumber and plywood. In both of these operations, only a minor fraction of the total log is utilized. In lumber manufacturing, as much as two-thirds of the log may end up as waste.

The first major steps toward using wood waste took place on the West Coast during the late 1940's and early 1950's when several of the larger lumber and plywood companies began chipping mill residues and using these chips to make pulp, hardboard, particle board, and silvichemicals. By 1958 the use of mill residues as a raw material for West Coast paper making had changed the whole complexion of the industry. Manufacturers once involved in only a single phase of the industry had grown into integrated firms, producing a full range of forest products. This integration not only utilized mill residues which would otherwise have been burned, but also allowed a firm to make selective choices in the use of its timber resources. Thus, a fully integrated western firm could use its high-grade Douglas fir logs to make exterior plywood, the bulk of its better grade logs to make lumber, and the waste from its sawmills and plywood mills to make pulp.

A major factor limiting this kind of integration, and thus timber utilization, was the requirement of substantial size for economic operations. Only the larger timber-based companies could afford to build expensive pulp and paper mills. Even the smallest pulp mill required a very substantial lumbering operation to provide sufficient chips from waste wood. A few medium-sized lumber producers manufactured and sold chips from waste wood, but chipping required substantial additional investment. Moreover, the chip supplier was at best in a marginal position, selling to a customer which could often increase its own chipping capacity as its needs grew. Many lumber mills in the West were too small and/or too remotely located to economically produce chips even if they desired to do so. Thus, large quantities of potentially usable wood waste were still being burned, and likely will continue to be, until the demand for chips greatly exceeds its present level.

Tax Situation

Income taxes for forest products companies which own and harvest their own timber tend to be substantially below the usual corporate rates. Not only are these companies granted a depletion allowance, but also the increase in timber value from growth—the difference between original cost and fair-market value at the time of cutting—is taxed at capital gains rates rather than as ordinary income. For the purpose of computing the capital gains tax, the cost basis of timber is the higher of the price paid or of its appraised value at March 1, 1913. Under the Internal Revenue code, timber is the only replenishable asset given this tax advantage, and as regrowth (the cost of which approaches zero) begins to be harvested, it too receives capital gains tax treatment.

With this tax structure, it is advantageous for a firm to employ a transfer pricing policy which transfers owned timber from the logging operation to the processing operation at the going market price rather than actual cost. This will show a disproportionately high indicated profit on the logging side of the business, to be taxed at capital gains rates. In turn, the mill end of the business will show a disproportionately low indicated profit, to be taxed as ordinary income. Consequently, there is a very real tax incentive for a company to harvest fee-owned timber if it has a low stumpage value relative to present fair-market value. This is usually the case with old-growth timber purchased some time in the past. If a company relies heavily upon timber purchased on cutting contracts from the government, usually at a cost close to the present market value (by definition), there will be little or no capital appreciation.

The rationale behind this tax structure is the government's goal of sustained-yield forestry. Since the cost basis of second-growth timber is low, a company is greatly encouraged to reseed land which has been cut over, or to farm new lands, thus increasing the potential timber resources to be available in the future.

MAJOR INDUSTRY SEGMENTS

Lumber

The lumber segment of the forest products industry is the oldest of the major product groups and by most standards the least dynamic. U.S. lumber output of 35.6 billion board feet in 1964 represented a slight gain over the previous several years, but was only a shade above the 34.6 billion board feet produced in 1919. The best year ever was 1909, when U.S. mills produced 44.5 billion board feet of lumber.

Some 54% of the total U.S. lumber output is produced in four states—Oregon, California, Washington, and Idaho—all of which are in the far West. Fifteen other states, primarily in the South, accounted for another 38%. The remaining 31 states produced only 8% of the total, with no one state adding as much as 1%.

The United States does not produce all of the lumber it consumes. In 1964 imports rose to about 15% of domestic consumption, compared with 10.2% in 1958. Canada accounted for 98% of all foreign lumber brought into the United States.

In marked contrast to the paper segment of the industry, lumber production is not concentrated in a small number of firms. The Weyerhaeuser Company, the largest lumber producer in the world, accounts for only about 4% of the U.S. production, and the next five largest firms each account for only about 2% of the total output for the industry.

There were over 33,000 lumber manufacturing units in the United States in 1964, the majority of which were very small. An estimated 88% of these sawmills (29,000) had annual capacities of less than 1 million board feet. This large number of mills produced only about 13% of total industry output. On the other hand, 2% of the sawmills (616), comprising the larger mills with annual capacities of more than 10 million board feet, produced about 55% of the total.

The preponderance of small firms in the lumber industry has been a direct consequence of the low investment required to get into the business. For approximately $55,000, an operator could purchase a circular saw and other incidental equipment, rent a building, and have enough working capital to get himself started in the lumber business. The minimum cost for a complete sawmill, however, was about $100,000, and a large full-scale operation could exceed $3 million in cost, according to a University of California forest economist.

While the large mills, with relatively constant annual capacity, were a continuous factor in the industry, the number of small mills in operation during any given year tended to fluctuate widely. In periods of poor profit expectations (i.e., low lumber prices), the smallest mills frequently shut down operations, planning to resume production when prices improved. Profit opportunities were affected by many variables, the most important of which was the over-all demand for lumber. This, in turn, was largely determined by the level of activity in the construction industry, since new construction accounted for three-fourths of lumber usage. In addition to the more general variations in demand, changes in the level of local stumpage costs and specific company manufacturing costs relative to current lumber prices also influenced profit opportunities for the small mills. In any specific area, the inflow and outflow of small firms was also affected by changes in timber ownership patterns, changes in demand in local markets, changes in the extent of by-product utilization, and changes in the output capabilities of competitive producing areas. In 1956, a Congressional study determined that the *annual* rate of entry of companies into the lumber industry was 21.7% of all companies then operating—highest for any industry in the nation.

In the far West, the number of small mills was increasing slightly in the Western Pine region, throughout a fairly narrow belt running through northern California, eastern Oregon and Washington, northern Idaho, and northwestern Montana (an area where timber was primarily owned by the U.S. Forest Service). To the west of this belt, however, in the Douglas Fir region, the total number of small mills was declining gradually. Concentration of the timber in the hands of a relatively small number of large private owners, together with competition for sawtimber from mills with inadequate supplies and from companies intending to use the timber for other purposes (e.g., telephone poles, piling, etc.), had decreased timber availability, pushed stumpage prices up, and reduced the chances for profitable operation by a small mill.

Lumber consumption.   Historical figures show that nearly three-fourths of the lumber consumed in this country was used for building and construction. Of this amount, half was used in new residential construction, 28% in nonresidential construction such as industrial plants, schools, hospitals, highways, and other public works, and the remaining 22% for maintenance and repair. 11% went to boxes and crating, a slowly declining usage because of increasing substitution of paperboard, plastics, and metal. All other consumption (15%) was accounted for by railroads, furniture manufacturers, and by a variety of such items as handles, boats, caskets, ladders, etc. While shifts in relative importance have occurred frequently among users within this category, it has remained a relatively constant percentage of total consumption over the past decade.

U.S. exports of lumber, virtually all to Canada and Mexico, have been relatively insignificant in recent years.

Lumber consumption by geographical area tends to follow patterns of growth in population and industrial activity. Thus, the construction boom on the West Coast and the continued development in the Lake and Central states has benefited western lumber producers in particular. (Total U.S. consumption figures are summarized in Exhibit 4.)

Lumber distribution.   Two factors have significant influence on the distribution of lumber in the United States. First, lumber has many of the characteristics of a commodity product; thus it is very difficult for a manufacturer to establish any kind of consumer franchise. Price, service, and personal relationships are the basis upon which most sales are made. Second, most lumber manufacturing is concentrated in areas that are remote from the major population centers. It is nearly impossible, therefore, for most manufacturers to sell their output locally, and thus they must turn to a nationwide market. This nationwide market is reached most economically through a network of some 6,000 lumber wholesalers who have become over the years the most significant factor in lumber distribution.

The role of the lumber wholesaler.   The lumber wholesaler basically serves as an intermediary between the customer (lumber yard or building contractor) and the producing mill. He is sometimes likened to a specialist in the stock market—that is, he acts as an expert in the mechanics of the market and is instrumental in keeping market operations on an orderly basis. His main contact with producers is by phone, although he is occasionally visited by mill representatives.

On receiving an order, the wholesaler normally calls five or six lumber producers (with whom he has a standing relationship) to obtain price and delivery quotations. Assuming that species, grade, and delivery times are comparable, price normally becomes the basis upon which the sale is made. Prices are usually quoted on a carload basis and quantity upcharges are incurred only when wholesalers purchase less than carload quantities. This is a relatively infrequent occurrence.

Once the order is placed, the lumber is shipped directly from the mill to the retailer or builder, even though the wholesaler takes title to the shipment. For his services, the wholesaler takes a 5% functional discount off the quoted price.

In addition to purchasing against firm orders, the wholesaler often buys for his own account and tries to improve upon the 5% discount by reselling the lumber at a higher price than he paid. He may order the lumber shipped for delivery within two to four weeks to a distant distribution point. Then he will try to sell the lumber while it is en route, either at some point along the way or to markets beyond the delivery point.

A wholesaler is relatively unlimited in his radius of operation. Theoretically, he may buy a carload of lumber from any producer and sell it to any retailer or builder in any other part of the country. In practice, most wholesalers restrict themselves to specific geographical areas where they are particularly familiar with market conditions and with customers.

Despite their extensive use of wholesalers, many lumber producers believe them to be a necessary evil. Some producers try to save part of the 5% functional discount by selling directly to large builders. An increasing trend to this kind of selling has been noted, beginning in the late 1950's. Some wholesalers have retaliated by not placing orders with producers who were known to be selling direct. If this action became widespread, it could be damaging to these producers, unless they could sell all of their output directly. This would be very difficult, even for large lumber manufacturers.

Canadian lumber supply. The three major markets for Canadian lumber were Canada itself, the United States, and Great Britain. The relative importance of these markets has been changing significantly during the post-World War II years, as Canadian exports to the United Kingdom have decreased significantly on both a relative and an absolute basis. Loss of market position in the United Kingdom has resulted from lower cost lumber supplies from Finland and the U.S.S.R. The relative change in distribution is shown below:

Percentage Distribution of British Columbia Lumber Shipments, 1947-1964

	1947	1964
Total shipments	100%	100%
Canadian consumption	46%	32%
United States	12%	50%
United Kingdom	28%	8%
Other	14%	10%

exhibit 4

NOTES ON THE FOREST PRODUCTS INDUSTRY

U.S. Lumber Consumption by Use

(million board feet)

	Building and Construction	Boxes and Crating	Industrial	Railroad	Export	Total Consumption	Per Capita	Softwood Lumber	Per Capita	Hardwood Lumber	Per Capita
1929	20,137	4,645	4,230	3,622	3,197	35,831	268	28,905	215	6,926	53
1930	13,820	4,038	3,255	3,052	2,352	26,517	196	21,475	150	5,042	37
1931	9,672	3,358	2,290	2,059	1,701	19,080	140	15,424	113	3,646	27
1932	6,469	2,425	1,425	1,641	1,156	13,116	96	10,647	78	2,469	18
1933	8,135	2,549	1,614	1,582	1,281	15,160	111	12,385	91	2,775	20
1934	7,969	2,661	1,670	1,832	1,349	15,481	112	12,774	93	2,707	19
1935	10,898	3,221	2,150	1,732	1,313	19,314	141	16,086	118	3,228	23
1936	14,012	3,664	2,518	2,156	1,284	23,634	174	19,824	147	3,810	27
1937	14,613	4,002	2,760	2,287	1,443	25,106	183	21,062	155	4,044	28
1938	13,667	3,840	2,542	1,478	977	22,504	166	19,180	142	3,324	24
1939	16,637	4,054	2,754	1,889	1,104	26,438	193	22,392	164	4,046	29
1940	20,357	4,295	2,994	1,929	972	30,547	224	26,169	192	4,378	32
1941	22,876	5,142	3,820	2,396	693	34,927	256	28,995	213	5,932	43
1942	25,958	9,138	4,742	2,209	463	42,510	312	34,555	254	7,955	58
1943	15,744	14,142	4,956	2,108	310	37,260	270	29,157	211	8,103	59
1944	11,920	15,241	4,706	2,145	360	34,372	246	26,401	189	7,971	57
1945	13,708	11,714	3,811	1,886	435	31,554	222	23,996	169	7,558	53
1946	20,910	5,724	4,482	1,757	648	33,521	232	25,766	178	7,755	54
1947	21,898	4,907	4,701	1,790	1,352	34,648	231	27,451	183	7,197	48
1948	25,571	3,993	4,378	1,962	647	36,551	245	28,976	194	7,575	51
1949	24,349	3,777	4,086	1,448	667	34,327	225	28,628	194	5,699	37
1950	30,879	4,291	4,842	1,609	518	42,139	274	34,664	226	7,475	48
1951	26,797	4,510	4,683	1,572	998	38,560	243	31,522	198	7,038	45
1952	28,372	4,690	4,771	1,582	735	40,150	251	32,795	205	7,355	46
1953	27,025	4,414	4,903	1,713	644	38,699	238	31,305	193	7,394	45
1954	28,628	4,092	4,465	1,276	723	39,184	237	32,608	197	6,576	40
1955	30,877	4,208	4,558	1,445	844	41,932	249	33,451	199	8,481	50
1956	25,563	4,537	4,915	1,446	767	41,228	241	33,346	195	7,882	46
1957	25,885	4,011	4,348	1,294	811	36,349	208	30,234	173	6,115	35
1958	26,704	4,235	4,587	890	728	37,144	209	30,833	174	6,311	35
1959	29,803	4,344	4,707	1,002	788	40,644	225	34,242	190	6,402	35
1960	27,261	4,094	4,436	1,050	861	37,702	204	31,391	170	6,311	34
1961	n.a.	n.a.	n.a.	n.a.	755	35,541	193	29,063	158	6,478	35
1962	n.a.	n.a.	n.a.	n.a.	793	38,615	207	31,129	167	7,486	40
1963						38,800					

Sources: Columns 1, 2, and 3: National Lumber Manufacturers Association.
Column 4: Association of American Railroads.
Columns 5-11: Department of Commerce.

Total shipment of softwood lumber from Canada to the United States reached 5.8 billion board feet in 1964, and had a total value of about $482 million.

The Plywood Segment of the Industry

Over the 19 year period following World War II, plywood was the fastest growing segment of the forest products industry. Plywood production showed a gain in all but one of these years, with the total increase being more than 700%, compared with gains of 100% in paper and 25% in lumber over the same period. Exhibit 5 shows the growth in plywood production for the period 1956–1964.

In the early 1960's, the United States produced annually about 55% of the world output of plywood, all but 1% of which was consumed domestically. Similarly, Canada, which produced 6% of the world's plywood, consumed all but 3% of its own output domestically, in sharp contrast to its heavy exports of lumber.

As can be seen in Exhibit 5, plywood production is divided into two categories —softwood and hardwood—with softwood being by far the more important. Hardwood plywood is used principally for furniture, paneling, and other decorative items. It is a highly specialized product whose domestic production is spread among some 500 small plants, scattered widely over the country. Softwood plywood, on the other hand, has become increasingly important as a major material for the construction industry in the United States, and this trend is expected to continue in the future.

In 1964 the production of softwood plywood was concentrated in 163 plants. Three leading plywood producers accounted for nearly one-third of total output. Georgia-Pacific led in plywood production with about 12% of the industry total, followed closely by U.S. Plywood and Weyerhaeuser, which each accounted for about 10%.

The minimum cost to build a full-scale economic softwood plywood mill, capable of producing more than 30 million square feet per year, was estimated at $2 million. The peeler lathe represented the largest single outlay in such a plant, and approximately 150 employees were required.

In addition to this capital requirement, two other factors tended to restrict the number of firms engaged in plywood manufacture. One was the requirement for high-quality logs (primarily of the Douglas fir species), which were owned by relatively few people. The other was the need for a network of distribution warehouses, to assure movement of a large quantity of plywood. Each of the three leading plywood firms had both extensive prime timber reserves and their own distribution system.

Five western states—Oregon (88 mills), Washington (33 mills), California (19 mills), Montana (6 mills), and Idaho (5 mills)—accounted for about 96% of total U.S. softwood plywood production in 1964. The remaining 4% was scattered among ten southern states, all of which were newcomers to the industry. Prior to 1964, virtually all softwood plywood was produced in the far West; 90% of these mills utilized large-size Douglas fir timber as their raw material. By 1964, however, several firms had proven the commercial possibility of plywood made from cheap, plentiful, southern pine timber. This breakthrough touched off a wave of new plywood plant construction in the South. At the end of 1964, 30 new plants were under construction in this area, and it was estimated that southern plants would account for about 2.2 billion feet of capacity by the end of 1966 (about 15% of U.S. output).

exhibit 5

NOTES ON THE FOREST PRODUCTS INDUSTRY

U.S. Softwood and Hardwood Plywood Production: 1956–1964

(million square feet)

| | Softwood Plywood | | Hardwood Plywood | | |
	Production	No. Plants	U.S. Production	Net Imports	Consumption
1964	11,678	163	1,598	1,944	3,542
1963	10,216	155	1,414	1,616	3,030
1962	9,216	155	1,231	1,436	2,667
1961	8,577	157	1,089	1,096	2,185
1960	7,816	154	944	1,013	1,957
1959	7,828	143	977	1,316	2,293
1958	6,440	122	804	906	1,710
1957	5,460	123	791	841	1,632
1956	5,240	123	887	695	1,582

Source: American Plywood Association, U.S. Department of Commerce, U.S. Tariff Commission.

Cost factors. Plywood manufacturing costs reflected stumpage prices of the raw material to a greater degree than lumber manufacturing. Because only high-grade, uniform diameter logs were suitable for plywood, Douglas fir "peeler" logs commanded about a 50% price premium over sawlogs. Nonetheless, labor costs remained the single greatest factor in plywood cost. In recent years, few significant technological advances had occurred in plywood production techniques, and increases in labor productivity had not kept pace with increases in wage rates. Average mill output of 90-95 square feet per man hour had remained relatively constant over the past 20 years. These relatively high fixed unit costs had tended to make plywood especially susceptible to the wide price swings which occurred with modest shifts in demand.

Plywood distribution. Approximately 75% of all softwood plywood was used in the construction industry. Residential construction (45% of all usage) consumed an average of 1500 square feet of plywood for each new single-family home. The major nonconstruction uses (25%) included furniture, paneling, cabinet work, boats, signs, shelving, etc.

More than three-fourths of the total Douglas fir produced was consumed in the Lake, northeastern, and western states. Douglas fir plywood's higher value per unit of weight allowed it to be shipped greater distances than Douglas fir lumber before being placed at a price disadvantage relative to substitute materials, such as southern pine lumber, plastics, and metal.

Plywood prices, on the average, were substantially more volatile than lumber, occasionally fluctuating 25% or more from one year to the next. Price movements tended to follow the level of construction activity, as well as the price of those types of lumber which could substitute readily for plywood. Exterior grades, whose water repellent characteristics rendered them less susceptible to replacement by substitution, tended to be more sensitive to changes in the level of supply than other grades.

Unlike lumber, which was usually shipped directly from the mill to either contractors or retail lumber yards in carload lots, most plywood sales were made from intermediate warehouses located in the major market areas. This was because a carload lot of plywood consisted of over 1 million square feet, both a larger quantity and a higher value than most customers could handle comfortably. Hence, the large number of wholesalers without warehouse facilities, who were the mainstays of lumber sales, were relatively unimportant in plywood sales. The comparatively small number of lumber wholesalers with warehouse facilities were eagerly sought after by plywood producers. Both to provide wider distribution and better control of sales and service effort than was being obtained through wholesalers, the largest plywood manufacturers chose to sell directly to customers from their own network of owned (or leased) warehouses. One of these companies had indicated that such control over the sale of their own output was the only way they could establish product differentiation and insulate themselves from extreme price competition. Others pointed out that since all softwood plywood was inspected, graded, and stamped by an official industry organization, whose job it is to establish and maintain quality standards, it was impossible to discern manufacturing differences within a given grade. Hence, they argued that plywood was sold on a commodity basis to an even greater degree than lumber, price and service being the only inducements which a manufacturer could offer. In the highly competitive plywood market, they believed an important service advantage was achieved through distribution from their own warehouses, using the company's own salesmen. They stated, however, that such an arrangement was practical only for a very large producer.

Thus, although lumber and plywood were sold to many of the same customers, these two products tended to be sold by the larger producers through quite different channels. As the importance of plywood grew, there was an indication of an incipient trend among the biggest companies to by-pass the wholesaler completely and to sell both plywood and lumber from their own regional warehouses with their own sales forces.

The Paper Segment of the Industry

The pulp and paper segment of the forest products industry, all by itself, ranked among the top ten U.S. industries in the value of its products. It employed about half a million people, and the paper segment's total assets in 1964 were estimated at $11.9 billion. Over the ten year period ending in 1964, annual domestic paper production increased 37%, from 30.4 million tons to 41.8 million tons. During this same period, annual per capita use of paper increased 24% from 386 lbs. to 479 lbs.

Paper manufacture was characterized by heavy investment in capital equipment and by a high degree of automation. A single paper machine, costing as much as $25 million, operated by only four workers per shift, could produce as much as $22 million in annual revenue. Some of these machines were as long as a football field, stood three stories tall, and put out a half-mile of paper a minute. The biggest machine could manufacture as much as 300,000 tons of paper per year.

Because of the high capital requirements, the bulk of the industry's basic paper making capacity was concentrated in fewer than 75 firms. International Paper Company, the world's largest paper manufacturer, accounted for about 10% of total U.S. paper production in 1964, where the next two largest paper making firms, Crown Zellerbach Corporation and St. Regis Paper Company, each produced about 5% of U.S. output. The next five firms, West Virginia Pulp and Paper Company, Mead Corporation, Scott Paper Company, Kimberly Clark Corporation, and Union Bag-Camp Paper Corporation, each produced more than 2% of the U.S. paper output; and the top ten companies accounted for about 40% of total domestic paper production. The remaining 60% was produced by approximately 60 companies, none of which accounted for as much as 2% of the total.

In addition to these few basic paper producers, there were a very large number of smaller paper converters and processors. These companies' sales, investment, and employment were included in industry figures because of the large value added by their operations.

The manufacturing process. The paper making process had two principal stages: the first involved converting wood to pulp, and the second the conversion of pulp to paper. Ideally, pulp and paper making facilities should be located together, with pulp in slush form being pumped with high efficiency through pipes from one operation to the other at very low cost. There were, however, a relatively large number of paper mills which did not have adequate pulp making facilities to match their paper making requirements. These mills purchased market pulp to make up their deficiencies. Market pulp was sold in sheet form, requiring drying, matting, baling, and handling operations which were unnecessary in an integrated operation. Finally, after delivery to the mill, the bales had to be broken and individual sheets fed into the beaters in order to convert the dry sheets to slushy, free-flowing fibers.

Pulp manufacture. Pulp was a crude fibrous cellulose raw material which, after suitable treatment, could be converted into paper, paperboard, or rayon. Wood pulp was produced by: (1) mechanically grinding up logs (groundwood pulp); (2) chemical fibrization of wood chips (sulfate, sulfite, or soda pulp);

or (3) by a combination of chemical treatment and mechanical grindings (semi-chemical pulp).

Sulfate pulp, which accounted for about 60% of 1964 total U.S. pulp production, could be used in making most grades of paper. It was particularly suitable for producing packaging materials—heavy brown wrapping papers and paperboard. Since 1950, virtually all new pulping facilities had been constructed to utilize the sulfate process, both because recovery of chemicals made it a lower-cost process than sulfite, and because technological advances had made it possible to produce a good bleached (white) sulfate product. Sulfite pulp (representing about 13% of total U.S. pulp output) was once the most prevalent process. The pulp was light in color and was especially well suited for the higher grades of writing and printing papers. Groundwood pulp (15% of total) was much cheaper to produce than chemical pulps, since only about 7% of the raw material was lost in processing vs. 55% or more in the chemical processes. But its low strength and coarse appearance limited its use to newsprint and low-grade tablet paper. The semichemical process (12% of total) was developed primarily to utilize hardwoods which were not well-suited to the sulfate or sulfite processes. Semichemical pulp extracted a high yield from the wood input and produced a stiff, resilient paper best suited to corrugated medium, insulating board, egg cartons, and similar formed or molded products.

Waste paper was also an important source of fiber, being used primarily for filler stock. Reusage of waste paper represented about 30% (9 million tons) of the industry's fiber needs in 1964.

The cost of entering the pulp making business was high. Estimates in the late 1950's, gathered from various industry sources, placed the initial capital investment for a pulp mill at somewhere between $50,000 and $75,000 per ton of daily output, exclusive of supporting forest lands. Many persons believed that the smallest economic size for a pulp mill was in the range of 350 to 400 tons a day, making $20 million a minimum capital requirement. Even such a small mill involved upwards of two years to construct and bring on stream.

Paper manufacture.   Paper was made by matting together wet cellulose fibers (the pulp obtained from one of the processes indicated above) to form a thin sheet of material which, when dried, had the desired strength, absorption, color, and flexibility specifications. In the modern day paper mill, the process began in the beater, where pulp fibers, suspended in water, were mechanically cut, split, and crushed. During the beating stage, the fibers developed strong adhesive properties. When the pulp had been beaten and the necessary dyes, sizings, and resins added, the stock was refined and then allowed to flow onto the paper making machine. The most widely used machine was the Fourdrinier, a machine that matted the fibers on an endless fine mesh screen, removed most of the excess water, and then dried the newly formed paper by passing it between a long series of steamheated cylinders.

The required capital investment for even a modest-sized paper mill was high, but not as great as was required for a pulp mill. As will be seen, there was a wide range of paper products that a firm could choose to make. And the choice of product line was the major determinant of the cost of entry. Paper mills designed to turn out huge quantities of a standardized product, such as newsprint, might cost as much as $20 million. On the other hand, a low-capacity mill, designed to make short runs of a specialty like high-grade writing papers, could be built for less than a million dollars. The greatest restriction on construction of a paper making operation of the latter type was the limited markets available for its output, rather than the magnitude of the investment.

The market for pulp and paper products.   Only a small amount of pulp production (less than 10%) was bought and sold on the open market. Pulp markets are considered briefly, however, because some individual firms derived substantial income from pulp sales.

Pulp markets.   In 1964, domestic production of wood pulp totaled 30.4 million tons, the bulk of which was consumed by integrated mills in manufacturing their own paper. The remainder was sold as market pulp to nonintegrated paper mills or to integrated mills which could not supply their own pulp in sufficient amounts. In addition to pulp purchased from domestic sources, U.S. paper manufacturers imported 2.8 million tons of pulp in 1964, virtually all from Canada.

Prior to World War II, imported pulp (principally from Scandinavia) supplied some 25% of U.S. requirements. The cutoff of Scandinavian supplies early in the war, however, stimulated the development of southern U.S. pulp capacity (which rose from 3.4 million tons in 1939 to 5.7 million tons in 1946), as well as increasing the reliance on Canadian suppliers. The importance of Canadian pulp was reduced considerably in the postwar period with the continued expansion of southern facilities, which, by 1958, had an estimated annual capacity of more than 16 million tons. This rapid development of pulp capacity in the South was based primarily on an abundant supply of low-cost raw material (pine pulpwood) which could be pulped by the relatively inexpensive sulfate process.

Exports overseas, mainly to Europe, the United Kingdom, and Latin America, had become an increasingly important outlet for U.S. market pulp. Nonetheless, pulp exports in 1964 were less than one-fourth the tonnage imported. An upward trend in pulp exports was anticipated as the newer nations of the world increased their consumption of paper products and as increasing European demand outstripped locally available raw material supply.

Within each of its various classifications—e.g., groundwood, sulfate, sulfite, semichemical—pulp was essentially an undifferentiated commodity, sold primarily on a price basis. And, since the movement of most market pulp was into regions where the supply was short, the freight rates from supplier to purchaser became the major factor in defining potential sales areas.

Paper products and their markets.   The conversion of pulp to paper results in a list containing several hundreds of products. For industry reporting purposes, however, a distinction is made among products classified as (1) paper, (2) paperboard, and (3) building paper and board. The major products falling into each of these categories are discussed below. Exhibit 6 provides production data for each product class over the past seven years. The difference between U.S. production and consumption of paper and paperboard products is accounted for primarily by imports of newsprint from Canada.

Newsprint in 1964 was the only important paper line in which imports accounted for the major portion of the domestic supply. Although U.S. mills had doubled their capacity since 1950, slightly more than 70% of the domestic newsprint consumption was still supplied from Canada (however, almost 20% of the Canadian newsprint capacity was owned by U.S. producers).

The deficit position of U.S. newsprint manufacturers dates back to 1913, when the tariff on newsprint was removed. This was a time when domestic pulpwood supplies were becoming scarce (before the development of U.S. capacity in the South), and the importing of Canadian newsprint enabled U.S. paper makers to utilize their nearby raw materials for the production of more profitable types of paper. As a result, output of newsprint in the U.S. declined from 1,684,000 tons in 1926 to only 719,800 tons in 1944, a drop of 57%.

Following World War II, several large U.S. companies reentered the newsprint market as a result of the development of the pulp and paper industry in the South around an ample supply of low-cost timber, as well as the rising freight rates charged Canadian suppliers.

Two factors influenced newsprint consumption. The first was the total rate of newspaper circulation (numbers of copies); the second was expenditures for newspaper advertising, which was the primary determinant of the number of pages per copy. Except for minor setbacks in 1952 and 1953, U.S. newspaper circulation has grown steadily. Newspaper advertising lineage was more volatile, since advertising expenditures tended to vary with general economic conditions. Per capita consumption of newsprint has changed little, remaining at about 80 lbs. per person over the past five years.

Most newsprint was sold direct to publishers on long-term-assured-supply contracts, which provided for price changes in response to changes in general industry levels.

In 1964, excess capacity remained a problem in the newsprint segment of the paper industry, and price concessions of one type or another (e.g., absorption of freight costs by manufacturers) were expected to be the rule rather than the exception over the near term.

Printing papers were used primarily by commercial printers for advertising copy, greeting cards, and business forms (about 50% of printing paper output); by periodical publishers (about 40% of output); and by book publishers (about 10% of total output). Many grades of printing paper were available, ranging

exhibit 6

NOTES ON THE FOREST PRODUCTS INDUSTRY

U.S. Paper and Paperboard Production

(thousand tons)

Actual Production Figures	Newsprint	Printing	Fine	Coarse	Tissue	All Other Paper	Total Paper	Containerboard*	Boxboard*	Other Paperboard†	Total Paperboard	Total Paper and Paperboard	Construction Paper and Board	Wet Machine Board	Total Paper, Paperboard, Construction Paper and Board, Wet Machine Board
1955	1,459	3,938	1,450	3,687	1,761	610	12,905	7,244	4,407	2,392	14,044	26,949	3,228	179	30,356
1956	1,620	4,304	1,575	3,948	1,860	683	13,990	7,451	4,530	2,390	14,372	28,362	3,070	147	31,579
1957	1,807	4,033	1,516	3,655	1,912	659	13,581	7,337	4,513	2,331	14,182	27,763	2,886	138	30,787
1958	1,726	4,037	1,535	3,613	1,945	642	13,497	7,259	4,533	2,445	14,237	27,734	3,055	121	30,910
1959	1,924	4,509	1,759	3,999	2,128	752	15,071	8,232	4,911	2,829	15,972	31,043	3,340	145	34,528
1960	2,004	4,700	1,776	3,957	2,201	760	19,399	8,187	4,895	2,845	15,927	31,326	3,194	175	34,695
1961	2,054	4,701	1,924	3,997	2,312	844	15,833	8,661	5,008	3,059	16,727	32,560	3,236	155	35,951
1962	2,098	4,910	2,038	4,197	2,424	912	16,579	9,299	5,265	3,283	17,847	34,426	3,407	162	37,995
1963	2,113	5,269	2,131	4,241	2,577	919	17,250	9,642	5,415	3,541	18,598	35,848	3,557	141	39,546
1964	2,137	5,620	2,247	4,349	2,717	980	18,050	10,371	5,593	3,977	19,941	37,991	3,749	136	41,842
Growth Rate 1964-55, %	4.3	4.0	5.0	1.8	4.9	5.4	3.8	4.1	2.7	5.8	4.0	3.9	1.7	3.0	3.6

*Domestic use.
†Includes all exports in paperboard.

Sources: American Pulp & Paper Association, National Paperboard Association, Donaldson, Lufkin & Jenrette.

from low grades, similar in composition to newsprint, to high grades made from linen rags and bleached sulfite pulps. In between were grades made from bleached sulfite or sulfate pulp, mixed with soda pulp and waste paper, or with small amounts of groundwood pulp.

Printing papers were sold by the mills to two basic types of customers: one was the volume user, such as a large periodical or book publisher; the other was the paper merchant, or jobber, who was the middleman in the distribution of paper to a multitude of smaller publishers and commercial printers.

The large volume user was primarily interested in a reliable supplier with the proven ability to produce to exacting standards and the facilities to provide technical assistance when unusual problems arose. Quality of product was a crucial factor, because the printing surface of the paper was an important variable in the efficient operation of a press, as well as in the appearance of the finished work. For these reasons, most transactions between paper producers and large volume users were based on long-standing relationships.

The typical paper merchant handled printing papers as part of a very wide product line. A single paper manufacturer rarely supplied more than 10% of a merchant's line. Furthermore, the paper was often produced to the merchant's specifications and bore the merchant's trade name. Under these circumstances, manufacturers tended to become highly dependent upon the merchant for sales to the small users who, in the aggregate, consumed more than 50% of the total production of printing papers. When buying from a manufacturer, the paper merchant expected equivalent pricing and negotiated with alternative suppliers primarily on the basis of quality and service differences.

Printing paper prices tended to move in the same direction as paper prices generally. However, the long-term contractual arrangements between paper manufacturers and publishers tended to keep prices relatively stable. Little new capacity in this segment of the paper industry was added during the major expansions of the 1950's.

Fine papers consisted of writing papers (including bond, ledger, and envelopes) made from chemical wood pulps and to a small degree from rags; bristols (index and post cards); and thin papers (cigarette and carbonizing papers). Writing papers accounted for 75% of total fine paper output.

Fine paper was distributed in the same general manner as printing papers. Sales to converters, who used large volumes of roll stock to make business forms, envelopes, tablets, etc., were usually direct, while sales of bond paper and other finished stock were made through paper merchants. Several manufacturers, such as Oxford and Hammermill, had established consumer franchises for their branded bond papers, but a good share of fine papers were sold under the trade name of the paper merchant. For standard grades of bond paper, price was the most important variable in the sale. For the specialty grades, quality and service took on an added importance.

Sanitary papers consisted of household and sanitary products, such as toilet tissue, cleansing tissue, paper towels, table napkins, and sanitary napkins. The demand for these papers, related closely to population growth and improved living standards, had demonstrated a strong growth trend since World War II. The manufacture of sanitary papers was somewhat more complex technically than production of other papers. Bigger and more expensive facilities were required.

Marketing was on a completely different basis from other paper products, since broad consumer distribution through markets, drugstores, etc., was required. Traditionally, this vastly different distribution requirement had discouraged the entrance of new producers, and profit margins generally had stayed above the industry average.

In 1964, Scott Paper Company was the dominant U.S. factor in the toilet tissue and paper towel field, whereas Kimberly-Clark Corporation was the principal producer of cleansing tissue and sanitary napkins. The manufacture of paper table napkins was somewhat less concentrated, with a number of large integrated producers, in addition to many small mills and converters.

Coarse paper or kraft paper, as it was often called, was the strong brown paper used primarily for paper bags and for wrapping. It was made principally of un-bleached sulfate pulp.

Until recently, growth in coarse paper sales had been aided importantly by the development of multiwall bags, made up of two to six layers of stout paper. Reflecting distinct cost advantages, these containers had captured markets formerly held by cotton and burlap bags. In 1964, about 20% of total U.S. kraft paper production was converted into multiwall shipping sacks. The largest usage for these containers was the chemical industry (principally for packaging fertilizers), followed by agricultural producers and the building materials industries.

Most multiwall bags were produced in converting plants owned by pulp and paper manufacturers. Bag sales were made directly to the user by the manufacturer's sales force, with price and service being the major determinants in securing an order.

A trend toward bulk shipment of cement and fertilizers, and the entry of polyethylene into the heavy duty bag market, were factors which might slow the growth in multiwall bag consumption in the years ahead.

Grocery bags and other paper bag production consumed slightly over 29% of the 1964 output of coarse paper. Demand for grocery and variety bags, which was geared primarily to consumer spending, has been fairly stable. Most coarse paper manufacturers converted their own bags and sold them through paper merchants or directly to food chains and food wholesalers. Price was the major factor in the sale.

Another important use for coarse paper was in the manufacture of converting papers such as asphalting papers, gumming stock, and envelopes. About 28% of total coarse paper production went into such converting papers. Converters normally purchased coarse paper in large rolls, directly from the paper manufacturer, on a price basis. There was no clear-cut trend in demand for these papers because the end uses of the converted paper were so varied.

Coarse paper was also used extensively as a wrapping medium (16% of coarse paper output), much of which was sold through paper merchants. For this use, however, competition from polyethylene had been strong, and there had been no growth in wrapping paper consumption in recent years.

The remaining 4% of coarse paper production was in waxed paper, glassine, greaseproof, and vegetable parchment varieties.

Paperboard was the name given to paper which was .009 inches or more in thickness, and whose other characteristics were more closely akin to board than to more flexible materials. About 80% of U.S. paperboard production was consumed for packaging; most of the remainder was used in the construction industry.

Paperboard used to make containers was generally of a combined type; i.e., the outer and inner layers consisted of different pulp stocks. Containerboard could be either solid or corrugated. In solid boards, the space between the two outer faces was filled completely with filler chip, made from waste paper stock. Corrugated board had between the outer faces one or more layers of intermediate corrugated material, called "medium." The outer faces of both types were called "liners" or "linerboard." Most linerboard was made from unbleached sulfate pulp. Corrugating medium was generally a mixture of wastepaper and semi-chemical pulp. In 1964, rolls of linerboard accounted for 40% of all paperboard production, and rolls of corrugating medium added another 15%. These rolls were processed by container plants into shipping containers meeting users' specifications.

Knocked-down folding boxes, such as those used to ship groceries, comprised 17% of paperboard output. Folding boxes were shipped flat, to be set up by the user at his plant. Folding box board was made economically from either sulfite or sulfate pulp.

Preformed and assembled "setup" boxes, such as those used in department stores, consumed about 9% of U.S. paperboard output. Setup box board could be made from groundwood stock, although liners made from bleached chemical pulp were often used to improve their appearance.

The remaining paperboard output went to a wide variety of special uses, such as packaging of individual food items (milk, butter, cereal, etc.) and cardboard.

In 1964, about three-fourths of the companies owning mills which converted pulp to paperboard also owned facilities for processing their paperboard output into containers and boxes. Thus paperboard production was closely tried to the demand for containers. Container sales were divided 20% to produce growers (fresh fruits and vegetables) and 80% to industrial users (20% of which went to food canners and packers).

The sale of shipping containers was a fiercely competitive business in the late 1950's and early 1960's, primarily because the integrated producers were often willing to take low prices for the finished product in order to keep their paperboard mills (which had very high fixed costs) running at full capacity. This practice allowed integrated companies to show over-all profits by combining substantial gains at the paper mill level with breakeven or loss operations at the converting level. Nonintegrated converters were able to survive under these conditions only by concentrating on specialty types of containers, which were free from commodity-type pricing, or by merging with integrated firms.

Building Paper and Board—Building paper was a general term applied to thick papers used in building construction. Sometimes the paper was mixed with asbestos (to be used as sheathing paper), with felt (used for heat insulation), or with tar or asphalt (for roofing materials).

Building boards included rigid materials such as wellboard, plasticboard, gypsum board, and many types of insulating boards. These were generally visible as exterior or interior wall covering. Flexible building board was usually inserted between studs and joists as insulating material and hence had much softer surfaces and more pliable form.

Paper and paper board manufacturers generally sold paperboard roll stock directly to building material converters, for processing into building papers and board. Since these products generally were highly standardized, they sold primarily on the basis of price and assured delivery.

Profit determinants.   Profits in the paper segment of the forest products industry were directly related to the percentage of mill capacity employed. Attaining consistently a high percentage throughput was extremely difficult for the industry, however, because new pulp and paper capacity could not be added gradually in response to demand. A new mill required about two years to construct, and, when it came on stream, there was a sudden, sizeable addition to output. The large investment involved in a new facility (often as much as $30 million to $40 million) placed fixed costs at a very high level. Moreover, the demand for paperboard tended to be relatively elastic. With the breakeven point often being as high as 75% of capacity, price reductions to increase throughput were frequently economic for the paperboard manufacturers. This same high throughput requirement was only slightly less critical to producers of other grades of paper.

Exhibit 7 shows capital expenditures for new facilities and modernization of old facilities for the paper industry in recent years, and the resulting relationship between capacity and production.

Coming off a decade of prosperity following World War II, the pulp and paper industry engaged in extensive capital spending which resulted in severe overcapacity in 1957. Between the peak profit year of 1956 and the recession which followed two years later, the industry's operating level fell from 96% to 79.8% of capacity, and industry profits declined from $680 million to $434 million. Overcapacity persisted through 1963, and price weakness continued throughout the period. In 1964, capacity was more in line with demand and prices firmed somewhat. The major concern in 1964 was that the industry was about to overbuild again, as it had in 1956. To some degree this was inevitable, since no major firm could afford to risk losing market share through lack of capacity when its competitors were increasing their productive capabilities by substantial additions.

THE WORLD SITUATION

The U.S. pulp and paper industry was a net importer of about 1.3 million tons of wood pulp and some 5.5 million tons of newsprint in 1964, while it was a net exporter of about 1 million tons of other grades of paper and board.

There was little question that both manufacturing and distribution of pulp and paper would become much more international in scope for U.S. firms in coming years. Per capita paper consumption in the United States had risen 24% in the period 1954–64 (to 479 lbs.). The comparable figure for some other countries included: Sweden, 357 lbs.; Great Britain, 230; West Germany, 205; France, 146; Japan, 136; Italy, 98; Spain, 44; Russia, 38; Central and South America, 33; and Africa, 7.5. As standards of living in these countries rose, demand for virtually every grade of paper was expected to increase. As foreign demand increased, the U.S. pulp and paper industry appeared certain to benefit, since North American timber resources were the largest supply suitable for paper making in

exhibit 7

NOTES ON THE FOREST PRODUCTS INDUSTRY

Pulp, Paper, and Paperboard
Domestic Capital Expenditures

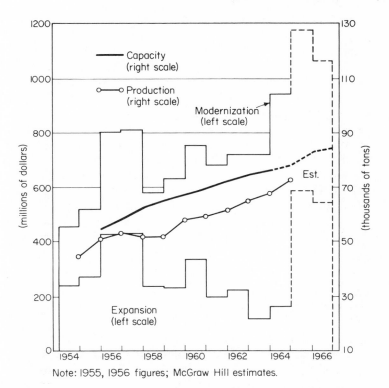

Note: 1955, 1956 figures; McGraw Hill estimates.

the world. Other major timber stands in the world were in Scandinavia, Africa, Latin America, and Russia. Scandinavian producers were believed to be nearing peak output, and rising labor costs in other countries enabled the capital-intensive U.S. producers to become fully competitive in world markets. Timber which grew in the tropical climates of Africa and Latin America thus far had proven too hard and too high in resin content to make suitable pulp. Even if the timber characteristics could be solved, political considerations made it unattractive to invest in these areas the large amount of capital necessary for efficient pulp production.

The U.S. Forest Products Industry,

PART II: COMPETITIVE STRATEGIES
OF EIGHT SELECTED COMPANIES

Part I of this note was concerned with examining the principal environmental forces within the forest products industry which affect strategic choices. This second part of the note is concerned with the ways in which a number of individual companies in the industry have reacted to the environment and how well they are performing.

Eight companies, representing a wide range of strategies, are discussed here in some detail. Exhibit 1 summarizes important characteristics of these companies plus those of the other top 50 U.S. and Canadian companies in 1966 forest products sales. Exhibits 2 through 8 show comparative financial data for the eight representative companies, plus Boise Cascade Corporation, for a ten year period.

Mergers, extensive diversifications, and heavy capital expenditures have caused marked shifts in position among the top companies over the past decade.

INTERNATIONAL PAPER COMPANY

This company and its subsidiaries comprised the largest papermaking and forest products organization in the world, with $1.4 billion in 1966 sales. It accounted for 11% of the industry paper and paperboard output and 3% of available market pulp.

Products. International Paper produced a full line of lumber, plywood, and paper products. Pulp and paper output in 1966 totaled 6,386,288 tons, of which 40.6% was bleached and unbleached paperboard, 19.6% newsprint, 21.8% other papers (book and bond paper, specialty papers, etc.), and 18.0% market pulp. International also converted 1,266,835 tons of its paper and paperboard production into shipping

---

© 1967 by the Board of Trustees of the Leland Stanford Junior University.

containers, milk cartons, folding cartons, labels, and multiwall and grocery bags.

In 1966, lumber and plywood operations, chiefly carried on by the Long Bell Division, resulted in an output of 188,992,000 board feet of lumber, 341,843,000 square feet of veneer and plywood, and 134,311,000 square feet of insulating board.

Markets. Paperboard products, which were not converted in the company's own plants, were sold to jobbers and to the manufacturers of containers (folding cartons, shipping containers, milk cartons, etc.). Newsprint was sold directly to newspapers throughout the United States. Book and bond paper, including rotogravure paper, various grades of salesbook and tablet paper, papers for magazines, telephone directories, and catalogs, and miscellaneous printing papers, were sold directly to publishers and manufacturers, and through paper distributors. Pulp was sold directly to other paper producers.

The Long Bell Division wholesaled the major portion of its lumber, plywood, and manufactured lumber products to independent lumber yards and building material dealers, predominantly in the midwestern agricultural states. The remainder was sold directly to the public from its own retail building material stores and lumber yards. The building material stores also marketed paints, wallpaper, hardwood, and other products.

Plants. International's annual primary production capacity was estimated at 6.4 million tons in 1966. The company operated 20 mills in the U.S. and seven in Canada. Kraft paper was primarily produced in nine southern mills, located near large areas of southern pine. These mills regularly produced all of their own sulfate pulp requirements, and also produced excess pulp for other companies. Northern mills were chiefly engaged in the manufacture of white papers, although these grades were also made to a lesser extent in the southern mills. Three Canadian plants, with an annual capacity of 960,000 tons, accounted for the bulk of the company's newsprint output. In addition, the company had two new plants in the southern United States which added another 230,000 tons to annual newsprint capacity. Market pulp was produced in both Canadian and southern mills.

International owned 49 converting plants located throughout the United States. Eleven additional converting facilities were operated in Canada, Germany, Israel, Italy, Greece, Mexico, Venezuela, Colombia, Puerto Rico, and Ecuador.

Timber holdings. Timberland reserves totaled 23 million acres at the end of 1966. 70% of these holdings were in Canada, of which 1.4 million acres were owned in fee, and 14.6 million acres were held under government license. In the United States, 6.4 million acres were owned in fee, and 354 thousand acres were leased.

The company. International Paper was organized in 1898 as a consolidation of companies accounting for approximately two-thirds of the newsprint capacity of the North American continent. By the end of World War I, however, its position had deteriorated to the point where it produced only one-fifth of the

exhibit 1

NOTES ON THE FOREST PRODUCTS INDUSTRY

Fifty Largest Products Companies
(ranked by 1966 forest products sales volume)

Name and Headquarters	1966		Product Mix		Facilities and Locations	Timberlands	Degree of Integration and Other Characteristics
1. International Paper New York, New York	Sales Net income Total assets	$1,450.1 105.2 1,304.6	Paper Paperboard Newsprint Other Pulp Converted Paper Products 1,267 M Tons Lumber 189 mil. bd. ft. Plywood 342 mil. sq. ft. Insulating Board 134 mil. sq. ft.	6.4 mil. tons 41% 19% 22% 18%	20 mills in U.S. and 7 in Canada. Kraft products primarily produced in southern states. White paper in both northern and southern mills. Newsprint and pulp produced in three Canadian mills. Converting plants throughout U.S., Canada, and other.	Owned 7,700,000 acres and had cutting rights on an additional 15,000,000 adres. 70% in Canada. U.S. holdings in southeast, northeast, and West.	World's largest paper producer. Bulk of converted products made from company produced paper and paperboard.
2. U.S. Plywood—Champion Papers, Inc. New York, New York	Sales Net income Total assets	$1,029.5 43.3 797.9	Plywood Lumber Other wood and building related Paper related products	31% 12% 16% 46%	26 plywood plants (primarily in the West), 23 sawmills (primarily in the West), 12 veneer and prefinished panel mills, 4 door plants, 8 particleboard plants, 35 paper related plants, 17 others, 216 warehouses in U.S. and Canada.	Owned 5.8 billion board feet in California, Oregon, Washington, Montana, New Hampshire, Virginia, North Carolina, South Carolina, and Canada. Owned or controlled 32 billion board feet plus tens of millions of cords of younger timber.	World's largest plywood distribution organization. Important paper producer. Produced 55% of plywood it sold
3. Weyerhaeuser Tacoma, Washington	Sales Net income Total assets	$ 838.8 79.2 996.9	Lumber Containers Pulp Paperboard Softwood plywood Hardwood products Manufactured panels Paper Logs, chips, and timber	25% 24% 11% 7% 9% 5% 2% 12% 5%	39 lumber and plywood mills; 16 other wood products plants. 14 pulp and paperboard mills. 6 printing and writing paper plants. 52 container and carton plants.	2,800,000 acres owned in Douglas Fir region. 800,000 acres owned in Southern Pine region.	Largest U.S. producer of timber products. Highly integrated throughout entire product line. Self-sufficient in timber.
4. Crown Zellerbach San Francisco, California	Sales Net income Total assets	$ 763.9 53.7 873.9	Paper Paperboard Newsprint Printing paper Tissues Industrial paper Lumber 360 mil. bd. ft. Plywood 256 mil. sq. ft.	27% 21% 11% 12% 29%	14 pulp and paper mills, 33 packaging and converting plants, 5 chemical products plants, 9 lumber and plywood mills. Plants primarily in the West and Canada.	Owned 769,000 acres in Washington and Oregon. Owned or controlled 920,000 acres in B.C. and 480,000 acres owned or leased in Louisiana and Mississippi.	The dominant West Coast paper company. 60% of pulpwood from own timberlands.

#	Company	Financials ($ millions)	Products	%	Facilities	Timberland	Notes
5.	St. Regis Paper, New York, New York	Sales $700.1; Net income 38.7; Total assets 725.8	Kraft pulp Corrugated boxes Printing and fine paper Multiwall and textile bags Flexible packaging Lumber and plywood Envelopes, paper plates, etc. Boxes Glassine and greaseproof papers Other (including plastics)	20% 17% 12% 10% 10% 10% 7% 5% 3%	22 paper mills, 116 paper converting plants, 25 plants making other products. Facilities located throughout the U.S. and in 18 foreign countries. Four mills were joint ventures, several foreign operations were partially owned.	5,794,720 acres owned or controlled in the following areas: Northeast 1,154,207 Great Lakes 170,921 Southeast 1,590,183 Northwest 703,642 Canada 2,175,767	40-45% of timber requirements from own timberlands. Bulk of paperboard requirements produced internally.
6.	Georgia-Pacific, Portland, Oregon	Sales $659.2; Net income 50.3; Total assets 958.0	Plywood Pulp, paper, and board Lumber Chemicals and minerals Other	34% 34% 11% 15% 6%	23 plywood and veneer plants, 17 paper and paperboard mills, 22 box and container plants, 24 lumber mills, 10 chemical plants, 9 gypsum, and 14 others.	3,500,000 acres in western and southeastern U.S., most timberland located in Washington and Oregon.	Largest producer of fir plywood. Second largest lumber producer. Third largest gypsum producer. 70% of lumber needs from own controlled land. 34% of paper and paperboard converted in own plants. Active in mergers and acquisitions, including Bestwall Gypsum in 1965.
7.	Mead Corporation, Dayton, Ohio	Sales $633.3; Net income 27.1; Total assets 456.9	White paper Paperboard Wholesale paper Educational products	28% 31% 31% 10%	6 white paper mills, 7 paperboard mills, 21 container plants, 7 other converting plants, 13 other plants.	Owned or controlled 4,560,000 acres.	Most pulpwood was purchased. 20% of pulp requirements for white paper purchased. Majority of paperboard output consumed in own converting plants.
8.	Kimberly-Clark Corporation, Neenah, Wisconsin	Sales $622.5; Net income 38.7; Total assets 571.5	Sanitary paper Book and fine paper Industrial paper Lumber, pulp, and miscellaneous	45% 25% 14% 16%	13 pulp mills, 32 consumer products mills, 10 industrial products mills, 19 other paper mills, 8 lumber products mills, 4 seedling nurseries. Throughout the U.S., Canada, Mexico, France, Puerto Rico, England, Germany, South Africa, Australia, Holland, Japan, Philippines, Venezuela, El Salvador, Malaysia.	Owned substantial acreage in Wisconsin, Minnesota, Michigan, Alabama, California, and Canada.	Largest producer of cellulose wadding and second largest producer of coated book paper.

Name and Headquarters	1966		Product Mix		Facilities and Locations	Timberlands	Degree of Integration and Other Characteristics
9. Bowater Paper Corporation, Ltd. London, England	Sales Net income Total assets	$ 530.0 82.3 710.0	Newsprint Packaging Magazine, coated, packaging, and other paper Market pulp Other	43% 16% 24% 12% 5%	Pulp, paper, and board mills in Tennessee, South Carolina, Canada, France, and England. U.S. plants produce kraft sulfite pulp, newsprint, and hardboard.	Harvesting rights on more than 6,000,000 acres in British Columbia.	Owned 8.5% of world newsprint capacity and 10.5% of combined U.S. and Canadian capacity. Tennessee mill was largest domestic newsprint mill.
10. Scott Paper Philadelphia, Pennsylvania	Sales Net income Total assets	$ 490.7 44.6 548.4	Toilet tissues, paper towels, household wax paper, plastic wrap, facial tissues, paper napkins, industrial wipers, windshield wipers, apparel and industrial polyurethane foams, plastic and paper cups, sanitary napkins, converting and printing papers. Also visual aid and reproduction equipment and materials.		19 plants in 11 states, including pulp and paper mills, converting plants, plants for plastic cups and other plastics, films, and equipment.	Owned or had cutting rights on 300,000 acres in Washington, Oregon, and British Columbia. 2,035,000 acres in Maine and eastern Canada. 425,000 acres in Alabama and Mississippi.	Largest domestic producer of toilet tissues, paper towels, and household wax papers. Most pulpwood purchased. Self-sufficient in pulp.
11. Boise Cascade Boise, Idaho	Sales Net income Total assets	$ 489.2 17.0 524.5	Lumber and plywood Pulp and paper Wholesale and retail Insulite Home construction Other	18% 60% 9% 6% 3% 4%	14 lumber mills, 7 plywood mills, 9 pulp and paper mills, 19 container plants, 6 multiwall and special products plants, 5 envelope plants, 92 retail and 13 wholesale outlets, 10 wood converting and house plants.	Owned 1,291,000 acres. Cutting rights on additional 4,758,000 acres.	25% of timber requirements from own timberlands. Bulk of paperboard supplied internally. 46% of wholesale and retail requirements purchased internally. Acquired Minnesota and Ontario Paper Company in January, 1965.
12. MacMillan, Bloedel, Ltd. Vancouver, B.C.	Sales Net income Total assets	$ 473.5 42.5 641.7	Lumber, plywood, building Newsprint Pulp, paper Container	48% 29% 19% 4%	4 sawmills in B.C. 2 newsprint, 3 pulp, 5 container, 2 plywood, 2 shingle, 1 door, 1 kraft paper, 1 paper bag, 1 roofing materials, 2 fine paper plants and three others throughout Canada.	Owned or controlled 3,500,000 acres in Canada. Bought less than 30% of requirements on market.	Company also conducted a worldwide merchandise business in timber products.
13. Container Corporation of America Chicago, Illinois	Sales Net income Total assets	$ 460.4 34.2 388.0	Corrugated and solid fibre shipping containers Folding cartons, fibre cans, and plastic products Paperboard, pulp, and waste paper	47% 35% 18%	14 paperboard mills, 28 container factories, 13 carton factories, 11 fibre can plants, 5 plastic plants, 6 waste paper facilities, 27 plants in Latin America and 18 in Europe.	Owned 584,000 acres in northern Florida and southern Georgia.	Largest independent paperboard container company. Estimated 25% of pulpwood own timberlands and 8% of paperboard from own plants.
14. American Can Company New York, New York	Sales Net income Total assets Forest products sales (est.)	$1,369.7 71.6 1,087.1 450.0	Metal and fibre cans Milk and other paperboard containers including Dixie cups Other	58% 27% 15%	146 plants in U.S., Canada, and Puerto Rico and American Samoa. Including 7 paper and plate plants, 22 paper packaging and tissue plants, and 13 milk container plants.	Cutting rights on 2,550,000 acres in eastern Canada and ownership and control of 570,000 acres in eastern Canada and eastern U.S.	World's leading producer of metal containers. Paper operations were completely integrated from forests to the consumer. Sales offices in more than 100 cities.

No. / Company	Financials		Products	%	Plants	Properties	Remarks
15. Domtar, Ltd. Montreal, Quebec	Sales	$ 430.1	Building materials	20%	27 building material, 28 chemical plants, 7 consumer product plants, 21 pulp and paper mills, 14 packaging and bag plants.		Had diversified extensively in last ten years through acquisition.
	Net income	24.2	Chemicals	17%			
	Total assets	506.4	Paper and pulp	63%			
	Forest products sales (est.)						
16. Continental Can Company, Inc. New York, New York	Sales	$1,339.2	Metal and composite containers	56%	170 total plants. 74 metal container plants, 58 paper product plants, 32 plastic plants. Paper product plants include 18 container plants, 15 folding carton and fibre drum plants, 11 paperboard mills.	Owned or leased 1,300,700 acres in 6 southeastern states.	Largest producer of fibre drums and third largest producer of paper containers and paper packaging.
	Net income	70.9	Paper products and containers	32%			
	Total assets	957.4	Glass and plastic containers	9%			Most paperboard requirements produced internally.
		430.0	Other	3%			
			Paper products include corrugated boxes, folding cartons; kraft bags and wrapping paper; boxboard and container board; fibre drums, paper plates, and cups.				
17. Diamond International New York, New York	Sales	$ 368.5	Paperboard, packaging, molded pulp, and commercial printing	65%	3 match plants, 4 molded packaging plants. 31 packaging and printing plants, 8 lumber mills. 77 building material stores on both coasts.	Owned 377,000 acres in California and Idaho. 167,000 acres in Minnesota, Maine, Montana, and New York.	Dominant factor in U.S. match industry. Had diversified extensively in the last ten years.
	Net income	29.0	Lumber, wood products, and retail operations	24%			
	Total assets	258.0	Matches and miscellaneous	11%			
18. West Virginia Pulp and Paper New York, New York	Sales	$ 360.4	Primary production 1,534,000 tons		6 paper mills, 15 corrugated box plants, 3 bag plants, 2 folding carton plants, 2 chemical plants. Paperboard and corrugated container plant in Brazil.	Owned 1,067,000 acres.	Most pulpwood purchased. Estimated 75% paperboard needs were obtained internally.
	Net income	22.9	Containers, boxes, and bags, 523,000				Owned 56% of U.S. Envelope.
	Total assets	309.8	Chemical products, 111,000 tons Production estimated at 50% printing and conversion, 50% container board and kraft				
19. Union Camp New York, New York	Sales	$ 323.8	Approximately half of sales in bags and containers. Balance in bleached and unbleached paper and board products, lumber and chemical by-products.		5 principal paper processing plants, 24 converting plants. Lumber mills in Georgia and Virginia. 6 chemical plants.	Owned or held options to buy 1,650,000 acres in Southeast.	Converted nearly half of paperboard output.
	Net income	29.6					Largest producer of paper bags and sacks in U.S.
	Total assets	383.3					
20. Flintkote New York, New York	Sales	$ 303.8	Building materials	49%	Approximately 180 plants and mines, mostly in U.S. and Canada.	Owned 16,000 acres in Mississippi and California.	Building materials include roofing, shingles, insulating board, siding, cement, etc.
	Net income	12.4	Paperboard products	17%			
	Total assets	293.2	Industrial products and paving materials	17%			
			Composition floor coverings and adhesives	12%			
			Pipe and conduit	5%			
21. Evans Products Company Portland, Oregon	Sales	$ 282.1	Building products	71%	13 building material plants, 31 wholesale and 25 retail building material distribution centers.	Owned or controlled cutting rights to 4 billion board feet of timber in Washington, Oregon, and Canada.	n.a.
	Net income	5.3	Transportation equipment	29%			
	Total assets	209.4					
22. Hammermill Paper Erie, Pennsylvania	Sales	$ 259.4	Primarily bond paper, mimeo bond, duplicator, ledger, safety, bristol, offset, opaque, cover, and translucent paper. Also envelope converting. Extensive wholesale operations.		15 pulp and paper and envelope plants, primarily in the East.	Owned or controlled 265,000 acres, primarily in the East.	Largest producer of fine papers.
	Net income	12.2					Bulk of pulpwood is purchased. In 1966, acquired Carter Rice Storrs and Bement Inc., a wholesale distributor.
	Total assets	188.0					

Name and Headquarters	1966		Product Mix	Facilities and Locations	Timberlands	Degree of Integration and Other Characteristics
23. Potlatch Forests, Inc. Lewiston, Idaho	Sales Net income Total assets	$ 255.4 11.2 267.0	Lumber (million bd. ft.) 594.6 Plywood (million sq. ft.) 393.5 Pulp (thousand tons) 408.9 Paperboard (thousand tons) Fine paper (thousand tons) 232.4 246.6	10 lumber mills, 2 plywood mills (Idaho), 1 pulp mill (Idaho), 4 paper and paperboard mills in Idaho, Minnesota, and California, 1 pulp specialties plant in California, 2 milk carton plants in California and Missouri, 4 corrugated box plants, and 7 folding carton plants.	Owned 441,000 acres in Idaho, 115,000 acres in Washington, 529,000 acres in Arkansas, and 235,000 acres in Minnesota.	Estimated 60% of timber requirements from own timberlands and 50% of pulp and paper production consumed internally. In 1964, merged with Northwest Paper, integrated paper producers.
24. Brown Company New York, New York	Sales Net income Total assets	$ 212.7 3.9 191.0	Packaging and converted paper 28% Paperboard stock products and matches 23% Cultural and converting papers 18% Paperboard 15% Paper towels and tissues 5% Plywood 5% Other 6%	Principal mills: 2 in New Hampshire, 1 in Michigan. Plus 15 other plants and converting facilities.	4,500,000 acres in Maine, New Hampshire, Vermont, and Ontario. Also Canadian Crown timber leases.	Integrated producer of pulp paperboard, and paper. Acquired KVP Sutherland Paper Company in 1966.
25. Abitibi Paper Company, Ltd. Toronto, Canada	Sales Net income Total assets	$ 211.2 15.9 264.2	Newsprint (thousand tons) 890.8 Printing and fine paper (thousand tons) 158.4 Bleached sulfite pulp (thousand tons) @5.1 Board (thousand tons) 206.5	14 mills in Ontario, Manitoba, and Quebec.	25,000 square miles controlled in Ontario, Manitoba, and Quebec.	54% of sales in U.S. 36% of sales in Canada.
26. Tenneco Corporation Houston, Texas	Sales Net income Total assets Forest products sales	$ 182.8	Integrated oil operations 42% Packaging 28% Chemicals 26% Other 4%	Packaging corporation division: 10 paper mills, 30 container plants, 9 carton plants, 5 moulded pulp plants.	Packaging corporation controlled 200,000 acres in Michigan. 51% owned subsidiary owned 271,000 acres in southeast.	Owned 51% of Tenneco Pulp and Paper Company. Also held an important interest in Fibreboard Paper Products Company.
27. Simpson Timber Seattle, Washington	Privately held. Sales estimated	$ 200.0	Important producer of lumber, plywood, and kraft paper	Mills in coastal Washington and Oregon.	Substantial holdings in Western Washington and Oregon.	Primarily a lumber producer but also held interest in Simpson Lee and other paper operations.
28. Olin Mathieson Chemical Corporation New York, New York	Sales Net income Total assets Forest products sales (est.)	$1,117.1 66.7 1,162.6 182.0	Chemicals 25% Packaging 17% Metals 21% Squibb 22% Winchester Western 15% Packaging includes cellophane, polyethylene, kraft paper, containers and cigarette paper, and hardwood flooring.	Packaging division: 16 plants including pulp and kraft paper mills, converting, plants for corrugated boxes, shipping containers, wrappers, paper, multiwall bags, printing paper, cigarette paper, 2 sawmills, a wood treating plant, and a hardwood flooring mill.	540,000 acres in Louisiana and Arkansas.	n.a.
29. Owens-Illinois, Inc. Toledo, Ohio	Sales Net income Total assets Forest products sales (est.)	$ 908.0 54.2 862.6 180.0	Forest products division: primarily containerboard and corrugated containers. Also multiwall bags, fibre cans, and plywood.	26 glass container plants, 12 plastic products plants, 5 paperboard plants, 20 corrugated box plants, 1 multiwall bag plant, 11 consumer and technical products plants, 1 plywood mill, and 5 fibre can plants.	Owned or leased 1,500,000 acres in Florida, Georgia, Michigan, Wisconsin, Virginia, Louisiana, Texas, and The Bahamas.	Largest domestic producer of bottles and other glass containers. Self-sufficient in pulpwood. Owned 31% interest in Owens-Corning Fibreglass Corporation.

#	Company		($ millions / figures)		Facilities	Notes
30.	Rayonier New York, New York	Sales Net income Total assets	$ 171.2 20.3 287.4	Pulp and paper, 1,022,700 tons Chemical cellulose tons Papermaking pulp tons Lumber—246 million bd. ft.	6 pulp mills in Washington, Georgia, Florida, British Columbia. 2 sawmills in British Columbia, 3 silvichemical plants. Grays Harbor Paper Company (2/3 owned) operated a fine paper mill in Washington. Owned and leased 391,115 acres in Washington and 694,251 acres in Florida and Georgia. Also held cutting rights on large acreage in British Columbia.	World's leading producer of rayon pulp. Traded its spruce and Douglas fir trees with plywood companies for hemlock. Only U.S. producer of bleached sulfite pulp from southern pine using company developed process.
31.	Consolidated Bathurst, Ltd. Montreal, Quebec	Sales Net income Total assets	$ 165.9 17.7 314.2	Primarily newsprint and other paper products; also lumber.	5 paper mills in Quebec and 2 saw mills in Ontario and 1 in Quebec, 5 multiwall bag plants. Owned 19,500 square miles in Eastern Canada.	Exported 65% of pulp and paper in U.S.
32.	Bemis Company, Inc. Minneapolis, Minnesota	Sales Net income Total assets Forest products sales (est.)	$ 245.2 6.5 143.0 165.0	A broad line of paper, burlap, plastics and textile bags and other forms of flexible packaging, including a molded cellulose material; plus packaging accessories and paper specialties. Also made equipment for plastics industry.	2 cotton mills (Tennessee and Alabama), 3 paper mills (New Hampshire, Vermont, and Illinois), 1 woven paper mill (Missouri), 3 paper specialty plants (Missouri, New York, and Arkansas), 17 converting plants, and 9 others. None	A leading manufacturer of flexible packaging materials.
33.	Inland Container Indianapolis, Indiana	Sales Net income Total assets	$ 154.8 9.9 110.5	Corrugated containers and kraft linerboard accounted for almost 85% of sales. Balance was paperboard products and glass containers.	Three 50% owned kraft linerboard and corrugating medium plants in Georgia and Alabama. 25 box plants in Indiana, Pennsylvania, Ohio, Michigan, Virginia, Wisconsin, Georgia, Florida, Kentucky, Texas, Illinois, Maryland, and New Jersey. 866,000 acres owned and 136,000 leased in Southeast.	Third largest shipper in U.S. fibre box industry.
34.	Riegel Paper New York, New York	Sales Net income Total assets	$ 146.6 7.9 132.3	Packaging products and machinery 50% Paperboard 16% Bleached kraft pulp 16% Industrial materials and papers	11 flexible packaging plants in New Jersey, Indiana, New York, Georgia, North Carolina, Pennsylvania, Virginia, Missouri, Texas, and Tennessee. 4 paper mills in New Jersey. Pulp and paperboard mill in North Carolina. Packaging equipment plant in Illinois. Owned or leased 335,387 acres near North Carolina pulp mill.	Used 42% of pulp production and sold the remainder.
35.	Price Company Limited Quebec, Canada	Sales Net income Total assets	$ 143.6 12.0 268.0	Newsprint 69% Paperboard and kraft 12% Paper for resale 11% Suffite pulp 5% Lumber 3%	4 pulp and paper mills in Quebec producing newsprint, paperboard, and boxes. 1 pulp and newsprint mill in Newfoundland. 1 sawmill in Quebec. Owned 186 square miles. Holds under license 8,200,000 square miles of timber in Quebec, and owned or leased 7,500 square miles in Newfoundland. Owned 194,000 acres. Also leased 117,000 in Maine.	Bulk of newsprint sold in U.S. Self-sufficient in pulpwood.

Name and Headquarters	1966		Product Mix		Facilities and Locations	Timberlands	Degree of Integration and Other Characteristics
36. Standard Packaging New York, New York	Sales Net income Total assets	$ 143.2 1.2 101.7	Business services Packaging products Consumer products Mill products	38% 22% 22% 18%	21 plants mostly in northeast.		Most pulpboard obtained from own timberlands. Most paperboard output consumed in packaging and consumer products plants. Groundwood pulp purchased for Maine and Vermont operations.
37. Fibreboard Paper Products San Francisco, California	Sales Net income Total assets	$ 143.0 4.8 142.6	Wood pulp, paperboard, folding cartons and boxes Smooth-surface floor coverings, gypsum products, asphalt roofing, shingles, lumber, and plywood	75%	4 pulp and paperboard mills in California, 2 in Washington, 14 container plants in California, Colorado, Hawaii, Arizona, Oregon, and Washington, 11 building products plants in Oregon, California, Nevada, and Colorado. 6 others.	Owned 100,000 acres in California, Washington, and Nevada.	Leading paperboard producer on the West Coast. Most wood chips and pulpwood purchased externally.
38. Hoerner-Waldorf Corporation St. Paul, Minnesota	Sales Net income Total assets	$ 140.0 11.1 118.1	Principally made corrugated containerboard, kraft, and boxboard which it sold or converted into containers. Also flexible packaging and wrapping paper.	25%	26 plants mainly in North central United States	Owned 36,000 acres in Michigan.	Sales principally in North central, midwestern, and southwestern United States.
39. Great Northern Paper Company Bangor, Maine	Sales Net income Total assets	$ 123.9 12.5 219.6	Newsprint Linerboard Specialty and printing papers	35% 28% 37%	2 pulp and paper mills in Maine. 1 kraft mill in Georgia.	2,208,000 acres owned in Maine. Owned or leased 178,000 acres in Georgia, Alabama, and Florida.	Accounted for 16% of domestic newsprint production. 50% of Maine mill's requirements from own timber and 10% of Georgia mills.
40. Nekoosa-Edwards Paper Company Port Edwards, Wisconsin	Sales Net income Total assets	$ 120.7 6.3 141.6	Business papers Printing papers Technical papers Other	64% 17% 13% 6%	3 pulp and paper mills in Wisconsin and 1 in New York. Merchants in 28 locations in 15 states.	Owned 237,000 acres.	Manufactured 60% of paper sold and purchased balance—principally fine papers.
41. Consolidated Papers, Inc. Wisconsin Rapids, Wisconsin	Sales Net income Total assets	$ 119.2 10.6 117.7	In thousand tons: Enamel papers Packaging papers Other papers Paperboard Paperboard products Sulfite pulp	364 27 2 16 30 12	9 plants in Wisconsin.	Owned or controlled 261,598 acres in Wisconsin, Michigan, and Minnesota, and 374,291 acres in Ontario, Canada.	n.a.
42. Longview Fibre Company Longview, Washington	Sales Net income Total assets	$ 114.0 13.3 105.6	Pulp, paper, and paper products, containerboard, corrugated and solid fibre containers. Also sells logs.		Main plant at Longview produced pulp, bleached and unbleached kraft paper, linerboard, and corrugated medium. 8 container plants in Washington, California, Massachusetts, Wisconsin, Iowa, and Minnesota.	360,000 acres owned in Douglas Fir region.	Purchased sawmill residuals for pulp requirements. Pulp and paperboard requirements obtained internally. 80% of sales made direct to customers mainly on West Coast.

No. & Company	Financials ($ millions)	Products	%	Principal Plants	Timberland	Remarks
43. Masonite Corporation, Chicago, Illinois	Sales $109.4 Net income 9.1 Total assets 122.5	Unfinished hardboard, exterior siding, prefinished hardboard for interior walls, pegboard perforated panels, plastic coated "Marlite," and prefab panels.		Principal plants: 1 plant to Mississippi, 1 plant in California, and 12 other plants.	Owned 322,867 acres in Mississippi, 75,050 acres in California, and 10,000 acres in Pennsylvania.	Largest domestic producer of hardboard, accounting for an estimated 75% of total output. Most timber purchased from farmers, wood lot owners, and jobbers. However, timber was also sold to others.
44. Lily-Tulip Cup Corporation, New York, New York	Sales $107.7 Net income 7.8 Total assets 89.1	Hot and cold paper beverage cups and nested paper containers for use in the serving and packaging of food and beverages. 600 different sizes, types, and styles. Plus 100 related plastic items.		5 main plants in Missouri, New Jersey, California, Georgia, and Canada.	None.	One of the two largest producers of paper cups and nested paper containers. Much of bleached paperboard requirements from joint venture company with International Paper Company.
45. Federal Paper Board Company, Bogota, New Jersey	Sales $107.6 Net income 3.6 Total assets 80.3	Folding cartons and paperboard Glassware and corrugated containers Miscellaneous	73% 26% 1%	11 paperboard mills in Connecticut, Illinois, Virginia, Ohio, Maryland, Pennsylvania, and North Carolina. 9 folding carton plants in Connecticut, Illinois, Massachusetts, Pennsylvania, Georgia, and North Carolina. 1 glass factory and corrugated container plant in Ohio. 2 corrugated container plants in Maryland and Pennsylvania.	None.	38% of paperboard output converted internally. Also purchased paperboard for conversion. 33% of shipping cases used by glass division.
46. American Forest Products, Inc., San Francisco, California	Sales $101.9 Net income 2.0 Total assets 75.7	Lumber, moulding, and other building materials, veneer; paper, wood, and corrugated boxes, unfinished furniture and plastic containers. Operated lumber yards.		14 sawmills, 7 container plants, 1 green veneer mill, 1 paper mill, 4 furniture manufacturing plants in New Jersey, Georgia, and Illinois. 3 pallet plants, 1 plywood mill, 1 fencing plant. Extensive distribution.	Owned 2,160,000,000 board feet in the West.	n.a.
47. Warren (S.D.) Company, Boston, Massachusetts	Sales $101.2 Net income 9.8 Total assets 102.8	Specialty producer of printing papers, including coated and uncoated bonds, magazine, and bible papers.		3 pulp and paper mills in Maine, New Hampshire, and Michigan.	150,000 acres in Maine are owned.	Most pulpwood and rag purchased externally. Some pulp purchased externally.
48. Oxford Paper, New York, New York	Sales $97.3 Net income 8.1 Total assets 119.2	Magazine paper Commercial printing paper Book paper Converting paper (for envelope, business forms, maps, etc.)	40% 20% 24% 16%	One pulp and paper mill each in Maine, Massachusetts, and Ohio.	400,000 acres owned in Maine, New Hampshire, and New Brunswick.	Purchased 94% of pulpwood needs externally. Obtained all pulp internally.
49. Dennison Manufacturing Company, Framingham, Massachusetts	Sales $87.4 Net income 5.3 Total assets 57.5	General stationery supplies Custom paper products Specialty papers Machinery and equipment	44% 29% 17% 10%	3 principal plants in Massachusetts. Others in Illinois, California, Michigan, and Quebec.	None.	Products included binders, pads, "eye-ease" paper, gummed labels.
50. Maryland Cup Corporation, Owings Mills, Maryland	Sales $85.1 Net income 6.8 Total assets 72.1	Manufactured paper cups and containers, paper and plastic straws, paper book matches, ice cream cones, and plastic cups and containers.		28 plants, the majority of which were on the East Coast.	None.	Sales concentrated on food sold from vending machines and for restaurant use.

industry's newsprint output. Following management changes, newsprint production was concentrated in Canada, near low-cost timber supplies, manufacture of kraft pulp and paper was begun, and extensive electric power development was constructed in Canada and New England. In 1937, the capital structure was simplified, the utility interests were divorced, and manufacturing activities were concentrated on kraft paper in the southern U.S. and on newsprint in Canada.

In 1956, International Paper actively entered the lumber and plywood business with the acquisition of the Long Bell Lumber Company. The merger, made through an exchange of common stock, resulted in the addition of approximately 500,000 acres of timber woodlands on the West Coast, 97% of which was located in Washington, Oregon, and California. Lumber mills, plywood plants, and wood processing facilities obtained in this merger were located chiefly in the Pacific Northwest. The company later obtained other lumber facilities in several central southern states.

In 1958, International acquired the Lord Baltimore Press through an exchange of stock. Lord Baltimore was a producer of folding cartons and labels used to package various household products, including cosmetics, medicinal products, tobacco, and confectionery and frozen food specialties. Antitrust regulations had restrained International from further mergers.

International had a very strong financial condition in 1966. Postwar expansion had been financed with funds generated from internal sources. At the end of 1966, the company negotiated a $180 million loan, of which $65 million was drawn down in 1966. This constituted the first significant long-term borrowing in recent history.

Capital spending in the early sixties had been aimed primarily at increasing operating efficiency, rather than toward expansion of existing capacity. However, by the mid-1960's the emphasis was shifting toward expansion of existing mills and construction of new complexes. Major complexes were built at Gardiner, Oregon, in 1964 and Androscoggin, Maine, in 1965. The expansion program for 1966 and 1967 was expected to add, on an annual basis, 700,000 tons of new primary paper capacity.

Capital expenditures totaled $199.9 million in 1966, up from $125.22 million in 1965.

U.S. PLYWOOD—CHAMPION PAPERS INC.

Following the 1966 merger of United States Plywood with Champion Papers (effective February 28, 1967), the surviving corporation reported consolidated *pro forma* 1966 sales of $1,029 million, making it the second largest company in the forest products industry.

Products.   Following the merger, activities were conducted through two groups, coinciding with the predecessor companies.

U.S. Plywood Group made, purchased, and sold Douglas fir and southern pine plywood (softwood), hardwood plywoods, patented particleboard, hardboard, various plywood specialties, doors and related components, veneers, cabinets, paper sticks for lollipops, and lumber. It also purchased and sold a complete line of adhesives, wood finishes and preservatives, and various laminated products, including metal panels. Trade names included Duraply, Weldwood, and Novoply.

Champion Paper Group was a major producer of pulp and paper. It had five divisions.

Paper Division made pulp, paper, and plastic and clay coated paperboards produced from bleached and semibleached pulps. Papers produced were used for many kinds of printing and graphic charts, and for a wide variety of converting purposes, such as production of envelopes, tablets, and business papers. The paperboard made was used for fabrication of containers for liquid, dairy, meat, and bakery products, and in the packaging of other consumer products. It had developed processes for making both machine coated and cast coated quality papers. The cast coated was made under own patents and sold under names Kronekote and Colorcast. The paper division accounted for approximately 48% of net sales.

Distribution Division engaged in the wholesale distribution of fine and industrial papers, commercial stationery products, and office equipment and supplies, as well as school supplies and maintenance and janitorial supplies and chemicals, throughout the U.S.

Packages Division produced packages and packaging materials for the bakery and food industries and for a wide range of other consumer products. It also made and sold thermoformed plastic containers and wax paper, and prints, laminates, and coated flexible packaging materials.

Milk Container Division converted polyethylene coated paperboard into milk cartons, and distributed these products.

Envelope Division made and sold a broad line of envelopes.

Sales in U.S. Plywood's 1966 fiscal year (April 30) of $533 million were divided as follows: softwood plywood, 31%; hardwood plywood and related products, 27%; lumber, 12%; doors, 5%; fir specialties, 5%; miscellaneous, 20%.

The breakdown of 1965 tonnage for Champion was as follows: printing papers, 54%; writing papers, 17%; kraft and sulfite papers, 9%; full chemical pulpboard 17%; specialties, 3%.

Markets. U.S. Plywood's most distinguishing characteristic was its strong wholesaling organization, which sold the company's products to various users of plywood in Canada and the United States from 161 wholly owned distribution warehouses in 43 states and 7 provinces. Canadian facilities were principally owned and operated by Weldwood of Canada, a 74% owned subsidiary. These units in the U.S. and Canada, which had numbered only 21 in 1945, were strategically located in major markets so that the company could take advantage of national advertising.

The Champion Group maintained 55 sales offices and warehouses in 27 states and in the District of Columbia, as well as in principal cities in Canada.

Together, the two groups employed more than 2,000 salesmen.

Plants.   The U.S. Plywood Group had 90 manufacturing and processing plants located in the U.S. and Canada. In 1966 these consisted of 26 plywood mills, 23 lumber mills, 12 prefinished panel and veneer mills, 8 hard and particle board plants, 4 door plants, and 17 miscellaneous plants. These plants provided 1.7 billion square feet of plywood, 850 million board feet of lumber, and 365 million square feet of Novoply and particleboard. This output was only sufficient for the supply of 55% of U.S. Plywood's captive distribution of softwood plywood.

Champion Paper Group had pulp and paper mills (annual capacities) at Canton, N.C. (400,000 tons of pulp and 450,000 tons of paper and board), Pasadena, Tex. (288,000 tons of pulp and 225,000 tons of paper and board), and Hamilton, Ohio (198,000 tons of paper); 5 milk container plants; 10 folding carton and flexible packaging plants; 10 envelope plants; and 7 plants for miscellaneous products.

Timber holdings.   Over 5.3 billion board feet owned for manufacture of plywood and allied products; also owned were about 628,400 acres, plus long-term cutting rights on about 300,000 additional acres, for manufacture of paper and allied products. Total owned or controlled timber exceeded 32 billion board feet.

The company.   U.S. Plywood started business as a plywood distributor, opening its first distribution unit in New York City in 1919. The company expanded its chain of distributing warehouses out of earnings, and took over management of its first manufacturing plant in 1932.

Until the middle 1950's, however, USP was primarily a merchandiser of timber products, rather than a producer. Although the company was a large producer of plywood, it still had to buy the great majority of its requirements from others. Additionally, it distributed an even larger volume of other building materials made by other producers.

In the 1960's, USP was moving away from this position; marketing and distribution network had been supplemented by expanding raw material and manufacturing facilities. As a result of a number of acquisitions, timber reserves increased from 3 billion board feet in 1953 to an estimated 5.3 billion board feet in 1966. The number of manufacturing plants grew from 33 to 125 during this period, and in 1966, over three-quarters of the company's sales (including 55% of fir plywood needs) originated with company owned mills. The most recent important acquisitions included the following.

In September, 1963, USP purchased substantially all of the assets of McCloud River Lumber Company, subject to certain of its liabilities, for approximately $41 million in cash. McCloud's properties were located principally in Northern California and consisted of a large integrated lumber facility and approximately 2 billion feet of timber owned or under contract.

On May 21, 1965, USP acquired the operating subsidiaries and corporate name of Lewers & Cooke Ltd., Honolulu, in exchange for 235,345 common shares at rate of one share for each two shares of Lewers & Cooke stock.

In June, 1965, USP acquired Mengel Wood Industries, Inc., in exchange for 77,609 common shares.

On May 31, 1966, USP acquired Dee, Oregon division of Edward Hines Lumber Company for over $8 million.

In 1966 USP acquired assets of West Coast Plywood Corp. for 109,000 common shares, and assets of Del Mar Industries Inc. and Union Lumber Co. for 85,000 common shares.

During the period from fiscal 1954 through 1961, U.S. Plywood's sales had risen steadily and more than doubled, reflecting the dramatic growth in plywood demand. Earnings, however, had been highly variable. Erratic price movements had been characteristic of the building materials business, and U.S. Plywood had been particularly vulnerable to fluctuating prices, because it depended wholly upon this market.

During the mid-1960's, the company was deliberately increasing the proportion of finished and semifinished items in its product mix in an attempt to differentiate its products and reduce sensitivity to wholesale price movements in the basic building commodities. Substantial research in new materials, new combinations of materials, new applications of current products, and increased consumer advertising were being conducted.

The February 28, 1967, merger of Champion into U.S. Plywood was accomplished through the issuance of 6,395,398 shares of $1.20 convertible preferred stock plus 2,558,159 shares of common. The following figures are presented so that the full importance of this merger on U.S. Plywood's performance and position can be seen.

1966	U.S. Plywood	Champion	Consolidated
Sales	$552,251,000	$477,215,000	$1,029,466,000
Earnings	21,687,000	21,622,000	43,309,000
Earnings/share	3.18	3.31	3.74

Consolidated capital expenditures were $37.2 million in 1966, down from $59.8 million in 1965.

WEYERHAEUSER COMPANY

This company is the largest lumber producer in the U.S. In 1966, it accounted for approximately 4.6% of total U.S. lumber production and about 2.3% of total U.S. production of pulp. Total sales of $838 million in 1966 placed it third among all companies in the forest products industry.

	1966	1957
Lumber	25%	41%
Containers and cartons	24	28
Paper	12	—
Pulp	11	18
Softwood plywood	9	4
Paperboard	7	8
Hardwood products	5	—
Logs, chips, and timber	5	—
Manufactured panels	2	1
	100%	100%
Total sales	$847,944,000	$426,980,000

Products.   Weyerhaeuser was most often cited as an example of the completely integrated forest products company. Presented below are product breakdowns for 1966; figures for 1957 are also shown to illustrate the changes in product mix which have occurred as the company extended its by-product utilization.

Markets.   Weyerhaeuser served a nationwide market and also sold to customers throughout the world.

Sales of lumber and plywood were made by the company's own sales force direct from mills and through company operated distribution centers. The major portion of the company's volume was in sales to retail lumber dealers and contractors, but sales were also made to furniture and fixture manufacturers, millwork houses, cabinet makers, woodworking plants, and other industrial customers.

Pulp and paperboard were sold domestically to paper mills and converters through the company's own specialized sales organization (separate from lumber and plywood group). Sales of all product lines outside the U.S. reached $76 million in 1966.

Sales of shipping containers, milk cartons, and folding cartons were made direct to industrial consumers by a third sales division.

Plants.   Weyerhaeuser owned the following major facilities:

Sawmills and plywood mills	39
Pulp, paper, and paperboard mills	14
Folding carton plants	9
Milk carton plants	7
Shipping container plants	36
Research labs	5
Printing and writing paper mills	6
Others	16

These plants were located in 27 states, Canada, Belgium, Italy, Malta, West Germany, France, Scotland, South Africa, Venezuela, Guatemala, Philippines, Jamaica, and Puerto Rico.

In addition, the company owned and operated extensive logging railroad facilities, a fleet of oceangoing ships to transport lumber, and substantial terminal and dock installations.

Timber holdings.   In 1966, Weyerhaeuser owned approximately 3.7 million acres of timberlands, 2.8 million acres of which were located in the Pacific Northwest, most of these having been acquired early in this century for under $10 per acre. Holdings in the northwest alone were estimated to constitute 60 billion board feet of sawtimber, making Weyerhaeuser the largest sawtimber owner in the country. The stumpage value of this timber was between $30 and $35 per thousand board feet. Additionally, leases and cutting rights added another 9 million acres in Canada, Southeast Asia, and the United States.

Weyerhaeuser also owned 800,000 acres of pulpwood forests in North Carolina, Mississippi, and Alabama. In 1960, through the acquisition of the Roddis Plywood Company, the company added 100,000 acres of hardwood timber in Costa Rica, Eastern Canada, and the United States. 1966 acquisitions also added cutting rights on 750,000 acres in Malaysia and the Philippines.

The company.   The Weyerhaeuser Company began operations with a small sawmill at Rock Island, Illinois, in 1860. It remained a very small lumber company until 1900, when Frederick Weyerhaeuser purchased 900,000 acres of forest land from Northern Pacific Railroad builder James Hill for $5 million.

During the years between 1900 and 1950, Weyerhaeuser remained primarily a manufacturer of lumber and plywood, although the company also operated two sulfite pulp mills established in the early 1930's. As lumber prices began to fall with the subsiding of the postwar housing boom, Weyerhaeuser sought ways to make fuller use of its vast resources and to lessen its dependence upon the construction cycle. A sulfate pulp mill, utilizing mill residues, was established at Longview, Washington, in 1948, and a container board plant was built in Springfield, Oregon, in the following year. In the years that followed, Weyerhaeuser undertook considerable internal expansion designed to gain greater utilization of its vast timber resources. Between 1958 and 1962, capital expenditures for gross additions to plants, equipment, and roads totaled $185.1 million. An additional $23.8 million was expended for timber and timberlands. This total of $208.9 million was financed entirely from cash resources of the company.

As a supplement to its internal integration program, Weyerhaeuser made several acquisitions during the 1950's and early 1960's. In 1954, the company expanded its paper business with the formation of the R-W paper Company (a joint venture with the Rhinelander Paper Company). This operation consisted of a paper plant in Longview, Washington, with an annual capacity of 10,000 tons of glassine and greaseproof papers. The following table lists the company's major acquisitions during the period from 1957 to 1966.

1957	Kiechkhefer Container Co.	Shipping containers, milk cartons, paperboard
	The Eddy Paper Corporation	Shipping containers, folding cartons, paperboard
1960	Rilco Laminated Products	Laminated beams and trusses
	Roddis Plywood Corporation	Softwood and hardwood plywood, doors, and hardwood specialties
1961	Hamilton Paper Company	Printing and writing paper
1962	Crocker Burbank & Company	Industrial specialty paper
1965	Merritt Diamond Mills, Ltd. (purchased by a jointly owned affiliate)	Sawmills (3) and timberlands
	Welsh Panel Company	Hardwood plywood
1966	A. DeWeese Lumber Company	Lumber, plywood mills, and timber holdings
	Bay Timber Company (Maylasia) Basilan Lumber Corporation (philippines)	Included harvesting rights on 750,000 acres

The value of acquired facilities during the years 1958–1962 totaled $45.7 million, and that of timberlands totaled $2.2 million. These acquisitions were effected principally by the use of 1,325,697 treasury shares acquired by the company in the open market, and through the issuance of 601,996 authorized but unissued shares. Total outstanding in 1963 was 30,622,000 shares.

By the end of 1962, Weyerhaeuser had arrived at a high level of integration. The company's western pulp mills obtained nearly all of their wood chip requirements from company owned sources, about one-half coming from sawmill residuals and the remainder from whole logs (primarily of species not suitable for lumber sales). Sixty-two per cent of the output of the company's pulp mills was consumed internally for the manufacture of paper and paperboard. In addition, 74% of the output of its paperboard mills was used in its own conversion plants in the manufacture of containers and cartons. Prior to 1957, almost all of the company's output of pulp and paperboard had been sold to other manufacturers for conversion to finished products.

Weyerhaeuser had consistently been a leader in forestry research. Chemical by-products, pressed fiber stems, and new containers had been three traditional areas of concentration. In 1962, the research facilities of the Martin-Marietta Company were acquired. Major projects included a wood quality study, the economic aspects of second-growth timber, and a tree-and-seed improvement program.

Weyerhaeuser had been very conservatively financed. Through 1963, it had not used long-term debt, and in that year working capital stood at $117.4 million and capital expenditures were $37 million, financed entirely from internal funds. During the preceding 11 year period earnings showed relative stability, $46 million in 1953 and $44 million in 1963.

In contrast, since 1963 management followed a less conservative pattern. Long-term debt stood at $203 million at year-end 1966 and working capital was increased to $216.4 million. 1966 capital expenditures reached $124 million and the company was following a program of buying treasury stock on the market and had accumulated 591,964 shares. Earnings increased substantially during this period, from $67.6 million in 1964 to $83.4 million in 1965, and dropping off to $79.2 million in 1966.

In 1965, Mr. George H. Weyerhaeuser, Jr., took over the job of president and chief executive officer from Mr. Norton Clapp, who became chairman of the board. Mr. Weyerhaeuser had been one of three executive vice presidents.

CROWN ZELLERBACH CORPORATION

This company is the second largest North American pulp and paper producer, representing about 5% of total domestic paper and paperboard produced. It is exceeded in size by the International Paper Company, and is the major pulp and paper producer west of the Rockies. Sales of $763.9 million (1966) placed it fourth in size in the forest products industry.

Products. Crown Zellerbach and its subsidiaries produced unbleached and bleached groundwood, sulfite, and sulfate (kraft) pulps, most of which were made into a wide range of paper products in the company's own paper mills. A major portion of paper output was converted in CZ's own plants into bags, multiwall shipping sacks, facial and toilet tissues, and process paper such as waxed paper and gummed tape. The trade names Zee and Chiffon were used for household tissues, towels, and other consumer items.

Output of paper products totaled 2,258,391 tons in 1966; 21% of this output represented newsprint, 11% other printing papers, 29% industrial and business papers, 12% tissue and sanitary papers, and 27% paperboard. In addition, 360 million board feet of lumber and 256 million square feet of plywood were produced, and 737 million board feet of saw logs and peeler logs were sold.

In addition to the products it manufactured, the company, through its merchandising subsidiaries, distributed products of more than 1,000 other manufacturers, consisting mainly of printing papers, wrapping papers, stationery, notions, school supplies, and sanitary products.

Markets. Crown Zellerbach concentrated its marketing efforts in the western part of the United States. Newsprint was supplied regularly to more than 400 daily and weekly newspapers in the 11 western states. Coated book paper was sold in the West to magazines, including the West Coast printing of *Life* and *Time*.

Other printing papers were sold for telephone directories, magazines, brochures, pamphlets, various commercial printing work, etc. Products of the Gaylord division (containers) account for the company's major sales east of the Rockies.

Crown Zellerbach sold industrial products direct to users, such as newspapers and converters. Printing, wrapping, and other commercial papers were sold through paper merchants, while consumer products were sold direct to grocery chains or through wholesalers. Sixty-seven sales offices served 26 states, 5 Canadian provinces, and 60 foreign market areas for Crown Zellerbach paper products. Zellerbach Paper Company, a major subsidiary, distributed the company's commercial paper products in California. Lumber and plywood were sold through lumber wholesalers.

Plants.   Crown Zellerbach owned a total of 14 pulp and paper mills in 1966, with a combined annual capacity of 2,808,000 tons of kraft, groundwood, and sulfite pulp. Eight were located on the West Coast, two in British Columbia, one in Ohio, two in Louisiana, and one in New York. A total of 33 packaging and converting plants were owned and/or operated throughout the United States, Canada, South Africa, and El Salvador. Crown Zellerbach operated five chemical products plants, nine lumber and plywood mills in the U.S. and Canada, and nine building supply outlets in Canada.

Timber holdings.   At the end of 1966, Crown Zellerbach was the third largest private timber owner in the United States. Its holdings included 814,000 acres in Oregon and Washington and 487,000 acres in Louisiana and Mississippi (plus 175,000 acres under lease). In addition, Crown Zellerbach owned or controlled 1,010,000 acres of timberlands in British Columbia. The company's total timber holdings contained in excess of 30 billion board feet.

The company.   Crown Zellerbach was formed by the merger of two old-time small paper companies in 1928, a local retail paper business in San Francisco (started in the 1870's) and a small paper mill at Willamette Falls, Oregon (established in 1889).

Soon after its formation, Crown Zellerbach began acquiring forest lands to assure a constant supply of pulp. At first, timber holdings were regarded merely as a raw material supply for pulp and paper. Following World War II, however, the company added a wood products division to improve the utilization of timber cut. By 1962, the wood products division accounted for approximately 10% of sales. In that year, two-thirds of Crown's pulpwood requirements were supplied from company owned forests.

Much of Crown Zellerbach's expansion occurred through merger and acquisition. In the late 1920's the company bought a half-interest in Fibreboard Products, which was sold in 1956 at a significant profit. The Canadian Western Lumber Company and St. Helen's Pulp and Paper Company were acquired in 1953, and the Waide Paper Company of St. Louis was acquired in 1956. Crown expanded on a geographic basis in both manufacturing and marketing with its acquisition of the Gaylord Container Company late in 1955. Gaylord manufactured and converted paperboard in the South and marketed throughout the eastern United States.

There had also been internal growth. During the 1950's, Crown Zellerbach built a packaging plant at St. Louis and a coated paper products mill at St. Francisville, Louisiana (as a joint venture with Time, Inc.). The company recently entered the international field by the establishment of a joint venture kraft specialties mill in the Netherlands.

The St. Helen's Pulp and Paper acquisition was opposed by the Justice Department, and in 1958 the FTC ordered Crown Zellerbach to divest itself of this company.

This ruling was subsequently upheld by the U.S. Supreme Court, and in May, 1964, St. Helen's was sold to Boise Cascade Corporation. It was estimated that the sale would have little effect on Crown's over-all sales volume.

In 1963 a major expansion was begun, including a $40 million Louisiana pulp and paper mill completed in 1966; a $30 million joint venture expansion of coated printing papers capacity which was to be completed in 1967; a $45 million California joint venture, completed in 1966; and a $90 million Oregon complex which was to be completed in 1967.

Postwar expansion was financed in large part from internal sources. Crown's total debt/net worth ratio stood at .47 in 1966.

Capital expenditures during 1966 were $117 million, versus $108 million in 1965 and $61 million in 1963.

Crown Zellerbach had increased net income from $23.9 million in 1952 to $39.3 million in 1963 and $53.7 million in 1966. 1966 earnings per share stood at $3.44, compared with $2.50 in 1963 and $2.34 in 1952.

ST. REGIS PAPER COMPANY

St. Regis was the third largest paper company in the United States, and the largest domestic producer of multiwall paper bags. The company accounted for about one-fifth of domestic multiwall bag output. 1966 sales of $700 million placed St. Regis fifth largest in the forest products industry.

Products. In 1966, St. Regis produced 1,533,313 tons of pulp, 1,340,084 tons of kraft and other paper and board, and 393,601 tons of printing and fine papers. 956,943 tons of paper and board were converted into multiwall bags, containers, waxed papers, and other products in the company's own plants. In addition, 392,549,000 board feet of lumber were produced.

Sales amounting to $700 million in 1966 were broken down approximately as follows: corrugated, folding, and setup boxes, 22%; kraft pulp, paper, and board, 20%; printing and fine papers, 12%; multiwall and textile bags, 10%; lumber and plywood, 10%; flexible packaging, 10%; school supplies and related items, 7%; glassine and greaseproof papers, 3%; and other products, 6%.

Markets.   The company converted most of its basic paper and paperboard production into a wide range of industrial and commercial products sold through paper merchants and jobbers. Pulp, which was produced in excess of the company's needs, was sold to other paper manufacturers. Plastics, lumber, and building products accounted for minor fractions of sales and were sold through brokers and wholesalers.

Plants.   In 1966, St. Regis operated 22 paper mills, 116 paper converting plants, and 25 plants making other products. These plants were located in the U.S. and 18 foreign countries.[1]

Printing and fine papers	6
Kraft paper	9
Specialty papers	3
Boxboard	4
Bags	19
Flexible packaging	11
Boxes	59
Packaging materials	19
Consumer paper products	8
Food processing equipment	3
Chemicals	6
Lumber, plywood, and building products	14
Packaging machinery	2

Timber holdings.   At the end of 1966, St. Regis owned in fee or controlled through timber purchase agreements a total of 3,618,953 acres in the U.S. and 2,175,767 acres in Canada. The company's holdings of timber had grown substantially between 1956 and 1966, in conjunction with an aggressive acquisition program.

The company.   The St. Regis Paper Company began operations in 1901 as a producer of newsprint. Until 1913, this was the company's major product. At that time, newsprint production was discontinued, and the company placed its emphasis upon other groundwood printing and publication papers. From this base, St. Regis expanded into multiwall bags, corrugated shipping containers, folding cartons, and flexible packaging. Then, in 1956, the company embarked upon a major expansion program. During the next five years its diversification by acquisition added lumber and plywood, glassine and greaseproof papers, bread wrappers and waxed paper products, frozen food wrappers, cellophane and polyethylene wrappers, wooden, corrugated, folding, and setup boxes, plastics and

---

[1] Foreign operations were largely confined to converting facilities.

other chemicals, food processing equipment, and school supplies. A total of 32 companies were acquired, largely through the issuance of stock. The number of shares outstanding more than doubled during this period. Since 1961, growth was largely financed by reinvested earnings and borrowed funds.

Sales almost doubled between 1957 and 1966, and net profit increased from $22 million to $39 million (35% of the improvement in earnings between 1961 and 1966 came from changes in accounting for depreciation and consolidation of subsidiary earnings). Capital expenditures in 1966 were $87 million, as compared with $22 million in 1963. In 1966, the total debt/net worth ratio stood at 0.42.

GEORGIA-PACIFIC CORPORATION

Georgia-Pacific was the nation's largest producer of plywood, accounting for 11.4% of total domestic softwood plywood production in 1966 and over 10% of hardwood plywood production. The company was also the second largest lumber producer (after Weyerhaeuser) and an important manufacturer and distributor of paper and container board (3% of the U.S. industry output), hardboard, and forest product chemicals. With 13% of the domestic gypsum product production, it ranked third largest in the U.S. Sales volume of $659 million in 1966 made G-P the nation's sixth largest forest products company.

Products. Georgia-Pacific produced a full line of lumber and plywood products. Pulp and paper products included kraft paper, kraft linerboard, and converted coarse paper products such as corrugated boxes, sheets, displays, newsprint, grocery bags, and sacks and multiwall bags and fine printing and specialty papers, plus some tissue paper products. A variety of chemical products were produced as well as a full line of gypsum products.

Output in 1966 was broken down as follows: plywood and plywood specialties, 34%; pulp, paper, paperboard and newsprint, 34%; lumber 11%; minerals and chemicals, 15%; other products such as hardboard, flakeboard and various building materials, 6%. Approximately 34% of paper and paperboard production was used in Georgia-Pacific's own converting plants.

Markets. Georgia-Pacific products were sold to 65,000 accounts located primarily in the U.S., but also in 54 foreign countries.

Plywood and other building products were sold through 95 distribution centers operated by the company in the principal marketing areas of 44 states. Most of these facilities were under lease arrangements. Sales from the centers were made by company salesmen to retail lumber dealers and industrial accounts.

Pulp and paper stock, chemicals, and other specialty products were sold through 53 U.S. sales offices and to contacts in 54 foreign nations. Newsprint sales were made to approximately 100 newspapers in the northeastern part of the U.S.

Lumber was sold through six principal company-operated sales offices directly to retail yards, contractors, and industrial users.

Plants.   In 1966, Georgia-Pacific and its subsidiaries operated 119 mills and plants with combined annual capacities of about 2.2 billion square feet (⅜ inch basis) of plywood, veneer, and hardboard, 547 million board feet of lumber, 1,642,000 tons of kraft pulp, paper and container board, and 292,502 tons of dry chemicals and 4,450,000 gallons of liquid chemicals. The plants were broken down by products as follows: lumber, 24; plywood, 21; pulp and paper, 17; converting, 22; chemical, 10; gypsum, 9; and other, 16.

Timber holdings.   Georgia-Pacific was the second largest private sawtimber owner in the United States. Its holdings included 3.5 million acres located in the U.S., Canada, and Brazil. These holdings, together with others which it controlled, contained an estimated combined total of 35 billion board feet of timber. Approximately 70% of the company's log requirements came from Georgia-Pacific controlled land.

Minerals.   Georgia-Pacific owned the underlying mineral rights on approximately 85% of its fee lands in the U.S. The company had coal reserves estimated at 240 million recoverable tons and gypsum reserves of 167 million tons. Coal was mined under lease to 25 coal companies and provided 1966 royalties of $990,000. Natural gas leases added another $215,000 in royalties. Gypsum resources were held for supplying the corporation's nine gypsum plants.

The company.   The Georgia Hardwood Lumber Company was incorporated in Georgia in 1927, and grew steadily to a sales level of $4 to $5 million per year by 1942. Assets at that time were stated at under $1 million.

Prior to the 1940's, the company had relied upon the forests of the southeast for its resources. After World War II, however, timber suitable for the production of lumber and plywood became increasingly scarce in the South, forcing the company to purchase more and more of its requirements from the West Coast. In 1947, the company embarked upon a full-scale westward expansion.

The C. D. Johnson Lumber Company of Oregon was acquired in 1951 for $16.8 million. This purchase included 66,000 acres of old-growth Douglas fir in the Siletz River Basin. Following this acquisition, the name of the company was changed to the Georgia-Pacific Company, and a few years later the company's corporate headquarters were moved from Augusta, Georgia, to Portland, Oregon.

Georgia-Pacific continued to expand through the 1950's in Oregon and northern California, although it also expanded operations into West Virginia and other Appalachian states. In the northwest, Georgia-Pacific acquired an additional billion board feet of timber reserves in 1955, 8 billion in 1956, and 3 billion in 1959. In 1962, the company acquired the Crosset Company, which added 560,000 acres of timberland in Arkansas and Louisiana.

In 1958, Georgia-Pacific entered the paper business and soon became a major manufacturer of kraft paper for packaging use. Entry into the packaging business was accomplished by the acquisition of several paper bag and sack companies and also by the construction of Georgia-Pacific's own plants for kraft paper and corrugated containers.

Georgia-Pacific's expansion into paper was made largely to improve by-product utilization. For example, its paper mill at Toledo, Oregon, was supplied with waste wood chips by pneumatic pipeline from its Springfield plywood factory.

In 1963, the company acquired the St. Croix Paper Company, a producer of newsprint and specialty papers and owner of 619,000 acres of timberland; Vanity Fair Paper Mills, a producer of tissue, toweling, and waxed paper; and the Fordyce Lumber Company, owner of 165,000 acres of timberland. In July, 1963, Georgia-Pacific merged with Puget Sound Pulp and Timber Company, a producer of various pulps, papers, and chemicals. Puget and its chief subsidiary owned or controlled more than 10 billion board feet of timber.

From 1962 to 1966, Georgia-Pacific spent approximately $175 million to add about 2 million acres containing more than 10 billion board feet of timber.

In 1965, Bestwall Gypsum Company was merged into Georgia-Pacific in exchange for 2,258,720 shares of convertible stock. Bestwall manufactured gypsum board, wallboard, lath papers, plasters, sheathing, roofing felt, boxboard, and newsprint.

During the period from 1954–1966, the company exhibited an extraordinary record of growth. Sales grew from $30 million in 1954 to $659 million in 1966, earnings from $1.8 million to $50.3 million.

Georgia-Pacific's major product during that period—plywood—exhibited exceptional increases in domestic consumption, but it should be noted that other plywood companies did not improve earnings to nearly the same degree as Georgia-Pacific. By purchasing timber properties with borrowed money and scheduling repayment of the loans with income generated from harvesting part of the acquired timber, the company expanded its timber holdings enormously without significantly increasing the number of common shares outstanding. In most cases, profits from the timber sold exceeded the interest paid on the debt. Furthermore, these profits were taken as capital gains, thus lowering the company's effective tax rate. This program entailed a high debt load; the total debt/net worth ratio stood at 1.03 in 1966.

During the years between 1962 and 1966, Georgia-Pacific spent approximately $390 million for the construction of 11 modern sawmills, eight pine plywood plants, two veneer plants, a new particleboard plant, three corrugated fibre box converting plants, two paper bag converting plants, a tissue and toweling plant, a milk carton plant, three chemical facilities, two 500-ton bleached kraft pulp plants at Samoa, California, and Woodland, Maine, for expanding the daily capacity of the Toledo, Oregon, unbleached kraft pulp, paper, and containerboard mill from 600 to 900 tons, and for the continued program of remodeling and updating facilities and equipment to enable the corporation to minimize the unit cost of production in all phases of its operations.

Georgia-Pacific's total plywood operation was estimated to have the lowest breakeven point among the major companies in the industry.

SCOTT PAPER COMPANY

Scott was the world's largest producer of sanitary paper for home, industrial, and personal use. Its 1966 sales of $491 million placed it tenth among companies in the forest products industry.

Products.   Scott's product line included toilet tissues, paper towels, household wax paper, plastic wrap, facial tissues, paper napkins, industrial wipers, windshield wipers, plastic and paper cups, and sanitary napkins. It also made sulfite and sulfate specialty papers and converting and printing papers. Consumer product brand names include Scot Tissue, Waldorf, Softweve, ScotTowels, Confidets, Scotties, Lady Scott, and Cut-Rite, and accounted for approximately 70% of total sales volume.

Markets.   Scott sold consumer items to over 6,600 direct purchasers, primarily wholesale distributors, chain stores, department stores, and jobbers. Specialty and converting papers were sold directly to converters. Printing papers were sold through paper merchants to the printing trade. Export sales were carried on in 110 foreign countries. Sales of Scott affiliates in foreign countries were approximately $100 million in 1966. The company followed a policy of developing consumer recognition and demand for its products through extensive promotions of brand names.

Plants.   The company owned 19 plants ranging from integrated mills to converting plants. Plants were located in eleven states and in Nova Scotia. Annual combined capacity in 1966 exceeded 2.6 million tons of paper.

Timber holdings.   Timber resources were estimated to be in excess of 2.6 million acres. These included owned and leased land in New Hampshire and Maine (835,000 acres), Eastern Canada (1,200,000 acres), Washington and British Columbia (360,000 acres), and Alabama and Mississippi (425,000 acres).

The company.   Founded in 1879, the company had chosen to emphasize consumer products in the conviction that demand in this segment was more stable than in other segments of the paper industry. Scott had concentrated its expenditures on promoting sales for its consumer products, and on the introduction of new items. Recent additions to the product line included paper cups, sanitary napkins (Confidets), and urethane foam specialties. In discussing new product philosophy, the Chairman stated: "The woman shopper is our boss. Unlike many companies which develop a new product and then proceed to introduce it, we at Scott start with the consumer and work back."

Scott began its backward integration in 1936 with the formation of the Brunswick Pulp and Paper Company (a joint venture with the Mead Corporation), in order to provide an assured supply of pulp. In 1945, the company purchased the Automatic Machinery Company, the manufacturer of Cut-Rite wax paper. In 1951, Soundview Pulp and Paper—the world's largest producer of bleached sulfite paper—was merged into Scott. In 1960, however, the Federal Trade Commission ordered Scott to divest itself of the latter company, as well as two smaller acquisitions made during the 1950's.

Scott had made major steps to build up its international organization, notably through the formation of the Bowater-Scott Company in 1956. This was a joint venture in the U.K. with the Bowater Paper Company. By 1966, Scott affiliates in foreign countries employed 5,000 people in 13 countries manufacturing 200 different paper products. Most of these affiliates were 50-50 joint ventures with nationals of the countries involved.

In 1963, the company planned an expansion program of manufacturing facilities. Capital expenditures were increased from $23 million in 1963 (for plant and timber resources) to $73 million in 1966. Major additions and modernization of facilities were made, especially at the Mobile, Alabama, and Nova Scotia, Canada, locations.

In 1965, the company acquired the Plastic Coating Corporation and the Tecnifax Corporation. These companies added new products and markets to the Scott family. These companies produced and sold visual aid, office copying, and engineering reproduction equipment, paper, films, and materials.

In May, 1967, Scott merged with the S.D. Warren Company for 4.7 million shares of Scott common stock. Warren had 1966 sales of $100 million and produced high-quality technical and printing paper.

During the ten year period ending in 1966, Scott had had continuously increasing sales, and earnings set new record highs in each year except 1966. In this period, sales grew at an annual compound rate of 6% and net profit after tax as a per cent of sales had been maintained at an average of 9.1%.

CONTAINER CORPORATION OF AMERICA

This company was the largest manufacturer of corrugated and solid-fibre shipping containers and folding cartons in the world. It ranked second in U.S. paperboard production and in the manufacture of fibre cans. Shipments of containers and folding cartons accounted for about 7 and 8%, respectively, of total industry output, while paperboard fabrication represented 5.7%. With 1966 sales of $460 million, it ranked thirteenth in the forest products industry.

Products. Although Container Corporation was primarily a converter, the company also manufactured substantial quantities of paperboard both for its own consumption and for sale to others. Total volume in 1966 exceeded 1.7 million tons, broken down as follows: corrugated and solid fibre shipping containers, 47%; folding cartons, fibre cans, and plastic products, 35%; paperboard, pulp, waste paper, etc., 18%.

Markets. CCA sold its products throughout the world to manufacturers, packagers, and shippers of a wide range of products. In the United States, the company had approximately 10,000 customers. Sales outside the U.S. accounted for 24% of 1966 company sales and 22% of earnings. CCA had a dominant market position in each of the foreign countries where it had facilities.

Plants. In 1966, CCA owned 77 plants within the United States, broken down as follows: paperboard mills, 14; shipping container factories, 28; folding carton factories, 13; paper stock processing plants, 6; fibre can factories, 11; plastics factories, 5. These plants were located in 55 cities in 24 states throughout the United States. In addition, 45 plants were owned in West Germany, Italy, Mexico, Colombia, Venezuela, and the Netherlands.

Timber holdings. CCA owned or had timber cutting rights on a combined total of 584,000 acres of timberland in northern Florida and southern Georgia.

The company. Container Corporation of America was established in 1926 to consolidate several paper mills and box companies. Since that time, it grew to become a world leader in paper packaging, design, and marketing.

By spending its money on "creative packaging services" as an aid to customers' merchandising requirements, rather than on raw material production, Container remained primarily a converter of paper products. Management believed that it avoided some of the price weakness in pulp, pulpwood, and paperboard in the 1960's by concentrating capital expenditures on the expansion of foreign operations and on domestic marketing effort instead of on expanding mill operations and timber ownership. The company did, however, increase timber resources in 1965 and 1966 from 405,700 acres in 1964 to 584,209 acres in 1966. During the mid-1960's CCA continued expansion of converting facilities and capital expenditures reached $44 million in 1966, up from $24 million in 1962.

In 1964 the company expanded in the plastic container area with the acquisition of shares of the Delaware Barrel and Drum Company, Inc. Again in 1965, CCA used shares to purchase Mullery Paper Packages, Inc., a St. Paul, Minnesota, converter and marketer of paperboard cartons and fibre cans.

The company had placed a heavy emphasis on packaging research. Annual expenditures exceeded $3 million and were carried out at four locations. Research activities included studies on combining paperboard with plastics and other materials, on increasing consumer convenience, and on improved packaging systems and procedures.

Container Corporation had realized a strong growth in sales (6% compound rate, 1962–1966) and a stronger growth in earnings (13% for the same period).

This improvement in earnings resulted in a 1966 return on invested capital of 16.8%, as compared with 14.2% in 1965 and 12.9% in 1964.

In 1966, total long-term debt/net worth ratio stood at .31.

exhibit 2

NOTES ON THE FOREST PRODUCTS INDUSTRY

Relative Changes in Sales Volume of Nine Selected Companies

(1957–1959 = 100)

Year	Container	St. Regis	Crown Zellerbach	Int'l. Paper	Scott Paper	Boise Cascade	Georgia-Pacific	U.S. Plywood[1]	Weyerhaeuser
1966	159	165	157	147	172	583	402	430	195
1965	140	149	143	132	161	513	351	397	168
1964	135	145	136	129	149	431	293	200	154
1963	122	140	126	118	130	260	275	160	135
1962	119	136	121	113	124	209	198	142	126
1961	114	133	115	108	117	164	155	126	114
1960	113	126	114	105	110	156	135	109	107
1959	111	119	108	106	104	150	117	115	107
1958	100	96	97	95	100	87	93	100	95
1957	89	85	94	99	96	63	90	85	98
1956	95	87	95	100	95	42	74	84	102

[1]Effective February 28, 1967, Champion Papers, Inc., was merged into U.S. Plywood, Champion's results have been excluded in order to maintain comparability.

Source: Standard & Poor's *Standard Corporation Descriptions.*

exhibit 3

NOTES ON THE FOREST PRODUCTS INDUSTRY

Capital Expenditures of Nine Selected Companies

(in millions of dollars)

Year	Container	St. Regis	Crown Zellerback	Int'l. Paper	Scott Paper	Boise Cascade	Georgia Pacific	U.S. Plywood	Weyerhaeuser
1966	44.03	87.34	117.21	199.93	64.91	95.68	118.30	37.22	101.87
1965	36.54	71.50	108.35	125.20	55.30	51.45	125.10	59.82	115.06
1964	30.37	37.72	95.92	114.28	64.76	59.98	93.50	24.67	87.15
1963	36.55	22.71	60.52	93.68	31.89	12.24	62.75	15.21	36.55
1962	23.97	24.28	53.30	79.35	22.98	8.43	134.75	15.95	58.32
1961	19.52	36.30	33.00	70.30	38.48	10.65	19.28	8.00	66.23
1960	17.64	49.22	39.04	101.12	40.35	7.03	16.12	11.56	57.64
1959	17.77	19.80	38.97	64.96	20.14	8.17	15.20	14.21	35.56
1958	22.05	14.38	22.91	68.15	14.25	—	13.34	6.77	37.55
1957	37.18	37.61	54.99	93.72	42.13	—	26.11	10.95	56.84
1956	21.15	40.14	70.32	137.31	33.85	—	119.23	11.18	70.62

Source: Standard & Poor's *Standard Corporation Descriptions.*

Year	Container	St. Regis	Crown Zellerbach	Int'l. Paper	Scott Paper	Boise Cascade	Georgia Pacific	U.S. Plywood	Weyerhaeuser
1966	11.4[1]	10.9	12.9	12.3	11.5	20.8	13.4	6.1	9.3
1965	9.7	10.7	13.5	8.6	11.0	13.9	16.4	10.1	11.8
1964	9.4	6.2	13.2	8.4	14.5	19.5	14.3	9.8	9.9
1963	11.6	3.7	9.1	7.6	8.5	9.8	12.9	7.6	4.5
1962	8.5	4.2	8.7	6.7	6.4	7.4	41.4	10.2	8.4
1961	7.4	6.5	5.7	6.2	11.0	14.5	7.5	5.2	10.1
1960	7.2	9.3	7.0	9.3	12.2	10.8	7.6	8.4	10.3
1959	7.9	4.3	7.3	6.5	6.7	—	6.9	12.7	7.0
1958	10.4	3.4	4.5	7.2	4.9	—	7.6	6.6	7.9
1957	22.0	9.9	11.2	10.6	15.0	—	14.7	12.0	12.4
1956	16.0	13.7	15.8	17.1	13.2	—	70.5	13.2	21.4

[1] Estimated.

Definition: Total capital expenditures during the fiscal year divided by gross property at the end of the fiscal year.

Source: Figures used in the calculations are from Standard & Poor's *Standard Corporation Descriptions.*

exhibit 4

NOTES ON THE FOREST PRODUCTS INDUSTRY

Profit Margins of Nine Selected Companies

(operating income as a percentage of sales)

Year	Container	St. Regis	Crown Zellerbach	Int'l. Paper	Scott Paper	Boise Cascade	Georgia-Pacific	U.S. Plywood	Weyerhaeuser
1966	18.8[1]	12.5	16.3	17.5	21.0	11.3	20.6	11.1	17.8
1965	18.0	11.5	16.0	17.0	20.8	12.2	21.3	11.4	19.1
1964	16.8	10.9	17.2	17.1	20.9	12.6	21.2	11.7	19.1
1963	16.2	11.1	17.0	16.1	22.6	11.2	20.1	9.7	16.1
1962	15.9	12.0	17.6	16.8	22.2	9.8	20.0	9.7	16.7
1961	15.9	10.6	17.3	17.3	22.9	6.6	20.0	10.3	17.4
1960	15.2	11.8	17.6	19.5	22.8	7.7	24.3	8.3	22.3
1959	16.2	15.3	18.5	20.9	21.8	10.0	26.2	11.6	28.1
1958	14.6	15.4	17.6	20.0	21.0	8.6	26.1	12.0	27.3
1957	14.0	17.6	17.9	21.0	20.8	7.7	25.0	8.4	27.2
1956	15.6	19.0	21.5	22.4	21.0	7.7	19.0	9.7	28.8

[1] Estimated.

Definition: Operating income is defined as the balance left from sales after deducting operating costs, selling, general, and administrative expenses; local and state taxes; and provision for bad debts and pensions; but before other income and before deducting depreciation charges, debt service charges, if any, Federal taxes, and any special reserves.

Source: Standard & Poor's *Standard Corporation Descriptions.*

exhibit 5

NOTES ON THE FOREST PRODUCTS INDUSTRY

Net Income of Nine Selected Companies

(1957–1959 = 100)

Year	Container	St. Regis	Crown Zeller- bach	Int'l. Paper	Scott Paper	Boise Cascade	Georgia- Pacific	U.S. Plywood	Weyerhaeuser
1966	209	159	151	134	196	472	461	398	146
1965	166	147	133	113	207	503	422	367	153
1964	141	110	131	104	186	415	332	183	124
1963	115	80	110	89	159	205	262	137	81
1962	114	87	109	86	143	140	176	120	72
1961	111	79	103	92	137	85	138	110	67
1960	104	90	113	91	124	94	140	68	88
1959	119	123	110	107	109	156	130	118	111
1958	92	90	93	92	97	84	92	123	91
1957	89	87	96	101	95	59	78	59	98
1956	110	104	141	110	98	33	68	76	119

Source: Standard & Poor's *Standard Corporation Descriptions.*

Net Income as a Percentage of Sales (%)

Year	Con- tainer	St. Regis	Crown Zeller- bach	Int'l. Paper	Scott Paper	Boise Cascade	Georgia- Pacific	U.S. Plywood	Weyerhaeuser
1966	7.4	5.5	7.0	7.3	9.1	3.5	7.6	4.2	9.5
1965	6.7	5.6	6.8	6.8	10.3	4.2	8.0	4.2	11.6
1964	5.9	4.4	7.0	6.5	10.4	4.1	7.5	4.2	10.2
1963	5.3	3.3	6.4	6.1	9.8	3.4	6.3	3.9	7.6
1962	5.4	3.7	6.6	6.1	9.2	2.9	5.9	3.9	7.2
1961	5.5	3.4	6.5	6.9	9.3	2.2	5.8	4.0	7.5
1960	5.2	4.1	7.2	7.1	8.9	2.6	6.9	2.6	10.4
1959	6.1	5.9	7.5	8.1	8.3	4.4	7.4	4.7	13.2
1958	5.6	5.6	7.1	7.9	7.8	4.2	6.6	5.6	12.1
1957	5.7	5.9	7.3	8.3	7.8	4.0	5.8	3.1	12.7
1956	6.6	6.8	10.8	8.9	8.3	3.4	6.1	4.1	14.8

Definition: Net income is the net profit after all charges as reported by the company.

Source: Standard & Poor's *Standard Corporation Descriptions.*

exhibit 6

NOTES ON THE FOREST PRODUCTS INDUSTRY

Earnings Per Share * of Nine Selected Companies

Year	St. Container	Crown Regis	Int'l. Zellerbach	Scott Paper	Boise Paper	Georgia Cascade	Pacific	U.S. Plywood	Weyerhaeuser
1966	3.06	2.99	3.44	2.40	1.53	1.48	2.63	3.74	2.60
1965	2.42	2.81	3.03	2.02	1.63	1.62	2.50	3.41	2.72
1964	2.06	2.14	2.98	1.85	1.47	1.26	2.30	3.99	2.21
1963	1.71	1.65	2.68	1.58	1.35	0.92	1.68	2.42	1.44
1962	1.71	1.72	2.52	1.56	1.23	0.67	1.42	2.14	1.28
1961	1.68	1.61	2.33	1.71	1.19	0.41	1.13	1.96	1.22
1960	1.57	1.91	2.56	1.74	1.16	0.45	1.26	1.23	1.59
1959	1.83	2.98	2.51	2.03	1.03	0.75	1.30	2.55	2.00
1958	1.41	2.41	2.11	1.75	0.92	0.55	0.97	2.68	1.64
1957	1.36	2.53	2.18	1.94	0.89	0.40	0.92	1.24	1.76

*The above records of earnings per share have been adjusted in prior years for all stock splits and stock dividends.

Source: Standard & Poor's *Standard Corporation Descriptions.*

exhibit 7

NOTES ON THE FOREST PRODUCTS INDUSTRY

Dividends on Common Stocks of Nine Selected Companies

(% of net income)

Year	St. Container	Crown Regis	Int'l. Zellerbach	Scott paper	Boise Paper	Georgia- Cascade	Pacific	U.S. Plywood	Weyerhaeuser
1966	40.9	46.8	58.1	51.7	65.3	15.5	34.2	37.4	53.8
1965	47.5	49.8	66.0	61.9	57.0	12.3	31.7	36.7	44.1
1964	48.5	65.4	62.1	62.7	60.8	15.8	32.4	40.1	54.3
1963	54.4	89.7	72.0	66.5	61.5	21.7	34.7	43.6	83.3
1962	48.5	81.4	72.9	67.3	65.0	29.6	39.2	51.0	93.8
1961	53.6	87.0	70.4	61.4	63.0	48.8	49.8	78.4	98.4
1960	63.7	73.3	54.0	57.5	64.7	38.5	41.8	—	75.5
1959	54.6	46.5	65.2	48.3	66.6	19.9	34.9	39.2	55.0
1958	74.1	57.9	77.6	54.9	72.7	27.3	38.0	37.3	60.9
1957	73.5	61.3	75.3	48.5	74.6	30.9	40.2	76.1	56.8
1956	47.4	60.1	51.0	42.6	66.5	36.8	33.8	61.7	47.6

Definition: Fiscal year dividends paid per share, divided by net earnings per share of common stocks.

Source: Figures for these calculations are from Standard & Poor's *Standard Corporation Descriptions.*

exhibit 8

NOTES ON THE FOREST PRODUCTS INDUSTRY

Price-Earnings Ratios of Nine Selected Companies

Year	Continental		St. Regis		Crown Zellerbach		International		Scott Paper	
	High	Low	High	Low	High	Low	High	Low	High	Low
1966	12.4	8.7	14.8	8.9	16.4	10.5	14.6	9.9	26.0	16.6
1965	15.3	12.1	13.6	10.9	19.9	15.5	17.9	14.0	24.6	20.2
1964	16.9	13.9	16.8	13.8	22.2	17.1	20.6	16.4	27.4	22.7
1963	20.5	13.8	23.7	17.0	24.2	18.0	22.9	16.5	28.4	23.0
1962	16.9	10.1	22.9	13.1	24.2	15.2	24.4	14.5	34.8	20.3
1961	17.6	12.9	25.7	19.6	26.1	15.5	22.4	17.3	40.5	23.8
1960	18.5	12.8	29.1	16.1	19.4	14.1	25.6	16.0	27.4	21.0
1959	16.8	13.7	18.9	14.2	21.9	18.2	22.8	17.9	28.5	23.5
1958	22.4	12.6	19.4	10.8	25.3	18.8	22.4	15.6	27.2	20.3
1957	15.3	12.1	19.1	9.3	24.5	16.8	17.7	13.3	24.1	19.4
1956	13.9	10.6	19.1	12.9	19.8	14.2	20.5	4.0	27.2	20.6

Year	Boise Cascade		Georgia-Pacific		U.S. Plywood		Weyerhaeuser	
	High	Low	High	Low	High	Low	High	Low
1966	25.3	11.6	20.9	11.5	14.7	7.8	16.5	10.8
1965	18.6	14.4	20.8	16.2	14.2	10.9	18.1	14.2
1964	19.3	13.3	21.4	14.4	15.4	10.7	21.0	13.7
1963	19.0	11.6	18.9	14.7	14.0	8.9	23.8	17.3
1962	15.9	1.1	22.8	11.8	12.6	8.9	27.7	17.5
1961	28.0	18.3	35.1	24.8	13.7	11.1	33.4	25.9
1960	28.6	16.5	25.6	17.8	21.1	17.1	25.6	18.9
1959	16.7	10.2	22.3	15.6	11.4	7.7	24.4	19.9
1958	12.7	6.6	21.4	10.8	8.0	4.9	29.6	19.2
1957	—	—	14.7	9.2	14.9	9.9	23.2	17.0
1956	—	—	17.3	7.6	16.0	10.0	20.5	16.5

Definition: High and low calendar year market prices divided by net earnings per common share.

Source: Figures used in the calculations are from Standard & Poor's *Standard Corporation Descriptions.*

part III

DETAILED ANALYSIS, PLANNING, AND DEPLOYMENTS IN COMPLEX, MULTIDIVISIONAL ENTERPRISES

chapter 7

Planning

Corporate Strategy

It should be clear to the reader that we conceive of a strategic plan as a broad, ever-changing program of corporate emphasis and resource deployment which responds to, and initiates upon, the competitive environment in which the company operates.

We do *not* advocate any detailed, idealized plan which is rigorously enforced and rigidly implemented over an extended time period. Plans must be flexible, "written in pencil," so that they can be adapted to changes in conditions. They must be limited to what is practical and feasible. Only those alternatives should be considered which are within the competence of persons presently in key positions (or realistically available) and are acceptable to them. Moreover, we must live within the financial and other resource constraints on the company. Hence, we inevitably concentrate on those *few* items which affect the *basic* character of the enterprise, ignoring the multitude of activities which do not affect the company in a major way. We accept some inefficiencies in operations as a necessary tradeoff for superior strategic effectiveness.

Strategic planning, to us, has a limited time perspective. It is primarily a matter of continually balancing the requirements for satisfactory performance *today* with the anticipated requirements for assuring satisfactory performance in the *future*. A company will enjoy continued success only as a result of its adjusting well to constantly changing customer needs, product and process technologies, and competitive practices. We must continually question the validity for the future of those emphases, methods, and policies which have been the basis of our success in the past.

Unfortunately, our planning can rarely be neat, complete, or definitive. Most of our choices must be qualitative rather than quantitative; they must be tentative judgments, rather than precisely calculated probabilities.

Most mathematical techniques currently available are far more appropriate to *operating* problems than to *strategic* issues. As Ansoff [1] points out, the conflicts between short-run and long-term profit requirements, the conflicts in interest among owners, employees, and other "stakeholders," partial ignorance of alternative opportunities and their potentials, the limited resources available for allocation, the synergistic possibilities of new combinations, and the unreliability of long-term cash flow projections combine to render quantitative "solutions" to strategic problems not only misleading but also highly dangerous. Perhaps the greatest future hope lies with Forrester's "Industrial Dynamics" models. But even Forrester concedes that "strategic problems are perhaps of the 100th order of complexity while the most sophisticated computers are presently capable of only the 10th order." [2]

Strategic planning is not just a statement of a company's aspirations. It also includes what must be done to make those aspirations a reality. The company's viewpoint must remain sufficiently flexible for a new plan to be substituted for the old one whenever conditions change or new information allows a more accurate perception of the situation.

Despite the need for flexibility, a company should *never* be without an explicit strategic plan. Only by active planning can it hope to initiate upon the environment and shape its own destiny. An explicit plan allows management to respond quickly and effectively to opportunities which arise unexpectedly. It enables managers to choose more wisely among the continual tradeoffs which must be made among desirable, but conflicting, outcomes and attributes.

Strategic planning goes far deeper than most budgeting procedures. Budgeting is an excellent means of planning and monitoring *operating* activities, but a budget, by its very nature, emphasizes *internal* performance within a *given* strategic framework. As a basis for strategic planning, budgets (especially those generated at the divisional or unit level) tend to focus on improving the performance of those activities in which the unit is presently engaged. Strategic planning, on the other hand, is *externally* oriented. It must concern itself with the basic direction and purpose of the activity: Are we using our resources most effectively?

---

[1] H. Igor Ansoff, *Corporate Strategy* (New York: McGraw-Hill Book Company, 1965).
[2] Jay W. Forrester, "The Structure Underlying Management Processes," in *Evolving Concepts in Management* (New York: Academy of Management, 1964).

Could we improve our performance by major changes in existing policies or major redeployments of our resources? Budgeting tends to limit one's thinking to his own unit's activities; strategic planning *obliges* one to view the unit from the perspective of the total company.

STEPS IN PLANNING CORPORATE STRATEGY

In earlier chapters we described a strategic plan as consisting of: (a) an explicit definition of the desired future *scope* of the company; (b) an explicit identification of the basis on which the company desires to differentiate itself from its competitors (its *competitive advantage*); (c) an explicit statement of the desired future performance *specifications;* and (d) an explicit statement of the planned *allocation of resources* over the foreseeable future.

These four elements comprise a statement of the intended direction, purpose, and character of the company. Such a strategic plan should be fully honored, until a new plan—to be honored as fully—is substituted. Regardless of the frequency of revision, no company should ever be without this basic understanding of where it is headed and how it intends to get there.

In this chapter, normative in its approach, we propose six sequential steps in planning strategy: (1) environmental analysis; (2) resource analysis; (3) identifying competitive advantages; (4) defining scope; (5) establishing performance specifications; and (6) resource procurement and deployment. Note that we do not start with a "statement of objectives," as is so frequently prescribed. Rather, we begin with establishing the reality limits and opportunities for the enterprise. Thus begins a continuous cycle of analysis, planning, deployment, reanalysis, replanning, redeployment, and so on.

Step 1: Environmental Analysis

Chapters 5 and 6 discussed at some length the kinds of questions a company's top management should continually ask themselves as they monitor their environment. We proposed that management should first try to identify future opportunities and threats within the company's *existing* product line and customer list. We urged an analysis of the life-cycle stages of major product groups and of the supply/demand/price characteristics of those products. We suggested a careful search for signs of change in customer needs or desires, especially as related to technological progress or development. Abandoning any arbitrary industry boundaries, we proposed looking closely for the potential emergence of substitute products or services, or for new competitors expanding from other bases. Our basic goals were to find: (a) new opportunities for present *products* (with new customers, geographical expansion, or new applications); (b) new opportunities to serve existing *customers* with new products or services or in new geographical locations; and (c) the major future *threats* to market position and profit margins.

After this first round of analysis of familiar products and customers has been completed, an alert management should look for new opportunities in other product/market areas. Recognizing the inevitable obsolescence of existing products, they should always be attempting to extend their present technological competences. Each major product grouping which lies within the company's ability should be explored for feasibility. Is its market potential sufficiently large to justify the risk of a new venture? How much better do we have to be than entrenched competitors in order to establish ourselves effectively? For how long and at what cost can an advantage be maintained? How long a lead time must be considered from starting research or development to the time when a genuine market impact can be created? How much capital will be required to support the venture over this time span?

Only a handful of companies, such as IBM, Xerox, Sears Roebuck, and Boise Cascade, have deliberately and consistently sought such new opportunities. More often, even among well-managed companies, basic changes in corporate strategy have developed only as a result of encountering massive problems. For example, DuPont's historical diversification into new products was a direct reaction to a market downturn in its basic line (gunpowder) and the threat of large excess capacity. General Motors' move to tightly integrated operations under Sloan was a reaction to excessive inventories and operating losses which had developed under Durant. Standard Oil Company's (New Jersey) major move into a complete, vertically integrated producing, transporting, refining, and marketing organization developed in reaction to earnings reductions and market conditions of acute shortages in some activities and serious oversupply in others.

No environmental analysis would be complete without close examination of competitors' activities, especially in new product development. This is why virtually every case in this book has extensive information about competitive companies. Moreover, major changes in government policy or activity—not only in the United States, but throughout the world—must be continually monitored for creation of potential opportunities and threats for the firm.

Step 1, then, can be thought of as identifying the major product/market opportunities—present and future—for company effort. It also provides warnings as to which present activities should be considered for deemphasis or ultimate withdrawal.

Step 2: Resource Analysis

In addition to environmental analysis (step 1), Chapters 5 and 6 also presented specific ways of analyzing and evaluating the resources presently or potentially available to a company. We suggested a series of questions for identifying major strengths and weaknesses in financial condition, market position, management competence, technical capability, physical facilities, and susceptibility to external pressures. We urged an orderly review of products, markets, processes, personnel, and facilities.

Some companies have great unused financial strength. Not only do these companies hold cash far in excess of their current requirements, but they also have vast untapped borrowing power which adds enormously to the funds potentially available for future opportunities. Some other companies are persistently cash hungry. There are always more opportunities for management to pursue than there are resources available to support them. Yet funds are somehow always generated whenever a sufficiently attractive opportunity arises.

This same relationship seems to occur in consideration of personnel resources. Defensively-oriented companies appear to have more than sufficient qualified personnel to carry out their current scope of operations. On the other hand, aggressively opportunistic companies seem to regard development and availability of qualified personnel as the most crucial constraint on their future activities.

Physical facilities are often a great competitive strength, while at other times these heavy fixed investments have appeared as severe weaknesses. In the airline industry, we saw the purchase of advanced capital equipment as providing competitive advantages which lasted only until the rest of the industry became similarly equipped. Financing these capital-intensive activities became a major constraint on company development.

Chapters 5 and 6 also provided some guidelines for evaluation of products and of market position. Company reputation, position, and technical competence should be reviewed continually vis-à-vis competitors, customers, suppliers, relevant governmental bodies, and so on.

This assessment of company strengths and weaknesses provides the basis for the planning of future strategy.

Step 3: Identifying Competitive Advantages

From environmental analysis (step 1) we can identify the major potential opportunities for the firm. From analysis of its present (and potentially available) resources (step 2) we can narrow the range of feasible alternatives. Matching future opportunities against present resources provides some indication of the *attractiveness* of major change in strategic posture. Future threats relative to resources provide some measure of the *urgency* of such change.

The most appropriate direction for future corporate strategy will be one in which the company can favorably differentiate itself from its competitors. The company must possess a meaningful *competitive advantage* if it is to be effective in the marketplace. Clarity in definining the nature of this advantage (step 3) enables the company to concentrate its resources on those elements crucial to future success.

An explicit definition of company strengths leads to the first of the principles of strategic planning to be presented in this chapter.

Rule #1: always lead from strength. Competitive strengths should be exploited as far as possible. They should provide the basis for future strategic action. For example, Mitchell Nursery's close proximity to orchardists gave it an excellent basis for serving all the basic supply needs of its customers.

Most companies spend the bulk of their time and resources on attempts to bolster and reduce competitive *weaknesses*. Virtually all of the steps taken by Pioneer Brass in the (B) case are this kind of defensive patching-up of weaknesses. Although attention to inefficiency is desirable for all companies, such a strategic emphasis is appropriate only to a company which is situated (and chooses to remain) in a fully matured industry. In addition, a defensive emphasis tends to be most prevalent among very large companies. It is easy to see the need for defensive repairing of weakness, but it takes greater courage to exploit new offensive opportunities inherent in the company's competitive strengths.

A second principle follows logically from the first.

Rule #2: the basic strategy for all companies should be to concentrate resources where the company presently has (or can develop readily) a meaningful competitive advantage. Corporate security, stability, survival, growth, and profitability all stem from being able to serve an important need better than anybody else. As explained in Chapter 5, a competitive advantage can take many forms; without some such distinctive competence, no company can induce customers to do business with it. Having established such an advantage, a company should marshal all of its resources in developing and extending it as far as is economically feasible. As Drucker pointed out in the article quoted in Chapter 6,[3] "the areas of greatest potential should be given the fullest resource support —in quantity and quality—before the next promising area gets *anything*." Thus, discretionary capital should be invested only in exploiting a present competitive advantage or in building a new one for the future.

A well-integrated offensive strategy demands some measure of control over the company's environment. Market control can result from a consumer franchise for a proprietary product line (sales on the basis of preference for perceived differentiable product characteristics or for personalized services rendered) or from ownership or control of final distribution or consumption units (sales based on contribution to over-all corporate profitability). If a company has nondifferentiable products or nonpersonalized services to customers, price, reciprocity, availability and convenience, or personal relationships become the basis on which one supplier is chosen over another. None of these represents a very meaningful long-term competitive advantage in the marketplace for an industrial company. Retailers or distributors, however, may find them sufficient for establishing an effective advantage over competitors.

Of course, market domination is not the only way to exercise control over the company's environment. Chapter 5 indicated more than 15 possible competitive advantages. The principal ones included:

---

[3] Peter F. Drucker, "Managing for Business Effectiveness," *Harvard Business Review,* Vol. 41, No. 3 (May-June 1963), p. 59.

1. *Preferential marketing position* (as indicated above) through: proprietary product line; brand franchise; long-term reputation and acceptance; superior services or facilities.
2. *Technological superiority* expressed in: outstanding performance characteristics of products; exceptional price-quality-value relationships; excellence of product design; leadership in product innovation, patent protection, and so on.
3. *Preferential supply position* through: ownership of low-cost or scarce raw materials; control of intermediate processing or servicing units.
4. *Physical advantages* expressed in: superior logistics; convenient, available locations; or outstanding facilities.
5. *Financial capability:* providing the resources for massive investment (especially significant for capital-intensive industries or where market entry is at high cost); unusual skills in creative financing and negotiating.
6. *Personnel competences:* especially in conceptual thinking and managerial performance, but also in highly personalized, nonmanagerial skills such as selling, producing, creating, trading, merchandising, and accounting.
7. Low-cost, high efficiency *operating skill* in manufacturing (becoming the lowest cost producer in the industry) and/or distribution (where there may be high efficiency in transportation, logistics, and inventory management). Note that we are concerned here with industrial engineering, data processing, and other process-management *skills,* and not just with heavy investment in capital equipment.

Clear definition and exposition of a company's competitive advantage becomes the "unifying concept" around which all strategic planning turns. Building on these strengths increases the likelihood of future success and enhances the probability of a long-term competitive edge.

Step 4: Defining Scope

Steps 1 and 2 analyzed the company's environment and resource availability. Step 3 obliged the company to determine and articulate what kind of competitive advantage it would attempt to establish. Now we are ready for explicit definition of the future scope of the company's activities, which is the fourth step in refining the nature of the company's over-all mission. The product/market segments in which the company plans to participate need to be clearly articulated in order to guide resource allocation decisions, appropriate skill development, and search and evaluation of new ventures or potential acquisitions, and to facilitate continual pruning and divestment of obsolescing products and shrinking markets.

The key idea is not to achieve broad, over-all coverage, but to establish relative emphasis, priorities, and selectivity among alternatives. In general, concentration on a very limited number of carefully defined product/market segments will bring the greatest success. Concentration produces the best understanding of present and future needs of customers and of desired future product characteristics, and assures that adequate resources will be available to exploit them.

Unless the corporate definition of desired competitive advantages and product/market scope is clear, it is impossible for divisions (or other units) to perform as effective parts of a unified whole. Without such definitions, individual units tend to perceive threats and opportunities in a self-serving, partial manner which is divisive in nature and potentially destructive to the welfare of the total organization. Divisional acquisitions and new investments then tend to be made on a wholly *ad hoc* basis, while potential divestments are postponed indefinitely. Clear-cut definition of *which* products, *which* customers, and *which* channels of distribution will receive the primary emphasis not only guide central resource allocation, but also free divisional management to plan operations with confidence. Interdivisional collaboration, direction, and cooperative contribution are thus dependent on clear definition of corporate scope.

This same point needs to be made regarding the relative emphasis put upon the various *functional* activities *within* each division. For example, a unit whose competitive advantage lies in its technological superiority needs to support and emphasize a large research and development group, and to pick markets which are responsive to demonstrable product performance; e.g., Morgan Corporation's engineers dominated the complex tube technology and sold to sophisticated engineers who appreciated their ingenuity. However, Morgan would have had a very difficult time in the consumer microwave oven business. Oven sales would have to be based on very different distribution channels and different appeals to buyers who would not understand or appreciate the technical differences between Morgan's oven and competitors'. Hence, in this instance, limiting the division's scope to product/market segments which demanded and understood high technology performance was most likely to produce successful results.

A unit whose real competitive advantage lies in its preferential market position may well emphasize its sales organization, customer service, or sales promotion activities, giving only minimal support to other functions. Here, scope should be limited to product/market segments most susceptible to this kind of appeal. Tupper's concentration on the home party distribution concept, limiting sales to a very narrow product line, is a good example.

Some companies, like Rexall, have tried to choose product/market segments primarily on the basis of their growth potential. However, participation in high-growth markets is no panacea, since these are usually the markets where competition is most intense. While all may prosper for a while, shakeouts inevitably occur. Such markets seldom yield long-term profits to the company which does not possess a meaningful competitive advantage. For example, basic petrochemical production has been one of the fastest growing U.S. industries. Rexall has managed to stay in the forefront of process improvement, but so have most of Rexall's important competitors. Lacking any real competitive advantage in this fast growing industry, Rexall has had to work very hard to make even modest returns on its massive investment in petrochemical production. The same situation has been true in such other high-growth industries as pharmaceuticals, semiconductors, and data processing equipment. These industries present extremely high risks for the marginal producer who lacks any real advantage over well-entrenched competitors, and yet must spend heavily to keep up technically or perish.

Careful identification and definition of product/market scope reduces the time necessary for decisions on acquisitions, new investments, and divestments. It provides a guide for the integrated direction of the enterprise. The assertion by a company that it will "go into anything that's honest and will show a good profit" tacitly assumes that there is no *managerial* requirement for the central corporation—only that it have the financial strength to make the necessary *investments*. Such a philosophy presumes that each "investment" will be self-sustaining and will operate effectively without corporate assistance. It assumes that the whole is no more or less than the sum of the various parts, and denies each unit the potential contribution of mutual support.

It is worth noting that the majority of the nation's most successful companies have defined their product/market scopes very narrowly; e.g., DuPont's historical emphasis on products of nitrocellulose (a focus on *technology*), General Motors' heavy concentration on automobiles (a *product* emphasis), Standard Oil's commitment to products of petroleum (a focus on a single *raw material*), and Sears' concentration on retail merchandising (specializing in a particular *customer category*). Most multiproduct companies originally specialized in a single market segment, in conversion of a single raw material, or in the exploitation of a single technology. As they became increasingly multimarket and multinational in scope, many of the most successful companies divisionalized so that each division could retain a relatively narrow scope, despite a broad total spectrum of over-all corporate activity (e.g., General Motors, IBM, Morgan, Rexall, Boise Cascade).

These observations bring us to another principle of strategic planning.

Rule #3: the narrowest possible product/market scope should be selected for each unit consistent with unit resources and with market requirements. No products should be included in the line which are not *required* by the market segment. Any lines producing a substandard return should be phased out. Marketing departments frequently claim that "the complete line is essential in order to make sales." If this is true (which it usually is *not*), substandard items should either be subcontracted out and purchased for resale, or the deficits charged as sales promotion expense.

It's remarkable how *unessential* these "essential" items can become when their losses are charged against the marketing department's budget. A progressive company should be willing to vacate small or marginal product/market segments, allowing some other supplier to fill this need, while they concentrate efforts on more fruitful segments. In general, the larger the company's resources, the broader the product/market scope that can be pursued satisfactorily. A small company with limited resources would do well to define its scope extremely narrowly and then try to dominate completely its chosen segment. (The small company's most limiting feature is often its shortage of skilled management personnel. These key people should be concentrated in a very narrow scope so that a real competitive advantage can be established and maintained.)

Successful companies ordinarily have a great number of alternatives available in defining scope. They also have adequate time to explore the alternatives, and usually sufficient money to pursue them. But their very success makes it hard for many to change from historically fruitful products, markets, or procedures. Old, entrenched values, past results and relationships, tend to thwart any basic change in company scope. Unsuccessful companies, on the other hand, are often in such critical condition that drastic retrenchment, rather than creative change, is frequently most appropriate.

Thus, while new and creative definition of scope should be carried forward continuously, strong forces are at work in most companies to resist change and perpetuate old patterns. It takes continuous management effort to preserve a flexible, viable approach to defining scope.

Step 5: Establishing Performance Specifications

Once we have determined a company's major opportunities (step 1) and limitations (step 2), identified what its future competitive advantage will be (step 3), and defined its scope (step 4), we are *finally* ready to talk about *objectives*. To do so earlier would have actually interfered with effective planning. Postponing consideration of objectives until this stage enables us to establish specific measurements, and guards against vacuous "creed" statements or over-emphasis of a particular functional point of view (see Chapter 2). To achieve commitment, goals must be visible and progress measurable.

As indicated in Chapter 4, numerical performance specifications can usefully be established for the company's desired rate of growth, market penetration, profitability, and survival capacity. Such quantification serves two indispensable functions. First, it provides target objectives for all to try to achieve. Second, it gives some precision to decisions on resource allocation, including prospective acquisitions and divestments, within the limits of the previously designated scope and competitive advantage.

An additional dimension in objective-setting might be to establish targets in terms of key personnel. Qualified people are frequently the most limiting factor in a company's growth because of their scarcity and their influence upon outcomes. Thus, "people-based" criteria might well be used in parallel with financial or numerical criteria. Such factors might include: (a) "growth" in numbers and competency of management personnel; (b) "market share" of the best qualified people in the industry; (c) "profits" per individual or profits per management unit (the basis of the profit center concept); and (d) degree of managerial ability as an index of "survival capacity." [4]

---

[4] The author is indebted to Mr. Nick Newman, President of American Community Stores Corp., for this analogy. Mr. Newman has been a pioneer in the managerial use of people-centered criteria.

The dimension that proves to be the limiting factor in a company's development must be given top priority. For example, a company in a fast-growing industry which seeks to hold or increase its market share (i.e., is experiencing rapid sales growth) soon finds that the *availability of cash*—to provide working capital and finance the product development and sales efforts which assure future profits—will be its main constraint. Companies in fully mature industries may find that they are accumulating *excessive* financial resources, instead of seeking new product/market segments for investment. For these companies, *cost reduction* and minimizing investments in old areas, while promoting new ones, becomes an important challenge. "In-between" companies situated in vigorous, but well-established, maturing industries, have a broader range of choice. They can seek to *increase sales*—through price changes, expanded product lines, improved product performance and design features, improved sales organization, distribution, service, promotion, or field inventory availability. They can seek to *reduce costs* by simplifying and standardizing the product line, introducing more labor-saving equipment, or simplifying processes and procedures. Or they can seek to *increase return on investment* by reducing the capital employed—either through aggressive debt management or through better control of inventories, material flow, space, and equipment utilization.

The rate of growth of the industry, relative to the rate of change in the number of firms competing, raises the key questions of market share and profitability. If the growth in competition is small relative to growth in industry demand, there is room for everyone. But if the proliferation of firms is more rapid than growth in market size, the individual firm must decide whether it will try to force out weaker competition by growing aggressively, or be willing to settle for a lower growth rate in order to protect competitors' survival. The best interests of very large companies under Justice Department scrutiny are often served by the latter course!

A decision not to expand an existing product/market segment at least the same rate as the industry is growing is tantamount to a decision to withdraw from that segment. A profitable phasing out of these activities is then called for, with a consequent reinvestment of the funds so generated into other segments of the newly chosen company scope.

Step 6: Procuring and Allocating Resources

The first two steps in the planning process have identified opportunities (step 1) and limits (step 2). In steps 3 and 4, we defined our desired competitive advantage and our preferred product/market scope. In step 5 we set desired performance targets. Now we are ready to allocate our resources and elaborate the defined strategy. Unless corporate resources are gathered and deployed in a manner consistent with the previously determined competitive advantage, scope, and performance specifications, all of the planning is for naught. These earlier determinations set the boundary limits and the general direction for over-all resource deployment.

We are now obliged to be quite specific in detailing each of the seven basic strategic variables introduced in Chapter 3. We should be able to define precisely: (1) the market segment(s) which will be pursued; (2) the products and services (and their specifications) which will be offered, developed, or discontinued; (3) the channels of distribution and promotion which will be utilized; (4) the pricing policies and quality/price tradeoffs which will be followed. We should keep in mind that careful market segmentation and concentration of our resources on the segments chosen are crucial to corporate success. We must choose which customers we will seek to please, how we will reach them, what we will offer them, and which competitors we will challenge.

By now, we should also be able to state clearly: (5) our investment policy on capital expenditures and our criteria for purchases or divestment; (6) the means by which our strategy will be financed and the limits which must realistically be placed on outlays; and (7) the key people who will be needed to carry out the strategic program.

Detailed definition of these seven strategic variables will refine substantially the broadly stated direction indicated earlier. But as we have said many times, a strategic plan is a *timed* sequence of *conditional* moves in resources *deployment*. Establishment of *emphasis* and *priorities* is the heart of such a plan. It is essential that a timetable of major moves be established, and that the resource requirements and availabilities be clearly spelled out. We suggest a program of implementation and elaboration as follows:

1. Having determined where our over-all product/market emphasis is going to be placed, we analyze all other activities and product lines to determine *when* and *how* these extraneous investments will be sold, liquidated, or phased out. Funds generated from gradual liquidation or outright sale should be estimated and scheduled over the likely time periods required. Key persons released from these activities should also be identified, and the probable dates of their availability noted.

2. Now we must calculate the requirements for investment in personnel, plant capacity, marketing effort, product development, and so on, necessary to establish and ensure the desired competitive advantage for each unit which will be emphasized. We must be sure that such outlays are adequate to achieve the performance targets previously defined.

3. Contrasting these requirements, over time, with the capital and personnel resources presently available, plus those which will be generated from operations and those which will become available from phasing out of extraneous activities, highlights shortages and excesses. Excesses provide new opportunities for further development. Shortages demand new financing and/or extensive head-hunting. They may suggest the desirability of a merger or acquisition to provide the necessary resources and/or shorten the time lag before the company can become an important factor in the market-place.

4. What we have left is, in essence, a critical path problem—scheduling personnel and activities in such a sequence that performance targets are met and resource availability matches requirements. The scarcity or unavailability of

crucial resources may oblige a change in the basic plan, or at least in the timing sequence.

THE FINAL PLAN

Our final strategic plan consists of:

1. A one or two page statement of desired *competitive advantage, scope,* and performance *specifications.*
2. One or two pages specifically detailing the seven strategic variables (market policy, product policy, distribution policy, pricing policy, investment policy, financing policy, and key personnel placement policy) which give substance to the earlier statement.
3. Three documents which schedule the necessary resource procurements and allocations:
   (a) A *timetable* of major strategic moves, which should indicate not only the sequence of major events but also the lead time required before each action can be made effective. It should also indicate specific times for measuring progress and reviewing plans.
   (b) A *funds flow* analysis tied to the strategic timetable. This document should indicate the sources and application of funds necessary to support the various planned events. (In addition, sufficient reserves should always be maintained to capitalize on unanticipated opportunities or to guard against unexpected adversity.)
   (c) A *manning table* indicating the key persons (and where they will come from) necessary to carry out the proposed strategic moves. Such a table should also indicate specific assignments to individuals for the various planned activities.

These three documents specify the allocations of time, funds, and executive attention, and highlight the sequences, the emphases, and the priorities. To produce these documents properly, agonizing decisions and tradeoffs must be made among competing alternatives. When this has been done, we have a viable set of documents which can be circulated throughout management to guide current decisions and future action.

Changing the Details of the Strategic Plan

We have talked many times about the need for frequent *change* in strategic plans. This is especially true for these three documents, whose detail may change from day to day.

The entire strategic planning process needs to be recycled regularly:

1. Whenever new opportunities or threats appear because of a major change in environment, resource position of the company, or key management or ownership complement.

2. Whenever results differ sharply from target performance specifications.
3. Periodically—say, once each year, regardless of whether there have been any important changes. This step is necessary to avoid creeping bureaucracy, to educate newer members of management in the importance and techniques of strategic planning, and to assure that key strategic questions are continually kept in the forefront by all management personnel. This is an especially effective device for identifying and emphasizing synergistic opportunities among units, and for creating an over-all corporate atmosphere.

Disinvestment Decisions

Even if no major additions or acquisitions are contemplated, annual review provides an opportunity for questioning whether a unit should be divested or cut back. Withdrawal from a dying market or a disadvantageous position is just as important as making a new investment or acquisition. If such disinvestments are not made, the company rapidly proliferates an enormous number of largely unrelated, marginal activities.

This brings us to another basic rule.

Rule #4: a unit whose future earning power (discounted at the company's current cost of capital) is less than its liquidation value should be sold as quickly as possible. The original amount invested in the venture, or its current book value, are meaningless when an operation becomes marginal or worse. Investment or book value must be treated as sunk costs. The future flow of funds should be compared with whatever funds flow can be generated by selling the venture. If the present value of estimated future earnings is less than the amount for which the unit can be sold, the appropriate course of action is obvious. Assumptions underlying projections of future earnings must be carefully scrutinized and vigorously challenged in situations which have spotty or marginal records.

Arthur Comas casts a refreshing light on the frequently necessary but always difficult disinvestment decision. He says:

> Disinvestment decisions within a context of corporate development planning are among the most difficult and emotionally-loaded issues that must be faced. If acquisitions are made to diversify *away* from existing product lines or businesses, there must obviously be some lines of business or assets that have matured to the point where prospects are dim. Logically, the reverse process of directing the flow of new funds to projects which promise the highest yield is the most desirable course of action.
>
> There are several unhappy connotations, however, surrounding the word "disinvestment." To some, it implies failure, surrender, an inability to compete with one's business peers. Or it runs counter to the growthmanship ethic of a free enterprise system. Or it smacks of the unpatriotic: loss of job opportunities that can threaten the economy of an area.
>
> Furthermore, there have indeed been instances where a disinvestment has

resulted in unfortunate consequences. It may have been a "bail out" where customers, lenders, suppliers, and the community have been left holding the now empty bag. And it may also have been the end result of a "raid"—unnecessary, haphazard, reckless, and unconscionably damaging to others.

The alternatives available to management for ultimate disposition of an unsatisfactory investment are normally these:

a) To hold and hope.
b) To invest more money to improve the investment.
c) To sell it as a package.
d) To liquidate gradually over time.

To hold and hope reflects the normal resistance and inertia among operating units to disinvesting any assets, however poor the current earnings or the outlook. Stating the company's financial and strategic investment criteria at frequent intervals will help raise questions about individual projects or assets for analysis. The general rule is that an asset should be sold when its liquidation value is greater than its earning power capitalized at the company's cost of capital. In looking at the valuation base, both original cost and present depreciated book value are irrelevant, as they represent sunk costs. The only relevant valuation on the realizable value of an asset is, of course, the current market value of that asset.

Investing more money to improve an investment may be a valid decision—or it may represent wishful thinking. One method of identifying disinvestment candidates is to analyze each request for additional funds for "modernization" or "replacement of facilities." It may well be that such requests indicate a very favorable return on the incremental investment, while the basic facility (or business) is not worth improving or even saving.

To sell a business (or division) as a package is by no means rare. Scanning periodic listings of mergers and acquisitions, such as the monthly summary issued by NICB, indicates that a significant portion of parties involved are complete units or sub-divisions of medium and large corporations. Disposing of these units is largely a problem of identifying that purchaser whose future performance would be most enhanced by the acquisition. By selecting a few target purchasers, not only is the risk of upsetting current operations by widespread advertising restricted, but the highest potential bidder can often be identified and approached on the basis of his own strategic goals.

In many cases, *liquidating gradually over time* is the best and most profitable way to implement a disinvestment decision. The key, of course, is to make provision for the gradual reassignment or relocation of personnel. Gradual liquidation involves the deliberate surrender of market position over a period of time, perhaps by maintaining high prices and accepting a declining share of the market. It may also involve the recapture of goodwill built up (and expensed) during the life of the business. In many ways it represents the ultimate payout for R&D, sales development, and organization investments which have been treated as expense items over the life of a product.

Implementing disinvestment decisions should involve a *planned* and *orderly* procedure which will result in the greatest possible profit and liquidity for the firm commensurate with the firm's responsibilities to stockholders, employees, customers, vendors, and its community. If rigorous corporate planning goes into its strategy for growth, the strategy for disinvestments should be equally thoughtful and consistent.[5]

STRATEGIC MODE

An important refinement of the concept of strategic planning is the choosing of a basic mode in which future company development will proceed.

For the small to medium-sized company, as discussed previously, a *niche* strategy is essential to long-run success. The company must dominate the market segment(s) it serves, and should concentrate its efforts and resources on preserving and extending its competitive advantages. This is the lowest risk strategy that a company can follow.

As the company grows, opportunities occur for *horizontal expansion*. Growth is achieved by widening the product line offered in present markets or by opening new markets for present products or services. The new markets can represent either geographical expansion or development of new classes of customers in existing locations.

The medium to large-sized firm often has attractive opportunities for *vertical integration*. Here the company attempts to grow by adding units closer to the final end-use market (forward integration) or to its original raw material sources (backward integration). This mode may be an attempt to optimize the utilization of natural resources, or an effort to improve the economic utility of existing production or marketing facilities. On the other hand, it may merely seek to reduce the number of steps between producer and user, with the consequent gain of the intervening profit increments, e.g., owning captive outlets for existing output.

A fourth basic mode goes under the euphemistic label of *diversification*. Here growth is achieved by entry into new markets with products or services different from the present line.

Diversification (as is also true of vertical integration and horizontal expansion) can be achieved through either internal corporate development or acquisition of existing firms. It is generally more desirable to buy an existing firm than to "bootstrap" one's way into a new product/market segment. The highest risk strategy is entry into new markets with new products against entrenched competition. Not only does entry by acquisition provide a "running start" by an established organization, it also provides entry without increasing of industry capacity. Even in growth industries like petrochemicals and corrugated paper, we have seen sharp erosion in prices and profits whenever new capacity comes on stream and creates surpluses of supply.

Diversification, in contrast to integrated growth, puts the company into un-

---

[5] Arthur P. Comas, *Corporate Strategy Development: Disinvestment Decisions* (Boston, Mass.: The Boston Consulting Group, 1967).

related product/market segments. Two basically different ways of administering diversified multibusiness organizations are beginning to emerge. Both are frequently classified under the misnomer *conglomerate,* but it is important to distinguish between them. The first type operates very much like a *holding company.* It will invest in anything which provides a satisfactory financial return, and provides little central direction of, or intrusion into, the affairs of the operating units. Little commitment is felt by any of the units toward the parent, and vice versa. Strategies are developed individually by the operating units with little or no concern for potential conflicts or synergisms among units. (General Electric operated this way in the 1950's, under its celebrated "decentralization plan.") Castle & Cooke is an almost classic example of a holding company in action. Rexall puts its operating units through a series of far more rigorous reporting practices than does Castle & Cooke; but it, too, leaves each of the basic units as an autonomous operation, from a strategic point of view. Ling-Temco-Vought, Inc. (LTV) is perhaps the most spectacular performer in this class of companies.

The second type of diversified multibusiness is becoming known as a *free-form corporation.* The basic distinction between the free-form company and the holding company is that the former strongly influences the strategic direction of its operating units. Central management controls the allocation of funds, key manpower, and executive attention among the various operating units. It may force feed one division and drastically prune another. Most importantly, it continually reassesses each unit in terms of the appropriateness of its total divestment from the corporation or its combination with another unit. This flexibility of capital investment is the essence of effective corporate strategy. Free-form companies aggressively seek synergistic connections among the operating units. Avoiding rigorous enforcement of the profit center concept, to which the holding company is tied, the effective free-form company finds ways to "bend" its internal bookkeeping so as to give due credit to any unit which benefits other units or which benefits the total corporation beyond its own profit contribution. Whenever short-term unit profits require action which is likely to affect adversely the long-term profitability of the total corporation, central management will insist on an alternate course. However, accommodations can be made in corporate accounting which do not penalize the unit manager's profitability showing. Among our present case collection, Boise Cascade and Applied Power are the best examples of effective free-form multibusinesses. Litton, Textron, Boise Cascade and American Standard are other companies which fit this pattern. High financial sophistication, coupled with a well-developed general management point of view, are the hallmarks of an effective free-form multibusiness.

Strategic Behavior

Regardless of which strategic mode seems most appropriate for a particular company at a particular point in time, there are a number of universal axioms which tend to apply despite differences in the type of industry (capital intensive, labor intensive, or materials intensive), the volatility of the industry (price sensitivity, rate of growth, maturity), and the structure of the industry (oligopolistic, fragmented, or broadly distributed).

For the large company, it is essential that management keep its eye on the relative concentrations and proportions of its various activities. It is easy to overemphasize what is new and different today, or what has been most difficult recently, and to lose sight of the fact that the bulk of the company's assets are committed to another activity.

A. *"Planning is crucial."* Without planned direction, people tend to allocate their time and resources according to which activities occur most frequently or are most troublesome, rather than those which are most productive.

B. *"Give up the crumbs."* The large company should not try to get the last dollar of profit out of an item or the last percentage point of market share. These increments are always more costly than capturing larger shares of other market segments. The big company should be content to dominate the principal product lines and to service the most important customers, leaving the peripheral business to smaller competitors, who can service the small-volume segments more efficiently.

C. *"Preserve company strength and stability."* Discretionary capital should be invested only in exploiting a present competitive advantage or building a significant, new advantage. Consideration should be given to the value—beyond present financial return—of an established competitive base. For this reason, a higher profit criterion should be placed on new activities than on the continuance of old ones. Nonetheless, investment should be made in improving or upgrading present operations only if the promise of return on the investment is at least as large as the target specification for the entire company, or if the company is sufficiently strong in the particular market segment that it stands to gain far more than its competitors from any technological improvement.

Frequently, more money can be made for the company through discontinuing marginal or submarginal activities than by investing heavily in new ventures. Lines should be phased out which are below standard. Essential but unprofitable items should not be manufactured, but purchased for resale.

It should be noted that large companies are especially vulnerable to public and governmental pressures. Perpetuation of the company, husbanding of its reputation and relationships, and acceptance of its responsibility in community and national economic and social affairs should be attended to continually. While these factors are often a deterrent to swift or decisive action, they are also the large company's greatest sources of strength.

For the small company, competing against very large ones, a more opportunistic behavior may be more appropriate. An excellent analogy can be drawn to guerilla warfare.[6] Essentially, the guerilla works on a relatively short time

---

[6] The author is indebted to Mr. Homayoun Sanati, Managing Director, Pars Paper Company, Ltd., Teheran, Iran, for some of the basic ideas in this analogy.

horizon, tries to maintain the initiative, and counts on his superior knowledge of the terrain (market) and populace (customers) to enable him to respond more quickly, more creatively, and more effectively than his larger and better financed opponent. The rules include:

A. *"Attack when the enemy retreats."* The small company should not attempt any form of direct competition until it has developed some special advantage over the giant. It should select only those markets in which the products, outlets, locations, and services can be so segmented that the small company can choose a unique basis on which to compete. Thus, when the "enemy retreats" (withdraws from a market or leaves a void) the market segments not being satisfied can be identified and selected for the "attack." The definition of scope for a small company should be based upon the identification of market niches where competition is either absent or has little or no strength—e.g., American Motors' definition of the need for compact cars at a time when the industry leaders were steadily increasing the size of their automobiles; LaPlant-Choate's specialization in dozer blades.

B. *"Do not take full advantage of all opportunities."* Maintain some reserves and preserve key strength against possible retaliation. If a major confrontation takes place, the small firm will be able to choose among a large number of alternatives, because it will still have uncommitted resources. (E.g., American Motors' low break-even point made it possible to operate profitably in 1960, even if volume were reduced or prices had to be dropped. Additionally, management minimized expenditures for equipment and arranged for extensive subcontracting, thereby conserving cash and increasing future debt capacity.)

C. *"Be as inconspicuous as possible."* If the market segment can be captured without calling attention to the company's success, the likelihood of retaliation is reduced. Thus, the small company should deploy its limited resources in ways which do not invite direct counterdeployment by competitors with vastly larger resources.

If the "enemy" waits a long time before responding to the "attack," it is possible that the small company can develop a permanent advantage through the development of a brand franchise, customer loyalty, market reputation, or an entrenched distribution system.

Except in a rapidly expanding market, the small company which wants to grow without inviting retaliation must seek to develop new products, new markets, new locations, or new services rather than try to expand volume in products or markets in which the giants are active. (E.g., American Motors' entry into European and South American markets offered sales expansion opportunities in which it did not compete with the principal factors in its major market.)

D. *"Respond quickly."* The small firm must be *more* responsive than its larger competitors to changes in demand within a chosen market segment if it is to continue to satisfy the market. It must be continually alert to additional product-service opportunities which arise within that market, so that new competitors are discouraged from entry.

In the early years of the association with Caterpillar, LaPlant-Choate responded readily to every change in emphasis suggested by Caterpillar (discontinue wagons, specialize in dozer blades) and thereby precluded Caterpillar's seeking a second source of supply. On the other hand, American Motors did not perceive that the market demand which they had defined in 1956 (for the 100 and 108 inch wheelbase compacts) had added other requirements by 1960 (more powerful engines and sportier appearances). Ford recognized this trend and hurt American Motors more with their new compacts than if they had chosen to produce cars more like the Rambler.

E. Frequently, there is insufficient time to develop a privileged market position before the enemy counterattacks. In this case, *"Retreat when the enemy attacks."*

The small company must be prepared to give up something in order to preserve its basic advantages. For example, American Motors was willing to subsidize dealers and reduce its profit margins in order to maintain volume in the face of General Motors and Ford competition.

Direct confrontation should be avoided, and the small firm should try to conserve its competitive strengths during a retreat. It should take whatever steps are necessary to maintain customer loyalty, distribution channels, financial community relationships, sources of supply, or any other variable crucial for success on the chosen "battlefield." (The special bonuses which American Motors gave its dealers preserved the distribution system which had been so vital to the company's success.)

For "the competing Lilliputian," a good offense may be the best defense. He needs to have great physical mobility to move swiftly, clear concepts and criteria to guide his choices, and ingenuity in selecting opportunities which capitalize upon his strength and enable him to maintain the initiative. These are potential advantages which are often difficult for the giant to match.

Relationship Between Military and Business Strategy

There is a key similarity between military and business strategy: In neither case is the end goal destruction of the enemy. Both the business firm and the military unit seek only to achieve the most favorable future relationship with the "enemy," at the least risk and lowest costs.

The business firm, like the military unit, should be trying to convince competitors of its superiority, the objective being to make the competitors accept certain constraints on their behavior: abandoning a market segment, not fighting for a customer or a product, foregoing product or process innovation, not expanding capabilities or capacities.

It is not important that the fact of superiority be demonstrated. It is sufficient that competitors *believe* that the firm can outcompete them. This can be done by establishing a lower cost structure; a preferred market position or brand franchise; superior service activities and personnel; or superior standing with important customers. If a firm can bind its customers to it, through superior service or value, it can dominate that market segment. Then it can force the full impact of market fluctuations on its competitors while maintaining a stable level of operations for itself. It can oblige its competitors to chase the marginal business —having to expand rapidly in good times and contract sharply in poor times— only if it is strongly entrenched in a low-cost, high acceptance position.

MODIFYING THE BASIC STRATEGIC PLAN

Ordinarily, plans may be prepared several years in advance, with the first year's schedule and cash flow documented in great detail, and subsequent years progressively less detailed. They will not normally include administrative aspects necessary to carry out the strategy—what the chief executive must do to influence performance throughout the company. This comes as a further step and includes design of the organization structure and work flow; recruitment, selection, placement, evaluation, and promotion of personnel; establishment of performance standards, limits, controls, rules, and routines; administration of rewards and punishments; and management's own personal behavior.

The wise chief executive does not expect the plan to be very detailed at top management level. The plan must fit the capabilities and motivation of company members, as well as the practical limits and opportunities of corporate resources. Adjustments for these factors are best left to lower levels, close to the points where they will be activated. Not only are self-esteem, recognition, contribution, and commitment of members involved. In a complex enterprise, the persons best qualified to modify a plan are often quite remote from the organization location and level from which the plan originated. A growing group of chief executives has come to *expect* and *demand* that subordinates exercise independent judgment and initiative in modifying strategic plans.

As Anthony points out:

> Several authors state that the aim of control is to assure that the results of operations conform as closely as possible to plans. We emphasize that such a concept of control is basically inconsistent with [our] concept. . . . To the extent that middle management can make decisions that are better than those implied in the plans, top management wishes it to do so. And the middle managers can in fact make better decisions under certain circumstances; to deny this possibility is implicitly to assume that top management is either clairvoyant, or omniscient, or both, which is not so.
>
> Since no one can foretell the future precisely—that is, since people are not clairvoyant—it follows that in some respects actual events will differ from the assumed events that the plans were designed to meet. Even if plans are revised frequently, the preparation and communication of revisions take time, and the revised plans therefore cannot be up-to-date in the literal sense of this term. Top management wants middle management to react to the events that actually occur, not to those that might have occurred had the real world been kind enough

to conform to the planning assumptions. Therefore top management does *not* necessarily want operations to conform to plans.

Furthermore, since people are not omniscient, their plans do not necessarily show the best course of action; they merely show what was thought of as best when the plan was made. Subsequently, someone may think of a way to improve on the plan; indeed, it is quite likely that he will do so as the facts and alternatives become clearer. If he does, he should act accordingly. For this reason, also, top management does *not* necessarily want operations to conform to plans.[7]

Rigidities in strategic planning frequently originate with specialist staff planners who have identified themselves personally with the product of their handiwork. As Tilles points out, this tendency has been a real deterrent to explicit strategic planning in many companies:

> One of the major difficulties in developing a statement of corporate strategy is that in most companies, the attempt to do so coincides with the beginning of a formal planning effort. As a result, all of the complex conceptual and procedural issues related to the corporate future tend to get bound up with the first groping efforts to work out a viable mission and program for the corporate planning activity.
>
> The most common causes of difficulty are the premature establishment of a formal planning department and the separation of the responsibility for the future of the company from the responsibility for managing current operations.
>
> Strategic planning is not what the planner does. It is what the management does. If the management finds that it is so deeply involved in the process that it requires some additional assistance, a planning officer may provide this. But to view the planner as synonymous with planning is to assume that a statement of corporate strategy remains a document rather than a creed.[8]

---

[7] Robert N. Anthony, *Planning and Control Systems: A Framework for Analysis* (Boston, Mass.: Division of Research, Harvard Business School, 1965), pp. 28-29.

[8] Seymour Tilles, "Making Strategy Explicit," *op. cit.* One of a series of informal statements on corporate strategy prepared by members of the staff of The Boston Consulting Group. © The Boston Consulting Group, Inc., 1968. Reproduced by permission.

Boise Cascade Corporation (A-1):
1913-1957

INTRODUCTION

When Robert V. Hansberger became president of the Boise Payette Lumber Company (predecessor to the Boise Cascade Corporation) in 1956, the company owned three sawmills, all located in the state of Idaho. In 1959 it had ten sawmills scattered across the states of Washington, Idaho, and Oregon.

The company produced a little more than 100 million board feet of lumber in 1956, compared with 504 million board feet in 1959 (thus ranking Boise among the three largest softwood lumber producers in the country).

It operated six wholesale building material plants in 1956 and nine in 1959. The company's retail division in 1956 had 78 retail stores which sold building materials. In 1959, the number of retail outlets had increased to 108.

Between 1956 and 1959, the company also entered into a substantial number of new operations. These included a plywood plant, a millwork plant, a soil conditioner plant, a multiwall paper bag factory, two textile packaging plants, four concrete block plants, seven concrete pipe plants, sixteen ready-mix concrete plants, eight sand and gravel mining operations, one pumice mine, eight stone and clay products warehouses, and one prestressed concrete plant. During the same period of time, the company constructed a 150 ton a day pulp and paper mill, and built two corrugated container converting plants.

The operating results achieved during Mr. Hansberger's first three years as president of Boise Cascade were impressive by any standard. Sales had risen 250% to $126,000,000

Case material of the Stanford Graduate School of Business is prepared as a basis for class discussion only. Cases are not designed as illustrations of either correct or incorrect handling of administrative problems or decisions.

© 1964 by the Board of Trustees of the Leland Stanford Junior University.

while earnings were up 370% to $5,600,000. Earnings per share were up 122% to $3.02 per share, and the market price of Boise shares had increased 254% to $46 per share.

EARLY HISTORY OF BOISE PAYETTE

The history of Boise Payette was not always as bright as it had been for the period 1956–1959. Started in 1913 as a joint venture by six families and their associates, Boise Payette produced substantial profits in its early years. Net profit in 1917 was $1,523,000 on a capital investment of $12,620,000, and in 1920 profits exceeded $2,000,000. After suffering losses in 1921 and 1922, the company recovered in the following year, recording profits in excess of $1,500,000. Much of the success during these years was credited to the company's 72 retail lumber yards, which provided a controlled outlet for a substantial proportion of the lumber produced by Boise Payette mills. But then the picture changed abruptly. From 1924 to 1929 the company lost money in all but one year, 1925, when earnings were $408,000 (sales and net income figures for the years 1913–1944 are presented in Exhibit 1).

Of the several reasons given for Boise Payette's depressed condition in the twenties, the main one was that the company could not economically reach the major U.S. lumber markets. Like other companies located in the Inland Empire (now part of the Western Pine region), Boise Payette experienced unusually high costs in harvesting its timber, much of which could be gotten out only by uphill hauls that defied the equipment of the mid-twenties. The problem was further complicated because Boise Payette had been forced to invest large sums in installations, such as gradings and bridges, which were often closed by winter snows or washed out by spring floods. And finally, there was an unfounded, but strong prejudice against the yellow-wood of the ponderosa pine, Boise's primary timber resource.

Suffering all of these adversities, Boise Payette had to compete for eastern markets against coastal timber (in the Douglas Fir region) where the trees grew densely on relatively gentle terrain. These trees were harvested cheaply and shipped to the major markets in the East, by sea through the newly opened Panama Canal, at low freight rates. Furthermore, the Douglas fir, so predominant in the coastal area, was the most widely accepted tree species used for lumber.

The same general conditions, that is, production costs and railroad rates, put Boise Payette in an unfavorable competitive position in the Middle West markets vis-à-vis southern pine lumber, which was produced in the southern states.

All of these factors came to bear at once when the lumber markets the company could reach conveniently by truck and rail, which were largely limited to Idaho, Utah, southern Wyoming, and western Colorado, became especially weak as the country edged into a nationwide depression.

As conditions worsened under full impact of the depression, the company

exhibit 1

BOISE CASCADE CORPORATION (A-1)

Summary of Boise Payette Sales and Earnings, 1913–1944

Year	Net sales (in thousands of $)	Net income after taxes (in thousands of $)
1913	2,097	(113)
1914	2,571	(534)
1915	2,161	1
1916	2,846	310
1917	2,776	1,523
1918	2,872	698
1919	3,170	840
1920	5,349	2,119
1921	1,698	(533)
1922	2,758	(205)
1923	4,427	1,569
1924	4,472	(112)
1925	4,360	408
1926	3,717	(23)
1927	3,077	(271)
1928	3,518	(32)
1929	3,820	(283)
1930	3,037	(572)
1931	5,454	(2,572)
1932	2,520	(2,788)
1933	3,565	(487)
1934	4,030	(865)
1935	6,034	(342)
1936	8,651	(123)
1937	9,686	501
1938	6,834	(612)
1939	8,036	(255)
1940	10,285	512
1941	13,453	1,257
1942	16,768	1,241
1943	16,487	982
1944	15,273	1,171

sustained losses in 1930–1932 which averaged $2,000,000 per year. In the face of these desolate operating results, Boise Payette's general manager resigned in 1931. The company's president died the following year.

Dr. E.P. Clapp, a practicing Illinois physician, became the company's new president. A series of deaths in his family in the 1920's had left Dr. Clapp responsible for a very substantial investment in the company, and he felt obliged to take an active part in the company's affairs. He had been a company director since 1924 and hence was closely familiar with the company's activities. The position of general manager was filled by Mr. S.G. Moon, a Wisconsin man with 30 years' experience in the lumber business, who, as one of the originators of the Barber Lumber Company, a precedessor to Boise Payette, knew the region well. Moon had similarly been a director of Boise Payette since 1914.

The period 1931–1934 was one of acute crisis in which Messrs. Clapp and Moon had to exert themselves to the utmost. Many of the retail yards were closed down, never to reopen. When a bank at Burlington, Iowa, failed, $100,000 of Boise Payette funds were on deposit. The First National Bank of Boise also closed. The company had considered taking out its money earlier, but had not for fear that it would create a run on the bank and that Boise Payette would be blamed for the failure. For part of 1931 and all of 1932 and 1933, the Emmett mill was shut because of overhauls and repairs, combined with the depression. Meanwhile, the Barber mill, also intermittently closed, cut its last readily available timber and in 1934 was dismantled.

By cutting back expenses and retrenching wherever possible, however, Clapp and Moon were able to pull Boise Payette through the depression. But when the recession of 1937 again placed the company in a losing position, some of the major officers and stockholders became convinced that Boise Payette should harvest the profitable stands of timber it owned within easy reach of its mills and then liquidate the remainder of its holdings.

The nature of the company's ownership played an important role in this attitude toward liquidation. In 1937, the original six families held about 90% of the company's common stock. Three of these families, with combined holdings of between 55–60% of the shares, had intermarried and reportedly acted fairly cohesively. The remaining families acted independently of the others and of one another. Boise Payette stock was not the major holding of any of the six families. It was noted, moreover, that the other more substantial holdings of the families required most of their time and attention. It was not surprising, therefore, that the owners were somewhat anxious to rid themselves of a relatively unimportant company that had proven difficult to operate and had shown uncertain earning power.[1]

Consequently, in 1936–1937 Boise Payette's management, with encouragement from the company's owners, and help from the U.S. Forest Service, had all of their timber holdings evaluated and mapped out for selective logging and eventual liquidation. In the process, all trees were given marks indicating "cut" or "leave." At the same time, management began an extensive effort to improve customer acceptance for ponderosa pine,[2] Boise Payette's largest standing timber resource,

---

[1] In the 1950's, even though there was family control, the company was ·clearly operated independently in the interest of sound planning for the company. From 1957 to date the family stock holdings have become smaller in relation to the total in view of the many acquisitions, as hereafter set forth.

[2] Characteristic of ponderosa pine was its yellowish wood. While ponderosa was equally serviceable in a wide range of building uses, its color mistakenly caused some people to believe it inferior in quality to other common softwoods.

and white fir, which theretofore had been sold only in small quantities. Recalled a principal marketing executive, "We had to work hard. We had to market everything we could through our own retail yards. We had to force them to take it (ponderosa pine) even though they wanted Douglas fir."

The arrival of World War II, and the resulting appeal by the War Production Board for increased production of lumber, disrupted Boise Payette's plans for orderly liquidation. In meeting the government's urgent plea for lumber, the company cut a large part of its timber reserves. Having little opportunity to negotiate timber purchases from the National Forests, it had to take the best of its own timber within easy reach, emerging from the war with badly depleted resources. Moreover, the seemingly large wartime pretax profits, $472,000 in 1945 and $1,276,000 in 1946, were taxed at high rates under the excess profits schedule. The company's management summed up the war time situation with this statement:

> The company had known, since the country's need for lumber became insistent under wartime conditions in 1941, that it was sacrificing at least one-half of its annual output of logs at a tremendous loss in order to be able to say that it was putting forth a hundred per cent effort. Others did likewise, no doubt, but with this difference—they will be in business long enough to make good their losses with further production, sales, and profits. The Boise Payette Company will not have that opportunity. It disposed of an irreplaceable wasting asset and will go out of the lumber manufacturing business earlier than it otherwise would have had to if the war had not occurred. . . . It could not go out and buy any portion of its timber and log requirements to produce its full quota but was compelled to use up its reserves of low-cost stumpage and pay the highest taxes in the history of the United States to boot.

It was near the end of the war that the mottoes "cut out and get out" and "liquidate by '48" became commonplace within the company. Another study of the company's resources, begun in 1944 and continued into 1945, concluded that it would be neither feasible nor economical for the Boise Payette Lumber Company to operate its remaining stands of virgin timber on a "sustained-yield basis."[3] Management recognized that only through very wide-scale, systematic purchases of federal and state timber could Boise Payette continue to operate indefinitely.

Yet another element in the determination to "cut out and get out" was the advanced age of the principal officers. Dr. Clapp's health failed after the war, and he retired in 1946. Soon after, Moon's vigor declined. Other executives reportedly were growing elderly and tired.

---

[3] Study conducted by Harold J. McCoy, borrowed from other activities of the Weyerhaeuser associates to make a study of the possibility of permanent operation. The Executive Committee of Boise Payette gave McCoy his instruction August 10, 1944. He gained the assistance of Regional Forester W. B. Rice of the National Forest Service, Ogden, Utah.

The final factor in the decision to "liquidate by '48" was the financial position of the shareholding families. Between 1935 and 1946, the company officers had chosen to pay out as return of capital, rather than reinvest, the large cash holdings which had accumulated through depletion and depreciation. (All earnings similarly were paid out in dividends.) This action resulted in a $27 per share return of capital on outstanding no-par stock that had dropped in market value to $11 per share during the depression. Deaths and subsequent transfers of the company stock to descendants had reduced the price of record for most shareholders to 0 by 1947. Consequently, when substantial earnings per share were realized in 1947, and appeared likely to continue for the subsequent three years during the cutout of accessible timber, the issue of liquidation became imminent. Tax laws prevented the company from holding these earnings as cash without additional taxation, and reinvestment of this cash within the Boise Payette corporate work was less attractive than other opportunities available. Distribution of these earnings as dividends would have been taxed at a 90% rate for virtually all shareholders, which was equally undesirable. Under these circumstances, there was great incentive for the owners to liquidate Boise Payette and withdraw funds at capital gains rates.

Late in 1947, Boise Payette management expanded the company's retail and wholesale operations by paying $5,000,000 in cash for the capital stock of the Merrill Company of Salt Lake City, Utah, establishing it as a wholly owned subsidiary. This move was made both to strengthen the nontimbering aspects of the business for a possible spinoff, and also to utilize some of the accumulated excess cash. The Merrill Company properties included the Morrison-Merrill Company, which operated a wholesale lumber business and a mill work factory in Salt Lake City, and a lumber distributing operation consisting of 39 retail yards in Idaho, Utah, and Wyoming.

Nevertheless, Boise Payette still looked to an early termination of its timber activities. Its manager of manufacturing stated in 1947:

> At the current rate of production, the remaining estimates of cut and available timber will only provide logs for a little better than three years of continued operations. As the retail yard division has shown profits for 28 out of its 31 years, it might be expected to continue to do well after the liquidation of logging and manufacturing.

Impartial observers in 1947 indicated that the policy of liquidating the company made for improper treatment of labor. They claimed that this policy fostered internal bickering, for employees felt no loyalty to an institution about to die.

Methods of cutting timber reportedly became highly selective; the practice became to take the best trees and discard the rest. One officer stated that the tired men in the top management instructed their land supervisor to make a quick, rough job of realizing the company assets by selling off the properties.

His instructions were to get rid of this land as fast as he could, and he did. Some good bargains were put on the block. We begged people to buy. It was cutover land, but it sure had a lot of virgin timber left up in the corners. The loggers did what they pleased. They were just getting their operation over with. They were trying to clear it up and forget about it.

In 1947, the company operated at full capacity its large sawmill at Emmett and its newer and much smaller mill at Council, Idaho, the two having combined annual production of more than 101,500,000 board feet. The timber for the mills was drawn from the company domain of 172,000 acres, containing a rated 776,000,000 board feet of timber. About one-third of this timber had been placed in the "cut" and two-thirds in the "leave" category by management's timber cruisers.

A CHANGING TREND, 1948–1956

In the midst of this liquidation procedure, some general changes in the lumber industry in 1948 caused Boise Payette's owners to re-examine their previous decision to liquidate the company's timber holdings. Before World War II, the softwood industry had been a 95% pine and Douglas fir economy. When wartime prices became frozen, however, many companies had found it undesirable to continue to cut their resources of prime timber. And, with demand high, it became possible to market other species of wood previously overlooked because of the seemingly endless supply of pine and Douglas fir. By 1947–1948, therefore, species such as white fir, birch, spruce, and hemlock, which were available in huge quantities, had gained strong market acceptance. Consequently, after the war, Boise Payette management found that pine logs represented only about 50% of the total cut. The mixed species, previously overlooked, were abundantly available in timber stands where most of the pine had been removed.

Another factor involved logging methods. Prior to 1939–1940, logging was carried on by horses and railroads, thus leaving vast amounts of timber economically inaccessible. With the advent, after the war, of efficient trucks and tractors, it became possible to harvest much of the previously inaccessible timber. Together, these two factors provided major additional prime timber resources to Boise Payette land previously thought to be of little value.

This accessibility of additional marketable timber, in combination with a 1944 change in the tax laws, which allowed profits taken in the cutting of timber to be taxed at the capital gains rate rather than as ordinary income, offered new opportunities to the stockholding families.

In 1948, a new and younger board of directors was elected. These Boise Payette owners brought in a new team of top managers—Norton Clapp (Dr. Clapp's son) as president and John Aram as general manager—to see what they could do to salvage the company. Mr. Clapp represented the ownership interests, as had his father. Mr. Aram was hired from Potlatch Forests, Inc. (another company on which the Boise Payette owners had controlling interest), where he had risen over a ten year period from an inexperienced college graduate to head of the manufacturing division.

Messrs. Clapp and Aram, from the beginning of their administration, sought ways to rescue Boise Payette from liquidation and to assure its continuance as a prime lumber producer on a permanent basis. In spite of the additional timber stands which became newly marketable following the war, the company required substantial additional timber for sustained operations. The company's own timber seemed badly depleted, little private timber could be bought, and the U.S. Forest Service seemed unfriendly, following Boise Payette's alleged "wasteful" forestry practices in the period preceding 1948. In fact, members of the Forest Service publicly announced that they preferred to assist small mills in the area, on the grounds that they provided more employment per thousand feet of lumber than did Boise.

John Aram set to work in 1949 to reorganize the company's land and forestry management and its public relations image. His fundamental position was that "Boise Payette timber, reorganized and conserved, could be combined with timber purchased from other sources to make the company an efficient, profitable, and *permanent* unit." He ordered the company to hold on to large acreages of cutover forest while waiting for new growth to mature, because grazing revenues rendered such land self-supporting.

At this time, Aram hired George Hjort, a graduate of the University of Idaho's forestry school, to cruise the company's timber. Hjort and Vern Gurnsey, another forester, made a study of Boise Payette's lands and discovered that there was three to four times more marketable timber available than had been reported previously.

Next, Aram announced throughout southern Idaho that Boise Payette was definitely going to continue manufacturing lumber. He wrote to another executive in the firm:

> I have met with the Forest Service of the Payette National Forest and the Boise National Forest. Meetings have been held with the Forest Timber Sales official and with the Regional Forester, Mr. Rice. In these conversations the following points have been expressed.
>
> 1. Boise Payette Lumber Company is in production to stay.
> 2. The board of directors understands and recognizes their economic responsibility to the communities in which we operate.
> 3. Boise Payette Lumber Company management can cooperate and will demonstrate cooperation with the United States Forest Service.
> 4. As head of the land and logging departments, I am in a new field. My intention is to give good effective service, but I need the advice and help of the Forest Service. Their criticisms and suggestions regarding our practices are always welcome.

5. We have responsibilities to employees, communities, stockholders, and customers that demand continued operation.
6. Our plans are to buy a certain volume of green or rough dry lumber from small operators and to give them technical help that make their operations efficient.
7. We hope to work toward high utilization of our timber stands and resources.

Aram and Clapp then withdrew from the market all the parcels of Boise Payette land being advertised for sale. Pending disposals were cancelled. Aram began to lay down a long-range program of selective cutting and tree farming. He appealed for advice to the University of Idaho, the Western Pine Association, and the Forest Service.

Under Aram's management, conservation became an important factor. Boise Payette, before, during, and after the war, had been accused of showing a definite disregard for conservation. The great Boise and Payette National Forests lying adjacent to Boise Payette's holdings had offered a sharp contrast to the company's indiscriminate logging practices. But under Aram's guidance Boise Payette lands were officially certified as a Western Tree Farm in 1950. New logging instructions were issued and enforced. Boise Payette management pledged itself to keep its "lands in continuous production . . . to harvest a crop of timber every 50 years."

Timber produced by the tree farms was not enough, however, to supply Boise Payette's mills adequately. The company still needed to obtain steady deliveries of timber from the National Forests, which surrounded its mills on three sides. But because of Boise Payette's past practices, the government was reluctant to help the company. The relationship that had existed between the government and Boise Payette in the mid-1940's was summarized in this anonymous statement:

. . . (While they were cutting out their stands) there was no purpose to get along with the government. When they got down to where they didn't really need government cooperation anymore and couldn't make any more exchanges of timber, the attitude was, "Why, the hell with it. Treat 'em as rough as you can." So they treated the government people like a bunch of crooks. This was done, I suppose, by one or two (lumbermen) who weren't big enough to look over the hill.

Aram's task, consequently, was to induce the local Forest Service to make large sales of timber to Boise Payette. Federal officials, operating under a policy of favoring the smaller mills, had broken the administration of the National Forests into what Aram called "small working circles." Aram indicated to the Forest Service people that he did not want to destroy the small mill, but that he believed that some were inefficient. He argued that wherever government timber was scattered over wide distances, small mills could not harvest it as efficiently as large concerns with better equipment.

To help encourage a change in the government's attitude, Boise Payette gave the Forest Service men a helping hand whenever possible. When a devastating fire broke out in the hills of the Payette National Forest, Aram called a halt to all Boise Payette's logging and milling operations and dispatched 350 men to the scene of the fire. Soon thereafter, Aram announced that "Wholehearted cooperation with Forest Service officials in fire fighting has won their goodwill."

Meanwhile, changes were occurring in Boise Payette's marketing and manufacturing operations. The company established its "Tru-Grade" trademark to encourage the building of a quality image for Boise Payette products. By-products, such as manufactured chips (sold to a paper mill) and packaged paneling,[4] were produced and sold. The company began to load boxcars mechanically. All existing facilities were evaluated as part of an extensive capital improvement program.

Aram continued to work hard at improving the company's relationship with the government. In cooperation with the Forestry Service in 1955, Boise Payette helped arrest an infestation of pine butterfly and spruce budworm which threatened to kill practically all of the ponderosa pine in southwestern Idaho. The leaders of the Southern Idaho Forestry Association, following the emergency action against the pests, urged authorities in Washington to expedite the sale of public timber, for much of it badly needed cutting and was heavily diseased. When the problem of financing the necessary access roads was brought up, members of the Association volunteered to lobby energetically for the appropriations.

Sufficient federal money was obtained to enable the Forest Service to build roads up many previously unexplored canyons. Systematic explorations from these new roads verified the suspicion that much of this remote timber had, in fact, become badly diseased and should be cut at once. In this way, private forest owners and government agencies began working together effectively.

Through continued cooperation with the Forest Service and self-policing of its own timber activities, Boise Payette was able, over time, to establish a relationship with the government which assured the company the opportunity to purchase and harvest economically public timber.

Concurrent with Aram's efforts to secure timber resources adequate to insure continued lumbering operations, he and the rest of Boise Payette's management began to consider the company's entrance into the paper business. They had observed in the early 1950's a trend toward greater by-product utilization in other companies, and realized that before too long Boise Payette could be at a competitive disadvantage. Timber surveys of Boise Payette lands revealed, however, that there was not enough by-product (wood waste) available in southern Idaho to support a 400 ton per day pulp mill, then considered to be the minimum size economical facility. Management, therefore, requested an eastern consultant to study ways in which Boise Payette might enter the paper business. The consultant confirmed the notion that a 400 ton per day pulp mill was the minimum feasible facility and did not suggest other possible courses of action.

---

[4] High-grade paneling which was finished at the mill and packaged 10 to 12 boards to a carton for protected shipment to the marketplace.

In the meantime, Mr. Aram, who had become Boise Payette's president in 1955, announced his resignation to accept a position as assistant to the president of the Weyerhaeuser Company. Still convinced that Boise Payette had to get into the paper business, Aram spent part of his remaining time with the company searching for a replacement who was skilled in paper making. One of the men to whom Mr. Aram talked was Mr. R. V. Hansberger. Mr. Hansberger's name was submitted by Mr. Glenn Lloyd, legal counsel and board member of Boise Payette. Mr. Lloyd was also counsel for several of the controlling families, and among other distinguished activities was Chairman of the Board of Trustees of the University of Chicago. Messrs. Lloyd and Hansberger served together on the board of Voi-Shan Industries in Chicago, and, through this relationship, Lloyd had learned of the latter's role in the successful construction and operation of a 120 ton per day pulp and paper mill in Portland, Oregon.

In considering Mr. Hansberger's candidacy as president of Boise Payette, the board of directors asked how he would accomplish the company's entrance into the paper business. Mr. Hansberger explained the steps required to manufacture paper from saw mill residues, but warned that before Boise Payette could consider even a 120 ton per day paper mill it would have to expand greatly its lumber operations to generate adequate wood waste. The directors reacted enthusiastically to the program presented by Mr. Hansberger, and, in 1956, invited him to develop the means for implementing it. Caught up in this challenge, Mr. Hansberger, then 36 years old, became president of Boise Payette.

BOISE PAYETTE'S NEW PRESIDENT

Mr. Hansberger's interest in paper manufacturing began in the early 1950's, while he was with Container Corporation of America. He and an associate at Container Corporation saw that many of the smaller lumber companies in the northwest desperately needed a way, such as paper making, to utilize fully the by-products of the timber that they were cutting and milling. A characteristic of unintegrated lumber operations was that only one-third of each tree ended up as usable lumber. The sawmill industry was heavily populated by small unintegrated firms. Unlike the larger lumber companies—Weyerhaeuser, Potlatch, Georgia-Pacific—which already were integrated in 1953, the small operators could not generate sufficient waste wood (which could be converted to chips) to operate the standard 400 ton a day mill. Moreover, these same companies could not cut timber for the express purpose of converting it to chips, because the end product would cost two or three times that of chips manufactured from waste wood.

Hansberger and his associate thus envisioned a small mill—120 ton per day mill vs. a 400 ton per day unit—as the answer to the needs of a group of the smaller lumber companies who were anxious to utilize their waste wood in this manner. The two men designed a mill which could be built for about $6 million and then sought to borrow about $5 million of the total, the balance being advanced by the group of lumber companies they approached. In going after the money, they sought certification of the project by an outside consultant. They approached a recognized consulting engineering firm in the field, but failed to gain acceptance of their concept. The paper mill engineer assigned to the project believed that the new design was too radical a departure from the design of traditional paper mills, and he refused certification. He claimed, for instance, that the venturi scrubber [5] included in the plans was not a proven component, and found also that the plans had not provided for "a chain link fence to surround the plant site."

Mr. Hansberger and his associate remained convinced that their mill would work and approached directly a midwestern insurance company for backing. The insurance company accepted the concept and agreed to extend the money as soon as the cost estimates were certified. A young design engineer from the Pacific Northwest, who was not bound by tradition, visited the site, reviewed the plans, and certified that the plant was workable and the estimates accurate. Subsequently, the mill was built for less than the original estimates and the operation proved even more efficient than expected.

The newly formed company was called Western Kraft and it was soon after its beginning that Hansberger was approached by Boise Payette.

Concerning his new assignment, Mr. Hansberger related:

> When I accepted the presidency of Boise Payette, I was confident that I could learn the fundamental principles of the lumber business. I was convinced that the lumber industry by itself was dead and that we had to look instead at the entire forest products industry. Consequently, we had to do a great number of things which would enable us to share the cost of lumber with other products. We needed to get into a vigorous program providing greater use of by-products of timber operations.
>
> It is important at this point to realize that timber in the West has its most important primary value as lumber. This is not true in the southern part of the country where the small, hard timber has less value as lumber, and whole trees are made directly into pulp. In the West, therefore, the waste from lumber manufacturing, and not the whole tree, became the raw material for the pulp industry.
>
> Research also demonstrated that pulp and paper are just two of the many potential uses of waste wood. Laboratory technicians have developed such other by-products as particleboard, hardboard, soft board, and sheathing plywood, which can make use of low-grade logs.
>
> However, our detailed study of the pulp and paper situation as it existed in the Intermountain area made it apparent that our company, with its three Idaho

---

[5] The venturi scrubber allowed the recovery of chemicals used in paper making process. The system was relatively new in 1957 and not yet commercially accepted throughout the industry.

sawmills and 165,000 acres of free timberland, was not economically large enough to take full advantage of the by-product utilization program that we had in mind.

"INTEGRATED GROWTH," 1956–1959

To implement his program of "integrated growth," Mr. Hansberger faced the problem of locating sufficient additional timber to support the operation of a small pulp and paper mill. He concluded that, geographically, Boise Payette could expand only by acquiring timber similar to its own. He had established that the wood chips manufactured from timber species available to Boise Payette were better suited for pulp than were wood chips from the Douglas fir of the coastal region. More important, he believed that expansion west of the Cascades would spread the company's operations over too great an area, and consequently narrowed his search to the Western Pine region.

In recalling the company's quest for additional timber, Mr. Hansberger referred to a map similar to the one shown as Exhibit 2. The blacked-in areas on the map designate government owned forests as they exist within the total forested areas of the western states. The strip of government lands running through western Washington and western Oregon demarks roughly the crest of the Cascade range. The privately owned forest lands west of the Cascades were controlled primarily by companies such as Weyerhaeuser, Crown Zellerbach, U.S. Plywood, Georgia-Pacific, and International Paper. Potlatch Forests, Inc., owned extensive forest acreage in central and northern Idaho, but the remaining privately held forest lands east of the Cascades were owned by a number of small- to medium-sized firms.

An extensive survey of the area east of the Cascades revealed that two firms— the Valsetz Lumber Company and The Cascade Lumber Company—seemed ideally suited for supplementing the timber holdings of Boise Payette. The Valsetz Lumber Company owned timber lands in northeastern Oregon (area B on map), and The Cascade Lumber Company had timber holdings along the eastern slope of the Cascades (area C on map). The timber holdings of these companies added to its own (area A on map) would give Boise Payette control of a nearly continuous band of timber stretching from southern Idaho to south central Washington, as well as close access to substantial U.S. forest lands.

THE CASCADE ACQUISITION

When Boise Payette made merger overtures to Cascade and Valsetz, the latter gave a definite "no" answer. However, the owners of the Cascade Lumber Company entered into merger negotiations. Cascade's facilities consisted of four

exhibit **2**

BOISE CASCADE CORPORATION (A-1)

Western Forests

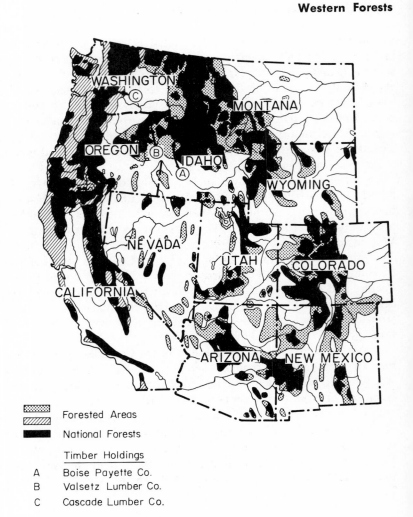

Forested Areas

National Forests

Timber Holdings

A   Boise Payette Co.
B   Valsetz Lumber Co.
C   Cascade Lumber Co.

sawmills in south central Washington, at Yakima, Ellensburg, Naches, and Gold-endale, three retail yards at Yakima, Ellensburg, and Naches, and five retail subsidiaries (approx. 75-80% equity) in Washington located at Pasco, Kenewick, Othello, Connell, and Goldendale.

Comparative data on the facilities of the two companies showed:

	Boise Payette	Cascade Lumber
Fee timber acreage	165,000	192,000
Annual cut potential (feet)	250,000,000	206,000,000
Lumber production (feet)		
1952	90,292,000	103,259,000
1953	106,707,000	98,643,000
1954	109,424,000	96,039,000
1955	120,145,000	99,856,000
1956	115,586,000	121,927,000
Mill sales ($)		
1952	$ 8,397,000	$10,610,000
1953	9,364,000	10,940,000
1954	9,415,000	11,199,000
1955	11,109,000	13,099,000
1956	10,673,000	13,288,000
Wholesale sales ($)		
1952	$12,078,000	*
1953	12,056,000	*
1954	11,656,000	*
1955	14,781,000	*
1956	14,328,000	*
Retail sales ($)		
1952	$15,774,000	†
1953	15,494,000	†
1954	13,745,000	†
1955	16,279,000	†
1956	16,126,000	$ 2,136,676

*No wholesale operation.
†Not available.

In the proxy statement to Boise Payette shareholders, Mr. R.V. Hansberger explained the proposed Cascade acquisition as follows:

Your directors have concluded, after studying alternative means of further development, that the company cannot progress as it should in managing its timberland unless it works out some economically feasible means which will justify the costs of accumulating and processing additional quantities of wood wastes incident to growing, harvesting, and converting sawtimber. These woods can be profitably used in making various kinds of by-products, provided they are continually available in sufficient quantity to justify the necessary investment in by-product facilities of adequate economic size.

At the present time Boise Payette does not have access to sufficient trees to assure a continuing supply of enough wood wastes to justify the installation of suitable by-product facilities. It has made a long study of the best way to gain such access.

Cascade Lumber Company has 192,000 acres of timberland located in an excellent timber growing area in south central Washington, and four sawmills. Cascade is in much the same position as Boise Payette in its need for additional by-product facilities. While the timberlands and mills of the two companies are separated by some distance, they were connected by direct railroad and highway routes. Your directors believe the combination with Cascade Lumber Company will be a big step toward meeting the needs and achieving the objectives of both companies.

The acquisition was accomplished in April, 1957, through an exchange of shares between the two companies. Boise Payette shareholders agreed to exchange 36,800 shares of a newly created $50 par preferred stock for the outstanding Cascade preferred stock on a one for one basis, and 375,220 shares of $10 par common stock [6] for the outstanding common stock of Cascade (a rate of 25.7 shares of Boise Payette Common for each share of Cascade Common stock outstanding). As a result of the combination, the surviving firm was named the Boise Cascade Corporation.

Comparative financial statements for the two firms at the time of the combination are presented as Exhibit 3.

As of March 31, 1957, there were approximately 304 shareholders of Boise Payette. Most of the directors and executive officers, together with members of their immediate families, were beneficial holders or holders of record of a substantial number of common shares. On the same date there were about 15 common stockholders and 29 preferred stockholders of Cascade.

Five of Cascade's six directors became directors of Boise Cascade. Mr. James D. Bronson, Cascade's president, relinquished his operating responsibilities. Mr. S.B. Moser, vice president and treasurer of Cascade, remained in an operating capacity, eventually becoming general manager of Boise Cascade's Western Timber Division. Both of these men were named to Boise Cascade's board of directors. The other three board members representing the Cascade interests were Messrs. Warren Bean, Lester Lewis, and David Bronson.

---

[6] The over-the-counter quotations for Boise Payette common stock on the date of the Cascade acquisition were $13 bid and $14 asked. Monthly high and low bid quotation for the period August, 1957, to December, 1959, and the bid and ask quotations on the dates of important acquisitions, are provided in Exhibit 6 of Boise Cascade Corporation (A-2).

exhibit 3

BOISE PAYETTE LUMBER COMPANY AND CASCADE LUMBER COMPANY

Summaries of Consolidated Earnings

(in thousands)

	Year Ended December 31				
	1952	1953	1954	1955	1956
Boise Payette Lumber Co. and subsidiaries					
Net sales	$31,221	$32,049	$30,143	$35,882	$34,902
Other income (net)	520	347	461	410	470
Cost of goods sold and expenses	29,106	30,723	28,324	33,052	32,977
Provisions for taxes on earnings	1,302	777	1,104	1,660	1,201
Net earnings	1,333	896	1,176	1,580	1,194
Per common share					
Net earnings	$1.52	$1.02	$1.34	$1.81	$1.37
Dividends	.60	.50	.50	.50	.50
Cascade Lumber Co. and predecessor Companies (including equity in retail subsidiaries)					
Net sales	$10,610	$10,940	$11,199	$13,099	$13,288
Other income (net)	76	48	294	115	84
Cost of sales and expenses	9,747	10,400	10,597	11,794	12,371
Provision for taxes on income	310	240	255	511	251
Net earnings	629	348	641	909	750
Net earnings available to common stock[1]	$ 537	$ 256	$ 549	$ 817	$ 658
Per common share[2]					
Net earnings	$38.36	$18.29	$39.21	$58.36	$45.07
Dividends	10.71	7.14	7.14	8.93	10.47

[1]Net income available to the common stock has been determined after providing dividends on the preferred stock during each period on the basis of the shares of preferred stock outstanding at December 1, 1956.

[2]Adjusted to give effect to a common stock dividend in 1955.

Pro Forma Combined Summary of Earnings

Net sales	$41,831	$42,989	$41,342	$48,981	$48,190
Other income (net)	596	395	755	525	554
Cost of sales and expenses	38,853	41,123	38,921	44,846	45,348
Provision for taxes on income	1,612	1,017	1,359	2,171	1,944
Net earnings applicable to common stock	$ 1,870	$ 1,152	$ 1,725	$ 2,397	$ 1,852
Net earnings per share (based on 1,244,970 shares[1])	$1.50	$ 93	$1.39	$1.93	$1.49

[1]Since December 31, 1956, Boise has acquired 9,000 shares of its own stock.

exhibit 3 (cont.)

BOISE PAYETTE LUMBER COMPANY AND SUBSIDIARIES

Consolidated Balance Sheets
December 31, 1956

Assets

Current assets		
Cash		$ 3,138,901
Receivables (less allowances of $295,687)		3,643,997
Mortgage loans held for resale, principally at cost		2,277,597
Inventories at lower of cost or market:		
Yard inventories (first in, first out method)	$ 5,940,820	
Mill inventories (last in, first out method)	2,116,909	8,057,729
Total current assets		$17,118,224
Timber and timberlands at cost (less allowances for depletion)		2,088,751
Real estate held for resale at cost		919,587
Property, plant, and equipment at cost	$11,088,763	
Less: allowances for depreciation	5,930,193	5,158,570
Other assets		841,530
Total assets		$26,126,662

Liabilities

Current liabilities		
Current portion of notes payable to banks		$ 400,000
Accounts payable		1,572,091
Accrued liabilities		711,506
Federal and state income taxes		1,012,735
Total current liabilities		$ 3,696,332
Timber purchase contracts, payable as timber is cut		609,080
Notes payable to banks (excluding current portion), 3 3/4% payable $400,000 annually through 1961, and $1,000,000 final payment in 1962		2,600,000
Stockholders' equity		
Capital stock, par value $10 a share, authorized and issued 875,000 shares	$ 8,750,000	
Earnings retained for use in the business	10,539,500	
	$19,289,500	
Less 5,250 shares capital stock in treasury at cost	68,250	19,221,250
Total liabilities and shareholder's equity		$26,126,662

---

exhibit 3 (cont.)

CASCADE LUMBER COMPANY

Balance Sheet—December 31, 1956

Assets

Current assets		
Cash and U. S. securities	$ 237,393	
Receivables	570,625	
Inventories, at lower of cost or market, principally on a last in, first out cost basis	1,807,966	
Prepaid expenses, etc.	435,025	$ 3,051,009
Investment in subsidiaries not consolidated		45,838
Equity in underlying book value of subsidiaries totals $164,152.07		
Timber and timberlands at cost (less depletion)		6,575,687
Property, plant and equipment at cost	$ 4,944,197	
Less: reserves for depreciation	1,782,786	3,161,411
Other assets		229,870
Total assets		$13,063,815

Liabilities

Current liabilities		
Current maturities of long-term debt	$ 447,189	
Accounts payable	313,886	
Accrued liabilities	528,813	
Reserve for income taxes	196,447	
Total current liabilities		$ 1,486,335
Long-term debt		
3 1/2% note payable	$ 4,946,035	
4 1/2% note payable	1,200,000	
Miscellaneous	172,925	
Less: current portion shown above	(447,189)	
Total long-term debt		5,871,771
Net worth		
Common stock, par value $100 per share, issued and outstanding 14,600 shares	$ 1,460,000	
Preferred stock, 5%, par value $50 per share, issued and outstanding 36,800 shares	1,840,000	
Paid-in surplus	84,000	
Earned surplus	2,321,709	5,705,709
Total liabilities and net worth		$13,063,815

Boise Cascade Corporation (A-2): 1957-1959

Following the 1957 merger of Boise Payette and Cascade Lumber Company [see Boise Cascade Corporation (A-1)], the newly formed Boise Cascade Corporation, having now secured sufficient timber resources to support a small pulp and paper mill, was able to select a location and commence construction. The chosen site was at Wallula, in southeastern Washington, near Walla Walla, and between the timber holdings of the old Boise Payette and Cascade companies. The Wallula location, on the Columbia River, had plenty of available water and was sufficiently isolated that the chemical odors indigenous to pulp manufacture did not affect residential areas. Construction was begun in 1957 on a 150 ton per day pulp and paper mill, patterned after the one previously built by Western Kraft. The mill was designed to produce unbleached kraft linerboard for shipping containers and bag paper, the most attractive products for the kinds of chips available.

Special attention was given to future expansion in selecting the plant site and in designing the pulp and paper mill. The mill construction was planned so that walls could be easily knocked out and the entire structure expanded. Mr. Hansberger's plans in 1957 called for continued acquisition of timber and sawmills. The only factor limiting the size of the mill in 1957 was the amount of raw material economically available as waste wood from the sawmills already owned by Boise Cascade.

When Mr. Hansberger committed Boise Cascade to the production of kraft linerboard in 1957, he acknowledged that the entire pulp and paper industry was just entering a phase of excessive overcapacity. He was convinced, however, that Boise Cascade could not, in the long run, consistently maximize its return on investment unless the company adopted a vigorous program of by-product utilization.

POTLATCH YARDS ACQUISITION

Before the end of 1957, Boise Cascade entered negotiations for the purchase of Potlatch Yards, Inc., of Spokane. Mr. Hansberger described this acquisition as a move to expand Boise Cascade's retail operations in Washington following the recent acquisition of sawmill capacity in that area. Potlatch Yards owned 41 retail yards selling lumber and other building materials throughout the state of Washington and in northern Idaho. Summary financial statements appear as Exhibit 1. Potlatch Yards also was in the ready-mix concrete and concrete products business through two partially owned subsidiaries.

Pre-Mix Concrete, Inc. (51% owned by Potlatch Yards), operated ready-mix plants in Kennewick, Pasco, Richland, and Othello, Washington. The financial history for Pre-Mix alone was:

Operating Results—Years Ended March 31

	Net Assets	Sales	Net Income	Dividends
1953	$175,053	$1,308,401	$50,274	$30,000
1954	190,715	956,804	27,662	12,000
1955	198,725	1,149,160	44,010	36,000
1956	242,673	1,049,815	3,949	—
1957 (2/28)	301,356	1,112,639	58,682	—

Graystone, Inc., 50-51% owned by Potlatch Yards, had eight concrete product plants located in Seattle and other communities in western Washington. It manufactured and sold concrete pipe, blocks, septic tanks, other case concrete products, and ready-mix concrete. Graystone financial history was:

Operating Results—Years Ended Dec. 31

	Net Assets	Sales	Net Income	Dividends
1952	n.a.	$3,420,000	$ 80,000	none
1953	n.a.	3,155,000	23,300	none
1954	n.a.	3,411,000	5,000	none
1955	$ 915,340	4,042,663	22,156	none
1956	1,099,045	5,094,938	185,496	none

Under the terms of the acquisition, which became effective in July, 1957, 46,680 shares of Boise Cascade stock were exchanged for the 99,360 outstanding shares of Potlatch Yards stock.

As of March 20, 1957, there were approximately 270 shareholders of Potlatch Yards. Most of the directors and executives of Potlatch Yards were substantial holders of common stock.

exhibit 1

BOISE CASCADE CORPORATION (A-2)

Summaries of Consolidated Earnings

(in thousands)

	Year Ended December 31				
	1952	*1953*	*1954*	*1955*	*1956*
Potlatch Yards, Inc., and wholly owned subsidiary[1]					
Net sales	$6,644	$6,007	$6,379	$7,565	$7,020
Other income (net)	67	69	171	104	73
Cost of sales and expenses	6,633	6,100	6,360	7,496	7,228
Provision for taxes on income	27	(6)	48	66	(45)
Net income	51	(18)	142	107	(90)
Per common share					
Net income	$ .52	$(.19)	$1.43	$1.08	$(.90)
Dividends	.25	—	.25	—	—

[1]The consolidated net income is the result of operations of the yards for 1952 through 1955 from various yard fiscal year closings and for 1956 from the various yard fiscal year closing dates in November and December, 1955, to December 31, 1956; and the income and expense of the general office for the calendar years.

Boise Cascade Corp. and subsidiaries					
Net sales	$41,831	$42,989	$41,342	$48,981	$48,190
Other income (net)	596	395	755	525	554
Cost of sales and expenses	38,853	41,123	38,921	44,846	45,348
Provision for taxes on income	1,612	1,017	1,359	2,171	1,452
Net earnings	1,962	1,244	1,817	2,489	1,944
Net earnings applicable to common stock	$ 1,870	$ 1,152	$ 1,725	$ 2,397	$ 1,852
Net earnings per share (based on 1,224,970 shares)	$1.50	$ .93	$1.39	$1.93	$1.49

Since December 31, 1956, Boise Cascade has acquired 9,000 shares of its own common stock.

Pro Forma Combined Summary of Earnings
(based on above summaries)

Net sales	$48,475	$48,996	$47,721	$56,546	$55,210
Other income (net)	663	464	926	629	627
Cost of sales and expenses	45,486	47,223	45,281	52,342	52,576
Provision for taxes on income	1,639	1,001	1,407	2,237	1,407
Net earnings	2,013	1,226	1,959	2,596	1,854
Net earnings applicable to common stock	$ 1,921	$ 1,134	$ 1,876	$ 2,504	$ 1,762
Net earnings per share (based on 1,294,650 shares)[†]	$1.48	$ .88	$1.44	$1.03	$1.36

[†]Since December 31, 1956, Boise Cascade has acquired 9,000 shares of its own common stock.

388

Assets

Current assets		
Cash	$ 194,055	
Receivables	1,009,326	
Inventories	1,904,585	
Total current assets		$3,107,966
Investments, at cost		81,599
Land, buildings, and equipment		
Cost	1,541,798	
Less: depreciation reserve	795,532	
Net book value		746,266
Prepaid expenses and other assets		87,520
Total assets		$4,023,351

Liabilities

Bank loans	$ 960,000	
Accounts payable	302,991	
Incentive bonuses	13,055	
Federal and state income taxes	2,384	
Other accrued taxes	44,660	
Total current liabilities		$1,323,090
Stockholders' equity		
Capital stock, authorized		
100,000 shares, par		
value $5.00 per share;		
issued and outstanding		
99,360 shares	496,800	
Contributed capital in		
excess of par value of		
capital stock issued		
at organization	645,030	
Contributed capital in		
excess of par value of		
capital stock sold	194,100	
Earned surplus	1,364,331	
Total stockholders' equity		2,700,261
Total liabilities and		
shareholders' equity		$4,023,351

The retail outlets of Potlatch Yards were assimilated into the Boise Cascade operation. The concrete operations continued to operate as subsidiaries. Mr. Hansberger decided to keep the 50% and 51% interests in the subsidiaries, since these building materials tied in with Boise Cascade's wholesale and retail operations. In 1956, Boise's retail division had already entered the concrete business through operation of ready-mix facilities in Idaho.

CONSTRUCTION OF CONTAINER PLANTS, 1957–1958

Concurrent with the construction of the pulp and paper mill at Wallula, Boise Cascade management sought to establish markets for the mill's future end product, kraft linerboard. Construction was started in 1957 of a container plant at the Wallula mill site. This plant was to convert kraft linerboard into corrugated con-

Current assets		
Cash		$ 3,376,294
Receivables, less reserves		4,214,622
Mortgage loans held for		
resale, less reserve		2,277,597
Inventories		9,865,695
Total current assets		$19,734,208
Timber and timberlands		8,664,438
Real property held for resale		919,587
Property, plant, and equipment	$16,032,960	
Less: reserve for depreciation	7,712,979	8,319,981
Other assets		1,552,263
Total assets		$39,190,477

Liabilities

Current liabilities		
Current maturities of		
long-term debt		$ 847,189
Accounts payable		1,885,977
Accrued liabilities		1,240,319
Reserve for income taxes		1,209,182
Total current liabilities		$ 5,182,667
Long-term debt (exclusive		
of current portion)		9,080,851
Stockholders' equity		
Capital stock, $10 par value;		
authorized 1,500,000 shares		
issued 1,250,220 shares		$12,502,200
Convertible preferred stock		
5%, par value $50 per		
share, issued 36,800 shares		1,840,000
Earned surplus		10,653,009
Less: 5,250 shares of capital		
stock in the treasury, at cost		(68,250)
Total shareholders' equity		$24,926,959
Total liabilities and		
shareholders' equity		$39,190,477

tainers for use by local food processors. The area surrounding Walla Walla, Wallula, and Pendleton was the largest green pea producing center in the country and there was no container facility in the vicinity.

In 1958, the company began construction of a second container plant in Burley, Idaho, the center of Idaho's potato growing and processing country. Both plants were scheduled for startup in 1958, somewhat before the Wallula mill would be producing paper to supply them. In the meantime, they were to purchase their raw materials from other sources.

AMES HARRIS NEVILLE ACQUISITION

Boise Cascade's program of "integrated growth" continued with the acquisition in late 1958 of the Ames Harris Neville Company of San Francisco. The Ames

Harris Neville operation was threefold. The company produced aluminum furniture, textile products, and multiwall bags. The multiwall bag operation, which accounted for about 35% of Ames Harris Neville's sales, was of primary interest to Boise Cascade because it was a sizeable user of the kind of paper that was to be produced at the Wallula mill. In the proxy statement that proposed the Ames Harris Neville acquisition, R.V. Hansberger stated:

> For the past year, the management of Boise Cascade has been studying ways of entering the field of manufacturing paper bags in order to provide a market for the highly profitable bag paper to be produced by our new paper mill. Ames Harris operates a modern paper bag plant in Berkeley, California, and sells multiwall paper bags throughout 11 western states. Your directors and management, after a thorough study of the alternatives available, have concluded that the acquisition of Ames Harris by exchange of stock is the best way to enter the paper bag industry.

In addition to the paper bag operation, Ames Harris had two textile plants in San Francisco and Portland (50% of sales volume), and an aluminum furniture plant in Glendale, California. The San Francisco plant was used for producing cotton and burlap bags, polyethylene bags, and canvas products. The bulk of these products were sold in the agricultural market. The plant at Portland, Oregon, produced burlap and cotton textile bags, sleeping bags, and miscellaneous canvas products such as tarpaulins and irrigation dams.

The Glendale, California, plant produced aluminum furniture and miscellaneous canvas products (15% of sales) which were sold by specialty salesmen in the 11 western states.

The terms of the acquisition, which became effective on September 2, 1958, required Boise Cascade to exchange 80,007 shares of its common stock for the outstanding shares of stock of Ames Harris at the rate of three shares of Boise Cascade common stock for each outstanding share of Ames Harris stock. To accomplish the acquisition, Boise Cascade increased its authorized number of common shares from 1,500,000 shares to 1,700,000 shares. Although the 80,007 shares to be issued for Ames Harris would not result in Boise Cascade having more than 1,500,000 shares outstanding, the extra shares were needed to meet conversion provisions of an earlier acquisition. Comparative financial statements for the two companies at the time of the proposal are presented as Exhibit 2.

In July, 1958, there were 108 shareholders of the 26,669 shares of Ames Harris common stock. Approximately 74% of the outstanding stock was held by members of the Ames and Harris families. Of Ames Harris' nine directors only Mr. Alan Ames, who was the company's president, was elected to Boise Cascade's board. Mr. Ames also continued in an operating capacity as general manager of the multiwall operation.

Soon after the acquisition, Boise Cascade liquidated the aluminum furniture business and sold the plant for something more than book value. The textile operation was kept intact in order to take advantage of its tax loss carryback.

exhibit 2

BOISE CASCADE CORPORATION AND AMES HARRIS NEVILLE

Summaries of Income (000 omitted)

Assets	*December 31, 1957*	*June 30, 1958*
Current assets		
Cash	$ 4,420,792	$ 1,897,895
Receivables, less reserves of $482,271 and $485,582	5,641,901	8,081,086
Construction advances and mortgage loans held for resale	1,337,777	1,657,058
Inventories at lower of cost or market		
Yard inventories (first in, first out method)	$ 7,848,863	$ 8,910,269
Mill inventories (last in, first out method)	3,892,132	1,416,942
Total current assets	$23,141,465	$21,963,250
Timber and timberlands, at cost less depletion	7,667,545	7,409,043
Real estate held for resale, at cost	793,893	931,569
Property, plant, and equipment, at cost	20,467,846	23,890,620
Less: reserves for depreciation	11,312,601	11,657,809
	$ 9,155,245	$12,232,811
Other assets	2,031,440	2,789,864
Total assets	$42,789,588	$45,326,537

Liabilities		
Current liabilities		
Current portion of long-term debt and short-term borrowings	$ 960,142	$ 2,955,224
Accounts payable	2,196,137	2,033,013
Accrued liabilities	1,398,679	1,689,461
Federal and state income taxes	685,611	569,232
Total current liabilities	$ 5,240,569	$ 7,246,930
Long-term debt, excluding current portion	9,553,370	9,537,856
Stockholders' equity		
5% convertible preferred stock par value $50	$ 1,840,000	$ 1,840,000
Common stock, par value $10	13,137,950	13,137,950
Paid-in surplus	522,556	522,556
Earned surplus	12,495,143	13,041,245
Total stockholders' equity	$27,995,649	$28,541,751
Total liabilities and stockholders' equity	$42,789,588	$45,326,537

Assets		
Current assets		
Cash	$ 217,905	$ 237,406
Notes and accounts receivable, less allowances for losses ($104,646 and $128,265 at respective dates)	1,216,487	1,931,199
Inventories of raw materials, work in process, and finished products (priced at the lower of cost or market on the basis of first in, first out)	3,038465	3,168,364
Balance available to suppliers under letters of credit	94,631	121,713
Prepaid expenses	35,111	51,920
Total current assets	$4,602,599	$5,510,602
Investments and deposits		
Property, plant, and equipment		
Buildings and equipment	3,242,026	3,263,988
Less: accumulated depreciation and amortization	1,448,588	1,517,715
	$1,793,438	$1,746,273
Land	486,146	486,146
	$2,279,584	$2,232,419
Unamortized cost of company pension plan	50,909	45,917
Total assets	$6,959,652	$7,815,498

Current liabilities		
Notes payable to bank, unsecured	$ 534,456	$1,723,649
Liability under letters of credit	341,157	136,732
Accounts payable	467,803	466,687
Directors and stockholder	8,229	10,660
Expense and other accruals	161,319	232,865
Current portion of long-term debt	100,000	300,000
Total current liabilities	$1,612,964	$2,870,593
Long-term debt due after one year		
5% notes payable		
to bank, secured (due in annual		
installments, maturing in 1962)	1,200,000	1,000,000
Provision for company retirement plan	147,423	136,770
Lessee's deposit held as a		
performance bond	9,600	9,600
Deferred rental income	1,600	1,600
Stockholders' equity		
Stated capital	2,719,200	2,719,200
Common capital stock		
authorized 35,000 shares of		
$100 par value, of which		
27,192 have been issued.		
Shares outstanding aggregate		
16,669, and 523 shares		
have been reacquired and are		
held as treasury shares.		
Retained earnings		
Appropriated for the		
unamortized cost of pension plans	50,909	45,917
Unappropriated	1,217,956	1,031,818
Total shareholders' equity	$3,988,065	$3,796,935
Total liabilities and		
shareholders' equity	$6,959,652	$7,815,498

Year Ended December 31

	1948	1949	1950	1951	1952	1953	1954	1955	1956	1957
Ames Harris Neville Co.										
Net sales	$11,397	$10,389	$11,608	$15,183	$12,758	$11,157	$10,893	$11,646	$11,731	$12,165
Other income (net)	30	287	20	15	94	14	8	(45)	(55)	(72)
Cost of sales and expenses[1]	10,977	10,579	10,944	14,458	12,914	11,168	10,910	11,783	11,670	12,662
Provision for taxes on income	171	33	277	368	—	2	—	—	—	—
Net income or (loss)	279	64	407	372	(62)	1	(9)	(182)	6	(569)
Per common share										
Net income or (loss)	$ 10.26	$ 2.35	$ 14.96	$ 13.70	$(2.29)	$ .02	$ (.35)	$(6.66)	$ .22	$(20.94)
Dividends	7.50	4.00	7.25	7.25	—	2.75	1.50	1.00	—	—

[1]Beginning in 1953, cost of sales and expenses were charged annually for approximately $10,000 for amortization of the estimated total cost ($200,000) of a pension plan adopted in 1948. The proportion of such cost applicable to the years 1948 to 1952 was charged to retained earnings.

Unaudited

	1948	1949	1950	1951	1952	1953	1954	1955	1956	1957
Boise Cascade Corporation and subsidiaries										
Net sales	$35,873	$33,662	$42,091	$40,238	$41,831	$42,989	$41,342	$48,981	$49,210	$53,032
Other income (net)	477	313	375	443	596	395	755	279	522	610
Cost of sales and expenses	28,706	29,101	36,312	36,969	38,853	41,123	38,921	44,600	46,327	50,772
Provision for taxes on income	2,969	1,813	2,571	1,595	1,612	1,017	1,359	2,171	1,471	1,004
Net income (including special credit of $275,000 in 1957)	4,675	3,061	3,583	2,117	1,962	1,244	1,817	2,489	1,934	2,141
Net income applicable to common stock[1]	$ 4,583	$ 2,969	$ 3,491	$ 2,025	$ 1,870	$ 1,152	$ 1,725	$ 2,397	$ 1,842	$ 2,049
Net income per share (based on 1,313,795 shares)	$ 3.49	$ 2.26	$ 2.66	$ 1.54	$ 1.42	$ .88	$ 1.31	$ 1.82	$ 1.40	$ 1.56

[1]Net income available to the common stock has been determined after providing dividends on the preferred stock during each period on the basis of the shares of preferred stock outstanding at December 31, 1957.

Pro Forma *Combined Summary of Income*
(based on above summaries)

	1948	1949	1950	1951	1952	1953	1954	1955	1956	1957
Net sales	$47,270	$44,051	$53,699	$55,421	$54,589	$54,146	$52,235	$60,627	$60,941	$65,197
Other income (net)	507	600	395	458	690	409	763	234	467	538
Cost of sales and expenses	39,683	39,680	47,256	51,427	51,767	52,291	49,831	56,383	57,997	63,159
Provision for taxes on income	3,140	1,846	2,848	1,963	1,612	1,019	1,359	2,171	1,471	1,004
Net income (including special credit of $275,000 in 1957)	4,954	3,125	3,990	2,489	1,900	1,245	1,808	2,307	1,940	1,572
Net income applicable to common stock	$ 4,862	$ 3,033	$ 3,898	$ 2,397	$ 1,808	$ 1,153	$ 1,716	$ 2,307	$ 1,848	$ 1,480
Net income per share (based on 1,393,802 shares)	$ 3.49	$ 2.18	$ 2.80	$ 1.72	$ 1.30	$ .83	$ 1.23	$ 1.59	$ 1.33	$ 1.06

REVIEW OF ACTIVITIES, 1957–1958

By the end of 1958 Boise Cascade had taken several significant steps on its way to becoming an integrated forest products company. In a little over two years, with R.V. Hansberger as president, the company had:

—More than doubled its timber holdings.
—Increased lumber mill capacity from 320,000 board feet per eight hour shift to 725,000 board feet.
—Added 28 retail yards to its original 78.
—Completed one and started another box converting plant.
—Acquired a multiwall bag factory.
—Acquired a textile products facility.
—Begun construction on a pulp and paper mill to open in six months.

Sales during this period jumped from $34.9 million in 1956 to $72.7 million in 1958. Other items in the financial statement also changed. Boise Payette's 1956 balance sheet showed long-term debt of $2,600,000; at the end of 1958, long-term debt totalled $13,439,732 after deducting a current portion of $1,279,-791. The largest single item in the debt structure was a $6,000,000 loan arranged with seven banks to finance the construction of the Wallula pulp and paper mill. Minimum payments on the long-term debt were $1,279,791 in 1959; $2,580,000 in 1960; $2,605,000 in 1961; $3,230,000 in 1962; $2,355,000 in 1963; $1,980,000 in 1964; and $805,000 in 1965.

VALSETZ–TEMPLETON ACQUISITION

In June, 1959, Boise Cascade had the opportunity to complete its original quest for timber when it entered negotiations for acquiring the Valsetz Lumber Company and the Herbert Templeton Lumber Company, both of Portland and controlled by the same interests. Valsetz owned in fee 71,000 acres of timberland and operated sawmills in northeastern Oregon [area B, Exhibit 2 of Boise Cascade Corporation (A-1)] and at Lincoln, Washington. It also owned timberland and a new plywood mill in western Oregon which could provide a portion of the plywood requirements of Boise Cascade's wholesale and retail operations. The timber holdings in northeastern Oregon, located between the areas of the old Cascade and Boise Payette Companies, would give Boise Cascade the almost continuous belt of timber stretching from southern Idaho to eastern Washington it had originally sought. All of the Valsetz timber was within economic freight reach of the Wallula pulp and paper mill, thus providing ample by-product waste materials for future expansion of the mill.

Valsetz also owned 100% interest in the Valley and Siletz Railroad Company, which owned and operated about 41 miles of standard gauge railroad extending from Valsetz, Oregon, to Independence, Oregon, at the point of interchange with the Southern Pacific Company. It was a common carrier railroad, hauling various items including the products of the Valsetz mill. It also hauled logs and lumber for several other logging and lumber operations located along its line.

The Herbert A. Templeton Corporation distributed the products manufactured by Valsetz and several other mills. In Mr. Hansberger's statement to Boise Cascade's shareholders concerning the Valsetz and Templeton acquisition, he commented:

> In April of this year, Boise Cascade started operation of its new pulp and paper mill at Wallula, Washington. This mill is built to produce 150 tons per day initially and has been designed to facilitate expansion in the future. Raw material for this mill is now being supplied in the form of waste wood from Boise Cascade sawmills in Washington and Idaho and from other mills in Washington and Oregon. Valsetz owns timberlands and operates sawmills all within economic freight reach of our pulp and paper mill at Wallula. By-product waste wood materials from the operations of Valsetz's timberlands and sawmills can make an important contribution in providing raw material for the expansion of our paper mill when conditions warrant in the future.
>
> After careful study, your directors believe that the acquisition of Valsetz and Templeton will make an important contribution to the program of integrated development which Boise Cascade has been following for the past 2½ years in that it will provide inexpensive raw material for additional by-product utilization capacity in the future. In addition, Valsetz and Templeton have a long history of strong earning power which should further enhance Boise Cascade's earnings in the future.

The acquisition was accomplished in July, 1959, by exchanging 373,602 shares of Boise Cascade common stock for the outstanding shares of common stock of Valsetz and Templeton. Boise Cascade had to increase its number of outstanding shares from 1,700,000 shares to 2,100,000 shares to complete the acquisition. Comparative financial statements are attached as Exhibit 3.

About 75% of the outstanding stock of Valsetz and Templeton was held by members of the Templeton family. The remaining shares were held by employees, except for 140 shares held by the Trustees of Iowa College.

Mr. Hall Templeton, the president of Valsetz, and Mr. James E. Bryson, its executive vice president, were elected to Boise Cascade's board of directors. Mr. Bryson remained in an operating capacity as general manager of the plywood operations.

With this acquisition, Boise Cascade gained additional mill capacity of 330,000 board feet per day, about 50% of its previously existing mills. The plywood mill at Valsetz, Oregon, was capable of producing 100,000 square feet, ⅜" basis, per eight hour shift. The Valsetz sawmills at La Grande, Enterprise, and Joseph, Oregon, were combined with the mills of the old Boise Payette Company to form the eastern timber division. The sawmill at Lincoln, Washington, and the plywood mill at Valsetz, along with the old Cascade Company sawmills, comprised the company's western timber division.

exhibit 3

BOISE CASCADE, VALSETZ, AND HERBERT A. TEMPLETON

Summaries of Income

(000 omitted)

Year Ended December 31

	1949	1950	1951	1952	1953	1954	1955	1956	1957	1958
Boise Cascade Corporation and subsidiaries										
Net sales	$33,662	$42,091	$40,238	$41,831	$42,989	$41,342	$48,981	$49,210	$53,032	$72,734
Other income (net)	313	375	443	596	395	755	279	522	610	562
Cost of sales and expenses	29,101	36,312	26,969	38,853	41,123	38,921	44,600	46,327	50,772	68,800
Provision for taxes on income	1,813	2,571	1,595	1,612	1,017	1,359	2,171	1,471	1,004	1,460
Net income (including special credit of $275,000 in 1957)	3,061	3,583	2,117	1,962	1,244	1,817	2,489	1,934	2,141	3,036
Net income per share (based on 1,475,602 shares)[1]	$ 2.07	$ 2.43	$ 1.43	$ 1.33	$ .84	$ 1.23	$ 1.69	$ 1.31	$ 1.45	$ 2.06

[1] Net income per share is stated on the basis of the number of shares of common stock outstanding at December 31, 1958, adjusted for the conversion of 36,800 shares of 5% convertible preferred stock into 73,600 shares of common stock on or before April 23, 1959.

	1949	1950	1951	1952	1953	1954	1955	1956	1957	1958
Valsetz Lumber Company										
Net sales	$3,256	$4,269	$4,276	$4,474	$8,376	$9,895	$19,011	$18,555	$17,937	$17,464
Other income and (expense), net	318	77	36	17	(50)	(71)	62	(37)	(15)	—
Cost of goods sold and expenses	2,806	3,137	3,425	3,434	7,176	8,357	15,818	16,890	16,787	16,101
Net income (loss) before taxes, from operation of railroad	86	94	37	(55)	8	68	366	273	278	208
Federal and state taxes on income	278	507	364	387	455	648	1,474	644	397	500
Net income	576	796	560	615	703	887	2,147	1,257	1,016	1,071

	1949	1950	1951	1952	1953	1954	1955	1956	1957	1958
Herbert A. Templeton Corporation										
Net sales		$12,249	$13,595	$15,095	$14,928	$20,337	$31,121	$32,382	$30,369	$28,999
Other income (net)		9	32	28	24	15	—	(10)	(5)	6
Cost of goods sold and expenses		12,016	13,329	14,862	14,716	20,109	30,708	31,911	30,131	28,659
Provision for taxes on income		113	161	140	125	133	229	248	121	181
Net earnings		129	137	121	111	110	184	213	112	165

Pro Forma *Combined Summary of Income*
(based on above summaries)

	1949	1950	1951	1952	1953	1954	1955	1956	1957	1958
Net sales[2]	$36,918	$55,392	$54,800	$58,376	$63,170	$63,363	$83,377	$83,565	$85,668	$103,089
Other income (net)	717	555	548	586	377	767	707	748	868	776
Cost of sales and expenses[2]	31,907	48,248	50,414	54,125	59,892	59,176	75,390	78,546	82,020	97,452
Provision for taxes on income	2,091	3,191	2,120	2,139	1,597	2,140	3,874	2,363	1,522	2,141
Net income (including special credit of $275,000 in 1957)	3,637	4,508	2,814	2,698	2,058	2,814	4,820	3,404	3,269	4,272
Net income per share (based on 1,849,204 shares)	$ 1.97	$ 2.44	$ 1.52	$ 1.46	$ 1.11	$ 1.52	$ 2.61	$ 1.84	$ 1.77	$ 2.31

[2] Sales of lumber and lumber products by Valsetz to Templeton in 1950 through 1958 have been eliminated.

Assets		Liabilities	
Current assets		*Current liabilities*	
Cash	$ 3,052,418	Notes payable to banks and	
Receivables, less reserves of $623,888	9,719,897	current portion of	
Construction advances and mortgage loand		long-term debt	$ 4,087,148
held for resale	1,619,876	Accounts payable	4,506,709
Inventories at lower of cost or market,		Accrued liabilities	2,631,933
including $4,281,307 determined by the		Federal and state income taxes	1,247,230
last in, first out method	17,783,964	Total current liabilities	$12,473,010
Total current assets	$32,176,155	Long-term debt, excluding current portion	13,439,732
Timber and timberlands, at cost less		Shareholders' equity	
depletion	6,443,061	5% convertible preferred stock,	
Real estate held for resale, at cost	1,016,014	par value $50	1,840,000
Property, plant, and equipment, at cost $31,975,394		Common stock, par value $10	14,020,020
Less: reserves for depreciation 15,059,627	16,915,767	Paid-in surplus	1,576,592
Other assets	1,423,118	Earned surplus	14,624,751
Total assets	$57,974,115	Total shareholders' equity	$32,061,363
		Total liabilities and	
		shareholders' equity	$57,974,115

Assets		Liabilities	
Current assets		Current liabilities	
Cash	$ 729,162	Notes payable	
Accounts receivable		Installments due within one year on	
Associated companies	633,881	long-term notes	$ 181,475
Employee stock purchases	29,977	Other	245,012
Others	143,356		$ 426,487
Notes receivable, associated company	200,000	Accounts payable—trade	773,537
Inventories, at lower of average		Accrued wages and expenses	602,778
cost or market		Federal and state taxes on income,	
Logs	1,161,831	estimated	734,981
Lumber	2,121,751	Total current liabilities	$ 2,537,783
Veneer	27,539		
Factory stock	265,835	Long-term notes, less amounts	
Operating supplies	61,261	due within one year	
	$ 3,638,217	Payable in equal annual	
Deposits under timber cutting		installments to 1974	
contracts	342,423	Mortgage notes	2,096,560
Prepaid expenses	275,155	Other	63,066
Total current assets	$ 5,992,171	Payable under loan agreement	1,462,500
		Total long-term debt	$ 3,662,126
Due from employees under stock			
purchase agreements		Stockholders' equity	
less amounts		Common stock, par value	
receivable within one year	117,787	$100 per share	
		Authorized—75,000	
Property, plant, and equipment, at cost		Issued—34,807	3,480,700
Plants and equipment	12,527,036	Capital received in excess	
Accumulated depreciation	7,797,120	of par value	90,384
	$ 4,729,916	Excess of book value of net assets of	
Plant sites	187,017	subsidiary at date	
Truck roads, less amortization	330,775	of acquisition over cost of investment	212,793
Timber and timberlands, less depletion	2,606,853	Retained earnings	4,020,733
Total assets	$13,964,519	Total stockholders' equity	$ 7,804,610
		Total liabilities and	
		stockholders' equity	$13,964,519

Assets		Liabilities	
Current assets		Current liabilities	
Cash	$ 13,804	Notes payable to Valsetz Lumber Company	$ 200,000
Accounts receivable, less allowance		Accounts payable	473,609
for losses of $47,215	1,154,519	Provision for taxes on income	92,910
Log and lumber advances	15,479	Total current liabilities	$ 766,519
Notes receivable	85,432	Stockholders' equity	
Total assets	$ 1,269,234	Preferred stock, par value $100,	
		authorized 1,000 shares	
		outstanding 1,000 shares (Note)	$ 100,000
		Common stock, par value $100,	
		authorized 500 shares,	
		outstanding 250 shares	25,000
		Retained earnings	377,715
		Total stockholders' equity	$ 502,715
		Total liabilities and	
		stockholders' equity	$ 1,269,234

Note: In May, 1959, all of the outstanding preferred stock was contributed to the corporation and cancelled.

ADDITIONAL DEVELOPMENTS IN 1959

The impact of starting a pulp and paper mill in April, 1959, and the ever increasing expansion of the company, forced Boise Cascade to seek additional funds in 1959. The company again turned to debt financing through the John Hancock Mutual Life Insurance Company. Mr. Hansberger summed up the company's need for financing by saying: "We had expanded so much that we found we just didn't have enough funds. We had mortgaged our cash flow well into the future (so) we went after a $14,000,000 line of credit from John Hancock Mutual Life Insurance Company on a 20 year program." Hansberger explained further that financing through debt had not been easy to sell to Boise Cascade's board. Never before in its history had the company been so deeply in debt. Before completing the John Hancock loan, Hansberger made a barnstorming trip of about a month during which he explained to the major shareholders why this financing was needed and how the company would handle the debt.

At the end of 1959 the company's debt structure appeared as follows:

Note payable to insurance company, 5½%, under loan commitment of $14,000,000 available until December, 1961, payable in equal annual installments from 1965 to 1979	$ 4,000,000
Notes payable to banks, unsecured:	
4 3/4%, payable in annual installments of $1,200,000 to 1964	6,000,000
4 1/4%, payable in quarterly installments of $82,500 to 1969	3,217,500
3 3/4%, payable in annual installments of $400,000, with final payment of $1,000,000 in 1962	1,800,000
Notes payable, secured by certain timber and timberlands:	
3 1/2%, payable as timber is harvested, with minimum payment of $530,000 in 1960, increasing $25,000 annually with final payment in 1965	3,362,378
4 1/2%, bank loan, payable in annual installments of $150,000 to 1965	900,000
Notes payable, secured by certain plants and equipment:	
5%, payable in annual installments of $300,000, with final payment of $400,000 in 1963	1,300,000
2 1/2%, payable in annual installments of $139,770 to 1974	2,096,560
Other	932,342
	$23,608,780
Less: current portion	3,185,354
	$20,423,426

Concurrent with growth through acquisition, Boise Cascade management committed substantial capital dollars to internal expansion and improvement. In 1958, for instance, Boise Cascade's capital expenditures of $9,100,000 exceeded by $500,000 the amount spent during the entire five year period 1953–1957. And in 1959 the company expended another $8,000,000 for capital projects. Of this amount, $3,554,482 was invested in completing the Wallula mill. Other projects included the addition of more dry kilns at several sawmills, the rebuilding of a sawmill destroyed by fire at Council, Idaho, and the construction of a corrugated shipping container plant near Denver, Colorado.

In the company's annual report for 1959 Mr. Hansberger gave the following summary of Boise Cascade's operations over the three years he had been with the company:

> For the past three years we have been following a program of integrated expansion—that is, expansion which is closely related to something else we do. The program was adopted because it appeared to offer the best return on investment opportunities for the future.
>
> Our first step in this program was to increase our timber and timberland resources. Those expanded resources then made it possible to make investments designed to increase the utilization of our timberlands. Our pulp and paper mill, designed to utilize by-product waste wood, started operations in March of 1959. During these past three years, we have also made capital improvements to increase the efficiency of our existing operations. Although our program of integrated expansion was undertaken with the long-range future in mind, it has already produced significant results.

As cited previously, the results to which Mr. Hansberger referred were indeed impressive. They included a 250% increase in sales, a 370% increase in earnings, a 122% increase in earnings per share, and a 254% increase in the market price per share of Boise Cascade common stock (comparative income statements and balance sheets for the years 1945–1959 appears as Exhibits 4 and 5). Exhibit 6 gives stock price data. Exhibit 7 shows Boise Cascade's area of operations at the end of 1959.

Looking to the future, Mr. Hansberger believed that the company's program of integrated expansion would open up increasing opportunities for the continued development of Boise Cascade.

exhibit 4

BOISE CASCADE CORPORATION (A-2)

Fifteen Year Summary of Income and Expense

(in thousands)

	1959	1958	1957	1956	1955	1954	1953	1952	1951	1950	1949	1948	1947	1946	1945
Income: net sales	$126,085	$72,734	$53,032	$34,902	$35,882	$30,143	$32,049	$31,221	$30,848	$32,166	$26,295	$28,224	$13,008	$9,570	$7,788
Other income	996	1,138	1,028	470	409	460	347	530	398	323	310	429	155	163	325
Total income	$127,081	$73,872	$54,060	$35,372	$36,291	$30,603	$32,396	$31,751	$31,246	$32,489	$26,605	$28,653	$13,163	$9,733	$8,023
Costs and expenses															
Costs and expenses	113,448	66,452	48,964	30,541	31,086	26,786	29,317	27,845	27,063	27,105	21,718	21,805	8,711	7,105	6,408
Depreciation and depletion	4,013	2,348	1,808	1,942	1,491	1,116	997	869	996	534	441	403	408	354	390
Taxes other than income taxes*				494	474	421	409	403	414	350	319	234	160	140	156
Interest expense†	1,062	576	418												
Federal and state income taxes	2,942	1,460	1,004	1,201	1,660	1,104	777	1,302	1,296	1,932	1,591	2,459	1,561	858	597
Special credit	—	—	(275)	—	—	—	—	—	—	—	—	—	—	—	—
Total costs and expenses	$121,465	$70,836	$51,919	$34,178	$34,711	$29,427	$31,500	$30,419	$29,769	$29,921	$24,069	$24,901	$10,840	$8,457	$7,551
Net income	5,616	3,036	2,141	1,194	1,800	1,176	896	1,333	1,477	2,568	2,535	3,751	2,322	1,276	472
Net income per common share after preferred dividends†	$3.02	$2.19	$1.61	$1.37	$1.81	$1.34	$1.02	$1.52	$1.68	$2.94	$2.90	$4.28	$2.64	$1.46	$.54
Common stock dividends paid per share†	$ .60	$ .60	$ .50	$ .50	$ .50	$ .50	$ .50	$ .50	$ .50	$ .60	$ .60	$ .60	$ .60	$1.50	$1.20

*Figures not available.
†Amounts in thousands except for † lines.

BOISE CASCADE CORPORATION (A-2)

Fifteen Year Summary of Financial Position

(in thousands)

	1959	1958	1957	1956	1955	1954	1953	1952	1951	1950	1949	1948	1947	1946	1945
Current assets															
Cash	$ 5,258	$ 3,052	$ 4,421	$ 3,139	$ 1,973	$ 2,064	$ 2,400	$ 1,866	$ 1,324	$ 1,716	$ 2,585	$ 1,996	$ 678	$ 2,324	$ 2,195
Receivables, less reserves	13,207	9,720	5,642	3,644	3,993	3,463	3,758	3,968	3,542	4,237	1,995	2,733	1,253	857	651
Mortgage loans held for resale	1,872	1,620	1,337	2,277	3,804	1,838	—	—	—	—	—	—	—	—	—
Inventories	23,380	17,784	11,741	8,058	7,938	7,630	7,525	7,708	8,478	6,944	4,999	5,857	2,439	1,333	1,142
Total current assets	$43,717	$32,176	$23,141	$17,118	$17,708	$14,995	$13,683	$13,542	$13,344	$12,898	$10,579	$10,586	$ 4,369	$ 4,515	$ 3,988
Timber and timberlands	9,326	6,443	7,668	1,480	1,090	715	792	1,227	1,336	1,202	573	659	716	973	1,015
Real estate held for resale	743	1,016	794	920	942	292	—	—	—	—	—	—	—	—	—
Property, plant, and equipment,															
Less: reserves	26,744	16,916	9,155	5,159	4,221	4,168	4,123	3,777	4,181	3,872	3,257	2,980	874	834	1,190
Other assets	1,655	1,423	2,031	841	742	591	728	756	754	668	688	882	4,475	948	741
Total assets	$82,185	$57,974	$42,789	$25,518	$24,703	$20,761	$19,326	$19,302	$19,615	$18,640	$15,097	$15,107	$10,434	$7,270	$6,934
Current liabilities															
Notes payable and current portion of long-term debt	$ 4,085	$ 4,087	$ 960	$ 400	$ 2,350	$ 300	$ 500	$ —	$ 600	$ —	$ —	$ 900	$ —	$ —	$ —
Accounts payable	4,670	4,507	2,196	1,572	1,040	932	506	703	543	647	179	391	852	316	157
Accrued liabilities	4,741	2,632	1,399	712	1,271	1,028	912	992	1,064	577	512	532	259	284	227
Federal and state income taxes	2,835	1,247	686	1,013	1,512	1,113	758	1,339	1,477	1,932	1,595	2,345	1,568	858	651
Total current liabilities	$16,331	$12,473	$ 5,241	$ 3,697	$ 6,173	$ 3,373	$ 2,676	$ 3,034	$ 3,684	$ 3,671	$ 2,287	$ 4,168	$ 2,779	$ 1,458	$ 1,035
Long-term debt	20,423	13,440	9,553	2,600	—	—	—	77	86	163	46	185	76	30	80
Shareholders' equity	45,431	32,061	27,995	19,221	18,530	17,388	16,650	16,191	15,845	14,806	12,764	10,754	7,579	5,782	5,819
Total liabilities	$82,185	$57,974	$42,789	$25,518	$24,703	$20,761	$19,326	$19,302	$19,615	$18,640	$15,097	$15,107	$10,434	$7,270	$6,934
Common shareholders' equity* per share	$24.48	$21.56	$19.92	$22.10	$21.08	$19.86	$19.02	$18.50	$18.10	$16.82	$14.58	$12.28	$8.66	$6.62	$6.64

*Amounts in thousands except for * lines.

Any discrepancy in figures due to rounding out of thousands.

exhibit 6

BOISE CASCADE CORPORATION (A-2)

Common Stock Price Data

1957			*1959*	
August	17 3/4 - 18		January	30 - 31 3/4
September	16 1/2 - 18		February	31 1/4 - 36
October	14 1/2 - 16 1/2		March	36 1/2 - 42 1/2
November	14 1/2 - 15 1/2		April	37 - 39 1/2
December	14 1/4 - 15		May	39 1/2 - 48
			June	45 1/2 - 49 1/2
1958			July	45 1/2 - 51
January	14 3/4 - 15		August	49 - 55 1/2
February	14 3/4 - 15		September	49 - 51
March	16 3/8 - 16 3/4		October	46 1/2 - 51
April	16 5/8 - 17 1/8		November	45 1/2 - 47
May	17 - 21 7/8		December	43 - 46 1/4
June	21 1/4 - 23 1/4			
July	22 - 23 1/2			
August	24 1/2 - 26 1/4			
September	26 - 27 7/8			
October	27 1/4 - 28			
November	27 - 28 3/4			
December	29 - 30 1/4			

Source: Blyth and Company, Inc.

Important Dates

		Bid	Asked
April 26, 1957	Execution of agreement and plan of reorganization with Cascade Lumber Company.	13	14
May 28, 1957	Memorandum agreement with Potlatch Yards, Inc., with respect to merger of Potlatch and Boise Cascade.	16	17
July 31, 1958	Execution of agreement and plan of reorganization with Ames Harris.	22 1/4	23 1/4
June 10, 1959	Execution of agreement and plan of reorganization with Valsetz Lumber Company.	49	50 1/2

Source: Company records.

exhibit 7

BOISE CASCADE CORPORATION (A-2)

Area of Operations: 1959

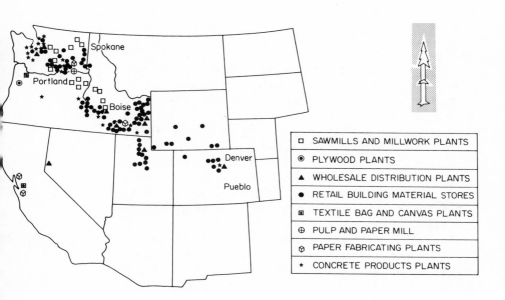

□	SAWMILLS AND MILLWORK PLANTS
◉	PLYWOOD PLANTS
▲	WHOLESALE DISTRIBUTION PLANTS
●	RETAIL BUILDING MATERIAL STORES
▣	TEXTILE BAG AND CANVAS PLANTS
⊕	PULP AND PAPER MILL
⬡	PAPER FABRICATING PLANTS
★	CONCRETE PRODUCTS PLANTS

Hallack and Howard Lumber Company

In November, 1959, just four months after the purchase of Valsetz-Templeton, the management of Boise Cascade seriously interested in another acquisition. Boise had been informed by an investment broker in Denver, Colorado, that the majority of stockholders of the Hallack and Howard Lumber Company were interested in selling their stock. He indicated that this stock could probably be purchased at its book value. Hallack and Howard's facilities included sawmills at Winchester, Idaho, and South Fork, Colorado, a lumber remanufacturing plant at Englewood, Colorado, a railroad serving the Winchester mill, a retail yard at Arvada, Colorado, and a specialty millwork plant in Denver.

Boise Cascade entered into negotiations with the management of Hallack and Howard, and, in January, 1960, obtained options to purchase all of the outstanding common stock of the company at a price of $41 per share. These options were to be exercised during the last week in January, subject to the approval of Boise's board of directors. The total purchase price of Hallack and Howard would be $5,500,000.

Boise Cascade's management believed that this was a bargain price, and a formal proposal to purchase Hallack and Howard was submitted to the board of directors. The remainder of this case presents the text of that proposal. Exhibit 1 shows the location of the Hallack and Howard facilities
. . . .

RESUME OF OPERATIONS

Winchester Sawmill

This sawmill, backed up by 103 million board feet of timber, is in excellent condition, but because of the competitive

---

© 1964 by the Board of Trustees of the Leland Stanford Junior University.

exhibit 1

HALLACK & HOWARD CORPORATION

Properties

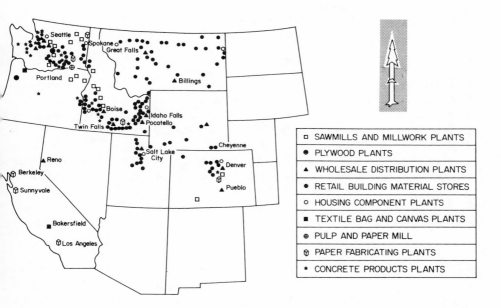

□	SAWMILLS AND MILLWORK PLANTS
●	PLYWOOD PLANTS
▲	WHOLESALE DISTRIBUTION PLANTS
•	RETAIL BUILDING MATERIAL STORES
○	HOUSING COMPONENT PLANTS
■	TEXTILE BAG AND CANVAS PLANTS
⊕	PULP AND PAPER MILL
⊕	PAPER FABRICATING PLANTS
✳	CONCRETE PRODUCTS PLANTS

situation on timber in its area, is being operated on a liquidation program. Our best estimates are that the mill will be liquidated within four to five years. It has a capacity to produce 30 million board feet per year, and during the liquidation program will produce minimum profits of approximately $600,000 per year.

South Fork Sawmill

This sawmill is located in southern Colorado; on the two-shift basis it can produce approximately 25 million board feet per year. It depends upon the Forest Service for its source of timber, but is operating in an area where there is no competition and is presently buying all the spruce timber it needs at appraisal prices. Hallack and Howard has expended considerable money in constructing a modern sawmill, but at this point, because of logging problems, has been unable to produce a profit at this mill. Due to the short logging season and the inefficiencies in logging, they are unable to produce enough logs to keep the mill running at capacity, and the cost of logs produced is exorbitant.

Craig Mountain Railroad

This railroad is a common carrier operating between Winchester, Idaho, and the switching point on the Union Pacific and Northern Pacific. As the originating carrier on all lumber shipped from the Winchester mill, which allows it to take a higher portion of the freight revenue, it has been a profitable operation. However, its life is limited by the life of the Winchester mill.

Colorado Mill & Lumber Company

This company operates a small head rig, green chain, and planer at Englewood, Colorado. This company was acquired by Hallack and Howard in August, 1959, principally for the purpose of supplying surfaced air-dried spruce boards to the Denver retail market, thereby freeing up the South Fork mill production for shipment into the midwest market at a better sales realization. Colorado Mill & Lumber Company has a net operating loss carried forward of approximately $125,000. This company owns cutting contracts from which it sells timber to gypo operators. The gypos saw the timber into cants and deliver the cants to the Englewood mill, where they are broken down into boards. The gypos are paid a set price for cants delivered.

Arvada Lumber Company

This company operates a profitable retail yard at Arvada, Colorado, a suburb of Denver. Hallack and Howard has acquired options for additional land in this rapidly growing suburban community. It is their intention to remodel the yard and provide additional parking and storage area.

Valley Building Supply

Approximately four years ago, Hallack and Howard acquired all of the outstanding stock of Valley Building Supply, a wholesale building materials company, located in Pueblo, Colorado. To date, this operation has never operated at a profit, but has managed to build up its volume to a figure in excess of $1,000,000 per year. It is located on owned land with plenty of space. This company serves western Kansas and Nebraska, southern Colorado, and northern New Mexico and Arizona.

Denver Operation

The Denver operation and headquarters of Hallack and Howard is located in the downtown industrial area on approximately 17 acres of owned land. The land has an estimated fair value of approximately $600,000. The physical layout of the properties does not lend itself to a modern type of mechanized wholesale operation. In addition to the head office and a lumber brokerage operation, this location operates as a wholesale and retail building materials business and contains one of the largest specialty millwork plants west of the Mississippi. Over-all, the volume handled out of the Denver location amounts to approximately $9,000,000.

BOISE CASCADE'S PLANS FOR OPERATING HALLACK AND HOWARD LUMBER COMPANY

Basically, Hallack and Howard fits very naturally into our sawmill, wholesale, and retail businesses. It would be our intention to retain their present businesses, splitting off Hallack and Howard divisions into their counterpart divisions in Boise Cascade Corporation. Our preliminary plans with respect to each of the Hallack and Howard divisions are set forth below. It should be recognized, however, that these plans are preliminary in nature and are subject to change depending upon further knowledge we gain in the future as to the operations of these divisions. (See Exhibits 2-4.)

1. The sawmill divisions of Hallack and Howard at Winchester, Idaho, and South Fork, Colorado, would become the operating responsibility of Mr. Hjort of the Idaho Lumber Division. The Winchester mill would be operated on an accelerated liquidation basis, cutting out all of the fee timber over a period of four to five years. The operating management of the South Fork sawmill would be changed, and we would defer the decision as to whether or not we should close this mill, depending upon how well the new management does.
2. Colorado Mill & Lumber Company, Arvada Lumber Company, and the retail business of the Denver operation would be put into our retail division, thereby strengthening our position in the Colorado retail building materials market.
3. New warehouses would be constructed at the Pueblo wholesale operation and a steel distribution center would be established at that point to operate under the retail division. Morrison-Merrill will operate the wholesale building materials business in Pueblo, thereby putting them into new markets in southern Colorado, northern New Mexico, and Arizona, and strengthening their position in western Kansas and Nebraska.
4. A complete investigation and cost study would be prepared on the Denver millwork plant. If this investigation proves we should be out of the millwork business and that we are not making adequate return on investment, then the decision will be made to liquidate this operation.
5. The Denver wholesale operation will be combined with the wholesale operation of Morrison-Merrill & Company in Denver. At this time, it is anticipated that, in 1961, a new wholesale distribution point for the combined companies would be located at some point in the suburbs of Denver. It ap-

exhibit 2

HALLACK & HOWARD CORPORATION

Balance Sheets—November 30, 1954–1959

	1954	1955	1956	1957	1958	1959
Current assets						
Cash	$ 196,616.46	$ 292,177.41	$ 201,576.78	$ 405,762.57	$ 159,408.59	$ 608,649.52
Marketable securities	894,934.23	746,256.85	718,619.04	954,957.69	985,949.10	1,108,570.64
Accounts and notes receivable		1,071,129.25	871,965.47	637,581.07	956,728.17	901,474.06
Less: allowance for doubtful receivables	(200,909.77)	(200,909.77)	(194,694.12)	(189,033.50)	(189,882.73)	(191,293.20)
	$ 769,500.03	$ 870,219.48	$ 677,271.35	$ 448,547.57	$ 766,845.44	$ 710,180.86
Inventories	1,063,832.12	1,208,738.43	1,392,811.06	1,042,440.61	1,142,763.27	1,256,681.56
Deposits	32,383.07	44,008.48	24,292.54	25,334.53	16,580.42	54,427.73
Prepaid expenses	27,684.21	45,031.60	29,091.72	37,079.08	220,548.53	25,355.83
	$2,984,950.12	$3,206,432.25	$3,043,662.49	$2,914,122.05	$3,092,095.35	$3,763,866.14
Current liabilities						
Accounts payable	$ 753,578.62	$ 563,654.04	$ 456,681.71	$ 216,617.41	$ 266,884.40	$ 360,702.63
Dividend payable	52,746.13	65,942.67	66,042.67	66,142.67	66,302.67	66,522.67
Accrued expenses	114,851.07	126,198.77	157,923.07	130,612.12	147,761.53	216,746.27
Federal taxes on income (net of U.S. Tax notes in 1954) (est.)	81,204.00	218,000.00	150,000.00	75,500.00	56,628.43	79,908.14
State taxes on income, (est.)	20,150.00	20,000.00	25,000.00	14,000.00	11,959.69	30,000.00
	$1,022,529.82	$ 993,795.48	$ 855,647.45	$ 502,872.20	$ 549,536.72	$ 753,879.71
Working capital	$1,962,420.30	$2,212,636.77	$2,188,015.04	$2,411,249.85	$2,542,558.63	$3,009,986.43
Notes receivable, due after one year	25,000.00	7,125.00	295,000.00	245,000.00	204,200.00	200,000.00
Investments	1,240,810.15	1,232,062.78	616,549.51	638,967.14	706,851.87	606,385.16
Timber	194,595.36	174,440.09	155,346.15	128,350.31	146,050.18	143,687.81
Plant, property, and equipment	3,072,455.67	3,218,704.84	3,802,620.95	2,980,907.07	4,060,613.94	4,150,000.00
Less: allowance for depreciation	(1,737,370.47)	(1,908,272.98)	(1,958,096.12)	(2,187,220.06)	(2,362,930.55)	(2,578,419.65)
	$1,335,085.20	$1,310,431.86	$1,844,524.83	$1,793,687.01	$1,697,683.39	$1,571,580.35
Stockholders' equity	$4,757,911.01	$4,936,696.50	$5,099,435.53	$5,217,254.31	$5,297,344.07	$5,531,639.75

pears as though this operation would be under the management of Mr. Schmidt, the present president of Hallack and Howard Lumber Company, who would report to Mr. Montgomery.

exhibit 3

HALLACK & HOWARD CORPORATION

Stockholders' Equity at October 31, 1959

	Denver	Winchester	South Fork	Valley	Book Value—October 31, 1959 Total
Current assets					
Cash	$ 417,000	$ 42,000	$ 14,000	$ 27,000	$ 500,000
Marketable securities	1,116,000	—	—	—	1,116,000
Accounts receivable—net	823,000	25,000	68,000	120,000	1,036,000
Notes receivable	17,000	—	—	—	17,000
Inventory	900,000	115,000	68,000	138,000	1,221,000
Prepaid expenses	9,000	9,000	18,000	4,000	40,000
Cash surrender value of insurance	102,000	—	—	—	102,000
	$3,384,000	$191,000	$168,000	$289,000	$4,032,000
Current liabilities					
Accounts payable and accrued liabilities	$ 324,000	$ 89,000	$ 30,000	$ 55,000	$ 498,000
Reserve for income taxes	200,000	—	—	—	200,000
	$ 524,000	$ 89,000	$ 30,000	$ 55,000	$ 698,000
Working capital	$2,860,000	$102,000	$138,000	$234,000	$3,334,000
Investment in subsidiaries					
Arvada Lumber Company	95,000	—	—	—	95,000
Colorado Mill & Lumber Company	230,000	—	—	—	230,000
Craig Mountain Railway Company	—	(19,000)	—	—	(19,000)
Fee timber and timberland	—	176,000	—	—	176,000
Timber cutting deposits	20,000	—	13,000	—	33,000
Plant, property, and equipment—net	637,000	316,000	613,000	6,000	1,572,000
Notes receivable	215,000	—	—	—	215,000
Stockholders' equity	$4,057,000	$575,000	$764,000	$240,000	$5,636,000

SUMMARY OF FAIR VALUE OF
HALLACK AND HOWARD LUMBER COMPANY

Hallack and Howard Lumber Company was operated in the wholesale building material business since the turn of the century, and at one time was considered one of the major wholesale building material firms in the west. Over the last 20 years, however, through weak management, the company has been on the downgrade. The age of the company in itself is an important factor, in that many of its capital assets are recorded at an original cost figure, substantially below the fair value of such assets today. This factor, coupled with the fact that the company has been accumulating cash funds and investing them in Blue Chip securities over a period of years, tends to make the acquisition of Hallack and Howard at book value a bargain purchase, whether treated from the standpoint of liquidating

exhibit 4

HALLACK & HOWARD CORPORATION

Statements of Net Income for the Years Ended November 30, 1955–1959

	1955	1956	1957	1958	1959
Sales	$10,946,592.31	$9,457,091.29	$8,113,151.55	$8,866,759.67	$9,660,000
Less: discounts	(147,359.14)	(130,548.57)	(106,413.42)	(108,410.16)	(110,000)
Cost of sales	$10,799,233.17	$9,326,542.72	$8,006,738.13	$8,758,349.51	$9,550,000
	(9,654,414.52)	(8,160,681.57)	(6,954,045.91)	(7,696,522.63)	(8,906,599)
Gross profit	$1,144,818.65	$1,165,861.15	$1,052,692.22	$1,061,826.88	
Selling, general, and administrative expenses	(751,402.15)	(843,026.09)	(809,462.54)	(873,161.94)	
Net operating profit	$ 322,835.06	$ 243,229.68	$ 188,664.94	$ 643,401	
Other income	202,990.73	200,727.02	145,547.02	151,548.01	63,553
Other expense	(16,705.04)	(8,674.99)	(7,308.09)	(13,606.53)	(164,102)
Net income before taxes on income	$ 514,887.09	$ 381,468.82	$ 326,606.42	$ 542,852	
Taxes on income (est.)	(236,325.04)	(189,691.40)	(100,943.38)	(85,000.00)	(148,000)
Net income	$343,377.15	$ 325,195.69	$ 280,525.44	$ 241,606.42	$ 394,852

all the assets or merely the liquidation of assets which have a value in excess of their value to us as operating properties.

Exhibit 5 sets forth the fair value of stockholders' equity in Hallack and Howard Lumber Company, which is approximately $2,300,000 in excess of book value.

exhibit 5

HALLACK & HOWARD CORPORATION

Adjusted Fair Value of Stockholders' Equity

at November 30, 1959

Book value of stockholders' equity at 11-30-59		$5,531,640
Adjustments to fair value		
To write value of securities up	$ 388,000	
Adjustment of log inventory at Winchester pond to reflect a value of 20,000 at $40.00	800,000	
Adjustment of LIFO inventories to current cost	363,000	
Adjustment of investment in subsidiaries to book net worth	30,000	
Adjustment of timber and timberlands to reflect a volume of 103,000[1] with a wholesale price of $30 for pine and $10 for mixed and land at $10 per acre	1,797,000	
To set up the value of the completed road system at Winchester	206,000	
Adjustment of Denver wholesale property to fair value	300,000	
To write down South Fork sawmill property to fair value	(300,000)	3,584,000
		$9,115,640
Less: Federal Income Tax on adjustment		(1,245,750)
Adjusted fair value of stockholders' equity at 11-30-59		$7,869,890

[1]Thousand board feet.

DISCUSSION OF CASH PAYOUT AND TAX PROBLEMS

We are offering to pay a price of $41 per share on the 133,045⅓ shares of Hallack and Howard common stock outstanding, which amounts to approximately $5,455,000. Certain of the options we obtained call for a three year payout of the purchase price. On this basis, the cash payout for the common stock will be $3,250,000 in 1960, $1,160,000 in 1961, and $1,210,000 in 1962. Attached hereto is Exhibit 6, which is a summary of cash flow for 1960 through 1964. From our review of this cash flow, it is apparent that Boise Cascade can purchase all of the outstanding common stock of Hallack and Howard Lumber Company with no dollar investment on the part of Boise Cascade. At the end of three years, that company will have generated enough funds to pay off the purchase price of the stock. The principal items involved in obtaining this powerful cash flow for the payment of the purchase price are set forth below:

1. Hallack and Howard has marketable securities on which we can realize approximately $1,700,000 upon disposal.
2. The Winchester operation, which on a liquidation program will be cutting 100% fee timber with a low tax cost basis, will produce a cash flow of over $600,000 per year over the next three to four years.
3. The Denver plant is located on valuable real estate, which should be sold during 1960 for a minimum amount of $600,000. The management of Hallack and Howard has expressed the opinion that values of $1,700,000 can be realized from the sale of this property.
4. Hallack and Howard Lumber Company is operating with present cash balances of $550,000, which is $300,000 in excess of its operating cash requirements.

In acquiring the common stock of Hallack and Howard, it is our intention to handle the transaction taxwise in such a manner that the maximum cash flow after income taxes will be realized during the first three years subsequent to the acquisition. Therefore, it is our intention to immediately liquidate Hallack and Howard Lumber Company on February 1, 1960. The liquidation would take place under the Internal Revenue Code Section 332-2, whereby there is no recognition of gain or loss, and the purchase price paid for the stock becomes the cost basis of the net assets acquired in liquidation. By so doing, the tax cost basis of the marketable securities is equivalent to their market value at February 1, 1960, and we will be in a position to sell these securities with no income tax involved. In taking such a course of action, the only disadvantage to Boise Cascade will be that it will be unable to claim capital gain on timber cut during 1960, in that the holding period for capital gains treatment on such timber will not become effective until January 1, 1961. The tax benefit lost is substantially equivalent to the tax benefit realized on the sale of the marketable securities, and the net result will be no additional tax cost to Boise Cascade Corporation. It is felt, however, that from an operating standpoint, it is highly advantageous to liquidate Hallack and Howard Lumber Company and fold its divisions into the counterpart divisions of Boise Cascade Corporation.

CONCLUSION

The management of Boise Cascade Corporation recommends to the Board of Directors that the acquisition of all of the outstanding common stock of Hallack

exhibit 6

HALLACK & HOWARD CORPORATION

Summary of Boise Cascade Corporation Cash Flow for 1960 thru 1964

Re: The Purchase of Hallack & Howard Lumber Company

	1960	1961	1962	1963	1964
Net income					
Winchester sawmill	$ 600,000	$ 600,000	$ 600,000	$ 500,000	$ 100,000
South Fork sawmill	50,000	100,000	100,000	125,000	125,000
Craig Mountain Railway Company	20,000	20,000	20,000	10,000	—
Colorado Mill & Lumber Company	30,000	50,000	75,000	100,000	100,000
Denver wholesale	55,000	—	—	—	—
Arvada retail	10,000	20,000	20,000	20,000	20,000
Valley Building Supply wholesale	75,000	75,000	75,000	75,000	75,000
New wholesale plant	—	25,000	50,000	75,000	100,000
	$ 840,000	$ 890,000	$ 940,000	$ 905,000	$ 520,000
Depletion	50,000	50,000	50,000	—	—
Depreciation	125,000	165,000	165,000	95,000	95,000
Sale of securities	1,700,000	—	—	—	—
Sale of life insurance	105,000	—	—	—	—
Sale of Denver wholesale properties	—	600,000	—	—	—
Collection of Abrahamson note	40,000	40,000	40,000	—	—
Federal Income Tax refund	75,000	—	—	—	—
Cash balances acquired from Hallack and Howard	500,000	—	—	—	—
	$3,435,000	$1,745,000	$1,195,000	$1,000,000	$ 615,000
Use of cash					
Purchase of Hallack and Howard common stock	$3,250,000	$1,160,000	$1,210,000	—	—
New warehouse for Valley Building Supply	—	40,000	—	—	—
Land purchase and remodel at Arvada retail yard	35,000	—	—	—	—
Construction of new wholesale plant and cost of moving	—	500,000	—	—	—
Increase in inventories and receivables	—	—	—	$ 200,000	$ 50,000
Capital expenditures for replacements	—	—	—	150,000	50,000
	$3,285,000	$1,700,000	$1,210,000	$ 850,000	$ 100,000
Increase (decrease) in cash	$ 150,000	$ 45,000	$ (15,000)	$ 650,000	$ 515,000
Beginning cash balance	—	150,000	195,000	180,000	830,000
Ending cash balance	$ 150,000	$ 195,000	$ 180,000	$ 830,000	$1,345,000

Note: No increase in working capital for receivables and inventory is projected during 1960 to 1962 since earnings have been projected on a conservative basis and there will be a reduction in inventory due to combining with Morrison-Merrill & Company.

and Howard Lumber Company by Boise Cascade Corporation be approved. The advantages to be obtained by such an acquisition are summarized below:

1. The acquisition will be paid over three years, and the funds to be used will come from the cash flow of the Hallack and Howard properties and will not require any funds out of Boise Cascade's own cash flow.
2. For a period of four years, the earnings of Boise Cascade Corporation will be increased approximately 48¢ per share as a result of this acquisition.
3. For a period of four to five years, the chips produced by the Winchester sawmill of Hallack and Howard Lumber Company can augment the chip supply of Cascade Kraft Corporation.
4. The wholesale and retail operations of Hallack and Howard will strengthen Boise Cascade's present retail and wholesale operations in the Colorado area.
5. It appears that many of the personnel and management of Hallack and Howard will be retained and that these people will enhance and strengthen our management and sales organizations in Colorado.
6. For some time we have been interested in rounding out our lumber sales program to include substantial amounts of Engleman spruce lumber. The acquisition of the South Fork sawmill will give us a substantial volume of spruce to sell through our lumber sales organization and will give us immediate experience in logging and production in the Colorado spruce area, which at some future date could lead to establishment of a stronger position in this area for exploitation of cheap spruce stumpage, either in the lumber field or pulp and paper field.

Boise Cascade Corporation (A-3): 1960-1961

After 1959's record performance, 1960 operating results were a sharp disappointment. Although sales were up slightly, earnings were down 40%. Earnings per share dropped from 1959's $1.51 to $.91 in 1960. Stock prices dropped from $23 to $17.50/share.[1]

Management attributed this drop in earnings primarily to the sharp decline in lumber prices during the year. Housing starts were down 17%, and generally high interest rates restricted commercial and industrial construction. The price decline was especially severe in ponderosa pine and the mixed species which comprised an important part of Boise's output.

The decline in home construction activity, which began in 1960, persisted throughout 1961. According to Mr. Hansberger, this industry situation continued to have a depressing effect on sales volumes and prices for several of Boise Cascade's principal products. Total company sales in 1961 were up 5% to $137,630,731, but net income at $3,051,145 was 9% lower than in 1960. Per share earnings dropped from 91¢ in 1960 to 82¢ in 1961. Market price of shares held at $17½/share. Comparative balance sheets and income statements for 1960–1961 are presented as Exhibits 1 and 2. Exhibit 3 shows Boise Cascade's area of operations at the end of 1961.

THE MAJOR EVENTS OF 1960 AND 1961

Despite the downturn in earnings, capital expenditures continued at a high rate. The 1960 program of expenditures for internal improvements was in excess of $7 million.

---

[1] Per share earnings have been adjusted to reflect the two for one stock split which occurred in May of 1960. Market price before the split was approximately $43/share; $21/share in May, following the split.

BOISE CASCADE CORPORATION (A-3)

Consolidated Income Statement
(for years ended December 31, 1960 and 1961: in thousands)

	1961	*1960*
Net sales	$137,631	$131,182
Other income	1,307	913
	$138,938	$132,095
Cost of goods sold	109,899	103,466
Depreciation	3,523	3,826
Depletion	937	911
Selling, general, and administrative expense	18,648	17,645
Interest expense	1,880	1,617
Federal and state income taxes	1,000	1,265
	$135,887	$128,730
Net income	$ 3,051	$ 3,365
Net income per common share*	$.82	$ .91
Per share cash dividend on common stock*	$.40	$ .35

*Adjusted for two for one stock split in May, 1960.

Major expenditures included the beginning of an extensive $2.7 million modernization program for the company's sawmill in Yakima, Washington, the construction of concrete plants in Boise, Mountain Home (Idaho), and Seattle, the expansion of the company's prestressed concrete plant at Redmond, Washington, and the beginning of a project to increase the capacity of the Wallula pulp and paper mill from 200 to 375 tons per day.

Throughout 1961, the emphasis on internal growth and improvement of existing facilities continued. Capital expenditures for the year, totaling $10,649,-270, were concentrated in the company's lumber and paper operations. Major projects included: beginning construction of a plywood plant in Yakima, Washington; commencing operation of a corrugated container plant in Sunnyvale, California (this plant converted kraft linerboard produced at the Wallula mill); and completing the expansion of the Wallula mill to the projected 375 tons capacity (the expansion required a shutdown of almost a month, the mill resuming operation late in December).

In April, the Monarch Lumber Company, which owned 37 retail lumber yards, two wholesale building material plants, and six ready-mix concrete plants, all in Montana, was purchased in a cash transaction, reportedly for 50% of book value. Montana brought to seven the number of states served by Boise Cascade retail outlets.

exhibit 2

BOISE CASCADE CORPORATION (A-3)

Financial Condition
(at December 31, 1960 and 1961: in thousands)

	1961	1960
Working capital		
Current assets		
Cash	$ 6,701	$ 5,735
Receivables, net	17,002	16,042
Mortgage loans held for resale	772	1,604
Inventories	26,972	23,750
Total current assets	$51,447	$47,132
Current liabilities		
Current portion of long-term debt	$ 6,245	$ 4,134
Accounts payable	4,211	4,462
Accrued liabilities	4,774	4,107
Federal and state income taxes	1,380	1,105
Total current liabilities	$16,610	$13,808
Total working capital	$34,837	$33,324
Fixed assets		
Timber and timberlands, at cost less depletion	$ 9,148	$ 9,124
Real estate held for resale	1,151	812
Property, plant, and equipment, net[1]	35,302	29,467
Other assets	2,014	1,843
Total fixed assets	$47,615	$41,246
Total working capital and fixed assets	$82,452	$74,570
Sources of working capital and fixed assets		
Long-term debt	$33,177	$27,441
Shareholders' equity[2]	49,275	47,129
Total sources of working capital and fixed assets	$82,452	$74,570

[1] Reserves for depreciation 1960—$26,723,361; 1961—$28,756,390.
[2] Common shares outstanding 1960— 3,720,808; 1961—3,758,408 (adjusted for two for one stock split in May, 1960).

The impact of Boise Cascade's substantial capital expenditure program and a reduced cash flow from profits in 1960 and 1961 prompted the borrowing of an additional $8,500,000 during 1961 from the John Hancock Mutual Life Insurance Company.

At the end of 1961, Boise Cascade's debt position was:

Notes payable to insurance company, unsecured, 5½% and 5 4/5%	$22,500,000
Notes payable, secured by certain timber, plants, and equipment, 2 1/2% to 6%	5,582,875
Notes payable, unsecured, 3 3/4% to 6%	11,339,815
	$39,422,690
Less: current portion	6,245,339
	$33,177,351

Minimum payments on long-term debt were $6,245,339 in 1962; $3,510,590 in 1963; $3,206,269 in 1964; $2,867,142 in 1965; and annually thereafter at averages of $1,971,680 to 1970; $1,477,463 to 1979; and $460,000 to 1981.

At December 31, 1961, the corporation and its subsidiaries also were lessees of mobile equipment, retail yards, wholesale warehouses, and other properties under leases which had terms extending for periods up to 25 years. The aggregate prospective rental payments for 1962 approximated $2,790,000 of which $1,580,000 represented commitments by the parent company on facilities which had been pledged by subsidiaries to secure long-term debt.

Looking back at the events of 1960 and 1961, Mr. Hansberger believed that the company's program for "integrated growth" had been severely tested by reduced demand and declining prices. He was convinced that without this program, which increased the interrelationships of the various company activities, the drop in net income would have been much greater.

Mr. Hansberger commented that, in 1961, Boise Cascade was moving continually closer to the point at which it could gain maximum utilization of its basic resources:

> What integration means in actual daily practice can be illustrated in the building of a home. It is possible to finance, design, and build a home through the facilities of just one company, Boise Cascade. Our Construction Finance Company will provide the financing for the home, the company's architects will design it, and the retail sales division will provide the necessary materials, from lumber grown on company timberlands and manufactured by its sawmills.
>
> In addition, a Boise Cascade enterprise will pour the concrete for the basement from ready-mix trucks, and the concrete pipe for the sanitary system will be made by another subsidiary. And the first groceries brought over the threshold by the new homeowner can be carried in containers manufactured and printed in a Boise Cascade plant, from paper produced by a Boise Cascade paper mill, from wood chips which came from a Boise Cascade sawmill.

The effects of "integrated growth" on the nature of the firm were significant. Whereas wholesale and retail activities represented 74% of the company's sales

exhibit 3

BOISE CASCADE CORPORATION (A-3)

Area of Operations, 1961

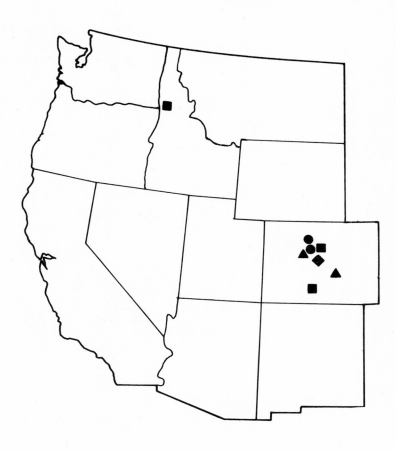

■ Sawmill
◆ Millwork Plant
▲ Wholesale Distribution Plant
● Retail Building Material Stores

in 1956, this figure had dropped to 38% in 1961. In the meantime, lumber and plywood sales had increased as a per cent of the total and several new product categories had appeared. The tables in Exhibit 4 show the shifting relationship of major lines from 1957 to 1961.

exhibit 4

BOISE CASCADE CORPORATION (A-3)
Sales Trends by Products
(as per cent of total company sales)

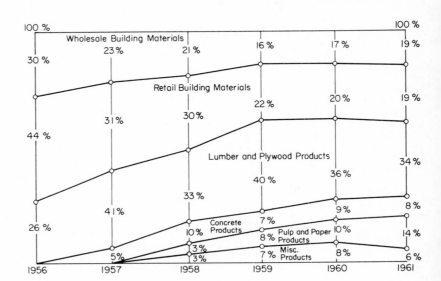

table 2

Net Income—as a Per Cent of Sales
(before taxes)

	1957	*1958*	*1959*	*1960*	*1961*
Lumber and plywood	7.1	11.3	13.3	6.0	6.0
Wholesale	3.0	3.7	2.0	2.3	4.0
Retail	5.5	7.7	6.5	2.8	3.8
Paper	—	(2.2)	1.8	8.0	8.5
Concrete	5.7	6.2	5.0	3.5	(1.1)
Miscellaneous	—	(.2)	2.9	6.2	2.6

LOOKING AHEAD

The downturns in earnings of 1960 and 1961 despite increased sales had emphasized Boise's heavy dependence on the construction industry for the major portion of corporate profits, and management was extending every effort to diversify operations. In the 1961 annual report, Mr. Hansberger made these comments about the coming year:

> While we anticipate a modest improvement in lumber prices during 1962, we do not predict a major increase in home construction activity for several years. However, our program of integrated growth, which is now approaching a stage of initial maturity, has brought about a diversification of our operations in several large new industries. This diversification not only tends to offset the effects of the cycles of the construction industry, but it also provides growth opportunities of its own.

Foremost in management's thinking were: (1) increased emphasis on paper products, which, although suffering price pressures of their own, were independent of the building cycle; (2) the possibility of extended activity in the recreation industry; (3) backward integration from the successful merchandising operations into manufacture of major products presently purchased for resale.

Boise already had a modest stake in the burgeoning recreation industry through its Ames Harris Neville subsidiary, which manufactured tents, sleeping bags, and water bags, and also distributed a general line of sporting goods. This multibillion dollar industry was especially important in the Pacific Northwest, with its myriad outdoor recreational opportunities. Camping, boating, and sporting goods items were perceived as a natural complement to building materials in Boise's 129 retail centers.

The excellent showing of Boise's wholesale division in 1961, in the face of lower profits by every other division except retail, highlighted the relative independence of this operation from fluctuations in lumber prices. The established position which Boise held in wholesaling and retailing, with a 1961 sales base of approximately $50 million, made attractive the possibility of the company's supplying more of its own requirements. Acquisitions of companies manufacturing such products as paint, wallboard, glass, and aluminum doors and windows were being considered as a major avenue for subsequent profitable growth.

Return on Investment by Product Line
(1957–1961: % of book value before taxes)

Product Line	1957	1958	1959	1960	1961
Lumber and plywood	9.5	17.0	22.6	9.4	8.2
Wholesale	9.5	15.0	7.0	10.6	15.4
Retail	10.1	15.0	17.0	6.1	7.6
Paper	—	(5.6)	1.4	11.5	8.3
Concrete	9.4	23.0	17.4	9.2	(.3)
Miscellaneous	—	(.3)	22.0	13.9	6.6

Capital Expenditures by Product Line
(in thousands)

Product Line	1953-57	1958	1959	1960	1961
Lumber and plywood	$5,452	$1,772	$—	$3,840	$3,886
Paper	—	5,990	3,554	1,884	4,962
Wholesale	426	455	—	128	86
Retail	1,618	672	—	188	201
Concrete	—	—	—	817	1,036
Other	1,022	211	—	172	478
Total	$8,518	$9,100	$8,174	$7,029	$10,649

Number of Employees by Product Line

Product Line	1956	1957	1958	1959	1960	1961
Lumber and plywood	750	1,641	1,752	3,049	3,302	3,193
Paper	—	50	300	575	605	669
Wholesale-retail	500	1,000	1,050	1,000	1,143	1,382
Concrete	50	516	500	600	557	544
Other	18	18	18	281	721	357
Corporate	65	75	80	100	150	179
Total	1,337	2,834	3,716	5,505	6,521	6,337

Columbia River Paper Company

Early in 1962, while Boise Cascade's management was considering the various growth alternatives available to the company, an opportunity arose to purchase the Columbia River Paper Company of Portland, Oregon. Boise Cascade executives had had an interest in Columbia River for the past three years, but negotiations had not reached a serious stage until late in 1961.

Columbia River Paper Company was in the fine paper business, its product line consisting primarily of bond and writing papers, including quality mimeograph paper, ledger papers, and various types of duplicating papers. Reportedly the company accounted for about 40% of the fine paper production on the Pacific Coast and approximately 7% of the total U.S. production. A substantial portion of the company's sales were made in the Los Angeles and San Francisco areas to a relatively small number of customers, most of whom bought the paper in roll and sheet form for subsequent conversion into consumer products (tablets, writing papers, envelopes, adding machine tapes, etc.). The Pacific Coast in total was a deficit area for fine papers, producing only two-thirds of its requirements. Consequently, Columbia River competed against eastern producers as well as those in the West.

The proposed purchase agreement called for Boise Cascade to purchase for cash all of the outstanding common stock of Columbia River. A tentative price of $1,765 a share for the 34,028 outstanding shares was agreed upon. Needing board approval for a transaction of this size, Mr. Hansberger submitted the following document to Boise Cascade's board of directors.

Report to the Board of Directors of Boise Cascade Corporation on Proposed Acquisition of Columbia River Paper Company

Within the last four years Boise Cascade has entered the paper industry and now operates the following plants in the coarse paper segment of the industry:

1. A kraft linerboard pulp and paper mill at Wallula, Washington, which has a daily capacity of 375 tons.
2. Four corrugated shipping container plants located at Wallula, Washington; Burley, Idaho; Golden, Colorado; and Sunnyvale, California. These plants have a combined capacity of 120 million square feet of corrugated board per month.
3. Two corrugated sheet plants at Los Angeles, California, and at Edmonton, Alberta.
4. A multiwall paper bag factory in Berkeley, California, which consumes approximately 1,000 tons per month of multiwall bag paper.
5. A folding carton factory in Spokane, Washington.

exhibit 1

COLUMBIA RIVER PAPER COMPANY

Properties

exhibit 2

COLUMBIA RIVER PAPER COMPANY

Comparative Summary Income Statement
(for the years ended December 31, 1951–1960 and five months ended May 31, 1960 and 1961)

	5 Mos. Ended May 31		For Years Ended December 31									
	1961	1960	1960	1959	1958	1957	1956	1955	1954	1953	1952	1951
Net sales	$10,372	$11,260	$25,440	$24,983	$21,919	$22,533	$23,691	$23,675	$20,644	$21,852	$24,203	$26,577
Cost of goods sold	8,146	8,431	18,157	17,338	15,973	16,060	15,339	16,331	15,171	16,582	17,343	17,580
Gross profit	$ 2,226	$ 2,829	$ 7,283	$ 7,645	$ 5,946	$ 6,473	$ 8,352	$ 7,344	$ 5,473	$ 5,270	$ 6,860	$ 8,997
Selling, general and administrative expenses	742	632	2,548	2,359	1,964	1,946	1,878	1,874	1,897	1,872	1,745	1,610
Profit from operations	$ 1,484	$ 2,197	$ 4,735	$ 5,286	$ 3,982	$ 4,527	$ 6,474	$ 5,470	$ 3,576	$ 3,398	$ 5,115	$ 7,387
Other income (expenses), net	83	142	343	281	95	305	37	377	689	32	(230)	(401)
Income before income taxes	$ 1,567	$ 2,339	$ 5,078	$ 5,567	$ 4,077	$ 4,832	$ 6,511	$ 5,847	$ 4,265	$ 3,430	$ 4,885	$ 6,986
Provision for income taxes	843	1,125	2,217	2,891	2,070	2,430	3,102	2,922	1,988	1,528	2,831	4,616
Net income	$ 724	$ 1,214	$ 2,861	$ 2,676	$ 2,007	$ 2,402	$ 3,419	$ 2,925	$ 2,277	$ 1,902	$ 2,054	$ 2,370
Included in above expense categories are:												
Depreciation[1]	n.a.	n.a.	$ 795	$ 703	$ 659	$ 649	$ 657	$ 621	$ 590	$ 549	$ 521	$ 480
Depletion[1]	n.a.	n.a.	136	19	24	119	245	302	245	350	201	n.a.

Note: The above statement excludes the operations of Opaco Lumber and Realty Company, which is to be held by its present owners. The operations of Columbia Steamship Company, Limited, which have also been excluded, are not significant.

[1]Depreciation and depletion as shown above are for the consolidated operations of the company and accordingly include certain indeterminate amounts of depreciation and depletion attributable to the operations of Opaco Lumber and Realty Company, which has been excluded from all other account categories.

Ever since entering the paper industry, Boise Cascade has had a keen interest in the fine paper segment of the paper industry, and accordingly, has had an interest in acquiring the Columbia River Paper Company for the past three years. Columbia River operates two fine paper mills at Salem, Oregon, and Vancouver, Washington, which have a combined capacity of 300 tons per day (see Exhibit 1). Columbia also owns in fee over one billion feet of prime standing timber located on approximately 87,000 acres of timberland in the states of Oregon and Washington. Columbia River Paper Company income statements for the period 1951–1960, and its balance sheet for the year ended December 31, 1960, are presented as Exhibits 2 and 3.

Columbia is not in the lumber or plywood business as is Boise Cascade, and consequently has had to rely upon purchased by-product wood chips from others and whole logs for its raw material. Over the years Columbia has taken very little of its raw material from its own timberlands, preferring to hold them in reserve for possible future needs. Under Boise Cascade ownership, the Columbia mills can rely for their future needs upon not only the Columbia lands but the lands owned by Boise Cascade in the Valsetz area and the timber from Boise Cascade's fee ownership on over 550,000 acres in the area immediately to the east of the Cascade Mountains. Acquisition would permit Boise Cascade to liquidate the mature timber now standing on the Columbia timberland, thereby rapidly reducing the debt incurred in the acquisition and releasing additional acres for new timber growth. In addition, as Boise Cascade replaces the hemlock logs now consumed by Columbia with by-product wood chips from its sawmill and plywood operations, the raw material costs for the Columbia operation will be reduced. Boise Cascade's current consumption of logs is in excess of one-half billion board feet per year. Approximately one-third of these logs are furnished by Boise Cascade's fee owned timberlands.

Boise Cascade has conducted an intensive investigation of the Columbia River operation for the past eight months. Following are a few of the principal advantages accruing to Boise Cascade from this proposed acquisition:

1. The fine paper industry is a stable industry and a growth industry, and this is particularly true in the western United States. The acquisition of Columbia River as an existing operation is the least expensive way to enter this industry.
2. The products of Columbia River are relatively immune from the vicissitudes of the building materials industry. Because Boise Cascade is now heavily committed to the building materials industry, the addition of Columbia River would provide us with a desirable offset to the cyclical and seasonal fluctuations in the demand and prices for our building materials products.
3. A substantial portion of the timber standing on Boise Cascade lands and in the general areas of Boise Cascade's present operations is unusually valuable raw material for paper pulp. The highest value for this material is *not* obtained in using it to manufacture coarse paper. But in contrast, the use of this material in the manufacture of fine paper will enable us to develop maximum economic value from these white wood species.

exhibit 3

COLUMBIA RIVER PAPER COMPANY

Balance Sheet as of December 1, 1960
(000 omitted)

Assets

Current

Demand deposits and cash on hand	$ 2,486
Time deposits	5,550
Short-term securities at cost and accrued interest	2,643
United States Treasury bonds	24
Customers' accounts and notes receivable	2,928
Other receivables	31
Inventories	
Finished merchandise	2,116
Work in process	248
Raw materials and supplies	3,037
Total current assets	19,063

Investments in capital stocks

Affiliated companies	614*
Nonaffiliated companies	147

Property, plant, and equipment

Buildings, equipment, and facilities	24,545
Less: allowance for depreciation	(12,461)
Timber and timberland, net of depletion	8,967
Other land	825

Other assets

Prepaid expenses	236
Claims, deposits, advances, etc.	418
	$37,354

Liabilities

Current

Trade accounts payable	$ 1,160
Accrued expenses	
Taxes, other than taxes on income	158
Wages	215
Dividends payable	373
Federal and state taxes on income	582
Total current liabilities	1,090
	$3,205

Capital

Capital stock	$ 4,626
Surplus	
Capital	472
Earned	29,051
	$37,354

*This account represents the company's investment in Opaco Lumber and Realty Company and Columbia Steamship Company, Limited.

4. The addition of the Columbia River timber and timberland will provide our profitable Valsetz operation with permanent life, whereas at the present time it faces probable early liquidation with the cutout of its limited timber reserves.
5. The acquisition of Columbia River will increase the net earnings accruing to the Boise Cascade common shareholders.

While the acquisition of Columbia River is a very substantial undertaking for Boise Cascade, and would result in a very large additional debt burden, the unique advantages resulting from the acquisition justify its undertaking.

During the past five years Boise Cascade has expended over $37 million of capital to improve and expand its operations. The opportunities to make these expenditures on an attractive return on investment basis have been provided by the growth of the past five years. In 1962 most of the major projects which have been undertaken in recent years will have been completed, and accordingly our rate of capital expenditures will drop substantially, as well as our debt.

Also during our recent years of growth, we have improved and streamlined our organization. The improvements made in recent years and the basic strength of the corporation have been quite vigorously tested during the past year and one-half with the severe recession of the building materials industry. In spite of substantial reductions in demand and prices for certain principal product lines, we have been able to stay well in the black and continue with internal improvements. Consequently we feel that we are now in an excellent position organizationally and financially to undertake the Columbia River acquisition.

Method of Acquisition

We have reached agreement with the management of Columbia River on the form and price of the acquisition, subject to further approvals. This agreement provides for a purchase price for the Columbia common stock of $1,765 per share. The total outstanding shares are 34,028, making the total purchase commitment for the common stock $60,059,000.

Included in the acquisition is a subsidiary of Columbia River (Opaco) which owns valuable land and a retail lumber yard operation in Las Vegas. Studies made by Boise Cascade and by an independent appraiser indicate that the liquidation value of Opaco is substantially above the $2.2 million included in the over-all purchace price to cover the addition of Opaco.

Columbia River also has outstanding, in addition to its common stock, 47,768 shares of preferred stock. This stock is callable at a price of $102.50 per share, or approximately $4.9 million. We plan to call this stock with cash provided by the liquidation of certain quick assets now owned by Columbia.

The proposed method of providing the funds required to acquire the Columbia common stock is outlined below:

Cash Needed

		Thousands
Purchase price of Columbia common (34,028 shares at $1,765)		$60,059
Less: assets to be immediately liquidated		
Short-term securities	$7,890	
Other assets including Opaco	3,067	
	$10,957	
Less: cost of calling outstanding preferred stock at $102.50	4,898	
Net internal funds provided by Columbia		6,059
Cash to be provided for the acquisition		$54,000

Cash Provided

	Thousands
Long-term borrowing	$49,500
Sale of preferred stock	4,500
Funds provided	$54,000

In order to isolate the financing of the Columbia River acquisition from Boise Cascade's present financing, we have formed a new wholly owned subsidiary— Boise Cascade Paper Corporation (a Delaware corporation). This corporation will acquire the common stock of the Columbia River Paper Company. Columbia River will then be merged into the Boise Cascade Paper Corporation. Boise Cascade will exchange certain assets which complement the assets of Columbia River for equity in the new subsidiary. These assets will be the 28,000 acres of timberland and 120 million board feet of timber now owned by Boise Cascade's Valsetz division. In addition, Boise Cascade proposes to contribute either its Valsetz plywood operation located in Valsetz, Oregon, and its ownership in the Valley and Siletz Railroad, or in the alternative, Boise Cascade will use one of its present subsidiaries, Ames Harris Neville, as the acquiring subsidiary. The present book value of all of the Valsetz assets, including associated working capital, is $4.2 million, and the fair value is approximately $9 million. If the alternative course is pursued, the book value of the Ames Harris assets, together with the Valsetz land and timber, is $4.3 million, and the fair value is also approximately $9 million.

As additional equity, the new subsidiary will issue $4.5 million of preferred stock. This preferred stock will be sold as a private placement through Blyth & Co., Inc., and be retired by Boise Cascade over a period of seven years, starting in 1964, by a sinking fund agreement. This preferred stock will carry a dividend rate of 6% or less. The additional funds needed to complete the acquisition will be provided through the liquidation of unessential assets in Columbia River and through the borrowing of $49.5 million.

Of the $49.5 million borrowed, it is proposed that $29 million be provided in the form of seven year bank loans carrying an interest rate of 5½%. These bank loans can be rapidly reduced through the liquidation of the mature timber now standing on the Columbia River and Valsetz timberlands. Two banks, the Chase Manhattan Bank and The Bank of America, have already indicated a strong interest in providing the bank portion of the total borrowing.

The $20.5 million of additional borrowings are to be provided in the form of a long-term insurance loan, with payments to be made over a ten year period starting in the eighth year after the bank debt has been retired.

The security available for the $49.5 million of borrowings is:

1. The mature timber of Columbia and Valsetz lands, having a present wholesale value of $26 million and a retail value of $37.5 million.
2. The Columbia and Valsetz soil and young growth, having a present value of $8 million, estimated value in 1972 of $15.8 million, and an estimated value in 1982 of $25 million.
3. The asset values of the two fine paper mills of Columbia, having a conservative present value of $25 million, and the asset values of the Valsetz Plywood Plant, together with the Valley and Siletz Railroad, which have an estimated asset value of $2.5 million.
4. A take or pay cutting contract by Boise Cascade covering the Columbia and Valsetz timber.

The Boise Cascade Paper Corporation will also have $4.5 million of preferred stock equity and net working capital of approximately $9 million.

The consent of the John Hancock Mutual Life Insurance Company will be required to permit Boise Cascade to form the new subsidiary and transfer certain of its assets to this new company. This matter has already been discussed with John Hancock, and a formal consent has already been submitted to them. Boise Cascade's take or pay cutting contract with its subsidiary will provide to the Boise Cascade Paper Corporation a minimum of $2.9 million per year for ten years.

Columbia River Assets

The Columbia assets acquired in the proposed transaction can be considered to be broken down into four principal categories: the paper mills together with the necessary working capital, the standing timber, the timberland, and the other miscellaneous assets to be liquidated.

Paper mills. The paper mills, in our opinion, are worth $25 million. The working capital needed to operate these mills, including a very adequate cash balance of $2.5 million, is approximately $7 million. The earnings from the operation of the mills alone are conservatively projected to amount to from $4 to $6 million before tax per year over the next 15 years. Because of the stability and future growth in the fine paper industry, this income is usually reliable and, together with depreciation, can easily service interest and debt retirement as well as substantial capital improvements. In our cash flow projections we have built-in yearly capital expenditures of $1.2 million. It is our opinion that expenditures of this amount are more than adequate to maintain the Columbia mills in a peak competitive condition. This is particularly true in view of the heavy capital expenditures made by Columbia itself in recent years. Our capital projections have also provided for an effluent pond and a recovery system for the Vancouver mill of Columbia. The need for these expenditures is somewhat questionable at this time, but in order to be conservative, liberal estimates have been included in the estimate for capital requirements for future years.

Standing timber. The value allocated to the standing timber of Columbia in our projections is $14 million. The retail value for this timber, which we conservatively estimate can be obtained over the next ten years (to be confirmed by independent foresters), is approximately $33 million. The $14 million allocated cost for the timber amounts to a stumpage value of slightly less than $12 per thousand. We feel that the liquidation of this timber can be accomplished in seven years or less, but our projections have provided the flexibility of a ten year liquidation. It should be pointed out that, at our cost basis on this timber, the entire value could easily be sold at any time we wish to liquidate the $25.5 million of debt associated with the Columbia timber. The immediate or wholesale liquidation of the Columbia land and timber (not including Valsetz land and timber) is estimated at $28.6 million.[1] The corresponding present liquidation value estimated for the Valsetz land and timber is $5.4 million.

Timberland. Because of our Valsetz operation, we are quite familiar with the Columbia land and timber, much of which lies immediately adjacent to our Valsetz holdings. The Columbia and Valsetz timberland represents some of the finest timberland in the nation. The value allocated to the Columbia timberland in our computations is approximately $6.6 million. We have asked the independent forestry consulting firm of Mason, Bruce & Girard of Portland, Oregon, who are familiar with the Columbia River timber and timberland, to prepare for us estimates of growth values on the Columbia and Valsetz lands over the next 20 years. It is their opinion that the soil and young growth values of the Columbia and Valsetz holdings combined is $8 million at present. Since most of the mature and merchantable timber for both acreages lies on a small percentage of the total acreage (approximately 30%), much of the timberland area is

---

[1] All estimates to be confirmed by independent consulting firm.

already well stocked with regrowth. During the cutout period of the mature timber, the acres involved in this cutout will not produce very much growth over the decade from 1962 to 1972. However, after this cutout, all of the acres involved will be producing incremental value. For this reason Mason, Bruce & Girard estimates the incremental growth value for the decade between 1972 and 1982 to be somewhat higher than for the period of the next ten years. They have developed an estimated incremental value of growth added to the timberland for the period of 1962 to 1972 of $783,000 per year. This means that in 1972 the land value will have increased from $8 million to about $15.8 million. The incremental growth value for the period between 1972 and 1982 is estimated to be $9.2 million. This additional growth would make the land value $25 million in 1982.

In establishing these values, no recognition has been given to the effect of inflation or to the fact that scarcity of privately owned timberland is likely to drive up timberland values in the next 20 years. Additionally, no recognition has been given to the fact that thinning might well produce higher growth rates than those used in establishing the values indicated. It should also be noted that the growth values have been substantially discounted from retail values. The discount used ranged from a high of 73% for younger age classifications to 47% for the older classifications. This appears to be a very conservative discount.

In the income projections which we have developed for the Columbia operation, we have given no recognition to income from timber growth, since the land or timber would have to be sold to realize these values. But it should be noted that the Columbia and Valsetz lands represent one of the special and unique values in the proposed transaction. Additionally, they are readily salable at any time in total or in part.

Miscellaneous assets to be liquidated. These assets exist in two principal categories: (1) Assets which can and should be immediately liquidated, such as investments, notes receivable, life insurance policies, and Opaco, amounting to a conservative liquidation value of approximately $3.1 million, and (2) Miscellaneous real estate and assets in the Oregon area not needed for the Columbia operations. A conservative liquidation estimate for these assets is $1 million. However, we estimate that it might take as much as a year to accomplish this liquidation.

While the acquisition of Columbia River, for cash, is a major undertaking for a company of the size of Boise Cascade, we strongly feel that the important advantages justify the acquisition. And although the debt appears very large in the total picture, a major portion of this debt is attributable to the acquisition of mature timber which can be safely and quickly liquidated with margins to spare at any time over the next ten years, either at retail values or at wholesale values which would retire more than their proportionate share of debt.

Boise Cascade Corporation (A-4):
1962-1963

Following disappointing earnings results in 1960 and 1961, Boise Cascade recovered dramatically in 1962 and 1963. Net income in 1962 of $5 million was up 66% from 1961, resulting in an increase from $.82/share in 1961 to $1.35/share in 1962. Sales for this same period increased 27% from $137 million to $175 million.

The upward trend continued in 1963, when the company announced net income of $7.4 million on sales of $218 million, representing gains of 46% and 25% respectively, from the comparable period in 1962. Per share earnings increased from $1.35 in 1962 to $1.85 in 1963. Financial statements for 1962 and 1963 are presented as Exhibits 1 and 2. Exhibit 3 provides operating results by product group.

Commenting on the gains made in 1962 and 1963, Mr. Hansberger said:

> . . . we have absorbed the shock of a drastic drop in lumber prices, and in addition, we have absorbed the initial costs of placing in operation many major new plants. Boise Cascade is now soundly positioned upon an expanding product and earnings base. This rising trend in our results should continue in the future. A principal reason for this self-assurance is that our growth has exposed countless opportunities for self-improvement. We are determined to continue to take full advantage of these opportunities.

MAJOR EVENTS OF 1962

In March of 1962, Boise's board of directors approved the purchase of the Columbia River Paper Company, effective April 1 of that year. Columbia River was acquired by a

---

wholly owned subsidiary of Boise Cascade, the Boise Cascade Paper Corporation, as proposed in the Columbia River Paper Company case. The purchase of Columbia River for a cash price of approximately $64 million had been financed through Boise Cascade Paper Corporation wholly with borrowed funds.[1] These funds were obtained principally from four banks (The Chase Manhattan Bank, Bank of America N.T. & S.A., First National Bank of Chicago, and First National City Bank) and from two insurance companies (New York Life Insurance Company and John Hancock Mutual Life Insurance Company).

In May, 1962, Boise began operation of its new Yakima plywood mill, which was said to be one of the most efficient in the industry. The addition of this mill, which increased the company's plywood capacity from 59 million to 130 million square feet per year, reportedly enabled Boise Cascade to make more economic use of certain types of timber in central Washington than if these logs had been converted into lumber.

The company also began a major sawmill modernization program at Yakima which was scheduled for completion in February, 1963. The program included addition of a third head rig (band saw) and other improvements at a total cost of $2 million.

At Emmett, Idaho, company engineers built and installed a pushbutton lumber grader and trimmer, reportedly a major advance in lumber manufacturing technology. The system allowed a worker to punch, trim, and grade instructions into an electronic memory as the lumber passed by him on a conveyor. Subsequently, the stored information activated a trimmer which automatically cut the lumber to size and a grade printer which marked the grade on each board.

The major event at the Wallula paperboard mill was the completion of construction which increased the rated capacity from 200 to 375 tons per day in

---

[1] The equity base for the formation of Boise Cascade Paper Corporation was provided primarily by transferring to it the assets of Boise Cascade's Valsetz plywood mill (valued at about $5 million). This mill planned to use Columbia River's timber to sustain its operation. Boise Cascade added further to this base by borrowing $4,500,000 from the Chase Manhattan Bank and in turn loaning it to Boise Cascade Paper Corporation (to be subordinated to all other debt). Boise Cascade also entered into a timber cutting contract with Boise Cascade Paper which guaranteed the latter a cash inflow of about $37 million over the next several years from the harvesting of timber.

With its credit thus established, Boise Cascade Paper Corporation borrowed $49,700,000 from four banks and two insurance companies. About $30 million of the total was with the banks, at 5¾%, with installments to be paid over seven to eight years. These loans were secured by the timber cutting contracts previously mentioned and would be liquidated as the timber was harvested. The remaining $20 million was insurance company money, at 5½%, to be paid over an 18 year period. This portion of the loan was secured by the physical assets of Columbia River, notably the two paper mills. To complete its requirements for the purchase of Columbia River, Boise Cascade Paper borrowed an additional $10 million of short-term, unsecured funds from the Chase Manhattan Bank. By the end of 1962, the indebtedness related to the acquisition had been reduced by $21 million. The retirement was accomplished by using excess liquid assets of Columbia River to the amount of $9 million; by selling nonoperating properties of Columbia for $5 million; and by applying $7 million of funds generated under the terms of the timber cutting contract.

exhibit 1

BOISE CASCADE CORPORATION (A-4)

Statement of Consolidated Income
(for the years ended December 31)

	1963	*1962*
Income		
Net sales	$218,095,935	$175,074,534
Other income, less deductions	1,264,918	940,830
	$219,360,853	$176,015,364
Costs and expenses		
Cost of goods sold	$166,786,114	$136,349,802
Depreciation	6,846,238	5,028,154
Depletion	3,197,774	1,787,041
Selling, administrative, and general expense	26,827,010	21,599,022
Interest expense	4,314,374	4,022,258
Federal and state income taxes	4,000,000	2,174,000
	$211,971,510	$170,960,277
Net Income	$ 7,389,343	$ 5,055,087
Net income per common share	$1.85	$1.35
Cash dividends per common share	.40	.40
Net income as a % of common shareholders' equity	11.43%	9.57%
Sales volume		
Paper, thousand tons	245	180
Lumber, million board feet	635	600
Plywood, million square feet (3/8")	259	117

Note: Other income includes gains of $500,000, net of income taxes, from operations disposed of in 1963, and $305,000, net of income taxes, from operations disposed of and property sold and leased back in 1962.

January. Startup problems, related to speeding up the paper machine substantially, limited the mill output throughout most of the year. Nevertheless, the added capacity resulted in an output of 108,000 tons for the full year, compared with 79,505 tons in 1961.

Capital expenditures for the year totaled $8.4 million, $4.8 million of which went into lumber and plywood operations. Softwood lumber production for the year rose to 600 million board feet from 579 million board feet in 1961, despite the phasing out of three marginal sawmills at South Fork, Colorado, and Goldendale and Kettle Falls, Washington. At year end, the company's paper capacity, including Columbia River, had grown to 250,000 tons per year. In a continuing

exhibit 2

BOISE CASCADE CORPORATION (A-4)

Financial Condition

(as of December 31, 1962 and 1963: in thousands)

	1963	*1962*
Working capital		
Current assets		
Cash	$ 5,213	$ 7,077
Receivables, net	27,221	23,633
Mortgage loans held for resale	2,892	804
Inventories	36,027	32,809
Total current assets	$ 71,353	$ 64,323
Current liabilities		
Notes payable to bank and current portion of long-term debt	$ 11,794	$ 13,079
Accounts payable	12,505	6,110
Accrued liabilities	8,454	8,060
Federal and state income taxes	2,531	1,112
Total current liabilities	$ 35,284	$ 28,361
Total working capital	$ 36,069	$ 35,962
Fixed assets		
Timber and timberlands, at cost less depletion	$ 22,685	$ 25,395
Real estate held for resale, at cost	--	845
Property, plant, and equipment, net	66,362	58,925
Other assets	5,339	3,255
Total fixed assets	$ 94,386	$ 88,420
Total working capital and fixed assets	$130,455	$124,382
Sources of working capital and fixed assets		
Other liabilities	$ 1,938	--
Long-term debt	63,815	$ 71,548
Shareholders' equity	64,663	52,834
Total sources of working capital and fixed assets	$130,456	$124,382

exhibit 3

BOISE CASCADE CORPORATION (A-4)

Operating Performance by Product Line, 1962

Net Sales as a Per Cent of Company Sales Before Intercompany Eliminations

	1963	1962
Lumber and plywood	33.6%	31.8%
Coarse paper	17.7	13.6
Fine paper	15.6	10.8
Wholesale	23.5%	16.7
Retail		15.8
Concrete products	4.3	6.3
Miscellaneous	5.3	4.9

Net Income of a Per Cent of Product Line Sales Before Taxes

	1963	1962
Lumber and plywood	7.5%	6.7%
Coarse paper	9.4	9.4
Fine paper	16.1	10.9
Wholesale	1.9	1.2
Retail		4.1
Concrete products	(0.4)	(0.5)
Miscellaneous	(1.2)	.7

Return on Investment—Net Income Before Taxes as a Per Cent of Assets at Book Value

	1963	1962
Lumber and plywood	13.8%	10.7%
Coarse paper	15.2	11.2
Fine paper	14.3	11.6
Wholesale	6.1	4.7
Retail		9.4
Concrete products	(1.0)	(1.2)
Miscellaneous	(3.2)	1.3

effort to "weed-out" operations which could not produce an adequate return on investment, 18 retail yards were sold or closed in 1962. The addition of two new yards during the year brought the total number to 113.

MAJOR EVENTS OF 1963

Late in February Boise Cascade announced the acquisition of the assets of the Columbia Envelope Company of Chicago in exchange for 75,000 shares of Boise Cascade common stock. Columbia Envelope produced a wide line of envelopes for business and institutional users. Its plant facilities, which were highly automated, operated 24 hours a day, six days a week, to produce about 36 million units each week.

Columbia Envelope Company differed from other manufacturers because it produced most of its envelopes by the "side seam" method, a converting process that enabled envelopes to be made directly from paper rolls. Most envelopes were manufactured by the "diagonal seam" method in which the rolls of paper had to be converted to sheets prior to being made into envelopes. In addition to the economy of omitting the sheeting requirement, the side seam method reportedly was a substantially faster and lower cost process. Columbia's President, Mr. Arthur Bermingham, Jr., had designed and built the necessary equipment, which was believed to be unique in the industry and gave the company its competitive advantage.

In 1962, the Columbia Envelope Company purchased 8,000 tons of paper, 6,500 tons of which were of grades produced by Boise's fine paper mills. By 1965, Boise management planned to supply the envelope operation with at least 5,000 tons of its paper requirements from the company's own mills.

Based on the $23.50 per share market price of Boise Cascade common stock at the time the acquisition was negotiated (Jan. 7, 1963), the purchase price for Columbia Envelope was about $1.76 million. The $200,000 excess of this price over the value of the assets was to be amortized against income over a period of about six years. Columbia Envelope's net income, which had been $160,000 in 1961 and $205,000 in 1962, was projected to reach $225,000 (net of amortization) by 1963.

In May, 1963, Boise Cascade purchased a plywood mill from Georgia-Pacific Corporation for "in excess of a million dollars" cash. This plant at Independence, Oregon (near Columbia River's timber), increased Boise's annual softwood plywood capacity by 140 million square feet. The sale resulted from Georgia-Pacific's having depleted its timber needed to support the mill, whereas Boise had substantial timber holdings nearby.

May also saw the closing of the Hallack and Howard millwork operation in Denver. In 1962, this operation lost close to $500,000 and management saw no potential in its continued existence.

In June several of Boise Cascade's major competitors in lumber and plywood were shut down by a strike. For several months thereafter Boise realized increased prices for its lumber and plywood output. In July and August, plywood prices were up about $20 per thousand square feet (to $85) and the price of pine lumber had increased from $86 to $90 per thousand board feet. By September the strike was over, and plywood prices quickly returned to $64 per thousand square feet. Lumber prices, which had not risen as high as plywood prices, eased somewhat less.

Boise continued to expand its plywood capacity in 1963, announcing in September that it would build a new plywood mill at Elgin, Oregon, and expand its Yakima plywood mill. The Elgin facility was to cost $2,500,000 and would require six months to build. When finished, it would produce, on a ⅜ inch basis, about six million feet of plywood per month. The Yakima mill expansion represented an investment of $1 million and would add about three million square feet per month (⅜ inch basis) to the mill's existing output of six million feet per month.

In a joint statement with the Crown Zellerbach Corporation, late in 1963, Boise officials announced their intent to purchase Crown's St. Helen's Pulp and Paper Company properties, subject to FTC approval. The St. Helen's facilities, which consisted of an integrated pulp and paper mill, with accompanying timberlands, produced a range of printing and sanitary papers. Crown Zellerbach had been under attack by the Justice Department and the FTC since acquiring the property in 1953. After a lengthy court fight, Crown was ordered to divest. Boise was the apparently preferred purchaser, providing the FTC ruled that such an acquisition was in the public interest.

Boise Cascade moved into the international picture in late 1963 when it signed a contract to provide management for the Industria Papelera Centio Americana mill at Escuintla, Guatemala. The Guatemalan mill operated two paper machines producing about 35 tons of mixed paper grades a day. The mill did not manufacture its own pulp. Industria Papelera was owned by the Chase International Investment Corporation, the Central National Corporation, and two Guatemalan families. The management contract included an option whereby Boise Cascade might acquire a substantial stock interest in the company. According to Boise management, "the venture should provide excellent learning experience as well as an opportunity to develop a profitable Central American business."

Near the end of 1963, Boise Cascade added nine paperboard converting plants and a 53% interest in a jute mill [2] to its existing operations. The jute mill, located at Monroe, Michigan, and five of the converting plants (located at Monroe, Michigan; Waterbury and Stratford, Connecticut; Newton, North Carolina; and LaPorte, Indiana) were gained through acquisition of the Waterbury Corrugated Container Company through an exchange of stock. In separate acquisitions, the company added converting plants in St. Paul, Minnesota; Dallas, Texas; and Los Angeles. In November, 1963, the company started up a newly built converting plant in Kansas City. Through the addition of these facilities, Boise was attempting to enter selectively packaging markets where the company was not yet an important factor.

As Boise Cascade moved into 1964, it did so with confidence. This attitude is best expressed in the following statement made late in 1963 by Mr. Hansberger before the Los Angeles security analysts:

As a newly constituted inhabitant of the forest products industry, Boise Cascade is a very immature company which cut its teeth and trained its people in the midst of some of the toughest competition seen in the building materials

---

[2] Pulp and paper mill that produced paperboard from waste paper. Paperboard produced by this process lacks the strength of paperboard produced from wood fibers, but is adequate for many packaging requirements.

industry and in the paper industry for many years. For this reason, although the net income of the pulp and paper industry as a whole for the first six months of this year declined 1% over the same period last year, we were able to carve out an additional share of the market for our paper products and increase their contribution to our total sales and profits.

Accordingly, we feel that from now on all signs point up, and we are much aware that we have only begun to develop our potential. An indication of this is our present earnings trend, which should continue in the future. Our newness makes precise earnings predictions difficult, but it appears that our earnings for 1963 should well exceed those for 1962.

We serve two basic industries, home construction and paper. Both are huge industries, and we are a tiny factor in both. But most significant to us is the fact that both are growth industries. Boise Cascade is uniquely well structured and positioned to participate in this growth.

But let me give you some specific observations about our future.

We are still burning waste wood at five of our twelve mills and much waste wood in our timber lands. Consequently, our paper operations will grow substantially in the future. We now operate an envelope factory in Chicago and a paper mill in Guatemala and we are looking toward becoming even more national and international in our production and sale of paper and paper products. Such growth will better utilize our timber resources and make us increasingly effective against our larger competitors.

I'm sure that you have heard how extremely competitive and how overbuilt the plywood industry has become, and it has. But the fact is that a modern, automated plywood plant is a money maker at the lowest plywood prices and utilizes at a profit logs which lose money in a sawmill.

We have four modern plywood plants now, and we are planning the construction of two more.

The per capita consumption of lumber is declining, and competition from Canada is impressive. And yet we are optimistic about the lumber business. This is not because we expect to reverse the declining per capita use of lumber, nor do we expect the Canadians to withdraw from American markets in a sudden wave of international altruism. Instead we expect that there will be much less lumber produced in the future. Many lumber producers have become noncompetitive today and are leaving the industry, since they are primarily producers of a single product. This trend will accelerate. In addition, a greater part of our timber resources will be much more properly used in the manufacture of paper and plywood, leaving fewer logs for sawmills. But these logs will be much better suited for lumber and capable of producing better grades of lumber. Today, a high proportion of the lumber flowing through a sawmill is sold at a substantial loss.

Better lumber and less lumber will command better and more stable prices and find more sustained acceptance in the market place.

An additional factor will be the production of more advanced end products from lumber. Today, lumber is a coarse raw material for many other end products and is shipped to remote markets at high freight rates. And the freight must be paid on that portion discarded as waste by the converter customer. In the future, more of this lumber will be fabricated into more sophisticated products having a higher value per pound before being shipped to distant markets.

We have made a start in this direction with the addition of finger-joining to make long pieces out of short pieces, laminated wood beams, wood windows, furniture parts, and prefabricated home components. We are far ahead of the Canadians in these areas and with our market know-how, we can increase this lead.

Packaging will have increasing competition from substitute materials. In order to prepare for this challenge, and to lead the way, we are currently manufacturing and developing new polystyrene foam packaging and building materials at our Auburn, Washington, facility.

Our development activities have already produced a number of profitable new products and processes and we are enthusiastic about accelerated results in this area. Our wholesale, retail, and housing components divisions provide us with a quick application for new developments.

But, most of all, we base our future on our people. Our unique approach to the acquisition and development of our people has already provided us with a youthful and ambitious organization. In the face of tough established competition, they created the framework of a sound new forest products corporation while they were yet greenhorns. They ought to be hard to beat now that they have had a little experience.

Boise Cascade Corporation (B):

Management Philosophy; Corporate Organization [1]

INTRODUCTION

Boise Cascade, with Mr. Robert V. Hansberger as president, operated under a concept which he called "centralized decentralization." In 1965, following a series of reorganizations and consolidations of previously separate groups and operations, the company was divided into five autonomous operating units: the Timber and Wood Products Division, the Paper Division, the Merchandising Division, the Mando Division, and the Kingsberry Homes Division. (See Exhibit 1.) Accountability for operations was wholly in the hands of the respective Division vice presidents. Each division was accounted for separately as a "profit center" and was evaluated on the basis of its return on the dollars employed by it.

Hansberger believed that not only was it important for each division to have independent operating authority and profit responsibility, but also that the activities of the various divisions should be closely coordinated in order to maximize overall corporate earnings. He indicated that he had tried to build a strong central staff to assure integrated corporate response without destroying the independence of the operating divisions. He and three staff officers—Mr. William D. Eberle (vice president and secretary), Mr. Robert W. Halliday (vice president and treasurer), and Mr. Don J. Black (development director) —formed what Hansberger called the "president's office." Any member of this group, in the absence of the others, could speak for, and commit, the entire company in operating matters. Hansberger explained that the "president's office" concept provided a vehicle for swift confirmation of decisions which was so essential to a company that was moving as rapidly as Boise Cascade. He was quick to emphasize, however, that there was within this concept no intent to usurp the authority of the group vice presidents. "To the contrary," he

---

© 1965 by the Board of Trustees of the Leland Stanford Junior University.

[1] Organization includes units which are not discussed until Boise Cascade Corporation (A-5), page 474.

exhibit 1

BOISE CASCADE CORPORATION (B)

Organization (1965)

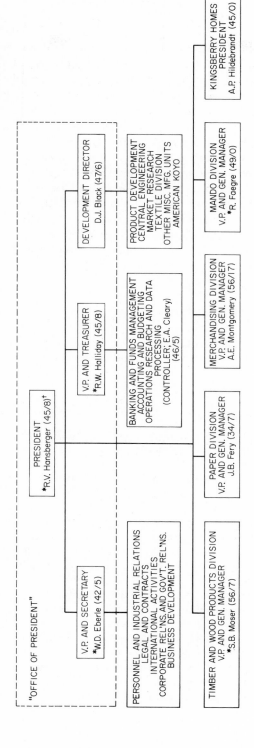

PRESIDENT
*R.V. Hansberger (45/8)†

"OFFICE OF PRESIDENT"

V.P. AND SECRETARY
*W.D. Eberle (42/5)

V.P. AND TREASURER
*R.W. Halliday (45/8)

DEVELOPMENT DIRECTOR
D.J. Black (47/6)

PERSONNEL AND INDUSTRIAL RELATIONS
LEGAL AND CONTRACTS
INTERNATIONAL ACTIVITIES
CORPORATE REL'NS. AND GOV'T. REL'NS.
BUSINESS DEVELOPMENT

BANKING AND FUNDS MANAGEMENT
ACCOUNTING AND BUDGETING
OPERATIONS RESEARCH AND DATA
PROCESSING
(CONTROLLER; E.A. Cleary)
(46/5)

PRODUCT DEVELOPMENT
CENTRAL ENGINEERING
MARKET RESEARCH
TEXTILE DIVISION
OTHER MISC. MFG. UNITS
AMERICAN KOYO

TIMBER AND WOOD PRODUCTS DIVISION
V.P. AND GEN. MANAGER
*S.B. Moser (56/7)

PAPER DIVISION
V.P. AND GEN. MANAGER
J.B. Fery (34/7)

MERCHANDISING DIVISION
V.P. AND GEN. MANAGER
A.E. Montgomery (56/17)

MANDO DIVISION
V.P. AND GEN. MANAGER
*R. Faegre (49/0)

KINGSBERRY HOMES
PRESIDENT
A.P. Hildebrandt (45/0)

* Directors.

† First number after name indicates age; second number indicates years with Boise Cascade.

indicated, "we try to encourage independence on the part of our people. Our purpose in corporate headquarters is to guide the direction of the company as a whole and to establish a climate where things get done quickly."

Although the men who operated Boise Cascade, and the staff which supported them, represented a wide range of age and experience, the youth and vigor of the organization was apparent to any observer. The average age of the company's top management was 46 in 1965, and the average age of the company's 166 key managers was 43. Of these men, 26 were originally with the Boise Payette Lumber Company. Another 75 came to the company from business schools, colleges, and other outside sources, and 65 were brought in with acquired companies.

Mr. Hansberger explained that, throughout Boise Cascade's acquisition program, he had consistently taken the stand that the personnel of the acquired companies would be given every opportunity to show their abilities. He indicated that, in almost every acquisition, he was gratified with the way in which the people had adapted to Boise's way of operating and had been able to make significant contributions.

MANAGEMENT PHILOSOPHY

Boise Cascade's management philosophy was closely tied to four interrelated concepts: corporate objectives, corporate organization, individualism, and salary administration.

Corporate Objectives

Mr. Hansberger explained that the first thing he did when he joined Boise Payette was to look at a statement of the company's objectives.

> It [the statement of objectives] took about two pages and consisted of a list. It said things like the purpose of the company is "to provide maximum service" or "to sell highest quality products to our customers" or "to be nice to employees." I think somewhere in the list there was something said about making money or return on investment. They [owners and management] were good citizens—very much so—and this was consistent with the concept that Boise Payette was a family company. Well, we felt, or "I" felt, at the time—I hope it is "we" now—that in this economic warfare which is business, to be successful you have to have a pretty single-minded purpose. If you try to pursue a whole list of objectives you end up compromising in almost every one or every pair of them. And the people in the organization really don't have any yardstick for performance unless you give them an overriding objective to which all of the other things are subordinated. So we tried to define what it was that we wanted most to do and we came up with this statement: *we wanted to consistently obtain a maximum return on investment.* Now there are a few compromises involved in that too, but it is pretty simple, pretty direct, and that is all there is to it. And

all these other things that we believe in—good public relations, good relations with our employees, growth, good quality products and service—are all subordinate to this one objective. The compromises that we make, then, are in the second level, and we try to make them so that they consistently give us maximum return on our investment.

Now this is why we got into integrated growth. Eight years ago integration was one of the ways to achieve a better return on investment. At that time we were burning up waste wood, and not getting the real economic value out of the company's forests. Paper production was a very valuable method by which we could get this return; but to get it we had to grow first.

At the beginning, I don't think we adequately merchandised this change in concept of objectives. We were too busy acquiring companies that had timber manufacturing facilities. Even now, I think the change on the surface appears to be slight and it looks like just a rearranging of the priorities on the list. I would like to think, however, that this change is very fundamental.

At the end of 1960 and early in 1961, we held a series of meetings with our division people to help sell the change in concept and, furthermore, to learn about division problems and their relationships within the corporate group. In all of these meetings we tried hard to emphasize the meaning of the return on investment concept. And, I should add that we put in the word "consistently" because it is in that word that we find the value of public relations and so on. We don't like our people to do something in one particular year if it hurts us in the future. We want this whole thing to be consistent.

We believed that this concept in itself was probably the best one that would identify the decisions that our people made with the appetites of the people who own the company. And these were increasingly becoming public shareholders at that time. We now have over 15,000 shareholders compared to 300 eight years ago.

Another thing that we want people to recognize is that they can get good returns on their investment not only by improving profit but by shrinking investment. In decentralized operations we don't know where the poorly used assets are. Our foremen, plant managers, superintendents, and group managers are in a much better position to know when an asset is not being used or is being poorly used. So we want to get this concept down to them. Then, when the foreman walks by the machine he hasn't been using for a few months, we want him to say, "Well, now, our return on investment may be improved if we just get rid of this machine and get the money back into the company." There are times, for instance, when we could improve the return by taking a lower profit if the investment involved goes down faster than the profit goes down. And with the opportunities ahead for our company, the fact that these dollars come back to our corporate treasury is wonderful. Up to now, we have been so short of dollars that we have had to turn down capital projects that time after time could have made 50–100% after tax. We don't have any concern about employing our cash. In fact, right now I think we are turning down projects unless they will pay out in four or five months. Now this is working money pretty hard, and is why it is critically important that the concept of return on investment gets down in the organization. And I will repeat, I don't think we have done that job well enough yet. I don't think that it is deep enough in the organization or completely understood yet. Although the concept is very simple to state—it just takes a few words—I think its application is pretty complicated.

Mr. Hansberger went on to explain that the company's control system was set up to implement the return on investment concept. The performance of each group and its component units was measured by return on investment. Hansberger believed that this was the only way to evaluate accurately how each unit was doing. The investment figure assigned to each measurable unit was determined by assigning a "true" value to each asset and calculating the return on the total assets employed. If, for instance, the true value or the liquidation value of an asset was higher than its book value, then the manager responsible was charged with the higher amount in calculating return on assets. Corporate overhead was not allocated to the group in this process. Assistance from staff functions was available to the groups on request and charged out as used. Each month managers received a statement of operating results with their names shown next to their responsibilities. "We are really nailing down these fellows as individuals," remarked Hansberger, "and I think in the long run it will make better businessmen out of us. It will make us the same kind of businessmen that the old entrepreneurs of the past were."

Organization

According to Mr. Hansberger, Boise Cascade's organization plan was consistent with its objectives because it divided the company into measurable units, with each unit leader responsible for his return on investment. Because each manager was responsible for his own return on investment, there were occasional conflicts regarding transfer of products between units. If two groups became involved in a stalemate about transfer prices, one of the men in the office of the president would resolve the issue according to what he believed was best for the company. He explained, however, that this rarely happened. He added:

> With very few exceptions, and I think for pretty good reasons, we try to give our people freedom as to where they buy and where they sell. Our retail division, for instance, can buy from competitors of our wholesale plants. Our sawmills can sell to our own wholesale division as they see fit. But we do ask them to give first refusal to our own division. For example, if one of our sawmills in Idaho has a surplus stock of a certain kind of lumber and marks it down $10 a thousand, we ask them to talk to Morrison-Merrill, our wholesale company, first. Now, Morrison-Merrill doesn't have to buy it because they might be able to buy the same line cheaper from a competitive sawmill; it is up to Morrison-Merrill whether they buy it or not. We think that unless you do this, you can't really measure these fellows, because at the end of the year they have an alibi. You can't tell them that their job is to make maximum return on their investment and "oh, by the way, you have to sell Boise Cascade lumber." Now the

people in the groups can negotiate, and they always have a competitor to measure their negotiations against.

Occasionally we run into some real problems and actually we have more trouble in relating divisions than we do with outside competitors. Our fellows are pretty competitive. They are vying for company dollars for expansion. Thus we get into some very interesting problems, and at times we have to make an exception to our policy. In most cases, however, the differences in opinion are resolved by the group managers involved.

Another of Mr. Hansberger's organizational concepts involved the "president's office." He believed that the management of a growing company like Boise Cascade had to be capable of making quick decisions which took the entire company into account. Because the company was so spread out, however, a question of availability arose. Many times the president couldn't be reached for a decision. So Mr. Hansberger explained:

We developed a new kind of concept of what the president's office was. Today I think the president's office is thought of—not universally in the company —as four people, any one of whom can make a decision which will bind the others. If the other members of the president's office don't like the decision, they will give the man who made the decision hell. But the line man who wants the decision will get the answer quickly. The president's office consists of myself and three of our staff officers: Don Black, development director; Bob Halliday, the treasurer; and Bill Eberle, our secretary. Now each of these fellows is a specialist, and most of their decisions are made in their area of specialty. But if one of them is the only member of the corporate staff available when a decision must be made outside of his specialty, he has the authority to give an answer which is binding. Now, he must evaluate the request for a decision and it is possible that he may not feel qualified to make it. Nevertheless, over a period of time we have made a lot of decisions that otherwise would have been delayed. My job is to keep the other three fellows and myself in tune so as a group our thinking is somewhat the same, and I think we have begun to think very much alike. This doesn't mean that we don't have arguments. We have all kinds of them. But we know enough about the group philosophy so that a line man can call one of these fellows and get an answer. Now usually he will call him anyway, in his own area. If a line man has an accounting problem, he wouldn't talk to me, even though he reports to me on the chart. He would call Bob Halliday, and Bob would give him an answer, and I may never know about it. If there was a disagreement between one of these line men and one of the staff people, they have recourse to me. This happens once in a while, but not very often. It is happening less and less. But you see, when one or two of us are on the road, there is somebody here to make decisions.

We started the concept in about 1960. At first, it was very confusing. I think it is much less so now. It is quite unusual for staff people to have this much authority, and it works only if these people all live together in the same place, meet together frequently, argue together, and talk together. This we think is important and is one of the reasons why I feel our organization has centralized decentralization. I think that without coordination here, our decentralization of authority and responsibility just wouldn't work. We are finding it advantageous to have most of our division managers here, too, even though we have decentralized to them a very major responsibility for their area.

One might argue that our division managers should be out in the field where they can carry out their line operating function, but we think not. At first we thought the other way, but today we see our division managers as having two jobs. They have to spend a certain amount of time relating to the other staff functions and to the general direction of the company which is changing from time to time, and then they have to spend time in the field with their people. But the fact that they are here means that their people out in the field can be much stronger men and they have to be, and this is what we want. It just means that when you pull a division manager back, you just have to have a stronger man left out in the field. Remember these men that we pull into the home office decentralize too. They are responsible for operations all over the West. They have to have strong general managers in their areas. We have under these division managers, mind you, not a sales manager and production manager; we have a series of general managers left behind—rounded out businessmen.

Individualism

Mr. Hansberger believed that, to be successful within his concept of managing a business enterprise, Boise Cascade employees had to have a strong sense of individualism. He did not want people in the company who were not willing to accept responsibility for their actions or for their failures to act. Hansberger indicated, in keeping with this attitude, "we encourage our managers to make decisions and we expect them to make mistakes. But we would rather have our people make a lot of decisions—with a high batting average—than to not make decisions for fear of being wrong."

Excerpts from a statement on individualism by Mr. Hansberger to all Boise Cascade employees, in the Christmas, 1961, edition of Boise Cascade's quarterly house organ, follow:

> . . . There is an increasing school of thought that centralization of planning, of providing, of directing, and of guiding the individuals in our society is more efficient. But what the students of this school do not seem to appreciate is that this centralization weakens the very foundation of our society.
>
> Centralization is dangerous, not so much because centralists are dangerous, but because centralism weakens our most important value, our individualism. We simply cannot direct the activities of all of the people in our society from a central point without losing respect for individuals and without individuals losing their own self-respect. And this applies to the operation of schools, companies, labor unions, and governments—in fact, to all sectors of our society.
>
> Most certainly it applies to corporations such as Boise Cascade. And as you know, we try very hard in the operation of Boise Cascade to decentralize a maxi-

mum of authority throughout the corporation with a minimum of inhibiting restrictions. The proper balance between the two is important and most difficult to find. We are always striving to do this better.

But the trend in our American society is the reverse of the trend within Boise Cascade. The drift is toward ever larger and more powerful agencies in industry, labor, and government. Unless this trend is arrested, we will find at some point in the future that we shall have unconsciously destroyed the force which made us strong—our individualism.

I think the answer lies not in destroying the centralists. Their motives are not evil and the damage they do is not deliberate. The answer lies in individualism itself.

Too many of us, who are busily engaged in the intoxicating opportunities of individualism, have not recognized the responsibilities that must go with these privileges. We simply cannot practice unbridled individualism without also assuming the responsibilities for the consequences of what we do. And this applies not only to individuals but to other organizations in our society, including corporations.

The pursuit of individualism has given America industrial might such as the world has never known before. But if we are to protect the opportunities for this type of growth in the future, we must also accept the responsibilities for the consequences of our actions. And we must not only assume these responsibilities, but we must conduct our pursuit in such a manner that the individual rights and opportunities of others are protected—and we must do this without losing the great incentive power of individualism.

America needs her rugged individualists, and we especially need them now. But these individualists, whether they be persons or corporations, need to adopt twelve months' worth of Christmas spirit if their individualism is to survive.

Salary Administration

Mr. Hansberger believed that salary administration was closely tied to his ideas about corporate objectives, organization, and the role of the individual within the company. He indicated that it would be extremely difficult to implement his concepts unless the company was willing to reward its people in accordance with their performance. Consequently, there were no salary levels established for *positions* in the company where the individual's income exceeded $7,200 a year. Instead, salaries applied to *persons* and were determined by an evaluation of the professional ability of the individual.

"Like most policies," said Mr. Hansberger, "this one has had its tests. Not long ago a general manager three levels down in the organization had a personality clash with a salesman working for him and fired the man. Now we saw some potential in the man who was fired and worked it out so he was hired by another group. His new general manager wanted to lower the man's salary on the justification that he would have to learn a new phase of the business. But our salary policy states 'salaries apply to persons, not positions' and furthermore that 'it is the responsibility of the company to assign positions to individuals which properly suit and challenge their abilities.' So we stepped in and disallowed the reduction in salary."

Hansberger also pointed out that salary administration was used to accomplish the objective of higher return on investment. Year-end bonuses were awarded at least partially on the basis of return on investment for the operating groups. However, it was not necessary for a reporting unit to have a high return on investment for its members to receive bonuses. An important criterion was improvement over previous performance. Thus, there was always an incentive to do better, even if a unit was in a loss position.

Throughout the month of June, each year, the annual salary review meetings of the Boise Cascade Corporation were held at the company's home office in Boise. During these meetings the general managers of each of the company's major groups or sections presented their salary recommendations to the Salary Review Committee, consisting of Messrs. Eberle, Halliday, and Black. These recommendations had been determined previously by the general managers and their subordinates jointly.

Each salaried person in the company making over $7,200 a year was reviewed individually, and a list of persons making less than $7,200 was audited. Employees in the "over $7,200" category were reviewed annually, this review coming in midyear. Those earning less than $7,200 were reviewed twice a year, in January and June. Any increase of 10% or less did not require approval by the Committee, although the increase could be questioned. Increases exceeding 10% required Committee approval. In all cases, salaries were given a final review by Mr. Hansberger, and he reserved the right to make any change he believed necessary.

Control Procedures

Implementing the plans, procedures, and budgets utilized by the corporation to coordinate and control its far-flung, diversified operations also consumed a significant portion of the time of the top management. These procedures appear in some detail later in this case.

CORPORATE ORGANIZATION

As indicated in Exhibit 1, the corporation operated with a four-man key corporate staff, all headquartered in Boise, and five autonomous operating divisions, each headed by a corporate vice president. Two of these division heads (Robert Faegre, general manager of the Mando Division, and A. P. Hildebrandt, president of the Kingsberry Homes Division) had joined Boise Cascade in late 1964 or early 1965, when their companies had been acquired. Mr. Faegre had been president of Minnesota and Ontario Paper Company for the preceding nine years, and Mr. Hildebrandt had been president of Kingsberry Homes Corporation for six years prior to the acquisition by Boise.

Mr. Moser had been running the former Cascade Lumber Company properties since 1953 (Western Timber Division), before taking responsibility for the entire corporate timber and wood products activities in 1964. Mr. Fery had headed the paper group since 1958, and Mr. Montgomery the merchandising operations since 1955. Brief biographical data on these nine key men are given below.

The Corporate Staff

Robert V. Hansberger, president and director, was born in 1920, on a farm in Worthington, Minnesota. He attended Worthington Junior College, receiving an AA degree in 1940, and then went on to the University of Minnesota, where he received a BME degree, with distinction, in 1942.

Mr. Hansberger stayed at the University of Minnesota as an instructor in engineering until the end of 1942, when he entered the Navy as an Ensign. He became engaged in torpedo design, and, by war's end, he was serving as the Chief of the Mechanical Design Section, Naval Ordnance Laboratory, in Washington, D.C.

After graduation from Harvard Business School (MBA, with great distinction, 1947), he joined Container Corporation of America, as assistant to the executive vice president, became a division chief engineer in 1950, later managed the company's national sales accounts, and in 1953 was appointed corporate director of the budget.

Mr. Hansberger left Container Corporation in 1954 to become vice president of Western Kraft Company of Albany, Oregon, and president of its affiliated Western Sales Company of Portland. At Western Kraft he played a major role in the design and construction of the industry's first economical pulp and paper mill with a capacity of less than 400 tons per day. This mill, which was rated at only 120 tons/day, completely changed existing notions of economies of scale and led directly to Hansberger's appointment as president of the then Boise Payette Lumber Company in 1956.

Mr. Hansberger and his wife, Klara, whom he married in 1942, have two daughters, aged 11 and 14. He is an ardent fisherman, hunter, and skier. He is also president of the Boise Art Association and the Boise Industrial Foundation, and is a director of a Boise hospital, of the Idaho Chamber of Commerce, and of the Associated Industries of Idaho.

In addition, he is chairman of the board of Fairway Products Corporation, a director of Idaho Power Company, First Security Corporation (banking), Sportsman's Golf Corporation, and VSI (missile and aircraft components). He serves as director or trustee of the Aspen, Colorado, Institute for Humanistic Studies, Pacific University, and Whitman College.

Mr. Hansberger was concerned that Boise Cascade might tend to lose some of the spirit and flexibility which characterized its operations as it continued to grow in size. He pointed out that the company would almost inevitably grow larger, since growth in the *value* of the company (as measured by return on investment, earnings per share, and price per share) nearly always required growth in size. He emphasized, however, that growth in size was definitely not an objective per se. In order to reduce the problems of growth in size, Hansberger was devoting considerable effort to improving internal communications. In addition to maintaining an atmosphere of informality, he was planning to institute seminars, in which he would personally hold informal discussions with 20 or 30 employees at a time. He also stressed the importance of the company's internal publications as a means of communication.

Mr. Hansberger explained that he spent about 60% of his time working with his subordinates within the company. This included personal contacts in Boise at the plants as well as telephone contact. Approximately 25% of his time was spent outside the company, making speeches, attending meetings, etc. The remainder of his time was devoted to acquisitions, major financing, and his relationships with the board of directors.

Eventually, Mr. Hansberger thought that he might like to get back into teaching or possibly enter politics. In the fall of 1961, a group of Idaho Republican leaders had tried to interest Mr. Hansberger in running for the U.S. Senate. Hansberger had indicated that the thought of public office had interested him, but he had felt many challenges unresolved within Boise Cascade, and he had decided against such a move.

The following comments about Mr. Hansberger are typical of those told the casewriter by various members of Boise Cascade management:

> His greatest ability is that of managing people. He has intelligence, imagination, and a dynamic personality which he uses to stimulate others. He is willing to delegate responsibility and possesses the facility to evaluate performance fairly.

> The company will always grow under Hansberger. He has surrounded himself with two or three sharp men and they have put the company together and know where they are going with it. If Hansberger weren't a strong leader, however, he would be dominated by his staff.

> Bob Hansberger gives clear-cut definitions of what is expected and then won't bother you if the job is getting done. He has tremendous perception of problems, is a dynamic worker, and is so down to earth with people it is disarming.

> Hansberger has thought so much about policy and the direction that this company must take that he has stored in his mind answers to most of the questions that come up. Everything seems to fit into place when he gives an answer.

> He will back up a decision made by a subordinate even if he disagrees. He will call the person off to the side and tell him where he was wrong, but will stick by the decision.

> In my opinion Bob Hansberger is 90% modest. This is very significant when you consider that I think most people are about 2% modest.

William D. Eberle, vice president and secretary, and a director of the company, born in 1923, is a native of Boise, Idaho. He earned his AB in Social Science at Stanford University in 1945, and served in the U.S. Navy as a Lieutenant until 1946. Eberle continued his education at Harvard, receiving his MBA in 1947 and his LL.B. in 1949. From 1950 to 1960, he was a partner in the leading Boise law firm of Richards, Haga, and Eberle, joining his father and his brother. As corporate counsel for Boise Payette, he was elected to the board of directors in 1952. In 1960, Eberle withdrew from his law practice to join Boise Cascade as full-time corporate secretary and director. He was elected a vice president as well in 1961. Eberle has been very active in Idaho politics, serving as a member of the Idaho House of Representatives since 1953. He was selected as Majority Leader in 1957, became Minority Leader in 1959 when the Democrats captured control of the House, and in 1961 was named Speaker of the House when the Republicans once more regained the majority. Eberle's many activities included directorships in the Idaho Tuberculosis Association, the Children's Home Society of Idaho, the Boise United Fund, and the Bank of Idaho. He also was president of the Idaho Citizens for Education, and was Chairman of a Citizens Council commissioned by the governor to propose legislation regarding child welfare in the state. Eberle was named Boise Jaycees' "Man of the Year" in 1959. Additionally, he has controlled and operated as personal business interests the Boise taxi service, the Hertz Rent-a-Car franchise, and Boise's two largest hotels. Mr. Eberle is married and has three sons and a daughter.

Eberle estimated that he spent approximately 45% of his time on his regularly assigned duties as secretary of the company, and about 25% of his time in evaluating potential acquisitions and related financial matters. The remainder was spent on "corporate problems," including committee meetings, operating issues, etc. Eberle stressed, however, that his involvement in operating problems was only to the extent of discussion and suggestion. "Members of the corporate staff," he said, "ask questions and make suggestions, but do not give orders." Group managers frequently sought his advice on personnel, legal, public relations, and operating problems. He explained that he had to know a great deal about operations, because as a member of the president's office he was expected to commit the corporation if a choice of alternatives had to be made in Mr. Hansberger's absence.

In discussing acquisitions, Eberle indicated that "initial overtures usually come from companies wishing to be acquired, although each year we seek out one or two ourselves. Boise Cascade receives over a hundred acquisition proposals a year, and does elaborate work on at least 15 of these. If a company warrants serious consideration, one or more members of the president's office personally carry out the initial negotiations. This usually involves a visit by one of these individuals to the facilities of the company in question. The appearance of a top Boise Cascade officer at this early stage has definite strategic advantage in future negotiations."

Mr. Eberle indicated that if, following this initial contact, the prospect looked attractive, a complete investigation was conducted by that operating group which would absorb the prospect company if it were acquired. Also, at this time independent auditors would check all financial statements, legal and tax aspects would be explored, and alternative methods of financing the acquisition would be investigated. If the operating group felt the acquisition would be profitable, the proposal came back to the corporate staff for final consideration and negotiation. Eberle explained that Mr. Hansberger, Mr. Halliday, and he then worked as a team of the proposal. "Bob Hansberger has the background of an engineer, Halliday of an accountant, and myself of a lawyer. Each contributes to the analysis of operations, finance, setting the value, cash flow, and working out the approach and method of acquisition. With this done, one of us will complete the negotiations. Charles McDevitt [1] and Ed Cleary [2] continually check detail and prepare for the closing."

Eberle stressed that Boise Cascade's basic rationale in its acquisition program was to become an economically integrated forest products company. He stated, however, that the company was also in the building materials industry and that this provided a second base for integration.

"Through our acquisition activities," he said, "we have gotten ourselves into a sound program of integration. Not only do we have expanded production of a growing line of products, but also we have been expanding our activities in various levels of distribution and of raw material supply. This whole process puts tremendous pressure on our cash position. By using a little imagination, however, we have always been able to generate the money we need for an investment that looks promising. Sometimes we have to turn down an opportunity because it comes at the wrong time psychologically or organizationally, but not for lack of money."

Eberle stressed that the company followed a very strict policy with respect to its relations with the Federal Government. Not only were all merger negotiations conducted with an eye toward the Anti-trust Division of the Justice Department and the Federal Trade Commission, but also Boise Cascade's management stressed that all of the company's operations were scrupulously conducted in strict accordance with the law.

Eberle believed that Boise Cascade's greatest competitive advantage was "our basic flexibility and our ability to move faster than other companies on acquisitions." He felt that the company's major problem in future years would be maintaining opportunities for the growth of Boise Cascade's people.

Mr. Hansberger described Eberle as ". . . brilliant and self-disciplined. He has a strong legal background, and his judgment and education are extremely valuable to us. We hired Bill in 1960 because we were using him so much and for so many things as our legal counsel that we thought we had better put him on our payroll and get full benefit of his talents."

Robert W. Halliday, vice president and treasurer, was born in 1920 in New Haven, Connecticut. He was educated at Yale University, where he received

---

[1] Assistant secretary and corporate counsel.
[2] Comptroller.

his BS in Economics in 1941. Halliday joined Arthur Andersen & Company in 1941, spent 1942–1945 in the U.S. Army, and returned to Arthur Andersen after the war. After 11 years of public accounting, during which he earned a CPA and developed a high level of experience in taxation, auditing, and timber accounting, he was chosen as controller of Pacific Mercury Electronics Company in 1956. Later that year he was invited to join Boise Payette as controller by the same management group that was simultaneously hiring Hansberger as president. He and Hansberger arrived on the Boise scene at about the same time and began to work together to strengthen control over the loosely operated company.

Mr. Halliday viewed his staff job with Boise Cascade as one of maintaining a close watch over the control function and tax problems. About 50% of his time was spent in this area. He explained that the control function consisted of preparing budgets and determining accounting methods to be used in preparing cost and financial statements. The basic accounting system consisted of responsibility accounting interwoven with various cost systems, such as process costing and standard costs. The budgetary control procedure was maintained in his office, with emphasis being given to deviations from budget and its effect on operating profits and cash flow. "I watch for deviations from the budget," he said, "and then try to hit the trouble spots and help them out. This way we are able to treat problems early and keep them from growing."

On tax problems, Halliday was continually involved in regulating the various activities of the company so as to maximize corporate cash flow. The severe pressure which the company's expansion had put on its cash position made this function extraordinarily important, and the diverse and complicated tax structures of the company's many activities demanded unusual skill.

Halliday spent about 25% of his time on acquisitions; this involved working closely with Hansberger and Eberle in the general evaluation of opportunities open to Boise Cascade. When an opportunity looked attractive, he would put together discounted cash flow schedules, compute present value of various assets, and make recommendations concerning the best way to implement proposed acquisitions from a tax viewpoint and from the standpoint of impact on the company's cash flow.

The remainder of his time was spent in committee meetings, counseling group managers, and on operating problems (visiting plants, etc.).

Halliday was pressing for centralized accounting, even though Hansberger was not sympathetic to this move because of the heavy costs involved. "I believe," he said, "with the continued progress being made in computers that the centralized accounting approach is inevitable because it will mean reduced accounting costs, speedier preparation of operating statements and reports, and greater flexibility in analysis of costs and marketing information. By centralizing, the company will be able to secure computer capacity to enable it to gain the benefits of linear programming and the operations research approach on many of its problems. At this point in time, feasibility studies do not indicate an adequate return on investment from a complete, centralized accounting system. Therefore, we have planned this program of centralization in steps. In June of 1962 an IBM 1401 system was installed. This system was proven out in a feasibility study and gives an adequate return on investment. When data transmission equipment from the operating plants to Boise can be justified, the final step will be taken to centralize accounting in Boise. At present it appears that this step is several years down the road."

Mr. Halliday found excitement in the company's many-faceted, fast moving operations, and kept in intimate touch with all of the major problems of the various divisions. Division general managers frequently sought him out for tax advice and for help in cost controls on regulating cash flow.

Halliday thought that Boise Cascade's greatest competitive advantage was its ability to move quickly on acquisitions. He believed that the major problem facing the company in 1965 was to develop an effective plan of action for the merchandising division. "In the future," he said, "our greatest problem will be to maintain our rate of growth in earnings and in the quality of our people." Mr. Halliday indicated that the company might even consider expanding into other industries, some day in the distant future, if earnings growth became limited in the forest products industry. To maintain growth in the quality of people, Halliday felt Boise Cascade should continue bringing in a number of good, young people who would bloom within ten years. "At the rate this company will grow," he added, "we desperately will need people who can step into responsible positions."

Hansberger described Halliday as being: "Hard driving, ambitious, and always outspoken. Bob has a brilliant and quick mind. At times we have to slow him down to substantiate some of his conclusions for us. He's a real expert in accounting and taxes."

Mr. Halliday is married and has a son and three daughters.

Don J. Black, development director and general manager of the manufacturing group, was born in Idaho Falls, Idaho, in 1917. After receiving an AB in Engineering from Stanford University in 1940, he joined the Carnation Company as a management trainee. In 1942 he became an industrial engineer with Pabco Products, Inc. Black advanced with Pabco as production planning manager in 1947, assistant general plant manager in 1951, and general works manager in 1952. From 1954 to 1955 he was a consulting industrial engineer, and in 1956 he became assistant to the executive vice president of Stone Enterprises. Black joined Ames Harris Neville in 1957 as manager of manufacturing and engineering, and became a part of the Boise Cascade organization via the Ames Harris acquisition in late 1958. He was named Boise Cascade's director of development and also general manager of the manufacturing group in 1960.

Although Mr. Black had complete responsibility for the manufacturing group, he spent approximately 80% of his time in the development function. He said that this was possible only because he had such able men managing the three sections of the manufacturing group. "Development," he said, "is broken down into two areas—process improvement and new product development." He explained that the former was traditionally the more important area for Boise Cascade, since forest products were generally merchandised as commodities rather than as proprietary products. Thus, Boise Cascade had made major efforts to cut costs at its mills and to obtain fuller utilization of its trees. As a result, Boise's Yakima plywood mill was one of the most efficient in the country, and Mr. Black believed that the company's new plywood mill at Elgin, Idaho, would be even more efficient. He also referred to efforts at the Wallula paper mill, where the company's required investment for expanding paper making capacity was running only $50,000 per daily operating ton, as compared with an industry average of well over $65,000 per ton. Black stressed that process improvement was carried out at every level of Boise's operations from the forest to the customer.

Black felt that process development would continue to grow in importance, but that product development was also becoming an area of significance with the evolvement of many plywood and lumber specialties. "We now find ourselves looking at about a dozen new products at any one time," he said. "Today we have five under active development and evaluation." Black explained, however, that new products required extensive merchandising support when they were introduced, and that Boise Cascade presently lacked this type of product promotion ability except in the intermountain area.

The annual budget for corporate level research and development was about $250,000. Approximately half of this went into product development. In addition, each operating group carried out its own process and product development and the aggregate development expenditures at that level were close to $1 million.

Mr. Black offered two explanations for the relatively small size of his budget. He said there was little justification for spending large amounts for research and development when Boise was still turning down merger offers from companies with proprietary products. He also pointed out that Boise Cascade did a great deal of research on a joint basis with larger (noncompetitive) companies when products of mutual interest were under consideration. In this way, Boise Cascade could avail itself of the large research staffs and facilities of other companies, while minimizing the risk to itself. "Here," he explained, "the relationship is much more important than the number of dollars involved."

The development staff consisted of approximately 35 people in 1963. About 20 of these were members of the central engineering staff providing technical service to the operating groups. The product development staff consisted of seven persons, operations development had five, and three were in market research.

Black saw Boise's major competitive advantage as "a strong motivating force and an atmosphere of decentralized growth, which gives us flexibility and a high speed of reaction."

He saw two major problems facing Boise Cascade in future years. The first was to find more qualified people to explore opportunities which were presently "right in front of our noses." The second was to continue growth in earnings, without getting so large that speed and flexibility were lost.

Mr. Black, according to Mr. Hansberger, was "a very flexible and hard working person. He has excellent judgment and can grasp quickly the total situation. Don has a good engineering background to go along with his other qualities, and we can rely on him for effective management of a diversified operation."

Steven B. Moser, vice president, Timber and Wood Products Division, and a director of the company, was born in Seattle, Washington, in 1908. After graduating from the University of Washington in 1928, he joined Lewis-Bean Company of Seattle and worked in sales and administration until 1941, when he was called into the Navy. He was discharged in 1945 as a Lt. Commander, and in 1946 joined the Cascade Lumber Company as secretary-treasurer and director. Moser was elected vice president and treasurer of Cascade in 1953. When Boise Payette and Cascade merged in 1957, Moser was chosen to continue operating the Cascade sawmills and was elected a vice president and a director of the parent company. In Yakima, Washington, the headquarters first of Cascade and then of its successor Western timber section, Moser was a director of the Community Chest, the YMCA, and the Chamber of Commerce. He also belonged to the Association of Washington Industries and was a member of the Yakima Valley Advisory Board of the Seattle First National Bank.

In late 1964, Mr. Moser assumed responsibility for all lumber, plywood, and forest management activities of the company as general manager of the Timber and Wood Products Division, continuing its headquarters in Yakima.

Mr. Hansberger described Mr. Moser as one of the company's most capable executives. "When Steve was with Cascade Lumber Company he had not been assigned major operating responsibility. We put him in charge of Cascade's lumber operations after the merger and he grew rapidly into his job. He has excellent judgment and is keenly interested in the affairs of the company. He is highly effective also as a director of the company."

John Fery, vice president, Paper Division, was born in 1930, in Bellingham, Washington. He did this undergraduate work in business administration at the University of Washington and received his MBA from Stanford in 1955. Following graduation, Fery joined Western Kraft Company as assistant to Mr. Hansberger, then the executive vice president. In 1956, he was oppointed production manager. He was brought by Mr. Hansberger from Western Kraft to Boise Payette just before the Cascade merger in 1957, and served as assistant to the president while the new paper mill was being planned and constructed. In 1958, he was named general manager of the newly created Paper Division. Fery was elected a vice president of Boise Cascade in 1960. He also served as a Trustee of the Northwest Pulp and Paper Association.

Under his leadership, the Wallula mill was operated and expanded, and the 17 corrugated container plants constructed or acquired also came under his cognizance. When the St. Helen's pulp and paper mill was acquired from Crown Zellerbach in May, 1964, Fery was given responsibility for its operations. In late 1964, he also was assigned responsibility for the Columbia River (fine paper) mills, and for Columbia Envelope, Honolulu Paper Company, and Associated

Stationers. These changes placed all domestic paper operations in manufacturing, sales converting, and distribution under his direction.

Mr. Hansberger stated that Mr. Fery was ". . . ambitious and has a great affinity for responsibility. He is always asking for more responsibility and I appreciate this. In spite of all that we have given John to do, I don't believe that we have yet stretched his full capabilities."

E. A. Montgomery, vice president, Merchandising Division, was born in Minneapolis, Minnesota, in 1908. He majored in accounting at the University of Minnesota, and from 1931 to 1940 he held accounting and auditing positions with the Pure Oil Company, Ernst and Ernst, and the Merrill Company. In 1940, he was elected comptroller and treasurer of the Tri-State Lumber Company (retail lumber yards), and in 1949 became assistant general manager of the same company. Tri-State was acquired by Boise Payette in 1947. In 1955, Montgomery was elected vice president of Boise Payette in charge of the company's merchandising activities (retail and wholesale building materials yards). He was active in several trade associations, such as the National Retail Lumber Dealers Association and the Lumber Dealers Merchandising Institute.

Mr. Hansberger described Mr. Montgomery as ". . . having vast experience in merchandising. He knows the people in the industry. 'Monty' is analytical in approaching merchandising problems and works best under conditions of minimum supervision."

Robert Faegre, vice president, Mando Division, and a director of the company, was born in Minneapolis, Minnesota, in 1916. After graduating from Dartmouth College in 1938, he joined the Minnesota and Ontario Paper Company, with whom—excepting for four years in the U.S. Navy (1942–1946)—he has spent his entire business career. Starting as representative to the finish subsidiary of the Insulite Division (wood fiber insulation board), he served in various capacities in the Chicago and Minneapolis sales office of the Insulite Division, becoming assistant sales manager on his return from the service in 1946, as a Supply Corps Lieutenant.

In 1953, Mr. Faegre was named executive vice president and director of Minnesota and Ontario Paper Company, and in late 1955 he was named president of the parent company and its subsidiaries.

Upon the acquisition of Minnesota and Ontario Paper Company by Boise Cascade, Mr. Faegre was named a vice president and director of Boise and general manager of the Mando Division. He continues to serve as president of the Ontario—Minnesota Pulp and Paper Company, a wholly owned Canadian subsidiary.

Mr. Faegre serves as a director of the Northwestern National Bank of Minneapolis, Northwestern National Life Insurance Company, Employers Mutual of Wausau, Upper Midwest Research & Development Council, North Star Research & Development Institute, and the Keep Minnesota Green organization.

Additionally, he is very active in the paper industry, serving as: vice president of the American Paper & Pulp Association (also member of executive committee and board of governors; chairman of Technical Policy Committee); member of executive board, Canadian Pulp & Paper Association; trustee, The Institute of Paper Chemistry; member of board of governors, National Council for Stream Improvement; and member business committee, National Planning Association.

The Board of Directors

As a result of Boise Cascade's acquisition program, its board of directors in 1964 consisted primarily of individuals who had had major financial interests in the acquired companies, and thus were major shareholders of Boise Cascade stock. R. V. Hansberger believed that this was good.

> To have people who have an important personal stake in the company I think is healthy. Those people take a lot of interest in what we do. Our board meetings are very well attended. And if we have a matter, such as a major acquisition, and it requires a special meeting, we have it.

Hansberger had, however, changed the concept of the role played by the board of directors. He indicated that in each of the major companies forming Boise Cascade—Boise Payette, Cascade, Potlatch, Valsetz, and Ames Harris Neville—the respective boards had been quite active in operating matters. "We could not operate under similar conditions," he added, "because management couldn't wait to bring together a group of directors from all around the country each time a decision smelled like a major thing. Many times now we don't even have time to develop a written report." Hansberger explained that the board now was concerned primarily with major acquisitions and financial matters. The board reviewed capital improvement budgets, and changes in the debt structure; it approved acquisitions, dividend policy, bonuses, and stock options; and it recommended and approved compensation of officers.

"When it comes to operating decisions," said Hansberger, "we make the decision to the best of our ability and then let the board review our action and criticize the results."

The Boise Cascade board of directors had 12 members in 1964. During the height of the acquisition program, it had reached 16 members, but had been pared to what Hansberger considered a more manageable size.

The chairman of the board in 1964 was Mr. Gilbert Osgood. Mr. Osgood was a partner of an investment firm in Chicago and a representative of the original Boise Payette interests. He had been a director since 1952.

Other members (year first elected director in parentheses) were:

Mr. James D. Bronson—Orchardist, formerly president and important shareholder of the Cascade Lumber Company. (1957)

Mr. David E. Bronson—Attorney in Minneapolis, brother of James Bronson, and formerly an officer of Cascade Lumber Company. He was an important holder of Boise Cascade stock. (1957)

Mr. James E. Bryson—represented the Templeton family. He was currently general manager of Boise Cascade's western Oregon plywood mills. (1959)

Mr. William D. Eberle—vice president and secretary of the company. (1952)

Mr. Robert V. Hansberger—president of the company. (1956)

Mr. Glen Lloyd—senior partner in a leading Chicago law firm. (Mr. Lloyd, who represented the interests of an original Boise Payette family, was instrumental in bringing Mr. Hansberger to Boise Payette in 1956.) (1955)

Mr. Albert J. Moorman, Jr.—Attorney in San Francisco. Represented one of the original six interests in Boise Payette. (1955)

Mr. Steven B. Moser—had been vice president and treasurer of the Cascade Lumber Company. Currently vice president, Timber and Wood Products Division. (1957)

Mr. Theodore H. Smyth—represented the interests of one of the original Boise Payette family groups. An ex-airline pilot, Mr. Smyth was in the ranching business in Santa Barbara. (1952)

Mr. Hall Templeton—investor. Had been president and director of the Valsetz-Templeton combine. (1959)

Mr. E. D. Titcomb—had been secretary of Boise Payette. Represented one of the original family interests. Presently, president of Building Materials Manufacturing and Distribution Company in St. Paul. (1952)

The executive committee of the board consisted of Messrs. Osgood, J. Bronson, Templeton, Titcomb, Lloyd, and Hansberger. It met whenever action did not necessitate calling the full board together.

The merger with Minnesota and Ontario Paper Company in January, 1965, resulted in expanding the board to 15 members, adding the following former directors of Mando:

Mr. Robert Faegre—president of Minnesota and Ontario Paper Company (became Mando director 1953).

Mr. Robert J. Keith—executive vice president, The Pillsbury Company (became Mando director 1963).

Mr. John S. Pillsbury, Jr.—president, Northwestern National Life Insurance Company (became Mando director 1958).

MAINTAINING OVER-ALL COMPANY COORDINATION

Operating Budgets and Reports

The "key budget" was at the heart of Boise Cascade's control system. This budget was submitted by each of the operating groups each year, and included an annual forecast for the current year and the four subsequent years of income statements, balance sheets, and source and application of funds statements. (See Exhibits 2, 3, and 4.) Each key budget for the current year was then revised,

Division or Subsidiary	Actual 1962	1963	1964	1965	1966	1967
Volume						
Net Sales						
Operating Income						
Capital Gains on— Fee Timber						
Economic Timber						
Other						
Total Capital Gains						
Net Income Before Taxes						

as necessary, jointly by the group general manager and the Budget Committee (consisting of the budget director, C. H. Dietz, and Messrs. Hansberger, Halliday, Eberle, Black, and Cleary), and a final consolidation key budget was drawn up and approved for the entire company. Once the total was approved, monthly budget figures were drawn up by each group.

On the basis of forecasted cash generation, the company drew up its financing plans, and determined how much cash was available for investment in capital projects. Authorizations for Expenditures (AFE's) were then added to the key budgets as they were approved.

The key budgets were revised quarterly for purposes of cash planning and reports to the board of directors. Each operating group, however, was evaluated against the standards of its original key budget. The only way that an operating group might modify its key budget was to submit additional AFE's later in the year, or to elect to cancel or postpone plans on previously approved AFE's.

Because Boise Cascade operated on a responsibility accounting system, each group prepared the budgets for its own departments, which formed the basis for the group's consolidated key budget. Thus, each accounting unit in the company, including mill departments, sales units, staff departments, etc., had its own monthly responsibility budget statement.

Top management received formal accounting statements each month from the operating groups. The first of these to arrive was the Profit Estimate, which forecast sales and income for the current month, and gave brief explanations for anticipated major variances (see Exhibit 5). This report went to the budget director five days before the end of the month. The profit estimate was then forwarded to Messrs. Halliday, Eberle, and Hansberger.

On the eleventh day following the end of the month, Mr. Dietz received actual month-end balance sheets, income statements, and cash flows. These were analyzed carefully by Dietz and Halliday for any major variances, and a complete analysis of variance was done each quarter for major reporting units.

On the sixteenth or seventeenth day following the end of the month, consolidated statements were completed and forwarded to the president and the board of directors, along with statements of major variances. These consolidated statements were also sent to all group managers and the managers of major sections and divisions, so that each group could see how its performance stood in relation to that of other groups. The statements included forecasted and actual sales, income, and return on investment for each major reporting unit, along with the name of the individual responsible for that group's performance.

In addition to these summary reports, the corporate staff prepared detailed statements presenting budgeted vs. actual performance for individual departments, and these were distributed to all concerned, down to and including the foreman level of the reporting unit concerned.

Mr. Dietz pointed out that he, Halliday, Cleary, and Alden [3] followed cash flow reports particularly closely, because of their important implications for debt management, capital expenditures, and short-term borrowing needs. He added that, to a limited extent, management had the power to influence cash flow and income. For example, an increase in planned cutting of fee-owned timber, because of its tax treatment, would increase profits and reduce cash outflow in any given year.

Control Procedures

Members of the president's office stated that they were receiving sufficient information to follow accurately the performance of each group. Mr. Halliday pointed out that he usually didn't know how every department in every group was doing, but that it was unnecessary for him to have this information since it was the concern of group and department management.

Members of the president's office followed group performance very closely, but they never took direct action in the management of the group. If a departure

---

[3] Assistant treasurer.

exhibit 3

BOISE CASCADE CORPORATION (B)

Five-Year Balance Sheet Projection

Name of Division or Subsidiary	Actual December 31, 1962	December 31, 1963	December 31, 1964	December 31, 1965	December 31, 1966	December 31, 1967
Current Assets:						
Cash						
Receivables						
Inventories						
Total Current Assets						
Current Liabilities:						
Short Term Notes						
Payables and Accrued Expenses (excluding income tax)						
Total current liabilities						
Net Working Capital						

Net Property:					
Plant, Property & Equipment					
Logging Roads					
Property for Resale					
Timber & Timberland-Fee					
Total Net Property					
Timber Deposits					
Other Assets					
Net Assets					
Long-Term Debt					
Investment					
Changes in Investment:					
Net Income Before Taxes					
Cash Control					
Advances to Subsidiaries					

465

exhibit 4

BOISE CASCADE CORPORATION (B)

Five-Year Projected Cash Flow

Name of Division or Subsidiary: _____

Funds Provided:	Actual 1962	Budget 1963	Budget 1964	Budget 1965	Budget 1966	Budget 1967
Net Income Before Income Tax						
Provision for Depreciation						
Road Amortization						
Depletion of Fee Timber						
Cash Flow						
Additional Long-Term Debt						
Short-Term Bank Borrowings						
Decrease - Real Estate for Resale						
Decrease in Timber Deposits						
Net Book Value of Plant and						

Equipment Sold or Retired	
Net Book Value of Plant and	
Equipment Transferred	
Decrease in Other Assets	
Total Funds Provided	
Funds Applied:	
Capital Expenditures -	
Plant and Equipment	
Logging Roads	
Fee Timber and Timberland	
Total Capital Expenditures	
Increase in Working Capital -	
Cash	
Receivables	
Inventory	
Payables and Accrued Expenses excluding Income Taxes	

exhibit 4 (cont.)

Payment on Short-Term Loan									
Total Increase in Working Capital									
Payments on Long-Term Debt									
Cash Dividends Paid									
Decrease in Division Cash Control									
Decrease in Subsidiary Advances									
Total Funds Applied									

exhibit 5

BOISE CASCADE CORPORATION (B)

Profit Estimate: Monthly Report to Comptroller's Department

Subsidiary or Division _____

	Month of _____		
	Current Year		*Prior Year*
	Estimate	*Budget*	*Actual*
Net Sales (See Explanatory Note)	_____	_____	_____
Net Income before Taxes*	_____	_____	_____
Note: Plywood and Lumber Division Complete Below: Capital Gains - Fee	_____	_____	_____
Capital Gains - Economic Interest	_____	_____	_____
Total (Include in Net Income before Taxes)	_____	_____	_____

If Estimate differs 10% either way from budget or if capital gains—other than timber—included in net income before taxes represent more than 5% of net income before capital gains, explain below. If the space is not adequate, use reverse side.

_____

_____

_____

_____

_____

Notes: Last year's figures are to be actual (adjusted to comparable basis). Net sales means gross sales less discounts and allowances and should include the following: interdivision sales, log sales block sales, underweights and overweights, and by-products. Intra-division sales, intra-department transfers, lumber used, and consigned sales should be excluded from net sales.

Mail to Attention of C. H. Dietz

from budget occurred, a letter was written by Dietz or Halliday to the manager concerned, and copies were sent to Eberle and Hansberger. This letter would point out the discrepancy, and would normally ask for an explanation. (Frequently an explanation accompanied the original report, obviating the need for such follow-up).

In the case of serious or extended departures from budget, Halliday personally visited the operation concerned, to apprise himself of all the facts and try to identify the problem. Group management would be consulted continuously, but no member of the corporate staff would issue orders to make any changes. On the basis of what the members of the president's office knew about the problem, questions would be raised with the manager concerned and suggestions would be made.

One example of this control procedure may be illustrative: In March of 1962 it became apparent that the Eastern Wholesale Region, located in Denver, was falling far behind budgeted profits. Dietz and Halliday, who set out to gather the additional information necessary to analyze the departure from budget, felt that the problem lay with incompetent performance at the regional level. This was pointed out to Mr. Montgomery, the merchandising group general manager. As a group manager, Mr. Montgomery made the decision as to what corrective action should be taken to improve the region's profit showing. Although Halliday and Dietz felt that the regional manager should be replaced, Montgomery believed it was not in the best interests of the Wholesale Division to take such action at that time. When the poor profit showing continued through September, Mr. Montgomery was urged to take further action, and, at this point, replaced the regional manager. Montgomery stated at this time that, had he not concurred with Halliday's diagnosis, he would have felt under no compunction to take this action.

Intracompany Transfers

Boise Cascade's management felt that, while there were problems associated with decentralized control, these were to be expected if the company lived up to the spirit of its organizational philosophy. One such problem involved intracompany transfers. It was recognized that the over-all company was not optimally integrated in its operations, since groups frequently purchased from Boise's competitors products which were manufactured by other groups in the company. Nevertheless, management felt that the longer range interests of the company were served best by allowing group managers complete freedom of action, then holding them strictly accountable for rate of return on investment.

Exhibit 6 provides a breakdown of product flow within the company, showing both the theoretically optimum and the actual extent of intracompany transfers, including tradeoffs.

Halliday believed that the company would see some centralization of control in future years with the increasing use of computer programs. He indicated that divisions presently using programmed inventory control were convinced that it was increasing their rate of return.

exhibit 6

BOISE CASCADE CORPORATION (B)

	% of Output Sold to Other Divisions	% of Requirements Purchased Internally	% of Requirements which could Presently be Purchased Internally
Lumber and plywood group			
Lumber and plywood	10	—	—
Wood chips	50	—	—
Morrison-Merrill Div.	20	38	45
Bestway Building Centers Div.	0	44	80
Paperboard Mill Div.	95	45	55
		(of chip req'ts.)	
Container Div.	0	100	100
Business and Printing	2	9	9
Paper Section	(to Columbia Envelope)	(of chip req'ts.)	

He also foresaw increasing opportunities for linear programming of various operations in the company. Late in 1963 the company was evolving plans to program certain minor mill operations. Halliday felt that the day would come when linear programming would be used in the woods to maximize the profit received from any given stand of trees. The variables involved would include transportation costs from the woods to different mills, the operating costs of the mills involved, the most economic use for the tree (lumber, plywood, or paper), expected demand, prices, etc.

Communication of Objectives

Communications from the corporate staff to the group management were largely informal and not considered a problem, since most group managers were head-quartered at Boise. Communications from the president's office to middle management was said to be a concern only to the extent of insuring the understanding of Boise's management philosophy, especially the return on investment concept.

In order to measure the success of this objective, members of the Stanford Business School staff spoke with a number of line managers outside Boise. These included three retail store managers, a wholesale plant manager, a prestress concrete plant manager, and a ready-mix plant manager.

In all but one case, these managers had a clear idea of the return on investment concept; and, in most cases, the man directly under this manager also understood the concept. In every case, the managers stated that they were in complete control of their operation, and that they felt no interference from corporate management. Two of them mentioned, however, that they would appreciate more contact from management, and that management tended to forget about them. It was felt in all cases that these managers received all the necessary information to run their operations effectively.

About half of the people interviewed, including several workmen and first line supervisors, made reference to a Boise Cascade "spirit" which stemmed from the youthfulness and aggressiveness of the organization.

Capital Planning

In December of each year, Boise Cascade's top management group met to discuss capital expenditures for the coming five years. Although capital planning took place throughout the year both formally and informally, each operating group submitted five year project requests for the December meetings. These requests included estimates of cost, timing, and the return on investment for each proposal. The comptroller and the treasurer at the same time, prepared a five year cash flow forecast to determine availability of funds for these projects. At these meetings the over-all sums to be available to each group for capital expenditures were set.

After the forecasted totals were determined, but before final approval was granted on individual major projects, a detailed study of each proposal was conducted by the Operations Development and Analysis Department, under Mr. G. M. Wilhelm. Next, the proposal was brought before the company's Authorization for Expenditure Committee. This committee, consisting of Messrs. Eberle, Halliday, Wilhelm, Black, Alden, and Cleary, evaluated the detailed engineering analyses and estimates of rate of return for each project, as presented by Mr. Wilhelm. On the basis of discounted cash flow projections, an AFE was awarded to the most promising projects. A 20% rate of return was required for approval of any major project, and the criterion for minor projects was 30%. Projects of less than $5,000 could be given final approval by the AFE committee. Those involving expenditure of over $5,000 had to be approved also by Mr. Hansberger.

Once a major construction project was approved, a critical path analysis was drawn up by the Central Engineering Department, for the purposes of minimizing unnecessary and costly delays. Critical path analysis had recently been used in rebuilding the Number Four paper machine at Salem, Oregon. Four down-time days were eliminated in completing this job, with the resultant cost saving of over $30,000. A critical path analysis for the expansion of the plywood mill at Yakima, Washington, is shown in Exhibit 7. This program was scheduled for 273 days at a cost of over $1 million.

Each month, groups carrying out capital projects reported their progress to the Operations Development Department on a form shown as Exhibit 8. Large variations from original plan were reported to the AFE committee, and follow-ups were initiated.

exhibit 7

BOISE CASCADE CORPORATION (B)

Critical Path Analysis for Yakima Plywood Mill Expansion

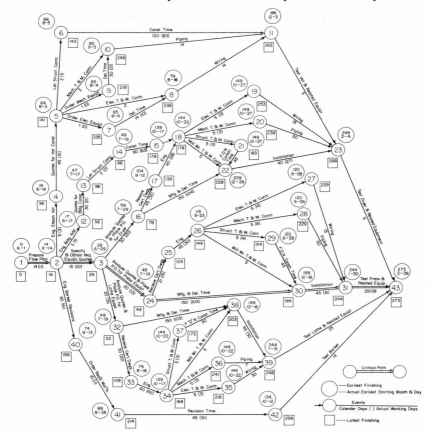

exhibit 8

BOISE CASCADE CORPORATION (B)

MAIL TO OPERATIONS DEVELOPMENT DEPT. BY 15th of MONTH

MONTHLY AFE REPORT (Omit Cents)

DIVISION _____

Month _____

AFE No.	Description	Approved Amount	Total Previous Expend's.	Current Month Expend's	Total Expend's.	Estimated Needed to Complete	Estimated Final Costs	Variances (Overruns) (Underruns)	Approved Amount	Total Expend's.	Estimated Needed to Complete	Estimated Final Costs
						CAPITAL				NON CAPITAL		
	Total											

Boise Cascade Corporation (A-5):

Company Development, 1964-1967

This case is intended to summarize the major developments in the company's history subsequent to the conclusion of Boise Cascade Corporation (A-4), 1963.

In the 1964–1967 period, enormous changes had taken place. Sales grew from $218 million in 1963 to $489 million in 1966, while profits went from $7.4 million to $17.0 million. In the first nine months of 1967, sales of $464 and earnings of $17.1 million augured well for a major increase in both measures over the previous year's performance.

Moreover in this three year period the company had grown geographically, in product and market diversity, and had sharply shifted its product mix. In 1966, 60% of the company's sales (over $290 million) was derived from paper making, as compared with 33% (or $72 million) in 1963. Plywood production was up from 259 million square feet to nearly 500 million. Building materials distribution, which was 22% of total sales in 1963, was down to only 9% in 1966. (See Exhibits 1 and 2.)

Earnings per share for 1967 were expected to more than double 1963's level, while the market price of the company's stock had increased from about $17 per share to over $42 in November, 1967.

The major events are reported chronologically in the pages which follow.

MAJOR EVENTS OF 1964

In a joint statement with the Crown Zellerbach Corporation, late in 1963, Boise officials announced their intent to purchase Crown's St. Helen's Pulp and Paper Company properties, subject to FTC approval. The St. Helen's facilities, which consisted of an integrated pulp and paper mill, with

---

accompanying timberlands, produced a variety of printing and sanitary papers. Crown Zellerbach has been under attack by the Justice Department and the FTC since acquiring the property in 1953. After a lengthy court fight, Crown was ordered to divest itself of the St. Helen's mill. Boise was apparently the preferred purchaser, providing the FTC ruled that such an acquisition was in the public interest.

On April 10, 1964, the Federal Trade Commission announced approval of the sale of Crown Zellerbach's St. Helen's pulp and paper mill to Boise Cascade. Boise took over operation of the mill on May 1, 1964, under the over-all cognizance of Mr. John Fery, vice president and general manager of the paper division.

Description of the St. Helen's Property
Before Sale to Boise

1. A kraft sulfate pulp mill with an annual capacity of 120,000 tons.
2. Integrated auxiliary facilities including a bleach plant (for bleaching pulp), a wood mill (for debarking and chipping logs), a chip supply and distribution system, appropriate steam, water, electrical, and water filtering systems, and a stock refining and preparation facility (for preparing kraft pulp for the manufacture of finer grades of paper).
3. Three paper machines, each separately housed, each integrated with supply lines from the pulp mill, and having a combined capacity of 120,000 tons/year.
4. Finishing rooms for the treatment of quality grades of paper.
5. A complete bag manufacturing facility.
6. Necessary warehouse, shipping, shop, dock, office, and laboratory facilities.
7. Two tracts of timber, totalling approximately 120,000 acres.

Products of the St. Helen's Mill

Machines No. 1 and No. 2, combined, produced about 87,000 tons of products ranging from lightweight kraft specialty papers to heavyweight bleached container and food board.

Machine No. 3 produced about 33,000 tons of napkin and tissue paper (facial and toilet). All of this was sold in the West by Crown's consumer products division and by Zellerbach Paper Company, Crown's wholesale paper distributing subsidiary.

These products had virtually no overlap with those produced at Boise's mills at Wallula, Salem, and Vancouver. Boise's various converting plants consumed about 20,000 tons/year of the types of paper manufactured at St. Helen's, which were currently being purchased from other paper producers. Of this total, about half the bag paper was consumed by the multiwall bag division, while the bulk of the remainder was in bleached board for the container division and kraft envelope stock for Columbia Envelope.

exhibit 1

BOISE CASCADE CORPORATION (A-5)

Statistical Review, 1959–1966

	1966	1965	1964	1963	1962	1961	1960	1959
Sales:								
Quantities shipped								
Paper, thousand tons								
Newsprint	280	274	276	—	—	—	—	—
Paperboard	196	159	144	134	108	79	—	—
Converting papers	189	158	123	31	17	—	—	—
Printing papers	123	98	93	38	7	—	—	—
Business papers	108	98	83	42	48	—	—	—
	896	787	719	245	180	79	72	41
Corrugated containers, million sq. ft.	3,037	2,479	2,215	1,112	920	702	404	504
Lumber, million bd. ft.	710	707	654	635	600	579	529	45
Plywood, million sq. ft.	602	474	398	259	117	60	51	—
Insulite building products, million sq. ft.	422	447	421	—	—	—	—	—
Sales mix								
Pulp and paper	60%	52%	48%	33%	25%	14%	11%	8%
Lumber	10	12	14	21	25	27	28	33
Plywood	8	7	6	7	3	2	2	2
Insulite	6	8	9	—	—	—	—	—
Distribution of building materials	9	12	13	22	29	36	37	38
Home construction	3	4	4	1	1	1	—	—
Other products	4	5	6	16	17	20	22	19
	100%	100%	100%	100%	100%	100%	100%	100%

Ratios

Net income as a % of sales	3.48%	4.26%	4.13%	3.39%	2.89%	2.22%	2.57%	4.41%
Net income as a % of common shareholders' equity	11.30%	14.62%	12.01%	11.43%	9.57%	6.19%	7.14%	12.36%
Current ratio	2.2 to 1	2.9 to 1	2.6 to 1	2.0 to 1	2.3 to 1	3.1 to 1	3.4 to 1	2.7 to 1
Cash flow as a % of long-term debt	19.01%	22.22%	27.34%	27.32%	16.59%	22.63%	29.53%	47.15%
Debt to shareholders' equity	1.01 to 1	.97 to 1	.70 to 1	.99 to 1	1.4 to 1	.67 to 1	.58 to 1	.45 to 1
Effective income tax rate	37.94%	33.72%	39.96%	36.18%	31.15%	26.25%	27.32%	34.41%

Resources

Employees	19,270	17,766	14,943	9,582	7,868	6,337	6,521	5,505
Assets per employee	$27,200	$23,690	$22,845	$17,297	$19,413	$15,632	$13,553	$14,920
Timberlands owned in fee (acres)	1,180,000	1,105,000	1,073,000	650,000	641,000	565,000	528,000	n.a.
Number of common shareholders	9,712	7,441	6,459	4,948	3,570	3,026	2,244	1,592
Number of preferred shareholders	8,036	8,310	9,442	—	—	—	—	—

Common share data

Common shares outstanding								
at year end	9,023,821	4,317,511	4,486,639	4,005,998	3,741,398	3,741,398	3,703,798	1,856,102
Average number outstanding	9,004,606	4,376,109	4,386,562	4,000,561	3,741,398	3,740,758	3,704,597	n.a.
Per common share								
Net income	$ 1.48	$ 1.62	$ 1.30	$ .93	$ .68	$ .41	$ .46	$ .76
% of increase from previous year	(9%)	25%	40%	37%	65%	(10%)	(40%)	38%
Cash flow	3.68	3.82	3.24	2.18	1.59	1.00	1.10	1.30
Dividends	.2375	.20	.20	.20	.20	.20	.175	.15
Equity	13.01	11.25	10.53	8.07	7.06	6.58	6.36	6.12

exhibit 2

BOISE CASCADE CORPORATION (A-5)

Financial Comparison, 1959–1966

Financial condition	1966 (000)	1965 (000)	1964 (000)	1963 (000)	1962 (000)	1962 (000)	1960 (000)	1959 (000)
Assets								
Current assets	$157,807	$144,273	$122,537	$71,353	$64,323	$51,447	$47,132	$43,717
Less: current liabilities	70,231	50,355	47,896	35,283	28,361	16,610	13,808	16,331
Working capital	87,576	93,918	74,641	36,070	35,962	34,837	33,324	27,386
Timber and timberlands	87,880	34,075	30,175	22,685	25,395	9,148	9,124	9,326
Property, plant, and equipment, net	240,597	218,801	175,484	66,362	58,925	35,302	29,467	26,744
Other assets	38,197	23,728	13,175	5,339	4,100	3,165	2,655	2,398
Total fixed assets	366,674	276,604	218,834	94,386	88,420	47,615	41,246	38,468
	$454,250	$370,522	$293,475	$130,456	$124,382	$82,452	$74,570	$65,854
Financed by								
Long-term notes payable	$193,909	$166,921	$117,127	$63,815	$71,548	$33,177	$27,441	$20,423
Other liabilities	67,590	31,350	9,852	1,978	—	—	—	—
Shareholders' equity	192,751	172,251	166,496	64,663	52,834	49,275	47,129	45,431
	$454,250	$370,522	$293,475	$130,456	$124,382	$82,452	$74,570	$65,854

Income								
Net Sales	$489,196	$420,059	$361,608	$218,096	$175,074	$137,631	$131,182	$126,085
Other income, less: deductions	3,270	2,852	1,973	1,265	941	1,307	913	996
	$492,466	$422,911	$363,581	$219,361	$176,015	$138,938	$132,095	$127,081
Expenses								
Materials, services, and other costs	$434,057	$368,096	$315,877	$193,613	$157,949	$128,547	$121,111	$113,448
Depreciation and depletion	19,849	19,198	17,081	10,044	6,815	4,460	4,737	4,013
Interest expense	11,146	8,629	5,726	4,314	4,022	1,880	1,617	1,062
Provision for income taxes	10,400	9,100	9,950	4,000	2,174	1,000	1,265	2,942
	475,452	405,023	348,634	211,971	170,960	135,887	128,730	121,465
Net income	$ 17,014	$ 17,888	$ 14,947	$ 7,390	$ 5,055	$ 3,051	$ 3,365	$ 5,616

Boise's Estimate of St. Helen's Value

An appraisal, conducted by Boise Cascade, estimated that the cost to build a new mill capable of producing an equal range and grade of products, exclusive of the No. 3 paper machine, would be well in excess of $35 million, and would require approximately two years and substantial startup costs to come on stream.

A cruise of the timberlands in 1962 indicated an estimated 1.1 billion board feet of mixed species with an approximate value of $17.3 million.

St. Helen's was a principal user of Douglas fir chips, which were produced by Boise's Western Oregon plywood mills, but which were not suited to Columbia River's sulfite process.

Essential Elements of the St. Helen's Purchase

1. Boise purchased all of the St. Helen's properties listed above, except for Machine No. 3 and the timberlands, for a price of $26 million plus the purchase of all inventories, supplies, materials, logs, etc., as of the closing date estimated at an additional $2 million.

    (Of this estimated $28 million, $6 million was to be carried on a noninterest bearing note payable to Crown five years from the closing date. $20 million of the balance was to be due in cash on the closing date and the remainder as soon after closing as an audited inventory was completed.)

2. Crown retained ownership of Machine No. 3 (the tissue machine) for a period of five years. At the end of that period, Crown was to have the option of selling the machine to Boise for $2.6 million or deferring sale for an additional three years (on two years' advance notice) and then selling the machine to Boise for $1.5 million. Both prices were to be increased by the cost of capital improvements during the period, less straight line depreciation of those improvements on a ten year life basis.

    During the five year period indicated, Boise was to furnish Crown with the necessary pulp to operate Machine No. 3 (estimated at 33-40,000 tons/year). Crown was obligated to pay Boise its costs of producing all of this pulp plus $20,500/month in lieu of depreciation charges. If there was to be an additional three years, the pulp price during that period was to be $30/ton more than Boise's costs.

3. All of the St. Helen's timberlands were to be sold to Boise on or before December 31, 1968. In the interim, Crown was to harvest 500 million board feet in accordance with a mutually agreed logging plan. The purchase price was to be $17.3 million, less the volumes removed by Crown at the unit values set in the 1962 cruise. (The net price was estimated to be approximately $11 million.)

4. Boise was obligated to supply a certain number of machine hours, for four years from the closing date on Machines No. 1 and No. 2, for the production of papers which Crown guaranteed to purchase.

St. Helen's Financing

The required $22 million in cash was supplied by a group of banks. This unsecured borrowing was backed up by the equity and earning power of Waterbury Corrugated Container Corporation, Columbia Envelope Company, and St. Helen's. It was estimated that this totally debt-financed purchase would be paid off in eight to nine years out of earnings.

OTHER EVENTS IN 1964

Purchase of Honolulu Paper Company, Ltd.

On June 26, 1964, Boise Cascade announced the purchase of Honolulu Paper Company, Ltd (HOPACO). HOPACO was a paper merchant or jobber and carried a complete line of industrial and fine papers. The company distributed stationery items, office furniture, office machines, and engineering supplies through three retail stores on Oahu and Maui; a staff of wholesale outside salesmen sold both industrial and fine papers to a wide variety of users. In addition, HOPACO produced and sold a relatively minor quantity of setup and folding boxes.

HOPACO had experienced substantial growth following World War II, increasing sales from $1 million just prior to the war to $8.4 million in 1963. The company had a total of 260 employees in 1964.

Acquisition of Associated Stationers Supply Company

Associated Stationers Supply Company, Inc., a Chicago based wholesale and retail office supply firm, became part of Boise Cascade on October 1, 1964. With annual sales of $16 million, Associated was said to maintain one of the largest and most inclusive inventories of office supplies in the industry. Its wholesale catalog included more than 15,000 different items in inventory. Associated had wholesale distribution warehouses situated in: Chicago, Illinois; Milwaukee, Wisconsin; Cincinnati and Cleveland, Ohio; Jacksonville, Miami, and Tampa, Florida; Charlotte, North Carolina; St. Louis, Missouri; Buffalo, New York; Nashville, Tennessee; and Atlanta, Georgia. The company also operated eight retail stores, serving the Chicago metropolitan area.

Under the terms of the acquisition agreement, Associated shareholders received one share of Boise Cascade stock for each four shares of Associated, representing a total of 88,490 new shares of Boise Cascade stock. Associated had 480 employees in 1964.

Purchase of Thermoplastics Industries, Inc.

In October, 1964, Boise Cascade announced the purchase of Thermoplastics Industries, Inc., of Brockton, Massachusetts, a small producer of plastic film products, machinery, and instrumentation for use in complex packaging. It was said that "Thermoplastics Industries' research capabilities in plastic films would complement and extend Boise Cascade's capability in packaging."

Acquisition of Kingsberry Homes Corporation

In November, 1964, Kingsberry Homes Corporation, one of the nation's leading manufacturers of factory-built homes, joined Boise Cascade. Kingsberry, with headquarters in Chamblee, Georgia, operated home manufacturing plants at Fort Payne, Alabama, and Emporia, Virginia. The two plants had a combined production capacity of 20 houses per day on a one shift basis. The company's line of homes included more than 90 basic models of single family residences and a group of four unit apartment houses. It had estimated sales of $16 million in 1964 and employed about 550 persons.

It was estimated that, in 1964, 20% of the single family houses built in the United States were manufactured homes of the type offered by Kingsberry.

Startup of Salem Container Plant

Boise Cascade added its seventeenth corrugated shipping container plant in June, 1964, with a new $1 million facility at Salem, Oregon.

Construction of Medium Mill

In midsummer, construction was begun on a $7,500,000 pulp and paper mill to produce corrugated medium—the fluted portion of a corrugated shipping container.

The medium mill, built adjacent to the company's kraft pulp and paperboard mill at Wallula, Washington, was programmed to produce 125 tons of corrugated medium a day, beginning in the fall of 1965.

Construction of an Envelope Plant at Allentown, Pennsylvania

At year-end, 1964, Boise management announced the beginning of construction of a new envelope manufacturing plant at Allentown, Pennsylvania. The 50,000 square foot plant, scheduled for startup by mid-1965, was to employ between 50 and 100 people.

Plywood Expansion

In April, 1964, Boise's new $2.5 million plywood mill at Elgin, Oregon, came into production and, in this same month, expansion was completed in plywood plants at Independence, Oregon, and Yakima, Washington.

Merchandising Change

The major change in Boise Cascade's merchandising group occurred in June, 1964, when the company's previously separate wholesale and retail divisions were combined at the regional level. In this way, the 15 warehouses of the wholesale division were expected to serve primarily as distribution centers for the company's 109 retail outlets.

Overseas Activities

Boise Cascade continued to expand its international activities in May, 1964, when management agreed to take over operations of a pulp and paper mill in the Philippines. A contract was signed in May to place the mill under the management control of Boise Cascade.

In October, 1964, Boise announced its intent to establish a multiwall paper bag plant in Costa Rica. The new company, Industria Nacional de Papel S.A. (INPASA), was a joint venture between Boise and Costa Rican interests.

Sale of Concrete Products Division

In late 1964, Boise Cascade sold its Washington concrete products division—at book value—to a corporation controlled by the various plant managers of the division. This division had sales of more than $11 million in 1964. All other concrete operations had been eliminated earlier in the year, except for the Boise Cascade Sand and Gravel Company, in Denver, Colorado.

Refinancing Program

In December, 1964, Mr. R. W. Halliday, vice president and treasurer of Boise Cascade, announced a major refinancing program which would make available $90 million for capital improvements during the next three years.

Two financial institutions—the John Hancock Mutual Life Insurance Company and the New York Life Insurance Company—were involved. Under this program, a new bond issue of $110 million was to be used to refinance Boise Cascade's existing debts and to improve its various operations.

"As part of this refinancing, we are able to stretch out our debt servicing requirements and receive a three year moratorium on debt payment," Halliday said. "Taking into consideration our cash flow and this moratorium, we are going to have $90 million available for capital expenditure for the next three years."

The following loan restriction governed the refinancing program:

a. Dividends were to be limited to 75% of earnings subsequent to the date of the refinancing.
b. A minimum working capital of $35 million would be maintained with the

provision that, in the event a division was sold, working capital could be reduced by a mutually agreed upon amount. The proceeds from such a sale could be applied either to the prepayment of the institutional notes within 60 days, or could, at the company's option and notice to the shareholders within 60 days, be committed for reinvestment by the company within a period of six months.

c. Principal value of lease commitments was limited to 20% of net assets, and annual payments on leases were limited to 13% of the total lease commitment permitted.

To provide an opportunity for additional borrowing in the future, a borrowing reserve factor was established, based on net asset values. The total long-term debt at any point in time was to be limited by the following percentage of long-term debt to net assets:

1965	65%
1966	60%
1967	60%
1968	55%
1969 and thereafter	50%

The Acquisition of
Minnesota and Ontario Paper Company

On December 16, 1964, the directors of Boise Cascade Corporation and of Minnesota and Ontario Paper Company (Mando) signed an agreement to merge Mando into Boise Cascade Corporation. Minnesota and Ontario was, directly and through its Canadian subsidiary, a manufacturer of newsprint, specialty papers, and building materials. Its 1964 net sales were $91,219,000.

The agreement of merger was approved by the holders of substantially more than the required two-thirds of the outstanding shares of common stock of each corporation in January 26, 1965.

The merger plan provided that Boise Cascade issue a share of cumulative, convertible preferred stock to the Mando shareholders for each share of their Mando common stock. This preferred stock carried an annual dividend of $1.40 per share, was callable at any time at a price of $40 per share, and had a preference of $40 per share in voluntary liquidation and $33 per share in involuntary liquidation.

Minnesota and Ontario was, directly and through subsidiaries, a manufacturer of newsprint, specialty papers, and building materials, the latter marketed under the brand name Insulite. Specialty papers manufactured included printing, packaging, and converting papers, such as groundwood printing and converting papers, coated-one-side label and release papers, bleached sulfate and sulfite converting papers, and bleached book and writing papers. Insulite manufacturing comprised a line of wood fibre insulation board, exterior siding products, interior finish products, and various industrial boards. The Insulite division also marketed a full line of hardboard products and a line of fiberglas insulating wool products produced by others. In 1963 newsprint sales represented 36% of total net sales, specialty papers 27%, Insulite 35%, and miscellaneous items, including subsidiary services, 2%.

Paper was manufactured at three plants, one at International Falls, Minnesota, and one at Fort Frances, Ontario, on the United States and Canadian sides, respectively, of the international boundary at the outlet of Rainy Lake, and one in Kenora, Ontario, at the northern outlet of Lake of the Woods. Insulite was manufactured at International Falls. The International Falls plant included a paper mill with an annual capacity of 82,000 tons of bleached kraft, sulfite, and groundwood specialty papers, and the Insulite mill with an annual capacity of 475 million square feet (one-half inch basis) equal to some 185,000 tons of insulation board and exterior siding products. The Fort Frances plant included newsprint and groundwood paper production facilities with an annual capacity of approximately 65,000 tons of newsprint and 60,000 tons of specialty papers. The Kenora plant was a completely integrated newsprint mill with an annual capacity of 220,000 tons.

Mando had acquired sites and announced plans for the construction of terminal warehouse facilities at South St. Paul, Minnesota, and Woodbridge, New Jersey, to provide faster delivery service to customers of its Insulite products.

Shipments in 1963 were: 254,578 tons of newsprint, 117,418 tons of specialty papers, and 163,676 tons of manufactured Insulite building products.

Newsprint was sold, usually under long-term contracts, by Mando's own sales organization to newspaper publishers in the upper midwestern states, principally Minnesota, Wisconsin, Iowa, Illinois, Indiana, Missouri, Kansas, Nebraska, and North and South Dakota.

Specialty printing and packaging paper sales were largely concentrated in an area in the midwestern states, which included Minnesota, Wisconsin, Iowa, Illinois, Indiana, Michigan, Ohio, Kentucky, Missouri, Kansas, and eastern Nebraska. Sales were made by the company's sales organization, and a substantial part were sold under long-term contracts.

Insulite products were sold and distributed widely, primarily through building material wholesalers and dealers. Insulite industrial insulation board products were also supplied in large volume to manufacturers of many end products, mainly in the building field.

Pulpwood Supply

In the United States Mando owned in fee approximately 315,000 acres of forest land in Minnesota and, through a contract with the United States Indian Service which was to expire in 1973 and contracts with the State of Minnesota and certain of its counties, had cutting rights on an additional 69,500 acres of forest land in Minnesota, all tributary to the International Falls plant. In addition, there was an area in Minnesota of approximately 3,550,000 acres of forest land, of which approximately two-thirds was publicly owned, tributary to the International Falls plant, from which Mando was able to purchase pulpwood.

In Canada the Canadian subsidiary had Crown timber concessions in Ontario, which were to expire in 1948 and carried provisions for 21 year renewals, in a forest area covering approximately 1,214,000 acres tributary to the Fort Frances plant, and in a forest area covering approximately 2,430,000 acres tributary to the Kenora plant.

In addition, the Canadian subsidiary had an agreement with the Province of Ontario, expiring in 1983, covering a forest area of approximately 1,200,000 acres, under which spruce and balsam pulpwood was reserved for use by the Fort Frances plant.

In addition to Mando's Crown timber concessions and provincial agreements, there were in Ontario approximately 400,000 acres of forest area tributary to the Fort Frances plant and approximately 700,000 acres tributary to the Kenora plant from which the Canadian subsidiary was able to purchase pulpwood. Pulpwood was also purchased from time to time in Manitoba and Saskatchewan.

MAJOR EVENTS OF 1965

During 1965, Boise Cascade continued to add to, and to consolidate, its activities. Organizationally, the paper activities of the Minnesota and Ontario Paper Company were made the responsibility of Mr. John Fery, vice president in charge of the paper group. A new building materials group was organized, consisting of the Insulite Division, Kingsberry Homes Division, lumber and plywood sales group, Components Division, and Building Materials Distribution Division (formerly the Merchandising Division), under vice president W. D. Eberle. Boise Cascade's research and development activities were realigned into four groups: a pulp-paper-fibre research center, a construction development group, a plastic-paper-packaging group, and a wood product development group. Mr. Eberle's responsibilities as corporate secretary were assumed by Mr. Charles F. McDevitt, who had been General Counsel since 1962.

The Paper Group

The Boise Cascade paper group continued to add to its activities in all areas. In September, 1965, a new 150 ton per day corrugating medium mill commenced production at Wallula, Washington. The mill was among the first in the United States to utilize softwood as a raw material and represented Boise's entry into production of this product.

The Kansas City, Missouri, box plant was expanded, and construction was begun on a new box plant to replace the existing facility in St. Paul, Minnesota. In December, negotiations were completed for part interest in a box plant in Vienna, Austria, marking the company's entrance into the European market.

Four envelope converting plants were added in 1965: two were newly constructed in Chicago, Illinois, and Allentown, Pennsylvania, and two were acquired in Pittsburgh, Pennsylvania, and Cleveland, Ohio.

During the year, the paper group sold its box and plastic bag plant in San Francisco to another major producer of these products, sold its facilities for producing camping equipment in Portland, Oregon, disposed of its multiwall bag plant in Berkeley, California, and moved its plastics research facilities to Brockton, Massachusetts.

Wood Products Group

In the building materials area, Boise Cascade continued to strengthen its position as a major producer of plywood with the acquisition of the Elk Lumber Company in Medford, Oregon. Additionally, a 49% interest was obtained in a Philippine Mahogany ("lauan") plywood mill located near Zamboanga, the Philippines, plus 100% of a plywood prefinishing plant at Torrance, California, to process the lauan. (The 49% interest was increased to 70.6% in 1967.)

The Elk acquisition included a plywood plant, a sawmill, and studmill, all located at Medford, Oregon, and considerable fee timber which the company agreed to purchase on cutting contracts over a ten year span. The marketing of Elk's output was assumed by the lumber and plywood sales group.

The lauan mill, located in Moro country six miles from Zamboanga Mindanao, the Philippines, consisted of a modern (1½ year old) plant, capable of producing 5,000 quarter-inch panels per day, and 25 year, renewable cutting rights on 85,000 acres of government owned timber. Because of the tropical climate, it was possible to harvest this timber on a 30 year continuous yield cycle, as opposed to the 80-120 year harvesting cycle in the northern United States. During the year, a $1.6 million expansion was begun to double the plant's output.

In July, the Getz-Roymac Company of Torrance, California, joined Boise Cascade. This company imported lauan plywood, which was prefinished in a 26,000 square foot plant at the rate of 1,000 panels per hour, using a highly automated, patented production process. The process embossed a V-groove, printed a pattern, applied color tone, and applied multiple coatings, all in one continuous production run. The Torrance plant purchased its raw material from the Zamboanga plant and other Philippine plywood producers, and marketed its output from a sales office located in San Francisco, California.

Near the end of 1965, negotiations were successfully concluded for the licensing to Boise Cascade of a patented Ford Motor Company process for curing paint on wood by an electron-beam process. The process could cure paint by irradiation in about six seconds.

In the Components Division, the Greeley, Colorado plant was closed, due to continuing low sales volume and recurring losses.

The Boise Cascade Merchandising Division was renamed the Building Materials Distribution Division, and Mr. James C. Hayes, previously general manager of the Central Region, was named Division general manager. His predecessor, Mr. A. E. Montgomery, was appointed corporate treasurer. The Distribution Division continued to consolidate its activities, closing or disposing of 27 retail lumber yards and one wholesale distribution branch, bringing the total operating at the end of the year to 15 distribution branches and 85 retail outlets.

The Boise Cascade Insulite Division completed a $12 million expansion, which had been initiated by Mando previous to its acquisition by Boise, with the construction of two terminal warehouses at South St. Paul, Minnesota, and Woodbridge, New Jersey, and the acquisition of 89 specially built railroad cars to transport the division's products to the warehouses. The expansion was made in an effort to speed up Insulite's service to its customers.

MAJOR EVENTS OF 1966

During 1966 Boise Cascade's primary emphasis was on internal improvements and expansion of facilities. Capital expenditures of $95.7 million were allocated to new plants and modernization and expansion of existing facilities. $55 million of this total was for the purchase of 426,000 acres of woodlands in the South. This timber was intended to supply a major part of the requirements for a complex of pulp, paper, lumber, and plywood mills that were planned for construction at DeRidder, Louisiana. These capital expenditures were financed by cash flow of $36.9 million and a new unsecured long-term loan at 5¼ % for an additional $25 million. At year end, Boise's long-term debt to equity ratio stood at one to one.

During the year, the company received delivery of an IBM 360/Model 40 computer, which was expected to allow expanded use of electronic data processing techniques. Besides routine management accounting and information systems, Boise had done extensive work in developing statistical models which were being used to obtain maximum realization from each log, as well as for scheduling machines at the company's pulp and paper mills. Boise had received national recognition in the industry for its computer applications, as well as for some creative programming that had been done for conversion from their older systems to the newer requirements of the IBM 360. These conversion programs had been so successful that they were being marketed, under a royalty basis, throughout the U.S. by Computer Sciences Corporation of Los Angeles.

Elsewhere in the company, $3.5 million had been budgeted during 1966 for research, development, and market development. A pilot plant in Boise had been completed for production of irradiated cellulose and polymer plastic combinations. This process, developed by the Ford Motor Company, was being used under exclusive license and allowed a superior bond between plastics and wood or paper. Initial applications for the pilot plant were in plastic-coated siding products.

In April, 1966, Boise Cascade split its common stock two for one and increased the dividend rate 25% to 25 cents for each new share.

Personnel Changes

During 1966, Mr. Robert W. Halliday, Boise's financial vice president, and Mr. John B. Fery, vice president in charge of the paper group, were elected to the board of directors to fill vacancies left by the resignation of Mr. Robert Keith (President of the Pillsbury Company), who had joined the board in the Mando acquisition, and Mr. David Bronson (Attorney), who had come onto the board with the merger with Cascade Lumber Company in 1956.

In September, Mr. W. D. Eberle, vice president and director, resigned to become President of American Radiator & Standard Sanitary Corporation (1966 sales $569 million). Mr. Eberle continued as a director of Boise Cascade.

Mr. Eberle's corporate responsibilities were assumed by Mr. McDevitt, while his management of the building materials group was temporarily undertaken by Mr. Hansberger.

Despite the major improvements achieved during the year, financial results were very disappointing. Although 1966 net income before taxes (of $27.4 million) was slightly higher than for 1965, an increase in the effective tax rate resulted in a 9% decline in earnings per common share. This decrease, the first since 1961, was attributed by management to the general U.S. decline in construction, with a corresponding softening in building material prices.

The Paper Group

During the year a new, $2.5 million corrugated shipping container plant was completed in West Memphis, Arkansas. This facility had a planned capacity of 360 million square feet of container board. Additionally, five existing corrugated container plants were expanded, with a resulting 30% increase in Boise Cascade's total capacity. Boise's 17 corrugated container plants were then able to produce 40 million containers per month. A grocery bag manufacturing company was acquired in 1966, greatly increasing Boise's bag output. A specialty bag manufacturer, producing decorative and specially printed paper bags and other decorative wrapping papers, was acquired.

Important capital expenditures were also made for existing paper mills. $4 million was spent to modernize and expand the printing and writing paper mills at Salem, Oregon, and Vancouver, B.C. A $1 million process and quality improvement program was completed at two newsprint mills.

Four new office supply and distribution centers were opened in the U.S.

and Canada during 1966. A new Roll Papers Division was formed, to sell directly and to distribute business and industrial forms, with four distribution centers located in Chicago, Dallas, Atlanta, and Kansas City. During the 1964 through 1966 period, Boise Cascade had spent a total of $150 million to upgrade paper making facilities and to develop distribution.

Building Materials

As with the paper group, building materials saw no dramatic changes in 1966. The sand and gravel operations in Denver were sold, and 12 of the company's 14 sawmills were upgraded with the expenditure of $1 million. During the year, building materials were distributed from ten company owned warehouses to 3,300 independent retailers and 88 company owned retail outlets. A major addition to the company's product line was realized with the completion of a $4.5 million particleboard plant at LaGrande, Oregon. This plant had a capacity of 160,000 square feet of particleboard per day.

In 1966, Kingsberry Homes completed its third plant, at Sigourney, Iowa. This $1.2 million, 104,000 square foot plant increased Boise Cascade's factory built home capacity to 5,300 homes per year. This plant was expected to serve a ten state market within 300 miles of the plant, producing 13 homes per week.

The most important acquisition during the year involved a 50% joint venture with R. A. Watt, a land developer and home builder in the greater Los Angeles area. The R. A. Watt Company had built 17,500 homes during the preceding 20 years, as well as 2 million square feet of industrial and commercial buildings and 1,000 apartment units. Sales in 1966 were $45 million. Boise's 50% interest was acquired for approximately 350,000 shares of Boise Cascade common stock. This purchase marked a major departure from the company's historical pattern of distributing building materials, components, and factory built houses to contractor customers. For the first time, Boise was now directly involved in on-site development and construction in the residential housing market.

MAJOR EVENTS OF 1967

During the first nine months of 1967, the downward trend of earnings was reversed. With earnings for the three quarters exceeding those of the full year 1966, management felt that Boise had successfully overcome the deleterious effects of the price weakness in building materials. The following chart summarizes financial results for this period.

During the year, Messrs. Fery, Halliday, and Moser, all of whom were already vice presidents and directors of Boise Cascade, were named executive vice presidents. The old "president's office," which used to consist of Messrs. Hansberger, Eberle, Halliday, and Black, was replaced by an expanded group referred to by Mr. Hansberger as "The Council." The council included Mr. Hansberger,

OPERATING HIGHLIGHTS

For the Nine Months Ended September 30

	1967	1966	1966	% Change in 1967
Net sales	$463,717,000	$415,075,000	$372,247,000	+25
Net income before taxes	25,523,000	26,366,000	21,382,000	+19
Net income	17,123,000	15,953,000	13,382,000	+28
Average number of common shares outstanding	10,241,197	9,395,024	8,995,024	+14
Net income per common share	$1.29	$1.28	$1.18	+ 9

the three executive vice presidents, Mr. McDevitt (vice president, secretary, and general counsel), Mr. Gordon Randall (director of organization and communication), and Mr. Robert J. Weston (general manager, building products). The council met once each month to discuss major corporate questions. Mr. Weston was named general manager of the building products group in March, 1967, with central responsibility for advertising, promotion, product management, market research, and product development for lumber, plywood, Insulite, prefinished panels, and other specialty products. (Originally hired in late 1966 to head the Insulite division, Mr. Weston had been marketing vice president for Temple Industries, a Texas building materials company.)

The Paper Group

At the end of 1967, a $34 million expansion of the St. Helen's pulp and paper mill was completed, yielding an increase in annual capacity of 65,000 tons. Plans for the expansion into the South were finalized for the DeRidder, Louisiana, pulp, paper, plywood, and lumber complex. During 1966 and 1967, Boise Cascade spent $89 million to obtain sufficient timber resources in Louisiana and Texas to satisfy the needs of this complex when it became fully operational in 1970. In addition to lumber and plywood facilities, the DeRidder facility was to include an $80-$90 million pulp and paper mill. One paper machine was intended for production of newsprint, while a second paper machine was to be committed to bag and specialty papers.

In June, Boise acquired the R. C. Can Company of St. Louis, Missouri, in exchange for 1,038,560 shares of Boise Cascade convertible preferred stock. This acquisition expanded Boise's participation in the container business. R. C. Can was a pioneer in the manufacturing and distribution of fibre and fibre-combination containers. Sales had grown rapidly from $2.5 million in 1952 to $31.4 million in 1962 and $54.3 million in 1966, while earnings increased from $1.3 million in 1962 to $2.7 million in 1966. 1967 sales were expected to reach $65 million. The rapid growth of R. C. Can began with the development of the spiral wound fibre container for refrigerated dough, and continued with the development of fibre-foil combination cans for frozen juice concentrates and for motor oil. At the end of 1967, R. C. Can produced a broad line of fibre cans manufactured from special papers, and/or combined with foil or plastic linings. R. C. Can also produced a line of plastic containers, used for packaging cottage cheese and similar products. Research activities in the development of new lower-cost fibre-based containers and machinery for their manufacture was continuing to expand rapidly the number of applications. At the end of 1966, the company had 23 manufacturing plants (8 of which were connected by direct conveyors to their customers), located in 11 states and employing 1,900 people. Sales of fibre-based containers to the food industry accounted for 48% of 1966 sales, while containers for the petroleum industry contributed another 35%. Eleven per cent of sales were of plastic containers, while the balance was of fibre containers to miscellaneous users. Fibre containers were distributed to 1,900 customers, usually located within 300 miles of the nearest R.C. plant. The largest single customer purchased 28% of R. C. Can's sales, while the second largest purchased another 8%. Sales of fibre products to the food industry were the most profitable for this company, and it was expanding its development efforts in this area. Test marketing was being conducted by a major food company on an R. C. Can developed container for coffee, while extensive research was being undertaken to develop containers which could stand the high pressures of beer and carbonated beverages.

Building Materials

In 1967, Boise Cascade completed a new 85 million square feet/year capacity plywood mill at Kettle Falls, Washington. Whereas 16 new plywood mills had been built in 1966 and 1967 by the total industry in the southern part of the country, this was the only western plywood mill built by any company during this period. During the same time span, 14 older western plywood mills were closed.

Substantial changes had been made within the Insulite organization. Mr. Weston's initial activities after joining Boise Cascade had concentrated on this group, resulting in substantial reductions in personnel and in overhead costs. With a low-cost manufacturing facility to back him up, Mr. Weston's Insulite marketing efforts were centered upon price competition in sidings and in the high volume styles of ceiling tiles which were introduced by leading competitors. While Insulite had been consistently unprofitable since Mando was acquired by Boise, this division had been turned around during 1967 and was making a significant contribution to Boise Cascade earnings.

The Shelter Group

Beginning with the 50% interest in R. A. Watt in 1966, Boise Cascade expanded its activities in land development and on-site residential construction with several acquisitions during 1967. A 50% interest was obtained for 125,000 shares of Boise common stock in Perma-Bilt Enterprises, Inc., a San Francisco area contractor with projects underway with a total value of $45 million. Permo-Bilt had built 10,000 homes in the preceding 15 years and was firmly established in California's second largest population center. In September the Boise interest in Perma-Bilt was increased to 100%.

In July, Boise completed negotiations to acquire U.S. Land Co. of Indianapolis, a major developer of lake-oriented resort properties. Common stock used in this acquisition was valued at more than $10 million. In its five years of existence, U.S. Land had sold 4,000 lots, varying in price from $2,000 to $20,000, in five major developments, each of which surrounded a 200 to 500 acre man-made lake. These developments were: a 1,700 acre project near Gary, Indiana, a 1,500 acre project near Chicago, a 1,300 acre project near Cleveland, a 2,500 acre project near Washington, D.C., and a 3,200 acre project outside San Francisco (in the foothills of the Sierra Nevada Mountains). 1967 sales were expected to exceed $20 million.

In August, Boise acquired Lake Arrowhead Development Company in exchange for 299,950 shares of Boise Cascade common stock. Lake Arrowhead was a year-round and second home development in the San Bernardino-Los Angeles area. Three thousand lots had been sold at this development since 1961, and lot sales in 1966 totaled $5.5 million.

In October, the remaining 50% interest in R. A. Watt was acquired for an additional $6 million in Boise Cascade common stock. In mid-1967 Watt announced a new lake-land homesite development called Lake Los Angeles, which was a 4,000 acre project located approximately 75 minutes from Los Angeles City Hall. Another major R. A. Watt project was a $38 million development on the Palos Verdes Peninsula.

In June, the managements of Boise Cascade and Divco-Wayne Corp. reached agreement to merge Divco-Wayne into Boise Cascade. Divco-Wayne was a leading manufacturer of travel trailers and mobile homes. It also produced mobile classrooms, dormitories, offices, and specialized automotive products, such as bodies for school buses and multi-stop trucks. In 1966, Divco-Wayne had sales of $109 million, profits of $3.9 million, and employed 4,300 people. Following this agreement, Boise Cascade purchased 27% of the outstanding shares of Divco-Wayne from a corporation controlled by Divco-Wayne's two top executives. However, the merger proposal was disapproved when put to a vote of Divco-Wayne directors, although management had recommended it. Subsequently, the purchase price was increased and an improved offer was submitted to the Divco-Wayne shareholders for vote in January, 1968. Boise Cascade management was highly optimistic that the new proposal would be approved.

Personnel and Organizational Changes

A major realignment of the building products group took place in May, 1967. Centralized sales management was established in Boise for all of the company's building products—lumber, plywood, Insulite, prefinished paneling, and specialty products—under Robert J. Weston, general manager of the building products group. In addition, Mr. Weston was responsible for the wholesale and retail building materials distribution yards for all wood products import-export activities and building material purchases for resale, as well as pricing, strategy, and product coordination between sales and manufacturing. Insulite manufacturing facilities also remained under Weston's control.

A separate group, timber and wood products, was separated out from the old building materials organization. Under executive vice president Stephen B. Moser, this group was charged with responsibility for the management of all of Boise Cascade's timberlands, forestry operations, and the various lumber mills, plywood mills, and other wood product manufacturing facilities.

Kingsberry Homes and the old Boise Components Division were separated from the building products group to form a new light construction group under Mr. J. B. Nowak, Kingsberry's president. It was anticipated that Divco-Wayne, when acquired, would also be part of this group.

The R. A. Watt, Perma-Bilt, U.S. Land Co., and Lake Arrowhead operations were combined under treasurer William M. Agee, to form a land and home development group.

R. C. Can Co. became part of the paper group, under executive vice president John B. Fery. Corporate vice presidents were named to head individual units within the paper group: the pulp and paper mills; the Packaging Division (corrugated shipping containers, bags, and specialty products); the R. C. Can Division; the Envelope Division; and the Paper Distribution Division (including paper merchant and office supply activities).

FACILITIES AND RESOURCES
(As of late 1967)

Boise expected 1967 sales to reach $750 million, providing that the merger with Divco-Wayne was consummated. In late 1967, operations were being conducted in 200 locations in 30 states and 6 Canadian provinces, as well as in several foreign countries. Employees numbered 26,000 and there were 23,000 shareholders in all 50 states and in several foreign countries.

Timber and Wood Products

Timber resources included 7.4 billion board feet of saw timber and 34.6 million cords of pulpwood. These resources were held on 1,291,000 acres of company owned land and on 4,758,000 acres of land on which Boise held long-term leases or cutting rights. Of this acreage, 4.2 million were located in the upper midwest and in Canada, 1.2 million acres were located in the Pacific northwest, .4 million acres were located in Louisiana and Texas, and .2 million acres were in the Philippines.

The following facilities were held by Boise Cascade for the conversion of the above timber resources into saleable building material products:

1967 Estimated Output	Manufacturing Facility
780 million board feet of lumber	14 sawmills operating 2 shifts
775 million square feet of plywood	8 plywood mills
	(55% sanded, 45% sheathing
41 million square feet of particleboard	1 particleboard plant
1.4 million interior wall panels	1 prefinished panel manufacturing plant
40 million square feet of Philippine mahogany plywood	1 Philippine mahogany plywood plant

In addition, the building materials group operated an Insulite plant, producing 420 million square feet (28% siding, 31% sheathing, 11% ceiling tile).

Total sales of building materials for 1967 were expected to be about $200 million, of which somewhat more than half were in lumber and plywood.

Building Materials Distribution

Building materials distribution had been contracting steadily in recent years. At the end of 1966, Boise Cascade operated 88 retail outlets and 11 wholesale distribution centers. On September 30, 1967, this number had been reduced to 60 retail and 9 wholesale outlets; by the end of October, this number had been cut to 26 retail and 7 wholesale locations.

Paper Making Facilities

Paper was produced by 21 paper machines located in 7 U.S. and Canadian plants. In 1967, production of paper was expected to reach 950,000 tons and purchases were expected to add another 225,000 tons to total paper sales. This capacity broke down roughly as follows: 285,000 tons newsprint; 206,000 tons paperboard; 202,000 tons converting papers; 137,000 tons printing papers; and 119,000 tons business papers. Total sales of paper and paper products were expected to reach $375 million in 1967. In May, 1969, Boise Cascade expected to own the 40,000 ton tissue machine at St. Helen's as part of the original agreement with Crown Zellerbach for purchase of the entire St. Helen's complex.

Packaging

Boise Cascade originally had viewed the manufacture of corrugated shipping containers as merely the means for achieving full capacity operations in the paper mills. By 1967, management's growing market orientation had led to the development of markets for containers that exceeded Boise's container board capacity by 125-150,000 tons. Corrugated shipping containers were being manufactured at 18 plants at the end of 1967. Four manufacturing plants were producing bags and other specialty products, while five envelope plants had an output that made Boise Cascade the second largest envelope producer in the country. Virtually all of these envelopes were being produced for the direct mail advertising market. In addition, R. C. Can division had 22 fibre-foil and plastic container plants located across the country.

Paper Distribution

Paper distribution expected to produce about $80 million in sales. Activities were divided into five separate units, as follows:

1. The Office Supply Division sold a wide line of merchandise. Ninety-five per cent of its volume was sold through 100 company employed salesmen. The remainder was marketed, principally in the Chicago area, through ten company owned retail stores.
2. Paper importing and merchandising operations were conducted in the New York City area, concentrated primarily in publishing and business papers. (This group did not sell any Boise Cascade produced paper.)
3. Wilson Stationers (Canada) sold 85% of its volume directly to industrial consumers and the balance through 22 company owned retail stores. (This group did not sell any Boise Cascade papers.)
4. Honolulu Paper Company distributed industrial papers and retail office supplies throughout the Hawaiian Islands.
5. The Roll Papers Division distributed business form papers through four distribution points. (This division sold 20,000 tons of Boise Cascade produced paper.)

Through these groups, Boise Cascade was, in 1967, one of the largest single factors in the office supply distribution business in both the U.S. and Canada. This network had been expanded to include 19 U.S. cities and was expected to be increased to about 30.

Light Construction

Kingsberry Homes Division had three manufacturing plants, with an annual capacity of 5,675 units, which were expected to produce 1967 sales of about $19 million. Kingsberry primarily served those contractors who build 50 homes per year or less. Most homes were built to retail in the $10-$40,000 range, with the bulk of sales being in units below $25,000. The average Kingsberry package was sold to the contractor for $4,200. In addition to this package, it was necessary for the contractor to supply foundation, masonry, and other heavy elements, plus, of course, all necessary construction labor. Planned expansion of two of Kingsberry's home manufacturing plants in 1968 was expected to increase capacity to 9,000 units per year.

The Boise Cascade Components Division had three manufacturing facilities with an estimated 1967 sales volume of $4.2 million.

Land and Home Development

This group was anticipated to have a 1967 sales volume of about $130 million. $70 million was expected to be in on-site building construction and sales (including the value of the land). $60 million was in sales of individual lots of recreational land. Operations were conducted in California, Illinois, Ohio, and Virginia, with plans for expansion into six new population centers. The on-site residential construction was carried on by R. A. Watt in the Los Angeles area and by Perma-Bilt Enterprises in the San Francisco area. Land development was mostly lake-oriented residential property (often second homes), and was conducted by Watt, Perma-Bilt, U.S. Land Co., and Lake Arrowhead Development Co. This group was expected to produce "several millions of dollars" in 1967 earnings.

During 1967, as part of its "growing commitment to the land and shelter requirements of an expanding population," Boise Cascade established a Department of Urban Renewal "to explore ways of serving cities embarking on substantial rebuilding programs." As Mr. Hansberger indicated, "with our interest in providing suitable housing for large numbers of people, Urban Renewal is a natural and related application of our resources and talents in the shelter building field." A nonprofit program had been commenced for the urban renewal of downtown Boise, Idaho, as an initial step into this field. A joint venture also had been established with a Negro businessman, Winston Burnett, for construction work in Harlem that was expected to make a substantial contribution to the New York City Negro community.

Financial

During 1967, debt had been increased by another $60 million, of which $21.6 million was in an issue of new convertible debentures. By the end of the third quarter, the number of common shares outstanding had increased to 10.2 million, up from 9 million at the end of 1966.

THE FUTURE

In late 1967, Boise Cascade management was going through one of its periodic self-examinations. In years past, the company had shifted its strategy and its character many times, sometimes in response to newly found opportunities, other times as a consequence of previous growth and momentum. Originally, it had been easy to define the company as a "forest products company." Later, it was possible to talk about "our commitments to paper and to building materials." But, in 1967, with sales nearing three-quarters of a billion dollars, some were beginning to talk about the company as if it were a "conglomerate."

President R. V. Hansberger had a somewhat different view. According to him,

> Boise Cascade is a state of mind. It is a company where management is flexible, intimate, and personal. We seek to give individual opportunities to all our people: to provide a free environment without restrictions. Over the years, there have been changes in our dimensions and in our product mix, but there has been no change in this essential philosophy. Nor has there been a change in our basic purpose: to provide our shareholders with a consistently higher value of ownership.
>
> We are going through a reorientation. We are cutting our umbilical cord to trees. We used to be a resource-oriented company. We got into conversion in order to use that resource adequately. Then, from being a converter of trees, we have become marketers. Our resource now is the market, not the tree. In fact, we are buying trees (at DeRidder) in a tight money market because we have a market opportunity, rather than vice versa. We are net buyers in container board because we can sell more than we make. We are increasingly developing specialties which the market wants, rather than just producing commodities. We start now with what does the consumer want—or what ought the consumer want.
>
> We see the same opportunities in the shelter market as we've had in paper. We are uniquely positioned to serve that market and to meet the growing problems of the cities: rehabilitation of the ghettos. We have a joint venture in Harlem; Kingsberry is active in urban redevelopment in Atlanta; our new Department of Urban Renewal is designing and will carry out the redevelopment of downtown Boise; Ray Watt is involved in redevelopment in Los Angeles. Our opportunities to serve and to create are limitless.
>
> Many people have asked why we have not been more active overseas. Our answer is simply that our opportunities at home have been greater than our resources for capitalizing on them. A few years from now we would expect to do more overseas—when there is real advantage in exporting our marketing and our managing skills.
>
> We have always tried to have a very explicit purpose and a clearly under-

stood strategy. We've made many acquisitions, but only when they made good sense in our ability to serve a market need. To buy something just because it's attractive financially leaves me cold! There must be some kind of unifying concept to what we're doing. And, while we have been flexible in changing that concept as conditions change in the world around us, we don't believe in destroying a concept we've been pursuing until we have something to replace it. So, we always have a strategy that we are following, but we are always searching for a better one.

If people who can't see the unifying concept want to call us a "conglomerate," that's their privilege. But certainly none of us here think of ourselves that way.

chapter 8

Corporate Strategy and Organizational Form

In previous chapters, as we described the concept of corporate strategy and the frameworks for identifying, evaluating, and planning strategy, much was inferred about organizational form and administrative behavior. This chapter will attempt to make explicit the more important of these inferences, in an attempt to sharpen and extend our understanding of the strategic process.

STAGES OF GROWTH AND DEVELOPMENT

Our former colleagues, Professors Bruce R. Scott and C. Roland Christensen of Harvard, originally pioneered the concept that companies move inexorably from simple organizational forms to increasingly more complex forms, as they grow in their market coverage, variety of products, and over-all size. They identified three distinct "stages" of organizational development, each with its own distinguishable characteristics.

Elaborating on the Scott-Christensen formulation, we have found it useful to think about organizations as falling into six different categories. These six categories, we submit, represent the basic alternative forms in which a company's actual strategic posture is developed. Depending on where the actual decisions and choices are made, companies can be classified as follows:

1. *The one man show*—all strategic and all operating decisions made centrally on the basis of first-hand knowledge.
2. *Management through assistants*—all strategic and all operating decisions made centrally, but relying at least in part on reported information.
3. *Functional management*—specialized operating decisions made by various functional managers; multifunctional operating decisions and all strategic decisions made centrally.
4. *Geographical dispersion*—some or all central unit functions replicated in other locations. Specialized functional operating decisions made centrally by functional managers and administered by assistants in the units. Multifunctional operating decisions made by regional managers. Strategic decisions and resource allocations made centrally.
5. *The holding company*—most strategic decisions and all operating decisions made individually by autonomous divisions or subsidiaries.
6. *The free-form company*—all operating decisions made individually by each division. Broad strategic decisions made centrally; detailed strategic decisions made in the units.

These six categories represent a spectrum of complexity, ranging from the simplest organizational form (the unitary *one man show*) to the most complicated (the *free-form company*). Management through assistants (Type 2) is a natural extension of Type 1. Types 3, 4, 5, and 6 represent increasingly complex ways of dispersing the natural conflict points and necessary decision requirements throughout the organization, rather than concentrating them wholly in the single central manager. Type 3 represents an attempt to increase the specialized competences of the company through division of labor on a *functional* or *process* basis. Type 4 divides the company on a *geographic* basis. And Types 5 and 6 are organized on a *product/market* basis. While these types have persisted because of their demonstrated effectiveness under past conditions, undoubtedly new organizational arrangements will be invented in the future.

1. *The one man show* is familiar to most everyone; it is the typical form for small business. Here, one man—"the boss"—is in personal contact with each of his employees, receives information from each of them directly, and instructs each of them individually. There is no need for intermediate supervision. The general management functions, the operating functions, the ceremonial functions, and many of the nonmanagerial work activities are all performed by the one person.

The one man show can be extremely efficient. Authority and responsibility are clear cut. All of the various functions and activities are integrated in a single mind. Confusion and lack of coordination can be minimized. If the boss is competent, this organizational form can be very satisfying to him. Although he must work hard and be continually available to his subordinates, he can take sustenance from his obvious indispensability, his assurance that "everything is under control," and from the high degree of dependence and adulation which his employees display towards him. This is the familiar paternalistic pattern, so prevalent in small businesses all around the world. It is usually accompanied by the boss's high personal involvement and commitment to each of the employees as "members of the family."

There are, however, some severe limitations on the one man show. First, it makes enormous demands on the boss. No one else can make a decision or commitment. Hence, the full burden of company performance rests on his conceptual ability and on his omnipresence. Second, it becomes unworkable when the company reaches a size of more than 40 or 50 employees. No one man can physically contact and direct that many individuals without sharply diminished effectiveness. Third, it does not develop any decision-making capabilities within the organization. The company must bring in an outsider or expire whenever "the boss" steps down. Mitchell Nursery is a classic example of the one man show. This case highlights how difficult it is, for a man who is deeply immersed in every detail of operations, to discern clearly the relevant strategic variables.

2. *Management through assistants*—In this organizational form, trusted "assistants" (who may carry such titles as Manager, Director, or Vice President) gather information and furnish it to "the boss" in digested form. The boss still makes all of the important decisions—both strategic and operating—and directs the assistants to carry them out. The assistants are expected to develop their own detailed plans and to administer them within their own bailiwicks, but there is no doubt about the severe limits on their discretion. This is a way of multiplying and extending the talents of "the boss," without really requiring him to change his basic behavior or mode of operations. Like the pure one man show, it induces dependency and discourages initiative, unless the boss is very aware of the impact of his own behavior and sensitive to his associates' needs. Pioneer Brass is a good example of management by assistants, as is LaPlant-Choate. In each of these instances, the chief executive made all of the major operating decisions, as well as the strategic ones, and looked to "assistants" to carry them out.

If the company limits itself to only a single principal location, and to only a narrow range of products, markets, distribution channels, and production processes, this mode can be quite effective until a company approaches perhaps as many as 500 employees. Increasing complexity in operations, expanding the number of employees, or adding a second major geographical unit, inevitably places such strains on the company's decision-making apparatus that "the boss" must choose between a basic change in organizational form (and especially in his own role) or a shrinking of the company to a size and simplicity where the old management through assistants can once more be effective. This is the most frequent reason why many chief executives sell their companies (or hire a new general manager and step aside) in the size range of 300–600 employees.

3. *Functional management*—In this organizational form, the functional managers—Sales Manager, Production Manager, Engineering Manager, Controller,

Personnel Manager, Purchasing Manager, etc.—make all of the necessary operating decisions and deal with all of the administrative responsibilities of their respective functions. Each receives from the General Manager only general directions and the basic prescribed requirements for contact with other units. All strategic issues are brought to the General Manager for his review. The General Manager receives summary performance data, reports and plans from the various separate functional managers, individually and collectively. On this basis, he sets the company's general goals, makes the strategic decisions, coordinates interfunctional activities, and dispenses rewards and punishments.

This organizational form requires sharply different behavior by the chief executive from the previous two. Here he must learn to truly delegate authority and to live comfortably with complete reliance on other people. No longer can he know all of the details of each operation. Nor can he achieve performance solely by the strength of his personal activity. Many general managers who are highly successful in running Type 1 and Type 2 companies become dismal failures in running a functional organization, which relies so heavily upon the competence and commitment of subordinate managers. Ideally, in this organizational form, the general manager will involve all of his functional managers deeply in strategic decisions which must be made. Not only is such collective involvement likely to produce better decisions than the General Manager could make alone, but also the difficult interfunctional coordination problems can be more readily understood and resolved. If the General Manager does not involve the functional managers as partners in the strategic planning process, the company probably should not be described as a functional management organization, but rather as management through assistants (Type 2).

The various functional managers inevitably find themselves in a position of conflict. To maintain the support of their subordinates, they must honor and fight for the values inherent in that function's point of view (see the discussion in Chapter 2 of "departmental" points of view). To maintain the confidence and support of their peers and their superior, they are expected to perceive, and to commit themselves to, the over-all good of the total enterprise. Frequently these views and commitments are incongruent. If the General Manager does not overtly direct the strategic posture of the company, inevitably the power balance among department heads will determine the values to be honored and the specification criteria to be pursued.

Functional management is the most prevalent form of organization for middle-sized, single unit companies. It is also the common form for individual single-location divisions of large, multidivisional firms. If the product/market scope of the company or the division remains sufficiently narrow, the functional management form can deal effectively with populations of several thousands.

This form has all of the advantages of specialization and division of labor, with only a single point required for integration, tradeoffs, and collaboration among units. However, if the company's scope broadens and the enterprise becomes involved in several unrelated markets, product lines or channels of distribution, the functional type organization soon breaks down. It lacks sufficient integrating devices to deal effectively with a broad scope, multiproduct, multi-market, multiple location strategy.

Within our present case collection, Morgan Corporation's Tube Department is a good example of a functional management firm (even though it exists as part of a much larger company). The department was able to formulate its own strategy, choose its own product development direction, and make its own product/market/distribution/price decisions.

4. *Geographical dispersion* represents the partial expansion of the single-location "functional management" form into two or more locations with some decision-making prerogatives. In this organizational form, clean separations are made among the various functional activities in the field units. Multiple manu-facturing units report to a central headquarters Production Manager. Multiple field sales offices report to a central headquarters Sales Manager, etc. Basic functional operating decisions and all strategic decisions continue to be made centrally, although implementation of operating decisions is delegated to field managers. A new layer of Regional Managers, usually reporting to the President, is held responsible for multifunctional coordination and operating decisions. However, in practice they usually have little direct authority and must achieve results primarily through personal influence and persuasion.

If the central functional managers are strong and competent and the regional managers flexible and skillful, and if the product/market scope of the company remains fairly narrow, this geographically dispersed form can function effectively for organizations of tens of thousands of employees. Indeed, some of the leading mining, steel, rubber, and oil companies are among the enterprises which have grown to very great size by dispersing operations, but retaining central control on a functional basis. The geographically dispersed form becomes very cumber-some, however, when it is desirable to unite the various functions in a given region (e.g., combining manufacturing, sales, and finance in a specific territory, in order to compete more effectively within that region against fully integrated local firms). Similarly, it breaks down when the company begins to sell inter-mediate products, in addition to its basic end products, where each unit is en-gaged in external transactions with customers.

The major airlines represent large populations organized on a basis of geo-graphic dispersion by function. This is an appropriate form for the very narrow scope most airlines have chosen—i.e., transporting passengers and cargo between airports—but becomes outmoded as companies like Pan American and TWA involve themselves in other types of businesses (hotels, missile center manage-ment, etc.).

5. *The holding company* is an organizational form composed of a number of separate, autonomous product/market units under a single corporate banner. Here, the chief executives of the various units act as if they were running com-pletely independent companies. Each unit makes both strategic and operating decisions with only tangential contact among units. The individual units may be

divisions or subsidiaries, wholly owned or only partially. Typically, each unit controls its own funds and makes its own investments. Central management may require certain dividend payments, or fees, and cash transfers; but, from the point of view of divisional management, this is not very different from the payment of taxes or interest or other nonoperating expenses. The extreme position would be that of Ling-Temco-Vought, where each unit has its own separate stock exchange listing. More common is the situation of the Signal Companies in which each operating unit has a separate (and different) board of directors and "floats on its own bottom." Rexall's rigorous accounting controls identify units which are not performing up to their own promised target specifications, but strategic decisions in each unit remain the full prerogative of the unit general manager. ITT takes one further step than Rexall by requiring divisions to produce annual strategic plans. However, the controls, rewards, and emphasis appear to be upon short-term profits and on "doing better what we're already involved in." Interunit collaboration or synergy is minimal.

In general, the holding company form is most appropriate where the businesses of the various units differ sharply from one another. It obliges only slightly more detailed knowledge of the individual businesses on the part of central management than is required by the manager of a mutual fund. It is relatively easy to administer, since all of the burden for performance is placed on the unit general managers. It allows great freedom to individual unit managers and provides extensive opportunities for them to gain a full range of strategic and operating experience. Its weaknesses are, first, that such an enterprise is essentially *undirected*. Over-all corporate emphasis, priorities and direction derive from the relative aggressiveness and vigor of the respective unit managers and the original relative sizes of their available resources. A strong unit manager with a large asset base will necessarily skew the over-all strategic posture of a holding company. Whether or not such an emphasis produces the most effective posture is largely a matter of chance. Secondly, about the only control mechanism which central management can exercise, if results are unsatisfactory, is to replace the general manager. If the basic problem is that the unit is in the wrong business (or has the wrong product/market scope), an entire procession of successive general managers is unlikely to correct the situation. Thirdly, the autonomy of the individual units usually is given a higher priority than is the potential which might exist for interunit synergy.

Usually a holding company form is created through a succession of mergers and acquisitions. Little or no attempt is made to reconstitute the units or to integrate their activities. Return on investment or impact on earnings per share is the usual criterion for such new acquisitions. It is assumed that the present record will continue (or be improved upon), with little active intervention being required on the part of central management. Under this form, a company can be in an unlimited number of businesses—all it needs to do is to make more acquisitions. Hence there are no limits on its size or characteristics.

6. *The free-form company* may be difficult for an outsider to distinguish

from the holding company form. Both are indiscriminately classified by the financial community as "conglomerates." Like the holding company, the free-form company has a number of divisions (or subsidiaries), each of which has a different product/market scope from the others. However, the free-form company usually has fewer divisional units (perhaps not more than half a dozen). Each unit is stimulated by central management to rigorously identify, evaluate, and plan its *own* strategic posture; but the final strategic plan for each unit is evaluated and revised in light of *total* enterprise commitments and objectives. Central management exercises a very strong influence on over-all corporate product/market scope determinations, competitive emphasis, performance specifications, and resource allocations. All resources are viewed as if in a common pot, and they are redistributed frequently to achieve desired emphasis and priorities. Each division represents a separable, well-defined product/market scope, but central management is continually looking for synergistic interconnections and obliging division managers to collaborate.

Into this category we would place such companies as Litton, Textron, IBM, Xerox, and American Standard.

The advantages of this organizational form are, first, that it allows for multi-market diversification without sacrificing resource concentration. Second, it focuses continuously on the key strategic issues—scope, competitive advantage, resource allocation—and is capable of cutting back or eliminating declining units, while pushing growth as far as possible in those units with the greatest opportunities. As such, it is the form best suited to optimum large-scale resource deployment. Third, it provides the same opportunities for individual learning and development as the holding company form, plus providing additional instructional experience in complex strategic planning.

On the other hand, a free-form posture is very difficult to sustain. It is easy for central management to slip toward a holding company form by over-proliferating divisional units or by abdicating strategic decisions to unit managers. It is very important for central management to maintain a delicate balance between freedom and control and to keep themselves clearly focused on the important strategic issues, while delegating the operating crises and urgencies. Such managerial skill is rare, but the companies indicated above demonstrate that it does exist!

SIGNIFICANCE OF ORGANIZATIONAL FORM

It should be clear to the reader that these six categories are not all inclusive. A number of half-way combinations can and do exist. Depending upon *how* most problems arise within a firm, different forms tend to emerge. In all of these, however, it is important to differentiate between where the *initiative* lies (in proposing an action) and where the *authorization* resides to approve or veto such a proposal. The initiative may come from above or below, but when we talk of key operating and strategic *decisions,* we are referring to the *authorizations* which put those proposals into action. When authorizations are not explicitly made, then the decision-making function is abdicated to whomever initiates a proposal. This is how organizations get out of control and suboptimize their potentials.

The six categories presented represent key modal points in a continuum of complexity and diversity in the decision-making, resource allocation process— what we have consistently called the process of planning and implementing corporate strategy. We have suggested that complexity increases with: (a) size and rate of change in the number of employees, the volume of transactions, and the quantities of assets, sales and cash flow involved; (b) variety of products, markets, and channels of distribution; (c) deconcentration of customers (moving from a very few customers—other departments or divisions, Government, a few large purchasers—to an increasingly diverse and multiple set of purchasers); and (d) geographical dispersion. Over-all coordination, direction, and control become increasingly more difficult as complexity and diversity increase.

BASIC OBJECTIVES

We have defined the six organizational categories in terms of (i) differences in the extent of their product/market scopes; and (ii) differences in the locus of their strategic decision making and resource allocation processes. It is our contention that specific characteristic values and objectives (what we have called "performance specifications") are typical of companies in each of the six organizational categories. Types 1 and 2 companies—the one-man show and its immediate extension, management through assistants—tend to place their major emphasis on assuring survival and, thus, on short-term profit performance. Types 3 and 4 companies, somewhat larger and more secure in their competitive environments, seem less concerned about survival and more concerned about stability and order—exercising fuller control and predictability over their activities —which now extend beyond a single person's capability for direct administration. Types 5 and 6, having developed some modicum of strength and stability, appear to be more concerned about increasing their resource bases, their power in the market place, and in diversifying their risks of market fluctuations. Type 5—the holding company concept—is essentially a defensive posture. It seeks to minimize conflict among units, between units and headquarters, and between the company and an unpredictable environment. The free-form company (Type 6), on the other hand, represents a more aggressive posture, seeking to maximize opportunity and to fully utilize its resources.

PERFORMANCE CRITERIA

It should also be noted that Types 1, 2, 3 and 4 organizations are most typically *resource-oriented* or *production-oriented* or *market-oriented.*

Types 1 and 2 organizations tend to be regulated by the personal likes and dislikes of "the boss" as regards the individual performance styles of his sub-ordinates.

Types 3 and 4 organizations tend to emphasize cost or expense centers—internal efficiency criteria—with most weight being given to the most powerful department's values.

Types 5 and 6 organizations tend to apply external effectiveness criteria through the establishment of individual profit centers.

Thus, the rewards and punishments administered throughout different companies tend to be a function of: the *person* in Types 1 and 2; the inter-departmental *power structure* in Types 3 and 4; and *abstract measurement* of profit or return on investment in Types 5 and 6.

STRATEGIC MODE

In Chapter 7 we described the four basic strategic modes of *niche development, horizontal expansion, vertical integration,* and *diversification.*

It should be clear that a Type 1 organization (one man show) is most appropriate to a *niche* strategy. Complexity is held at a low enough level that one person can cope with all the revelant variables. As previously noted, the major concern for such an organization is assuring its survival by maintaining flexibility and mobility.

A Type 2 organization (management through assistants) lends itself to an enlarged niche strategy or to a relatively straightforward *horizontal expansion*—either by geographic expansion or by developing new classes of customers in existing locations. Again, the basic concern is for survival and for maintaining personal control of activities.

The Type 3 organization (functional management) is especially well suited to a strategy of *vertical integration,* where for each unit except the terminal one, the volume of transactions is predominantly internal—i.e., with other units of the company. Here the emphasis shifts from survival to maintaining order and improving efficiency. Geographical decentralization of operating units can be easily accommodated by preserving their functional integrity and moving to a Type 4 organization.

Types 5 and 6 are two organizational solutions to the strategy of *diversification.* To be sure, in any geographically dispersed organization, there are many possible variations on the degree of centralization or decentralization of the various *operating* functions. But the basic distinction between Type 5 (holding company) and Type 6 (free form) is where and how the *strategic* choices of product/market scope, competitive emphasis, performance specifications, and resource allocations are made. Both types place major emphasis on growth—extending resources, markets and influence.

If some of the strategic choices are made centrally and some in the units—

e.g., planning in the units and resource allocation centrally—a hybrid organizational form can develop which is less effective than either Type 5 or Type 6. It is our argument that the entire strategic process should remain integrated—i.e., planning and implementation should not be separated organizationally. Thus a Type 5 holding company should try to maximize the effectiveness of each of the autonomous units. Even though it gives up its opportunities for synergy and cumulative emphasis, it is more important to simply assure that each unit's over-all objectives and performance specifications are consistent with the company's total targets than it is to monitor each decision. On the other hand, a Type 6 organization—requiring far greater administrative skill—should attempt to maximize results for the whole company, while deliberately sublimating the performance opportunities of specific units. Thus central management needs to be much more frequently involved with unit management in Type 6 than in Type 5.

It is our contention that each of the various strategic modes becomes administratively practical only under specific organizational forms. Direction, coordination, and control of a diversified company require either a holding company or free-form organizational structure. Vertical integration and horizontal expansion demands either a pure functional management or its logical extension, geographic dispersion. The single niche strategy requires the flexibility of the one-man show or its modification, management through assistants. Note, however, that the free-form company may, in fact, be pursuing a multiniche strategy!

We suggest that companies move inexorably from Type 1 to Type 2 to Type 3 organizations as size, complexity, and diversity increase. Thereafter, Types 4, 5, and 6 represent essentially different alternatives. Type 4 is appropriate for a large company with a narrow scope (e.g., a typical oil or mining company). Type 5 is appropriate for the large, diversified company that seeks a very broad entry into a large number of very different markets (e.g., ITT, Castle & Cooke, Rexall). While Type 6 is appropriate only to the company with the general management skills and strategic restraint to attempt to achieve overwhelming market leadership in a very few market segments (e.g., Boise Cascade, Textron, IBM, Applied Power).

STRATEGY AND STRUCTURE

In his provocative book *Strategy and Structure,*[1] historian Alfred Chandler investigated the changes over time in corporate strategy and organizational form of four large industrial enterprises: Du Pont, General Motors, Standard Oil Co. (New Jersey) and Sears, Roebuck. As a result of these studies, Chandler postulated that the choice of a strategy necessarily determines a company's structural arrangement. Our position is only slightly different: We argue also that the existing power structure, in the absence of overt direction, will determine the company's strategic emphasis. Moreover, if the forces for perpetuating a particular

---

[1] Alfred D. Chandler, *Strategy and Structure* (Cambridge, Mass.: MIT Press, 1962).

structural form are very strong, we postulate that that company necessarily has excluded itself from any basic change in strategic posture.

Chandler's study of the four companies confirmed that a change in structure is often slow in following a change in basic strategy. This was particularly true in periods of rapid expansion. The conclusion of the author about this was: Either the executives were too involved in day-to-day operating activities to appreciate or understand the long-range organizational needs of their enterprises, or else their training and education failed to sharpen their perception of organizational problems, or failed to develop their ability to handle them. Other possible reasons for the resistance of executives to administratively desirable changes were that structural reorganization threatened their own personal position, their power, or most important of all, their psychological security.

Following Chandler's concepts, we can see that Rexall Drug did not change its basic corporate strategy or its corporate structure during the years of the Great Depression and World War II. The "distinctive competence" of Rexall remained relatively constant until 1949, as did its key personnel. Rexall Drug, Inc. was an operator of 600 company-owned retail drugstores, and manufactured and distributed a line of drug and convenience products through 10,000 franchised "Rexall" drug stores. In 1949, Rexall suffered its first loss from operations. Management reacted to the loss situation by eliminating dividends, by reducing inventories, and by selling property. There was no particular change in either strategy or structure. These were primarily operating moves, rather than strategic ones. The strategy of Rexall began to change when the management moved to *diversify* operations rather than to continue to *integrate*. The structure began to change as Tupperware and other acquisitions were held as separate operating divisions, and new activities such as Riker and petrochemicals were created as separate autonomous units.

Fidelity Credit Corp. [on page 457] offers still another example of the relationship between strategy and structure. Fidelity developed a strategy that was highly responsive to the needs of its environment. However, the structure that emerged did not match the strategy. The consulting report noted that the most efficient structure to implement the strategy was to combine the two functions of consumer financing and car sales financing. However, as we saw, the markets for these two functions were different in the environment. There were differences in dollar amount of loans, credit evaluation, length of loan, and especially in the values of the personnel. The new structure had the effect of changing the basic strategy through changes in interpersonal relationships, and of limiting the company's capability to adjust effectively to the needs of the environment.

SKILL REQUIREMENTS

The characterization of the six different organizational forms also makes it possible to differentiate the skill requirements for managers in the various situations.

Type 1 companies require a man of very broad capabilities—conceptual, technical, and human. The success of the company rests entirely upon him personally.

Type 2 companies demand only slightly less from the top man, as some technical support is provided by assistants.

In Types 3 and 4 companies, the general manager requires strong conceptual and human skills, but technical proficiency can be provided by department managers. The department manager in turn, requires substantial human skill and some conceptual skill, in directing his own unit and relating it to other departments.

In Types 5 and 6 companies, the principal requirement for the general manager is strong conceptual ability. Division heads and department managers require skills which are analogous to Types 3 and 4 general managers and department heads respectively.

In a Type 6 company, the *field unit* managers are primarily involved in carrying on or personally supervising day-to-day activities. The manager operates within the framework of policies and procedures set by the departmental headquarters and the higher offices. The *departmental and divisional* executives may make some long-term decisions, but because their work is within a comparable framework determined by the general office, these executives' administrative activities tend to be tactical or operational. The *general office* executives make the broad strategic or entrepreneurial decisions as to policy and procedures and can do so largely because they have the final say in the allocation of the firm's resources—men, money, and materials—necessary to carry out these administrative decisions and actions.

The managers in the *field unit* are concerned with one function—marketing, manufacturing, engineering—in one local area. The executives in the departmental headquarters plan, administer, and coordinate the activities of one *function* on a broad regional and often national scale. Their professional activities and their outside sources of information concern men and institutions operating the same *specialized* function. The *divisional* executives deal with an *industry* rather than a *function*. They are concerned with all the functions involved in the over-all process of handling a line of products or services. Their professional horizons and contacts are determined by industry rather than functional interests. The executives in the *general office* have to deal with several industries or one industry in several broad and different geographical regions. Their business horizons and interests are broadened to range over national and even international economies.

Of course, the executives that are responsible for entrepreneurial decisions are not necessarily imbued with a long-term strategic outlook. Some executives responsible for resource allocation may very well concentrate on day-to-day operational affairs, giving little attention to changing markets, technology, sources of supply, and other factors affecting the long-term health of their company. Their decisions may be made without forward planning or analysis but rather by meeting in an *ad hoc* way every new situation, problem, or crisis as it arises.

They may *accept* the *goals* of their enterprise as *given* or *inherited*. Clearly, wherever entrepreneurs *act like managers,* they have failed to carry out effectively their role in the economy as well as in their enterprise.

THE ORGANIZATIONS OF THE FUTURE

Increasing complexity—both of companies which have grown to enormous size and diversity and of a rapidly changing environment in which parts become increasingly interdependent—is certain to make enormous demands upon organizations in the future.

Already, the profit center concept has become outmoded as an effective means of measuring or motivating unit performance. Its emphasis is on short-term consequences which are frequently transitory rather than upon basic shifts in competitive advantage. A number of far-sighted managers are already contending that changes in profits must be viewed together with changes in market share, changes in basic product cost, and the discounted present value of the unit's cash flow. This is certainly a far cry from the simple, single criterion of profit or return on investment! Yet it seems clear that such analysis avoids the gross misinterpretations of current performance which stem from conventional accounting practices. John Dearden [2] urges that profit evaluation be used to determine the effectiveness of the unit's strategy, rather than the effectiveness of the specific manager. Thus, he recommends evaluating unit performance at critical periods in its life cycle, rather than on a rigid annual basis and making such evaluation a full-blown study of the unit's strategy and not just its operating efficiency.

Such changes are coming. And so is the ever-growing trend towards "conglomeration." The Boston Consulting Group [3] makes an articulate and convincing case for conglomerates as the most effective organizational form in the future. They state:

> Conglomerates are the normal and natural business form for efficiently channeling investment into the most productive use. If nature takes its course, then conglomerates will become the dominant form of business organization, particularly in the U.S.
>
> This conclusion may seem surprising in view of the widespread criticism of the whole idea of a conglomerate. People do not seem to take conglomerates seriously as a more effective business organization form. Closed and mutual funds, which are a very dilute form of conglomerate, nearly always sell at a deep discount. Apparently even the anti-trust division of the Justice Department does not take conglomerates very seriously as an effective competitor.
>
> In a sense, almost all companies are conglomerates if they have more than a

---

[2] John Dearden, "Appraising Profit Center Managers," *Harvard Business Review,* (May–June 1968).

[3] "Conglomerates in the Future," The Boston Consulting Group, 1968.

single product. The designation "conglomerate," however, seems to be reserved for companies which have business interests so different that they are essentially independent except for their financial resources.

There is no difficulty in identifying Litton or Ling-Temco-Vaught as conglomerates. Textron is no longer so obviously composed of unrelated businesses. But General Electric is surely a conglomerate. Certainly Du Pont has only a limited interplay between its textile fibers and its automobile finishes. It too is a conglomerate.

There is an infinite range of relatedness and therefore characteristics of a conglomerate. However, all true conglomerates as distinct from holding companies of any kind have one major characteristic in common. They are able to control the internal allocation of financial resources. As a corollary every conglomerate has an ability to obtain financial resources which is a function of the characteristics of the firm as a whole rather than of the individual parts. This particular characteristic is of critical importance.

The conglomerate is able to carry the process of business evolution to one level higher in complexity. Instead of developing a family of products, it is able to develop a family of businesses. Every product goes through a sequence in which it is first a drain on corporate resources, then becomes profitable but is still a cash drain because of the reinvestment required, and finally becomes a generator of excess cash. This process is obscured in most businesses because of the overlap in stages of development between products. The smooth growth of a business may conceal the birth, development, growth and maturity of a long and complex series of products. Within a business the products are usually closely related.

But businesses as a whole go through the same cycle. They tend to be unprofitable when very new, profitable but undercapitalized when their growth is the fastest, and then generators of cash when they become successful, mature and slow growing. The problems change with maturity. The young fast growing business needs capital to take advantage of its potential growth and exploit its opportunity. The mature business has real problems of finding suitable investments for its cash flow.

The conglomerate is exceedingly well positioned to discharge the function of directing capital investment into the most productive areas. It can be far more efficient and effective than the public capital market is likely to ever be.

The top management of even a far-flung and diverse company is better equipped to appraise the potential and characteristics of a growing business than an outside investor. Such a company has staff research capability and the access to data that even the most detailed prospectus cannot provide to the general public.

This ability to divert and reinvest the cash flows of a mature business is very important. There is no reason to reinvest the profits of a business in further expansion of the same business merely because it has been successful in the past. General Motors is not the only successful company who would find it unwise or difficult to expand faster than its industry.

The U.S. tax structure characteristically severely curtails investment funds available for reinvestment, first if they appear as reported profits and again if they pass through the hands of shareholders as dividends. As a consequence, any corporate form which permits reinvestment expenditures to be treated as an expense instead of capitalized has a major advantage. This attrition of investable capital is the effect of a company paying a normal income tax and the stockholder paying taxes on dividends received before the funds are reinvested. The value of this advantage is not small. Income taxes would take away about half the reinvestable funds, if the cash flow is reported as a profit. If paid out in dividends before reinvestment, then only a fraction of this is left for reinvestment.

Any company which can treat its investments in growing businesses as an expense to be offset against other profit has a great advantage in terms of its cost of capital. Also any company which can obtain its equity from internally generated funds has a far lower effective cost of capital than if it obtained those funds outside from stockholders who can retain only a fraction of the proceeds they eventually receive in dividends.

The conglomerate is in an unexcelled position to obtain capital at the lowest possible cost and to put it to the best possible use. The question of course is: will it?

If conglomerates treat each of their divisions or units as separate and independent businesses, they fail to take advantage of their own strength. The traditional profit center concept of management has a fatal defect for a conglomerate. It concentrates attention on near term reported earnings rather than investment potential. This is why most successful conglomerates have been composed of mature businesses and have been notably inconspicuous for their success in incubating new businesses. Conglomerates must behave like investors, not operators if they are to achieve their great potential.

Experience curve theory dramatizes how great the potential really is for a conglomerate. This theory says that costs are a direct function of accumulated market share. It further says that investment in market share can have extremely high returns during the rapid growth phases of a product. As long as the growth rate exceeds the cost of capital every year in the future is worth more in present value than the current year. Today's losses therefore may be very high return investments, even if prices never go up, provided those losses protect or increase market share. If market share correlates with cost differential, then it can be translated into investment value.

If experience curve theory is correct, then the logical consequence of competition will be extremely low prices initially on new products. These prices will tend to be so low as to be pre-emptive. They will also be stable. The net result will be very large negative cash flows for a considerable period until costs decline to match the low price. This will be followed by even larger positive cash flows as costs continue their decline and volume continues to increase. This pattern is already visible in certain military procurement and in the pricing of commercial aircraft. Prices never go up, but costs do continue to go down. This produces the return of investment.

The conglomerate is eminently well suited for this kind of "expense investment." In fact, only a conglomerate can hold a portfolio of risks. Only the conglomerate can match positive and negative cash flows. Only the conglomerate can pair off the tax consequences of "expense investment." Only the conglomerate can accumulate and analyze the detailed information required to make a wise investment involving such massive initial negative cash flows.

Everything favors the conglomerate: tax laws, capital costs, sources of funds, breadth of business opportunity. This does not mean that conglomerates will automatically succeed. Their inherent advantage lies in their flexibility and many conglomerates are conspicuously lacking in flexibility. If the flexibility is not used, they are under a handicap. The individual business is given no advantage except uncertain financial backing. The corporate overhead structure can be a real burden if the conglomerate is managed as if each business were an independent and irreversible investment. There are quite a few lackluster conglomerates.

If the conglomerate is to realize its potential, it must have an investment and strategy development skill which goes well beyond the characteristic pattern of the independent business. Certainly some corporations are going to do this. Those that do are quite likely to be the preeminent and dominant firms of the future.

If this be true, and we think it highly likely, then the understanding and skillful implementation of Corporate Strategy will become the single most important characteristic of the successful company of the future.

Castle & Cooke, Inc.

Introduction

In 1965, Castle & Cooke, Inc., was ranked #312 among *Fortune* Magazine's 500 largest U.S. industrial corporations. This ranking placed it just behind such well-known companies as Sunbeam, McGraw-Hill, and Beech-Nut Life Savers, and just ahead of such companies as Gerber, Bell & Howell, and Schenley. Had the proportionate sales of its non-wholly owned subsidiaries been included, its ranking would have been nearly 100 places higher, alongside such familiar names as Libby, McNeill & Libby, Merck, Bristol-Myers, and Studebaker. Divisions or subsidiaries included the world's largest pineapple company (Dole), the world's second largest banana company (Standard Fruit), and the fourth largest U.S. packer of seafoods (Bumble Bee). Yet despite this preeminence, the parent company was little known outside Hawaii, its corporate headquarters and point of origin.

The reasons for the company's relative obscurity were primarily: (1) through most of its history, Castle & Cooke (C & C) had acted largely as a holding company; and (2) the integration and/or acquisition of some of the most important portions of the company had been relatively recent, i.e., in the last five years. In the 1960–1965 period, the character of the company had been undergoing great change. Still greater changes appeared likely in the future.

ABOUT THE CASES

This case series provides an opportunity for the student to identify past changes, to assess the present situation, and to become involved in planning the future strategy of this large and complex company.

Castle & Cooke, Inc. (A) describes the historical evolu-

---

tion of the company, highlighting the major strategic changes at different points in time. The student's task here is to evaluate the determinants of these changes and to assess the subsequent outcomes. This case also provides an over-all description of the company and its principal executives as of late 1965. These data can be used to identify the company's actual strategic deployment of assets and efforts at that time, and to appraise the opportunities and constraints which the company faced.

Then, cases on each of the five major operating units of the company follow: Dole, Standard Fruit, Bumble Bee, C & C's sugar interests, and Oceanic Properties (a major real estate development firm). In each instance, the student is asked to analyze that unit's resources, opportunities, and constraints, and to determine a strategy which would be most favorable to the future survival and growth potential of that unit.

Castle & Cooke, Inc. (B), the final case in the series, highlights the determination of C & C's chief executives to move the company toward greater integration and toward becoming more of an operating entity than had been true in the past.

The full series, then, allows the student to address the crucial questions of: where C & C's real competitive advantages lie; what its corporate scope, objectives, and strategy should be; what emphasis (positive or negative) should be given to present activities; what new activities should be entered into; what units should be combined or redefined; how the whole company should be organized and operated.

Castle & Cooke, Inc. (A)

SCOPE OF OPERATIONS

In late 1965, Castle & Cooke, Inc. (C & C) consisted of four operating divisions, an investment division, and 12 principal subsidiary companies. These divisions and subsidiaries, in turn, held majority interests in 31 other companies and had important investments in 14 more. Exhibit 1 shows the organizational relationships among these 62 corporate units.

Headquartered in Honolulu, Hawaii, the company's 1965 major concentration of assets and equity lay in five clusters of companies. Each of these five is described in detail in a separate case. These five, in order of asset size, were:

1. *Dole Co. and subsidiaries.* Dole, a wholly owned division, was the world's largest pineapple company, with acreage and plants in Hawaii, California, Oregon, and the Philippines.
2. *Standard Fruit and Steamship Co. and subsidiaries.* Standard, an 84% owned subsidiary, was the world's second largest banana company (after United Fruit), with major holdings in Honduras, Costa Rica, and Louisiana.
3. *C & C sugar interests.* These included the majority ownership in three Hawaiian plantations (Ewa, Waialua, and Kohala), and a 16% equity in the California and Hawaiian Sugar Refining Corp., operators of the U.S.'s largest cane sugar refinery at Crockett, California.
4. *Bumble Bee Seafoods and subsidiaries.* Bumble Bee, a wholly owned division, was the fourth largest U.S. packer of seafood products (after Van Camp, Star-Kist, and Booth Fisheries), with canneries in Oregon, Washington, Alaska, Hawaii, and Maryland.
5. *Oceanic Properties, Inc., and subsidiaries.* Oceanic, a wholly owned subsidiary, was one of the nation's largest real estate development firms, with important holdings in California, Hawaii, the Philippines, and Malaya.

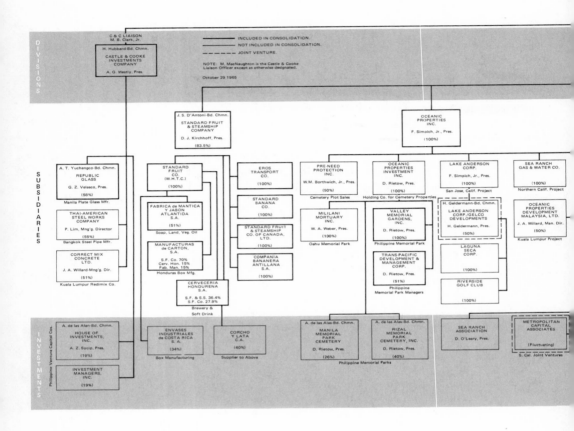

DIVISIONS

C & C LIAISON
M. B. Clark, Jr.

H. Hubbard-Bd. Chmn.
CASTLE & COOKE
INVESTMENTS
COMPANY

A. G. Westly, Pres.

————— INCLUDED IN CONSOLIDATION.
- - - - - NOT INCLUDED IN CONSOLIDATION.
——·——·— JOINT VENTURE.

NOTE: M. MacNaughton is the Castle & Cooke
Liaison Officer except as otherwise designated.

October 29 1965

J. S. D'Antoni-Bd. Chmn.
STANDARD FRUIT
& STEAMSHIP
COMPANY
D. J. Kirchhoff, Pres.
(83.5%)

OCEANIC
PROPERTIES
INC.
F. Simpich, Jr., Pres.
(100%)

SUBSIDIARIES

A. T. Yuchengco-Bd. Chmn.
REPUBLIC
GLASS
G. Z. Velasco, Pres.
(58%)
Manila Plate Glass Mfr.

THAI-AMERICAN
STEEL WORKS
COMPANY
P. Lim, Mng'g. Director
(55%)
Bangkok Steel Pipe Mfr.

CORRECT MIX
CONCRETE
LTD.
J. A. Willard-Mng'g. Dir.
(51%)
Kuala Lumpur Redimix Co.

STANDARD
FRUIT
CO.
(W.H.T.C.)
(100%)

FABRICA de MANTICA
Y JABON
ATLANTIDA
S.A.
(51%)
Soap, Lard, Veg. Oil

MANUFACTURAS
de CARTON,
S.A.
S.F. Co. 70%
Cerv. Hon. 15%
Fab. Man. 15%
Honduras Box Mfg.

CERVECERIA
HONDURENA
S.A.
S.F. & S.S. 36.4%
S.F. Co. 27.9%
Brewery &
Soft Drink

EROS
TRANSPORT
CO.
(100%)

STANDARD
BANANA
CO.
(100%)

STANDARD FRUIT
& STEAMSHIP
CO. OF CANADA,
LTD.
(100%)

COMPANIA
BANANERA
ANTILLANA
S.A.
(100%)

PRE-NEED
PROTECTION
INC.
W.M. Borthwich, Jr., Pres.
(50%)
Cemetery Plot Sales

OCEANIC
PROPERTIES
INVESTMENT
INC.
D. Rietow, Pres.
(100%)
Holding Co. for Cemetery Properties

LAKE ANDERSON
CORP.
F. Simpich, Jr., Pres.
(100%)
San Jose, Calif. Project

SEA RANCH
GAS & WATER CO.
(100%)
Northern Calif. Project

MILILANI
MORTUARY
INC.
W. A. Weber, Pres.
Oahu Memorial Park

VALLEY
MEMORIAL
GARDENS,
INC.
D. Rietow, Pres.
(100%)
Philippine Memorial Park

H. Geldermann-Bd. Chmn.
LAKE ANDERSON
CORP./GELCO
DEVELOPMENTS
H. Geldermann, Pres.
(50%)

OCEANIC
PROPERTIES
DEVELOPMENT
MALAYSIA, LTD.
J. A. Willard, Man. Dir.
(50%)
Kuala Lumpur Project

TRANS-PACIFIC
DEVELOPMENT &
MANAGEMENT
CORP.
D. Rietow, Pres.
(51%)
Philippine
Memorial Park Managers

LAGUNA
SECA
CORP.
(100%)

RIVERSIDE
GOLF CLUB
(100%)

INVESTMENTS

A. de las Alan-Bd. Chmn.
HOUSE OF
INVESTMENTS,
INC.
A. Z. Syclp, Pres.
(19%)

INVESTMENT
MANAGERS,
INC.
(19%)

Philippine Venture Capital Cos.

ENVASES
INDUSTRIALES
de COSTA RICA
S. A.
(34%)
Box Manufacturing

CORCHO
Y LATA
C.A.
(40%)
Supplier to Above

A. de las Alas-Bd. Chmn.
MANILA
MEMORIAL
PARK
CEMETERY
D. Rietow, Pres.
(26%)

A. de las Alas-Bd. Chmn.
RIZAL
MEMORIAL
PARK
CEMETERY, INC.
D. Rietow, Pres.
(40%)

Philippine Memorial Parks

SEA RANCH
ASSOCIATION
D. O'Leary, Pres.

METROPOLITAN
CAPITAL
ASSOCIATES
(Fluctuating)
S. Cal. Joint Ventures

520

exhibit 1

CASTLE & COOKE, INC. (A)

Organization Chart: 1965

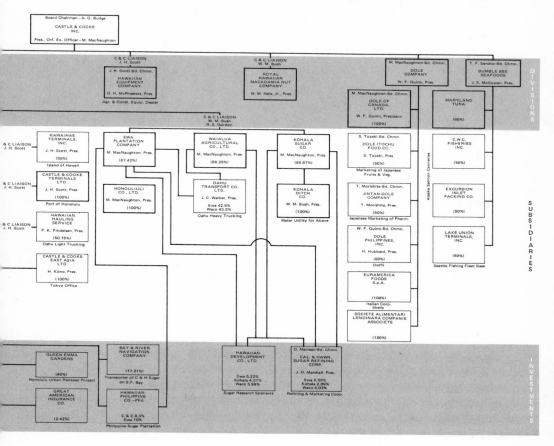

In addition to these five widespread operations, Castle & Cooke also conducted a number of smaller, local businesses in Hawaii. These included Castle & Cooke Terminals (a stevedoring firm), Hawaiian Equipment Co. (a distributor of heavy equipment for agriculture and construction), Royal Hawaiian Macadamia Nut Co. (a grower and marketer of macadamia nuts), and Oahu Transport Co. (an intrastate trucking concern).

Castle & Cooke also held important investments in a Philippine glass plant, a steel pipe manufacturer in Thailand, a concrete company in Malaya, and a major U.S. insurance company.

FINANCIAL DATA

For the fiscal year ending April 30, 1965, C & C recorded all-time highs in sales, earnings, and net worth. Although reported sales volume of $182.4 million was down slightly from 1964's previous record high of $185.5 million, the 1965 figures did not include C & C's pro rata share of the sales of Standard Fruit (which would have added about $26 million). The pro rata share of Standard's earnings was included in reported 1965 profits after taxes of $8.2 million, up from the previous year's record $7.8 million. This $8.2 million was in addition to a net capital gain of $9.2 million, realized on the sale of C & C's 24% interest in Matson Navigation Co. (Proceeds from this sale were utilized to purchase C & C's holdings in Standard Fruit.) Net worth was reported at $121.2 million, up from the previous year's high of $107 million. Exhibit 2 presents comparative income statements for the years 1955–1965, while Exhibit 3 presents balance sheet data for the same period. Exhibit 4 summarizes sales, earnings, and net worth figures for earlier years.

In 1965, C & C employed 18,000 people at peak employment periods, had more than 10,000 shareholders, and its shares were actively traded on the New York Stock Exchange.

The 1965 reported results, beyond omitting Standard Fruit sales, tended to understate the magnitude of the company's operations. The total *pro forma* 1965 sales volume of all of the companies in which C & C held a majority interest reached $267 million. Their *pro forma* total earnings exceeded $21 million before taxes, while total equity was in excess of $160 million. Exhibit 5 summarizes this fiscal 1965 *pro forma* financial data, indicating minority interest shares where appropriate.

Exhibit 5 also indicates the relative importance of C & C's various activities. As can be seen, Dole, Standard Fruit, and Bumble Bee (together with their subsidiaries) accounted for over $225 million in total sales in 1965 (84% of the total corporate activity), $14.7 in pretax earnings (81% of total), and 72% of stated book equity.

The addition of sugar interests and Oceanic Properties to the Dole, Standard,

exhibit 2A

CASTLE & COOKE, INC. (A)

Comparative Income Statements, 1955–1960
(in thousands)

| | Years Ending December 31 | | | | | |
	1955	1956	1957	1958	1959	1960
Income						
Agency fees	$1,477	$1,475	$1,582	$1,581	$1,650	$1,759
Dividends	1,201	1,318	1,482	1,073	2,024	2,558
Interest	55	56	64	69	66	57
Gross margin of subsidiaries	4,821	4,938	4,228	2,994	4,355	4,191
Equipment and other rentals	472	496	501	1,241	1,235	1,229
Miscellaneous (net)	(68)	234	125	164	231	298
Gain on sale of land	—	—	—	429	441	291
Total income	$7,957	$8,518	$7,981	$7,551	$10,004	$10,382
Operating expenses	5,112	5,467	4,962	5,101	5,724	6,447
Net income before taxes	2,845	3,051	3,019	2,450	4,280	3,935
Taxes						
Federal	881	988	950	640	1,139	823
Hawaii	84	91	75	100	109	121
California	—	—	—	1	—	1
Net income after taxes	$1,880	$1,973	$1,994	$1,710	$3,032	$2,991
Less minority interest in earning of subsidiary	3	—	—	—	—	—
Net income, Castle & Cooke, Ltd.	1,877	1,972	1,993	1,710	3,031	2,991

and Bumble Bee operations accounted for nearly 95% of total sales, 90% of pretax earnings, and 90% of total equity.

C & C has always followed very conservative accounting practices in valuing its major agricultural holdings. For example, growing crops and inventories were carried on the balance sheet at a modest, constant "static value." The "static value" of the growing sugar cane (a two year crop, which produced nearly $26 million in raw sugar in 1965) was stated at $3.5 million. The growing pineapple crop was stated at $1.8 million. These values were less than 20% of the crops' 1965 liquidation value. Inventories were shown at 1933 static values. Similarly, the company's extensive land holdings were carried at their original cost of $20.3 million. Of this total, about one-third represented land holdings in California, Oregon, the Philippines, Latin America, and elsewhere outside Hawaii.

exhibit 2B

CASTLE & COOKE, INC. (A)

Comparative Income Statements, 1962–1965
(in thousands)

| | Years Ending April 30 | | | |
	1962	1963	1964	1965
Revenues				
Food products, except sugar	$112,552	$122,983	$134,218	$136,798
Sugar	21,593	22,825	29,579	24,489
Merchandising	8,108	7,288	7,428	9,278
Service operations, including rentals	10,833	11,006	10,981	7,999
Gain on disposal of capital assets	494	615	1,116	1,231
Dividends, interest, and other	1,749	1,778	2,179	2,589
Total revenues	$155,329	$166,494	$185,502	$182,385
Costs and expenses				
Cost of products sold	110,368	122,195	126,318	125,760
Selling, service, general, and administrative	35,735	37,431	40,052	42,091
Total costs	$146,103	$159,626	$166,370	$167,851
Income before taxes	9,226	6,868	19,132	14,534
Federal and state income taxes	4,125	3,406	10,228	6,541
Income before minority interests	5,102	3,463	8,903	7,993
Less: minority interests	509	649	1,103	765
Net income	$ 4,592	$ 2,813	$ 7,801	$ 7,229
Special items to retained earnings net after tax gain on liquidation of Honolulu Oil Corp. stock	16,486			
Pro rata share of Standard Fruit earnings				931
Net after tax gain on sale of Matson stock				9,235

HAWAIIAN LAND

Hawaii comprises about 4.1 million acres, making it the forty-seventh largest state in area (slightly smaller than New Jersey and slightly larger than Connecticut). Of this, 1.75 million acres (43%) is owned by the state and federal governments. Castle & Cooke, with 154,000 acres, was, in 1965, Hawaii's third largest private land holder (after the Bishop Estate and Parker Ranch).

exhibit 3

CASTLE & COOKE, INC. (A)

Comparative Balance Sheet, 1955–1965
(in thousands)

	Year Ending 12/31						Year Ending 4/30			
	1955	1956	1957	1958	1959	1960	1962	1963	1964	1965
Current assets										
Cash	$ 2,162	$ 2,510	$ 2,105	$ 1,771	$ 1,408	$ 2,683	$ 7,777	$ 4,976	$ 4,648	$ 7,044
Marketable securities	1,176	2,069	2,832	2,645	1,359	1,566	4,548	682	1,028	10,083
Accounts receivable	2,286	2,485	1,611	2,316	2,117	2,984	20,681	22,224	20,347	31,198
Inventories	3,800	2,568	2,375	2,432	2,901	2,976	39,353	40,944	42,225	53,415
Prepaid expenses	92	57	63	121	191	370	2,287	2,377	2,289	3,421
Total current assets	$ 9,516	$ 9,689	$ 8,987	$ 9,285	$ 8,977	$10,580	$ 74,646	$ 71,202	$ 70,539	$105,161
Deduct current liabilities										
Accounts payable	3,073	3,593	3,251	3,513	3,096	4,192	2,874	9,858	4,926	10,434
Notes payable	850	800	812	753	2,074	2,751	13,651	13,149	15,230	22,111
Income taxes payable	908	963	859	464	944	810	5,617	2,030	5,551	10,915
Total current liabilities	$ 4,831	$ 5,355	$ 4,922	$ 4,730	$ 6,114	$ 7,754	$ 22,141	$ 25,037	$ 25,707	$ 43,459
Net current assets	$ 4,685	$ 4,333	$ 4,065	$ 4,555	$ 2,863	$ 2,826	$ 52,504	$ 46,164	$ 44,831	$ 61,701

	(1)	(2)	(3)	(4)	(5)	(6)	(7)	(8)	(9)	(10)
Growing crops—static value	5,300	5,300	5,300	5,300	1,000	1,000	1,000	1,000	1,000	1,000
Investments and advances to foreign subsidiaries	10,334	14,612	8,390	6,537	22,606	21,660	17,613	10,401	9,416	8,130
Land at cost	20,319	20,371	17,500	17,632	6,300	6,367	5,403	2,727	2,729	2,373
Buildings, machinery, and equipment (net)	62,212	40,782	39,977	39,503	6,014	5,714	5,432	4,889	5,062	5,313
Other assets	13,910	4,977	5,572	4,572	24	28	406	474	603	177
Deferred charges	—	—	—	—	—	—	—	66	105	82
Net assets	$173,777	$130,874	$122,904	$126,048	$38,771	$37,632	$34,409	$23,620	$23,249	$21,760
Deduct										
Long-term debt	7,200	10,215	9,352	10,232	3,569	3,799	1,490	750	1,000	—
Deferred income	2,774	1,025	538	533	—	16	446	—	—	—
Deferred income taxes	5,416	4,562	2,204	1,394	98	78	65	57	74	591
Reserves					—	8	8	9	9	35
Minority interests	37,177	8,137	8,634	11,050	—	—	—	—	—	—
Net assets	$121,210	$106,935	$102,176	$102,839	$35,104	$33,730	$32,401	$22,804	$22,166	$21,134
Stockholders' equity										
Capital stock	$ 25,989	$ 23,604	$ 23,488	$ 23,447	$16,026	$15,713	$15,404	$10,000	$10,000	$10,000
Capital in excess of par	8,033	1,587	1,463	1,427	1,327	673	—	396	396	396
Capital from acquisition of subsidiaries' stock	16,687	16,456	16,273	15,784	2,407	2,407	2,407	2,407	2,407	2,630
Retained earnings	71,788	66,571	62,235	62,198	15,522	15,099	14,590	13,070	12,378	11,088
	$122,497	$108,218	$103,459	$102,857	$35,282	$33,892	$32,401	$25,873	$25,181	$24,625
Less: Treasury stock	1,287	1,283	1,283	18	178	162	—	3,068	3,014	2,980
Stockholders' equity	$121,210	$106,935	$102,176	$102,839	$35,104	$33,730	$32,401	$22,805	$22,166	$21,134

Notes (aligned to columns):

- (1) Purchase of 55% of Standard Fruit and Steamship Co.
- (4) Merger of Dole and Bumble Bee into Castle & Cooke
- (5) Ownership in Bumble Bee now 60%
- (7) Helemaro merged increased ownership in Bumble Bee to 30%
- (9) Exchanged Hawaiian Tuna Peaches for 12% of Bumble Bee

exhibit 4

CASTLE & COOKE, INC. (A)

Summary of Sales, Earnings, and Net Worth
(in thousands)

Year	Div. & Int. Income	Il Other Income	Net Profit Before Tax	Net Profit After Tax	Net Worth
1895				$ 31	
1896				60	
1897				131	
1898				95	
1899				1,403	
1900				288	$ 2,205
1901				213	2,299
1902				94	2,297
1903			$ 161	160	2,398
1904	$ 113	$ 21	$ 134	133	2,451
1905	99	50	149	147	2,418
1906	113	—	—	150	2,417
1907	192	46	238	236	2,503
1908	265	59	324	322	2,625
1909	311	74	385	382	2,768
1910	379	55	434	427	2,955
1911	377	104	481	476	3,190
1912	341	70	411	404	3,354
1913	199	58	257	253	3,397
1914	304	(2)	302	299	3,496
1915	471	(48)	423	415	3,551
1916	821	139	960	951	4,082
1917	648	183	831	811	4,493
1918	546	(10)	536	498	4,711
1919	695	144	839	827	5,138
1920	1,073	288	1,361	1,314	5,838
1921	597	37	634	586	6,124
1922	536	68	604	584	6,384
1923	676	(27)	649	619	6,608
1924	898	95	993	948	6,636
1925	681	33	714	684	6,927
1926	752	88	840	807	7,315
1927	805	72	877	866	7,958
1928	1,013	85	1,098	1,094	8,469
1929	958	16	974	961	8,790
1930	859	(16)	843	840	9,258
1931	854	(58)	796	795	9,527
1932	615	(27)	588	577	9,765
1933	1,213	6	1,219	1,197	10,529

1934	805	223	1,028	985	10,928
1935	1,127	112	1,239	1,196	11,253
1936	1,907	128	2,035	1,939	11,578
1937	1,498	156	1,654	1,532	11,919
1938	1,259	39	1,298	1,236	12,245
1939	1,168	118	1,286	1,224	12,336
1940	1,121	6	1,127	1,079	12,591
1941	1,439	211	1,650	1,516	13,212
1942	1,220	3	1,223	1,129	13,764
1943	1,531	107	1,638	1,507	14,387
1944	1,348	167	1,515	1,354	14,912
1945	1,370	278	1,648	1,485	15,478
1946	1,128	430	1,558	1,360	15,967
1947	1,339	3	1,342	1,246	16,342
1948	1,215	(120)	1,095	1,043	16,866
1949	1,021	31	1,052	946	17,147
1950	1,617	749	2,366	1,816	18,137
1951	1,276	1,112	2,388	1,579	18,761
1952	902	513	1,415	1,046	18,698
1953	1,094	645	1,739	1,268	18,894
1954	1,152	202	1,354	1,087	21,729
1955	1,193	1,652	2,845	1,880	21,645
1956	1,274	1,777	3,051	1,973	22,166
1957	1,472	1,547	3,019	1,994	22,805
1958	1,078	980	2,450	1,710	32,400
1959	2,035	2,245	4,280	3,032	33,730
1960	2,558	1,377	3,935	2,991	35,104

exhibit 5

CASTLE & COOKE, INC. (A)

Selected Financial Data, April 30, 1965
(in millions)

Divisions and Subsidiaries (listed in order of total stated asset value)	C & C Ownership of Parent Entity (%)	Revenues		Assets		Equity		C&C's Share of Pretax Earnings Expressed as Return on Before-Tax Earnings		Assets (%)	Equity (%)
		1	2	1	2	1	2	1	2		
Dole Companies and subsidiaries	100.0	$101.5	$101.5	$ 82.8	$ 82.8	$ 62.2	$ 62.2	$ 6.4	$ 6.4	7.7	10.3
Standard Fruit and Steamship Co. and subsidiaries3	84.0	84.6	71.0	48.2	40.5	33.4	15.3	6.0	3.1	6.4	20.2
Sugar interests											
Waialua Agricultural Co.	66.3	10.4	6.9	12.4	8.2	10.4	6.9	1.8	1.2	14.6	17.4
Ewa Plantation Co.	67.4	8.1	5.5	10.0	6.7	8.5	5.7	.7	.5	7.5	8.8
Kohala Sugar Co. & Kohala Ditch	99.9	7.0	7.0	8.7	8.7	6.6	6.6	.1	.1	1.2	1.5
Total sugar interests		$ 25.5	$ 19.4	$ 31.1	$ 23.6	$ 25.5	$ 19.2	$2.6	$ 1.8	7.6%	9.4%
Bumble Bee Seafoods and subsidiaries4	100.0	34.0	32.5	22.6	21.9	18.1	17.4	2.9	2.8	12.8	16.1
Oceanic properties	100.0	1.9	1.7	10.0	9.9	4.0	3.6	.1	0	—	—
Transportation interests											
C & C Terminals	100.0										
OTC	85.0										
Kawaihae Terminals	55.0										
Hawaiian Hauling	33.3										
Total transportation interests		7.8	7.1	9.0	7.6	3.9	3.5	.5	.5	5.3	11.4
Hawaiian Equipment	100.0										
Royal Hawaiian Macadamia Nut Co.	100.0										
C & C Corporate and other		12.0	11.0	18.3	16.5	11.3	10.3	1.86	1.66		
C & C consolidated totals		$267.3	$244.2	$222.0	$202.8	$158.4	$131.5	$20.3	$16.2	8.0	12.3

1Total figures.

2C & C share of total.

3Figures based upon 53 weeks, ending January 2, 1965, computed on *pro forma* basis, after tender purchase of 9/65, in which Standard Fruit repurchased 100,000 shares of common stock at $26, and C & C purchased 177,000 shares and attained 84% ownership of common outstanding.
C & C share of revenues and assets is based on 84% of total. C & C share of equity is 84% of balance remaining after deducting $10.1 million of preferred stock and $5.1 million of minority interests in subsidiaries. C & C share of earnings is 84%

of balance remaining after deducting the pretax income applicable to minority interests and preferred shareholders.

4Asset, equity, and earnings figures include partners' shares in joint ventures.

5Investment does not include written-off accumulated losses of approximately $7 million.

6Not including $9,235,000 after tax gain on sale of Matson stock.

Note: Some of these figures are estimates by the casewriter wherever the appropriate data were not available in the desired form within the various companies.

This acreage, carried on the books at under $14 million, consisted of three major units (see Exhibit 6):

1. 42,000 acres on the island of Oahu (11% of the island's 380,000 acres) occupied an important portion of the central valley, running north from near Wahiawa, above Pearl Harbor, to Waialua on the windward coast. 80% of Hawaii's 750,000 people lived on this island. About 12,000 acres of this fee land was planted in pineapple (by Dole) and 5,000 in sugar cane (by Waialua Agricultural Co.), while the rest, over and above 60 acres of industrial land in the City of Honolulu, was pasture, mountainous watershed, or gulch areas.

exhibit 6

CASTLE & COOKE, INC. (A)

Properties in Hawaii

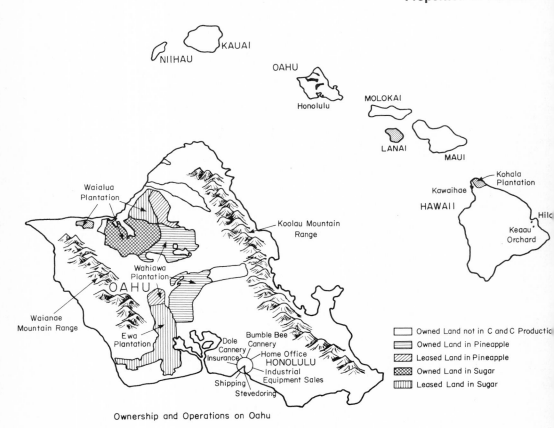

Ownership and Operations on Oahu

2. The entire 90,000 acres of the island of Lanai was owned by C & C. 15,000 acres were under cultivation (by Dole) in pineapple. Another 10,000 acres was flat, desert land. The remainder was mostly rough and mountainous.

3. A 20,500 acre parcel on the island of Hawaii was located on the northernmost tip. 10,500 acres were planted in sugar cane (by Kohala Sugar Co.), while the remainder was rugged mountains or arid flatland. Another 3,000 acres on Hawaii was just south of Hilo. 1,200 acres were planted in macadamia trees (by Royal Hawaiian), surrounded by dense jungle. These 23,500 acres comprised less than 1% of "the Big Island's" 2.5 million acres.

COMPARISON WITH OTHER COMPANIES

Exhibit 7 compares Castle & Cooke with other food packers among the *"Fortune 500 Largest Industrial Companies."* Although, as indicated above, C & C's accounting procedures do not make for strict comparability, the data do give a rough indication of C & C's relative performance. These data show a 1962–1965 average return on stated book equity of 7.2%/year for Castle & Cooke vs. an average of 8.9%/year for the six companies compared (Heinz, Calpak, Di-Giorgio, Hunt, Libby, Stokeley) and vs. 9.2%/year for all of the 500 *Fortune* industrial companies. According to C & C president Malcolm MacNaughton, "this is because we have had more capital tied up in operations (growing) than these other companies have. We must learn how to trade on our equity better, both in looking for acquisitions and in capturing better position in the marketplace."

COMPANY HISTORY

The history of Castle & Cooke is intertwined with the glamour and romance of the development of Hawaii. The story begins with the attempts of the Congregational Church in Boston to send missionaries to "the savage Sandwich Islands," starting in 1820. At this time sugar cane was already growing wild in the islands, and pineapple culture had begun as early as 1813.

In 1837, the seventh reinforcement of missionaries landed at Honolulu. Among the 32 pilgrims aboard was Samuel Northrup Castle, 28, formerly a school teacher and clerk, and Amos Starr Cooke, 27, who had studied for the ministry but had become a clerk. At this time, Honolulu had 6,000 residents, of which 350 were white. Initially, Brother and Sister Cooke ran a school for children of Island royalty, and Brother Castle acted as corresponding secretary for the mission and helped run the mission's depository (store).

When the British seized the Islands in 1843, S. N. Castle was instrumental in restoring the Island monarchy. Following his effort, King Kamehameha asked Brother Castle to become one of his advisors. This was the beginning of his political relations with three successive kings. In 1848, Amos Starr Cooke joined

exhibit 7

CASTLE & COOKE, INC. (A)

Comparative Financial Data

Selected Food Companies, Fortune "500," and Castle & Cooke, Inc.

Company	Total Reserves (millions) Latest Year¹ ($)	% Change Latest Year (%)	% Change Period² (%)	Total Latest Year¹ ($)	Total % Change Latest Year (%)	Total Period² (%)	Income after Tax Per Share Latest Year ($)	As % of Reserves Latest Year (%)	As % of Reserves Av. for Period (%)	As % of Equity Latest Year (%)	As % of Equity Av. for Period (%)	Stockholders' Equity (millions) Latest Year¹ ($)	Change² (%)
Cal Pack	410	6	4	18.0	13.0	6	1.68	4.4	4.3	9.9	10.8	183	6
S & W (Di Giorgio)	132	15	7	2.5	19.0	20	1.48	1.9	1.6	8.7	6.7	29	8
Heinz	488	5	10	14.5	17.0	4	2.71	3.0	3.3	7.5	8.2	194	9
Hunt	402	1	6	9.6	14.0	5	1.63	2.4	2.9	4.8	6.4	200	9
Libby	290	5	0	6.1	97.0	10	.93	2.1	1.3	6.0	6.0	73	6
Stokeley	205	1	6	4.4	38.0	7	1.43	2.2	2.1	6.3	4.1	96	2
Av.	—	5.5	5.5	—	33.0	8.7	—	2.7	2.6	7.2	7.3	—	6.7
Six Co. Weighted Av.	—	5.0	5.0	—	22.0	6.0	—	2.9	2.9	8.4	8.3	—	6.8
Fortune 500													
500 Co. Av.	—	8.7	6.8	—	16.2	10.6	—	5.0	4.4	10.5	9.2	—	—
Food Co. Av. (Pro Forma)	—	5.6	5.0	—	15.1	8.5	—	2.7	2.6	9.8	8.9	—	—
Castle & Cooke Consolidated													
1960-65	268	.2	5.5	9.5	3.1	14.53	3.71	3.5	2.5	7.7	5.6	123	10.5
1962-65	"	"	7.0	"	"		"	"	3.1	"	7.2	"	7.5

1 $000,000—calendar year 1964 or latest fiscal year.
2 Compound % change over period—latest five years or as stated.
3 Increase from a loss position.

S. N. Castle at the depository. Also in this year the $500 per year missionary salary was dropped, the church in Boston expecting the missionaries to be self-supporting. Brothers Castle and Cooke were asked to continue to run the depository on a commission basis, and in 1850 formed a partnership to operate the depository as a private merchandising business. At this time four firms were in existence in Honolulu that were later to become part of the "Big Five": Castle & Cooke, C. Brewer, R. C. Janion (which was later to become Theo H. Davies), and H. Hackfeld (which was later to become American Factors). During the 1850's the "agency system" began. This system, which is still active today, was created in order that a small plantation could have the benefit of a central office performing the nonagricultural business functions of purchasing, recruiting, warehousing, selling, arranging shipping, insurance, and loaning money.

1850–1875:
The Beginning of Extensive Agriculture

During the period 1850–1875, many sugar plantations were started. In these times, a shortage of plantation labor developed. Hawaiian natives had never taken to hard agricultural work, since they had known plenty by gathering ample food from the sea, from wild fruit trees, and from taro patches. Chinese laborers were brought in by the thousands. A total of 35,000 Chinese migrated to Hawaii under contract labor agreements, calling for less than $60/year, before China stopped this emigration.

Haiku plantation, on the island of Maui, was launched in 1858, as a stock company in which Castle & Cooke were investors, by Samuel Alexander (Brother Cooke's son-in-law) and Henry Baldwin. Initially Haiku spent many more dollars than it took in, but ultimately became one of the most successful plantations in the Islands. Castle & Cooke became agents for Haiku in 1866, by which time they were also agents for seven other plantations. It was in 1862 that the Reverend Elias Bond conceived of a sugar plantation on the Kohala peninsula of Hawaii as a way to employ his native flock, increase their well-being, and enable them to remain in the Kohala district. Castle & Cooke helped raise the capital for the Kohala plantation. It was 1865 before the first crop was harvested, and 1873 before Kohala was able to free itself of debt.

In 1868, the first shipment of 148 Japanese were imported, ultimately to be followed in 1885 by large waves of immigrants.

Following Brother Cooke's death in 1871, his son-in-law, J. B. Atherton, became a leading force in the Castle & Cooke enterprises. By 1874, the company had prospered greatly from its sugar interests and agency activities. By this time, it had become common practice for the agencies, which had accumulated substantial wealth, to loan money to the plantations. Castle & Cooke made loans to many plantations. One of these loans grew as high as $195,000. In four cases where Castle & Cooke had supplied financing to a plantation, Castle & Cooke eventually lost the agency for that plantation when the plantation merged with another in order to solve financial and operating difficulties.

1876–1900:
An Era for Improving Agricultural Operations and the Beginning of Pineapple in Hawaii

In 1876, Alexander and Baldwin conceived of the first of several major water development projects that were to bring financial prosperity to Hawaiian sugar plantations. Their program called for the construction of a system for capturing and conducting 40 million gallons of water per day from the hills to their Haiku plantation. Later similar water development projects were constructed at other sugar plantations, including Castle & Cooke's Kohala plantation.

The concept of developing major water resources was responsible for the founding of Ewa plantation on the arid Ewa plain of leeward Oahu in 1889. Unlike the previous water development projects, which had captured the heavy rainfall in the mountains and conducted it to low lying plantations, the Ewa project used 71 wells to pump 105 million gallons a day of the fresh water that flowed under the earth's surface to the sea.

During this period, the labor shortage continued, and a total of 20,000 Portuguese were brought in from Madeira and the Azores. For the first time, women and children accompanied the male laborers.

In 1882, Captain Matson made his first trip to Hilo, Hawaii, from San Francisco. During the next several years, Captain Matson purchased several other sailing ships, including one that carried passengers in addition to freight.

In 1885, Captain Kidwell brought a dozen pineapple plants from Florida to begin the first commercial pineapple plantation in Hawaii. The following year he brought an additional 1,000 plants from Jamaica. By 1892, 100,000 pineapple plants were growing near Pearl Harbor. At that time, Ewa plantation convinced Kidwell that the land could better be used to grow sugar cane, and he retired. Byron Clark, using some plants that had been discarded from Kidwell's then defunct operation, began another plantation near Wahiawa.

Between 1886 and 1906, 180,000 Japanese were brought in to work on the plantations. Of these, 126,000 ultimately returned to Japan.

Although Ewa was successful in growing cane, problems in the mill severely drained Castle & Cooke's resources to the point that in 1892 Bishop and Company bank refused to advance money to the company, and even refused to honor a check for $54. To save their Ewa investment, Castle & Cooke was forced to sell many of their other holdings, including the very profitable Haiku plantation.

Ewa finally came into its own in 1896 with a new crusher that solved the mill problems. Ewa's sugar yields reached undreamed of levels, and between 1895 and 1900 restored Castle & Cooke's waning fortunes. C & C stockholders, as individuals, then formed the Bank of Hawaii, ending the one bank domination of the Islands.

On December 28, 1894, Castle & Cooke incorporated with a capital stock of $600,000. For many years they had refused to do so because Brothers Castle and Cooke felt that a businessman should put his entire resources behind his business. J. B. Atherton was the first president, E. D. Tenney, Brother Castle's nephew, who had worked up from a laborer, became the corporate secretary, and W. A. Bowen (Tenney's cousin) became the treasurer.

A few years later, Alexander and Baldwin opened their own sugar agency to represent the sugar plantations in which they had an interest. In so doing, they took over three plantations that had been represented by Castle & Cooke. The formation of this agency established the fifth of the firms later to be known as the "Big Five."

During this period, Hawaiian sugar was sold at a continual disadvantage. On the East Coast of the United States, it was sold at a discount relative to sugar from other exporting countries, and on the West Coast, Claus Spreckles, who controlled and dominated the western sugar industry, dictated the price that he was willing to pay the Hawaiians for their raw sugar. In 1898, following extremely harsh demands on the part of Spreckles, the Hawaiian sugar agencies united to send their sugar to California Beet Sugar and Refining Company. This firm was 37½ % owned by Castle & Cooke, and 25% by C. Brewer, and became the forerunner of the California and Hawaiian Sugar Refining Company.

In its first full year of operation as a corporation, Castle & Cooke, Ltd., reported a profit of $31,000 on its $600,000 capital. In establishing the corporation, the partners exchanged some of their personal holdings in other companies for the stock of C & C, so that the firm itself held shares in a number of plantation companies and in the Honolulu Iron Works.

C & C's interest in Onomea plantation was sold in 1899 to C. Brewer, and the money was used to establish a new venture—the piecing together of various tracts of land on northern Oahu to form Waialua Agricultural Co., Ltd. Waialua was capitalized at $3.5 million, 40% of which was subscribed by C & C. The company ended up with 10,000 acres for sugar and another 12,000 acres, which ultimately was leased out to Dole, for pineapple cultivation.

At this same time, C & C withdrew from their original general merchandise business, selling the inventories to B. F. Dillingham, who previously had built Hawaii's first railroad. Now the young company could concentrate on its sugar agency business and on looking after its investments in various plantations and other Island enterprises. James B. Castle, son of S. N. Castle, had a great many ideas for aggressively changing the character of the firm. He envisioned an expansion of direct ownership in agricultural activities, as well as embarking into ranching, railroading, and other operations. These ideas were not accepted by President Atherton, who was more interested in maintaining the company as an agency and investor. In 1899, James B. Castle convinced the Castle Estate to buy a 63% interest in the Spreckles plantation on the island of Maui— Hawaiian Commercial and Sugar Company—for $2 million, which was considered to be a tremendous bargain for what was then the largest and most profitable plantation in the Islands. He then went to Castle & Cooke and offered this plantation to Atherton in exchange for a one-third interest in Castle & Cooke. Atherton and Tenney turned down this opportunity, which, when added to their other holdings, would have made C & C the leading company in the Hawaiian sugar industry. James B. Castle then walked across the street to present the same offer to his friend, J. P. Cooke, who was then head of Alexander and Baldwin. A & B agreed at once. This move reduced Castle & Cooke to fourth place among the five agencies in Hawaiian sugar.

1900–1930:
Pineapple, Shipping, Hotels,
and the Beginning of Labor Troubles

Pineapple. In 1901, James Dole organized the Hawaiian Pineapple Company. The company was capitalized with $20,000, $14,000 of which James Dole had raised in Boston, from whence he came, $5,000 in San Francisco from several merchandisers and marketers of canned fruit products, and the balance in Honolulu from the railroad company, lawyers, and suppliers who accepted shares in lieu of cash for their services and products. The young Harvard graduate had come to Hawaii two years before looking for a new business opportunity. In 1903, the firm canned 1,800 cases of pineapple. By 1905, the pack was 25,000 cases, and, in another two years, the pineapple company had outgrown its cannery near the plantation at Wahiawa. A new modern cannery was built in Honolulu, next to the can manufacturing plant that American Can had built to serve it in the industrial section of town.

Shipping. Just prior to the turn of the century, most of Captain William Matson's competition had been converting from sail-powered ships to coal-powered steamers. In 1901 Matson incorporated in order to make this conversion. In 1902, Matson had his first steam-powered ship, but, unlike those of his competition, his was oil-fired. Five years later, Captain Matson asked E. D. Tenney if C & C would take on the agency for his company. Mr. Tenney had taken over the management of Castle & Cooke, under President George Parmele Castle, who had succeeded J. B. Atherton. C & C invested in 429 shares of Matson Steamship Company and became Matson agent for the port of Honolulu. The following year Castle & Cooke invested $100,000 more in Matson to help finance a new ship. C. Brewer and Alexander and Baldwin also invested in Matson at this time. (Castle & Cooke purchased additional shares on the market in the 1920's until their ownership was about 16%.)

To insure a supply of oil for his ships, Captain Matson founded the Honolulu Oil Co., to own wells in California and operate a pipeline to the coast. Castle & Cooke invested $140,000 "as a gesture of friendship" for Captain Matson. This resulted in about a 4% interest.

At the beginning of World War I, the American-Hawaiian Steamship Company moved its fleet of freighters from the Pacific Ocean to the Atlantic, since at that time this business was more profitable. This created a tremendous opportunity for Matson to serve the needs of the entire Hawaiian economy. This was the beginning of Matson's near monopoly position as a West Coast–Hawaiian ocean transporter. By 1917, when Matson died, three of the other large sugar agencies which had also invested in Matson Steamship Company were Matson's agents on the other islands of Hawaii. By 1920, Matson was carrying 75% of the Hawaiian water freight. At the end of World War I, the Los Angeles Steamship Company was formed by purchasing three ships from the Alien Property Custodian for a very low price. Not only did this company sail to Hawaii at lower fares than those of Matson, it also served Hawaii from the port of Los Angeles, which Matson had previously refused to do. At first, this threat was ignored, as the new steamship company was perceived as being able to carry only a small volume of passenger business. But later, when the Dillingham interests teamed up with the company and solicited freight business, Matson realized that the Los Angeles Steamship Company could have a major affect upon their operations. Matson purchased an interest in the Inter-Island Steamship Co. to compete with the inter-island tours that had been initiated by the Los Angeles Steamship Company. Ultimately, in 1930, Matson bought out the Los Angeles Steamship Company.

In the 1920's, Matson built its first luxury passenger ship to carry 650 people. Later, when C. C. von Hamm's Territorial Hotel Company needed funds for expansion, Matson, Castle & Cooke, and others recognized this as a prime opportunity to invest in the luxury hotel business. The Royal Hawaiian Hotel was built at Waikiki to supplement the older Moana. Later, Matson bought out the other investors and became the sole owner of this chain.

Pineapple again.   When the pineapple industry was forming, Castle & Cooke had not been interested in investing any money directly. However, a venture of James B. Castle's, Castle & Kellogg Pineapple Company, had borrowed $203,000 from Castle & Cooke by 1908 and had placed them into pineapple regardless. Castle & Cooke also became involved indirectly in pineapple through their ownership in Waialua plantation, which, by 1916, was leasing 3,676 acres to Hawaiian Pineapple Company and another 4,315 acres to California Fruit Growers Association, predecessor to California Packing Corp.

In 1922, having explored other areas of the world for growing pineapple, Dole had negotiated a 12,000 acre prepaid lease for 17½ years from Waialua Agricultural Company. In return for the lease, plus $1.25 million cash, Dole gave Waialua a one-third interest in the pineapple company. $1,100,000 of these funds was used to purchase the island of Lanai, which was thought to be capable of growing pineapple on about 15,000 acres. At this time, Castle & Cooke was the agent and dominant shareholder in Waialua Agricultural Company.

Labor.   During this period, several groups of contract laborers had begun to form associations. In 1909, several thousands of Japanese sugar workers struck in the first major Hawaiian strike, but were defeated in their efforts. In 1919, the Federation of Japanese Labor and the Association of Filipino Laborers struck. Twelve thousand strikers were evicted from their plantation homes. They moved to Honolulu, where an influenza epidemic was raging, and 1,200 members of the strikers' families died. After three months, the Filipinos settled for a 30% pay increase; six months later the Japanese settled. Although this strike cost the planters $12 million, management still felt that it had the upper hand over labor. Three years later, 3,000 members of the Association of Filipino Laborers struck on the Island of Kauai. They asked $2 for an eight hour day. During this eight month strike, 12 policemen and 16 strikers were killed.

During this period, while E. D. Tenney was president of Castle & Cooke, he was also president of Matson Steamship Company, Hawaiian Trust Company, the Hawaiian Sugar Planters Ass'n., Ewa plantation, Waialua plantation, and Kohala plantation. He was also director of a dozen companies, including Theo H. Davies, in which C & C then owned a 25% interest.

1930–1950:
Hawaiian Pineapple Reorganization,
Castle & Cooke Proxy Fight, War, and Labor's Expansion

Pineapple.   The depression hit Hawaiian Pineapple very hard. Inventories had grown very large and 230 million plants were ripening in the field. They owed $3.5 million to banks, in addition to a $5 million term loan taken out in 1931. Dole made the mistake of canning all of the crops in the field and did not cut the prices of the pineapple inventory soon enough to reduce its size. It appeared that mainland companies were waiting for Hawaiian Pineapple to go bankrupt in order to capture the company at a depressed price. In order to keep the ownership in the Hawaiian Pineapple Company in Hawaii, Castle & Cooke called a meeting of the major investors in the company. At this meeting it was arranged that a new company would be formed to take over the assets and liabilities of the old Hawaiian Pineapple Company. The new company was capitalized with an additional $1.5 million of convertible preferred stock, which was underwritten by Castle & Cooke. Waialua Agricultural took its pro rated share of the issue, and Castle & Cooke wound up with the balance. With this reorganization, Castle & Cooke, together with Waialua Agricultural Company, owned more than 50% of Dole. Castle & Cooke then made Atherton Richards, a C & C executive, president of Dole, and James Dole became the chairman of the board. At the same time, Henry White, a Castle & Cooke officer, was named treasurer of Hawaiian Pineapple, but remained an executive of C & C.

Richards immediately began to develop the "Dole" label for Hawaiian pineapple. In 1934, the Hawaiian pineapple industry entered into a cooperative marketing agreement which embraced land, growing, and pricing restrictions. This agreement was later considered to be in violation of the anti-trust laws, and its members withdrew from the agreement. Atherton Richards' efforts to turn the

Hawaiian Pineapple Company around were successful, and, by 1935, the company was making substantial profits.

Shipping. In the late 1930's, the shipping and hotel businesses began to regain their former prosperity. During this period, C & C was both passenger and freight agent for Matson and was influential in the management of the hotels. In 1936, C & C bought out the Matson terminals operations and formed a stevedoring and terminal services company to serve Matson and other lines docking in Honolulu.

Proxy fight. In 1940, a public stockholder proxy fight took place between Atherton Richards and the rest of Castle & Cooke management. Although Atherton Richards had done very well as manager of the Hawaiian Pineapple Company, he had had many differences of opinion with the directors of Hawaiian Pineapple Company and the management of Castle & Cooke. Although Richards was unsuccessful in securing the necessary number of proxies to take over Castle & Cooke, his uncle, Frank Atherton, who had become president of Castle & Cooke when Mr. Tenney died in 1934, persuaded the other members of Castle & Cooke management to allow Richards to stay on as president of Hawaiian Pineapple Company, provided he did not cause any further trouble. A year later, new differences arose between Atherton Richards and the Castle & Cooke management, and Richards was replaced by Henry White.

It had been said that, while E. D. Tenney was president of Castle & Cooke, Alexander Budge had been the only man who would stand up to him and disagree. Although when Tenney died in 1934 he was succeeded by Frank Atherton, it was only another two years before Alexander Budge was appointed president of Castle & Cooke. Mr. Budge had joined the company as a young engineer in 1920, and had risen through the ranks to become the first president who was not descended from either of the founders.

Labor. In 1937, strikers on the island of Maui were aided for the first time by outside union organizers. The CIO and the Maritime Union backed the plantation workers in a short strike, which the workers won. At that time, the CIO began to organize the Hawaiian labor force. In 1940, the McBryde Sugar Co. workers voted to align with the CIO.

In 1941, the CIO won representation of 1,300 waterfront workers. At the same time, the A.F. of L. was trying to organize other segments of Hawaiian labor. They were successful in organizing some teamsters, utility workers, and craft unions. However, in December of 1941, when Pearl Harbor was bombed, the military ordered the unions to cease their organizing efforts. At that time martial law was declared, and the governor of Hawaii ceded authority. Most jobs were frozen, men and equipment were requisitioned by the Army, and land use was diverted. While in many respects life on the Islands continued as usual, civil liberties were definitely curtailed. The military brought in construction workers from the mainland to fill the severe wartime demand. These men were paid mainland wages, and, in addition, received bonuses for working in a hazardous area. However, working side by side were Island construction workers who were paid low Island wages and no war bonuses. Resentment fanned earlier union sentiments.

Immediately following the war, the ILWU swept the islands and organized 57 companies. Even companies that formerly had been independently unionized were converted to ILWU representation. Almost immediately, 28,000 sugar workers went out on strike for 79 days, seeking higher wages and a union shop. Average wage rates increased from $2.74 per day in 1938 to $8.00 per day in 1946. In this strike, no workers were evicted from their homes, but $20 million worth of sugar and $8.2 million in wages were lost.

In 1947, the ILWU faltered in dealing with the pineapple industry. The planters had offered an across the board increase to all workers. However, the ILWU would neither accept nor reject this offer until the fruit was ripening. When $60 million worth of fruit was ready to be canned, the union struck, asking for a 50% wage boost. Immediately, the union knew that they had lost. Public opinion was aroused to the point that Honolulu citizens volunteered to go out and pick pineapples in the fields. Employees of the pineapple company ignored their own pickets and went into the canneries to work. Four days later, the unions settled for less than the original industry offer. Nonetheless, it became apparent that the union was in to stay. Union leadership led political efforts at social reform, and captured half of the seats in the lower house. Citizen indignation against attempts to block legislative action and to break up large holdings caused the union to retreat from its dominant social role, and made clear that there were definite limits within which the public would support union action.

In 1949, one of the most important strikes in Hawaiian history took place. Waterfront workers struck for 179 days, tying up the entire Hawaiian economy. After President Truman had refused to invoke the Taft-Hartley Act and force the strikers back to work, the legislature of Hawaii passed new and more sweeping laws, the main provisions of which allowed the Territorial Government to take over the docks. Since Matson ships were completely tied up by this strike, Isthmian ships were used to handle the small amount of freight that did cross the Hawaiian docks. Some estimates of the strike cost ran as high as $100 million. It was said that "this strike finally cracked the Big Five" in showing that unified union strength and intelligent union management could outmaneuver and outlast the "Big Five" plus all the other pressures that were brought to bear against the union effort.

In 1946, 15 major Honolulu corporations had commissioned the firm of Ivy Lee and T. J. Ross to do a survey of the Hawaiian industry and social structure. The report made a number of hard-hitting recommendations, basically intended to increase the competition among major Hawaiian companies, in order to improve the image of these companies as well as that of Hawaiian industry in general. The report recommended that: 1) the leading companies in Hawaii should not hold stock in one another's companies; 2) public relations experts should be established in all of the major companies to represent these companies to the public; 3) a "Hawaiian Economic Foundation" be set up with the purpose of surveying the composition of the Hawaiian economy and determining the true role of the major companies in the economy; 4) interlocking directorates be eliminated; 5) the ownership of Matson should be divested from some of the "Big Five" in order to remove conflicts of interest; 6) the position of the Oriental be elevated through corporate opportunity for capable people from this racial group.

Castle & Cooke had already taken several of the steps recommended by this report. By 1945, they had sold their minority interests in Theo H. Davies Company, American Factors, Honolulu Iron Works, Hawaiian Cane Products, Inter-Island Navigation, and had sold 22,700 shares of Matson. A year later, they sold an additional 12,000 shares of Matson. Their sugar plantations began to publish annual reports which gave full explanations of their activities. The Hawaiian Pineapple Company began a large-scale employee education program to provide a full understanding of the Hawaiian pineapple business, its ownership, wage scales, and other aspects that previously had not been public knowledge.

1946–1960:
Concentration in Hawaii

By 1950, Castle & Cooke had passed through several different stages in its strategic posture. From its early mercantile beginnings, it had evolved into an agency for sugar plantations, and an important investor in the plantation properties. After the turn of the century, C & C had become a ship agency, as well as a plantation agency, drawing its earnings from commissions and fees.

In the 1920's and 1930's, the company had, almost unwillingly, found itself in the role of an investor in properties and stocks of companies over which it exercised no control, such as Honolulu Oil and Hawaiian Pineapple. Earnings from dividends, interest, and rent became the major source of income. The crisis at Hawaiian Pineapple had changed this, and C & C had become much more actively involved in influencing the management of the properties in which it was invested. Many of the stocks in which C & C held only minority interests were sold, and attention was centered on those investments in which the company had either the controlling interest or the agency contract.

Following World War II, the definition of C & C as a regional company began to crystallize. Under Mr. Budge's aegis, C & C's basic function became "to invest in and manage companies whose products and services are important to Hawaii." Castle & Cooke's new financial commitments were deliberately limited to "those which contributed to the business development of the Territory."

C & C's role as a holding company, controlling local Hawaiian enterprises and providing central financial and staff services to a group of relatively autonomous operating companies, became clear during this period. So long as a company performed well, it was allowed to pursue its own independent course. Additional capital investment had to be approved only when the requirement exceeded that company's depreciation reserves. Members of C & C's small staff were "liaison officers" to the various operating units, but performed little more than "overseeing" functions, so long as the unit operated smoothly. When a problem arose, or an investee company's profits turned to losses, all of C & C's talents were turned to finding the causes and taking remedial action.

In 1946, in line with the philosophy of strengthening the Hawaiian economy, C & C formed Hawaiian Equipment Co., in order to provide modern mechanical equipment for the sugar plantations. Two years later, the A. F. Stubenberg Co. was purchased for this company to give it the International Harvester franchise for the Islands.

Also in 1946, Waialua and Ewa, under C & C sponsorship, jointly formed a trucking company with the Dillingham family's Oahu R. R. Co. and Oahu Sugar Company (an American Factors holding) to haul sugar from the plantations to the shipping storage plant at the waterfront, and carry plantation supplies on the backhaul. This company, in which the two C & C plantations each owned 22.5%, became the Oahu Transport Co.

In 1948, the land holdings of Waialua, as well as their one-third stock ownership in Hawaiian Pineapple Company, was spun off into a new company, Helemano, and distributed to Waialua's shareholders. The effect of this spinoff was to return Waialua to the status of producing earnings from plantation operations, rather than from the rentals and dividends of its investment holdings.

Also in 1948, C & C bought 41% of Hawaiian Tuna Packers, Ltd. This company packed virtually all of the tuna that were caught in Hawaiian waters. In 1951, ownership was extended to 96.8%.

Another effort to develop additional industry to utilize the Islands' limited natural resources was the founding of the Royal Hawaiian Macadamia Nut Co. In 1949, C & C bought 1,000 acres of jungle land near Hilo and began development of Keaau orchard. By early 1951, more than 20,000 trees had been planted and an additional 2,000 acres of adjacent land purchased. It was anticipated that these nuts could compete with almonds, pecans, and walnuts, and a nationwide market could be developed. $100,000 per year was scheduled for planting expenses over a ten year period.

Hawaiian Pineapple Expansion

In 1948, the Hawaiian Pineapple Company, under president Henry White, purchased, for stock, the Barron-Gray Packing Co., of San Jose, California, the originator of fruit cocktail and a large private label packer. This acquisition marked the beginning of a major expansion into the packing of mainland fruits and vegetables, which culminated in the 1955 acquisition of the F. M. Ball Co., of Oakland, California, private label packers of peaches and tomato products, and Paulus Bros. Packing Co., of Salem, Oregon, private label packers of fruits and vegetables grown in that region.

In 1948, Hawaiian Pineapple also participated in a Mexican pineapple cannery venture, and began experimental plantings in Cuba as well. Both ventures were discontinued in 1950 because of poor fruit quality. The company then purchased the lands on Oahu for $10 million to expand growing capacity there.

During this period, Hawaiian Pineapple sustained a seven month strike on the island of Lanai.

Construction was begun on a large frozen pineapple concentrate plant in the Honolulu cannery.

Although Castle & Cooke owned important interests in Hawaiian Pineapple, it did not take an active part in management other than placing two men on the board of directors.

At this same time, C & C, concerned over the long-range prospects for profitable sugar production at Kohala, made funds available to that company for experimental pineapple plantings in areas previously devoted to sugar.

Other Activities

During this period, in line with its stated policy, C & C increased its investment in its other Hawaiian interests—Helemano, Waialua, Kohala, and Hawaiian Trust Co.

The company reported 1,000 shareholders in 1951, up from 19 in 1920, 26 in 1930, and 176 in 1940. By 1951, shares were traded over the counter in Honolulu, San Francisco, and Los Angeles. Until 1895, when the company incorporated, only nine persons had shared in C & C's ownership. When J. B. Atherton became a partner, he, Brother S. N. Castle, and Brother A. S. Cooke each held a third interest. By 1879, the Cooke interests had been sold to Castle and Atherton. The stock remained largely in the hands of descendants of the founders or in family trusts until the 1930's, when some of the trusts terminated. At that time, shares were divided among a number of beneficiaries, and trading in the stock spread ownership to general investors in Hawaii and on the mainland.

In 1951, after 100 years of operation, the company prided itself on its deep commitment to Hawaii and its active participation in the enterprises with which it was associated. "Business Enterprises in Which We Are Interested" included:

I. "Companies for Which We Provide Full Agency and Management Services" (percentage ownership in parentheses): Waialua (26%), Ewa (20%), and Kohala (89%), sugar plantations; Helemano (26%), holdings in Oahu land and 33.5% of Hawaiian Pineapple stock; Castle & Cooke Terminals (100%), Honolulu stevedoring; Hawaiian Equipment Co. (100%), plantation equipment dealer.

II. "Companies for Which We Provide Limited Agency Service": Matson (12.7%), Honolulu port and freight agent; Isthmian Steamship Co. (0) port and freight agent; Hawaiian Tuna Packers (96.8%); Kahua Ranch (0), Hawaiian cattle ranch.

III. "Companies in Which Our Management Participation is Limited to Representation on Boards of Directors": Hawaiian Pineapple Company

(15.8%); Honolulu Oil (4.3%); Bay and River Navigation Co. (17.2%), transporting sugar in San Francisco Bay; Home Insurance Co. of Hawaii (38.4%), underwriters and insurance agents in Hawaii.

Agency services were compensated for by sugar plantations to the extent of direct costs of services received, plus 2.5% of any net profit realized for the year. Shipping companies paid a negotiated commission only. By 1951, agency services included: advice and assistance on policy matters; specialized consultants to aid in agriculture, mechanical engineering, legislative assistance, industrial engineering; project cost and feasibility studies; industrial relations and public relations assistance; land negotiations, property taxes, and leases; complete tax service; financing; centralized purchasing, inventory control assistance; accounting records and analysis; freight service; traffic and routing service. While the range of services had grown, the concept and practice were roughly the same as 100 years before. The agency methods of bookkeeping and the agency ways of thinking about ownership in properties are reflected in Exhibit 2A, the detailed income statements for the 1955–1960 period.

Close identification of Castle & Cooke's fortunes with the prosperity of the Territory was the keynote of this era. By 1956, Hawaiian Pineapple had begun operation of a new $3 million can manufacturing plant, to supply all of the needs of its Honolulu cannery. Later, it also supplied Calpak's and Libby's pineapple operations. This plant, importing tinplate from Japan, was an immediate and consistent moneymaker. American Can Co., previously the Islands' sole supplier, was forced to reduce sharply its Honolulu canmaking operations, Hawaiian Tuna Packers remaining its principal important customer.

Castle & Cooke, together with Helemano, organized a new realty company to sell Helemano residential land in rural Oahu, in order to meet the demand for fee-simple homesites. (This venture was discontinued two years later, after the sale of a 145 acre parcel to a development group.) C & C's ownership in Kohala Sugar Co. was increased to over 99%, and it was consolidated with the parent. Both C & C and Helemano began open-market purchase of their shares, when available.

Although Hawaiian Equipment Co., Hawaiian Tuna Packers, the Macadamia Nut division, and Kohala all operated at a nominal profit, or at a loss, during this period, the Terminals business improved sharply, and dividends from other activities continued at former levels, despite lower earnings for Hawaiian Pineapple and the sugar plantations. Labor difficulties and low sugar prices continued as persistent problems.

The search for new business opportunities led C & C to join with Alexander and Baldwin and others in the formation of an electronics manufacturing and servicing company, Kentron Hawaii, whose business was primarily in TV tube service, in 1956. (This venture was sold in 1961.)

Also in 1956, Hawaiian Tuna Packers was merged with Columbia River Packers Association, Inc., whose Bumble Bee brand was well-known in tuna and salmon markets. (As a result of the merger, C & C received 12% of CRPA's stock.) Further, $1.25 million was invested jointly by C & C and Helemano in a 6,500 acre parcel of land in northern California, Blackhawk Ranch. The company's only significant investment outside Hawaii, this land purchase was held solely for its appreciation potential.

By 1958, C & C was becoming concerned over Hawaiian Pineapple's declining earnings, attributed to "excessive mainland fruit and juice packs and the competitive conditions fostered by this situation." Herbert C. Cornuelle, formerly vice president in charge of Hawaiian plantation and manufacturing operations, was named president, succeeding Henry White.

Other significant developments in 1958 (the year in which Hawaii finally achieved statehood) were: 1) The merger of Helemano into Castle & Cooke, which had the effect of increasing C & C's net worth by over 45%, its landholdings by 100%, and its direct ownership in Hawaiian Pineapple from 15% to 49%. Mr. Budge noted that, "for the first time . . . (C & C) . . . has become a substantial direct owner of land on Oahu through acquisition of the 27,290 acres formerly held by Helemano." 2) The acquisition of a 60% ownership in Columbia River Packer's Association, "the first time in the history of C & C that we have acquired a majority ownership position in a mainland firm." (This additional stock had become available when Transamerica Corp., the majority owner, was obliged to divest itself from operating industrial properties.) 3) The marketing of macadamia nuts on the mainland, under the "Royal Hawaiian" label. 4) The development of Kawaihae harbor, on the island of Hawaii, as a port where C & C could provide terminal facilities and from which Kohala could ship its sugar in bulk form.

By 1959, the limiting of company efforts to Hawaii, broken originally by Blackhawk and CRPA, had begun to shift still further. As Mr. Budge indicated at year-end, "jets in effect have made opportunities on the mainland and elsewhere more conveniently available to management and capital in Hawaii. . . . Long-established companies such as ours are reviewing their investments and traditional patterns of business to be in a position to participate in new growth possibilities here and elsewhere."

An important event in 1959 was the disposal by Matson of virtually all of its nonshipping assets, primarily stock in the Honolulu Oil Co. and the Waikiki hotels. The effect of this divestment, facilitated by the redemption of more than 600,000 shares of Matson capital stock, was to increase C & C's ownership in Matson to 23%. It also took C & C out of its indirect activities in the hotel and tourist business. Despite low sugar income (resulting from a costly strike in 1958), greatly improved earnings of Hawaiian Pineapple, plus strong performance from CRPA and Matson, enabled C & C to show the best earnings in history, $3 million after taxes. Although nearly two-thirds still resided in Hawaii, the number of shareholders had grown to 3,600.

At year-end, 1959, C & C's investments, based on market value of publicly held companies or book value of consolidated companies, was as follows:

Pineapple (holdings of Hawaiian Pineapple Co.)	33.6%
Shipping (holdings of Matson, C & C Terminals, Kawaihae Terminals, Bay & River Navigation)	23.1%
Sugar (holdings of Ewa, Waialua, Kohala, and C & H)	15.4%
Oil (holdings of Honolulu Oil Co.)	12.7%
Seafood processing (holdings of Columbia River Packers)	6.6%
Merchandising (Hawaiian Equipment Co.)	4.5%
Insurance (holdings of Home Ins. Co. of Hawaii)	3.2%
Misc. (holdings of Bishop Trust Co., Hawaiian Trust Co., Blackhawk, Kentron)	0.9%
	100.0%

Early in the year, a major investment banking house had discussed with C & C officials the possibility of selling these various holdings and producing a total cash return substantially in excess of either Castle & Cooke's stated book value or its current market value. After giving this proposal serious consideration, Castle & Cooke management concluded that the long-run interests of their shareholders could be better served by C & C's remaining as an operating entity than by liquidating. Thus, they turned to the task with renewed commitment.

Management Succession

For several years prior to 1959, Mr. Budge had been grooming younger members of management for greater responsibility. In 1957, William M. Bush (treasurer since 1944 and vice president since 1955), Malcolm MacNaughton (vice president since 1953), and Frederick Simpich, Jr. (secretary since 1949 and vice president since 1953), were elected to the board of directors. In 1958, Mr. MacNaughton was named executive vice president, Mr. Henry B. Clark, Jr., was elected treasurer, and Mr. Howard Hubbard was named controller. In December, 1959, Mr. Budge, then 67 years old, became chairman of the board and chief executive officer, after the longest presidency in the history of Castle & Cooke (23 years). Mr. MacNaughton, then 49, was elected president. Mr. John F. Murphy (director of industrial relations since 1946) was named vice president and secretary.

1960–1965:
Emergence as a "Food Company"

In 1959, 1960, and 1961, management was actively exploring opportunities for new investment beyond Hawaii. C & C was also intent upon increasing its directly managed ownerships and reducing its purely investment holdings. In January,

1961, as an important step in this direction, C & C directors authorized the merger of Hawaiian Pineapple (now renamed Dole Corp.) and of Columbia River Packers Association into Castle & Cooke. This merger had the effect of more than doubling C & C's indicated net worth (from $35.1 million to $78.1) and of increasing stated after tax earnings by over 70% (from $3 million to $5.2). More importantly, it obliged C & C to conceive of itself primarily as a "food company."

As Mr. Budge and Mr. MacNaughton indicated early in 1961, "Management and directors have agreed on the desirability of further steps that would be consistent with changing business conditions in Hawaii and would, at the same time, broaden the base of our investments in areas outside of Hawaii. . . . If C & C is to improve upon its relatively static earning capacity, the emphasis in our business direction should be away from that of an investment-agency concern to a company more firmly established in the food industry, which has experienced dynamic growth in recent years . . . the mergers with Dole and CRPA . . . will provide the company with a greater growth potential."

Although both Dole and CRPA, renamed "Bumble Bee Seafoods," continued to operate autonomously under their previous managements, the character of Castle & Cooke had been changed enormously. These two subsidiaries, overnight, jumped corporate sales volume from a reported $28 million for C & C to a consolidated $120 million.

During the following year, C & C also acquired majority control of Ewa Plantation Co. (after a "raid" on Ewa stock by a mainland investor) and consolidated both Ewa and Waialua (whose shares it had been accumulating for many years) with C & C results. The liquidation of the Honolulu Oil Co. in 1961 gave C & C about $16.5 million in cash, net after taxes. Investments in Kentron and Hawaiian Trust Co. were also eliminated. These funds were used in part to reduce the debt accumulated in the mergers, to purchase Ewa stock, and to finance the acquisition of Maryland Tuna Co. by Bumble Bee.

At this time also, Oceanic Properties, Inc., was established "to assess opportunities for acquiring and planning use of lands which have development possibilities in Hawaii or elsewhere. In addition, it was assigned the responsibility for planning long-range use of the 156,000 acres of owned land and the 46,000 acres leased by C & C and its affiliates in Hawaii." Mililani Memorial Park (a perpetual care cemetery in Central Oahu) was transferred to Oceanic, and Frederick Simpich, Jr., formerly vice president of C & C, was named president of Oceanic. C & C stock was listed on the Pacific Coast Stock Exchange in mid-1961, and claimed over 10,000 shareholders.

Meanwhile, Dole had committed itself to a 70% interest in an Italian fruit and vegetable processing venture, Euramerica, and to a major pineapple growing and canning venture on Mindanao, in the Philippines (Dolfil). Bumble Bee had entered into further joint ventures in Alaskan salmon canneries.

1963 earnings were off sharply, due primarily to a drastic decline in Dole earnings. Quarterly dividends were reduced to 30¢, from the previous 35¢.

Matson, in 1962, transferred its Honolulu freight agency functions from C & C to its own Honolulu office. Additionally, Matson, after a loss in calendar year 1961, suspended payment of dividends over most of C & C's fiscal years 1962 and 1963.

Dole, despite record sales, had disappointing profits for the second straight year. Mr. MacNaughton explained this apparent paradox. "Chronic overproduction and resulting distress pricing of important California canned products, notably peaches, fruit cocktail, pears, and tomato products, caused Dole's mainland facilities to operate at a loss. These severe marketing conditions also caused a weakening in canned pineapple prices during a part of the year as grocers reduced promotional effort on pineapple in favor of the lower-priced, competitive fruits. Dole countered these conditions with aggressive selling, advertising, and promotional programs, with the result that, although total pineapple industry sales were off slightly for the year, the Dole brand's share of the pineapple market was the highest in 15 years."

In May, 1963, Mr. Herbert Cornuelle resigned as president of Dole to become a vice president of the United Fruit Co. Mr. MacNaughton assumed the presidency of Dole, in addition to his C & C responsibility.

The 1963–1964 year produced record earnings of $7.8 million (vs. $2.8 million for the previous year). This strong record was attributed primarily to higher prices for Dole's pineapple and a generally firmer market for its mainland products. Another important contribution was made by unusually high sugar prices. During the year, C & C made investments in a new venture to construct a steel pipe plant in Bangkok (Thai-American Steel Works Co., Ltd.) and in Republic Glass Corp., of Manila, the only flat-glass producer in the Philippines. Oceanic Properties involved itself in a southern California shopping center, a Los Angeles medical building, and a 5,200 acre property on the northern California coast (Sea Ranch). Blackhawk Ranch was sold for a $2 million capital gain. Home Insurance Co. of Hawaii (in which C & C held a 41% interest) was acquired by Great American Insurance Co. of New York, taking C & C out of the insurance business, but leaving it with 75,000 shares (2.4%) in Great American. In March, 1964, C & C shares were listed for trading on the New York Stock Exchange.

Matson provided the most significant negative influence in 1964, by announcing that they would terminate their stevedoring contract with C & C Terminals, following-up the termination of the freight agency relationship in the previous year. This step required drastic cutbacks and reorganization in the Terminals operations, involving many hundreds of employees. Terminals management were determined to stay in business, despite the loss of the Matson account, and were successful (in obtaining the business of Isthmian Lines and its parent, States Marine). In the wake of this loss of Matson business, C & C, with urging by the U.S. Department of Justice, was able to sell its holdings in Matson, along with C. Brewer and other major holders. Alexander and Baldwin, the buyer of interests which, when added to its own, equalled 94% of Matson, paid C & C $14 million, for a net profit of $9.2 million after taxes.

In September of 1964, these funds with other cash were used to purchase a 55% common stock interest in Standard Fruit and Steamship Co. of New Orleans, one of the world's largest producers and shippers of bananas. This interest was expanded to 84% by a joint tender offer of Standard and C & C.

THE COMPANY AS OF LATE 1965

In late 1965, Castle & Cooke was still regarded by some as "a food company," by others as "a Hawaiian company," and as "an investment" and "agency management company" by others. In one sense or another, each of these was partially true. As indicated earlier (and in Exhibit 1), the company was organized into more than 60 separable units, a perplexingly complex maze of divisions, subsidiaries, and investments. Yet it was also possible to separate these activities into "clusters of operations" in order to simplify description and analysis. Exhibit 5 (page 529) separates out:

1. *Dole Co. and subsidiaries,* including Dole Philippines, two Japanese marketing subsidiaries (one for pineapple, the other for pineapple-derived bromelain enzyme and other pharmaceuticals), and the Canadian subsidiary. In 1965, this was the largest and most important company activity in terms of sales, assets, net worth, and earnings.
2. *Standard Fruit and Steamship Co. and subsidiaries,* including its shipping subsidiary companies, banana marketing companies, and the Costa Rican and Honduran plantations, beer, soft drinks, vegetable oil, and box plant subsidiaries. This was the second largest unit in 1965.
3. *C & C sugar interests,* which includes Ewa, Waialua, and Kohala plantations, plus the C & C interest in C & H Sugar Refining Co.
4. *Bumble Bee Seafoods and subsidiaries,* including all of its joint ventures in cannery and terminal facilities. These activities, which ranked fourth (after sugar) in assets and equity, constituted the third largest segment of C & C business in terms of sales and earnings.
5. *Oceanic Properties, Inc., and subsidiaries* include the various cemetery companies (Oceanic Properties Investment, Inc.), Hamilton (Lake Anderson), Sea Ranch, and the other properties formally assigned to Oceanic.

The remaining interests have been divided by the casewriter into three additional categories: *Transportation Interests; Investments;* and *Other Operating Companies.*

Transportation interests included:

1. *Castle & Cooke Terminals, Ltd.,* which performs stevedoring and terminal services for ships docking in Honolulu. Despite the major readjustment which this unit had to make in 1964–1965, following the loss of the Matson business, it was able to cut back sufficiently to remain profitable. It has modernized operations, reduced costs, and survived a reduction in force

from over 1,000 employees to about 400 in less than one year. On a net worth of about $1.5 million, C & C Terminals did about $5 million in billings in 1965 (down from $11 million the previous year), and earned about $300,000 before taxes.

2. *Kawaihae Terminals, Inc.,* which was a similar kind of company to C & C Terminals, operated at the port of Kawaihae on the island of Hawaii. In addition to warehousing and stevedoring, Kawaihae Terminals also maintained bulk sugar storage, oil storage, and other similar facilities. It was owned 55% by C & C, 45% by Theo H. Davies, Co., whose Hawaii plantations used the facility for shipping their raw sugars, as did C & C's Kohala. This operation had an investment of about $1 million and, after small losses in preceding years, earned about $22,000 before taxes in 1965 on volume of about $300,000.

3. *Ship Agency Division,* which provided husbanding services for ships docking in Hawaii, had nominal investment and earned about $75,000 pretax as commission on services performed.

4. *Oahu Transport Co.,* 85% owned by Wailua and Ewa (15% by American Factors), was Hawaii's largest common carrier trucker. On assets of about $6 million and net worth of about $2.3 million, it earned about $170,000 pretax on sales of about $2 million. Only about one-fourth of its business was in plantation transportation.

5. *Hawaiian Hauling Service,* 51% owned by C & C, 35% by Emory Air Freight, and 14% by a local trucker, provided small-volume trucking services to the Terminals and shippers. On an investment of $95,000, the company earned about $18,000. Sales volume was about $500,000.

Not included in these listings were the very substantial trucking units owned and operated by Dole or the Dole barge line—Isleways—which barged pineapple from the Lanai plantation to the Honolulu cannery.

Investments included all activities in which C & C had committed capital but which were not related to any other activity. These included:

1. *Bay and River Navigation Co.,* which barged C & H sugar around San Francisco Bay. C & C's 17.2% interest in this company represented an investment (at cost) of $94,000, and yielded dividends of $64,000 in 1965.

2. *Great American Insurance Co.,* a major U.S. underwriter. C & C's 2.42% interest (75,000 shares) had a $500,000 cost, but a 1965 market value in excess of $4.5 million, and yielded $180,000 in dividends.

3. *Republic Glass Corp.,* Philippine plate glass manufacturer. C & C's 58% share in this company was consolidated with the parent's return. On a net worth of about $2.5 million, and sales of about the same amount, this company showed profit before taxes of about $600,000.

4. *Thai-American Steel Works Co., Ltd.,* in Bangkok, Thailand, was 55% owned by C & C. In fiscal 1965, it had not yet begun production and C & C management was skeptical about future prospects, since Japanese competi-

tion had entered its markets. The company was capitalized at $1 million, plus C & C guarantees on its loans.

5. *Correct-Mix Concrete, Inc.,* of Kuala Lumpur, Malaya, was 70% owned by C & C, with an investment in excess of $500,000. It, too, had not yet begun production in fiscal 1965.

6. *Honouliuli Co., Ltd.,* was a wholly owned subsidary of Ewa Plantation Co., and was wholly invested in listed common stocks. On a cost value of $200,-000, it yielded dividends of $5,000 in 1965.

7. *House of Investments, Inc.,* in which C & C had a 19% interest, was a Philippine venture capital company. C & C's investment was about $400,000. It did not yield a return in fiscal 1965.

8. *Hawaiian-Philippine Co.,* in which C & C held 22.8% of the preferred stock, had been organized as a means of investing in Philippine sugar plantations. C & C's book investment of $166,000 yielded dividends of $12,000 in 1965.

9. *C & C Investments Co.* had listed equity of $1.4 million in 1965, after deducting the net worth of C & C Terminals, which it held as a subsidiary. This equity was primarily in land holdings—three acres of industrial land (leased to C & C Terminals) and 230 acres of agricultural land, all on Oahu. (C & C Investments in 1966 was made a division holding the stock of C & C's far-eastern investments. C & C Terminals and the land on Oahu in 1966 were held directly by C & C.)

Not included in these listings are C & C's 154,000 acres of fee-simple Hawaiian land. Carried on Dole's accounts at $8.3 million were 15,000 acres on Oahu, of which 5,300 acres were in pineapple cultivation, 1,650 acres were leased to tenants, and the balance was mostly in forest land. Dole also leased about 17,650 acres (9,750 from C & C), of which 10,000 were in pineapple.

Similarly, Lanai's 90,000 acres were carried on Dole's books at their $1.1 million cost. 15,800 acres were in pineapple cultivation.

Castle & Cooke carried its 27,000 acres of Oahu land at its cost of $2.9 million. Of this land, 9,750 acres were leased to Dole, 7,000 to Waialua, and 4,500 to other tenants.

Kohala's 20,500 acres, of which 12,700 were in sugar cane, were carried at $1.6 million.

Rentals from these properties were not fully reflected in the operating statements of the various companies. Similar agricultural acreage was being leased by Ewa, Waialua, Dole, and Kohala from others for rentals in the range of $15-$75/acre/year.

Other operating companies were Hawaiian Equipment Co. and Royal Hawaiian Macadamia Nut Co. Both of these companies were consolidated divisions of Castle & Cooke.

1. *Hawaiian Equipment Co.* had been started in 1946. It owned and operated sales and service facilities, on each major island, for trucks, tractors, and other agricultural and construction equipment. As the Hawaiian distributor

for International Harvester, it faced its major competition from Caterpillar and other heavy equipment dealers. While it had not been profitable in its early years, it earned a small profit subsequently, and sales and earnings had grown steadily since. In 1965, it had record sales of $7.5 million. On a book equity of $3.3 million and total assets of $4.6 million, it earned $300,000 before taxes, which was also a record high. Management saw slow, steady growth continuing for this company, to a possible saturation of about $12 million in sales volume by 1971.

2. *Royal Hawaiian Macadamia Nut Co.* had been started in 1949 as a new venture. 1,200 acres of jungle had been cleared and over 80,000 macadamia trees planted and nursed to maturity. When combined with another 365 acres being grown at Kohala and Waialua, these orchards make Royal Hawaiian the world's leading producer of macadamias. In a new $400,000 plant, the hard shells are cracked, and the nutmeats are sorted, roasted, and packed. While the company provides employment for 50 permanent employees and as many as 250 more during the peak season, it has not yet reached profitability. 1965 sales of $2 million accounted for about 60% of total world macadamia sales. On this volume (about 1.5 million pounds), the company showed a 1965 loss of about $150,000, a substantial reduction from previous years' losses. The high cost of the nut, and the very modest supply of product forecast to be available over the next ten years, make it questionable whether world consumption can reach as much as 5 million pounds. (Since it takes eight to ten years for a tree to come into economic bearing, the supply is highly predictable.)

Although the Royal Hawaiian brand has achieved nationwide distribution, the costs involved in the total venture have absorbed over $7 million investment in the 15 years of operation. 1965 book value, with these losses written off, was $700,000, and assets employed were about $2 million.

SUMMARY

This, then, was how the casewriter described Castle & Cooke in 1965: a company with great strengths, but still emerging from its historical roots and having yet to clearly define its future shape or character.

Castle & Cooke, Inc. (B) describes the central headquarters organization and some of the interests and objectives of key management as of late 1965.

BIOGRAPHIES OF THE
PRINCIPAL CASTLE & COOKE, INC. EXECUTIVES

Alexander G. Budge, 74, chairman of the board of Castle & Cook, Inc., was born in Grand Forks, North Dakota, on December 4, 1891. He entered the University of North Dakota, Grand Forks, before transferring a year later to Stanford University. He was graduated in 1912 from Stanford with an

AB in mechanical engineering and returned in 1959 to the University of North Dakota to receive an honorary degree of Doctor of Laws.

Following graduation, Mr. Budge joined the San Francisco firm of Charles C. Moore & Co. as a sales engineer. His duties with the company were interrupted by World War I, in which he served in France as an Ordinance Captain. After the war, he returned to Charles C. Moore & Co. before joining Castle & Cook, Inc., in 1920 as assistant secretary.

In 1924, Mr. Budge was named secretary, a position he held until 1930, when he was appointed vice president and secretary. He served in this capacity until 1935, at which time he became president.

It was during Mr. Budge's tenure as president that Castle & Cooke actively embarked upon a search for new, young talent from the mainland. This search ranks as one of Mr. Budge's outstanding contributions to Castle & Cooke. His belief was that the greatly increased investments of mainland companies in Hawaii and the resulting economic pressures, together with the slipping of sugar profits, created a demand for new men with fresh outlooks who were attuned to mainland business methods. Thus, Mr. Budge's policy became to procure "men who are different from myself in experience and temperament."

In December, 1959, Mr. Budge was named chairman of the board, Castle & Cooke, Inc. In addition to these duties, he is a director of the following companies: Waialua Agricultural Company, Kohala Sugar Company, Bumble Bee Seafoods, Inc., Dole Company, Ewa Plantation Co., and Oceanic Properties, Inc.

Malcolm MacNaughton is president and a director of the company. He joined the company in 1942 as assistant secretary. He was appointed vice president in 1953, executive vice president in 1957, and president in 1959. In addition to the company, he is president and director of Dole of Canada, Limited, Ewa Plantation Company, Kohala Sugar Company, and Waialua Agricultural Company, Limited. He is chairman of the board of directors of Dole Company, Dole Philippines, Inc., and Hawaiian Equipment Company. He is a director of Bumble Bee Seafoods, Castle & Cooke Terminals, Limited, Oceanic Properties, Inc., Royal Hawaiian Macadamia Nut Company, Standard Fruit and Steamship Company, Oahu Transport Company, Limited, Hawaiian Trust Company, Limited, California & Hawaiian Sugar Refining Corporation, Limited, House of Investments, Great American Insurance Company of New York, and American National Fire Insurance Company. He is also a director of Queen's Hospital, the National Health and Welfare Retirement Association, and the Honolulu Community Chest.

Mr. MacNaughton is a member of the executive committee of the Hawaiian Sugar Planters' Association and vice president of the Pineapple Growers Association of Hawaii. He is trustee of Reed College, Portland, Oregon, Nutrition Foundation, Inc., and the Hawaii Council on Economic Education. He is a director, the secretary, and treasurer, as well as a member of the executive committee of the Oahu Development Conference. Mr. MacNaughton is a member of the Advisory Council, Graduate School of Business, Stanford University. He is a member of the Newcomen Society in North America. Mr. MacNaughton is Honorary Consul of Thailand in Honolulu.

William M. Bush, 62, executive vice president and director of Castle & Cooke, Inc., was born in Scotland. He came to Hawaii in 1920 and joined the Hawaiian Electric Company as pricing clerk in charge of the billing section of the merchandise department. Upon resigning this position in 1924, he returned to school for two years at the University of Hawaii.

He joined Castle & Cooke in 1926 as assistant bookkeeper, was elected treasurer in 1944, and vice president in 1955. Since 1961, he has been executive vice president.

In addition to his day to day work with Castle & Cooke and its affiliates, Mr. Bush is a member of the Honolulu Chamber of Commerce, Hawaiian Sugar Planters' Association, and International Society of Sugar Cane Technologists. He is a past president and director of the Hawaii Medical Services Association and treasurer of Hawaiian Botanical Society.

John F. Murphy, 58, vice president and secretary of Castle & Cooke, was born in Worcester, Massachusetts. He was graduated from Holy Cross College in Worcester, Mass., in 1930, and did graduate work at New York University before leaving in 1934 to join the New York State Employment Service as head of the research section.

He came to Castle & Cooke in 1946 as director of industrial relations from the Industrial Relations Counselors of New York, where he had been employed since 1938. In 1959, Mr. Murphy was elected vice president and secretary.

In addition to his day to day work with Castle & Cooke and its affiliated companies, Mr. Murphy is a member of Hawaiian Sugar Technologists and Oahu Industrial Relations Association. He is president of the Honolulu Symphony Society and a member of the Honolulu Orchid Society and World Brotherhood.

Henry B. Clark, Jr., 50, is vice president and treasurer of Castle & Cooke. He was graduated from Northwestern University in Evanston, Illinois, in 1937, and received a Masters in business administration from Harvard Business School in 1940. Upon completion of graduate work, Mr. Clark served as a naval reserve officer until release from active duty as a Lieutenant Commander in 1945.

He joined Castle & Cooke in 1946 in the operation analysis department. He became head of that department, and, over the years, was elected assistant secretary, assistant treasurer, treasurer, and, in 1962, vice president.

In addition to his day to day work with Castle & Cooke and its affiliates, Mr. Clark is a director or trustee of the following organizations: Palolo Chinese Old Men's Home, Hawaii Committee on Alcoholism, Hawaii Mission Children's Society, Hawaii Preparatory Academy, the Tax Foundation of Hawaii, the Honolulu Chamber of Commerce, and Hawaiian Airlines.

Stanley Rosch, 47, Castle & Cooke controller, was born in New York, N.Y., June 8, 1918. He attended the City College of New York and was graduated in 1940 from Columbia University with a BBA degree. Later he did graduate work at George Washington University.

Before joining C & C in 1965 as controller, he was from 1956 to 1963 a partner with Haskins & Sells in both Honolulu and Los Angeles. Rosch is also controller of Ewa Plantation Company, Kohala Sugar Company, and Waialua

Agricultural Company. He is a member of the American Institute of C.P.A.'s, National Association of Accountants, and the Hawaii Society of C.P.A.'s.

Frederick Simpich, Jr., 54, president of Oceanic Properties, Inc., was born in New Franklin, Missouri. He attended the New Mexico Military Institute and the University of Pennsylvania.

Mr. Simpich joined the Dole Company in 1936 as an assistant to the treasurer before coming to Castle & Cooke in 1938. Three years of military service during World War II saw Mr. Simpich discharged as a Lt. Col., General Corps Staff, with the Bronze Star, Order of the British Empire, Croix-de-Guerre, and five battle stars.

Upon returning to Castle & Cooke following the war, he played an important role in readjustment of the company's postwar business operations. He became secretary in 1949 and was elected a vice president in 1953. He was elected president of Oceanic Properties, Inc., in 1961. Mr. Simpich is also a director of Castle & Cooke, Inc., Dole Company, Mililani Memorial Park, Inc., and Royal Hawaiian Macademia Nut Company.

William Quinn, 46, president and director of Dole Company, was born in Rochester, New York, on July 13, 1919. Mr. Quinn was graduated summa cum laude from St. Louis University in 1940 with a BS degree. He was graduated cum laude from the Harvard Law School in 1947 with an LLB degree. During World War II, Mr. Quinn served as an air combat intelligence officer with the naval reserve. He attained the rank of Lieutenant Commander.

Quinn came to Honolulu in 1947, the same year that he was graduated from law school, and joined the Honolulu firm of Robertson, Castle & Anthony. Mr. Quinn was made a partner in the firm in 1950.

In 1957, Quinn was appointed Governor of the Territory of Hawaii by President Eisenhower. When Hawaii achieved statehood two years later, he ran for the office and became Hawaii's first governor. He was defeated for re-election by Democrat John A. Burns in November, 1962.

Mr. Quinn returned to law practice with the firm of Quinn and Moore and remained active in Republican activities. When he was elected executive vice president and director of Dole Company in June, 1964, Mr. Quinn ended his political career. He became Dole's president in 1965.

Mr. Quinn is a former member of the City Charter Commission and the Statehood Commission and a past president of the Honolulu Community Chest and the Honolulu Community Theatre. He is a director of Biship Trust Company.

Donald J. Kirchhoff, president of Standard Fruit and Steamship Company, was born in St. Louis, Missouri, in 1925. He is a graduate of Miami University of Ohio and the Harvard Business School. From 1949 to 1953 he was an accountant with the Kroger Company, and from 1953 to 1956 he was controller with National Food Stores of Michigan, Inc.

He joined Standard Fruit and Steamship Company in 1956 as manager of the new Operations Analysis Department, and served in that capacity until 1958, when he was appointed assistant to the president. In 1960, he was appointed general manager of the Honduras Division, with headquarters in La

Ceiba, and later was elected vice president in that capacity. In 1962, he was elected executive vice president of the company and returned to the general hadquarters in New Orleans, Louisiana. In November, 1964, he was elected to the board of directors and in the same month of that year was elected president of Standard Fruit and Steamship Company when Castle & Cooke bought controlling interest in the company.

Thomas F. Sandoz, 64, chairman of the board and chief executive officer of Bumble Bee Seafoods, of Astoria, Oregon, was born in Mobile, Alabama. He attended public school in Astoria and joined Bumble Bee Seafoods (then the Columbia River Packers Association) in 1928 after a nine year period with Mason Ehrman & Co. as a salesman. He was elected president in 1950 and became chairman of the board in 1963, after having been a director since 1938.

Mr. Sandoz is also a director of Dole Company, Castle & Cooke, Inc., and the Pacific Power & Light Company and the First National Bank of Oregon, both of Portland. In addition, he is active as an advisor to various national and international fishery commissions.

John S. McGowan, 47, president of Bumble Bee Seafoods, was born in Los Angeles, California. He attended the public schools of Iwaco, Washington, and was graduated with a BS degree from the University of Oregon in 1940.

Mr. McGowan joined the sales department of Bumble Bee (then the Columbia River Packers Association) in 1946 after serving active duty as a Lieutenant in the naval reserve. He was named sales promotion manager in 1950, assistant secretary in 1952, and assistant vice president in 1955. He was elected vice president in 1957 and director and executive vice president in 1960. In 1963, Mr. McGowan was named to the presidency.

He is a director of the Chamber of Commerce of Astoria, Oregon, and the National Canners Association, in addition to serving as an advisor to several fishery commissions.

The Dole Company

The Dole Company was the world's largest producer and marketer of pineapple. The company owned two plantations in Hawaii, leased one in the Philippines, and owned and operated its own canneries in both locations. The company also owned and operated fruit and vegetable canneries in Salem, Oregon, and San Jose, California. Dole products were distributed mostly in the United States and Canada, through food brokers assisted by the company's marketing personnel. In fiscal 1965, Dole had sales of $98 million and after-tax earnings of $4.2 million.

REQUIREMENTS FOR GROWING AND CANNING PINEAPPLE

Climatological requirements for growing pineapple confine production to a few areas of the world. Ideally, temperature should range between 60 and 90 degrees Fahrenheit. Higher temperatures result in bland-tasting fruit, and lower temperatures retard growth. Pineapple thrives in slightly acid soil, with an annual 40-50 inches of rainfall evenly distributed throughout the year. Inadequate rainfall can be supplemented by irrigation, but excessive rainfall prevents sufficient sunlight from reaching the plant—a critical element in growing good pineapple. The pineapple industry has done a good job in controlling parasitic insects, but is still struggling to control plant diseases. Some plant diseases remain a problem to Hawaiian growers, but are not nearly as serious as they are in some other parts of the world.

Land Preparation and Planting

Land preparation for new planting of pineapple begins with the previous crop.

Most old fields are merely chopped down with a "stump cutter," and the plants are either burned or left to decompose as mulch. The leaves in some fields operated by large, sophisticated growers are sometimes harvested and chopped, dried and pelletized for cattle feed. A more recent development is the processing of the stump to produce the enzyme *bromelain*. After any of these alternatives, the field is plowed and disced smooth, then covered with 32-inch wide rows of black polyethylene film, spaced about two feet apart. As the film is laid, the soil underneath is fumigated and fertilized. Weeds are boom-sprayed with herbicides, while the film restricts the loss of moisture, heat, and fumigants.

Pineapple plants are started by inserting pieces of planting material through the plastic and into the soil at 12 inch intervals. Planting material, gathered from mature plants, may be: crowns—the top of a ripe fruit; slips—a young shoot growing just under the fruit; or suckers—a similar growth from the lower stump of the pineapple plant. An experienced man can plant about 9,000 slips or crowns (about a half-acre) in an eight hour shift.

Fruit Production

The first crop (called the "plant crop") ripens in 20-22 months. The plant crop produces one fruit per plant at the apex of the stem (at an average density of about 19,000 per acre), but the same plant is capable of yielding second and third crops more numerous than the first. These additional crops, called "ratoons," result from the plant's producing fruits on suckers branching off the main stem. The first ratoon crop ripens 13 months after the plant crop. It is maintained and harvested much like the plant crop. As many as 25,000 pineapples per acre can be yielded by the first ratoon crop. However, since the fruit from the ratoon crop is smaller than that produced by the plant crop, usually fewer tons per acre are realized. On most large mechanized plantations, only one ratoon crop is harvested. Then the field is razed and prepared for a new planting. In those instances when a second ratoon is allowed to grow, this crop follows the first ratoon by about 18 months.

The pineapple plant has no "season," and can be planted or harvested at any time of the year (after allowing the full growth cycle). However, the fruit tends to have somewhat different taste and color characteristics under differing time spans of sunlight, rain, warm days, cold days, etc.

During the growing period, the fields are sprayed with insecticides, irrigated, and fertilizer is applied as needed. The fields may also be sprayed once or twice with a hormone to force all the fruit sprayed to mature at roughly the same time. Although hormone "forcing" can predetermine the beginning of the ripening period within a two week span, ripening of the entire field usually will require six to eight weeks. The ripened fruit remains at its peak of quality for a very short time, so harvesting crews typically go through a field at least once a week during this period.

On mechanized plantations, workers follow large truck-mounted harvesters, selecting the ripe pineapples, picking them by hand, removing the crowns, and placing the fruit on a moving conveyor. The conveyor belt carries the pineapple to a bin mounted on the same truck. Bins subsequently are transported to the cannery. In addition to the long conveyors and large trucks, mechanized plantations also have substantial investments in other heavy equipment. For example, field preparation is done by large "crawler-type" tractors, and irrigation and fertilization are done with giant, specially designed spray rigs. These same operations are done in low labor cost areas of the world with little or no capital equipment by large numbers of hand laborers at roughly comparable over-all cost.

Cannery

On arrival at the cannery, the fruit is automatically sorted by size and by color (indicative of state of ripeness). Fruit of uniform size and color is conveyed to a "Ginaca machine," [1] which removes the shell, the core, and the ends of the pineapple in a half second's time. These machines feed the shelled and cored fruit to long trimming tables. Here, girls inspect the cylinders of fruit, and, by hand remove the "eyes," bits of shell, bruises, and imperfections with special knives. The Ginaca machines can be set to various thicknesses of cut in shelling. A thin cut leaves more fruit, but also more "eyes" and bits of shell to be removed than a thicker one. Thus the number of trimmers required is proportional to the thinness of the cut. The cylinders of fruit are then conveyed from the trimmers, through slicing knives, to the packers, who carefully grade each slice. Only perfect rings of the best color are eligible for cans of fancy grade sliced pineapple, and an effort is made to select all fruit which can qualify. Slices which do not meet the fancy standard are downgraded by the packers to a "choice" slice grade. All other slices (or partials) are cut into "tidbits." Any remaining pineapple is processed as "crushed." The solid pack pineapple slices are placed in cans, which are then mechanically filled with sugar syrup, sealed, heated for sterilization, and sent to the labeling room for labeling, casing, and palletizing.

Although there is a great deal of hand labor in the trimming, grading, and packing processes, the balance of the cannery operation can be highly automated. In highly mechanized canneries, more than one-half of the total labor force may be involved in the trimming, grading, and packing operations.

Secondary Products

Although sliced pineapple is the main product of the cannery, juice ordinarily constitutes an extremely important secondary product. Cores, the meat from the pineapple shells, and juice and scraps from the trimming tables are collected for

---

[1] Named for the inventor, Henry Ginaca, a Dole Co. engineer. These machines, now in use in all pineapple canneries throughout the world, revolutionized the industry with their fast, accurate peeling and coring capabilities.

juice. These materials are pressed, heated, centrifuged, and packed. Most juice is canned, but a portion may be concentrated and frozen. Some of the concentrate may be bulk-packed for later blending or reconstitution.

An equally important secondary product is "crushed" pineapple. A small amount of "crushed" pineapple is also packed as a frozen product.

By-Products

Uncanned juice can be converted into a sugar syrup by filtering, ion exchanging, and concentrating. In Hawaii, more than half of the sugar syrup required for packing sliced pineapple is derived from this ion exchange process. Sugar produced in this manner is generally cheaper than cane sugar in Hawaii, so excess Hawaiian juice is usually processed in this manner.

A second important by-product is cattle feed, made by shredding, pressing, and drying the shell material.

Two other by-products are commercially practical. The pineapple leaves can be shredded and pelletized as cattle feed, and the stump can be milled to extract the enzyme bromelain, which is used as an anti-inflammatory agent, a meat tenderizer, and a digestion aid. Each of these processes, however, requires a significant capital investment.

Fresh Fruit

Pineapples intended for fresh fruit sales are often grown specially. Smaller than average sized fruit is usually selected because consumers tend to buy whole pineapples by the unit, rather than by the pound. Fields planted specially for fresh fruit generally are planted at a very high density per acre, and are staged to yield mature fruit year-round.

Pineapple to be sold fresh is picked before it is fully ripe and is handled with special care to avoid bruising. It is then boxed, refrigerated, and shipped for consumption. The crowns are shipped with the fruit and are not available as planting material. Special handling and fast transportation schedules can get a fresh pineapple from Hawaii to the East Coast within 14 days after picking.

WORLD PINEAPPLE PRODUCTION

Differences in temperature, sunlight, and water conditions have created differentiable distinctions in fruit characteristics among the various producing areas. Hawaii's growing characteristics are nearly ideal, and resulting fruit quality is very high. However, Hawaii produces sweeter and larger fruit during the summer months than in other seasons. Acreage harvested "off season" does not necessarily yield less pineapple tonnage than summer harvests, but frequently yields fewer fancy slices per ton. The Hawaiian pineapple industry also relies heavily upon students to fill cannery labor needs, thus May through late August becomes an attractive time to harvest and pack from that point of view. In 1964, 85% of Hawaiian pineapple was canned during this period and employment increased from a year-round 6,800 to a seasonal peak of 21,550 cannery and field workers. In areas other than Hawaii, climatic and labor conditions allow for more uniform, year-round crop scheduling.

In many growing areas other than Hawaii, high temperatures result in bland-tasting fruit. While this fruit is adequate as a solid packed product, most of it is sold in the U.S. on a price basis under unpromoted brands or private labels, or is sold in the less discriminating foreign markets. The by-product juice resulting from packing this solid pineapple (normally about 700 pounds of juice per ton of fruit) is generally too bland and its acidity level too low for it to be saleable as a beverage product in any market. Sugar prices have generally been low in these countries, so it has not been advantageous to convert the juice to sugar through ion exchange. Therefore, no attempt is made to recover the juice in most non-Hawaiian producing areas. Non-Hawaiian producers have remained competitive largely because of low costs (e.g., Taiwan labor costs per ton are only 10% of Hawaiian). Also, some foreign canners have been able to extract 34-38% of total fruit weight as solid pack by slicing the husks thinly and using extensive hand labor to remove defects. This compares with a solid pack yield of only 25% for Hawaii. Prior to automation, just after World War II, Hawaiian canneries reportedly extracted a 40% yield of solid pack from each ton of fruit.

Pineapple is not as subject to great output fluctuations as other crops, and thus world volume can be very closely predicted for any given year. Solid pack canned pineapple production by all major world sources for selected years is shown in Exhibit 1. As indicated, Hawaii's share of world production has declined from 71% in 1950 to 49.7% in 1963.

Exhibit 2 shows similar figures for world production of canned pineapple juice. As indicated, non-Hawaiian sources of pineapple juice have not materialized to the degree that solid pack competition has. Although declining, Hawaii's share of the total market for pineapple juice remained above 75% in 1965. Other significant factors in juice production were the Philippines with 10%, Australia and South Africa with 3.5% each, and Puerto Rico with 2%. Taiwan and Malaya, important solid pack producers, were insignificant in the juice market because of the low quality of their product.

HAWAIIAN PINEAPPLE PRODUCERS

The Hawaiian Islands have 66,000 acres of land planted in pineapple. In 1965 six companies divided this acreage to produce about $120 million worth of pineapple products, or about 560,000 tons. Dole was the largest of these companies, with about half of the state's 1965 output and supplying about 35% of U.S. consumption. Plantations were on Oahu and Lanai, while the cannery was

exhibit 1

THE DOLE COMPANY

Known World Production of Canned Pineapple
(in 1,000 24/2 ½ case equivalents—45 lbs.)

Year	Hawaii	Singapore	Taiwan	South Africa	Philippines	Australia	Okinawa
1935	9,045	2,793	1,189	67	149	195	—
1940	8,200	1,921	1,614	19	1,073	393	—
1945	7,553	—	22	79	—	117	—
1950	11,314	734	204	272	1,127	569	—
1955	13,726	1,220	1,024	583	1,871	1,347	—
1956	13,211	1,753	1,132	796	1,457	1,164	—
1957	12,220	1,805	1,143	1,324	1,944	924	35
1958	12,863	2,015	1,744	1,541	1,397	1,162	143
1959	12,585	1,889	1,731	1,792	1,985	1,328	401
1960	13,240	1,919	2,227	1,835	1,610	1,107	659
1961	13,130	2,197	2,897	2,367	1,847	800	735
1962	13,177	2,355	2,710	2,069	1,988	1,052	721
1963	12,732	2,512	2,343	1,914	1,444	885	866

Puerto Rico & Continental U.S.	Mexico	Kenya	Martinique	Ivory Coast	Cuba	Other	Known World Production	Hawaiian % of Total
48	—	—	—	—	39	5	13,530	66.86
68	16	—	—	—	300	35	13,639	60.12
321	110	—	—	—	390	48	8,640	87.41
786	563	—	—	—	329	21	15,918	71.08
497	493	175	189	—	496	66	21,688	63.29
446	608	229	151	49	770	41	21,807	60.58
437	501	207	211	98	748	37	21,633	56.49
454	764	203	224	109	551	99	23,270	55.28
486	472	192	438	191	594	63	24,148	52.11
501	676	195	486	176	545	109	25,285	52.36
626	715	222	473	205	159	118	26,494	49.56
737	691	370	354	235	23	197	26,680	49.39
789	716	467	371	370	10	202	25,622	49.69

1 Includes Ivory Coast.

Source: Pineapple Fact Book/Hawaii, 1963.

in Honolulu. It employed a peak of 9,600 workers who earned total wages of $21.1 million to produce products sold primarily under the Dole label.

The second largest Hawaiian producer, with about 18% of Hawaii's production, was the California Packing Corporation (Calpak), which employed a peak of 4,600 workers who earned $7.4 million on its plantations on Oahu and Molokai and in its Honolulu cannery. Calpak sold worldwide through brokers, jobbers, and direct to merchants. Most of Calpak's output was packed under the Del-Monte label, which, in 1965, commanded about 18% of the U.S. market for canned pineapple. Both Dole and Del-Monte brand pineapple products had the reputation of being the highest, most uniform quality available, and sales efforts relied heavily upon brand promotion. Besides these Hawaiian plantations, Calpak had operated a pineapple plantation and cannery in the Philippines since the 1920's.

The third largest Hawaiian pineapple grower was Maui Pineapple Co., with about 13.5% of the state's production. This company, owned and operated by Alexander & Baldwin, had peak employment of about 2,700 workers who had earnings of $5.6 million. Virtually their entire output was sold under private label through the parent company.

Libby, McNeill & Libby was in 1965 the fourth largest pineapple producer in Hawaii, with about 12.5% of the output. Libby had plantations on Molokai, while its cannery was in Honolulu. Peak employment reached 1,500 workers who

exhibit 2

THE DOLE COMPANY

Known World Production of Canned Pineapple Juice
(in 1,000 24/2 ½ case equivalents—29.25 lbs.)

Year	Hawaii	Philippines	Australia	South Africa	Puerto Rico	Ivory Coast	Other	Total	Hawaiian % of Total
1935	4,531	—	—	—	21	—	—	4,552	99.54%
1940	11,982	560	—	—	34	—	3	12,579	95.25
1945	9,569	—	—	—	219	—	6	9,794	97.70
1950	13,699	1,914	324	n.a.	92	—	278	16,307	84.00
1955	13,960	735	419	375	120	—	274	15,883	87.89
1956	14,383	2,645	446	255	157	—	205	18,091	79.50
1957	11,699	3,222	616	469	201	n.a.	224	16,431	71.20
1958	14,020	1,115	833	396	237	173	273	17,047	82.25
1959	12,248	1,012	996	419	229	190	353	15,447	79.29
1960	12,856	1,446	997	349	391	278	419	16,736	76.82
1961	13,322	1,712	658	622	383	267	412	17,376	76.66

Source: Pineapple Fact Book/Hawaii, 1963.

earned $5.1 million. Libby's U.S. market share in pineapple had fallen steadily from 13% in 1957 to 6% in 1964. To offset this decline, Libby had reduced its costs by packing in lighter syrup and by purchasing Taiwan pineapple to sell under the Libby label along with its Hawaiian production. With lower costs and reduced margins, Libby was offering special prices to the trade, which, in 1965, appeared to have halted the decline in market share. Almost all of their output was sold under the Libby label by their own sales force.

Differing strengths and competitive advantages have been established. For example, Calpak was first to produce pineapple-grapefruit juice drink and it since has held a majority of that market. In contrast, Dole has traditionally sold more straight pineapple juice than both Calpak and Libby combined. While Dole has been the over-all national sales leader, in certain regions like the southeast Dole was a poor third to Calpak and Libby in solid pack pineapple. In 1965 Libby had captured much of the lower price, lower quality market, while Dole and Calpak continued to concentrate on the high quality, fancy pack market segment.

Besides Dole, Calpak, Maui Pineapple, and Libby, there were two smaller pineapple companies in Hawaii in 1965. Hawaiian Fruit Packers, who owned and operated a small plantation and cannery on the island of Kauai, were controlled by Stokely-Van Camp. Most of the cannery's output, which accounted for 2.5% of Hawaiian production, was sold under the Stokely label. Hawaiian Fruit Packers employed about 700 workers who earned $1.0 million.

The last producer of pineapple in 1965 was the Haserot Pineapple Company, which conducted a very small growing and canning operation on Maui. Most of its output, which accounted for the remaining .8% of the state's production, was sold in the Cleveland area through the parent's wholesale company. The Haserot Pineapple Company employed less than 400 workers who earned $.3 million.

By 1965, all other Hawaiian pineapple operations had been sold or merged into one of the six companies listed above, or had gone out of business, and the land had been converted to sugar cane production.

U.S. PINEAPPLE CONSUMPTION

More than half the pineapple grown in the world is consumed in the United States. The U.S. pineapple market has been a very high quality one and has been primarily in the fancy quality grades. Despite the demand for high quality, a large portion of this market is sold on a price basis. Private labeling contracts with the large chains have been a growing source of sales for major producers. However, private labels and unknown brands generally have been promoted on a price basis. Case allowances and advertising allowances have become commonplace in pineapple marketing. All of the foreign pineapple not packed under nationally advertised brands has been sold on a price basis. Under these pressures, the share of market held by the nationally advertised brands has been decreasing in recent years. However, although their percentage share of market has been declining, the Dole and Del-Monte labels have managed to maintain a consistently improving price level.

Industry sources have reported that U.S. canned pineapple prices tend to relate directly to the available supply of other canned fruit. Particularly, the price of canned pineapple is supposed to be related to the price of California cling peaches. This reasoning is based on the expectation that a large peach crop will prompt grocers to use peaches as loss leaders or promotional items, thus reducing the selling effort which might have been given to pineapple. Exhibit 3 shows the price and volume relationships between California cling peaches and Hawaiian sliced fancy pineapple for the periods 1947–48 through 1960–61.

exhibit 3

THE DOLE COMPANY

Canners' Domestic Movement of Cling Peaches and Pineapple

Marketing Year June thru April	California Cling Peaches (24 No. 2-1/2 Basis)		Hawaiian Pineapple Sliced Fancy (No. 1-1/2 F.O.B.)	
	Thousands of Cases	Dollars[1] per Case	Thousands of Cases	Dollars[1] per Case
1947 - 8	13,843	$4.78	10,112	$6.10
1948 - 9	12,382	5.10	11,684	6.80
1949 - 0	15,615	4.07	11,920	6.40
1950 - 1	14,287	5.17	13,032	6.80
1951 - 2	13,648	5.53	9,685	6.80
1952 - 3	14,351	5.32	11,695	6.85
1953 - 4	14,706	5.12	12,050	6.85
1954 - 5	14,086	5.17	12,743	6.90
1955 - 6	15,023	5.70	13,198	7.35
1956 - 7	15,008	5.35	12,101	7.40
1957 - 8	16,925	5.10	12,457	7.45
1958 - 9	13,886	5.36	12,779	7.75
1959 - 60	17,387	4.89	12,951	8.05
1960 - 1	15,984	4.36	13,100	8.05

[1] Based on weighted average canners' f.o.b. sales prices determined from canners' reports on their billings and invoices of sales f.o.b. cannery or dock (including brokerage, cash discount, and swell, label, and case allowances, but excluding any special or trade discounts and any prepaid charges included in delivery prices, such as freight and marine insurance). Prices adjusted to an industrywide common or nondifferentiated basis by modification for recognized price premiums conventional for certain brands.

Source: Sidney Hoos and George M. Kuznets, *Pacific Coast Canned Fruits F.O.B. Price Relationships, 1960-61,* California Agricultural Experiment Station, Giannini Foundation Research Report No. 246, July 1961, p.7 and p.8.

In 1965, nationally advertised canned pineapple was being sold to grocery stores in a variety of ways. Dole was selling through a nationwide system of brokers. Calpak was selling 45% of its pineapple through the company's own 600 man sales force, and 55% through brokers. Libby, which was selling directly to the supermarkets with its own 700 man sales force, employed brokers in special situations.

WORLD PINEAPPLE CONSUMPTION

In 1965, pineapple consumption for the rest of the world was somewhat less than U.S. consumption alone. The relative consumptions of the major pineapple-eating countries are shown in Exhibit 4. This exhibit shows the total consumption of each major market and the sources of supply for those markets. More than three-fourths of non-U.S. consumption is accounted for by five countries: West Germany, U.K., Japan, Canada, and France.

Consuming Country	Total Consumed	Home Grown	Imported	Taiwan	Singapore	U.S.
United States	13,698	10,809	2,889	928	430	2571
West Germany	2,671		2,671	689	160	854
United Kingdom	2,613		2,613	54	980	118
Japan	1,389		1,389	387		66
Canada	1,063		1,063		346	292
France	786		786			30
Australia	571	571				
Netherlands	387		387	119	4	173
Belgium-Luxembourg	339		339	98		165
Denmark	212		212	42	35	43
South Africa	189	189				
New Zealand	186		186		138	1
Sweden	185		185	2	2	106
Spain	157		157			42
Switzerland	117		117			117
Other (less than 100,000 cases) and reconciling	566	268	298	45	195	(107)
Totals	25,129	11,837	12,292	2,364	2,290	2,157

1Puerto Rico.

The sales pattern in these foreign markets differed in two important respects from the U.S. market: 1) tariff and quota restrictions tended to influence sources of supply for some of these countries; 2) this market historically has been a lower quality market than the U.S. domestic market.

Some countries' sources of supply are wholly related to their political alignment. For instance, Japan's supply comes almost entirely from Taiwan and Okinawa. (Japan has imposed a 55% ad valorem tariff on United States-grown canned pineapple, although fresh pineapple is admitted without tariff.) France has traditionally favored Martinique and the Ivory Coast, and these two sources dominate the entire French supply. The United Kingdom has imposed tariffs of 69¢ per pound on U.S.-grown pineapple in order to give preferential treatment to Commonwealth affiliated countries (primarily South Africa, Malaya, and Australia). Even Canada has given a 1.5¢ per pound benefit to Commonwealth suppliers over U.S.-supplying companies. Only in West Germany have U.S. producers found an important overseas market, unhampered by tariff discrimination. (Exhibit 5 gives a more complete picture of the world pineapple tariff structure.)

exhibit 4

THE DOLE COMPANY

**Sources and Consumption of Pineapple
(in 1,000 24/2 ½ case equivalents—45 lbs.)**

Philippines	South Africa	Okinawa	Mexico	Kenya	Martinique	Ivory Coast	Australia	Others and Reconciling
630	121		461	6			22	34
445		316	55	111		1	24	16
147	987			188			105	34
66		866						4
3	225		48				146	3
	10				371	369		6
51	9		6	1				24
49	1		1					25
14	23		1					
							71	(24)
53	16		3	2				1
			115					
	17		22	158			(59)	27
1,458	1.409	1,182	712	466	371	370	**309**	204

Source: Pineapple Fact Book/Hawaii, 1965.

exhibit 5

THE DOLE COMPANY

World Pineapple Tariffs

Tariffs on Pineapple Imported into U. S.	Per Pound
Prepared or preserved	0.75¢
Exceptions to full rate	
Cuba	0.55¢*
Philippines	0.22¢†
Canned pineapple juice	22¢/gal††

*No Cuban imports presently allowed.
†Philippine tariff preference scheduled to be eliminated by 1974 when current 0.22¢/lb. rate will increase by scheduled increments to full duty rate of 0.75¢.
††Exception to juice rate is Philippines, for which the applicable U. S. duty for 1965-67 is 40% of the duty, or equivalent of 9¢/gal.

Tariff Rates on U.S.
Canned Pineapple Exported to Selected Countries

European Common Market

Country	Ad Valorem Current Rate (1965 %)	Ad Valorem Ultimate Rate (1970 %)
France	31.5	25
West Germany	21.5	25
Benelux	25.0	25
Italy	18.7	25

Other Nations

Japan	55.0% ad valorem (less to Okinawa)
Spain	25.5% (approx.) ad valorem
Sweden	30 Kroner per 100 Kgs. (2.6 ¢ /lb.)
Switzerland	40 Sw. Fr. per 100 Kgs. (4.2 ¢ /lb.)
Canada	2 ¢ per lb. (none to 1/2 ¢ /lb. to British preferential nations)
U.K.	.69 ¢ per lb. (none to British preferential nations)

1British preferential nations include Australia, South Africa, and Malaysia.
2Less to preferred countries.

The quality difference between the U.S. domestic and foreign markets has been caused by two major factors. First, much of the supply of these foreign consumers has come from countries with climatic conditions which produce a slightly lower quality of fruit than the fancy Hawaiian. Secondly, Hawaiian producers historically have used the European market as a dumping ground for their choice and standard grades (below fancy). Some industry sources believe that European consumers could be educated to prefer the fancy grade if it were made available to them at reasonable prices.

The U.S. and foreign markets for fresh pineapple were still in the developing stage in 1965. For many years most of the U.S. supply of fresh pineapple had come from nearby Cuba (until this source was shut off), Puerto Rico, and Mexico. Until very recently, only limited quantities of fresh pineapple had been shipped from Hawaii on a regular basis. This market was now being developed, primarily by Dole, which was selling fresh pineapple under the "Royal Hawaiian Pineapple" label. Dole management believed that the U.S. housewife was only willing to pay about 49¢ for a pineapple, and thus was selling some of its smaller than average [2] pineapples in the U.S. fresh fruit market, while canning the larger ones. Availability of fresh fruit was so limited in Japan that the Japanese had been known to pay as much as $5 per pineapple. Exports to this market were limited by the extent of available refrigerated shipping space.

Solid pack pineapple prices appear to be very inelastic, as shown by Exhibit 3. However, the price-volume relationships of pineapple juice appear to be very sensitive. Industry sources have indicated that pineapple juice sales increased substantially with decreasing prices, or when disaster temporarily reduced the available supply of fresh orange juice. A new influence in the pineapple juice market has been the introduction of synthetic drinks, such as Awake and Tang. These very low cost products pose a potential threat to the price structure of the entire natural fruit juice market. (E.g., Hawaiian Punch, a major fruit-flavored canned drink competing in the juice market, manufactured by Pacific Hawaiian Company of Fullerton, California. Sales of Hawaiian Punch increased from $10.8 million in 1957 to $23.8 million in 1960, while Pacific Hawaiian's earnings grew from $497,000 to $1.4 million in the same period. In 1963 this company was purchased by R. J. Reynolds Tobacco Company for an undisclosed amount of cash.)

THE DOLE COMPANY

In 1901 James Dole began the Hawaiian Pineapple Company with $20,000 and a 12 acre pineapple plantation near the present Dole Wahiawa facility. With an initial pack of 1,893 cases in 1903, the new company was on its way. Production was rapidly increased to 25,000 cases in 1905, and by 1907 Dole had constructed a new cannery in Honolulu to accommodate the increased output. In the early years this new company acquired several small competitors, retaining all of their brand names. In 1915, with a pack of almost 800,000 cases, Hawaiian Pineapple hired their first salesmen. During the 1920's Hawaiian Pineapple prospered. In 1926 the company had its first 3 million case year and earned $2.3 million after taxes.

The depression caught James Dole off guard. In the face of a shrinking market and mounting inventories, Dole canned the new crop. By the time the company had lowered its prices to move this huge inventory, it was too late. 1931 operations resulted in a net loss of almost $4 million and, by 1932, the company was forced into reorganization. This resulted in Castle & Cooke, a major creditor,

---

[2] Large pineapples averaging around 8 pounds were deemed to be optimum in the cannery, whereas an average of 5 pounds per pineapple was viewed as preferable for the fresh fruit market.

taking control of the floundering company. Under the new Castle & Cooke management, the reorganized firm was once again profitable, with earnings varying between $2.5 and $3 million. The "Dole" label was introduced and the many other brands were deemphasized.

Henry A. White, who had come to Hawaiian Pineapple from Castle & Cooke at the time of the reorganization, became president in 1941. Under Mr. White, the company was operated very autonomously and embarked upon a program to acquire a full line of canned fruits and vegetables. In 1948, Barron-Gray Packing Company of San Jose was acquired, and in 1949 a pineapple cannery was constructed in Mexico (operations of which were discontinued the following year). In 1955, the expansion program was continued with the acquisition of F. M. Ball & Co. of Oakland and Paulus Bros. Packing Co. of Salem, Oregon. During the time that Mr. White was chief executive officer, sales rose to $81.5 million and net operating income fluctuated between a loss of $3.8 million in 1952 to a net profit of $5.4 million in 1950.

Mr. H. C. Cornuelle, who had been Mr. White's assistant and had been concerned primarily with sales promotion, succeeded Mr. White in 1958 and was president during the next five years. During his tenure, the Hawaiian Pineapple Company was merged into Castle & Cooke and the division name was changed to the Dole Company. In 1963, Mr. Cornuelle resigned to accept the vice presidency of United Fruit Company, and was succeeded by Malcolm MacNaughton, who was also president of the parent, Castle & Cooke. This was seen as a "move to bring Dole and Castle & Cooke closer together."

In 1964, Mr. MacNaughton brought in Mr. William Quinn as executive vice president, and made him president the following year. Mr. MacNaughton then resumed full-time responsibility as president of Castle & Cooke. Mr. Quinn, a practicing attorney, had been elected the first Governor of Hawaii when the Islands achieved statehood in 1958. He was recruited from his private law practice to become an executive of the Dole Company.

At the close of fiscal 1965 Dole earned $6,428,000 before taxes on net sales of a little over $98 million. Roughly $75 million was in Hawaiian pineapple products, while the remaining 25% of total sales came from canned fruits and vegetables produced at the two mainland facilities. This sales and earnings level was generated on an asset base of $81.7 million. Exhibit 6 shows recent financial and operating data for Dole.

Physical Facilities

In 1965, Dole's two Hawaiian plantations had approximately 30,000 acres under cultivation. The Wahiawa plantation, located on the island of Oahu, was the area where James Dole conducted the first successful Hawaiian pineapple plantings in 1901. Wahiawa had always been a high-producing plantation. It had plentiful water and access to a substantial labor supply, and in 1965 had 15,000

exhibit 6A

THE DOLE COMPANY

Balance Sheet as of April 30, 1965
(in thousands)

Current assets	
Cash and marketable securities	$ 6,317
Accounts receivable (net)	13,611
Due from divisions	20
Due from affiliates consolidated	350
Inventories	27,561
Other	1,421
Total current assets	49,280
Growing crops (at static value)	1,800
Investment in and advances to	1.932
foreign subsidiaries	20
Total investments	1,952
Land	9,770
Buildings, machinery, and equipment	53,212
Less: accum. depreciation	34,770
Net	18,442
Noncurrent receivables	484
Total long-term assets	32,448
Total assets	$81,728
Current liabilities	
Notes payable, including current	
installments on long-term debt	$ 3,313
Accounts payable	9,691
Due to divisions	1,834
Total current liabilities	14,838
Long-term liabilities	
Notes payable	3,816
Deferred income and other credits	876
Total long-term liabilities	4,692
Equity	
Retained earnings 4/30/1964	28,349
Intracompany equity	27,507
Intracompany deferred taxes	2,213
Intracompany profit	6,429
Cash advanced from divisions	(2,300)
Total shareholder equity	62,198
Total liabilities and net worth	$81,728

THE DOLE COMPANY

Financial Data
(in thousands)

	1965	1964	1963	1962	1961	1960	1959	1958	1957	1956	1955	1950	1946
Financial Condition													
Current assets	$49,280	$41,426	$42,042	$43,097	$42,097	$43,116	$44,950	$42,621	$43,345	$36,490	$23,271	$19,643	$18,367
Current liabilities	14,838	13,538	14,308	13,130	12,302	9,178	11,042	10,902	13,693	13,667	6,711	6,206	4,235
Working capital	34,442	27,888	27,734	29,976	29,975	33,938	33,908	31,719	29,652	22,823	16,560	13,437	14,132
Net plant	28,219	29,548	28,885	28,219	28,972	26,869	27,113	27,183	28,197	27,528	23,054	17,623	9,795
Other assets	4,236	4,772	2,338	1,848	1,863	1,705	1,968	2,175	1,964	2,414	8,084	3,099	2,438
Total assets	81,728	75,746	73,265	73,164	72,932	81,690	74,031	71,979	73,506	66,432	54,409	40,365	30,600
Long-term debt	4,692	6,675	7,850	9,025	10,200	10,975	11,750	12,500	13,604	10,396	10,750	0	0
Net worth	62,198	55,532	51,107	51,009	50,430	51,537	51,238	48,577	46,209	42,369	36,948	34,159	26,367
Income and Expenses													
Gross sales													
Hawaiian	67,751	57,082	51,940	47,463	48,948	50,941							
Blends and drinks	9,445	10,925	7,843	6,087	7,222	7,866							
Mainland	31,785	36,027	33,892	30,181	32,321	32,790							
Net sales—total	100,825	101,463	91,333	82,113	86,394	89,277	91,917	87,003	81,521	71,809	58,802	51,891	29,045
Net income before tax	6,429	9,255	(62)	1,256	1,116	5,352	8,991	5,659	2,947	5,441	2,808	8,875	4,499
Net income after a tax	4,216	4,425	98	579	631	2,577	4,241	1,904[1]	1,368[2]	2,493[3]	1,201[4]	5,354	2,367
Depreciation	2,493	2,544	2,380	2,504	2,377	2,274	2,356	2,138	1,573	1,409	1,395		672

[1]Excluding $1,355,000 special gain.
[2]Excluding $52,000 special gain.
[3]Excluding $159,000 special gain.
[4]Excluding $168,000 special gain.

exhibit 6C

THE DOLE COMPANY

Sales and Profits for Selected Years Prior to 1955
(in thousands)

Year	Net Earnings	Sales
1954	$1,877	$60,090
1953	3,144	59,108
1952	(1,632)	46,239
1951	3,521	54,719
1950	5,354	51,353
1949	4,636	52,719
1944		31,093
1940	3,199	
1938	2,251	
1937	3,275	
1936	2,596	
1935	1,338	
1934	950	
1931	(3,875)	
1926	2,329	
1923	2,760	

1 Net after special items.

acres planted in pineapple.[3] Trucks could carry its pineapples to the company's Honolulu cannery in less than an hour's time.

Wahiawa plantation was in the section of Oahu that was "greenbelted" by the Hawaiian legislature in 1962, and thus was zoned only for agricultural or conservation use. However, it appeared that Wahiawa lands might be in the path of future residential development. After completion of a proposed high-speed highway, this area would be only 15 to 20 minutes from downtown Honolulu. A zoning variance had already been obtained by Oceanic Properties, another Castle & Cooke subsidiary, to construct a new community, "Mililani Town," at the edge of the plantation nearest to Honolulu. The lands furthest from Honolulu were at relatively high elevation and were adjacent to Castle & Cooke's Waialua sugar plantation. Many agriculturalists believed that this land was more suitable to sugar cane production than to pineapples. Thus plantation management was under continual pressure to divert its highly productive pineapple lands to other uses.

---

[3] Dole owned in fee 15,000 acres at Wahiawa, of which 5,300 acres were in pineapple, 1,650 acres were leased to tenants, and 8,000 acres were in forest or gulch lands. In addition, Wahiawa leased 17,650 acres (9,750 from Castle & Cooke), of which 10,000 acres were in pineapple and the balance in forest.

exhibit 6D

THE DOLE COMPANY

Comparative Income Statement
(in thousands)

	4/30/65	4/30/64	4/30/63	4/30/62	5/31/61	5/31/60	5/31/59
Gross sales	$106,563	$102,546	$93,675	$83,731	$88,491	$91,597	$94,224
Less: Allowances	2,240	2,531	2,342	1,618	2,097	2,320	2,307
Ocean freight and insurance	5,846	n.a.	n.a.	n.a.	n.a.	n.a.	n.a.
Net sales	$ 98,476	$100,015	$91,333	$82,113	$86,394	$89,277	$91,917
Cost of sales							
Opening inventory	11,780	12,109	13,241	11,839	12,085	12,193	13,420
Cost of products manufactured							
Raw product production	12,849	12,621	12,016	10,308	12,239	11,195	10,567
Raw product purchased	8,900	8,893	10,527	11,347	9,028	8,867	9,751
Fruit transportation	2,292	2,452	2,657	2,413	2,339	2,135	2,240
Cannery (Honolulu)	25,859	28,931	29,848	26,496	27,929	26,246	24,791
Mill and by-products	446	569	516	478	521	461	434
Plants (mainland)	7,241	7,223	7,102	6,342	6,558	6,158	5,708
Fresh fruit	825	589	—	—	—	—	—
Total cost of manufacturing	$ 58,412	$ 61,279	$62,667	$57,384	$58,614	$55,062	$53,492
Warehouse and shipping	6,156	7,153	6,850	5,854	6,554	6,210	6,168
Total mfg. and distr.	$ 76,349	$ 80,542	$82,858	$75,077	$77,254	$73,466	$73,080
Less: Adjustments to inventory	1,779	1,937	103	123	54	124	96
Closing inventory	11,540	11,780	12,109	13,241	11,839	12,085	12,193
	$ 63,031	$ 66,824	$70,645	$61,713	$65,361	$61,257	$60,791
Cost of: Citrus products	5,269	6,385	4,472	3,380	3,438	6,243	6,254
Products purchased	3,320	790	1,328	1,143	2,332	2,673	1,746
Total costs	$ 71,619	$ 73,999	$76,446	$66,237	$71,131	$70,172	$68,790
Gross profit from sales	$ 26,857	$ 26,016	$14,887	$15,876	$15,263	$19,105	$23,127
Selling expenses	13,701	11,100	9,198	8,545	7,897	7,660	8,382
Administration and general	5,780	5,697	5,687	5,677	6,427	6,219	5,621
Total S, A, & G	$ 19,481	$ 16,798	$14,885	$14,222	$14,324	$13,879	$14,003
Net: operating profit	$ 7,376	$ 9,218	$ 2	$ 1,656	$ 939	$ 5,227	$ 9,123
Miscellaneous: Other revenue	732	1,302	1,066	815	1,192	925	719
Other charges							
Interest	624	625	878	858	807	652	695
Other	1,056	348	251	357	208	147	156
	$ (947)	$ 328	$ (64)	(400)	$ 177	$ 125	$ (132)
Net income before taxes	$ 6,429	$ 9,546	$ (62)	$ 1,256	$ 1,116	$ 5,352	$ 8,991

Lanai Plantation

Dole's second Hawaiian pineapple plantation was on the island of Lanai. This entire 90,000 acre island was purchased in 1922 by Dole for $1,100,000. Since then 15,000 acres of this once-barren island had been developed into a high-producing pineapple plantation. Most of the permanent employees of the Lanai plantation lived in Lanai City, a small isolated community. Seasonal laborers were brought in from other islands, as the Lanai population was inadequate to meet peak planting and harvesting requirements.

Lack of an adequate year-round labor supply had always limited the size of this plantation, as had the water supply. Available water was adequate for present production needs, but if more acreage was planted, more fresh water had to be developed. These same shortages of labor and water had also kept Dole from constructing a cannery on the island. Lanai's pineapples were trucked in bins to barges and then towed by Dole's wholly owned Isleways Barge Company to the Honolulu docks. There, the bins were trucked to Dole cannery, and handled in the same manner as Wahiawa bins.

Like Wahiawa, the Lanai plantation also offered possible future development opportunities. Lanai was only 60 miles from Honolulu and was considered an ideal location for a sportsman's resort. It was said that the waters off Lanai offered the best sports fishing in Hawaii. There were extensive horse riding trails, and wild game for the hunter was abundant. The island also had a small, scenic, palmstudded sand beach, and a small yacht harbor.

The two plantations employed a number of highly qualified, well-educated experts in the agricultural and engineering problems of the plantation. Dole engineers designed and built their own specialized equipment to aid in the planting, cultivation, and harvesting of pineapple. The agricultural experts had developed the farming aspects of the plantation into a highly scientific activity. They had learned the optimum ranges for the critical variables in producing pineapple and, through controlled experiments, had been able to identify the supplementary nutrients needed to bring inactive marginal land into production. The efforts of the staff employees were supplemented by the Pineapple Research Institute, an activity financed by all of the Hawaiian pineapple growers.

Honolulu Cannery

Dole's cannery in the Honolulu industrial district covered 50 acres, and was one of the world's largest. The older portions of the cannery and warehouse covered 39 acres. Another 90,000 square feet of warehouse had been completed in 1964. Through this plant more than 250 million pineapples were processed each year. Approximately three-fourths of this total was canned during the peak production season from mid-May through late August. The cannery was completely shut down for repairs and renovation each year between October and December. Fruit harvested during this period was traded with a competitor's cannery with a different shutdown period. Production began on a limited scale each January, but did not accelerate until late April, when heavy production began.

Besides the general cannery equipment described earlier, the Dole cannery had as its heart a complex conveyor system. The fruit was automatically graded by size and distributed to the proper Ginaca machine, yielding the largest possible cylinder of pineapple out of each fruit. The cannery used 17 miles of conveyor lines for its material handling. Following the high-labor stage of inspection, trimming, and grading, cans of pineapple were syruped, sealed, and sterilized automatically at the rate of 4,000 per minute. Then 11 labeling machines attached labels at the rate of 1,200 cans per minute. It took only 15 minutes for a pineapple to pass through the entire processing system. Solid pack pineapple was produced in six forms: slices, chunks, tidbits, cubes, spears and crushed.

The juice which was extracted from the cores and shells and retrieved from the trimming tables was processed in a $1 million production line completed in 1962. Adjoining this line, Dole also had a $1 million frozen juice concentrate plant where the single strength juice was evaporated to concentrate it for sale in other forms. The concentrated product was either packed in six-ounce cans for sale as frozen juice or in seven-gallon cartons to be shipped to the mainland for later reconstitution. These bulk shipments of concentrated pineapple juice were blended with orange juice, grapefruit juice, etc., to produce popular pineapple juice blends. Some of this reconstitution was performed by copackers; some was reconstituted in Dole's San Jose plant.

The cannery was linked by conveyors to Dole's own adjacent can manufacturing plant. This $4.6 million facility, built in 1955, had 12 can manufacturing lines producing nearly 500 million cans per year. (This production was about half of the theoretical maximum operating capacity on a 24 hour/365 days a year basis.) The can plant supplied not only all of Dole's needs, but those of Libby and Calpak as well. In return for the 200 million cans required by Calpak and Libby for their Hawaiian pineapple operations, these companies supplied the equivalent volume to Dole's mainland canneries from their own canmaking facilities in California. In addition, Dole's Philippine pineapple cannery was to be supplied cans in collapsed form from Calpak's Mindanao pineapple cannery, 300 miles away. In 1965, these can manufacturing activities contributed approximately 50% of Dole's total pretax earnings. Cans vary in value according to size and could be expected to range from 3¢ to 10¢ for those used in the pineapple industry.

In 1965, the can plant was capable of manufacturing seven different diameters of cans. It was currently producing 11 different height and diameter combinations. Height changes were relatively minor. The addition of a totally different can diameter required the expenditure of several thousand dollars for tooling. New types would require substantially greater investment.

Maintaining an adequate labor force in the cannery and on the plantations was a continually increasing problem. Hawaii's growing economy was putting increasing demands on the labor force for nonagricultural type jobs.

Dole's Hawaiian facilities employed 3,200 people on a regular year-round basis, with an additional 6,400 workers for peak summertime needs. All of these workers were unionized by the ILWU. In the past Dole had experienced some labor difficulties, especially on the island of Lanai. In 1951, a strike of Lanai employees lasted for seven months. Relations at this plantation had been improving in recent years and productivity was increasing.

Labor relations at the Wahiawa plantation and at the cannery in Honolulu had been considerably better than at the Lanai plantation. However, the can manufacturing plant has experienced a number of short walkouts, and labor relations there appear to be extremely sensitive.

The custom in the Hawaiian pineapple industry has been for labor negotiations to be carried on directly between top manufacturing management and the union, without the services of an intervening personnel department. Dr. Melvin Levine, vice president for Hawaiian operations, personally has handled Dole's part in industrywide negotiations, assisted by his key managers and the Hawaii Employers Council.

Dolfil

In 1963, Dole organized a subsidiary, Dolfil, Inc., to produce pineapple in the Republic of the Philippines. Dolfil was expected to have 15,000 acres in pineapple cultivation on the island of Mindanao, 650 miles from Manila. The location was selected, after considering other possible growing areas around the world, as part of a long-term plan for developing low cost production to supplement or partially replace Hawaiian operations whose land values could not justify agricultural usage indefinitely. Dole's parent, Castle & Cooke, had established business relations with members of the Philippine business and political community. Moreover, Calpak had been producing pineapple in the Philippines successfully since the 1920's, and Dole management felt that they should be able to do the same.

Dolfil was capitalized as a joint venture, with 20% ownership in the hands of Philippine partners, who put up $1 million in cash. For their 80% ownership, Dole supplied slips for planting material valued at $4 million and underwrote a $22 million, ten year loan from the Bank of Hawaii, which was also guaranteed by Castle & Cooke. The technicalities of this financing made it necessary for Dolfil to be owned 80% directly by Castle & Cooke rather than through Dole. Nevertheless, Dolfil was operated as a part of Dole, and Dolfil's president reported to Mr. Quinn.

This $27 million commitment was expected to produce low cost sources of canned pineapple; to diversify Dole's sources geographically against vagaries in labor, weather, and shipping; to make it possible to free pineapple lands for higher and more profitable usage; to benefit from legislated inconsistencies in shipping rates which made it cheaper to ship from the Philippines to the East Coast of the U.S. and to Europe than to ship from Hawaii; and to provide entry into markets in the Orient, especially Japan.

The Dolfil operation was intended to supply approximately one-third of Dole's eventual pineapple needs. It was set up to sell 100% of its export output to Dole at a fixed price, with the profits from agriculture and manufacturing distributed among the partners (the Philippine nationals and Castle & Cooke). Dole was then to sell this output through their own marketing organization, and to make their profits from this function. (Dolfil was to do its own marketing in the Philippines.)

As of September, 1965, with construction of the cannery and plantation community largely completed, initial costs at Dolfil had substantially exceeded budget. Preliminary canning runs were conducted on the first pineapple crop, and this output was being subjected to stringent quality and taste tests.

A special committee had been set up to determine the can sizes and products which should be planned and tooled for in the Dolfil operation. This group included members of Dole's marketing, manufacturing, and long-range planning functions. They developed a linear programming model, using known information about Hawaiian operations, and approximations for the Dolfil operation and for aspects of Hawaiian operations that had not been quantified. Because of the 80% ownership in Dolfil by Castle & Cooke, rather than by Dole itself, it was decided that the program should be written to maximize profits to Castle & Cooke. This was the first time that management thinking had been directed toward maximizing the parent's profit rather than toward maximizing the profits of the Dole Division of Castle & Cooke. In 1966 Dolfil was expected to produce and can significant quantities of pineapple products. Dole executives were making plans for what product mix should be canned and for how it would be marketed.

Mainland Facilities

On the mainland, Dole had two physical facilities for the canning of fruits and vegetables. At Salem, Oregon, Dole packed about two million cases per year. The most important crop was green beans, accounting for about a million cases per year. Then followed pears, plums, cherries, blackberries, and boysenberries. The cannery was in operation each year from mid-June to the end of October. Production began with about 200,000 cases of cherries. Then followed pear processing of about 450,000 cases. Since pear canning in recent years has rarely covered total costs, pear canning was interrupted by the more profitable processing of about 250,000 cases of plums during the two to three weeks when this fruit was available. Six ripening rooms enabled the Salem plant to hold the pears for latter canning. Bean packing was the major activity through late summer and fall.

Dole management considered this cannery to be an efficient, low cost producer. Production was conducted in a modern building built in 1948 with a net book value of about $1.5 million. Average annual pretax earnings were relatively consistent at about $400-$500,000 per year. About 75 people were employed on a year-round basis, while seasonal labor increased this number to 1,200-1,400 during the packing season. Virtually all of the Salem cannery's output was packed for private labels. The remainder was marketed under unadvertised house labels, such as Blue Tag, Red Tag, White Tag, Green Tag, Richland, and Far West.

Dole's other mainland canning facility was a much larger operation, located in San Jose, California, having a net book value of about $2.6 million. There Dole packed fruit cocktail, apricots, fruit salad, peaches, pears, carrot juice, apricot and pear nectar, and artichoke hearts. This facility was operated on a July to September peak season. Full capacity was reached only while fruit cocktail was being packed, during a seven week period beginning about August 1. A very low level of activity continued into the fall, with the packing of carrot juice, artichoke hearts, and the reconstitution of pineapple-grapefruit drink.

Fruit cocktail was by far the most important item packed in San Jose, accounting for nearly 75% of the facility's total output. The three million cases of fruit cocktail packed by Dole each year represented about 20% of the total U.S. supply. Most of the fruit cocktail was packed for private labels, as was virtually all of the other output of the San Jose cannery. Over the past decade fruit cocktail prices have been very volatile, since the product has been subject to strong competition from substitutes, such as canned cling peaches. In times when the price of peaches has been low, Dole has lost as much as a million dollars in a single year on the sale of fruit cocktail. The other lesser items packed have shown small but consistent profits, with the exception of pears.

In 1965 the San Jose cannery was adding a new low calorie line of peaches, pears, fruit cocktail, and pineapple to be sold under the Dole label.

The San Jose cannery employed 100 year-round people, with peak employment reaching almost 2,000 during the seven week fruit cocktail season. The Dole Company corporate marketing activities were also housed in this facility. About 250 office workers were employed, mostly in the Marketing Division, but including some who handled the clerical work of the cannery.

All of the mainland facilities were postwar purchases. The San Jose plant, purchased by Dole in 1948 from Barron-Gray Packing Company, was then, as now, the world's largest canner of fruit cocktail. In 1955 Dole purchased the F. M. Ball Company of Oakland and the Paulus Bros. Packing Company of Salem, Oregon. Paulus Brothers was then the world's largest packer of Queen Anne cherries. The F. M. Ball Company, primarily packers of peaches and tomato products, was closed in 1963. It had been unprofitable due to the chronic oversupply and continual low prices of its major packs. Equipment of the F. M. Ball Company was dismantled and shipped to the new Dolfil operation in the Philippines, and the building was sold. While further cutbacks in mainland canning activities have been under continual consideration, management concern for the economic security of their "more than 3,000 mainland employees" has weighed heavily in favor of continuation. San Jose executives have also argued persuasively that their facility makes an important incremental contribution to corporate overhead. The realizeable sale value of these properties was deemed to be very low relative to their cost. Moreover, future mainland pack plans were being forecasted as profitable.

Production Control

From an agricultural standpoint, it is very difficult to reduce pineapple production volume to adjust to fluctuations in market demand. The two year growth cycle of the first crop and the year and a half required for ratoons commit the grower to a fixed volume at any point in time. Very rarely does any external information from the cannery or from marketing influence the way in which the plantations are planted. However, since it needs to be closed for modernization and maintenance, the cannery can impose deadlines for final fruit delivery.

Dole plantation managers have believed that since the marginal costs of production were relatively low, and since long-range projections were likely to be inaccurate, the risks incurred in deliberate reduction in crop size were likely to be far more substantial than the risks of overproduction in the event that market consumption actually turned down. If consumption were to fall sharply, the plantation managers have argued that it would be wise at that time to let the fruit rot in the fields. This would do no damage to the fields, and since ratoons would begin to develop, the fields would not be thrown out of cycle. Thus the tendency has been for each plantation to put as much land as possible into production.

A recently developed problem has been determining how much acreage should be planted for production of fresh fruit. Since the optimum size of fruit for the fresh market was believed to be considerably smaller than that best suited for canning, different varieties were planted and given differing agricultural treatment. These included differences in planting density, since the size of the fruit produced tended to vary inversely with the density of plants. Because marketing experience with fresh pineapple was very limited, it was difficult to forecast what the future requirements would be.

Until 1961, according to management, Dole was a "production oriented" company. Major decisions were made strictly on the basis of optimizing production or manufacturing variables. The cannery accepted all the fruit the two plantations could grow, and made no choices for the plantations except to specify deadlines for final fruit delivery prior to cannery shutdown and the maximum time allowed between harvesting and the delivery. The cannery management, in turn, attempted to optimize the percentage yield of fancy grade sliced pineapple from the tonnage delivered. Whole fruit or pieces of pineapple that could not meet the fancy sliced criteria were downgraded to choice and standard grades or to crushed, tidbits, chunks, or spears categories. It was not deemed necessary to forecast demand by categories, since it appeared that all of the fancy sliced pineapple which could be produced could be sold at current or higher prices. Therefore, it was expected that the greater the percentage of fancy sliced pineapple produced, the more net revenue for Dole.

The change in 1961 from a "production oriented" company to a "marketing" company was noted by many members of management, including president William Quinn, Dr. Melvin Levine, Mr. Laurence Hogue, and Mr. Harry Bleich. Dr.

Levine had joined Dole in the Technical Division after receiving a Ph.D. in Bio-Chemistry. He had worked up through quality control and manufacturing to responsibility for all Hawaiian operations. Mr. Hogue had been employed by Barron-Gray Packing when that company was purchased by Dole. Subsequently he had managed the Salem facility, after which he became the controller of Dole. He was named head of mainland operations in the fall of 1965. Mr. Bleich came to Dole in 1961 as vice president of Marketing. During the previous 25 years he had high level marketing experience with C & H Sugar Company. In 1961, these men reported, the company experienced shortages of some product categories relative to demand (notably crushed), while the price of fancy sliced had to be reduced in order to move the heavy inventories. Consequently, a new system of production control was established whereby marketing made estimates of what they could sell in a given year and translated these estimates into formal, written requirements for the year's pack plan. By 1965, this procedure had been modified only slightly. The initial requirements were sent from the San Jose marketing division to the Honolulu cannery to be analyzed by key management personnel. Dr. Levine, Mr. Daniel Phelan, head of manufacturing in Hawaii, and Dr. Charles Mumaw, head of the Honolulu cannery, analyzed the plan in light of their knowledge of fruit size expected and the capacity of the cannery to produce the different mix of products ordered. Based on manufacturing constraints, they determined a revised pack plan which was returned to the marketing personnel for their analysis. Changes that had to be made were noted in San Jose, and a revised plan was returned to Honolulu. This process continued until the requirements and capabilities of the two functions were satisfied.

After the final pack plan was established, and the cannery began operations for the season, cannery production control staff endeavored to produce slightly more fancy sliced products than the pack plan called for. As one member of management indicated, "they can later downgrade products if they have too much fancy sliced, whereas if they don't have enough it's impossible to upgrade once the pineapple's been crushed or chunked."

At the cannery, staff members of Production and Quality Control held brief daily meetings to review the previous day's performance. At these meetings, measurements of yield extracted, volume of each cut of fruit per ton input, volume of each quality type per ton input, and other measurements of production control and efficiency were presented in chart and graph form. Discussion generally seemed to be confined to identifying and explaining why a given difference existed. Correction methods appeared to be clearly understood by all involved.

Production by grade and product categories was reviewed periodically by top division management and compared against projected volumes to date and against the desired pack plan. If an imbalance between cumulative output and pack plan indicated a need for downgrading (i.e., packing more fruit in the categories other than fancy sliced), such decisions were generally made at these meetings. Also discussed would be cost data and coordination between the cannery and the plantations. Participating in these sessions would be Mr. Quinn, Dr. Levine, Dr.

Mumaw, Mr. Phelan, Dr. George Felton (head of the Technical Division), Mr. Karl Manke (staff agriculturalist), controller John Gale, and Mr. Thomas Cleghorn and Mr. William Aldrich (managers of the two Hawaiian plantations). Others in the company were invited to attend whenever topics requiring special knowledge were discussed.

Marketing

Dole's marketing organization was headed by Mr. Harry Bleich, vice president of marketing. Mr. Bleich reported directly to president Quinn in Honolulu, although Mr. Bleich and his staff were located on the mainland, headquartered at the San Jose cannery site. Mr. Bleich had his marketing organization divided into three principal line departments and three minor specialized selling departments. The three major departments were: 1) Product Planning, headed by Mr. C. G. Trundle; 2) Sales, headed by Mr. C. J. Patterson, Jr.; and 3) Marketing Services, headed by Mr. R. H. Hamilton. The other departments represent areas requiring special attention and had been removed from the three general department areas. The other departments were: 1) management of fresh fruit sales, under Mr. G. D. Crabb; 2) management of the general export trade, under Mr. R. H. Smith; and 3) European marketing, under Mr. G. W. LaBorie.

Mr. Bleich had structured the division in this way "in order to change Dole sales into a modern marketing organization. Under the old system, general sales management made all of the decisions. Under the new system, the decisions are made by experts in their individual fields." As an illustration, Mr. Bleich cited Product Planning, "where Mr. Trundle has assigned the responsibility for the various products in the line to individual product managers." Separate product managers had been established for the catagories: 1) pineapple and pineapple juice; 2) fruit cocktail and pineapple-grapefruit drink; and 3) frozen and miscellaneous other products. In addition, the director of Product Planning was responsible for advertising services, merchandising services, and home economics.

The Sales Department, which was the largest of the three major units, was responsible for: 1) sales development and trade relations; 2) sales of corporate brands, including both the Dole brands and the lesser known non-nationally advertised house labels; and 3) sales of private label packs.

The third department, Marketing Services, included responsibility for traffic, distribution, market information, and coordination of marketing with production. The costs of running the marketing function amounted to approximately 13% of sales in recent years.

Product Planning

The Product Planning Department developed the programs by which sales personnel attempted to strengthen the position of Dole products in the marketplace.

This activity encompassed advertising, specific promotional programs, and the solving of other problems related to individual product lines.

Since Mr. Bleich had taken over the marketing function, Dole advertising had taken the form of "use ads," where pineapple was pictured in use, as part of a specific dish or meal. Such ads were often joint promotions with other manufacturers. For example, Dole and a cake mix manufacturer might jointly sponsor the pineapple upside-down cake displayed with accompanying pictures of the respective ingredient packages. Advertising expenditures in 1965 amounted to $4.6 million, of which approximately 60% was spent specifically on pineapple products, 35% on mainland products, with the balance used for Canadian and other special promotions. In 1965 other promotional allowances amounted to $1 million in addition to price protection of $2 million.[4]

New Products

Product innovations were the responsibility of the New Product Division, headed by Mr. E. Feigon, who reported directly to Mr. Quinn. This division was located in San Jose and worked closely with the product managers in developing new items. It conducted (or contracted out) its own consumer research and sales tests of new products. After these tests were completed, recommendations were made to the Marketing Division. New products accepted by Marketing, and approved by Mr. Quinn, were then market tested by the Product Planning and sales departments to determine their potential before entering them into the regular product line.

Sales

The company had three basic selling jobs to perform: 1) sales of Dole brand packs; 2) fresh fruit; and 3) private label and house label merchandise.

Dole brand products were sold by a nationwide system of 94 food brokers, who employed a total of 1,000 salesmen. Most brokers handled a number of noncompetitive grocery products. These brokers were directed by a line sales organization, composed of a director of sales, four regional sales managers, and nine district sales managers. Specialized assistance was provided the line selling organization by a sales service manager and three regional sales service representatives for institutional and industrial products, and by a frozen food sales manager and three frozen food service representatives, who provided specialized knowledge in their respective fields. This sales force directed and assisted the brokers in selling Dole products, in planning promotions, and in troubleshooting problems. Brokers in the U.S. received a commission of 2.5% on all sales (foreign sales commissions were 5% of sales). 1965 brokerage amounted to $2.5 million.

---

[4] Price protection assured the grocer that any reduction in the price of an item would be applied to any inventories he had on hand which had been purchased at the higher price.

Hegblade-Margueles, a fresh fruit distributor, was exclusive distributor for all Dole fresh pineapple sales and had been principally responsible for developing this business. Their extensive experience in selling perishable fruits throughout the U.S. had provided Dole with the organization and techniques necessary to enter this market. Initially, Dole had insisted on selling their fresh pineapples unbranded. However, after they had demonstrated clearly that the pineapples would be of uniformly high quality at the time of sale to the consumer, a branding program was developed under the Royal Hawaiian Pineapple label. The Dole name was reserved for the canned products sold through brokers. (Royal Hawaiian was also the trade name used for the sale of macadamia nuts, produced by another Castle & Cooke division.) 1965 sales of fresh pineapple reached 12,000 tons (about 5% of total Dole production). This segment was expected to grow rapidly to as much as 40,000 tons by 1970.

Private label sales were consummated partly by direct selling and partly through Dole's private label brokers. A dozen chains bought directly, and accounted for about $12 million in 1965 sales volume. The balance of the private label business, accounting for $24 million in 1965, was handled by four Dole private label sales managers, who directed approximately 30 private label brokers. Only about 10% of Dole's pineapple production was sold under private label. Thus, the principal volume (80%) of the private label sales was composed of mainland-canned, nonpineapple products. As the private label buyer controlled his own label, he placed his orders with the canner that currently offered the best price. As a consequence, the private label business was characterized by both announced and unannounced prices, all subject to confirmation by the seller. Dole management believed that, in general, they received as high a price for their pack as any other private label packer. Because of their uniformly high quality, Dole usually did not have to resort to the "trading prices" that some private label purchasers demanded of lower quality producers.

While the great proportion of Dole sales were made in the U.S., a program was developed in 1962 to increase the marketing of Dole products in Europe. Until that time, the European market had been looked upon only as an outlet for surplus pineapple products, with particular emphasis on the choice and standard grades that were not marketed under the Dole label in the domestic market. In 1963 plans were made to increase the distribution of the Dole label in Europe, in anticipation of expanded pineapple supplies from the Philippines. In 1965, sales approximated one million cases of canned pineapple, juice, fruit cocktail, and peaches, and represented a market penetration of approximately 15% in these products.

Export Sales management explained that in the European market the Dole label was not well-known, while Libby was well-accepted in the U.K., and both Libby and Del-Monte were established labels in Scandinavia. Europe was thought to be wholly a solid pack (and primarily sliced) pineapple market. Virtually no juice was sold. Most of the solid pack pineapple consumed in Europe was of choice or standard grade, with very little fancy grade being sold. Even Dole made 50% of its European sales in its choice and standard grade labels. Thus, the great majority of European imports were from non-Hawaiian sources.

In 1965, Dole sold 36% of the total Hawaiian solid pack (including Canada). Dole also sold 21% of the total Hawaiian juice exported outside the U.S. These were substantially smaller shares of Hawaiian production than Dole sold domestically.

In recent years, Dole sales had grown rapidly in the Netherlands and some inroads had been made in West Germany. Most Dole European volume was accounted for by the two countries.

European retail prices for solid pack choice and standard grade pineapple were reported to be comparable to U.S. prices for fancy grade. However, tariffs and freight charges reduced the prices received by Dole in Europe to from half to three-quarters of the domestic price realization. (See Exhibit 7 for selected freight charges.)

exhibit 7

THE DOLE COMPANY

Ocean Freight Rates between Selected Pineapple Producing Areas and the United States and Europe
(dollars per case of 24/2 ½ Sliced Pineapple at 53 lbs./case)

| | U. S. Port Destination | | Northern Continental |
Source	West Coast ($)	East and Gulf Coast ($)	Europe ($)
Hawaii	0.44	0.75	.94
Philippines	0.53	0.63	.53
Taiwan	0.64	0.75	.66
Australia	0.78	0.97	.65
Malaya	0.76	0.73	.48
South Africa	0.76	0.47	.34
Brazil	1.94	0.93	.74

Note: In 1965 Dole shipped approximately 100,000 short tons of canned products from Hawaii to the West Coast, 130,000 short tons total to the East and Gulf Coasts, and about 15,000 tons to Europe.

Japan, unlike Europe, was regarded as a fancy quality market. However, Japanese tariffs of 55% ad valorem and quota restrictions on foreign pineapple made it difficult for Dole to compete with duty free Okinawan canned production. Consequently, little volume had been achieved in that country, but substantial opportunities existed for fresh pineapple.

Marketing Services

Marketing services included traffic, distribution, market research, and production planning. The traffic group was responsible for moving products from cannery locations to final destinations, including arranging for any warehousing required and handling all claims. This group had pioneered the "expendable standardized pallet," a system by which loads were permanently palletized from cannery to final store destination to facilitate handling. The pallet could then be destroyed or retained by the customer for his own use. Savings in handling costs not only justified the discarding of the pallet but even made possible a reduced price for customers ordering in pallet load quantities. A study of the over-all flow of Dole products resulted in the booking of "forward shipments" between Honolulu and the mainland. By guaranteeing an annual tonnage of business to the steamship companies, prescheduled by specific quantities and sailings, Dole was able to obtain freight rate reductions which have saved more than $1 million per year over previous scheduling methods. 60% of the output of the Honolulu cannery was booked in this manner in 1965, yet ocean freight still amounted to almost $6 million. Total freight, warehousing, and distribution expenses have been approximately 12% of sales in recent years.

The distribution group handled the problems of inventory control for all Dole products. Warehouse stocks at the canneries and at intermediate consolidation points came under their cognizance. Orders could be placed with the canneries or other warehouses whenever stocks in a particular location fell below predetermined standard levels.

The marketing information group conducted surveys, sales analyses, economic studies, and any other type of marketing intelligence activities which were required by product planning or sales. The group relied heavily upon information regarding supermarket sales supplied by the Nielsen service. However, since this service did not include information on sales to the U.S. government or sales to institutional consumers, much of the group's time was spent in gathering such data. The group also hired and supervised consultants who conducted research studies requested. A major task of the marketing information group was the extensive analysis of Dole sales and Dole broker performance, both relative to the performance of competitors and to a calculated index of indicated market potential.

The marketing information group was also responsible for developing the basic pack plan for the Honolulu cannery. Planning the pineapple pack began by taking into account the history of pineapple price and supply relationships, competitors' production history, developments in the economy, and trends in purchasing. This information was used to develop a five year U.S. forecast by customer type (i.e., grocer, institution, government, etc.) and by geographical region. This forecast showed both the total potential for each type of pineapple product in each market segment and also the share of that market which Dole could reasonably be expected to capture. Segments of these forecasts, divided geographically, were then sent to each sales area to be examined by the brokers and by the regional sales offices. The men in each regional area compared the forecast with their own firsthand market knowledge. Differences were noted and revised plans prepared. These plans then became the basis for the pack plan for the Honolulu cannery. From the final pack plan, budgets and *pro forma* operating statements were prepared. These provided the basis for ordering labels, tin plate, and other supplies, and for planning the necessary cash and manning requirements.

Pricing

Historically, all pricing decisions had been made solely by the Marketing Division. In turn, marketing was the only division that had ever been placed on a profit center basis. According to president Quinn, Dole generally had been a price follower. However, he felt that in 1965 the Marketing Division was taking a look at more basic economic data and approaching the marketplace more aggressively in pricing decisions. They were then considering factors such as the size of the competitive crops and the levels of their inventory when they made such decisions. This was especially true during calendar 1965 in reducing the price of pineapple juice and fruit cocktail to move lagging inventories. Solid pack pineapple list prices had been more or less stable, although product movement frequently was stimulated by temporary "buying allowances" off of list prices. Generally, the customers were required to qualify their "buying allowances" by featuring the products in special sales promotions of special displays. Dole was continually seeking ways "to accomplish competitive independence, and to 'unhinge' both pricing and merchandising strategies from those of our competitors."

Harry Bleich, in describing Dole pricing policy, reported: "Pricing recommendations start right here! They have to, because we are the ones who know what the market will bear and what price is needed to move slow stock. We also have the data and the facilities to calculate the impact of changes in ocean or rail freight rates and to judge how they or other factors should affect our pricing. Further, we must estimate not only the effect on our customers, but also consider the effect of the alternatives available to our competitors. Marketing must also appraise the influence of pack volumes, inventories, and product disappearance, through sales and consumption, in order to properly evaluate pricing strategies."

Some members of management felt that, as a small factor in the total canned fruit and vegetable market, Dole could not afford to be a price leader. According to Mr. Bleich, giants like Calpak, Libby, or Hunt had a distinct advantage in that they could easily reduce prices on selected products, such as pineapple, or in selected markets, and, because of their great size and diversification, that portion of their business would not affect their over-all results significantly. He pointed out that any Dole-initiated price reduction could be swiftly countered by these giants, which would hurt Dole greatly and destroy any advantage the company might have gained by the reduction. He felt that this was especially applicable to mainland fruits and vegetables, "where Dole's limited market share and absence of brand franchise precluded any possibility of price leadership." He felt Dole's role in pineapple should be to be the initiator of price increases when appropriate, rather than to be the leader in price reductions.

Dole's experience in competing with lower quality pineapple was offered to support this conclusion. Even with block shipments of private label Taiwan pineapple being sold to grocers at as much as 50% below the regular Dole or Calpak price, Dole had not yet found it necessary to reduce prices to move their pack. Substantial gains in market share had been registered by foreign imports. Until recently, most of these gains reportedly had been at the expense of Libby's branded pineapple and of private label and house label Hawaiian packs. However, in 1965, market positions had begun to shift: Libby's sustained $1 per case price differential (below Dole and Calpak) had restored their market share to about 9%; foreign imports continued to gain; private label Hawaiian pineapple continued to lose position; and Calpak suffered a significant reduction in market share. Dole's share was off only slightly, and management was "watching very carefully to see how far the Libby label would carry a reduced quality product—one positioned somewhere between the low quality foreign pack and the high quality of Dole and Calpak."

Dole thinking on pricing policy also was influenced by the size and price of a current year's peach crop. As Mr. Hogue said, "Pineapple and peaches are not closely related, but fruit cocktail sales are closely related to peach prices." He explained that 50% of the cost of fruit cocktail ingredients was in cling peaches. Thus, not only did the cost of fruit cocktail vary with peach prices, but peaches were an obvious direct substitute product for fruit cocktail. Mr. Bleich carried the peach-pineapple price argument one step further, saying, "The movement of pineapple is influenced by the supply and movement of peaches. Hoos' authoritative study [5] proves these fruits are related."

Exhibit 8 presents the recent trends in price received for principal Dole products.

Data Collection

Dole financial data were collected and analyzed both at San Jose (marketing) and at Honolulu (production). Each location used a different accounting method for the preparation of these data. The San Jose offices used an IBM 1401 computer in accounting for mainland fruits and the analysis of all aspects of company-wide marketing. The Mayhew system of cost accounting was used at San Jose. This system had been chosen because all West Coast canneries were standardizing on it, and it was hoped that such uniformity would provide a more realistic and comparable base from which canners bid for their supplies of fruits and vegetables.

---

[5] See Exhibit 3.

exhibit 8

THE DOLE COMPANY

Average Prices for Major Products
(different can sizes have been converted to comparable standard cases)

Product (in order of 1965 dollar sales volume)	Price per Standard Case						
	1965	1964	1963	1962	1961	1960	1959
Solid packed pineapple	$4.79	$4.39	$4.96	$5.07	$5.21	$5.23	$5.03
Pineapple juice	2.45	1.76	1.88	1.81	1.91	2.21	2.35
Fruit cocktail	4.76	5.23	4.49	4.74	5.00	5.08	5.45
Frozen citrus blends	4.42	4.45	4.00	3.97	3.66	3.67	3.95
Pineapple citrus drink	2.88	2.89	2.41	2.43	2.47	2.61	2.71
Beans	4.00	4.07	4.03	4.26	4.21	3.99	3.95
Peaches	4.54	4.66	4.19	4.24	4.30	4.38	4.64
Frozen concentrate juice	5.34	4.17	4.76	4.68	4.34	4.29	4.05
Pears	5.44	6.49	4.80	5.43	5.51	5.11	5.61
Tomato products	3.69	3.62	3.54	3.70	3.40	3.08	3.04

Note: Tomato products had the fourth highest sales volume until 1963, when the F.M. Ball Co. cannery was shut down.

This accounting function was under the direction of Mr. Hogue, who felt the data generated, while not as complete or as timely as he would prefer, nonetheless were adequate to control operations effectively. He received performance versus budget information on all items on a monthly basis.

Accounting in Honolulu was under the direction of Mr. John Gale, who in late 1965 became corporate controller. Mr. Gale had joined the Castle & Cooke controller's department in late 1961 and was transferred to Dole in March, 1965. In Honolulu a contributive margin system of accounting was used to generate the necessary information. This system, instituted three years ago, was the same as the one which was used by Bumble Bee Seafoods. Under this accounting method, sales of each product line were reported and the direct costs for each product were allocated against its sales. The function of this system was to provide incentives to the marketing people to stress sales of those products with the best profit margins. Since Dole's board of directors was not thoroughly conversant with this system of reporting, the controller's department prepared additionally a conventional profit and loss statement for use by the directors and for other external purposes.

Since mid-1965, all of Dole's Honolulu data processing was being performed by Castle & Cooke's data processing group. This group handled the routine accounting needs of all Castle & Cooke's Honolulu-based operations.

Over the years, there had been considerable internal dissatisfaction with Dole's data collection and reporting. Total costs had been approximately $1 million per year. There were complaints of reports being too late to be useful, reports generated but not used, and desired information not being available. The manufacturing group's pressing needs for daily process information had led to formation of a unit that did the necessary production and quality control data processing by hand so that it could be available every morning for analysis of the previous day's operations.

As a result of these data handling problems, in 1965 Dole hired Strong, Wishart & Associates, management consultants specializing in systems and procedures analysis, to do a nine month study covering both San Jose and Honolulu. It was anticipated that the consultants would provide direction for alleviating the data collection and analysis problem. President Quinn felt that it would be important for him to have monthly profit and loss information for every product. These data were not available in usable form in 1965. This was because static prices for the season's pack were used in the mainland accounting system. While this was useful in advance planning, it resulted in misleading conclusions whenever price fluctuations occurred during the year. Moreover, static inventory values were employed in the Honolulu system, which produced inaccurate cost of goods sold information. Management was concerned that abandoning the static inventory procedure would require a stated increase in valuation, which might have serious income tax consequences in the year in which the change took place.

Capital Expenditures

Operating budgets and capital budgets were prepared by each department. These were reviewed by the respective divisional managements and then sent to the budget department. The budget department consolidated departmental and divisional requests, compared these data with comparable data for previous years, and suggested changes or modifications to the requesting department. The budget department prepared and presented the final consolidated budget at budget review sessions, attended by Mr. Quinn, Mr. Bleich, Dr. Levine, Dr. Felton, and Mr. Hogue. The final decisions on operating expenditures by various divisions were made by Mr. Quinn after full discussion with his division heads. Actual performance was reviewed and compared to budget at least once each quarter. Similar procedures were followed for capital budgeting, except that final approval of these expenditures rested with the Dole board of directors.

For many years capital expenditures for the total company had been given blanket approval to the extent of the previous year's depreciation. This procedure had made all profits available for distribution as dividends. However, since Dole had become a division of Castle & Cooke, there no longer was any formal dividend requirement. Mr. Quinn felt that, as a guideline, "Dole should probably plan future expenditures to the extent of its anticipated cash flow less one-half to two-thirds of its profit." Mr. Gale had also expressed the desire to get away from the historical pattern of having capital expenditures equal to depreciation, so that planning could be based wholly on company needs and opportunities.

The Mainland Facilities Issue

In 1948, Mr. Henry White, then president of Hawaiian Pineapple Company (Dole's predecessor company), argued strongly that Hawaiian Pineapple Company was exceedingly vulnerable and that its growth would be severely limited if confined only to the single product line. Consequently, he believed that the company's future growth and strength depended on its offering a broad line of canned fruits and vegetables, such as Calpak or Libby were able to do. Such a broad line, he argued, would supply the sales basis to support a large, expert marketing staff which would remove the company's competitive disadvantage. The first step in this direction was the acquisition of the Barron-Gray Packing Co. in San Jose. This company had been a consistent moneymaker, primarily through its premier position in fruit cocktail, a product first developed by Barron-Gray which commanded a premium price.

Subsequent steps to broaden the product line were the acquisition of the Paulus Bros. Packing Co. in Salem, Oregon, and F. M. Ball & Co. in Oakland, California, in 1955. By this time, profits from the Barron-Gray operation had declined sharply, as nonpineapple products under the Dole label had had difficulty in gaining shelf space and market position. Mr. White believed that these results clearly demonstrated the need for a broader line and thus sought Paulus Brothers' cherries and bean pack and Ball's tomato and peach packs for inclusion under the Dole label.

When the board of directors of Hawaiian Pineapple, uneasy with the Barron-Gray results, refused to authorize the raising of new capital for acquisitions, Mr. White raised the money by selling (to Weyerhauser Co.) the Dole corrugated box plant in Honolulu. This facility, the only significant box plant in Hawaii, had been a consistent moneymaker, and the sale produced enough money to continue Dole's diversification.

In retrospect, some of the managers with long service analyzed these moves as "believing that all we needed were the production facilities, that the Dole label was so well-accepted that it could be transferred immediately to other basic products. Henry badly underestimated the cost of building distribution and acceptance for these new products."

By 1957, the attempt to broaden the Dole line had been abandoned. Virtually all of the mainland production was packed for private label sales, and Dole brand items other than pineapple and fruit cocktail were withdrawn from the market. Mr. White himself withdrew from the company, and Mr. Herbert C. Cornuelle was elected president.

In 1965, Mr. Quinn and others frequently questioned the advisability of continuing to operate the mainland facilities. Mr. Bleich and Mr. Hogue cited many reasons for retaining the mainland operations. The most important of these was the argument that these activities contributed more than $1 million per year to corporate overhead, notably marketing and accounting services. A second argument was that, by having a diversified product line, they were often able to ship in cost-savings quantities, whereas if they had had only pineapple to ship, virtually all shipments would have had to go in less than carload lots. According to Mr. Bleich, even with the present line, Dole is still at a shipping disadvantage compared to a canner like California Packing Company. Whereas Calpak made almost all shipments in carload lots, Dole is fortunate if it can ship a mixture of carload and trailer load quantities. Dole does take advantage of opportunities to combine shipments with other small canners, in order to benefit from carload shipment rates.[6]

According to Mr. Bleich, the basic problem with mainland products was that "Dole never developed a consumer franchise for these products. From the beginning, marketing never had sufficient advertising funds to develop and maintain brand recognition and loyalty." Mr. Bleich anticipated that it would require an expenditure of at least $50 million over a ten year period to introduce and maintain a full line of branded products. As an indication of the tremendous competition the company faced, he cited that General Foods had spent more than $23 million just on the introduction of Tang, a single product.

In 1965, the Dole marketing group was hopeful that a low calorie line of canned fruits—including pears, peaches, fruit cocktail, and pineapple—under the Dole label would provide profitable volume for the San Jose facility. It was estimated that between 40-45% of the present customers of syruped canned fruits would actually prefer low calorie variations. A move into this relatively new product area with Dole branded products was felt to be an easier way to develop additional consumer franchises than competing with conventional food lines, which were already well-entrenched. In 1965, these low calorie products had been introduced with an initial exposure in seven major market areas. In the following year, Dole expected to expand marketing of these branded low calorie fruits into areas serving 80% of the total U.S. population, and $1.5 million in advertising and promotion had been budgeted for these products. To support this effort, the cannery was packing low calorie canned fruits only under the Dole label, and had refused several private label bids for such products.

Other Plans for the Future

In 1965, Dole management was actively seeking other opportunities for growth in sales and profits. Since U.S. per capita consumption of pineapple had declined about 10% during the past ten years, they felt that increasing their share of the

---

6 According to the Dole marketing services manager, cross-country shipments of products were always in rail car lots and sometimes benefited from special rates for shipping in 9-15 car lots. Pineapple products were generally not combined with private label shipments. Some mainland products were combined (or "enclosed") with other canners' products. Mainland products only helped freight charges in going from warehouses or concentration points to customers. Here many products could be combined to make up trailer loads.

pineapple market could occur only at their competitors' expense, and therefore could be very expensive. As reported earlier, they believed Calpak and Libby to be much better able to withstand severe price competition in pineapple than Dole. They saw several alternative means of expanding Dole sales: 1) to increase marketing efforts for pineapple in areas where Dole penetration was below the national average, such as the southeast; 2) to enter totally new geographic markets for pineapple, such as Japan and Europe (made necessary if the Dolfil output was to be sold); 3) to enter totally new product areas.

In 1962, during Mr. Cornuelle's tenure, Dole had purchased 75% of an Italian joint venture to pack and distribute canned fruits and vegetables in Europe. This venture, Euramerica Foods, S.P.A., had been established "to get an operating foothold in the European Common Market." In 1965, the venture was terminated at a loss. According to Mr. MacNaughton, "The investment was a mistake. . . . In retrospect, it appears the desire to make a commitment became great enough to overbalance a careful judgment as to the particular advantages or disadvantages of a plant situated in the Po Valley area. Principal products of the area are tomatoes, which at best are a highly competitive and small profit margin item. Longer profit items, such as peaches and pears, are not of outstanding quality.

"Our errors here have been an inadequate appraisal of the facility at the outset, inadequate understanding with our partner, and the failure to develop such an understanding. Instead of continuing to work closely with our partner, thus providing him with Dole management and knowhow, we left him alone, subjected only to occasional visits and correspondence. While this has been an expensive error, I believe that we have learned from it and I am satisfied our more recent investments in the Pacific area have been studied carefully and continue to get thorough attention."

New Products

Development of mass markets for fresh pineapple appeared to be the most promising future activity for Dole. In addition to shipments and sales of whole pineapples, experiments were underway to establish the possibility of chilling and extending the shelf life of half-pineapples in polyethylene packages. A further step was to deoxidize and chill fresh pineapple spears in plastic wrapping. It appeared that flavor and color could be held for 45-60 days under these conditions, versus 20 days for fresh pineapples in the shell.

Investigations were underway in 1965 to determine the market potential for a line of cakes which included Dole fruits, e.g., pineapple upside-down cake, etc. Initial test marketing was conducted on fruit upside-down cake. Mr. Quinn felt that Dole would need a full line of cakes in order to command frozen food space in the supermarket. The test marketing therefore included pineapple, peach, apple, and fruit cocktail upside-down cake. (Results showed pineapple outselling the others by a three to one margin.) Mr. Quinn was enthusiastic about initial test results, but felt other items should receive higher priority.

Another new product area, arising from Dole's newly gained experience in handling fresh pineapple, was the possibility of exporting fresh mangoes, papayas, and other native Hawaiian fruits for mainland consumption.

A most promising start was being made on pineapple packed in its own juice, rather than in sugar syrup. It was hoped that this less sweet pack would appeal to the young adult market. Preliminary market data had suggested that a preponderance of purchases of canned pineapple in heavy syrup were by persons over 35.

Mr. Quinn considered Dole as having competence as: 1) an agricultural producer of anything; 2) food processors—of canned, fresh chilled, and frozen; 3) a food marketer any place in the world. He indicated that Dole was interested in exploring any product, process, or market opportunities that were "reasonable."

Many members of management indicated that Dole's past success was primarily attributable to their market reputation in pineapple. As many said, "Dole and pineapple are synonymous." Mr. Gale considered this the company's key competitive advantage, since quality differences between Dole and Calpak products were difficult to establish. Mr. Hamilton felt that, besides the strength of the Dole name, Dole provided its customers with faster service with fewer errors than the competition. Some management sentiment was divided between those who advocated concentration on pineapple products only and those who favored product diversification.

Relations with Castle & Cooke and its Divisions

During the years when Henry White was president of Hawaiian Pineapple, the company was run as a totally independent entity. Even though Castle & Cooke had effective stock control, Mr. White was able to act very autonomously in setting the direction that Dole took in major investment and divestment decisions. When Mr. Cornuelle succeeded Mr. White in 1958, Castle & Cooke and Dole moved somewhat closer together. However, much of the thinking in the upper levels of Dole management remained strongly influenced by their past autonomy.

After the 1961 merger of Dole into Castle & Cooke, there was little doubt where the balance of power lay. The C & C influence became more apparent two years later, when Mr. Cornuelle resigned to accept the position of executive vice president of the United Fruit Company, and was succeeded by Castle & Cooke's president, Malcolm MacNaughton. With Mr. MacNaughton holding the presidency of both Castle & Cooke and its Dole division, he concentrated his efforts "on proving to those fellows that we weren't so tough to get along with."

In the following year, Mr. MacNaughton appointed Mr. William Quinn first to the executive vice presidency of Dole and then to the presidency, allowing Mr. MacNaughton to devote his full efforts to the presidency of Castle & Cooke. With the Dole presidency filled by Mr. MacNaughton's hand-picked choice, a man who had had no previous contact with the old Dole loyalties, it appeared that future liaison would be closer between the Dole division and C & C headquarters than had been true in the past.

During the past few years, the geographical separation of marketing management from the Dole corporate headquarters has presented growing difficulties in the efficient management of a marketing oriented company. The marketing people believed that it was essential for them to be based near the market. Most of the major canners were located on the West Coast. Similarly, most private label sales of fruits and vegetables were consummated by the San Francisco buying offices of the principal chains. Mr. Quinn felt that it was crucial to his effectiveness to be in close touch with the marketing group. He also thought that marketing-manufacturing coordination would benefit from physical proximity.[7] But he believed that Dole company headquarters should be located in Honolulu in order to remain in close contact with headquarters personnel of Castle & Cooke.

In the fall of 1965, the controller's office of Dole was moved from San Jose to Honolulu, and the formal organization was changed so that the new Dole controller (Mr. Gale) was responsible not only to Mr. Quinn, but also to Mr. Stanley Rosch, the controller of Castle & Cooke.

Dole's relationships to Castle & Cooke were further complicated by Dolfil. Operations of this company, 80% owned by Castle & Cooke, were the responsibility of Dole. Initially Dolfil's president, Mr. Howard Hubbard (formerly Castle & Cooke vice president and controller), had reported directly to Castle & Cooke president MacNaughton. After a few months, he was directed to report to Mr. Quinn. By the end of 1965, all of the Dolfil operations were being guided by Dole's principal executives.

It appeared to some members of Castle & Cooke management that there might be possible economies in joint warehousing and, perhaps, even selling, between Bumble Bee Seafoods and the Dole Company. Dole management indicated that while Bumble Bee was reluctant to integrate their operations with those of Dole, some joint warehousing was being initiated and a common broker was being tried out in the New York market.

Another avenue for integration was the possibility of Dole's joining with Standard Fruit Company in the joint marketing of fresh bananas and pineapples, to utilize Standard's extensive facilities for handling fresh fruit and their experience in marketing these products. Dole's plantation lands in the Philippines and their contacts in Japan provided other possible opportunities for joint action with the Standard Fruit Company. It appeared practical for Standard Fruit to grow bananas at the Dolfil plantation, and to ship both bananas and pineapples as fresh fruit to Japan. The same opportunities appeared feasible for Dole to grow pineapple on Standard's Central American lands, which would be a more economical location from which to ship fresh pineapple to East Coast and Gulf ports.

---

[7] In early 1966, Mr. Bleich, director of marketing, was moved to Honolulu "in order to achieve greater coordination between divisions of the company, and to facilitate management decisions."

Standard Fruit and Steamship Company

Standard Fruit and Steamship Company, of New Orleans, is one of the world's largest producers and marketers of bananas. The company owns and operates extensive plantations in Honduras and Costa Rica, and maintains permanent agronomy, buying, processing, and shipping facilities in Ecuador. Over a billion pounds of bananas were shipped from these countries in 1965 in the company's fleet of ten large, chartered refrigerated ships, to company owned and operated terminals in New York, New Orleans, and Long Beach for distribution throughout the U.S. and Canada. Subsidiary companies in Honduras and Nicaragua produce cartons, beer, soft drinks, salad and cooking oils, margarine, and soap, and make a significant contribution to sales and earnings. In calendar 1965, Standard Fruit had all-time record high sales of $97 million. After tax, earnings were $4.5 million on assets of $48 million. In 1964, Castle & Cooke, Inc., purchased, for cash, 52% of the company's common stock from the founding D'Antoni family and others. In late 1965, under a joint tender offer by Standard Fruit and Castle & Cooke, the latter's ownership was increased to 84%. Subsequently, Standard Fruit has continued to operate relatively autonomously, retaining its original corporate structure and its independent stock listings.

WORLD BANANA INDUSTRY [1]

Growing areas for bananas include a major part of the world's tropic zone, and extend from Asia and Africa to Central and South America, including many of the tropical islands south of the Tropic of Cancer. The banana plant requires warm

---

[1] This note draws heavily from information presented in the *FAO Monthly Bulletin of Agriculture Economics and Statistics,* Vol. 13 (December 1964), pp. 10-16.

weather, frequent rain, and rich soil for healthy growth. Given the necessary climatic and soil conditions, a banana plantation can be brought into continuous production within ten months after the first planting. As many as 1,000 plants can be grown on a single acre, and annual yields can range from 6-25 tons per acre, depending on variety and climate. Banana production is usually relatively stable year-round, seasonal variations being limited to approximately ± 25% of normal volume. The occurrence of seasonal peaks, however, varies in accordance with geography and climate; e.g., Ecuador, the world's leading producer, harvests its greatest output between January and May, while Honduras's output is on a continuous eight month cycle, which moves the peak harvest period to a different time each year.

Each banana shoot grows only a single stem of bananas during its lifetime. However, a healthy plant continuously grows new shoots, each of which could mature and bear fruit. The accepted practice on banana plantations is to allow each plant to maintain three shoots, each sequenced to mature at a different time. Thus, if in a particular area the plant requires nine months to bear fruit, the grower will allow only a single shoot to grow during the plant's first three months. At this point, he will allow one additional shoot to develop, while cutting back all other new sprouts for an additional three months. This process is continued so that, as a stem of ripe bananas is harvested from a plant, there will be a new shoot just developing, a shoot which is one-third mature, and another which is two-thirds mature. Plants are similarly sequenced so that harvesting of bananas can proceed on every day of the year. As the bananas mature the diameter of the individual banana fingers is measured with calipers. When the fingers achieve a predetermined diameter, the shoot bearing the stem of bananas is cut down by hand, and the stem, made up of many "hands" and weighing 60-120 pounds, is removed and transported manually to the wagons which will carry it to the packaging shed. There, the stem is washed, inspected, and boxed for shipment.

Once a plantation is established, the grower is largely committed to a series of relatively fixed costs. He must cultivate, spray, harvest, wash, pack, and transport his bananas to market when they are ready, regardless of the prevailing price. He cannot accelerate output materially in times of high prices, nor can he reduce output significantly when prices are low.

There is no known limit to the life of a banana plant, but disease and/or wind damage have limited most plants to between five and twenty-five years of production. For many years the control of Sigatoka Leaf Spot was very costly, but since the late 1950's new techniques of control with orchard spray oil have reduced this expense. Panama Disease, a fungus attacking the root system of the banana plant, is its most serious current enemy and has caused substantial damage in many of the well-established banana producing regions of the world. There is no known prevention or cure for this disease, and its incidence has caused a number of banana growers to abandon the universally accepted, good-yielding, historically successful variety known as Gros Michel, in favor of new varieties which are more resistant to Panama Disease. The high-yielding Giant

Cavendish, introduced by Standard Fruit, or the Valery, which is United Fruit's name for the comparable variety, is both disease-resistant and excellent in its growing and taste characteristics. However, sufficient planting material to bring these new varieties into production has not been generally available. As a result, only those growers who have had the research facilities to develop the new resistant strains and the nursery facilities to produce sufficient seed material have been able to convert their old, established plantations and thus reduce the risk of destruction from Panama Disease. Standard Fruit has wholly converted its large plantations in Costa Rica and Honduras, while United Fruit is converting its plantations as rapidly as possible. Virtually all of the Ecuadorian production is in Gros Michel. Ecuador's advantage has been sufficient virgin areas to replace the limited inroads of Panama Disease. But Ecuadorian planters also are attempting to convert to the newer varieties.

Because the banana plant grows in a topheavy form, it is also very vulnerable to wind damage. Wind storms have been known to completely flatten entire plantations. In 1961, the damage from Hurricane Hattie to Guatemala banana production was so severe that a major industry factor like Standard Fruit chose to discontinue operation of its devastated plantations in that country. Heavy wind damage has plagued most banana producing regions and has instigated much research into new varieties that are less vulnerable.

World Production of Bananas

Present world banana production for export is approximately 4.4 million tons per year. Exhibit 1 presents trends in export volume for principal areas of world banana production. This exhibit clearly indicates the dominance of Central and South America, with 65-70% of world production. The banana export trade is the backbone of the economies of most of the major producing countries. For all producing nations, it is an important source of foreign exchange.

The most significant increase in world production in recent years has come from Ecuador. Ecuadorian banana plantings have reached 350,000 acres, and exports have grown from 120,000 tons in 1949 to 1.4 million tons in 1964, which now constitute nearly one-third of total world exports. The Ecuadorian government has played an important role in supporting the industry's extraordinary growth through road building projects and a favorable political climate, including governmental price support. Further banana export expansion to 1.7 million tons is planned by the Ecuadorian government by 1973. Efforts are also being made to reduce costs by eliminating marginal production areas, continuing the improvement of roads and port facilities, and encouraging the formation of cooperative production and marketing societies.

Important expansion has also taken place in present or former colonial areas, which have received preferential tariff treatment in supplying the consumption requirements of the mother country; e.g., Guadeloupe, Martinique, the Windward Islands, Somalia, Ivory Coast, Guinea, and the Canary Islands. Under the Con-

exhibit 1

STANDARD FRUIT AND STEAMSHIP COMPANY

Trends in World Banana Exports
(in thousands of tons per year and as a percentage of world trade)

					Exporting Area								
	South America		Central America		Jamaica and Windward Islands		Guadalupe and Martinique		Africa and Canary Island		Asia and Pacific		Estimated World Total
Period	Tons	%	Tons	%	Tons	%	Tons	%	Tons	%	Tons	%	Tons	%
1924 - 1928	316	15	1,168	54	324	15	—	—	190	9	161	7	2,159	100
1934 - 1938	459	17	1,290	47	418	15	68	3	297	11	183	7	2,715	100
1948 - 1952	586	23	1,273	50	120	5	120	5	419	16	47	2	2,565	100
1953 - 1957	1,072	32	1,232	37	222	7	147	4	608	18	72	2	3,353	100
1958 - 1962	1,567	36	1,351	31	274	6	267	6	785	18	135	3	4,379	100

Source: FAO Journal (December 1964), p. 10.

vention of Association with the European Economic Committee (EEC), all tariffs from historically and politically affiliated countries are being eliminated progressively through 1970, while a tariff of 20% ad valorem is being established on imports from nonaffiliated countries. The EEC has given the Federal Republic of Germany a special duty-free quota on bananas for up to an ultimate maximum annual importation of about 300,000 tons from nonaffiliated countries. Germany thus represents the only major market in the EEC for which most Central and South American bananas can compete on an equal basis.

Further expansion of banana production is planned for Jamaica and the Windward Islands, whose exports are geared to consumption in the U.K. The Jamaican government is being assisted by the United Fruit Company and its British subsidiary, Elders & Fyffes, Ltd., in raising annual output by 35% to a total of about 250,000 tons.

The Canary Islands, with a preferential position in the Spanish market, is also expanding banana production. Large-scale commercial production in Southeast Asia, aiming at the Japanese market, is being considered actively by major producers. Such development would represent a completely new factor in the world supply pattern.

Other factors which may increase the banana supply available for export are potential reductions in export taxes in major producing countries and the growing adoption of box-packaging. Box-packaging has greatly reduced damage in transit, thus increasing the net saleable tonnage from a given amount of production, as well as allowing use of previously underweight stems.

In the Turbo area of Colombia, new lands, well-suited to banana cultivation, are being developed by private producers under contract to the United Fruit Company. It is estimated that the Turbo region will be producing for export about 10 million bunches (220,000 to 275,000 tons) by 1968, doubling current Colombian supply.

Some formerly important producing countries, such as Mexico, Nicaragua, and Cuba, lacking the research support of the large exporting companies or of government agencies, have seen disease and neglect reduce their banana export volume to an insignificant level.

Exhibit 2 shows the recent trends in banana export volume for the major producing countries and gives some indications of the importance of the banana trade to each nation's total economy.

Other Factors Affecting
Supply from Various Nations

The large exporters operate their own shipping fleets in order to control these costs and to increase their market flexibility. Other buyers hire ships individually for specific journeys. Thus the large exporter has a heavy fixed investment in ship operations, in addition to plantations and terminals, which obliges him to ship continuously. This is an important element in the banana economy of Costa Rica, Honduras, and Panama.

Shipping costs may vary from as little as 8% to as much as 20% of the landed value of the bananas, depending on the distance between the consuming and producing areas. Ecuador, on the west side of South America, is 1,000 miles or more further from New York or Europe than the banana producing countries in Central America, the Caribbean, or the eastern coast of South America. Thus Ecuadorian growers' prices, while determined by week to week world banana supply and demand, are affected during periods of plentiful supply by the high shipping costs.

Besides shipping costs, the various producing countries differ in the time at which the grower establishes his profit or loss. In Ecuador and Colombia, all bananas are produced by independent growers and sold at auction on the open market. Growers' profit or loss is thus determined at the export dock. In Honduras, Costa Rica, and Panama, most production is either from plantations owned and operated by the large banana exporters (United Fruit, Standard Fruit) or from growers under contract with, or leasing from, these companies. Since there is no open market bidding in these areas, contract prices tend to be relatively stable, and the profit or loss for the exporter is not known until the final import price is determined at the port of entry.

Weekly fluctuations in production volumes can usually be predicted within a

exhibit 2

STANDARD FRUIT AND STEAMSHIP COMPANY

Banana Export Volume and Values for Each of the Principal Banana-Producing Nations
(volume in thousands of tons and value in thousands of U.S. dollars)

Country	1959 Volume	1959 Value	1960 Volume	1960 Value	1961 Volume	1961 Value	1962 Volume	1962 Value	1963 Volume	1963 Value	Value of 1963 Banana Exports as a % of that Country's Exports
Ecuador	1,157	$89,700	1,171	$89,800	1,083	$80,900	1,145	$88,500	1,394	$107,400	65%
Honduras	395	32,254	399	28,790	473	39,505	416	35,372	378	33,072	40
Panama	320	23,520	290	18,160	298	20,020	276	11,754	328	13,724	24
Costa Rica	235	22,269	300	24,960	254	18,546	321	21,167	287	22,677	25
Brazil	234	4,370	266	4,561	270	3,799	238	3,228	226	2,924	0.2
Colombia	224	13,876	210	13,687	226	14,055	162	10,174	223	13,942	3
Dominican Rep.	112	6,075	200	11,322	187	11,769	190	11,788	n.a.	n.a.	7
Jamaica	169	13,844	172	13,462	175	13,692	163	12,633	184	13,563	7
Ivory Coast	59	4,335	80	5,156	101	8,483	135	11,537	147	14,130	61
Cameroon	64	3,783	40	2,379	56	3,324	141	8,345	130	7,670	n.a.
Martinique	144	14,680	139	13,319	151	15,019	166	15,274	128	12,429	n.a.

1 Based upon 1962 export value.

Source: Trade Yearbook, Vol. 18 (Rome: Food and Agriculture Organization of the United Nations, 1964), pp. 179-180.

range of $\pm$ 10%; however, even this range of variation is substantial enough to create large price movements. At present, total world production available for export only modestly exceeds total consumption by importing nations, but major export supply/import demand imbalances may occur at any time in an individual area. The FAO study predicts increases in world banana supply at a rate at least equal to that of the past five years (an approximate compound rate of growth of 5% per year). FAO also expects Mexico to reenter the banana export market, by growing bananas sufficiently close to the United States border that shipment by truck would be practical. The FAO projections suggest a 1970 available supply for export of about 6.7 million tons.

Importing Countries

Some 85% of world banana exports are presently absorbed by the United States and Western Europe. Japan and Argentina, the only other significant markets, add another 11%. Exhibit 3 shows major trends in banana imports by geographical area.

The general level of banana consumption by nation appears to be most closely related to national income levels. However, variations in consumption in some countries, like the United Kingdom, which for many years has maintained banana importing ties with Jamaica, tend to occur with production fluctuations in the supplying region. From 1945 to 1962, Japanese consumption was restrained artificially by import restrictions, imposed to maintain a balance of payments. In the year following relaxation of the import regulations, banana consumption tripled. Japan is regarded as having great potential for substantial additional increases in the future.

Exhibit 4 shows the worldwide export-import flow of bananas. These flows reflect the many elements influencing banana procurement; e.g., shipping costs, political ties, tariffs, quotas, and the supply/demand equilibrium. Figure 1 is a map of major world production and consumption areas.

Exhibit 5 presents the national per capita consumption in the principal consuming countries, suggesting both variation with income level and a possible per capita "saturation" ceiling. Exhibit 6 plots per capita consumption against average income level for each country, to indicate the degree to which these two variables are related. Countries farthest above the regression line, like Argentina, Chile, Spain, and Portugal, reflect especially low retail price levels and, thus, higher than expected consumption. Countries farthest below the regression line, like Japan, Italy, Greece, and Finland, show the effects of import restrictions, which have artifically held back consumption. The FAO concludes from these data, that "in most countries, per capita consumption tends to level out in the region of 9 to 10 kilograms [20-22 pounds]. This is indicated by the experience of the United States, Canada, and Argentina, where consumption has remained around this figure despite very different income levels. New Zealand would appear to be an

exhibit 3

STANDARD FRUIT AND STEAMSHIP COMPANY

World Banana Imports
(in thousands of tons)

Region/Country	Average 1924 - 28	Average 1934 - 38	Average 1948 - 52	Average 1953 - 57	Average 1958 - 62	1963 (Preliminary)
Western Europe[1] (total)	481	815	722	1,365	1,974	2,178
Germany, Fed. Rep. of	63	130	64	255	494	523
France	83	188	225	303	398	398
Italy	2	21	17	46	99	176
Netherlands	18	34	15	38	68	79
Belgium - Luxembourg	9	25	41	55	71	73
Total EEC countries	176	398	363	698	1,129	1,249
United Kingdom	250	335	162	333	385	402
Spain	28	28	110	144	194	216
Sweden	9	13	33	58	54	59
Switzerland	6	7	14	24	47	59
Portugal	n.a.	11	28	41	46	55
Austria	1	1	0	10	29	36
Denmark	1	4	3	30	30	33
Norway	6	8	2	14	29	28
Other Western Europe	n.a.	9	6	14	20	26
North America[1] (total)	1,492	1,489	1,591	1,781	2,071	1,870
United States	1,425	1,431	1,478	1,623	1,891	1,694
Canada	64	56	110	155	174	165
South America[1] (total)	83	202	198	225	284	297
Argentina	66	176	153	186	226	n.a.
Chile	10	15	23	20	28	n.a.
Uruguay	6	11	23	19	25	n.a.
Africa	2	17	22	38	44	n.a.
Asia[1] (total)	110	146	22	47	82	n.a.
Japan	109	134	14	27	60	282
Hong Kong	n.a.	n.a.	2	19	22	n.a.
New Zealand	13	13	11	25	35	33
World Total[1] (excluding U.S.S.R. and Eastern Europe)	2,181	2,682	2,566	3,494	4,507	4,769

[1] Data by nation and continent do not reconcile due to rounding.

[2] Decline from 1958-62 average is attributable to a longshoremen's strike in January and wind damage to Central American plantations in March and June.

Source: Official data as supplied to FAO and national trade statistics, 1963.

exhibit 4

STANDARD FRUIT AND STEAMSHIP COMPANY

Principal Sources of Bananas Imported by Selected Countries

Importing Country	*Principal Sources of Bananas*
United States Canada Germany, Fed. Rep. of Netherlands	Central and South America
Scandinavian Countries	Central America, Canary Islands
France	Martinique, Guadeloupe, Ivory Coast, Madagascar
Spain	Canary Islands
Portugal	Politically associated sources only
Italy	Somalia, Ivory Coast, Canary Islands, French Caribbean, Ecuador
United Kingdom	Jamaica, Windward Islands, Dominican Republic, Brazil
New Zealand	Countries within Oceania (Fiji, Western Samoa, Tonga)
Chile	Ecuador
Argentina	Brazil

figure 1

STANDARD FRUIT AND STEAMSHIP COMPANY

Major World Production and Consumption Areas

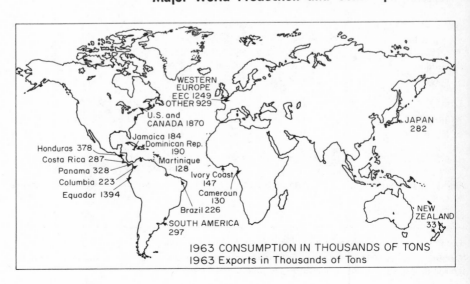

WESTERN EUROPE
EEC 1249
OTHER 929

U.S. and CANADA 1870

Jamaica 184
Dominican Rep. 190

Honduras 378
Costa Rica 287
Panama 328
Columbia 223
Equador 1394

Martinique 128

Ivory Coast 147

Cameroun 130

Brazil 226

SOUTH AMERICA 297

JAPAN 282

NEW ZEALAND 33

1963 CONSUMPTION IN THOUSANDS OF TONS
1963 Exports in Thousands of Tons

exhibit 5

STANDARD FRUIT AND STEAMSHIP COMPANY

Annual Per Capita Consumption of Bananas in Selected Countries
(in pounds)

Country (arranged in order of est. 1963 rank)	Average 1934-38	Average 1948-52	Average 1953-57	Average 1958-62	1963
New Zealand	16.1	11.7	22.6	27.7	n.a.
Argentina	25.7	17.8	19.1	22.0	n.a.
Switzerland	3.5	5.7	9.4	17.4	20.4
United States	23.1	19.8	20.2	21.6	19.8
Uruguay	10.8	18.7	14.7	19.1	n.a.
Germany, Fed. Rep. of	4.0	2.6	10.1	18.3	18.0
Canada	9.6	14.5	19.4	19.1	17.6
France	5.3	10.3	13.9	17.4	16.7
Sweden	3.5	7.3	15.8	14.5	15.6
Belgium—Luxembourg	5.9	8.8	12.3	15.4	15.2
Norway	5.5	1.1	7.9	16.3	14.9
United Kingdom	13.6	6.8	13.0	14.7	14.9
Denmark	2.0	1.3	13.6	13.2	14.1
Spain	3.3	7.7	10.3	12.8	13.8
Netherlands	7.9	2.9	7.0	11.9	13.6
Portugal	2.9	6.6	9.5	10.6	12.3
Austria	.2	.2	2.9	8.1	10.1
Ireland	4.2	3.7	5.1	6.6	8.8
Chile	5.9	7.3	5.7	7.5	n.a.
Italy	.9	.7	2.0	4.0	7.0
Japan	3.7	.4	.7	1.3	5.9
Finland	1.5	.2	3.1	4.6	5.7
Syria	n.a.	2.2	3.3	3.7	n.a
Algeria	1.5	1.5	2.0	3.1	n.a.
Morocco	.9	.7	1.8	1.8	n.a.
Tunisia	2.0	1.1	1.1	1.3	n.a.

Source: FAO Journal (December 1964), p. 13.

exception, with per capita consumption of 10 to 12 kilograms [22-26 pounds]." [2]

Exhibit 7 presents an FAO model of projected banana import demand by geographical area for 1970, assuming retail prices remain constant at average 1960–1962 levels. As indicated, total world demand is expected to reach 6.3 million tons by 1970, representing an increase of 32% over 1960–1962, or a compound rate of growth of about 3% annually (vs. 5.9% during the preceding decade).

---

[2] *FAO Journal* (December 1964), p. 14.

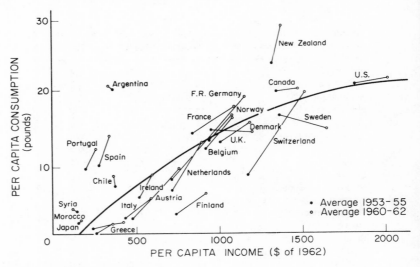

Source: FAO Journal (December 1964), p. 14.

Possible reductions in retail price levels might increase this consumption rate materially. While the price elasticity of bananas tends to be greatest in countries where the retail price is high, as in Italy and Japan, and least in countries where banana prices are comparatively low, as in the United States and Germany, elasticity appears to decrease as per capita income rises. Thus, on a market by market basis, FAO forecasts that a 10% reduction in average retail price by 1970 would result in an increase in consumption of about 550,000 tons (8.7%) over the projected demand, to a possible total of 6.85 million tons.

It appears unlikely that any significant future increases in per capita banana consumption can be expected in the United States, either as a result of income growth or reduced prices. A similar "saturation level" of per capita banana consumption in Canada, Argentina, Uruguay, and New Zealand will likely hold consumption increases to population growth rates in these countries as well.

Per capita banana consumption in Western Europe can be expected to rise somewhat, but the rate of expansion is declining markedly. West German and United Kingdom imports, for example, have been relatively constant for the past two to three years. On the other hand, significant increases in consumption can be anticipated in Italy, Greece, the rest of Southern Europe, and in the low income countries of the Near East and North Africa. The potential of the

exhibit 7

STANDARD FRUIT AND STEAMSHIP COMPANY

Estimated 1970 Import Demand for Bananas *

Item	North America	EEC	Mediterranean	Rest of Western Europe	South America	Near East and North Africa	Japan	Rest of World²	Total
(a) Average annual consumption, 1960-62 (thousand tons)	2,030	1,186	272	628	280	41	282	36	4,754
(b) Average annual per capita consumption, 1960-62 (lbs.)	20.1	13.6	8.1	14.1	13.0	2.4	5.9	22.0	13.4
(c) Expected population growth to 1970 (compound rate per annum)	1.8	0.8	0.9	0.6	2.1	2.5	1.1	2.2	1.3
(d) Expected increase in real per capita income (compound rate per annum)	2.0	4.5	4.5	3.0	2.0	2.0	5.0	1.5	—
(e) Income elasticity⁴	0.1	0.5	1.0	0.5	0.4	2.0	1.5	0.1	—
(f) Estimated total consumption,⁵ 1970 (thousand tons)	2,424	1,593	436	766	366	70	561	45	6,261
Average annual rate of increase in total consumption (compound)									
Between 1948-52 and 1953-57	2.3	14.0	7.7	16.0	2.5	10.8	( )	18.0	6.4
Between 1953-57 and 1958-62	3.0	10.1	6.4	4.2	4.9	7.0	( )	6.9	5.2
Estimated between 1960-62 and 1970	2.0	3.3	5.4	2.3	3.0	6.3	8.0	2.4	3.1

1Excluding U.S.S.R. and Eastern Europe and a number of minor importing countries for which income data were not available.

2Mainly New Zealand.

31963.

4FAO judgment of expected change in per capita banana consumption which would result from a change in per capita income.

5Computed from the combined factors of population growth plus consumption change due to increase in income.

$$f = \left[(a)\, (1 + \frac{c}{100})^9 \right] \times \left[1 + (e) \left((1 + \frac{d}{100})^9 - 1 \right) \right]$$

6Not relevant due to restriction of imports prior to 1962.

Source: FAO Journal (December 1964), p. 15.

Japanese market is considerable, and this country could conceivably have an effective import demand of about 550,000 tons by 1970, or about 9% of estimated 1970 world consumption.

Imports into countries with centrally planned economies which presently preclude bananas, such as Eastern Europe, offer additional possibilities. Eastern Europe, as a moderately high income area, has the capacity to import substantial quantities of bananas, should controls be relaxed. For example, if per capita consumption of bananas in Eastern Europe and the U.S.S.R. were to rise from its present negligible level to half the current Western European average, import requirements would be on the order of one million tons per year.

Price Movements

Since the mid-1950's, world wholesale prices of bananas have been under steady downward pressure. Wholesale prices of bananas coming into the United States have fallen from an average of 7.4¢/lb. in 1958 to 5.7¢/lb. in 1963, the largest single price decline for any country or for any other five year period. In some countries, such as France, prices have increased on an absolute basis, but, after accounting for inflationary influences, the real price of bananas has declined in these countries, as elsewhere.

Exhibit 8 illustrates the retail prices of bananas in the principal importing countries between 1955 and 1963. The stability of these annual averages masks the often substantial week to week fluctuations, but does indicate considerably

exhibit 8

STANDARD FRUIT AND STEAMSHIP COMPANY

Average Retail Prices of Bananas in Specified Countries, 1955–1963
(U.S. cents per pound)

Country	1955	1956	1957	1958	1959	1960	1961	1962	1963
Netherlands	16.5	16.5	17.2	15.4	14.0	14.5	14.6	n.a.	n.a.
United States	17.1	16.8	17.3	17.3	17.1	16.0	16.0	16.3	16.5
Germany, Fed. Rep. of	19.9	17.0	17.0	16.5	15.4	15.4	15.4	15.7	17.5
United Kingdom	19.3	18.7	19.9	19.8	18.3	18.6	19.0	18.0	17.3
France	n.a.	n.a.	n.a.	n.a.	16.9	16.9	17.4	18.2	19.0
Belgium	19.6	19.7	20.6	19.7	17.9	18.3	17.7	18.3	19.1
Canada	20.0	20.1	20.7	20.6	20.4	19.5	18.7	18.7	19.4
Denmark	22.4	21.4	20.9	21.7	21.6	21.4	21.4	n.a.	n.a.
Norway	22.9	22.2	22.0	22.4	23.0	22.8	23.7	25.4	25.4
Italy	29.3	34.8	34.8	34.8	34.8	33.0	29.3	25.6	25.6

Source: FAO Journal (December 1964), p. 13.

less price volatility at the retail level than at wholesale. Price differences from country to country, e.g., between Germany and Italy, help to explain the variations in per capita consumption by nation discussed earlier.

Logistics Impact

The logistics of ship movement are an important influence on market price. Each shipload of bananas, from present-day, large, refrigerated, special purpose ships, represents a volume which, by itself, is sufficiently large to affect the wholesale price at the port of entry. Therefore, exporters try to schedule their ship arrivals among the various receiving ports so as to seek the most favorable current supply/demand conditions. When a ship reaches port, its bananas are sold to specialized banana wholesalers or jobbers, or directly to large chain store buyers. No exporter presently performs this intermediate step in U.S. distribution. Because the product is highly perishable, and refrigerated storage to prolong ripening and wait out temporary supply/demand imbalances is both expensive and limited in effectiveness to a maximum of seven days, and because ship delays or holdovers are very costly, each shipload is generally sold while en route to the port. Prices are bid by wholesalers, jobbers, and chains, on solicitation by the exporter, and will vary in proportion to each one's current and previously contracted for wholesale and retail inventories in the region, relative to his expectations of near-term supply volume. Since the time required to carry the bananas from the various exporting countries to the major importing ports is great, supply and demand relationships can change materially in a specific port of destination while the cargo is en route.

In addition to this uncertainty regarding import market price, exporters also, as indicated previously, face wide fluctuations in the price of product purchased from independent growers. With only a few days' latitude in when he harvests his fruit, the grower cannot wait out temporary price movements. Therefore, the supply available to any port at the time of loading can be closely estimated, and a price can be negotiated which relates supply to available ship capacity at that port. Often negotiations take place only hours in advance of loading. In Ecuador, where the entire banana industry is in the hands of independent growers, the negotiated price must also be above the minimum set by the government. This floor tends to accentuate the price fluctuations, since exporters can and do reroute their ships and sharply reduce or increase their Ecuadorian purchases at any point in time, depending on the relative price and availability in competitive producing areas.

U.S. Consumption and Price Movement

Over-all 1965 food sales in the U.S. were estimated at $62 billion, of which produce accounted for 8% (or about $5 billion). Within the produce sector, bananas ranged second only to potatoes in number of tons sold, and were first in dollar volume with 11% ($550 million). While at one time U.S. banana consumption was wholly of the Gros Michel variety, it is estimated that 40% of present U.S. consumption is now of the newer Giant Cavendish or Valery varieties.

With fairly steady week to week demand, and per capita consumption apparently near saturation level, U.S. retailers have been able to hold their prices at a reasonably constant average level (recently approximately 17¢/lb., but with a week to week range of 10-19¢/lb.).

Industry sources indicate that, over this full price range, for any extended period, consumption will vary within only ± 20%. However, a 10¢/lb. price is estimated to generate, for short periods of time, up to three times as much demand as generated by the "normal" 17¢/lb. price. These same sources suggest the existence of an apparent "ceiling" of 20¢/lb., beyond which demand falls off sharply as consumers switch to alternative products.

Principal Banana Trading Companies

In an industry whose prices are independently volatile at both the point of export and the port of entry, operating margins fluctuate substantially. As a result, the number of companies participating at any one time in the banana trade varies considerably. Whenever profit margins increase, due to diverging export and import prices, a number of small operators enter the market to bid for unconsigned bananas. These exporters hire space on refrigerated tramp steamers or enlist out of service vessels, and bring bananas into the port of entry for sale to wholesalers, without having to provide any supporting services. In 1965, there were six regularly participating importers serving the United States banana market, plus about a dozen small nonregulars who were active from time to time. In 1965, the two major importers, United Fruit Company and Standard Fruit Company, together accounted for about 83% of total U.S. imports of bananas. Both were major plantation operators. The next most important importer, Pan American Fruit Company, held approximately 7% of the U.S. market. Pan American had become a permanent participant in the banana trade by combining the resources of a half dozen small nonregulars, and purchased most of its fruit from independent growers. Next in size among the regularly participating companies was West Indies Fruit Company, which accounted for about 4% of the U.S. market. The two other regulars were Parker Banana Company, which had a small plantation of its own, and Thatcher Fruit Company, which limited its import operations to the state of Florida. Between them, Parker and Thatcher accounted for only 1% of the 1965 U.S. total import volume. In 1965 the nonregulars were responsible for the remaining 5% of U.S. imports.

The European market in 1965 was served primarily by a very small number of large, financially strong banana wholesalers in each major importing country. These wholesalers had established relations with independent growers and bought both on contract and at auction. While some of these wholesalers owned or operated some plantations and ships, all controlled most distribution within their respective markets. Thus the major American banana companies can be thought of primarily as *exporters,* selling and delivering their products to the ultimate distributors, while the European companies can be thought of primarily as *importers,* buying the products from the growers, contracting the shipping, but then performing all of the ultimate distribution functions. In recent years, United Fruit has acquired ownership in four large European wholesalers and has established working relationships with others. In 1965, Standard Fruit also began developing such relationships in Europe.

United Fruit Company

United Fruit Company, in 1965, was the largest banana company in the world. With headquarters in Boston, Mass., United began operations in 1870 and expanded rapidly by buying many small banana growing companies, originally in Jamaica and Costa Rica, but ultimately extending to many of the major banana producing regions of the world. For many years United completely dominated the U.S. market. Through acquisition of Elders & Fyffes, Ltd., in 1910, it also took an important position in the U.K. In 1951, United Fruit's profit after tax was $50 million on gross sales of $314 million, most of which were in the U.S. Their dominant position enabled them to enjoy wide profit margins, while providing only the necessary growing and export functions. They were pioneers in plantation improvement and in shipboard temperature and humidity control, which greatly improved the quality of the bananas that reached the market place. Once landed, the bananas were then sold to specialized wholesalers with little company follow-up required.

Standard Fruit Company in the mid-1950's began to offer ripening and merchandising help to the wholesalers, as a means of breaking into the U.S. market. During this period, Standard built up impressive capabilities in all areas of growing, shipping, and marketing bananas, while United Fruit did little in response. When Panama Disease began taking a heavy toll of banana plants in the Central American plantations, Standard Fruit started to develop a new disease-resistant strain, achieving success several years ahead of United Fruit. Also during this period Standard Fruit introduced a concept of boxing bananas on the plantations, precooling them, and shipping them directly to the grocery stores without additional packaging or handling. United Fruit, again, did not react immediately to this development, but maintained their shipments of bananas on the stem until customer pressure obliged a change to the more convenient boxes. (In 1965, shipment in boxes had replaced the old method of shipping stems for nearly 100% of U.S. banana imports.)

By 1960, after tax profits of United Fruit had declined to a little over $2 million, and a new president was hired as part of a major reorganization "to bring United Fruit back on its feet." A broad scale program was instituted for replanting the company's Central American plantations with the new, disease-resistant Valery variety. Extensive facilities for plantation boxing were established.

Although United began selling in European markets at the turn of the century and had purchased their first distributor, Elders & Fyffes, Ltd., in 1910, it was not until 1955 that they began a concerted effort to strengthen and expand their foreign sales. They began by adding a French foreign affiliate to the Elders & Fyffes subsidiary. In 1960 they set up a new distributor in the Netherlands and began sales in Germany. The following year they established German "associates" and commenced sales to Finland. By 1963, United's Netherland subsidiary had established distribution in Austria and Switzerland as well as in the Netherlands. They had purchased the outstanding stock of B. M. Spiers & Son of Belgium and had begun a Japanese company in joint venture with six of Japan's largest trading companies. United supplies its foreign affiliates from the free market where possible (Germany from Latin America) and from politically tied regions where necessary, as in the case of Cameroun and Jamaica for consumption in France and the United Kingdom respectively.

By 1963, United Fruit had extended its marketing assistance to wholesalers all the way to branding their bananas ("Chiquita") and conducting a consumer advertising program, estimated to cost $3.5 million annually.

In 1965, United Fruit grew approximately two-thirds of its U.S. market requirements. Much of this production came from plantations owned by United Fruit, but operated by tenants. This trend toward leasing plantations to former operating personnel has been explained as helping to reduce production costs, as well as improving political relations with the various countries involved.

In 1958, the U.S. Justice Department obtained a consent decree against United's alleged monopoly position in the U.S. banana market. Under this decree, United Fruit is required to present a plan of divestiture of production capability of at least 9 million stems per year. The plan is due June 30, 1966, and must be implemented by 1970. (Standard Fruit Company is explicitly excluded from the "suitable" list.)

A summary of United Fruit operating data from 1954 to 1965 is presented in Exhibit 9. These data indicate clearly that, although important steps have been undertaken to improve United's competitive position, earnings performance remains well below the level of the 1950's.

Appendices A and B present two articles summarizing United Fruit activities during 1965. As indicated here, the substantial improvement in 1965 has been attributed to reduce operating costs associated with the conversion to the Valery variety of bananas.

Exhibit 10 compares operating results of United Fruit and Standard Fruit over the past ten years. These data show Standard's growing market penetration, but emphasize United's continuing great size and scope.

STANDARD FRUIT AND STEAMSHIP COMPANY

The company was founded in 1890 in New Orleans, La., primarily as a steamship company, to import bananas from Honduras. In 1926, the present name was

exhibit 9

UNITED FRUIT COMPANY

Ten Year Performance Data

Year	Total Assets	Shareholders' Equity	Sales	Earnings	Dividends
1965			$379,851,000	$17,268,000	
1964	$318,112,704	$271,941,605	333,415,000	704,560	$ 3,610,316
1963	324,592,373	283,261,564	329,910,481	458,298	4,814,758
1962	337,793,670	298,948,510	319,786,983	11,005,888	5,330,515
1961	331,373,181	295,324,101	311,320,593	8,920,911	4,340,742
1960	337,641,183	291,123,306	304,421,213	2,171,094	6,532,773
1959	383,761,341	354,234,609	312,921,474	12,087,670	8,745,772
1958	386,339,033	356,471,831	324,385,946	22741,575	24,081,523
1957	395,914,113	358,150,274	342,324,549	31,454,756	26,296,866
1956	401,378,829	355,032,593	343,693,168	30,283,130	26,324,991
1955	390,134,309	350,456,743	333,242,952	33,539,366	26,324,991
1954	391,870,657	343,357,084	323,542,138	31,459,780	26,324,991

Year	Employees		Tons Produced of Products		
	Tropical	Other	Bananas	Cacao	Palm Oil
1963	42,963	9,873	1,217,744	4,886	12,750
1962	39,357	9,945	1,272,043	6,893	10,865
1961	39,690	10,328	1,295,372	6,146	8,389
1960	50,284	9,925	1,282,258	6,614	7,901
1959	65,737	10,079	1,121,669	6,813	7,938
1958	68,982	10,378	1,090,060	4,690	7,849
1957	78,990	11,163	1,117,944	4,661	5,586
1956	83,760	11,142	1,149,420	4,008	5,782
1955	81,670	11,169	1,063,670	4,904	4,275
1954	81,958	10,335	1,077,686	4,929	3,412

1 Preliminary.

2 Plus special charge against income of $8,414,203.

substituted for the original Vaccaro Bros. & Co., and shares became publicly available. The company grew bananas on its own plantation in Honduras and sold them wholly through banana wholesalers and jobbers in the U.S. and Canada.

In 1953, Dr. Joseph S. D'Antoni, son of one of the founders, became president. Under his aegis the company grew from $50 million in sales in 1953 to $63 million in 1961 and $84 million in 1964. During this time the company's operating base was changed from Honduras, Ecuador, Haiti, Guatemala, and Panama to Honduras, Ecuador, and Costa Rica, and the transportation facilities were transformed from an old seven ship company owned fleet to a modern fleet of ten chartered

exhibit 10

STANDARD FRUIT AND STEAMSHIP COMPANY

Major Factors in the U.S. Banana Trade

		1955	1956	1957	1958	1959	1960	1961	1962	1963	1964	Est. 1965
Sales												
Total company in $ millions (all products, all regions)	United	333	344	342	324	313	304	311	320	330	318	380
	Standard	51	51	58	55	54	54	63	69	70	85	97
In thousand tons of bananas shipped to U.S.	United	1,064	1,149	1,118	1,090	1,122	1,282	1,295	1,272	1,218	n.a.	980
	Standard	275	300	354	348	352	368	371	375	426	484	602
	Other	304					460		465			300
U.S. market share % (Estimated)	United	64	62	59	61	58	58	59	49	49	47	51
	Standard	16	17	19	19	18	17	19	23	24	27	32
	Other	20	21	22	20	24	25	22	28	27	26	17
Earnings:												
Pretax in million	United	58.1	54.1	52.6	37.7	20.9	2.9	12.3	16.3	2.4	4.5	30.1
	Standard	6.8	3.1	2.2	(.2)	1.2	(6.6)	1.9	8.1	4.3	6.0	8.1
After tax in $ million	United	33.5	30.3	31.5	22.7	12.1	2.2	8.9	11.0	.5	.7	17.3
	Standard	3.8	2.0	1.6	(.8)	.2	(7.6)	.6	5.7	2.4	3.5	4.5

ships.[3] In November, 1964, Dr. D'Antoni relinquished his duties to Mr. Donald Kirchhoff, who had been executive vice president since 1962, and Dr. D'Antoni remained as chairman of the board.

Over the years, Standard Fruit expanded its operations from Honduras to include Guatemala, Ecuador, Costa Rica, and Nicaragua. In calendar 1965, Standard Fruit had sales of $97.4 million and net earnings of $4.5 million. Although bananas comprised the company's major crop, it had modest additional sales of coconut and grapefruit. Since 1963, Standard had also been experimenting in the growing of pineapples. At the end of 1965, the company owned approximately 700,000 acres in Central and South America. In addition, the company has majority interests in Honduras subsidiaries in the brewing and soft drink field and vegetable oil industry.

Exhibit 11 summarizes operating results for the past ten years. It should be noted that 1961, 1962, and 1963 net profits reflect the substantial loss carry-forward from 1960's disastrous results "caused by low selling prices and an enormous oversupply of bananas." 1963 earnings were considered by management to be somewhat lower than "normal." Exhibits 12 and 13 provide a more complete picture of the company's current financial position.

Mr. Kirchhoff explained 1960's huge loss as follows:

The loss in 1960 was the culmination of problems that the Standard Fruit Company had been dealing with for a number of years. In the main, there were two factors involved.

The first of these was the necessity to switch to a banana variety resistant to Panama Disease, inasmuch as Standard did not have suitable virgin lands to continue Gros Michel production. While the variety selected (Giant Cavendish) was a fine producer and the fruit quality at the plantation was good, these bananas were much more subject to bruise from the handling processes required to get the bananas to market. During the period when Standard first had large quantities of Giant Cavendish (1954–1955) there was a shortage of Gros Michel, and it appeared Cavendish would be a profitable item even in stem form. However, its deficiencies in terms of appearance by the time it reached the consumer were quite obvious.

As Gros Michel production increased from the country of Ecuador, the Cavendish became more and more a marginal commodity on the market. Standard had recognized this problem even when the item was quite profitable and began, in the middle '50's, to experiment with packaging. The eventual result of these experiments was, of course, the cardboard cartons now used

---

[3] On January 3, 1966, Standard Fruit received a new ship, MV Augustenburg, as a replacement for one of its older vessels. This latest addition to the company's refrigerated fleet was 450 feet long, had a cruising speed of 21 knots, and had a deadweight capacity of 7,000 tons when fully loaded (approximately 117,000 boxes). (2,700 gross wt., 2,300 net wt. —banana deadweight.) Four additional larger (3350 gr. tons, 145,000 boxes), faster (23 knots) ships are on order.

exhibit 11

STANDARD FRUIT AND STEAMSHIP COMPANY

Summary of Operating Results, 1955–1965

	1965	1964	1963	1962	1961	1960	1959	1958	1957	1956	1955
Sales of products and services to customers (000)	$97,412	$84,569	$69,763	$68,578	$63,444	$53,888	$54,212	$55,084	$57,766	$51,245	$51,261
Net income (loss) after taxes (000)	4,512	3,537	2,364	5,714	603	(7,750)	234	(833)	1,605	2,039	3,815
Earnings per share—preference stock	49.73	33.30	22.25	53.78	5.67	—	2.20	—	15.11	19.20	35.91
Earnings per share—common stock1	4.55	2.92	1.93	5.10	.27	—	—	—	.95	1.37	3.04
Dividends per share declared—preference stock	4.60	4.20	8.25	2.25	—	1.50	3.00	4.40	5.60	5.60	5.60
Dividends per share—(declared) common stock	.40	.30	—	—	—	—	—	.35	.65	.65	.65
Capital expenditures (000)	3,036	3,873	4,320	2,233	1,648	4,935	3,310	2,799	3,824	3,663	2,692
Net working capital (000)	14,349	16,562	14,442	13,206	10,765	4,134	12,701	12,992	14,225	16,323	16,988
Current ratio	2.9	3.6	3.6	3.1	3.4	1.4	4.4	5.1	4.7	5.6	4.9
Long-term debt (000)	313	563	1,570	646	4,646	—	—	—	—	—	—
Total shareholders' equity (000)	34,100	36,080	33,307	31,619	25,620	27,663	36,056	35,141	36,811	36,489	35,732
Book value per share—common stock2	27.17	23.06	20.44	18.84	13.17	15.10	23.04	22.17	23.75	23.44	22.73
Number of 40 lb. boxes of bananas imported (000)	—	20,128	12,236	12,044	10,069	2,403	29	—	—	—	—
Total bananas imported millions of pounds)	1,204	969	853	750	743	736	704	697	708	599	550

1Computed on net profit after deducting dividends declared (1955-59 and 1964-65) or accrued (1960-1963) on participating preference stock.

2Computed after allowance for redemption price of $110 per share for participating preference stock. (All computations based on number of shares outstanding at end of year.)

throughout the industry. However, it was not until late 1960 that we were able
to begin shipping substantial commercial quantities of packaged bananas.

The other factor was that, during the period of the '50's, the entire banana
industry began to change in Central America, not only due to the inroads of
disease, but also because of the pressures of social legislation, unionization, and
nationalism. The industry, which had been a very profitable but a paternalistic
and somewhat inefficient operation, was not able to abruptly change with these

exhibit 12

STANDARD FRUIT AND STEAMSHIP COMPANY
AND SUBSIDIARY COMPANIES

at January 1, 1966 and January 2, 1965

Assets	1965	1964
Current assets		
Cash	$ 2,702,939	$ 2,651,075
Time certificates of deposit	5,050,000	7,050,000
	$ 7,752,939	$ 9,701,075
Receivables, less allowances for doubtful accounts		
Trade	2,513,299	2,096,053
Other	1,435,544	1,099,070
Inventories, at lower of cost or market	8,893,118	8,769,181
Unterminated voyage expense—net	213,620	265,099
Prepaid expenses	1,183,143	1,120,979
Total current assets	$21,991,663	$23,051,457
Investments and other assets		
Miscellaneous investments, at cost or less	2,108,706	1,667,030
Advances and long-term receivables, less allowances for doubtful accounts	1,405,472	1,285,159
	$ 3,514,178	$ 2,952,189
Fixed assets, at cost		
Land	$ 1,956,464	$ 1,998,073
Cultivations, railroad, buildings, and equipment		
Outside United States	49,294,365	47,778,658
Domestic	1,161,573	1,463,083
	$52,412,402	$51,239,814
Less: amortization and depreciation	30,772,294	29,511,115
	$21,640,108	$21,728,699
Deferred charges	$ 259,652	$ 504,791
Total assets	$47,405,601	$48,237,136

Liabilities and Shareholders' Equity	1965	1964
Current liabilities		
Accounts payable and accrued liabilities	$ 4,848,873	$ 4,595,597
Portion of long-term debt payable within one year	250,000	250,000
Dividends payable	196,762	227,951
Estimated federal and foreign taxes on income less: foreign government securities	2,357,310	1,415,439
Total current liabilities	$ 7,652,945	$ 6,488,987
Long-term debt		
5% note (payable quarterly until 1968)	312,500	562,500
Minority interests in subsidiaries	$ 5,349,756	$ 5,105,419
Shareholders' equity		
Capital		
Cumulative $3 participating preference stock of no par value. Authorized 129,388 shares, issued 106,234 shares	$10,092,230	$10,092,230
Common stock of $2.50 par value. Authorized 1,500,000 shares, issued 1,074,336 shares	2,685,840	2,685,840
Capital in excess of par value of common stock (no change during the year)	3,799,480	3,779,480
	$16,577,550	$16,577,550
Statutory appropriations of foreign earnings	739,422	735,791
Retained earnings	22,428,493	18,786,431
	$39,745,465	$36,099,772
Less: common stock in treasury, at cost, 1965—187,588 shares, 1964—16,518 shares.	4,088,660	19,542
Preference stock in treasury, at cost, 1965—15,520 shares, 1964—none	1,556,405	
	$34,100,400	$36,080,230
Commitments and contingent liabilities		
Total liabilities and net worth	$47,405,601	$48,237,136

new developments. As a consequence, it was possible for anyone to purchase bananas—Gros Michel bananas, the more preferred variety at that time—in Ecuador at a lower cost than either of the large companies could produce bananas for in Central America. These purchases required little or no investment. Therefore, 1960, the last year of substantial imports of stem Cavendish bananas, found the Standard Fruit Company with a high cost product that was unable to compete successfully in the market place with the lower cost Ecuador Gros Michel.

The development of the box and the introduction of more efficient methods in the producing divisions was the answer which resulted in the change in our profit picture.

exhibit 13

STANDARD FRUIT AND STEAMSHIP COMPANY
AND SUBSIDIARY COMPANIES

	1965	*1964*
Sales of products and services to customers	$97,412,495	$84,569,442
Amortization, depreciation, and abandonment of fixed assets	2,800,301	2,590,849
All other operating costs and expenses	86,798,122	76,282,701
	89,598,423	78,873,550
Operating income	7,814,072	5,695,892
Other income—net of other expenses	302,582	289,960
	8,116,654	5,985,852
Estimated federal and foreign taxes on income	2,872,000	1,805,000
	5,244,654	4,180,852
Minority interests in net income of subsidiaries	733,123	643,788
Net income for the year	$ 4,511,531	$ 3,537,064

Standard Fruit's Foreign Facilities

In the 1890's, when the Vaccaro Brothers began operation, most activities were based in Honduras. Today, Honduras is still the company's most important banana growing area. In 1965, the total acreage owned and leased by Standard Fruit in Honduras was 250,000 acres, most of which was undeveloped. Eleven and a half thousand acres were under banana cultivation, 3,800 were devoted to coconut production, 400 were being used for citrus crops, and 12,000 acres were devoted to livestock pasture.

In addition to agricultural activities, Standard holds interests in a number of other enterprises in Honduras. The company owns and operates: a 300 mile diesel railroad; power and telephone facilities; dairies and ranches; 64% of a major beer and soft drink bottler; 51% of a soap, lard, and vegetable oil plant; and 88% of a corrugated box plant. The Honduras operations employ a total of 6,000 people, 97% of whom are Honduran nationals.

In 1956, Standard Fruit began operations in Costa Rica. In 1965, 5,000 acres were under cultivation for production of bananas and 2,000 people were employed. In addition, Standard also had a 34% interest in a corrugated box plant in Costa Rica. Whereas in Honduras the historical situation has required Standard to supply all housing, transportation, storekeeping, and other services, the company's more recent entry into Costa Rica has not required the same degree of company performed services.

The third major source of Standard Fruit bananas has been open market purchases in Ecuador. During the past 15 years, Standard Fruit has augmented its own production with purchases from independent banana growers. In 1965, one-half of total Standard Fruit sales of bananas was purchased in Ecuador, and half came from company owned plantations in Honduras and Costa Rica.

Ecuadorian activities were handled by 75 employees, concerned mainly with helping the local growers in technical growing problems, and in packing bananas in boxes. Standard has helped set up more than 100 banana boxing plants in Ecuador and has established nonexclusive contracts with many Ecuadorian growers. These contracts provide a working relationship between the exporter and the grower, but bind neither to any specified volume or price.

Standard Fruit and Steamship Company operates a wholly owned subsidiary, the Standard Fruit Company, which conducts all of its business activities in Central and South America. This subsidiary is incorporated as a Western Hemisphere Trade Corporation. As such, it has a U.S. tax rate of up to 14% less than the normal corporate tax rate. In order to qualify for this treatment, the Western Hemisphere Trade Corporation must transact all business in the Western Hemisphere (including the West Indies and Puerto Rico but *excluding* Hawaii); it must have 90% of gross income derived from the "active conduct of a trade or business"; and 95% of its gross income (over a three year period) must be derived from sources outside the U.S. This final definition is complicated, and transfer prices and other qualifications must be established with the approval of the Internal Revenue Service.

Over the years, Standard Fruit has had operations in other parts of Central America, but has discontinued these plantations because of heavy damage from Panama Disease or wind storms. The company also has holdings of 400,000 acres in Nicaragua. However, land ownership in Central and South America does not imply values in any way similar to those in the U.S., since more than two-thirds of the land in these areas is jungle or mountainous area, not put to any productive use.

Mr. Robert H. Smith, vice president in charge of all banana growing operations, felt that there were a number of things that Standard Fruit could do to improve its competitive position. He felt his department's efforts should be concentrated on:

1. Increasing the percentage of Giant Cavendish variety in the over-all mix of bananas being imported.
2. Reducing spoilage in boxing and handling.
3. Increasing labor efficiency.
4. Beginning heavier rebuilding of soils to combat declining land efficiency.
5. Increasing the percentage of purchased bananas in Central America, as contrasted with bananas grown on company plantations.

6. Increasing the percentage of local nationals employed in each major location.
7. Decreasing dependence on Ecuador as a source of bananas.

Mr. Smith indicated that this program should reduce average banana procurement costs. He felt it would also decrease the company's dependence on any one country for supply, and thus improve Standard Fruit's relations with the governments of other Central and South American countries.

Mr. Smith and the other members of his production management group take an active role in plantation management and keep abreast of growing developments throughout Central and South America. Research and development facilities in Honduras, Costa Rica, and at corporate headquarters in New Orleans have enabled Standard Fruit to lead in many of the recent technical developments in the banana industry. For example, the Standard research group, as indicated earlier, was responsible for the commercial development of the Giant Cavendish banana for the North American market, which has proved to be not only more resistant to Panama Disease and wind damage, but also more productive than the previously predominant Gros Michel. This group also developed and introduced the concepts and techniques for precooling and boxing bananas, a concept which has revolutionized industry practice.

Transporting Bananas

In past years, Standard Fruit owned its own ships, and was continually battling high cost, inefficiency, and obsolescence. Today the company charters its entire fleet of ships, under terms of one to five years. These ships, with an average age of approximately two years, comprise one of the most modern and efficient refrigerated fleets in the world. All of these ships in this fleet are approximately the same size, designed for maximum flexibility in choice of routes and for ease of cargo handling. The logistics of ship movements depend heavily on regularity of discharge in the United States and Canada, and supply factors on company owned plantations in Central America.

Standard's fleet of ships unloads principally at three company terminals at: New York City, servicing the East and Northeast; Long Beach, California, servicing the 11 Western states; and New Orleans, servicing the Middle West and South. Each terminal is equipped with specially designed gantries, conveyors, and other material handling equipment to provide efficient unloading of the banana cargo. Discharges are also regularly scheduled at Newark, N.J., Baltimore, Md., and Gulfport, Miss., at other than company operated facilities. Strikes and other unusual circumstances occasionally necessitate docking in other ports, but virtually all "normal" volume proceeds through the abovementioned terminals.

Most of the import requirements of the Honduras plantations are carried on company ships. However, the ships to Costa Rica always return empty, since any ship carrying general cargo must wait its turn at the limited dock facility of the major port. This frequently takes more than three days.

Marketing

Traditionally, there have been three levels of distribution for bananas in the United States. The first level is composed of the eight or nine banana importers, the most important of which are United Fruit and Standard. These importers, in turn, have sold their cargos directly to a group of specialized banana jobbers, who maintained the handling, ripening, and storage facilities necessary to transform green bananas to saleable produce. The jobbers then sold the ripened bananas to the third level of distribution, the retail grocery stores. The advent of plantation boxing, together with the steady growth of grocery chains, has tended to reduce the jobber's activity. In 1965, 32% of bananas imported into the U.S. were sold directly to chains.

While jobbers remain the principal customers of the importers, Standard has tended to concentrate on direct selling to the chains, who in 1965 accounted for 44% of the total U.S. grocery volume. Of the 957 buyers who purchased bananas directly in 1965, more than 500 were served by Standard Fruit. This concentration has followed naturally from Standard's boxing program, terminal construction, and specialized organization to help customers perform their own ripening.

The sale of a banana cargo generally is negotiated while the ship is still at sea. Terms are usually F.O.B. port of discharge, with the customer taking responsibility for subsequent shipping, ripening, and distribution. From the time the bananas leave the plantation, they are held at a constant 56 degree temperature, under controlled humidity conditions. Under these conditions, the ripening cycle, using catalytic gas such as ethylene, generally takes about 18 days from the time the bananas were harvested. However, by varying temperature, ripening can be accelerated or retarded by five days either way. Once ripe, bananas have a shelf life of only three to four days in the grocery store. Since none of the importing companies accept product returns, it is incumbent upon the customer to monitor the process carefully in order to prevent spoilage. Prior to plantation boxing, elaborate inspection techniques and extensive controlled environments were necessary. Few retailers were willing to incur the additional expense, risk, and handling, and relied on jobbers for processing. Boxing, however, has greatly reduced these requirements, and Standard has concentrated on giving the chain operators the technical support necessary to perform the ripening function themselves.

Standard Fruit maintains 30 sales offices in the United States and Canada to serve their customers. Salesmen, in cars equipped with two-way radios, cover daily all the major outlets in the country. These men provide technical service to the customer and also keep Standard Fruit management apprised of developing market conditions throughout the country. This timely information is used to direct ship movements so as to take maximum advantage of market opportunities.

Standard Fruit's marketing head, R. Bruce Paschal, has described bananas as a "commodity which can be differentiated only to a moderate extent by quality." Consequently, he has operated on the basis that "the only way to build sales volume without cutting prices is to provide service to the customer." Thus,

Standard Fruit's marketing approach has been one of helping the grocer with all of the problems he faces in the marketing of bananas. It was this basic desire that fostered the boxed banana program. In this program, which is more costly on a per pound basis than bananas sold on the stem, Standard Fruit was able to prove that the increased cost was more than offset by subsequent savings in handling, ripening, and net saleable product.

Standard's salesmen maintain daily contact with all principal accounts. These salesmen are knowledgeable and equipped to help solve any problem that may arise in banana handling and ripening. In addition to this on-the-spot problem solving, Standard Fruit runs clinics for customers on banana processing and marketing techniques. In 1964, the company conducted a total of 150 such clinics. This service by technically qualified Standard Fruit employees begins with the design and operation of customer ripening rooms, and covers the entire gamut of grocery store produce management through final display and promotional efforts.

When the boxing program was first introduced, sales efforts were concentrated on demonstrating the cost savings to the customer through use of boxed bananas. Since United Fruit has followed in converting to box packs, Standard has lost this differentiation, but continues to instruct customers as to the best methods for handling and merchandising bananas. Since most grocers maintain buying relationships with more than one source of supply, Standard's attempts to build customer loyalty have centered on providing these technical services, as well as on providing certainty of supply in times of high demand and low availability.

Although United Fruit has been branding its bananas since 1963, Standard Fruit management have not been enthusiastic about following such a program. In the early 1960's, Standard Fruit made market tests of branded bananas. The results of these tests showed banana sales increasing initially, but beginning to tail off and return to their former level after about one month's sales. They argue further that although United has achieved some indicated success with their "Chiquita" brand, Standard is not in a comparable position to support the advertising necessary to develop a national brand franchise. While Mr. Paschal has been negative on the placing of stickers on each banana, Standard is investigating the future possibility of marketing "hands" of bananas in labeled plastic bags. At present such "shrink films" are too expensive to make this method attractive, but Mr. Paschal is quick to point out that the cost of such new packaging techniques is being reduced each year. Standard Fruit does, however, brand the boxes in which the bananas are shipped to the grocer with their trade names—"Cabana" and "Tropipac." This branding is viewed as taking advantage of extensive relationships with grocers, without requiring extensive consumer promotion.

Coordination of Production, Shipping, and Sales

Coordination (or scheduling) of production, shipping, and marketing of the highly perishable bananas is a continuous operation. Many people were involved in Latin America, in the marketing system, and in New Orleans, where the information flow was centered. Weekly production estimates from company owned plantations in Honduras and Costa Rica formed the basis of the schedule, or short-term operating plan. These were related to the company's normal pattern of six major unloadings per week in the U.S. (usually two in New York, three in New Orleans, and one in Long Beach) as well as for European requirements. Then the tentative volume of additional fruit, to be purchased and shipped from Ecuador, was determined. Expected market conditions were relayed daily from sales offices, and determined final volumes.

According to Mr. D. W. Furbee, company controller, the schedule was laid out to optimize short-term profit. Once determined, it was immediately relayed to all of the people involved. Many factors, such as bad weather at sea, delays in port, or productivity changes, could require several schedule changes within a single day. Full ship utilization, both from the point of view of time and capacity, was a constant goal. However, market conditions and varying Central American production at times precluded 100% utilization of the fleet of ten ships.

It was considered very important by company management that persons making day to day scheduling decisions had current knowledge of the operating conditions and limitations in the various areas affected. The members of management traveled extensively, constantly keeping abreast of changing circumstances, both in company operations and in industry conditions. Such information was also mandatory for longer-range planning and for modification of previously made plans.

Mr. Furbee has made an extensive analysis of all components of costs of the banana business which breaks down each part of the costs of goods sold into its fixed and variable components. Since the company's agricultural commitment is much larger in a country such as Honduras, where all bananas come from company owned plantations, than it is in Ecuador, where the entire supply is purchased from independent growers, the fixed cost of a banana cargo varies considerably for different sources of supply. These differences are partially offset by adding in shipping costs, which, because of the necessity to operate the fleet at close to full utilization, must be considered as relatively fixed. After including all costs from plantation through marketing, Mr. Furbee indicated sizeable differences from country to country, with Honduras having variable costs of 26%, Costa Rica 40%, and Ecuador 70%. With this kind of analysis, Mr. Furbee was able to indicate average operating margins and anticipated incremental profit or loss resulting from each purchase–shipping–marketing decision.

Because of the importance of bananas to the economy of the major producing countries, the company is obliged to spend much time in government relations. National governments are often very volatile. In one year, the governments of two of the three countries providing bananas to Standard Fruit underwent complete changes. During Standard Fruit's history, it has witnessed 55 revolutions in Honduras alone. Operating under such conditions requires that Standard's management keep fully appraised of political developments in Central and South America. In addition, the company is seeking more diversification in banana sources, in order to reduce its heavy dependence on a single country, such as Ecuador. It is also increasing the participation and ownership by nationals in the plantations and other activities which Standard Fruit operates, in order to make the company's involvement in these countries more desirable to the governments and their people. In areas other than Ecuador, Standard has been setting up responsible farmers as independent banana growers, under ten year fixed price contracts, with Standard providing agricultural assistance.

The Outlook for the Future

In developing projections of future sales and earnings, management has forecast a number of industry trends. Principal among these are the conclusions that: 1) average unit revenues will decrease by about 1¢ per box each year from the present average price; 2) direct plantation costs will tend to decrease slightly, as the result of improved practices over the next five years; 3) shipping costs will decline slightly; 4) costs of operating terminals in the U.S. will remain approximately the same; 5) unit marketing, general, and administrative costs will decline slightly. Based upon these assumptions, total costs per box are estimated to decline over the next five years by approximately 4.5%, while revenues per box decline by approximately 1%. Assuming that Standard can hold its present market share, the company's U.S. sales are estimated to grow by about 10% over the next five years, while earnings are expected to grow at about 10% per year. After tax earnings of approximately $1.2 million each year from the nonbanana subsidiaries in Honduras and Costa Rica, which have been included in past earnings reports, are expected to continue at about the same level.

By 1970, Standard Fruit also expects to have penetrated markets in Europe and Japan. Entering the European market is expected to be very difficult, since European banana wholesalers have strongly resisted inroads by new participants in the past. However, Standard was able to establish a working relationship with a group of Western European wholesalers in November, 1964, and hopes to be able to expand these activities. United Fruit Company has preceded Standard in European marketing and, as of 1965, United Fruit had approximately 40% of that portion of the market which was not committed politically to a particular source of supply. Standard Fruit management feel that the introduction of higher quality bananas by Standard Fruit will be well received, which, when combined with the kind of service which Standard is presently offering in the U.S., will help them to develop strong relationships with the European banana wholesalers and distributors. Management's goal for 1966 is for Standard Fruit to have developed sufficient business to justify one shipment per week to Europe. It is anticipated that this area could add approximately $500,000 to company profits by 1970.

The company views the Japanese market as grossly undersupplied, and believes that it will be important to develop a source of bananas for Japanese consumption somewhere in the South Pacific. Currently, management is contemplating the possibility of growing bananas in the Philippines.[4]

Present management feels that the most the company will ever be able to earn from the banana business is about $10 million per year after taxes. Therefore, Standard Fruit has begun developing alternative sources of revenue, in addition to their diversified activities in Honduras. They are presently growing coconuts, grapefruit, and pineapple. Indications are that coconuts probably will not offer great profit opportunities, but that grapefruit and pineapple may contribute significantly. Grapefruit grown in Honduras is presently being exported to Europe. Experimental cultivation of pineapple in Honduras was started in the early 1960's. Commercial plans for production have not yet been solidified, but management feels that, by 1970, pineapple sales might contribute an additional ½ to ¾ million dollars of profit.

Integration with Castle & Cooke

In September of 1965, Castle & Cooke increased its ownership in Standard Fruit to 84%. Mr. Kirchhoff spoke of many opportunities for integration between Standard Fruit and Castle & Cooke, utilizing Standard Fruit's assets and specific competences, and listed five key areas in which he felt Standard Fruit could contribute to Castle & Cooke.

1. Standard Fruit's marketing group for distribution of perishable commodities is second to none.
2. Standard maintains an excellent staff of trained agriculturalists and agricultural researchers.
3. Standard has lands and facilities in labor surplus areas which are close to major world markets.
4. Standard Fruit's steamship company has both the knowledge and facilities for transporting cargos. Standard Fruit is presently shipping bananas northbound and has excess space for other cargos southbound. It may be possible that Standard shipping services can be combined with Castle & Cooke shipping needs.
5. Standard Fruit offers representation in Latin America. We can distribute products to this market of 275 million people, thus offering substantial growth opportunities. Our existing good government relations are essential for success in such endeavors.

---

[4] In early 1966, Standard Fruit committed $7.5 million to establish a banana plantation on Mindanao, the Philippines, several miles from Dolfil. This includes $2 million which was planned for a box manufacturing plant to support the plantation.

appendix A

United Fruit Indicates It Had 4th Period Net,
Against Year-Ago Loss [1]

Year's Profit and Sales Spurted;
Cost-Cutting Program is Cited;
Further Gain Forecast for '66

United Fruit Co. earned an indicated $4,135,000, or 52 cents a share, on indicated sales of $98,293,000 in the fourth quarter of 1965.

In the like 1964 quarter the company had an indicated loss of $1,370,000 on indicated sales of $78,598,000. Indicated results are obtained by subtracting nine-month from full-year figures.

The banana producer and shipper reported net income for the year of $17,-268,000, or $2.17 a share, on sales of $379,851,000. In 1964 United Fruit had net operating income of $705,000, or 9 cents per share, on sales of $333,415,000. It also had nonrecurring income of $444,779, or 6 cents a share, in 1964.

A substantial part of the gain in earnings is attributable to an expense reduction program, said John M. Fox, president. "We look for continued cost improvement in 1966, although we can't expect to show as much improvement this year as we did last," he said. He declined to predict sales or earnings for 1966.

Other factors cited by United Fruit in the 1965 gain: The company grew more bananas in 1965 and consequently had to purchase fewer to supply customers, and its shipments weren't lowered by a maritime strike as they were in the summer of 1964. The increase of $46,436,000 in sales resulted from increased volume in North America and Europe, Mr. Fox said. Banana prices in the fourth quarter of the year averaged about 7% below a year earlier.

The company continues to increase plantings of the Valery banana, a low-growing variety that resists disease and wind damage. Mr. Fox said about 55% of the company's Central American banana acreage now is planted to the Valery type, and the company expects an increase to about 65% during this year.

United Fruit will be prepared to present a plan of divesture to the Federal court of Louisiana by June 30 under terms of an anti-trust consent decree signed with the Justice Department, Mr. Fox said. Under the terms of the decree United Fruit is to divest itself of enough assets to set up a competitor.

---

[1] From *The Wall Street Journal*, February 9, 1966, p. 10. Reprinted with permission of the publisher.

UNITED FRUIT CO. AND SUBSIDIARIES

Preliminary report for the year ended Dec. 31:

	1965	1964	1963
Earned per share	$2.17	a-$.09	a-$.06
Net sales	379,851,000	333,415,000	329,910,481
Taxes	12,875,000	3,800,000	1,975,000
Net income	17,268,000	a705,000	a-458,298
Capital shares	7,960,925	8,022,925	8,022,925

a-Excludes nonrecurring profit from sale of tropical properties of $444,779, or 6 cents a share, in 1964, and $1,115,882, or 14 cents a share, in 1963.

appendix B

"A Winning Streak in the Banana Game" [1]

*President John Fox's First Year as Chief
is United Fruit's Best in Seven*

. . . the company completes the best year since 1958 when sales of $324,-000,000 produced net of $22,700,000 or $2.60 a share. In the first nine months of 1965 sales rose 10% while net vaulted to $1.65 a share from 26¢.

Comparisons for the whole year should prove even more favorable because, president Fox declares, for the first time in three years "we don't expect to lose any money in the fourth quarter." But as for specific results in the final quarter, which "has been such a horror down through the years," John Fox will only say "its going all right." Some Wall Street pundits reckon 1965 earnings as high as $2.

At any rate, the final tally will undoubtedly be a tidy recovery from 1964 earnings of $700,000 or 9¢ a share, realized on sales of $333,000,000. The previous year was worse—an alltime low of 6¢ a share on roughly the same volume. To contrast with a happier time, back in 1950 UF earned $7.49 a share on $312,000,000 sales.

The 1965 fruits are hardly the result of one year's labors. The company began to revamp its operations in 1959 when Thomas Elbert Sunderland, formerly

---

[1] From *Investor's Reader* (New York: Merrill Lynch, Pierce, Fenner, & Smith, Inc., January 5, 1966), pp. 13-15, reprinted with permission of the publisher.

legal vice president of Standard Oil of Indiana, took over as UF president and chief executive. Sunderland, now chairman, brought John Fox into the company in 1961, shortly after Coca-Cola bought Minute Maid which Fox had headed.

When John Fox joined UF in 1961, it had just begun planting the newly developed Valery banana which is resistant to Panama Disease, one of the tropical scourges which, along with blowdowns and competition, have laid UF profits low for a dozen years.

One of John Fox's first projects was to develop a box in which Valery bananas could be shipped from Central and South America, since they have thinner skins and more brittle stems than other varieties. Consequently they do not ship well on the stem as bananas have always been shipped. UF Valery bananas are now packed in boxes which are actually easier for wholesalers to handle and make possible branding of fruit.

UF labels all its first-class fruit "Chiquita." The proportion of fruit arriving at market which qualifies for this label has risen to 92% of total sales in 1965 from as low as 70% a few years ago. In consequence, John Fox allows, UF gets "a little better prices" than others since it is known for dependably supplying first-class fruit.

In addition, Valery plants have a shorter growing cycle and can be planted closer together. As a result Valery-planted acreage yields 2-to-2½ times as much fruit as land planted with older varieties.

John Fox estimates 54% of UF's own production in 1965 was from Valery plants. He expects the proportion to rise to around 66% in '66. UF buys about half the fruit it sells from independent producers.

FORCED PEELING

Under a consent decree United Fruit must have a plan in the hands of the Justice Department by mid-1966 to divest itself of assets capable of producing 9,000,000 stems of bananas annually. John Fox reveals he would prefer to sell the assets outright for cash rather than spin them off as a separate company.

The improvement in 1965 results was due to a number of factors besides better bananas. John Fox says "the second most important factor has been the general over-all tightening up of operations and improvement of efficiency" under the direction of executive vp Herbert Cornuelle who came to UF in 1963 from the presidency of Dole Corp.

In addition, John Fox allows, "it was a year in which the breaks of the business went our way." During the stevedore strike early in the year UF was able to obtain injunctions to unload fruit and avoid losses. "It was the first time a strike of that nature hasn't crippled the company." Then in 1965 maritime strike "hit our competition badly during the summer. Our contract had a different termination date. We were in operation during the whole period."

STEADIER COSTS

Also, "weather has been in our favor. We have not been hit as severely by blow-downs. What has happened in 1965 is that our costs have gone down faster than the price structure." Asked if he feels the year's margins were about as good as they can get, John Fox replies: "Not by any means. I think we can do better."

One of the chief executive's great hopes is to find ways to raise per capita consumption of bananas which already account for 1% of total grocery store sales and 10% of produce department sales. He cracks: "What I'd like to find is something that has the sock to it that Vitamin C has."

While John Fox is interested in further diversification of the company which already produces sugar, vegetable oil, cocoa and freeze-dried foods and is engaged in the cargo and communications business, he maintains: "Our position in the world market is so strong we will be with bananas for the rest of time. Our interest is to superimpose other businesses on this one. It's not an easy thing to use as a building block."

HEAVY RESERVES

However, UF is financially well-fixed to make acquisitions. President Fox estimates cash reserves to be "at least $50,000,000, probably more." In the last several years the company has been spending some of its cash to reacquire common stock. In 1963 it acquired 426,000 shares through a tender offer; in 1965 it bought another 63,000 on the open market.

The nearly 8,000,000 shares still outstanding trade on the Big Board right around the 1965 high of 28, up from 16 earlier in the year and nearly twice the alltime low registered in 1960. The stock's record high of 73⅝ was reached in 1951 before Panama Disease, the weather man, a sudden jump in Ecuadorian banana production, and the Justice Department began pinching UF's profits.

Bumble Bee Seafoods, Inc.

Bumble Bee Seafoods is one of the four largest seafood packers in the United States. In fiscal 1965, it earned a pretax $2.8
million on revenues of $34 million, and showed a net worth
of $17.4 million. Sales of canned albacore (white meat) tuna
generated almost two-thirds of 1965 total sales, while canned
Pacific salmon sales accounted for about one-fourth. The
remainder came primarily from sales of canned light meat
tuna, crabmeat, pet food, and shrimp, and from direct sales
of fresh and frozen seafood products.

Bumble Bee Seafoods was merged into Castle & Cooke in
1961, as the culmination of a relationship beginning in 1956.
In 1965, Bumble Bee accounted for 15.5% of Castle & Cooke
sales, 15.8% of the parent's pretax earnings, and 16.3% of
total corporate net worth. Mr. Thomas F. Sandoz, chairman
of the board, and Mr. John McGowan, Bumble Bee's president, directed company affairs from headquarters in Astoria,
Oregon.

THE WORLD FISHING INDUSTRY

The fishing industry provides one of the world's basic food
sources. Exhibit 1 summarizes the volumes and sources of
the world fish supply, as of 1962. As indicated, the principal
fishing areas of the world were located in the northwestern
Pacific, near Japan; in the northeastern Atlantic; and in the
East-Central Pacific, off the coast of Peru.

Exhibts 2 and 3 show the changes in recent years of the
worldwide distributions among fishing areas and among the
types of fish caught. Japan remains the largest fish producing
nation in the world, and its catch has increased substantially
over this period. Since 1958, however, Peruvian production
has grown enormously, primarily in herring and sardines for
grinding into fish meals and solubles. Similar gains are shown
for Red China.

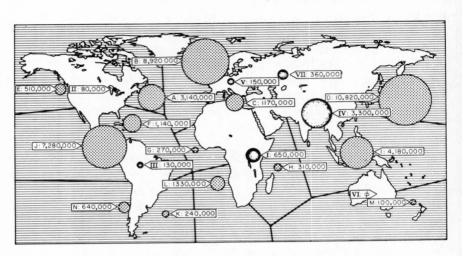

MARINE AREAS ⊛	FRESHWATER AREAS ◯
Atlantic, Northwestern . . . . A	Africa I
Atlantic, Northeastern . . . . B	America, North II
Mediterranean and Black Sea C	America, South III
Pacific, Northwestern . . . . D	Asia IV
Pacific, Northeastern . . . . E	Europe V
Atlantic, Western–Central . . . . F	Oceania VI
Atlantic, Eastern–Central . . . . G	U.S.S.R. VII
Indian Ocean, Western . . . . H	
Indo-Pacific Area I	
Pacific, Eastern–Central . . . . J	
Atlantic, Southwestern . . . . K	
Atlantic, Southeastern L	
Pacific, Southwestern . . . . M	
Pacific, Southeastern . . . . N	

Source: FAO Yearbook of Fisheries Statistics (1962).

Exhibit 3 shows that world catches of fish varieties other than herring and sardines increased only modestly during the 1956–1962 period. The catch of tuna and similar species has increased gradually to 2.2 million tons, but still accounted for only about 5% of the 44 million metric tons of 1962 world fish production. Only 500,000 tons (1.1%) of salmon and related species were landed in 1962, down slightly from 1956.

As shown in Exhibit 4, most of the fish catch was consumed fresh (36%),

exhibit 2

BUMBLE BEE SEAFOODS, INC.

**Catch of Fish, Crustaceans, Mollusks, etc.
(for the six largest producing countries)**

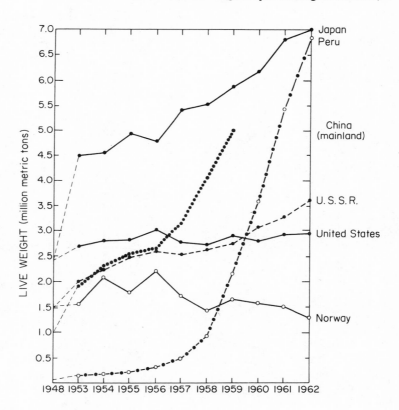

Source: FAO Yearbook of Fisheries Statistics (1962).

frozen (9%), or cured (17%) form; 27% was reduced to meal for fertilizer. Only 9% of the annual catch was canned each year over the 1957–1962 period.

Exhibit 5 shows that herring, sardines, and anchovies comprised the largest volume group of canned fish in 1962, about 500,000 metric tons (12.5%) out of a 4 million ton total. Canned tuna represented 400,000 tons (10%), while canned salmon amounted to 160,000 tons (4%).

Exhibit 6 shows total U.S. production of canned seafoods for the 1958–1963 period. As can be seen, tuna was by far the most important product in the U.S. pack (52% of 1963 total), followed by salmon (25%) and various shellfish

exhibit 3

BUMBLE BEE SEAFOODS, INC.

Catch of Fish, Crustaceans, Mollusks, etc.
(by groups of species)

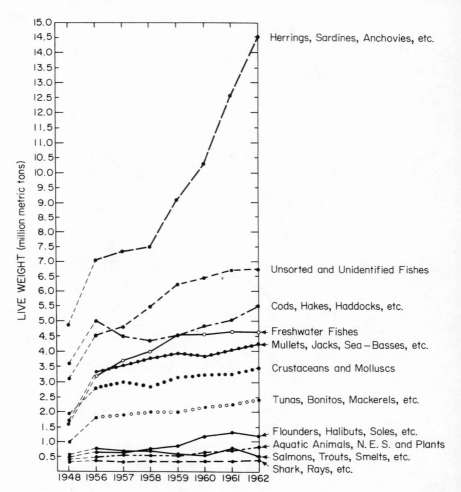

Source: FAO Yearbook of Fisheries Statistics (1962).

(17%). Of the U.S. tuna pack, about one-third was sold as "white meat" (albacore), while two-thirds was "light meat" (bluefin, skipjack, yellowfin). 70% of the white meat albacore was sold as solid pack, while more than 90% of the light meat tuna was sold in flake or chunk form. Almost all salmon was sold as solid pack, with "pink salmon" (hump back, chum) comprising about 75% of the catch, and "red salmon" (chinook, sockeye, coho) about 25%.

exhibit 4

BUMBLE BEE SEAFOODS, INC.

Disposition of World Catch

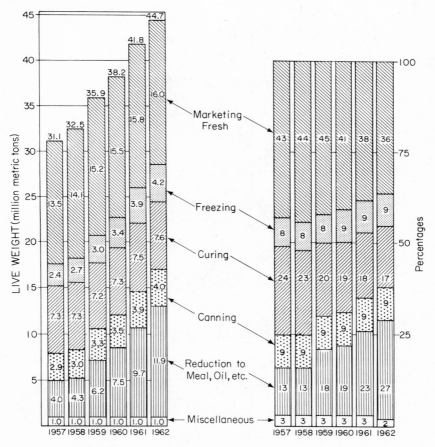

Source: FAO Yearbook of Fisheries Statistics (1962).

Comparison of year to year data for the pack of different fish varieties demonstrates one of the most perplexing problems which faces canners and marketers of seafood. Sizeable fluctuations occur in the size of the annual catch, and thus, the volumes canned (e.g., Pacific Pilchard available for packing dropped from 46,000 tons in 1958 to less than 2,000 tons in 1963). Not only do these great changes in available volume create sharp price fluctuations from year to year, but they also create great uncertainty as to whether adequate quantities of each kind of fish can be supplied to the consuming public on a continuous basis.

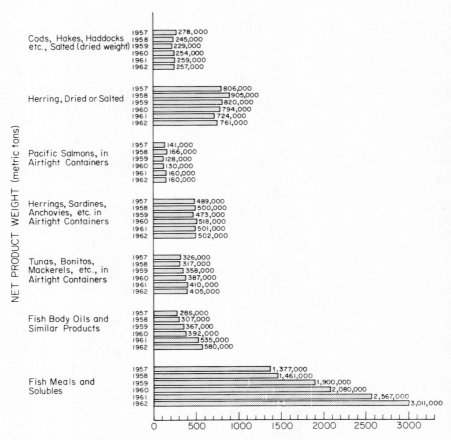

NET PRODUCT WEIGHT (metric tons)

Cods, Hakes, Haddocks etc., Salted (dried weight)
- 1957: 278,000
- 1958: 245,000
- 1959: 229,000
- 1960: 254,000
- 1961: 259,000
- 1962: 257,000

Herring, Dried or Salted
- 1957: 806,000
- 1958: 905,000
- 1959: 820,000
- 1960: 794,000
- 1961: 724,000
- 1962: 761,000

Pacific Salmons, in Airtight Containers
- 1957: 141,000
- 1958: 166,000
- 1959: 128,000
- 1960: 130,000
- 1961: 160,000
- 1962: 160,000

Herrings, Sardines, Anchovies, etc. in Airtight Containers
- 1957: 489,000
- 1958: 500,000
- 1959: 473,000
- 1960: 518,000
- 1961: 501,000
- 1962: 502,000

Tunas, Bonitos, Mackerels, etc., in Airtight Containers
- 1957: 326,000
- 1958: 317,000
- 1959: 358,000
- 1960: 387,000
- 1961: 410,000
- 1962: 405,000

Fish Body Oils and Similar Products
- 1957: 286,000
- 1958: 307,000
- 1959: 367,000
- 1960: 392,000
- 1961: 535,000
- 1962: 580,000

Fish Meals and Solubles
- 1957: 1,377,000
- 1958: 1,461,000
- 1959: 1,900,000
- 1960: 2,080,000
- 1961: 2,567,000
- 1962: 3,011,000

0   500   1000   1500   2000   2500   3000

Source: FAO Yearbook of Fisheries Statistics (1962).

Exhibit 7 shows the source and volume of U.S. imports of each type of canned fish over the same period, and Exhibit 8 shows U.S. exports. Domestic canned seafood consumption, which has been equal to the pack available, is summarized in Exhibit 9. Total U.S. per capita consumption of canned seafood has remained relatively constant at about 4.2 pounds per year over this period, as has consumption of fresh and frozen seafood at about 5.9 pounds per year.

Comparing Exhibit 9 with Exhibit 5 also shows that the U.S. ordinarily consumes a little more than half of the world supply of canned salmon and nearly

exhibit 6

BUMBLE BEE SEAFOODS, INC.

**U.S. Production of Canned Seafoods
(thousand metric tons)**

	1958	1959	1960	1961	1962	1963
Pacific salmon						
Alaska	64.7	38.7	57.7	69.9	75.6	57.7
Red (Chinook, sockeye, coho)	14.0	15.8	28.1	31.1	19.7	14.1
Pink (chum, pink)	50.7	22.9	29.6	38.8	55.9	43.6
Oregon and Washington	16.4	14.8	5.6	10.4	7.0	13.8
Red (chinook, sockeye, coho)	12.9	7.1	4.4	6.3	4.5	4.8
Pink (chum, pink)	4.5	7.7	1.2	4.1	2.5	9.0
Herring, sardines, anchovy	68.5	34.1	33.8	17.6	25.8	18.6
Pilchard	46.2	15.5	12.6	9.6	3.0	1.2
Herring	22.3	18.6	21.2	8.0	22.8	17.4
Tuna, bonito, skipjack	122.9	124.6	132.7	141.9	152.5	148.8
Albacore (solid)	18.9	20.8	24.5	24.5	26.2	33.7
(flakes, chunks)	7.4	7.6	12.6	10.6	14.6	15.1
Lightmeat (solid)	13.1	11.7	9.4	10.4	13.7	6.2
(flakes, chunks)	75.6	77.5	86.0	94.9	97.7	93.2
Bonito and others	7.9	7.0	.2	1.5	.3	.6
Crustaceans and mollusks	35.9	40.3	35.6	39.3	43.6	48.5
Crab	1.4	1.4	2.0	2.4	2.7	3.6
Shrimp	6.6	6.4	6.4	4.3	6.1	7.4
Lobster	.1	.2	.2	.2	.2	.2
Conch and clam	20.0	19.4	21.4	24.0	25.7	27.1
Oysters	5.4	5.9	5.3	5.8	5.6	6.5
Squid						
Total U.S. canned						
seafood production	308.4	252.5	265.4	279.1	304.5	287.4

Source: FAO Yearbook of Fisheries Statistics, 1963.

half of the canned tuna, but only about 10% of the world's canned herring, sardines, and anchovies.

Much of U.S. tuna production utilizes both domestic fresh tuna and imported frozen tuna as its raw material. This frozen tuna, mostly from Japanese sources, is not shown in the U.S. import figures (Exhibit 7) since it is processed by domestic fish canners and is included as U.S. production.

The large volume of frozen fish and the small volume of canned seafoods imported into this country can be attributed in some measure to the tariff structure. Tariffs range from no duty on fresh and frozen tuna to 12.5% ad valorem for canned tuna in brine and 35% on canned tuna packed in oil. Should the importation of canned tuna in brine in any year exceed 20% of the previous year's U.S. pack, the duty on the excess would increase to 25%.

exhibit 7

BUMBLE BEE SEAFOODS, INC.

U.S. Canned Seafood Imports from Country Indicated
(thousand metric tons)

	1958	1959	1960	1961	1962	1963
Pacific salmon						
Canada	4.4	.6	.4	.9	.9	.2
Japan	—	.7	—	—	—	—
Total salmon	4.4	1.3	.4	.9	.9	.2
Herring, sardines, anchovy						
South and South West Africa (pilchard)	.7	.2	1.7	4.1	4.9	3.5
Canada (sea herring, kipper snacks)	.2	.2	.4	.5	.5	.5
Denmark (herring, sardines, anchovy, sprats)	.5	.7	.7	1.5	1.6	.5
Norway (herring, sardines, sprats)	8.6	8.8	9.0	10.4	12.1	9.8
Portugal and Spain (pilchard, anchovy)	6.0	6.4	6.5	7.1	7.3	6.1
United Kingdom (herring)	.4	.7	.6	1.0	1.0	.6
Total herring, sardine, anchovy	16.4	17.0	18.9	24.6	27.4	21.0
Tuna, bonito, skipjack						
Peru (tuna, bonito—in oil)	5.6	6.7	4.8	4.9	4.1	2.2
Portugal (tuna—in oil)	.2	1.0	.8	1.3	1.2	.9
Japan (albacore in brine)	12.6	9.6	9.4	16.2	12.0	13.2
(light meat in brine)	7.6	10.1	10.1	4.9	8.9	8.7
Total tuna, bonito, skipjack	26.0	27.4	25.1	27.3	26.2	25.0
Crustaceans and mollusks						
South and South West Africa (rock lobster)	.4	.1	.2	—	.1	.1
Japan (crabmeat)	2.6	3.1	1.9	1.9	1.5	2.1
(shrimp, prawns, lobster)	.1	.1	.1	.1	.5	.4
(oysters, clams, abalone)	2.0	2.3	2.4	3.0	3.1	3.3
Mexico (abalone)	2.4	2.2	2.8	2.6	3.1	3.8
Total crustaceans and mollusks	7.5	7.8	7.5	7.6	8.3	9.7

Source: FAO Yearbook of Fisheries Statistics, 1963.

The very nature of the salmon resource, with its variation in the cycles and the extent of the runs, has made it difficult to make accurate predictions on future catches. Much constructive work has been done in recent years by the state agencies, U.S. Fish & Wildlife Service, and industry supported research programs toward more accurate prediction projections. The yardsticks being used on these projections are escapement records on the parent run, lake survival

exhibit 8

BUMBLE BEE SEAFOODS, INC.

U.S. Exports of Canned Seafood and Fish
(thousand metric tons)

	1958	1959	1960	1961	1962	1963
Sardines	8.4	17.6	9.6	3.5	3.6	1.7
Tuna	.1	.1	.2	.1	.2	.1
Crab and shrimp	1.0	1.3	1.6	1.1	1.0	1.5
Squid and other Mollusks	2.8	4.4	3.7	2.3	4.4	4.4
Total U.S. exports	12.3	23.4	15.1	7.0	9.2	7.7

Source: FAO Yearbook of Fisheries Statistics, 1963.

exhibit 9

BUMBLE BEE SEAFOODS, INC.

U.S. Availability of Canned Seafood
(thousand metric tons)

	1958	1959	1960	1961	1962	1963
Salmon	85.5	65.5	63.7	81.2	83.5	71.7
Herring, sardines, anchovies	84.9	51.1	52.7	42.2	53.2	39.6
Tuna	148.8	151.9	157.6	169.1	178.5	173.7
Crustaceans, mollusks	39.6	42.4	33.1	43.5	46.5	52.3
U.S. total	358.8	310.9	307.1	336.0	361.7	337.3
Average annual U.S. per capita consumption: 4.2 lbs.						

Source: Constructed from Exhibits 6,7, and 7.

of the fry, downstream ocean migrant counts, and tagging of maturing fish on the high seas. At best, due to the wide variables in nature, there will always be seasonal variations in the runs.

Conservation

Catching enough fish to provide man with needed food, but not so much that it threatens future seafood crops, has long been a major objective of the U.S. commercial fishing industry. Perpetual yield, however, requires concerted efforts among fishermen to exercise good judgment, and catch fish in ways that assure continued abundance by maintaining adequate balances of natural forces.

In recent years, certain runs of Columbia River salmon have been destroyed and others depleted as a result of the construction of a number of large multiple-purpose dams on the Columbia and its main tributaries. Other factors, such as pollution and unregulated fishing by Indians in sections of the river closed to commercial fishing, have also contributed to the depletion of certain runs.

Fish Procurement

Most U.S. fish packers obtained their basic supply either from their own fleets, manned by company employed fishermen paid on incentive, or from independent fishermen who had committed their catch to the packer. A canner purchasing from an independent fisherman usually made advance arrangements for the entire year's output of the man's boat. Fishermen usually remained with the same canner year after year. Their relationship often became interdependent through credit extended by the packer to the fisherman for the purchase or modernization of his boat. Almost all U.S.-produced fish was delivered under these contractual arrangements. For example, all salmon caught commercially off Alaska and Washington was for the account of that cannery with which the particular fishing crew had either employment or a firm commitment before sailing. Pacific salmon had a very short season, running from May through August. Alaskan king crab was caught in the same waters as Alaskan salmon, by the same fishermen, in the October-April season.

Tuna and other species, produced worldwide, tended to be more available on an open market basis. However, the two largest U.S. packers of tuna had found it desirable to arrange long-term contracts with individual fishing boats, covering the major portion of their annual pack, rather than risk shortages of product or uncontrollably high prices. In recent years, each had opened overseas processing facilities.

The albacore white meat tuna was caught year-round in the temperate areas of the Pacific. Some 30-40% of U.S. requirements were caught by U.S. fishermen. Light meat tuna, also available year-round, came principally from warmer regions, with U.S. fishing boats accounting for about 60% of U.S. requirements. Canners supplemented their catch by purchasing and importing fish caught by fishermen of other nations—mainly Japan. Fish caught by Japanese boats in the South Pacific and Indian Ocean were sometimes landed in Japan, and, at other times, at transshipment points such as the island of Mauritius, Penang (Malaysia), the New Hebrides, and the Fiji Islands. Upon being landed, the fish were then inspected in port before being shipped to U.S. canneries on refrigerated ships. The purchase price of foreign fish was reported to be very sensitive to U.S. demand. Prices tended to fluctuate inversely with the inventories held by packers and with forecasts of the size of the local catch. Open market tuna were generally auctioned on a daily basis, and were often purchased as much as 90 days in advance of the anticipated canning date. White meat albacore tended to command a slight premium over the light meat varieties.

About 85% of seafood packing costs were direct costs. Of this 85%, about two-thirds was in raw material. The other third was made up of labor, packing oils, cans, and cases. With so much of total cost in the price of fish purchased or contracted for, management had to be extremely sensitive to the supply and demand relationships affecting prices of their raw material.

U.S. Tuna Packers

In 1965, Van Camp, Star-Kist, Bumble Bee, Westgate California, and California Packing Corporation (Calpak) were the five principal factors in U.S. tuna packing and marketing. Though Van Camp Seafood Co. also packed sardines, mackerel, cat food, and nonedible fish products, it had been the largest U.S. tuna packer for many years. Van Camp sold approximately 30% of all tuna consumed in the U.S. Seventy-five percent of tuna sold in the U.S. was under nationally advertised labels, and Van Camp's two major brands, "Chicken of the Sea" and "White Star," accounted for 40% of such nationally advertised sales. Almost 60% of Van Camp's estimated $80 million business was in sales of canned branded tuna.

Until the late 1950's, Van Camp was totally dependent upon southern California fishing fleets to supply its needs. Van Camp had since developed receiving and processing stations in American Samoa, Puerto Rico, Ecuador, Peru, Sierra Leone, and Ivory Coast. A fish reduction plant in Peru manufactured anchovies into fish meal fertilizer, producing an annual sales volume of $10 million. The major portion of Van Camp's consumer business was packed by three canneries in southern California, one in American Samoa, and one in Puerto Rico. The income from Samoan and Peruvian facilities was temporarily tax exempt in 1965, which enabled Van Camp to carry most of its operating income into net profit. In 1963, Van Camp Seafoods merged with the Ralston Purina Company. Industry sources estimated that a value of $70 million was placed on Van Camp in this transaction.

Star-Kist Foods, Inc., was the second largest selling nationally advertised brand of tuna in the U.S. Star-Kist's activities were very similar to Van Camp's. Besides canned tuna, Star-Kist sold sardines, mackerel, bonito, cat food, fish meal, fish oils, and tuna pies and casseroles. Tuna was marketed under the "Star-Kist" trade name and accounted for approximately two-thirds of total company sales of about $75 million. Most Star-Kist sales were made in the U.S., but 9%, mainly fish meal, bonito, sardines, and mackerel, were made overseas. In 1960, Star-Kist expanded into Puerto Rico, with a 6,000 case per day tuna cannery and a fish meal reduction plant. Star-Kist also operated six anchovy fish meal reduction plants and a tuna and bonito cannery in Peru. Total investment in Peru was estimated at $3.3 million. In 1963, Star-Kist constructed a tuna cannery, cold storage, and reduction plant in American Samoa. Earnings were exempt from Puerto Rican and American Samoan taxes until 1970. In 1963, Star-Kist was purchased by the H. J. Heinz Co. for an estimated $48 million.

Bumble Bee Seafoods was, in 1965, the third largest factor in the domestic tuna market. A regionally advertised brand, Bumble Bee had concentrated its efforts in only a few major markets. By having as much as 50% penetration in some markets, they maintained an approximate 8% share of the total U.S. canned tuna market, despite being completely without distribution in some markets. Their position in albacore tuna (white meat) and salmon in these markets was even stronger than their over-all record.

Westgate California Co., a fourth factor in the domestic tuna market, manufactured and sold tuna under the "Breast of Chicken" brand. Westgate did not allow public access to their financial and operating data, but industry sources estimated their market share at about 5%.

The other major participant in the domestic tuna market was Calpak, selling under their Del-Monte brand. Del-Monte had re-entered the tuna market in only the past few years. Because they did not have an existing sales volume, Del-Monte was obliged to present substantial promotions in order to get supermarket distribution. Its special efforts had been centered on light meat tuna products.

U.S. Salmon Packers

In 1965, the main participants in the U.S. salmon market were Alaska Packers' Assoc., a subsidiary of California Packing Corp. (selling under their Del-Monte label), Bumble Bee Seafoods, Pacific American Fisheries, selling under the Demming label, Libby, McNeill & Libby, New England Fisheries, and Peter Pan Seafoods, selling under the Double Q label. None of these marketers had full national coverage in canned salmon.

The marketing of canned salmon differed from tuna marketing in two important respects: 1) the supply of salmon was much more limited; and 2) there were many more small independent canners of salmon and no truly dominant large factors. Because of the small supply and the lack of national advertising, canned salmon has not been a regular promotional item in the grocery store. A large catch of one type of salmon is often offset by small crops of others, resulting in price differences that may shift consumer demand from one type of salmon to another. But the over-all canned salmon supply, equal to the total annual catch, is readily absorbed. Major packers have been reductant to promote salmon for fear that increased demand might outrun the relatively small supply, resulting in a current or future out of stock situation that would invalidate the promotional efforts.

The Pacific salmon is caught from Oregon north to Alaska during the summer season, while the fish are entering the rivers to spawn. Salmon does not freeze well and must therefore be processed immediately at nearby canneries. Many small canneries are located near the salmon fishing grounds. Most operate for a very short time during the season. Most salmon are caught by fishermen in packer owned boats or by independent fishermen with long-term relationships with individual canneries.

An opening price for salmon is usually set each year by one of the principal packers. Others will follow this price or may offer more, if they wish to increase their share of the available supply. In Alaska, the opening price generally applies through the whole season. On the Columbia River, however, a higher price is paid at the beginning of the season, when more fancy quality salmon is caught, and the price declines during the season as the percentage of select salmon in the catch declines. Other price differences may occur because of the differing benefits which packers give their fishermen, including terms of financing purchase or modernization of their boats, health and accident insurance, etc.

By the end of 1965, Bumble Bee had become one of the two most significant factors in the U.S. salmon packing industry, producing about 11% of the total pack. In 1959 Bumble Bee, together with Ward's Cove Packing Company, purchased all of the Alaska salmon canneries and facilities of Libby, McNeill & Libby. Early in 1964, Bumble Bee and Ward's Cove jointly purchased a salmon cannery at Alitak, on the South end of Kodiak Island, from Pacific American Fisheries, Inc. In 1965 Pacific American announced its withdrawal from the fish packing business to become a closed end investment company, at which time Bumble Bee and Ward's Cove jointly acquired Pacific American's one-third interest in Excursion Inlet Packing Company, which operates a salmon cannery at Excursion Inlet in southeastern Alaska. The remaining two-thirds of Excursion Inlet was already jointly owned by Bumble Bee and Ward's Cove. The combined Bumble Bee–Ward's Cove pack was estimated to be about 22% of the total 1965 volume of U.S. canned salmon. Ward's Cove's 50% share of the output of the four joint venture Alaskan salmon canneries was sold largely to Libby, McNeill & Libby, and was, in 1965, Libby's principal canned salmon source.

Packs of the other major factors as a percentage of the total 1965 U.S. canned salmon production were as follows: Peter Pan Seafoods, 13%; Alaska Packers' Assoc. (a subsidiary of California Packing), 12%; New England Fisheries, 11%. The balance was divided among several dozen small independent canners.

Operating Results

Exhibit 10 gives selected operating data for the six largest U.S. canned seafood companies. These data, for 1960 and 1962, are for the last years before four of the six companies were merged into larger parent companies. (Booth Fisheries, while third largest, is not strictly comparable with the other five firms, since its production is mainly in the sale of canned and frozen shrimp, scallops, and fillets, rather than tuna or salmon. It is included to give some idea of the relative profitability of such specialties.)

Bumble Bee's criteria of success have been percentage return on sales and on net worth *before taxes*. Against these criteria, Bumble Bee's performance, as shown, has been better than that of any of the other major companies. However, both Star-Kist and Van Camp, by utilizing Puerto Rican and American Samoan

exhibit 10

BUMBLE BEE SEAFOODS, INC.

Comparison of Major U.S. Canned Seafood Companies
(in millions of dollars and in percentages)

	Van Camp[1] Yr. End May 31		Star-Kist[2] Yr. End May 31		Booth Fisheries[3] Yr. End Apr.27-28		Bumble Bee[4] Yr. End Apr. 30		Alaska Packers[5] Yr. End Feb. 28		Pacific-Amer. Yr. End Feb.28	
	1962	1960	1962	1960	1962	1960	1962	1960	1962	1960	1962	1960
Sales	$73.5	$57.1	$67.8	$62.3	$56.7	$48.3	$29.8	$23.3	$16.6	$14.5	$14.6	$15.4
Net worth	19.6	15.7	19.0	16.0	12.2	10.9	12.1	7.4	15.2	14.5	11.7	10.6
Earnings before taxes	5.2	2.7	2.1	.8	2.7	1.9	3.7	2.0	8.5	.4	1.4	.9
Earnings after taxes	3.2	1.9	1.9	.7	1.2	.9	1.7	.9	.4	.3	.7	.9
Before tax return on												
Sales	7.1%	4.7%	3.1%	1.3%	4.8%	3.9%	12.5%	8.6%	6.5%	2.9%	9.6%	5.9%
Net worth	26.5	17.2	11.0	5.0	22.1	17.4	30.7	27.1	7.6	2.9	12.0	8.5
After tax return on												
Sales	4.4	3.3	2.8	1.1	2.1	1.9	5.7	4.0	2.7	2.1	4.8	5.9
Net worth	16.4	12.1	10.0	4.4	9.8	8.3	14.1	12.6	3.1	2.1	6.0	8.5
Effective tax rate	38.4	29.1	8.2	16.1	53.6	50.2	54.5	53.4	48.0	27.0	49.4	0.0

1 Division of Ralston Purina Company.   4 Division of Castle & Cooke.
2 Division of H.J. Heinz Company.   5 Tax loss carry forward.
3 Division of Consolidated Foods.   6 Withdrew from seafood canning in 1965.

locations, have greatly reduced their effective tax rates. As indicated, these steps have converted their lower before tax performance into much more favorable after tax results.

BUMBLE BEE SEAFOODS

Bumble Bee Seafoods has grown steadily over the years. From a sales volume of $1 million in 1932, revenues have climbed to a 1965 total of $34 million. Exhibit 11 indicates the 1955–1965 history of sales and earnings, while Exhibit 12 shows the balance sheet as of April 30, 1965.

As shown, sales have increased steadily over the decade. Earnings, which dropped sharply in 1963 and 1964, appeared to be recovering in 1965, although still below 1962 and 1961 levels. Major investments since 1961, primarily for the

exhibit 11

BUMBLE BEE SEAFOODS, INC.

Financial and Operating Data

	4/30/65	4/30/64	4/30/63	4/30/62	4/30/61	4/30/60	12/31/58	12/31/57	12/31/56	2/31/55
Sales ($ millions)										
Bumble Bee(including sales of Maryland Tuna)	$34.0	$31.2	$30.0	$29.8	$27.9	$23.3	$20.6	$18.8	$16.4	$15.0
Earnings ($ millions)										
Before tax	2.7	1.7	2.2	3.7	2.9	2.0	1.9	1.6	1.5	1.1
After tax	1.5	.8	1.0	1.7	1.4	.9	.9	.8	.7	.6
After tax including Maryland Tuna	1.6	.9	1.0							
Return on sales (%)										
Before tax	7.9	5.5	7.3	12.5	10.5	8.6	9.0	8.7	9.3	7.5
After tax	4.7	2.9	3.3	5.9	5.1	4.0	4.2	4.1	4.4	3.7
Total assets ($ millions)	$19.8	$18.3	$19.1	$16.5	$14.0	$14.8	$12.7	$12.7	$10.4	
Including 60% of Maryland Tuna	21.9	19.9	20.7							
Shareholders' equity ($ millions)	16.4	14.0	13.2	12.1	8.5	7.4	6.5	8.3	8.1	6.5
Including 60% of Maryland Tuna	17.4	15.0	14.0							
Return on equity (%)										
Before tax	15.5	11.3	15.7	30.7	34.5	27.1	28.7	19.7	18.8	17.3
After tax	9.2	6.0	7.2	14.1	16.8	12.6	13.3	9.2	8.8	8.4

purchase of the Pacific American salmon canneries and the acquisition of the Maryland facility, have reduced return on equity more sharply than return on sales. Nonetheless, fluctuations in Bumble Bee earnings have been less extreme than for most of its competition. Only Van Camp Seafoods has shown steadily increasing earnings. Otherwise, an erratic record has been more typical of the industry. For example, Star-Kist's earnings have dropped as much as 50% in a single year. Pacific American Seafoods and Alaska Packers' Assoc. have had intermittent years of net losses. Bumble Bee had endeavored to realize pretax profit on sales of 7.5-9%. In the past ten years, annual pretax earnings have averaged 8.7%. A graphical representation of Bumble Bee's sales and profit history for the past six years is shown in Exhibit 13, prepared by the Bumble Bee staff.

exhibit 12

BUMBLE BEE SEAFOODS, INC.

**Balance Sheet
(April 30, 1965)**

Assets	
Current Assets	
Cash	$ 415,738
Accounts receivable	1,349,810
Inventories	
Finished	
Canned	8,031,469
Frozen	15,499
Unprocessed fish	789,946
Materials and Supplies	952,372
Total inventories	$9,789,286
Advances to affiliates	2,849,180
Prepaids	113,971
Total current assets	$14,517,985
Other assets and investments	
Accounts receivable—fishermen	957,921
Less: Reserve for losses	156,030
	$ 801,891
Investment in affiliated	
companies	1,202,852
Note receivable from affiliate	150,000
Other noncurrent receivables	559,509
Property, plant, and equipment	
Original cost	7,340,941
Less: Accum. depr.	4,740,999
Net book	$ 2,599,942
Total assets	$19,832,179

Liabilities and stockholders' equity

Current liabilities	
Notes payable to bank	$ 2,145,267
Accounts payable	
Trade	626,600
Fishermen	453,369
Accrued payrolls, taxes	207,284
Total current liabilities	$ 3,432,520
Equity accounts	
Intracompany equity	4,000,000
Intracompany deferred tax	219,773
Retained earnings, May 1, 1964	9,982,186
Intracompany profit for year	2,697,700
Cash advanced to Castle & Cooke	(500,000)
Retained earnings, April 30, 1965	$12,179,886
Total equity accounts	$16,399,659
Total liabilities and equity	$19,832,179

Note: April 30 should be low inventory time of year because it is at end of selling season and before new runs are to be packed.

Physical Facilities

In 1965, Bumble Bee operated nine strategically located canneries (see Fig. 1): one at the mouth of the Columbia River (Astoria, Oregon); one on Puget Sound (Bellingham, Wash.); one in the Hawaiian Islands (Honolulu); one on Chesapeake Bay (Cambridge, Md.); one in Southern Alaska (Excursion Inlet, near Juneau); one in Cook Inlet, Alaska (Kenai); one on Kodiak Island (Alitak); and two on the northern side of the Alaska Peninsula (Naknek and Ekuk) on Bristol Bay. The Honolulu, Cambridge, and Astoria canneries primarily packed tuna, while the Bellingham and Alaska canneries packed salmon. Astoria also packed significant quantities of salmon, and Alitak was also an important canner of crabmeat.

Most of Bumble Bee's light meat tuna was packed in Honolulu, where skipjack and yellowfin were the native tuna varieties. Astoria and Cambridge tended to concentrate on albacore (white meat). Exhibit 14 summarizes important information on these facilities.

The basic methods of processing canned tuna were quite different from those used in the canning of salmon. As a consequence, the type of equipment used for processing tuna was entirely different from the equipment used in the processing

exhibit 13

BUMBLE BEE SEAFOODS

Sales and Profit

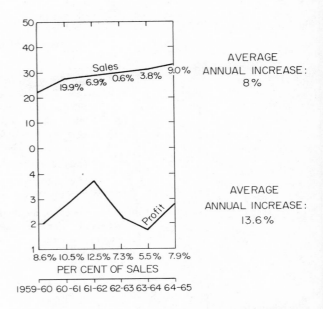

AVERAGE
ANNUAL INCREASE:
8%

AVERAGE
ANNUAL INCREASE:
13.6%

of salmon, except for sealing the cans, sterilizing, and labeling. Bumble Bee has standardized the equipment used in its three tuna canneries to a marked degree. The same is true of the equipment used in the salmon canneries. In both cases, the company utilizes the most advanced automatic equipment available.

The salmon canneries had an exceedingly short season. For example, in Bristol Bay, 75% of the 1965 catch was packed within 12 days, and the total catch was canned within one month. This short run, typical of salmon, required that employees be flown in for temporary service. During this period, the cannery worked at peak capacity around the clock. The tuna canneries were able to extend their packing seasons with frozen fish. Given adequate refrigerated storage, it was practical for a tuna cannery to pack year-round.

Although much of Bumble Bee's output was canned in older plants, they had been modernized by installation of special conveyorized cleaning and trimming tables and by the use of high speed (240 cans per minute) sealing equipment. These canneries were staffed largely by women, who performed the high labor input tasks of cleaning, trimming, and packing. The composition of the work group at each plant varied widely from region to region. The Honolulu workers were mainly Hawaiians of oriental descent, many of whom were related to

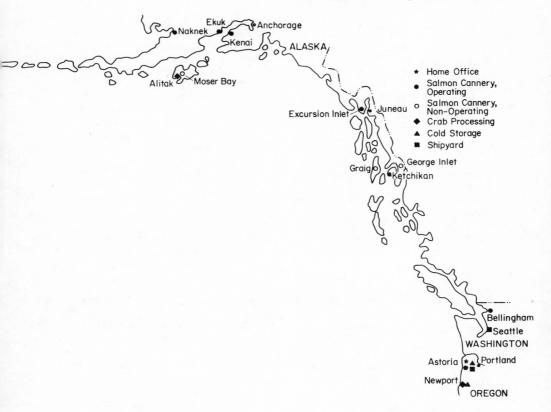

figure 1

BUMBLE BEE SEAFOODS, INC.

Major Facilities: Oregon, Washington, Alaska

the fishermen. The Cambridge, Md., tuna plant was in a largely Negro area. The short season of the Alaskan facilities required some temporary workers to be imported, but utilized mostly Alaskans. While Bumble Bee had had no labor supply problems, Mr. Hendrickson believed it would be difficult to add a second shift in plants with year-round production, such as Astoria, Oregon. Such canneries were staffed mainly with housewives, reluctant to work during hours when their husbands were at home.

The size of cold storage facilities determined tuna cannery flexibility. The larger these facilities, the greater the freedom of choice that Mr. John Gizdavich, head of Bumble Bee's foreign fish procurement, had in when to buy or ship frozen tuna for that cannery. Similarly, large frozen fish inventories created flexi-

Cannery Location	Average Annual Output (cases)	Per cent Nonlocal Pack	Nonlocal Source	Other Products	Tuna
Astoria, Oregon	30-50,000 salmon 750-900,000 tuna	50-80%	Japanese exports (Pacific Fishery)	Salmon eggs, shad, shad roe, smoked sturgeon, pet food	July - Oct.
Naknek, Bristol Bay, Alaska	20-175,000 salmon	0	None	—	—
Bellingham, Washington	20-65,000 salmon	0	None	Salmon eggs	—
Excursion Inlet, Alaska	40-200,000 salmon	0	None	Salmon eggs	—
Honolulu, Hawaii	350-500,000 tuna	30-65	Japanese exports (Pacific Fishery)	pet food, fish meal	May - Oct.
Kenai, Cook Inlet, Alaska	15-95,000 salmon	0	None	—	—
Ekuk, Alaska	30-140,000 salmon	0	None	Salmon eggs	—
Cambridge,	250-450,000 tuna	65-85	Japanese exports (mostly Atlantic Fishery	Pet food	June - Sept.
Alitak, Kodiak Is., Alaska	50-175,000 salmon 80,000 crab	0	None	Salmon eggs	—

1 Varies year to year and is subject to availability of supplies (30-60 days).

2 Ward's Cove Packing Co. in 1965 was wholly owned by the Brindle family of Seattle, Washington. Its principal holdings were the 50% partnerships with Bumble Bee in the four Alaskan canneries indicated (purchased from Libby and Pacific American in 1959 and subsequently) and in the moorage and warehousing facilities in Seattle (Lake Union Terminals), which the two partners purchased from Libby in 1960. Its sales volume was estimated at $3 million, and consisted primarily of private label sales of their share of the canneries' output.

exhibit 14

BUMBLE BEE SEAFOODS, INC.

Summary of Production Facilities, 1965

Salmon	Shutdown Period	Peak Employment	Per cent Owned	Year Acquired	How Acquired
May 1-Sept. 15	1	500	100	1899	Original cannery
June 20-July 25	July 26-June 19	265	100	1939	Built by Bumble Bee
June 25-Sept. 15	Sept. 16-June 24	100	100	1946	Built on leased ground by Bumble Bee
June 25-Sept. 1	Sept. 2-June 24	140	50	1950	Originally joint venture with Pacific American, now with Ward's Cove2
—	1	200	100	1956	Purchased from Castle & Cooke
June 25-Aug. 15	Aug. 16-June 24	140	50	1959	Purchased from Libby, joint venture with Ward's Cove
May 21-July 25	July 26-May 20	200	50	1959	Same as above
—	1	150	60	1962	Joint venture—Taiyo Gyogyo3
June 15-Mar. 30	Mar. 31-June 14	165	50	1963	Purchased from Pacific American, joint venture with Ward's Cove

3Taiyo Fishery in 1965 was the largest-scale fishing enterprise in Japan. It owned and operated 729 fishing vessels and was also a major wholesaler of fish products. A widely held public company, Taiyo had sales for the year ending January, 1965, of nearly 100 billion yen ($250 million). Its profits of 1.7 billion yen ($4.2 million) produced about 10% return on net worth. Sales were divided: 58% commercial transactions (wholesaling); 30% sales of own fish catch; 9% fish processing; 3% other. Average monthly production during 1964 was: whaling operations, 12,000 tons; canned salmon, 10,000 cases; canned crab, 9,000; dragnet catch (mostly herring, sardines, etc.), 11,000 tons; tuna and mackerel catch, 4,000 tons.

bility in production scheduling, as well as making it possible for the cannery to wait out temporary high price levels for raw material without shutdown. Astoria had cold storage facilities equivalent to two months' production. Cambridge's facility was even larger. Honolulu's cold storage facilities, however, were equivalent to less than one month's production.

All capital expenditures for Bumble Bee's physical facilities were subject to approval by top management. Mr. Hendrickson said that, although there was no specified cutoff rate, he could not recall ever having submitted a proposal that had not paid for itself in less than five years. He indicated that Bumble Bee historically had been conservative, but realistic, in expanding into new areas. For example, new canning locations, such as Cuba and Brazil, had been investigated and turned down because of the existing political climate.

The Bumble Bee Headquarters

In 1965, Bumble Bee headquarters in Astoria, Oregon, housed most key management personnel, including Mr. Thomas Sandoz, Mr. McGowan, president, Mr. H. William Larson, marketing vice president, Mr. J. D. Hendrickson, senior vice president—production, Mr. John Gizdavich, vice president—tuna procurement and sales, and other members of Bumble Bee's organization. These men had offices in an unimposing, informal, two story, frame building on the waterfront. This arrangement allowed for quick, easy, and frequent communication among group members.

In Honolulu, Mr. Herbert Hart was general manager of Hawaiian Tuna Packers, while vice president John Supple was resident manager of the Maryland facility, and vice president R. B. Hendrickson supervised Alaskan operations.

All major decisions regarding purchasing, pricing, and production scheduling are approved by Mr. Sandoz and Mr. McGowan. Mr. McGowan stated: "To achieve maximum potential profits in this business, it is essential that top management have a knowledge of both production and sales. Sales decisions cannot be made alone on the basis of what seems to be attractive from a marketing standpoint, but rather must take into consideration as well the supply and replacement cost situations." Mr. McGowan further elaborated that both he and Mr. Sandoz keep close touch with the company's marketing activities.

Mr. Sandoz added that good inventory management was also crucial to continued profitability. He explained that inventory decisions could be very risky, since inventory carrying costs added $1.25 to $1.50 per case per year, and year to year price fluctuations could be much larger.

Mr. McGowan was in daily contact with his key subordinates, who kept him informed of the major developments in the functions. Mr. McGowan thus maintained a constant interplay between production and sales. Through his continuous emphasis on estimating the profitability of each decision, based upon daily cost data and information on market conditions, he kept each department sensitive to its impact on the others. For example, Mr. Larson would not change prices based solely on competitive marketing practice, nor would Mr. Gizdavich purchase a shipment of frozen fish based solely on cost.

According to Mr. McGowan, the location of the company's headquarters in remote Astoria had many advantages. "It is true that we are somewhat isolated from the headquarters of our major salmon and tuna competitors, which are centered in Seattle, Washington, and Terminal Island, California, respectively. As a consequence, we concentrate on our own objectives rather than being preoccupied with the activity of our competitors." Mr. Hendrickson added, "One always knows what your competition is paying for fish because the prices paid local fishermen are posted and negotiations with our foreign tuna suppliers generally reveal the prices currently being paid by others. So, there is no disadvantage to us in being off by ourselves." Mr. McGowan commented wryly that "Bumble Bee is not totally without sources of rumors, since it has offices in Seattle and other centers."

History

Mr. Sandoz indicated that the basic philosophy guiding the company when he joined in 1928 was still Bumble Bee's marketing philosophy in 1965. He stated, "Quality is nothing more than basic honesty." When Mr. Sandoz joined what was then called Columbia River Packers' Assoc., the company had three canneries, $1 million in sales, and was selling approximately 60 different brands of canned salmon.

Mr. Sandoz became sales manager in 1933. At that time, the finest salmon were being packed under the "Bumble Bee" label. Sales of this one brand had grown more rapidly than any of the other 60, and Bumble Bee had begun to acquire a reputation as "the quality salmon packer." In 1933, Mr. Sandoz became "the first Bumble Bee employee to actually call on the trade." Over the next few years, one after another of the 60 brand names was dropped and their sales volume was picked up by the "Bumble Bee" label. Bumble Bee maintained the quality standards that had created its reputation and acceptance, and did not provide special allowances and deals. Expansion was slow; it generally followed a pattern of deeper penetration into individual markets in which Bumble Bee was already selling well.

Albacore tuna was discovered off the coast of Oregon in 1938, and Columbia River Packers pioneered the packing of this fish in the northwest, in addition to their regular salmon pack. This new product was introduced to the market under a second quality label, "Cloverleaf," until management was certain that they could produce tuna worthy of the "Bumble Bee" label. Housewives made a ready transference from quality salmon to quality tuna, and Bumble Bee tuna gained quick acceptance in the areas where the company had previously held strong market position in canned salmon.

Subsequently, the company expanded its salmon packing facilities by building an Alaskan cannery in Bristol Bay (1939), which greatly increased the pack.

Astoria facilities were expanded to pack the Oregon tuna, as well as Columbia River salmon.

After World War II, a third salmon cannery was built on Puget Sound (1946). Over the next ten years, the company concentrated on building strong market demand for its limited volume salmon and albacore pack. New York and New England became the company's principal markets, and virtually all sales promotion and production was directed to these areas. These efforts resulted in very strong brand acceptance and market penetration in these limited areas. In 1950, business had developed to the point where another Alaskan cannery was established.

In 1956, the company began its relationship with Castle & Cooke. C & C had purchased a portion of Hawaiian Tuna Packers in 1948, and the balance in 1951. "This company required a volume of 200-300,000 cases of tuna in order to break even," according to HTP management. "Since Hawaii could only absorb about 75,000 cases, the balance had to be sold on the mainland. But such small volume could not be adequately promoted or distributed. So we looked for someone else to do our marketing. Columbia River Packers was a natural. Their demand for tuna was growing, and we represented a high quality source of supply. For us, they were good people to do business with—honest, straightforward, and quality-minded."

In 1956, Hawaiian Tuna Packers was sold to Columbia River Packers for stock in the latter company. This sale left C & C with an 11% interest in CRPA. When a major block of CRPA stock became available in 1958, C & C's further purchase gave it a 60% interest.

In 1959, together with Ward's Cove, CRPA bought the Alaskan salmon packing and Washington terminal facilities of Libby, McNeill & Libby to provide for their expanding sales.

In 1961, CRPA was merged into Castle & Cooke. The company name was changed to Bumble Bee Seafoods, but operations remained autonomous. A new tuna cannery as big as Astoria was constructed in Maryland in 1962, as a joint venture with a major Japanese fishing company which provided the facility's raw material from Atlantic and other sources.

In 1963, Mr. John McGowan, formerly executive vice president (and before that, vice president with responsibilities which included liaison between production and marketing), succeeded Mr. Sandoz as president. The latter became chairman of the board and chief executive officer. In 1964, Bumble Bee and Ward's Cove jointly purchased from Pacific American Fisheries a salmon cannery at Alitak, on the South end of Kodiak Island: and in 1965, the remaining interest in Excursion Inlet Packing, which formerly was owned one-third each by Pacific American, Ward's Cove, and Bumble Bee.

By 1965, Bumble Bee's business had changed substantially. Tuna accounted for nearly two-thirds of Bumble Bee's 1965 sales. Albacore alone produced more than twice the volume which the company had realized from salmon in any previous year. Exhibit 15 shows Bumble Bee production of tuna and salmon for the years 1950, 1955, 1960, and 1965. As can be seen, the company's production

exhibit 15

BUMBLE BEE SEAFOODS, INC.

Production and Percentage of Total Production for Tuna and Salmon
(calendar years)

	1965	1960	1955	1950
Albacore tuna:				
U.S. albacore production	$ 5,538,233	$ 4,052,026	$2,342,653	$1,681,131
Imports	1,600,857	769,619	660,333	600,000
Total	$ 7,139,090	$ 4,821,645	$3,002,986	$2,281,131
Bumble Bee production	1,285,118	965,665	434,300	311,952
Percentage of Total	18.0%	20.0%	14.5%	13.7%
Light meat tuna:				
U.S. light meat production	11,488,915	$11,183,022	$7,385,461	$7,721,887
Imports	991,794	1,694,905	1,033,143	1,133,787
Total	$12,480,709	$12,877,927	$8,418,604	$8,855,674
Bumble Bee production	320,578	289,769	99,895	126,308
Percentage of total	2.6%	2.3%	1.2%	1.4%
Salmon:				
U.S. production	$ 3,541,187	$ 2,912,016	$3,286,885	$4,274,462
Bumble Bee production	395,158	240,405	163,702	154,972
Percentage of total	11.2%	8.3%	5.0%	3.6%
Alaska Packers Association	n.a.	$459,037	$284,766	$282,462
Percentage of total		15.8%	8.7%	6.6%
Pacific American Fisheries	(facilities have been	$312,955	$299,053	$393,446
Percentage of total	sold to Bumble Bee and Ward's Cove)	10.7%	9.1%	9.2%
New England Fish Co.	n.a.	$191,419	$186,089	$269,550
Percentage of total		6.6%	5.7%	6.3%

Estimated.
Note: Cases of canned tuna on a standard basis of 48–1/2 #; cases of canned salmon on a standard basis of 48–1# .

has consistently emphasized albacore (white meat), rather than other tuna varieties (light meat). Bumble Bee has built a commanding position in this relatively small (less than one-third of total) but premium price segment of the U.S. tuna market. The tonnage of light meat tuna packed has grown to nearly half that of salmon, while salmon itself has grown steadily (doubling volume in 15 years vs. tuna's quadrupling).

Exhibit 16 gives a dollar breakdown of 1965 Bumble Bee sales volume and indicates management's expectation of sales growth over the next five years, forecasting roughly the same product mix as in the past.

Product	1965	Est. 1970	Percentage Increase
Albacore tuna (white meat)	$17.2	$23.8	+ 39%
Light meat tuna	4.1	6.3	+ 54
Salmon	9.4	13.4	+ 42
Crab	1.1	3.2	+187
Pet food	0.9	2.0	+122
Fresh and frozen	0.9	1.2	+ 33
Shrimp	0.2	0.5	+300
Other	0.1	0.1	zero
Total	$34.0	$50.5	(Avg.) 48%

Exhibit 17 shows historical sales data on the company's product mix, in cases sold for 1950, 1955, and 1960–1965. It also includes price information for major items during this period. These figures do not correspond with those of Exhibit 15, since Exhibit 15 reports only cases *packed* under Bumble Bee ownership, while Exhibit 17 includes Bumble Bee sales of cases purchased from other packers (primarily salmon). Minor discrepancies arise from the Exhibit 15 data being on a calendar year basis and Exhibit 17 showing fiscal years.

Marketing

Aggregate information of Bumble Bee's total sales and product mix can be misleading. Bumble Bee Seafood's explicit strategy over the years has been to market intensively in only a few of the most densely populated regions of the U.S. In these areas the company has attempted both to achieve a quality reputation that would command a premium price, and also to acquire and hold the major portion of the quality segment in each market for its principal products. According to Mr. Sandoz, 80% of the total U.S. albacore sales is concentrated in five or six metropolitan markets.

Exhibit 18 presents geographical distributions of Bumble Bee's total sales by product. As can be seen, Bumble Bee had nearly 60% of its total sales concentrated in the New York-New England region. More than three-quarters of its albacore tuna was sold there, but less than half of its salmon and only 20% of its light meat tuna. These figures clearly show Bumble Bee's dominance of the

exhibit 17

BUMBLE BEE SEAFOODS, INC.

Total Case Sales for Selected Years

| | Year Ended April 30 | | | | | | Calendar Year | |
	1965	1964	1963	1962	1961	1960	1955	1950
Cases sold: "As they run"								
Abacore tuna	1,315,073	1,131,633	1,105,357	1,086,506	1,012,372	861,766	433,872	311,113
Light meat tuna	358,171	336,694	362,812	352,953	326,635	300,360	179,025	108,187
Salmon	560,996	517,683	486,499	477,557	499,297	392,137	354,670	373,585
Miscellaneous	100,728	91,061	71,092	62,136	56,687	72,106		
Tuna pet food	171,160	159,791	96,324	47,146	15,038	3,375		
Total	2,506,128	2,236,862	2,122,084	2,026,298	1,910,029	1,629,744	983,568	826,609
Average price—major items: (weighted by volume)								
Fancy white meat tuna 48 1/2lb.	$15.34	$15.35	$15.17	$15.54	$14.89	$17.35	$15.09	$16.63
Chunk light meat tuna 48 1/2lb.	12.22	12.49	12.10	12.00	11.14	11.06	11.27	12.30
Red salmon 48/1 lb.	40.25	37.31	34.07	34.87	34.73	36.06	31.00	28.94
Pink salmon 48/1 lb.	22.05	23.02	25.25	27.89	25.64	23.56	22.47	23.55
Price range—major items: (not including promotional allowances)								
Fancy white meat tuna 48 1/2lb.	16.25- 15.25	16.25- 15.25	16.25- 15.00	16.25- 15.25	16.25- 14.50	16.25- 15.25	16.00- 15.00	17.00- 15.00
Chunk light meat tuna 48 1/2lb.	12.50- 11.00	13.50- 11.50	13.50- 11.50	13.50- 11.50	13.00- 11.00	11.50- 11.00	13.00- 11.00	12.50
Red salmon 48/l lb.	41.00- 40.00	40.00- 37.00	38.00- 34.00	36.00- 34.00	37.00- 33.00	37.00- 35.00	33.00- 29.00	—
Pink salmon 48/l lb.	23.00- 22.00	24.00- 22.00	28.00- 23.00	28.00- 25.00	28.00- 24.00	24.00- 22.00	23.00- 21.00	23.50

high quality market in white meat tuna, and, to a lesser extent, in salmon. They also emphasize the strategy of high penetration of a few selected urban markets. Bumble Bee's "Coral" brand accounted for 80% of Hawaiian tuna consumption. Major market shares in white meat tuna and salmon were reached in Portland, Miami, Washington, D.C., Los Angeles, and Baltimore. Unlike its competitors, Bumble Bee has concentrated on premium quality products, and promoted them actively only in a few urban areas.

Management saw three possible ways to achieve further sales growth: 1) penetrate further with existing products into existing markets (i.e., increase present share of present markets); 2) addition of products to the Bumble Bee product line (i.e., add new products in present markets); and 3) marketing in peripheral regions of already successful city markets, thus effecting continuous market penetration in regions between existing centers of Bumble Bee sales (i.e., promote existing products in new additional markets). In 1965, they were pursuing all of these directions.

exhibit 18

BUMBLE BEE SEAFOODS, INC.

Geographical Composition of Bumble Bee Sales
(in thousands of cases and thousands of dollars)

| | Year Ending 12/31 | | | | Year Ending 4/30 | | | | | | |
| | 1950 | | 1955 | | 1960 | | | | 1965 | | |
Market served	Cases	% of Total	Cases	%of Total	Cases	%of Total	Cases	%of Total	Dollars	%of Total	Cumulative % of Total
New York											
Albacore tuna	138	44	184	43	441	51	700	55			
Light meat tuna	20	19	12	7	43	14	58	16			
Salmon	145	39	149	42	163	41	178	32			
Miscellaneous	7	20	2	10	22	30	129	48			
Total	310	38	348	35	669	41	1,064	42	$14,270	42.0	42.0
New England											
Albacore tuna	58	19	86	20	201	23	295	22			
Light meat tuna	15	14	16	9	22	9	23	4			
Salmon	32	8	51	14	48	12	67	12			
Miscellaneous	4	13	3	18	24	32	18	7			
Total	109	13	156	16	295	18	403	16	5,830	17.2	59.2
Honolulu									1,246	3.7	62.8
Portland, Ore.									1,114	3.3	66.0
Miami									1,040	3.1	69.1
Washington, D.C.									980	2.9	72.0
Los Angeles									820	2.4	74.4
Baltimore									791	2.3	76.8
Cleveland									632	1.9	78.6
Philadelphia									577	1.7	80.3
Other									6,700	19.7	100.0
Total									34,000	100.0	

Since Bumble Bee was not a dominant factor in the total fish industry, it did not tend to function as the industry price leader. Traditionally, this role had fallen to Van Camp. Bumble Bee had been able to develop sufficient consumer franchise that, in the markets where it was strongest, it could command a 1-2% premium per case over Van Camp and Star-Kist for its white meat tuna. Thus, Bumble Bee was somewhat less vulnerable to price competition than its competitors, and frequently refused to match minor price cuts.

Historically, tuna had always been an important promotional item to grocers, and 80% to 90% of canned tuna was purchased by housewives on some kind of special promotion. In general, Bumble Bee followed competitors' specials and promotional allowances, but they were rarely obliged to equal the dollar amount of such allowances. For example, Bumble Bee might have to give $1.00 per case allowance to maintain volume when their competition was giving a $3.00 promotional allowance.

Bumble Bee further demonstrated its independent pricing policy by continuously assessing the relationship among fish availability, operating costs, and market conditions. While it was rarely the first to reduce prices, it often led the industry in price increases. Management indicated that whenever it was determined that they were replacing their inventories at a higher cost than previously, they would consider a price increase. To cut back on supply would mean to lose market position, while to hold the price line would mean to reduce profitability. Close relationships among the various functional departments enabled the management group to reach balanced resolutions between these conflicting outcomes.

Mr. McGowan believed that Bumble Bee had a competitive advantage in pricing because of its method of procurement. "Since only 30 to 40% of albacore tuna requirements can be supplied domestically, Bumble Bee has developed the ability to gauge its purchases to its sales needs. In contrast, our major competition is located in southern California, where the warmer climate provides a local catch of light meat tuna. These companies have working relationships for purchasing the entire output of their fishermen, which often produces more fish than is currently desired. Thus, these firms have to gear their marketing to uncertain production output. Bumble Bee works in just the opposite manner, gearing our purchases to evolving market conditions. But Bumble Bee can't totally ignore the actions of our competition, since white meat tuna sales and prices are somewhat sensitive to the price of light meat tuna."

Brokers

Most Bumble Bee sales were made through a system of 51 food brokers, 49 of whom were large multiple-line companies representing several noncompeting food manufacturers. One broker in New York City and one in Portland, Oregon, had only two or three lines. According to Mr. McGowan, "This concentrated effort has led to exceptional progress on our line."

These brokers, scattered across the U.S. (see Fig. 2), had large wholesale and retail merchandising organizations which Bumble Bee believed were "tops" in their areas. Most brokers maintained a warehouse consignment of Bumble Bee products from which to service their market. All brokers surveyed each customer's credit activities and were required to uphold Bumble Bee prices and discount terms. Brokers conveyed current Bumble Bee prices, advertising, and promotional offerings to all grocery trade in their area. They were expected to spend adequate time in presenting sales programs and arranging for advantageous, attractive shelf displays of Bumble Bee products. In return for these services, brokers received 3% of collected sales.

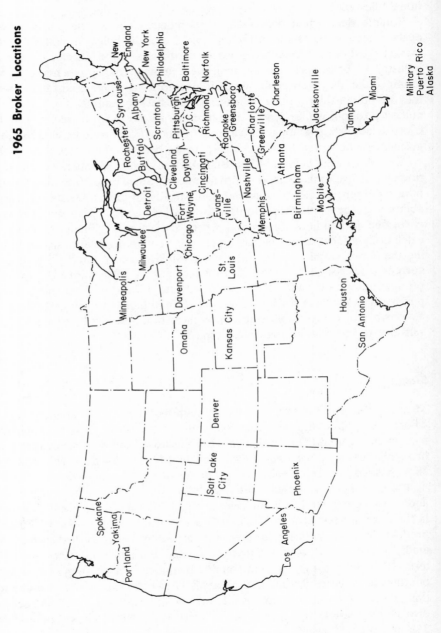

figure 2

BUMBLE BEE SEAFOODS, INC.

1965 Broker Locations

New
England

New York
Philadelphia
Baltimore
Norfolk

Charleston

Jacksonville

Miami

Tampa

Military
Puerto Rico
Alaska

Rochester
Syracuse
Albany
Scranton
Pittsburgh
D.C.
Richmond
Roanoke
Greensboro
Charlotte
Greenville
Atlanta
Birmingham
Mobile

Buffalo
Cleveland
Dayton
Cincinnati
Nashville
Memphis

Detroit
Fort
Wayne
Evans-
ville

Milwaukee
Chicago

Minneapolis

Davenport

St.
Louis

Omaha

Kansas City

Houston

San Antonio

Denver

Salt Lake
City

Phoenix

Spokane
Yakima
Portland

Los Angeles

Bumble Bee brokers were visited four times a year by either the sales vice president, sales manager, or district sales manager. Time was spent with the broker's management and with his wholesale, retail, and chain salesmen. Regular news bulletins informed brokers of developments in prices, promotions, and products between visits.

An eight man sales force supplemented the brokers' activities, working directly with both broker and retailer. Sales promotion was supported by advertising programs in major sales areas. Historically, advertising expenditures had averaged between 1% and 2% of sales. The New York metropolitan area, Bumble Bee's largest market, had 1965 advertising expenditures of 1.2% of sales. Most smaller markets had expenditures more nearly 2% of the region's sales. According to Mr. Sandoz, margins on tuna are too competitive to support large advertising expenditures. He indicated that Bumble Bee had demonstrated the excellence of its name by substantial growth without the benefit of heavy advertising. He contrasted this growth with that of the White Sar Brand, which had required intensive advertising and which Columbia River Packers had sold to another producer.

Direct Sales

Although the Bumble Bee sales effort was primarily through brokers, in three market areas Bumble Bee sold direct: Seattle, San Francisco, and Honolulu. Mr. McGowan said that direct sales were employed only in special situations.

Direct sales efforts in the San Francisco area were begun in the early 1960's, because Bumble Bee was dissatisfied with the brokers' efforts there.

Mr. McGowan believed that substantial progress in the distribution and sales volume of Bumble Bee products in any marketing area, and particularly new markets, required consistent sales and merchandising pressure at the retail level. "We were unable to obtain this from the brokers who formerly represented us in the Bay area. Since establishing our own sales force, we have made steady progress. We have our greatest opportunities to break into a new market when there are management changes in the major chains or when the chains adopt a new emphasis on quality."

The Seattle sales office was opened in 1965, to improve the quality of the company's sales coverage in western Washington. Additionally, because of its proximity to Bumble Bee's headquarters, the Seattle sales office served as a training ground for young salesmen.

Other nonbroker volume included export sales (mostly of salmon), but was limited to about 2% of total cases sold.

Marketing Policies

Management attributed the success of their sales effort to the uniform high quality of their canned products and to the excellent service they provided. Their policy was to never let any item they sold run out of stock. They refused to undertake a new product unless there were reliable resources to assure a continuous supply. For this reason, Bumble Bee had not been enthusiastic about shrimp canning, a crop which has been subject to wide fluctuations in the past. Both Mr. McGowan and Mr. Sandoz felt it was foolish to spend time and money developing consumer acceptance of a new product and then have the resource fail and be out of inventory.

Mr. Sandoz indicated that the most important criterion for success was the figure on the bottom line of the income statement. He saw no value in entering any new market or in bringing out any new product that would not result in increased company profit. He said, "Too many companies in this industry are more conscious of their sales volume than of their return on sales."

Carefully analysis of the light meat tuna business gave Bumble Bee little incentive to expand this phase of its operations under the circumstances which have existed the past several years.

Another management yardstick was that it did not pay the company to attempt to enter a new market area unless it could reasonably be expected that Bumble Bee would capture a fair share of the market and be able, through its production, to sustain and supply this market continuously.

The Future

Mr. Sandoz indicated that, at the time of the merger with Castle & Cooke, C & C had added $2 million to the working capital of Bumble Bee, which had been used for plant acquisition and expansion. This was the only new money that had been put into the capital of the company since it was established as Columbia River Packers' Association in 1899. All expansion and acquisition since that time had been accomplished entirely with internally generated funds. Mr. Sandoz served as a director of Castle & Cooke; Mr. Budge, chairman of the board, and Mr. MacNaughton, president of Castle & Cooke, served on Bumble Bee's Board. Through these contacts, a close liaison between company operations and Castle & Cooke policy programs was maintained.

Mr. Sandoz believed that "full responsibility for the division's operations and profit performance should be centered in the division's management, and that this management should be held responsible by Castle & Cooke. At the same time, major policy decisions and capital expenditures should be cleared with the parent company." It was also his belief that full responsibility for marketing should lie with the division's management. The close liaison that was maintained between production and marketing by the division's management permitted the making of timely decisions which were a contributing factor to the company's success. They saw opportunities for increasing their share of U.S. salmon packs and market, and for increasing Bumble Bee's share of the albacore tuna market. Bumble Bee's investment and participation in their subsidiary salmon packing operations tended to assure these projections.

Castle & Cooke Sugar Interests:

Ewa Plantation Company;

Waialua Agricultural Company, Ltd.;

Kohala Sugar Company

Castle & Cooke, Inc., has had a long and continued interest in the sugar business. The company's founders invested individually in several early Hawaiian sugar plantations, and the company itself later participated in financing a number of these same companies.

In 1966 Castle & Cooke was agent for and held ownership in three sugar companies—the Ewa Plantation Company, and the Waialua Agricultural Company, Ltd., on the island of Oahu, and the Kohala Sugar Company on the island of Hawaii.[1] The three companies had a combined annual production of 180,000 tons of raw sugar, representing about 15% of the total output for the Hawaiian Islands. For the year ended April 30, 1965, sugar revenues of $24.5 million represented about 9% of Castle & Cooke's total sales.

The industry environment within which the sugar plantations operated placed some unique limitations on management's normal prerogatives. For this reason a review of the sugar industry will precede further description of Castle & Cooke's sugar interests.

---

[1] The Kohala Sugar Company was a wholly owned subsidiary. Castle & Cooke had a 67.4% interest in the Ewa Plantation Company and a 66.25% interest in the Waialua Agricultural Company. Outstanding shares of Ewa and Waialua stock were traded on the Honolulu Stock Exchange. On February 11, 1966, 105 shares of Ewa stock were traded at $28¼. On February 14, 1966, 45 shares of Waialua stock traded at $19½.

© 1966 by the Board of Trustees of the Leland Stanford Junior University.

BACKGROUND DATA ON THE SUGAR INDUSTRY

Sugar is produced in almost every area of the world. Because it is considered by many as an essential food, most of the principal countries have government programs designed to provide a supply adequate for their population. This desire for a guaranteed supply of sugar causes about 70% of the world output to be consumed in the countries where it is produced, and another 20% to have relatively assured markets.

Consequently, the concepts of a "world market" and a "world price" for sugar refer to that 10% of the world production which does not have a place in the system of one of the great sugar consuming nations.[2] For this reason, only a few paragraphs of this note will be devoted to world production and consumption of sugar. Where the world situation does influence the U.S. sugar industry, it will be indicated.

Virtually all of the commercial sugar throughout the world comes from two sources—sugar cane and sugar beets. The chemical composition of refined sugar obtained from these sources is identical. About 55% of the world output of sugar comes from sugar cane and the remaining 45% from sugar beets. Cane is grown in tropical and semitropical areas, sugar beets in the more temperate zones.

The manufacturing process for cane and beet sugar is basically the same, except in the stage during which the juice is extracted. In processing sugar cane, extraction is done mechanically by pressing the cane between heavy rollers which squeeze out the juice. In processing sugar beets, the juice is extracted by passing slices of the beet against a stream of hot water which diffuses the sugar through the membranes into the surrounding water. Subsequent stages of clarification and evaporation of the juice, crystallization, and centrifuging are the same in principle.

During the centrifuging stage, sugar can either be held as raw sugar or processed into refined sugar. Raw sugar contains about 2.5% nonsugar and molasses, is nonperishable, and bulk handles easily. Sugar is produced in its raw form whenever the product must be shipped to distant markets. Raw sugar is subsequently refined in factories close to major market areas.

World production of sugar is summarized in Exhibit 1. The United States and its territories produced about 10% and consumed about 13% of the world sugar output in 1965. Per capita consumption in the U.S. has averaged slightly under 100 pounds annually in recent years, compared with a world average of 38 pounds per person per year.

---

[2] The "world price" for sugar tends to be an artificial figure because it represents the homeless 10% that has to find a buyer as best it can. In periods when sugar is in adequate supply throughout the world, the "world price" is often the distressed price and is not truly representative of the price at which most transactions are taking place.

Year	World*	U.S.†
1963	37.83	96.7
1962	37.73	96.0
1961	38.93	95.0
1960	37.76	93.9
1959	35.81	94.4
1958	35.58	93.7
1957	34.33	93.9
1956	32.96	96.7
1955	31.80	93.7
1954	30.90	92.1
1953	30.33	96.6

Sources: *Lamborn's Sugar Market Report.

+Willett & Gray.

THE U.S. SUGAR INDUSTRY

Almost from the beginning of government in the United States, the sugar industry has been regulated. For a period of 145 years, from 1789 to 1934, it was protected and regulated almost solely by tariff duties. The tariff system was replaced in 1934 when passage of the Jones-Costigan Act provided specific sugar quotas for various domestic and foreign areas. The subsequent passing of the Sugar Act of 1937 continued the quota system and also provided the model for present-day sugar legislation.

Under the quota provisions of the Sugar Act, Congress specifies who shall grow each pound of sugar sold in the United States. The quota is based on an estimated U.S. consumption level and assigned about two-thirds to domestic growers and one-third to foreign growers.

The most recent extension of the Sugar Act was signed into law on October 22, 1965, and covers the period 1966 through 1971. Quotas were based on an annual estimated U.S. consumption of 9.7 million tons of sugar and were assigned as shown at the top of page 669.

The new quota represented a 580,000 ton increase in the domestic share, with mainland beet growers gaining 375,000 tons and mainland cane growers the remaining 205,000 tons. The quotas for Hawaii, Puerto Rico, and the Philippines remained unchanged.

Quotas for other specified foreign countries were established as percentages of the requirements remaining after the quotas for domestic areas and the Philippines were established. Also changed was the method of allocating the 1,635,000 ton Cuban quota which was being withheld in the absence of diplomatic relations between Cuba and the U.S. Beginning in 1966, this quota was to be assigned on

exhibit 1

CASTLE & COOKE SUGAR INTERESTS

World Sugar Production (Centrifugal)
Centrifugal Sugar (Raw Value):[1] Production in Specified Countries
(average 1955–1956 through 1959–1960, annual 1962–1963 through 1964–1965[2])

Continent and Country	Average 1955-56 through 1959-60 1,000 short tons	1962-63 1,000 short tons	1963-64 1,000 short tons	1964-65[3] 1,000 short tons
North America (cane unless otherwise indicated)[1]				
Canada (beet)	151	153	173	175
Mexico	1,380	1,870	2,089	2,368
United States				
Continental (beet)	2,088	2,598	3,100	3,350
Continental (cane)	572	853	1,185	1,300
Hawaii	1,013	1,101	1,150	1,150
Puerto Rico	1,036	990	989	950
Virgin Islands of the U.S.	11	11	15	16
British Honduras	12	31	38	43
Costa Rica	44	96	101	127
El Salvador	51	68	72	85
Guatemala	70	152	158	160
Honduras	17	30	32	38
Nicaragua	61	111	105	120
Panama	25	40	54	63
Cuba	5,883	4,211	4,000	4,500
Dominican Republic	883	847	970	1,000
Guadeloupe	146	185	184	198
Haiti	61	67	70	75
Jamaica	419	542	531	582
Martinique	83	102	68	79
West Indies				
Barbados	183	214	181	202
Leeward and Windward Islands[4]	94	76	72	81
Trinidad and Tobago	205	255	254	280
Total North America	14,488	14,603	15,591	16,942
South America (cane unless otherwise indicated)				
Argentina	906	858	1,157	1,063
Bolivia	11	55	77	83
Brazil	3,110	3,576	3,606	3,939
British Guiana	330	355	308	375
Chile (beet)	40	81	118	119
Colombia	297	449	399	485
Ecuador	93	149	130	170
Paraguay	30	38	43	45
Peru	800	904	882	915
Surinam	10	12	13	15

Uruguay (beet and cane)	27	57	44	70
Venezuela	205	292	339	378
Total South America	5,859	6,826	7,116	7,657

Europe (beet unless otherwise indicated)

Austria	282	286	355	347
Belgium and Luxembourg	393	383	402	525
Denmark	353	225	403	450
Finland[5]	38	49	57	53
France	1,571	1,795	2,218	2,277
Germany, West	1,590	1,635	2,230	2,241
Greece[6,7]	0	29	42	66
Ireland	126	151	159	174
Italy	1,271	1,099	1,007	1,018
Netherlands	490	503	461	625
Portugal				
Azores and Madeira	13	13	16	19
Spain (cane and beet)	470	529	448	560
Sweden[5]	314	239	262	327
Switzerland	40	33	50	60
United Kingdom	818	836	978	998
Total West Europe	7,769	7,805	9,088	9,740
Albania[7]	12	14	12	13
Bulgaria[7]	137	169	170	170
Czechoslovakia[7]	860	1,112	1,191	1,270
Germany, East[7]	804	790	822	815
Hungary	332	468	512	525
Poland	1,152	1,464	1,570	1,800
Rumania	244	337	343	400
Yugoslavia	219	272	375	360
Total East Europe	3,760	4,626	4,995	5,353
Total Europe	11,529	12,431	14,083	15,093
U.S.S.R. (Europe and Asia)	5,632	6,600	6,350	9,000

Africa (cane unless otherwise indicated)

Ethiopia	35	69	73	76
Egypt	340	381	421	472
Congo (Leopoldville)	31	49	40	33
Kenya[7]	29	39	44	45
Tanganyika	28	44	58	65
Uganda[7]	89	124	140	150
Malagasy Republic	55	102	129	130
Mauritius	612	587	808	614
Mozambique	165	203	210	204
Reunion	219	225	280	250
Rhodesia	9	94	129	180
South Africa, Republic of[8]	989	1,277	1,359	1,479
Other Africa	93	171	177	191
Total Africa	2,694	3,365	3,868	3,889

Asia (cane unless
otherwise indicated)

Iran (beet and cane)	119	180	198	195
Turkey (Europe and Asia) (beet)	408	467	565	725
China, mainland (cane and beet)	836	900	1,150	1,200
Taiwan	963	873	860	815
Burma	38	72	60	60
India	2,737	2,979	3,449	3,800
Indonesia	903	648	725	703
Japan (beet; incl. cane beginning 1959-60)	86	225	256	258
Pakistan	174	223	324	360
Philippines	1,356	1,714	1,920	2,000
Thailand	102	147	194	234
Other Asia (cane and beet)	111	363	343	415
Total Asia	7,833	8,791	10,044	10,765

Oceania (cane)

Australia	1,428	2,000	1,934	2,017
Fiji	210	279	331	330
Total Oceania	1,638	2,279	2,265	2,347
World total (cane)	29,379	31,805	34,065	36,333
World total (beet)	20,294	23,090	25,252	29,360
World total (cane and beet)	49,673	54,895	59,317	65,693

1Centrifugal sugar, as distinguished from noncentrifugal, includes cane and beet sugar produced by the centrifugal process, which is the principal kind moving in international trade. 2Years shown are crop-harvesting years. For chronological arrangement here, all campaigns which begin not earlier than May of one year, or later than April of the following year, are placed in the same crop-harvesting year. The entire season's production of each country is credited to the May/April year in which harvesting and sugar production began. 3Preliminary. 4Includes Antigua, St. Kitts, St. Lucia, and St. Vincent. 5Beginning with this issue, excludes sugar from imported beets. 6No sugar produced prior to 1961-62. 7Production relates to calendar years for the first of the two years indicated in crop-year heading. 8Includes Swaziland. 9Includes Khandsari.

Source: Foreign Agricultural Service, U. S. Department of Agriculture. Prepared or estimated on the basis of official statistics of foreign governments, other foreign source materials, reports of U. S. Agricultural Attaches and Foreign Service Officers, results of office research, and related information.

a temporary country by country basis. It had been previously filled by competitive imports of raw sugar.

The Sugar Act extension further provided that any increase in national consumption between 9.7 million and 10.4 million tons would go to foreign producers. If total consumption should exceed 10.4 million tons, domestic beet and mainland cane growers would receive 65% of the increase and foreign producers the remaining 35%. Beet growers in this case would receive 75% of the increased domestic quota.

Per Capita Consumption of Sugar

	Tons
Domestic beet producers	3,025,000
Hawaii cane	1,110,000
Florida and Louisiana cane	1,100,000
Puerto Rico	1,140,000
Virgin Islands	15,000
Total "domestic" quota	6,390,000
Philippines	1,050,000
Mexico	348,501
Dominican Republic	340,925
Brazil	340,925
Peru	272,013
British West Indies	136,000
Ecuador	49,770
French West Indies	42,970
Argentina	42,000
Haiti	18,731
Venezuela	17,000
Other West Hemisphere	182,242
Australia	162,152
China	67,431
India	64,861
South Africa	48,000
Others	90,479
Total "foreign" quota	3,310,000
Total U.S. quota	9,700,000

Through the administration of the Sugar Act, the Secretary of Agriculture can normally stabilize the price of sugar at a predetermined level. In 1965–1966 the parity was pegged at $6.87 per hundred pounds, raw value. The base consumption level of 9.7 million tons used in the act was selected as the estimated demand–supply level which would produce this price. If demand increased to a level over 9.7 million tons, the growth factor allowing foreign suppliers to sell more sugar to the U.S. would compensate for the imbalance.[3] If demand fell below 9.7 million tons, the Secretary of Agriculture had the power to reduce the quotas of the domestic beet and mainland cane growers. Offshore producers in this situation would still be guaranteed their quota as established by the act.

Growers were encouraged to abide by the quotas by a section of the act which provided benefit payments to sugar cane and beet growers in the United States, Puerto Rico, and Hawaii for complying with the quotas and for meeting certain

---

[3] During the first two months of 1966 the Agriculture Department increased the import quota for foreign-produced raw sugar by 100,000 tons in response to a nationwide increase of 15¢ a hundred pounds for refined sugar. At the time of the announced increase in the foreign quota, the price of raw sugar was $6.94 a hundred pounds, compared to the established parity price of $6.87. The price per hundred pounds of refined sugar, including the 15¢ increase, ranged from $9.65 in the midwest to $10.50 in the northeast.

stipulated conditions regarding wage and labor standards set by the government. The schedule of compliance payments is presented below:

**Government Benefit Payments
(in terms of short tons—raw value)**

Size of Crop	Benefits per Hundred Weight*	Size of Crop	Benefits per Hundred Weight*
0- 350 tons	$0.800	3,000- 6,000 tons	$0.525
350- 700 tons	0.750	6,000-12,000 tons	0.500
700-1,000 tons	0.700	12,000-30,000 tons	0.475
1,000-1,500 tons	0.600	More than 30,000 tons	0.300
1,500-3,000 tons			

*Benefits to domestic growers of sugar cane and sugar beets.

Source: U. S. Dept. of Agriculture.

Compliance payments have averaged about 68¢ per hundred pounds, ranging from 46¢ in Hawaii, where most of the production was on large farms, to 79¢ in the beet area, where small farms prevailed.

These payments are financed by an excise tax of 50¢ per hundred pounds placed on all refiners in the United States, whether they process domestically grown or imported sugar.

For the U.S. sugar industry the quota system means greater stability in both production and prices. This stability, however, has resulted in typically higher sugar prices in the U.S. For the 15 years between 1951 and 1965 the U.S. price had been below the world price only four times (see Exhibit 2). The most recent trend reversal was in 1963, when a series of events severely cut the Cuban sugar output and world supplies were further reduced by poor beet sugar crops in Europe. In face of a world demand which was increasing about two million tons annually, this abrupt change in supply caused the world price to jump from an average of 2.97¢ per pound in 1962 to an average of 8.48¢ per pound in 1963. At the same time, however, with many foreign producers diverting their U.S. shipments to the world market, U.S. prices increased from 5.56¢ in 1962 to 7.28¢ in 1963. Similar sharp increases in world prices, rather than significant decreases in U.S. prices, accounted for the other occasions when the world price of sugar rose above the U.S. price. With the establishment of specific foreign quotas under the 1965 extension of the Sugar Act, the sharp rise in U.S. prices was not expected to occur again. The act provided that foreign quotas would be reset each year; therefore, if a country chose not to fill its U.S. quota in favor of selling sugar at a higher world price, it would be unlikely to receive the same sugar quota in future years, when the U.S. price normally could be expected to be above the world price.

exhibit 2

CASTLE & COOKE SUGAR INTERESTS

U.S. and World Prices

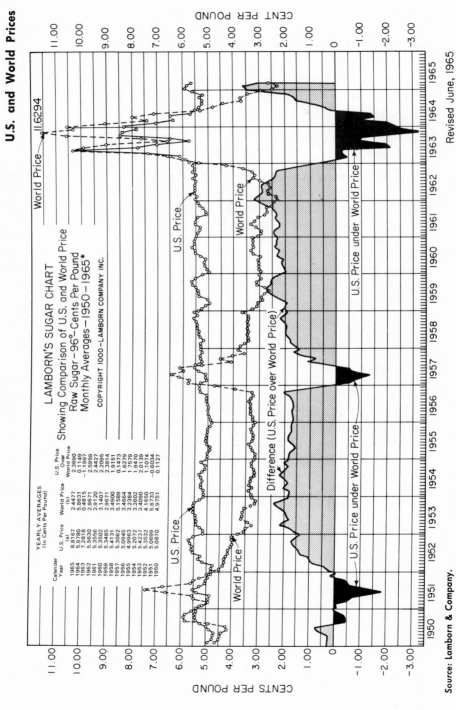

LAMBORN'S SUGAR CHART

Showing Comparison of U.S. and World Price
Raw Sugar–96° Cents Per Pound
Monthly Averages–1950–1965*

COPYRIGHT 1000–LAMBORN COMPANY INC.

Calendar Year	YEARLY AVERAGES (In Cents Per Pound)		
	U.S. Price (a)	World Price (b)	U.S. Price Over World Price
1965	8.8167	2.4477	2.3690
1964	5.9780	5.8631	0.1149
1963	7.2818	0.4815	-1.1997
1962	5.5630	2.9671	2.5959
1961	5.3556	2.9120	2.4427
1960	5.3502	3.1407	2.2095
1959	5.3485	2.9671	2.3814
1958	5.4131	3.4900	1.9151
1957	5.3062	5.1589	0.1473
1956	5.0945	3.4664	1.6279
1955	4.9963	3.2384	1.7579
1954	5.2072	3.2602	1.9470
1953	5.4237	3.4090	2.0139
1952	5.3532	4.1650	1.1074
1951	5.0699	5.6733	-0.6034
1950	5.0870	4.9751	0.1127

World Price ·· 11.6294

U.S. Price

World Price

U.S. Price

World Price

U.S. Price

World Price

Difference (U.S. Price over World Price)

U.S. Price under World Price

U.S. Price under World Price

U.S. Price under World Price

CENTS PER POUND

CENT PER POUND

1950 1951 1952 1953 1954 1955 1956 1957 1958 1959 1960 1961 1962 1963 1964 1965

Revised June, 1965

Source: Lamborn & Company.

THE STRUCTURE OF THE U.S. SUGAR INDUSTRY

Exhibit 3 summarizes the basic structure of the U.S. sugar industry. It will be noted that various segments of the industry have their own unique characteristics, the more important of which are discussed below.

Beet Sugar

In contrast to the cane sugar segment of the industry, all beet sugar consumed in the U.S. comes from raw material grown and processed on the mainland. Sugar beets are grown in 23 states and processed into beet sugar in 15 states. Beet sugar production by states is summarized in Exhibit 4.

For the most part, the beet sugar processors have chosen not to become involved in growing beets, but have sought to assure their raw material supply by locating plants in the center of the beet growing areas.[4] Exhibit 5 lists the beet processing companies and the location of their plants. Exhibit 6 shows the growth in beet sugar production in the U.S. for the period 1913 to 1964.

Beet sugar factories purchase their beet requirements largely from independent growers under annual purchase contracts. The price paid depends on the sugar content of the beets and the net received by the manufacturers from the sale of refined sugar. Under this arrangement the growers and processors share in the effects of price fluctuations; but even more important from the standpoint of the processors, a portion of the lower returns that may result from price cutting tactics and special promotions is passed back to the growers.

The beet sugar industry is further characterized by the exclusive use of single stage processing plants run at peak capacity during a 120 day harvesting season. The refined beet sugar they produce is stored in silos to await shipment to markets. Even though many of the beet processing factories are located at some distance from their markets, the highly developed transportation system in this country has facilitated this operation.

Cane Sugar

The structure of the cane sugar segment of the industry is somewhat more complicated than the beet sugar segment because it involves imported sugar. Since it is not practical to ship refined sugar to the U.S., cane sugar processing is done in two stages. The first stage, that of making raw sugar, takes place in the widely

---

[4] Because it requires seven tons of sugar beets to produce one ton of refined beet sugar, and because of the danger of spoilage, it is uneconomical for a grower to ship beets any distance to a processor.

exhibit 3

CASTLE & COOKE SUGAR INTERESTS

Structure of the U.S. Sugar Industry

Growing Area	Quota 1966 (tons)	Raw Material (cane or beets) Grown by—	Processing
Mainland beet: 1,395,000 acres harvested in 1964	3,025,000	24,000 independent growers who sell under contract to beet processors. Sugar beets are grown in 23 states with the largest share of the crop coming from the 11 western states. Beet sugar harvest lasts from late October until late February.	Because it is possible to build processing plants relatively close to both the source of the beets and major market areas, sugar beet processing is done in a single step process. Refined beet sugar is produced in 67 plants located in 19 states. In 1966, 12 companies were actively engaged in producing and selling refined beet sugar.
Mainland cane: Florida (1965 production 535,000) 221,000 acres harvested in 1964	1,100,000	13 independent sugar cane farms harvest November through February.	Raw sugar is produced at 20 mills in Florida and at 48 mills in Louisiana. The raw sugar is then sold to one or more of the 17 cane refining companies (excluding the Calif. & Hawaiian Sugar Refining Corp.) on the U.S. mainland. These companies operate a total of 27 refineries located mainly in the southern and eastern states. In addition to refining the raw sugar produced in Florida and Louisiana, these U.S. companies refine all the raw sugar (exclusive of the major share of Hawaiian raw sugar) shipped to the mainland from offshore and foreign lands.
Louisiana (1965 production 533,000) 325,000 acres harvested in 1964		2,500 independent sugar cane farms harvest September through December.	
Hawaiian cane: 110,759 acres harvested in 1964	1,110,000	90% of Hawaii's sugar cane is grown by 25 plantation companies. The remaining 10% is grown by 1,200 independent farmers. Harvest is from April through December.	Raw sugar is produced at 25 mills owned by the plantation companies. Cane from independent growers is processed by these same mills. About 70% of Hawaiian raw sugar is refined by C & H Refinery at Crockett, California. Remainder is sold as raw sugar to other refiners on U.S. mainland.
Puerto Rico: 303,142 acres harvested in 1964	1,140,000	15,000 independent cane farms. Harvested January through April.	Raw sugar is produced at 30 mills in Puerto Rico. Quota sugar for U.S. markets is sold to U.S. sugar refiners.
Foreign	3,310,000	All foreign imports are of cane sugar grown mainly by independent farmers.	Raw cane sugar is produced in the foreign country and sold to the U.S. cane sugar refining industry.
Summaries	9,700,000	All beet sugar consumed in the U.S. comes from sugar beets grown in the U.S. 11.1% of sugar consumed in the U.S. is supplied from cane grown on the mainland, 11.3% from cane grown in Hawaii, 11.3% from cane grown in Puerto Rico, and 34% from cane grown in foreign lands.	Approximately 31% of refined sugar consumed in the U.S. is beet sugar, all of which is processed on the mainland. All cane sugar consumed in the U.S. is refined here. About 84% of raw cane sugar refined on the mainland comes from offshore lands.

*Reflects increased prices in 1963 caused by world shortage of sugar.

Source: Casewriter exhibit.

exhibit 4

CASTLE & COOKE SUGAR INTERESTS

Beet Sugar Production in the U.S.
(1960–1961 to 1964–1965: hundredweight, refined)

State	1964-65[1]	1963-64	1962-63	1961-62	1960-61	Average 1960-61 to 1964-65	Percent
California	18,496,960	15,533,039	12,341,809	11,220,361	11,199,155	13,758,265	26.56
Colorado	9,791,997	9,576,942	9,329,527	8,023,431	9,360,635	9,216,507	17.79
Idaho	6,204,540	6,294,089	5,814,389	5,009,416	4,349,073	5,534,302	10.68
Nebraska	3,681,454	2,826,031	2,293,158	2,998,120	3,662,624	3,292,277	6.36
Washington	3,598,999	3,679,881	3,540,854	3,196,520	2,325,728	3,268,396	6.31
Minnesota	3,438,494	4,110,663	3,174,141	3,429,054	3,700,586	3,570,588	6.89
Montana	3,348,200	3,348,059	2,675,036	2,520,298	2,679,618	2,914,242	5.62
Michigan	2,914,383	2,797,056	2,349,925	2,298,608	2,276,325	2,527,259	4.88
Oregon	2,447,882	2,520,414	2,145,347	1,977,216	1,602,067	2,138,585	4.13
Wyoming	2,167,448	2,325,611	1,631,221	1,840,246	1,842,122	1,961,330	3.79
Utah	1,539,180	1,555,103	1,216,439	951,643	1,481,139	1,348,701	2.60
Texas	1,275,000	—	—	—	—	255,000	.49
Ohio	1,231,423	1,289,921	1,165,779	830,386	1,038,232	1,111,148	2.14
Iowa	619,259	605,077	551,302	466,879	238,854	496,274	.96
South Dakota	350,237	369,994	338,985	328,091	331,719	343,805	.66
Wisconsin	—	—	—	189,578	178,682	73,652	.14
Total	61,105,456	57,831,880	48,567,912	45,279,847	46,266,559	51,810,331	100.00
Total— Short tons raw value	3,269,142	3,094,006	2,598,383	2,422,472	2,475,261	2,771,853	

1 Partly estimated.
Source: United States Beet Sugar Association, Washington, D.C.

Statistics by crop year, which is for spring planting and fall harvesting in first year named, except in Imperial Valley of California, where figure is for fall planting in first year named and spring harvesting in following year. Sugar beets are grown also in Illinois, Indiana, North Dakota, New Mexico, and Texas, and processed in plants located in states listed above.

scattered domestic and offshore growing areas. The second, or refining stage, occurs on the U.S. mainland near the major ports of entry.

Because of the geographical separation in the two stages of producing refined cane sugar, the cane sugar refining business has, for the most part, developed independently of raw sugar production. Production of raw cane sugar by major geographical area is summarized in Exhibit 7. Exhibit 8 lists the cane sugar refining companies and the location and capacity of refineries in the U.S. It can be seen that three refineries, all of which are in Louisiana, are attached to a raw sugar mill. The other major exception to the independent development of the two stages of processing is the California and Hawaiian Sugar Refining Corporation, which has a direct relationship with the raw sugar producers in Hawaii. The details of this arrangement will be discussed later.

Excluding the abovementioned exceptions, the cane sugar refiners purchase their raw sugar requirements either on the open market or through contractual arrangements with raw sugar producers. The world's largest market for raw sugar trading is New York. Here are located the principal buyers and sellers, or their agents, of raw sugar for the U.S. domestic market. An organized market for raw sugar transactions is provided by the New York Coffee and Sugar Exchange, which functions in the same manner as other major commodity exchanges.

In summary, the beet sugar segment of the U.S. sugar industry is entirely domestic. Sugar beets are grown by independent farmers and sold to processors who manufacture refined beet sugar in single process plants. The processors then sell refined beet sugar through normal channels to consumers and industrial users.

The production of cane sugar, on the other hand, occurs in two stages: Raw sugar is produced in mills which are located in the far-flung cane growing areas such as Puerto Rico, Hawaii, the Philippines, Florida, and Louisiana, and is then refined in factories on the U.S. mainland.

A description of the Hawaiian segment of the cane sugar industry, with special emphasis on its unique features, follows.

THE HAWAIIAN SUGAR INDUSTRY

Sugar is the largest industry in Hawaii. The value to the Hawaiian economy of the raw sugar and by-products produced there has been estimated at $165,000,000 annually in recent years, and invested capital in the industry is said to be about $200,000,000.

The sugar industry provides full-time employment for about 12,500 persons who earn a total payroll of approximately $65,500,000 per year. About 5.5% (233,000 acres) of Hawaii's total land area is utilized in growing sugar cane. More than half of this land is owned by the sugar companies; the rest is leased from governmental agencies or private owners.

Hawaii's annual sugar production amounts to roughly one-fifth of that grown under the American flag, one-ninth of U.S. consumption, and one-fiftieth of world production.

The Hawaiian sugar industry began in 1835 when three young New Englanders founded Ladd and Company at Koloa on the island of Kauai. Previous attempts to grow and mill cane had been undertaken, but these ventures had all failed. Ladd and Company's first crop produced 12 tons of cane which yielded 2.5 tons of saleable sugar.

By 1838 there were 20 animal power and two water power mills in the Ha-

exhibit 5

CASTLE & COOKE SUGAR INTERESTS

Major U.S. Beet Sugar Processors, Their Plant Locations, and Daily Beet Slicing Capacity (as of 1964)

Company	Daily Beet Slicing Capacity (tons)
Great Western Sugar Company	
Brighton, Colorado	1,950
Eaton, Colorado	1,750
Ft. Collins, Colorado	last operated in 1955
Ft. Morgan, Colorado	2,350
Greeley, Colorado	1,700
Longmont, Colorado	3,200
Loveland, Colorado	3,000
Ovid, Colorado	2,050
Sterling, Colorado,	1,600
Windsor, Colorado	1,700
Billings, Montana	3,900
Lovell, Wyoming	1,750
Bayard, Nebraska	1,950
Gering, Nebraska	2,000
Mitchell, Nebraska	1,950
Scottsbluff, Nebraska	3,100
Presque Isle, Maine	to be completed 1967
Findley, Ohio	1,500
Fremont, Ohio	1,500
	33,150
Holly Sugar Corporation	
Alvarado, California	2,700
Carlton, California	6,000
Dyer, California	1,700
Hamilton, California	1,700
Tracy, California	2,700
Delta, Colorado	1,700
Hardin, Montana	1,800
Sidney, Montana	2,300
Torrington, Wyoming	3,000
Worland, Wyoming	1,700
Hereford, Texas	6,000
	31,300
American Crystal Sugar Company	
Clarksburg, California	2,600
Rocky Ford, Colorado	3,200
Missoula, Montana	1,500
Mason City, Iowa	2,400
Chaska, Minnesota	1,850
Crookston, Minnesota	3,900
Moorhead, Minnesota	3,900
East Grand Ford, Minnesota	2,800
Grand Island, Nebraska	1,200
Drayton, North Dakota	5,000
	28,150

Company	Daily Beet Slicing Capacity (tons)
Amalgamated Sugar Company	
Nyssa, Oregon	6,275
Nampa, Idaho	4,780
Rupert, Idaho	3,040
Twin Falls, Idaho	3,835
Lewiston, Utah	1,815
	19,745
Utah-Idaho Sugar Company	
Moses Lake, Washington	6,250
Toppenish, Washington	3,750
Idaho Falls, Idaho	3,000
Garland, Utah	2,500
West Jordan, Utah	1,700
Centerfield, Utah	last operated in 1961
Layton, Utah	last operated in 1961
Belle Fourche, South Dakota	1,800
	19,000
Spreckles Sugar Company	
Phoenix, Arizona	to be completed in 1967
Manteca, California	2,900
Spreckles, California	7,200
Tracy, California	3,600
Mendota, California	3,800
	17,500
Michigan Sugar Company	
Sebewaing, Michigan	2,000
Corrollton, Michigan	1,700
Croswell, Michigan	1,200
Caro, Michigan	1,600
	6,500
Union Sugar Div. of Consolidated Food Corp.	
Betteravia, California	4,700
Monitor Sugar Div. of Robt. Gage Coal Co.	
Bay City, Michigan	3,200
Buckeye Sugar, Inc.	
Ottowa, Ohio	1,600
National Sugar Manufacturing Co.	
Sugar City, Colorado	1,200
Pepsi-Cola Company	
Auburn, New York	to be completed in 1966

Source: American Beet Sugar Companies, 1963-64, United States Beet Sugar Association, January 1964.

exhibit 6

CASTLE & COOKE SUGAR INTERESTS

Sugar Beets: Acreage, Production, Season Average Price per Ton Received by Farmers, and Value; Production of Beet Sugar and Other Products (U.S. 1913–1964 *)

	Sugar Beets						Beet Sugar and Pulp			
	Acreage Planted 1,000	Acreage Harvested 1,000	Average Yield Per Acre Short	Production 1,000	Price3 Dollars	Farm Value3 1,000	Sugar produced (chiefly refined) 1,000	Molasses pulp 1,000	Dried pulp 1,000	Moist pulp 1,000
Year	acres	acres	tons	short tons	Per Ton	Dollars	short tons	short tons	short tons	short tons
1913	635	580	10.1	5,886	5.69	33,491	733	—	—	—
1914	515	483	11.6	5,585	5.45	30,438	722	—	—	—
1915	664	611	10.7	6,511	5.67	36,950	874	—	—	—
1916	78	665	9.4	6,228	6.12	38,139	821	—	—	—
1917	807	665	9.0	5,980	7.39	44,192	765	—	—	—
1918	690	594	10.0	5,949	10.00	59,494	761	—	—	—
1919	890	692	9.3	6,421	11.74	75,420	726	—	—	—
1920	978	872	9.8	8,538	11.63	99,324	1,089	—	—	—
1921	882	815	9.5	7,782	6.35	49,392	1,020	—	—	—
1922	606	530	9.8	5,183	7.91	41,017	675	—	—	—
1923	732	657	10.7	7,006	8.99	62,965	881	—	—	—
1924	936	816	9.2	7,508	7.95	59,689	1,090	—	—	—
1925	781	648	11.4	7,381	6.39	47,137	913	—	—	—
1926	746	677	10.7	7,223	7.61	54,964	897	74	78	—
1927	756	721	10.8	7,753	7.67	59,455	1,093	89	76	—
1928	698	644	11.0	7,101	7.11	50,477	1,061	64	75	—
1929	772	688	10.6	7,315	7.08	51,804	1,018	111	48	—
1930	821	776	11.9	9,199	7.14	65,698	1,208	150	60	1,458
1931	760	713	11.1	7,903	5.94	46,948	1,156	99	75	1,112
1932	812	764	11.9	9,070	5.26	47,705	1,357	116	134	1,340
1933	1,036	983	11.2	11,030	5.13	56,599	1,642	141	134	1,715
1934	945	770	9.8	7,519	5.16	38,776	1,160	130	92	1,198
1935	809	763	10.4	7,908	5.76	45,565	1,185	125	74	1,454
1936	855	776	11.6	9,028	6.05	54,636	1,304	157	73	1,543
1937	813	753	11.6	8,759	5.26	46,101	1,283	166	51	1,600
1938	985	925	12.4	11,497	4.65	53,478	1,674	219	105	1,858
1939	993	918	11.7	10,781	4.76	51,342	1,641	175	98	1,711
1940	971	912	13.4	12,194	5.11	62,287	1,758	182	110	1,676
1941	796	755	13.7	10,342	6.43	66,522	1,488	176	102	1,257
1942	1,048	954	12.2	11,685	6.84	79,905	1,617	149	134	1,390
1943	619	550	11.9	6,547	8.81	57,674	935	92	62	1,009
1944	633	555	12.1	6,718	10.60	71,156	979	72	99	923
1945	775	713	12.1	8,616	10.20	87,539	1,191	121	95	1,142
1946	905	802	13.2	10,582	11.10	117,840	1,422	153	127	1,446
1947	968	879	14.2	12,503	11.80	148,080	1,719	203	91	1,834
1948	800	694	13.6	9,424	10.60	99,639	1,280	199	76	1,385
1949	768	687	14.8	10,196	10.80	110,369	1,461	204	96	1,389
1950	1,014	925	14.6	13,535	11.20	151,293	1,878	293	113	1,777
1951	758	691	15.2	10,482	11.70	122,483	1,448	231	88	1,764
1952	719	665	15.3	10,169	12.00	121,970	1,407	253	67	1,593
1953	794	745	16.2	12,084	11.60	140,364	1,697	324	100	1,641
1954	964	876	16.1	14,082	10.80	152,151	1,909	355	164	1,823
1955	798	740	16.5	12,228	11.20	136,477	1,625	354	108	1,368
1956	831	785	16.6	12,993	11.90	155,087	1,837	428	106	1,378
1957	918	880	17.7	15,530	11.20	174,261	2,050	480	138	1,538
1958	935	891	17.0	15,150	11.70	177,807	2,056	484	158	1,372
1959	955	905	18.8	17,015	11.20	191,186	2,187	591	148	1,482
1960	977	957	17.2	16,421	11.60	190,109	2,291	613	152	1,298
1961	1,129	1,077	16.4	17,704	11.20	197,547	2,247	712	131	1,276
1962	1,182	1,103	16.5	18,254	12.80	233,243	2,417	676	316	1,393
1963	1,285	1,235	18.9	23,328	12.20	285,011	2,893	1,004	183	1,560
1964	1,460	1,395	16.8	23,368	11.90	278,079	3,069	n.a.	n.a.	n.a.

1Most years from 1913 to 1923 include a small unknown quantity of beets grown in Canada for Michigan factories.
2Basis of crop year including beets planted in previous fall in California and Arizona.
3Includes production incentive payments which were payments made to producers of sugar beets and sugar cane by the Commodity Credit Corporation during the period of government price control in World War II, to stimulate production, but excludes Sugar Act payments.
4Preliminary.

Source: Agricultural Marketing Service and Statistical Reporting Service, U.S. Department of Agriculture (June 1965).

waiian Islands. Total export of the Islands was two tons, worth about $200. Between 1841 and 1855 the sale of Hawaiian sugar abroad averaged 240 tons, and it was not until the beginning of the Civil War that Hawaiian sugar shipments passed 1,000 tons a year.

In 1860 the first of more than 140,000 Japanese laborers arrived to furnish the manpower for the burgeoning industry. Ten years later the Reciprocity Treaty between the Kingdom of Hawaii and the U.S. helped lead to the first 100,000 ton crop in 1886.

Additional workers brought to Hawaii from China, Korea, the Philippines, Europe, and the mainland helped the growth of the industry. In 1932 Hawaii recorded its first 1,000,000 ton crop, only to have a quota imposed under the Jones-Costigan Act in 1934, which has held Hawaiian production close to the 1,000,000 ton level since. Exhibit 9 summarizes the trend of cane sugar production in Hawaii for the period 1908–1964.

Sugar Production in Hawaii

In 1965 the Hawaiian sugar industry was composed of 25 plantation companies, located on four major islands in the Hawaiian group. Sugar production by island in 1964 [5] was:

Island	Tons Sugar
Hawaii (11 plantations)	426,618
Kauai (8 plantations)	265,718
Maui (3 plantations)	264,896
Oahu (4 plantations)	221,538

The 25 plantation companies normally account for about 93% of the sugar cane grown on the islands and for all of Hawaii's production of raw sugar. Work on the Hawaiian sugar plantations is divided into two divisions, the field and the mill. Field work consists of preparation of the soil, planting the crop, weeding, insect control, irrigation, and harvesting. Because there is little seasonal change in temperature in Hawaii, planting, growing, and harvesting of cane take place throughout the greater part of the year. The principal unique feature is the scheduling of these operations so that a steady flow of ripe sugar cane will reach the mill.

Sugar is milled and processed into raw sugar directly on each plantation. The mills usually operate on a six day, 24 hour a day basis for nine to ten months a year. Mill shutdowns occur during the heavy rainy season, normally in January, February, and March, because at this time the fields are too muddy to bear the

---

[5] Production in 1964 was from 26 plantations. Two plantations were merged in 1965, reducing the total to 25.

exhibit 7

CASTLE & COOKE SUGAR INTERESTS

Production of Raw Cane Sugar by Geographical Area Under U.S. Quota System
(1945–1964:* short tons, raw value)

Area	1945	1946	1947	1948	1949	1950	1951	1952	1953	1954
Domestic beet	1,042,544	1,378,640	1,574,262	1,656,319	1,487,314	1,748,701	1,730,180	1,559,505	1,748,993	1,802,491
Mainland cane	416,887	444,746	382,803	455,411	557,894	517,985	460,306	552,506	513,315	500,759
Hawaii	740,061	632,852	842,244	714,333	768,634	1,144,930	941,129	971,672	1,087,301	1,039,700
Puerto Rico	902,660	866,914	968,545	1,013,175	1,090,733	1,052,706	959,231	983,359	1,118,171	1,082,032
Virgin Islands	3,907	4,823	2,744	4,287	4,363	10,694	6,306	6,297	12,250	10,424
Philippine Islands										
Quota sugar	—	—	—	251,622	524,803	473,614	705,522	860,123	932,116	973,968
Nonquota sugar	—	—	—	—	—	—	—	—	—	—
Global quota sugar	—	—	—	—	—	—	—	—	—	—
Cuba2	2,802,959	2,282,393	3,942,900	2,927,096	3,102,629	3,264,303	2,946,306	2,981,896	2,759,313	2,717,418
Other Foreign										
Quota sugar	87,416	46,353	44,732	61,892	51,565	61,396	12,666	50,772	111,011	113,264
Nonquota sugar	—	—	—	—	—	—	—	—	—	—
Global quota sugar	—	—	—	—	—	—	—	—	—	—
Total	5,996434	5,656,721	7,758,230	7,084,135	7,587,935	8,274,329	7,761,646	7,966,130	8,282,470	8,240,056

Area	1955	1956	1957	1958	1959	1960	1961	1962	1963	1964
Domestic beet	1,797,327	1,955,252	2,070,694	2,239,852	2,241,164	2,164,692	2,607,166	2,415,182	2,964,790	2,698,514
Mainland cane	499,623	601,369	637,172	680,552	577,595	619,047	783,611	787,354	1,072,202	905,511
Hawaii	1,052,004	1,091,282	1,060,000	630,175	976,845	884,788	1,044,858	1,084,179	1,032,541	1,110,000
Puerto Rico	1,079,562	1,134,769	920,000	823,034	957,853	895,784	980,176	904,030	875,245	792,788
Virgin Islands	9,942	12,535	14,753	6,093	12,302	6,954	16,184	10,751	15,000	15,856
Philippine Islands										
Quota sugar	977,375	981,765	930,000	980,000	980,000	979,783	962,403	1,073,763	1,194,833	1,171,090
Nonquota sugar	—	—	—	—	—	—	—	182,401	0	0
Global quota sugar	—	—	—	—	—	—	—	—	—	46,269
Cuba	2,861,937	3,090,680	3,127,028	3,440,844	3,218,723	2,393,663	0	0	0	0
Other foreign countries:										
Quota sugar	118,524	127,122	215,353	281,215	280,809	434,208	363,510	1,336,799	1,649,734	1,421,462
Nonquota sugar	—	—	—	—	—	1,187,487	2,974,275	1,404,773	0	0
Global quota sugar	—	—	—	—	—	—	—	597,989	1,710,648	947,717
Total	8,396,294	8,994,774	8,975,000	9,081,765	9,245,291	9,526,406	9,732,183	9,797,211	10,514,993	9,109,207

1Quotas not in effect September 11 to December 31, 1939, and April 13, 1942, to December 31, 1947.

2Data exclude following quantities shipped to U.S. for refining and reshipped to other countries under international allocations: 1942, 144,000 tons; 1943, 466,000 tons; 1944, 262,000 tons; 1945, 337,000 tons; 1946, 368,000 tons, and 1947, 230,000 tons. Also excludes invert molasses (sugar equivalent) produced and shipped in lieu of raw sugar at request of U.S. government as follows: 1942, 316,466 tons; 1943, 260,977 tons; 1944, 700,914 tons.

3Excludes first ten tons imported.

4Excludes 238,277 tons shipped to United Kingdom in exchange arrangements to conserve shipping.

5Prior to 1953 there was no restriction in direct-consumption imports from full-duty countries.

Source: Agricultural Stabilization and Conservation Service, U.S. Department of Agriculture (June 1965).

exhibit 8

CASTLE & COOKE SUGAR INTERESTS

The U.S. Sugar Refining Industry on the Mainland

Region	Name of Company	Location of refinery	Melting Capacity per 24 hours sh.
Eastern	The American Sugar Refining Co.	Baltimore (Maryland)	1,750
		Boston (Massachusetts)	1,000
		Brooklyn (New York)	1,800
		Philadelphia (Pennsylvania)	1,750
	The National Sugar Refining Co.	Long Island City (New York)	2,000
		Philadelphia (Pennsylvania)	2,000
	The Sucrest Corp.	Brooklyn (New York)	n.a.
	Pepsi-Cola Co.	Long Island City (New York)	400
	Refined Syrups & Sugard, Inc.	Yonkers (New York)	1,150
	Revere Sugar Refinery	Charlestown (Massachusetts)	1,500
Southern	Savannah Sugar Refining Corp.	Port Wentworth (Georgia)	1,250
	Imperial Sugar Co.	Sugar Land (Texas)	1,125
	The American Sugar Refining Co.	Chalmette (Louisiana)	2,000
	Colonial Sugars Co.	Gramercy (Louisiana)	875
	Henderson Sugar Refinery, Inc.	New Orleans (Louisiana)	*
	Godchaux Refining Corp.	Reserve (Louisiana)	1,250
	The South Coast Corp.	1Mathews (Louisiana)	500
	Southdown Inc.	1Houma (Louisiana)	325
	J. Aron & Co., Inc.	1Supreme Louisiana)	650
Western	California & Hawaiian Sugar Refining Corp.	Crockett (California)	3,250
Central	Industrial Sugars Inc.	St. Louis (Missouri)	n.a.
	The Sucrest Corp.	Chicago (Illinois)	500

1Attached to a sugar mill.
*No longer operates as a refinery, but has sugar toll—refined in another refinery.

Source: Casewriter exhibit.

weight of the heavy harvesting equipment. The labor force continues to be used, however, in maintenance and repair work.

In contrast to many cane growing areas where the harvest takes place annually, the Hawaiian sugar crop is allowed to mature for 22 to 24 months to assure maximum sugar content. This longer growing period, made possible by Hawaii's climate, has produced record crops averaging more than ten tons of sugar per acre for the entire industry. Adjusted back to an annual basis, the average of five tons of sugar per acre represents about twice the yield achieved in most of the other sugar producing areas of the world.

exhibit 9

CASTLE & COOKE SUGAR INTERESTS

Cane Sugar: Production in Hawaii, 1908–1964

Production Year[1] (Beginning Oct. 1st, ending Sept. 30th)	Tons sugar per acre	Tons cane per ton sugar	Total cane land area (acres)	Acreage harvested[2] (acres)	Average yield per acre short tons	Production short tons	Converted to 96° raw value[3] (short tons)	Equivalent refined[4] (short tons)	Raw value 96° sugar made per short tons of cane (pounds)	Recovery of equivalent refined sugar from cane ground[5] (percent)
1908-1909	5.14	7.42	201,641	106,127	38.2	4,050,000	645,738	610,048	270	12.59
1909-1910	4.81	7.78	209,469	110,247	37.4	4,122,000	529,940	495,282	257	12.02
1910-1911	5.16	7.94	214,312	112,796	41.0	4,623,000	582,196	544,120	252	11.77
1911-1912	5.34	7.75	216,345	113,866	41.4	4,711,000	607,863	568,109	258	12.06
1912-1913	4.90	7.99	215,741	113,548	39.1	4,445,000	556,654	520,249	250	11.70
1913-1914	5.54	8.01	217,470	112,700	4.44	5,000,000	624,165	583,345	250	11.67
1914-1915	5.75	7.96	239,800	113,164	45.8	5,184,393	650,970	608,397	251	11.74
1915-1916	5.17	8.14	246,332	115,419	42.1	4,859,424	596,703	557,679	246	11.48
1916-1917	5.57	7.98	247,476	117,468	4.44	5,220,000	654,388	611,591	251	11.72
1917-1918	4.86	8.34	246,813	119,785	40.5	4,855,804	582,192	544,117	240	11.21
1918-1919	5.07	7.81	239,844	119,679	39.6	4,744,070	607,174	567,465	256	11.96
1919-1920	4.91	7.98	247,838	114,105	39.2	4,473,498	560,379	523,730	251	11.71
1920-1921	4.83	8.53	236,510	113,056	41.2	4,657,222	546,273	510,547	235	10.96
1921-1922	4.98	8.23	228,519	124,124	41.0	5,088,062	618,457	578,010	243	11.36
1922-1923	4.85	8.23	235,134	114,182	39.9	4,559,819	554,199	517,954	243	11.36
1923-1924	6.42	7.91	231,862	111,581	50.7	5,661,000	715,918	669,097	253	11.82
1924-1925	6.47	8.06	240,597	120,632	52.2	6,297,000	781,000	730,000	248	11.59
1925-1926	6.58	8.07	237,774	122,309	53.1	6,495,686	804,644	752,020	248	11.58
1926-1927	6.68	8.41	234,809	124,542	56.1	6,992,082	831,648	777,258	238	11.12
1927-1928	7.00	8.37	240,769	131,534	58.6	7,707,330	920,887	860,661	239	11.17
1928-1929	7.16	8.05	239,858	129,131	57.7	7,447,494	925,140	864,636	248	11.61
1929-1930	7.02	8.36	242,761	133,840	58.7	7,853,439	939,287	877,858	239	11.18
1930-1931	7.43	8.33	251,533	137,037	61.9	8,485,183	1,018,047	951,467	240	11.21
1931-1932	7.57	8.38	251,876	139,744	63.4	8,865,323	1,057,303	988,155	239	11.15
1932-1933	7.34	8.05	254,563	144,959	59.1	8,566,781	1,063,605	994,045	248	11.60
1933(Oct.1-Dec.31)	—	—	—	—	—	—	127,317	118,990	—	—
Production Year Beginning Jan.1										
1934	7.14	8.33	252,237	134,318	59.5	7,992,260	959,337	896,596	240	11.22
1935	7.82	8.67	246,491	126,116	67.8	8,555,424	986,849	922,309	231	10.78
1936	7.97	8.80	245,891	130,828	70.1	9,170,279	1,042,316	974,149	227	10.62
1937	7.46	9.32	240,833	126.671	69.5	8,802,716	944,382	882,619	215	10.03
1938	6.92	9.39	238,302	135,978	65.0	8,835,370	941,293	879,732	213	9.96
1939	7.18	8.66	235,227	138,440	62.2	8,600,543	994,173	929,154	231	10.79
1940	7.16	8.76	235,110	136,417	62.7	8,557,216	976,677	912,802	228	10.67
1941	7.24	9.04	238,111	130,768	65.5	8,559,797	947,190	885,244	221	10.34
1942	7.58	9.10	225,199	114,745	69.0	7,918,342	870,099	813,195	220	10.27
1943	7.79	9.24	220,928	113,754	71.9	8,185,400	885,640	827,719	216	10.11
1944	7.99	8.95	216,072	109,522	71.5	7,832,185	874,947	817,725	223	10.44
1945	7.96	8.98	211,331	103,173	71.4	7,371,158	821,216	767,509	223	10.41
1946	8.06	8.83	208,376	84,379	71.1	6,002,127	680,073	635,596	227	10.59
1947	7.72	9.11	211,624	113,020	70.3	7,942,216	872,187	815,146	220	10.26
1948	8.35	9.03	206,550	100,042	75.4	7,542,613	835,107	780,491	221	10.35
1949	8.76	8.44	213,354	108,794	73.9	8,045,941	955,890[6]	893,375	238	11.10
1950	8.78	8.51	220,383	109,405	74.7	8,174,821	960,961[7]	898,114	235	10.99
1951	9.09	8.51	221,212	109,494	77.4	8,477,201	995,759	930,636	235	10.98
1952	9.44	8.52	221,990	108,089	80.4	8,693,920	1,020,450	953,712	235	10.97
1953	10.15	8.19	221,542	108,337	83.1	9,003,967	1,099,316	1,027,421	244	11.41
1954	10.02	8.75	220,138	107,480	87.75	9,431,781	1,077,347	1,006,889	228	10.68
1955	10.74	8.66	218,819	106,180	92.94	9,867,978	1,140,112	1,065,525	231	10.79
1956	10.28	9.01	220,606	106,956	92.65	9,909,990	1,099,543	1,027,633	222	10.37
1957	10.16	8.71	221,336	106,742	88.51	9,447,647	1,084,646	1,013,710	230	10.73
1958	9.09	9.87	221,683	84,136	89.77	7,552,750	764,953	714,925	203	9.47
1959	8.33	9.66	222,588	110,371	85.31	9,416,225	974,632	910,891	207	9.67
1960	9.03	9.20	224,617	103,584	83.15	8,613,317	935,744	874,546	217	10.86
1961	10.09	8.78	227,027	108,320	88.58	9,595,342	1,092,481	1,021,033	228	11.39
1962	10.31	8.76	228,926	108,600	90.36	9,812,580	1,120,011	1,046,762	228	11.41
1963	10.25	9.12	231,321	107,436	93.39	10,033,969	1,100,768	1,028,777	219	10.97
1964	10.64	8.9	233,145	110,759	94.76	10,495,175	1,178,770	1,101,678	225	11.23
1965	—	—	—	—	—	—			—	—
1966	—	—	—	—	—	—			—	—

[1]From 1908-1933, acreage harvested represents summation of plantation crop years and does not necessarily correspond to the period Oct. 1 to Sept. 30.

[2]The average growth of a crop is from 22 to 24 months. Only a portion of the total acreage in cane is harvested each year.

[3]Converted in accordance with Sugar Regulations, Series 1, No. 1 U. S. Department of Agriculture. Agricultural Adjustment Administration, issued February 18, 1935, or Section 101(h) of the Sugar Act of 1948 or corresponding provisions of its predecessors, as the case may be.

[4]1 ton of sugar, 96° test is assumed to be equivalent to 0.9346 ton of refined.

[5]Based on tonnage of cane used.

[6]Includes 2,369 tons raw value sugar produced from volunteer cane for which no acreage shown.

[7]Includes 2,690 tons raw value sugar produced from volunteer cane for which no acreage shown.

Source: Hawaiian Sugar Planters' Association, June 1965.

Sugar cane is a giant, hardy perennial plant belonging to the grass family. It resembles bamboo in that it has a joint every six to eight inches along the stalk. Mature cane grows to a height of 10 to 20 feet. Once planted it will continue to spring up each year from buds (or "ratoons") on the stalk of the plant. In Hawaii it is customary to grow from two to four ratoon crops of cane on a field before it is completely replanted.

Ratoon crops are started after the field is harvested. Existing furrows which are broken down by the harvesting machines are reshaped, irrigation water and fertilizer are applied, and the new growth is started from the old root system. The field is checked several months after the ratooning operation and sections that have not grown back are replanted.

When a whole field is to be planted, the soil is plowed to a depth of 20 inches and turned over to give it maximum aeration. In planting, a 20 inch length of cane cut from an eight to nine month old stalk is placed horizontally in the furrow, covered with two to four inches of soil, and irrigated. Nearly all of the planting and ratooning operations are accomplished by mechanical means.

An important part of a plantation's planting program involves the continuous introduction of new varieties of cane. When a particular variety of cane is grown over a period of ten years or so, microorganisms in the soil begin to overcome the plant and reduce its growth, and consequently its yield of sugar. Plantation managers combat this deterioration in yield by experimenting each year with several hundred new varieties of cane [6] (however, on each plantation two or three varieties with proven characteristics for that plantation comprise the bulk of the growing crop). Seldom do more than one or two varieties a year emerge as strong candidates to replace existing commercial canes. However, the process of finding new varieties is essential to maintaining high crop yields over an extended period of time. In 1965, 38% of the Hawaii production was in one variety and 17% in the second most prevalent.

Major activities during the sugar cane's growth cycle include weed control, irrigation, and the application of fertilizers. Weed control is important for the first few months of growth while the field is "closing-in," or becoming high enough to shade out any weed growth. Weeds are primarily controlled through the use of herbicides. The application of irrigation water and fertilizers is controlled by continuous analysis of plant and soil conditions.

Water is the most important single ingredient affecting the yield of sugar cane crops. Under normal rainfall conditions an irrigated field will produce about two times as much cane as an unirrigated field. The higher yields from irrigation are the result of the greater quantity of water available and, equally important, the

---

[6] New varieties of cane for testing on the plantations are developed by the Experiment Station of the Hawaiian Sugar Planters' Association. Each year the Station produces as many as a million new crosses of cane, starting from seed which is produced from the cane tassel or flower. The unique growing characteristics of each plantation are taken into consideration by the Experiment Station in its development of cane varieties.

ability to control the timing of the application of water. On the average, more than a ton of water is required to produce a single pound of sugar.

As the cane reaches maturity, water and plant food are withheld to stop growth. When the plant stops growing the sunlight energy will no longer cause the production of cellulose in the plant, but instead will support a conversion to sucrose. Timing can be crucial at this stage of the growth cycle, because the objective is to produce as much sucrose as possible but to harvest the plant before it dies.

Sugar cane is harvested by machines which break the stalks off at the ground and tumble the severed cane into rows. Large grab cranes then load the cane onto 40 ton cane haulers for transport to the mill. In Hawaii the fields are burned before harvesting to remove much of the dead leaves and trash. Burning does not damage the cane stalk in which the sugar producing juice is stored.

In 1964 the Hawaiian sugar plantations averaged about 95 tons of sugar cane per acre harvested. The range for the industry was from a low of 59 tons of cane per acre to a high of 117 tons. The low yields were primarily from plantations with unirrigated fields.

Most of the field work that has been described is done by machines. Labor requirements are for irrigation crews, herbicide spraying crews, machine operators, and field supervisors.

When the newly harvested cane reaches the mill it is lifted onto a moving conveyor and is passed under jets of water to remove any debris brought in from the field with the cane. The sugar cane is then chopped into short sections and carried through high-pressure roller mills which crush the sugar bearing juices from the stalks. Sugar cane contains about 87% juice and 13% plant fibre, which is called bagasse. Bagasse is normally used as a fuel for the mill boilers, although it can be used to make wallboard and paper. In Hawaii, however, bagasse has been used primarily for fuel because the demand for paper has not been deemed large enough to justify the substantial investment in an economic-size pulp and paper making facility.

The crushing operation will normally extract in excess of 95% of the available juice; however, this figure varies depending on the efficiency of the particular mill. After the juice has been extracted it goes through clarifying, filtering, evaporating, crystallizing, and centrifuging processes to become raw sugar. About 12 pounds of raw sugar and three pounds of molasses are produced from each 100 pounds of cane processed. This output is equivalent to an industry average of about 10.6 tons of sugar per acre harvested. In 1964 the yields of the individual plantations ranged from 6.61 tons per acre to 14.28 tons per acre.

Most of the raw sugar produced by the plantation mills is trucked to seaport terminals from which it is shipped to the mainland to be processed into refined sugar. Molasses is also shipped to the mainland, where it is sold for livestock feed.

In the cane sugar refining operation a series of centrifuging and filtering steps remove the 2.5% of molasses that remains in raw sugar after the milling process. One ton of raw sugar is required to produce .9346 ton of refined sugar. About

95% of the Hawaiian produced raw sugar is shipped to the U.S. mainland for refining. The remaining 5% is refined in a small plant on the island of Oahu for Hawaiian consumption.

The Agency System

All but two [7] of the Hawaiian sugar companies are represented by agencies or parent companies in Honolulu. Exhibit 10 lists the plantation companies and their 1964 output, and shows the agency relationships. Controlling interest in all but one sugar company [7] is held by agencies. The agencies are often referred to as "factors" and offer a variety of services to the sugar company, such as executive management, industrial relations, industrial engineering, public relations, specialized staff, financing, accounting, tax, buying, and shipping.

The agency system in Hawaii developed when many of the plantation companies were in their infancy and could not justify hiring specialists to handle each of the many facets of their business. As a result the plantations turned to the established companies in Honolulu, which were in a strategic position to check the arrival of ships, to negotiate space for cargoes, to follow through on sales and collection, and to handle many other business needs. This division of functions permitted an advantageous specialization, with the plantations concentrating on production and the agencies concentrating on the commercial problems of the industry.

The rapid expansion of the sugar industry during the Civil War and again following the Reciprocity Treaty in 1876 brought the agencies into even greater prominence in the industry. The agencies had begun to invest in the industry by extending long-term loans to planters to cover production costs, and these, if the crops or market were poor, had frequently been converted into part ownership. The planters were generally struggling farmers living from hand to mouth and with inadequate resources. The agencies, on the other hand, had a diversified business, some had surplus capital, and all had access to capital supplies. Hence they had the capital the planter lacked, and exigencies of nature and the market brought the two together.

The agency system further led to horizontal integration of the industry. In a continued effort for efficiency, the number of plantations was reduced from 90 in 1883 to 38 in 1938 and to 25 in 1965.

By 1966, the agency system in Hawaii had remained intact with the exception of C. Brewer and Company, the second largest of the island sugar producers. In 1956, upon acquiring a controlling interest in each of its ten sugar plantations, C. Brewer gave up the agency system in favor of a subsidiary arrangement under

---

[7] The Gay and Robinson and Grove Farm Co., Ltd., plantations on the island of Kauai. Sugar production of these plantations represented approximately 5% of the total output of the Hawaiian sugar industry. Waimea Sugar Mill Co., Ltd., is represented but not controlled by American Factors, Ltd. Production is approximately 5,000 tons. Cane grown on the Waiamea Plantation is ground by Kekaha Sugar Co., Ltd.

exhibit 10

CASTLE & COOKE SUGAR INTERESTS

Agency Relationships and Production of Hawaiian Sugar Companies, 1964

	Tons
Alexander & Baldwin, Inc.	
Hawaiian Commercial & Sugar Co.	176,170
Kahuku Plantation Company	20,254
McBryde Sugar Company, Ltd.	29,400
Total	225,824
American Factors, Ltd.	
Kekaha Sugar Co., Ltd.	49,532
Lihue Plantation Co., The	74,848
Oahu Sugar Co., Ltd.	73,677
Puna Sugar Co., Ltd.	51,599
Pioneer Mill Co., Ltd.	58,248
Waimea Sugar Mill Co.,	4,666
Total	312,570
C. Brewer & Co., Ltd.	
Hawaiian Agricultural Co.	46,144
Hilo Sugar Co., Ltd.	32,012
Hutchinson Sugar Co., Ltd.	31,906
Kilauea Sugar Co., Ltd.	17,707
Olokele Sugar Co., Ltd.	31,066
Onomea Sugar Co.	34,776
Paauhau Sugar Co., Ltd.	24,091
Pepeekeo Sugar Co.	60,337
Wailuku Sugar Co.	30,478
Total	308,517
Castle & Cooke, Inc.	
Ewa Plantation Co.	54,503
Kohala Sugar Co.	43,992
Waialua Agricultural Co., Ltd.	73,104
Total	171,599
Theo. H. Davies & Co., Ltd.	
Hamakua Mill Co.	27,811
Laupahoehoe Sugar Co.	46,403
Honokaa Sugar Co.	27,547
Total	101,761
Bishop Trust Co., Ltd.	
Gay & Robinson	18,563
Total	18,563
Grove Farm Co., Ltd.	
Grove Farm Co., Ltd.	39,936
Total	39,936
Grand Total	1,178,770

Source: Hawaiian Sugar Planters' Association.

which the parent company began providing all services at cost rather than on the typical fixed fee basis. At the same time, corporate management began exerting much greater influence over the day to day operations of the plantations.

The Cooperative Nature of the Hawaiian Sugar Industry

Another feature of the Hawaiian sugar industry is the arrangement for marketing all of the island's sugar output. The Hawaiian sugar companies are the sole shareholders of the California and Hawaiian Sugar Refining Corporation, Ltd., a cooperative whose refineries at Aiea, Oahu, Hawaii, and Crockett, California, convert the plantation-produced raw sugar into refined sugar for sale on the islands and the mainland. This type of marketing arrangement makes the 25 island plantations noncompetitive with one another so far as sugar and molasses is concerned.

Because they are noncompetitive, the island sugar producers have cooperated extensively to advance the technology of growing sugar cane and manufacturing raw cane sugar in Hawaii. To aid in the mutual development of the industry, the plantation companies established a producers' cooperative known as the Hawaiian Sugar Planters' Association (HSPA) in 1895. The Association is a nonprofit, agricultural organization financed by Hawaii's 25 sugar plantations, and administered by an executive committee composed of sugar company representatives.[8]

In addition to serving as a clearing house for exchanging information about sugar technology, the HSPA carries on such activities as industrial relations and public relations, and through its Washington, D.C., office represents the industry in all of its government relationships.

The major activity of the association, however, is the HSPA Experiment Station, a $2,500,000 (about 70% of the HSPA budget) per year operation which employs 275 scientists, technicians, and other staff members to work on all phases of sugar technology. The station's ten departments range from those concerned with sugar cane chemistry and sugar cane genetics to departments whose major functions are mechanization of field work and the training of plantation personnel in field and factory techniques.

Through the combined efforts of the plantation companies and the HSPA to improve sugar technology on the islands, the Hawaiian sugar industry has gained a worldwide reputation for efficiency of operation. It ranks highest in the world in tons of sugar produced per acre (Exhibit 11) and is said to have the lowest loss of sugar from insect damage. Mechanization of field work has resulted in a higher level of productivity for Hawaiian field workers than for their counterparts

---

[8] The HSPA functions as a producers' cooperative in much the same manner as the California and Florida Citrus Growers' Associations. The product is sold under a single brand name (e.g., "Sunkist") with the growers working together to improve production technology.

exhibit 11

CASTLE & COOKE SUGAR INTERESTS

Yield of Sugar per Harvested Acre
(short tons, raw value)

	Louisiana	Florida	Hawaii	Puerto Rico	Beet Area
1951	1.15	3.14	9.09	3.38	2.22
1952	1.64	3.60	9.44	3.50	2.30
1953	1.72	3.38	10.15	3.07	2.45
1954	1.94	3.43	10.02	3.28	2.34
1955	1.96	3.42	10.74	3.23	2.33
1956	2.12	4.28	10.28	3.26	2.50
1957	1.76	4.18	10.16	2.74	2.51
1958	2.02	3.96	9.09	2.85	2.48
1959	1.76	3.77	8.83	3.15	2.57
1960	1.84	3.26	9.03	3.11	2.58
1961	2.34	3.70	10.09	3.38	2.23
1962	1.86	3.33	10.31	3.27	2.33

Yield of Sugar per Acre of Foreign Countries
(1956 or 1957, short tons, raw value)

Argentina	1.06	Dominican Republic	1.57	Philippines	2.90
Australia	3.63	India	1.12	Peru	8.66
Brazil	1.09	Indonesia	5.93	Taiwan	4.52
Cuba	2.09	Mexico	2.44		

Source: U.S. Department of Agriculture.

in other domestic areas (Exhibit 12) and probably in the world, if data from other areas were available.

Despite its high ranking in the measures mentioned, the Hawaiian sugar industry has been long plagued with a poor record of earnings. Rapidly increasing labor costs in face of relatively constant price levels for sugar is said to have been the major contributing factor. Exhibit 13 shows the post-World War II wage trend for Hawaiian field workers compared with field workers in the other domestic producing areas.

Exhibit 14 shows that increases in wages between 1946 and 1964 have more than offset gains in worker productivity. Consequently, in terms of field labor costs

exhibit 12

CASTLE & COOKE SUGAR INTERESTS

Man-Hours of Fieldworkers per Ton of Sugar Produced (raw value)

	Hawaii	*Beet*	*Louisiana*	*Florida*	*Puerto Rico*
1946	33.24	46.00	117.62	59.52	166.20
1947	31.30	43.40	148.60	68.04	150.78
1948	30.54	40.80	112.14	59.16	139.82
1949	27.32	38.40	94.50	47.84	111.66
1950	25.86	36.00	77.14	42.46	108.74
1951	24.18	33.40	101.70	34.04	109.26
1952	23.00	33.00	65.52	26.04	111.56
1953	23.42	31.80	59.12	23.48	115.56
1954	21.06	33.80	55.86	24.46	99.34
1955	17.42	31.80	56.20	24.80	95.28
1956	17.30	28.00	48.82	22.36	89.92
1957	16.46	27.60	53.22	21.86	93.34
1958	18.02	24.60	47.52	21.86	96.76
1959	16.90	21.40	50.86	21.57	88.62
1960	16.72	20.60	41.56	23.24	86.32
1961	13.76	20.80	31.68	23.82	80.30
1962	13.76	20.38	38.64	25.03	77.28
1963	13.56	19.50	31.46	22.50	80.881

1 Revised.

Source: U.S. Department of Agriculture.

per ton of raw sugar produced, Hawaii has been transformed from the lowest labor cost domestic area to a high cost area.

The significant increase in wages is attributed largely to the successful efforts of the International Longshoremen's and Warehousemen's Union (ILWU) to organize the Hawaiian sugar workers shortly after the end of World War II. The Hawaiian sugar industry had been particularly vulnerable to union organization for several reasons: First, the group of workers were accessible and identifiable because of the plantation system and the year-round nature of their employment. Second, the industry was particularly vulnerable to strike action. An industrywide strike not only affects production during the strike but, because of the two year cane growing cycle on the islands, for several years after.

The ILWU resorted to industrywide strike tactics in 1946 and again in 1958. While in each strike the economic consequences for workers were seriously felt, the Union has emerged as the established bargaining unit for the sugar workers.

exhibit 13

CASTLE & COOKE SUGAR INTERESTS

Weighted Average Earnings * of Fieldworkers
(dollars per hour)

| Hawaii | | | | | | | Puerto |
	Earnings	Fringe	Total	Beet	Louisiana	Florida	Rico
1946	0.586	0.147	0.733	0.751	0.372	0.586	0.254
1947	0.776	0.123	0.899	0.782	0.389	0.634	0.305
1948	0.955	0.140	1.095	0.816	0.414	0.669	0.344
1949	1.056	0.185	1.241	0.850	0.428	0.667	0.343
1950	1.089	0.195	1.284	0.888	0.444	0.667	0.348
1951	1.127	0.235	1.362	0.938	0.454	0.714	0.370
1952	1.204	0.251	1.455	0.939	0.493	0.842	0.393
1953	1.303	0.269	1.572	0.938	0.523	0.888	0.416
1954	1.372	0.339	1.711	0.940	0.550	0.880	0.439
1955	1.448	0.405	1.853	0.943	0.564	0.885	0.437
1956	1.469	0.448	1.917	0.979	0.629	0.914	0.454
1957	1.538	0.482	2.020	1.036	0.667	0.952	0.494
1958	1.597	0.571	2.168	1.065	0.692	0.984	0.504
1959	1.753	0.521	2.274	1.094	0.710	0.991	0.497
1960	1.794	0.557	2.351	1.117	0.765	1.051	0.524
1961	1.939	0.605	2.544	1.132	0.786	1.105	0.552
1962	2.003	0.734	2.737	1.160	0.826	1.131	0.568[2]
1963	2.100	0.750	2.850	1.220	1.121	1.300	0.656[2]
1964	2.248	0.750	2.998	1.290	1.070	1.380	0.693

[1]Fringe benefits of from 2 to 19 cents per hour for areas other than Hawaii not included.
[2]Revised.

Source: U.S. Department of Agriculture.

THE CALIFORNIA AND HAWAIIAN
SUGAR REFINING CORPORATION

Established in 1906, the California and Hawaiian Sugar Refining Corporation (C and H) was reorganized in 1921 in California under a 50 year charter. The entire capital stock is owned wholly by the 25 Hawaiian plantation companies—151,785 shares (par value $100 each). The per cent of ownership in C and H was roughly equivalent to the share of total Hawaiian sugar production attributable to each plantation.

exhibit 14

CASTLE & COOKE SUGAR INTERESTS

Field Labor Costs per Ton of Sugar Produced
(1946–1964: raw value)

	1946	1964	Change Dollars	per cent
Hawaii (including fringes)1	$24.36	$38.85	+$14.49	+59
Hawaii (excluding fringes)	19.48	19.13	+ 9.65	+50
Puerto Rico	42.21	54.03	+11.82	+28
Florida	34.88	36.98	+ 2.10	+ 6
Louisiana	43.75	43.44	.31	1
Beets	34.55	24.64	9.91	29

1Hawaii is the only area for which the U.S.D.A. releases fringe benefits figures. For other areas, noncash benefits (not included above) are stated to range from 2 to 19 cents per hour.

Source: U.S. Department of Agriculture.

C and H acts as the cooperative marketing organization for its 25 plantation–stockholders. It contracted with each plantation member, through a Standard Sugar Marketing Contract, to receive and market on the mainland all the raw sugar production of the members not required in Hawaii. Similarly, the member contracted to deliver all of its sugar production to C and H as marketer. C and H, as a result of its operation, returned to the members the difference between the proceeds of all sales and the sum of its operating expenses, the amount declared as a dividend on the capital stock of the corporation, and withholdings for a capital reserve fund to finance capital expenditures.

The amount withheld to pay dividends was normally equal to the 8% of stated capital, which is the maximum a cooperative is allowed to pay its members. This sum was paid directly to the plantation–stockholders in proportion to their ownership in C and H.

Inventories are considered in the settlement formula. They are valued at the anticipated net sales price minus all expenses to the time of final sale, and the resulting estimated net value was included in the final settlement. If the inventory value was overestimated or underestimated, the difference was adjusted the subsequent year.

The foregoing method pertained specifically to sugar. For molasses, a separate contract and a similar procedure, excepting withholdings for dividends and capital reserves, are followed.

The major operating property owned by C and H was a sugar refinery located at Crockett, California. The Crockett plant, which was in 1965 the largest cane sugar refinery in the world, had a daily capacity of 3,600 short tons of raw sugar and was equipped to produce a complete assortment of packaged granulated and soft (brown) sugars, as well as bulk granulated, liquid, and invert sugars for industrial use. The refinery employed about 1,500 people.

C and H also owned a small refinery at Aiea, on the island of Oahu. This refinery had a maximum daily capacity of 205 short tons of raw sugar and was equipped to produce granulated sugars only. The Aiea refinery was intended primarily to fill Hawaii's requirements for sugar.

In 1956 C and H acquired a 25.2% interest in the Imperial Sugar Company of Sugarland, Texas. Imperial operated a medium size cane sugar refinery (about one-third the capacity of the C and H refinery at Crockett) at Sugarland, and marketed cane sugar primarily in Texas and the surrounding area. Subsequent to the C and H purchase of an interest in Imperial, the two companies entered into a long-term contract whereby C and H sold most of its surplus raw sugar to Imperial. Sales within the terms of the contract represented about 25% of Hawaii's production and almost completely filled Imperial's requirements for raw sugar. The C and H surplus of raw sugar resulted from limitations of refining capacity, inability of the available market to absorb refined sugar, and price considerations.

Deliveries of raw sugar to Imperial were shipped direct from Hawaii on ships owned by the Reynolds Metals Company. The Reynolds ships hauled alumina [9] from processing plants in Texas to aluminum reduction plants near Portland, Oregon, deadheaded from Portland to the Hawaiian Islands, and then carried raw sugar to the Imperial refinery on the return trip to Texas.

C and H Management

C and H was operated as a separate company with its own management group. The Hawaiian plantation companies were represented on the C and H board of directors, usually by the chief executive and one other officer from each of the agency companies. Board meetings were typically devoted to reviewing C and H operations and to discussing future strategies and plans.

Refined Sugar Marketing

C and H sold refined sugars under the brand name "C and H" in a complete assortment of granulated, confectioners, powdered, browns, cubelets, and crystal tablets.

The primary C and H marketing area was defined as the eight western states shown in Exhibit 15. In recent years about 60% of the company's sales were made in this area.

Its secondary marketing area included the central states west of the Mississippi

---

[9] Alumina, a granular substance having the appearance of refined sugar, bulk handles in a similar fashion to raw sugar.

exhibit 15

CASTLE & COOKE SUGAR INTERESTS

C and H Marketing Areas and Freight Rate Disadvantages

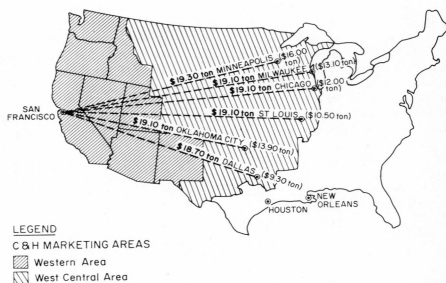

LEGEND

C & H MARKETING AREAS

▨ Western Area

▧ West Central Area

Figures in Brackets are Freight Rates from Houston or New Orleans.
Bold Figures are Freight Rates from San Francisco.

River and the Chicago area. Sales in this territory gave rise to additional freight absorption costs because customers paid only the freight from the nearest cane sugar refining point, New Orleans or Houston, while C and H paid the freight costs from San Francisco. The freight disadvantages for C and H are also shown on Exhibit 15. The actual cost of freight absorptions for C and H, along with other costs associated with the physical distribution of Hawaii's sugar production, are presented in Exhibit 16. The warehousing costs shown in the exhibit were the result of having to maintain local supplies in public warehouses to provide quick service to the trade.

Competition varied for C and H by areas. To aid in the description of these differences, Exhibit 17 shows the distribution of cane and beet refineries throughout the United States. In the area east of the Rocky Mountains, competition was primarily from Rocky Mountain and Colorado beet companies. Cane sugar supplies in addition to those of C and H entered this territory from refineries in

exhibit 16

CASTLE & COOKE SUGAR INTERESTS

Physical Distribution Costs for C and H

Year	Ocean Freight and Insurance to Crockett	Additional Cost of Shipping Raws Thru Canal to East Coast	Freight Absorption for Shipping Refined Sugar to Mainland Customers	Distribution Warehousing
1954	$ 9,772,000	$1,499,000	$2,839,000	$1,095,000
1955	10,945,000	1,667,000	3,025,000	831,000
1956	10,556,000	1,463,000	3,409,000	960,000
1957	10,346,000	1,123,000	3,677,000	1,016,000
1958[1]	7,738,000	821,000	2,867,000	1,034,000
1959	6,913,000	1,374,000	3,317,000	1,025,000
1960	5,712,000	1,055,000	3,236,000	889,000
1961	6,347,000	1,674,000	3,514,000	977,000
1962[1]	6,547,000	2,558,000	3,180,000	939,000
1963	6,230,000	849,000	3,029,000	808,000

[1]Figures include freight absorptions and warehousing costs on sugar purchased to supplement Hawaiian sugar during the strikes.
Source: Hawaiian Sugar Planters' Association.

Louisiana. In the Chicago area the Atlantic Coast cane refineries were also strong competitors.

In the far West, where C and H was the only cane sugar refiner, competition was with the beet growers. As shown in Exhibit 17, this was the one area of the country that produced a surplus of refined sugar. In California alone, combined production of refined cane and beet sugar, totaling 1,640,000 tons in 1964, exceeded consumption of about 600,000 tons. The supply-demand level was even more out of balance in the other, less densely populated western states, where local sugar consumption equalled about one-third of the total sugar produced. The situation was made even more difficult for C and H because much of this overcapacity was the result of expanded beet sugar quotas in the West following the break in relations with Cuba. Between 1960 and 1964, beet sugar production in California was allowed to increase by approximately 375,000 tons, compared to an increase in cane sugar production of about 50,000 tons. While much of this increased quota was meant to fill midwestern and eastern deficits, the quota does not specify where the sugar is to be sold. Consequently, California beet sugar producers did everything possible to sell their output locally to avoid added freight costs.

Exhibit 18 compares beet sugar and cane sugar deliveries in California and the western states for the years 1955 and 1964. Cane sugar deliveries have nearly

exhibit 17

CASTLE & COOKE SUGAR INTERESTS

Location of Beet Sugar Processors and Cane Sugar Refineries in the U.S.

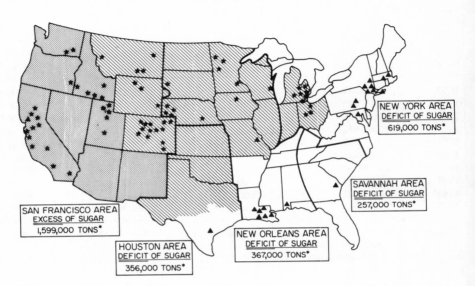

NEW YORK AREA
DEFICIT OF SUGAR
619,000 TONS*

SAVANNAH AREA
DEFICIT OF SUGAR
257,000 TONS*

SAN FRANCISCO AREA
EXCESS OF SUGAR
1,599,000 TONS*

NEW ORLEANS AREA
DEFICIT OF SUGAR
367,000 TONS*

HOUSTON AREA
DEFICIT OF SUGAR
356,000 TONS*

LEGEND

C & H MARKETING AREAS

☒ Western Area

◩ West Central Area

★ Beet Factories

▲ Cane Refineries

• Estimated Figures

exhibit 18

CASTLE & COOKE SUGAR INTERESTS

Beet and Cane Sugar Deliveries in California and the 11 Western States (1955 and 1964)

	1955 (CWT)	1964 (CWT)	Change (CWT)	%
Eleven western states				
Beet sugar deliveries	13,091,057	17,737,665	+4,646,608	+35
Cane sugar deliveries	8,722,314	9,801,658	+1,079,344	+12
Total	21,813,361	27,539,323	+5,725,952	+26
California				
Beet sugar deliveries	7,713,465	11,609,610	+3,896,145	+50
Cane sugar deliveries	6,813,061	7,550,698	+ 737,637	+11
Total	14,526,526	19,160,308	4,633,782	+32
Total U.S.				
Beet sugar deliveries	33,631,811	50,448,199	+16,816,388	+50
Cane sugar deliveries	112,721,367	125,624,663	+12,903,296	+11
Total	145,353,178	176,172,862	+29,719,684	+21

Source: Agricultural Stabilization and Conservation Service, U.S. Department of Agriculture.

kept pace with increases in cane sugar production, but have not kept pace with the over-all increases in consumption. Beet sugar, on the other hand, has increased its market share, particularly in California, but at the same time it appears increases in deliveries have not kept pace with over-all increases in beet sugar production. Exhibit 18B shows cane and beet sugar deliveries throughout the United States for the year 1964.

Competition for sugar sales further breaks down into various market segments. Exhibit 19 shows deliveries by type of product or business of buyer for the years 1955 and 1964. This data indicates that the industrial market has become the largest user of sugar and has increased substantially in recent years, compared with a net decrease in deliveries to the nonindustrial market. This trend is explained largely by a growing demand for premixed, convenience products to which sugar is added by the manufacturer and not by the housewife.

Exhibit 20 presents the same data broken down by beet and cane for the year 1964. It shows strong consumer preference for cane sugar, which accounted for about 75% of all deliveries to nonindustrial users and 81.5% of all deliveries in consumer-size packages. Comparable figures in 1955 show cane sugar with 81%

CASTLE & COOKE SUGAR INTERESTS
Deliveries of Sugar in Continental U.S.
by Primary Distributors
(calendar year 1964: hundredweights) [1]

State and Region	Cane Sugar Refiners	Beet Sugar Processors	Importers of Direct Con- sumption Sugar	Mainland Cane Sugar Mills	Total
New England					
Connecticut	1,239,022	14,631	27,230	1,250	1,282,133
Maine	627,324	6,763	7,900	—	641,987
Massachusetts	4,956,405	73,139	187,471	1,500	5,218,515
New Hampshire	356,800	—	—	—	356,800
Rhode Island	457,078	—	32,392	—	489,470
Vermont	217,113	49,311	—	—	266,424
Subtotal	7,853,742	143,844	254,993	2,750	8,255,329
Mid-Atlantic					
New Jersey	7,350,499	154,577	782,543	2,300	8,289,919
New York	15,691,218	633,979	891,769	14,220	17,231,186
Pennsylvania	11,589,137	474,189	887,551	—	12,950,877
Subtotal	34,630,854	1,262,745	2,561,863	16,520	38,471,982
North Central					
Illinois	8,629,671	10,560,627	800	67,833	19,258,931
Indiana	3,787,587	1,899,448	—	2,000	5,689,035
Iowa	519,799	1,684,766	—	9,200	2,213,765
Kansas	452,593	859,471	—	3,600	1,315,664
Michigan	2,689,397	3,658,175	—	—	6,347,572
Minnesota	449,903	2,015,429	—	8,000	2,473,332
Missouri	2,589,423	1,965,820	—	44,214	4,599,457
Nebraska	263,722	1,061,063	—	6,900	1,331,685
North Dakota	2,070	335,803	—	—	337,873
Ohio	6,070,435	2,283,544	3,070	2,002	8,359,051
South Dakota	29,866	352,869	—	—	382,735
Wisconsin	1,202,782	2,311,301	—	5,400	3,519,483
Subtotal	26,687,248	28,988,316	3,870	149,149	55,828,583

uthern					
abama	2,670,931	—	—	19,113	2,690,044
kansas	1,053,615	100,508	—	3,687	1,157,810
laware	1,045,189	—	14,965	—	1,060,154
strict of Columbia	314,193	—	33,608	—	347,801
rida	2,930,132	—	396,174	738,118	4,064,523
orgia	5,794,201	—	1,255	12,890	5,808,346
ntucky	2,383,061	67,957	—	200,002	2,471,020
uisiana	3,556,241	—	—	104,108	3,660,349
ryland	4,161,674	35,666	386,184	—	4,583,524
ssissippi	1,577,822	—	—	13,355	1,591,177
rth Carolina	3,964,605	2,150	93,341	5,520	4,065,616
lahoma	1,142,088	369,078	—	405	1,511,571
uth Carolina	1,630,484	—	6,171	—	1,636,655
nnessee	3,788,191	1,679	—	850	3,790,720
xas	6,934,899	1,700,700	6,643	75,843	8,718,085
ginia	2,767,728	19,600	264,122	6,000	3,057,450
st Virginia	936,008	18,291	13,190	—	967,489
Subtotal	46,651,161	2,315,629	1,215,653	999,891	51,182,334
stern					
ska	36,469	22,733	—	—	59,202
zona	432,187	255,160	—	—	687,347
lifornia	7,550,698	11,609,610	93,142	1,600	19,255,050
orado	97,980	1,117,697	—	1,510	1,217,187
ho	52,337	335,576	—	—	387,913
ntana	30,327	315,598	—	—	345,925
vada	72,640	51,499	—	—	124,139
w Mexico	103,998	182,896	—	—	286,894
gon	642,745	1,272,096	42,215	—	1,957,056
h	84,016	640,238	—	800	725,054
shington	693,380	1,853,307	40,628	—	2,587,315
oming	4,881	81,255	—	—	86,136
Subtotal	9,801,658	17,737,665	175,985	3,910	27,719,218
Grand total	125,624,663	50,448,199	4,212,364	1,172,220	181,457,446

ported as produced or imported and delivered, except liquid sugar, which is on a sugar
ds content basis.

rce: Agricultural Stabilization and Conservation Service, U.S. Department of
iculture.

exhibit 19

CASTLE & COOKE SUGAR INTERESTS

Refined Sugar Deliveries by Type of Product or Business of Buyer in the U.S.
(1955 and 1964: hundredweights)

Product or Business of Buyer (hundredweights)	1955	1964	Change	% Change
Industrial				
Bakery, cereal and allied products	17,550,447	21,632,908	4,082,461	+23
Confectionery and related products	13,167,386	17,300,533	4,133,147	+31
Ice cream and dairy products	5,968,977	8,762,287	2,793,310	+47
Beverages	17,968,897	28,010,904	10,042,007	+56
Canned, bottled, frozen foods, jams, jellies, and preserves	13,036,164	17,065,360	4,029,196	+31
Multiple and all other food uses	5,523,651	7,170,701	1,647,050	+29
Nonfood products	1,038,870	1,223,905	185,035	+18
Subtotal	74,254,392	101,165,596	26,911,204	+36
Nonindustrial				
Hotels, restaurants, institutions	714,060	1,382,049	667,989	+94
Wholesale grocers, jobbers, sugar dealers	55,173,163	47,437,890	-7,735,273	-14
Retail grocers, chain stores, supermarkets	22,248,677	24,111,851	1,863,174	+8
All other deliveries, including deliveries to government agencies	1,477,683	2,683,725	1,206,042	+81
Subtotal	79,613,583	75,615,515	-3,998,068	-5
Total deliveries	153,867,975	176,782,111	22,813,136	+15
Deliveries in consumer-size packages	52,945,759	53,966,121	1,020,362	+2

Source: Agricultural Stabilization and Conservation Service, U.S. Department of Agriculture.

of the nonindustrial market and 84% of the deliveries in consumer-size packages. The dominant position of cane sugar in the nonindustrial market stems from a long-standing consumer preference for cane sugar. Beet sugar processors have not chosen to challenge the cane sugar image at the consumer level, but instead have offered their product at a slightly lower price. The increase in the beet sugar share of the consumer market would indicate that this tactic has met with some success.

Industrial users do not share the same preferences for cane sugar and consequently make their purchases primarily on a price basis. The major exception is in the production of beverages, where beet sugar has had a tendency to cause some streaking in clear liquids.

Of concern to both cane and beet sugar markets was the increased use of artificial sweeteners. In recent years many industrial users of sugar have shown

exhibit 20

CASTLE & COOKE SUGAR INTERESTS

Sugar Deliveries by Type of Product or Business of Buyer, and by Type of Sugar
(calendar year 1964, U.S.:* hundredweights)

Product or Business of Buyer	Beet (total) Hundredweight2	Cane (total)	Imported D.C. (total)	Total All Sugar	Beet	Cane
Industrial						
Bakery, cereal, and allied products	7,246,358	13,933,614	452,936	21,632,908	181,783	2,249,299
Confectionery and related products	4,396,224	12,451,771	452,538	17,300,533	135,196	2,809,367
Ice cream and dairy products	3,339,143	5,145,350	277,794	8,762,287	1,292,114	3,956,400
Beverages	6,269,007	21,469,572	272,325	28,010,904	2,472,079	13,717,045
Canned, bottled, frozen foods, jams, jellied, and preserves	8,169,481	8,118,040	777,839	17,065,360	2,865,362	4,201,764
Multiple and all other food uses	2,801,061	4,228,823	140,817	7,170,701	112,206	843,960
Nonfood products	117,619	1,068,926	37,358	1,223,905	6,092	460,461
Subtotal	32,338,893	66,416,096	2,411,607	101,166,596	7,064,832	28,238,296
Nonindustrial						
Hotels, restuarants, institutions	75,936	1,293,538	12,575	1,382,049	5,729	70,397
Wholesale grocers, jobbers, sugar dealers	11,457,779	34,481,209	1,498,902	47,437,890	252,763	148,365
Retail grocers, chain stores, supermarkets	5,368,440	18,445,779	287,632	24,111,851	78,695	99,842
All other deliveries, including deliveries to government agencies	1,212,999	1,469,072	1,654	2,683,725	18,725	816
Subtotal	18,115,154	55,699,598	1,800,763	75,615,515	355,912	319,420
Total Deliveries	50,454,047	122,115,694	4,212,370	176,782,111	7,420,744	28,557,716
Deliveries in consumer-size packages (less than 50 lbs.)	9,978,091	43,988,030	325,236	54,291,357	—	—
Deliveries in bulk (unpackaged)	15,885,965	21,482,985	0	37,368,950	—	—

1Represents approximately 97.4% of deliveries by primary distributors in continental United States.

2Reported as produced or imported and delivered, except liquid sugar, which is on a sugar solids content basis.

Source: Agricultural Stabilization and Conservation Service, U.S. Department of Agriculture (June 1965).

an increasing tendency to replace a portion of their sugar requirements with other sweetening agents. This trend was greatly intensified in 1963 because of high sugar prices. Apparent market acceptance of products sweetened with synthetics and the development of improved sweeteners has led to a continuation of this trend.

Most of the synthetic sweeteners are used by soft drink manufacturers, who for years have been the sugar industry's number one industrial customer. The Association of American Bottlers of Carbonated Beverages reports that in 1964, 11% of sales were sweetened by synthetics, compared with less than 1% in 1958. Some estimate that as much as 50% of soft drink sales will ultimately be low calorie, synthetically sweetened, beverages.

The total sales of synthetic sweeteners in 1963 amounted to 2,250 tons. On the basis of sweetening power, this displaced about 270,000 tons of sugar. The amount of synthetics used in 1964 was estimated at 4,750 tons, equivalent to 360,000 tons [10] of sugar. Some market analysts predict sales of synthetic sweeteners will reach the equivalent of 750,000 tons of sugar by 1968.

The C and H Market Positions in 1965–1966

The C and H marketing situation in 1965–1966 could be summarized as one of trying to increase sales in markets which would bring the highest return to the Hawaiian sugar producers.

The most obvious was the consumer market in the western states, and in particular, in California. According to C and H management, the company's greatest strength in this market was its well-entrenched consumer franchise. Years of advertising and promotional efforts had gone into establishing the "C and H" brand and the slogan, "pure cane sugar from Hawaii." In addition to its strong brand identification, the company claimed to offer a more complete line of consumer products than the competing beet processors. While the company did not release market share figures, it was believed that these efforts had established C and H as the dominant brand in California. In the other, more fragmented, western markets, the company's position was believed to be more irregular. The major beet sugar companies competing for the California market were the Spreckles Sugar Division of the American Sugar Refining Company and the Holly Sugar Corporation. The largest of the beet sugar processors, Great Western Sugar Company, operated factories mainly in Colorado and Nebraska.

As was pointed out earlier, several factors limited the future development of the western market. One was increased competition caused by rapidly expanding beet sugar production in the area. Another was the general downward trend in the sale of sugars to nonindustrial users, although in California this trend was partially offset by an increasing population.

At best, however, one could conclude C and H faced a difficult task in im-

---

[10] Some of the popular, newly developed sweeteners do not have the same sweetening powers as those previously used.

proving its consumer sales in the western states. The alternatives included consumer sales in the central states and industrial sales in the western and central states. C and H operated at a disadvantage in the highly priced sensitive industrial markets because the company was in direct competition with western beet processors who were able to pass a portion of any lower net proceeds from sugar sales back to the independent beet growers. By contrast, lower net proceeds to C and H resulting from price action were borne directly by the Hawaiian plantation companies.

During 1965 C and H called in a well-known management consulting firm to review its marketing operations. The results of this study have not been made public, but apparently it did not recommend any basic changes in C and H strategy. This would mean that C and H could be expected to do everything possible to maintain its strong consumer franchise in California and to attempt to increase its brand identification in other major western and central markets. Sales to industrial users would be continued, with special emphasis on markets that did not invoke high freight costs.

CASTLE & COOKE'S SUGAR OPERATIONS

Three of Hawaii's 25 sugar plantations were controlled by Castle & Cooke in 1965: Ewa Plantation Company (67.42%); Waialua Agricultural Company, Ltd. (66.25%), and Kohala Sugar Company (99.9%). Revenues from the plantation companies were $24,500,000 for the year ending April 30, 1965, $29,600,000 in 1964, and $20,300,000 in 1963. Net income was $1,450,000 in 1965, $2,897,000 in 1964, and $1,715,000 in 1963. The substantial increase in revenues and income in 1964 were the result of unusually high prices in 1963 caused by the previously mentioned world shortage of sugar. During 1963 the returns from C and H to the plantations averaged $150 per ton, compared with a more normal return of $127 per ton in 1964.

Exhibit 21 compares the operations of the three plantation companies for the period 1948–1965. Individual financial statements for the three companies, covering the period 1962–1965, are provided as Exhibits 22, 23, and 24.

The Relationship of the
Plantation Companies to Castle & Cooke

The three plantation companies were listed as consolidated subsidiaries of Castle & Cooke, Inc., but were operated as separate corporations under the traditional agency concept. Each plantation company had its own board of directors and published its own annual report to its shareholders.

Mr. Malcolm MacNaughton, President of Castle & Cooke, held the title of president of each of the plantation companies, and Mr. W. M. Bush, executive vice president of Castle & Cooke, was a vice president of each. Both served as direc-

	1948	1949	1950	1951	1952	1953	1954	1955
Tons raw sugar manufactured								
Ewa	43,000	57,000	59,000	60,000	59,000	62,000	61,000	61,000
Waialua	60,000	61,000	65,000	67,000	67,000	55,000	66,000	64,000
Kahala[3]	38,000	37,000	42,000	44,000	41,000	50,000	42,000	44,000
Total	141,000	155,000	166,000	171,000	167,000	167,000	169,000	179,000
Total for Hawaiian sugar industry	835,000	956,000	961,000	996,000	1,020,000	1,099,000	1,077,000	1,140,000
Net return from C & H per ton ($—calendar year) sugar only	n.a.	$ 108	$ 114	$ 117	$ 124	$ 123	$ 119	$ 116
Cost per ton at market ($)								
Ewa	$122	$ 103	$ 101	$ 101	$ 109	$ 107	$ 110	$ 110
Wialua	105	104	93	98	108	116	116	116
Kahala	123	129	113	111	136	123	127	126
Industry high	140	133	146	157	150	132	143	131
Industry low	102	95	93	96	107	99	110	100
Earnings[4] after taxes ($000)								
Ewa	4	543	904	824	719	696	656	597
Waialua	n.a.	621	1,091	818	671	519	478	408
Kahala	(50)	(200)	315	409	82	365	178	120
Total	n.a.	$ 964	$ 2,310	$ 2,051	$ 1,372	$ 1,580	$ 1,312	$ 1,125
Shareholders' equity ($000)								
Ewa	8,230	8,495	8,836	9,149	9,361	9,494	9,757	10,169
Waialua	n.a.	8,925	9,264	9,478	9,645	9,710	9,829	9,868
Kahala	5,879	5,329	6,119	6,546	6,567	6,289	6,431	6,098
Total	n.a.	$23,249	$24,209	$25,073	$25,573	$25,493	$26,017	$26,135
Net return on shareholders' equity (%)								
Ewa	—	6.4%	10.1%	9.0%	7.7%	7.3%	6.7%	5.9%
Waialua	n.a.	7.0	12.0	8.6	7.0	5.4	4.9	4.1
Kahala	(.8)%	(3.4)	5.2	6.3	1.2	5.8	2.8	2.0
Total	n.a.	4.1%	9.6%	8.1%	5.4%	6.2%	5.0%	4.3%
Acres harvested								
Ewa	4,001	4,307	4,230	4,302	4,315	4,332	4,345	4,333
Waialua	4,794	4,895	4,723	4,894	4,833	3,662	4,898	4,781
Kahala	6,799	6,681	6,630	6,526	6,409	6,839	6,592	6,325
Total	15,594	15,883	15,573	15,722	15,557	14,833	15,835	15,439
Total for Hawaiian sugar industry	100,000	109,000	109,000	109,000	108,000	108,000	107,000	106,000
Tons sugar per acre harvested								
Ewa	10.8	13.2	14.0	13.9	13.6	14.3	14.2	14.1
Waialua	12.4	12.4	13.8	13.8	14.0	15.1	13.5	13.4
Kahala	5.3	5.2	5.9	6.5	6.0	6.9	6.1	6.7
Industry average	8.3	8.8	8.8	9.1	9.4	10.2	10.0	10.7
Industry high	12.4	13.3	14.0	14.0	14.0	15.1	14.2	15.5
Industry low	4.2	4.7	3.2	4.8	6.0	7.0	6.1	6.7

[1] Results in 1958-60 severely affected by 1958 strike of Hawaiian sugar workers.

[2] Earnings for the year ended April 30, 1964, reflect higher sugar prices during the calendar year 1963

[3] Includes sugar produced from cane supplied by independent growers.

exhibit 21

EWA, WAIALUA, AND KOHALA SUGAR PLANTATIONS

Comparative Data
(including selected industry data, 1948–1965)

1956	1957	1958[1]	1959[1]	1960[1]	1961	1962	1963	1964[2]	1965
58,000	61,000	27,000	35,000	44,000		52,000	50,000	62,000	57,000
64,000	63,000	52,000	56,000	58,000		65,000	65,000	75,000	74,000
47,000	49.000	29,000	50,000	42,000		44,000	37,000	42,000	49,000
169,000	173,000	108,000	141,000	144,000		160,000	152,000	179,000	180,000
1,100,000	1,085,000	765,000	975,000	936,000	1,092,000	1,120,000	1,101,000	1,179,000	
$ 118	$ 121	$ 122	$ 120	$ 120		$ 127	$ 155	$ 127	$ 132
$ 115	$ 113	$ 182	$ 164	$ 135		$ 125	$ 133	$ 134	$ 126
115	121	128	131	126		116	119	119	116
120	120	158	122	141		124	150	151	136
135	137	187	171	169		142	150	172	157
108	108	113	110	109		109	107	119	116
649	711	(238)	(139)	101		365	627	953	400
652	482	341	134	410		742	958	1,844	964
323	313	(224)	249	(72)		323	130	102	86
$ 1,624	$ 1,506	$(121)	$ 244	$ 439		$ 1,430	$ 1,715	$ 2,897	$ 1,450
10,670	10,901	10,603	10,423	10,180		10,526	9,939	9,709	9,549
11,183	11,200	11,300	11,200	11,300		11,379	10,304	10,856	11,172
6,398	6,711	5,892	6,141	6,100		6,016	6,145	6,248	6,333
$28,251	$28,811	$27,795	$27,764	$27,580		$27,921	$26,388	$26,813	$27,054
6.0%	6.5%	(2.2)%	(1.4)%	1.0%		3.5%	6.3%	9.8%	4.2%
5.8	4.3	3.0	1.2	3.7		6,5	9.3	18.4	8.7
4.7	4.7	(3.8)	4.1	(1.2)		5.4	2,1	1.6	1.4
5.7%	5.2%	(.4)%	.9%	1.7%		5.1%	6.5%	10.8%	5.4%
4,329	4,424	4,233	4,359	4,228		3,935	4,054	4,594	4,550
4,969	4,870	4,393	5,221	4,941		4,729	4,676	5,467	5,261
5,704	6,150	3,668	6,567	6,090		7.107	6,852	6,824	7,047
14,992	15,444	12,294	16,147	15,259		15,771	15,582	16,885	16,858
107,000	107,000	84,000	110,000	104,000	108,000	109,000	107,000	111,000	
13.4	14.0	6.3	8.0	10.5		13.1	12.3	13.6	12.6
13.0	13.0	11.9	10.8	11.7		13.7	13.9	14.0	14.2
7.7	7.4	7.8	7.4	6.6		6.3	5.3	6.1	7.0
10.3	10.2	9.1	8.8	9.0		10.3	10.2	10.6	—
13.4	14.7	13.0	13.3	12.6		13.8	14.6	14.3	—
7.6	7.2	6.3	6.2	6.0		5.9	5.1	6.1	—

[4] Returns from molasses sales and from compliance payments add about $12.50 per ton to plantation revenues.

Source: Company records, Hawaiian Sugar Producers' Association.

exhibit **22A**

EWA PLANTATION COMPANY

Statement of Income and Retained Earnings

For the Years Ended April 30

	1965	1964	1963	1962
Income				
Sugar	$7,175,187	$ 9,171,403	$6,855,918	$6,247,108
Molasses	273,536	586,295	446,341	351,082
Sugar Act compliance	447,066	460,721	442,048	451,881
Dividends	89,119	89,119	109,369	111,394
Others—net	31,712	20,088	29,937	45,689
Total	$8,016,620	$10,327,626	$7,883,613	$7,207,154
Costs				
Employment				
Salaries and wages	3,491,716	3,588,847	3,136,614	2,994,891
Payroll taxes	127,875	126,513	106,716	102,351
Pensions and group insurance	200,072	229,276	190,049	188,855
Medical and dental plan—net	175,877	175,551	138,316	114,106
Village facilities—net	101,890	110,909	50,247	27,374
	$4,097,430	4,231,096	$3,621,942	$3,427,577
Materials, supplies and services				
Materials and supplies used	1,146,190	1,063,191	922,769	927,428
H.S.P.A. assessments	144,885	167,533	141,318	150,000
Electricity and other svces. purch.	508,310	620,858	475,641	457,361
	$1,799,385	$ 1,851,582	$1,539,728	$1,534,789
Rent on plantation land	237,244	971,947	417,312	422,660
Depreciation and amortization	401,692	399,851	374,090	370,342
Marketing of sugar and molasses	539,371	592,565	494,470	503,208
Gross income tax	56,034	103,983	111,601	129,007
Real property tax	101,689	105,852	99,378	94,382
Special projects	103,735	84,810		
Total	$7,336,580	$ 8,341,686	$6,658,521	$6,481,965
Income before income taxes	680,040	1,985,940	1,225,092	725,189
Income taxes				
Federal	251,354	938,161	543,209	328,000
State	28,535	94,466	55,000	32,000
Total	$ 279,889	$ 1,032,627	$ 598,209	$ 360,000
Net income	400,151	953,313	626,883	365,189
Retained earnings, beginning of year	6,622,471	6,288,157	6,117,054	6,098,740
	$7,022,622	$ 7,241,470	$6,743,937	$6,463,929
Deduct:				
Dividends—per share 1965,$1.00; 1964,$3.50; 1963,$2.25; 1962,$1.60	174,180	618,999	455,780	346,875
Retained earnings, end of year	$6,848,442	$ 6,622,471	$6,288,157	$6,117,054

Source: Company records.

exhibit 22B

EWA PLANTATION COMPANY

Facts in Brief

For the Years Ended April 30

	1965	1964	1963	1962
Earnings and dividends				
Net income	$ 400,151	$ 953,313	$ 626,883	$ 865,189
Per share	2.47	5.45	3.27	1.69
Dividends	174,180	618,999	455,780	346,875
Per share	1.00	3.50	2.25	1.60
Financial position				
Cash due from agent, and				
marketable securities	$ 88,755	$1,574,412	$ 873,463	$1,046,241
Inventory of supplies	484,547	435,874	422,568	422,080
Noncurrent assets	963,326	1,267,618	1,174,845	2,066,516
Capital stock outstanding, shares	161,950	174,785	191,442	216,477
Book value per share	58.97	55.55	51.91	48.62
Number of stockholders	710	721	766	838
Other financial data				
Payroll				
Sugar production	3,465,887	3,434,731	3,136,614	2,994,891
Other operations	428,913	344,768	273,304	282,285
Total payroll	$ 3,894,800	$3,779,499	$3,409,918	$3,277,176
Number of employees	694	677	695	709
Taxes				
Sugar production	$ 565,487	$1,368,977	$ 915,903	$ 685,739
Other operations	76,225	74,101	71,651	71,171
Total taxes	$ 641,712	$1,443,078	$ 987,554	$ 756,910
Additions to plant and property	509,724	424,111	476,565	481,642
Cost per ton at market	126.15	133.97	131.99	125.45
Cultivating				
Acres under cultivation	9,112	8,930	8,647	8,591
Acres planted	1,910	2,777	2,240	958
Acres ratooned	2,986	2,681	1,745	2,915
Million gallons water	33,042	31,178	26,214	29,354
Harvesting				
Acres harvested	4,550	4,594	4,054	3,935
Tons cane per acre	101.71	111.14	103.38	112.36
Tons cane per ton sugar	8.05	8.16	8.38	8.58
Tons sugar per acre	12.63	13.63	12.33	13.10
Tons sugar per acre month	.555	.564	.497	.523
Average crop age (months)	22.75	24.18	24.83	25.04

Manufacturing				
Tons cane ground—net	462,178	506,886	418,766	441,488
Tons cane ground per hr.—net	134.72	129.89	121.30	126.53
Tons sugar	57,338	61,632	50,066	51,453
Tons sugar per day	356	356	327	332
Tons molasses produced	17,246	18,795	18,548	19,150
Weather				
Rainfall at mill (inches)	17.03	13.50	38.81	21.87
Day degrees at mill	5,090	5,697	5,430	5,503

Source: Company records.

tors of the individual plantations. While Mr. MacNaughton was the titular head of the plantations, Mr. Bush had specific responsibility for maintaining corporate liaison with the three plantation managers, who were charged with operating the properties. Mr. Bush described his function as one of keeping informed of developments relating to the business of the plantations, but not of becoming involved directly in day to day operations. He was available to the plantation managers at any time to discuss operating matters and to provide whatever assistance he could in bringing the resources of Castle & Cooke to their aid. Mr. Bush further served as a member of the C and H board of directors and, in that capacity, represented the sugar marketing interests of Castle & Cooke and the plantations.

The separate boards of directors of the three plantation companies were composed mostly of Castle & Cooke executives. The Ewa Plantation Company directors included Mr. MacNaughton, Mr. Bush, Mr. A. L. Castle (a director of Castle & Cooke), Mr. E. C. Bryan, the Ewa plantation manager, and three outside directors: Mr. Kenneth Char (President of Aloha Airlines), Mr. N. R. Gilliland (representing the Bishop Trust Co.), and Mr. Allen Renton.

The directors of the Waialua Agricultural Company were Mr. A. G. Budge, chairman of Castle & Cooke's board, Mr. MacNaughton, Mr. Bush, Mr. A. L. Castle, Mr. H. K. L. Castle (vice president and director of Castle & Cooke), Mr. Gilliland, Mr. J. H. Midkiff (retired manager of Waialua and a director of Castle & Cooke), Mr. H. J. W. Taylor, manager of Waialua, and Mr. H. W. B. White, an associate of Mr. H. K. L. Castle, and Mr. A. B. Lau.

The Kohala Sugar Company's directors were Mr. MacNaughton, Mr. Bush, Mr. Budge, Mr. B. Howell Bond (a descendant of the plantation's founder), Mr. H. B. Clark, Jr. (vice president and treasurer of Castle & Cooke), Mr. H. J. W. Taylor (manager of the Waialua plantation), and Mr. Alvan C. Stearns (manager of Kohala).

The outside directors on the Ewa and Waialua boards represented the interests of minority shareholders.

Approval of annual budgets and review of operating results were the major functions of the plantation companies' directors. Capital expenditures within the plantation's annual depreciation allowance were normally accepted without question, while projects requiring funds in excess of depreciation funds required

WAIALUA AGRICULTURAL COMPANY, LTD.

Statement of Income and Retained Earnings

For the Years Ended April 30

	1965	1964	1963	1962
Income				
Sugar	$ 9,276,450	$11,475,257	$8,575,666	$7,856,294
Molasses	297,451	686,255	460,151	341,605
Sugar Act compliance	558,671	549,393	548,437	522,633
Dividends	73,184	73,184	93,434	95,459
Other—net	114,182	94,366	47,033	30,468
Total	$10,319,938	$12,878,455	$9,724,721	$8,846,459
Costs				
Employment				
Salaries and wages	$ 3,532,801	$ 3,644,243	$3,102,730	$3,012,172
Payroll taxes	122,797	134,978	102,856	102,578
Pensions and group insurance	219,666	244,989	222,000	216,289
Dental plan	17,736	17,550		
Medical plan—net	170,260	165,266	146,437	146,808
Village facilities—net	22,139	15,061	21,338	11,197
	$ 4,085,399	$ 4,222,087	$3,595,361	$3,489,044
Materials, supplies, and services				
Materials and supplies used	1,342,357	1,450,522	1,232,736	1,154,225
H.S.P.A. assessments	200,183	208,798	193,954	184,754
Water, electricity, and other svces.	807,900	890,418	687,940	670,908
	$ 2,350,440	$ 2,549,738	$2,114,630	$2,009,887
Rent on plantation land	563,232	553,614	528,762	511,708
Depreciation and amortization	601,797	602,733	581,115	561,793
Marketing of sugar and molasses	747,276	779,755	693,415	683,533
Gross income tax	82,804	143,096	145,937	158,627
Real property tax	125,034	129,388	123,384	97,404
Total	$ 8,555,982	$ 8,980,411	$7,782,604	$7,511,996
Income before income taxes	$ 1,763,956	$ 3,898,044	$1,942,117	$1,334,463
Income taxes				
Federal	718,736	1,858,386	892,184	616,605
State	81,351	195,167	92,000	61,877
Total	$ 800,087	$ 2,053,553	$ 984,184	$ 678,482
Net income	963,869	1,844,491	957,933	741,518
Retained earnings, beginning of year	6,853,363	6,062,937	5,845,916	5,559,808
	$ 7,817,232	$ 7,907,428	$6,803,849	$6,301,326
Deduct:				
1964,$2.25; 1963,$1.50; 1962,$.80	452,857	1,054,065	740,912	455,410
Retained earnings, end of year	$ 7,364,375	$ 6,853,363	$6,062,937	$5,845,916

[1] Includes extraordinary net income of $85,537 from sale of real estate.

Source: Company records.

WAIALUA AGRICULTURAL COMPANY, LTD.

Facts in Brief

For the Years Ended April 30

	1965	1964	1963	1962
Earnings and dividends				
Net profit	$ 963,869	$1,844,491	$ 957,933	$ 741,518
Per share	2.13	4.00	2.03	1.35
Dividends	452,857	1,054,065	740,912	455,410
Per share	1.00	2.25	1.50	.80
Balance sheet				
Cash, demand notes, and				
marketable securities	$2,368,627	$3,082,351	$1,052,298	$1,623,633
Inventories	517,397	534,020	473,450	483,517
Working capital	2,700,578	2,654,016	1,485,913	2,683,919
Capital stock outstanding				
shares	452,857	461,632	471,916	550,747
Book value per share	24.67	23.52	21.84	20.66
Number of stockholders	1,265	1,295	1,339	1,457
Other financial data				
Payroll				
Sugar production	3,532,801	3,644,243	3,102,730	3,012,172
Other operations	273,508	262,189	257,144	271,366
Total payroll	$3,806,309	$3,906,432	$3,359,874	$3,283,538
Number of employees	686	688	682	706
Taxes				
Sugar production	$1,130,722	$2,461,014	$1,356,362	$1,068,610
Other operations	37,496	36,712	35,046	37,318
Total taxes	$1,168,218	$2,497,726	$1,391,408	$1,105,928
Additions to plant and property	952,264	551,663	599,661	448,872
Cost per ton at market	116.38	119.46	119.32	115.92
Cultivating				
Acres under cultivation	10,930	10,812	10,565	10,370
Acres planted	2,137	2,858	2,509	2,575
Acres ratooned	3,181	3,329	2,442	2,388
Million gallons water	27,668	28,499	23,096	24,148
Harvesting				
Acres harvested—irrigated	5,014	5,268	4,644	4,682
Acres harvested—unirrigated	323	312	91	109
Tons cane per acre	111.05	116.44	115.74	112.50
Tons cane per ton sugar	7.85	8.29	8.32	8.22
Tons sugar per acre	14.15	14.04	13.91	13.68
Tons sugar per acre month	.616	.596	.581	.575
Average crop age (months)	22.98	23.57	23.93	23.78

Manufacturing				
Tons cane ground—net	579,338	629,916	542,681	533,718
Tons cane ground per hour—net	174.13	179.16	166.47	160.20
Tons sugar	73,519	75,174	65,223	64,804
Tons sugar per day	477	461	415	400
Tons molasses produced	20,198	21,757	20,121	20,732
Weather				
Rainfall at mill (inches)	41.57	27.39	49.62	35.77
Day degrees at mill	4,248	4,605	4,463	4,197

[1]For irrigated crop only.

Source: Company records.

special study and justification for board approval. As a general rule, approval was given to all projects which were deemed necessary to keep existing plants and equipment operating efficiently, as well as to any projects which were expected to return at least 15% on investment after taxes, on a discounted cash flow basis. All capital expenditure proposals were initiated by the plantation managers, reviewed by a committee of Castle & Cooke executives, and, if approved, then submitted to the plantation's board of directors.

The plantation managers were primarily concerned with obtaining the greatest possible net tonnage of sugar at the lowest possible cost. Because the C and H marketing arrangement took sales and pricing functions out of the hands of the plantation managers, plantations tended to be cost centers, rather than profit centers. Cost per ton of sugar produced was the result of the total acreage of cane harvested, the tonnage yield of cane produced per acre, the total agricultural cost, the sugar content per ton of cane, and the efficiency of the mill in extracting juice from the cane. The measure of tons of sugar per acre, which took account of nearly all of the above listed factors, was used as the principal nondollar measure of a plantation's performance. As will be seen, it was difficult to use this criterion to compare plantations, because of the very different growing conditions that existed among locations.

The typical organization of the Castle & Cooke plantations is presented below:

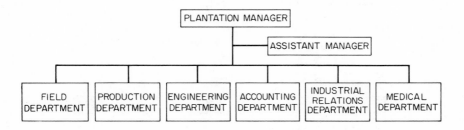

KOHALA SUGAR COMPANY

Statement of Income and Retained Earnings

	For the Years Ended April 30			
	1965	1964	1963	1962
Income				
Sugar	$5,883,474	$5,954,557	$4,863,269	$5,235,689
Molasses	194,676	363,096	290,639	220,797
Sugar Act compliance	375,161	332,176	340,844	365,794
Dividends	35,008	35,008	35,008	35,008
Disaster tax relief[1]	350,000			
Other—net (loss)	(11,884)	16,044	(46,609)	(41,442)
Total	$6,826,515	$6,700,961	$5,483,231	$5,815,726
Costs				
Employment				
Salaries and wages	2,923,098	2,794,611	2,392,371	2,355,351
Payroll taxes	136,987	128,032	101,652	96,869
Pension and group insurance	195,457	115,260	103,308	124,035
Dental plan	2,1200	20,413		
Medical plan—net	137,939	140,168	125,758	126,354
Village facilities—net	107,689	80,469	90,569	59,240
Total	$3,522,370	$3,278,953	$2,813,658	$2,761,849
Materials, supplies and services				
Materials and supplies used	1,533,141	1,408,817	1,260,031	1,258,037
H.S.P.A. assessments	123,021	112,578	103,805	111,194
Water, electricity, services	604,405	624,584	562,355	469,008
	$2,260,567	$2,145,979	$1,926,191	$1,838,239
Less: processing and overhead				
recovered from planters	108,451	57,149	94,102	63,952
Total	$2,152,116	$2,088,830	$1,832,089	$1,774,287
Rent on plantation land	27,476	31,935	27,447	29,622
Depreciation and amortization	288,059	285,379	303,153	319,888
Marketing of sugar and molasses	486,460	454,985	394,621	469,848
Gross income tax	52,329	74,981	88,700	101,379
Real property tax	73,008	58,830	58,511	26,921
Miscellaneous project	42,980	61,787	—	—
Total	$6,644,798	$6,335,680	$5,518,179	$5,492,794
Income before income taxes	181,717	365,281	(34,948)	323,132
Income taxes				
Federal	90,000	248,000		
Federal—refund			164,147	
State	6,000	15,000		
	$ 96,000	$ 263,000		
Net income	$ 85,717	$ 102,281	$ 129,199	$ 323,132

[1]Disaster relief received from the State to cover the drought loss years of 1962 and 1963. Kohala experienced a $141,281 loss from sugar operations for the year ended April 30, 1965, compared to a $365,281 pretax profit for the prior fiscal year.

Source: Company records.

exhibit 24B

KOHALA SUGAR COMPANY

Facts in Brief
(for the year ended April 30)

	1965	1964	1963	1962
Earnings				
Net profit	$ 85,717	$102,281	$129,199	$323,132
Per share	.34	.41	.52	1.29
Balance sheet				
Cash, demand notes and				
marketable securities	$ 16,719	$ 16,894	$ 18,038	$ 19,160
Inventories	472,550	447,445	445,943	465,230
Working capital	551,351	498,913	281,177	73,441
Capital stock outstanding,				
shares	250,000	250,000	250,000	250,000
Book value per share	25.53	24.99	24.58	24.07
Number of stockholders	8	8	8	8
Cultivating				
Acres under sugar cultivation	13,046	13,250	13,253	13,287
Acres planted	2,825	3,566	2,311	2,262
Acres ratooned	5,122	3,908	4,744	5,410
Million gallons water	10,915	13,308	12,298	13,905
Harvesting				
Acres harvested	7,047	6,824	6,852	7,107
Tons cane per acre	70.43	58.27	46.26	54.59
Tons cane per ton sugar	10.01	9.48	8.69	8.21
Tons sugar per acre	7.02	6.13	5.32	6.26
Tons sugar per acre month	.313	.275	.246	.279
Average crop age (months)	22.46	22.78	21.75	22.52
Manufacturing				
Tons cane ground—net	496,339	397,660	316,993	387,999
Tons cane ground per hour—net	95.38	88.56	79.96	96.25
Tons sugar	49,414	41,806	36,566	44,451
Tons sugar per day	199.25	195.35	185.61	233.95
Tons molasses produced	14,636	12,804	12,163	13,921
Weather				
Rainfall at Hawi (inches)	54.06	36.96	36.94	30.41
Day degrees at Hawi	23.83	2.504	2,801	2,873

Source: Company records.

At Ewa and Kohala the field department was responsible for cultivating, planting, growing, and harvesting the plantation's sugar cane crop. The production department was responsible for the milling operation which converted the harvested cane into raw sugar. The remaining departments provided general support for the field and mill activities. At Waialua harvesting was included under the production department.

Under the agency system the plantations relied on Castle & Cooke's corporate staff for a number of services, such as executive management, industrial relations, industrial engineering, public relations, specialized staff, tax, accounting, purchasing, insurance, and banking. Additional services could be purchased as needed at the discretion of the plantation manager.

Much of the technical assistance for the plantations was provided by the HSPA Experiment station on a fee per ton of sugar basis. Joint venture projects to solve special problems of the individual plantations were often undertaken with the Experiment Station on a shared cost basis.

Transportation of sugar and molasses to the Honolulu docks for the Ewa and Waialua plantations was provided by the Oahu Transport Company, Ltd. (OTC). OTC owned and operated a bulk sugar warehouse on the Honolulu docks in addition to its fleet of trucks. The company's original purpose was to haul raw sugar and molasses from all Oahu sugar plantations to the warehouse to await shipment to the C and H refinery at Crockett. OTC subsequently began operating as a common carrier to avoid empty backhauls. By 1965, revenues from the common carrier phase of the business represented more than 50% of the company's $2,000,000 a year business. The Ewa and Waialua plantations each owned a 42.5% interest in OTC; the remaining 15% interest was owned by an American Factors Company sugar plantation on the island of Oahu.

The Kohala Sugar Company operated its own fleet of trucks which hauled raw sugar 30 miles to Kawaihae Terminals, Inc., a bulk sugar, molasses and freight facility on the western coast of the island of Hawaii. Kawaihae Terminals was jointly owned by Castle & Cooke (55% interest) and Theo H. Davis (45% interest). It had been built in 1958 specifically to handle bulk sugar shipments for the C & C and Davies sugar plantations located on the northern tip of the island. Previously raw sugar had to be hauled 80 miles or more, at great cost to the plantations, to a similar facility at Hilo, Hawaii. The Hawaiian and Federal Government had developed the harbor at Kawaihae, providing the deep water port necessary for this type of facility. Ships stopping at Kawaihae carried raw sugar directly to the C and H refinery at Crockett.

Ewa Plantation Company

The Ewa Plantation Company was located in the community of Ewa on the southern (leeward) side of the island of Oahu near Pearl Harbor, about 15 miles west of Honolulu. The town of Ewa, with a population of 3,500 people, depended largely on the plantation for livelihood. The Ewa Plantation employed about 670 workers on a year-round basis, most of whom were housed in company built and owned homes. (Ewa was prohibited from selling these houses to their residents by terms of the plantation lease.)

The plantation was started in 1890 by W. R. Castle and his father, Samuel Northrup Castle, one of the original founders of Castle & Cooke. Ewa has been a consistently profitable operation under normal conditions and has paid a dividend each year since 1896, with the exception of 1959, the year following the costly industrywide strike of the ILWU Hawaiian sugar workers.

In 1965, the plantation covered 10,000 acres, about 9,000 of which were under cultivation. All of its lands were leased (virtually all from the James Campbell Estate). The Campbell Estate lease was scheduled to expire on December 31, 1978, and did not carry in it any provision for renewal.

Because of its location on the relatively dry, leeward side of the island, the Ewa plantation depended heavily on irrigation in order to produce high crop yields. Water requirements were pumped from more than 65 artesian wells, which produced about 150 million gallons per 24 hour period (about one and one-half times the amount of water used by the city of San Francisco in one day). By using overhead irrigation rigs in fields that were too rocky to accommodate efficient furrows, Ewa had been able to place its full 9,000 cultivated acres under irrigation.

The mill at Ewa had a 24 hour grinding capacity in excess of 3,000 tons of cane, and was capable of producing more than 61,000 short tons of raw sugar per season. (In 1965 Ewa was getting a ton of sugar from about eight tons of cane.) The mill was in round-the-clock operation five days per week, for about 170 days each year. The plantation had regularly yielded about 60,000 tons of sugar from its annual harvest until the 1958 strike, when sugar production dropped to 27,000 tons. 1964 production was 61,600 tons, while in 1965, operating a fewer number of days, the plantation produced 57,300 tons.

Because Ewa relied so much on irrigation, it was more severely affected by the 1958 strike than most of the other Hawaiian plantations. Lack of care in the fields not only had ruined the 1958 crop, but also, because of the two year growing cycle, had seriously affected the cane that was scheduled for harvesting in 1959 and 1960. The losses incurred were such that Ewa was one of two island plantations to qualify for "mutual support funds" from the Hawaiian sugar industry in 1959.[11] The amount of support, before Ewa's own proportionate regular assessment and contribution to the fund, was $500,000, which reduced the company's operating loss to $317,000. A refund of $179,000 in Federal income taxes further reduced the loss to only $138,000, but this experience clearly demonstrated Ewa's vulnerability to labor disruption.

By 1962, Ewa's sugar yields per acre appeared to be returning to prestrike levels, which historically had been among the highest in the industry. A setback

---

[11] The HSPA, acting as a producers' cooperative, insured its members against disaster by collecting an annual assessment from each plantation, based on its tonnage output. These "mutual support funds" were then dispensed by the HSPA Executive Committee whenever a plantation (or plantations) underwent extraordinary circumstances.

for the year ended April 30, 1965 (from 13.6 tons of sugar per acre to 12.6) was said to have been due chiefly to the harvesting of a significant volume of immature cane, in order to provide seed for a larger planting program than had been usual in previous years. This was necessitated by the desire to convert as much acreage as possible from an old variety, whose productivity was slowly declining, to a new variety which appeared to be most promising for Ewa's water, soil, and climatic conditions. The measure of tons of sugar per acre month, which takes into account differences in crop age, had remained about the same, thus substantiating this explanation.

The Ewa Plantation Company was managed by Mr. E. C. Bryan. Mr. Bryan had been brought up in the sugar industry, and had been assistant manager of the plantation for many years prior to his promotion in 1962, when the previous manager died. In addition to the task of bringing the plantation's production back to prestrike levels, Mr. Bryan also had to contend with replacing the volume produced from about 400 acres of prime sugar growing lands that were being lost to highways and similar public facilities. Part of this land had been replaced by leasing and converting adjoining former pasture lands to sugar production. Additional land that was considered as unsuitable for sugar was being reclaimed by a continuing program of pumping in new layers of top soil from the residues that clung to the harvested cane and were brought into the mill. This soil was washed from the cane, concentrated into a heavy mud, and then pumped to the thin soil, coral lands below the mill. Here it was mixed with the bagasse waste and leaf trash produced in cane milling, which were in excess of the mill's fuel requirements, and spread by the plantation's bulldozers when they were not employed in harvesting.

In a further attempt to increase plantation revenues, Mr. Bryan had established a department of diversified agriculture in 1963. This department was charged with finding uses for lands not suited for sugar cane culture and not yet reclaimed. By 1965, about 150 acres of coral wasteland and swampy pastures had been brought under cultivation, and the department had about 4,000 banana plants and 35,000 papaya trees coming into bearing. Most of the bananas and papayas produced by this effort were purchased by the Dole Company for use in its new Tropikai Fruit Pack. Other such areas were planted to forage crops for sale to a neighboring cattle feeding operation.

Another attempt to increase revenues was the establishment in 1965 of a plant to process cane stripping into cattle feed. The strippings, consisting of the leaves left on the cane after it was burned and hauled to the mill, were a chronic mill nuisance since they had to be removed from the cane and disposed of before the cane could be milled.

Mr. Bryan indicated that the cattle feed and diversified agriculture programs had limited potential volume, but he expected that these operations would produce about $150,000 in pretax earnings, on a continuing basis.

Long-range planning for Ewa was clouded somewhat by the lease term which was due to expire in 1978, and the reluctance of the trustees of the Campbell Estate to make long-term commitments at this time in view of the rapid urbanization of the leeward side of the island of Oahu. In 1965 the Campbell Estate was getting $1,000/acre rental in areas used for nonagricultural purposes versus $75/acre for sugar land. Ewa, being relatively close to Honolulu and adjacent to Pearl Harbor, had substantial potential for future nonagricultural development. Some members of Castle & Cooke management were becoming disenchanted with the profit and growth opportunities in sugar, and were arguing against renewing the lease. Others were uncertain as to whether or not the Ewa lease could be extended, even if Castle & Cooke did want to continue to operate the plantation. A further important factor was that the adjacent Oahu Sugar Company, owned by American Factors, was presently losing and would continue to lose land to urban use, and should have, by 1978, sufficient capacity to grind a substantial portion of Ewa's annual production if Ewa were to cease milling operations.

Under the circumstances, management considered it prudent to accumulate funds over the remaining life of the lease either for dissolution or for rehabilitation if the lease could be renewed. During a corporatewide profit planning session in September, 1965, Mr. Bryan presented a plan indicating the requirements for phasing out operations by 1978. In brief, the plan proposed limiting capital expenditures to the bare minimum required to keep the plantation running. (The existing lease called for the reversion of the mill and its equipment to the landowner at the time of lease termination, and prohibited removal of stationary capital items.) The growing crop was planned to be phased out during the last two years of the lease by harvesting the cane after only 12 to 14 months of growth. If no new employees were engaged, normal attrition and retirement would reduce the work force gradually to only 300 people during the last years of the lease. It was felt that there would be ample opportunities for these older, experienced people in other Castle & Cooke activities, or else that an early retirement program could be adopted.

Mr. Bryan projected that the plan would accumulate $15 million in cash by 1978, even after allowing for annual dividend payments equal to 60% of earnings. On the other hand, if the lease were renewed and the future of the plantation assured, Mr. Bryan estimated that Ewa could produce pretax earnings of at least $1 million per year on an indefinitely continuing basis. If management chose to phase out the Ewa operation, an important facilitating factor would be the willingness of the Union to negotiate the orderly removal of the crop during the final two years of the lease.

Waialua Agricultural Company, Ltd.

The Waialua Agricultural Company, Ltd., was incorporated in 1898, with Castle & Cooke playing a major role in its formation. The company was reorganized in 1948 and its assets were divided into: 1) a company holding all of the stock in Hawaiian Pineapple Company, Limited (now Dole) and all of the sugar and pineapple lands except for 200 acres containing the factory and Puuiki Village, and 2) a sugar company. Later the land investment company (Helemano) was merged into Castle & Cooke. Following the reorganization, the Waialua plantation operated primarily on leased lands, like Ewa. In 1965 Waialua had 10,930 acres under cultivation.

Waialua was one of the "showplace" plantations on the Islands. Its location on the windward side of the island of Oahu, 25 miles from Honolulu, placed it favorably in regard to rainfall and other important weather conditions. Furthermore, rainfall was supplemented by the company's own irrigation system, which was capable of furnishing 110 million gallons of water per day, from 19 pumping stations and 99 artesian wells. In addition, rainfall runoff stored in the Wahiawa reservoir, a facility controlled by Castle & Cooke and favorably situated to serve Waialua and Dole, was sufficient to irrigate 4,800 acres of Waialua cane by gravity flow of purchased water.

The significance of these favorable conditions is seen in the plantation's crop yields. In terms of tons of cane produced per acre and tons of sugar produced per acre, Waialua consistently ranked among the top three of Hawaii's 25 plantations. These high yields meant more sugar revenue per employee and a larger base for distributing factory overhead. Compared with its sister plantation at Ewa, which was itself one of Hawaii's better yielding plantations, Waialua produced 30% more tons of sugar in 1965, with the same number of employees and only 18% more land under cultivation.

The Waialua plantation was managed by Mr. H. J. W. Taylor, who previously had been manager of Castle & Cooke's Kohala plantation. Mr. Taylor moved from Kohala to Waialua in 1958, the year of the industrywide strike. Compared to other plantations, Waialua survived the strike in fairly good condition. Normal rainfall partially sustained the growing crop during the strike, thus limiting the decline in sugar produced in 1958 to the forced shortening of the milling operation. While production in the field was somewhat below normal in 1959 and 1960, Waialua's growing crop was relatively unaffected when compared with Ewa. Even during the strike, Waialua was able to show a profit.

During the early 1960's, Mr. Taylor began a program of increasing the plantation's sugar production by planting cane on additional lands, subleased from Dole, above the regular fields. These new fields were unirrigated, because it was not economically justifiable to pump water to the higher elevations. However, normal rainfall on these higher lands was substantially greater than that on the low lying regular fields. While yields from this land were well below those of the irrigated fields (about 8 tons of sugar per acre vs. 14 tons from irrigated lands), production was considerably cheaper, because unirrigated fields did not incur the costs of furrowing or water application. Also, these flat, unfurrowed fields made planting and harvesting much easier.[12]

The amount of sugar produced from the unirrigated fields represented a small share of the 1965 total production of the plantation (about 2,500 tons compared

---

[12] Some of the unirrigated land in cultivation in 1965 was not accessible by cane carrier and, thus, was not used to grow cane for processing in the mill. This land was used to grow seed-cane, however, so that it was not necessary to take other, high-yield land out of production for this purpose.

to 71,000 tons from irrigated fields), but according to Mr. Taylor it made an important profit contribution. He reasoned that any additional tonnage of cane produced, so long as it did not exceed the mill's existing grinding capacity, would provide marginal revenue that otherwise would be lost. In 1965, grinding capacity was in excess of 4,000 tons of cane per day.

In 1965, the unirrigated lands were only available to Waialua on a short-term basis since Dole wished the flexibility of putting this acreage into pineapple production, if that were necessary to meet market demand.

Mr. Taylor projected no significant change in earnings between 1965 and 1970. Pretax profits were expected to remain close to $2 million per year, producing an after tax approximate 8% return on shareholders' equity. These estimates were based on Mr. Taylor's belief that there was little opportunity to improve significantly the plantation's already excellent yield of sugar per acre or its cost per ton of sugar. All of Waialua's leased land was currently under cultivation, so there was limited opportunity to increase the acreage farmed. Mr. Taylor indicated that a $2 per ton increase in sugar prices over those which he had projected (based on past history) would bring the return on equity up to about 10%, but he held little hope for such increases.

Major capital improvements at Waialua in 1965 included the initiation of construction of a new boiler system at an estimated cost of $2 million. The boiler project was tied to an air pollution problem created by an open field burning of bagasse and strippings left over after the cane milling operation. The plantation had been under considerable pressure from local residents, Hawaii's governor, and the Board of Health to control the fly ash and smoke from this operation. The cost of the fly ash arrestor and incinerator required to eliminate the air pollution had been estimated at $1.6 million in capital expenditures, plus $100,000 per year in additional operating costs. Rather than follow this course of action, Waialua management had determined that an additional $1.1 million investment would increase the mill's power generating capacity sufficiently to require burning all bagasse produced in the milling operation. Although a relatively inefficient boiler generator system was required to consume the total bagasse volume, this alternative made it unnecessary to install the fly ash arrestor and incinerator. The cost savings in power and operating expenses expected from the new boiler system (including the $100,000 per year savings from not having to operate the fly ash arrestor and incinerator) anticipated that the project would pay back in six to seven years the 1.1 million dollars required above the $1.6 million deemed unavoidable in order to meet the Board of Health's standards. Waialua's directors had approved the expenditure in 1965, and expected construction to be completed in 1966.

Kohala Sugar Company

The original Kohala Sugar Company was the oldest of Castle & Cooke's three sugar plantations, having been incorporated in 1863. It had been established in a remote section on the northern tip of the island of Hawaii, as the result of a missionary's attempt to provide steady employment for his congregation. The Reverend Elias Bond had solicited help from Samuel N. Castle, one of Castle & Cooke's founders, in establishing a sugar plantation at Kohala. Mr. Castle had helped with the initial financing, and Castle & Cooke had become the agent for the new plantation. The present Kohala is a combination of five sugar plantations. Halawa Plantation lands were split between Kohala and Niulii in 1929. Hawi Mill and Plantation Company's properties were merged into Kohala at the end of 1930, and Niulii and Union Mill Plantations were acquired and merged into Kohala in 1937. In 1965, Kohala was still an isolated community on the largest land mass of the Hawaiian chain. The nearest city of any size was Hilo, located some 80 miles to the east.

Access to Kohala was over a long, winding, mountainous road, from the route joining Hilo, on the east coast, with Kawaihae on the west. Kohala's hauling costs had been reduced with the construction of the federally supported harbor at Kawaihae, but were still above those of most plantations on other islands. In 1965, it was anticipated that a state and federally financed road would be constructed at sea level between Kawaihae and Hawi. If built, this road would substantially reduce driving time both to Kawaihae and to other more populated areas on the Island.

The Kohala plantation had always been at the mercy of nature. Its land was too porous to hold water for very long. Consequently, in years of heavy and consistent rainfall, the plantation had produced reasonable crop yields, but drought years reduced the crop to below break-even levels. The 20 mile long Kohala ditch, dug through rocky, mountainous terrain to bring rain water accumulation to the low lying plantation, was completed in 1906. Although the ditch's maximum flow of about 15 billion gallons a year enabled irrigation of about 5,000 of Kohala's 13,400 cultivated acres, this was less than half the amount of irrigation water available to the more prosperous Ewa and Waialua plantations. This maximum volume of water provided by the ditch was substantially reduced during the drought periods, when Kohala needed it most.

Because of this shortage of water, the future of the Kohala plantation had been continuously questioned throughout its 100 year history. The decision to keep the plantation operating had as one of its important elements management's concern for the more than 600 plantation employees, who, with their families, relied on the Kohala Sugar Company for their livelihood. Closing down operations would, in fact, have meant complete dislocation of the entire community, because its economy was solely dependent upon the plantation. Many of Kohala's employees were descendants of the original workers who had started the plantation in 1863; few had had an opportunity to learn any job skills other than those required in the growing and milling of sugar.

This was the situation confronting Mr. A. C. Stearns when he became plantation manager in 1958. The problem became more pronounced in the early 1960's, as the Kohala area suffered another extended drought. For the year ended April 30, 1962, the area measured 30.14 inches of rain, compared to a 74 year average of 51.5 inches. In 1962, annual rainfall dropped further to 25.7 inches, before increasing to 37 inches in 1963.

In an effort to compensate for this erratic pattern of rainfall, Mr. Stearns called upon the HSPA Experiment Station to conduct an intensive study of Kohala's water problem. The study concluded that, in view of Kohala's porous soil conditions, overhead irrigation would produce the same results as furrow irrigation with the expenditure of only one-third the volume of water in wet years and only one-sixth the furrow volume in dry years. The study further indicated that deep wells drilled on Kohala's land would have a high probability of success in reaching previously untapped water resources.

Following the recommendations of the study, Mr. Stearns, with the support of the plantation's board of directors, embarked on a long-range water development program by installing overhead irrigation units in selected fields. By 1965, 3,500 of the plantation's 4,900 irrigated acres were utilizing the overhead system. The plantation's remaining 8,350 acres of cultivated land were unirrigated.

While Mr. Stearns believed that the results of the overhead irrigation program had been encouraging, he saw it as only the beginning of a long-range effort to finally produce a continuously adequate return on the plantation's assets.

The program envisioned by Mr. Stearns included: 1) a continuation of substituting overhead irrigation for furrows, designed to bring total irrigated acreage to 7,700, thereby increasing estimated sugar production to 57,000 tons per year on existing lands (as against an historical average of 36-44,000); 2) an increase in mill capacity to accommodate the increased production; and 3) the eventual addition of new irrigated acreage as additional water resources were developed through deep wells. He anticipated, ultimately, a fully irrigated plantation, with as much as 15,000 acres under cultivation, producing 64,000 tons per year.

The total cost of this program over the ten year period, 1965–1975, was estimated at $10 million, an amount that exceeded accumulated depreciation by $4 million. $2.5 million of the total program cost was committed in 1965, with the balance subject to later review. Because the largest expenditures of capital would be required in the factory to increase capacity, in drilling wells for new sources of water, and in additional overhead irrigation facilities, a time lag in production improvement of three years or more was projected. Profit expectations, therefore, were minimal for the first five years (a cumulative $320,000 before taxes), producing an anticipated average annual return on investment of less than 1%. In 1972 pretax earnings of $500,000 were forecast, increasing steadily to $1 million by 1975. In that year, and thereafter, return on investment was expected to be 10.6%. These calculations were based on modest annual increases in sugar prices, exclusive of molasses proceeds and compliance payments over the preiod (from 1964's $126 per ton to an estimated $145 per ton by 1975), as well as on continually decreasing plantation costs (from $136 per ton in 1965 to $126 per ton in 1975).

Mr. Stearns expressed concern over the poor earnings projected for the next five years, but believed that the alternative of making no improvements at all was far less attractive over the long run. Previous attempts to find alternative uses for the 13,400 production acres of land [13] owned by the plantation had been inconclusive. Pineapples were successfully grown on a section of the land in the early 1950's, but the project had been abandoned because of "uncertain market conditions and the difficulty in keeping the fruit in good condition while it was transported to the Dole cannery on Oahu." A small number of macadamia trees were being raised on the plantation in 1965, but Mr. Stearns indicated that poor tree growth in some areas dimmed the future of this project. Some thought also had been given to the development of Mahukona as a resort area similar to Rockefeller's Mauna Kea Hotel, about 30 miles down the coast, but the land required was a relatively small number of acres and was presently unsuited for cultivation.

Late in 1965, Kohala's directors had approved the expenditure of $1.6 million for the installation of a new boiler to replace small and wornout units. The new boiler was designed to conform to the long-range plan for increasing the capacity of the cane mill from its present 2,500 tons of cane per day to about 3,500. This capacity was deemed adequate, under Kohala's conditions, to produce the ultimate 64,000 tons per year forecast in the plantation's long-range plan. Work on the project was to begin in 1966. No decision beyond this commitment had been made on the remainder of the expansion plan.

CASTLE & COOKE'S APPRAISAL OF THEIR SUGAR INTERESTS

Sugar was one of the oldest of Castle & Cooke's many activities. The traditions and ties of the old sugar agency relationship had had great impact on most of the company's procedures and on much of its past strategy. Although the company had diversified its holdings enormously, about one-sixth of Castle & Cooke's stated 1965 book value was in its sugar holdings ($19.2 million). If the true, rather than nominal, values of growing crops had been included, this equity value would have been over $34 million. Additionally, while neither Ewa nor Waialua owned real estate, Kohala's 20,500 acres of fee land was carried on its books at the original cost of $85 per acre, far below its true value. Total 1965 revenues from sugar and related operations of $25.5 million were 9% of Castle & Cooke's total, and produced $2.6 million (12.8%) of the parent company's pretax earnings. Before tax return on book investment averaged 9.4% for sugar and related activities vs. 12.7% for all other Castle & Cooke operations.[14]

---

[14] Values used were in part based upon reallocation by the casewriter of accounts shown in Exhibit 5, Castle & Cooke, Inc. (A).

[13] In 1965 Kohala had 13,400 acres under cultivation out of 24,700 owned or leased. Of this, 20,500 acres were owned in fee. The noncultivated 11,450 acres were primarily rough, steep, heavily forested mountain land at high elevations, or arid desert near sea level.

Increasing the profitability of sugar operations appeared to management to be much more a function of increased realization in sugar prices than of internal improvements in cost or of expanding output. Additional acreage suitable for sugar, if available near existing plantations on Oahu, was leasing in 1965 for upwards of $65 per acre per year. While about two-thirds of plantation costs were controllable, 1965 costs of producing a ton of sugar ranged from Kohala's $136 per ton to Waialua's $118 per ton. Thus, with this as a range, and 1965 sugar price realization at about a $130 level,[15] margins were viewed as being determined primarily by price level. For example, a 4% price increase for Ewa's production was estimated to increase the plantation's pretax profits by as much as 40%. Similarly, at Waialua it was estimated that yields of sugar would have to increase one-half ton per acre (4%) in order to give the profit equivalent of a $2 increase (1.5%) in price.

Each of Castle & Cooke's sugar properties, as indicated, has unique characteristics. Ewa, with its highly efficient mill and high fixed costs, could likely be a steady profit maker in most years and could double its profit performance in years of strong sugar prices. Waialua, with its favorable climatic conditions, could likely be an even more profitable plantation than Ewa. Kohala had always been a marginal plantation because of its limited water supply, and there was serious question as to whether even a $10 million investment could bring it to Ewa's or Waialua's performance levels.

In 1965, both Mr. Bush and Mr. MacNaughton felt a continuing commitment to sugar operation. Both believed that sugar culture was the highest and best available use of most of the plantation lands. Neither felt that any of the plantations could be sold at anything close to their book values because of the generally low returns on investment. Moreover, Ewa's before tax 1965 return of 7.1% on book value was below the average of 12.5% for all Castle & Cooke's operations, and Waialua's 17.4% was far above it. While Kohala remained a persistent problem, both men believed that the total sugar properties could provide a relatively certain and stable income flow. Furthermore, consolidated with Castle & Cooke, the plantation properties' equity could provide excellent collateral against which Castle & Cooke could borrow to finance other activities with greater profit potentials.

---

[15] Exclusive of molasses proceeds and compliance payments.

Oceanic Properties, Inc.

EARLY DEVELOPMENT OF OCEANIC PROPERTIES

Dole and Castle & Cooke each had its own real estate department before their 1961 merger. Corporate headquarters of Castle & Cooke included a group which served the real estate needs of the C & C plantations and other land holdings. This group handled rental agreements, condemnation proceedings, zoning and other government relations, and other requirements resulting from holding land.

The Dole real estate group performed the same functions and was considering the upgrading of land values through development. The Dole group had surveyed real estate opportunities in Hawaii and on the mainland, and had concluded that a large residential community could be developed on Dole's fallow Oahu pineapple land. The most attractive location appeared to be on the Wahiawa plantation, about 20 minutes from Honolulu.

Development plans for this project, then named Waipio New Town, were well along by 1960, but activities were temporarily suspended during the merger proceedings. After the merger, all land service and development activities of the two companies were combined in a new company called Oceanic Properties, Inc. Chosen as president of the new company was Frederick Simpich, Jr., a vice president of Castle & Cooke. Mr. Simpich had been involved in the supervision of C & C's shipping and terminal activities, the Royal Hawaiian Macadamia Nut Co., and various other corporate responsibilities. He and Malcolm MacNaughton had had roughly parallel careers in C & C in the 15 years following the end of World War II, and were regarded as the "new generation" of top management.

Mr. Simpich's staff in this new real estate development activity initially included Mr. Donald D. Rietow, Mr. J. K. Palk, and Mr. Alfred A. Boeke. Mr. Rietow, formerly in charge of Dole's real estate operations, was named vice presi-

---

dent and general manager of Oceanic Properties. He was responsible for naming Mr. Boeke to the Oceanic staff, and later recommended the transfer of Mr. Warren G. Haight to Oceanic.

Mr. Haight had been performing economic analysis and planning functions for Dole in Honolulu over the nine years prior to joining Oceanic in May, 1964. Mr. Boeke had been hired by Mr. Rietow during the Dole survey of mainland real estate opportunities. Mr. Boeke, a practicing architect and community planner, had both taught and engaged in real estate planning on the mainland before his appointment to the Dole staff.

Mr. Palk, a native of Oahu and a trained attorney, had been in charge of the Castle & Cooke real estate section and had long experience in providing services to Castle & Cooke's land holdings.

Oceanic Properties was established as a wholly owned subsidiary of Castle & Cooke with an original equity of $2.6 million. Castle & Cooke executives indicated that "this financing arrangement was merely temporary and that someday additional capital would be provided such that Oceanic would be self-sustaining within its own cash flow and available borrowing power."

A CHANGE IN DIRECTION AND CONCEPT FOR THIS NEW COMPANY

Oceanic Properties was formed to carry out the land objectives of Dole and Castle & Cooke on a unified and more efficient basis.

The Castle & Cooke land department was basically oriented to developing and serving the company's Hawaiian agricultural lands. Almost all these agricultural lands were far from existing population centers, so that development to higher use appeared unlikely over the near future. Moreover, while Castle & Cooke had studied many local opportunities, it had never elected to acquire any additional Hawaiian land holdings that were not adjacent to existing holdings or related in use to existing properties.

On the other hand, the Dole real estate department was actively pursuing non-agricultural land development in Hawaii. At the time of the merger with Castle & Cooke, Dole had two projects on Oahu well underway. The first was the Waipio residential community mentioned earlier. The second was Mililani Memorial Park,[1] located near the Waipio site. The Memorial Park project was put into operation before the temporary cessation of real estate activity preceding the Dole–C & C merger in 1961, but the Waipio project at that time was only in the preliminary planning stages.

---

[1] A memorial park is a cemetery without tombstones, providing guaranteed perpetual care through the diversion of a share of proceeds to a trust fund. All headstone markers are imbedded flush with the land contour for ease of upkeep, providing a simple and neat appearance to the park.

After the merger had been completed and the new land development company formed, the Waipio project was resumed and given high priority. This was in November, 1961. In April, 1962, before the project had proceeded much further, the Hawaiian legislature enacted "greenbelt" zoning laws, which "froze" all existing land usage in Hawaii as of that date. These regulations specified that large areas of land, then in agricultural, watershed, or forest reserve use, were to be kept in those same uses in the future. This action was a hard blow to Oceanic Properties, since their Waipio lands were in agricultural use at that time and thus could not be converted to residential development.

The combination of this "Greenbelt freeze" and the fact that no other Castle & Cooke lands were both properly zoned and suitably located for immediate development forced Oceanic Properties to change its sphere of activities. Although the Oceanic staff continued to work with the state legislature on zoning requirements and variances, work on the Waipio project was halted, and the attention of the company shifted to areas outside Hawaii.

NEW CONCEPT OF OCEANIC PROPERTIES

The concept of Oceanic Properties as a worldwide real estate development company, limited neither to C & C land holdings nor to Hawaii, evolved from the 1962 Greenbelt restrictions and the flexibility given management with the advent of jet planes. Mr. Simpich set the stage for the new concept by providing many ideas for possible activities and by setting the guidelines for Oceanic investments.

One of the first constraints imposed required that Oceanic Properties, Inc., carry on the image of all other Castle & Cooke businesses, and "should continue the tradition of Castle & Cooke quality" in all of its real estate activities. This desire for quality implied a definite selectivity in Oceanic Properties' operations, as well as continuation in business for an unlimited time.

Mr. Simpich also sought diversification as a goal in the selection of possible projects. He defined diversification as having several aspects: geography, type of project, market appealed to, and length of development cycle. By 1965, Oceanic had in fact committed itself to a group of projects that met all of these criteria. Mr. Simpich believed that this diversification would season his staff and enable them to learn where the profit opportunities lay, so that they could concentrate their future activities in these areas.

Mr. Simpich stated his conviction that "it is more economic and efficient to operate through a small central staff and employ consultants as volume dictates, rather than staffing up for all eventualities." Mr. Haight added that, "in a business as cyclical as the construction and development industry, using a small staff with supplementary consulting help enables a firm to chop off its overhead [consultants] quickly in any declines of the economy." Thus, Mr. Simpich had his small staff engaged in selecting real estate development opportunities and working together to determine the use and economics of each project. Then, when an actual commitment was made, additional personnel were engaged to handle that project's detailed development.

By 1965, some codification in procedures had evolved in project selection. Before any project was launched, an initial proposal of land purchase, use to be pursued, and economic justification of the project was prepared by the staff and presented to the Oceanic board of directors. This board was composed of: Mr. A. G. Budge—chairman of the board of Castle and Cooke; Mr. Malcolm MacNaughton—president of Castle & Cooke; Mr. W. M. Bush—executive vice president of Castle & Cooke; Mr. H. B. Clark, Jr.—vice president of Castle & Cooke; Mr. Howard Hubbard—vice president of Castle & Cooke; Mr. Donald D. Rietow—vice president of Oceanic Properties; Mr. George B. Paulus—Salem, Oregon, director of Dole, and former owner of Paulus Bros. Packing Co. (now part of Dole); and Mr. R. H. Wheeler—director of Castle & Cooke, and president of Andrade & Company (Honolulu clothier). Few of these men had had a great deal of experience in real estate development, but all were deeply imbued with the Castle & Cooke tradition of quality. At least one member of the board personally visited and examined carefully each property under consideration and all details of the proposed plan. He then reported his recommendations to the total board.

To most board members, the Oceanic Properties activity was considerably different from the other businesses with which they were familiar. Mr. Simpich pointed out that the rest of Castle & Cooke's businesses were concerned with preserving their physical assets and developing earnings from asset use. Oceanic, on the other hand, had to sell its assets, or consume them, in order to generate earnings.

According to Mr. Simpich, Oceanic was unique among C & C operations in several important ways:

1. Since each project was independent and had a limited life, earnings from a single project or from all projects in one year could not be annualized to give an indication of future profitability.
2. There was considerably more risk in the real estate business than in the other activities of Castle & Cooke, and the extent of the risk was much more difficult to assess.
3. Many real estate projects were conceived as operating at a loss or break-even until the original investment was paid back. Such projects produced their profits in the form of value remaining in the project after payback but before the sale of the total property. This remaining value, "the residual," was not readily handled in normal accounting procedures or accurately reflected in traditional return on investment analysis; neither was the pre-planned "break-even" operation.

These unique characteristics made it difficult for Oceanic's board of directors to know how to assess prospective projects relative to other C & C activities. To date, virtually all projects that have been presented to the board have been approved after discussion and examination of the project information. Mr. Simpich indicated that a cutoff rate on proposed projects was a 15% return on invested capital after taxes over the life of the project as determined by discounted cash flow techniques.

After the project was approved by the board, the corporate staff would develop detailed plans and financial arrangements, hire an architect, and sometimes consultants. They then engaged a permanent staff to take over the project and conduct its development through completion. This staff received a budget and an operating plan from the corporate staff. The staff's project manager then developed his own detailed operating plans within these constraints. There has been no clear-cut procedure as to the point in a project's development at which the corporate planner, Mr. Boeke, turns over the responsibilities to the project manager. Oceanic did not expect to do the actual construction of these projects. It was anticipated that the developed land would be sold to independent builders under master plan site and architectural restrictions, or that Oceanic would joint venture construction of a project with a large-scale builder.

Functions of Key Management

President Simpich "started this organization at 80 miles an hour," say his associates, who call "him a man of enormous energy and many ideas. His creative ability and his desire for diversification among projects have set the company's tone." As a result, the corporate staff has been kept busy considering the many projects Mr. Simpich has assembled.

In 1965, Mr. Simpich was spending much of his time away from his Honolulu headquarters, visiting Oceanic's widespread projects. Much of his attention was devoted to the largest project—Hamilton—near San Jose, California.

Mr. Simpich considered timing of a project as one of the most crucial aspects of Oceanic's land development operations. He said, "since we deal with the time value of money, most of our mistakes have been in failure to gauge time properly." Projects are evaluated with present value techniques, and some projects have life expectancies of more than 20 years. Thus, errors in accurately forecasting timing, when discounting at rates of 20 and 30%, can make enormous differences in the calculated present values of the projects.

In 1965, Mr. Alfred A. Boeke was vice president in charge of planning. He viewed Oceanic properties as a leader in the sophisticated use of real estate planning techniques. In describing Oceanic's procedures, Mr. Boeke indicated that any real estate project should start with a basic social or market need in the area. He felt that Oceanic's job was to conceive developmental plans to satisfy the need and, in doing so, to increase the value of the land. After initial plans were made, and the most desirable alternatives selected, they were then checked for economic feasibility. Mr. Boeke felt that the estimation of market demand was the only truly subjective aspect of the various elements included in this economic analysis.

In describing his job, Mr. Boeke said that good planning resulted in a smooth time progression of continuously increasing value. "Any plan must, in its initial stages, attract customers, yet it must also allow flexibility over time for adapting to changes in purchasing patterns. Additionally, good planning often results in decisions that will reduce short-term profit but will benefit total long-run profits."

As an example, he cited reserving the best "view sites" in a project for later development of high-rise apartments rather than using them in the early stages of development for single family residences. By sacrificing some short-term profits in land sales, the entire project thus could achieve a much higher long-run value with the higher use of these sites in later years. "Since land values will increase due simply to urban growth, planning adds a second level of value. Good planning makes development not just the consumption of land, but permanently enhances the value of the area."

In 1965, Mr. Warren Haight was financial vice president and treasurer, and was in charge of both the controllership and economic analysis functions. Mr. Haight often counterbalanced Mr. Boeke's aesthetic point of view by introducing the economic limits and requirements in planning decisions.

Techniques for meaningful measures of discounted cash flows were the backbone of Mr. Haight's economic analysis. He felt that the over-all feasibility of a project should be measured by such discounted cash flows, and that the various assumptions within projections could also be tested for sensitivity by the same methods. This analysis could then be applied against Oceanic's potential investment, including both equity and guarantees, to determine the anticipated return on investment for the project.

After analysis of the discounted cash flow and return on investment, Mr. Haight evaluated the various risk variables (market potential, prospective competition, credit availability, possibility of war, etc.) before the project was presented to the board of directors.

The entire sequence of analytical techniques had to be quick, since "land deals" often were fleeting, and each project required an entirely separate analysis. Oceanic Properties has adapted an existing computer program to help prepare discounted cash flows for some of the longer and more complicated projects.

Mr. Haight admitted that some projects were not readily adaptable to these techniques. An example would be a new field like development of second homes, where there is inadequate data for determination of prices and absorption rates. In these instances, Oceanic had to revert to break-even analysis and subjective judgment. However, Mr. Haight believed that "seat of the pants" development days were over. He explained that the postwar land boom allowed practices that were now putting many developers out of business.

After the board approved a project with the supporting economic plan and detailed budget, Mr. Haight's controllership function took over monitoring the project. Daily and weekly reports were submitted to him, and monthly financial reports were due ten days after the close of the month. Any major changes in a project plan were subjected to the same kind of cash flow analysis methods used in development of that plan.

Besides monitoring individual projects, the controllership function included supervision of cash availability for the entire company. Short-term needs for funds were often provided for by an overdraft from Castle & Cooke. All debt financing in the past has been negotiated by Mr. Simpich and Mr. Haight.

Mr. J. K. Palk, vice president, was in charge of providing real estate services to plantations and other land holdings of Castle & Cooke. Half of his work was directly related to providing such services, while the other half was in support of the development activities of Oceanic Properties.

Mr. Palk agreed with Mr. Simpich that one of the biggest potential problems in land development was that of prolonging the time schedule. He believed that simply putting a building on land would not insure a successful real estate project, but, instead, the company should work with the state and local governments to show that greater economic benefit would be achieved by such development. Mr. Palk cited the Waipio project as an example. Mr. Palk, other members of Oceanic Properties' staff, and outside consultants working with the government spent almost three years proving that the Waipio land would provide an increased over-all benefit to the state if converted from agricultural to urban use. Even though Oceanic was successful in getting the necessary zoning changes to continue with the Waipio project, Mr. Palk felt that it would be increasingly difficult in Hawaii to convert such agricultural land to other uses. Mr. Palk's legal background had been very useful in getting zoning changes and project approvals for the Waipio project and others, especially the Central Business District.

The half of Mr. Palk's activities that involved providing service to the plantations included handling zoning problems, condemnation, taxes, purchase and sale of land, leasing, and other problems. Oceanic Properties charged the plantations on a time basis for the services provided.

Mr. Donald Rietow in 1965 was vice president and general manager. However, he indicated that under a president as dynamic and dominant as Mr. Simpich, the general manager role was merely titular. Consequently, Mr. Rietow had taken over total responsibility for all of the memorial parks owned and operated by Oceanic Properties, and was giving this activity his major attention. Nonetheless, he remained one of the five key members of Oceanic management, and his experience and opinions were important influences in development decisions.

Since most real estate development projects were long-range with very modest cash flows in the early years, Mr. Rietow explained that a real estate company needed a source of funds to carry its operations until it had many projects maturing continuously. Thus he viewed the cemetery activities as Oceanic's method of providing adequate short-term cash flow, and as the source of early profits per share.

Mr. Rietow believed that Oceanic should be able to add one new memorial park each year in different locations around the world. New locations for memorial parks had to meet several criteria: 1) existing cemeteries in the area should either be full or poorly maintained; 2) the market should be affluent enough to afford burial on a purchased plot (e.g., in some areas of the world a burial plot was rented for five years; then the remains were removed to a remote location in order to make room for a new burial); 3) the country's religion and traditional practices should provide a social need for cemeteries.

Mr. Rietow believed that, once a desirable location had been identified in a foreign country, it was best for Oceanic to find a local businessman or lawyer to work as a partner in acquiring the land and arranging the necessary zoning changes. Almost always, rezoning was required in establishing an area as a cemetery. Not only did such changes frequently arouse neighboring land owners, but also, the political bodies responsible for zoning administration frequently obliged deft or unusual working relationships. Because of foreign languages, unfamiliar customs, and very sensitive political conditions, Mr. Rietow had engaged a local partner in each of Oceanic's foreign memorial park activities.

In some areas, local ownership of a memorial park was required by law to be greater than 50%. In these cases, Oceanic has kept control by establishing a management company for the park in which Oceanic had majority ownership. Such financial arrangements could be very attractive to the memorial park holding company and extremely lucrative for the management company. The management company typically was compensated with a fee, plus a percentage of the gross sales, plus a percentage of the net profit.

The management company took over control of activities after the memorial park was in operation, with all construction and landscaping completed. This company supervised the sales and management activities, which varied widely with local custom. In some areas specialized salesmen did nothing but sell plots in the memorial parks. In other places, such as in Manila, salesmen often sold many products, including insurance, toothbrushes, and cemetery plots.

Mr. Rietow felt that the sales efforts of Oceanic memorial parks had to be dignified in order to preserve the Castle & Cooke corporate image. On Oahu a handsome brochure supplemented the salesmen's efforts. It included pictures of facilities and a dignified commentary describing the need for advance planning of burial needs.

Oceanic Holdings and Developments

Memorial parks. Mililani Memorial Park was Oceanic Properties' first memorial park. It was on Oahu near the Waipio development. It was started with an original cash investment of $250,000 in fiscal 1960 along with a substantial subsequent debt commitment, and it had accumulated an earned surplus of $1.6 million in 1965, and had long- and short-term liabilities of about $2 million. This park was planned to grow to 140 acres when 10 to 25 years old. In 1965, it had 50 acres in operation.

The ten man sales force was armed with the sales brochure mentioned above, and with an understanding of the carefully researched geographic location and ancestral background of prospective buyers. A memorial plot of 26 square feet sold for $240 at Miliani. Another $30 bought an annuity for perpetual care of the plot. With increasing demand over the next few years, Mr. Rietow anticipated the sale price might rise to as much as $600 per plot. Besides burial plots, this park derived revenue from catering facilities and a multidenominational mortuary.

Mr. Rietow recently changed the name of Mililani Memorial Park to Oceanic Properties Investment Company. This change was made so that the existing "inside" board of directors could be maintained for ownership purposes, and a new "outside" board of directors for sales purposes could be employed. This outside board in 1965 had members who were both knowledgeable and influential, and could aid in the sales efforts of the Mililani park.

Mr. Rietow has used Mililani as a pace setter to evolve innovations for both physical development and management of parks so these procedures can be used at other Oceanic parks.

In 1965 Oceanic Properties also had investments in two memorial parks in the Philippines. Manila Memorial Park had 209 acres and was completed in May, 1964. While this park was begun with an Oceanic equity investment of only $500 for a 26% stock ownership, plus a $9,500 loan at 11%, it was expected that Oceanic would underwrite the subsequent loan requirements for the park's development. The second Philippine memorial park was in Quezon City north of Manila, and was called Holy Cross Memorial Park. This 79 acre park, 51% owned by Oceanic Properties, was still under construction in 1965.

Mr. Rietow commented that one of his major functions was to work out the necessary financing for these parks. Both parks were managed by Trans-Pacific Management Company, 51% owned by Oceanic Properties. Trans-Pacific received a fixed fee from each park, plus 10% of gross sales, plus 8% of the net profit. Trans-Pacific Management Company earned for Oceanic Properties $75,000 after taxes in its first year. Exhibit 1 shows anticipated net earnings over the next five years of Oceanic Properties memorial park activities.

exhibit 1

OCEANIC PROPERTIES, INC.

Projected After-Tax Earnings of Present Memorial Park Activities (in thousands)

	1966	1967	1968	1969	1970
Mililani Memorial Park	$185	$185	$185	$185	$185
Mililani Mortuary	(35)	0	5	10	15
Manila Memorial Park					
Holy Cross Memorial Park	115	340	340	340	340
Trans-Pacific Management Company	100	100	100	100	100
Total after tax earnings	$365	$625	$630	$635	$640

Waipio.[2]   Although Waipio was the first major development project of the new Oceanic Properties company, its development was held up for almost three years, as indicated above, because of the land use freeze imposed by the new Greenbelt laws. As a result, in 1965 construction still had not begun on the Waipio project, although the first 705 acre increment (of the 3,000 acres to be developed over a ten year span) had been approved for conversion to residential use. The first increment was expected to include a 705 acre residential community and a 150 acre golf course. To get the necessary zoning, Oceanic Properties had to promise to provide a house of at least 1,100 square feet, on at least 6,000 square feet of fee simple land, to sell for less than $16,000. The first increment of development will include 50 to 75 houses to meet this minimal requirement. After initial sales, Oceanic planned to upgrade the houses slightly to include a some-what more luxurious interior and other refinements. This project is still in the formative financing stages. One possibility is a $2.5 million equity contribution from Oceanic, $5.5 million equity contribution from an outside source(s), which would cover total estimated capital requirements except for midyear peaks, which would be covered by short-term construction loans. Another possibility is $2.5 million in equity from Oceanic, and a long-term loan commitment (possibly with interest only payable in the first few years), in the range of $5 to $7 million, from an institutional and/or corporate source. When finished, Waipio would be a complete community, with its own shopping centers, schools, industrial parks, and recreational facilities.

Central Business District.   Another large Hawaiian project underway in 1965 was the redevelopment of a major business block in downtown Hono-lulu. This Central Business District (CBD) project was to be the U.S.'s first known condominium business development, encompassing one entire block in the heart of Honolulu's business district, and was under Oceanic's over-all management. When completed, this $22 million project would include a 21 story, 11,000 square foot per floor tower (Castle & Cooke corporate head-quarters were to be in the top three floors), a 12 story, 6,000 square foot per floor tower, and a 6 story tower housing the main offices of the Bank of Hawaii. The remaining 52% of the surface area of this redeveloped block was to be left in open plaza. $4 million in equity was provided by the land and building con-tribution of the condominium members, and the remaining $18 million in the form of a 25 year mortgage was guaranteed by the members in proportion to their ownership.

There were two major problems encountered in the planning stages of the CBD. The first, and by far the most difficult, was to get all land owners in this block to agree to join the condominium and then to determine the basis for valuation of their land. When one land owner, the Bishop Trust Company, did

---

[2] In late November, 1965, Oceanic Properties announced that the name of its proposed new community near Waipio, Oahu, would be "Mililani Town," and that construction on an 18 hole, 72 par golf course would begin January 1, 1966.

not want to enter this agreement, Oceanic Properties was able to arrange a land exchange between the Bishop Trust Company and the Bank of Hawaii. The bank had not been a land owner in this block but wanted to be part of the condominium.

The other land owners who agreed to be part of the CBD were American Savings and Loan with 6.3%, Wilcox Development Corporation (Brewer Estate) with 14.6%, Territorial Savings and Loan with 6.3%, and Castle & Cooke with 27.9%. The Bank of Hawaii held the remaining 44.6% interest in CBD.

The problem of valuation was solved by all land contributors agreeing to accept an independent appraiser's evaluation of their present land and buildings, and thus the proportionate contribution each made to the CBD. The value of Castle & Cooke's headquarters building and the land under it, $1.16 million, represented C & C's equity in the redevelopment project.

A second, and lesser problem, was obtaining a zoning variance, since the project deviated from the Honolulu bulk-height zoning law. Even though this was the first major project to help overhaul the obsolete downtown Honolulu business district, the zoning request met considerable resistance. Though the resistance was finally overcome and the variance granted, members of management said it indicated a basic problem still existed in the city's image of the "Big Five" companies.

Oceanic Properties, as project manager for the CBD, was to receive a fee of 4% of the total cost of the CBD project. At the end of 1965, planning and zoning requirements had been arranged, financing agreements had been signed with Morgan Guaranty Trust Company, present occupants of the block were finding new temporary quarters, and demolition was expected to begin shortly. CBD was expected to be completed in April, 1968.

The Sea Ranch.   The Sea Ranch was a 5,200 acre tract on California's Sonoma County coast, about two and one-half hours' drive north of San Francisco. It was to contain mostly second homes for Bay Area residents and was expected to take 10 to 25 years to complete. Present plans called for the construction and sale of luxurious condominium apartments and of house lots for building similarly high-priced individual residences. An over-all architectural plan had been completed which required all construction to meet certain standards of quality and architectural style in keeping with the natural beauty of the area. Mr. Simpich stated: "The undertaking at Sea Ranch has been to develop the best of all possible plans in the expectation that people will pay for the perpetuation of natural beauty, and that we will be rewarded accordingly."

Oceanic management saw Sea Ranch as a project in which the company would be obliged to provide the total equity requirements of about $4 million. Since lending institutions had had little experience with second home real estate projects, they were reluctant to finance improvements and construction until a definite sales pattern was established for luxury second homes in this region. Plans called for selling at least 100 lots per year, which was expected to return Oceanic Properties equity within seven years. At that time Oceanic anticipated a residual of 3,200 acres with an estimated value of $2.8 million. Financing methods for returning the equity contribution earlier than originally anticipated were being investigated.

Mr. Haight believed that this project was one of the most difficult to analyze with cash flow techniques (because of the large number of unknown variables), but he felt that it could yield a calculated "present value" return of about 33% after taxes on Oceanic's investment.

By September, 1965, Oceanic had constructed six model homes and ten condominium apartments, a sales office, and a restaurant at the Sea Ranch site, and had completed sales of 61 lots ranging in price from $7,500 to $13,000 each, including utilities.

Oceanic management believed that this type of project was still so new that, even with the initial sales performance, they could not tell if an adequate market existed, or, if it did exist, just what kind of extra facilities would be demanded (i.e., golf course, air strip, etc.).

Hamilton. The Hamilton project, located within the city limits of San Jose and Morgan Hill, California, was an ambitious plan for the construction of a totally new complete city, with all necessary service and industrial facilities. This 11,500 acre development was expected to be developed over 20 to 30 years, with an eventual population of about 100,000 residents.

The Hamilton project was a joint venture owned 50% by Lake Anderson Corporation (an Oceanic subsidiary), and 50% by Gelco Corporation (owned by Mr. Harlan Gelderman, a California real estate developer). Mr. Gelderman had located the ranch properties which comprised the site, obtained the necessary purchase options, and worked extensively with the city of San Jose in order to obtain the necessary zoning approvals for the project.

Mr. Gelderman obtained options to purchase this land, which he then sold to the joint venture for $1,000 per acre. Except for payments of $150,000 per year for the first three years, he was restricted from receiving further payment for the options until after the joint venture was operating at a profit. Besides the joint venture's $11 million obligation to Mr. Gelderman, Castle & Cooke had itself guaranteed a $2 million line of credit for four years and additionally had guaranteed the first five years of land payments to the sellers of the two ranches.

Obtaining long-term financial arrangements was a crucial element in the success of this enormous project, which was expected to be self-supporting. As Mr. Simpich indicated in the Oceanic Properties' 1965 annual report:

> Early in 1965 explorations were begun looking toward a source of long-term low-cost financing, the ideal source being an industrial concern who might "seed" the project by putting a plant on the property. At the close of the period under review, the detailed cash flows required in the presentation to such lenders were still in preparation. Collaterally, efforts were initiated in Congress to retain

proposed "New Town" financing sections that were being strongly opposed by the Council of Mayors, the Home Builders Association, the National Association of Real Estate Boards, and the insurance industry. The provisions were being supported by no one except the FHA. Through our efforts, language in acceptable form remained in the bill as it emerged from Committees in both Houses. (It has since been passed and signed in that form.) The availability of this legislation should prove very helpful in the negotiation of San Jose financing in the year ahead.

Mr. Simpich had been instrumental in the conceptance adoption of "New Town" legislation by the federal government, and it appeared that the Hamilton development might qualify for up to $12 million of financing through the FHA. However, since total requirements for funds were expected to be near $20 million, Oceanic Properties hoped to find, as an equity partner, a large U.S. industrial corporation, such as a diversified electric manufacturer or electronics firm. Additionally, Oceanic anticipated using improvement district bonding for much of the utility improvements. Through Mr. Gelderman's efforts, this project was expected to qualify under the 1915 California improvement district laws, and thus would be backed by the full faith and credit of the City of San Jose and would carry minimum interest rates. $11 million was anticipated to be obtained through the sale of improvement district bonds on major improvements. The remainder might be obtained through a major institutional and/or corporate lender in the form of debt or equity. The amount of Castle & Cooke and Oceanic equity to remain in the project in the future was dependent upon the nature of the long-term financing. Oceanic management indicated that they did not wish to ask Castle & Cooke for additional capital for this project. Instead, they preferred to raise capital either through debt issues or by taking in a sizeable equity partner, or both.

Gelso and Lake Anderson Corp. each had certain responsibilities in this development project. As Mr. Simpich indicated, "physical planning, financial analysis and control, external financing, and federal government relations have been assumed primarily by Oceanic. Relationships at the local and state level, internal financing, and marketing have been assumed by Gelco." By the end of 1965, about $350,000 had been spent on planning activities.

Oceanic Properties was using a computer simulation of the project to test out various assumptions of building costs, land densities, and marketing plans to determine the variables necessary to provide adequate cash flow and return on investment. Preliminary results indicated that the extra cost involved in building on the slopes of the site was likely to be a delaying factor in long-term profitability, considering present urban development and land demand in the San Jose area. It appeared that, after the first five years of development activities, this project could have residual value to Oceanic of $7.6 million. At the end of 1965, the Hamilton project was still in the planning and financial arranging stages. Construction had not yet been scheduled.

Wilshire Medical Center. Another real estate man, Mr. Walter Scott, was working with Oceanic Properties in Southern California in in 1965. Mr. Scott had found a property next to the Good Samaritan Hospital in Los Angeles and had entered into a joint venture with Oceanic for construction of a 15 story medical office building, containing more than 100 medical suites. Mr. Scott was a partner in this venture, to the extent of 47% of any profit realized, the William A. Staats & Co. investment firm was a 5% partner, and Oceanic held a 48% interest. Oceanic provided $375,000 of the initial equity of $395,000 plus advances of $200,000 and a guarantee of $1.5 million for loans. Construction of this $8 million building was completed ahead of schedule, at a cost $150,000 below budget estimates.

At the end of 1965, the joint venture was actively involved in leasing the Wilshire Medical Center. Ultimate sale of the building as an investment trust to some or all of the occupying doctors was anticipated. Such a sale required a positive cash flow, which was obtainable at about 67% occupancy. The major difficulty in leasing to the many doctors interested in occupying spaces adjacent to Good Samaritan Hospital was that most had existing lease obligations at other locations. Consequently, Oceanic management felt that it was only a matter of time until the building was fully occupied, but was disappointed at the rate at which leases were being sold.

Mr. Simpich believed that, once a satisfactory level of occupancy was achieved, the building could be sold for a profit of between $500,000 and $1,000,000. Mr. Haight indicated that he would like to see Oceanic with at least one project like this medical center under development at all times.

Orange County Shopping Center. A second Southern California partnership with Walter Scott was a joint venture for the development of a "regional shopping center," at the corner of Lincoln and Tustin streets in Orange County. By the end of 1965 the venture had signed leases with several tenants, including Safeway, Safeway Super S, Union Oil, and Bank of America. Besides these leases, enough long-term financing of $1,175,000 had been arranged to return the $100,000 equity contribution of Oceanic Properties. Oceanic Properties planned to continue development of this shopping center until it was fully mature, and then to sell it to a financial institution. Such a sale was not anticipated for at least five years.

Queen Emma Gardens. Queen Emma Gardens was an urban renewal apartment project in Honolulu. It included 587 apartment units, and housed approximately 1,500 persons. The project was completed late in 1964 and has been fully occupied since January, 1965. This project was cited by the HHFA as "the most successful urban renewal project in the United States." 40% of this $12.5 million project was owned by Castle & Cooke, and had involved an equity contribution of $200,000 and a loan of $450,000 for working capital. Although Queen Emma does not enjoy a large return on investment from its operation, it is expected to yield a handsome capital gain when it is sold (anticipated at five to ten years).

Kuala Lumpur.   Because of Castle & Cooke's partnership with Ahong Construction Company in a concrete mix plant in Malaysia, Oceanic Properties was able to join this Malaysian firm in a joint venture to construct twelve 16 story luxury apartment buildings in Kuala Lumpur. Oceanic had invested $260,000 for the purchase of land for this project, but basic differences subsequently developed between Castle & Cooke and Ahong, and, as of 1965, it appeared likely that the apartment buildings would not be undertaken until Oceanic's position with the Ahongs could be resolved.

Oceanic management had hoped that this experience in Kuala Lumpur might position them to participate in future government housing in that area when the Malaysian government succeeded in writing an FHA-type law for their country. As of the end of 1965, however, the Oceanic management was somewhat reluctant about following through in Kuala Lumpur. In discussing problems of government in Malaysia and Singapore, Mr. Palk said that Oceanic would be much safer to confine its current operations to the United States. Others in management felt that projects such as the Kuala Lumpur project were both too small, and too far away to receive adequate attention from Oceanic Properties' management.

Future Projects and Areas for Development

Although the past history of Oceanic Properties indicated clearly that its growth was being inhibited by difficulty in attracting competent personnel to staff new projects and by inadequate capitalization, Oceanic's management in 1965 was actively exploring several areas of future development. On the windward side of Oahu, Oceanic was considering a joint venture with a family who owned 4,500 acres ideally located for a prime residential community.

They also had under consideration a resort development on the island of Lanai, wholly owned by Dole. While reductant to enter the tourist business, Oceanic management believed that a joint venture with an experienced hotel operator might be attractive. If a suitable partner could be found who would take prime responsibility for the management and development of a hotel, Oceanic management felt they could develop a highly desirable range of peripheral facilities around the hotel complex.

Due to the monetary limitations imposed by Castle & Cooke, Oceanic has entered into exploratory discussions with several potential real estate development partners. Oceanic management believed that they could provide needed services to selected railroads, ranchers, and other large land holders in converting their lands to higher use and value.

In 1965, Oceanic entered into agreement with two such companies to inventory their land and to determine what land, if any, offered real estate development potential. Since these companies had very limited experience and staff competence in real estate, Oceanic was in an excellent position to aid in this evaluation.

Oceanic and a large paper manufacturer were considering joint development of a second home project on timber lands in Oregon. On a shared-cost basis, they were conducting a market study to determine if adequate demand existed

Oceanic and a large oil company were investigating jointly the development of a 300 acre site owned by the latter in Los Angeles county. This site, bought for oil refinery use, was valued at $120,000 per acre. A third possible joint venture existed on the Monterey Peninsula on 200 acres of land belonging to another large land owner.

Mr. Simpich also saw big long-term potential in Australia. With the continuous development and improvement of desalinization techniques, he felt that some day it might be possible to convert the arid areas of western Australia into fertile food production areas for the millions of people in Asia and the South Pacific.

However, with the existing mix of projects and maturity dates, management expected that most new projects initiated during the next five years would be short-term ventures. Increased emphasis was also anticipated on the managing of projects on a fee basis, such as the CBD, more cemetery developments, and joint ventures with industrial firms, like those with the paper company and the oil company mentioned above.

Operating Results

Financial results for fiscal 1961–1965 are shown in Exhibits 2 and 3. As previously stated, these conventional accounting reports do not portray Oceanic's activities very satisfactorily. Residual values in existing projects and contracted management fees are not reflected either in Oceanic equity or in Oceanic profitability.

Oceanic Properties has treated each of its development ventures as a separate and unique project. The method of financing has varied with the particular characteristics of each development. For example, it was necessary to provide all of the equity in the Sea Ranch project, while the Wilshire Medical Center was very highly leveraged, with a $395,000 equity supporting an $8 million building. The Waipio project is expected to be self-financing through use of FHA loans after development begins. The San Jose project, Hamilton, will probably require the use of public bonds and a joint venture with a large industrial firm.

With these different kinds of projects and the different financing methods, Oceanic Properties has subjected itself to widely varying degrees of risk. In all of its activities it has been restricted severely by its limited capital base. As Mr. Simpich indicated:

> As originally conceived, Oceanic was to have a capital of $4,000,000 to $5,000,000, much of it in land at book rather than market value. Various con-

exhibit 2

OCEANIC PROPERTIES, INC.

Consolidated Statement of Loss and Retained Earnings
(April 30, 1962–1965)

	1962	1963	1964	1965
Revenues				
Cemetery plot sales		$784,214	$260,378	$780,487
Other sales		225,675	186,595	145,932
Management fees			20,000	241,395
Finance charges and interest income				
From affiliated companies		253	6,818	3,101
From others	$ 1,500	183,984	162,885	231,205
Land service income				
From affiliated companies	80,050	95,580	153,278	171,433
From others		2,740	20,734	7,500
Commissions				
From affiliated companies			7,600	25,000
From others			2,500	24,390
Rentals and pasturing fees			31,861	26,294
Gain on sale of capital assets				
(net)		2,934	(55)	98,956
Other		39,320	29,741	39,597
Total revenues	$ 81,550	$1,334,700	$862,335	$1,795,650
Costs and expenses				
Cost of sales		225,010	184,708	226,301
Selling, service, general, and administrative expenses (including depreciation—1965, $71,185; 1964, $62,835)	297,179	1,044,463	1,001,917	1,470,855
Total	$297,179	$1,269,473	$1,186,625	$1,697,156
Income (loss) before income taxes	(215,629)	65,227	(324,290)	98,494
Federal and state income taxes[1]	—	168,856	(62,873)	203,890
	($215,629)	($103,623)	($261,417)	($105,396)
Minority interests				74,532
Net loss	(215,629)	(103,623)	(261,417)	($179,928)
Retained earnings, beginning of year	—	1,006,083	902,454[2]	641,037[2]
End of year	($215,629)	$902,454	$641,037	$461,109

[1]Tax liabilities have resulted from:(1) receipt of income payments on cemetery plot sales under long term installment contracts, and (2) earnings of subsidiary companies with net earnings for the year

[2]Retained earnings appear as the result of consolidating memorial park activities as of 4/30/1963.

exhibit 3

OCEANIC PROPERTIES, INC.

Consolidated Balance Sheets *
(1962–1966)

	April 30, 1962	April 30, 1963	April 30, 1964	April 30, 1965	April 30, 1966
Current assets					
Cash	$112,000	$ 255,000	$ 375,000	$ 192,000	$ 61,000
Marketable securities	—	50,000	—	—	
Accounts receivable					
From affiliated companies	38,000	14,000	45,000	—	
From others (less:allowance for doubtful accounts)	2,000	—	—	—	
	—	984,000	952,000	1,107,000	3,121,000
Notes receivable—trade	—	202,000	20,000	167,000	54,000
Inventories[2]	—	967,000	1,015,000	579,000	21,000
Prepaid expenses	5,000	17,000	19,000	18,000	22,000
Total current assets	$156,000	$2,489,000	$2,427,000	$2,062,000	$ 3,279,000
Deduct current liabilities					
Accounts payable					
To affiliated companies	267,000	66,000	208,000	688,000	—
To others	34,000	116,000	86,000	314,000	47,000
Notes payable, including current portion of long-term debt[3]					
To affiliated companies	—	4,000	89,000	298,000	308,000
To others	—	—	276,000	1,300,000	396,000
Income taxes payable	—	245,000	250,000	291,000	6,000
Total current liabilities	$302,000	$ 431,000	$ 908,000	$2,891,000	$ 757,000
Working capital (deficiency)	($146,000)	$2,058,000	$1,518,000	($829,000)	$ 2,522,000
Investment					
Equity in limited partnership		304,000	307,000	267,000	
Other companies—at cost	422,000	35,000	47,000	360,000	946,000
Advances to foreign affiliates	—	—	282,000	567,000	
Land—at cost	—	43,000	2,780,000	2,873,000	2,877,000
Buildings, machinery, and equipment (net)	71,000	401,000	859,000	877,000	641,000
Construction in progress	108,000	276,000	—	—	2,568,000
Noncurrent receivables and other[4] (less: allowance for doubtful receivables)	1,000	2,293,000	1,688,000	2,514,000	863,000
	$445,000	$5,408,000	$7,480,000	$6,629,000	$10,417,000
Deduct					
Noncurrent portion of long-term debt					
To affiliated companies	—	423,000	302,000	230,000	
To others	—	722,000	2,803,000	2,358,000	2,181,000
Deferred income and other credits	—	453,000	316,000	259,000	387,000
Deferred income taxes[5]	—	1,206,000	798,000	623,000	
Minority interests in Philippine Memorial Park activities	—	—	—	77,000	—
	0	$2,805,000	$4,219,000	$3,548,000	$ 2,568,000
Net assets, representing stockholders' equity	$455,000	2,603,000	3,261,000	3,081,000	7,850,000
Stockholders' equity					
Capital stock	1,000	1,000	1,000	1,000	1,000
Additional paid-in capital	670,000	1,700,000	2,619,000	2,619,000	9,824,000
Retained earnings	(216,000)	902,000	641,000	461,000	(1,975,000)
Stockholders' equity	$455,000	$2,603,000	$3,261,000	$3,081,000	$ 7,850,000

[1]The consolidated financial statements include all significant operating subsidiary companies. Trans-Pacific Development and Management Corporation, a newly organized company, is included for the first time for the year ended April 30, 1965. The accounts of this foreign subsidiary are translated at appropriate rates of exchange.

[2]Inventories consisted of:

(in $000)

	1965	1964	1963
Cemetery plots (at cost)	565	894	842
Livestock (at cost)		114	113
Other	14	7	12

[3]Notes payable and long-term debt at April 30, for each year, consisted of the following:

(in $ 1,000)	1965 Current	1965 Noncurrent	1964 Current	1964 Noncurrent	1963 Current	1963 Noncurrent	1962 Current	1962 Noncurrent
To affiliated companies	$ 298	$ 230	$ 89	$ 302	$37	$ 423	$267	0
To others	1,300	2,358	276	2,803	4	722	0	0
	$1,598	$2,588	$365	$3,105	$41	$1,145	$267	0

[4]Noncurrent receivables and other assets consisted of:

(in $1000)	1965	1964	1963
Development projects in progress	$1,216	$ 401	$ 216
Contracts receivable on cemetery sales	1,033	1,246	2,032
Notes receivable	192		
Other	73	40	45

*After deductions for reserve for Endowment Care Fund of $791.

[5]Deferred income taxes are indicated for cemetery plot sales financed by long-term installment contracts.

[6]Additionally, the companies were contingently liable as guarantors of loans made to associated joint ventures of $2,000,000 in 1965.

siderations and events have resulted in its operating in these initial years from a much lower base. At the close of the fiscal year the management developed a forecast of capital needs in the amount of about $5,000,000 for consideration by the Board and ultimate recommendation to Castle & Cooke. It was then suggested that the capital could be provided in the form of cash, guarantee of debt, transfer of nonagricultural land, or sale of an equity interest in Oceanic. This question remained unresolved at the year-end [1965].

In early 1966 a refinancing of Oceanic properties was accomplished through the transfer of accounts between Castle & Cooke and Oceanic, resulting in an effective recapitalization of Oceanic to $9.8 million. The effects of this refinancing are shown in the January 31, 1966, balance sheet in Exhibit 3. Working capital was increased to a positive $2.5 million from an $800,000 deficiency, by eliminating notes and accounts payable by Oceanic to Castle & Cooke. Oceanic gained an additional $1.5 million in net assets by Castle & Cooke's assuming $1 million of

exhibit 4

OCEANIC PROPERTIES, INC.

Five-Year Projection
(in thousands)

	1966	1967	1968	1969	1970
Anticipated revenues					
O.P., Inc. (management fees)	$ 387	$ 491	$ 323	$ 261	$ 270
Sea Ranch	1,324	1,170	1,305	1,527	1,903
Mililani Memorial Park	—	100	100	100	100
Lake Anderson Corp.	—	—	500	300	500
Wilshire Medical Center	1,500	—	—	—	—
Total revenues	3,211	1,761	2,228	2,188	2,773
Cost of sales					
O.P., Inc.	853	765	803	843	885
Sea Ranch	1,417	911	1,033	929	1,101
Wilshire Medical Center	233	—	—	—	—
Total costs	2,503	1,676	1,836	1,772	1,986
Income before taxes	$ 708	$ 85	$ 392	$ 416	$ 787
Dividend exclusion		(72)	(333)	(340)	(510)
Profit before net operating					
loss deducted	708	13	59	76	277
Tax loss carry forward	(1,154)	(445)	(432)	(373)	(297)
Taxes payable	0	0	0	0	0
Net income after tax	708	85	392	416	787

Residual value of Sea Ranch at the end of five years—$2,767,000.
Residual value of Hamilton (lake Anderson Corp.) at the end of five years—$7,600,000.

Oceanic's long-term debt obligations and transferring $.5 million to Oceanic in fixed assets. The result of all of these transactions was to assign to Oceanic a cumulative operating deficit of $2 million and a final net asset figure of $7.8 million.

Based on existing land development projects only, the Oceanic Properties staff projected substantial profit contributions to Castle & Cooke for the next five years, as shown in Exhibit 4. Despite the high risks and the constraining demands for current cash flows, several members of Oceanic's management predicted that, within 10 to 15 years, Oceanic Properties could become Castle & Cooke's most important revenue producer.

Castle & Cooke, Inc. (B):

Corporate Organization and Development

In late 1965, Castle & Cooke's corporate headquarters staff, including all clerical employees, numbered fewer than 200 persons. It was organized in roughly the same way in 1965 as it had been for the previous 50 years, with a very small group of officers, each a technical specialist in one of the important agency functions, and each supported by a small staff of experts in subspecialties. Exhibit 1 shows the corporate organization chart as of November, 1965. On this chart is indicated the scope of responsibilities for each man, as well as the directorships and officerships he held in the various affiliated or subsidiary companies.

AGENCY ORGANIZATIONS

This "agency" form of organization had developed naturally from the needs of the remote, outlying sugar plantations which the company had served since very early in its history. The plantation operators in those days looked to their agents to arrange shipping, supplies, financing, sales contracts, technical guidance, assistance in the recruitment of labor, and the conducting of negotiations with the monarchy. By providing a technically specialized central staff, the agency was able to furnish each plantation with a broader range and higher grade of expert talent than any one of them alone could afford. The agencies saved their clients money by reducing overhead and manpower requirements, and, through their special competences and contacts, provided services which the client plantations could not have performed effectively for themselves.

Consolidated purchasing, industrial relations activities, accounting, tax accounting and negotiations, public relations (and representation before governmental bodies), operations

---

analysis, insurance, and shipping arrangements had continued as C & C agency functions in 1965. In addition, staff consultants were available to the client companies for assistance in industrial engineering, civil engineering, and other specialized projects.

Inherent in the agency relationship (whether it be an advertising agency, a management consulting firm, a real estate management firm, or whatever) is the autonomy of the client. Thus the individual boards of directors of C & C's various companies (rather than the agency) were viewed as the appropriate bodies for decision-making relative to their respective operations. (The most noteworthy characteristic of Exhibit 1, which is indicative of the degree to which the agency form persists, is the great number of directorships or officerships held by each principal executive.)

The autonomous client, operating with central agency assistance, was both a desirable and necessary situation for the agency in its representation of companies in which there were substantial ownership interests other than the agency's. To give an advantage to one client at the expense of another would have been morally reprehensible. And to find mutual advantages for different companies with different ownerships and objectives was not only difficult, but also could place the agent in delicate "conflict of interest" situations. Therefore the agency companies tended to view each operation as a completely separate and independent entity.

The agency relationship tended to be most advantageous to all concerned when the client companies were relatively small. When a client became large enough to perform economically the agent's functions itself, there was little reason to continue the relationship (as Matson demonstrated in 1963 and 1964).

In the early days in Hawaii, client plantations frequently transferred their business from one sugar agent to another, even as many mainland businesses do today with insurance agencies, advertising agencies, and the like. Even though the agent might hold an important ownership interest in the plantation, he still might lose the account. (Indeed, in 1963 and 1964, Castle & Cooke lost the Matson ship agency account and the terminals agency account, despite a 23% ownership of Matson.)

Agency relationships also tended to oblige the client company to regard itself as a wholly independent entity, regardless of the extent to which the agency held ownership. (The independence of Hawaiian Pineapple [Dole] in its various investment and strategy decisions is a relevant example.) Similarly, these relationships tended to make the agent regard his role primarily as one of solving the client's problems. Thus the agency's director(s) on a client company's board tended to take the scope and objectives of the client as fixed and unchanging, and concentrated their efforts on helping the client to operate smoothly, rather than on effecting drastic changes in the company's strategy. In Hawaii, moreover, the formation of the C and H Sugar Refining Co. by the plantations in 1905 gave the sugar marketing responsibility wholly to that organization. Thus the agencies tended to concentrate their expertise primarily upon the production and financial problems of their clients, and to leave sales activities to C and H.

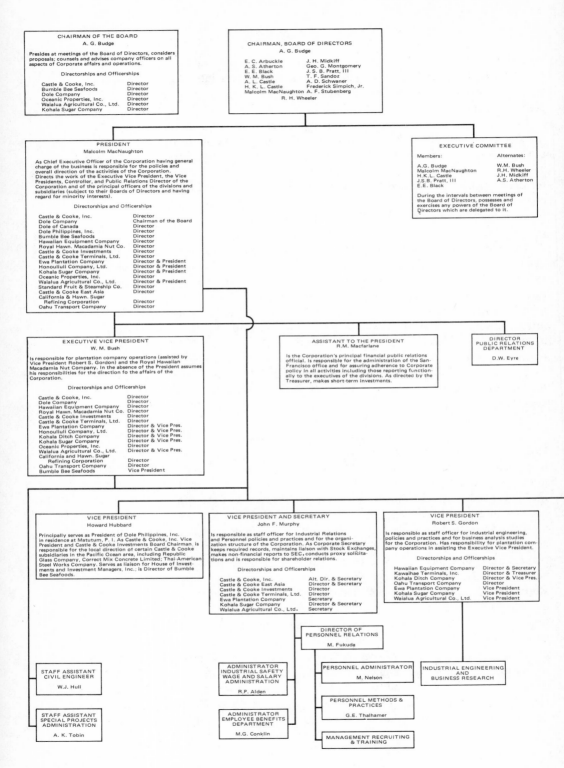

CHAIRMAN OF THE BOARD
A. G. Budge

Presides at meetings of the Board of Directors, considers proposals; counsels and advises company officers on all aspects of Corporate affairs and operations.

Directorships and Officerships

Castle & Cooke, Inc.	Director
Bumble Bee Seafoods	Director
Dole Company	Director
Oceanic Properties, Inc.	Director
Waialua Agricultural Co., Ltd.	Director
Kohala Sugar Company	Director

CHAIRMAN, BOARD OF DIRECTORS
A. G. Budge

E. C. Arbuckle	J. H. Midkiff
A. S. Atherton	Geo. G. Montgomery
E. E. Black	J. S. B. Pratt, III
W. M. Bush	T. F. Sandoz
A. L. Castle	A. D. Schwaner
H. K. L. Castle	Frederick Simpich, Jr.
Malcolm MacNaughton	A. F. Stubenberg
R. H. Wheeler	

PRESIDENT
Malcolm MacNaughton

As Chief Executive Officer of the Corporation having general charge of the business is responsible for the policies and overall direction of the activities of the Corporation. Directs the work of the Executive Vice President, the Vice Presidents, Controller, and Public Relations Director of the Corporation and of the principal officers of the divisions and subsidiaries (subject to their Boards of Directors and having regard for minority interests).

Directorships and Officerships

Castle & Cooke, Inc.	Director
Dole Company	Chairman of the Board
Dole of Canada	Director
Dole Philippines, Inc.	Director
Bumble Bee Seafoods	Director
Hawaiian Equipment Company	Director
Royal Hawn. Macadamia Nut Co.	Director
Castle & Cooke Investments	Director
Castle & Cooke Terminals, Ltd.	Director
Ewa Plantation Company	Director & President
Honouliuli Company, Ltd.	Director & President
Kohala Sugar Company	Director & President
Oceanic Properties, Inc.	Director
Waialua Agricultural Co., Ltd.	Director & President
Standard Fruit & Steamship Co.	Director
Castle & Cooke East Asia	Director
California & Hawn. Sugar	
Refining Corporation	Director
Oahu Transport Company	Director

EXECUTIVE COMMITTEE

Members:	Alternates:
A.G. Budge	W.M. Bush
Malcolm MacNaughton	R.H. Wheeler
H.K.L. Castle	J.H. Midkiff
J.S.B. Pratt, III	A.S. Atherton
E.E. Black	

During the intervals between meetings of the Board of Directors, possesses and exercises any powers of the Board of Directors which are delegated to it.

EXECUTIVE VICE PRESIDENT
W. M. Bush

Is responsible for plantation company operations (assisted by Vice President Robert S. Gordon) and the Royal Hawaiian Macadamia Nut Company. In the absence of the President assumes his responsibilities for the direction fo the affairs of the Corporation.

Directorships and Officerships

Castle & Cooke, Inc.	Director
Dole Company	Director
Hawaiian Equipment Company	Director
Royal Hawn. Macadamia Nut Co.	Director
Castle & Cooke Investments	Director
Castle & Cooke Terminals, Ltd.	Director
Ewa Plantation Company	Director & Vice Pres.
Honouliuli Company, Ltd.	Director & Vice Pres.
Kohala Ditch Company	Director & Vice Pres.
Kohala Sugar Company	Director & Vice Pres.
Oceanic Properties, Inc.	Director
Waialua Agricultural Co., Ltd.	Director & Vice Pres.
California and Hawn. Sugar	
Refining Corporation	Director
Oahu Transport Company	Director
Bumble Bee Seafoods	Vice President

ASSISTANT TO THE PRESIDENT
R.M. Macfarlane

Is the Corporation's principal financial public relations official. Is responsible for the administration of the San Francisco office and for assuring adherence to Corporate policy in all activities including those reporting functionally to the executives of the divisions. As directed by the Treasurer, makes short-term investments.

DIRECTOR PUBLIC RELATIONS DEPARTMENT
D.W. Eyre

VICE PRESIDENT
Howard Hubbard

Principally serves as President of Dole Philippines, Inc. in residence at Matutum, P. I. As Castle & Cooke, Inc. Vice President and Castle & Cooke Investments Board Chairman is responsible for the local direction of certain Castle & Cooke subsidiaries in the Pacific Ocean area, including Republic Glass Company, Correct Mix Concrete Limited; Thai-American Steel Works Company. Serves as liaison for House of Investments and Investment Managers, Inc.; is Director of Bumble Bee Seafoods.

VICE PRESIDENT AND SECRETARY
John F. Murphy

Is responsible as staff officer for Industrial Relations and Personnel policies and practices and for the organization structure of the Corporation. As Corporate Secretary keeps required records, maintains liaison with Stock Exchanges, makes non-financial reports to SEC, conducts proxy solicitations and is responsible for shareholder relations.

Directorships and Officerships

Castle & Cooke, Inc.	Alt. Dir. & Secretary
Castle & Cooke East Asia	Director & Secretary
Castle & Cooke Investments	Director
Castle & Cooke Terminals, Ltd.	Director
Ewa Plantation Company	Secretary
Kohala Sugar Company	Director & Secretary
Waialua Agricultural Co., Ltd.	Secretary

VICE PRESIDENT
Robert S. Gordon

Is responsible as staff officer for industrial engineering, policies and practices and for business analysis studies for the Corporation. Has responsibility for plantation company operations in assisting the Executive Vice President.

Directorships and Officerships

Hawaiian Equipment Company	Director & Secretary
Kawaihae Terminals, Inc.	Director & Treasurer
Kohala Ditch Company	Director & Vice Pres.
Oahu Transport Company	Director
Ewa Plantation Company	Vice President
Kohala Sugar Company	Vice President
Waialua Agricultural Co., Ltd.	Vice President

DIRECTOR OF PERSONNEL RELATIONS
M. Fukuda

STAFF ASSISTANT CIVIL ENGINEER
W.J. Hull

ADMINISTRATOR INDUSTRIAL SAFETY WAGE AND SALARY ADMINISTRATION
R.P. Alden

PERSONNEL ADMINISTRATOR
M. Nelson

INDUSTRIAL ENGINEERING AND BUSINESS RESEARCH

PERSONNEL METHODS & PRACTICES
G.E. Thalhamer

STAFF ASSISTANT SPECIAL PROJECTS ADMINISTRATION
A. K. Tobin

ADMINISTRATOR EMPLOYEE BENEFITS DEPARTMENT
M.G. Conklin

MANAGEMENT RECRUITING & TRAINING

exhibit 1

CASTLE & COOKE, INC. (B)

Organization Chart: November 1965

DONATIONS COMMITTEE

Administers Corporate donations policy. Makes recommendations for corporate donations for those divisions and subsidiaries located in the State of Hawaii.

H. B. Clark, Jr., Chairman	D. W. Eyre
R. S. Gordon	W. P. Hodgins
R. H. Wheeler	

FINANCIAL RESOURCES COMMITTEE

Advises on and assists in the coordination of plans for medium and long-term debt commitments of the Corporation and its divisions and subsidiaries where corporate credit is involved. Assists in appraisal of alternate sources of such funds, and counsels on the relative merits of proposals for borrowing.

H. B. Clark, Jr., Chairman	D. W. Furbee
J. R. Gale	W. G. Haight
W. N. Siegmund	S. Rosch, ex officio

ORGANIZATION COMMITTEE

Makes and reviews studies and proposals for development of the organization of the Corporation to assure that functions and relationships are established to facilitate attainment of corporate objectives, to provide for optimum use of personnel and for definition of responsibility, authority and accountability.

John F. Murphy, Chariman

PLANTATION COMMITTEE

For Ewa, Kohala and Waialua, reviews capital expenditure budgets and makes recommendations to plantation Boards. Reviews operating budgets, appraises major programs for profit improvement and counsels operating management.

W. M. Bush, Chairman	H. B. Clark, Jr.
R. S. Gordon	Malcolm MacNaughton
J. F. Murphy	J. H. Scott

PROFIT PLANNING COMMITTEE

Develops and coordinates the use of methods of gathering data and making projections for short and long-term estimating of profit. Assists in the establishment of profit goals, in the evaluation of profit projections and profit performance, and in the determination of potential deviations from forecast objectives.

Stanley Rosch, Chairman	Allen V. Cellars
D. W. Furbee	John R. Gale
S. P. McCurdy	H. B. Clark, Jr., ex officio

SIGNING AUTHORIZATION

In addition to the officers of Castle & Cooke, Inc. shown on the chart, the following officers, who are in most instances officers of divisions or subsidiaries of the Corporation, have the authority to sign documents for the Corporation. Such documents generally relate to transactions of the division or subsidiary of which these officers are an employee or an officer.

J. K. Palk, Assistant Treasurer	G. C. Shervey, Assistant Treasurer
H. B. Benner, Assistant Secretary	A. V. Cellars, Assistant Secretary
J. R. Farley, Assistant Secretary	R. M. Macfarlane, Assistant Secretary
H. M. Richards, Assistant Secretary	

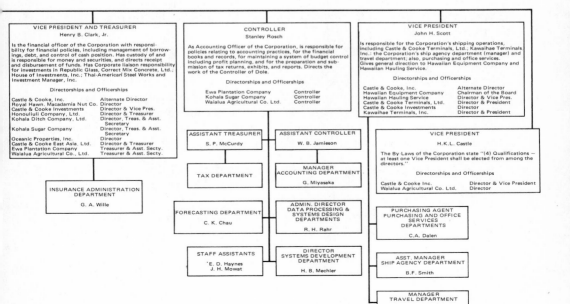

VICE PRESIDENT AND TREASURER
Henry B. Clark, Jr.

Is the financial officer of the Corporation with responsibility for financial policies, including management of borrowings, debt, and control of cash position. Has custody of and is responsible for money and securities, and directs receipt and disbursement of funds. Has Corporate liaison responsibility for investments in Republic Glass, Correct Mix Concrete, Ltd., House of Investments, Inc.; Thai-American Steel Works and Investment Manager, Inc.

Directorships and Officerships

Castle & Cooke, Inc.	Alternate Director
Royal Hawn. Macadamia Nut Co.	Director
Castle & Cooke Investments	Director & Vice Pres.
Honouliuli Company, Ltd.	Director & Treasurer
Kohala Ditch Company, Ltd.	Director, Treas. & Asst. Secretary
Kohala Sugar Company	Director, Treas. & Asst. Secretary
Oceanic Properties, Inc.	Director
Castle & Cooke East Asia, Ltd.	Director & Treasurer
Ewa Plantation Company	Treasurer & Asst. Secty.
Waialua Agricultural Co., Ltd.	Treasurer & Asst. Secty.

INSURANCE ADMINISTRATION DEPARTMENT
G. A. Wille

CONTROLLER
Stanley Rosch

As Accounting Officer of the Corporation, is responsible for policies relating to accounting practices, for the financial books and records, for maintaining a system of budget control including profit planning, and for the preparation and submission of tax returns, exhibits, and reports. Directs the work of the Controller of Dole.

Directorships and Officerships

Ewa Plantation Company	Controller
Kohala Sugar Company	Controller
Waialua Agricultural Co. Ltd.	Controller

ASSISTANT TREASURER
S. P. McCurdy

TAX DEPARTMENT

FORECASTING DEPARTMENT
C. K. Chau

STAFF ASSISTANTS
'E. D. Haynes
J. H. Mowat

ASSISTANT CONTROLLER
W. B. Jamieson

MANAGER ACCOUNTING DEPARTMENT
G. Miyasaka

ADMIN. DIRECTOR DATA PROCESSING & SYSTEMS DESIGN DEPARTMENTS
R. H. Rahr

DIRECTOR SYSTEMS DEVELOPMENT DEPARTMENT
H. B. Mechler

VICE PRESIDENT
John H. Scott

Is responsible for the Corporation's shipping operations, including Castle & Cooke Terminals, Ltd., Kawaihae Terminals, Inc.: the Corporation's ship agency department (manager) and travel department; also, purchasing and office services. Gives general direction to Hawaiian Equipment Company and Hawaiian Hauling Service.

Directorships and Officerships

Castle & Cooke, Inc.	Alternate Director
Hawaiian Equipment Company	Chairman of the Board
Hawaiian Hauling Service	Director & Vice Pres.
Castle & Cooke Terminals, Ltd.	Director & President
Castle & Cooke Investments	Director
Kawaihae Terminals, Inc.	Director & President

VICE PRESIDENT
H.K.L. Castle

The By-Laws of the Corporation state "(4) Qualifications — at least one Vice President shall be elected from among the directors."

Directorships and Officerships

Castle & Cooke Inc.	Director & Vice President
Waialua Agricultural Co. Ltd.	Director

PURCHASING AGENT PURCHASING AND OFFICE SERVICES DEPARTMENTS
C.A. Dalen

ASST. MANAGER SHIP AGENCY DEPARTMENT
B.F. Smith

MANAGER TRAVEL DEPARTMENT
J. Clancy

CASTLE & COOKE IN 1965

In late 1965, Mr. MacNaughton and other key executives were raising serious doubts about the effectiveness of this organization structure for the conduct of their operations. Not only had the company become deeply involved in companies whose major activities were highly market-dependent (e.g., Dole, Standard Fruit, Bumble Bee), but also each was of sufficient size that it economically could carry on virtually any functions it required. Furthermore, there appeared to be important opportunities for combination and integration, which would greatly strengthen over-all operations and increase total corporate profitability.

There were nine principal corporate officers in late 1965:

Alexander G. Budge, 74, chairman of the board since 1959, had joined the company in 1920 as assistant secretary, after graduating in engineering from Stanford University. He served as president from 1936 to 1959, seeing the company through important stages in its growth and development. In 1965, he did not concern himself actively with operations of the various units, but was viewed by his colleagues as "a wise and steadying influence on the company," Mr. Budge viewed C & C's past success "as the result of a highly competent staff, working together well." He saw a current need to "digest the major mergers of preceding years, consolidate and develop personnel, and provide seasoning to the central staff."

Malcolm MacNaughton, 56, president and director, was a native of Portland, Oregon, where his father had been president of the leading bank, publisher of the local newspaper, and president of Reed College. A graduate of Stanford Business School, Mr. MacNaughton joined Castle & Cooke in 1942 as assistant secretary. He became a vice president in 1955, executive vice president in 1957, and president in 1959. Mr. MacNaughton spent much of his time traveling about C & C's far-flung operations, working with the mainland financial community, and participating in important industry activities. His colleagues referred to him as "a sharp mind," "quick-on-the-draw," "incisive and decisive." He viewed the recent past with some satisfaction, but felt there was much still to be done. He indicated, "we're not nearly as much an operating company as I want to see us become over the next 3–4 years. We have great opportunities to make attractive returns on our investments. We have experienced, qualified, imaginative people. There's no reason why we can't become a major factor in the food business."

William M. Bush, 62, executive vice president and director, had joined the company in 1926 as a bookkeeper. He came to Hawaii in 1920 from his native Scotland. Treasurer from 1944 to 1958, he was named vice president in 1955, and executive vice president in 1961. He devoted most of his time to the problems and operations of C & C's three sugar plantations and to the C & C companies on whose boards he served. He was regarded by his colleagues as "canny," "careful," "thorough," "a wonderful human being." He viewed C & C's future as one requiring "great transitions from old ways of doing things" and involving the "retraining and assimilation of a lot of people."

John F. Murphy, 59, vice president and secretary, joined the company in 1946 as director of industrial relations, after building a national reputation in labor relations in New York. He was elected vice president and secretary in 1959, as well as continuing his industrial relations activities. Since his arrival in Hawaii, Mr. Murphy had been the major industry spokesman in union negotiations for the sugar industry and on the waterfront. In 1965, much of his time was devoted to contract negotiations, but he had additionally been assigned the responsibility for organization planning. He was regarded by his associates as "a quietly competent, gentle man," "sensitive and persuasive," "hard-working and dedicated." He himself viewed his new assignment as a great opportunity to contribute to C & C's future development and growth.

Henry B. Clark, Jr., 50, vice president and treasurer, joined the company in 1946 as a business analyst, after having graduated from the Harvard Business School, and having served five years as a navel officer during World War II. He was elected treasurer of C & C in 1958 and a vice president in 1962. "Polished," "personable" Mr. Clark, "a real team man," spent much of his time assuring adequate availability and flow of funds for corporate headquarters and the plantation companies, looking after insurance and leases, investments, and relations with shareholders and the financial community. He was very active in Honolulu civic affairs and was a director of a number of important non-C & C Hawaiian companies. He noted the "dramatic change in the character of the company which has taken place over the last 10 years, as we've moved from a strictly Hawaiian company to a greatly diversified one, with interests all over the world." He viewed C & C as being "in a number of speculative businesses" and saw a need to "protect, and continue to develop, the opportunities in which we are presently involved."

Stanley Rosch, 48, controller, joined the company in 1965. He had previously been a partner in a Honolulu auditing firm, and then with Haskins & Sells, in Honolulu and Los Angeles, since 1956. He had become intimately familiar with C & C as its external auditor, and had been handpicked by Mr. Howard Hubbard, previous controller and a C & C vice president, "to develop uniform accounting systems and policies throughout Castle & Cooke." Mr. Rosch viewed his job primarily as "being a translator: reporting the information to the operating people which they need in order to manage in a form that needs no interpretation. Accounting is a service department. Information often does not come from the divisions on time or in the right form. I want to see management reports properly designed, with accurate information, prepared with appropriate frequency, with minimum effort. We ought to be doing some systems studies, and also conducting internal audits, as a check on policies and accountabilities."

Howard Hubbard, 53, vice president, had joined Dole in 1936, and later transferred to C & C, where his work was primarily in accounting and fiscal matters. He was named controller in 1958 and vice president in 1962. In mid-1965, after Mr. Rosch's appointment, Mr. Hubbard was transferred to the Philippines to become president of Dolfil and "to look after C & C's other Asian investments."

John H. Scott, 50, vice president in charge of shipping operations, had been with C & C since 1935. He became personnel officer for C & C Terminals in 1949, Terminals manager in 1954, and vice president for all C & C shipping operations in 1962. Hawaiian-born Mr. Scott, "dedicated," "hard-working," "with considerable line operating experience," looked after most of the C & C transportation activities. He had had some trying times in adjusting to the loss of the Matson business, but had managed to retain most of his key personnel and to rebuild a profitable ship agency and terminal operation. In 1965, he also supervised the central purchasing function, which Mr. Hubbard had previously performed. Mr. Scott saw great future profit opportunities for C & C in providing an integrated intrastate transportation service, as well as entering into Island-mainland shipping. He saw "transportation as a major segment for the company's future growth, along with food products and land development."

Robert S. Gordon, 49, vice president, joined Castle & Cooke in 1952 as director of industrial engineering. A graduate of MIT and a native of Massachusetts, Mr. Gordon had served as a naval officer during World War II, and had joined Libby, McNeill and Libby in Honolulu as an industrial engineer in 1946. In addition to providing industrial engineering services and feasibility studies on new projects or major capital expenditures for the various client companies, he assisted Mr. Bush in directing the affairs of the C & C sugar plantations. He took a particular interest in the planning function, in formalizing corporate procedures and direction, and in management development and recruiting.

Liaison with Subsidiaries and Divisions

Each of these men also had a "liaison relationship" with one or more of the various operating companies. As Mr. MacNaughton wrote in mid-1965:

> A company as large, diversified, and geographically dispersed in its operations as ours functions best with decentralized operating management. This type of organization requires establishing well-defined lines of communication so that the president and other executive officers are adequately informed on operations and the managers of the subsidiaries and divisions have ready access to advice

and assistance on their problems. Members of staff departments, such as industrial relations, public relations, industrial engineering, and others, also benefit from established lines of communication.

A primary "executive contact" and an alternate (to act in the primary's absence) was assigned to each affiliated company. Mr. MacNaughton's memo continued:

Certain areas of responsibility have been well-known heretofore, others have not been as clear, and some are new. For this reason, we list below in alphabetical order the various affiliates, and opposite each the executives and their alternates who will serve as contacts.

Bumble Bee Seafoods	*Executive Contacts*
T. F. Sandoz, Board Chairman	Malcolm MacNaughton
John S. McGowan, President	Howard Hubbard
Castle & Cooke Investments	Howard Hubbard
	A. Gordon Westly
Castle & Cooke Terminals, Ltd.	
Edmund Jensen, Vice President & Manager	John H. Scott
	Howard Hubbard
Dole Company	
William F. Quinn, President	Malcolm MacNaughton
	W. M. Bush
Ewa Plantation Company	
E. C. Bryan, Vice President & Manager	W. M. Bush
	R. S. Gordon
Hawaiian Equipment Company	
O. H. McPheeters, President & Manager	John H. Scott
	R. S. Gordon
Hawaiian Hauling Service, Ltd.	
Paul K. Findeisen, President	John H. Scott
	Howard Hubbard
Honouliuli Co., Ltd.	W. M. Bush
	Henry B. Clark, Jr.
Kawaihae Terminals, Inc.	
Kent Bowman, Vice President & Manager	John H. Scott
	R. S. Gordon
Kohala Ditch Co., Ltd.	
A. C. Stearns, Vice President	W. M. Bush
	J. K. Palk

Kohala Sugar Company
A. C. Stearns, Vice President & Manager   W. M. Bush
                                                  R. S. Gordon

Mililani Memorial Park, Inc.
Donald D. Rietow, President & General Manager   Frederick Simpich, Jr.

Oahu Transport Co., Ltd.
J. C. Walker, President   W. M. Bush
                                                  R. S. Gordon

Oceanic Properties, Inc.
Frederick Simpich, Jr., President   Malcolm MacNaughton
                                                  W. M. Bush

Royal Hawaiian Macadamia Nut Company
W. M. Hale, Jr., President   W. M. Bush

Standard Fruit & Steamship Company
Donald J. Kirchhoff, President   Malcolm MacNaughton
                                                   L. H. Hogue

Waialua Agricultural Co., Ltd.
H. J. W. Taylor, Vice President & Manager   W. M. Bush
                                                   R. S. Gordon

Boards of Directors

As indicated earlier, the individual boards of the various affiliated companies
tended to be the decision-making bodies for each of the various units. Directors'
meetings of most of the smaller companies were held monthly. These meetings
rarely lasted longer than an hour, and, frequently, three or four would be scheduled in a single morning. Meetings of the directors of Castle & Cooke, Dole, Standard Fruit, Bumble Bee, Oceanic, and the three plantation companies normally were
held quarterly.

Castle & Cooke's board of directors consisted of 16 men. Three (Mr. Budge,
Mr. MacNaughton, and Mr. Bush) were active in C & C central management.
Two (Mr. F. Simpich, president of Oceanic, and Mr. T. F. Sandoz, chairman of
Bumble Bee) headed important divisions of C & C. Six represented important
ownership blocs (Messrs. A. L. Castle, Mr. H. K. L. Castle, Mr. A. S. Atherton,
Mr. J. S. B. Pratt, III, president of Hawaiian Trust Co. [all representing heirs of
the founders]; Mr. A. D. Schwaner, who had sold his family's F. M. Ball Co.
cannery to Dole, and Mr. A. F. Stubenberg, who had sold his company to
C & C's Hawaiian Equipment Co. subsidiary). Two were former C & C employees
(Mr. G. G. Montgomery, chairman of the board of Kern County Land Co., and
Mr. J. H. Midkiff (retired manager of Waialua). The remaining three, Mr. R. H.
Wheeler, Honolulu clothier, Mr. E. C. Arbuckle, Dean of the Stanford University

Graduate School of Business, and Mr. E. E. Black, Honolulu contractor, were "outside" directors.

The 14 man *Dole board* included six members of the Castle & Cooke board (Messrs. Budge, MacNaughton, and Bush from corporate headquarters, Mr. Simpich, Mr. Sandoz, and Mr. Schwaner). Besides Mr. Schwaner and Mr. R. C. Paulus (who had sold his family's Salem, Oregon, cannery to Dole), neither of whom was active in Dole management, and the four principal operating officers of Dole (Messrs. Quinn, Bleich, Levine, and Hogue), there were three "outside" directors (Mr. L. Jenks, Honolulu attorney; Mr. Robert Sato, Honolulu clothier; and Mr. R. B. Brown, Associate Dean of the University of Hawaii's School of Business).

The 12 man *Standard Fruit board* included only one C & C director, Mr. MacNaughton, along with Dole vice presidents Hogue and Levine. Three were Standard officers (Dr. D'Antoni, Mr. Kirchhoff, and Mr. Smith), while the other six were important shareholders or "outside" directors in the New Orleans business community.

Bumble Bee Seafoods' 11 man board included Mr. Budge, Mr. MacNaughton, and Mr. Hubbard from C & C headquarters, the three top Bumble Bee officers (Messrs. Sandoz, McGowan, and J. D. Hendrickson), and five "outside" directors from the Pacific Northwest. Thus, there were three C & C directors on this board.

Oceanic's 9 man board included five C & C directors (Messrs. Budge, MacNaughton, Bush, Simpich, and Wheeler), two C & C officers (Messrs. Clark and Hubbard), Mr. George Paulus (brother to R. C. Paulus), and Mr. Donald D. Rietow, Oceanic vice president and president of the various memorial park activities.

The three plantation boards each included Mr. Budge, Mr. MacNaughton, and Mr. Bush, and the manager of the particular plantation company. Additionally, Kohala and Waialua each had one former manager. Ewa had three representatives of important minority shareholders interests, plus one "outside" director, as did Waialua, while Kohala had Messrs. Clark, Hubbard, and Murphy in lieu of the minority interests, and Waialua's manager as the "outsider."

About 20% of C & C's capital stock was voted by various trusts, heirs, etc. Another 10% was controlled by operating officers and directors. The balance was widely held by more than 10,000 shareholders.

Beginnings of Change

In late 1965, Mr. MacNaughton had initiated a number of steps to change the organizational relationships. In a late September meeting of management personnel from all of the various affiliated companies, he made the following remarks:

> We need to ask ourselves, "what kind of a company are we?" We are a food company, but we are also in all kinds of other things: glass, trucks and heavy

equipment, a railroad, a brewery, a pipe plant. I believe we ought to look at any opportunity that's honest where we can make a good return.

As of now, no company [in C & C] has any right to any money that company generates. We have to look at who gets it from the bottom line figure of Castle & Cooke. You fellows are all in competition for the use of the money. In other words, if you show that with funds you develop, you can earn more money for Castle & Cooke than Company B over here can, you can hold on to it and even expect to get some of Company B's money. That's the way it has to work out. The romance in this is gone as far as we're concerned, and we have got to work the whole thing on a coordinated basis.

We sometimes tend to get a little oversatisfied. We need exposure to new ways of thinking. New questions must be asked and new answers found.

Since the merger of Castle & Cooke, Dole, Bumble Bee, and the emergence of Oceanic Properties, we have put together some of our corporate activities. These actions were discussed at the time of the merger and, in fact, were listed as one of the economies of merger. The moves have been:

1. Castle & Cooke and Dole Purchasing have been united.
2. Al Tobin, Bill Hull, and Bob Gordon [engineering specialists] have become available to all companies as need may arise.
3. All corporate tax counsel has been united at the Castle & Cooke level.
4. While Oceanic Properties with its expanded effort was an outgrowth, it did unite all effort on lands then owned.
5. Gradually, nearly all of Castle & Cooke's and Dole's data processing and accounting work has been centralized at Castle & Cooke.
6. Insurance management has been centralized and coverage grouped; this has produced some substantial savings.
7. Similar treatment has been given benefit plans with consequential savings.

In the main these moves have been accomplished without too much discomfort to those engaged in the services. No one has immediately lost a position by dint of these moves. Normal turnover and attrition, however, already have and will continue to produce substantial payroll savings. Yet the moves have not gone far enough if we are to accomplish maximum economic results through centralization of management control. Particularly is this true of Dole and Castle & Cooke, which have the bulk of their operations here in the islands. In this interest I propose to establish a single controller's department with Stan Rosch at its head. Bill Jamieson will continue as assistant controller with offices at Castle & Cooke, reporting on this company's operations. John Gale will become controller of Dole and will remain in Honolulu, also reporting directly to Stan. Larry Hogue will continue in San Jose as a vice president of Dole in charge of all mainland operations except marketing.

As we gain experience with this unification, it may prove advantageous similarly to realign Bumble Bee controller functions. Remember the purpose of moves such as these is not to enlarge Castle & Cooke, but wherever possible to better coordinate over-all effort in the interest of most effective control and operating economies.

In addition to his duties as corporate controller, Stan henceforth will act as chairman of a new committee, the Castle & Cooke Profit Committee. The responsibility of this committee will be to make profit projections and to establish profit goals. The committee will work closely with the various divisions and subsidiaries, but with the approval of the president will have the responsibility of making the final profit estimate.

The treasurer's department will be treated similarly. We not only are developing, but have already developed, a major money management problem. Each company or division has seasonal borrowings or balances of substantial proportions. In addition, there is term debt at Bumble Bee, at Dole, Dolfil, Oceanic, and Castle & Cooke. It is essential that control be centralized so as to develop an over-all long-range debt plan and to minimize interest costs. We should have no fear of debt, but we must know where we are going. Properly managed debt can enhance considerably our common share earnings and, therefore, the value of our equity.

While I have stated the controller at Dole will report to Stan Rosch as the Castle & Cooke corporate controller, he also will continue to work as he now does with the various operating units of the Dole division. Bill Quinn, as president, and the operating heads will get the same performance reports they have found necessary and valuable in the past. The same relationship will hold for the Dole treasurer and the Bumble Bee treasurer, the treasurers for the plantation companies, Royal Hawaiian, and Oceanic. The operating companies or divisions will continue their own banking connections on seasonal borrowings but will report on them to the Castle & Cooke treasurer. The Castle & Cooke treasurer, however, will begin to be responsible for arranging all term financing.

This fall we will establish a new responsibility called Corporate Organization. This responsibility will belong to John Murphy, vice president for industrial relations and corporate secretary. He will assume this in addition to his present duties. Others of his choice already within the companies will assist him. The objective is to have some one office responsible for continuing to plan how best our various branches or businesses may fit one to another and how lines of authority and accountability most effectively may be drawn. These are relations that never will be final. Necessarily they must change. We will not stay abreast without work on them being done continuously. The office will not have the right of decision. It will consider and recommend. It will be those in charge of the affected areas who will decide.

Out of this work also will come a better opportunity to begin to standardize or make uniform our personnel plans and practices and to develop corporate industrial relations policy. Some progress has been made on these matters but not as much as we must.

You will note I have spoken so far only of service or staff functions. Line activities have not been mentioned. We have found it best to establish operating companies or divisions as profits centers and to establish considerable authority. These units have been asked to stand or fall on performance. The record indicates this has been a good plan to follow. It has occurred to me, however, we might have some modification, and I would like to have you begin to think about it. Growing and packing pineapple is quite different from catching or buying and packing fish. Macadamia nut culture and processing does not have anything to do with bananas or sugar, but all of these products have to be brought to market and to be sold. For the most part they are all brought to the same market, the continental United States, yet presently we have separate marketing organizations for Dole, Bumble Bee, Royal Hawaiian, and Standard Fruit. Some of us sell direct. Some of us sell through brokers. In most instances the brokers are different. Some of us have a market research department and some of us do not.

I ask would we be better off if:

1. We had a single marketing department with various major divisions and the product divisions thereunder as does General Foods?
2. Would we be better off if Dole, Bumble Bee, and Royal Hawaiian all used the same brokers?
3. Would we be better off if we had our own selling offices in certain large markets where we dominate, such as New York City, or markets where we may have been weak, such as San Francisco for Bumble Bee?
4. Would a single marketing division produce operational savings by dint of:
   a) Less personnel?
   b) More carload shipments?
   c) Consolidated warehousing?
5. Would the present Dole market research department expand to become a helpful tool to other units? As now structured, this is not likely.
6. Would Dole's present new products department similarly prove useful?
7. Would the Dole technical division under George Felton be helpful to Bumble Bee, for example?

As of now, I have no conclusions for these questions, and they are not new with me. We have asked them of ourselves before in discussion and in management meetings. They represent the type of thinking we must do if we are to progress most profitably. Put yourselves to them.

Now I would like to talk about people within our organization. I am satisfied we have a good team and in the main we get along rather well together. Frequent exposure to other companies leads to this conclusion. Already, however, we have grown too large to enjoy the casual relationship between persons and operations or departments that has characterized Hawaiian business for many years. We must begin to define more clearly lines of responsibility and authority. This will be a task for the office of corporate organization to lead, but this officer cannot do it alone or with only the support of his assistants in office. It best can be done with positive help from you line people who are responsible for making the company go—for making it profitable. You can instruct him in your problems and how you believe your functions must be executed so that John and his assistants can understand and place them in the proper perspective as related to other line activities.

On the other hand you staff people, whether the corporate organization office or any other staff office, cannot wait for line people to come to you for help. It will not work. If effective, they are too busy. They will find their own solutions and leave you behind. You must establish regular times and means for contact so that you become not only acquainted with what goes on in the line areas but get to know the processes so well you could in fact perform them.

In speaking of relationships, let me offer a caution. We do not want to permit them to become overly strict. For me as Castle & Cooke president to be the single source of information to Castle & Cooke personnel on affairs at a division and have this information obtained only from the division president is wrong and a waste of time. Communication must be open at all levels to attain the most effective action in the shortest time. Further, good communication will foster personal relationships and development which will produce a strong management team.

Applied Power Industries, Inc. (A)

In the fiscal year ending August 31, 1965, Applied Power Industries, Inc., recorded the most successful performance in the company's 55 year history. Sales exceeded $22 million, and profits after taxes were in excess of $1.25 million, both substantial increases over the previous record years of 1963 and 1964. (See Exhibits 1 and 2 for summary of operations and financial statistics for the past 15 years.)

Headquartered in Milwaukee, Wisconsin, Applied Power manufactured and distributed a wide line of hydraulic equipment for the automotive, industrial, and construction markets. Its activities were conducted by over 700 persons employed in four operating divisions: Blackhawk Manufacturing Company; Blackhawk Industrial Products Company; the Dynex Company; and Applied Power International. Each of these divisions was headed by a general manager, who was also a corporate vice president. The small central management staff, under the direction of president and treasurer Philip G. Brumder, consisted of the corporate director of manufacturing, James Ryan, director of research and development, Joseph Johnson, director of corporate planning, Frank Bloomquist, the company controller, John Wermuth, and the assistant to the president, Edward Brabant. Parts and Service for BMC and Enerpac was a separate profit center headed by G. H. Goehrig, Jr. (see Exhibit 3 for simplified organization chart).

Blackhawk Manufacturing Company (BMC), the largest of the operating divisions, accounted for almost one-third of 1965 sales volume. It manufactured and sold two broad lines of hydraulic equipment to the automotive service market. One line, "Blackhawk Lifting Equipment," included a wide range of hydraulic jacks and related lifting items, primarily for trucks or for use in commercial garages. This line was sold directly to very large accounts and in smaller quantities

---

exhibit 1

APPLIED POWER INDUSTRIES, INC. (A)

World Consolidated Operations Summary
(thousands of dollars)

Fiscal Year Ending	Net Sales	Cost of Products Sold	Engineering	Selling	Administrative	Total	Depreciation and Amortization	Interest	Earnings Before Tax	Net Earnings	Net Working Capital	Fixed Assets Addition
12/31,51	$ 6,463	$ 4,395				$1,524	$ 86	$ 35	$ 423	$ 229	$2,122	$122
12/31/52	8,369	5,949				2,052	115	39	215	(4)	1,909	641
8/31/53[1]	5,560	3,985		$1,045	$ 540	1,585	95	47	(147)	(104)	1,615	87
8/31/54	7,046	5,060		1,008	444	1,452	133	70	352	192	2,070	52
8/31/55	7,918	5,484		1,166	378	1,544	139	42	721	358	2,945	65
8/31/56	9,492	6,171		1,637	729	2,366	143	43	801	438[2]	3,158	202
8/31/57	10,674	7,034	$598	1,465	847	2,910	200	52	499	101	2,980	799
8/31/58	10,877	7,000	602	1,646	893	3,141	249	87	436	132	3,036	132
8/31/59	12,298	7,824	680	1,638	1,278	3,596	269	66	591	279	3,302	98
8/31/60	14,996	9,426	771	2,202	1,565	4,538	299	102	653	311	3,300	362
8/31/61	14,465	8,667	657	2,588	1,710	4,955	332	113	448	204	3,529	149
8/31/62	15,889	9,499	781	2,823	1,917	5,521	317	118	452	267	3,553	243
8/31/63	16,680	9,548	970	2,724	1,775	5,469	298	95	1,285	582	3,994	217
8/31/64	19,434	10,974	880	3,047	2,146	6,073	290	84	2,048	935	4,785	350
8/31/65	22,854	12,733	906	3,348	2,785	7,039	351	83	2,744	1,353	5,544	603

1 Eight months.
2 Includes $104,000 from sale of the hand tool business.

exhibit 2

APPLIED POWER INDUSTRIES, INC. (A)

World Consolidated Statistics

Fiscal Year Ending	Common Shares Year-End	Net Earnings	Dividends	Book Value	% Return Year End Equity	Cost of Products Sold	Engineering	Selling	Administrative	Total	% Earnings Before Tax	% Net Earnings	Net Sales	Net Earnings
12/31/51	200,000	$1.03	$ .15	$13.79	7.5	68.0				23.6	6.5	3.5	12.7	9.5
12/31/52	200,000	(.14)	.15	13.50	(1.0)	71.2				24.5	2.6	(0.3)	29.0	Loss
8/31/53	200,000	(.56)	—	13.57	(6.2)	71.7		18.8	9.7	28.5	(2.7)	(1.4)	(00.3)	Loss
8/31/54	200,000	.87	.20	14.03	6.2	71.8		14.3	6.3	20.6	5.0	2.7	(15.5)	Loss
8/31/55	200,000	1.67	.30	15.50	10.8	69.3		14.7	4.8	19.5	9.1	4.5	12.4	86.3
8/31/56	200,000	2.08	.30	17.28	12.0	65.0		17.2	7.7	24.9	9.5	4.6	19.9	22.6
8/31/57	200,000	.39	.48	17.19	2.3	65.9	5.6	13.7	7.9	27.2	4.7	0.9	12.5	(77.0)
8/31/58	200,000	.54	.30	17.43	3.1	64.4	5.5	15.1	8.2	28.8	4.0	1.2	1.9	30.6
8/31/59	200,000	1.28	.30	18.41	6.9	63.6	5.5	13.3	10.4	29.2	4.8	2.3	13.1	111.8
8/31/60	200,000	1.44	.30	19.55	7.4	62.9	5.1	14.7	10.4	30.2	4.4	2.1	21.9	11.4
8/31/61	200,000	.90	.30	20.16	4.5	59.9	4.5	17.9	11.8	34.2	3.1	1.4	(03.5)	(34.4)
8/31/62	184,550	1.32	.30	22.05	6.0	59.8	4.9	17.8	12.1	34.8	2.8	1.7	9.8	30.7
8/31/63	187,550	2.98	.60	24.23	12.3	57.2	5.8	16.4	10.6	32.8	7.7	3.5	5.0	118.0
8/31/64	207,750	4.42	1.00	26.62	16.9	56.5	4.5	15.8	11.0	31.3	10.6	4.8	16.5	60.6
8/31/65	210,285	6.43	1.50	31.23	20.6	55.7	4.0	14.6	12.2	30.8	12.0	5.9	17.6	44.7

1 Eight months.
2 Related to annualized sales for fiscal 1953.
3 Includes $.52 from sale of hand tool business.

4 Includes 3.0% from sale of hand tool business.
5 Includes 1.1% from sale of hand tool business.

exhibit 3

APPLIED POWER INDUSTRIES, INC. (A)

Organization Chart: August 31, 1965

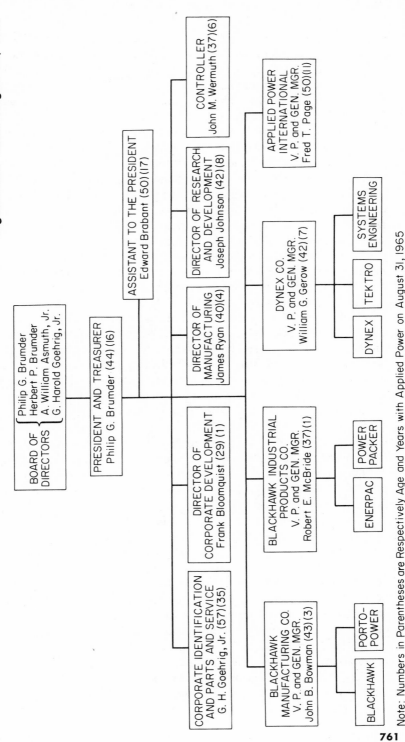

BOARD OF DIRECTORS
Philip G. Brumder
Herbert P. Brumder
A. William Asmuth, Jr.
G. Harold Goehrig, Jr.

PRESIDENT AND TREASURER
Philip G. Brumder (44) (16)

ASSISTANT TO THE PRESIDENT
Edward Brabant (50)(17)

CONTROLLER
John M. Wermuth (37)(6)

DIRECTOR OF RESEARCH AND DEVELOPMENT
Joseph Johnson (42)(8)

APPLIED POWER INTERNATIONAL
V. P. and GEN. MGR.
Fred T. Page (50)(11)

DIRECTOR OF MANUFACTURING
James Ryan (40)(4)

DYNEX CO.
V. P. and GEN. MGR.
William G. Gerow (42)(7)

SYSTEMS ENGINEERING

TEKTRO

DYNEX

DIRECTOR OF CORPORATE DEVELOPMENT
Frank Bloomquist (29) (1)

BLACKHAWK INDUSTRIAL PRODUCTS CO.
V. P. and GEN. MGR.
Robert E. McBride (37)(1)

POWER PACKER

ENERPAC

CORPORATE IDENTIFICATION AND PARTS AND SERVICE
G. H. Goehrig, Jr. (57)(35)

BLACKHAWK MANUFACTURING CO.
V. P. and GEN. MGR.
John B. Bowman (43)(3)

PORTO-POWER

BLACKHAWK

Note: Numbers in Parentheses are Respectively Age and Years with Applied Power on August 31, 1965 through a nationwide network of automotive supply distributors and jobbers. The second line, "Porto-Power," consisted of an assortment of specialized hydraulically powered tools and attachments for use in repairing automobile collision damage. Porto-Power was sold primarily through specialized bodyshop and automotive paint supply distributors. In both lines, BMC was the recognized leader in the industry, with more than 30% in lifting equipment and 50% in CDR.

Blackhawk Industrial Products Company (BIPCO) accounted for somewhat less than one-fourth of 1965 sales volume. BIPCO also had two main lines of hydraulic equipment: "Enerpac" products included pipe benders, pumps, cylinders, jacks, and a variety of other standardized portable hydraulic tools for use in maintenance, production, construction, and testing applications. This line of catalogued items for pulling, pushing, bending, straightening, clamping, and testing operations was marketed through a selected group of mill and contractor supply distributors. The "Power Packer" line consisted of items similar to Enerpac's, but specifically modified and adapted to meet the hydraulic power requirements of original equipment manufacturers. These were all custom items, sold directly to the manufacturer for incorporation in his product.

The Dynex Company was the smallest of the four divisions in sales volume, accounting for 15% of the total, but its activities were by far the most technologically sophisticated. Its major line, "Dynex," offered specially designed hydrostatic transmission systems, primarily to mobile equipment manufacturers for incorporation in their products. "Systems Engineering" performed contract product design and development work for manufacturers building prototype equipment involving complex advanced hydraulic technology. Both lines' products and/or services were sold directly to the manufacturer by the division's sales engineers, often on a competitive bid basis. The "Tektro" line in the U.S. offered a specially designed version of the Dynex piston pump for sale to persons constructing industrial equipment through hydraulic and pneumatic component distributors. The Tektro line was not a significant portion of 1965's business, but it was the intention to develop over the long pull a broad line of components for this market, including various types of valves, pumps, and accessories. Applied Power would then have a wide coverage of the mobile and industrial markets—from the very sophisticated Dynex activity, through the Tektro and Power Packer product groups, to the relatively unsophisticated Enerpac line.

Applied Power International was the company's fastest growing division, and accounted for nearly 30% of total sales in 1965. This division sold and manufactured the products of the other three divisions in overseas markets, as well as acting as the exclusive private label distributor, in the countries it served, for other firms manufacturing complementary hydraulic components or automotive service equipment. In 1965, Applied Power International had sales, service, and manufacturing facilities in England, Switzerland, France, Germany, Holland, Mexico, and Canada, and was negotiating for joint venture companies in selected locations in Asia, Africa, and South America.

COMPANY HISTORY
1920–1950:

The Formative Years

Applied Power Industries, Inc., had its real beginning with Herbert P. Brumder, the youngest of the 11 children of George Brumder, outstanding Milwaukee publisher, businessman, and civic leader. After graduation from the University of Wisconsin, Herbert Brumder spent a short period as a bank teller, then as a laborer building rubber tires and tubes in companies in which his father had large stock holdings. Subsequent to his father's death in 1910, he looked after real estate interests of the George Brumder estate and worked for a time for the North American Press, then owned by the estate.

In 1920, Herbert Brumder, together with two of his brothers and a brother-in-law, made a large loan to the American Grinder Manufacturing Company, founded in Milwaukee in 1910. As a part of the loan agreement, the lenders received a small block of stock in the company, with an option to purchase substantially more. Herbert Brumder became treasurer of the company in order to supervise the loan. Operating losses put the company in serious financial difficulty in 1922, and matters grew increasingly worse through 1923. At the end of that year, Herbert Brumder, then 38 years old, purchased the controlling interest in the company and took over its management as president. At this time, the company was manufacturing a line of hand tool grinders, a series of automotive socket wrenches, and was beginning to produce circulating water pumps for automobile engines.

In 1924, after taking over American Grinder, Herbert Brumder made an extensive tour of automotive product distributors, saw the need for water pumps to improve the performance of the Ford model "T," and began to emphasize production of the pumps, while reducing the volume of grinder business. This move put the company in the black, and in 1925, American Grander recorded sales of $818,000 and profits of $37,500 (a return on investment of about 13%).

In 1925, in recognition of the reduction of grinders to less than 10% of sales, and the rise of water pumps to nearly 50%, Herbert Brumder changed the name of the company to Blackhawk Manufacturing Company, a nonconfining label under which he felt he could manufacture freely any products he felt appropriate.

By 1927, Ford Motor Company began to manufacture its own water pumps, and Blackhawk's pump business declined rapidly. Herbert Brumder immediately sought a substitute product which could be sold through Blackhawk's established automotive products distributors. In Los Angeles, he found a small company manufacturing the first economic, trouble-free hydraulic jack for automotive service use. Purchasing the company, Mr. Brumder moved strongly into promot-

exhibit 4

BLACKHAWK MANUFACTURING COMPANY

Operating Summary for Selected Years, 1925–1950

	1925	1930	1935	1940	1945	1950
Net sales	$818,660	$1,057,132	$1,401,191	$2,257,573	$5,016,987	$5,107,908
Cost of sales	554,318	689,115	827,029	1,435,635	3,396,617	3,286,205
SAE and other	224,250	375,048	352,697	511,200	791,086	1,446,503
Taxes	2,600	–	49,750	116,322	610,000	166,000
Net profit	37,491	(7,030)	171,715	194,415	219,283	209,200
Shareholders' equity	298,999	579,815	611,750	1,091,842	1,810,718	2,903,692
Net sales— breakdown by product						
Pumps	400,480	43,031	–	–	–	–
Grinders	59,405	–	–	–	–	–
Wrenches, etc.	358,775	501,279	398,532	530,522	1,081,426	454,537
Hydraulic jacks	–	512,822	962,450	1,669,168	2,414,214	1,712,073
Parts and repairs	–	–	40,210	57,883	291,204	325,914
Porto-Power	–	–	–	–	1,230,143	1,722,677
Hydraulics for original equipment manufacturers	–	–	–	–	–	892,708
Total	$818,660	$1,057,132	$1,401,191	$2,257,573	$5,016,987	$5,107,908

ing hydraulic jacks in the automotive market. At a cost of over $50,000 he ran a pioneering series of advertisements in the *Saturday Evening Post,* showing a little girl jacking up an auto with one finger. Gradually, consumer demand obliged skeptical distributors to carry Blackhawk's jack line. The jacks proved very successful and quickly substituted the needed volume to compensate for the almost complete drying up of pump sales.

Through the Depression, Blackhawk held its own financially, showing only small losses in its worst years. By 1935, sales had reached $1.4 million, and profits registered $172,000, for a 28% return on equity. Roughly two-thirds of these sales were in jacks and related products, while the balance was in the old automotive wrench line.

Sales grew rapidly thereafter, primarily in jacks and related items, reaching $2.25 million by 1940, while profits approximated $200,000 each year. World War II put the company into defense manufacture and swelled sales volume to over $5 million, although excess profits taxes held earnings to the old $200,000 level.

In 1935, Herbert Brumder again began to search for new products to substitute for the declines he anticipated in defense business. In visiting automotive distributors and their customers—garages and service stations—he learned that some customers were adapting Blackhawk's hydraulic jacks to straightening auto frames and bodies which had been damaged in collisions. A small company in Ohio was beginning to develop a prototype. Sensing an opportunity, Mr. Brumder put his personnel to work on the development of hydraulically powered tools and attachments to be used specifically for damage repair. These units, labeled Porto-Power, were failures in a preliminary market test, but Mr. Brumder persisted in bringing the line out through Blackhawk's distributors. By 1950, they had exceeded jacks and related units in sales volume.

This success led to seeking other specialized applications of Blackhawk's basic hydraulic jack competence. Pipe and conduit benders for the construction industry, plus cylinders and pumps for industrial manufacturing applications and for inclusion in more complex products, were developed and marketed in the late 1940's. (An operating summary for selected years during this period appears as Exhibit 4.)

1951–1961:
Reorganizing and Redirecting

By 1950, Herbert Brumder, then aged 65, had begun to withdraw from intimate, continuous direction and operation of the business, and to turn more and more responsibility over to his son Philip.

Philip was the youngest of Herbert P. Brumder's three children. The oldest son, Herbert E. Brumder, after graduating from college in 1939, went to work for the Pressed Steel Tank Company of Milwaukee, manufacturer of heavy metal drums, cylinders, and other containers. This company, owned and operated by the Brumder family since 1923, had two plants in the Milwaukee area and another in western Pennsylvania. Herbert E. Brumder, three years Philip's senior, became president of this company in 1950. Philip's sister married, in 1940, a man who subsequently became president of a tool products manufacturing firm in Milwaukee. Neither brother nor sister had ever taken an active interest in the affairs of Blackhawk.

Philip G. Brumder, then 30 years old, was named executive vice president of Blackhawk Manufacturing Company in 1951, and president in 1952. From that point forward, he was in full operating control of the company. Philip graduated in industrial administration from Yale University in 1941, and was married on December 6 of that year. Following World War II, he worked in a variety of jobs in Blackhawk in manufacturing, accounting, and sales, familiarizing himself with the various aspects of the business. He and his wife have five children, two boys and three girls, ranging from Philip, Jr. (born 1943), to mixed twins (born 1954).

The crises of the early fifties. In 1951, as executive vice president, Philip Brumder conducted an extensive financial analysis of the various segments of the business—the first such study of costs and profitability by product that had ever been undertaken in the company. This study showed that the Porto-Power collision damage equipment was very profitable, but that its high earnings performance had masked the fact that the rest of the company's products (primarily jacks and hand tools) were either just breaking even or losing money. Moreover, it was clearly indicated that Blackhawk was losing market position in both its basic jack business and its historic automotive hand tools line, a market in which Blackhawk had been prominent for many years.

Philip Brumder described the situation as follows: "For years we had been a sales-dominated company. Product specifications were based solely on operating performance, without regard for manufacturing cost. There was no financial control or analysis: it was viewed as unnecessary because of obvious over-all corporate success and limited competition. But the market situation in hydraulic jacks and automotive hand tools was beginning to change. Other manufacturers were making good quality products, getting wide distribution, and exerting severe price pressures. Our jack costs were very high. Much of our machining had to be subcontracted. We were selling lots of jacks; but, because of price competition we weren't making much money in them."

1952: new Sheboygan plant. To improve the manufacturing costs of hydraulic jacks, a new plant was set up in 1952 in Sheboygan, Wisconsin, employing special high production automatic equipment and utilizing low-cost floor space. All jack manufacturing was moved from the company's old, inefficient West Allis (Milwaukee) plant with the intent of cutting costs and increasing capacity, thus reducing subcontract work.

The engineering department was placed on a "crash program" to redesign the basic jack line for ease of manufacture and low cost. Engineering was stretched thin—having to redesign the entire line and also to set up the new plant. High startup and moving costs, together with the extraordinarily high engineering expense, resulted in a sharp reduction in operating earnings (from $423,000 pretax to $215,000 pretax). Special tax assessments wiped out the earnings and resulted in a slight after tax loss.

By 1953, the Sheboygan jack plant was in high volume production, but sales was having difficulty to moving the output. Inventories began to accumulate alarmingly and reached a level of $3 million. Jack inventory turnover was down to a 1.6 times rate. Hand tools were at a one time turnover level.

Attempts at reorganization. In 1952 and 1953, Philip Brumder made repeated attempts to reduce overhead and costs of manufacturing. It became increasingly apparent to him that engineering and manufacturing management were unwilling to risk conflict with the sales department through simplifying the product line and redesigning units to cut manufacturing costs. When the needed changes were not forthcoming, Mr. Brumder fired the vice president of engineering, the chief engineer, and the manufacturing manager. The indicated changes were initiated immediately by those promoted.

He then moved to focus attention on the critical areas by breaking out a separate hand tool division, with its own general manager, engineering and marketing departments, and manufacturing facility (at West Allis), and retaining the hydraulic tools division, under the existing central management structure. However, all sales were handled by a single sales force under the vice president of sales reporting to the president. A third division, very small in size, was created at the same time, to handle OEM hydraulics. This division was headed by a manager who had direct charge of engineering and sales, but not manufacturing, which was retained in the old structure.

He also attempted to change automotive products distribution from a small number of semiexclusive distributors to a large number of nonexclusive distributors, who, in turn would sell on a nonselective, nonexclusive basis to dealers. Resistance from the sales department was so strong that he decided not to force this change and withdrew it.

At this same time, the CIO Steelworkers' Union moved to supplant the AFL Machinists' Union in the company's plants. Philip Brumder personally negotiated a new contract with the CIO, accepting a union shop and union security in exchange for assurances of improved work standards and productivity.

Weak accounting procedures and lack of useful financial information moved Mr. Brumder to bring in a large national public accounting firm for assistance on budgetary controls and other management systems. One of the outcomes of this study was a change in the fiscal year from December 31 to August 31. The eight months' results from January to August, 1953, indicated a pretax loss of $147,000. High inventory levels had required extensive bank loans. At August 31, the company had more than $2.2 million in 90 day notes outstanding (vs. a total net worth of $2.8 million), which became a matter of considerable concern to the banks.

The move to rebuild. In 1954, Mr. Brumder hired Fred T. Page, who had had substantial accounting, financial, and marketing experience with Phillips Lamp and Ford International, as controller and director of commercial development. One of Mr. Page's first assignments was to make an extensive market study of jack distribution. This study demonstrated persuasively that Blackhawk was closing itself off from the major portion of its market by its exclusive distributor policy. Page recommended that the company go nonexclusive and selected about 6,000 of the 20,000 automotive supply distributors as ones to try to get to carry the Blackhawk line. As an inducement for new distributors who already had satisfactory jack suppliers, he proposed that Blackhawk provide a *complete* line (not offered by any competitor), buying items on private label which the company did not produce currently.

These policies proved effective in moving inventories; by year-end, the company was solidly back in the black. Earnings before taxes were $352,000. Bank loans had been reduced to $800,000.

1955 saw earnings double to a pretax $721,000. Manufacturing costs were lowered by subcontracting on make or buy calculations. General price increases throughout the industry improved gross margins and helped assure the profitability of the resale of purchased units to round out the jack line. The short-term loans of the company were refinanced with the bank and an insurance company and converted to long-term debt. By year-end, bank borrowings had been eliminated.

1955:
Dynex Formed

During this year, the company received a number of inquiries regarding high pressure piston pumps. Sensing a new product line opportunity, Mr. Brumder brought in the consulting firm of Welling & Woodard to make a market study and pinpoint the specific market opportunities and requirements. He then hired three men having long experience in this technology with the leading company in the industry, Vickers Division of Sperry Rand Corporation. These men were established as the key personnel for a new Dynex division, charged with studying applications and developing a product development program. In what was described as a "difficult" and "painful" experience, the new division was created—to build a new organization, a new management group, develop new products, with no orders, except for a modest continuing requirement to provide a special hydraulic pump and valve circuit for Bucyrus Erie cranes that dated back to 1948.

1956:
Hand Tool Business Divested

In 1955, the Welling & Woodard firm recommended the sale of Blackhawk's hand tool business, which had been unprofitable for some time. Sales were down to less than $1 million per year, and inventories were running at about $500,000. Welling

& Woodard assisted in the sale of Blackhawk's fixtures, inventories, and brand name on hand tools for about $650,000 to the New Britain Machine Company. Despite the loss of the hand tool business, 1956 sales increased 20% to a new all-time high of $9.5 million, while earnings after taxes reached $438,000, including a $104,000 nonrecurring gain from the sale of the hand tool business, the last remaining segment of the company's original product line.

During 1956, the company experienced a series of minor work stoppages and slowdowns which were protested to the Union without any apparent effect. Finally, when a major walkout occurred, Mr. Brumder laid off all employees involved for one week as a disciplinary action. Although the Union protested bitterly, the action was made to stick as an enforcement of the contract.

1957–1961:
Sales Growth and Profit Regression

1957 and 1958 saw earnings fall as sales increased. The "two-step" distribution of jacks was introduced and was expected to account for about 25% of distributor volume. The whole industry had followed suit. While volume had increased markedly, the anticipated savings in selling expense, inventory turnover, and overhead had not materialized. Thus, while jack costs were improving, profits were dropping under intensive price competition.

The earnings decline was also due in part to a rapid increase in expenses connected with the expansion of the Dynex division. The Dynex division was moved in 1957 from the former automobile showroom spaces it had been occupying into its own new building in Pewaukee, Wisconsin, built at a cost of $575,000. When business in high pressure piston pumps, motors, valves, and cylinders was not as good as expected, hand pump and cylinder manufacture (now Power Packer) was moved into the new Pewaukee plant from West Allis.

1958:
Industrial Division Formed

Following a study of industrial products applications conducted by Mr. Page, again using Welling & Woodard as a resource, the old hydraulic tools division was completely separated into two units in 1958: the automotive division, manufacturing and selling the Porto-Power and jack lines; and the industrial division, manufacturing and selling hydraulic tools to the factory and construction markets.

William Gerow, who had been hired as manager of the service department in 1957, and who had reduced costs in that department sharply and placed it on a separate profit center basis, was selected by Mr. Brumder to head up the new industrial division. By 1959, the division had its own separate manufacturing plant (at Columbus, Wisconsin), its own engineering staff, its own controller and accounting staff, and its own sales force. This resulted in broadening the product line and distribution, increasing sales volume and selling prices, and reducing manufacturing costs. He added to the product line, replaced the old manufacturing manager transferred from West Allis (with a new man, James Ryan), increased the sales force, and by 1960 had sales volume over $2.4 million and earnings after taxes of $197,000 in his division.

This performance, while greatly improving the situation in the industrial division, was insufficient to counteract continued price erosion in automotive jacks, and total corporate profits still fell below the 1956 level.

Meanwhile, the Dynex division continued to show heavy losses. Mr. Brumder relieved the general manager and assumed the title himself. During this period, "committee management" by the operating heads of departments reportedly led to many separate activities and little coordination.

1960:
International Division Started

In 1960, following an extended trip by Mr. Page and Mr. Brumder exploring opportunities in Europe, an International division was formed with Mr. Page as general manager. Although the company had sold its products in the export market through agents since the 1920's, this was the first attempt at direct marketing abroad. Blackhawk's London agent, who had been covering all of Europe, was also a licensee for manufacturing the Porto-Power line. Negotiations with this agent continued his manufacturing license, and created a new wholly owned marketing subsidiary of Blackhawk in England with the agent as general manager. The sales force that had been handling the Blackhawk line was hired by the new subsidiary. Direct control of marketing on the Continent was initiated with a new Blackhawk subsidiary in Geneva.

1950–1962:
Changes in Physical Facilities

1960 also marked the end of manufacturing in the West Allis plant, as Porto-Power and service jack manufacturing was moved out to a manufacturing plant in Hebron, Illinois. At this time, separate marketing managers were set up within the automotive division for: (1) lifting equipment, and (2) Porto-Power. These men had direct control over product development and marketing for their respective product lines.

In 1962 service jack manufacture was shifted from Hebron to Sheboygan, consolidating all jack manufacture there. The shipping department was closed in West Allis, in favor of the various outlying plants.

1961:
Personnel Changes

In late fiscal 1961, Mr. William Gerow, having met most of the major challenges in the industrial division, accepted an attractive offer to become vice president and general manager of a larger division of a big company. Mr. Brumder assumed the title of general manager, but left marketing and engineering in the hands of the Enerpac sales manager, Paul Moore. Mr. Moore had joined the company in 1954, worked with Mr. Page on the jack study and the industrial products study. He had become the first (and only) sales manager of the industrial division, had set up its sales force and established its distribution.

At the same time, Mr. Brumder appointed the director of manufacturing engineering for Dynex as the general manager of that division. It was stated later that, while this man "had the best concept of what was going on," he did not get along well with either his subordinates or Mr. Brumder. The appointment "brought stability to the situation," but "autocracy" and "unrest" were reported in the division.

1961:
Name Change

In 1961, the corporate name was changed to *Applied Power Industries, Inc*. The old Blackhawk Manufacturing Company (BMC) name was assigned to the automotive division, and the industrial division became Blackhawk Industrial Products Company (BIPCO).

According to Mr. Brumder, the name was changed in order to reflect the expanded concept of the scope of the company's operations. He wished to avoid having the company regarded primarily as an automotive jack company (where the Blackhawk name had won recognition). Also he wanted to divorce the company from association with the Blackhawk hand tool line, that had been sold in 1956. His concept was to develop strong trade names for individual product groups—e.g., Enerpac, Power Packer, Dynex, etc.—while providing a comprehensive parent label that was not a trade name.

The corporate symbol, to be applied to all product lines, combined an engineering force vector arrow with the hexagon which had been used earlier by Blackhawk.

1962–1965:
Consolidation and Expansion

In 1962, John B. Bowman was hired as vice president of corporate planning, with specific instruction to restudy the automotive portion of the business.

Mr. William Gerow, dissatisfied with his new venture, was rehired as general manager of the industrial division.

1962: Dynex restructured. The Power Packer hand pump and cylinder product line was transferred from Dynex to the industrial division, and its manufacturing operations were moved from Pewaukee (the Dynex plant) to Columbus (the industrial division plant). This move was considered desirable because the

Power Packer line was based on adaptions and modifications of the Enerpac hydraulic tool line, for installation as simple hydraulic actuating devices on other manufacturers' products (OEM). Dynex technology and selling was based on complex applications of sophisticated powered pumps, valves, motors, and transmissions, which was less appropriate to Power Packer marketing than the Enerpac orientation.

A few months later, Mr. Brumder fired the general manager of the Dynex division and moved William Gerow to general manager of Dynex, as well. BIPCO was going well and Dynex was in a serious loss position, so Gerow moved into Dynex full time and confined himself to "financial and marketing study, planning and review of BIPCO." To simplify his control of both operations, he split the Dynex controller, John Wermuth, between the two divisions as well.

According to Mr. Gerow, "Phil was having a hard time communicating with the previous manager. He [the manager] didn't like to be subservient, and he had a different concept of strategy from Phil's—one that didn't fit the company's goals. The old timers were becoming upset by the seeming conflicts in direction. My immediate objectives were: (1) to calm the people down and hold on to the ones we wanted; and (2) to cut out the fat and minimize the losses. We had a messed up organization—too many people in manufacturing, sales, and engineering; too many chiefs."

Gerow made a substantial reduction in force, including many major organizational replacements and advancements. The product line was simplified, quality control and product engineering refocused, sales direction was divided up among technical specialists in specific markets. Within six months, overhead had been reduced to $250,000, and Dynex was in the black for the first time since its founding.

1963: BMC restructured.   In 1961, 1962, and 1963, sales and profits in the lifting equipment (jacks and related units) segment of BMC had declined sharply. Losses were recorded in each year. Similarly, the Porto-Power (collision damage repair) segment—always profitable—had suffered a sharp drop in earnings. This division had been managed, since 1959, by a cousin of Mr. Brumder's. This man, who had been with the company since 1950, was described as very brilliant but somewhat theoretical. In 1963, he bought a distributor firm, left Applied Power, and John Bowman was appointed general manager.

Bowman, with Mr. Brumder's support, recombined divisional marketing and engineering management. The two sales forces were combined into a single force calling on both automotive supply distributors (lifting equipment) and paint and body shop distributors (Porto-Power). The Hebron plant was closed, and Porto-Power assembly was moved to the Columbus (BIPCO) plant, with the assistance of Mr. Ryan, who had been brought into BMC as acting manufacturing manager, in addition to his responsibilities in BIPCO.

Ryan also, on request from Bowman, "fixed manufacturing." Tooling efficiency and control was improved at Sheboygan. A consolidated warehousing, fabricating, assembly, and shipping unit was established at Bareboo, Wisconsin, reducing the amount of work being subcontracted, following a restudy of make/buy alternatives.

Bowman put engineering and quality control on strict programs for product improvement, reducing functional failures in the field, and hired a new chief engineer. A new controller was hired, and a separate product planning unit was established.

Within a year, profits had been restored to the lifting equipment segment and earnings of Porto-Power increased sharply.

1963–1965: rapid international expansion.   After minor startup losses in 1960 and 1961, the International division, under Fred Page, grew rapidly in sales and earnings. Page's basic concept was to establish Applied Power International as a full-line, strong marketing force in all major world markets for the company's products. His approach was to develop individual marketing subsidiaries selling in separate highly developed countries (England, Germany, France, Canada, etc.) and manufacturing subsidiaries strategically located to produce items for a number of different countries. Joint venture marketing or manufacturing companies were to be established in countries where wholly owned subsidiaries were not feasible for political or other reasons (Mexico, Japan, Australia, etc.). Subsequently, he obtained overseas rights to lines of various manufacturers on a private label basis.

1964–1965:
Major Events

In 1964, Robert E. McBride, formerly vice president–marketing of Colt Firearms Division of Fairbanks Whitney Company, was hired as general manager of the industrial division (BIPCO), releasing William Gerow for full attention to the Dynex division.

Also in 1964, the company was recapitalized. The 2,000 shares of second preferred stock were called and redeemed at par. The 10,015 shares outstanding of old Class A (nonvoting) common stock were exchanged for 100,150 shares of new Class A (nonvoting) common. All 2,000 outstanding shares of first preferred stock and 8,800 shares of old Class B (voting) common stock were exchanged for 101,000 shares of new Class B (voting) common. Appropriate changes were made in retained earnings and paid in capital accounts to reflect the elimination of preferred stock and the establishment of the new common at $7.50 par. Class A stock was owned by key employees, by a few persons outside the company, and by members of the Brumder family. Options on Class A stock were granted to some 31 "manager-shareholders." Almost all of the Class B (voting) stock was owned by Mr. Brumder, his brother, sister, and father. Mr. Brumder personally owned more than 50% of the outstanding voting stock.

In 1965, a new plant was established in Camden, Tennessee, to manufacture hydraulic transmissions for the Dynex division. Anticipated as a low-cost operation to meet competition on production items, Camden went into operation in the summer of 1965. It was expected that the manufacturing and assembly of standard items would be done at Camden, leaving Pewaukee primarily as a systems engineering, product development, and prototype manufacturing facility. Manufacture of special parts and Dynex assembly would also be retained at Pewaukee.

THE HYDRAULIC POWER INDUSTRY

The hydraulic power industry manufactures products for transmitting and controlling power through the use of pressurized fluids within an integrated circuit. A typical circuit consists of a pump, valving, cylinders or hydraulic motor, and suitable reservoir for the fluid. Linear circuits using cylinders are employed for positioning, forming, bending, clamping, and similar functions, whereas rotary circuits employing hydrostatic transmissions are used for driving wheels, tracks, propellers, conveyors, etc. In 1964, sales of hydraulic components amounted to over $566 million in the United States, an increase from $365 million in 1957.

The hydraulic power industry sells in several markets, including the industrial machinery, aerospace, marine, military, and mobile equipment markets. Generally, components are customized for each market, although some overlap occurs, such as the possible use of common pumps by industrial and mobile equipment manufacturers.

In a typical hydraulic circuit the pump is driven by hand, a gas engine, or electric motor. The pump delivers fluid in proportion to its driving speed to a valve which directs the fluid to a cylinder for positioning or a motor for rotation. The main advantages of a hydraulic drive as compared with mechanical or electrical drive are: the adjustable speed control, large power capacity in a small space, ability to perform complex sequencing functions easily, speed of performing operations, and remote control capability.

Hydraulic systems range from simple hand pumps, such as used to pump up a barber chair, to complete automation control systems used for machining engine blocks without human intervention. In power they range from fractional horsepower levels to several hundred horsepower, and a few systems exist on large ships with up to 3,000 horsepower.

Simple, Lower Horsepower Units

The simplest hydraulic units are hand powered hydraulic jacks. These devices use a fluid under pressure to move a piston in and out, and then hold a given position, thus raising or lowering a weight resting on the piston. These units compete directly with mechanical jacks, which are generally cheaper and simpler to manufacture, but which require much greater input force to raise a given weight than do the hydraulic units.

Automotive jacks comprise the largest and most familiar usage of hydraulic hand jacks. Virtually all passenger automobiles are outfitted with low-cost mechanical automotive jacks, but trucks and other large mobile equipment require hydraulic jacks to deal efficiently with their greater weights.

About 30 companies competed in the automotive jack business. Of these, only seven manufactured hydraulic automotive jacks, and four of these (Applied Power Industries, Inc.; Walker Manufacturing Company; Hein-Werner Corporation; and Auto Specialists Manufacturing Company) reportedly accounted for more than 90% of total annual sales volume. Applied Power Industries, Inc., Hein-Werner, and Walker Manufacturing did not manufacture automotive jacks (although they purchased others for resale under private label). Auto Specialists (AUSCO) was the nation's largest mechanical automotive jack manufacturer.

According to The Jack Institute, national trade organization, total automotive jack sales since 1955 had averaged about $21 million per year (ranging from a low of $18.8 million in 1958 to a high of $23 million in 1965). Of this, about 25% was believed to be in hydraulic hand jacks and another 25% in hydraulic service jacks, such as one-end lifts, transmission jacks, wheel dollies, and similar units for use by garages and service stations. In addition to Applied Power, Hein-Werner, AUSCO, and Walker, Weaver Manufacturing Company (division of Dura Corporation) was a significant market factor in hydraulic service jacks, front-end lifts, transmission jacks, and similar products. These five companies reportedly accounted for over 95% of sales volume in these lines.

The basic hydraulic jack unit had not changed in design since conception. Innovations such as transmission jacks (1950), one-end lifts (1954), and wheel dollies were the result of meeting automotive service demands after they had appeared. Future developments in combining air actuation and hydraulic lifting to obtain the advantages of both are predicted, but little market activity had been detected.

Low profits margins in automotive jacks had resulted from the inability to differentiate products. Selling prices were held down by intense competition and by the markups required for the different channels of distribution. In 1965, the majority of jack manufacturers reportedly were dissatisfied with their current return on investment. However, wholesalers reportedly were enjoying a good profit (30% gross) because of high retail price levels and deferred payment schedules. Problems of trade-in of old jacks, servicing of existing models, and promoting jack sales reportedly had hindered wholesalers' interest in the relatively small proportion which jacks represented of their total sales volume. Exhibit 5 indicates the *major channels* of distribution from manufacturer to users of automotive jacks.

The Blackhawk Manufacturing Company (BMC) division of Applied Power was, in 1965, the most important single factor in the hydraulic automotive hand jack business. It also made and marketed air-activated hydraulic units for the automotive market.

exhibit 5

APPLIED POWER INDUSTRIES, INC. (A)

Major Channels of Distribution

Auto collision damage repair equipment (CDR) was somewhat more complex than the automotive jack units. These units combined low horsepower hydraulic pumps (activated manually or, more frequently, by compressed air) with cylinders that had been specially fitted with attachments appropriate to the straightening out of damaged automobile bodies and the straightening of frames.

These units were sold to body shops and garages, primarily through specialized body shops and auto paint distributors. The total annual domestic market was estimated at under $4 million, and only two manufacturers—Applied Power, through its BMC division, and Hein-Werner—were significant factors. Of the two, BMC, with its Porto-Power trademarked line, was, by far, the largest and best-known in the trade. BMC had pioneered the market, while Hein-Werner had followed several years later by purchasing the small Ohio company that had developed the original product concept.

Profit margins were very comfortable in this highly specialized product line, but required full lines of relatively low volume items and specialized sales and service aids to distributors.

Other Low Horsepower Units

Portable units. An enormous range of specialized applications for simple, portable, low horsepower hydraulic units and attachments exists wherever pushing, pulling, pressing, bending, clamping, straightening, and lifting operations are required. However, the total U.S. market for such devices was estimated at under $6 million in 1965. No single family of applications accounted for as much as $1 million.

Applied Power, through its Blackhawk Industrial Products division (BIPCO), was the dominant factor in this market. Its Enerpac line included a broad spectrum of portable hydraulic pumps—hand, air, and electrically operated, hydraulic cylinders, accessories, and attachments, plus combined "sets" of pumps, cylinders, accessories, and attachments for specific applications. This catalogued line was sold through an extensive network of industrial equipment and contractor supply distributors. Repair parts and service were provided by over 100 factory-trained franchised units—primarily general line, hydraulic service companies.

Only in the pipe-bending applications had Enerpac encountered meaningful competition, where a construction equipment manufacturer (Greenley) had captured more than 50% of the market. In all other important applications, Enerpac's market share has been 65% or better, and profit margins have been very comfortable.

Hydraulic Components Incorporated as Parts of Other Equipment

Low horsepower hydraulic components are incorporated in a very wide range of mobile and industrial equipment. The total 1965 market was estimated at approximately $15 million, of which more than $10 million was self-manufactured by the equipment manufacturers incorporating the units. The balance was split among more than a dozen hydraulic component producers.

Applied Power participated in this market through its BIPCO division's Power Packer line. Power Packer sold pumps, cylinders, and jacks, similar in technology and design to Enerpac's and BMC's lines, to OEM customers. Most applications required special engineering and adaptations for a specific product. They usually represented low potential volume uses with little competition and wide margins. As volume grows, the threat of competition or self-manufacture by the OEM would become very real. In 1965, Power Packer had little important competition in the market segments it served, excepting in its largest volume category—hydraulic cylinders for tilting truck cabs. Here BRIMCO had made a serious challenge to capture this market. Power Packer competed to a lesser degree with Hein-Werner, Ausco, Greenley, and others.

Medium Horsepower Components

In contrast to the limited sales volume of the low horsepower hydraulic components, those in the range of 10-50 horsepower had a 1965 market potential estimated in excess of $150 million. Medium horsepower components, such as vane pumps or gear pumps, were predominantly simple design, high volume, mass produced products. They were manufactured primarily by large companies such as the Vickers division of Sperry Rand, Sundstrand, Cessna, New York Air Brake, a division of American Brake Shoe, Bendix, Thompson Ramo Wooldridge, Borg-Warner, Houdaille, etc., and were sold primarily to OEM customers through direct sales efforts. These customers were in the farm equipment, earth moving, material handling, aircraft construction, railroad, marine, and machine tool markets.

Cessna and Vickers dominated the portion of the OEM mobile market that was sold on the basis of price, while Vickers dominated the OEM portion of the machine tool market. Another part of the hydraulic market, which was equal in size to the medium horsepower OEM market, was in selling to the industrial user. This market was composed of manufacturers who bought medium horsepower components to aid in their own manufacturing processes. Industrial users were supplied by 2,000 hydraulics distributors, none of which was a significant factor in the industry. No single hydraulics manufacturer dominated either the industrial user market or controlled a large percentage of the hydraulics distributors. Applied Power did not compete in the medium horsepower market.

Vickers was reported to be the major source of profits for its giant parent.[1]

Heavy-Duty Units

Hydraulic units in the 50-150 horsepower range were predominantly extremely complex, special purpose units. The total 1965 domestic market was estimated at

---

[1] *Fortune*, April, 1965, p. 123.

$25 million. Primary factors in the market were Vickers, Sunstrand, and Cessna.

Heavy-duty units were predominantly complicated piston pumps capable of variation in both speed and direction of oil flow from a single power source.

Applied Power participated in this market through its Dynex division. Because quantities were small and end uses were very heterogeneous, much special engineering and sales development activity was necessary for each sale. Two to five years lag time from customer contact to delivery of product was common. Products in markets offering substantial sales potential were subject to extensive competition or being manufactured by the customer as soon as his requirements reached important volume.

Operating results for a few representative companies in this industry are summarized as Exhibit 6. Most of the larger companies had such widely diversified operations that their hydraulics business was not separable from reported totals. Most of the smaller companies were privately held and did not report financial statistics.

Applied Power Performance: 1960–1965

Exhibit 7 summarizes Applied Power corporate and divisional financial statistics from 1960 to 1965. As can be seen, the company showed steady and rapid improvement in sales and earnings since 1962. 1963, 1964, and 1965 were successively all-time record years in both sales and earnings. In 1965 every division showed profitability increases over 1964.

CORPORATE DIRECTION AND CONTROL

Although Mr. Philip Brumder had, at various times, served directly in the management of each of Applied Power's operating units, he preferred to maintain direction and control of the corporation primarily through financial plans and reports, and had added a second level of control by using strategic plans. This mode of operation had given the company a distinctively "profit oriented" or "financial" character, as compared with the "sales" character it possessed under Mr. Herbert Brumder.

Financial Controls

Applied Power had an extensive, formal, and thorough system of accounting and reporting. The system was based upon annual profit planning. Each year, by divisions, the division general manager, division controller, corporate controller, and Mr. Brumder jointly determined sales and profit goals for that division for each of the next three years.

From these targets, plans were developed by the division management into a detailed budget for achieving these results. Anticipated *pro forma* balance sheets

exhibit 6

APPLIED POWER INDUSTRIES, INC. (A)

Financial Statistics for Selected Companies

A. *Hein-Werner Corporation, Waukesha, Wisconsin*
Produced hydraulic jacks, collision-damage repair units, pumps, valves, rams, etc.

	Net Sales	Income Taxes	Net Earnings	Earnings Per Share[1]	Dividends Paid	Cash Dividends Per Share	Net Worth	Shares Outstanding	Book Value Per Share[1]	working Capital
1955	$ 5,222,954	$414,000	$378,643	$1.36	$278,829	$1.00	$2,571,725	278,829	$ 9.22	$2,086,286
1956	5,579,759	480,000	403,090	1.51	275,819	1.00	2,551,507	266,789	9.56	2,086,232
1957	5,277,851	447,000	428,542	1.61	266,789	1.00	2,713,260	266,789	10.17	2,274,205
1958	5,259,691	250,000	215,582	0.81	266,789	1.00	2,662,053	266,789	9.98	1,686,618
1959	7,691,733	221,000	195,034	0.73	266,789	1.00	2,490,667	266,789	9.34	1,986,462
1960	6,893,594	194,000	252,339	0.93	40,782	0.152	2,699,838	271,881	9.93	2,158,765
1961	6,437,253	346,000	305,253	1.07	71,269	0.252	2,928,882	285,076	10.27	2,124,139
1962	7,174,362	459,000	409,815	1.44	285,076	1.00	3,053,621	285,075	10.71	2,220,244
1963	8,052,927	680,000	585,984	2.01	289,921	1.00	3,406,648	290,926	11.71	2,525,586
1964	10,597,766	900,000	847,025	2.64	298,547	1.002	3,954,447	320,413	12.34	2,836,368

[1]Based on the number of shares outstanding at the end of the year.　　[2]Plus a 10% stock dividend in 1964, 5% in 1961, and 2% in 1960.

B. *American Brake Shoe Corporation*
(all figures in millions)

Mass producer of hydraulic pumps, motor controls, presses, systems, primarily for aircraft, marine, railroad, and mobile equipment controls. Active R&D department in hydraulics. Have recently developed: transmissions for mobile equipment, new piston pumps, new servo-valves, high speed pumps. Constructing in 1965: new hydraulic piston pump plant and new valve pump facility.

	1958	1959	1960	1961	1962	1963	1964
Total sales	$138	$168	$165	$166	$195	$215	$241
Net earnings	4.8	7.7	5.7	5.4	7.0	7.4	9.8
Estimated Sales in hydraulics	14	20	21	29	46	46	51

C.Borg-Warner Corporation—Funded debt: $9,995,000;
Pfd. 86,743 shares, $3.50 Cum., $100 Par;
Com., 9,251,683 shares, $5 Par.

Year	Net Sales	Operating Income	Net before Taxes	Net Income	Net Working Capital	Current Ratio Assets to Liabilities
1954	$380.3	$56.93	$48.9	$24.46	$114.1	2.6-1
1955	552.2	95.06	84.8	41.08	145.7	2.5-1
1956	598.7	84.30	71.7	35.84	182.5	3.0-1
1957	608.5	82.81	71.0	34.08	190.2	3.3-1
1958	533.0	58.49	45.9	21.14	190.4	3.7-1
1959	649.9	96.89	84.5	39.31	201.6	3.1-1
1960	586.9	68.03	55.9	27.21	206.9	3.9-1
1961	584.7	63.41	49.8	23.43	202.5	3.7-1
1962	658.9	83.25	68.5	33.0	211.1	3.4-1
1963	688.5	92.78	79.5	31.71	229.7	3.5-1

Per share figures are adjusted for 3 for 1 stock split in 1955. Includes all major domestic and Canadian subsidiaries except B-W Acceptance Corporation; also includes Byron Jackson from 1955 and York Corporation from 1956.

D.*Webster Electric Company, Racine, Wisconsin.* Manufactured communication equipment, telephone components, ignition transformers, heating products, hydraulic pumps, products, and systems. ($000)

Fiscal Year Ends 12/31	Net Sales[1]	Income Taxes	Net Earnings[1]	Earnings Per Share[2,5]	Cash Dividends	Cash Dividends Per Share[2,5]	[1]Net Worth	Total Assets	Working Capital
1957	$ 9,476		$303.7	$ .81	$160.9	$.38			
1958	8,371		158.0	.42	135.2	.32			
1959	9,403		349.2	.89	140.2	.32			
1960	8,019		109.7	.28	126.5	.28	$4,446.5	$5,340.7	$3,368.5
1961	10,123		408.2	1.16	86.9	.27	3,781.7	6,041.5	3,460.1
1962	9,800	$179.3	236.8	.70	84.6	.27	4,087.5	6,103.3	3,387.2
1963	11,081	336.6	386.4	1.11	90.8	.27	4,431.6	6,473.3	3,625.8
1964	13,064	522.6	637.8	1.75	143.8	.41	4,871.6	7,914.7	4,467.6
1965	13,701	704.0	705.2	1.92	205.7	.56	5,596.6	8,753.2	4,512.6

[1]1964 and prior years adjusted to reflect consolidation of foreign subsidiaries.

[2]Adjusted to reflect 4.3 stock split in 1965.

[3]Includes extraordinary gain and tax loss carry forward on acquisition of subsidiary. 1965 includes consolidated foreign subsidiaries, 1964 and prior include investments at cost. Hydraulic components account for about 50% of total sales.

[4]Includes extraordinary losses on disposition of product lines.

[5]Earnings per share and cash dividends per share for Racine Hydraulics & Machinery, Inc., and Oilgear Company are adjusted to make comparable.

E.*Racine Hydraulics & Machinery, Inc., Racine, Wisconsin.* Manufactured metal cutting machines, railroad maintenance tools, hydraulic pumps, valves, controls, gauges, power units, pressure boosters, couplings, and accessories. ($000)

Fiscal Year Ends 12/31	Net Sales[1]	Income Taxes	Net Earnings[1]	Earnings Per Share[2,5]	Cash Dividends	Cash Dividends Per Share[2,5]	[1]Net Worth	Total Assets	Working Capital
1957	$ 5,268.0		$308.0	$1.20			$2,233.0		$1,501.0
1958	3,999.0		28.0	.08			2,647.0		1,580.0
1959	4,682.4	$232.0	192.3	.54			2,764.7	$ 3,977.8	1,687.5
1960	6,581.3	398.0	281.9	.95	$124.8	$.38	2,967.3	5,015.3	1,569.2
1961	5,857.6	7.0	(19.9)	(.09)	132.7	.38	2,825.3	5,310.6	2,298.6
1962	7,412.4	328.6	280.6	.70	147.6	.38	3,125.7	6,135.1	2,775.4
1963	8,648.6	397.6	425.6	1.07	148.8	.38	3,419.9	6,814.0	3,021.8
1964	11,282.4	670.0	636.9	1.61	150.2	.38	3,960.2	8,406.8	2,980.8
1965	14,552.8	907.0	871.9	2.10	213.7	.48	4,671.1	10,568.8	3,584.9

[1]Retroactively adjusted to reflect merger with Sarasota Precision Products inc., at 9/30/60. Hydraulic components accounted for 80.85% of total

F. *The Oilgear Company, Milwaukee, Wisconsin.* Manufactured hydraulic power pumps, motors, transmissions, cylinders, valves, and controls. ($000)

Year									
1957		$ 587.0	$ 519.6	$1.17	$266.4	$ .60	$6,523.1		$3,345.0
1958		188.0	125.9	.29	177.6	.40	6,471.4		3,737.1
1959		745.0	607.0	1.37	266.4	.60	6,877.4	$ 8,453.4	4,239.4
1960	$ 8,311.3	921.0	755.9	1.66	337.4	.75	7,375.9	8,637.5	4,653.5
1961	7,421.0	619.0	517.0	1.14	282.9	.62	7,619.5	8,771.4	4,902.6
1962	8,589.6	835.0	688.7	1.52	339.5	.75	7,968.7	9,430.2	5,460.9
1963	9,488.0	1,002.0	834.0	1.84	453.5	1.00	8,370.7	10,134.9	5,896.1
1964	10,750.5	1,165.0	1,048.5	2.31	488.3	1.07	8,930.9	10,809.0	6,493.7
1965	12,169.5	1,465.0	1,443.9	3.18	726.2	1.60	9,645.6	11,779.9	6,857.9

G. *Greer Hydraulics, Inc., Los Angeles, California.* Manufactured hydraulic accumulators, valves and accessories, aircraft hydraulic test systems, and power units.

Year									
1962	$4,497.6								
1963	4,781.0	0	$151.9	$ .28	0	0	$ 966.1	$2,134.5	$1,138.2
1964	5,611.9	0	716.0	1.34	0	0	1,709.4	2,069.1	1,327.8
1965	5,415.8	0	702.1	1.27 (ave)	$138.7	$.25	2,389.9	2,833.3	1,427.1

[1] Net operating loss carry forward.

exhibit 7

APPLIED POWER INDUSTRIES, INC. (A)

Summary of Operating Performance, 1960–1965
Total Corporation and by Operating Divisions
(in thousands)

	Net Sales (Year ending 8/31)	Net Earnings (after tax)	Bank Borrow	Total Shareholders' Investment at Year-end	Return on Shareholders' Investment	Total Invested Capital[1] at Year-end	Return on Invested Capital[1]
Total corporation							
1960	$14,996	$ 311		$4,255	7.4%		
1961	14,465	204		4,403	4.5		
1962	15,889	267		4,439	6.0		
1963	16,680	582		4,820	12.3		
1964	19,434	935		5,287	16.9		
1965	22,854	1,353		6,568	20.6		
Blackhawk Manufacturing Company							
Porto-Power							
(Collision damage repair equipment)							
1960	$2,960	$144				$1,380	9.8%
1961	3,260	273				1,560	20.7
1962	2,910	92				1,510	6.1
1963	2,570	153				1,180	11.9
1964	2,340	197				870	20.0
1965	2,390	242				810	32.0
Lifting equipment							
(jacks, etc.)							
1960	$5,520	$ 14				$2,130	.5%
1961	4,380	(82)				2,120	(8.3)
1962	4,470	(14)				1,980	(.7)
1963	4,130	(17)				1,900	(.9)
1964	4,450	61				1,800	3.5
1965	4,880	142				1,830	7.8
Blackhawk Industrial Products Company							
Enerpac							
(portable pumps, cylinders, etc., sold through distributors)							
1960	$2,410	$197				$820	26.7%
1961	2,450	215				800	30.2
1962	2,850	313				790	44.1
1963	2,800	372				640	55.8
1964	2,980	317				740	55.0
1965	3,720	470				900	64.9
Power Packer							
(OEM pumps, cylinders, etc.)							
1960	$1,400	$200				$490	40.9%
1961	1,110	133				520	26.3
1962	1,130	109				350	24.8
1963	1,130	124				290	38.1
1964	1,300	212				300	77.6
1965	1,700	264				430	80.9

The Dynex Company
Dynex division
(high HP complex special pumps and cylinders)

1960	$1,304	$(133)				$1,216	(10.9%)
1961	1,185	(137)				1,103	(12.4)
1962	1,876	(60)				1,124	(5.3)
1963	2,177	56				1,057	5.2
1964	2,369	54				1,240	4.4
1965	2,750	38				1,698	2.2

Engineering systems
(contract engineering and prototype development)

1960	$209	$(17)				$110	(15.5%)
1961	396	(19)				120	(15.8)
1962	198	(71)				73	(97.3)
1963	449	20				101	19.8
1964	732	57				264	21.6
1965	743	7				186	3.8

Applied Power International Division
(overseas sales and manufacturing)

1960	$ 983	$(15)	$127	$ 22	(69.8%)	$ 333	(4.5%)
1961	1,512	(13)	270	51	(25.7)	561	(2.3)
1962	2,366	7	349	49	14.3	1,275	.5
1963	3,427	112	670	45	248.0	1,991	5.6
1964	4,894	245	615	241	101.7	2,588	9.4
1965	6,478	314	650	800	39.2	3,748	8.4

Parts and service
(Separate profit center since 1957)

1960	$ 853	$127		$357	32.8%		
1961	858	100		399	25.1		
1962	856	83		360	22.8		
1963	897	96		385	24.9		
1964	931	149		284	50.2		
1965	1,008	183		249	68.6		

1Inventories, accounts receivable, and net fixed assets.

and income statements were constructed from these same assumptions. This procedure was followed every year and was completely reviewed and updated by the general manager and Mr. Brumder every four months (each third of the year).

Exhibit 8 combines domestic and international sales figures to show total corporate sales by type of product for relevant divisions.

Exhibit 9 shows worldwide consolidated balance sheets for Applied Power for the period 1959–1965.

Exhibits 10 and 11 show rate of growth in sales and net earnings per share for Applied Power for the period 1958–1965.

At the corporate level John Wermuth, the controller, reporting directly to Mr. Brumder, kept him apprised of any developments or deviations from plan. Mr. Wermuth also communicated, through the division controllers, information and decisions affecting division finance or policies. Mr. Wermuth worked with Mr. Brumder in determining what information was needed centrally, and in what form and frequency. In turn he brought to the division controllers the specifica-

exhibit 8

APPLIED POWER INDUSTRIES, INC. (A)

Sales
(thousands)

	1960	1961	1962	1963	1964	1965
Collision damage repair						
Blackhawk Manufacturing Co.,	$2,960	$3,260	$2,910	$2,570	$2,340	$2,388
International	748	1,240	1,444	2,223	2,790	3,383
Total sales	$3,708	$4,500	$4,354	$4,793	$5,130	$5,771
Lifting equipment						
Blackhawk Manufacturing Co.	5,520	4,380	4,470	4,130	4,450	4,883
International	164	188	214	317	405	570
Total sales	$5,684	$4,568	$4,684	$4,447	$4,855	$5,453
Enerpac						
BIPCO	2,410	2,450	2,850	2,800	2,980	3,722
International	65	57	603	647	1,024	1,495
Total sales	$2,475	$2,507	$3,453	$3,447	$4,004	$5,217
Dynex						
Dynex	1,304	1,185	1,876	2,177	2,369	2,751
International	—	—	20	94	283	245
Total sales	$1,304	$1,185	$1,896	$2,271	$2,652	$2,996
Tektro						
Dynex	—	—	—	—	—	38
International	—	—	—	4	84	272
Total sales	—	—	—	$ 4	$ 84	$ 310
All other						
Domestic*	$2,166	$2,364	$2,384	$2,476	$2,963	$3,448
International†	12	24	88	146	313	513
Total sales	$2,178	$2,388	$2,472	$2,622	$3,276	$3,961

*Primarily Power Packer, systems engineering, parts and service.
†Primarily other automotive items, plus parts.

tions of this uniform reporting system and insured that the desired procedures were carried out.

Each division controller was responsible to both the division general manager and to Mr. Wermuth. He was expected to maintain all of the normal bookkeeping, payroll, and accounting functions for the division. In addition, he was expected to keep Mr. Brumder informed through Mr. Wermuth of deviations from the

exhibit 9

APPLIED POWER INDUSTRIES, INC. (A)

World Consolidated Balance Sheet
(for years ending August 31: nearest $000)

Assets	1959	1960	1961	1962	1963	1964	1965
Current							
Cash	$ 231	$ 259	$ 241	$ 229	$ 529	$ 400	$ 417
S/T Investments	—	—	—	—	100	1,135	447
A/R and N/R	2,146	2,741	3,496	3,321	3,494	3,800	4.531
Inventories	2,737	2,660	2,313	2,770	2,752	2,969	3,593
Prepaid expenses	62	62	101	98	73	148	102
Total current	$5,176	$5,722	$6,151	$6,418	$6,948	$8,452	$9,090
Other assets	211	228	43	22	30	—	—
Life insurance	—	—	155	162	170	177	185
Fixed assets	1,492	1,554	1,375	1,303	1,222	1,282	1,552
	$6,879	$7,504	$7,724	$7,905	$8,370	$9,911	$10,827

Liabilities and net worth	1959	1960	1961	1962	1963	1964	1965
Current							
N/P—unsecured	$ 375	$1,027	$1,227	$1,198	$ 676	$ 727	$ 722
A/P and accounting exp.	1,111	951	1,089	1,458	1,546	1,941	1,907
Taxes on income	288	293	206	109	633	896	811
Note—current port.	100	150	100	100	100	103	106
Total current	$1,874	$2,421	$2,622	$2,865	$2,955	$3,667	$ 3,546
Def. for. taxes	—	—	—	—	—	216	324
5% domestic note	1,000	850	750	650	550	450	350
6% foreign note	—	—	—	—	—	50	39
Net worth							
Capital stock	822	822	834	839	855	1,558	1,577
Add. pd-in capital	—	—	—	14	60	770	753
Retained earnings	3,183	3,411	3,532	3,718	4,165	3,200	4,238
Less: treasury stock	—	—	(14)	(181)	(215)	—	—
Total net worth	$4,005	$4,233	$4,352	$4,390	$4,865	$5,528	$ 6,568
	$6,879	$7,504	$7,724	$7,905	$8,370	$9,911	$10,827

plan or other major developments. In this dual role it was frequently necessary for the division controller to develop more detailed analysis of costs and variances for his own division general manager than was required for central reporting. The emphasis in central reporting was upon the profit or loss figures. Deviations within sales and costs categories were not considered of great concern, so long as the profit goal was achieved.

Every month, complete reports were submitted from all divisions and were compared with the plan. Any major deviations would be explained at the monthly

exhibit 10

APPLIED POWER INDUSTRIES, INC. (A)

Rate of Growth in Sales

1958–1965

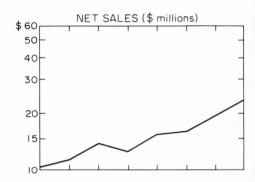

management meeting, attended by all division general managers and the central corporate staff. The identification of deviations was expected to provoke the division general manager to take the necessary action to reach the planned financial goals.

Cash planning was done at the corporate level after consolidating all individual plans. Excess cash was invested in Treasury Bills, and cash borrowings were negotiated with the banks directly by Mr. Brumder. Although each division controller maintained a separate checking account, the needs for cash were coordinated centrally.

Divisionalization

Another key concept in Mr. Brumder's direction of the company was the separation of the company into relatively autonomous "profit center" divisions. As early as 1953, he divided the company into two divisions—one for hand tools, the other for hydraulic units. When high horsepower systems development work was commenced in 1955, Dynex was established as a separate division. Similarly, automotive and industrial products were separated in 1957, and international activities were begun as a separate division in 1960.

Mr. Brumder explained that Applied Power was involved in serving many industries. He indicated, "We need to have our business adapt to the markets' needs while using our resources effectively and profitably. To do this, I think

exhibit 11

APPLIED POWER INDUSTRIES, INC. (A)

Growth in Net Earnings per Share

1958–1965

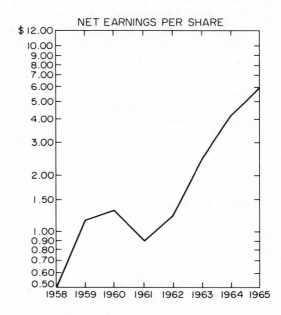

NET EARNINGS PER SHARE

we need to have competent businessmen concentrating on each market segment. In this way, we compensate for whatever lack exists in top management.

"In the past five years we have worked hard to make this approach to management work. We've improved our measurements and reports so we know what's happening. We've made management changes to be sure of competent business direction in each division. And now we're working at improving our over-all corporate planning. We need deliberate strategies for growth."

Strategic planning in Applied Power was often the result of market research done by outside consultants as well as by members of the corporate staff. Mr. Brumder indicated that such information was crucial for the development of product strategies for each division. He explained, "If these studies were conducted at the direction of corporate headquarters in cooperation with the division, this process would provide corporate influence for the future direction for the division. With adequate knowledge of a product's market environment, strategic planning could provide not only the general direction for division development, but also could be used for establishing a specific timetable for accomplishment of important elements of the plan." This then was the evolving facet of control which supplemented the traditional financial reports. Not only was a manager expected to achieve the established profit goals—he was also measured by his ability to meet the schedule of his strategic plan. Mr. Brumder indicated financial controls without strategic planning could result in short-term profit maximization at the expense of a favorable long-term growth in earnings per share.

Within the constraints of the annual profit plan (and its "thirdly" updating), Mr. Brumder believed in giving his division general managers as complete autonomy as possible. Each of the general managers reported to the researcher that he had the freedom to do "just about whatever [he] wanted." Each also indicated that "Phil is good about rewarding good performance. He's also pretty tough on poor performance. There's been a real turnover here on men who couldn't perform." General managers received as much as $30-35,000 base salary, plus substantial bonuses based on individual performance, in addition to stock options.

Shareholder-Managers

Mr. Brumder had recapitalized the company in early 1964 "in order to provide stock ownership opportunity for those top level people who have a direct influence on profits." Some 31 "shareholder-managers" owned shares and/or stock options in the company. In the aggregate, these options, after exercise, would amount to 30% of the company's Class A (nonvoting) stock. A general manager's share could run as high as 5%, while lesser employees would be scaled down to as little as 1/10 of 1% on the total Class A ownership.

Each shareholder-manager was allotted a total number of options on a ten year installment purchase contract. Each year, he was obliged to buy 10% or more of his allotment at a price determined by an outside investment banker. (In 1964, the price set was $23.25/share vs. a book value of $26.62.) In the event a shareholder-manager left the company, he was obliged to resell his purchased shares to the company at an independently determined price, and his outstanding options were cancelled.

Marketing—Finance—Production

Mr. Brumder indicated that each of his general managers had had substantial marketing experience. Although two were engineers, all were selected at least in part for their "marketing orientation."

Mr. Brumder felt this orientation was the appropriate counterbalance to his own "financial orientation."

Although the company had been completely divisionalized financially and into separate sales and engineering forces, manufacturing was not completely divisionalized. Instead, each plant performed similar operations for whatever division(s) used those components or products. Thus, the Sheboygan plant (under BMC) produced all of the jacks manufactured for BMC sales, and also made the comparable component units for Enerpac and Power Packer.

The Columbus plant (under BIPCO administration) was entirely an assembly operation. It did work for Porto-Power (BMC), Enerpac, Power Packer, and Service. Bareboo (under BMC) did work for both BMC and BIPCO.

However, each plant has been assigned to the division taking the majority of its output.

Only Dynex, with its Pewaukee and Camden plants, did not do work for other divisions. James Ryan, corporate director of manufacturing, coordinated operations among the various plants by working through the respective division manufacturing managers.

Mr. Brumder's Concept of the Company

Mr. Brumder believed strongly in autonomous divisions, headed by competent, marketing oriented, businessmen who would seek out opportunities within their product and market segments within the constraints of the over-all profit plan and general long-range goals. He hoped to develop worldwide strategies for each product and market segment and to exploit its potential as far as possible.

He also believed in the smallest possible central staff: a controller to provide the necessary financial data for direction and control, a manufacturing director to assure manufacturing competence and economies among the divisions, a director of R & D to undertake projects which were outside the present product definitions of the divisions, and a director of corporate development to undertake special studies, evaluate acquisition opportunities, and generally assist the president in seeing that planning was adequately performed and coordinated throughout the company.

He defined the strategy of his present business as finding "niches" in the automotive service market, in the industrial tool market, and in the fluid power market big enough for Applied Power to become the most important factor, yet small enough that they would be relatively insignificant to the big manufacturers, e.g., Vickers, Bendix, *et al*. He defined these niches as "relatively small, specialty businesses, frequently requiring long product lines and complex distribution, so that they are unattractive to the mass-producers." He, his director of corporate development, Frank Bloomquist, and the division managers were actively seeking to identify as many of these potential inches as possible. He did state that the company would be interested in larger-sized niches, as Applied Power gained in strength over the years.

Even without acquisitions or significant additions in the company's divisional line-up, he anticipated a continued rapid growth in sales and earnings, but hoped to improve "coordinated companywide planning on a corporate worldwide basis (as distinct from a division, segment, or regional basis), in order to direct the company resources toward those opportunities that will best optimize the value of the stock over the long pull."

Applied Power Industries, Inc. (B-1):

The Blackhawk Manufacturing Company

The Blackhawk Manufacturing Company (BMC) was, in 1965, the largest and the oldest of Applied Power's four operating divisions. 1965 sales volume was $7.3 million. Net profit (after tax) was $384,000 for an over-all return on investment of 14.6%.

This division accounted for 31.8% of Applied Power's total corporate sales, 28.4% of corporate net earnings, and 40.3% of corporate net worth.

BMC was the automotive division of Applied Power. As such, it served the $6-9 billion auto "aftermarket" (all automotive parts and equipment except that going into new cars). The aftermarket was composed of four major categories: (1) parts (which comprised about 85% of the total); (2) accessories; (3) supplies and chemicals; and (4) service equipment. BMC's product line was wholly within the service equipment segment (items used to *service* automobiles), which was estimated at about $350 million annually.

BMC offered two product lines to the service equipment market: (1) the Blackhawk line of *lifting equipment;* and (2) the Porto-Power line of *collision damage repair equipment* (CDR). Of the two, the CDR line was much smaller in sales (1965: $2.4 million vs. $4.9 million) and investment (1965: $.8 million vs. $1.8 million), but much more profitable (1965: $242,000 vs. $142,000) than the lifting equipment line.

The importance of these two lines to the total corporation is emphasized when International sales, which were not included under BMC, but handled separately under the International division, were added. (The International division licensed or subcontracted the manufacture of some part of both lines overseas and exported the balance to meet their own sales requirements in the various countries served.) As can be seen from Exhibit 1, while declining in relative im-

exhibit 1

APPLIED POWER INDUSTRIES, INC. (B-1)

Lifting Equipment and CDR Equipment Sales, 1960–1965
(in millions of dollars and as a percentage of divisional sales)

	1960		1961		1962		1963		1964		1965	
	$	%	$	%	$	%	$	%	$	%	$	%
BMC lifting equipment	5.5	(65)	4.4	(57)	4.5	(61)	4.1	(61)	4.4	(66)	4.9	(67)
International lifting equipment	0.2	(20)	0.2	(15)	0.2	(9)	0.4	(11)	0.5	(10)	0.6	(8)
Total corporate	5.7	(38)	4.6	(32)	4.7	(30)	4.5	(27)	4.9	(25)	4.5	(20)
BMC-CDR equipment	3.0	(35)	3.3	(43)	2.9	(39)	2.6	(39)	2.3	(34)	2.4	(33)
International CDR equipment	0.7	(70)	1.2	(80)	1.5	(62)	2.2	(65)	2.8	(57)	3.4	(47)
Total corporate	3.7	(25)	4.5	(31)	4.4	(28)	4.8	(28)	5.1	(26)	5.8	(25)
Total lifting and CDR												
BMC	8.5	(100)	7.7	(100)	7.4	(100)	6.7	(100)	6.7	(100)	7.3	(100)
International	0.9	(90)	1.4	(95)	1.7	(71)	2.6	(76)	3.3	(67)	4.0	(55)
Total corporate	9.4	(63)	9.1	(63)	9.1	(58)	9.3	(55)	10.0	(51)	11.3	(49)

portance over the years, lifting and CDR equipment in 1965 still accounted for almost half of the sales of the total corporation and nearly two-thirds of the International division's sales volume.

BMC had approximately 200 employees. About 105 were in manufacturing, located in the 51,000 square foot Sheboygan plant (60 miles north of Milwaukee), and in the 20,000 square foot Baraboo plant. Thirty were field salesmen and field sales managers, and another 50 made up the engineering (7), accounting (15), purchasing (4), and central office forces. Division headquarters were in the same building with corporate headquarters.

The division general manager, John B. Bowman, was also a corporate vice president. Bowman, 44, had joined the company in 1962 after more than 15 years in industrial marketing. After a year and a half as director of corporate planning, he had been named general manager of BMC in the summer of 1963, following the withdrawal of his predecessor. Bowman had made a number of significant moves to reduce costs and increase margins. As a result, lifting equipment went from a loss position in the years ending August 31, 1961, 1962, and 1963, to healthy profits in 1964 and 1965. In the CDR line, a sharp profit decline in 1962 was reversed in 1963, and strong increases were shown in 1964 and 1965.

THE "TURN-AROUND"

Mr. Bowman indicated a series of steps which he felt had achieved the turn-around.

1. He had recombined divisional marketing and engineering management. Where previously, lifting equipment and CDR had each had their own sales forces, sales management, and engineering departments, Mr. Bowman had merged the two with significant cost savings. (Divisional manufacturing and finance had always been unified.)
2. He had placed all engineering and manufacturing efforts toward "fixing" and "eliminating" products which were failing in customers' operations because of poor design or construction (notably the service jack.)
3. "Jim Ryan fixed manufacturing." Mr. Bowman had called in Ryan (corporate director of manufacturing) and given him a free hand. As a result, the Sheboygan plant's tooling efficiency had been greatly improved. The Baraboo plant had been established for assembly, shipping, and minor fabrication. Make or buy decisions had been restudied and "sourcing out" had been reduced. And the Hebron, Illinois, plant had been closed, and Porto-Power assembly moved to BIPCO's Columbus plant.
4. A new controller was hired, and Mr. Bowman was now receiving the kinds of data he personally felt most important for directing and controlling the division.
5. Product planning had been established as a separate unit reporting to the general manager, rather than as a part of each of the two product-marketing segments. During 1961–63, virtually all of the division's product development efforts had gone into "Atar"—a unit for automatic transmission analysis and repair. While Atar was reportedly an "engineering success" which "demonstrated to Detroit our sophistication as equipment makers," it proved too expensive to construct and too complex to operate to be a commercially practical product. The restructuring assured Mr. Bowman of closer contact with projects all through their development periods, as well as control over which items reached project status, and the Atar project director was selected as the new product development manager.
6. Mr. Bowman hired a new chief engineer to take over the total engineering responsibilities for the division.

In the summer of 1965, Mr. Bowman was operating without a general sales manager. In January, the former sales manager had resigned to take a much bigger job with Stewart-Warner Corporation, and Mr. Bowman had been carrying on the sales management function as well as general management. Although he had been seeking a new man assiduously for nearly a year, he had not found anyone who met his standards of ability and experience. With the hiring of the new sales manager, the entire management staff of the division would have been replaced since Mr. Bowman became general manager.

LIFTING EQUIPMENT

[The Blackhawk line of lifting equipment was designed primarily for use by service stations, garages, automobile dealers, repair shops, and truck fleet operators.]

Product Line

BMC's lifting equipment sales in 1965 were divided roughly half in hydraulic hand jacks and half in service jacks, one-end lifts, transmission jacks, safety stands, cranes, dollies, mobile lifts, mechanical jacks, jack oil, etc.

According to Mr. Bowman, the bulk of the line's profits came from the sale of hydraulic hand jacks and transmission jacks. The other items barely held their own, and some showed losses. He felt that the heavy manufacturing investment made in 1952 at Sheboygan in special-purpose, high-speed machine tools made BMC the lowest cost producer of hydraulic hand jacks in the industry. As a result, BMC had captured a significant share of the total market, with only Hein-Werner also having a significant share, and the balance being split among a half dozen companies.

BMC's hand jack market was split five ways:

- One part to OEM customers (GM, Ford, Chrysler) for standard equipment on their new trucks.
- A second part to a few very large retail chains (e.g., Sears, Western Auto, etc.) for resale.
- A third part to automotive supply jobbers.
- The fourth part to warehouse distributors, who handled inventories for the jobbers.
- The balance to smaller chains, oil companies, government agencies, etc.

The other items in the lifting equipment line were sold almost entirely through the automotive supply jobbers and warehouse distributors. More than 25,000 small jobbers, averaging less than $150,000/year sales volume, were the major factor in automotive aftermarket distribution. Jobbers normally sold extremely wide lines of parts, accessories, supplies, and equipment at manufacturers' catalog prices to garages, service stations, shops, and retailers. They operated on a standard 30% margin off list, but frequently received other concessions from manufacturers which improved this markup. Prepaid freight, delayed dating on accounts receivable, and extended time periods for "cash" discounts were common in the trade.

Warehouse distributors commonly operated on a 15-20% margin off the price sold to the jobber. Large jobbers frequently "redistributed" inventories to smaller jobbers, and claimed the additional warehouse distributor margin from the manufacturer.

BMC sold to the warehouse distributors and jobbers through a nationwide, regionalized sales force of 25 men, plus three "missionaries" or troubleshooters, under the direction of a field sales manager. Previous to 1958, BMC had sold only hand jacks and service jacks through a limited number of semiexclusive distributors. Subsequently, the full-line concept was adopted, and nonexclusive distribution was established. This resulted in a "two-step" policy (i.e., selling directly to both distributors and jobbers) which was common in other automotive items, but previously had not applied to jacks (primarily because of the relatively small volume in jacks). At this same time, BMC also expanded direct sales (house accounts) to the chains, oil companies, and other national and regional accounts.

It was uneconomic for each manufacturer to make limited runs of all of the various types of mechanical and hydraulic jacks, yet many dealers demanded a full line under a single label. As a result, most manufacturers bought parts or special units for resale under their own brands. BMC sold a limited number of hydraulic units to competitors and purchased the mechanical jacks which were required to round out the line.

Vigorous competition has held lifting equipment prices at levels which have not advanced materially since World War II.

Manufacturing

The Sheboygan plant performed all of the critical machining operations with expensive, automated, multi-operation machine tools, and purchased its castings and minor parts. This plant produced all of the basic jack units for the entire company, operating on a two shift basis.

Following machining of parts, the products were assembled by hand, painted, and tested. Rejects could usually be reworked. Even though the building was old and equipped mostly with used tools, the manufacturing staff considered the Sheboygan plant to be the lowest cost operation in the country for the manufacture of comparable hydraulic units. Periodically, the staff analyzed all competitive jacks made anywhere in the world to determine what kind of changes in design and quality would alter their competitive posture from cost, marketing, and performance viewpoints. The output of the Sheboygan plant was limited by the availability of skilled machinists and the capabilities of existing vendors, but potential capacity was estimated to be nearly double the 1965 production level. The Baraboo plant assembled service jacks and other units on a one shift basis, and performed warehousing and shipping functions for the entire BMC division.

Most products were manufactured for inventory, since distributors and jobbers demanded immediate shipment. It was estimated that at least 95% of all orders had been shipped within four days of receipt.

Exhibit 2 presents financial data for the lifting equipment line. These and other data were prepared for each line annually, and revised every third, by Mr. Brumder and each divisional general manager. Data were always included on the preceding five years, the present year, and the forecast for the next three years. For purposes of this case, the forecasted years have not been included.

COLLISION DAMAGE REPAIR EQUIPMENT

[Blackhawk's Porto-Power line of collision damage repair equipment was the best-known name in the CDR field.]

exhibit 2

APPLIED POWER INDUSTRIES, INC. (B-1)

Unit Financial Profile by Years
(thousands of dollars)

Lifting Equipment	1960	1961	1962	1963	1964	1965
Net sales	$5,518	$4,378	$4,468	$4,132	$4,449	$4,880
Net profit	14	(82)	(14)	(17)	61	(142)
Net working capital	1,630	1,623	1,612	1,571	1,537	1,687
Net fixed assets	499	500	366	329	260	234
Total investment	2,129	2,123	1,978	1,900	1,797	1,921
Average % return on investment	.5%	(8.3%)	(.7%)	(.9%)	3.4%	(7.4%)
Total net cash flow	$ 182	$ (76)	$ 131	$ 61	$ 164	n.a.

Porto-Power						
Net sales	$2,963	$3,258	$2,911	$2,568	$2,343	$2,390
Net profit	144	273	92	153	197	242
Net working capital	1,267	1,448	1,388	1,118	838	726
Net fixed assets	116	115	123	66	36	28
Total investment	1,383	1,563	1,511	1,184	874	754
Average % return on investment	9.8%	20.7%	6.1%	11.9%	20.0%	33.1%
Total net cash flow	$(175)	$ 93	$ 144	$ 480	$ 507	$ 367

Sales were made primarily through body shop distributors who provided the full range of supplies (notably auto paints) and equipment for this very specialized market. "Two-step" distribution was not utilized in this market.

Authorized service and repair franchises were established in key cities for CDR and lifting equipment.

BMC frequently found it necessary to offer easy payment terms on its expensive units, such as working through the distributor and providing bank-rate financing.

According to Mr. Bowman, the regular Porto-Power line, while having enormous growth overseas, was not likely to grow as much domestically. Units lasted a long time and major product improvements were infrequent. This standard line of pumps, rams, hoses, and tubes for light work he viewed as a relatively stable market. But he saw a bright future for big, portable frame straighteners as well as heavy duty units for truck service and repair.

During 1965, Porto-Power was attempting to establish a body shop planning service for car dealers. They were showing auto dealers how to install well-designed total body shop repair units, and helping them plan and schedule work through the units. BMC hoped to demonstrate that for a total equipment investment of $11,000 for a six stall, three man operation, auto dealers could anticipate $95,000 worth of business annually with a net profit before taxes of around

$20,000. In such an installation, Porto-Power units would have a value of about $3,000. BMC was working with Ford Motor Company on the installation of such units in a number of Ford dealerships in 1965–66. Many dealers had steered clear of body work as it proved to be costly and specialized, and BMC hoped to alter this situation through the new program.

BMC was also working with deVilbiss, the leading manufacturer of spray painting units, in the design and operation of the complete body shop units.

Body Panels

During 1962–65, in an attempt to widen the line of products sold to body shops, BMC had begun to manufacture and distribute replacement panels for fender rust out and collision damage. As Mr. Bowman explained it, this venture was "disastrous." Changes in winter road maintenance methods and materials were reducing rust outs. Plastic filling was coming in to accommodate minor collision damage repair. A fixed investment in tooling of over $100,000/year appeared necessary in order to keep up with current automobile models. Sales never exceeded $400,000, while break-even was estimated at $1 million. In retrospect, it appeared that the size of the market (about $5 million) had been seriously overestimated, and that, to be successful, a panel manufacturer would have to capture about 40% of it. As it became increasingly clear that substantial sales would not be forthcoming and that panel promotion was "only pulling away effort from Porto-Power," Mr. Bowman moved to extricate BMC from the panel business. In mid-1965, he sold the entire operation.

The combination of getting out of the panel business, closing the Hebron, Illinois, plant, and closer control of inventories had halved the total investment in Porto-Power from 1962 to 1965, while doubling profits.

The Future

Mr. Bowman looked for big changes to take place in automotive aftermarket distribution, similar to changes which had already taken place in food distribution, hardware, and household goods. He anticipated the company's becoming more oriented to its ultimate market—car dealers, garages, and service stations—than to the automotive distributors and jobbers to whom BMC currently sold so much of its output.

He looked for a long-run limitation of investment in lifting equipment and increased activity in other diagnostic and service equipment situations. He indicated he was currently exploring some 27 different classifications of automotive service equipment for possible additions to the line (e.g., wheel-balancing, engine analysis, front-end alignment, dynamometers, etc.). He saw BMC's major competitive advantages as laying in equipment lines requiring substantial service and training capability, for which BMC had an excellent reputation in the trade.

Applied Power Industries, Inc. (B-2):

Blackhawk Industrial Products Company

Blackhawk Industrial Products (BIPCO) had its beginning in 1957 when a separate industrial marketing group was formed with its own catalog. Two years later, in 1959, BIPCO was separated from the automotive division and given full division status. In 1965, sales for the division were $5.4 million, with after tax profits of $734,000 for a return on investment of 55%.

These results showed BIPCO as providing 24% of total Applied Power sales, 54% of earnings, and operating on 20% of the corporate investment (see Exhibit 1 for detailed operating statistics).

The hydraulics market can be stratified into several broad categories of size and use, as described in Applied Power Industries, Inc. (A). BIPCO operated in the hand pump (fractional horsepower) and small power pump (under ten horsepower) range. Its selling and engineering activities had been separated into two segments—Enerpac and Power Pack.

Enerpac served users of portable industrial tools, a domestic market of about $7 million annually, and held a very important position in the market. In 1965, this division earned $470,000 on $3.7 million sales and on an indicated investment of $900,000. Total sales of this division were more than $5 million, after adding foreign sales of Enerpac products. In 1965, the Power Packer segment was about half the size of Enerpac. 1965 sales were $1.7 million and earnings after taxes were $264,000 on an indicated investment of $430,000. Foreign sales of $180,000 barely altered this picture.

BIPCO had about 120 employees. Sales accounted for 16 people, 15 of whom worked for Enerpac and one for Power Packer. Enerpac also employed two engineers, while Power Packer had only one.

The 51,000 square foot Columbus, Wisconsin, plant sub-

---

exhibit 1

APPLIED POWER INDUSTRIES, INC. (B-2)

**Unit Financial Profile by Years
(thousands of dollars)**

Power Packer	1960	1961	1962	1963	1964	1965
Net sales	$1,404	$1,114	$1,129	$1,134	$1,303	$1,700
Net profit	200	133	109	124	212	264
Net working capital	341	389	329	267	284	291
Net fixed assets	146	131	16	18	16	17
Total investment	487	520	345	285	300	308
Average % return on investment	40.9%	26.3%	24.8%	38.1%	77.6%	85.5%
Total net cash flow	$ 195	$ 100	$ 284	$ 184	$ 197	$ n.a.

Enerpac						
Net sales	$2,415	$2,447	$2,855	$2,800	$2,980	$3,720
Net profit	197	215	313	372	317	470
Net working capital	761	759	739	598	707	658
Net fixed assets	56	45	50	38	31	56
Total investment	817	804	789	636	738	714
Average % return on investment	26.7%	30.2%	44.1%	55.8%	55.0%	65.9%
Total net cash flow	$ 112	$ 228	$ 328	$ 525	$ 215	$ 471

contracted all of its parts and assembled components for Enerpac, Power Packer, part of the collision damage repair segment of BMC, and some for International. (The latter supplied most of its requirements from its European facilities.) Almost all of the production was of standard catalog items, being manufactured for inventory. Inventory turnover had been rapid (six times/year), and the plant had held Enerpac's back orders to less than five days. In contrast, Power Packer's large runs of special items had lead times varying from two weeks to five months because of the uncertainties and irregularities in their receipt of orders.

In 1965, Robert E. McBride, 38, was the general manager of the BIPCO division of Applied Power. After graduating in industrial management from M.I.T., Mr. McBride worked for 16 years for General Electric Company in sales and engineering management of several small operating units. He then worked for a year for Colts' Fire Arms as vice president of marketing. Since joining BIPCO in 1964, he had concentrated most of his time on planning the future direction of his division and the product needs for his two segments. Mr. McBride had felt that, because of already high market penetration in existing lines, the best avenue for future growth was through new products. He, therefore, was prepared to increase the engineering staff substantially and to undertake economic analysis and test marketing in the near future. He was assigned the task of looking for acquisition prospects for lines fitting close to the Enerpac and Power Packer segments.

HISTORY

In 1957, Mr. Fred Page, then controller and director of corporate development, Mr. Paul Moore, hired by Mr. Page for market analysis work in the industrial market, and Welling & Woodard, a management consulting firm, began a study of the market opportunities for industrial hydraulics. Two years later, these products were formally established as the Blackhawk Industrial Products Company, with William Gerow as general manager, and Paul Moore as sales manager. The Power Packer product line had been shifted in 1957 to the Dynex plant in Pewaukee, which had excess capacity.

BIPCO was established by separating Enerpac marketing and manufacturing from the automotive division, establishing a separate purchasing department, and beginning to manufacture in the Columbus plant. Mr. Moore hired a sales force of eight men and a division controller was employed. By 1960, the separation was complete, and Mr. Gerow took steps to assure BIPCO's separate profitability. He raised prices, cut manufacturing costs and vendors' prices. A new manufacturing manager was located, and several products were added to the line.

In 1961, Mr. Gerow left the company for another job, and Mr. Brumder personally took over as general manager. The division was operating smoothly, and Mr. Brumder was required to be active only during the first three months after Mr. Gerow had left.

For the balance of 1961, the division ran without a full-time general manager. Sales and engineering were handled by Mr. Moore for Enerpac. Power Packer was transferred from Dynex to BIPCO, along with it its marketing manager, Mr. David Brown. Mr. Gerow returned as general manager in 1962, and the Power Packer manager, Mr. Brown, was replaced by Mr. Tom Goulet. Two months later, Mr. Gerow took over the general manager's function at the Dynex division in addition to his BIPCO responsibilities. Mr. Gerow split the time of John Wermuth, the Dynex controller, between Dynex and BIPCO, and had him prepare financial plans and controls for BIPCO, enabling him to supervise BIPCO on an "exception reporting" basis.

1964 witnessed considerable change at BIPCO. Lawrence Lopina was hired as controller, Lore Frost took over the Power Packer segment from Mr. Goulet, who was transferred to head Applied Power's Canadian operations, and Robert McBride was hired as the first full-time general manager since 1961.

In 1965, the division was still organized in two profit centers—Enerpac and Power Packer—each with its own sales and engineering staffs. There were also two service centers—manufacturing and finance. All four of these centers, plus a staff assistant for business development, Robert Spath, reported to the general manager.

ENERPAC

[The Enerpac product line included pipe benders, pumps, cylinders, jacks, and a variety of other standardized portable hydraulic tools for use in maintenance, production, construction and testing applications.] Most product applications were accomplished by employing special attachments for a particular job. The Enerpac marketing concept had been to dominate a large number of specialized markets, through broad distribution and specially adapted tools.

In 1965, more than three-fourths of the Enerpac line was in hoses, parts, pumps, rams, pipe benders, oil, jacks, couplers, and electric pumps. The balance was in hand jacks, knock out punches, maintenance sets, pullers, double acting cylinders, and a number of other items.

In general, the products enjoyed a very healthy gross margin. Pipe benders had lower than average margins because considerable competition was being offered by Greenlee in the electrical equipment supply area. Greenlee was reported to have sales of approximately $20 million, of which about $2 million was estimated to be in items competitive with Enerpac. They had a good product, strong distribution, and generally sold at lower prices than Enerpac. That portion of Enerpac business which was awarded on the basis of bids was most vulnerable to this competition.

Enerpac tried to set its prices on the basis of the value of the product to the user in the functions it performed. However, competition sometimes precluded this flexibility of pricing policy. Enerpac maintained simple, uniform pricing for each item, regardless of where and how it was used, with no discounts or bargaining. Average unit price was about $65, with some sets selling for as much as $1,500.

Enerpac sold through several types of distributors: mill supply, warehouse, electrical supply, building contractor supply, laboratory supply, etc. Fifteen salesmen split the country on the basis of geography and population, even though management recognized that marketing competence was based on familiarity with the function to be performed, rather than a specific industry or geographical region. Much of Enerpac's sales effort was concentrated on the ultimate customers, trying to pull the product through the distribution channels and to increase Enerpac's knowledge of the markets' requirements. In 1965, Ohio was the leading geographic market for Enerpac, with the northeast and Texas following. Sales had been assisted by an advertising program of about 4.5% of sales.

Enerpac excelled in its distribution system. The number of channels and outlets covered was considerably larger than any competitor's coverage. Management felt that generally they had a better knowledge of customer needs than did competition and that their products performed better in relation to size.

While in 1965 the most important use of Enerpac products was in factory applications, it was anticipated that in the future the construction industry would make much wider use of hydraulic tools. Laboratory and test system applications were other emerging use areas.

POWER PACKER

The Power Packer product line was composed of units similar to those of Enerpac. These products differed primarily in that some had special adaptions unique to specific OEM customers. This division tried to sell systems rather than components, which were much more competitive. However, about one-fourth of the Power Packer business was in components which were standard products of other Applied Power segments. Only one new product had been developed in Power Packer in recent years.

In 1965, about half of Power Packer sales were in hand pumps. The remainder was in power pumps, cylinders, standard and modified jacks, and accessories and valves.

Very healthy gross margins had been maintained in most of the product line, with the exception of jacks. The most important single use of Power Packer products was in truck tilt cabs. Although Power Packer had almost all of this market in 1965, BRIMCO and Auto Specialties Company posed a growing future competitive threat. Most other applications were small volume and had not met serious competition on a system basis. They were, however, always vulnerable on an individual component basis. In addition, any systems that developed into sizeable sales volume were subject to manufacture by the customer in his own facilities or replacement by a more sophisticated hydraulic system.

In 1965, the business was split among 39 large customers (net worth of $500,000 or more) and 400 smaller users. The two largest single sales items were direct sales to the government and to a large mobile equipment manufacturer, each accounting for about 7% of total sales. The small customers were frequently unaware of alternative sources of supply and somewhat dependent upon Power Packer for engineering assistance. As a result, the customer list had changed little over the years.

Management estimated that 1965 Power Packer distribution was about 75% direct to OEM. The balance was through distributors and service stations, or in service and repair parts.

The division used 32 distributors, ten of whom did more than 80% of the distributor business. The one man sales force covered the entire country.

Power Packer appeared to have as its competitive edge the long-established reputation of company and product with a group of long-time customers. In addition, there was some carryover from prospects' knowledge and experience with other Applied Power product segments. The low turnover of customers had enabled Power Packer to establish strong positions in some markets, such as in the truck tilt cab market.

Current areas that were receiving Mr. Frost's attention were the building of a group of sales representatives supported by application engineers, the improvement and enlargement of the catalog, and "wrapping up the tilt cab business." In the future, he hoped to extend the segment further into the industrial tool business.

Two obstacles to future growth of this segment were the limitations of the pumping systems in the product line and the existing product manufacturing relationships. In 1965, customers whose products were being upgraded from hand systems to power systems were not able to make the transition with Power Packer units. However, if Power Packer were to develop small power operated systems, they would compete with the large, automated companies such as Vickers, Cessna, Sundstrand, etc.

The second obstacle, as reported by Mr. Frost, was the result of the manufacturing facility not being specifically set up to handle Power Packer's needs. Because most of the Columbus output was used to replenish the rapidly turning inventories of CDR and Enerpac, large blocks of time were not readily available to run Power Packer orders. These could not be inventoried, because of their special characteristics. Additionally, many jobs required special foundry work before Columbus could even begin assembly. The resulting delays, two weeks to five months, were likely to cause large customers to give serious thought to self-manufacture, since Power Packer offered little more than an assembly operation. This feeling was not shared by Mr. Ryan, corporate director of manufacturing.

Applied Power Industries, Inc. (B-3):

The Dynex Company

The Dynex Company division was organized as two separate profit centers—the commercial segment and the systems engineering segment. William G. Gerow, vice president of Applied Power and general manager of the Dynex Company, was directly responsible for both segments of the business. Mr. Wesley Master, one of the three original men hired to form the Dynex division in 1955, was responsible to Gerow for the total management of the systems engineering segment as well as for the engineering activities of the commercial segment. Each segment had its own sales force and own engineering staff, but shared manufacturing, financial, and office staffs, and a joint 55,000 square foot, modern plant in Pewaukee, Wisconsin. Because of Mr. Master's dual role, engineering time could be, and was, frequently shifted back and forth between segments to satisfy current requirements. Much of the sales effort in both segments was market development work, and was heavily dependent upon extensive engineering assistance. About 60% of total divisional engineering time was classified as sales support.

Of 1965's total divisional sales of $3.5 million, 79% was in the commercial segment. This segment also accounted for 84% of the division's $45,000 pretax profits and 92% of the division's total investment of $1.8 million.

MARKETS AND PRODUCTS

Whereas BIPCO and BMC focused their product activities on a limited number of relatively simple, linear applications of low horsepower hydraulics, Dynex's product capability was much broader and more complex. Commercial units were both linear and rotary, with power ratings of as much as 150 HP. "Split-flow"—different outputs from a single pump—was a

---

© 1966 by the Board of Trustees of the Leland Stanford Junior University.

Dynex specialty. Systems engineering offered advanced technology competence in high-pressure hydraulic systems and sophisticated design capability for special applications. Virtually all of its work was on development contracts or prototype construction.

The big market (estimated at over $100 million) for high-powered rotary hydraulic pumps was, in 1965, satisfied primarily by low-pressure gear pumps and vane pumps. Dynex had deliberately chosen not to compete in these types, and had confined their activities to high-pressure axial piston pumps, much more complex units with a far smaller market demand.

The major manufacturers of gear and vane pumps were large companies such as Vickers, Cessna, Sundstrand, and New York Air Brake. All were heavily tooled to manufacture high-volume, low-cost, hydraulic units.

Although the axial piston pumps could perform any function that the low-pressure gear or vane pumps could, their much more complicated design was inherently more expensive to produce. In addition, the small size of the market for axial piston pumps precluded automated production. Therefore, the axial piston pump generally found markets only where it had unique performance advantages.

The most important advantage of high-pressure systems was that they could be much smaller in size and weight than low-pressure systems of comparable performance capability. For example, a 100 ton force could be applied at 6,000 psi (high-pressure) with a cylinder only six inches in diameter, while at 1,000 psi (low-pressure), a 16 inch diameter would be required. In addition, the oil flow of Dynex's axial piston pumps could be divided so that a single pump could do several jobs. Each pump could provide variable flow at one point and constant flow at another. Alternatively, two or more different pressures could be maintained with one pump.

Thus, the high-pressure, axial piston pumps were purchased primarily for applications where a single pump could replace several pumps, or where size was a crucially limiting factor.

About two-thirds of Dynex commercial sales were of standard products that were manufactured to catalog specifications. The balance of the commercial segment's sales volume resulted from special engineering modifications to the standard line. . . .

Engineering systems sold development work based largely upon the same technology that was incorporated in the commercial line.

The standard commercial product line was concentrated in a series of hydraulic axial piston pumps, ranging from 50-150 HP and operating at up to 10,000 psi working pressure. Dynex also made hydrostatic transmissions (consisting of a pump and motor) which converted linear fluid flow to rotary output motion. In addition, they made (or supplied from other divisions or companies) the necessary valves, controls, and cylinders which, when combined with Dynex pumps or transmissions, comprised a total system.

Although some systems engineering units might include standard commercial products, systems was not explicitly limited by the Dynex line in its product development work. It was not uncommon for all components for a specific systems project to be specially produced by hand or purchased from other companies.

Most of the Dynex commercial units were sold to the mobile equipment market. In 1965, the most important single product in the line was a transit mixer drive system (the unit that turned the drum on a mobile concrete mixer). This unit, which sold at a price just under $1,000, comprised a considerable portion of the commercial segment's sales. Dynex had pioneered this market and had solved the many difficult engineering problems involved. In mid-1965, it appeared as if a low-cost pump and motor could be adapted to the system Dynex had developed, and that vane pump producing competitors might try to sell complete drive system units below Dynex's costs.

Another major product line (and one in which low-pressure vane pumps could not compete) was in lifting units for certain types of cranes. By using high-pressure pumps for the drive system and reducing the weight of structural components through the use of hi-tensile steel, cranes could be safely operated from truck bed mountings which would have required crawler tractor mounting for support if a heavier hydraulic unit were employed. This was also a market that Dynex had pioneered and developed over an extended time period.

Another potentially important product area was the powering of auxiliary axles on mobile equipment. In this case, hydraulics replaced complicated and expensive mechanical linkages by using a hydrostatic transmission to drive either a gear reducer on the wheel or a pinion gear on the axle.

TEKTRO

In 1964, Mr. Gerow and Mr. Brumder hired a consulting firm to study product opportunities for Applied Power in the whole range of fluid power components sold through air-hydraulic distributors. This study had convinced the company that adding pneumatic capability was not the best way to establish Applied Power in this distribution channel. It was decided to enter this market with low-cost, Dynex-developed pumps, with the opportunity to add valves and other fittings subsequently. It was also decided to develop this segment with the brand name of "Tektro." This was in keeping with the corporate strategy of having separate identification for different markets. Because of the similarity of technology, Mr. Gerow was to head up this activity. The long-range plan intended was to develop this into a completely separate division.

DYNEX MARKET DEVELOPMENT AND SALES

Mr. Gerow hoped to develop Dynex's hydraulic transmission systems into a much more important line. He looked for opportunities to increase his systems business, as opposed to selling "loose" pumps and valves. He wanted to avoid competing on a component basis for mass market applications where the drive problems were technically simple and price was the major basis for production differentiation. Instead, he hoped to find markets where the functions were technically difficult, and problem solution, not price, was the basis for competition.

Direct sales forces were employed for both commercial and systems. Prospective buyers were generally selected on the basis of potential improvement in their products if hydraulic power transmission were to be utilized instead of mechanical. If the improvement could be made by adapting existing Dynex products, the sales effort was conducted by the commercial segment. However, if the potential adaptation had never been developed, systems might solicit the customer for a research and development contract on the project. In 1965, commercial sales were made by five field salesmen. They were assisted by two field servicemen, and whatever engineering help that proved necessary. Sales effort was rarely aimed at existing users of hydraulic systems, most of whom were in old, proven technologies adequately served by simple gear or vane pumps. If a development were to open up an exceptionally large market (for example, replacing mechanical automotive transmissions with hydrostatic), Dynex sales executives expected that intense competition from Vickers, Sundstrand, Cessna, and the other large hydraulics mass producers would occur immediately. It was also likely that present powers in mechanical transmissions, e.g., Rockwell-Standard and Dana, would enter the hydrostatic transmission market if and when it matured.

Therefore, the Dynex strategy had been to concentrate on areas of relatively small potential sales volume and complex engineering requirements so as to avoid competing with the large companies who were supplying the volume users. This concentration had resulted in an average two to five years lead time requirement between the original customer contract and production. Even so, unless they were able to create a unique advantage, or unless the market did not get large enough to invite competition, Dynex could not be sure of holding whatever markets it had developed.

Six mobile equipment manufacturers, located in the Milwaukee area, accounted for more than 50% of Dynex's sales. The balance of the volume was evenly distributed among manufacturers of mobile and industrial equipment located in the midwest and mid-Atlantic states.

Systems sales were conducted by a group of five men, who were also assisted by the engineering staff. Most research contracts were negotiated in two parts: (1) a feasibility and exploratory study to see if the project was worth pursuing and to give experience upon which to base the cost of part two; (2) a full-scale development resulting in a final system. These contract prices were negotiated (or bid) at a profitable level, since the system resulting from contract work remained the property of the customer and could not be marketed to their competition.

Systems customers were sought primarily from large companies. Competition was from consulting engineers, as well as from the large hydraulics firms which competed with commercial.

Engineering

The engineering department was staffed by about 50 people, half of whom were engineers, with the balance providing drafting, clerical, and secretarial support. This group was the backbone of Dynex, since products were more sophisticated than most customers' knowledge and required substantial engineering content in product design, sales, and customer education. Most of the engineers had worked for one or more of the very large U.S. hydraulics companies. Engineering management had not found recent engineering graduates to be as practical or knowledgeable for Dynex work as the experienced men attracted from the large companies.

Facilities

Dynex manufacturing was performed in two plants in 1965. The higher volume machining and assembly was performed at a small plant in Camdem, Tennessee. The recent move to this plant was designed to take advantage of the lower wage rates in the area and of an attractive building lease. All of the rest of the machining, assembly, and testing was done at the Pewaukee headquarters. In addition, this location also housed the research and development laboratories, engineering, and office facilities.

Manufacturing utilized standard types of machine tools at both locations. In addition, some specialty work was subcontracted to firms uniquely equipped for this type of work.

Finance

Financial reports for the two segments are included as Exhibit 1.

As can be seen, both segments had a history of unprofitability until 1963. Even then, earnings had been well under the levels achieved by other Applied Power divisions.

exhibit 1

APPLIED POWER INDUSTRIES, INC. (B-3)

Unit Financial Profile by Years
(thousands of dollars)

Dynex	*1960*	*1961*	*1962*	*1963*	*1964*	*1965*
Net sales	$1,304	$1,185	$1,876	$2,177	$2,369	$2,750
Net profit	(133)	(137)	(60)	56	54	38
Net working capital	660	638	597	564	775	840
Net fixed assets	556	465	527	493	465	719
Total investment	1,216	1,103	1,124	1,057	1,240	1,559
Average % return on investment	(10.9%)	(12.4%)	(5.3%)	5.2%	4.4%	2.4%
Total net cash flow	$ 206	$ 164	$ 81	$ 123	$ 129	n.a.

Systems	*1960*	*1961*	*1962*	*1963*	*1964*	*1965*
Net sales	$209	$396	$198	$449	$732	$743
Net profit	(17)	(19)	(71)	20	57	7
Net working capital	77	87	40	68	232	155
Net fixed assets	33	33	33	33	32	64
Total investment	110	120	73	101	264	219
Average % return on investment	(15.5%)	(15.8%)	(97.3%)	19.8%	21.6%	3.2%
Total net cash flow	$ 79	$ 29	$ 24	$ 8	$106	n.a.

Applied Power Industries, Inc. (B-4):

Applied Power International

In 1965, the International division was the youngest and fastest growing division of Applied Power. From its inception in late 1959, sales had grown steadily to over $6 million in 1965, with earnings after taxes of $314,000. Exhibits 1 and 2 show relevant financial information for the division. Whereas the other divisions of Applied Power had developed around building and selling a *product* line or a special technology, the International division had concentrated on developing a sales and distribution organization of "broad market competence." Management had felt that "how you do business is more important than the product itself." As a consequence, their efforts had been aimed at obtaining control of an outstanding marketing organization in each of the major markets in the world, then supporting it with local manufacturing where appropriate.

THE GENERAL MANAGER

Fred T. Page, 50 years old in 1965, was president of Applied Power International and general manager of all foreign operations. He was also a vice president of the parent company. He joined the then Blackhawk Manufacturing Company in March of 1954, after working nine years for Philips' Lamp, in accounting, finance, and international marketing, and one year for Ford International, where his work brought him in close contact with a number of the smaller operating units.

Mr. Page began at Applied Power as corporate controller and director of commercial development. In the latter position he was given the assignment of improving the lagging business in hydraulic jacks. His study and subsequent recommendations completely changed the marketing concept from exclusive distribution of a limited product line to selling a full line of

---

© 1966 by the Board of Trustees of the Leland Stanford Junior University.

exhibit 1

APPLIED POWER INDUSTRIES, INC. (B-4)

Sales Data before Intercompany Eliminations
(thousands of dollars)

Area by Product	1960	1961	1962	1963	1964	1965
Europe and Africa Sales:						
CDR	$480	$996	$1,176	$1,795	$2,347	$2,943
Lifting	26	50	62	44	82	127
Tune-up						115
Other auto					94	134
Enerpac			525	586	758	1,144
Power Packer			67	80	106	152
Dynex			20	91	277	239
Tektro					73	242
Service and unclassified				29	47	52
Total sales	506	1,046	1,850	2,625	3,784	5,153
Net profit a.t.	(13)	—	25	151	297	368
Western Hemisphere Sales:						
CDR	60	60	65	236	245	252
Lifting	70	70	77	201	246	365
Tune-up						
Other auto		2		2	5	
Enerpac	20	20	25	21	193	264
Power Packer					17	27
Dynex				2	3	5
Tektro						16
Service and unclassified	6	7	9	10	10	17
Total sales	156	159	176	472	719	946
Net profit a.t.	2	14	27	39	75	42
Far East Sales:						
CDR	205	186	202	194	195	188
Lifting	70	70	77	69	78	78
Tune-up						
Other auto		3		6	18	
Enerpac	40	40	48	40	73	87
Power Packer			4	1	1	1
Dynex				1	3	1
Tektro				4	11	9
Service and unclassified	6	8	9	15	12	15
Total sales	321	307	340	330	391	379
Net profit a.t.	6	65	72	81	87	58

automotive lifting equipment on a semiexclusive basis to a much larger number of distributors.

A later project was the analysis of markets for the industrial application of Blackhawk's automotive products. Following this study, the applications destined for the industrial market (Enerpac) were separated from the automotive division and set up as a new Industrial Products division.

In 1959, Mr. Page and Mr. Brumder spent six weeks in Europe, evaluating the market opportunities for Blackhawk products. Shortly afterwards, the International division was formed, with Mr. Page as general manager.

Mr. Page had formulated extensive and specific written programs for each country and each continental area, and kept detailed current records of all International's activities to assure that these programs were proceeding as planned. He had personally hired all of the original employees in his division, and he continued to maintain close contact with all of his key people around the world.

BRIEF HISTORY

In 1959, Mr. Brumder and Mr. Page set up a Panamanian corporation as a vehicle through which they could repatriate foreign earnings in the form of dividends. At the same time, they negotiated a new arrangement with the English firm that had been distributing and manufacturing Blackhawk products as a licensee for many years. This agreement gave Applied Power a full-time sales force in the U.K. and an overseas manufacturing facility. In 1960, a sales office was opened in Geneva. Sales and manufacturing facilities in Holland and France followed in 1961. The Dynex line was added in the United Kingdom in 1962. German distribution began in 1963. Mexican operations were started in 1964.

In order to reduce the risk of foreign operations, individual corporations were formed for each activity. As of 1965, there were 11 such corporations and two branch operations employing a total of 216 people. None of the people outside of corporate headquarters were American except for the Canadian manager.

EXPRESSED NEED FOR BROADER LINE

By comparing the degree of market saturation which had been achieved by Applied Power products in the U.S. to the estimated foreign sales potential, the International division management in 1962 had predicted that sales in Europe of existing products would tend to plateau at about $7.5 million by 1969. On the basis of this forecast, corporate management agreed to allow International to expand its sales activity beyond the then existing Applied Power lines. Mr.

Page and his staff began looking for U.S. manufacturers of hydraulic components which would be complementary to Applied Power's, and were without good foreign distribution. Specifically, he looked for relatively small, privately owned, highly successful companies, with good product acceptance, whose organizations would welcome the additional volume which International could provide them by distributing their products in new markets. As of 1965, the division had exclusive overseas marketing agreements with seven such companies: Webster Electric, Bruning, Beckett-Harcomb, Republic Valve, Milwaukee Cylinder, Oil Dyne, and Sanbar. In each case, the agreement gave Applied Power complete foreign marketing rights of the company's products for a specified length of time, as well as the right to comanufacture those same products abroad on a 50-50 joint venture basis.

PRODUCTS

These companies were experienced in the manufacture and application of air and hydraulic pumps, motors, valves, couplings, cylinders, accumulators, miniaturized systems, and machine tool feeds. This group of products was combined to form an important segment of the Tektro brand name. All of these products were either labeled Tektro or Tektro–(company name) (e.g., "Tektro-Bruning"). The Tektro concept was to supply, from one supplier (Applied Power), a complete group of compatible components that could be combined to satisfy the industrial user's and original equipment manufacturer's entire hydraulic system requirements. By far the biggest portion of International's sales in the industrial user hydraulic market, however, came from the proprietary Enerpac line.

This industrial hydraulics business, while very fast growing, was not nearly so large in 1965 as International's volume in the automotive market. This market was served with the Porto-Power line of collision damage repair equipment, the Blackhawk line of lifting equipment, as well as some non-Applied Power products. The International division purchased for resale, under the Blackhawk name, car alignment equipment, air chisels, impact wrenches, sanders, and wheel balancers. The division also sold Performance Test Equipment, a complete line of meters and instruments for analyzing and adjusting internal combustion engines, under the Blackhawk name. This line was the result of a joint venture agreement with Allen Electric similar to the ones negotiated with the partners in the Tektro line.

The balance of the Applied Power International product line included Dynex products, which were being sold in some volume in Great Britain, and Power Packer, which had had a slow start overseas.

While Enerpac and Porto-Power were responsible for most of International's 1965 sales, management believed that Tektro and Performance Test Equipment held real growth potential for the future.

exhibit 2

APPLIED POWER INDUSTRIES, INC. (B-4)

Sales Data before Intercompany Eliminations
(thousands of dollars)

Product by Area	1960	1961	1962	1963	1964	1965
CDR						
Europe	$ 480	$ 996	$1,176	$1,795	$2,347	$2,943
Far East	205	186	202	194	195	188
Western Hemisphere	60	60	65	236	245	252
Total	$ 745	$1,242	$1,443	$2,225	$2,787	$3,383
Lifting						
Europe	26	50	62	44	82	127
Far East	70	70	77	69	78	78
Western Hemisphere	70	70	77	201	246	365
Total	$ 166	$ 190	$ 216	$ 304	$ 406	$ 570
Tune-up						
Europe						115
Far East						
Western Hemisphere						
Total						$ 115
Other auto						
Europe					94	134
Far East		3		6	18	
Western Hemisphere		2		2	5	
Total		$ 5		$ 8	$ 117	$ 134
Enerpac						
Europe			525	586	758	1,144
Far East	40	40	48	40	73	87
Western Hemisphere	20	20	25	21	193	264
Total	$ 60	$ 60	$ 598	$ 647	$1,024	$1,495
Power Packer						
Europe			67	80	106	152
Far East			4	1	1	1
Western Hemisphere					17	27
Total			$ 71	$ 81	$ 124	$ 180
Dynex						
Europe			20	91	277	239
Far East				1	3	1
Western Hemisphere				2	3	5
Total			$ 20	$ 94	$ 283	$ 245

Tektro						
Europe					73	247
Far East				4	11	9
Western Hemisphere						16
Total				$ 4	$ 84	$ 272
Service and unclassified						
Europe				29	47	52
Far East	6	65	72	81	87	15
Western Hemisphere	2	14	27	39	75	17
Total	$ 8	$ 79	$ 99	$ 149	$ 209	$ 84

DIVISION ORGANIZATION

A substantial number of existing and projected vehicle registrations in a particular country, and a strong local economy, had been the major determinants of which countries warranted Applied Power International's entry.

New markets were started with minimum capitalization to limit risk and retain financial mobility. Wherever possible, local debt financing was employed to hold down equity and dollar requirements. Young "entrepreneur type" men were sought for general management for each company and the area offices. When possible, men who had been either general managers or sole proprietors in their prior work experience were chosen.

Both the United Kingdom and French operations had begun with existing companies. The English firm had been the distributor of Blackhawk products and the French firm had manufactured and sold its own product line for automotive body alignment.

The marketing methods employed by each region differed according to the particular demands and customs of that environment. In 1959, in France, International had one existing distributor, on an exclusive basis. In 1965, there were more than 100 Applied Power distributors in France. In Germany, only a limited distribution system for hydraulics existed, so the primary sales effort was conducted directly with the customer.

Pricing decisions were also related to local conditions. In order to make it convenient for the customer to purchase from Internation, Applied Power products were priced in the country's local currency, F.O.B. a local freight basing point.

MANUFACTURING

The initial investment in any area was largely limited to inventory and accounts receivable. As sales of a product grew, local manufacturing was seriously considered. Quarters were leased initially, and operations usually began by importing components from the U.S. Later, subcontracting was evaluated. At times, Applied Power produced components in its own plant to prove to the subcontractors that certain costs were obtainable. If a vendor could supply a component for less than 90% of the standard variable Applied Power cost, a contract was awarded. The decision whether to manufacture the component locally rather than purchase it was based upon discounted cash flow analysis. In the past, those investments for self-manufacture which were made had had 12 to 18 month payouts.

If a desirable sales agreement with a U.S. company was about to expire, Applied Power sometimes exercised its right to jointly manufacture that product abroad. The subsequent joint investment in manufacturing facilities was felt to tie the partner more closely to Applied Power, and assured a continuing flow of new products and technical developments, as well as providing low-cost components. Applied Power continued to retain the marketing responsibility.

In 1965, the International division had manufacturing facilities in England, Holland, Canada, and Mexico for Applied Power products, and also had foreign manufacturing operations in joint venture with Allen Electric and with Webster Electric.

CONTROLLING THE ORGANIZATION

The International division was divided into three major subareas: Europe and Africa, Far East, and Western Hemisphere. Within each area, the next level of responsibility was the country. Each year, top management reviewed with area and local management the plan developed and submitted by the local management. This plan began with a sales forecast by product and by country, and carried through operating budgets for each function. It concluded with *pro forma* financial statements. After discussion and revision, this plan represented the operating performance guide for the local company, the area manager, and the corporate management. This plan was reviewed formally at least three times per year and was the basis for daily control. Each area reported its performance by product and function each month, within eight days after the close of the month. These figures were compared to the annual plan to determine areas needing special attention. Within the plan and policy limits, each area operated fairly autonomously. As long as the profit goal was achieved, minor variances in the details of the plan were not criticized. However, the plans of all areas were watched very closely by headquarters. The book of all plans was consulted 30-40 times per month. Area managers and company managers all had duplicates of the appropriate section of the plan book to assure understanding and consistency. Information about local conditions was communicated to and from all areas, averaging twice daily, by letter, cable, or telephone. Control was facilitated further by travel of the area managers to Milwaukee and of corporate management to all locations.

In addition to the profit plan, corporate management developed a four point program of those crucial steps needing to be accomplished by each key individual in the coming year. Performance was then evaluated on the basis of both achieving the profit and investment goals and in accomplishing those steps deemed necessary for future growth and profits.

GROWTH

From an initial investment of $41,000, the International division had grown to a net worth of more than $800,000, after buying out the original English partner for $150,000. The growth rate from internally generated funds and local debt indicated financing support for a future growth of about 40% per year compounded, after paying dividends of 25% of profits to Applied Power (1965 dividends were $165,000 and return on total assets employed was 14.6%).

International management planned growth from four key sources:

1. Geographic expansion of present operations. Present plans called for operations in South Africa, Australia, India, and Argentina. Other possible areas considered for the future included Japan, Italy, Spain, and Sweden. The greatest limiting factor to this expansion was the ability of securing desirable partners or employees for management of these operations.
2. Expanding the product line for local needs. This included finding specific market requirements that could be easily met by adding a product, e.g., the distribution of a French wheel balancer in England to satisfy such a need.
3. Addition of a whole new segment to the product line for sale through the present marketing organization, i.e., the selling of automotive performance test equipment.
4. Growth through finding and selling new applications of existing products, e.g., Enerpac applications for the English mining industry.

Mr. Brumder felt a great deal was yet to be gained from Applied Power International's operations by an effective marrying of the specialized marketing and technical know-how existing in the U.S. product/market oriented divisions with the International division's overseas operating organization. He felt the product line staff directly under Mr. Page could never develop the strength equaling that in the U.S. divisions, and that in the future the U.S. divisions must be mobilized in some fashion to perform worldwide staff functions in strategic planning and product and market development.

"Admittedly," he said, "this would be extremely difficult because of the complexities inherent in the multitude of geographic, economic, trade practice, and other differences existing in the various areas and countries of the world. Since the overseas line organization structure was created to specialize by geographic and national areas, the problem of bringing product line marketing and technical specialization to the market place would be additionally difficult, particularly when much of the overseas local business organizations were still quite small."

Mr. Brumder also felt strongly that Applied Power could end up by default as virtually two separate companies, one U.S. and the other international, unless the marrying process was brought about. In his words, this would be "a shameful waste of painstakingly developed know-how and resources." He felt that because of lack of certain product line knowledge overseas, many current profitable opportunities in Applied Power's present lines were being overlooked. At the same time, efforts were being made to develop business in lines in which the company had virtually no experience. He felt a good start in correcting this situation would be a high degree of planning coordination between U.S. division, the International division, and the corporate staff.

Another area where worldwide staff direction would be fruitful, according to Mr. Brumder, was in the manufacturing and supply function. He already had James Ryan heavily involved in the study of this situation.

One last major area of interest to Mr. Brumder was to create a worldwide uniform financial accounting, planning, and control function under the direction of the corporate controller.